BASIC

CHESS ENDINGS

By

REUBEN FINE

AUTHOR OF

Modern Chess Openings, *Revised Edition*
Chess the Easy Way

DAVID M^CKAY COMPANY, INC.

NEW YORK

17

ISBN: 0-679-14002-6
Printed in the United States of America

Dedicated

to the Memory of

DR. EMANUEL LASKER

PREFACE

The unprecedented success of MODERN CHESS OPENINGS led me to believe that a similar work on the endings would be welcomed by the chess world. Despite the great and increasing importance of this part of the game there is still relatively little literature on it.

In this book I have tried to present a handy guide for the practical player. Throughout I have concentrated upon those aspects of the ending which occur most often in over-the-board play. Virtually no problems have been included; those which are cited might quite conceivably have come up in a tournament or match game.

I wish to express my grateful thanks to Mr. Irving Chernev for kindly allowing me to use his excellent library. I must also beg my wife's pardon for heartlessly thrusting the typing of the manuscript upon her.

CONTENTS

CONTENTS

INTRODUCTION

The great importance of the ending has often been recognized, especially in recent years. Yet even masters have had to learn practically everything from bitter experience because the standard material available has been scattered in a thousand different, and often inaccessible, places.

Because of the lack of similar material, I have tried to do two things in this work. In the first place the standard positions which come up time and again have been given at great length. Every experienced player simply must know these: they are as indispensable to further proficiency in the endings as a knowledge of the scales is to the performance of a symphony in music, or the mastery of the alphabet to the reading of novels. In the second place I have at the same time tried to make this a useful book of instruction for the more advanced phases of the ending. With this in mind I have given a large number of rules which are at times incorrect from a strictly mathematical point of view, but are nevertheless true by and large and are of the greatest practical value.

The diagrams and their discussion form the bulk of the book. To facilitate reading and reference the solutions have been printed in bold face type, thus setting them off from the rest of the text. Examples and illustrations which are not diagrammed will be of value chiefly to the student who wishes to perfect his knowledge of any branch of the endgame.

While it is manifestly impossible to present more than a small portion of the endings which come up in practical play, I have tried to solve this problem by the use of *typical positions*. Illustrations taken from master games have been selected only because they are representative of large numbers of similar endings.

Consequently, to use the material given here in the analysis of any particular ending, one must first examine that ending to see what category it will fit into and then compare it with the appropriate position or positions. The endings have been classified first according to the kind of material on the board, then according to the amount, and finally according to the nature of the Pawn position. However, in endings with more than three Pawns on each side, the amount of material is usually irrelevant and has not been considered. Thus, to find an ending with Rook and two Pawns vs. Rook and one Pawn, one must consult the appropriate part of the chapter on Rook and Pawn endings, where cases with exactly the same number of Pawns are given. But in an ending with Rook and seven Pawns vs. Rook and six Pawns, one must turn to the part on material advantage in Rook and Pawn endings, and then to the section where that particular type of Pawn position is discussed. While space limitations have unfortunately made it impossible to present more complicated cases where both sides have many pieces, the principles and rules given are equally applicable to all endings.

Only two special symbols have been used. "White" and "Black," where they do not refer to any specific players, denote the superior and inferior sides, respectively. E.g., in endings with R vs. Kt, the side with the Rook is always "White," the side with the Knight always "Black." This facilitates general discussion. The " = " sign has been used to denote a drawn position, rather than mere general equality.

BIBLIOGRAPHY

Berger's THEORIE UND PRAXIS DER ENDSPIELE is the classic and has been invaluable throughout. This monumental work is the compendium of all previous research up to 1921. Other general works which have come in handy from time to time are: I. Rabinovitch, ENDSPIEL; Un Amateur de l'Ex U. A. A. R., FINS DE PARTIE; and Sutherland and Lommer, 1234 MODERN ENDGAME STUDIES.

For Bishop and Knight endings F. Reinfeld's two booklets have been suggestive. For Rook and Pawn endings, Spielmann's articles in L'Echiquier, 1929 and 1930, F. Reinfeld's two booklets and Grigorieff's article in the Yearbook 1937 have all been helpful.

Chapter I

THE ELEMENTARY MATES

In this chapter we shall consider the question of pieces checkmating a lone King. The minimum material required in general is either a) one Queen; b) one Rook; c) two Bishops; d) Bishop and Knight; e) three Knights. With two Knights a mating position is possible, but cannot be forced. Against one Knight or one Bishop the defender cannot lose even if he wants to. However, two Knights can in most cases force checkmate when the defender has one or more Pawns (See Chapter III). Similarly, in certain special positions Bishop or Knight vs. Pawn or Pawns can mate.

To checkmate White must drive the Black King to the edge of the board. A Queen or Rook can then administer the coup de grace anywhere along the last rank or file, but with Bishop and Knight or two Bishops or three Knights one must further chase the King into the corner.

1. THE QUEEN

Before proceeding with the exact moves in this and the other cases we shall enumerate the final mating positions which we are striving to obtain. With the Queen there are basically two types of mate: White K at Q6, Black K at Q1. a) Q—Q7, b) Q—QR8 (QKt8, KB8, KKt8, KR8). The mate can be forced in at most ten moves from any position, but in general requires a smaller number.

In No. 1 nine moves are necessary. *1 K—Kt2!, K—Q4; 2 K—B3, K—K4* (or 2 .... K—K3; 3 K—Q4, K—B3; 4 Q—K4, K—B2; 5 K—K5!, K—Kt2; 6 K—B5, K—B2; 7 Q—Kt7ch, K—K1; 8 K—K6, K—B1; 9 Q—B7 mate); *3 Q—KKt6, K—B5* (Or 3 .... K—Q4, 4 Q—K8, K—Q3; 5 K—B4, K—B2; 6 K—B5, K—Kt2; 7 Q—Q7ch, K—R3; 8 Q—K7!, K—R4; 9 Q—R7 mate, but here not 8 Q—QB7?? stalemate!); *4 K—Q4, K—B6; 5 Q—Kt5, K—B7* (or 5 .... K—K7; 6 Q—Kt2ch); *6 Q—Kt4, K—K8; 7 K—K3, K—B8; 8 Q—Kt7* (again not 8 Q—Kt3?? Stalemate), *K—K8; 9 Q—Kt1,* or *9 Q—R1* mate.

1

(If the White King is originally at QKt2 in No. 1, the mate will last ten moves, since either King or Queen will have to make one useless move.)

There are two types of stalemate to watch for:

1. Black King at QR1, White Queen at QB7 or QKt6 (and similarly for the other three corners);

2. Black King at QR3, White King at QB5, Queen at QB7 (Black to move in both cases).

No. 1

White to play; mates in 9.

No. 2

White to play; mates in 16.

2. THE ROOK

There is only one type of mating position here, although it may occur on any square on the edge of the board. It is: Black K at QKt1, White K at QKt6, R—KR8 (KKt8, KB8, K8, Q8). The mate requires at most 17 moves, although again in most cases it can be done much more quickly.

No. 2 corresponds to No. 1. The shortest road to Rome is *1 K—Kt2, K—Q5; 2 K—B2, K—K5* (if 2 .... K—B5; 3 R—Q1. White's first problem is to force Black to the side of the board); *3 K—B3, K—K4; 4 K—B4, K—K5; 5 R—K1ch, K—B4* (5 .... K—B5; 6 K—Q5, K—B6; 7 R—K4); *6 K—Q4, K—B5; 7 R—B1ch, K—Kt4* (If 7 .... K—Kt6; 8 K—K4, K—Kt5; 9 R—Kt1ch, K—R5!; 10 K—B3, K—R4; 11 K—B4, K—R3; 12 K—B5, K—R2; 13 K—B6, K—R1; 14 K—B7, K—R2; 15 R—R1 mate); *8 K—K4, K—Kt3!; 9 K—K5, K—Kt4; 10 R—Kt1ch, K—R5* (or 10 .... K—R4; 11 K—B4 and continues as in the note to Black's seventh move); *11 K—B5, K—R6; 12 K—B4, K—R7; 13 R—Kt3* (13 R—QR1, K—Kt7! would not be as accurate. But not here 13 .... K—R6; 14 R—R2!, K—R5; 15 R—R2 mate),

K—R8; 14 K—B3, K—R7; 15 K—B2, K—R8; 16 R—R3 mate. Again with the White R at Q Kt2 in No. 2 one more move is necessary.

The most common stalemate is Black K at QR1, White K at QB6, R at QKt7. The only other one that is possible is Black K at QR1, White K at QB8, R at KR7 (or anywhere else along the seventh rank).

3. TWO BISHOPS

To mate here the King must be driven into a corner. The final posi-

| No. 3 | No. 4 |

White to play; mates in 18.　　Black to play; White mates in 33.

tion will then be Black K at QR1, White K at QB7, B at QKt6, B—K4 (KR1, KKt2, KB3, Q5, QB6, QKt7) mate. Or Black K at QR2, White K at QB7, B at QKt7, B—QB5 (QKt6, Q4, K3, KB2, KKt1) mate. Another mating position is possible: Black K at QR4, White K at QB5, B at QKt5, B—Q2 mate. But this cannot be forced. Checkmate requires at most 18 moves.

In No. 3 the maximum number is necessary. *1 B—Q1, K—K6; 2 K—Kt2, K—Q7; 3 B—QB2, K—K6; 4 K—B3, K—B6* (Or a) 4 .... K—K7; 5 B—Kt5, K—B6; 6 K—Q2, K—Kt5; 7 B—K3, K—B6; *8* B—KB5, K—Kt7; 9 K—K2, K—Kt6; 10 B—Kt5, K—Kt7; 11 B—B4, K—Kt8; 12 K—B3, K—B8; 13 B—Q2, K—Kt8, 14 K—Kt3, K—B8; 15 B—Q3ch, K—Kt8; 16 B—K3ch, K—R8; 17 B—K4 mate. b) 4 .... K—B5; 5 B—Q3, K—B6; 6 K—Q4, K—Kt5; 7 B—K1, K—B6; 8 B—Q2 as in a)); *5 K—Q4, K—Kt5; 6 B—K1, K—B6; 7 B—Q3, K—B5; 8 B—K4, K—Kt4; 9 K—K5, K—Kt5; 10 B—KB2, K—Kt4* (Or 10 .... K—R6; 11 K—B4, K—R7; 12 K—B3, K—R6; 13 B—Q3, K—R7; 14 B—B1, K—R8; 15 B—K3, K—R7; 16 K—B2, K—R8; 17 B—Kt2ch, K—R7; 18 B—B4 mate); *11 B—KB5, K—R3; 12 K—B6, K—R4; 13 B—K6, K—R3; 14 B—Kt4, K—R2; 15 K—B7, K—R3; 16 B—K3ch, K—R2; 17 B—B5ch, K—R1; 18 B—Q4* mate.

There are two types of stalemate:
1. Black King at QR4, White K at QB5, Bishops at QKt5, QKt2.
2. Black King at QR1, White King at QB7, Bishops at QKt6, QB2.
Two Bishops of the same color cannot administer mate; a mating position is not even conceivable. The same holds true of nine (or more!) Bishops all of one color.

4. BISHOP AND KNIGHT

This is the most difficult case. The King must be driven into a corner of the same color as the Bishop, with the mating position Black K at QR1, White K at QKt6, Kt at QR6, B—K4 mate, or Black K at QKt1, White K at QKt6, B at QKt7, Kt—QR6(Q7) mate. Two other mating positions are possible, but cannot be forced. a) Black K at KKt1, White K at KR6, Kt at KKt6, B—Q5 mate. b) Black K at Q1, White K at Q6, B at Q7, Kt—B6 (K6, KB7, QKt7) mate. In an unfavorable position the mate may require as many as 34 moves.

The mate may be divided into two parts. First the Black K is forced to the wrong corner (i.e., not of the same color as the B), and it is then driven to the other side. Thus in No. 4 (which requires 33 moves) after *1 .... K—B3* (White to play begins with 1 Kt—Kt3ch and gets there more quickly. 1 .... K—B5; 2 B—B7ch leads to much the same variations); *2 Kt—Kt3, K—Q3* (2 .... K—Q4; 3 K—Kt5, K—Q3; 4 K—B4, K—K4; 5 Kt—B5, K—B4; 6 K—Q5, K—Kt4; 7 B—B3, K—B4; 8 Kt—K6, K—B3; 9 B—K4, K—K2; 10 K—K5, K—B2; 11 Kt—B4, K—Kt2; 12 B—Q5, K—R2; 13 K—B6, K—R1; 14 Kt—Kt6ch, K—R2; 15 B—K6 and continues as in No. 5); *3 K—Kt5, K—Q4; 4 B—B7ch, K—K4* (if 4 .... K—Q3; 5 B—B4, K—K4; 6 K—B5, K—K5; 7 K—Q6, K—B4; 8 B—Q3ch, K—B3; 9 Kt—Q2, K—B2; 10 Kt—B4, K—B3; 11 Kt—K5, K—Kt2; 12 K—K7, K—R1; 13 K—B6, K—Kt1; 14 Kt—B7 and again continues from No. 5); *5 K—B5, K—B3; 6 B—B4, K—K4; 7 Kt—Q2, K—B5; 8 K—Q6, K—B4* (If 8 .... K—K6; 9 Kt—Kt3, K—B5; 10 B—Q3, K—Kt4; 11 K—K5, K—R3; 12 K—B6, K—R4; 13 B—B5, K—R5; 14 K—Kt6, K—Kt6; 15 K—Kt5, K—B6; 16 B—B2, K—K6; 17 K—Kt4, K—K7; 18 K—B4, K—B7; 19 B—Q1, K—K8; 20 B—B3, K—B7; 21 Kt—Q4 etc., as in No. 5. On 9 .... K—K5 instead of 9 .... K—B5 here the variations are similar. One always gets to No. 5 or to one of the variations included there.); *9 B—Q3ch, K—B3; 10 Kt—B3, K—B2; 11 K—K5!, K—Kt2* (11 .... K—K2; 12 B—B4 and continues as in No. 5); *12 Kt—Kt5, K—Kt1!; 13 K—B6, K—B1; 14 Kt—B7, K—Kt1* and now we have the basic No. 5, where the problem is to chase the King over to the other side. *15 B—B5, K—B1; 16 B—R7!, K—K1; 17 Kt—K5, K—Q1* (better than 17 .... K—B1; 18 Kt—Q7ch, K—K1; 19 K—K6, K—Q1; 20 K—Q6, K—K1; 21 B—Kt6ch, K—Q1; 22 Kt—B5, K—B1; 23 B—

Q3, K—Q1; 24 B—Kt5, K—B1; 25 B—Q7ch, K—Kt1; 26 K—B6, K—R2; 27 K—B7,K—R1; 28 K—Kt6, K—Kt1; 29 Kt—R6ch, K—R1; 30 B—B6 mate); *18 K—K6* (18 B—K4 is also good and leads to much the same kind of variations: 18 B—K4, K—B2; 19 Kt—B4, K—Q2; 20 K—B7, K—Q1; 21 B—B6, K—B2; 22 B—Kt5, K—Q1; 23 K—K6, K—B1; 24 K—Q6, K—Q1; 25 Kt—R5, K—B1; 26 B—Q7ch, K—Kt1; 27 K—B6, K—R2; 28 Kt—Kt7, K—R3; 29 K—B7, K—R2; 30 B—Kt5, K—R1; 31 Kt

No. 5

White to play mates in 19.

—Q6, K—R2; 32 Kt—B8ch, K—R1; 33 B—B6 mate), *K—B2* (or 18 .... K—B1; 19 Kt—Q7, K—Kt2; 20 B—Q3, K—B1; 21 B—Kt5, K—Q1; 22 Kt—B5 and continues as in the note to Black's 17th move); *19 Kt—Q7, K—Kt2* (or 19 .... K—B3; 20 B—Q3! and now

a) 20 .... K—B2; 21 B—Kt5, K—B1; 22 K—Q6, K—Q1; 23 Kt—B5, K—B1; 24 B—Q7ch and again we are on familiar ground: the note to Black's 17th move.

b) 20 .... K—Kt2; 21 K—Q6, K—B1; 22 Kt—B5, K—Kt1 (or 22 .... K—Q1; 23 B—Kt5 as above); 23 K—Q7, K—R2; 24 K—B7, K—R1; 25 K—Kt6, K—Kt1; 26 B—R6 and mates in two: 26 .... K—R1; 27 B—Kt7ch, K—Kt1; 28 Kt—Q7.); *20 B—Q3, K—B3; 21 B—R6, K—B2; 22 B—Kt5, K—Q1; 23 Kt—Kt6, K—B2; 24 Kt—Q5ch, K—Q1; 25 K—Q6, K—B1; 26 K—K7, K—Kt2; 27 K—Q7, K—Kt1; 28 B—R6, K—R2; 29 B—B8, K—Kt1; 30 Kt—K7, K—R2* (or 30 .... K—R1; 31 K—B7, K—R2; 32 Kt—B6ch, K—R1; 33 B—Kt7 mate); *31 K—B7, K—R1; 32 B—Kt7ch* (not 32 Kt—B6?? Stalemate!), *K—R2; 33 Kt—B6(B8) mate.*

Stalemate positions are of three kinds:
1. With the Bishop: Black K at Q1, White K at Q6, B at Q7;
2. With the Knight: Black K at QR1, White K at QB7, Kt at QB6;
3. With both: Black K at QR2, White K at QB7, Kt at QKt4, B at K4.

5. THREE KNIGHTS

Here again Black has to be chased into the corner, although mating positions on other squares on the edge of the board are also possible. The final mate is: Black K at QR1, White K at QKt6, Kt's at QR6, Q6, QB7. In general not more than 20 moves should be required.

In No. 6 the procedure is as follows: *1 Kt(Kt2)—B4ch, K—Q4* (1 .... K—B5; 2 K—Kt2 would only hasten the end. Black must try to stay in the center of the board as long as possible); *2 K—Kt2. K— B4; 3 K—B3, K—Q4; 4 Kt(B2)—K3ch, K—B4; 5 Kt—K4ch, K—B3; 6 Kt—K5ch, K—B2; 7 K—Q4, K—Q1; 8 K—Q5, K—K2; 9 Kt— B5ch, K—Q1; 10 K—Q6, K—K1; 11 Kt—B5, K—B1* (or 11 .... K— Q1; 12 Kt—K6ch, K—B1; 13 K—B6, K—Kt1; 14 Kt—Q6, K—R2; 15 Kt—QB7, K—Kt1; 16 Kt—Q7ch, K—R2; 17 Kt(Q6)—Kt5 mate); *12 K—Q7, K—Kt1; 13 K—K7, K—R2; 14 K—B7, K—R1; 15 Kt—K6, K—R2; 16 Kt—Kt5ch, K—R1; 17 Kt—Kt6 mate.*

From the final position we see why two Knights cannot do the trick. Suppose the Kt at B5 were missing in the mate. Then on 16 Kt— Kt5ch, Black could have replied .... K—R3, for if the other Kt had been covering that square it could not have been able to go to Kt6 on the next move.

Thus in No. 7 no mate can be forced, Black unwilling. E.g., a) *1 .... K—R1; 2 Kt—B7ch, K—Kt1; 3 Kt—R6ch, K—R1; 4 Kt—Kt5 stalemate.* b) *1 Kt—QB4, K—R1; 2 Kt—K5, K—Kt1; 3 Kt—Q7* (or 3 Kt—B7 stalemate), *K—R1; 4 Kt—Kt5, K—Kt1; 5 Kt—B6ch, K— B1!* etc., not 5 .... K—R1??; 6 Kt—B7 mate).

No. 6	No. 7

White to play; mates in 17. | Draw.

Chapter II

KING AND PAWN ENDINGS

The Pawn, as Philidor put it, is the soul of chess, and we can add that in the ending it is nine-tenths of the body as well. All endgame play revolves about Pawns, how to evaluate their placement, how to manoeuvre with them, when to exchange them. Positions where there are no Pawns occur very rarely, and when they do are usually of a simple character. Endings with pieces not only require a knowledge of correct Pawn play, but also demand an evaluation of the corresponding Pawn ending in order to be able to answer the question of whether to exchange or not.

In view of all this, the present chapter is in every sense fundamental. Fortunately, a good deal of work has been devoted to the subject, so that the reader can readily secure an adequate grasp of everything that is needed for practical play. In addition it should be borne in mind that 95% of the endings which come up are subject to exact calculation.

The classifications of this chapter have been made quantitatively, i.e., according to the number of Pawns on each side. One should never lose sight of the fact that to win in materially even positions, or to draw (or win) when one is a Pawn behind, unusual circumstances must prevail.

There are three basic concepts which will be referred to time and again: opposition, triangulation, and gaining a tempo. Readers who are unfamiliar with these should first turn to Parts IX and X of this chapter (Pages 77–80).

I. KING AND PAWN VS. KING

The problem here is whether the Pawn can queen or not. If the Black King cannot catch the Pawn, it can queen and we have an elementary win. A simple way to determine whether the Black King can reach the queening file is the

Rule of the Square: Draw a square on the board, using the distance from the Pawn to the eighth rank (except that if the Pawn is on the second rank, the square should be drawn from the third) as the side.

7

No. 8. White to move.   **No. 9. Black to move.**

 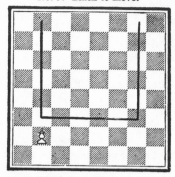

Draw if the Black King is inside the square. Win if the Black King is not inside the square.   Draw if Black can move inside the square. Win if Black cannot move inside the square.

If the Black King is inside this square, with White to move, or can reach it with Black to move, then he can stop the Pawn. If not, the Pawn promotes and Black is lost (Nos. 8 and 9).

Where the Black King is on the queening file or can reach it the win depends on whether White can drive him off the file or not. This in turn depends on who has the opposition.

There are two basic positional types here: one with the White King behind his Pawn, the other in front of it. In the first case (No. 10) the game is always a draw because Black need never relinquish the opposition. Thus: *1 P—Q5ch, K—Q3; 2 K—Q4, K—Q2; 3 K—K5, K—K2; 4 P—Q6ch, K—Q2; 5 K—Q5, K—Q1!* (essential); *6 K—K6, K—K1; 7 P—Q7ch, K—Q1; 8 K—Q6* stalemate. Note that Black can never

No. 10   **No. 11**

Draw.   White wins.

lose if he always moves straight back (keeping the opposition). E.g., if he had played 5 .... K—K1?? (diagonally instead of vertically or straight back) he would have been forced to abandon the queening square after 6 K—K6, K—Q1; 7 P—Q7, K—B2; 8 K—K7, when White's long-thwarted Pawn realizes all his ambitions.

In the second case (White King in front of the Pawn) the result depends on the relative King positions. In No. 11 White wins with or without the move: *1 P—K3* (Now he has the opposition), *K—Q3; 2 K—B5, K—Q2; 3 K—B6, K—Q1; 4 P—K4, K—Q2; 5 P—K5, K— K1; 6 K—K6* (again securing the opposition. 6 P—K6??, K—B1 would only draw), *K—Q1; 7 K—B7* and the Pawn queens. Or 1 .... K—B3; 2 K—Q5, K—K2; 3 K—K5, etc., as above.

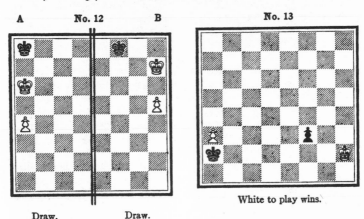

A   No. 12   B   No. 13

White to play wins.

Draw.   Draw.

The rule is that if the White King is two or more squares in front of his Pawn he always wins; if he is one square in front of his Pawn he wins only if he has the opposition. Thus in No. 11a, White: K at K4, P at K3; Black: K at K3, White to move draws, but Black to move loses. One important exception must be noted: when the White King is on the sixth rank he always wins regardless of whose move it is.

The above discussion does not apply to a RP, which is always a draw if the Black King can reach B1, Kt1, or R1. In No. 12A the Black King can never be driven out of the corner, while in No. 12B the White King has the pleasant choice of stalemating either himself or his opponent. E.g.:*1 P—R6, K—B2; 2 K—R8, K—B1; 3 P—R7, K—B2* stalemate; or 1 K—Kt6, K—Kt1; 2 P—R6, K—R1; 3 P—R7 stalemate. A simple rule to remember in the ending with the RP is that if Black's King can reach B1 he draws, while if White's King can reach Kt7 he wins.

II. KING AND PAWN VS. KING AND PAWN

Although all wins here are special cases, a number of them are of vital practical importance. There are four reasons why White may be able to win: 1. He queens ahead of his opponent (but one of the Q vs. P endings which are drawn —Q vs. RP or BP— does not ensue); 2. He queens with check; 3. Both sides queen; White mates or wins the Queen; 4. White wins the Pawn and the Black King cannot get back in time, or the Black King can reach the queening file but White retains the opposition.

1. WHITE QUEENS FIRST

Ordinarily this is quite simple. The White Pawn promotes and captures the Black Pawn fairly quickly unless that Pawn is on the seventh. Black can then usually draw with a BP or RP; for a full discussion see Chapter VIII, pages 522–524.

Sometimes, however, the task is quite complicated when Black's Pawn is far advanced. Thus in No. 13 (H. Rinck, 1922) if Black's K can reach K7, which he might do by gaining a tempo through an attack on the White P a draw would result. The solution is *1 P—R4, K—Kt6; 2 P—R5, K—B6* (if 2 .... K—B5; 3 P—R6, K—Q6; 4 P—R7, P—B7; 5 P—R8 = Q, P—B8 = Q; 6 Q—R6ch); *3 K—Kt1!!!* (but not 3 P—R6?, K—Q7!!; 4 P—R7, P—B7; 5 K—Kt2, K—K7 =, or 3 K—Kt3?, K—Q5!!; 4 P—R6, K—K6; 5 P—R7, P—B7 =), *K—Q5; 4 P—R6, K—K6; 5 K—B1!* and the White Pawn queens while the Black one is blockaded. Note that the White K must be able to actually occupy the queening square in time, so that if it had been at R3 originally the ending would have been drawn. E.g., No. 13a (Réti, 1922) White: K at KR8, P at QB6; Black: K at QR3, P at KR4. White to play and draw. 1 K—Kt7, P—R5; 2 K—B6, K—Kt3 (or 2 .... P—R6; 3 K—K7, P—R7; 4 P—B7 =); 3 K—K5!!, P—R6; 4 K—Q6 and both Pawns promote.

2. WHITE QUEENS WITH CHECK

This requires no special elaboration in the general case; it merely reduces to the Q vs. P ending. Sometimes, however, it is necessary to manoeuvre the Black K into a position where it will be checked by the new Q. E.g., No. 13b (Duras, 1905) White: K at QKt4, P at QKt2; Black: K at KR3, P at KKt2. White to play and win. 1 K—B5!, K—Kt3 (or 1 .... P—Kt4; 2 P—Kt4, P—Kt5; 3 K—Q4!, K—Kt4; 4 P—Kt5, P—Kt6; 5 K—K3, K—Kt5; 6 P—Kt6, K—R6; 7 P—Kt7, P—Kt7; 8 K—B2, K—R7; 9 P—Kt8 = Qch); 2 P—Kt4, K—B2; 3 P—Kt5, K—K2; 4 K—B6!, K—Q1; 5 K—Kt7!!, P—Kt4; 6 P—Kt6, P—Kt5; 7 K—R8, P—Kt6; 8 P—Kt7, P—Kt7; 9 P—Kt8 = Qch.

3. BOTH SIDES QUEEN; WHITE EITHER MATES OR WINS THE QUEEN

We have already seen examples of this in Nos. 13 and 13b, where the Black Q was born but to die. There is one important ending where both sides Queen and White can then mate. This is No. 14, many variants of which frequently occur. The solution is: *1 P—B7, P—R7; 2 P—B8=Q, P—R8=Q; 3 Q—B3ch, K—Kt8* (or 3 .... K—R7; 4 Q—Kt3 mate); *4 Q—K3ch, K—B8* (4 .... K—Kt7; 5 Q—K2ch, K—Kt8; 6 K—Kt3, transposing back into the main variation); *5 Q—B1ch, K—Kt7; 6 Q—Q2ch, K—Kt8; 7 Q—K1ch, K—Kt7; 8 Q—K2ch, K—Kt8; 9 K—Kt3!!!* and Black must give up his Q to ward off immediate mate, only to suffer the same fate one move later.

A
White
wins

No. 14

No. 15

White to play wins.

C
Whoever moves
loses

B
draw.

Something less common is No. 14a, White: K at QB7, P at QKt6; Black: K at QR3, P at KR6. White to play and win. 1 P—Kt7, P—R7; 2 P—Kt8=Q, P—R8=Q; 3 Q—Kt6 mate.

4. WHITE CAPTURES THE PAWN

This of course is a win only if after capturing the Pawn the Black King is too far away, or the White King retains the opposition. An example of the first is No. 14b, White: K at KB7, P at QR6; Black: K at QKt7, P at QR2. White to play and win. 1 K—K6, K—B6; 2 K—Q5!! (but not 2 K—Q6, K—Q5; 3 K—B6, K—K4; 4 K—Kt7, K—Q3; 5 K×P, K—B2=), K—Kt5 (2 .... K—Q6; 3 K—B6, K—K5; 4 K—Kt7, K—Q4; 5 K×P, K—B3; 6 K—Kt8); 3 K—B6, K—R4; 4 K—Kt7, K—Kt4; 5 K×P, K—B3; 6 K—Kt8 and wins. Or a similar example, No. 14c (Dobias, 1926), White: K at K4, P at KB2; Black: K at QKt4, P at KKt3. White to play and win. 1 K—Q4!!,

K—B3; 2 K—K5!, K—B4; 3 P—B4!, K—B5; 4 K—B6, K—Q5; 5 K×P etc. But here if 1 K—Q5?, K—Kt5!; 2 K—Q4, K—Kt6!; 3 P—B4, K—B7=, or 1 K—B4?, K—B5; 2 K—Kt5, K—Q4; 3 K×P, K—K5!; 4 K—Kt5, K—B6=.

An example which utilizes the results of No. 14c is No. 14d (Grigorieff, 1925), White: K at KKt8, P at QR2; Black: K at KKt3, P at QR6. White to play and draw. 1 K—R8!! (but not 1 K—B8?, K—B3! and the White King does not get back to QB2), K—B4; 2 K—Kt7, K—K5; 3 K—B6, K—Q6; 4 K—K5, K—B7; 5 K—Q4, K—Kt7; 6 K—Q3, K×P; 7 K—B2.

Where both Kings are near the Pawns the commonest cases are shown in No. 15. In 15A, Black to move has to abandon the P at once; White to move must first play *1 K—B7*. Then after *1 .... K—R1; 2 K×P* we are back to No. 11. In 15B, the game is drawn because Black can keep the opposition: *1 K—R6, K—B2; 2 K—R5, K—B1!* (anywhere except Kt2); *3 K×P, K—Kt2* and nothing can be done. The same type of draw holds good if we move all the pieces and Pawns back one or two ranks, but not if we move them up one rank, since that gives No. 15A. In 15C whoever moves must lose a P, after which he cannot even get to the queening file. E.g., *1 .... K—Q6; 2 K×P, K—Q5; 3 K—Kt4, K—Q4; 4 K—Kt5, K—Q3; 5 K—Kt6, K—Q2; 6 K—Kt7, K—Q3; 7 P—Kt4, K—Q4; 8 P—Kt5* etc.

Various applications of these ideas occur time and again. E.g., in No. 15d (Compare with No. 15C) White: K at KKt4, P at K3; Black: K at QB6, P at K5, whoever moves wins. 1 K—B5! (but not 1 K—B4??, K—Q6! and Black wins), K—Q6; 2 K—B4. Or No. 15e, White: K at QKt7, P at K4; Black: K at KR2, P at K3. White to play wins. 1 P—K5! (but not 1 K—B6, K—Kt3; 2 K—Q7?, K—B3; 3 K—Q6, P—K4; 4 K—Q5, K—B2!=. 15B), K—Kt3; 2 K—B6, K—Kt4!; 3 K—Q7!, K—B4; 4 K—Q6 and wins —15C. Or No. 15f (Cf. 15A), White: K at QKt2, P at K3; Black: K at QR5, P at K5. Black to play and win. 1 .... K—Kt5 (He has the opposition); 2 K—B2, K—B5; 3 K—Q2, K—Kt6; 4 K—K2, K—B7; 5 K—B2, K—Q7 etc. Or finally No. 15g (Kling and Horwitz, 1851), White: K at K6, P at K2; Black: K at K1, P at K2. Draw. 1 P—K3 (or 1 P—K4, K—Q1; 2 K—B7, P—K4!=15B), K—Q1; 2 P—K4 (2 K—B7, K—Q2!; 3 P—K4, K—Q3=), K—K1; 3 P—K5, K—Q1; 4 K—B7, K—Q2 and now 5 K—B8 draws, but 5 P—K6ch??, K—Q3! loses (15C).

Where the Pawns are on adjoining files a sacrificial drawing combination is sometimes available. Thus in No. 16 (Duclos, 1904, also Salvioli) after 1 .... K—Kt3; 2 K—B4, K—B3; 3 K×P, K—K3; 4 K—B4, K—B3; 5 P—B3 White wins (No. 11), but instead *1 .... P—K6!!* draws: *2 P×P, K—Kt3; 3 K—B4, K—B3; 4 K—K4*, K—K3= holds the game. For this stratagem to be successful the Black K

No. 16

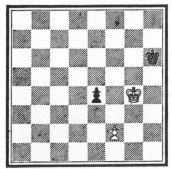

Black to move draws.

No. 16A

White wins.

must not be too far away. E.g., No. 16a (Dedrle, 1921) White: K at QB2, P at QKt2; Black: K at KB3, P at QR5. White to play and win. 1 K—Kt1!, P—R6!; 2 P—Kt3! (not P—Kt4), K—K3; 3 K—R2, K—Q4; 4 K×P, K—B4; 5 K—R4, K—Kt3; 6 K—Kt4 and White has the opposition.

III. KING AND TWO PAWNS VS. KING

This is always a win unless the Black King can capture both Pawns, or capture one and stop the other (which defense is rarely possible). It is important to consider the following points in play with two Pawns.

1. Connected passed Pawns should be kept one rank apart until the King approaches. If the back Pawn is captured by Black, the front one queens. If neither Pawn is captured, one will be escorted by the King to the eighth rank. There is only one special case that presents any difficulty: No. 16A. Here the win can only be achieved by sac-

No. 17

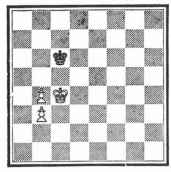

White wins.

rificing the RP at the proper moment, i.e., when it will permit the White K to occupy R6 or B6. Thus: *1 K—Q5, K—R1; 2 K—B5, K—Kt2; 3 P—R8= Qch, K×Q; 4 K—B6, K—Kt1; 5 P—Kt7, K—R2; 6 K—B7* and mates in three.

2. Doubled passed Pawns should not both be advanced. The extra Pawn is decisive only because it furnishes a vital tempo at the critical moment. Thus in No. 17 the solution is *1 P—Kt5ch, K—B2* (1 . . . . K—Kt3; 2 K—Kt4); *2 K—B5, K—Kt2; 3 P—Kt6, K—Kt1; 4 K—B6,*

K—B1; 5 P—Kt7ch, K—Kt1; 6 P—Kt4! (to the rescue!), *K—R2; 7 K—B7, K—R3; 8 P—Kt8 = R!* (Q would stalemate. 8 P—Kt5ch and then 9 P = Q is of course perfectly all right). It follows from this analysis that if the Pawns are on the fifth and sixth ranks no win can be forced. E.g., No. 17a, White: K at KB5, P's at K5, K6; Black: K at K2. 1 .... K—K1!; 2 K—B6, K—B1; 3 P—K7ch, K—K1 and now the only tempo move, 4 P—K6 stalemates. Pawns on the fourth and fifth always win, but with KtP's a little finesse is required. No. 17b, White: K at QB5, P's at QKt4, QKt5; Black: K at QB2. 1 P—Kt6ch, K—Kt2; 2 K—Kt5, K—Kt1; 3 K—B6, K—B1; 4 P—Kt7ch, K—Kt1 and now the winning move is either 5 K—B5!!, K×P; 6 K—Kt5!, or 5 P—Kt5, K—R2; 6 P—Kt8 = Qch!!, K×Q; 7 K—Kt6 and White has the opposition in both cases. But 5 P—Kt5, K—R2; 6 P—B7??, or 6 P—Kt6ch??, K—Kt1 both draw. Two (or more) RP's always draw

3. *Disconnected passed Pawns* must, unless they are very far apart, be supported by the King at the earliest convenient moment. Further, unless one can queen by force they should be kept on the same rank.

Pawns that are one file apart (No. 18A) can mutually defend one another. *1 .... K—R4; 2 P—B5!* or *1 .... K—B4; 2 P—R5!* White's K can then approach and escort one P to the eighth. If White's P were at R2 instead of at R4, 1 .... K—B4 would draw. Again, Black to play moves 1 .... K—Kt2, and if then 2 P—R5?, K—R3, or 2 P—B5?, K—B3! and a P is lost. The P's must be kept on the same rank.

Pawns that are two files apart (No. 18B) win unaided if they are on the fifth (White to move), sixth or seventh ranks (either side to move), can mutually defend one another if they are both on the second, but

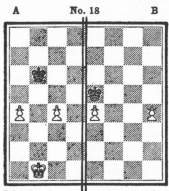

A   No. 18   B

Black plays,
White wins.

Unless the White
King is nearby
both Pawns can
be captured
by Black.

win only with the support of the King if they are on the third or fourth or fifth (Black to play and attacking one of the Pawns). Thus in No. 18B, if the White K were at QR1 and could not move away the game would be drawn: *1 P—R5, K —B3!; 2 P—R6, K—Kt3,* or *2 P— K5ch, K×P* and Black has time to capture both P's. The same holds true when the P's are on the third rank. But when the P's are on the second rank neither can be captured, for then the other could advance two squares and be beyond the reach of the enemy K. However, it would be fatal for either P to move before the White K has come to assist. When the P's are on the fifth rank (White to play), one must queen. E.g., move all the pieces up one rank in No. 18B, 18c, White P's at K5, KR5; Black: K at K3. White to play wins by 1 P—R6, K—B2; 2 P—K6ch!, K—Kt3; 3 P—K7, etc. But Black to play could afford to capture the KP and still get back to the other P in time. It is obvious that when the Pawns are on the sixth or seventh they queen by force even if Black has time to capture one of them.

Pawns that are three files apart queen by force unless they are both on the third and fourth ranks and Black to move can capture one of them. But again if they are not on the same rank this may not hold. E.g., No. 18d, White P's at Q4, KR2; Black: K at Q3. 1 .... K—Q4 enables Black to capture the QP and still stay in the square of the RP.

Pawns that are four or more files apart promote in any position without the aid of the King; once more assuming that they are kept on the same rank.

No. 19	No. 20

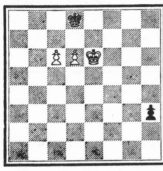 

White to move wins; Black to move draws.	Black to play draws; White to play wins.

IV. KING AND TWO PAWNS VS. KING AND PAWN

This is of course a win in general, but there are quite a few exceptions. We shall classify the cases according to the nature of White's Pawns.

CASE 1. WHITE HAS TWO CONNECTED PASSED PAWNS

The White Pawns defend one another at K4, Q5, e.g. (or in any similar diagonal position), while the White King has time to gobble up the remaining Black Pawn. If however, the Black Pawn is beyond the range of the White King the outcome depends on how soon White can force a Queen. E.g., in No. 19 White to move wins by *1 P—Q7, P—R7; 2 K—Q6, P—R8 = Q; 3 P—B7* mate. Or even 1 P—B7ch, K—B1; 2 K—K7, P—R7; 3 P—Q7ch, and queens with check. But if it is Black's turn to move there is no time for the above mating variation and White must take the draw after *1 .... P—R7* by *2 P—B7ch, K—B1; 3 K—K7, P—R8= Q; 4 P—Q7ch, K×P; 5 P— Q8= Qch.*

CASE 2. WHITE HAS TWO DISCONNECTED PASSED PAWNS

This is essentially the same as K+2 P vs. K (see No. 18 and discussion) unless White's King must lose valuable time to stop the Black Pawn; or unless the White King cannot catch the Black Pawn at all, in which case the outcome depends on who queens first. Sometimes Black can afford to get out of the square of a passed Pawn in order to aid in the promotion of his own Pawn. E.g., in No. 20 Black to move draws by *1 .... K—Kt5!; 2 P—Q6* (this would win if there

No. 21   No. 22

White wins.   White wins.

were no Black Pawn), *2 .... K—Kt6!; 3 P—Q7, P—B7; 4 K—K2, K—Kt7; 5 P—Q8= Q, P—B8= Qch.* Note that if White had been able to bring his King to KB1, he would have won.

In the above two cases White wins without any trouble except for a few problem positions. This is however not so in the remaining cases, which are consequently of more interest.

CASE 3. WHITE HAS ONLY ONE PASSED PAWN
A. HIS PAWNS ARE SEPARATED

Normally this is a simple win. White uses his passed Pawns as a decoy to lure the Black King away from the other side, captures Black's Pawn and the ensuing ending with K+P vs. K is routine (No. 21). This illustrates the well-known "outside passed Pawn" reduced to its simplest elements. The moves might be *1 P—Kt5ch, K—Kt3; 2 K—Kt4* (not essential here, but sometimes it is advisable to gain this extra move), *K—Kt2; 3 K—B5, K—B2; 4 K—Q5, K—Kt3; 5 K—K6, K×P; 6 K—B6* etc.

The more complicated examples in this case occur only when the Pawns are one file apart, so that the White King must do considerable manoeuvring. In No. 21a (Berger), White: K at QR4, P's at QR2, QB4; Black: K at QR3, P at QB4, the correct continuation is 1 K—R3!, K—Kt3!; 2 K—Kt2!, K—R4; 3 K—Kt3, K—Kt3; 4 K—B3, K—R4; 5 K—Q2!, K—R5; 6 K—K3, K—R6; 7 K—K4, K—R5; 8 K—Q5, K—Kt5; 9 P—R3ch. Note that here after 1 K—Kt3, K—R4; 2 K—B3?, K—R5 White can only draw, for if 3 K—Kt2, K—Kt5; and if 3 K—Q3, K—Kt5!; 4 P—R3ch, K×P; 5 K—K4, K—Kt6!; 6 K—Q3 (but 6 K—Q5?, K—Kt5! loses), K—Kt5 etc.

With center Pawns White can sometimes win only by choosing the right moment to sacrifice his Pawn. Thus in No. 22 (Berger) the main variation is *1 K—K4, K—B4; 2 P—Q4ch, K—Q3; 3 K—K3* (an example of *triangulation:* White wishes to play K—Q3 only when the Black King is at Q4, for else Black could reach K5), *K—B3; 4 K—Q2, K—Q3; 5 K—B3, K—B3; 6 K—B4, K—Q3; 7 P—Q5, K—Q2* (or 7 .... K—K4; 8 K—B5, K×P; 9 P—Q6, K—K3; 10 K—B6); *8 K—B5, K—B2; 9 P—Q6ch, K—Q1!; 10 P—Q7!!, K×P; 11 K—Q5* and now White has the opposition, which is decisive here since he captures the Pawn on the sixth rank. In No. 22a (Berger), White: K at Q5, P's at Q3, KB6; Black: K at Q2, P at KB2 the lack of elbow room saves the day for Black. The QP can only be sacrificed on the seventh, when White's opposition is useless. However, with the P at Q2 instead of Q3, White has an extra tempo and can win by attacking the KBP: 1 K—K5, K—B3; 2 K—B5, K—Q3; 3 K—Kt5, K—K4; 4 P—Q3!, K—K3; 5 P—Q4, K—Q4; 6 K—R6, K×P; 7 K—Kt7 etc.

Again, where the King is behind the passed Pawn in some cases a draw is possible. E.g., No. 22b (Rabinovitch); White: K at K2, P's at QB4, K3; Black: K at KB4, P at QB4. Draw. 1 K—B3, K—K4; 2 P—K4 (or 2 K—K2, K—K5; 3 K—Q2, K—K4; 4 K—Q3, K—B4; 5 P—K4ch, K—B5!), K—Q5!! (not 2 .... K—K3??; 3 K—B4, K—B3; 4 P—K5ch, K—K3; 5 K—K4 etc.); 3 K—B4, K×P; 4 P—K5, K—Kt6!! (again not 4 .... K—Q 4?; 5 K—B5, P—B5; 6–8 P—K8= Q, P—B8=Q; 9 Q—Q7ch, K—B4; 10 Q—B7ch); 5 P—K6, P—B5;

Draw.
Win with White Pawn at KR5, Black Pawn at R3.

No. 24

White wins.

6 P—K7, P—B6; 7 P—K8=Q, P—B7 and draws because it is a BP (See No. 545). No. 23 is the only other important exception to the general rule that an outside passed Pawn with one remaining set of Pawns always wins. The Black King has time 'to capture the QRP and return to KB1, when the draw is clear: *1 K—B4, K—R4; 2 K—Q5, K×P; 3 K—K5, K—Kt4; 4 K—B5, K—B3; 5 K—Kt5, K—Q2; 6 K×P, K—K1; 7 K—Kt6, K—B1.* With the White Pawns at KR5 or KR6 White wins, since his King can occupy Kt7; with the Black Pawn at KR5 or KR6 the game is still a draw.

In No. 24 (Bayer, 1911) there is a set of RP's, but White can nevertheless force the win: *1 K—Q4, K—Q3; 2 P—B5ch, K—B3; 3 K—B4, K—B2; 4 K—Q5, K—Q2; 5 P—B6ch, K—B2; 6 K—B5, K—B1; 7 K—Q6, K—Q1; 8 P—B7ch, K—B1; 9 K—B6, P—QR4; 10 K—Kt6, P—R5; 11 P—R3* and now Black must abandon the queening square. If Black had played P—R4, White would have countered with P—R4 and then won the Pawn, thus: *1 K—Q4, P—R4; 2 P—R4, K—Q3; 3 P—B5ch, K—B2; 4 K—Q5, K—Q2; 5 P—B6ch, K—B1; 6 K—B5, K—Kt1* (or 6 .... K—B2; 7 K—Kt5, K—Q3; 8 K—Q6); *7 K—Kt6.* The only drawing position here is No. 24a, White: K at QKt6, P's at QR2, QB6; Black: K at QKt1, P at QR6, White to play, for the Black QRP can only be captured at the expense of the White QBP. It is

No. 25

Black to move draws; White to move wins.

No. 26

White wins.

interesting to note that with the Pawns up one square White still wins.
Thus: No. 24b. White: K at QKt6, P's at QR3, QB6; Black: K at
QKt1, P at QR5. White to play: 1 K—R5!, K—B2; 2 K—Kt5 and
now Black must either allow the White Pawn to queen, or abandon his
own Pawn.

Two other variants of this ending are shown in Nos. 25 and 26.
In No. 25 (Grigorieff) Black forces his opponent to waste a priceless
Pawn tempo: *1 .... K—B2!; 2 K—Kt5, K—K3!; 3 P—R3* (or A),
K—B2; 4 K—B5, K—K1!; 5 K—K6, K—B1; 6 P—R4 (or 6P—B7,
P—R3; K—B6, P—R4!; 8 K—Kt6, P—R5=), *K—K1* (now Black
must not move the Pawn); *7 P—R5, K—B1; 8 K—K5, K—B2;
9 K—B5, K—K1!; 10 K—K6, K—B1; 11 P—B7, P—R3.* Draw.
Variation A: 3 P—R4, K—B2; 4 K—B5, K—B1!; 5 K—K6, K—K1;
6 P—R5, K—B1; 7 P—B7, P—R3. Draw.

In No. 26 (game Fahrni-Alapin) the win is accomplished by a
triangulation manoeuvre by which White succeeds in reaching the
diagrammed position with Black to move: *1 K—Q5, K—B1; 2 K—B4,
K—Kt1* (or 2 .... K—Q1); *3 K—Q4!* (the key move), *K—B1; 4 K—
Q5, K—B2* (or .... K—Q1; 5 K—Q6 and White has the opposition);
5 K—B5, K any; 6 K—Kt6, winning the RP. This ending in point of
fact always wins, except for the special case mentioned in No. 23.
E.g., even with the Black King relatively well placed a conclusive
sacrifice will still be available: No. 26a, White: K at QB2, P's at QR4,
QB3; Black: K at QB5, P at QR4. White to play and win. 1 K—Kt2,
K—B4; 2 K—B1!, K—Q4 (2 .... K—B5; 3 K—B2 and proceeds as in
the main variation. Note that White triangulates in order to get to
the original position with Black to play); 3 K—Q2, K—K5 (3 ....
K—B4; 4 K—Q3, K—Q4; 5 P—B4ch, K—B4; 6 K—B3 etc., as in
No. 24); 4 K—K2, K—Q4; 5 K—Q3, K—B4; 6 P—B4!!, K—Kt5;
7 K—Q4, K×RP; 8 K—B3!!, K—R6; 9 P—B5, P—R5; 10 P—B6,
K—R7; 11 P—B7, P—R6 (11 .... K—Kt8; 12 K—Kt4); 12 P—
B8=Q, K—Kt8; 13 K—Kt3 and it is all over.

B. HIS PAWNS ARE UNITED

Again this is ordinarily a quite simple win. In the model position
No. 27 White need only try to attack the QP by going around to the
other side of the board. Black will eventually be unable to keep up
with him because he has to stay inside the square of the passed KP.
*1 K—K3, K—K3; 2 K—Q3, K—Q2; 3 K—B3, K—B3; 3 K—Kt4,
K—Kt3; 5 K—R4* and now 5 .... K—R3 would allow the P to queen,
while after *5 .... K—B3; 6 K—R5, K—B2; 7 K—Kt5, K—Q2; 8 K—
B5, K—K3; 9 K—B6* the P cannot be held.

From this model we can see under what circumstances there are
drawing chances for the person who is a Pawn behind. When the

No. 27

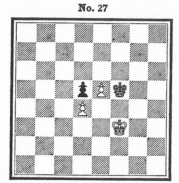

White wins.

No. 28

Draw. Position with all pieces and Pawns one file to the left is also a draw.

White King attacks the Pawn Black must have sufficient leeway to move his King. Consequently, when the Black Pawn is on the second rank, the passed White Pawn on the seventh, the game is drawn if Black's King is on the R or Kt files, but lost otherwise. Thus in No. 28, *1 K—K5, K—Kt1; 2 K—B6*, is stalemate but in No. 29 after *1 K—B5, K—Q2; 2 K—Kt5, K—K1; 3 K—R6, K—Q2; 4 K—Kt7, K—K1; 5 K—Kt8* Black has a move with his King and loses.

In No. 30 there are two winning methods, one as above (No. 29) and the other by sacrificing the Pawn at the proper moment: *1 K—Q4, K—K2; 2 K—B4, K—Q3; 3 P—K7!, K×P; 4 K—B5, K—Q2; 5 K—Q5* (now he has the opposition), *K—K2; 6 K—B6*, etc.

It is only when neither of these winning methods (squeezing out the Black King, or sacrificing the Pawn to get the opposition) is available

No. 29

White wins. Similar positions with White Pawns at K6, Q7; Q6, B7; B6, Kt7; B6, Q7 also win.

No. 30

White wins. This Pawn configuration wins anywhere except on the Rook file.

that Black can draw. Thus if he had a RP in No. 30 he would draw, because White has the choice of trying to force the Black King off the board or giving up the KtP to get to an ending of K+RP vs. K.

We have already seen (No. 27) that with the Black Pawn on the fourth rank White always wins. If the Black Pawn is a RP, White captures it, if necessary, by advancing his own at the right moment. There is, however, a trap to be avoided. No. 27a: White: K at QB5, P's at QR4, QKt5; Black: K at QKt2, P at QR4. White to play. 1 P—Kt6??, K—R3! only draws (2 K—B6 stalemate), but 1 K—Q5, K—B2; 2 K—K6 still wins: 2 .... K—Kt2; 3 K—Q7, K—Kt3; 4 K—B8 (or 4 K—Q6), K—R2; 5 K—B7, K—R1; 6 K—Kt6, etc.

With the Black Pawn on the fifth rank there is nothing to gain by sacrificing the passed Pawn, for with the Pawns on the fourth or third

No. 31

No. 31A

White wins; Win in all similar positions except Nos. 31A and 31b.

Draw.

ranks Black can always keep the opposition after his Pawn has been captured. However, the first method (as in No. 27) is applicable except for some special positions. These occur when Black has the opposition, and can prevent the White King from approaching his Pawn, or when Black can afford to let the White Pawn queen, because the resulting position is drawn.

The general case is exemplified in No. 31, where White to play wins even though Black has the opposition: *1 K—B2, K—B4; 2 K—Q2, K—Q3; 3 K—K2, K—K3; 4 K—B3, K—K4; 5 K—Kt3, K—B3; 6 K—B4, K—K3; 7 P—K5*, etc.

Two exceptions due to the presence of a BP are seen in the next two examples. In No. 31A Black to move draws by *1 .... K—Q5; 2 K—Q2* (if 2 K—B2, K—K4; 3 K—Kt2, K—B3; 4 K—R2, K—Kt3!; 5 K—R3, K—Kt4; draw), *K—B5; 3 K—B2, K—Q5; 4 K—Kt3, K—Q4!*

(but not 4 .... K—K6? see Variation A); *5 K—Kt4, K—Q5!; 6 K—Kt5, K—K6; 7 P—Kt5, K×P; 8 P—Kt6, K—K7; 9 P—Kt7, P—B6; 10 P—Kt8=Q, P—B7* Draw. See Chapter VIII No. 545.

Variation A: 4 .... K—K6?; 5 P—Kt5, K×P; 6 P—Kt6, K—K7; 7 P—Kt7, P—B6; 8 P—Kt8=Q, P—B7; 9 Q—Kt2!, K—K8; 10 K—B3!, P—B8=Q; 11 Q—Q2 mate.

In No. 31b Black draws by keeping the opposition: White: K at KKt1, P's at QB3, QKt4; Black: K at KKt2, P at QB5. Black to play and draw. 1 .... K—B2; 2 K—B2, K—K3! (distant opposition); 3 K—Kt3 (or 3 K—K2, K—B3!; 4 K—Q2, K—K3), K—K4! (diagonal opposition); 4 K—Kt4, K—K5; 5 K—R4, K—B5 (or 5 .... K—Q6, as above); 6 K—R3, K—B4; 7 K—Kt2, K—K5; 8 K—Kt1, K—B4! (distant opposition). This drawing variation can also be found in No. 31A.

No. 32

White wins.

No. 33

White wins; Win in any similar position without a RP.

Finally, we come to those positions where Black's Pawn is on the sixth rank. Here if Black ever has a chance to capture the backward White Pawn he draws with ease. However, in the general case, No. 32, this is not possible. After *1 K—B1, K—B5* (or 1 .... K—Kt6; 2 K—Q1, K—Kt7; 3 P—K4 and the King is outside the square); *2 K—Q1, K—Q4; 3 K—K1, K—K4; 4 K—B2, K—K5; 5 K—Kt3, K—K4; 6 K—B3* the Black Pawn is untenable. A draw is possible only in such special cases as No. 32a, White: K at KB1, P's at KKt2, KR3; Black: K at KB5, P at KKt6. 1 .... K—K6; 2 K—K1 (if 2 K—Kt1, K—B5!), K—Q6; 3 K—Q1, K—K6!; 4 K—B2, K—B7, etc., or No. 32b, White: K at QB1, P's at QR2, QKt3; Black: K at QB6, P at QR6. Black plays K—Q6—B6 and if White's King goes off to the right K—Kt7 draws.

C. HIS PAWNS ARE DOUBLED

This is a draw whenever Black's King is in front of the Pawns, for White must give one up to be able to capture the Black Pawn.

CASE 4. WHITE HAS NO PASSED PAWN

Black has drawing chances only when the position is blocked, or when the White Pawns have advanced too hastily, or when the White King is in a backward position.

It is convenient to divide these endings into those with blocked Pawn positions and those with fluid Pawn positions. The latter are more elastic, generally present fewer difficulties and are often reducible to a blocked type, so that we shall consider such inelastic positions first.

With the Black Pawn on the second rank, White always wins easily unless there is a RP on the board. In No. 33 Black's King must not leave the square of White's King Pawn. In view of this reduced mobility White can get the opposition and win Black's Pawn: *1 K—Kt5, K—Q3* (1 .... K—Kt2?; 2 P—Q6); *2 K—B4, K—B2; 3 K—B5, K—Q1; 4 K—Kt6* (4 K—B6 is also good), *K—B1; 5 K—B6, K—Q1; 6 K—Kt7, K—K1; 7 K—B7, K—B1; 8 K—Q7* (or 8 P—Q6, PXP; 9 K—Q7, P—Q4; 10 P—K7ch), etc. Note that there are two ways for White to win: either by capturing Black's Pawn, or by queening his own advanced Pawn. Where Black has a RP neither of these is possible, so that a draw results. No. 33a: White: K at KB5, P's at KKt5, KR6; Black: K at KB2, P at KR2. 1 K—K5, K—Kt3; 2 K—B4, K—B2; 3 K—B5, K—Kt1; 4 K—B6, K—R1 and the best that White can do is claim a moral victory. When Black has a KtP and White a RP, again the draw can be held: No. 33b, White: K at KB5, P's at KKt6, KR5; Black: K at K2, P

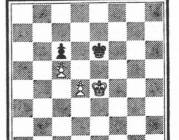

No. 34

White to move draws; Black to move loses; Draw in any case with RP's.

at KKt2. 1 K—K5, K—B1; 2 K—K6, K—Kt1; 3 K—K7, K—R1; 4 P—R6, K—Kt1!! (but not 4 .... PXP, 5 K—B7); 5 P—R7ch, K—R1; 6 K any, stalemate.

With Black's Pawn on the third rank White can in general win only if he has the opposition, while if there are RP's he cannot win at all. In No. 34 one can try *1 K—B4, K—B3; 2 K—Kt4,* when 2 .... K—Kt3?; 3 P—Q5! would lose, but *2 .... K—K3!; 3 K—B4, K—B3!* (not 3 .... K—Q4?; 4 K—K3, K—K3; 5 K—K4, when White has the opposition) draws. Black to move must allow the Pawn advance or lose his own Pawn: *1 .... K—B3; 2 P—Q5!* or *1 .... K—Q2; 2 K—B5!, K—K2; 3 K—K5* and now that he has yielded the opposition Black must ultimately lose his BP. However, if Black has a RP, No. 34a, White: K at QB4, P's at QR5, QKt4; Black: K at QB3, P at QR3 the opposition is useless, for after *1 .... K—Q3; 2 P—Kt5, P×Pch; 3 K×P, K—B2* Black can only lose by a brainstorm.

The same conclusions hold when Black's Pawn is on the fourth or fifth ranks: in general White can win only if he has the opposition, while with RP's on the board he cannot win at all.

It should be noted that the concept of distant opposition (i.e., where more than one square separates the two Kings) plays an important role in endings of this type. Thus in No. 34 on 1 K—K3, Black can only draw by either *1 .... K—K2!* or *1 .... K—B2*, but not *1 .... K—B3?; 2 K—B4, K—K3; 3 K—K4*, or *1 .... K—Q4; 2 K—Q3, K—K3; 3 K—K4*.

Why the Pawn position should be kept elastic is now abundantly clear. Whenever the Pawns are blocked White's winning chances diminish, at times they even vanish. One apparently insignificant tempo often makes all the difference in the world. The well-known composer Kling once illustrated this principle graphically in No. 35. With White's Pawn at R3 the game would be drawn regardless of whose turn it was to move, but in the diagrammed position White can win. There are two threats that Black must guard against: one is getting the opposition, the other is exchanging the RP for the KtP while Black's King is still on the K file. By utilizing both these possibilities White decides the game: *1 K—B3, K—K4* (on *1 .... K—Q5* or *1 .... K—Q3; 2 K—Kt3* wins, while if *1 .... K—K3; 2 K—K4* is the answer); *2 K—Kt3, K—B3; 3 K—Kt2!, K—B2* (or *3 .... K—K4; 4 K—B3, K—Q5; 5 K—Kt3*, or *3 .... K—K4; 4 K—B3, K—B3; 5 K—K4, K—K3; 6 P—R3!*, as in the main variation); *4 K—B2, K—B3; 5 K—Kt3!, K—Kt3* (forced); *6 K—B3, K—B3; 7 K—K4, K—K3; 8 P—R3* and White has the opposition.

If we turn to the general position where White Pawns have an abundance of living and moving space, we find that the win is routine, provided only such Pawn moves as are essential to White's plan are made. Thus in No. 36 the first objective is the occupation of K6 by the King: *1 P—K3, K—Q3; 2 K—B5, K—Q4; 3 P—Q3, K—Q3; 4 P—K4, K—Q2; 5 K—K5, K—Q1; 6 K—K6, K—K1.* Next White must bring his King to either K7 or B7: *7 P—K5* (or P—Q4), *K—B1; 8 K—Q7, K—B2.* Finally he must win the KP. *9 P—Q4, K—B1; 10 P—K6.*

The dangers of a premature advance of the Pawns may be seen in No. 36a, White: K at KB4, P's at Q4, K4; Black: K at KB3, P at K3. Black to move draws by *1 .... P—K4ch!; 2 P×Pch, K—K3;* while

White to move must resort to the manoeuvre 1 K—K3, K—K2; 2 K—Q3, K—Q3; 3 K—B4, K—B3; 4 P—K5! to win. Again, in No. 36b, White: K at K4, P's at KB4, KKt4; Black: K at K3, P at KB3, even the move does White no good. E.g., 1 K—Q4, K—Q3; 2 K—B4 (or 2 P—B5, K—B3; 3 K—B4, K—Q3!=), K—B3 and if 3 K—Kt4, K—Q4. This is likewise true when the Pawns are on the second or third ranks, but not when they are on the fifth, for then P—B6ch would win (No. 33). On the other hand, if White's Pawn were at KKt2, the position would be won because of the extra tempo: No. 36c, White P at KKt2, other pieces as in No. 36b. White wins. 1 K—Q4, K—B4 (if 1 .... K—Q3; 2 P—Kt4!, K—K3; 3 K—B5, K—K2; 4 K—Q5, K—Q2; 5 P—B5, K—K2; 6 K—B6, K—B2; 7 K—Q6, etc.); 2 K—K3, K—Kt5 (2 .... K—K3; 3 K—K4, P—B4ch; 4 K—Q4,

No. 35   No. 36

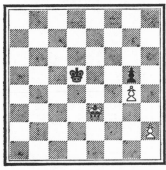 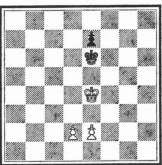

White wins (Draw if P is at R3).   White wins.

K—Q3; 5 P—Kt3! is hopeless for Black); 3 K—K4, K—R5! (not 3 .... K—Kt6; 4 K—B5!); 4 K—B3! (but not 4 K—B5?, K—Kt6!!; 5 K×P, K×BP!=), P—B4!; 5 K—B2!! (but not 5 P—Kt3ch?, K—R6!; 6 K—B2, K—R7!=), K—Kt5; 6 P—Kt3, K—R4 (6 .... K—R6; 7 K—B3, K—R7; 8 P—Kt4); 7 K—B3!, K—Kt3; 8 K—K3, K—B3 (8 .... K—R4; 9 K—Q4, K—Kt5; 10 K—K5); 9 K—Q4 and White wins because he has the diagonal opposition.

Now we can see that there are only two types of position where White has any difficulty: when he has only one Pawn move at his disposal, and when there are RP's on the board. However, neither of these conditions leads to a forced draw, so that further distinctions must be made.

Where White has only one Pawn move, assuming normal King positions, he can win when he has at least one center Pawn, but can often do no more than draw when he has no Pawn on the King and Queen

No. 37

White wins.

files. It is always better for Black to have his Pawn as far advanced as possible.

The crucial positions here are Nos. 37 and 38. In No. 37 White must reserve his Pawn advance (P—Q5) until it gives him the opposition: *1 K—B3* (not 1 K—B4?, P—Q4 ch!), *K—Q2; 2 K—Kt4, K—B3; 3 K—R5, K—Kt2; 4 K—Kt5, K—B2; 5 K—R6, K—B3; 6 P—Q5ch!, K—B2* (or 6 .... K—B4; 7 K—Kt7, K—Q5; 8 K—B6, K—K4; 9 K—B7); *7 K—R7, K—B1; 8 K—Kt6, K—Q2; 9 K—Kt7.* Here too a premature advance of the QP would have ruined White's winning chances, e.g., 1 K—B3, K—Q2; 2 P—Q5, K—B2!, and Black draws (See No. 34).

When White has Pawns on the Bishop and Knight files, with only one Pawn move, if Black's Pawn is on the B file he can usually draw, but if it is on the Knight file he will as a rule lose. The variations with the BP are illustrated in No. 36b above. With a KtP Black loses, because of the threat of a Pawn sacrifice which hamstrings the White King in No. 36b does not exist here. Thus in No. 38 White to play wins by *1 P—Kt3*, for if *1 .... K—B4; 2 K—Q3* and if *1 .... K—Q5; 2 P—B3*, while with Black to play *1 .... K—B5* (if 1 .... K—Q5; 2 P—B4! wins); *2 K—Q3, P—Kt6; 3 P—B3, K—B4; 4 K—K3, K—K4; 5 P—*

No. 38

White wins; draw if Black's Pawn is at B5.

No. 39

White wins.

B4ch, etc., decides. With the Pawns further advanced the winning idea is exactly the same.

Where one or both sides have RP's, the results form exceptions to the general rule. When there are two RP's, White can only win if his King is advantageously placed, and if he has an adequate reservoir of Pawn moves.

The win in No. 39 is highly instructive: *1 K—Kt4, K—Kt3; 2 P—Kt3,* and now:

a) *2 .... P—R3; 3 P—R3!.*

1. *3 .... K—B3; 4 K—B4, K—Kt3; 5 K—Q5, K—Kt4; 6 K—Q6, K—Kt3; 7 P—R4* (7 K—Q7 is also good, but not 7 P—Kt4??, P—R4=), *K—R4* (or 7 .... P—R4; 8 K—Q5 followed by capture of the RP, or 8 .... K—Kt2; 9 P—R5 and again the RP is lost); *8 K—B6, K—Kt5; 9 K—Kt6, K×P; 10 P—R5!* and the White Pawn will queen.

2. *3 .... P—R4ch; 4 K—B4, K—B3; 5 P—R4, K—Kt3; 6 K—Q5, K—Kt2; 7 K—B5, K—R3; 8 K—B6, K—R2; 9 K—Kt5.*

b) *2 .... K—R3; 3 K—B5,*

1. *3 .... K—R4; 4 P—R4!, K—R3* (or 4 .... P—R3; 5 K—B6, as in a)1.); *5 K—B6, K—R4; 6 K—Kt7, P—R3; 7 K—R7.*

2. *3 .... K—Kt2; 4 K—Kt5, K—R1!; 5 K—R6, K—Kt1; 6 P—Kt4, K—R1; 7 P—Kt5, K—Kt1; 8 P—R3!* (P—R4 draws: White must play his Pawn to Kt6 only when Black's King is at R1), *K—R1; 9 P—R4, K—Kt1; 10 P—R5, K—R1; 11 P—Kt6, P×P; 12 P×P, K—Kt1; 13 P—Kt7* and Black's King must abandon the queening square.

Why the White King must be sufficiently advanced may be seen from three examples. No. 39a, White: K at KB2, P's at KKt2, KR2; Black: K at KB5, P at KR5. This is a draw, for on 1 P—R3, K—K5; 2 P—Kt3 (using the winning manoeuvre of No. 38), P×Pch; 3 K×P, K—B4, while 1 K—K2, K—K5 likewise leads to nothing. Similarly, in No. 39b, White: K at KB2, P's at KKt2, KR2; Black: K at KB4, P at KR2, Black to move plays 1 .... K—B5!; 2 P—R3, P—R3!; 3 P—Kt3ch, K—B4; 4 K—B3, P—R4!, transposing to No. 39a, while if White is to move, 1 K—B3, P—R4!; 2 P—R3, K—K4; 3 P—Kt3, K—B4 (again we have No. 39a) or 1 K—Kt3, K—Kt4; 2 P—R3, P—R3; 3 K—B3, K—B4; 4 P—Kt4ch, K—Kt4; 5 K—Kt3, K—B3; 6 P—R4, K—K4; 7 K—B3, K—B3!; 8 K—B4, K—K3! and White can only win by foul means, for fair ones fail. On the other hand, in No. 39c, White: K at K5, P's at KKt2, KR2; Black: K at KKt4, P at KR2, the win is quite simple: 1 K—K6, K—Kt3; 2 P—R3, P—R3 (or 2 .... K—Kt4; 3 P—Kt3); 3 P—Kt3 and we are back to No. 39, a) 1.

Now we can also see why it is so essential for White to have a number of Pawn tempi at his disposal. In the crucial position with White's

King at R6 and Black's King at Kt1 (or R1) the win is possible only if at the critical stage (No. 40) it is Black's turn to move. This explains why Nos. 40a, White K at KKt5, P's at KKt4, KR4; Black: K at KKt2, P—KR2 is a draw, for after 1 .... K—R1!; 2 K—R6, K—Kt1 there is no way in which White can gain a tempo, while the straightforward Pawn advance leads to No. 40 with Black to move. Similarly, in No. 40b, White: K at KB5, P's at KKt5, KR5; Black: K at KKt2, P at KR2, the game is a draw because any Pawn move results in an ending already established as drawn (1 P—R6ch, K—R1 is No. 33a, 1 P—Kt6, P—R3 is No. 30).

No. 40	No. 41

White to move draws; Black to move loses.   White wins.

To sum up, in positions of type No. 39, White can win only if his King can reach R6 and he can secure No. 40 with Black to play.

With KtP vs. RP and KtP, the ending is almost always lost for Black. In the general case, No. 41, on *1 .... K—B5; 2 K—K2, K—K5; 3 P—Kt3, P—Kt4; 4 P—R3, K—B4; 5 K—Q3!* White has the opposition. (5 .... K—K4; 6 K—K3, K—B4; 7 K—Q4!); while after *1 .... P—Kt4; 2 K—Kt3, K—B3; 3 K—Kt4, K—Kt3; 4 P—R3,* again the opposition is decisive.

If Black does not move his Pawn at all, we get to No. 41a, White: K at KKt5, P's at KKt4, KR4; Black: K at KB2, P at KKt2, when 1 K—B5, P—Kt3ch (or 1 .... K—B1; 2 K—Kt6, K—Kt1; 3 P—R5); 2 K—K5!, K—K2; 3 P—Kt5! (No. 34) decides.

However, even here White must be careful not to exhaust his Pawn moves too early. In No. 41b, White: K at KB5, P's at KKt5, KR5; Black: K at KB2, P at KKt2 Black to play draws by 1 .... P—Kt3ch!; while White to play can at best chase Black's King into the corner, where the Nubian monarch can safely go to sleep: 1 K—K5,

K—K2; 2 K—B5, K—B2; 3 P—Kt6ch, K—Kt1; 4 K—K6, K—R1, etc. (No. 33b). With his Pawns on the fifth rank, White can only win in No. 41c, White: K at KB5, P's at KKt5, KR5; Black: K at KR2, P at KKt2. Now if 1 .... P—Kt3ch; 2 K—B6!, P×P; 3 K—B7!, while if 1 .... K—Kt1 (or 1 .... K—R1; 2 K—K6, K—Kt1; 3 K— K7); 2 K—K6, K—R2; 3 K—B7, K—R1; 4 K—B8!! (but not 4 P— R6, K—R2!!!, drawing), K—R2; 5 P—Kt6ch, K—R1 (or 5 .... K— R3; 6 K—Kt8); 7 P—R6 and mates in two.

Ordinarily, if the Black King is far away from his Pawn, White can simply advance his Pawns and queen. An exception which presents

No. 42 **No. 43**

White wins. White wins.

some difficulty is seen in No. 42 (Rabinovitch). If it were Black's turn to move, he would either have to abandon the pressure on White's BP (.... K—R4), when K—B6 decides, or desert the KtP, when P— B5 forces a Queen. Consequently, White to play must manoeuvre to lose a move. This can easily be done for if Black goes to the sixth rank, P—B5 queens White's Pawn.

Thus White can win by *1 K—K4, K—R5* (if 1 .... K—R4; 2 K— B5); *2 K—Q5!!, K—R4* (2 .... K—Kt5; 3 K—K5); *3 K—Q6!, K— Kt3* (3 .... K—R5; 4 K—K7); *4 K—K7, K—Kt2; 5 P—B5, K—Kt1; 6 P—B6.*

We come now to endings where White's Pawns are neither connected nor passed. Again, if his King is in a favorable position, and if he has an adequate number of Pawn tempi, White can win. The idea is as usual either the capture or the advantageous exchange of Black's Pawn. No. 43: *1 P—K4!, K—K3; 2 P—K5!, K—K2* (2 .... P—Q3; 3 P×P, K×P; 4 K—B4, K—B3; 5 P—B3 and White has the opposition); *3 K—Q5, K—K1; 4 K—Q6, K—Q1; 5 P—B4, K—B1* (or 5 ....

K—K1; 6 P—K6!); *6 K—K7, K—B2; 7 P—B5, K—B1* (or 7 ....
K—B3; 8 K—Q8); *8 P—B6!, P×P; 9 P—K6, P—B4; 10 K—B8.
P—B5; 11 P—K7, P—B6; 12 P—K8= Qch.* To try to win by out-
flanking the Black King would allow a curious draw: 1 P—K4, K—B3;
2 K—K5, K—B4; 3 K—B6?, K—Q5; 4 P—K5, K—Q4!; 5 P—B3,
K—K5!! (not 5 .... K—B5; 6 K—K7, K—Q4; 7 K×P, K×P; 8 K—
B6! and wins); 6 P—B4, K—Q5; 7 K—K7, K×KP!=.

In general, White can win such endings only if he can attack Black's
Pawn from the side (i.e., P at Q2, White K at K7 or B7). This in turn
is possible only if he can occupy the square in front of the Black Pawn,
White to play, with at least one tempo to spare. Thus, if his Pawn
moves are exhausted, or if his King is disadvantageously placed, the
draw is inevitable. In No. 43a, White: K at Q3, P's at QB3, K3;
Black: K at QB3, P at Q3 Black to move draws by 1 .... K—Q4!
for if 2 P—B4ch, K—B4; 3 P—K4 (3 K—B3, P—Q4), K—Kt3!; 4
K—Q4, K—B3 and White can get no nearer. However, White to
move wins by 1 K—Q4!, K—B2 (1 .... P—Q4; 2 P—B4, P×P; 3
K×P. See No. 11); 2 K—Q5, K—Q2; 3 P—B4, K—K2; 4 K—B6,
K—K3; 5 K—B7, K—K2; 6 P—K4! (if this tempo were not available,
the game would be drawn, e.g., K—Kt6, K—B3! or K—B8, K—K1
or K—Kt7, K—B2. Black can always hold the distant opposition on
the rank), K—K3; 7 K—Q8, K—K4; 8 K—Q7. Or No. 43b, White:
K at Q2, P's at QB2, K2; Black: K at QB4, P at Q2, Black to move
draws by 1 .... K—Q5; while White to move wins by 1 K—B3!, with
variations similar to those in No. 43, i.e., 1 .... K—Q4; 2 K—Q3,
K—B4; 3 P—K4!, P—Q4 (3 .... K—B3; 4 K—Q4, K—Q3; 5 P—
K5ch, is No. 43); 4 P—K5, or 3 .... P—Q3; 4 K—B3, P—Q4 (4 ....
K—B3; 5 K—Q4 is the same as No. 43a; White has two tempi with
his BP); 5 P×P, K×P; 6 K—Kt4.

A curious special case which resembles the variation in the note to
White's 6th move in No. 43a, is No. 43c: White: K at KKt2, P at
KB3; Black: K at Q8, P's at K4, KKt4. Black to play wins by 1 ....
K—K7, but White to play can hold the draw by 1 K—R1!!, K—K7;
2 K—Kt2, or 1 .... K—K8; 2 K—Kt1, or 1 .... K—Q7; 2 K—R2,
or finally 1 .... K—B7; 2 K—Kt2! (the only move—2 K—R2, K—
Q7!! and 2 K—Kt1, K—B8!! both lose), K—B6; 3 K—Kt3, and White
can always keep the distant opposition.

As is to be expected, when White has a RP this type of ending is
drawn. The most favorable position which White can possibly force
is No. 43d, White: K at QKt6, P's at QR5, QB5; Black: K at QKt1,
P at QKt2, Black to play. Then 1 .... K—B1! (but not 1 .... K—
R1?; 2 K—B7, K—R2; 3 K—B8, K—R1; 4 P—R6! as in No. 43); 2
K—R7, K—B2; and to carry out the winning manoeuvre of No. 43

White must either move his King to the zero file or suspend it in mid-air.

Finally, we come to the case where White has a doubled Pawn. Where all the Pawns are on the same file, in the model example No. 44, White wins both with and without the move: A. *1 .... K—B3; 2 K—K5, K—B4; 3 P—Q4ch, K—B5* (3 .... K—B3; 4 P—Q3); *4 P—Q5, K—B4; 5 P—Q3* followed by *K—Q6.* B. *1 K—B4, K—B3; 2 P—Q4, K—Q3* (or 2 .... P—Q3; 3 P—Q5ch, K—Kt3; 4 K—Q4, K—Kt4; 5 P—Q3!, K—Kt5; 6 K—K3!!, K—B4; 7 K—K4, K—Kt3;

No. 44　　　　　　　　　No. 45

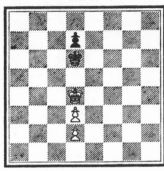

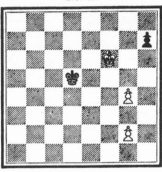

White wins.　　　　　　　　Draw.

8 K—B5, K—Kt4; 9 K—K6, K—B4; 10 P—Q4ch); *3 P—Q5, K—K4* (if 3 .... K—B2; 4 K—B5, P—Q3ch; 5 K—Kt5, K—Kt2; 6 P—Q3); *4 K—B5, K—K5; 5 P—Q6, K—K4; 6 P—Q3!, K—K3; 7 P—Q4, K any; 8 K—Kt6, K—K3; 9 K—B7.*

It is clear that a win is possible only if White can force the position in variation B above after his 7th move, with Black to play, or the corresponding position at some other point on the file. This gives us as the crucial test, whether in No. 44a, White: K at K5, P's at Q6, Q4; Black: K at QB3, P at Q2, White or Black is to move. However, it should be noticed that when all the Pawns are on the Kt file, the lack of elbow room for Black's King makes the draw inevitable. Applying the test gives a simple solution to almost all such endings with doubled Pawns. In No. 44b, White: K at Q3, P's at Q4, Q5; Black: K at Q1, P at Q2, 1 P—Q6! leads after 1 .... K—B1; 2 K—K4, K—Kt2; 3 K—B5!, K—B3 (or 3 .... K—Kt3; 4 K—B6); 4 K—K5, to No. 44a. In No. 44c, (Grigorieff, 1935), White: K at KB4, P's at KB3, KB6; Black: K at Q4, P at KB2. Black to play would draw by 1 .... K—

K3; 2 K—Kt5, K—K4!; 3 P—B4ch, K—K3 (again No. 44a, this time White to move). However, White to play can win by an elegant manoeuvre: 1 K—B5 (not 1 K—Kt5, K—K4!), K—Q3; 2 P—B4, K—Q2; 3 K—Kt4!, K—K1; 4 K—R5, K—B1; 5 K—Kt5!! (now Black is forced to pick one side, when White goes to the other), K—Kt1; 6 K—B5, K—R2; 7 K—K4!, K—R3; 8 K—Q5, K—Kt3; 9 K—K5, etc.

Where the White and Black Pawns are on adjoining files a new type of threat arises. The possibilities of this kind of ending are illustrated in No. 45 (Flohr-Ragosin, Moscow, 1935). Strange though it may seem, the fact that there is a RP makes no difference whatsoever; the above analysis holds no matter what files the Pawns are on. Black to play moves *1 .... K—K5!; 2 K—Kt5, K—K6!!; 3 K—R6, K—B5!!; 4 P—Kt5, K—B4!!* (4 .... K—Kt5; 5 P—Kt3!, K—B4; 6 K—R5, see No. 45a); *5 P—Kt3, K—Kt5* or *5 K—R5, K—B5,* with an easy draw in either event. The traps that are to be avoided are illustrated in two variants. In No. 45a, White: K at KR5, P's at KKt5, KKt3; Black: K at KB4, P at KR2, White to play can only draw: 1 K—R4, K—K5! (but not 1 .... K—Kt3??; 2 K—Kt4, K—B2; 3 K—R5, K—Kt2; 4 P—Kt4 as in No. 45b); 2 K—Kt4, K—K4; 3 K—R5, K—B4. If, however, Black must move, his King must go away, when P—Kt6 wins. No. 45b shows why a chess player should be aggressive, even when the game is in its last throes. White: K at KKt5, P's at KKt4, KKt3; Black: K at KKt2, P at KR2. 1 K—R5, K—Kt1 (or 1 .... P—R3; 2 P—Kt5, see No. 11); 2 K—R6, K—R1; 3 P—Kt5, K—Kt1; 4 P—Kt6, K—R1!; 5 P—Kt7ch!, K—Kt1; 6 P—Kt4—the extra tempo has carried the day.

This concludes our consideration of endings with two Pawns against one. Disregarding for the moment the many special cases, we may sum up our discussion by saying that *the side who is a Pawn ahead always wins unless the Pawn position is blocked, or almost blocked, and he does not have the opposition.* Exceptions to this rule occur most often when there are RP's, occasionally with KtP's, and almost never with B or center Pawns.

V. KING AND TWO PAWNS VS. KING AND TWO PAWNS

Other things being equal, this ending is a draw. But the phrase "other things" covers a multitude of chess sins, so that it is worth our while to subject this type of position to a more careful analysis, especially since the ideas and possibilities which these finales exhibit are typical of all King and Pawn endings with even Pawns. Thus the conclusions may be readily extended to more general cases.

As above, we can classify the possible endings according to the number and kind of passed Pawns. It should be remembered that doubled Pawns are in effect no better than a single Pawn.

CASE 1. WHITE HAS TWO CONNECTED PASSED PAWNS

A. Black also has two connected passed Pawns. The idea of such an ending is the same as that of a horse race—whoever gets there first wins. Normally, however, both Kings can stop the advance of the opposing Pawns, which then cannot advance without further support. Thus, in No. 46, neither side can make any progress. Both play K—R4 and K—Kt3 and draw either by agreement or by exhaustion. Trivial though it may appear, the salient fact which this example illustrates is fundamental: *Two connected passed Pawns, unsupported by their King, can make no headway against the opposing King.*

No. 46

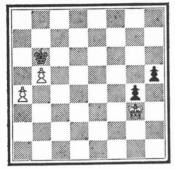

Draw.

No. 47

White to play queens after at most three Black Pawn moves, or mates after at most four Black Pawn moves.

It follows that such endings can be won only when White can bring his King up and force a Queen ahead of his opponent.

To carry through such a winning manoeuvre when Black likewise has passed Pawns White must have his Pawns relatively far advanced —at least the fifth rank with Black's Pawns still on the second—and he must be able to get his King near his Pawns without allowing the Black Pawns to get out of bounds.

Consequently, before doing anything else we must determine how long it takes two Pawns with the help of the King to promote. In No. 47, which we may regard as a typical position (if White has a RP, the corresponding position is even worse for Black, since he will be mated right after White queens) *1 P—Q6ch* will force a Queen in at most three moves, Black to play, or four moves, White to play (which of course amounts to the same thing): *1 P—Q6ch, K—Q1* (1 .... K—Q2 and 1 .... K—K1 lead to similar variations, while 1 .... K—B2 and 1 .... K—B1 both shorten Black's agony by two moves); *2 P—K6* (or variation A), *P—R4; 3 K—B6, P—R5; 4 K—B7, P—R6; 5 P—K7ch, K—Q2; 6 P—K8 = Qch.*

Variation A: *2 K—K6, P—R4; 3 P—Q7, P—R5; 4 K—Q6, P—R6; 5 P—K6, P—R7; 6 P—K7* mate.

As a result of the above analysis, we can see that if White's Pawns and King are all on the fourth rank, it will take him at least six moves to queen, if on the third nine moves. Since an unimpeded Pawn can promote in five moves we may conclude that in general White cannot win if his Pawns are not beyond the fourth rank, but that he can win if his King is well placed, if his Pawns are on the fifth rank and if Black cannot queen in less than four moves.

With these points in mind it is a relatively easy matter to determine when it is feasible to abandon the square of an opponent's Pawn and when not. In addition, two simple rules will be found useful in this and similar endings: 1. Always advance your Pawns as far as possible; 2. Always try to block your opponent's Pawns.

In No. 47a (Behting, 1900). White: K at KB4, P's at K7, KB6; Black: K at KB2, P's at QB2, Q5 we see how effective advanced Pawns are. White to move wins by 1 K—B3! (to lose a tempo; the point will be obvious in a moment), K—K1 (or 1 .... P—B3; 2 K—B4!!), 3 K—K4, P—B4; 4 K—Q5!! (threatening mate in two beginning with K6; we see now why White had to lose a tempo and force the Black King back to K square), K—Q2; 5 K—B4, K—K1; 6 K×P!!!, P—Q6; 7 K—Q6 (again intending K—K6), K—B2; 8 K—Q7 and Black is one move too late.

In No. 47b (Horwitz, 1879), White: K at KB3, P's at Q4, K5; Black: K at KKt4, P's at KB4, KKt3 shows why blockaded Pawns are such a serious handicap: 1 .... K—R3 (if 1 .... P—B5; 2 P—Q5, K—B4; 3 P—Q6 and wins the BP); 2 K—B4!, K—Kt2; 3 P—Q5, K—B2; 4 K—Kt5, K—K2; 5 P—K6 (White has made two Pawn moves, Black none), K—K1 (or 5 .... K—Q3; 6 K—B6!); 6 P—Q6, K—B1; 7 K—B6 and concludes quickly.

B. When Black has two disconnected passed Pawns the result depends on the relative positions of the Pawns and Kings. We have seen (No. 18) that if two Pawns are one file apart, they can defend one another, if they are two files apart they are usually lost unless they are on the fifth or sixth ranks, while if three files apart one cannot be prevented from queening. These considerations determine the outcome of the endings now under discussion: if the White King can merely hold the Pawns (one file apart) the game is a draw; if he can capture one (two files apart, on third or fourth ranks) he wins; if he cannot catch up with them (three or four files apart) he loses. In addition, one must remember that it is sometimes possible to let the enemy Pawn run away and come to the aid of one's own. We can record a number of model positions: No. 47c, White: K at Q4, P's at KKt4, KR3; Black: K at KKt4, P's at QKt4, Q3. Draw. White moves K—Q4— Q5, Black K—R5—Kt4. If the Pawn position is more favorable, as in No. 47d, White: K at QB4, P's at KB6, KKt6; Black: K at KB1, P's at QKt3, Q3, White can win by 1 K—Q5, P—Kt4; 2 K—K6!, P— Kt5; 3 P—Kt7ch (or 3 P—B7), K—Kt1; 4 K—K7, P—Kt6; 5 P— B7ch. In No. 47e, White: K at KB4, P's at K4, Q4; Black: K at K2, P's at QKt5, KR5 the Black Pawns are too well placed, so that White must lose. Conversely, in No. 47f, White: K at KB3, P's at QKt5, QB6; Black: K at QB2, P's at Q3, KR3, White to play wins by 1 K—

No. 48   No. 49

White wins.   White wins.

B4!, K—Kt3 (if either Pawn moves it will be captured); 2 K—B5!, K—B2; 3 K—B6!!, K—Kt3; 4 K—K6, K—B2; 5 K—Q5, P—R4; 6 P—Kt6ch, K×KtP; 7 K×P, P—R5; 8 P—B7.

CASE 2. WHITE HAS ONE PASSED PAWN

If Black also has a passed Pawn the outcome will depend on which Pawn is farthest from the other set of Pawns. In other words, whoever has the outside passed Pawn wins. Thus in No. 48 the White RP advances until the Black King is forced to desert his QBP, and then both Black Pawns are captured. *1 P—R5, K—B3; 2 P—R6, K—Kt3; 3 P— R7, K×P; 4 K×P, K—Kt2; 5 K—Q6, K—B1; 6 K—K6, K—Q1, 7 K×P, K—K2; 8 K—Kt6* etc. As in the case of K+2P vs. K+P, if there is a set of RP's Black's drawing chances are considerably enhanced.

However, the outside passed Pawn is an advantage only when the other Pawns may be captured. Thus in No. 49 Black loses because

White has a *protected passed Pawn,* which the Black King must watch. Consequently White can capture the Black KtP at his leisure and then win on the other side (No. 27). If the Pawn were nearer home here, e.g., at Q4 Black could draw without any trouble, since he can defend his Pawn and stay in the square of White's KtP at the same time. An exception to this rule occurs when either the White or Black Pawns are too far advanced. E.g., in No. 48a, White: K at KKt4, P's at KB5, KKt6; Black: K at KB1, P's at KB3, KR3 White can afford to abandon the square of the RP by a very ingenious stratagem: 1 K—B4, K—K1 (if the RP ever moves while the White King can still catch it it will be lost); 2 K—K4, K—K2; 3 K—Q5, K—B1; 4 K—Q6!, K—

No. 50

No. 51

White wins. Draw No. 50a with Black Pawns at QKt3, QB3.

White to play wins; Black to play draws.

Kt1; 5 K—K7!!, P—R4 (or 5 .... K—Kt2; 6 K—K6!); 6 K×P, P—R5; 7 P—Kt7, P—R6; 8 K—Kt6 and mates in two.

Where Black does not have a passed Pawn, he loses if his two Pawns are blocked by White's one but draws if they are not. In No. 50 *1 P—R5, K—Kt4; 2 K—K4* followed by the capture of both Black's Pawns decides quickly, but if the Black Pawns were at QKt3 and QB3 (No. 50a) the result would be a draw, since on 1 P—R5, K—Kt4; 2 K—K4, K×P; 3 K—K5, K—Kt5; 4 K—Q6, P—B4! forces the exchange of the last Pawn.

We can draw two important conclusions from the above: 1. an outside passed Pawn wins when the opponent's Pawns are capturable;

2. a protected passed Pawn almost always wins.

In general, subject to inevitable problem exceptions, these **rules hold** for all King and Pawn endings.

CASE 3. NEITHER SIDE HAS A PASSED PAWN

Here there are only two winning possibilities, either a sacrifice to force a passed Pawn, or an advantageous King position. The first is seen in No. 51. White to play forces a passed KtP by *1 P—Q5;* Black to play can prevent this by *1 .... P—Q4* which draws.

The second possibility (advantageous King position) is far more important. This advantage can be of two kinds: either the White King is nearer the Pawns, or White has the opposition. If there is a great deal of difference in the relative positions of the two Kings, e.g., if the White King in No. 51 were at K6, then White would simply capture all Black's Pawns. The ending presents special interest only if the

No. 52   **No. 53**

White wins.   White to play wins; Black to play draws.

Kings are close to one other. Where feasible, the winning method is reduction to a more simple ending, either by capturing a Pawn, or by securing a passed Pawn which is way ahead of its rival. In No. 52 we have one of the more difficult cases: *1 K×P, K—B4; 2 K—R6, K—B3* and now *3 P—R5!* forces Black to either allow the White King to escape to the other side, or permit the Pawn to queen. No. 52a (from a game Von Der Lasa-Mayet, two of the celebrated "Seven Pleiades") presents another type of problem. White: K at KKt3, P's at QKt4, Q4; Black: K at KKt8, P's at QB2, QKt3. Here when White captures a Pawn, Black will also capture one, so that the question becomes one of leading to a won ending with K+P vs. K+P. With this in view White proceeds as follows: 1 .... K—B8 (White to move wins by either 1 P—Q5 or 1 K—B3, but not 1 P—Kt5); 2 K—B3, K—K8; 3 K—K3, K—Q8; 4 K—Q3, K—K8; 5 K—B4, K—Q7; 6 K—Kt5, K—B6; 7 P—Q5, K—Q5; 8 K—B6, P—Kt4; 9 K×BP!, K×P; 10 K—Kt6, K—B5; 11 K—R5. It is an interesting commentary on the state of chess a century ago that this game, conducted by two of the foremost experts of the time, was drawn.

We come now to the most difficult case of all, that where both Kings are near the Pawns, but White has no greater superiority than the opposition or a slightly more favorable position.

In No. 53 we have an example of the effectiveness of the opposition. White plays *1 K—K4* and poor Black is on the horns of a dilemma. If he tries *1 .... P—Q4ch*, then *2 K—B4, K—K2* (or *2 .... P—B4; 3 P—Q4, K—B3; 4 P—B3!*); *3 K—B5, K—B2; 4 P—Q4, K—K2; 5 K—Kt6, K—K3; 6 P—B4, K—K2; 7 P—B5* costs him the BP. And if he adopts a do-nothing attitude with *1 .... K—K2*, then *2 K—B5, K—B2; 3 P—Q4, K—K2; 4 P—Q5, K—B2; 5 P—B3, K—K2; 6 K—Kt6* again offers him no consolation. Note here that if the White Pawn were at KB3 instead of KB2, the opposition would do him no good.

A few more illustrations will show the proper method of exploiting the opposition under different circumstances. No. 53a, White: K at KB2, P's at K2, KKt4; Black: K at KB2, P's at K2, KKt4. 1 K—K3, K—B3; 2 K—Q4, K—K3; 3 K—K4, K—B3; 4 K—Q5, P—K3ch (or 4 .... K—B2; 5 K—K5); 5 K—Q6, K—B2; 6 P—K4, K—B3; 7 P—K5ch, K—B2; 8 K—Q7 wins the KP. A fairly common case is No. 53b, White: K at Q4, P's at QKt4, KKt4; Black: K at Q3, P's at QKt4, KKt4. Black to play loses, since he must allow either K—K5 or K—B5, while White to play draws by 1 K—K4 (but not 1 K—Q3??, K—Q4), K—K3; 2 K—Q4, K—Q3! etc. An unusual application of the distant opposition is seen in No. 53c, a problem by Grigorieff. White: K at KB8, P's at QKt4, KR4; Black: K at Q8, P's at QKt4, KR4. It is clear that White can only capture the RP at the expense of his QKtP. He therefore tries to make his opponent dizzy by 1 K—K7!. If now 1 .... K—K7??; 2 K—K6!! White has the distant opposition, so that Black must commit himself first as to which Pawn he will attack and in that event White can go to the same side and win a Pawn first. E.g., if 2 .... K—B6; 3 K—B5, K—Kt6 (3 .... K—K6 would be too late now); 4 K—Kt5. Thus 2 .... K—K8 is best, but then comes 3 K—K5!, K—K7; 4 K—K4!, K—K8; 5 K—K3!! and now Black must speak up like a man and lose a Pawn accordingly. But instead of blundering by 1 .... K—K7?? he can keep the distant opposition for himself by 1 .... K—K8!!; 2 K—K6, K—K7!; 3 K—K5, K—K6!, when White must leap while Black looks, instead of vice versa as above. After 4 K—B5, K—Q5 or 4 K—Q5, K—B5 the draw is routine.

A curious use of the opposition is seen in No. 53d. White: K at KB7, P's at KKt4, KR3; Black: K at KR2, P's at KKt4, KR3. Black to move is forced to try 1 .... P—R4 (for 1 .... K—R1; 2 K—

Kt6 is hopeless), but is bowled over by the surprising rejoinder 2 P—R4!!, P×RP (or 2 .... P×KtP; 3 P×KtP); 3 P—Kt5, P—R6; 4 P—Kt6ch, K—R3; 5 P—Kt7, P—R7; 6 P—Kt8=Q and mates next move. This, however, is only an exception to the more general case No. 53e, White: K at K7, P's at KKt3, KR3; Black: K at KR3, P's at KKt2, KR2, where White can win a Pawn but not the game. After 1 K—B7, P—Kt4; 2 K—B6, P—Kt5!; 3 P—R4 (3 P×P stalemate), K—R4; 4 K—B5, P—R3; 5 K—B4, K—Kt3; 6 K×P, P—R4ch we have our old friend No. 34.

A doubled Pawn for Black is a serious handicap, but it is only fatal if White has an adequate reserve of Pawn moves or has the opposition. Thus in No. 53f, White: K at QB3, P's at QKt2, Q2; Black: K at QKt4, P's at QB3, QB4, White to play wins by 1 P—Kt3, K—R3; 2 K—B4, K—Kt3; 3 P—Q3 (thus two Pawn tempi were necessary), while Black to play draws by 1 .... P—B5! (now there are no Pawn tempi); 2 K—Q4, K—Kt5; 3 K—K5, K—Kt6; 4 K—Q4, etc.

VI. KING AND THREE PAWNS VS. KING AND TWO PAWNS

With any normal and most abnormal Pawn positions it is easier to win with 3 Pawns vs. 2 than with 2 Pawns vs. 1. We may take No. 54 as the general case. It is highly instructive to note that such endings are in general won by reducing them to simpler cases. With Black to move, if a) *1 .... K—B2; 2 P—Kt6ch, K—Kt1* (2 .... P×P; 3 RP×Pch gives us No. 33); *3 K—K6, K—R1; 4 K—B7, P×P; 5 P—R6!, KtP×RP; 6 P×P* (Compare No. 33a). Or b) *1 .... P—Kt3; 2 RP×P, P×P; 3 P—B6ch, K—K1; 4 K—K6*, etc., as in No. 30. Finally, with White to move, *1 P—Kt6, P×P; 2 RP×P* (see a)), or here *1 .... P—R3; 2 K—K4, K—B3; 3 K—B4, K—K2; 4 K—K5, K—K1; 5 K—K6, K—B1; 6 K—Q7, K—Kt1; 7 K—K7, K—R1; 8 P—B6, P×P; 9 K—B7* and mates in two. The advantage of the added material may be seen from the fact that if White's BP and Black's KtP were missing, the ending would be a draw.

Where White has an outside or protected passed Pawn the win is even easier. E.g., No. 54a, White: K at Q5, P's at QR3, QKt4, QB5; Black: K at Q2, P's at QR3, QKt4. 1 P—B6ch, K—B2; 2 K—B5, K—B1; 3 K—Kt6, K—Kt1 and now either 4 K×P, K—B2; 5 K×P, or 4 P—B7ch, K—B1; 5 K—B6!, P—R4; 6 P×P, P—Kt5; 7 P—R6, P—Kt6; 8 P—R7, P—Kt7; 9 P—R8=Q mate.

Black has drawing chances in such endings only in four cases:
1. He can block the Pawn position permanently;
2. He can exchange enough Pawns to force one of the more elementary draws;
3. He has a protected passed Pawn;
4. He can bring about stalemate.

1. is illustrated in No. 55, a position which could have occurred in the game Kmoch-Van Scheltinga, Amsterdam, 1936. White to play would win at once by 1 K—B4. But Black to play can draw by *1 .... K—B4!; 2 K—B3, K—K4!!*. If now 3 P—R5, K—B4 and the Pawn is lost, while if *3 K—Kt4, K—K5!; 4 P—R5, P—B4ch; 5 K—Kt3, K—K6; 6 P—R6, P—B5ch* and both Pawns queen simultaneously.

This blockade of the Pawns must go hand in hand with the superior or at least equal King position. Thus in No. 55a, White: K at QKt2, P's at QKt4, KR2; Black: K at KKt2, P's at QR2, QKt4, KR2 (taken from the second match game Botvinnik-Loewenfisch, 1937), Black scores an easy victory by 1 .... K—B3; 2 K—B3, K—K4; 3 K—Q3, K—Q4. But if it were White's turn to move, he could

<table>
<tr><td align="center">No. 54</td><td align="center">No. 55</td></tr>
<tr><td></td><td>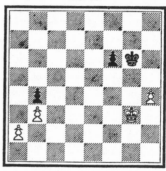</td></tr>
<tr><td align="center">White wins.</td><td align="center">Black to play draws.</td></tr>
</table>

draw by 1 K—B3, when Black can just manage to save the day by going after the RP. With both Kings in the center, and no reserve Pawn moves, e.g., No. 55b, White: K at Q3, P's at QKt4, KR4; Black: K at Q4, P's at QR3, QKt4, KR4, if Black is to move White has the opposition and can draw, despite the extra Black Pawn. E.g., 1 .... K—B3; 2 K—B3, K—Kt3; 3 K—Kt3, P—R4; 4 P×Pch, K×P; 5 K—R3 (No. 23), or 1 .... K—Q3; 2 K—Q2!! and White maintains the distant opposition.

Where the extra Pawns are badly isolated but not passed it is often impossible to rectify this unfortunate placement by exchanges. E.g., No. 55c (Lolli), White: K at KR3, P's at QKt3, Q3, KB3; Black: K at KR4, P's at QB4, K4. Draw. 1 K—Kt3, K—Kt4; 2 K—B2, K—B5 or (Black to play) 1 .... K—Kt4; 2 K—Kt3, K—B4; 3 K—B2, K—B5; 4 K—K2, K—Kt4; 5 K—K3, K—B4; 6 K—Q2, K—B5; 7 K—B3, K×P; 8 K—B4, K—K6=.

No. 56 illustrates the second kind of drawing chance. After *1 ....
K—B6!* (but not 1 .... P—B5—see variation A); *2 K—Kt1* (or 2
K—K1, P—B5; 3 P×P, K×P; 4 K—K2, K—Kt5; 5 K—K3, K×P;
6 K—B4, K—R6 and draws), *P—B5* White can either lose a Pawn by
3 P×P, K×P; 4 K any, K—Kt5 or reduce to a well-known draw by
3 K—R2, P×Pch; 4 P×P, K—Kt5. Variation A: 1 .... P—B5;
2 K—Kt2, P—B6ch (or 2 .... P×P; 3 K×P!, K—K4; 4 P—B3,
K—B4; 5 K—Kt2, K—K4; 6 K—B1!, K—B4; 7 K—K2, K—B5;
8 K—B2, K—K4; 9 K—K3, K—B4; 10 P—B4, K—Kt5; 11 K—K4,
K×RP; 12 K—B3!, K—R6; 13 P—B5, P—R5; 14 P—B6, K—R7;
15 P—B7, P—R6; 16 K—B2! and mates in three); 3 K—R3!, K—B4;
4 P—Kt4ch!!, P×Pch; 5 K—Kt3, etc. A simpler but more common

No. 56	No. 57

Black to play draws.	Draw. Win No. 57a with Black's protected passed Pawn on the QB file.

case is No. 56a (Walker, 1841), White: K at QB1, P's at KB3, KKt3,
KR3; Black: K at KB4, P's at KKt4, KR4. Black to play draws.
1 .... P—R5!; 2 P×P, P×P; 3 K—Q2, K—B5; 4 K—K2, K—Kt6!;
5 K—K3, K×RP; 6 K—B2!, K—R7; 7 P—B4, P—R6; 8 P—B5,
K—R8; 9 P—B6, P—R7; 10 P—B7 stalemate.

No. 57 is an example of the third type of drawing possibility.
Here the two passed Pawns do White no good: he cannot afford to
leave the square of the Black KtP. Only if Black's protected passed
Pawn were on the QB file or further east could White do better than
draw. In that case, e.g., No. 57a, White: K at QB3, P's at QKt4,
KKt3, KR2; Black: K at KR6, P's at QKt4, QB5, White can by skillful manoeuvring force one Pawn to the sixth, and can then afford to
leave the square because he will mate shortly after queening: 1 K—
Q4, K—Kt5; 2 P—R4, K—R4; 3 K—K3, K—Kt5; 4 K—K4, K—R4;

5 K—B4! (still in the square), K—Kt3; 6 P—Kt4, K—Kt2; 7 P—R5!, K—R3; 8 K—K4!, K—Kt4; 9 K—B3 (triangulation), K—R3; 10 K—B4, K—Kt2; 11 P—Kt5, K—B2; 12 P—Kt6ch, K—Kt2 and now 13 K—Kt5, P—B6; 14 P—R6ch, K—Kt1 (or 14 .... K—B1; 15 K—B6, P—B7; 16 P—R7); 15 K—B6, P—B7; 16 P—R7ch, K—R1; 17 K—B7 and mates in a few. The crucial question in all such positions is what will happen if White leaves the square of Black's protected passed Pawn. It is worth noting that No. 57a is a win only because of the mating threats, which in general are not available if one of the passed Pawns is not on the Rook file. E.g., No. 57b, White: K at QKt3, P's at QR4, KB3, KKt4; Black: K at KB5, P's at QR4, QKt5, is drawn.

In general, the mobility of the Pawns is more important than their number. Two connected passed Pawns are more valuable than "sextuplets," six Pawns on one file. This is why White in a blocked position can win only if he can get his Pawns moving, which usually can happen only if he has the opposition.

When White's plus Pawn is doubled, he can win only if he can reduce to a won ending with 2 P's vs. 1 P by an appropriate exchange, or if he has the opposition. In No. 58 White to play wins because the exchange by *1 P—Q5ch* is favorable for him: *1 ....* P×P (Or 1 .... K—Q2; 2 P×Pch, K×P; 3 K—Q4, see No. 45a); *2 P×Pch, K—B3* (or 2 .... K—K2; 3 K—B5, K—B2; 4 P—B4, No. 34); *3 K—Q4!* (now Black must hurry back to the Queen's file, for 3 .... K—B4; 4 P—B4, K—B3; 5 P—B5 is immediately decisive), *K—K2; 4 K—B4, K—Q2; 5 K—Kt5, K—B2; 6 K—R6* and will soon win the QP.

On the other hand Black to play can force a draw by *1 .... P— Q4ch, 2 P×Pch* (or A), *P×Pch; 3 K—B4, K—B3* because he has the opposition.

A. *2 K—Q3, K—Q3* (not 2 .... P×Pch; 3 K×P, K—Q3; 4 K— Q3!!, K—Q4—if 4 .... P—B4; 5 K—B4!!! wins—; 5 P—B4ch and we have No. 37); *3 P—B5ch, K—K3; 4 K—K3, K—K2!; 5 K—B4, K—B3; 6 K—Kt4, K—Kt3; 7 K—R4, K—R3*. White can make no headway here because the exchange of his BP for Black's QP results in a draw (see No. 34).

Three connected passed Pawns can be stopped by a lone King, but he then has no tempo, so that if he is forced to move the Pawns advance. This is why three such Pawns, even though unsupported by the King, win against two. In No. 59, after *1 P—R4, P—R4; 2 P— Kt4, P—Kt4; 3 P—B4, P—R5; 4 K—R3* (now the Black King must move), *K—Kt3; 5 P—R5ch, K—R3; 6 P—B5, K—Kt4; 7 K—Kt4* (the key move), *K—R3; 8 P—B6, K—R2; 9 P—Kt5, K—Kt1; 10 P— Kt6* and queens shortly, for with two Pawns on the seventh he can sacrifice one and promote the other. An exception to this general rule is seen in No. 59a, White: K at KKt3, P's at QR6, QB6; Black: K at QKt1, P's at KB2, KKt5, KR4. Here Black loses because he cannot afford to move his King. 1 K—B4, P—B3; 2 K—Kt3, P—B4; 3 K—Kt2, P—R5; 4 K—R2, P—B5; 5 K—Kt1!!, P—B6; 6 K—B2, P—R6; 7 K—Kt3 and Black has fought nobly but in vain.

Similarly three connected passed Pawns, of which two are doubled, win against two in general. E.g., No. 59b, White: K at QB3, P's at KKt5, KR4, KKt3; Black: K at KKt3, P's at QKt4, QB5. White wins. 1 .... K—B4; 2 K—Q4, K—Kt3; 3 P—Kt4, K—Kt2; 4 P—R5, K—R2; 5 P—Kt6ch, K—R3; 6 K—B3!, K—Kt2; 7 P—Kt5, K—Kt1; 8 P—R6, K—R1; 9 P—Kt7ch, K—R2; 10 P—Kt6ch, K—Kt1; 11 K—Q4!, P—B6; 12 P—R7ch!!, K×KtP; 13 K×P

No. 58

White to play wins; Black to play draws.

No. 59

White wins.

followed by capturing the KtP, when the two passed Pawns decide.

Stalemate occurs chiefly in problems, but on rare occasions comes up in practice. Two examples: No. 59c (Rinck, 1912), White: K at KB2, P's at K2, KR4; Black: K at KR8, P's at Q3, KKt5, KR2. White to play draws. 1 K—Kt3!, P—R4; 2 P—K4!, K—Kt8; 3 P—K5!!, P×P stalemate. (If 3 .... P—Q4; 4 P—K6 and White wins.) No. 59d (Troitsky, 1923) White: K at QR3, P's at QB4, KB5; Black: K at KR1, P's at QB3, Q2, KKt2. White to play draws. 1 K—Kt4, K—Kt1 (or 1 .... P—Q3; 2 K—R5, P—Q4; 3 P×P, P×P; 4 K—Kt5, K—R2; 5 K—B5, K—R3; 6 K×P, K—Kt4; 7 K—K5=); 2 K—B5, K—B2; 3 K—Q6, K—K1; 4 P—B5!, K—Q1; 5 P—B6!!, P×P stalemate (but not 5 .... P—Kt4??; 6 P—B7 and wins).

VII. KING AND THREE PAWNS VS. KING AND THREE PAWNS

No. 60

White wins.

As mentioned above, endings with even Pawns are drawn unless one side has a clear positional advantage. In the case of 2 P's vs. 2 P's it was feasible to enumerate exhaustively all the possible combinations in which such superiorities occur. Here, however, such a classification would lead to an enormously complicated table of little practical value. It is more instructive to group the various types of positional advantage under seven headings:

1. White can force a passed Pawn and queen it;
2. White has an outside passed Pawn;
3. White has a protected passed Pawn;
4. White has a qualitative Pawn superiority;
5. White's passed Pawn or set of passed Pawns is qualitatively superior;
6. White's King is nearer the Pawns;
7. White has the opposition.

1. WHITE CAN QUEEN BY FORCE

There are of course many positions where the Black King simply is not near enough to stop the passed Pawn. But what we are chiefly interested in here is the more complicated case where there is as yet no passed Pawn. The type of position which most frequently occurs in practice is seen in Nos. 60 and 61. In No. 60 White to move queens by *1 P—B6, P×P; 2 P—Kt6!, P×P; 3 P×P.* If Black begins, then White can still win: *1 .... K—K3; 2 P—B6, P×P* (or A); *3 P—Kt6, P×P; 4 P—R6!!* and Black cannot get back in time.

A.: 2 .... K—Q3; 3 P×P, K—B2; 4 P—R6, K—Kt1. Now the win consists of three steps:

1. Winning the Black KRP;
2. Playing the K to Q5 and then sacrificing the P at Kt5 by P—Kt6;
3. Queening the White QKtP (if necessary capturing the Black QKtP first) as in K+2 P's vs. K.

It would not have helped Black to have played his P to QR3; P—B6 would still decide. He can only avoid the break by playing .... P—QKt3 earlier, blocking White's Pawns.

Another eventuality which sometimes comes up is seen in No. 61. The solution is *1 P—Kt6!!, BP×P; 2 P—R6!!!, KtP×P; 3 P—B6.* (Or 1 .... RP×P; 2 P—B6!, P(Kt2)×P; 3 P—R6). Black to move can prevent the break by *1 .... P—Kt3,* but both 1 .... P—R3; 2 P—B6! and 1 .... P—B3; 2 P—R6! are disastrous.

2. WHITE HAS AN OUTSIDE PASSED PAWN

Where there are only two Pawns for each side this is a win only if the Black Pawns are blocked. This is due to the fact that when the Black Pawns are mobile he can liquidate all the material on the board (except of course the Kings!). It is clear, however, that this drawing resource fails when there are more Pawns on the board, since at best only one pair of Pawns can be exchanged. E.g., in the model position No. 62, after *1 .... K—B3; 2 P—QR5, K—Kt4; 3 K—Q5, K×P; 4 K—K6, P—B4; 5 P×P, P×P; 6 K×P* the RP still guarantees White victory (compare No. 23). Even when the Pawns are close together and the Black King well placed White experiences little difficulty. No. 62a, taken from the game Breyer-Nyholm, Baden, 1914, White: K at Q2, P's at QB2, KKt2, KR3; Black: K at Q5, P's at K3, KKt2, KR3 shows this plainly. 1 .... P—R4; 2 P—R4, P—K4; 3 P—B3ch, K—K5 (or 3 .... K—B5; 4 K—B2); 4 K—K2, P—Kt3; 5 K—Q2, K—B5; 6 K—Q3, P—Kt4; 7 P×P, K×P; 8 K—K4, K—B3; 9 K—Q5! (but not 9 P—B4, K—K3; 10 P—B5, P—R5; 11 P—B6, K—Q3; 12 P—B7, K×P; 13 K×P, K—Q2; 14 K—B5, P—R6!! draw, since Black's King gets to KB1), K—B4; 10 P—B4, and now if 10 .... P—K5; 11 K—Q4!, K—B5; 12 P—B5, P—K6; 13 K—Q3, K—K4; 14 K×P, K—Q4; 15 K—B4, K×P; 16 K—Kt5, and wins.

No. 61

White to play wins; Black to play draws.

No. 62

White wins.

Black has drawing chances against an outside passed Pawn only when he can secure a Pawn position where he is always threatening to force a passed Pawn, so that White is either prevented from attacking the Pawns with his King or is forced to a disadvantageous simplification. How this works out in practice may be seen from No. 63 (Bogoljuboff-Fine, Zandvoort, 1936). At first sight it looks as though the White win is child's play, but a little analysis shows what difficulties White is up against. The game continued *1 .... K—B2; 2 K—Q3, K—K3; 3 K—K4, P—Kt3!; 4 K—Q4* (the direct advance 4 P—QR4, K—Q3; 5 P—R5, K—B4; 6 P—R6, K—Kt3 leads to a draw after 7 K—Q5, P—Kt4!; 8 P—B5—8 P×P transposes to what actually happened—, P—R4; 9 K—K6, P—R5; 10 K×P, P—Kt5;

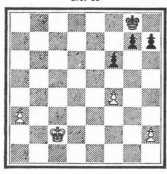

No. 63

Black to play. Draw.

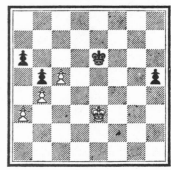

No. 64

White wins.

11 K—K6, P—Kt6 and they will queen simultaneously), *K—Q3; 5 K—B4, P—R3* (5 .... K—B3 is also good, but Black is now threatening to put an end to White's hopes by 6 .... P—Kt4 and if 7 P×P, RP×P!; 8 K—Q4, P—B4—B5); *6 K—Q4, K—B3* (now 6 .... P—Kt4?; 7 K—K4! would lose); *7 K—K4, K—Kt4; 8 K—Q5, P—Kt4!!* (the drawing manoeuvre); *9 P×P, BP×P!; 10 K—K5, K—R5; 11 K—B5, K×P; 12 K—Kt6, K—Kt5; 13 K×P, P—Kt5!!.* Drawn, since the Black King can get back to KB1. White could not have won by the preparatory P—KR3 at some earlier stage, since Black would then have exchanged everything by .... P—Kt4, ... P—R4 and .... P—Kt5. Again, we may obsreve that if Black had had blocked Pawns he could have resigned immediately.

Sometimes a potential outside passed Pawn is more dangerous than one which is actually on the board. This is seen in No. 63a (a problem by Troitsky), White: K at KKt2, P's at QR4, QB4, KB2; Black: K at KB4, P's at QKt2, KKt5, KR4. After 1 P—R5! (threatening P—

B5—B6), K—K4 is forced, when 2 K—Kt3, K—Q5; 3 K—R4, K×P; 4 K×P, K—Kt4; 5 K×P, K×P; 6 P—B4, P—Kt4; 7 P—B5, P—Kt5; 8 P—B6, P—Kt6; 9 P—B7, P—Kt7; 10 P—B8=Q, P—Kt8=Q; 11 Q—R8ch, K any; 12 Q—Kt8ch, wins Black's Queen.

For endings with an outside Pawn vs. a protected passed Pawn see 3.

3. WHITE HAS A PROTECTED PASSED PAWN

This is much stronger than even an outside passed Pawn, e.g., it can draw against two connected passed Pawns in most positions. Black can save himself only if he can prevent the White King from attacking his Pawns, which in turn is possible only if he can oppose the enemy King and at the same time remain in the square of the Pawn. Such a defense, however, is not often available.

It is worth reemphasizing that an outside passed Pawn is a handicap against a protected passed Pawn.

Again in No. 64 Black is hopelessly lost for White can win first his RP and then queen. *1 .... K—K4; 2 K—B3, K—B4; 3 K—Kt3, K—K4* (he must not leave the square of the QBP); *4 K—R4, K—Q4; 5 K×P, K—B3; 6 K—Kt5, K—Q4; 7 K—B5, K—B3; 8 K—K6, K—B2; 9 K—Q5, K—Q2; 10 P—B6ch, K—B1; 11 K—Q6, K—Q1; 12 P—B7ch, K—B1; 13 K—B6!, P—R4; 14 P×P, P—Kt5; 15 P—R6* and mates in two. However, if the Black Pawn were on any other file Black could draw, since his King would have sufficient manoeuverability to keep the White King out. E.g., No. 64a, Black P at KKt4, other pieces as in No. 64. Black to play draws: 1 .... K—K4; 2 K—B3, K—B4; 3 K—Kt3, K—K4; 4 K—Kt4, K—B3; 5 P—B6 (there is nothing else), K—K3; 6 K×P, K—Q3; 7 K—B6, K×P; 8 K—K6, P—R4!= or 8 .... K—Kt3; 9 K—Q6, P—R4= since Black's Pawn is on the fourth rank. This is the sole type of exception here to the rule that a protected passed Pawn wins. A position, similar to No. 64, which is rather difficult to force is No. 64b (Berg-Petrov, Kemeri, 1937), White; K at QKt2, P's at QR4, KKt2, KR4; Black: K at KR1, P's at QR4, QKt5, KKt2. Black wins. Black to play would decide immediately by 1 .... P—Kt4!; 2 P×P (2 P—R5, P—Kt5 and wins both K—side Pawns), K—Kt2; 3 K—Kt3, K—Kt3. After capturing both KtP's we have reduced to No. 27. White to play therefore must begin with 1 P—Kt4 (to answer 1 .... P—Kt4! by 2 P—R5=), when Black can only win by getting the distant opposition: 1 P—Kt4, K—Kt1; 2 K—B2, K—B2; 3 K—Q3, K—K3; 4 K—K4, K—Q3; 5 K—Q4, K—B3; 6 K—B4, K—B2!!; 7 K—Q3 (7 K—B3, the only square from which he can keep the opposition is impossible), K—Q2; 8 K—K2, K—Q3; 9 K—Q2, K—B4; 10 K—K3, K—B5; 11 K—Q2 (or 11 K—K4, P—Kt6, or 11 P—R5, K—Q4!; 12 P—Kt5, K—K4 and liquidates the K—side Pawns), K—Q5 and again after the exchange of White's KtP and RP for Black's KtP the win is simple.

4. WHITE HAS A QUALITATIVE PAWN SUPERIORITY

This occurs when the Black Pawns are blocked (also doubled), so that two Pawns are held in check by one. In effect White here has a potential outside passed Pawn, which means that since Black's Pawns are blocked he can force a quick decision. How this works out is seen in No. 65. On *1 .... K—B2; 2 K—B4, K—B3; 3 P—R4, K—B2; 4 K—K5, K—K2; 5 P—Kt5* White gives up his KtP to capture both KP and QP, while on *1 .... P—K4; 2 P×P, K—B2; 3 K—B4, K—K3; 4 P—R4, P—Q5; 5 K—K4, P—Q6; 6 K×P, K×P; 7 K—K3* White wins because he has the opposition (No. 35).

No. 65   No. 66

White wins.   White to play wins; Black to play draws.

A doubled Pawn is a serious handicap, but when all the Pawns are on one side it need not be fatal, for then there can be no question of two Pawns being held by one. In No. 65a (Flohr-Capablanca, Moscow, 1935), White: K at Q3, P's at K3, KKt3, KR2; Black: K at K3, P's at KB3, KB4, KR4, after *1 .... K—K4; 2 K—K2, K—K5; 3 K—B2, P—R5!; 4 P×P, P—B5!!, 5 P×P, K×P* the draw is obvious. White can only win here if he can force his King to KB4 with at least one tempo to spare.

5. WHITE'S PASSED PAWN OR SET OF PASSED PAWNS IS QUALITATIVELY SUPERIOR

By this we mean that the Pawns are either more mobile (e.g., Black's Pawns are doubled or disadvantageously isolated) or farther advanced. In general this works out in exactly the same way as the analogous case with K+2P's vs. K+2P's. No. 65b is an example from tournament practice—Stoltz-Nimzovitch, Berlin, 1928. White: K at Q2, P's at QR4, QKt5, KKt3; Black: K at K4, P's at Q5, KB4, KKt5. Nimzovitch won by the break 1 .... P—B5!; 2 P×Pch, K—Q3!!!; 3 P—R5, P—Kt6; 4 P—R6, K—B2!!; 5 K—K2, P—Q6ch and queens first.

6. WHITE'S KING IS NEARER THE PAWNS

This is important but not difficult. In the model position, No. 66 White to play wins at least two Pawns after *1 K—Q6,* while if it is Black's turn to move *1 .... K—B2* prevents the entrance of the White King. Sometimes, however, such positions present unusual difficulties, since the Black King is never too far away. E.g., in No. 66a (problem by H. Mattison), White: K at KKt3, P's at KB4, KKt2, KR2; Black: K at QR5, P's at KKt2, KKt3, KR3, after 1 P—B5! (not 1 K—B3, K—Kt4; 2 K—K4, K—B3=), K—Kt4!; 2 K—B4!! (2 P×P would only draw), K—B3 (.... P×P would doom his remaining Pawns); 3 K—K5, K—Q2; 4 P—B6!!, K—K1!!; 5 P×P, K—B2; 6 P—Kt8=Qch!, K×Q; 7 K—B6, K—R2; 8 P—Kt4, P—Kt4; 9 K—B7!, P—R4; 10 P—R4!! and wins (No. 53d).

Where the Pawn position is not yet blocked, it is essential for the inferior side to block it in such a way that he will not queen later than his opponent. This is normally simply a question of counting. In No. 66b (a problem by Grigorieff) White: K at QR4, P's at QR2, KKt3 KR3; Black: K at QB5, P's at QKt5, KKt4, KR4. 1 P—R4? loses, while 1 P—Kt4 draws. This result may be calculated in the following way. After fixing the Pawns on the King's side White must play his King to R5. Then .... P—QKt6, exchanges the QRP and QKtP's so that one must now count to see who will get to the other side first. With the Black Pawns at his KKt5 and KR4, it will take White's King, now at QR5, seven moves to capture the Pawn, one to get his King off the file, and four to queen, or twelve in all. The Black King, now at QKt6, will capture the White Pawn at KKt3 in five moves, and queen in four more, a total of nine (the fact that he will queen with check is unimportant here). But if White had played P—Kt4 on the first move, and fixed the Black Pawns at KKt4 and KR5, it would now take him six moves to capture the Pawn, and five more to queen, while Black needs six moves to capture the Pawn and four to queen, or a total of ten in all. Since White begins the race, the two Pawns promote simultaneously, so that a draw results.

7. WHITE HAS THE OPPOSITION

No. 67

White to play wins.

In the simpler cases this is no different from K+2P's vs. K+2P's (Nos. 53, 53a). An elegant illustration of the central idea is seen in No. 67, a problem by Dr. H. Neustadtl. *1 P—Kt4!, P—B4; 2 P—Q4!!!, P×QP* (or 2 .... P×KtP; 3 K—B6); *3 K—B6, P—Q6* (or 3 .... K—Q2; 4 K—K5, K—B3; 5 K—K6); *4 P×P, P—Q5; 5 K—B5, K—Q4; 6 K—B4, K—Q3; 7 K—K4, etc.*

Where the distant opposition is involved the play is often exceedingly complicated. To illustrate the idea when there are three Pawns we shall quote two more "natural" problems, No. 67a (K. Ebersz, 1935), White: K at K1, P's at QR4, KKt5, KR6; Black: K at K1, P's at QKt3, KB2, KR2. The solution is 1 K—Q2!, K—Q1 (1 .... K—Q2; 2 K—B3, K—K2; 3 K—B4!, K—K3); 2 K—K2!!, K—B1! (if 2 .... K—Q2; 3 K—B3, or 2 .... K—K2; 3 K—K3); 3 K—B3, K—Q2; 4 K—K3, K—B1 (or 4 .... K—Q1; 5 K—Q4, or 4 .... K—K1; 5 K—K4, or 4 .... K—K2; 5 K—K4, K—K3; 6 K—B4); 5 K—Q4, K—Q1; 6 K—K4!!, K—Q2 (Black is in zugzwang: on 6 .... K—K1; 7 K—B5, K—K2; 8 K—K5 or 7 .... K—B1; 8 K—B6 wins, while on 6 .... K—K2; 7 K—K5 is decisive); 7 K—Q5 and White has the opposition.

Another interesting example of the opposition with three Pawns on each side is No. 67b (Locock), White: K at QR1, P's at Q5, K4, KKt3; Black: K at KR1, P's at Q2, Q3, KKt5. After 1 K—Kt2, K—Kt2; 2 K—B3, K—B2!; 3 K—Q2!!, K—B3; 4 K—K2!!!, K—Kt3; 5 K—Q3! (the key position—Black must now allow either the advance of White's KP or the loss of his KKtP), K—B3 (5 .... K—Kt4; 6 K—K3); 6 K—Q4, K—B2; 7 P—K5, P×Pch; 8 K×P, K—K2; 9 P—Q6ch, K—K1; 10 K—B6!, K—B1; 11 K—Kt5, K—B2; 12 K—B5, K—Kt2; 13 K×P, K—B3; 14 K—R5, K—K3; 15 P—Kt4, K×P; 16 P—Kt5, K—K2; 17 K—R6, P—Q4; 18 P—Kt6 and promotes one move earlier.

A good deal of attention has been devoted to No. 68 and its innumerable offshoots. For our purposes it suffices to note that whoever moves wins. The main variation is *1 K—K2, K—Q2; 2 K—B3, K—B3; 3 P—R4, P—R4; 4 P—B4, P—B4; 5 K—Kt3!, K—Kt3; 6 P—Kt4, P—*

Kt4 (or 6 .... P—Kt3; 7 P—R5ch, K—R3; 8 P—B5, K—Kt4; 9 K—Kt2, P—Kt4 (or A); 10 K—Kt3, P—Kt5; 11 K—B2!, P—B5; 12 K—Kt2, P—R5; 13 K—Kt1!!, P—B6; 14 K—B2, P—R6; 15 K—Kt3 and now the Black King must move, when a White Pawn queens *A.:* 9 .... P—R5; 10 K—R2!, P—B5; 11 K—Kt1!!, P—Kt4; 12 K—Kt2, P—Kt5; 13 K—Kt1, etc., as above); *7 P—R5ch, K—R3* (7 .... K—Kt2; 8 P—B5); *8 P—B5, P—R5ch; 9 K—R3, P—B5* (or 9 .... K—Kt4; 10 K—R2, as in variation A in the note above); *10 P—B6, P—B6; 11 P—Kt5ch, K—R2; 12 P—B7!, P—Kt5ch* (or 12 .... K—Kt2; 13 P—Kt6, P—Kt5ch; 14 K—R2, P—Kt6ch; 15 K—Kt1, P—R6; 16 P—R6ch, K—B1; 17 P—R7); *13 K×KtP, P—B7; 14 P—B8= Q, P—B8= Q; 15 P—Kt6* mate.

No. 68

No. 69

Whoever moves wins.   White wins.

VIII. ENDINGS WITH FOUR OR MORE PAWNS ON EITHER SIDE

It would be pointless to work out elaborate analyses of these more complicated endings, since the principles exemplified have already been considered at sufficient length. Instead we shall make an attempt here to answer some of the more important questions which continually crop up in over-the-board play.

A. ONE SIDE IS A PAWN AHEAD

As indicated above, the win with material superiority becomes progressively easier with a larger number of Pawns. K+2P vs. K+1P presents less difficulty than K+1P vs. K; K+3P vs. K+2P is won more quickly and simply than K+2P vs. K+P. The reason for this is that the extra Pawn is used as a decoy to divert the attention of the enemy King, so that the greater the number of the remaining Pawns the more material White has to capture.

We have already seen that with two Pawns against three Black can only hope to draw under certain special circumstances. With three against four it is still worse. The standard position is No. 69 (Berger). White always proceeds by reducing to some case which is a well-known win. Black has five chief defenses:

a) *1 .... K—B5; 2 K—Q3, K—B4; 3 P—B4, K—B5; 4 P—R4, P—R3; 5 P—Kt4, K—B4; 6 P—R5, P×P; 7 P×P, K—B5; 8 P—Q5, P×P; 9 P×P, K—K4; 10 K—B4, K—Q3; 11 K—Q4* —Nos. 23, 24.

b) *1 .... P—B4; 2 P×P, P×P; 3 P—Kt3, P—R3; 4 P—R3, P— R4; 5 P—R4, K—K4; 6 K—K3, K—Q4; 7 K—Q3, P—B5ch* (or 7 .... K—Q3; 8 K—K4); *8 P×Pch, K—B4; 9 K—Q2!, K×P; 10 K—B2*—No. 26a.

c) *1 .... P—Kt4; 2 P—Kt4, P—R3; 3 P—R3, K—B5; 4 K—Q3, K—B4; 5 P—B4, K—K3; 6 P—B5, K—Q4; 7 K—K3, K—K3; 8 K—K4, K—K2; 9 P—Q5, P×Pch; 10 K×P*—No. 54a.

d) *1 .... P—R3; 2 P—Kt4, P—R4; 3 P×P, P×P; 4 P—R4, K— B5; 5 K—Q3, K—B4; 6 K—K3, K—K3; 7 K—K4, K—Q3; 8 P—B4, K—K3; 9 P—B5* and *P—Q5*, No. 24.

e) *1 .... P—R4; 2 P—R4, P—Kt4; 3 P×P, P×P; 4 K—K2, P— Kt5; 5 K—Q2, P—Kt6; 6 K—K2, P—R5; 7 K—Q2, K—Q4; 8 K—Q3, K—Q3; 9 K—B4, K—B3; 10 K—Kt4.*

With 5 vs. 4, or 6 vs. 5, the win is child's play.

We can summarize the winning process in endings with a Pawn ahead as follows:

1. Force a passed Pawn;
2. Sacrifice the Pawn at the right moment to get either
   a) a Pawn that queens by force;
   b) a sufficient preponderance of material;
   c) a win in one of the standard basic positions.

In most cases these rules are easily applied. But chess would not be the game it is if there were not numerous exceptions. Almost all of these are due to irregular Pawn structures. Even here, however, it seldom happens that Black can avert loss when White has more than three Pawns.

We can group the possible difficulties which White may encounter (assuming more or less normal King positions) under two headings— blocked Pawns (including doubled Pawns), and stalemate.

1. BLOCKED PAWNS

With the Pawns interlocked and offering no possibility of exchange, the problem becomes one of forcing the entry of the King. Now, the opposing King is always the obstacle here, so that the solution depends upon the proper use of the opposition. This applies then to what we may call a complete Pawn blockade.

If White has the opposition in such cases, he simply waits for Black to get his King out of the way and then marches in with the band going full blast. The position requires thought and analysis only when the direct and obvious methods fail. In such cases the weapon to be used is the *distant opposition.*

How this works out is seen in No. 70 (Lasker and Reichhelm, 1901). White wishes to get his King either to QKt5 or to KKt5. On the direct try 1 K—Kt2, K—Kt2; 2 K—B3, K—B2; 3 K—B4, K—Kt3; 4 K—Q3, K—B2; 5 K—K3, K—Q2; 6 K—B3, K—K2; 7 K—Kt3,

No. 70

No. 71

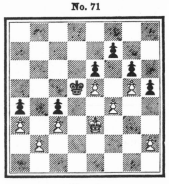

White to play wins; Black to move draws.   White wins.

K—B3; 8 K—R4, K—Kt3; he gets nowhere too quickly. Obviously a little finesse must be employed. In the above variation two observations may be made:

1. Black must never remain more than one file to the left of White on his march to the Queen's side, e.g., if the White King is on the K file, the Black King must be at least on the Q file.

2. Consequently, with the Black King at QKt3 and the White at QB4, Black to play loses, for 4 .... K—R3 is forced.

Let us carry the analysis one step further. With the White King at Q3 and the Black King at QB2, Black to play loses, since he must play to the Kt file to prevent K—B4—Kt5.

Again, one general point must be borne in mind. To have the opposition the Kings must be one square apart. And to have the distant opposition the Kings must be an odd number of squares apart. Now the solution is clear. *1 K—Kt1!, K—Kt2; 2 K—B1, K—B2;*

3 K—Q1, K—Q2 (3 .... K—B1; 4 K—Q2, K—Q2; 5 K—B3, K—B2; 6 K—Q3); *4 K—B2, K—Q1;* 5 K—B3, K—B2; 6 K—Q3 and Black is lost because he cannot keep the opposition by 6 .... K—Q2; 7 K—B4, etc.

Black to move can draw by *1 .... K—Kt2!!; 2 K—Kt1, K—R2!!!.* If then *3 K—Kt2, K—R1!,* or *3 K—B1, K—Kt2,* or *3 K—B2, K—Kt1,* and each time Black's King can remain at a distance of five, three, or one squares, White to move, so that Black always retains the opposition.

A winning method closely allied to that involving opposition is triangulation. Here there is a struggle for a certain vital point and because of the Pawn configuration one side has access to one more square than his opponent. Thus in No. 71 (taken from a game Neustadtl-Porges) White wants to occupy the square Q4. To do so he must first occupy K4, Black King at B4. He has two squares (K3 and B3) from which he can approach K4, while Black has only one. Thus he can reach his goal by *1 K—B3, K—B3; 2 K—K2!* (if 2 K—K4, K—B4; 3 P—R4?, K—Kt3!; 4 K—Q4, K—Kt4, the game is drawn—White must reserve his Pawn tempi), *K—B4* (2 .... K—Q4; 3 K—K3, K—B4; 4 K—K4); *3 K—B2, K—B3; 4 K—B3, K—Q4; 5 K—K3, K—B4; 6 K—K4, P—R5* (6 .... K—Kt3; 7 K—Q4, K—Kt4; 8 P—R4); *7 K—B3!, K—Q4; 8 K—K3!, K—B4; 9 K—K4, K—Kt4; 10 K—Q4, P—R6* (the first phase is ended: now White must win the KRP); *11 K—K3, K—B4; 12 K—B2!* (White is trying to get the diagonal opposition with his King at KB3 and the Black King at Q4), *K—Q4; 13 K—B3, K—B4; 14 K—Kt3, K—Q4; 15 K×P, K—K5; 16 K—Kt4* (second phase concluded; the final coup now follows), *K—K6; 17 K—Kt3, K—K5; 18 P—R4, K—K6* (18 .... K—Q4; 19 K—B3); *19 P—R5!, P×P; 20 P—B5!!, P×P; 21 P—Kt6, P×P; 22 P—K6, P—B5ch; 23 K—R2* and wins because he queens with check.

A complete Pawn blockade is less usual in actual play than positions where some Pawn exchanges are possible. Here the problem usually boils down to that of choosing the proper moment to exchange, where the "proper moment" means that in the ensuing position one will have the opposition or some other tangible advantage.

No. 72 (taken from a game Teichmann-Blackburne) is all the more interesting because it was adjudicated a draw. Black must sooner or later play .... P—R5. To capture would be senseless for White, since that would make the RP an outside passed Pawn. Consequently he must reply K—R3 when the Black Pawn advances. Black must then capture .... P×P, K×P, when he must lose a move by .... P—B4 to force the entry of his King to B5. As a result White can retreat K—Kt2 and after .... K—B5, K—B2 will have the opposition. Thus the first question is, at what point can Black advance his Pawn, capture the KtP and then force his King to B5 without the loss of a Pawn tempo? Clearly only when the Kings are at KKt3 and KB4, with White to move. This can be accomplished by playing the Black King to KB4 the moment White plays K×P.

The first step then is *1 .... K—B3; 2 K—R3, K—Kt3; 3 K—R2* (if 3 P—Kt4, P—R5 and if 3 P—B4, P×P; 4 P×P, K—B4), *P—R5; 4 K—R3, P×P; 5 K×P* (5 K—Kt2 is clever but useless: 5 .... K—B3; 6 K—R3, K—K4! and now White must capture), *K—B4; 6 K—Kt2* (on 6 K—B2, K—B5; 7 K—Kt2 even .... P—Kt5 wins), *K—B5; 7 K—B2, P—B4* (now 7 .... P—Kt5?; only draws after 8 P×P,

No. 72	No. 73
Black wins.	White wins.

K×P; 9 K—K3); *8 K—K2* (or 8 K—Kt2, K—K6; 9 K—Kt3, K—Q6; 10 K—Kt4, K×P; 11 K×P, K—Kt6; 12 P—B4, P—B6 and queens with check. 10 .... K—K7! is also sufficient here), *K—Kt6; 9 K—K3, K—R6!!!* (distant opposition: White cannot counter with the only move which keeps the Kings three squares apart, K—Q3); *10 K—K4* (10 P—B4, P—Kt5!), *K—Kt7!; 11 K—K3, K—B8; 12 K—K4, K—B7* and Black's extra Pawn on the Queen's side is decisive.

Another stratagem occasionally used to win with an extra Pawn is a sacrifice of one or two Pawns leading to a forced promotion. In No. 73 (correspondence game Berger-Bauer, 1889–1891), this is done by *1 P—B4!, P×P e.p.* (1 .... K—Kt4; 2 K—Kt3 is hopeless); *2 K—K3, K—Kt4; 3 P—R4!!, K×P; 4 P—Kt4, P×P; 5 K—Q3!!!* (the only winning move. If instead 5 P—R5, P—Kt6; 6 K—Q3, P—Kt7; 7 K—B2, K—B6; 8 P—R6, K—K7; 9 P—R7, P—Kt8=Qch!, 10 K×Q, K—Q8 and both sides queen), *P—R4; 6 P—R5, P—R5; 7 P—R6, P—R6; 8 P—R7, P—R7; 9 P—R8=Q,* followed by *Q—R1,* with a simple win (See No. 557).

A variant on this idea is seen in No. 73a, White: K at QKt3, P's at QR4, K4, KB3, KKt4, KR5; Black: K at QB4, P's at QKt3, KB3, KKt4, KR3. Here the win is achieved by 1 .... K—B3 (on 1 .... K—Q5; 2 K—Kt4 White queens first); 2 K—Kt4, K—Q3; 3 K—B4, K—B3; 4 P—B4!!, P×P; 5 P—K5!, P×P; 6 P—Kt5, P—B6; 7 K—Q3.

Another such position which also involves the exchange of queens after both Pawns have promoted is No. 73b, (Colle-Gruenfeld, Carlsbad, 1929). White: K at KKt3, P's at QR4, KB4, KKt5, KR4; Black: K at K6, P's at QR4, KKt3, KR4. White to play won by 1 P—B5, P×P; 2 P—Kt6, P—B5ch; 3 K—Kt2!!! (on any other move Black would draw the ensuing Q and P ending), K—K7; 4 P—Kt7,

<table>
<tr><td align="center">No. 74</td><td align="center">No. 75</td></tr>
<tr><td align="center"></td><td align="center"></td></tr>
<tr><td align="center">Black wins.</td><td align="center">White wins.</td></tr>
</table>

P—B6ch; 5 K—Kt3, P—B7; 6 P—Kt8=Q, P—B8=Q; 7 Q—B4ch, K—K8; 8 Q×Qch, K×Q; 9 K—B4. The Black King had to be forced to go on to the same diagonal as the future Queen.

A relatively simple device, yet nevertheless one which is frequently necessary, is that of sacrificing one or more Pawns to remove the blockade in order to penetrate to the other side of the board with the King. In No. 74 this is done by *1 P—KR4, P—B4; 2 K—B2, P—R4!; 3 K—K3, RP×P* (note that 3 .... BP×P; 4 P×P, P—R5?? is a hopeless draw, since the position is completely blocked); *4 P×P, P×P; 5 K—Q2, K—B2; 6 K—B2, K—B3; 7 K—Kt2, K—B4; 8 K—Kt3, K—Q5.*

When the defending side has a protected passed Pawn, the win is exceedingly difficult, sometimes impossible. If the Pawn defending the passed Pawn cannot be induced to get out of the way then the only winning possibility is (compare No. 57a) leaving the square to

guide one's own Pawns to queen. In No. 75 this is done by *1 P—Kt5,
K—Kt1; 2 P—R5, K—B1; 3 P—R6, K—Kt1.* Now White must lose a
move, so that when he plays his K to Q6 he will be threatening K—B7.
*4 K—Q4, K—R1; 5 K—B3, K—Kt1; 6 K—Q3, K—R1; 7 K—Q4,
K—Kt1; 8 K—B5, K—R1; 9 K—Q6, K—Kt1* (else 10 K—B7 mates);
10 K×P!, P—Q5; 11 K—B7, P—Q6; 12 P—K6 and queens with mate.

Where the plus Pawn is doubled, the win is usually long and difficult. Sometimes it is possible to sacrifice the Pawn to get the opposition or an otherwise won ending. No. 76 (taken from a game Spiess-
Buerger) is an example of this. The only way White can make any
progress is by *1 P—B4!, P×Pch; 2 K—R4!, K—K5;* and then *3 K—
Kt4!!, P—B6* (or 3 .... P—R4ch; 4 K×P, K—B6; 5 K—Kt5);

No. 76	No. 77
	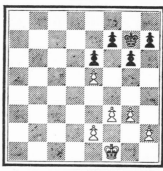
White to play wins; Black to play draws.	White wins.

4 P—KR4, P—R4ch (4 .... K—Q6; 5 K×P is equally hopeless)
5 K×P, K—B5; 6 K—Kt6 is decisive.

A similar idea is seen in No. 76a (Von Scheve-Walbrodt, Berlin,
1891), White: K at KKt3, P's at QKt4, QKt2, KB3, KB2, KR2;
Black: K at KKt4, P's at QKt3, K4, KB2, KKt3. The chief value of
the doubled QKtP here is that it gives White two extra tempi. Wal-
brodt won by 1 P—Kt5, P—B4; 2 P—B4ch!, K—B3; 3 P×Pch,
K×P; 4 K—B3, P—Kt4; 5 K—K3, K—Q4; 6 P—R3!, K—B4;
7 P—B4! Resigns, for if 7 .... P—Kt5; 8 P×P, P×P; 9 P—B5,
K—Q4; 10 K—B4.

Where no such sacrifice is feasible, as in No. 77 (this could have
occurred in Reshevsky-Fine, Nottingham, 1936—see No. 577) the
superior side must jockey for a vantage point from which he can liquidate his unfortunate twin, using the greater number of tempi which
his Pawn plus assures him. In this position the first advantage that

the extra Pawn confers is that Black cannot sit back and do nothing. For if he allows White's King to get to Q6, the advance P—K4, P—KB4, P—KKt4, followed by P—B5 will force Black to exchange and undouble White's Pawns. So he must play his King to the center. On the other hand, White cannot make any direct progress by playing his King to the center. Nor can he penetrate the Black position via KB4 and KKt5, since Black can play his Pawn to KR3. Consequently, he must force a further weakness in the Black position. After *1 .... K—B1* this can be done by *2 P—R4, K—K2; 3 K—Kt2, K—Q2; 4 P—R5!, K—B3* (or 4 .... P×P; 5 K—R3, K—B3; 6 K—R4, K—Q4; 7 P—B4, or 4 .... P—Kt4; 5 P—Kt4, K—B3; 6 P—B4!, K—Q4; 7 K—B3, K—Q5; 8 P—R6, K—Q4; 9 P—K3, P×P; 10 K×P!, K any; 11 K—Kt5, K any; 12 K—B6); *5 P×P, BP×P* (there's small choice in rotten captures. If 5 .... RP×P; 6 P—B4, K—Q4; 7 K—B3 followed by K—Kt4—Kt5 and either K—B6 or P—K4—B5, depending on the position of Black's King, is decisive). The rest is easier: *6 P—B4, K—Q4; 7 K—B3, K—Q5; 8 P—Kt4, P—Kt4* (if Black does nothing, then K—K3—Q3 followed by P—K4 and P—B5 will decide; while if 8 .... P—R3; 9 P—K3ch, K—Q4; 10 K—K2!!, K- -K5; 11 K—B2, P—Kt4; 12 K—Kt3!!! wins); *9 P×P!* (now 9 P—K3ch, K—Q4; 10 K—B2, K—K5; 11 K—Kt3, P—R3! only draws—e.g., 12 P—B5, K×P(K4); 13 P×P, K×P; 14 K—B3, K—K4! etc.), *K×P; 10 K—K3, K—Q4* (or 10 .... K—Q3; 11 K—B4, K—K2; 12 P—Kt6!, P×P; 13 K—Kt5, K—B2; 14 P—K4, K—Kt2; 15 P—K5, K—B2; 16 K—R6); *11 P—Kt6!, P×P; 12 K—B4, K—Q5; 13 K—Kt5, K—K6; 14 K×P, K×P; 15 K—B6, K—B6; 16 P—Kt5, K—B5; 17 P—Kt6* with a simple win.

The possibility of stalemate very rarely occurs in practical play, but it is still wise to be on one's guard against it. The most usual method of avoiding it is by underpromotion (promoting to less than a Queen), usually to a Rook. Sometimes, however, this is insufficient, and it is necessary to change the entire character of the position. In No. 78, e.g., the obvious 1 P—R5? only draws after 1 .... K—R3!; 2 P—R6, K—R4!!; 3 P—R7, P—R3!!!; 4 any, stalemate. Instead, *1 K—Q7* wins, even though Black queens: *1 K—Q7, P—R4* (if 1 .... K—R3; 2 K×P, K—R4; 3 K—Q7, P—R3; 4 P—B6); *2 P—R5, P—R5; 3 P—R6, P×P; 4 P—R7, P—Kt7; 5 P—R8=Q, P—Kt8=Q; 6 Q—B8ch, K—R2; 7 Q—B7ch, K—R1; 8 K×P!, Q—Kt3ch* (8 .... Q—K5ch; 9 K—Kt6, Q—K3ch; 10 P—B6, Q—K6ch; 11 P—B5); *9 K—Kt5, Q—K1ch; 10 P—B6, Q—Kt1ch* (10 .... Q—R4ch; 11 K—Kt6); *11 Q×Qch, K×Q; 12 K×P* and we have No. 17.

The circumstances under which Black can draw when he is a Pawn down have already been discussed in the case of 3P vs. 2P, but the conclusions reached there are just as applicable to all other Pawn endings. The most important points to be remembered are that doubled or immobile Pawns are the most serious handicap to the side who is trying to win, while a protected passed Pawn is almost a certain guarantee of a draw for the inferior side.

It cannot be too strongly emphasized that the mobility of Pawns is more important than their number. An elementary illustration of this is No. 79 (Horwitz, 1880), where White to move loses despite the fact that he is a Pawn ahead. *1 K—Q3, K—B5; 2 K—Q4, K×P; 3 K—K3* (3 P—K5, BP×Pch; 4 K—K4, K—R4), *K—R4* followed by playing his King around to the Queen's side and eventually to Q5, sacrificing the KtP (which has meanwhile tied the White King down to its square), and then capturing the KP and the QP.

No. 78   **No. 79**

White plays and wins.   White to move loses.

2. STALEMATE

Although stalemate defenses are a monopoly of problemists, problems with this theme are often very stimulating. We give three particularly striking ones here: No. 79a (problem by Prokop), White: K at KR3, P at KR6; Black: K at Q3, P's at QKt6, QB2, KB4, KB5, KKt4. 1 P—R7, P—Kt7; 2 P—R8=Q (or 2 . . . . P—Kt5ch; 3 K—R4, P—Kt8=Q; 4 Q—B6ch, K any; 5 Q×Pch, Q×Q stalemate); 3 Q—Q4ch. Black can only avoid perpetual check by going to the Kt file, when Q—Kt2ch forces the draw. No. 79b (problem by F. Lazard), White: K at QR4, P's at QR5, QKt5, QB4, K5, KKt5, KR4; Black: K at QR7, P's at QR2, QKt2, Q2, Q3, K2, KB2, KKt2, KKt3. 1 P—R5!, P×RP; 2 P—KKt6, BP×P; 3 P—K6, P×P; 4 P—B5, P×P; 5 P—R6, P×P; 6 P—Kt6, P×P stalemate! No. 79c (problem by Berger), White: K at KR2, P's at KB3, KKt2, KKt4, KR3; Black, K at QKt1, P's at QR3, KKt3, KKt4. 1 P—B4!!, P—R4; 2 P×P,

P—R5; 3 K—Kt3!, P—R6; 4 K—R4!!!, P—R7; 5 P—Kt3, P—Kt8=R stalemate.

B. MATERIALLY EVEN POSITIONS

The types of positional advantage in endings with an even number of Pawns have been enumerated in Part VI (K+3P vs. K+3P) and they in general likewise sum up all the cases where a win is possible despite numerical equality. Here we shall illustrate these principles with examples taken from more complicated positions.

a) *A Queen Is Forced.*

Endings where one side can force a passed Pawn and queen it

No. 80	No. 81

Black to play wins.	White wins.

usually involve Pawns on both sides of the board, which are freed by some sacrifice (Compare Nos. 51, 73). Such is the case in No. 80 (Gossip-Mason, Manchester, 1890). Black has two potential passed Pawns, one on the QR file and one on the KB file, so that he is bound to queen one of them: *1 .... P—Kt4; 2 BP×P, P×P; 3 P×P, P—R5; 4 K—Q3, P—R6; 5 K—B2, P—B5,* etc.

No. 80a (from an offhand game Stahlberg-Tartakover) is more complicated. White: K at K2, P's at Q4, KKt6, KR2; Black: K at K3, P's at QR2, QKt2, QB5, KKt2. White to play forces a Queen by 1 F—R4, P—R4; 2 P—R5, P—R5; 3 K—Q2! (Discretion is the better part of a Pawn ending), P—Kt4; 4 P—Q5ch, K—Q2; 5 P—R6, P—R6; 6 K—B2!, P—Kt5; 7 P×P, P—Kt6ch; 8 K—Kt1!, P—R7ch; 9 K—R1!, P—B6; 10 P—Kt8=Q Just in time!

No. 80b (Zubareff-Grigorieff, Leningrad, 1925) is an ending where Black queens a Pawn because the White King is too far away. White:

K at KB7, P's at QR4, QKt3, QB2, KB3; Black: K at QR3, P's at QR4, QKt3, QB4, Q5. 1 .... P—Kt4; 2 P×Pch, K—Kt3!! (to gain an all-important tempo); 3 K—K6, P—R5!; 4 P×P, P—B5; 5 P—B4, P—Q6 and queens when White's Pawn is on the sixth.

b) *The Outside Passed Pawn.*

The outside passed Pawn is practically certain to win when there are more than three Pawns on each side (unless of course the defender has a protected passed Pawn). No. 81 (Lasker-Allies, Moscow, 1899) is typical of thousands of such endings. After *1 P—KR4, P—R4; 2 P—Kt4, P—R5; 3 K—B2, P—R6; 4 K—K3, K—K3; 5 K—K4, K—B3; 6 P—B4, P—Kt3; 7 P—B3, K—K3; 8 P—R5, P×P; 9 P×P, K—B3; 10 P—R6, K—Kt3; 11 K×P* White can either queen in time or capture all of Black's Pawns.

Where both sides have outside passed Pawns or are threatening to acquire them careful calculation is required to see who gets there first in what is often a chessic "photo-finish." We can see this in No. 82 (Mueller-Rohde, correspondence). Black's potential passed Pawn on the King's side is a strong weapon, but his first job must be to block the White Pawns. For this purpose both 1 .... P—QR3 and 1 .... P—QKt3 come into consideration. Offhand 1 .... P—QKt3 looks better, but there seems to be nothing wrong with the other move. Only an exact calculation of all the possible consequences can enable one to decide which is better.

On 1 .... P—QR3; 2 P—R4!! (best. If 2 P—B5, P×P; 3 P—B6, K—Q3; 4 P×P, K—B2; 5 P—R6, P—B6; 6 P×P, P×P; 7 K—K3, P—Kt5 and queens first), P×P e.p. (On 2 .... P—R4?; 3 P—Kt6! turns the tables: 3 .... P—B6; 4 P×P, P×P; 5 K—K3, P—B7; 6 K×P, K—Q5; 7 K—B3, K×P; 8 K—K4!!, K—Kt4; 9 K—Q5, K×P; 10 K—B5!!, K—R5; 11 K—Q6, K—Kt4; 12 K—B7, P—R4; 13 K×P, P—R5; 14 K—R7, P—R6; 15 P—Kt7, P—R7; 16 P—Kt8=Qch); 3 P×KRP, P—B6; 4 P×P, P×P; 5 K—K3, P—B7; 6 K×P, K—Q5; 7 K—B3, K×P; 8 K—Kt4. White captures the KRP, Black the QRP. Although Black queens first, White's Pawn reaches the seventh, so that no win is possible (See No. 546).

Since White just manages to escape by the varnish of his pieces in the above variation, *1 .... P—QK*

No. 82

Whoever moves wins.

t3 must also be counted out with great care. *1 .... P—QKt3; 2 P×P* (2 P—R6, K—Q3), *P×P; 3 P—B5* (the only chance), *P× P; 4 P—Kt6, K—Q3; 5 P—Kt7, K—B2; 6 P—Kt8=Qch, K×Q; 7 K—K4, K—B2; 8 K×P, P—R4; 9 P—R3, P—B5!* and White can resign (No. 21).

On the other hand, if in the diagrammed position it were White's turn to move he could force a win by *1 P—B5!*, for if *1 .... K—Q4; 2 P—B6!, P×P; 3 P—Kt6, P×P; 4 P—R6!* and queens by force.

c) *The Protected Passed Pawn.*

Endings with a protected passed Pawn form an exception to the rule that the more Pawns there are on the board the easier it is to win. The additional Pawns either block the position or give the defender tactical counter-chances.

d) *Qualitatively Superior Pawn Position.*

The general Pawn configuration is an essential factor in all endings. Where there are not more than three Pawns on each side, one Pawn position is better than another only if there is some qualitative Pawn majority (one Pawn holding two, e.g.). In more complicated endings, such advantages are equally decisive, but other questions, such as the relative King positions and the number of reserve Pawn moves available, assume more importance.

Qualitative majorities are due either to doubled Pawns or to a blockade. In No. 83 (Loewenthal-Williams, London, 1851) we see the fatal weakness of doubled Pawns: Black forces an outside passed Pawn on the Queen's side and then sacrifices it to capture the Pawns on the other wing. Meanwhile the White majority is useless. The game continued: *1 K—K3, K—Q3; 2 P—B5, K—K2; 3 K—B3, P×P; 4 P×P,*

No. 83

Black wins.

P—QKt4; 5 P—Kt5, P×P; 6 P —Kt4, K—Q3; 7 K—K3, K—B3; 8 K—Q3, K—Kt3; 9 K—B3, K— R4; 10 K—Kt3, P—Kt5 and White soon resigned.

Weak Pawns are exploited by attacking them with the King. But the success of such an attack depends on whether the King can penetrate the defense put up, which in turn brings us back to the problem of the opposition. And the effectiveness of the opposition is in large measure determined by who has the extra tempo. E.g, in No. 84, the entrance of the Black King is made possible by the inferior (too far advanced) position of the White Pawns. After *1 .... K—B3, 2 K— K3, K—K4; 3 P—B4* it is clear that if the White King can be forced to move Black will mop up either on the Queen's side or on the King's side. The tempo move *3 .... P—Kt5* is for this reason decisive. On *4 K—K2, K—K5* keeps the opposition.

Very often handling the Pawns properly, i.e., in such a way that one keeps as many tempi as possible in reserve, is the decisive factor. No. 85 (Taubenhaus-Pollock, Bradford, 1888) is an instructive example of how to manoeuvre Pawns in conjunction with a qualitative majority. It has some of the typically complex problems which arise here, which is why we give the analysis in great detail. The problem for Black is

No. 84   No. 85

Black to play wins.   Black wins.

obviously that of forcing an entry with his King. To do this he must get rid of the White KP. Hence 1 .... P—Q4. It would be a bad blunder for White to exchange, since 2 P×Pch, P×P not only undoubles the Black Pawns but also gives Black a protected passed Pawn in the center. So he is reduced to marking time. Now, it is clear that the only winning continuation for Black must involve P×KP, since on 2 .... P—Q5; 3 K—Q3, P—B4; 4 P—B4 a complete blockade ensues. Further, after Black has played .... P×P his King will only be able to enter via Q4 and QB4. But this would allow White to capture both KP's and the KKtP, freeing his KRP. Consequently we must conclude that Black can only win by sacrificing the forward KP and forcing his King to K5. To do this he must have a position with his King at Q4 or KB4, his Pawn at QB5 and at least one extra tempo if it is his turn to move. Let us go on with the analysis: once Black has reached K5, the White King will go to K2, when Black must again have an extra tempo at his disposal in order to keep the opposition. Now we have the outline of the winning plan: to manipulate the Queen-side Pawns in such a way that he will have at least two extra tempi after an eventual .... P×P. It is necessary, then, to count out the Pawn moves. If White does nothing, Black has five Pawn moves (P—R5, P—QB4—QB5, P—QB3—QB4) when White has one remaining (P—QR3). If Black does nothing, White also has five Pawn moves (P—QR3—R4, P—QKt3, P—QB4—QB5) when Black has none remaining. This shows that Black cannot win by playing .... P×P immediately his Pawn gets to Q4: he must first force further weaknesses in the White position. By playing his QBP to QB5 and his QRP to QR5 he can set up an adequate tempo reserve. But the trouble is that as soon as he plays .... P—QB4, the reply P—B4!! draws. E.g., 1 .... P—Q4; 2 K—K3, P—B4; 3 P—B4!!, P×KP! (3 .... P—Q5ch blocks the position, while 3 .... P×BP; 4 K—Q2 is bad); 4 P—QR4! (the simplest), K—B3; 5 K—Q2! and Black cannot win because he has no reserve tempo—5 .... P—K6ch; 6 K×P, K—B4; 7 K—Q3, P—K5ch; 8 K—K2!, K—K4; 9 K—K3, P—B3; 10 P—Kt3.

We have now reached three important conclusions:

1. Black can only win by .... P×P;
2. He must first force further weakness in White's Q-side Pawns;
3. The minute he plays .... P—QB4 the reply P—QB4! destroys all his hopes.

If there is a win, then, it must begin with *1 .... P—Q4; 2 K—K3, P—R5,* when White will simply continue to mark time. What now?

No weakness has as yet been forced. It cannot be done by the advance of the BP, so the King must come to the rescue. *3 K—Q3, K—Q3; 4 K—K3, K—B4.* Now White is faced by a new problem: Shall he allow the Black King to occupy QB5 or shall he prevent it? If he allows it, it will eventually be apparent that he has drifted into a loss. E.g., 5 K—Q2, K—B5; 6 K—B2 (or 6 K—K3, P—R6), P×P; 7 P—Kt3ch, P×Pch; 8 P×Pch, K—Kt4!; 9 K—Q2, P—B4; 10 K—K3, P—B5; 11 P—Kt4, K—R5; 12 K×P, K—Kt6; 13 K—B5, K×P; 14 K×KtP, K—Q6; 15 P—R4, P—B6, etc.

It follows that White must prevent the inroad of the Black King by *5 P—Kt3, RP×P; 6RP×P.* After this exchange Black can afford to advance his QBP, since the reply P—QB4 can then be answered by .... P—Q5 (the position is no longer blocked) or even .... P×P (he has the needed tempo with .... P—QB3). *6 .... K—Q3; 7 K—K2, P—B4; 8 K—Q3* (there is nothing better: on 8 P—B4 both .... P—Q5 and .... P×P win, while on 8 P×P, K×P; 9 K—Q3, P—B5ch! is decisive: 10 P×Pch, K—B4; 11 K—K4, K×P; 12 K×P, K×P; 13 K—B5, P—B4 and queens first), *P—B3* (to

defend the QP and thus free the King); *9 K—K3, K—B2; 10 K—Q3*
(or 10 K—B2, K—Kt3; 11 K—Kt2, P—Q5! and both 12 P—B4 and
12 K—B2, P×P; 13 K—K3, K—Kt4; 14 K—Q3, K—Kt5; 15 K—B2,
P—B5 are equally hopeless), *K—Kt3; 11 K—K3, K—Kt4; 12 K—Q3,
P—Q5!* (the decisive break); *13 K—Q2* (13 P—B4ch, K—Kt5;
14 K—B2, K—R6 is no better), *P—B5!; 14 P×QP, KP×P; 15
P×Pch* (or 15 P—K5, P—B6ch; 16 K—Q3, P—B4 and the White KP
is lost), *K×P; 16 K—B2, P—B4.* We have reduced the ending to the
case of two connected passed Pawns against one lone Pawn, which is a
well-known win.

In this example we wish particularly to call the reader's attention
to the essential role which the Pawn tempi play. Any unnecessary
Pawn move on Black's part would have made the draw unavoidable.

One significant difference from the basic endings which the presence
of a number of Pawns (more than three) creates is the enhanced value
of center Pawns. In the more elementary cases a center Pawn is often
a serious handicap because the opponent then has potential or actual
outside passed Pawns. Where there is more material on the board
this fact is of much less importance, since usually neither King can get
through to the other's Pawns. In view of this one can see why center
Pawns are an advantage in the complicated cases. In No. 85, e.g., the
King was tied down because of the powerful center phalanx. But
when there is a passed Pawn it is preferable not to have it in the
center. For the strength of a passed Pawn is that it lures the opponent's King away from the other Pawns, so that the farther away it is
the stronger it becomes. E.g., in No. 85a (Pirc-Alatortzeff, Moscow,
1935) White: K at Q3, P's at QR3, QKt2, Q4, KB4, KKt2, KR2;
Black: K at Q3, P's at QR2, QKt3, KB2, KB4, KKt3, KR2 is a draw
precisely because the center Pawn merely gets in White's way and
does not hamper Black in the least. The game continuation was
1 .... K—Q4; 2 P—QR4, P—QR3; 3 P—QKt3, P—B3; 4 P—R4, P—
R3; 5 P—Kt3, P—Kt4; 6 K—K3, P×RP; 7 P×P, P—KR4; 8 K—
Q3, P—Kt4! and White can do nothing, e.g., 9 P×P, P×P; 10 K—K3
(10 K—B3?, K—K5! gives Black winning chances after 11 K—Kt4,
K×QP; 12 K×P, K—K5; 13 K—B4, K×P; 14 P—Kt4, K—K6;
15 P—Kt5, P—B5; 16 P—Kt6, P—B6; 17 P—Kt7, P—B7; 18 P—
Kt8=Q, P—B8=Qch, or if here 13 K—B5 instead of 13 K—B4,
then K×P, K—Kt5 and Black should still win the resulting Queen
ending), K—Q3; 11 K—Q2, P—Kt5!; 12 K—Q3, K—Q4, etc.=.

Although weak Pawns are a serious danger, they are not necessarily
fatal unless they are combined with an inferior King position. In No.
85b (Reinfeld-Fine, New York, 1940) White: K at Q2, P's at QKt3,
QKt2, K2, KB2, KKt3, KR2; Black: K at QR1, P's at QR4, QB4,
K3, KB2, KKt2, KKt4 White could have held the draw because his

King is not badly placed. After 1 .... K—Kt2; 2 K—B3, K—Kt3 3 K—B4, P—Kt5; 4 P—B3, P—B4; 5 P—B4 (now Black does not have an extra tempo), K—B3; 6 K—Q3, K—Q4 (6 .... K—Kt4; 7 K—B3 is useless. Black will first try to get a Pawn at K5, to deprive the White King of the square Q3); 7 K—B3, P—K4; 8 K—Q3 (not 8 P×P?, P—Kt4; 9 P—K3, K×P; 10 K—B4, K—K5 with a simple win), P—K5ch; 9 K—B3, K—Q3 (to answer K—B4 with K—B3); 10 K—Q2, K—B3; 11 K—B2? (this inaccuracy in time pressure loses. It is clear that Black must have two Pawn tempi to win, one to drive the King from QB3, the other to drive it from QB2. After 11 P—K3! Black would only have one tempo and so could only draw. Attempts such as .... P—B5 or .... P—R5 lead to nothing), K—Kt4!; 12 K—Q2 (or 12 P—K3, K—Kt5; or 12 K—B3, P—K6!; 13 K—Q3, K—Kt5; 14 K—B2, P—Kt3), K—Kt5; 13 K—B2, P—K6! (not 13 .... P—Kt3; 14 P—K3!, for if 14 .... P—B5; 15 P×P, K×P; 16 P—Kt3ch, K—Kt5; 17 K—Kt2=). Here White resigned, for if he goes after the KP, the Black RP will queen in at most six moves.

Most weak Pawn positions are not permanently inferior, unless there is an indissoluble doubled Pawn or a succession of isolated Pawns. Usually Pawn inferiority is relative to the amount of time available to straighten out the Pawns and bring up the King. This is quite obvious in a number of examples which have been quoted (see Nos. 76, 82, etc.). No. 86 (Böök-Fine, Warsaw, 1935) is another case in point. If White were an obliging fellow and went to sleep for a while, Black could set up his Pawns at QB3, QKt4 and QR5, his King at Q4, when his opponent's game in turn is hopelessly lost. But making one move at a time Black must both defend his KBP and prevent the entrance of the King on the Queen's side—an impossible task. After *1 .... K—B2; 2 K—K2, K—B3* (or 2 .... K—K3; 3 K—Q3, P—QKt4; 4 K—K4, P—Kt4; 5 P—Q5ch, K—Q3; 6 P—QKt4, P—B3; 7 P×P, K×P; 8 P—R4, K—Kt3; 9 P—R5!, P—R4; 10 P×Pch, K×P; 11 K—B5 and White queens when Black's Pawn is on the sixth); *3 K—Q3, K—B4; 4 K—B4, P—B3; 5 P—Q5, P×Pch; 6 K×P, K—Kt4.* Here there is a routine win by *7 P—B4, K—R5; 8 P—QKt4* but White is bedazzled by the fact that he can win a Pawn. The interesting continuation was 7 K—K5?, P—Kt4!; 8 P—QKt4, P—Kt3!! (this draws—the point will soon be seen); 9 K—K4, K—R5!; 10 K×P, P—KR4!!! (it was essential to have this Pawn protected); 11 K—K5, K—Kt6; 12 K—B6, K×P; 13 K×P, K×RP!; 14 P—B4 (on 14 K×P, K—Kt6 White would lose), P—R5 and White could do nothing in the Q and P ending.

Where one passed Pawn or set of passed Pawns is better placed than the opponent's the winning process (as in the case of 3 vs. 3) consists of blocking the enemy's counter-chances and advancing one's own

Pawns as far as they will go. In No. 87 (Euwe-Alekhine, 24th match game, 1935) White's only hope lies in manoeuvring his King-side Pawns into a position where the Black King will not dare to go to support his Queen-side Pawns. E.g., if he could get a passed Pawn or set up his Pawns at KB4, KKt5, KR5, the constant threat of P—R6 would confine the Black King to his bed. This can only be avoided by the exchange of the Black KP for the White KBP or the prevention of P—KB4. Consequently Alekhine played *1 .... P—K4!*. If now 2 P—B4, P×P; 3 P×P, K—B2 and Black can pick up all the White Pawns at his leisure. Again, if 2 P—KKt4, K—K2; 3 P—R5 and Black can manoeuvre his King to KB5, break with .... P—K5 and the capture of the KtP and RP, followed later by a similar liquidation

No. 86   No. 87

White wins.   Black to play wins.

of White's KP and BP. So White is lost if he cannot exchange the BP for the KP without breaking up his Pawn structure, i.e., if he cannot play P—KB4 and recapture with his King. But since the White King at KB4 is outside the square of a Black QKtP at QKt5 Black need only advance his QKt and QRP's. *2 K—B1, P—QKt4, 3 K—K2, P—QR4.* (In the game Alekhine unaccountably played 3 .... P—B4, when Euwe drew with 4 K—K3); *4 K—Q3, P—R5; 5 K—B3, P—B4; 6 P—Kt4, K—K2; 7 K—Q3, K—Q3; 8 K—B3, K—Q4; 9 P—R3, K—K3; 10 K—Kt2, P—Kt5; 11 P×P, P×P; 12 K—B2, K—Q4; 13 P—R5, K—B5; 14 K—Kt2, P—R6ch; 15 K—R2, K—B6; 16 P—Kt5, P—Kt6ch* with mate in a few.

A protected passed Pawn is qualitatively superior to an outside passed Pawn, and is generally a sufficient advantage to win. No. 88 is relatively difficult only because the Black Pawn is so far back. Still,

White, by making proper use of the greater mobility of his King (the Black King must not leave the Kt file) and the advanced position of his Pawn, can manage to score. *1 K—Kt4, K—Kt3; 2 K—R4, P— QR3* (or 2 .... K—Kt2, 3 K—Kt5, or 2 .... K—B3; 3 K—R5); *3 K—Kt4, K—B3; 4 K—B4, K—Kt3; 5 K—Q5!, K—Kt2* (if 5 .... P—QR4; 6 K—Q6!, P—R5; 7 P—K6 both Pawns promote but White captures Black's Queen by 11 Q—Kt8ch and 12 Q—R8ch); *6 K— Q6!, K—B1* (or 6 .... P—R4; 7 P—K6); *7 K—B6* (7 K—K7 is also good), *K any; 8 K—Kt6,* after which the rest is routine.

An outside passed Pawn can however draw against a protected passed Pawn under certain circumstances (see 3 vs. 3)—blockade, if it can remain in the square, and if the base of the protected passed

No. 88   No. 89

White wins.   Black to play.   Draw.

Pawn can be undermined. No. 88a (Tarrasch-Schiffers, Nuremberg, 1896) is an example of this last stratagem. White: K at QB5, P's at Q6, K3, KB4, KR2; Black: K at Q1, P's at QR2, K5, KKt3, KR2. 1 K—B6, K—B1 (in the game Schiffers played 1 .... P—KR3???; 2 P—KR4, P—KR4; when 3 K—Q5, K—Q2; 4 K×P, K×P; 5 K— Q4, K—B3; 6 P—K4, K—Q3; 7 K—B4, K—B3; 8 K—Kt4, as in No. 81, is decisive); 3 K—Q5, K—Q2; 4 K×P, K×P; 5 K—Q4, K—K3; 6 P—K4, P—QR4; 7 K—B5, P—Kt4!; 8 P—B5ch (8 P×P, K—K4; 9 P—R4 is also a draw), K—K4; 9 P—B6, K×P; 10 K—Q6 and the Pawns promote simultaneously.

Where there are two connected passed Pawns against two widely separated passed Pawns (or potential passed Pawns) the outcome al-ways depends on who can get there ahead of the other fellow. The principles with more than three Pawns on the board remain exactly the same as in the simpler case, but sometimes one must resort to certain finesses to get the Pawns through. No. 89 (Pillsbury-Tarrasch, Nuremberg, 1896) is of historical interest because Pillsbury has been severely criticized for exchanging Queens to get into this ending, although it should be a draw with best play. Black must either try to mobilize his own Pawns (1 .... P—QKt4) or blockade his opponent's (1 .... K—B2). In point of fact it makes no difference as far as the eventual result is concerned but on general principles one would play 1 .... K—B2 to prevent a White Pawn from reaching the seventh. That the game is a draw in any case is shown by the following variations: *1 .... P—QKt4; 2 P—R5!* (but not 2 P—Q6?, K—B2; 3 P—Q7, K—K2; 4 P—K6, P—QR4; 5 P—R5, P—Kt4; 6 K—Kt3, P—Kt5; 7 K—Kt4, P—R5; 8 K—B5, P—Kt6; 9 P×P, P×P; 10 K—Kt6, P—Kt7; 11 P—Q8=Qch, K×Q; 12 K—B7, P—Kt8=Q; 13 P—K7ch, K—B2; 14 P—K8=Q, Q—B4ch! and Black wins by forcing the exchange of Queens), *P×P* (if instead 2 .... P—Kt4?; 3 K—Kt3, P—R4; 4 K—Kt4, P—Kt5; 5 P—Q6 will decide for White); *3 K—Kt3, P—R4; 4 K—R4, P—Kt5; 5 P—Q6, K—B2; 6 P—Q7, K—K2; 7 P—K6, P—R5; 8 K×P, P—Kt6; 9 P×P, P×P; 10 K—Kt6, P—Kt7; 11 P—Q8= Qch, K×Q; 12 K—B7* and the Q and P ending cannot be won. If 1 .... K—B2; P—R5! at the right moment will force a drawn Q and P ending.

Tarrasch actually made an incredible blunder in the game. 1 .... P—QKt4; 2 K—Kt3, P—Kt5; 3 K—B4, P—Kt4ch??; 4 P×P, P×Pch; 5 K×P, and after 5 .... P—R4; 6 P—Q6, K—B2; 7 K—B5 it takes White only two moves to queen, while it takes Black four.

In No. 90 (Pillsbury-Gunsberg, Hastings, 1895) White does not have time to go to the aid of his Pawns with his King, but the threat of doing so forces Black to allow White an extra passed Pawn. *1 P—K4!, P×P; 2 P—Q5ch, K—Q3; 3 K—K3, P—Kt5; 4 K×P, P—R5; 5 K—Q4, K—K2* (5 .... P—B4; 6 P×P, P—Kt5; 7 P—B6 is much easier); *6 K—B4, P—Kt6; 7 P×P, P—R6; 8 K—B3, P—B4; 9 P×P, P—Kt5.* Now apparently Black queens right after his opponent, but because White's Pawns are already so far advanced he can manage to queen with check. *10 P—Kt4, P—R4; 11 P—Kt5, P—R7; 12 K—Kt2, P—R8= Qch; 13 K×Q, P—R5; 14 P—Kt6, P—Kt6; 15 P—Q6ch!, K×P* (or 15 .... K—B3; 16 P—

No. 90

White to play wins.

Q7, K—K2; 17 P—Kt7, P—Kt7; 18 P—Q8=Qch, K×Q; 19 P—
Kt8=Qch); *16 P—Kt7, K—B2; 17P—K 7, P—Kt7; 18 P—Kt8= Q
ch, K× Q; 19 P—K8= Qch.*

The rule has already been established that passed Pawns should be
advanced as far as possible. No. 90a (Berger) is an amusing illustration of the great strength of Pawns on the seventh. White: K at
KKt3, P's at QR5, QB6, QB7, Q6; Black: K at QB1, P's at QR3,
KB4, KKt2, KKt4, KR3. Because his Pawns have the Black King
all bottled up White can win by 1 K—B3, P—Kt5ch (or 1 .... P—
R4; 2 K—K3, P—R5; 3 K—Q4, P—R6; 4 K—B5, P—R7; 5 K—Kt6,
P—R8=Q; 6 P—Q7 mate!); 2 K—B4, P—R4; 3 K—K5, P—Kt6;
4 K—K6, P—Kt7; 5 K—K7, P—Kt8=Q; 6 P—Q7ch, K×P; 7 P—
Q8=Qch, K×P; 8 Q—Q7ch, K—B4; 9 Q—R7ch. However, Pawns
in general should not be advanced if that decreases their mobility
(compare No. 84).

e) *Better King Position and Opposition.*

The better King position goes hand in hand with the opposition. If
one King is so placed that the other has little or no mobility, Pawns
must be moved, and after these are exhausted either the extra tempo
or the opposition decides.

Sometimes it is necessary to exchange a number of Pawns before the
opposition is of any significance. Thus in No. 91 (Horwitz) first the
QBP is blockaded, then the QP is exchanged, and finally the BP must
fall, because with P's at QB4, QB5 and his King on the fifth White
always has the opposition. *1 .... K—Q2; 2 P—B4, P×P e.p.; 3
P×P, P—R6; 4 P—B4, K—B2; 5 P—K4, K—Q2; 6 P—K5, P×P;
7 K×KP, K—B3; 8 K—K6, K—B2; 9 K—Q5, K—Kt3; 10 K—Q6,*
etc.

No. 91

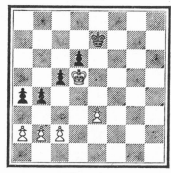

White wins.

The same exchange manoeuvre
is decisive when the opposing King
has been shunted off to some de-
serted part of the board and cannot
get back in time to challenge the
opposition. In No. 91a (Mason-
Englisch, London, 1883) White: K
at K3, P's at QKt4, QB4, KB3,
KKt3, KR2; Black: K at QR3, P's
at QB3, K4, KB3, KB4, KR2 on
1 P—Kt4 Black does not get back
in time after 1 .... P—B5ch, but
does after 1 .... P×P: 1 .... P
×P (For 1 .... P—B5ch see var
A); 2 P×P, P—R3; 3 P—R4, K—

Kt3; 4 K—K4, K—B2; 5 P—Kt5, B P×P; 6 P×P, P×P; 7 K×P, P—Kt5; 8 K—B4, K—Q3; 9 K×P, K—K4=

Variation A. 1 . . . . P—B5ch?; 2 K—K4, P—R3; 3 P—R4, K—Kt3; 4 P—Kt5, BP×P; 5 P×P, P×P; 6 K×P, P—Kt5; 7 K×P, P×P; 8 K×P, K—B2; 9 K—K4, K—Q3; 10 K—B5 and wins. (See No. 37).

A variant on this idea is the sacrifice of a Pawn to cramp the opponent's game and secure the opposition. This is seen in No. 91b (Horwitz), White: K at KR6, P's at QB3, Q4, K5, KB4; Black: K at Q1, P's at Q4, K2, KB2, KB4. Black to play can draw at once by 1 . . . . P—K3. But White to play wins with 1 K—K7 (not 1 P—K6, P×P; 2 K—Kt7, K—B2! and Black has the distant opposition), K—K1; 2 P—K6!, P×P; 3 K—Kt8 (Now White has the opposition), K—Q1; 4 K—B8, K—Q2; 5 K—B7, K—Q3; 6 K—K8, P—K4; 7 QP×Pch, K—K3; 8 K—Q8, K—B2; 9 K—Q7 (White still has the opposition), K—B1; 10 P—K6 or 10 K—K6.

The value of any King position is not absolute but relative to the Pawn skeleton. One King is almost always nearer a certain set of Pawns than the other, but it is only when we view the situation as a whole that we can determine which one is better placed. Then too we must consider whether a given advantageous post can be maintained, which of course again brings in the opposition. A Pawn configuration is relatively static, but a King position is mobile. E.g., in No. 91c (Loyd-Winawer, Paris, 1867). White: K at KB4, P's at QB4, K4, KKt4, KR4; Black: K at K3, P's at QB4, KB2, KKt3, KR3, there seems to be nothing wrong with White's game, yet after 1 . . . . P—Kt4ch!; 2 P×P, P×Pch; 3 K×P (on 3 K—B3, K—K4; 4 K—K3, P—B3! decides), K—K4; 4 K—R6, K×P; 5 K—Kt7 (if 5 P—Kt5, K—B5!—diagonal opposition—6 K—Kt7, K×P; 7 K×P, K—B4; or 6 K—R5, K—Kt6; 7 P—Kt6, P×Pch; 8 K×P, K—B5), P—B4!!; 6 P—Kt5, P—B5 and Black either queens with check (if the King goes to the B file) or exchanges Queens (if the King goes to the R file).

Where the superior side does not have the opposition, but would have it if his opponent were forced to move, a favorable result can often be attained by the skillful use of Pawns moves to get a position where one has an extra tempo. Of course, if the position is completely blocked nothing can be done. It is well to bear in mind that the opposition is effective only if a move to *either* side costs the opponent the game. Thus in K+RP vs. K White does get the opposition, but it is useless because Black can move in only one direction, and so cannot be driven away from the queening file. Similarly, in many cases of K+2P vs. K+P, with a RP on the board, whether White has the opposition or not was immaterial. In general, then, to be able to exploit the opposition, one must have a winning continuation against

all possible enemy King moves. An illustration is No. 92 (Berger). If it is White's play, then *1 K—Q5* (both 1 P—K5, P×P; 2 P×P, K—Q2; 3 K—Q5, P—Kt4; 4 P—K6ch, K—K2; 5 K—K5, P—KR4; 6 K—B5, P—Kt5; 7 K—Kt5, K×P; 8 K×P, K—B4= and 1 P—KR4, P—Kt3!; 2 K—Q5, K—Q2; 3 P—K5, P×P; 4 K×P, K—K2= are inadequate), *K—Q2; 2 P—K5, P×P* (what else? If 2 .... K—K2; 3 P×Pch!, P×P—3 .... K×P transposes back into the main variation—4 K—B6, K—K3; 5 K—Kt6, K—B4; 6 K×P, K×P; 7 K×P, K—K6—on 7 .... K—K5 White gives check; on 7 .... K—Kt5 or Kt4 the White King gets back to KB1—8 K—B5, P—B4; 9—12 P—Kt8 = Q, P—B8 = Q; 13 Q—K5ch, K—Q2; 14 Q—Q4ch, and exchanges queens in two moves, while if 2 .... P—B4; 3 P—K6ch, K—K2; 4 K—K5, P—Kt3; 5 P—R3!, P—R3!; 6 P—KR4, P—KR4; 7 K—Q5, K—K1; 8 K—Q6, K—Q1; 9 P—K7ch, K—K1; 10 K—K6 forces mate after 10 .... P—Kt4; 11 RP×P, P—R5; 12 P—Kt6 etc.); *3 K×P, K—K2* (again no choice: both 3 .... P—Kt3; 4 K—B6 and 3 .... P—R3; 4 K—B5, K—K2; 5 K—Kt6, K—B1; 6 P—B5, K—Kt1; 7 P—KR4, K—B1; 8 P—R5, K—Kt1; 9 P—B6, P×P; 10 K×BP, are equally useless); *4 K—Q5, K—Q2* (or 4 .... K—B3; 5 K—B6, K—B4; 6 K—Kt6, K×P; 7 K×P, P—Kt4; 8 K×P, P—Kt5; 9 K—B6, P—R4; 10 P—Kt5 and again White queens with check); *5 K—B5, K—B2* (we now have come back to the starting position with the sole difference that two Pawns are missing); *6 P—B5!!!* (this gives him the needed extra tempo), *P—R3* (if 6 .... P—Kt3; 7 P×P, P×P; 8 P—KR4); *7 P—R3!, P—KR4; 8 P—KR4, K—Q2; 9 K—Kt6, K—K2!!; 10 K×P, K—B3; 11 K×P, K×P; 12 P—R4* (12 K—B4, P—Kt4!; 13 K—Q4, P—Kt5 only draws, See No. 57), *P—Kt4; 13 P—R5, P—Kt5; 14 P—R6, P—Kt6; 15 P—R7, P—Kt7; 16 P—R8 = Q, P—Kt8 = Q; 17 Q—Q5ch, K—B3; 18 Q×P,

No. 92

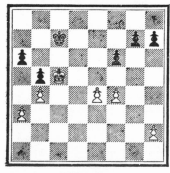

White wins.

Q—B8ch; 19 K—Kt6, Q—B7ch; 20 K—R6! with a fairly easy win (E.g., 20 .... Q—R7ch; 21 K—Kt5! and Black has no check.)

The interesting feature here is that in the diagrammed position it does White no good to have the opposition! For Black to play moves 1 .... K—Q2, when 2 K—Kt6? would be bad because of 2 .... P—Kt4, and now Black has an outside passed Pawn and will win. Before he can draw any profit from the opposition White must first clarify the position on the King-side. *1*

.... *K—Q2; 2 K—Q5, K—K2; 3 P—K5, P×P; 4 K×P, P—Kt3* (or 4 .... K—Q2; 5 K—Q5, P—Kt3); *5 P—R3, P—KR4* (5 .... P—R3; 6 K—Q5, K—B3; 7 K—B6 is no better—White queens with check); *6 P—KR4, K—B2; 7 P—B5!, K—Kt2; 8 P×P, K×P; 9 K—K6* and now the opposition on the King's side is decisive.

No. 93

Black to play. Draw.

Where the Pawns are far apart and there is a constant threat of creating a passed Pawn (as in No. 92) the win is neither easy nor certain. In No. 92a, White: K at Q5, P's at QR4, QKt3, QB5, KKt4, KR3; Black: K at K2, P's at QR4, QKt2, KB2, KKt2, KR3, the dominating position of the White King does him no good. With 1 .... P—KKt3 followed by P—KB4 at the proper moment (after White has played P—B6) Black is assured of equality.

Again, when the defending side has more reserve Pawn tempi and the win depends upon exploiting the opposition, the result is usually a draw. In this connection one of the few recorded Morphy endings is pertinent. No. 92b (Morphy-Loewenthal, 8th match game, 1858), White: K at KKt5, P's at QR4, QKt3, Q3, K4, KB5; Black: K at KB2, P's at QR2, QKt3, QB4, K4, KKt2. If the Black Pawn were at QR4 here, Morphy could have forcibly occupied the square KKt6: 1 K—R4, K—K2; 2 K—Kt4, K—B3 (2 .... K—B2; 3 K—Kt5); 3 K—R5, K—B2; 4 K—Kt5, K any; 5 K—Kt6 when P—B6 would have brought him a speedy victory. But because Loewenthal has two extra tempi, he can hold the game. The continuation was 1 K—R4, K—K2; 2 K—Kt4, K—B3; 3 K—R5, P—QR3; 4 K—R4, P—Kt3; 5 P—R5!, P×RP; 6 P×P, K×P; 7 K—Kt4 (Morphy's ingenuity is of no avail; his opponent still has the needed tempo), P—R5!; 8 P×P, P—R4. Here the game could have been abandoned as a draw, but Morphy took too many chances and lost.

The complexity of the conversion of a better King position into one where one has the opposition is illustrated in No. 93 (Bernstein-Fine, New York, 1940). The first winning plan which comes to mind consists of manoeuvring against the weak K-side Pawns. Thus, e.g., 1 .... K—B5; 2 K—B2, P—Kt5; 3 P×P, K×P; 4 K—Kt2, P—KR4; 5 K—B2, K—R6; 6 K—Kt1, P—R5; 7 K—R1 but now Black has reached a dead end. However, instead of 2 .... P—Kt5, 2 .... P—KR4 might have been tried: 3 K—K2, P—Kt5; 4 P×P, P×P; 5 K—

B2, K—Kt4; 6 K—Kt3, P—Kt3; 7 K—B2, K—R5; 8 K—Kt2, P—Kt4; 9 K—Kt1, K—R6; 10 K—R1, P—Kt6; 11 P×P, K×P; 12 K—Kt1. Thus this variation would also result in a draw but it furnishes a valuable hint for a winning scheme: if White's Pawns on the Queen's side were weakened, i.e., if his QBP were at QB3 the K could march over (after 12 K—Kt1) and gobble up a Pawn. Consequently Black's first effort is to induce a Pawn advance on the Q-side. *1 .... K—Q5; 2 K—Q2, P—QR4* (clearly Black can only force White to push up his QBP at the point of a gun: So instead the reverse of the first plan will be tried; weaken White's Q-side Pawns, force the White King to stand guard over them, exchange and finally shift over to the other wing. Why the QRP had to move up will soon be seen); *3 K—K2, P—Kt4; 4 K—Q2, P—B5* (If the Black Pawn were still at QR3, 5 QP×P, P×P; 6 P—Kt4 would draw); *5 KtP×P* (with this a draw can just be squeezed out. How the alternatives lose is highly instructive: *A.* 5 P—B3ch, K—Q4; 6 KtP×Pch, P×P; 7 P—Q4 (7 P×Pch, K×P; 8 K—B2, P—R5); K—K3; 8 K—K3, K—B4; 9 K—B2, K—B5; 10 K—K2, P—R4; 11 K—B2, P—Kt5; 12 P×P, P×P; 13 K—K2, K—Kt4; 14 K—B2, K—R5; 15 K—Kt2, P—R5; 16 K—R1, K—R6; 17 K—Kt1, P—Kt6; 18 P×P, K×P; 19 K—B1, K—B6; 20 K—K1, K—K6; 21 K—Q1, K—Q6; 22 K—B1, P—R6!; 23 P×P, K×P; 24 P—R4 (24 K—Kt1, K—Q7; or 24 K—Q1, K—Kt7), K—Kt5; 25 K—B2, K×P; 26 K—B3, K—Kt4. *B.* 5 P—B3ch, K—Q4; 6 QP×Pch, P×P; 7 K—B2, P—B4 (7 .... P×Pch would only draw); 8 P×Pch, K×P; 9 P—Kt3ch (or 9 K—Q2, K—Kt6; 10 K—B1, P—B5; 11 K—Kt1, P—R5; 12 K—B1, P—R6; 13 P×P, K×BP), K—Q4; 10 K—Q3, P—B5ch!; 11 K—B2, K—B4; 12 K—Kt2, P×P; 13 K×P, P—R5ch; 14 K×P, K—B5; 15 K—R5, K×P; 16 K—Kt6, K—Q6. Black gets there first. *C.* 5 K—K2, P—B6!! (the simplest); 6 P×Pch, K×P; 7 K—Q1, P—R5 and again White will have to give up two Pawns to stop the QRP.), *5 .... P×P; 6 P×P* (again best: on 6 P—B3ch, K—B4; 7 P—Q4ch, K—Kt4; 8 K—B1, K—R5; 9 K—B2, P—R4 and Black again penetrates to QKt6), *K×P; 7 K—K3, P—R5; 8 P—B4!!* (8 K—K4?, P—B4; 9 P—B4, P×P; 10 K×P, K—Q5; 11 P—R4, P—B5 is hopeless), *P×Pch* (or 8 .... P—B4; 9 P—Kt3ch!=); *9 K×P, K—Q5; 10 K—B3!!, P—R4!!* (the only chance: if 10 .... P—B4; 11 K—K2, P—B5; 12 K—Q2, P—B6ch; 13 K—B1!=); *11 K—K2, K—K5; 12 K—B2, K—B5; 13 K—Kt2* (White must not move any Pawns), *K—Kt5; 14 K—B2!, K—R6; 15 K—Kt1, P—R5* (the crucial position: if it were Black's move here he would win by 16 .... P—B4; 17 K—R1, P—B5; 18 P—B3, K—Kt5; 19 K—Kt2, P—R6ch; 20 K—B2, K—B5; 21 K—K2, K—K5; 22 K—K1, K—K6; 23 K—Q1, K—Q6; 24 K—B1, P—R6!); *16 K—R1, P—B4; 17 K—Kt1, P—B5; 18 P—B3, K—Kt5; 19*

K—B2, K—B5; 20 P—R3= for
White now has the opposition.

Where one side already has the opposition, other things being equal,
it is usually fairly simple to convert
it into the gain of material. In
No. 94 (Brinckmann-Rubinstein,
Budapest, 1929) it is clear that the
winning method will consist of first
forcing an entry on the King's
side, then driving the White King
from the first and second ranks,
following by exchanging the KtP's
and finally securing a sufficient
advantage on the Queen's side.
Thus before forcing the issue on the

No. 94

Black wins.

King's wing Black must make sure that he will be able to capture a
sufficient number of Pawns, or queen earlier on the Queen's wing. It
turns out that this is feasible *1 .... K—Kt5; 2 K—Kt1* (or 2 P—
KKt3, K—R6; 3 K—B3, P—Kt4; 4 K—B2, P—KKt5), *K—Kt6;
3 K—B1; P—Kt4; 4 K—Kt1, P—KKt5; 5 K—R1!, K—B7; 6 K—R2,
P—Kt5!* (but not 6 .... K—B8??; 7 K—Kt3, K—Kt8; 8 K×P,
K×P; 9 K—B4, K—B7; 10 K—K5, K—K7; 11 K×P, K—Q7;
12 K—B5, K×P; 13 K×P, K—Kt6!; 14 K—B5!, K×P; 15 K—Kt4!
and Black is lost); *7 BP×P, P—Q5; 8 P—Kt5, P—Q6; 9 P—Kt6,
P—Q7; 10 P—Kt7, P—Q8= Q; 11 P—Kt8= Q, Q—Kt8 mate.* But
such variations are not typical of the usual run of these endings.
What actually happened shows a winning method which can be more
often applied.

Instead of the above, Rubinstein chose a line which is less compli-
cated, but equally effective: *1 .... K—K5; 2 K—K2, P—Kt4; 3 K—
B2* (if now 3 K—Q2, K—B5; 4 K—K2, K—Kt6; 5 K—B1, K—R7;
6 K—B2, P—KKt5; 7 K—B1, P—Kt6), *P—Q5; 4 P×P, K×P;
5 K—K2, P—QKt5!; 6 K—Q2, P—Kt6; 7 P—B3ch, K—K5; 8 K—
K2, K—B5: 9 K—B2, K—Kt5; 10 K—B1, K—Kt6; 11 K—Kt1, P—
Kt5; 12 K—B1* (or 12 K—R1, K—B7; 13 K—R2, K—B8; 14 K—R1,
K—K7; 15 K—R2, K—Q7; 16 K—Kt3, K—B7, etc.), *K—R7; 13
K—B2, K—R8; 14 K—Kt3, K—Kt8; 15 K×P, K×P* and here Brinck-
mann resigned, since his Pawn will only be on the sixth when Black
queens.

Often a game is a draw or a win depending on who happens to have
the move, and Pawn moves cannot change the situation either way.
In No. 94a (Ed. Lasker-Maroczy, New York, 1924) White: K at K4,
P's at QR4, QKt3, QB2, Q5, KR3, KR5; Black: K at KB3, P's at

QR4, QKt5, QB4, Q3, KKt4, KR3, White loses if he has to play for after 1 K—Q3, K—K4; 2 K—B4, K—K5; 3 K—Kt5, K×P; 4 K×P, K—B3!; 5 K—R6, P—Q4; 6 P—R5, P—B5; 7 K—R7, K—B2; 8 P—R6, P×P; 9 P×P, P—Q5; 10 K—R8, P—Q6; 11 P—R7, P—Q7; 12 P—R4, P—Q8=Q mates next move. But Black to play can hold the draw by 1 .... K—K2! (not 1 .... K—B2; 2 K—B5, when White has the opposition); 2 K—Q3 (or 2 K—B5, K—B2—White has no extra tempi), K—B3!; 3 K—K4, for 3 K—B4??, K—K4! loses as above.

No. 95

Draw only if White fixes the Pawns on the King's side.

No. 96

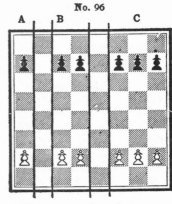

A   B   C

Whoever moves loses the tempo.

When one side has the opposition, but needs several extra tempi to exploit it properly, it is all-important to manoeuvre the Pawns properly. The consequences of neglecting a timely clarification of the Pawn position may be seen in No. 95 (Lissitzin-Alatortzeff, Moscow, 1935). *1 K—B3, P—QR4; 2 P—R4, P—R4; 3 K—Q3?* (this should not yet lose, but it deserves a question mark because 3 P—KKt4 would have removed all danger: 3 .... P×P—3 .... P—KKt3; 4 P—Kt5—; 4 P×P, P—B3; 5 P—R5, P—QKt3; 6 P—K4, P—K4; 7 K—Q3! etc.), *K—Kt5; 4 K—B2, P—QKt4* (he must first exchange, since 4 .... K—R6; 5 K—B3, K—R7; 6 K—B4! would be bad); *5 P×P, K×P!; 6 K—B3, K—B4; 7 K—Q3??* (now this is fatal. Both 7 P—Kt4 as above and 7 P—K4! would have held the position. E.g., 7 P—K4: *A.* 7 .... P—K4; 8 P—B4, P—B3; 9 K—Q3, K—Kt5; 10 K—B2, P—R5 (or 10 .... K—R6; 11 K—B3, P—Kt3; 12 K—B4, K—Kt7; 13 P—QKt4!, P—R5; 14 P—Kt5 and the Pawns promote at the same time); 11 P×P, K×P; 12 K—B3, K—Kt4; 13 K—Kt3, K—B4; 14 K—B3, P—Kt3; 15 K—Q3, K—Kt5; 16 K—K3 and

Black must take the draw with 16 .... K—B4, for if 16 .... K—B5??; 17 P—B5!!, P×P; 18 P×P, K—Q4; 19 P—Kt4!, K—Q3; 20 P—Kt5! wins for White. *B.* 7 .... K—Kt4; 8 P—B4, K—B4; 9 P—K5!, K—Kt4; 10 K—Q3, K—Kt5; 11 K—B2, P—R5; 12 P×P, K×P; 13 K—B3, K—Kt4; 14 K—Kt3=), *K—Kt5; 8 K—B2, K—R6; 9 K—B3, K—R7; 10 K—B2* (now 10 P—QKt4 would lose after 10 .... P×Pch; 11 K×P, K—Kt7; 12 K—B4, K—B7; 13 K—Q4, K—Q7; 14 K—K4, K—K7; 15 K—B4, P—B3!; 16 P—Kt4, P—Kt3!; 17 P×P (17 P—Kt5, P—K4ch; 18 K—K4, P×P!), P×P; 18 K—K4, K—B7; 19 K—B4, K—Kt7), *P—B4* (now it is perfectly clear why White's do-nothingness was fatal: Black has the requisite Pawn tempo); *11 K—B3, K—Kt8; 12 P—K4, P×P; 13 P×P, P—K4!; 14 K—Q3, K—Kt7; 15 K—B4, K—B7; 16 K—Q5* (the condemned man dines on a Pawn), *K×P; 17 K×P, P—R5* and White soon resigned.

IX. MANOEUVRING FOR A TEMPO

As most of the above examples indicate, the proper manipulation of Pawns to maintain as large a reserve as possible is often a vital consideration. While no rule can be given which can cover all positions, the elementary cases will be sufficient for a large percentage of the endings that do occur.

To gain a tempo it is disadvantageous to have to move first. Starting from the symmetrical position (No. 96) the person who does not move always retains an extra tempo, by simply copying his opponent's moves.

A. *1 P—R3, P—R3; 2 P—R4, P—R4.*

B. *1 P—B3, P—B3; 2 P—Q3, P—Q3; 3 P—B4, P—B4;* or 3 P—Q4, P—Q4.

C. *1 P—B3, P—B3; 2 P—Kt3, P—Kt3; 3 P—R3, P—R3; 4 P—B4, P—R4!* (not 4 .... P—B4; 5 P—Kt4!, P—R4; 6 P×RP, P×P; 7 P—R4); *5 P—Kt4* (or 5 P—R4, P—B4; or 5 P—B5, P×P; 6 P—R4, P—B5!; 7 P×P, P—B4), *P—R5!; 6 P—Kt5, P—B4;* or *6 P—B5, P—Kt4.*

From this last variation we can draw the all-important conclusion that *an exchange loses the tempo.*

Where the Pawns are not in a symmetrical position, one must generally determine who has the tempo by trial and error, always remembering however that in a symmetrical position whoever moves loses.

X. THE OPPOSITION

One of the most important considerations in Pawn endings is how to occupy certain squares with the King, or how to drive the enemy

King from a vital square. Because the Kings cannot approach one another directly, but must always be separated by a chessic *cordon sanitaire* the occupation of squares is determined by the Pawn position and by the position of the other King. Where no relevant Pawn moves are available, it depends solely on the relative positions of the two Kings, and of all such possible relative positions those involving the opposition are the ones of chief interest.

The simplest case is shown in No. 97, where whoever plays has to cede one of the two (presumably vital) squares he is holding. Thus *1 .... K—B3; 2 K—Q5,* or *1 .... K—Q3; 2 K—B5,* or *1 K—Q4,*

<table>
<tr><td align="center">No. 97</td><td align="center">No. 98</td></tr>
<tr><td>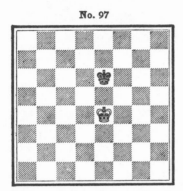</td><td></td></tr>
<tr><td align="center">Whoever is not on the move has the opposition.</td><td align="center">Whoever is not on the move has the distant opposition.</td></tr>
</table>

K—B4, or *1 K—B4, K—Q4.* If we imagine Pawns on the Q and KKt files we can see under what circumstances these squares are ordinarily vital. E.g., No. 97a, White: K at K4, P's at QB4, KKt4; Black: K at K3, P's at QB4, KKt4. Then if Black is to move, White has the opposition and wins, for on 1 .... K—B3; 2K—Q5 captures the QBP and similarly on the other side. But if White is to move the game is only a draw. For on 1 K—Q3, both K—B4, and K—Q4 are impossible, so that it does Black no good to have the opposition. Only if White makes the blunder 1 K—K3? is Black able to do anything, for he then replies 1 .... K—K4! and now he has an opposition that means something.

Direct opposition may be vertical (as in No. 97) or horizontal (White King at QB6 or KKt6) or diagonal (White King at KKt4 or QB4). All of these are equally effective as far as capturing squares is concerned, but whether they are a winning advantage or not depends on the Pawn position. Thus No. 97b, White: K at KKt4, P's at Q3,

K4; Black: K at K3, P's at Q5, K4. Black to play. White has the opposition and wins because the occupation of KB5 is decisive. 1 .... K—B3; 2 K—R5, K—B2; 3 K—Kt5, K—K3; 4 K—Kt6 (*horizontal opposition*), K—Q3; 5 K—B6, etc. But No. 97c, White: K at KKt4, P's at QB4, Q3, K4; Black: K at K3, P's at QB4, Q3, K4 Black to play, the opposition is useless because occupation of KB5 leads to nothing. 1 .... K—B3; 2 K—R5, K—B2; 3 K—Kt5, K—Kt2; 4 K—B5, K—B2=.

The *distant opposition* (No. 98) is an extension of the same principle. When two Kings are on the same file and an *odd number of squares apart* then whoever is not on the move has the distant opposition. The distant opposition is usually a potent weapon when the Pawn position is badly blocked or involved, and depends for its effectiveness not only on the occupation of certain specific squares but also on forcing the enemy King to go to or keep off certain files. Or again in No. 99 (Folbys, 1931) 1 K—B1 gives White the distant opposition (five squares away from the Black King). But clearly in order to win he must occupy either KB4, or QR6, and not merely QR5, for then Black's King could prevent further invasion. This means that when the White King gets to QR5, the Black King must be no nearer than QB2. In other words White must contrive to force Black to stay two files to his right. Thus the solution is *1 K—B1!, K—K2; 2 K—K1!, K—B2; 3 K—Q1, K—K2; 4 K—B2, K—K3* (if 4 .... K—Q2; 5 K—B3, K—B2; 5 K—Q2, K—Kt2; 6 K—K3, K—R3; 7 K—B4; K—R4; 8 K—K5!!, P—Kt5; 9 P×Pch, K×P; 10 K—Q6, K—R6; 11 K×P, K×P; 12 K×P, K—Kt6; 13 P—B6, P—R6; 14 P—B7, P—R7; 15 P—B8=Q, P—R8=Q; 16 Q×P and wins); *5 K—Q2, K—B3* (or 5 .... K—Q2; 6 K—K3, K—B2; 7 K—B4, etc.); *6 K—B3, K—K2; 7 K—Kt4, K—Q2; 8 K—R5, K—B2; 9 K—R6; K—Q1; 10 K—Kt7, K—Q2; 11 K—Kt6* and wins.

Other examples of the uses of the distant opposition may be found in Nos. 70, 67a, 67b, etc.

A problem which sums up all the advantages of the opposition is No. 100 (L'Hermet, 1914). The solution is *1 K—R2* (distant opposition) *K—Kt1; 2 K—Kt2, K—B1; 3 K—B2, K—K1; 4 K—K2, K—Q1; 5 K—Q2, K—B1; 6 K—B2, K—Kt1; 7 K—Kt2, K—R1; 8 K—B3* (a triangulation manoeuvre. White can now keep the distant opposition

No. 99

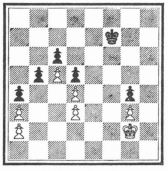

White to play wins.

at a distance of only three squares), *K—Kt2; 9 K—Kt3, K—R2* (if
9 .... K—B2; 10 K—R4 and reaches QR8); *10 K—B4; K—Kt3;*
11 K—Kt4, K—R2; 12 K—B5 (diagonal opposition), *K—Kt2; 13 K—*
Kt5, K—R2; 14 K—B6, K—Kt1; 15 K—Kt6, K—R1; 16 K—B7,
K—R2; 17 K—B8.

If one remembers the principle that with Kings on the same file,
rank or diagonal, when they are an odd number of squares apart whoever does not play has the opposition, manoeuvring in such position
becomes automatic. E.g., No. 100a, White: K at QB6, P's at QB4,
K4; Black: K at K3, P at Q3. White to play. Draw. 1 K—B7,
K—K2; 2 K—B8, K—K1, or 1 K—Kt7, K—B2!! (but not 1 .... K—

No. 100   No. 100A

White to play has the opposition and   White to play wins by triangulating.
must reach QR8 or QB8 in at most
17 moves.

K4?; 2 K—B7, or 1 .... K—B3; 2 K—B8!!, or 1 .... K—K2; 2 K—
B7); 2 K—Kt6, K—B3! (again not 2 .... K—B1?; 3 K—B6, K—K2;
4 K—B7) and White's extra Pawn is worthless.

Other examples of the opposition are almost everywhere in this
chapter.

Triangulation is a stratagem which is closely allied to the opposition.
It is feasible when one side has more squares available for his King
than his opponent. No. 100A is the typical case. If White approached
the Pawn directly by 1 K—K3? Black could reply 1 .... K—K4 and
White would have to retreat. But White has two avenues of approach
to K3 (Q2 and K2), while Black has only one to K4 (Q3). That is,
White can manoeuvre in the *triangle* Q2—K2—K3, while Black must
stick to the straight line Q3—K4. Consequently a tempo move by
White will do the trick. Thus: *1 K—Q2* and if *1 .... K—K4;*
2 K—K3, while if *1 .... K—B3,* likewise *2 K—K3,* winning the Pawn
in both cases.

Chapter III

KNIGHT AND PAWN ENDINGS

I. THE KNIGHTS ALONE VS. PAWNS

A lone Knight can only win against Pawns in certain problem positions where the enemy King is blocked by his own Pawns. What White is usually faced with is whether he can draw against one or two or more Pawns. To this question a definite answer can be given in practically every case which comes up in over the board play. We shall try to give this answer systematically here.

Knight against one Pawn is a draw whenever the Knight can reach any square on the queening file ahead of the Pawn (except QR1 with the RP). No. 101 is the crucial position. If Black tries *1 .... K—B7;* then *2 Kt—R3ch,* while on *1 .... K—R7; 2 Kt—Q2* is the rejoinder. Even if White were for some reason forced to move his Knight he could draw with *1 Kt—Q2ch, K—B7; 2 Kt—B4!, P queens; 3 Kt—R3ch.* Against a RP, No. 101a, White: K at KR8, Kt at QR4; Black: K at QKt4, P at QR4, the advance of the Pawn can also be prevented by 1 Kt—B3ch, K—Kt5; 2 Kt—Q5ch, K—B5; 3 Kt—Kt6ch, K—Kt4; 4 Kt—Q5!, or even 1 Kt—Kt2, K—Kt5; 2 Kt—Q3ch, K—B6; 3 Kt—B5, etc. Only when the Pawn is at R7 does White lose, for on .... K—Kt7 the only moves which do not put the Knight en prise are off the board. The worst place that a Knight can be is one square diagonally in front of the Pawn. E.g., No. 101b, White: K at KR8, Kt at QKt2; Black: K at QR1, P at QR5. On 1 .... P—R6 the Knight can no longer catch the Pawn.

When the Knight is at some distance away from the Pawn, or can for some other reason not get to a square on the queening file directly,

No. 101

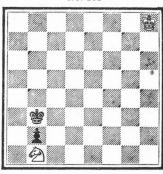

Draw.

81

he can very often get back in time by checking or threatening to check. This is the saving idea in No. 102 (Grigoreff, 1932) *1 .... Kt—B7!!* (1 Kt—Kt6 loses: 1 .... P—R6; 2 Kt—B4, P—R7; 3 Kt—K2ch, K—Q7; 4 Kt—Kt3, K—K8!), *P—R6; 2 Kt—Kt5, P—R7; 3 Kt— K4ch, K—B7* (or 3 .... K—Q5; 4 Kt—B2!! and Black must retreat to be able to approach the Knight, which gives White a breathing spell in which he can bring up his King: 4 .... K—B6; 5 K—Q6, K—Q7; 6 K—K5, K—K7; 7 Kt—R1!, K—B6; 8 K—Q4, K—Kt7; 9 K—K3, K×Kt; 10 K—B2 stalemate); *4 Kt—Kt3, K—Q8; 5 K—Q6, K—K8; 6 K—K5, K—B7; 7 K—B4=.*

A mate with Kt vs. P is possible only in the problem position No. 102a, White: K at QB1, Kt at Q3; Black: K at QR7, P at QR6. White to play. 1 K—B2, K—R8; 2 Kt—B1!, P—R7; 3 Kt—Kt3 mate.

No. 102   **No. 103**

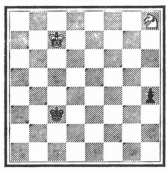

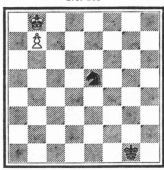

White plays and draws.   White wins. Draw if Pawn is on B, Q or K files. Win on KT or R files.

When the Pawn is on the seventh with the King right near, with a KtP or RP there are good winning chances, but with a center Pawn or BP there are not. In No. 103, Black to play is lost, for on *1 .... Kt—Q2ch; 2 K—B8!* (not 2 K—B7?, Kt—B4!=), *Kt—Kt3ch; 3 K— Q8* and queens. But in No. 103a, White: K at QB8, P at QB7; Black: K at KR8, Kt at KB4, after 1 .... Kt—K2ch (1 .... Kt—Q3ch?; 2 K—Q7, Kt—B5; 3 K—B6, Kt—K4ch; 4 K—B5, Kt—Q2ch; 5 K— Kt5); 2 K—Q8, Kt—B3ch; 3 K—K8, Kt—R2! we get back to No. 101.

Knight vs. two Pawns is likewise a draw in general, because a Knight can blockade two connected passed Pawns. In No. 104 the block is achieved by *1 Kt—B3!, P—Kt6* (or 1 .... P—B6; 2 Kt—Q4 or 1 .... K—R7; 2 Kt—Q2 or 2 K—K7); *2 Kt—Q2, P—Kt7; 3 Kt— Kt1.* If the Knight is anywhere near the Pawns such a manoeuvre is always possible provided the Pawns are not on the sixth or seventh.

No. 104

Draw.

No. 105

White to play draws; Black to play wins.

E.g., No. 104a, White: K at K7, Kt at QB1; Black: K at QB1, P's at KB4, K5. 1 .... P—B5 (White to play: 1 Kt—K2); 2 Kt—Kt3! (2 Kt—K2?, P—B6; 3 Kt—Kt3, P—K6 loses), P—B6; 3 Kt—Q2, P—B7; 4 Kt—B1.

Where the King is supporting the two Pawns, the game is tenable for the side which has the Knight only if his King is likewise on the scene. In No. 105 *1 K—Kt1* holds the position, for if *1 .... P—B7ch; 2 Kt×P*, if *1 .... P—Kt7; 2 Kt—Q1, K—Kt6; 3 Kt×KtP!* and finally if *1 .... K—Kt5; 2 Kt—Q5ch, K—B5; 3 Kt×P, K×Kt; 4 K— B1.* With Black to move in the diagrammed position *1 .... K—R7* is decisive, for on any Kt move *2 Kt—Q1* (e.g.), *P—Kt7ch* queens with check. Even when the Black King is not right near the Pawns, as in No. 105a, White: K at KR3, Kt at KB3; Black: K at KB2, P's at QKt4, QB5, he can still win by 1 .... K—B3; 2 Kt—Q4, P—Kt5; 3 K—R4, P—Kt6; 4 Kt—K2, P— Kt7; 5 Kt—B3, K—K4 and K—Q5.

If the King were off in some far corner here Black could clearly force a queen even if his Pawns were only on the fourth or fifth ranks.

Again there is a possible mating position with two Pawns: No. 106. If White begins, *1 Kt—B6, K—R8; 2 Kt—Kt4, P—R7; 3 K—B1, P— Kt4; 4 Kt—B2* mate. If Black begins, *1 .... K—R8* (or 1 .... P— Kt4; 2 Kt—B6, P—Kt5; 3 Kt×*

No. 106

White wins.

Pch, K—R8; 4 K—B1); *2 Kt—B6, K—R7; 3 Kt—Kt4ch, K—R8; 4 K—B1, P—Kt4; 5 K—B2, P—R7; 6 Kt—K3, P—Kt5; 7 Kt—B1, P —Kt6ch; 8 Kt×P* mate.

When the Pawns are disconnected they can be checked by the Knight only if they are one, two or three files apart. The outcome then depends on the relative King positions. With the Black King anywhere near the Pawns a draw is inevitable; with the Black King far away and the White King near the Pawns the Knight cannot hold back the tide. Two examples will suffice here. In No. 107 White to move draws by *1 Kt—B3, P—Kt7; 2 Kt—Kt1!* (not 2 K—K6, P— K7; 3 K—B5, P—Kt8 = Q; 4 Kt×Q, P—Kt8 = Q), *K—B2; 3 K—K6, K—B3; 4 K—K5,* etc. Black to play forces a Queen. Or as in No.

No. 107

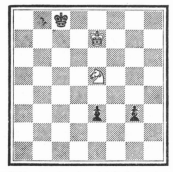

White to play draws; Black to play wins.

No. 108

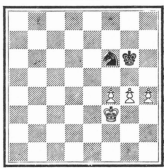

White plays and wins; Black plays and draws. Win for White if Pawns are on fifth or sixth ranks.

107a (problem by Grigorieff), White: K at K2, Kt at KR7; Black: K at K1, P's at QKt5, KR3, the King takes care of one Pawn, the Knight of the other: 1 Kt—B6ch, K—B2; 2 Kt—K4, K—K3; 3 K—Q3, K— B4; 4 Kt—Kt3ch, K—B5; 5 Kt—R5ch, etc.

Again there is a mating position with two disconnected Pawns: No. 107b (problem by Jaenisch), White: K at QB1, Kt at QB3; Black: K at QR8, P's at QR6, QB5. 1 Kt—Q5, K—R7; 2 K—B2, K—R8; 3 Kt—Kt4, P—B6; 4 K—B1, P—B7; 5 Kt×Pch, K—R7; 6 Kt—Q4, K—R8; 7 K—B2, K—R7; 8 Kt—K2, K—R8; 9 Kt—B1.

In No. 108 we have the critical position of the ending with Kt vs. 3 connected passed Pawns. White to play wins by *1 P—B5ch!* (not 1 P—Kt5, Kt—Q4!; 2 K—K4, Kt—K2!!; 3 K—K5, K—R4!!; 4 P—B5, K×P; 5 K—B6—or A—, Kt—Q4ch; 6 K—K6, K×P; 7 K×Kt, K×P. A. 5 P—Kt6, K—Kt4!; 6 P—Kt7, Kt—Kt1; 7 K—K6, Kt—

B3), *K—Kt2; 2 P—Kt5, Kt—Q4; 3 P—R5, Kt—B6* (for 3 .... K—B2; 4 P—R6, Kt—B6; 5 P—R7, K—Kt2; 6 P—Kt6, Kt—Q4 see No. 108b); *4 K—B4, Kt—K7ch; 5 K—K5, Kt—Kt6; 6 P—B6ch, K—Kt1; 7 P—R6!, Kt—R4; 8 P—Kt6, Kt—Kt6; 9 P—R7ch, K—R1; 10 P—B7.* From this we may infer that if the White Pawns are anywhere beyond the fourth rank, unless they are completely blockaded, they will be able to promote. This is borne out by two sub-variations: No. 108a, White: K at KKt4, P's at KR5, KKt5, KB4; Black: K at K3, Kt at KB2. White wins. 1 .... Kt—Q3; 2 P—R6, K—B2; 3 K—R5, Kt—K1 (or 3 .... K—Kt1; 4 P—Kt6, Kt—K5; 5 P—B5, Kt—B3ch; 6 K—Kt5, Kt—K5ch; 7 K—B4, Kt—B3; 8 P—R7ch, K—Kt2 transposing into 108b); 4 P—B5, Kt—Q3; 5 P—Kt6ch, K—B3; 6 P—R7, K—Kt2; 7 P—B6ch, K—R1; 8 P—B7. No. 108b, White: K at K5, P's at KB5, KKt6, KR7; Black: K at KR1, Kt at KB3. White wins. 1 .... Kt—R4 (or 1 .... Kt—Kt5ch; 2 K—K6, K—Kt2; 3 P—B6ch, Kt×P; 4 P—R8=Qch, K×Q; 5 K×Kt and White has the opposition./ Or 1 .... Kt—Q2ch; 2 K—K6, Kt—B1ch; 3 K—K7, Kt×RP; 4 P× Kt, K×P; 5 P—B6); 2 K—K6, K—Kt2 (or 2 .... Kt—B5ch; 3 K—K7—White must avoid stalemate possibilities—, Kt—R4; 4 K—B7); 3 K—K7, Kt—B5; 4 P—B6ch, K—R1; 5 P—Kt7ch! (not 5 K—B7?, Kt×P!), K×P; 6 K—B7.

But if it were Black's turn to move in the diagrammed position he could draw by *1 .... Kt—Q4; 2 P—R5ch* (2 K—K4, Kt—B3ch. 2 P—B5ch, K—B3; 3 K—K4, Kt—B6ch; 4 K—Q4, Kt—K7ch!; 5 K—K3, Kt—Kt6=), *K—R3!* (the most advanced Pawn must be blockaded. If instead 2 .... K—B3; 3 P—R6!, K—Kt3; 4 P—Kt5, Kt—K2; 5 K—Kt4 and wins, for 5 .... Kt—B4; 6 P—R7! costs Black his Knight); *3 K—K4, Kt—B3ch; 4 K—B5, Kt—Q4; 5 K—K5, Kt—K6; 6 P—Kt5ch, K×P; 7 K—B6, Kt—Q4ch=.*

To sum up: The three Pawns win if and only if at least two can reach the fifth rank. Black should always keep his King in front of the Pawns.

Where the three Pawns are disconnected (two connected) it requires little argument to show that the Knight cannot hold them back. Either the Knight must be sacrificed to stop one isolated Pawn, or it must blockade the two connected Pawns, when the White King after advancing his isolated Pawn to drive the Black King to the other side of the board will come to the support of his two passed Pawns. Against three isolated Pawns the chances of holding the game are somewhat better because the King can usually capture one, while the Knight holds the other two. However, even here the three Pawns should win as a rule. The type of drawing chance may be seen in No. 108c, White: K at KB4, Kt at Q1; Black: K at QKt5, P's at QKt3, Q7, KR5. White draws by 1 K—K3, P—R6; 2 K×P, P—R7; 3 Kt—B2, K—

Kt6; 4 K—K2!!, K—B7; 5 K—B3, P—Kt4; 6 K—Kt2, P—Kt5; 7 Kt—Kt4!, P—Kt6; 8 Kt—K3ch and we have the equivalent of No. 101.

Although two Knights against a lone King cannot mate, in certain positions two Knights vs. a Pawn can. This is due to the circumstance that the Knights can only mate by stalemating the King first and the extra Pawn leaves the King stalemated but gives the player two or three more moves, depending on where it is. The winning idea then consists of three steps: 1. Blocking the Pawn; 2. Confining the King to a corner where he must move back and forth between two squares; 3. Lifting the blockade at the appropriate moment, when the win is possible because for a short while stalemating the Black King is admissible.

<table>
<tr><td style="text-align:center">No. 109</td><td style="text-align:center">No. 110</td></tr>
<tr><td>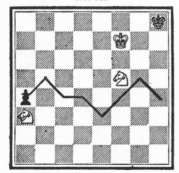</td><td>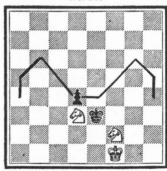</td></tr>
<tr><td style="text-align:center">Black to play. White wins if the Pawn
cannot cross the heavy line.</td><td style="text-align:center">Black to play. White wins if the Pawn
cannot cross the heavy line.</td></tr>
</table>

There is a vast literature available on this ending * but since the greater part has little or no relation to problems of practical play we shall only give the main results here (chiefly by Troitzky).

Once the King is in the corner, as in No. 109, mate can be given in six moves (White to play) or eleven moves (Black to play). *1 Kt—B4!, P—R6; 2 Kt—K5, P—R7; 3 Kt—Kt6ch, K—R2; 4 Kt—B8ch, K—R1; 5 Kt—K7* (or R4), *P—R8= Q; 8 Kt(Kt7 or R4)—Kt6* mate. We can see why a KtP may not be beyond the fourth rank, for if it queens at Kt8, on Kt—Kt6ch the rejoinder Q×Kt is available. If it is Black's move, on *1 .... K—R2;* White must first manoeuvre to get the diagrammed position: *2 K—B6, K—Kt1; 3 K—K7!, K—R1; 4 K—B8, K—R2; 5 K—B7, K—R1; 6 Kt—B4* and continue as above.

All this is relatively simple. Complications arise when the King is

* See Berger, Endspiel, pp. 433–446, for further analysis references.

in the center of the board (No. 110). The process of driving him into a corner is then long and involved, as a matter of fact it requires an extension of the ordinary 50-move rule. The main variation as given by Troitzky runs as follows: *1 .... K—B6; 2 K—K1, K—K6; 3 K— Q1, K—B6; 4 K—Q2, K—Kt7; 5 K—K2, K—Kt6; 6 Kt—K4ch, K—Kt5; 7 K—B2, K—B4; 8 K—B3, K—K3; 9 K—B4, K—Q4; 10 Kt—Q2, K—K3; 11 K—K4, K—B3; 12 K—Q5, K—B4; 13 K—Q6, K—B3; 14 K—Q7, K—B4; 15 K—K7, K—Kt3; 16 K—K6, K—Kt4; 17 K—K5, K—Kt3; 18 Kt—K4, K—Kt2; 19 Kt—Kt5, K—Kt3; 20 Kt—K6, K—B2; 21 Kt(K6)—B4, K—K2; 22 Kt—Kt6ch, K—Q2; 23 K—Q5, K—B2; 24 Kt(Kt6)—K5, K—Kt3; 25 Kt—B4ch, K—B2; 26 K—K5* (White must lose a move), *K—Q2; 27 K—B6, K—B2; 28 K—K7, K—B3; 29 K—K6, K—B2; 30 Kt(B4)—K5, K—Kt3; 31 K— Q5* (the same position as on the 24th move, only now Black must play), *K—R4; 32 K—B4, K—Kt3; 33 K—Kt4, K—Kt2; 34 K—Kt5, K—B2; 35 K—B5, K—Q1; 36 K—Q6, K—K1; 37 Kt—Kt4, K—B2; 38 K—Q7, K—Kt2; 39 K—K7, K—Kt3; 40 K—K6, K—Kt4; 41 Kt(Kt4)—K5, K— R4; 42 K—B6, K—R3; 43 Kt—Kt4ch, K—R4* (*43 .... K—R2; 44 K—B7*); *44 K—B5, K—R5; 45 Kt—B6, K—R6; 46 K—K5, K— Kt6; 47 K—K4, K—R5; 48 K—B4, K—R6; 49 Kt—K4, K—R5; 50 Kt—Kt3, K—R6; 51 Kt—B5.* Mate in fifteen!!: *51 .... K—Kt7; 52 K—Kt4, K—R7; 53 Kt—R4, K—Kt8; 54 K—Kt3, K—B8; 55 K— B3, K—Kt8; 56 Kt—KKt2, K—R7; 57 Kt(Kt2)—B4, K—Kt8; 58 K— K2, K—R7; 59 K—B2, K—R8; 60 Kt—R3, K—R7; 61 Kt—Kt5, K—R8; 62 Kt—K1, P—Q6; 63 Kt(K1)—B3, P—Q7; 64 Kt—K4, P—Q8=Ktch; 65 K—Kt3, Kt—K6; 66 Kt—B2* mate.

This ending actually occurred in a tournament game some years ago. And although Black was the well-known Hungarian grandmaster A. Lilienthal the game resulted in a draw. The position reached was No. 110a (Norman-Lilienthal, Hastings, 1934–'35), White: K at K8, P at QKt3; Black: K at K3, Kt's at K4, QKt5. The shortest road to victory is now *1 .... Kt—B2; 2 K—B8, Kt—Q3; 3 K—Kt7, K—B4; 4 K—R6, Kt—K1!; 5 K—R5!, Kt—Kt2ch; 6 K—R4, K—B5; 7 K— R3, Kt—B4; 8 K—Kt2, K—K6; 9 K—B1!, Kt—R5!; 10 K—K1, Kt—Kt7ch; 11 K—Q1, K—Q6; 12 K—B1, Kt—K6; 13 K—Kt2, Kt(K6)—B7!; 14 K—B1, K—K7; 15 K—Kt1, K—Q8; 16 K—Kt2, K—Q7; 17 K—Kt1, Kt—R6ch; 18 K—Kt2, Kt—Kt4!; 19 K—Kt1, Kt—Q6; 20 P—Kt4, Kt—B6ch; 21 K—R1, K—B7; 22 P—Kt5, Kt— B8; 23 P—Kt6, Kt—Kt6* mate.

When Black has more than one Pawn the two Knights win if they can reduce to a case of No. 110. The first step is to blockade the Pawns, the next to capture all but one. In No. 111 this can be done by *1 K—R3!* (diagonal opposition), *K—Kt4; 2 K—Kt3, K—R4; 3 K— B2!!, K—Kt4; 4 K—Q1!, K—B4; 5 K—K1, K—Q3; 6 K—B2, K—*

K3; 7 K—Kt3, K—B4; 8 K—R4!, K—B3; 9 K—Kt4, K—Kt3; 10 Kt—KB3, K—B3; 11 Kt—Kt3, K—K3; 12 K—Kt5, K—Q3; 13 K— B5, K—B4 (13 .... *P—Q5;* 14 K—K4!); *14 Kt×P, P—Q5; 15 Kt— Q3ch, K—B5; 16 K—K4* and we have No. 110.

Against three Pawns the Kt's are also successful: No. 111a, White: K at K3, Kt's at QB3, KB3; Black: K at KB3, P's at QB3, Q3, K3.

No. 111

No. 112

White plays and wins.   White wins.

1 K—B4, P—K4ch (1 .... K—Kt3; 2 Kt—K4, P—K4ch; 3 K—Kt4, K—Kt2; 4 Kt×P, P—K5; 5 Kt—K5, K—B3; 6 K—B4, K—K3; 7 Kt(Q6)—B4, K—Q4; 8 K—K3, P—B4; 9 K—Q2, etc.); 2 K—Kt4, K—K3; 3 Kt—Kt5ch, K—B3; 4 Kt(B3)—K4ch, K—K2; 5 K—B5, P—Q4; 6 Kt—B5, K—Q3; 7 Kt(Kt5)—K6, P—K5; 8 K—B4, K—K2; 9 K—K5.

Against four connected passed Pawns the Knights cannot set up an effective blockade, so that the result is a draw. More than four Pawns win against two Knights unless a reduction to a simpler draw is available.

II. KNIGHTS AND PAWNS VS. PAWNS

The Knight alone is not a sufficient advantage to win, but if there is a Pawn on the board it is. Naturally, Black can draw only if he can capture the Pawn. For this reason the Pawn should always be defended from the rear by the Knight, which will gladly sacrifice itself to let the Pawn achieve its ambition. In No. 112 Black can do nothing but shunt his King back and forth. White wins by bringing his King up to the support of the Pawn. When it reaches the sixth the King can either be driven away from the queening square by a Knight check, or White may win the opposition by a Knight move. *1 K—Kt2, K—Q3; 2 K—B3, K—K4; 3 K—B4, K—Q3; 4 K—Kt5, K—Q2;*

5 K—B5, K—B2; 6 P—Q6ch, K—Q1; 7 K—B6, K—B1 and now
both *8 Kt—K6, K—Kt1; 9 P—Q7* and *8 P—Q7ch, K—Q1; 9 Kt—
R3, K—K2; 10 K—B7* are adequate.

With the Knight in front of the Pawn a win is possible only if the
King is so near that the Knight can be sacrificed to get the opposition.
Thus, No. 112a, White: K at KR1, P at QKt3, Kt at QB7; Black: K
at K7 is a draw: 1 .... K—Q6; 2 Kt—Q5; K—Q5; 3 Kt—B4, K—B6;
or 2 P—Kt4, K—B5; 3 P—Kt5, K—B4; 4 K—Kt2, K—Kt3. But No.
112b, White: K at KR1, Kt at Q7, P at QB3; Black: K at KB6 is a
win: 1 Kt—B5, K—K6; 2 Kt—R4, K—Q6; 3 K—Kt2, K—B5; 4 K—
B3, K—Kt6; 5 K—K4!, K×Kt; 6 K—Q5.

One must be careful not to advance a Rook Pawn to the seventh

No. 113

Draw.

No. 114

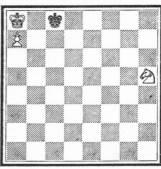

White to play draws; Black to play
loses. A Knight cannot gain a tempo.

too hastily. For in No. 113 it is too late to do anything but cry over
lost opportunities. Black simply moves his King back and forth. The
Kt cannot move without abandoning the Pawn; the King cannot ap-
proach without creating stalemate. On the other hand, in No. 113a,
White: K at QKt5, P at QR5, Kt at QB6; Black: K at QKt2, the
win is child's play: 1 P—R6ch, K—R1; 2 Kt—Kt4, K—R2; 3 K—B6,
K—R1; 4 K—Kt6, K—Kt1; 5 Kt—Q5, K—R1; 6 Kt—B7ch, K—
Kt1; 7 P—R7ch.

The fact that one cannot win a tempo with the Knight (as one can
with a Bishop, e.g.) is strikingly illustrated in No. 114. White to move
can never drive the King away from KB2—KB1, since he must always
approach both squares by giving check. With Black to move, however, *1 .... K—B2; 2 Kt—Kt7, K—B1; 3 Kt—K6, K—Q2; 4 K—
Kt7* is immediately decisive.

Knight and Pawn against Pawn is in general a win, but if the Black

King is too near the enemy Pawn and the White King too far away a draw may sometimes be unavoidable. If White has a passed Pawn he can defend it with his Knight and take care of his opponent's Pawn with his King, or vice versa. If there is no passed Pawn and the White King is near the Pawns, he can always capture the other Pawn with the help of his Knight. Difficulties crop up here only when the King cannot approach the Pawns in time, and when the Knight cannot prevent either the exchange or the capture of the last Pawn.

When the Pawns are on the same file, the Knight can defend the Pawn without subjecting himself to attack. Thus in No. 115 time to allow the approach of the White King is gained by playing *1 P— Kt4, K—Q4; 2 Kt—B5, K—B5; 3 Kt—R6, K—Q4; 4 K—Kt7,* etc.

No. 115

No. 116

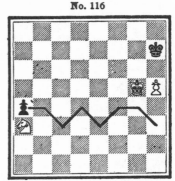

White wins.

White wins if the Black Pawn is not beyond the heavy line.

With Black to play, after *1 .... K—Q4; 2 K—Kt7, K—Q5; 3 Kt— B1!, K—K6; 4 Kt—Kt3!!, K—Q6; 5 Kt—R5, K—B7; 6 P—Kt4, K— B6; 7 Kt—B6, K—B5; 8 K—B6, K—Q4; 9 Kt—R5* (or 9 Kt—Kt8, K—B5; 10 Kt—R6), is decisive. That it is useless to leave the Knight at Q3 is clear in the diagrammed position. But even when the White King is right near the scene of action it is best to defend the Pawn from a more advanced post. It is never advisable to allow a simultaneous attack on Knight and Pawn. The danger here is due to the circumstance that one cannot gain a tempo with a Knight. Thus in No. 115a (Blackburne-Zuckertort, 1881), White: K at K2, Kt at K3, P at KKt4; Black: K at KB5, P at KKt3, Black to play can hold the draw by 1 .... K—Kt6; 2 K—Q1, K—B6; 3 K—Q2, K—B7 (Black maintains the opposition); 4 K—Q3 (if 4 Kt—B5, K—B6; 5 Kt—R6, K—B5), K—B6; 5 K—Q4, K—B5. Now 6 K— Q5 would still lead to nothing after 6 .... K×Kt; 7 K—K5, K—B6;

8 K—B6 (8 P—Kt5?? would lose: 8 .... K—Kt5; 9 K—B6, K—R4).
With White to move in the initial position, he could win by 1 K—B2,
P—Kt4 (or 1 .... K—K5; 2 Kt—Kt2); 2 K—K2, K—Kt6; 3 K—
Q3, K—B6; 4 K—Q4, K—B5; and now the sacrifice 5 K—Q5, K×Kt;
6 K—K5, K—B6; 7 K—B5.

With the Pawns on adjoining files the problem of gaining time for
the approach of the King is often more involved. In No. 115b, White:
K at KR8; Kt at QKt5, P at QKt2; Black: K at Q2, P at QR4, White
can only reach his goal by 1 Kt—Q4! (if 1 K—Kt7, K—B3; 2 Kt—
Q4ch, K—B4; 3 Kt—Kt3, K—B5!; 4 Kt×Pch, K—Kt5=), K—Q3;
2 Kt—Kt3!, P—R5 (if now 2 .... K—Q4; 3 Kt×P, K—B4; 4 Kt—
Kt3ch, K—B5; 5 Kt—B1); 3 Kt—R1!, K—Q4; 4 K—Kt7, K—Q5;
5 K—B6, K—Q6; 6 K—K5, K—Q7; 7 K—Q4, K—B8; 8 K—B3, and
the rest is simple.

Black's drawing chances are greatest when there are two RP's on
the board. For then the defense of No. 115 is inapplicable and White
can only prevent the capture of his Pawn if his King can protect the
Knight in time. With the Pawns on the same file, if the King gets
there in time, a win is possible. No. 115c, White: K at QB4, P at
QR2, Kt at QB3; Black: K at QKt7, P at QR6. 1 K—Q3, K—R8;
2 Kt—R4!, K×P (or 2 .... K—Kt8; 3 K—Q2, K—R8; 4 K—B1!,
K×P; 5 K—B2); 3 K—B2 and mates in four (No. 102a).

With a passed RP for White and an advanced passed Pawn for Black
the win depends on whether the King can afford to abandon his watch
over the enemy Pawn. In No. 116 it is permissible: *1 P—R6, K—Kt1;
2 K—Kt6, K—R1; 3 Kt—Kt5, K—Kt1; 4 P—R7ch, K—R1; 5 Kt—Q6,
P—R6; 6 Kt—B7* mate. Or, if the Black Pawn is at QB6 here we get
1 P—R6, K—R1; 2 K—Kt6, K—Kt1; 3 Kt—Q4, K—R1; 4 Kt—B6!,
P—B7; 5 Kt—K5, P—B8=Q; 6 Kt—B7ch, K—Kt1; 7 P—R7ch,
K—B1; 8 P—R8=Qch, K—K2; 9 Q—Q8ch, K—K3; 10 Q—Q6 mate.
If the Black Pawn is at QR6 he draws by a careful choice of the
square of retreat for his King: 1 P—R6, K—R1! (1 .... K—Kt1
loses by 2 K—Kt6, K—R1; 3 Kt—Kt4, K—Kt1; 4 P—R7ch, K—R1;
5 Kt—Q3, P—R7; 6 Kt—K5 and mate next move); 2 K—Kt6
(there is no way to win a tempo: if the White King is not at Kt6
Black will always play .... K—R2), K—Kt1; 3 Kt—Kt4, K—R1 and
now if 4 P—R7, P—R7= or 4 Kt—Q3, P—R7; 5 Kt—K5, P—R8=Q;
6 Kt—B7ch, K—Kt1; 7 P—R7ch, K—B1; 8 P—R8=Qch Q×Q.
If White has his Pawn on the seventh, so that Black's King is stalemated, he can only win if his Knight can mate in a few moves. E.g., in
No. 116a, White: K at KR6, P at KR7, Kt at QR6; Black: K at KR1,
P at QKt5 White to play can win by 1 Kt—B5, P—Kt6; 2 Kt—K4,
P—Kt7; 3 Kt—Kt5, P—Kt8=Q; 4 Kt—B7 mate, but Black to play
wins after 1 .... P—Kt6.

When Black has two Pawns against the Knight and Pawn White should again have no trouble. Two winning ideas are open to him: he can either manoeuvre to capture one Pawn, or he can give up his Knight to win both the opposing Pawns.

The first is seen in No. 117, Reti-Marshall, Baden-Baden, 1925. Black to move would have to give up either his QKtP or his KKtP, for on 1 .... K—Kt3; 2 P—Q6 the Pawn queens. The real problem is how to win with White to play. Clearly the idea would be to lose a move and get back to the diagrammed position with Black to play. This can be done by a triangulation manoeuvre: Black may not move his King away from the B file, while White may. *1 K—Kt3, K—B4; 2 K—B3, K—B3; 3 K—Kt4.*

No. 117   No. 118

White wins.   White plays and wins.

The other idea is seen in No. 118 (problem by Reti and Mandler, 1924). White can only force the entrance of his King by offering to sacrifice his Knight: *1 Kt—Kt1, K—Q7; 2 Kt—B3ch, K—Q6; 3 K—K1, K—K6; 4 Kt—K5, K—K5; 5 Kt—B4!, K—Q6; 6 Kt—Q2, K—K6; 7 Kt—B3, K—Q6; 8 K—B1, K—K6; 9 Kt—K1, K—Q7; 10 Kt—B2!!, K—Q8* (if 10 .... K×Kt; 11 K—K2 followed by K—B3 etc.); *11 Kt—Kt4, K—Q7; 12 Kt—Q5.*

The win is not always smooth sailing for White. Difficulties crop up when the opponent's Pawns are too far apart, when one's King is too far away, when the opponent's Pawns are too far advanced. In practice, however, such obstacles are rarely insurmountable, and one of the two winning ideas will be found to be applicable, provided the White Pawn can be defended either by the King or by the Knight.

A rare kind of winning possibility may be seen in No. 118a (problem by Skalicka and Schubert, 1930). White: K at KR7, P at KR5,

Kt at K2; Black: K at Q7, P's at QR5, KKt3. White to play. 1 P—
R6!!!, P—R6; 2 Kt—B3, K×Kt; 3 K—Kt8! (3 K×P??, K—Kt7!;
4 P—R7, P—R7 only draws (see No. 546), P—R7; 4 P—R7 and
Black's extra Pawn is his undoing.

Kt+P win against three Pawns only if the opposing Pawns can be
blockaded or isolated and subsequently captured. In any normal
position such as No. 119 this cannot be done, for Black forces the
exchange of the last Pawn by *1 .... P—R5ch; 2 K—B2, P—B4;
3 Kt any, P—Kt5.* Even if the Black Pawns were isolated he could
still hold the draw. E.g., No. 119a, White: K at KKt3, Kt at K3,
P at KR3; Black: K at KKt3, P's at K3, KKt4, KR4. 1 .... K—
B3; 2 K—B2, K—K4; 3 Kt—Kt2 (3 K—B3, P—Kt5ch), K—K5—no
progress can be made.

When one can win a Pawn and secure a passed Pawn it is better to
blockade the opposing Pawns with the Knight than with the King.
The reason for this is that the Knight alone cannot force the promotion
of the Pawns, but the King alone can if it can rely upon tempi which
the Knight gains. Thus in No. 119b (Kieseritzky, 1842), White: K at
QB2, Kt at QB3, P at KKt4; Black: K at K2, P's at QKt2, QB4,
KKt4, the obvious 1 Kt—K4, P—B5; 2 Kt×P, P—Kt4; 3 K—B3,
K—B3; 4 Kt—B3, K—Kt3= is inferior. Instead one should play
1 K—Q3, K—K3; 2 K—K4, K—Q3; 3 K—B5, P—B5; 4 K×P,
K—B4; 5 K—B5, P—Kt4; 6 P—Kt5, P—Kt5; 7 Kt—K4ch, K—Q5
(there is nothing better, e.g., 7 .... K—Kt4; 8 Kt—Q6ch, K—B4;
9 Kt×P, K×Kt; 10 P—Kt6 and queens with check); 8 P—Kt6,
P—Kt6; 9 P—Kt7, P—Kt7; 10 P—Kt8=Q; P—Kt8=Q; 11 Q—
Q8ch, K—K6; 12 Q—Q2ch, K—B6; 13 Q—B2 mate.

Where the Black Pawns are far advanced the Knight is often not
in a position to hold them. However, where they can be blockaded a
draw and sometimes even a win
will result. In No. 119c Del Rio,
1831), White: K at K1, P at KR4,
Kt at K3; Black: K at QKt5, P's at
QR7, QB2, KKt3 White draws by
1 Kt—B2ch, K—B6; 2 Kt—R1!,
K—Kt7; 3 K—Q2, K—Kt8 (3 ....
K×Kt is sufficient but dangerous,
see A.); 4 K—B3, K—B8; 5 K—
Kt3, K—Kt8.

A. 3 .... K×Kt; 4 K—B2,
P—B4! (4 .... P—B3? loses after
5 K—B1, P—B4; 6 K—B2, P—
B5; 7 K—B1, P—B6; 8 K—B2,
P—Kt4; 9 P—R5!, P—Kt5; 10—12

No. 119

Draw.

P—R8=Q, P—Kt8=Q; 13 Q×P mate); 5 K—B1, P—B5; 6 K—B 2, P—B6; 7 K—B1, P—Kt4! and if 8 P×P, P—B7; 9 K×P stalemate, while on 8 P—R5, Black queens with check.

Kt+P against more than three Pawns is at best a draw for White. When Black has three connected passed Pawns and the Knight can manage to blockade them (e.g., P's at QR4, QKt3, QB4; Kt at QKt5) and prevent the King from coming to the aid of the Pawns he can hold the game. Ordinarily this is too much to expect, so that we may set up the rule that three passed Pawns in an ending with nothing but Knight and Pawns are worth more than a Knight. Even with a bad structure (doubled, isolated) the Pawns may be successful. In No. 119d (Loewenfisch-Fine, Leningrad, 1937) White: K at KB2, Kt at K2, P at K3; Black: K at Q3, P's at QKt5, QKt6, K4, K5, the helplessness of a Knight against an army of Pawns is illustrated: 1 Kt—Kt3, K—Q4; 2 Kt—B1, K—B5; 3 K—K2 (or 3 Kt—Q2ch, K—B6; 4 Kt×Pch, K—B7); K—B6; 4 Kt—Q2, P—Kt7; 5 K—Q1, K—Q6; 6 Kt—Kt1, K×P; 7 K—B2, K—B7 and White resigned. Exceptions to this rule occur only when all the Pawns are blockaded, as in No. 119e (Ponziani, 1782) White: K at QB4, Kt at K3, P at QKt3; Black: K at QKt3, P's at QR4, QKt5, QB4, KB4. 1 Kt×P, P—R5!; 2 P×P, K—R4; 3 K—Kt3, P—B5ch only draws, but White can win with 1 Kt—Q5ch, K—R3; 2 Kt—B7ch, K—Kt3; 3 Kt—K6, P—R5; 4 P×P, K—R4; 5 Kt×P, P—B5; 6 K—Kt3, P—B6; 7 Kt— K4, K—Kt3; 8 K×P and we have No. 116.

Against more than three Pawns the Knight is totally helpless.

With Knight and more than one Pawn a draw is possible only if a number of Pawns are captured or exchanged, or the Black Pawns are so far advanced that the Knight is immobile. If the King can run loose among enemy Pawns defended only by a Knight, he can generally

No. 120

White wins.

manage to capture or exchange all of them. By luring the White King away from his Pawns and entering with his King Black then acquires excellent drawing chances. With Pawns on the sixth or seventh he may even have winning chances.

A blockaded position can only postpone the win or make it more complicated: it cannot assure a draw. In No. 120 apparently Black can hold the draw by K—Kt1 and K—R1 but White can force the Black Pawn out of the way by sacrificing his Knight. *1 Kt—Q6, K—*

Kt1; 2 Kt—K4, K—R1; 3 Kt—B6!, P×Kt; 4 K—B7. Or (Black plays) *1 .... K—Kt1; 2 Kt—Q6, K—R1; 3 Kt—K4, K—Kt1; 4 K—K8, K—R1; 5 Kt—B6, P×Kt; 6 K—B7.*

Here again three mobile Pawns are superior to a Knight. E.g., No. 120a (Bledow correspondence game 1843), White: K at Q3, Kt at QKt3, P's at KB3, KR3; Black: K at K4, P's at QR7, QKt5, KB5, KKt4, KR4. 1 K—K2 (or A. 1 K—B4, P—Kt5; 2 BP×P, K—K5!; 3 P—Kt5, P—B6; 4 P—Kt6, P—B7; 5 Kt—Q2ch, K—B5; 6 P—Kt7, P—B8=Qch!; 7 Kt×Q, P—R8=Q; 8 P—Kt8=Q, Q—R7ch. B. 1 Kt—R1, K—B4; 2 K—K2, P—Kt5; 3 RP×Pch, P×P; 4 Kt—Kt3, P×Pch; 5 K×P, K—K4 and the White King is tied down to the KB file, so that Black is free to go to the support of his Q-side Pawns),

No. 121

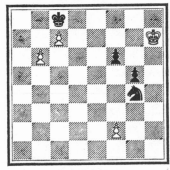

White plays and draws.

No. 122

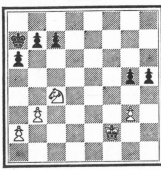

White wins.

K—B3; 2 K—Q3, P—Kt5; 3 BP×P, P×P; 4 P×P, K—Kt4; 5 K—K2, K×P; 6 K—B2, P—B6; 7 Kt—R1, K—B5; 8 Kt—Kt3, K—K5; 9 K—B1, K—Q4; 10 K—B2, K—B5.

In No. 121 (Troitzky, 1898) we have a pretty drawing manoeuvre where the King can attack the enemy Pawns. *1 P—B3!, Kt—K4; 2 K—Kt7, Kt×P; 3 K×P, P—Kt5; 4 K—B5, P—Kt6; 5 K—Kt4, P—Kt7; 6 K—R3!!!* and whatever Black promotes to will do him no good. E.g., 6 .... P—Kt8=R 7 P—Kt7ch, K×BP; 8 P—Kt8=Qch, K×Q stalemate or 6 .... P—Kt8=Ktch; 7 K—Kt2 and neither Knight can move.

How a Knight wins against Pawns in an ordinary over-the-board position may be seen in No. 122 (Nimzovitch-Alekhine, New York, 1927). *1 K—K3, P—B4* (if 1 .... P—QKt4; 2 Kt—Q2, P—R5; 3 P—KKt4!, P—R6; 4 K—B3, P—B4; 5 Kt—K4, P—B5; 6 P—Kt4!—one must keep as many Pawns as possible—, K—Kt3; 7 K—Kt3, K—B3; 8 Kt×P, P—B6; 9 Kt—B3!, K—Q4; 10 Kt—K1 and the passed Pawn is decisive); *2 P—R4, P—QKt4; 3 P×P, P×P; 4 Kt—Q2, K—Kt3; 5 Kt—K4, P—R5; 6 P—KKt4!, P—R6!; 7 K—B3, P—Kt5* (or 7 .... P—B5; 8 P—Kt4!, K—B3; 9 K—Kt3, K—Q4; 10 Kt—B3ch, K—Q5; 11 Kt×Pch, K—Q6; 12 Kt—R3, P—B6; 13 P—Kt5, etc.); *8 Kt×P, P—B5!; 9 Kt—K4!!, P×P* (9 .... P—B6; 10 Kt—B2); *10 P—Kt5, P—Kt7; 11 Kt—Q2, K—B4; 12 P—Kt6, P—R7; 13 K—Kt2, K—Q5; 14 P—Kt7, K—Q6; 15 P—Kt8 = Q, K×Kt; 16 Q—R2, K—B7; 17 Q—B4ch,* resigns.

From this example we can see that the winning method in such endings consists of three steps: 1. Weaken the enemy Pawns either by

No. 123   No. 124

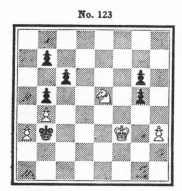   

Draw.   White wins.

blockade or a disadvantageous advance; 2. Force a passed Pawn in order to divert the enemy King; 3. Either queen the passed Pawn or establish a decisive material superiority in Pawns.

No. 123 (Zukertort) shows how Black can normally draw when his King manages to attack the enemy Pawns. In fact White can just draw by *1 K—Kt4, K×P; 2 Kt—Q3!* (if instead 2 K×P, K×P; 3 K×P, K—B6!; 4 P—R4, P—Kt5 Black queens with check, gives up his Queen for the RP and his remaining two Pawns decide), *K—Kt6; 3 K×P, K—B6; 4 K×P, K×Kt; 5 P—R4, P—B4; 6 P×P, P—Kt5; 7 P—R5* and both players queen.

Where no such counter-attack can be carried through the winning method outlined above is normally quite simple to execute. In a blockaded position, if no passed Pawn can be forced, material can be captured. E.g., No. 123a (Horwitz), White: K at K1, P's at Q2, K3, K5, Kt at KB1; Black: K at KKt5, P's at Q6, K5, K3. 1 K—B2,

K—B4; 2 K—Kt3, K×P; 3 K—Kt4, K—Q3; 4 K—B4, K—Q4;
5 Kt—Kt3. However, such block positions should be avoided for
Black to move here can win with 1 .... K—B6; 2 K—Q1, K—B7;
3 Kt—R2, K—Kt6; 4 Kt—B1ch, K—R6!; 5 K—K1, K—Kt7; 6 Kt—
R2, K×Kt and the advanced Black QP decides.

We have aready pointed out that two Pawns are not sufficient com-
pensation for a Knight, other things being equal. In No. 124 (Bot-
winnik-Thomas, Nottingham, 1936) even a strong protected passed
Pawn cannot save Black. Botwinnik scored by *1 P—Kt5, RP×P;
2 P×P, K—K2* (or 2 .... P×P; 3 Kt×Pch, K—B4!; 4 Kt—Kt4!,
P—R4; 5 P—Q5, P—R5ch; 6 K—B2, K—Kt5—or A.—; 7 P—Q6,
P—R6; 8 P—Q7, P—R7; 9 P—Q8=Q, P—R8=Q; 10 Q—Kt8ch,
K—B4; 11 Q—B7ch, K—K4; 12 Q—B4ch, K—K3; 13 Q×Pch, K—
Q2; 14 Q×Pch, etc. A. 6 .... K—K4; 7 P—Q6, K—K3; 8 Kt—Q5!,
K—Q2; 9 Kt—B3, P—Kt5; 10 Kt×P, K—B3; 11 K×P, P—Kt6;
12 K—Kt4, P—Kt7; 13 Kt—Q2, P—Kt3; 14 P×P, K×QP; 15 K×P,
K—B3; 16 K—Kt4, K×P; 17 K—B3, K—Kt4; 18 P—K4, K—Kt5;
19 K—K3); *3 P—Kt6* (threatening 3 Kt×Pch, P×Kt; 4 P—B6 and
queens), *K—Q2; 4 Kt—R5, K—Q1; 5 Kt—B6, P—R3; 6 Kt—Kt4,
P—R4; 7 Kt—B2, K—Q2; 8 K—R4, K—Q1; 9 K×P, K—K2; 10 K—
Kt4, K—K3; 11 K—Kt3, K—Q2; 12 Kt—R3, K—Q1; 13 Kt—B4,
K—Q2; 14 Kt—R5, K—K3; 15 Kt—Kt7ch, K—Q2; 16 Kt—B5, K—
B1; 17 K—B4!, K—Kt1; 18 K—K5, K—B1; 19 K—Q6, K—Kt1; 20
K—Q7, K—R1; 21 Kt—Kt3!, K—Kt1; 22 Kt—B1, K—R1; 23 K—B8*
resigns. For now he must play 23 .... P—B7, when the White King
comes all the way back and captures the BP, and the rest is elemen-
tary.

Two Pawns draw against a Knight only when the Pawn structure is
such that the enemy King is not in a position to attack the Pawns.
For a Knight, as we have seen, can defend Pawns, but cannot help one
to queen without the aid of the King. Thus when there are one or two
passed Pawns which cannot be adequately blockaded by the Knight,
a draw is very often the result. E.g., No. 124a (Charousek and Fahn-
drich-Halprin and Marco, Vienna, 1897), White: K at KB4, P's at
QR2, QKt2, QB2, K4, KKt5, KR5; Black: K at KB1, Kt at QB3, P's
at QR2, QKt3, QB2, KB2. Black to play. Draw. The game continuation was 1 .... K—Kt2 (If instead 1 .... Kt—Kt5, which is so
tempting, White cold-bloodedly replies 2 P—R6!, Kt×BP; 3 K—B5,
Kt—Q5ch; 4 K—B6, K—Kt1; 5 P—K5, P—B4; 6 P—R7ch!, K×P;
7 K×P, Kt—B6; 8 P—Kt6ch, K—R3; 9 P—Kt7, Kt×Pch; 10 K—
B8, Kt—Kt3ch; 11 K—B7, Kt—K2!; 12 K×Kt, K×P; 13 K—Q6,
K—B3; 14 P—R4!, K—B4; 15 P—R5 and the ending is drawn); 2 P—
B3 (now 2 .... Kt—Kt5 was a serious threat), Kt—K2; 3 P—K5,
P—QB3; 4 K—K4, P—QB4; 5 P—K6! (the decisive break after which

the draw becomes clear. Now the Black King will have to stay on the
K-side and the White King will be able to mop up on the other wing),
P×P; 6 K—K5, Kt—Q4; 7 P—B4 (hoping for a win. 7 K×P, Kt—
B5ch; 8 K—Q6 of course draws without any trouble), Kt—K6; 8 P—
Kt3, K—B2; 9 P—Kt6ch, K—K2; 10 K—B4, Kt—B4; 11 K—Kt5,
Kt—Q5; 12 P—R3 (on 12 P—R6, Black has a forced draw: 12 ....
Kt—B6ch; 13 K—Kt4, Kt—K4ch; 14 K—Kt5, Kt—B6ch=, while if
12 K—R6?, K—B3; 13 K—R7, Kt—B4; 14 P—R6, Kt—K2; 15 P—
Kt7, K—B2!; 16 K—R8, P—K4! and Black wins, for 17 P—R7 allows
17 .... Kt—Kt3 mate!), P—R3; 13 P—Kt4, P—R4; 14 P×P, P×P;
15 P—R4, Kt—B6ch; 16 K—R6, K—B1; 17 P—Kt7ch, K—Kt1;
18 K—Kt6, P—K4; 19 P—R6, Kt—R5ch; 20 K—B6, Kt—B6; and
the players agreed to a draw.

When two connected passed Pawns are far advanced they may often
win against a Knight, regardless of the total material strength. E.g.,
No. 124b (Petrov-Fine, Kemeri, 1937), White: K at Q6, P's at QR3,
QKt7, QB4, KKt2; Black: K at Q1, Kt at QKt1, P's at QR3, KB2,
KKt3, KR2. White wins despite the fact that he has only one Pawn
for the Knight. 1 .... P—QR4; 2 P—B5, Kt—R3; 3 P—B6, P—B4;
4 P—B7ch!, Kt×P; 5 P—Kt8=Q mate.

An advantage of two Knights when both sides have Pawns is so
overwhelming that drawing chances are to be found only in problems.

III. ONE KNIGHT AND PAWNS VS. ONE KNIGHT AND PAWNS

A. POSITIONS WITH MATERIAL ADVANTAGE

With a Pawn ahead the win with Knights on the board is by no
means as simple as in pure Pawn endings. Nevertheless the principles
which were established in Pawn endings, such as the value of outside
and protected passed Pawns, the necessity of preserving the mobility
of the Pawns, and many others are equally applicable here. In fact,
the outlines of the general winning process are exactly the same as for
the corresponding Pawn ending: force an outside passed Pawn, drive
the King towards it, and establish a decisive material superiority.
Where there are Pawns on both sides of the board, there is little difference in the conduct of the two types of finales. It is only when all
the Pawns are on one side of the board that we find new problems coming up.

Kt+P vs. Kt is generally a draw because the Knight can be sacrificed for the Pawn. To effect this sacrifice, however, Black must have
both King and Knight in favorable positions, i.e., covering the squares
on the queening file. When this is not the case White can usually win.
The most favorable files for the Pawn to be on are the Kt and R files.

If the Pawn manages to reach the seventh rank, and is supported by both King and Knight it can almost always queen. In No. 125 (Kling, 1867) White need only close the squares QB6 and Q7 to the Black Knight. If the Black King were off in some other part of the board, 1 Kt—B5, Kt—K4; 2 K—Kt6 would decide at once. Here some more manipulation is required. *1 Kt—Kt4, K—K4* (or 1 .... K—B2; 2 Kt—Q5ch, K—Q3 (or any); 3 Kt—Kt6, Kt—K4; 4 Kt—B4ch or 4 P—Kt8=Qch); *2 Kt—Q3ch, K—Q4* (or 2 .... K—K5; 3 Kt—B5ch, or 2 .... K—B4; 3 Kt—B5, Kt—K4; 4 K—Kt6); *3 Kt—B4ch, K—B3; 4 Kt—Kt6, K—Q4* (or 4 .... K—B4; 5 Kt—B8, Kt—K4; 6 K—R8, Kt—B3; 7 Kt—K6ch, K any; 8 Kt—Q8); *5 Kt—B8, Kt—K4; 6 K—Kt6, Kt—B3!; 7 Kt—Q7, K—Q3; 8 Kt—K5, Kt—Kt1; 9 K—R7,*

No. 125

No. 126

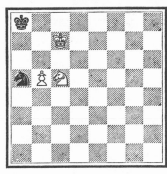

White wins.

White to play wins; Black to play draws.

K—B2; 10 Kt—B4, Kt—B3ch (if 10 .... Kt—Q2; 11 Kt—Kt6, Kt—Kt1; 12 Kt—Q5ch); *11 K—R8, Kt—Kt1!; 12 Kt—Kt6, Kt—R3; 13 Kt—Q5ch, K any; 14 K—R7* or *14 Kt—Kt4* and the Knight finally has to quit the neighborhood of the queening square.

The same idea is effective in the allied ending No. 125a (Von Scheve-Estorch, 1905) White: K at QKt6, Kt at QB7, P at QR6; Black: K at Q2, Kt at QB3. 1 Kt—Kt5, Kt—K2; 2 K—Kt7, Kt—B3 (or 2 .... Kt—B1; 3 Kt—R3, Kt—Q3ch; 4 K—Kt8, Kt—B1; 5 Kt—B4, K—Q1; 6 K—Kt7, K—Q2; 7 Kt—Kt6ch); 3 Kt—Q4, Kt—R4ch; 4 K—Kt8, Kt—B5; 5 P—R7, Kt—Kt3; 6 K—Kt7, Kt—R1!; 7 Kt—K6!! and Black resigns gracefully.

Another such position is No. 125b (Reti, 1929), White: K at QKt7, Kt at K4, P at QR6; Black: K at QR4, Kt at QKt4. 1 Kt—B5, K—Kt5; 2 K—Kt6, Kt—Q3; 3 Kt—K4, Kt—B1ch; 4 K—B7, K—Kt4!; 5 K—Kt7!, K—R4; 6 Kt—B5, Kt—Q3ch; 7 K—B7, Kt—Kt4ch;

8 K—B6, Kt—R2ch; 9 K—Kt7!, Kt—Kt4; 10 Kt—K4, K—Kt5; 11 K—Kt6, K—R5; 12 Kt—B3ch. Care must always be exercised in this type of ending, since the slightest misstep will allow the sacrifice of the Knight for the Pawn. Compare No. 125c (Reti, 1929), White: K at KKt5, Kt at K3; Black: K at KR7, Kt at KB7, P at KR6. Draw by 1 K—R4, K—Kt8; 2 Kt—Kt4, K—Kt7; 3 Kt—K3ch, K—R7; 4 Kt—B2, Kt—Q6; 5 K—Kt4, Kt—K4ch; 6 K—R4, Kt—B3ch; 7 K—Kt4, Kt—Kt4!; 8 Kt—K1!, K—Kt8; 9 Kt—B3ch!, K—Kt2!; 10 Kt—R4ch!, K—B7!; 11 Kt—B3! and Black can make no headway.

When the King is in front of the Pawn a win is possible only in certain special positions. Thus in No. 126 we set up a kind of Kt opposition: *1 P—Kt6, Kt—Kt2!; 2 Kt—K6!, Kt—R4* (or B4 or Q1. If 2 ....

No. 127

White wins.

No. 128

White wins.

Kt—Q3; 3 K×Kt); *3 K—B8!, Kt any; 4 Kt—B7* mate (or P—Kt7—Kt8=Qch). Black to move can hold the draw by *1 .... Kt—B5* for the same old reason: White cannot gain a tempo. E.g., *2 Kt—Q3, K—R2; 3 Kt—Kt4, K—R1; 4 Kt—Q5, K—R2; 5 Kt—K7, K—R1* (here Black to move loses); *6 Kt—B6, Kt—Kt3!!.* With a RP White has better winning chances, e.g., No. 126a (Von Scheve-Estorch, 1905), White: K at QKt6, P at QR5, Kt at QB5; Black: K at QKt1, Kt at Q1. 1 Kt—R6ch!, K—B1 (or 1 .... K—R1; 2 Kt—B7ch, K—Kt1; 3 P—R6); 2 Kt—B7, K—Q2; 3 P—R6, Kt—B3; 4 Kt—Kt5 and we have No. 125a.

With the Black King at some distance from the Pawn a win is possible even if it is all the way back because by constantly offering to exchange White can facilitate the advance of his Pawn. In No. 127 this is done by *1 Kt—K4, K×P; 2 Kt—Q2, K—Kt2; 3 Kt—B4, Kt—Kt8; 4 K—Q4!* (not 4 P—Kt5?, Kt—B6!; 5 P—Kt6, Kt—R5ch and draws),

K—B2; 5 P—Kt5, K—K2; 6 P—Kt6, K—Q2; 7 K—B5, Kt—B6;
8 Kt—K5ch, K—B1; 9 K—B6, Kt any; 10 P—Kt7ch, K—Kt1; 11 Kt—
Q7ch.

From No. 127 we can likewise see how Kt+2P's vs. Kt is won when
the Pawns are disconnected. One Pawn is sacrificed to enable the
other to advance. With two connected passed Pawns the win is even
simpler, since the Knight cannot even threaten to sacrifice, e.g., No.
127a, White: K at KKt4, Kt at KB4, P's at KKt5, KR5; Black: K
at KKt2, Kt at KB2. 1 Kt—K6ch, K—Kt1; 2 P—Kt6, Kt—K4ch;
3 K—B5, Kt—B6; 4 P—R6, Kt—R5ch (spite check); 5 K—B6, Kt—
B6; 6 Kt—Kt5, Kt—Q5; 7 P—R7ch, etc.

With Kt+2P vs. Kt+P the game is won if there is an outside passed
Pawn blockaded by a Knight or an advanced protected passed Pawn,
but drawn otherwise. In No. 128 (Mason-Reggio, Monte Carlo, 1903)
the finish was *1 Kt—B6, K—R5* (or 1 .... Kt—Q6ch; 2 K—Q4,
Kt×P; 3 Kt—K4ch); *2 P—Kt6, K—R6; 3 K—B5, K—Kt7; 4 Kt—*
K4, Kt—Q2; 5 P—Kt7, K—B6; 6 Kt—B6, Kt—Kt1; 7 Kt×P, Kt—
R3; 8 Kt—B6, K×P; 9 K—K5, K—K6; 10 K—Q5, K—Q6; 11 Kt—
Q7, K—B6; 12 K—B6 Resigns for there is no defense against K—Kt6.

It should be borne in mind that the really decisive factor here is the
far more favorable position of the White King. If the passed Pawn is
stopped by the King (e.g., BK at QKt2) White can do nothing, for
Black attacks the KBP with his Kt, and if the White Kt moves 1 ....
K—Kt3 captures the Pawn. A similar idea is seen in No. 128a (from
Botvinnik-Lissitzin, Moscow, 1935), White: K at QKt3, Kt at QB2,
P at KB3; Black: K at Q4, Kt at Q3, P's at QKt3, KB5. After 1
Kt—K1, K—Q5; 2 Kt—Kt2, K—K4; 3 K—Kt4, K—B4; 4 K—R4!
the draw is evident.

Where there is a protected passed Pawn an equally simple win is
available only in special cases. No. 128b (Horwitz, 1880), White: K
at K3, Kt at K6, P's at KB7, KKt6; Black: K at KR1, Kt at KB1, P
at KKt2. White to play wins. The solution is 1 Kt—B4, Kt—K3;
2 K—K4, Kt—B4ch; 3 K—Q5, Kt—K3; 4 K—Q6, Kt—B1; 5 K—K7,
Kt—K3; 6 Kt—R5; Kt—B1; 7 K—K8, Kt—K3 (or 7 .... Kt×P;
8 Kt—B4 or 7 .... Kt—Q2; 8 Kt×P!); 8 Kt—B6!, P×Kt; 9 P—
B8=Qch and mates in four. If, however, all the pieces and Pawns here
are moved back two squares (with the Black Kt at KB2 instead of
KB3) a draw would result. For if the King tried to approach, Black
would give up his KtP to capture his opponent's. Similarly, in a position without a passed Pawn with all the Pawns on one side, e.g., No.
128c, White: K at K3, Kt at KB3, P's at KB4, KKt4; Black: K at
KB3 Kt at K3, P at KKt3 Black's game is perfectly tenable. On
1 K—K4 there could follow 1 .... Kt—B4ch; 2 K—Q5, Kt—Q6 or
2 K—Q4, Kt—K3ch.

With Kt+3P vs. Kt+2P again an outside passed Pawn is a sufficient advantage, and again if all the Pawns are on one side the outcome
should be a draw. But the greater number of Pawns creates other possibilities. Three Pawns vs. one on one side, or two connected passed
Pawns should win. E.g., No. 128d (Tchekhover-Rabinovitch, Leningrad, 1934), White: K at K5, Kt at QR3, P's at KB5; KKt5, KR4;
Black: K at KB2, Kt at QKt6, P's at QR5, KR2. After 1 .... Kt—
Q7; 2 P—R5, Kt—B6ch; 3 K—B4, Kt—Q5; 4 P—R6!, Kt—B3;
5 Kt—B4, Kt—K2; 6 K—K5, Kt—B3ch; 7 K—K4, Kt—K2; 8 K—
B4, Kt—B3; White could have scored with 9 P—Kt6ch!, K—Kt1 (or
9 .... P×P; 10 Kt—Q6ch, K—B3; 11 Kt—K8ch); 10 K—Kt5, etc.

In No. 129 we have a position from a world's championship match

No. 129   No. 130

Draw.   White wins.

(Anderssen-Steinitz, 1866). The game continuation was 1 .... Kt—
K3; 2 Kt—K5ch, K—B4; 3 Kt—Q3 (3 Kt—B4 is preferable), P—Kt3;
4 Kt—K1, Kt—Q5ch; 5 K—Kt2, K—K5; 6 K—B1, P—B6; 7 K—
Kt1, P—Kt4; 8 K—R2, P—R4; 9 K—Kt3, Kt—B4ch (Here Steinitz
could have won by force: 9 .... Kt—K7ch; 10 K—R2, P—R5!;
11 Kt—B2, Kt—B5; 12 Kt—K3, K—Q6; followed by K—K7, when
the KBP cannot be defended); 10 K—R2, P—Kt5?; 11 P×P, P×P;
12 K—Kt1, K—Q5; 13 Kt—B2ch, K—Q6; 14 Kt—R3? (and here
Anderssen could have drawn with 14 Kt—Kt4ch, K—K7; 15 Kt—Q5,
P—Kt6; 16 Kt—B4ch, K—K8; 17 Kt—Q3ch, K—Q7; 18 Kt—B4
etc.), P—Kt6!; 15 Kt—Kt5, P—Kt7 followed by Kt—Q5—K7. The
variation played indicates that if Black can set up his Pawns at KB6
and KR5 either the White KBP or the White KRP will in the long run
be untenable. From this we can infer that White's best drawing
chance consists in advancing his own KBP and, in point of fact, anal-

ysis reveals no conclusive refutation of such a defense: Thus, *1 ....
Kt—K3; 2 K—Kt2!, K—B4; 3 P—B3!; P—Kt4* (3 .... K—Kt4;
4 Kt—K5, K—R5; 5 Kt—Kt6ch leads to nothing); *4 K—B2, Kt—B4;
5 Kt—K7ch, K—K3; 6 Kt—B6, K—Q4; 7 Kt—K7ch, K—B5; 8 Kt—
B5, P—R4; 9 Kt—Kt7, P—R5; 10 K—K2* and how Black can make
any progress is not clear. If the White Pawns were connected here
instead of being isolated Black would have no winning chances at all,
unless the position were such that he could force a decisive gain of
material.

However, Kt+4P vs. Kt+3P probably wins even when the Pawns
are all on one side. E.g., No. 130 *1 .... K—B3; 2 P—Kt3, K—K4;
3 Kt—B6ch, K—K3; 4 K—K3* and now there are three types of defense:

a) *4 .... K—Q2; 5 Kt—Q4, P—B3; 6 P—B4, K—K2* (Black is
paying passively); *7 P—R4, Kt—B2; 8 P—Kt4, K—Q2; 9 K—
Q3, K—K2; 10 K—B4, K—Q3; 11 P—Kt5, P×P; 12 RP×P,
K—K2* (if 12 .... P—R3; 13 P—K5ch, K—K2; 14 P×P,
Kt×RP; 15 K—Q5, Kt—Kt5; 16 Kt—B6ch, K—K1—or A—;
17 K—K6, Kt—K6; 18 Kt—Kt4, Kt—Kt7; 18 Kt—Q5 and
White will soon capture Black's last Pawn. A. 16 .... K—Q2;
17 P—K6ch, K—K1; 18 K—Q6, Kt—B3; 19 K—Kt4, Kt—
K5ch; 20 K—K5, Kt—B7; 21 Kt—Q5, Kt—Kt5ch; 22 K—Q6
and wins); *13 P—K5, Kt—Q1; 14 K—Q5, Kt—B2; 15 Kt—
B6ch, K—K1; 16 P—K6, Kt—R1; 17 K—K5, K—B1; 18 K—B6,
K—K1; 19 K—Kt7.*

b) *4 .... P—B4; 5 Kt—Q4ch* (5 P—K5, Kt—B2; 6 P—B4 is also
good), *K—B3* (if 5 .... K—K2; 6 P—K5, Kt—B5ch; 7 K—B4,
P—R3; 8 P—R4, Kt—Kt7; 9 Kt×Pch, P×Kt; 10 K×P, K—
B2; 11 P—B4, Kt—Q6; 12 P—R5, Kt—B7; 13 P—Kt4, Kt—
R6; 14 P—Kt5 and wins); *6 P×P, P×P; 7 K—B4, K—Kt3* (or
7 .... P—R3; 8 P—R3: White has the tempo); *8 K—K5, Kt—
B2ch; 9 K—K6, Kt—Q1ch; 10 K—K7, Kt—Kt2; 11 P—B4,
Kt—B4; 12 Kt—B3!, Kt—K5* (12 .... K—R4; 13 Kt—K5 fol-
lowed by K—B6 or Kt6); *13 Kt—K5ch, K—Kt2; 14 K—K6* and
wins a Pawn.

c) *4 .... P—Kt4; 5 Kt—Q4ch, K—B3; 6 P—B4, P×Pch; 7 P×P,
Kt—B5ch; 8 K—B2!, K—Kt2; 9 P—K5, K—Kt3; 10 K—K2,
Kt—Kt7; 11 K—B3, Kt—B5; 12 K—K4, Kt—Q7ch; 13 K—Q5,
Kt—B8; 14 P—B5ch, K—Kt4; 15 P—K6, P×Pch; 16 K×P,
Kt×P; 17 P—B6* and the Pawn cannot be stopped.

One of the chief drawing methods at the disposal of the defender is
that of reduction to a more elementary case, often by the sacrifice of
the Knight to get rid of the remaining Pawns. E.g., in No. 130a (Rie-
mann-Mieses, Leipzig, 1888), White: K at K3, Kt at KR6, P's at QR4,

KKt5; Black: K at K4, Kt at QKt5, P's at QR4, QB5, QB6 this can be done by 1 Kt—Kt4ch (in the game there occurred 1 Kt—B7ch?, K—Q4; 2 P—Kt6, P—B7; 3 K—Q2, P—B6ch; 4 K—B1, K—B5 followed by K—Kt6 and Kt—Q6 or R7 mate), K—B4 (or 1 .... K—K3; 2 K—K2, P—B7; 3 K—Q2, P—B6ch; 4 K—B1, K—B4; 5 Kt—K3ch, K×P; 6 Kt×P!); 2 K—Q4, K×P; (or 2 .... P—B7; 3 Kt—K3ch, K×P; 4 Kt×P, Kt×Ktch; 5 K×P, Kt—R6ch; 6 K—B5, K—B4; 7 K—Kt6, Kt—B5ch; 8 K—Kt5=); 3 K×P(B3)!, K×Kt; 4 K×P, Kt—B3; 5 K—Kt5=.

In more complicated positions a Pawn plus should win unless the defender succeeds in setting up a complete blockade. No. 131 (Reshevsky-Rellstab, Kemeri, 1937) is an instructive ending with a potential outside passed Pawn, which may be considered typical. Black brings

No. 131

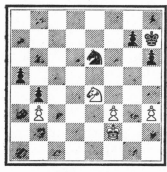

Black wins.

No. 132

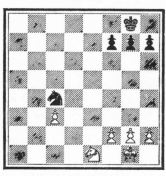

Black to play; White wins.

about the decision by first tying White's pieces down to watch the Q-side Pawns and then securing a winning superiority on the other wing. *1 K—K3, K—Kt3; 2 Kt—Q2, Kt—B4; 3 K—Q4, Kt—Kt2; 4 K—Q5, K—Kt4; 5 K—B6, Kt—Q1ch; 6 K—Q7, K—R5!!!* (the crux of the winning process: with the King so far away the Knight will not be able to stop both KRP and potential passed QKtP); *7 K×Kt, K×P; 8 K—K7, P—R4; 9 K—B7, P—KR5; 10 K×P, K—Kt6* (simpler 10 .... K—Kt7); *11 K—B6* (if 11 Kt—K4ch, K×P; 12 Kt—Kt5ch, K—Kt7; 13 K—B6, P—R5! etc.), *P—R6; 12 Kt—B1ch, K—B7; 13 Kt—R2, P—R5!; 14 P×P, P—Kt6; 15 P—B4, P—Kt7* and White resigned.

The nearer the outside passed Pawn is to the main group of Pawns the harder it is to win, but of the ultimate outcome there should never be any doubt. The principle is always the same: use the outside Pawn to divert the King and then secure a sufficient advantage on the other wing. Now, this "sufficient advantage" must be either in the form of two connected passed Pawns or two connected passed Pawns with the King favorably placed or one passed Pawn which can only be stopped by the sacrifice of the Knight.

In No. 132 (Keres-Reshevsky, Leningrad-Moscow, 1939) it is instructive to see how this transformation of a small material advantage into a larger one takes place. *1 . . . . K—B1; 2 K—B1, K—K2; 3 K— K2, K—Q3; 4 Kt—B2, K—K4; 5 Kt—K3, Kt—Kt7; 6 Kt—Q1, Kt— R5* (Black naturally cannot afford to exchange pieces); *7 K—Q3, K— Q4; 8 Kt—K3ch, K—B4; 9 Kt—B5* (forcing weaknesses in the opponent's Pawns structure), *P—Kt3; 10 Kt—R6, P—B4; 11 Kt—B7, K— Q4; 12 Kt—Kt5, Kt—B4ch; 13 K—K3, P—R3; 14 Kt—B3, P—Kt4; 15 P—Kt3, Kt—K5; 16 Kt—Q4, Kt×P(B6); 17 Kt×P, P—R4; 18 P— B4!* (the Pawns must first be fixed. In the game Keres continued with 18 Kt—Kt7, P—R5; 19 P×P, P×P; 20 P—B4, P—R6!; 21 Kt—B5, K—K3; 22 Kt—Kt3, K—Q4 and the favorable position of the Black King made it impossible for White to do better than draw), *P—Kt5* (or 18 . . . . P×Pch; 19 K×P, Kt—K5; 20 P—R4!, Kt—B3; 21 Kt—Kt7, K—Q3; 22 K—B5, K—K2; 23 K—Kt6. Or 18 . . . . Kt—K5; 19 Kt— K7ch); *19 Kt—Kt7, K—Q3* (19 . . . . P—R5; 20 P×P is hopeless); *20 Kt×P, K—K3; 21 Kt—Kt7ch, K—B3; 22 Kt—K8ch* and wins without much trouble.

Where no immediate outside passed Pawn can be forced, the winning process must begin with forcing weaknesses in the Pawn structure which are then exploited by the King. E.g., No. 131a (Fajans-Fine, New York, 1940) White: K at KB2, Kt at QB2, P's at QR2, QKt2, KB3, KKt2, KR2; Black: K at KB1, Kt at Q4, P's at QR2, QKt3, K3, KB2, KKt3, KR2. White to play. Black wins. 1 P—QR3 (if 1 Kt—Q4, Kt—Kt5; 2 P—QR3, Kt—Q6ch wins a Pawn), P—K4; (to immobilize the White Kt); 2 P—QR4 (to get out via R3 and Kt5), K—K2; 3 Kt—R3, P—B3; 4 P—KKt3, K—K3; 5 K—K2, Kt—Kt5; 6 Kt—Kt5, P—QR3; 7 Kt—B3, P—B4; 8 K—Q2, K—Q3; 9 Kt—K2, K—B4; 10 K—B3, Kt—Q4ch; 11 K—Kt3 (11 K—Q3, K—Kt5), P— KKt4; 12 P—R3 (White is in zugzwang: if 12 K—B2, K—Kt5; 13 P— Kt3, Kt—K6ch; 14 K—Kt2, Kt—B8; 15 P—R3, Kt—Q7, winning a Pawn), P—KR4; 13 P—R4, P×P; 14 P×P, P—B5; 15 K—B2 (15 K—R3, K—B5); Kt—K6ch; 16 K—Q3, Kt—Kt7; 17 K—K4, K— Q3; 18 Kt—B1, Kt×P; 19 Kt—Q3; Kt—Kt3; 20 K—B5, Kt—K2ch; 21 K—Kt5, K—Q4; 22 K×RP, K—Q5 etc.

Because the Knight is only effective at short distances it is often advisable to sacrifice it to divert the enemy King (See No. 131). Thus in No. 132a (Marco-Maroczy, Vienna, 1899) White: K at QB2, Kt at QB1, P's at QKt4, QB3, Q4; Black: K at K6, Kt at QKt7, P's at QR6, QKt4, QB3, Q4 the coup de grace is given by *1 . . . . Kt—Q6!!; 2 Kt—*

No. 133

Draw.

Kt3, Kt—K8ch; 3 K—Q1, K—Q 6!!!; 4 K×Kt, K×P; 5 Kt—R1!, K×QP! (5 .... K—Kt7?; 6 K—Q 2,K×Kt; 7 K—B1!, P—R7; 8 K— B2, P—B4; 9 QP×P, P—Q5; 10 P—B6=); 6 Kt—B2ch, K—B6; 7 K—Q1,P—R7; 8 K—B1,P—Q5; 9 Kt—R1, P—Q6; 10 Kt—B2, P—B4 and White resigned.

If he cannot force a favorable reduction by Pawn exchanges the best bet of the defending side is a blockade. This is much more effective than in the corresponding K and P ending because there is no possibility here of gaining the opposition by a Pawn sacrifice. In No. 133 (Botvinnik-Lissitzin, Moscow, 1935) the blockade is so strong that despite his protected passed Pawn Black can make no headway. Of course if he could exchange Knights his King could enter via QKt5 or KKt6 by means of the sacrifice of his QP. But before that this sacrifice would lead to nothing. After *1 K—Q2, Kt—Kt3* (1 .... K—B4; 2 Kt—Q3ch); *2 K—Q3, Kt—B1; 3 K—B4, Kt—K3; 4 Kt—Q3, Kt— Kt4* (on 4 .... Kt—B4; 5 Kt×Kt!!, P×Kt; 6 P—R5 draws, for after 6 .... K—Q2; 7 K—Q3, P—B5ch; 8 K×P, K—Q3; 9 K—Kt4, P— Q6; 10 K—B3, K—B4; 11 P—Kt6, P×P; 12 P×P, K×P; 13 K×P, K—Kt4; the diagonal opposition does Black no good: 14 K—B3, K— B4; 15 K—Q3, K—Kt5; 16 K—Q2! etc.); *5 Kt—K1, K—K3; 6 K— Kt4* (for the game continuation see A), *Kt—R6; 7 Kt—Q3, Kt—Kt8; 8 Kt—K1, K—B3* (or 8 .... Kt—K7; 9 K—Kt3, Kt—Kt6; 10 Kt— Q3, Kt—B8; 11 K—B2 and Black's King must not abandon the defense of the KP); *9 K—B4, K—Kt4; 10 K—Q5, K—R5; 11 K×P, K—Kt6; 12 K×P, Kt×Pch; 13 Kt×Kt, K×Kt; 14 P—K5=.*

A. 6 K—Q3, K—Q3; 7 K—B4, Kt—R6; 8 Kt—Q3, Kt—Kt8; 9 Kt—K1, K—K3; 10 K—Q3 (10 K—Kt4 draws as above), Kt—R6; 11 K—Q2, K—B3; 12 K—Q3, K—K2; 13 K—K2, K—Q3; 14 Kt— Q3, Kt—Kt4; 15 Kt—Kt2, Kt—B2; 16 Kt—Q3, Kt—Q1; 17 Kt— Kt2, Kt—Kt2; 18 K—Q2, Kt—B4; 19 K—B2, K—K3; 20 K—Q1, K—B3 but even here Black could find nothing decisive.

B. POSITIONS WITH EVEN MATERIAL

Again such positions are normally drawn but there is a wide variety of possible advantages which must be considered. These may conveniently be grouped under the three rubrics:

1. A better Pawn position;
2. A better King position;
3. A better Knight position.

It should not be supposed that the last two groups are completely independent of the first, since the value of any piece depends to a large extent on the Pawn structure. Often one can speak of an advantage only when two or three of these factors occur together.

1. BETTER PAWN POSITION

In practical play this type of advantage consists of one or more of four factors.

a) *Outside Passed Pawn.*

When there are pieces on the board such a superiority is usually overwhelming. It is even greater than in the corresponding endings without pieces for there as we have seen one protected passed Pawn can often draw against two outside passed Pawns, while with one out-side passed Pawn reduced material frequently gives Black excellent drawing chances.

The principles for exploiting an outside passed Pawn remain exactly the same no matter how many pieces there are on the board. The Pawn is advanced as far as possible. It must be stopped either by a piece or the King. In either case the other side is weakened, the King enters the breach and an adequate material superiority is established. If the Pawn is not sufficiently blockaded its advance and support will win a piece. Sometimes two passed Pawns on opposite sides of the board are just as good as a considerable material superiority.

No. 134 (Lasker-Nimzovitch, Zuerich, 1934) is a classical illustration. There are four parts to Black's winning plan: 1. fixing the Q-side Pawns; 2. blockading the KP with his Kt instead of his King; 3 ma-noeuvring his King to the Q-side; 4. finally going back to the K-side and forcing the promotion of his QRP.

1 .... K—B2; 2 K—B1, K—B3; 3 K—Q2, K—K4; 4 K—K3, P—KR4; 5 P—R3 (if 5 Kt—R3, Kt—B7ch; 6 K—B3, Kt—Kt5; 7 P—R3, Kt—Q6; 8 P—Kt4, Kt—K8ch; 9 K—K2, Kt—B7, winning

No. 134

Black plays and wins.

a Pawn), *P—R4; 6 Kt—R3, Kt—B7ch; 7 K—Q3, Kt—K8ch; 8 K—
K2, Kt—Kt7; 9 K—B3, Kt—R5ch; 10 K—K3, Kt—Kt3; 11 Kt—Kt5,
K—B3; 12 Kt—R7ch, K—K2; 13 Kt—Kt5, Kt—K4; 14 K—Q4, K—
Q3; 15 Kt—R3, P—QR5; 16 Kt—B4, P—R5; 17 Kt—R3, P—Kt3!!*
(to gain a tempo); *18 Kt—B4, P—Kt4; 19 Kt—R3, Kt—B3ch; 20 K—
K3, K—B4; 21 K—Q3, P—Kt5!* (Pawn exchanges are as a rule inad-
visable in such endings, but Nimzovitch had carefully calculated that
this would win); *22 P×Pch, K×P; 23 K—B2, Kt—Q5ch; 24 K—Kt1
Kt—K3; 25 K—R2* (25 K—B2, K—B5), *K—B5!; 26 K—R3, K—
Q5!!!; 27 K×P, K×P; 28 P—Kt4, K—B6; 29 P—Kt5, K—Kt7* and
Lasker resigned.

No. 134a (Botvinnik-Lilienthal, Moscow, 1936) shows how the outside Pawn is used to create a decisive material superiority. White: K
at KB2, Kt at QB8, P's at QR5, K4, KB3, KKt3, KR4; Black: K at
KKt1, Kt at KB3, P's at Q3, K3, KB2, KKt3, KR2. 1 .... Kt—K1
(or 1 .... P—Q4; 2 P—R6); 2 P—R6, Kt—B2; 3 P—R7, Kt—R1;
4 Kt×P, K—B1; 5 P—K5, K—K2; 6 K—K3, P—B3; 7 K—B4, P—
R3; 8 Kt—B8ch, K—B2 (8 .... K—Q2; 9 P×P); 9 K—K4, K—Kt2;
10 K—Q4, Kt—B2; 11 K—B5 and the Black Knight will soon be lost.

b) Protected Passed Pawn.

Unlike K and P endings this is not quite so strong here as an outside
Pawn. The reason is that the Knight is a natural blockader, i.e., it
loses little or no mobility by stopping such a Pawn, so that the King is
free to scare up effective counter-chances elsewhere (compare No.
132). Nevertheless where the base of the Pawn is securely defended a
protected passed Pawn is inevitably a powerful threat and will, other
things being equal, be enough to win. In No. 135 (Pillsbury-Gunsberg,
Hastings, 1895) the cramped positions of the Black pieces which the
threat of the advance of the White QBP has compelled make a reduction to a simpler ending possible. *1 P—B5!* (to win the QP and thus
have two connected passed Pawns in the center), *P—Kt4* (1 ....
KtP×P; 2 P×P, P×P; 3 Kt—B4); *2 Kt—Kt4!!, P—QR4; 3 P—
B6!!!, K—Q3; 4 P×P!!!!, Kt×P* (if 4 .... P×Kt; 5 P—K7, K×KP;
6 P—B7 and queens); *5 Kt×Kt, K×Kt; 6 P—K4!* and wins (No. 90).

c) Qualitative Pawn Majority.

Here two cases must be distinguished—doubled and blocked Pawns.
Where one side has two doubled Pawns held by one, or three held by
two without any chance to dissolve them one proceeds exactly as
though one were a Pawn ahead. Where, however, the Pawns are
blocked, this advantage is a minor one with Knights on the board
because the threat of freeing the Pawns compels the player to maintain

the blockade with either Kt or K, so that the opponent's pieces are in no way constricted.

d) Qualitatively Superior Pawns.

Here a better Pawn position is of value only in conjunction with a Kt and K which are advantageously posted. The examples have consequently been put under other headings, but could just as well have been included here (see in particular No. 134). In No. 136 (Maroczy-Marshall, Monte Carlo, 1903) a tactical finesse makes it possible for Marshall to capitalize on his strong center Pawn. *1 .... Kt×P!; 2 Kt×Kt, P—B5ch; 3 K—B2, P×Ktch; 4 K×P, K—K5!; 5 K—B2,*

No. 135

No. 136

White to play wins.   Black to play wins.

K—K6!!!; 6 K—Q1, K—B6; 7 P—R4, K×P; 8 P—R5, P—B5; 9 P—R6, P—B6; 10 P—R7, P—B7; 11 K—K2 (if 11 P—R8=Qch; 12 K—Q2, Q—Kt7ch), *P—Q6ch; 12 K—Q2, P—B8=Q; 13 P—R8=Q, Q—Kt7ch; 14 Q×Qch, K×Q; 15 K×P, K—Kt6* and wins. If White had had time to retreat to B2 or K2 with his King here, he could have drawn. Such combinations, however, are frequently available in Knight endings and one should always be prepared when opportunity knocks, even though that benevolent lady behaves differently on the chess board than in proverbs.

One other illustration will suffice to show how fleeting and uncertain a Pawn positional advantage often is in Knight endings. No. 136a (Horwitz, 1880): White: K at KR4, Kt at Q4, P's at Q5, K6, KB4, KKt4; Black: K at KR2, Kt at KR3, P's at Q3, K2, KB3, KKt3. Draw. 1 P—B5, P—Kt4ch? (1 .... P×P draws—see A); 2 K—R5, Kt—Kt1 (if 2 .... K—Kt2; 3 Kt—Kt5, Kt—Kt1; 4 Kt—B7, Kt—

R3; 5 Kt—K8ch, K—R2; 6 Kt×BPch and wins); 3 Kt—Kt5, K—Kt2 (3 .... Kt—R3; 4 Kt×P!) 4 Kt—B7, Kt—R3 (or 4 .... K—B1; 5 K—Kt6!, Kt—R3; 6 K×Kt); 5 Kt—K8ch, K—R2; 6 Kt×Pch, K—Kt2; 7 Kt—K8ch or 7 Kt—K4 with a simple conclusion in both cases.

A. 1 .... P×P; 2 P×P, K—Kt2 or 2 Kt×P, Kt×Kt; 3 P×Kt, K—R3; 4 K—Kt4, K—R2; 5 K—R5, K—Kt2.

If the Knight had originally been at KKt1, 1 .... P—Kt4ch would also have drawn here (no tempo can be gained). E.g. (with Kt at KKt1), 1 P—B5, P—Kt4ch; 2 K—R5, Kt—R3; 3 Kt—Kt5, Kt—Kt1; 4 Kt—B7, Kt—R3; 5 Kt—K8, Kt—Kt1 and White must retreat.

2. BETTER KING POSITION

We need not consider in detail those cases where one King is so far ahead of his rival that he can simply knock down all the Pawns as though he were a bowling ball among ninepins. Of more interest are positions where one King is only somewhat better placed and some skill is required to exploit this minimal superiority.

In complicated endings we must note a characteristic feature which occupies a minor place in Pawn endings: the value of a centrally posted King. When one King is at K4 or Q4 and the other at K2 or Q2 or even K3 or Q3 with only Pawns on the board, this in itself makes little differences, but with Knights or other pieces it is frequently the decisive factor.

In No. 137 (Keres-Rabinovitch, Leningrad-Moscow, 1939) the strong White King position makes it impossible for Black to avoid the loss of a Pawn. *1 P—Kt3, Kt—B4; 2 Kt—Q5, K—Q3; 3 Kt×KtP, Kt—K3ch; 4 K—K3, Kt—B2; 5 Kt—B8ch!, K—Q2; 6 Kt—R7, P—B3; 7 P×P* (Keres played 7 P—KR4, P×P; 8 RP×P, P—K4!; 9 P×P, Kt—K3; 10 Kt—Kt5, Kt×P; 11 Kt—Q4, P—R4; 12 K—B4, Kt—K3ch! and could only draw), *P×P; 8 Kt—Kt5, Kt—K3* (8 .... Kt×Kt; 9 P×Kt, K—Q3; 10 K—Q4, K—K3; 11 K—B5, K—Q2; 12 K—Q5 is hopeless); *9 P—QR3, Kt—B4; 10 Kt—Q4, P—Kt4; 11 P—B5* (Pawn exchanges should be avoided wherever possible), *K—Q3; 12 P—Kt4, P×P; 13 P×P, Kt—R3; 14 P—B5ch,* K—Q4; 15 P—B6! and the passed Pawns decide.

No. 137a (Belavienetz-Kan, Leningrad-Moscow, 1939) is another instance where a King on a central square dominates the board. White: K at QB4, Kt at QB1, P's at QR3, QKt4, K3, KB2, KKt2, KR3; Black: K at K4, Kt at Q4, P's at QR3, QKt3, K5, KB4, KKt4, KR4. Black wins. The game continued 1 Kt—K2, P—B5!; 2 P×Pch, Kt×P; 3 Kt—B3 (if Kt×Kt, P×Kt; 4 P—KR4—else .... P—R5—, P—B6; 5 P×P, P×P; 6 K—Q3, K—B5; 7 K—Q4,

K—Kt5; 8 K—K4, K×P; 9 K×P, K—R6; 10 K—B4, K—Kt7; 11 K—Kt5, K×P and Black will win the horse race); Kt×KtP; 4 P—Kt5. And here a simple conclusion was possible by 4 .... P×Pch! (instead of the complicated 4 .... P—R4 as actually played); 5 K×P, P—R5; 6 K×P, P—Kt5; 7 P×P, Kt—B5!; 8 P—Kt5 (or 8 P—R4, P—R6 and the Pawn cannot be stopped), P—R6; 9 P—Kt6, Kt×P; 10 Kt—K2, P—R7; 11 Kt—Kt3, K—B5; 12 Kt—R1 (or 12 P—R4, P—K6), K—B6; 13 P—R4, K—Kt7; 14 P—R5, K×Kt; 15 P—R6, K—Kt7; 16 P—R7, P—R8=Q; 17 P—R8=Q, Q—Kt8ch; 18 K any, K×P or 18 .... Kt—B5.

Another such example where centralization of the King is the decisive factor is No. 137b (Salvioli), White: K at Q3, Kt at Q6, P's at

No. 137   No. 138

White to play wins.   White plays and wins.

QR2, QKt3, QB2, KB3, KKt4, KR3; Black: K at QR2, Kt at KKt7, P's at QR3, QKt2, QB4, Q5, KKt2, KR3. White to play wins. 1 K—K4!, Kt—K8 (1 .... Kt—R5; 2 P—KB4, P—QKt4; 3 P—B5, followed by Kt—K8); 2 Kt—B5, Kt×QBP; 3 Kt×KtP, Kt—Kt5; 4 Kt—B5 and White's Pawns on the K-side cannot be stopped.

3. BETTER KNIGHT POSITION

Unlike a Bishop a Knight is at home in any Pawn structure, so that advantages of this type must be utilized immediately or they will dissipate into thin air. The superior Knight is always one which is nearer the Pawns and which can either force the gain of material or a serious positional weakness (blocked Pawns, e.g.).

In No. 138 (Alekhine-Andersen, Folkestone, 1933) the decisive manoeuvre begins with *1 Kt—Kt3!!, K—B1* (Black has no choice because his King is too far away from the Queen's side. If 1 .... Kt—K2;

2 Kt—R5, Kt×P; 3 Kt×P, Kt—B5; 4 Kt×P, Kt—Q6ch; 5 K—B2, Kt×BP; 6 P—QKt4!, K—B1; 7 P—QR4 and if 7 .... K—K2; 8 Kt—B8ch, while if 7 .... Kt—Kt5; 8 P—Kt5, Kt×P; 9 P—R5 and the QRP cannot be stopped); *2 Kt—R5, P—QKt3; 3 Kt—B6, K—K1* (Black is in an uncomfortable bind); *4 K—Q2, Kt—K2* (if the White King gets too near it will be all over); *5 Kt×P, Kt×P; 6 Kt—Kt5* (Alekhine has thus transformed his original superior Knight position into the more lasting advantage of a potential outside passed Pawn), *K—Q2; 7 Kt—Q4, P—Kt3; 8 P—QR4, Kt—B2; 9 K—B3, P—KKt4; 10 K—Kt4, P—Q4; 11 Kt—B3, P—B3; 12 Kt—Q4, K—Q3* (Hastens the end. But even after 12 .... K—K2; 13 P—R5, P×Pch; 14 K×P, K—Q2; 15 P—QKt4, K—B1; 16 K—Kt6 Black is hopelessly lost); *13 Kt—Kt5ch, Kt×Kt; 14 K×Kt, K—K4; 15 P—QKt4, P—Q5; 16 K—B4* and Black resigned.

Very often there is a choice between giving up a center Pawn and giving up a wing Pawn. Since the great strength of the outside passed Pawn has repeatedly been demonstrated, where one must choose, the center Pawn should always be the victim. However, one must remember that passive defense in Knight and Pawn endings is rarely successful. The most effective way of saving an apparently lost position is a vigorous counter-attack. Here as in Pawn endings lengthy and precise calculations are sometimes required. In No. 138a (Berger-Maroczy, Barmen, 1905) the draw can be achieved only by accurate counting. White: K at KKt1, Kt at K5, P's at QR2, QKt3, Q4, KR3; Black: K at KKt2, Kt at QB6, P's at QR2, QKt2, Q4, KR3. Drawn. White to play must clearly lose a Pawn. 1 Kt—Kt4 (1 P—QR4, Kt—K7ch; 2 K—B2, Kt×P; 3 P—Kt4, Kt—K3 is no improvement), Kt×P; 2 Kt—K3, Kt—B8? (2 .... Kt—B6 would win); 3 P—Kt4, Kt—K7ch; 4 K—B2, Kt×P; 5 Kt×P, K—Kt3; 6 K—K3, Kt—K3; and now 7 K—K4! draws by one tempo: 7 .... Kt—Kt4ch; 8 K—K5, Kt×P; 9 K—Q6, K—Kt4; 10 K—B7, P—Kt3; 11 K—Kt7, Kt—B5; 12 Kt—K3!, P—QR4; 13 P—Kt5!, Kt—K3; 14 K×P, P—R5; 15 Kt—B4, P—R4; 16 K—R5, P—R5; 17 K×P, P—R6; 18 Kt—Q2 (just in time), K—B5; 19 Kt—B1 =.

IV. TWO KNIGHTS AND PAWNS

The presence of the extra Knights practically never requires any change in the rules and principles which have already been set up. On rare occasions it is possible to get a bind on the opponent's position with two Knights which it is impossible to have with one. Such a case is seen in No. 139 (Marco-Maroczy, Vienna, 1899). With either Black Knight off the White King would be free to roam wherever he pleased, since there would be no constant threat against his Pawns.

But as it is he is completely tied up and is condemned to a useless career of royal dawdling. Maroczy wins by first advancing his Pawn to QR5 (so that if and when he captures the QRP he will have a protected passed Pawn nearer to queening) and then forcing an entry on the King's side. The winning process is highly original. *1 .... K—Q3; 2 K—K2, K—B2; 3 K—B2, K—Kt3; 4 K—K2, P—R4; 5 K—B2,* (5 P×Pch, K×P is worse), *P—R5; 6 K—K2, K—B2; 7 K—B2, K—Q3; 8 K—K2, K—K2; 9 K—B2, K—B2; 10 K—K2, K—Kt2; 11 K—B2, K—R2; 12 P—Kt3* (this makes no difference), *K—R3; 13 K—K2, P—KB4; 14 P×P, P×P; 15 K—B2, K—R4; 16 K—K2, P—B5; 17 P×P, P×P; 18 K—B2, K—Kt4; 19 K—K2, K—R5; 20 K—B2, K—R6!; 21 Kt—Q3* (there is no alternative; on 21 K—K2, K—Kt6 forces a Kt move, for if then 22 K—Q3, K—B7); *Kt—B7; 23 Kt×Pch, K—R5; 24 Kt—Q3* (if 24 Kt—Kt6ch, K—Kt4; 25 Kt—K5, Kt(B5)× RP; 26 Kt×Kt, Kt×Kt; 27 Kt×P, Kt—B5 and the Pawn queens), *Kt(B7)×RP; 25 Kt×Kt, Kt×Kt; 26 Kt—B1, Kt—Kt8; 27 Kt—R2, K—R6; 28 K—K3, K—Kt6; 29 P—KB4, K—Kt5; 30 P—B5* (White is in zugzwang), *K×P* and the outside passed Pawn decides (No. 132a)

No. 139

Black wins,

Chapter IV

BISHOP AND PAWN ENDINGS

I. BISHOP VS. PAWNS

The general results here are pretty much the same as in Knight endings. Bishop vs. one or two Pawns is a draw (unless the Pawns are so far advanced that they can no longer be stopped) while Bishop vs. 3 Pawns is a draw or win depending on the relative positions of the Pawns.

Except for some unusual cases the Bishop draws against one Pawn if it can cover any square on the queening file which the Pawn must cross. A win for the Pawn is possible only when the King blocks the action of his own Bishop or when the Pawn can gain a move by checking. In No. 140 (Allgaier, 1795) we have the second case: *1 .... P—Q6ch; 2 K any, P—Q7* and 3 .... P queens. Unless White's Bishop has just come from QKt8 and captured at K5, any normal play by White would have drawn the move before, so that this type of win is either luck or the result of a reduction from some more complicated ending. In No. 140a (Kling and Horwitz, 1853), White: K at QR5, P at QKt6; Black: K at QB3, B at KKt3 there is no check and consequently Black can get back in time. 1 K—R6, B—K5!; 2 P—Kt7, K—B2; 3 K—R7, B×P. Stalemate! No. 140a would be drawn with the Bishop anywhere on the board but K square.

With two Pawns against the Bishop there is more chance to win. If the Pawns are not beyond the fourth rank, there should be no difficulty drawing, but if the Pawns are beyond the fourth rank the outcome depends on whether the King is able to stop one Pawn

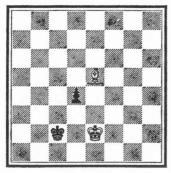

No. 140

Black plays and wins.

while the Bishop takes care of the other. An exception to this general rule is seen in No. 141 (problem by H. Otten) which we have included to show how a King can get in the way of his own piece. The solution is *1 P—R5, B—B1; 2 K—Q5, B—R3; 3 P—Kt5ch!!, B×P* (or 3 .... K×P; 4 P—R6); *4 K—K4, B—R5; 5 K—B3!* and the Pawn marches on. If the Black King here had been anywhere else near either Pawn the draw would have been obvious.

With two Pawns on the fifth the King positions decide. E.g., No.

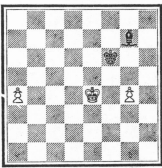

White plays and wins.

141a (Salvioli, 1887), White: K at KR5, B at K2; Black: K at KKt8, P's at QR5, Q5. Black wins. 1 B—B4, P—R6; 2 K—Kt4, K—B7!; 3 K—B4, P—Q6; 4 K—K4, P—Q7; 5 B—Kt3, P—R7 etc. Pawns two files apart (as here) cannot be stopped by a Bishop in any position once they are on the fifth rank or beyond. If they are one file apart (e.g., QR5 and QB5) they can be stopped by a Bishop at QKt2 or QKt4 and if three files apart (QR5, K5) by a Bishop at QB1 or QB5. Thus the most favorable position for the Pawns is to be two or four or more files apart from one another. This has been seen in No. 141a and is also clear in No. 141b (Kling and Horwitz), White: K at QKt5, B at QB3; Black: K at Q4, P's at QB5, KB4. Black to play wins by 1 .... P—B5; 2 K—Kt4, P—B6; 3 B—K1, K—Q5; 4 K—R3, P—B6; 5 K—R2, K—Q6; 6 K—Kt1, K—K7; and if 7 B×P, P—B7 while if 7 B—R4, K—Q8. With the Black Pawn at KR4 here the game is also a win, but if it is at either K4 or KKt4 the result is a draw.

Two connected passed Pawns can be stopped by the Bishop unless they are both on the sixth. E.g., White Pawns at K4, Q4, Black plays 1 .... B—KB3 and if 2 P—K5, B—Kt2 or 2 P—Q5, B—K4 and the Pawns cannot advance. But if they are at K6, Q6, then on 1 .... B—KB1; 2 P—K7 forces a queen. With connected Pawns one must always advance that Pawn which is not on the same color as the Bishop, else they will be blockaded immediately. In No. 141c (Kling and Horwitz, 1853) we have a case where blockaded Pawns do not win despite the proximity of the King. White: K at Q8, B at KR3; Black: K at Q3, P's at KKt6, KB7. 1 B—Kt2!, K—K4; 2 K—K7, K—Q5; 3 K—K6, K—K6; 4 K—K5, K—K7; 5 K—B4 and the Kings will have to battle it out alone.

With three connected passed Pawns a win is possible only if all three Pawns can succeed in crossing the fourth rank (except for certain special cases). The defense always consists of blockading the Pawns, and this is not feasible if the Pawns are too near the queening square. No. 142 is the model position. White's Bishop is so favorably placed that the Black Pawns must soon come to a halt. If *1 .... P—B6ch; 2 K—B2, K—B5; 3 B—Q8, P—R6; 4 B—B7ch* (not 4 B×Pch?, K—Kt5!!! and wins), *K—Kt5; 5 B—Kt3,* or *1 .... K—R4; 2 B—Q6* (to prevent 2 .... P—Kt5), or *1 .... K—B4; 2 B—Q8.*

That the position of the Bishop is all-important is shown by No. 143 (Horwitz, 1880). Here *1 .... K—B4* (for 1 .... P—B6ch see A) is decisive because the Bishop has too little freedom of action to stop the Pawns. *2 B—R5* (or 2 K—R3, P—B6; 3 B—B2, K—K5; 4 B—Kt6, K—Q6; 5 K—R2, K—K7; 6 K—Kt1, P—Kt5), *P—Kt5; 3 B—Q8, P—R6ch; 4 K—R2, K—K5; 5 B—Kt6, K—B6; 6 B—B7,*

No. 142　　　　　　　　　　　　　No. 143

Draw.

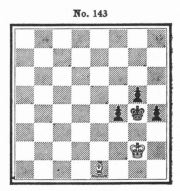

Black to play wins.

K—K6; 7 B—Kt8, P—B6; 8 K—Kt1, K—K7; 9 B—Kt3, P—R7ch; 10 K×P, P—B7; 11 B×P, K×B; 12 K—R1, K—Kt6!

A. 1 .... P—B6ch is much inferior: 2 K—Kt1!!! (the only drawing move, if, e.g., 2 K—B2, P—R6; 3 K—Kt1, K—B5!; 4 B—Q2ch, K—B4; 5 B—K1, K—K5; 6 B—Kt3, K—K6; 7 K—B1, P—Kt5; 8 B—Kt8, P—B7; 9 B—R7ch, K—B6; 10 B×P, P—R7), K—B4 (2 .... K—B5; 3 B—Q2ch); 3 B—R5, P—Kt5; 4 B—Q8, P—R6; 5 B—B7, K—K5; 6 K—B2 and here Black can do nothing.

When the Pawns are on the sixth or seventh ranks the battle is hopeless. E.g., No. 143a (Kling and Horwitz, 1853) White: K at KKt1, B at K1; Black: K at KR6, P's at K7, KB6, KKt7. Black manoeuvres his King to Q8, then wins the Bishop by promoting KtP and KP and finally queens his BP. Or No. 143b, White: K at KKt1, B at QKt4; Black: K at KKt6, P's at KB5, KKt5, KR6. Here 1 ....

P—B6??; 2 B—Q6ch, K—R5; 3 K—B2 only draws, but 1 .... K—B6; 2 K—R2, K—K7, as in No. 131 is sufficient.

On the other hand it is easy to see that with the Pawns further back none of the above methods can be carried out. No. 143c (Berger, 1890), White: K at KKt2, B at Q1(ch); Black: K at KKt5, P's at KB5, KKt4, KR5. Draw. 1 .... K—B4; 2 K—R3, K—K5; 3 K—Kt2, K—K6; 4 B—Kt4, and now 4 .... P—B6ch; 5 B×P, P—R6ch; 6 K—Kt3 leads to nothing. Or No. 143d (Berger, 1890) White: K at KKt2, B at Q1; Black: K at KB4, P's at KB5, KKt4, KR4. Draw. 1 .... P—Kt5; 2 B—B2ch, K—K4; 3 K—B2, P—R5; 4 B—Q1!, K—B4; 5 B—B2ch, K—B3; 6 B—K4, P—R6; 7 B—B6, P—Kt6ch; 8 K—B3, K—Kt4; 9 B—Q7, P—R7; 10 K—Kt2, P—B6ch; 11 K—R1, P—B7; 12 B—R3, K—B5; 13 B—B1, K—K6; 14 B—R3, K—K7; 15 B—B1ch, K—K8; 16 B—R3, P—B8=Q; 17 B×Q=. No. 143e (Berger, 1890), White: K at KKt3, B at K2; Black: K at KKt4, P's at KB4, KKt3, KR4. 1 .... K—B3; 2 B—B3, K—K4; 3 K—R4, K—B3; 4 B—B6, K—K3; 5 K—Kt5=.

The essential point in all the examples is this: if the Pawns can be blockaded before two reach the seventh the ending is a draw; if not it is a win (except for the RP which allows certain stalemate possibilities). It makes no real difference whether the Pawns are on center or side files (again with the exception of the stalemate in No. 143d).

Three isolated Pawns (or two connected and one isolated) are, unlike the similar Knight ending, not stronger than three connected Pawns. They win when one Pawn can reach the sixth, but draw otherwise. Thus No. 144 (Handbuch) is a draw because the QKtP is too far back. *1 .... K—B4* (or 1 .... P—K5; 2 K—B4, K—B4; 3 K—Q4, P—Kt4; 4 B—Q6, P—Kt5; 5 B×P, K—B5; 6 B—K1, K—B6; 7 B—R4, P—K6; 8 K—Q3 and Black is at a standstill); *2 K—B4!* (2 K—Kt6?, P—K5!; 3 K—B5!, P—Kt4; 4 K—Q4, P—Kt5; 5 B—R2, P—Kt6; 6 K—B3, P—K6; 7 K×P, P—K7; 8 B—Kt3, K—K5 loses for White), *K—K5; 3 K—B5, P—Kt4; 4 B—R2!* (not 4 K×P, K—Q5! followed by .... P—K5 and .... K—K6), *P—Kt5; 5 K—B4, P—QKt6; 6 K×P, K—Q5; 7 K—B2, P—K5; 8 K—Q2=.*

But if we consider a position such as No. 144a, White: K at QKt1, B at KKt3; Black: K at KB4; P's at QKt6, K4, KKt5, where White has no time to delay capture of the KtP, Black can force a pretty decision by 1 .... P—K5; 2 K—Kt2, P—K6; 3 K×P, K—K5; 4 K—B2, K—B6; 5 B—Kt8, P—Kt6; 6 K—Q1, P—Kt7; 7 B—R2, K—B7!! and White is in zugzwang. Or again in No. 144b, a problem by Dr. Lewitt, White: K at KB3, P's at QKt2, QKt5, KR6, Black: K at QR4, B at QKt3, the advanced Pawns are irresistible. 1 K—K4, B—Q1; 2 P—Kt6!!, K—R3!! (2 .... K×P; 3 K—B5); 3 K—K5, B—Kt4; 4 P—R7, B—B8; 5 K—Q6, B×P; 6 K—B7, B—K4ch; 7 K—B6,

B—B3; 8 P—Kt7, K—R2; 9 K—B7, and one Pawn will queen.

Four or more Pawns clearly win against a Bishop, unless they are doubled or so far back that they can be captured at will. However, two Bishops win against four Pawns. Berger gives the following position: (No. 144c), White: K at KB3, B's at QKt5, KB2; Black: K at K3, P's at Q4, K4, KB4, KKt4. White wins. The main variation is 1 B—B5, P—K5ch; 2 K—K3, P—B5ch; 3 K—Q4, P—Kt5; 4 B—B6, P—K6; 5 B×Pch, K—B4; 6 K—Q3, K—Kt4; 7 B—K7ch, K—B4; 8 B—K4ch, K—K4; 9 B—Q8, K—Q3; 10 B—B5, P—Kt6; 11 B—K4, K—K4; 12 B—B7ch and wins all the Pawns. Against the plan of first blocking the Pawns and then winning them Black is defenseless.

No. 144

Draw.

No. 145

Draw.

II. KING, BISHOP AND PAWNS VS. KING,
WITH AND WITHOUT PAWNS

Bishop and Pawn always win against a lone King unless the Pawn is a RP and the Bishop is of the wrong color, i.e., does not command the queening square. In No. 145 White can do nothing because he cannot chase the Black King out of the corner. After *1 K—Kt5, K—Kt2; 2 P—R6ch, K—R1; 3 K—Kt6, K—Kt1; 4 B—K5ch, K—R1* the best White can do is stalemate. On the other hand if the Bishop were on white, of the right color, the win would be child's play. No. 145a, B at Q3 instead of Q4 in No. 133. 1 K—Kt5, K—Kt2; 2 B—K4ch, K—R2; 3 P—R6, K—Kt1; 4 K—Kt6 and queens in two moves.

To draw against a Bishop of the wrong color the Black King must either actually be in the corner or be able to reach it. In No. 145b (Troitzky, 1896) White: K at K3, B at KR3, P at KR5; Black: K at K1, White to play can win by 1 B—K6!, K—K2; 2 P—R6!!, K—B3; 3 B—B5!!!, K—B2; 4 B—R7, K—B3; 5 K—B4, K—B2; 6 K—Kt5,

K—B1; 7 K—B6, etc. Another application of this rule will be seen in No. 147b.

There is one position with a KtP which completes the list of cases where B+P do not win against a lone King. No. 145c (Mouret, 1838) White: K at QR4; Black: K at QKt2, P at QKt5, B at QR7. After 1 .... P—Kt6; 2 K—R3, K—B3; 3 K—Kt2, K—B4; 4 K—R1 the Black Bishop cannot move and the Black King cannot come too near without stalemating.

With B+P vs. P we have pretty much the same state of affairs: simple win unless there is a RP with a Bishop of the wrong color and the opposing King can creep into the corner. In general the extra material is only a handicap for the defender. Thus, as we shall see, when he has one KtP against B+P the game is generally but not always a draw, while with a doubled KtP the game is usually lost.

There are two winning possibilities when extra Pawns are added to positions such as No. 145: one is shutting the Black King out of the corner; the other is forcing a Black Pawn to sacrifice itself to the White RP and thereby transform it into a KtP.

In No. 146 (Kling and Horwitz, 1851) we have the first case. If White attacks the Black Pawn directly Black will have time to get back to QR1. The problem then is to keep the Black King at a respectable distance from the QR file. The solution is *1 B—B4!, K—Kt7; 2 K—Kt4!!* (if 2 K—K4, K—R6; 3 K—Q5, K—Kt5; 4 B—R2, K—B4; 5 K—B6, K—K3 and White is no nearer his goal), *K—B7; 3 B—B1, K—K7* (if 3 .... K—Kt7; 4 B—K3, K—B8; 5 K—B3, K—K8; 6 B—B4, K—Q8; 7 K—K3, K—B7; 8 K—Q4, K—Kt6; 9 B—Q6); *4 K—B4, K—Q8* (or 4 .... K—Q6; 5 B—K3, K—B5; 6 K—K5, K—Kt6; 7 B—B5, K—B5; 8 K—Q6, K—Q6;

9 K—Q5, K—B6; 10 B—Q6, K—Q6; 11 K—B5, K—K5; 12 B—R2); *5 B—K3, K—B7; 6 K—K5, K—Kt6; 7 B—B5, K—B5; 8 K—Q6, K—Kt4; 9 K—Q5, K—R4!; 10 K—B6, K—R3; 11 B—K3, K—R4; 12 K—Kt7, K—Kt4; 13 B—Kt6, K—B5; 14 K—B6, K—Kt6; 15 B—B5, K—B5; 16 B—K3, K—Kt6; 17 B—B1, K—B5; 17 B—Kt2!!!* (the point), *K—Kt6; 19 K—Kt5!* and wins.

With Black to move White has a much harder time. For a long while, as a matter of fact, it was held that he could actually draw but

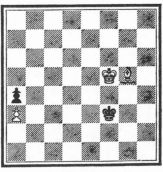

No. 146

White wins.

in 1928 Rauser demonstrated that this opinion was incorrect. White can win by *1 .... K—Kt6; 2 B—B6!, K—B6* (if 2 .... K—R6; 3 K—B4, K—R7; 4 K—B3, K—R6; 5 B—Kt5, K—R7; 6 K—Kt4, K—Kt7; 7 B—B4 as in the main variation); *3 B—K5, K—K6; 4 B—Kt2!!!* (the only winning move. If 4 B—Kt8?, K—Q5!; 5 K—K6, K—B4; 6 K—Q7, K—Kt3 and draws, e.g., 7 K—B8, K—B4; 8 K—B7, K—Q4!; 9 K—Q7, K—B4; 10 B—B7, K—Kt4!, etc.), *K—Q6* (or 4 .... K—B6; 5 B—B1, K—Kt6; 6 B—Kt5, K—B7; 7 K—B4, K—K7; 8 K—K4, K—B7; 9 B—B4); *5 K—K5, K—K6* (if instead 5 .... K—B5; 6 K—Q6, K—Kt4; 7 B—Q4, K—B5; 8 B—B5, K—Kt4; 9 K—Q5, again as in the main variation above); *6 B—B1ch, K—B6; 7 K—B5!, K—Kt6; 8 B—Kt5, K—B6* (or 8 .... K—R6; 9 K—B4); and we have come back to the diagrammed position with White to play: *9 B—B4.* The key to this ending is to be found in No. 147 (Rauser, 1928). It makes no difference whose turn it is to move, but if the Black King can manage to reach any square behind the heavy line before his Pawn is captured (but not more than two files away from the White King) he can draw; if not he loses. In No. 147 itself the solution is *1 B—R2, K—Q5; 2 K—Q6, K—B5* (2 .... K—K5; 3 K—B5, K—B4; 4 K—Kt5, K—K3; 5 K×P, K—Q2; 6 K—Kt5, K—B1; 7 K—B6 and wins); *3 K—B6, K—Kt6; 4 B—Q6, K—B5; 5 B—B5, K—Kt6; 6 K—Kt5.* Black to move: *1 .... K—B6; 2 K—B5, K—K6; 3 B—Kt2!, K—Q6; 4 K—K5, K—K6; 5 B—B1ch, K—B6; 6 K—B5, K—Kt6; 7 B—Kt5, K—B6; 8 B—B4* and we have come back to No. 146.

If the Black Pawn still has moves Black loses unless his King is in the corner. E.g., No. 147a (problem by Teichmann), White: K at QR6, P at QR2, B at KKt3; Black: K at QB1, P at QR5. White wins.

No. 147

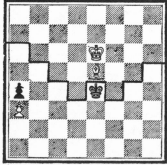

White wins if the Black King is not in the zone marked off by the heavy line.

1 K—Kt6, K—Q2; 2 K—Kt7, K—Q1; 3 K—B6!, K—K2!; 4 B—B7, K—K3; 5 B—Q6, K—B4 (or A); 6 K—Q5, K—B3; 7 B—Kt4, K—B2; 8 K—Q6, K—K1; 9 B—R5, K—B2, 10 B—Q8, K—K1; 11 B—R4, K—B2; 12 K—Q7, K—Kt3; 13 K—K6, K—R4; 14 B—K7, K—Kt3!; 15 B—B6, K—R3!; 16 K—B5, K—R2; 17 B—Kt2, K—Kt1; 18 K—K6, K—B1; 19 B—B6, K—Kt1; 20 K—K7, K—R2; 21 K—B7, K—R3; 22 B—K7, K—R4; 23 K—B6, K—R3; 24 B—B8ch, K—R4; 25 P—R3, K—Kt5; 26 B—R6 and Black's King cannot

get out of the losing zone.

A. 5 .... K—B3; 6 K—Q7, K—B4; 7 K—K7, K—K5; 8 K—K6, K—Q5; 9 B—R3, K—B5; 10 K—Q6, K—Q5; 11 B—Kt2ch, K—K5; 12 K—K6, K—B5; 13 B—B6, K—Kt5; 14 K—K5, K—R4; 15 K—B5, K—R3; 16 B—Kt2, K—R2; 17 K—B6, K—R3!; 18 B—B1ch, K—R4 (or 18 .... K—R2; 19 K—B7, K—R1; 20 B—R6, K—R2; 21 B—Kt7, P—R6; 22 B—B8); 19 P—QR3 and again we have No. 147.

Another illustration is No. 147b (Duras, 1908) White: K at KR1, B at QR3, P at QR2; Black: K at KKt2, P at Q2. White to play wins. 1 B—Kt4!, K—B2 and after 2 P—R4, K—K3 (or 2 .... K—K1; 3 P—R5, K—Q1; 4 B—Q6, K—B1; 5 P—R6); 3 P—R5, K—Q4; 4 P—R6, K—B3; 5 B—R5! Black's Pawn moves will soon be ex-

No. 148   No. 149

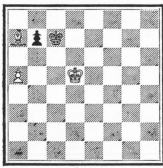   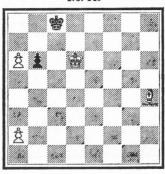

White wins.   Draw.

hausted and his King will have to abandon the square of White's RP.

When the Bishop is of the right color, the only point that need be borne in mind is that the White Pawn should be allowed freedom if it is still at its original square. The trap position to be avoided is No. 147c (Lolli, 1763), White: K at QKt1, P at QR2; Black: K at Q6, B at Q5, P at QR6. This is a draw no matter who begins. E.g., 1 .... K—B6; 2 K—B1!, B—K6ch; 3 K—Kt1, K—Q6; 4 K—R1 and 4 .... K—B7 is stalemate. If the Black Pawn were still at QR5, No. 147d, White: K at QKt1, P at QR2; Black: K at Q6, B at Q5, P at QR5, it would all be over in a few moves. 1 .... K—B5; 2 K—B1, K—Kt5; 3 K—Kt1, K—R6; 4 K any, K×P.

When Black has a KtP White can win if he can get to position No. 148 (Paulsen-Metger, Nuremberg, 1888). One must be careful to avoid various traps here, e.g., 1 K—B5?, P—Kt3ch=(2 B×Pch, K—Kt2, No. 145; 2 P×Pch, K—Kt2, No. 145c), or 1 K—B4?

P—Kt4ch!!. But White can win with *1 K—Q4!!, K—B3* (or a) 1 ....
P—Kt4 (or 1 .... P—Kt3); 2 P—R6, K—B3; 3 K—B3, K—Q2;
4 K—Kt4, K—B3; 5 K—R5. b) 1 .... K—Q2 (or .... K—Q1, ...
K—B1); 2 K—B5, K—B2; 3 K—Kt5, P—Kt3; 4 P—R6!!); *2 B—
Kt6!, K—Q3* (2 .... K—Kt4; 3 K—Q5, K—R3; 4 K—Q6); *3 K—B4,
K—B3; 4 K—Kt4, K—Q3; 5 K—Kt5, K—Q2; 6 K—B5, K—B1;
7 B—R7, K—B2; 8 K—Kt5, K—Q2; 9 B—Kt8, K—B1; 10 B—R2,
K—Q2; 11 K—Kt6.*

With the Black King snugly in the corner the game is a draw
regardless of where White's pieces are. In the most favorable case,
where Black has a KtP, the Pawn may be forced to move by stalemating the King but even that leads to nothing, for if White captures

No. 150

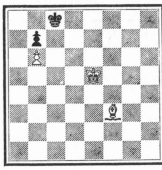

Draw.

No. 151

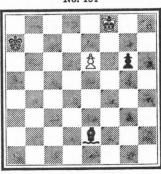

White to play draws!

Black is stalemated, while if he goes by Black gives up his Pawn and
transposes into No. 145. Even with two RP's, as in No. 147 (Kling
and Horwitz, 1851) nothing can be done. *1 P—R4, K—Kt1; 2
B—B2, K—R1!* (not 2 .... K—R2??; 3 P—R5, K×P; 4 P×P;
and wins); *3 K—B7, K—R2; 4 P—R5, K—R1!; 5 P×P* stalemate
(or 5 B×P stalemate. Or 5 K×P, K—Kt1 and the extra White
Pawn makes no difference).

With two KtP's we can have a position similar to that with a RP.
In No. 150 no win is possible because of the constant stalemate threat.
E.g., *1 K—Q6, K—Kt1; 2 K—Q7, K—R1;* and now 3 K—B7 is
stalemate, while *3 B—B6* is met coldbloodedly by *3 .... K—Kt1!.*
If White had a Bishop on Black squares he could not even approach
with his King. Black would simply move his King back and forth
from B1—Q2 and nothing could budge him.

Except for these special cases one can draw with P vs. B+P only
if the opponent's Pawn can be captured. As a rule this is out of the

question but sometimes it can be managed. In No. 151 (Problem by
Reti, 1928) White wards off defeat by first forcing Black to guard his
Pawn with his Bishop and then queening to remove the support of the
Black Pawn. *1 K—K7!!, P—Kt4; 2 K—Q6, P—Kt5; 3 P—K7,
B—Kt4, 4 K—B5!* (gaining the tempo necessary to get to the square
of the KtP), *B—Q2; 5 K—Q4, K—Kt3; 6 K—K4, K—B3; 7 K—B4,
K—Q3; 8 P—K8=B.*

Since a Bishop is worth approximately three Pawns, B+P vs.
2 P's is in general a win. However, the added Black material, as is to
be expected, creates many more drawing possibilities for the defender.

Again a RP and B of the wrong color must be sharply distinguished

No. 152   **No. 153**

White to play wins.   White wins.

from the general case. Here too if the Black King can reach the
corner the game is usually drawn. But if Black has a doubled KtP or a
KtP with a RP, the extra Pawn is a severe handicap because it ruins
his stalemate defense and allows White to transform his RP into a KtP.

In the most difficult position, No. 152 (Kling and Horwitz, 1851),
White proceeds by stalemating the Black King. *1 B—Q2* (to answer
1 .... K—R4 with 2 P—R3), *K—B2* (or 1 .... K—Kt2; 2 K—Q6,
K—Kt3; 3 B—K1, K—Kt2; 4 B—R4, K—Kt3; 5 B—Q8ch, K—Kt2;
6 B—B7, K—R1!; 7 K—B6, K—R2; 8 B—Q8, K—R1!; 9 K—Kt6,
K—Kt1; 10 B—B7ch, K—B1; 11 K—B6 and 1 .... P—Kt6 is
forced when 12 P×P, P—Kt5; 13 B—Q6 is decisive); *2 B—Kt5,
K—Q2; 3 K—B5, K—B2; 4 B—R4, K—B1; 5 K—Kt6, K—Kt1;
6 B—Kt3ch, K—B1* (6 .... K—R1; 7 B—B4 and 7 .... P—Kt6 must
come); *7 B—B4, K—Q2; 8 K×P, K—B1; 9 K—Kt6, K—Q2; 10 K—
Kt7, K—K3; 11 K—B6, K—K2; 12 B—Q6ch, K—Q1; 13 K—Kt7*
and Black cannot get back.

With RP and KtP the same idea is decisive. In No. 153 (Walker, 1841) the crucial stalemate position is brought about by *1 K—Q4, K—Q3; 2 K—K4, K—K3; 3 K—B4, K—B3; 4 B—B5, K—B2; 5 K—K5, K—Kt1* (if 5 .... K—K2; 6 B—K6, K—B1; 7 K—B5, K—K2; 8 B—R2, K—K1; 9 K—Kt6, K—B1; 10 B—Kt3); *6 K—K6, K—B1; 7 B—Kt6, K—Kt1; 8 K—K7, K—R1; 9 B—B2, K—Kt1; 10 B—Q3, P—Kt4* (or 10 .... K—R1; 11 K—B7, P—Kt4; 12 P×P e.p.); *11 P×P e.p., K—Kt2* (11 .... P—R4; 12 K—B6) *12 K—K6, P—R4; 13 K—B5.*

There are many variations on this theme. E.g., No. 153a (Horwitz, 1885), White: K at QB5, B at KB4, P at QR3; Black: K at QR2, P's at QR5, QKt4. White wins. 1 K—B6, K—R1 (on 1 .... K—R3; 2 B—K3 mates in five: 2 .... K—R4; 3 B—B5, P—Kt5; 4 P×Pch, K—R3; 5 B—Kt6, P—R6; 6 P—Kt5 mate); 2 K—Kt6, P—Kt5; 3 P×P, P—R6; 4 P—Kt5, P—R7; 5 B—K5, P—R8=Q; 6 B×Q etc. But if Black's Pawn had been at QR3 here instead of QR5 he could draw: 1 K—B6, P—R4; 2 B—K3ch, K—R1; 3 B—Kt6, P—Kt5; 4 P—R4, K—Kt1 and now stalemate does White no good because his RP can never become a KtP.

Even with a greater number of Pawns, the crucial point is whether Black has a KtP which can be used to transform the White RP. E.g., No. 153b (Frankfurter Schachzeitung, 1886), White: K at QB6, B at KKt1, P at QR3; Black: K at QR3, P's at QR2, QR5, QKt4, K4, KKt5, KKt7. White wins. 1 B—B2! (not 1 B—K3, P—Kt6; 2 B—Kt1, P—Kt5!; 3 P×P, P—R6; 4 B—K3, P—Kt8=Q and Black wins), P—Kt6; 2 B—K3, P—Kt5 (or 2 .... K—R4; 3 B×P, P—Kt5; 4 B—Kt6ch and mates in two); 3 P×P, P—Kt8=Q (or 3 .... P—R6; 4 B—Q2 and mate next); 4 P—Kt5ch, K—R4; 5 B—Q2 mate. Or No. 153c (Walker, 1841), White: K at QKt1, B at KKt6, P at KR5; Black: K at K4, P's at QB4, QB6, KKt2, KR3, to which the solution is 1 K—B2, K—Q5; 2 B—Q3, P—B5 (or 2 .... K—K4; 3 K×P, P—Kt4; 4 P×P e.p., K—B3; 5 K—Q2; P—B5; 6 B—B2! and White wins the RP and then queens—he always has an unlimited number of tempo moves with his Bishop); 3 B—Kt6, K—K4; 4 K×P, K—Q4; 5 B—B7ch, K—B4; 6 B×P, K—Q3; 7 K—Q4, K—K2; 8 K—K5, K—B1; 9 K—B5 and we have No. 153.

As we have seen, Black loses when he has KtP+RP only when the RP is ahead of the KtP, so that he cannot offer to exchange without transforming the White RP. Similarly, Black cannot lose with a Pawn on some other file in conjunction with a KtP, provided as usual that his King can reach the corner. Thus in No. 153d (Kling and Horwitz, 1851), White: K at QKt4, B at QB5, P at QR2; Black: K at QKt2, P's at QB3, QKt4 the extra BP makes no difference whatsoever, for if the White Bishop moves it can be sacrificed at once, while if the

White Bishop does not move we have in effect the ending of K+B+ RP vs. K+KtP. E.g., 1 K—R5, P—Kt5; 2 K—R4, K—R3; 3 B— K3, P—B4; or 1 P—R3, K—R3; 2 K—B3, K—R4; 3 K—Q4, K—R3; 4 K—K5, K—Kt2; 5 K—Q6, K—B1; 6 B—Kt6, P—B4; 7 K—B6, P—B5; 8 B—K3, P—B6, etc.

Where there is no RP Black can only draw under certain special circumstances. In the general case, No. 154, where White already has a passed Pawn, the extra tempo which the Bishop provides makes all the difference. As the reader will recall, the White Pawn here can be forced to the seventh, but if there is nothing else on the board White must move his King, and stalemate his opponent. Thus all that

No. 154   No. 155

White wins.   White wins.

is needed is one tempo so that the win here is *1 B—Kt5* (but not 1 K— B6??, P—Kt6!; 2 K—Kt5, P—R6 and Black wins), *P—R6; 2 B—B4, K—Q2; 3 K—B5, K—Q1; 4 K—B6, K—B1; 5 P—Q7ch, K—Q1; 6 B—Kt3, K—K2; 7 K—B7.*

A passed Pawn should either be supported by the Bishop at a distance, so that that piece retains enough mobility, or—and prefer- ably—by the King. In No. 154a (Troitzky, 1895) we have an ex- ception which proves the rule. White: K at Q5, P at KKt7, B at KR6; Black: K at KB2, P's at KR2, K2. White can only win by 1 P—Kt8= Qch!, K×Q; 2 K—K6, K—R1; 3 K—B7, P any; 4 B—Kt7 mate. Black to move could draw by 1 .... P—K4!; 2 K×P (2 P—Kt8= Qch, K×Q; 3 K—K6, P—K5 likewise leads to nothing), K—Kt1 and White can only gnash his teeth because his Bishop is tied down. On the other hand, if the White King were at KR6, the B at K5, the win is elementary. On 1 .... K—Kt1 the Bishop plays back and forth until the Black King is again forced to move.

Where the White Pawn is not passed, the winning method consists of first blockading the Black Pawns (so that no Pawn exchange is feasible) and then capturing them with the King. No. 155 is typical. *1 B—B4, P—Q4* (1 .... K—B2; 2 P—B5); *2 P—B5, K—R3; 3 K—Q4, K—Kt2* (or 3 .... K—Kt4; 4 B—K3, K—Kt5; 5 K—K5, K—B5; 6 K—Q6, K—Kt4; 7 B—B2); *4 K—K5, K—B2; 5 K—K6 dis ch, K—B1; 6 B—K5, K—Kt2; 7 K—Q6.*

Exceptions to the rule that B+P wins against 2 P's (in addition to the case where the P is a RP and the B of the wrong color) may be grouped under three headings:

1. The Pawns are so far advanced that they can be used to divert the Bishop or King and enable the King to capture White's Pawns.

No. 156   No. 157

White to play draws.   Whoever moves wins.

2. The Pawns are so far advanced that they queen. Here Black wins.
3. The White King cannot approach without allowing an exchange of Pawns.

1. ADVANCED PAWNS DRAW

No. 156 (Reti, 1928) is a beautiful illustration of this theme. *1 K—B6!!* (1 P—R7?, K—Kt2; 2 K—K6, K×P loses), *B—R4* (if 1 .... K—Kt3; 2 K—Q7, B—R4; 3 K—K6, B—B6; 4 P—Q7, B—R4; 5 P—R7!); *2 K—Q5, B—B6; 3 P—R7, P—B4* (3 .... K—Kt2; 4 K—K6!, K×P; 5 P—Q7); *4 P—Q7, K—K2; 5 P—Q8= Qch, K×Q; 6 K—K6!!!, P—B5; 7 K—Q5, P—B6; 8 K—B4!, B—R1; 9 K—Q3* and the Pawn cannot be saved.

A somewhat analogous case where one passed Pawn suffices to draw is seen in No. 156a (Alapin-N.N., 1907), White: K at KB2, P's at QR5, KR2; Black: K at KB3, B at KR6, P at KR2. 1 P—R6, B—B1; 2 P—R7, B—Kt2; 3 K—Kt3; K—Kt4; 4 K—R3, K—B5 (4 .... K—R4; 5 K—Kt3. If Black does not venture out with his King White will simply stick to his two squares Kt3 and R3); 5 K— R4, K—B6; 6 K—R5, K—Kt7; 7 K—R6, B—K5; 8 P—R8=Q.

2. ADVANCED PAWNS WIN

We have already seen that Pawns which are two, four or more files apart are most dangerous against a Bishop. This is again the case in No. 157 (Handbuch, 1st Edition). Black wins by *1 .... P—B5; 2 B—Q4* (2 K any, P—B6; 3 K any, P—B7), *P—KB6; 3 K—B6, P—B6; 4 K—K5, P—B7; 5 B—K3, P—B7* and one Pawn must promote. White to play can win both Pawns by *1 K—B6, P—B5; 2 K— B5, P—KB6; 3 K—B4, P—B6; 4 K×P, P—B7; 5 B—K3.*

3. PAWN EXCHANGE UNAVOIDABLE

In No. 157a (Walker, 1841), White: K at QB3, B at K3, P at QB4; Black: K at QKt2, P's at QKt3, QB3, White's only winning chance is 1 K—Q4, when 1 .... K—R3!; 2 K—K5, P—B4; 3 K—Q5, P—Kt4 is sufficient. Black must not play .... P—B4 too soon here: E.g., 1 K—Q4, P—B4ch??; 2 K—Q5, K—R3; 3 K—B6, K—R4; 4 B×P! etc. Compare No. 155.

B+P vs. 3P is still theoretically favorable for the Bishop but because of the reduced material the Pawns offer excellent drawing and at times even winning chances, so that the result depends largely on the relative position of the Kings and Pawns.

Where White has a passed Pawn, if Black has three connected passed Pawns on the fourth rank or beyond he can draw, while if they are on the third or second they lose. No. 158 is another one of those positions where the outcome is determined by whose move it is. After *1 .... P—B5* the Pawns cannot be stopped, e.g., *2 B—Kt6, P—R5; 3 B—R5, P—R6; 4 B—B3, P— R7; 5 K—Kt5, P—Kt5; 6 B—R1, P—B6.* On the other hand *1 B×P, P—Kt5; 2 B—Q6, P—Kt6; 3 B—R3, P—R5; 4* B—Kt2 does blockade the Pawns and force a

No. 158

Whoever moves wins.

quick conclusion. With the Pawns on the third rank, No. 158a (Pawns at QR3, QKt3, QB3, other pieces as in No. 158) they can be stopped after 1 .... P—B4 (or 1 .... P—Kt4; 2 B—B5!!, P—R4; 3 B—Kt6!, P—R5; 4 B—B5); 2 B—B4, P—B5; 3 B—B7, P—Kt4 (or 3 .... P—B6; 4 B×P, P—B7; 5 B—K3, P—R4; 6 B—B1); 4 B—R5.

Of course if the White King in No. 158 had been anywhere near the Black Pawns, a draw would have been certain.

If Black has three disconnected passed Pawns, they can again in general be stopped only if they are not beyond the fourth rank. E.g., No. 158b, Black's Pawns at QR4, QKt4, Q4, White's Bishop at K3. 1 B—Kt6, P—R5; 2 B—B5. But again if the Black Pawns are far apart even on the fourth rank the Bishop cannot hold them. No. 158c, Black's Pawns at QR4, QKt4, KB4; White's Bishop at K3. 1 B—Q2, P—R5!; 2 B—B1, P—Kt5 etc. Or 1 B—Kt6, P—R5; 2 B—B5, P—B5.

In rare cases White can allow his opponent to queen in order to set up a mating position. Thus in No. 158d (Salkind, 1916), White: K at QKt5, B at KR7, P at KR6; Black: K at QKt7, P's at QR6, QKt5, KB2, the dramatic finish is 1 B—B2!!, P—R7; 2 P—R7, P—R8=Q; 3 P—R8=Qch, K—R7; 4 B—Kt3ch!!, K—Kt8; 5 Q—R7ch, K—Kt7; 6 Q—B2ch, K—R6; 7 B—Q5!, Q—B1ch; 8 K—R5 and mates soon.

It is in general easier to win if the White Pawn is not passed, for a Bishop can easily blockade two Pawns. The winning process is then exactly the same as in B+P vs. 2 P's—blockade the enemy Pawns, then either capture all of them or capture the most important and queen one's own Pawn. White's task is thus much easier if Black has already blockaded his Pawns or is obliging enough to do so. In No. 159 (Walker, 1841) the problem is relatively difficult (Walker gives it

as a draw). *1 K—K2, K—R6; 2 B—Kt5, K—Kt6; 3 K—K3, K—Kt7; 4 B—R4!, K—R6; 5 B—K1, P—Kt6* (or 5 .... K—R7; 6 K—B4, K—R6; 7 B—Kt3, P—B4; 8 P×P e.p., P—K4ch; 9 K×P); *6 K—B4!, P—Kt7; 7 B—B2* followed by K—Kt5—B6.

No. 159

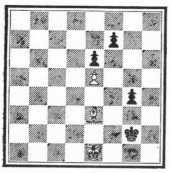

White to play wins.

The classification of the defender's drawing and winning chances given above (p. 126) is also valid here. The only difference is that the extra material increases the number of exceptions to the dictum that White wins. The case of B+RP vs. 3 or more P's, B of the wrong color, differs in no essential respect from that of B+RP vs. 2 P's, so that it need not be considered here.

1. ADVANCED PAWNS DRAW

In No. 160 Black is threatening .... P—R8=Qch, so that White must begin with *1 B—B6*. Then 1 .... K—Kt5?; 2 P—Kt5!, K—B5; 3 K—R3 would lose. But there is an ingenious resource in *1 .... P— Kt4!!; 2 B×P, K—Q5; 3 B—B6ch, K—K5; 4 P—Kt5, K—B4; 5 K×P, P—R8= Q.* No. 160a (Reti, 1929) has a different drawing idea: blocking the Bishop. White: K at QR8, P's at QB7, Q5, KKt4; Black: K at KB3, B at QR3, P at KR3. 1 P—Q6! (not 1 K—R7, B—B1; 2 K— Kt8, B×P), K—K3; 2 P—Q7!!!, K×P; 3 K—R7, B—K7; 4 K—Kt8, B—R3; 5 K—R7, B—B1; 6 K—Kt8 and Black cannot gain the needed tempo.

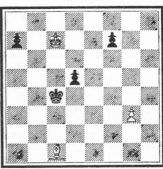

No. 160   No. 161

Draw.   Black to play wins.

2. ADVANCED PAWNS WIN

Unless the Pawns are on the sixth or seventh ranks they need the support of the King to be able to advance against a Bishop. This allows the opponent's King to capture a Black Pawn or to come back in time to stop the passed Pawns. All this goes to show that such endings cannot be solved by applying a priori rules, but always require exact calculation.

E.g., in No. 161 (Flohr-Thomas, Hastings, 1935–'36) Flohr has sacrificed a piece to get this position and in point of fact wins by only one tempo. The conclusion of the game was *1 .... P—Q5; 2 K—Q6, P—R4; 3 P—Kt4, P—R5; 4 P—Kt5, P—Q6; 5 K—K7, P—R6!; 6*

B×P, P—Q7; 7 K×P, P—Q8= Q; 8 B—K7, K—Q4; 9 P—Kt6, Q—
B6ch; 10 B—B6, Q—B4!; 11 P—Kt7, Q—K3ch and Black resigned.
If, however, it had been White's turn to play in the diagrammed posi-
tion he could have saved himself by 1 K—Q6, P—Q5; 2 K—K7, P—
R4; 3 K×P, P—R5; 4 P—Kt4, P—Q6; 5 P—Kt5, P—R6; 6 P—Kt6,
P—R7; 7 B—Kt2, P—Q7; 8 P—Kt7, P—Q8= Q; 9 P—Kt8=Q.

A win for White is out of the question here, e.g., 1 K—Q6, P—Q5;
2 K—K5?, K—B6!; 3 K—K4?, P—R4; 4 B—B4?, P—Q6!; 5 K—K3,
K—B7 and again the Pawns are victorious.

When the King is far away, two disconnected passed Pawns are often
a greater advantage than connected ones. This is clear from the above

No. 162   No. 163

White to play wins.   White wins.

example, where if the Black Pawn were at QB4 instead of QR2, after
1 .... P—Q5; 2 K—Q6 would draw without any trouble. No. 161a
also illustrates this point. White: K at QR8, P at KR5, B at KKt6;
Black: K at K2, P's at KR3, KKt2, K5. After 1 .... P—K6; 2 B—
Q3, P—Kt4!; 3 P×P e.p., P—R4 one Pawn must queen. If the Black
Pawn had been at KB3 originally the outcome would have been a
draw.

No. 162 (Reti, 1922) is another beautiful example of the play of dis-
connected Pawns against a Bishop. *1 K—Q4!!!, K—B7; 2 P—R4,
K—Kt6; 3 K—K3!!, B—Kt5!; 4 P—Kt5!, K×P; 5 P—Kt6!!* (threat-
ening 6 P—R6), *B—B1; 6 K—B4, K—R4; 7 K—K5, K—Kt4; 8 K—
Q6, K—B3; 9 K—B7, B any; 10 P—R6* and queens in two moves.
Another such delectable morsel by Reti (1922) is No. 162a, White: K
at K5, P's at QR4, QKt5; KR4; Black: K at KB7, B at KB6, P at
QR2. The winning idea is similar. 1 K—B5!!! (1 K—B4, B—K7!!=),

B—K7 (or A); 2 K—B4!! and now Black is in zugzwang! If 2 ....
B—Q6; 3 P—KR5, B—K7; 4 P—R6, B—Q6; 5 P—R5, while if 2 ....
B—B6; 3 P—QR5 or 2 .... K—Kt7; 3 K—Kt5.

A. 1 .... K—K6; 2 P—QR5, K—Q5; 3 P—Kt6, P×P; 4 P×P,
K—B4; 5 K—B4!!! (the key move), B—Q4 (or 5 .... B—B3; 6 P—
R5, K×P; 7 P—R6) 6 K—K5, B—B6; 7 P—R5! and again both
Pawns cannot be stopped.

Connected passed Pawns must be supported by the King, for they
can easily be blockaded by a Bishop. With the King, however, they
are quite powerful and always win unless the opposing King can approach too quickly. In No. 163 (Charousek-Caro, Berlin, 1897) Black
loses because he cannot approach the dangerous BP which cramps his
Bishop's mobility with his King, but White must be careful not to allow a blockade of his Pawns. *1 K—B6!, K—K2; 2 P—Kt5, K—K3* (or
2 .... K—K1; 3 P—R4, K—K2; 4 P—R5, K—K1; 6 P—R6, K—K2;
7 P—Kt6); *3 P—R4, K—K4; 4 P—R5, K—Q5; 5 P—Kt6* and queens
in a few moves. The freedom of the Pawns is all-important here. Thus
1 P—Kt5, B—Kt2; 2 P—R4? (2 P—R3! still wins) would only draw
after 2 .... P—R3!; 3 P—Kt6 (or 3 P×P, B×P; 4 P—R5, B—B1;
5 K—B6, K—K2; 6 K—Kt6, K—Q3); P—R4; 4 K—B5, K—Q2;
5 K—Kt5, K—Q3; 6 K×P, K—B4.

Where there is a choice as to whether one should set up connected or
disconnected passed Pawns, the proximity of the King and the rank
the Pawns are on always decide. In No. 163a (from Horwitz, 1884),
White: K at QKt7, B at QB2, P at QR3; Black: K at KKt2, P's at
QR4, QKt4, QB5 the Black King is so far away that connected Pawns
will be useless. Consequently only disconnectedones come into con-
sideration and they do in fact win. 1 .... P—R5!; 2 K—Kt6, P—
Kt5!; 3 P×P, P—R6; 4 B—Kt1,
P—B6 etc. White to play could
have won by forcing connected
Pawns: 1 K—Kt6, P—Kt5; 2 P—
R4!, P—Kt6; 3 B—Q1!, P—Kt7; 4
B—B2 and the Bishop is of the
right color.

3. PAWN EXCHANGE UNAVOIDABLE

This case is of frequent occur-
rence when the side with the Bishop
only has one Pawn which is not
passed. In No. 164 the KP is first
blockaded, then exchanged. *1 ....
P—K3; 2 K—Q4, P—B3.* White

No. 164

Draw.

could win this position only if Black's Pawns were played to KKt3 and K3, for the exchange by .... P—B3 would then be out of the question and the White King could enter via KKt5 and KB6, as in No. 159.

Four Pawns are somewhat superior to B+P. With all the P's on one side we get to B vs. 3 P's after one P is exchanged, which is a draw in most positions (See No. 142), but with four connected passed Pawns if the Black King can succeed in blocking the White passed Pawn he should win. E.g., No. 164a, White: K at QKt1, B at KB5, P at KKt4; Black: K at KKt4, P's at QR4, QKt4, QB4, Q4. Black wins. 1 B—K6, P—Q5; 2 B—Q7, P—Kt5; 3 B—Kt5 (if 3 K—B2, P—B5; 4 B—K6, P—B6; 5 B—Kt3, K×P; 6 K—Q3, K—B6; 7 K×P, K—K7), K×P; 4 K—B2, K—B6; 5 K—Q3, K—B7; 6 K—Q2, P—Kt6!; 7 B—B4, P—R5; 8 B—K6, K—B6; 9 B—B7, K—K5; 10 B—B4, P—Q6; 11 K—B3, P—Q7; 12 B—K2, K—K6; 13 B—Q1, P—B5; 14 B—R5, P—R6 and wins.

With the Pawns doubled or blockaded the side with the Bishop should at least draw. But again advanced Pawns form an exception. In No. 165 (Reti, 1929) White can win by *1 K—Q3!!, K—Kt6; 2 K—K3, K—R5; 3 K—Q4, K—Kt5* (or A); *4 K—K4, B—Q1; 5 K—K5, P—Kt3; 6 P—Q6, B—R4; 7 P—B5, K×P; 8 P—B6!!, B—B6ch* (or B); *9 K—Q5!!!, B×P; 10 K—K6, B—Q1; 11 K—B7, K—B4; 12 K—K8, B—R4; 13 P—Q8= Q* and the second Pawn queens ahead of Black's.

A. 3 .... B—Q1; 4 P—Kt6!, K—R4; 5 P—B5, B—B3ch; 6 K—B5, K—Kt4; 7 K—Q6, B—Q1; 8 K—K6.

B. 8 .... K—R3; 9 K—K6, B—Q1; 10 K—B7, P—Kt4; 11 K—K8, B×P; 12 P—Q8=Q, B×Q; 13 K×B, P—Kt5; 14 K—K7, P—Kt6; 15 P—Q7, P—Kt7; 16 P—Q8=Q, P—Kt8=Q; 17 Q—R8ch and captures the Black Queen.

Again we occasionally see unusual stalemate combinations here.

No. 165

White plays and wins.

No. 165a (Berger), White: K at QB3, B at QR6, P at QKt2; Black: K at KKt1, P's at QR4, QKt6, Q4, KR6. Draw. If 1 .... P—R7; 2 B—Kt7!!, P—R8=Q; 3 B×Pch!!!, Q×B stalemate. If 1 .... P—R5!; 2 B—Kt7, P—Q5ch; 3 K—Kt4!, P—Q6 (or 3 .... P—R6; 4 K×RP followed by K×KtP, while on other moves the capture of both Pawns is likewise an adequate defense); 4 K—B3!, P—R6; 5 P×P and White will win.

With two Pawns and the Bishop, Black must usually have the full equivalent of the Bishop (three Pawns) to be able to draw, otherwise the extra Pawn makes a Pawn exchange much less meaningful, since White can still retain enough material to win. The method when Black has less than five Pawns, is to either win several Pawns or to force a passed Pawn which cannot be stopped. Just how this is done in any particular case cannot be described by any general rule, but the outlines of the procedure are always quite clear. Here we shall confine our attention to some more difficult cases.

No. 166

Draw.

The problem of blockading the opponent's Pawn comes up when one's King is stalemated by the opponent's King, which can only be forced to move when all Pawn moves are exhausted. Such is the case in No. 166 (Horwitz, 1880). We have already seen (No. 158) that a Bishop can blockade three Pawns on the second or third ranks, but here the blockade cannot be brought about in as straightforward a manner as usual because Black's QRP is at R3, that is, not subject to attack. If, e.g., *1 B—Kt3, P—B4; 2 B—B7, P—B5; 3 B—R5, K—B1; 4 B—B3, K—B2!* and White can only draw since 5 B—Kt4??, P—Kt3!; 6 B—Q2, P—R4!!; 7 B—B3, P—R5; 8 B—Kt4, P—Kt4 wins for Black. (But if the Black Pawn had been at QR2 originally, the Pawns could have been stopped by 1 B—Kt3, P—B4; 2 B—B2!, P—Kt3; 3 B—Kt3, P—R3—3 .... P—Kt4; 4 B—B2—; 4 B—B7, P—Kt4; 5 B—Q6, P—B5; 6 B—Kt4.)

There apparently is a win with *1 B—B2!!* (to prevent the immediate advance of the BP), *P—R4* (or 1 .... P—Kt3; 2 B—Kt3, P—B3; 3 B—B7, P—Kt4; 4 B—Q6!, P—R4; 5 B—B7, P—R5; 6 B—Q6; or 1 .... K—B1; 2 B—K3, K—B2; 3 B—B5, P—Kt3; 4 B—K7 etc.); *2 B—B5!* the point: White had to occupy this critical diagonal at the earliest possible moment—now only Pawn moves are possible. If now 2 .... P—R5 (if 2 .... P—Kt3; 3 B—K7 wins a Pawn, while if 2 .... P—B3; 3 B—K7, P—R5; 4 B—B5, as in the main variation); 3 B—K7 (White must not allow a Pawn to stay on Black for more than one move. 3 B—Kt4??, P—Kt3; 4 B—K7, P—B4!; 5 B×P! only draws), P—B3 (3 .... P—Kt3; 4 B—Q8, P—Kt4; 5 B—K7); 4 B—B5, P—Kt3 (other attempts are equally useless); 5 B×P, P—R6; 6 B—Q4, P—R7; 7 B—R1, P—B4; 8 B—Kt2, P—B5; 8 B—B3, K—B1; 9 P—B7!, K×P; 10 B—Kt7 and after he has given up all his Pawns Black will still have to release the White King. But Black can draw by *2 .... P—Kt4!!!*, for if *3 B—K7, P—Kt5!; 4 B×P* etc.

To win enemy Pawns once they are blockaded is normally fairly simple, since King and Bishop are in effect battling against a King. Where there is danger, however, of losing one's own Pawns complications arise. Thus in No. 166a (problem by A. Havasi), White: K at QB4, B at QB1, P's at KKt2, KKt3; Black: K at KB4, P's at QB3, QB4, Q3, KKt4 White's first thought must be to defend his own Pawns. He wins by 1 B—K3, K—Kt5; 2 B—B2, K—B4; 3 B—Kt1!, K—Kt5 (if 3 .... K—K5; 4 P—Kt4); 4 B—R2, K—B4; 5 P—Kt4ch, K—K3; 6 B—Kt3, K—K2; 7 B—K1, K—K3; 8 B—Q2, K—B3; 9 P—Kt3! (the winning tempo), K—Kt3; 10 B—R5, K—B3; 11 B—Q8ch, K—Kt3; 12 B—K7 and now Black's Pawns go the way of all wood.

Occasionally certain unusual drawing possibilities come up which can be overcome with careful play. In No. 167 the solution is at once clear if one bears in mind that with the Black KKt and KB P's off the board the game would be a draw. Consequently, 1 B×P? would be a mistake because of 1 .... P—Kt6; 2 B—K4, P—Kt7! Instead a win can be achieved by *1 K—Q7, P—Kt6* (or 1 .... P—B5; 2 B×P, P—B6; 3 B—R3!, P—B7; 4 B—B1); *2 B—Q5, P—B5; 3 B—B3, P—Kt7* {if 3 .... K—R1; 4 K—B7 and mates); *4 B×P, P—B6; 5 B—B1, P—B7; 6 K—Q8, K—R1; 7 B×P!!, K—Kt1* (7 .... P×B; 8 K—B7 and mate in two); *8 B—B1, K—R1; 9 B—Kt2, K—Kt1; 10 K—Q7, K—R1; 11 K—B7, P—B8 = Q; 12 B×P* mate. For the position without Black's King's side Pawns see No. 168.

The same problem—that of avoiding a theoretical draw—is seen in No. 167a (Herbstmann, 1928), White: K at K2, B at KB8, P's at QR5, QKt5; Black: K at QB4, P's at QR2, Q3. 1 P—Kt6!, P×P; 2 P—R6, K—B3; 3 B—K7! (3 B×P?, P—Kt4; 4 B—B5, P—Kt5; 5 K—Q3, P—Kt6; 6 K—B3, K—B2!; 7 B—R7, K—B3! and draws because White has no time for 8 K—B4), K—B2; 4 B×Pch!! (4 B—Q8ch?, K—Kt1!), K—B3; 5 K—Q3, P—Kt4; 6 B—B5, K—B2; 7 B—R7, K—B3; 8 K—B3, P—Kt5ch; 9 K×P and wins. Or a common case with RP's: No. 167b (from Alekhine-Tylor, Nottingham, 1936), White: K at QKt1, B at QR4, P's at KKt4, KR4; Black: K at Q4, P's at KKt3, KR2. White to play must merely avoid the ending with B+RP, i.e., he must exchange his RP. This can be done by 1 B—K8!!, K—K4; 2 P—R5, K—B3 (or 2 .... P×P; 3 B×P!. On 2 .... P—Kt4; 3 B—Q7 holds everything until the King gets there); 3 P×P, P×P; 4 B—Q7, etc.

Finally we must again note those cases where one cannot prevent the opponent from queening, but can set up a mating position with Queens on the board. No. 167c (Dr. Lewitt, 1917), White: K at Q3,

P's at KKt5, KR6, B at QKt5; Black: K at QKt6, P's at QR5, QKt5, KKt3, KR2. White can only score by the pretty manoeuvre 1 B—K8, P—R6; 2 B×P, K—Kt7 (if 2 .... P×B; 3 P—R7, P—R7; 4 P—R8 = B!!, but not 4 P—R8 = Q?, P—R8 = Q; 5 Q×Q stalemate. Or 2 .... P—R7; 3 B—B7ch, K—Kt7; 4 B×P, K×B; 5 P—Kt6, and if 5 .... P—Kt6; 6 P—Kt7, queening with check); 3 B—B7, P—Kt6; 4 P—Kt6, P×P; 5 P—R7, P—R7; 6 P—R8 = Qch, K—Kt8; 7 B×P(Kt3), P—R8 = Q; 8 B—B2ch, K—R7; 9 Q—Kt8ch, K—Kt7; 10 Q—Kt7ch, K—R7; 11 Q—B7ch, K—Kt7; 12 Q—B6ch and mates by checking successively at B6—K6, K5, Q5, Q4, B4, B3, Kt3.

The cases in which Black can draw when he has less than three Pawns for the Bishop are again the same as those given above (p. 126)

No. 167

White wins.

No. 168

Draw.

—special positions with the RP, advanced Pawns, Pawn exchange forced. As is to be expected, these stratagems are much less effective when White has two Pawns. Thus the exchange of one Pawn still has not solved Black's drawing problem, while against advanced Pawns White can often sacrifice the Bishop and emerge with a won Pawn ending.

No. 168 (Kling and Horwitz, 1851) is a special position with the essential characteristic of RP+B of the wrong color—the King cannot approach without stalemating. And in addition any such attempts as *1 B×P, K×B,* or *1 B—K2, K—R1; 2 B×P, P×B!* lead to a drawn Pawn ending (No. 30). There remains only the idea which worked in the similar Kt ending (No. 120): *1 B—Kt2, K—R1; 2 B—B6* but Black dispels all illusions by coolly replying *2 .... K—Kt1!*

An analogous case where 2 P's draw against B+2P's is No. 168a, White: K at K2, P's at QKt3, QB2; Black: K at K5, B at KB5, P's at QKt5, QB6. This is in effect the same as No. 150 with B+P vs. P—the King cannot be driven out of the corner. E.g., 1 K—Q1, K—K6; 2 K—K1, K—B6; 3 K—Q1, K—B7 stalemate. The only difference here is that a Bishop on White squares would do the trick for Black, and this was not so in the other example.

Advanced Pawns draw more rarely against a Bishop when there are a larger number of Pawns on the board and when they do, the play is generally more involved. Some of the added difficulties are seen in No. 168b (Reti, 1928), White: K at KKt7, P's at Q4, KB4, KKt5; Black: K at Q2, B at QR4, P's at QB3, K3. White draws. If the White QP and Black QBP were missing, 1 K—B7, B—B6; 2 P—Kt6 would draw at once. But now the draw must be brought about by 1 K—B7, B—B6; 2 P—Q5!!! (2 P—Kt6?, B×P and it is all over), BP×P (if 2 .... KP×P; 3 P—Kt6, P—B4; 3 P—B5 and White wins); 3 P—Kt6, K—Q3; 4 K—B8!, B—Kt7; 5 K—B7, B—R1; 6 K—Kt8, B—B3; 7 K—B7 and Black can make no headway because he cannot advance his passed Pawn without blocking the diagonal of his Bishop. In No. 168c we have another stalemate theme (H. Lommer, 1933), White: K at K4, P's at QKt5, Q5, K6, KR4; Black: K at KR4, B at KB3, P's at QB2, K2. The solution is 1 P—Q6!, BP×P (if 1 .... KP×P; 2 K—Q5, K×P; 3 K—B6, B—Q1; 4 K—Q7 and wins); 2 P—Kt6, P—Q4ch; 3 K—B5!! (3 K×P, B×P; 4 P—Kt7, B—Kt6 would lose —Black still has a Pawn), B—Q5; 4 P—Kt7, B—R2; 5 P—Kt8=Q!, B×Q stalemate.

An exchange of Pawns is a saving manoeuvre (when there are less than three P's for the Bishop) only when the superior side has a doubled Pawn. We see this in No. 168d (Burn-Marco, Vienna, 1898), White: K at KKt3, P's at QR2, QB3, KKt2, KR3; Black: K at Q4, B at KB4, P's at KR3, KR4. Draw. After 1 K—R4, B—Kt3; 2 P—R4, K—B5; 3 P—Kt4, P×P; 4 P×P, B—K1; 5 K—Kt3, B×P; 6 P—Kt5, P×P; 7 K—Kt4 a draw was agreed to. Had Black here tried 5 .... K—B4 (instead of 5 .... B×P) the answer would have been 6 K—R4, K—Kt3; 7 P—B4!, B—B2; 8 K—Kt3, B×P; 9 P—Kt5, P—R4; 10 P—Kt6! and the Black RP cannot be held.

No. 169 (Fine-Kevitz, New York, 1936) is what may be called a normal position in this type of ending—the three Pawns draw against the Bishop. The continuation was *1 K—B6, K—K5; 2 K×P, B×P; 3 P—R4, K—Q4; 4 P—R5, K—K3* (4 .... K—B4; 5 K—Q7, K—Kt4?; 6 P—B5, K×P; 7 P—B6, K—Kt5; 8 K—K7, loses for Black); *5 K—Kt7, B—Q4ch; 6 K—B7!* (6 K—Kt6, K—Q3; 7 P—R6, B×P; 8 P—R7, B—B6; 9 K—R5, K—B2 is inferior), *B—B5* and the game was called a draw. That every Pawn played its part here, even the despised doubled Pawn, is shown by the fact that if we remove the White Pawn at KKt2 in the diagram, White will lose. For after 1 K—

B6, B×P; 2 K×P, K—K5; 3 P
—R4, K—B6!; 4 P—B5, K×P; 5
P—B6, K—B5; 6 P—R5, K—K4;
7 P—R6, K×P; 8 P—R7, B—Q4
the Pawn is stopped and Black will
soon queen.

Clearly the result of such endings
depends on the relative positions
of the Pawns, Kings and Bishop.
In practice, it is "normally" a draw
even though the side with the Bishop
does not win as often as the side
with the Pawns.

No. 169

White to play draws.

No. 169a (Cochrane-Staunton,
London, 1842) has some instructive
errors in the handling of both Bishop and Pawns. White: K at QR6,
P's at QR4, QKt6, QB6, KKt2, KR3; Black: K at QB1, B at Q7, P's
at QR4, KR5. White to play could have forced a speedy conclusion
by 1 P—Kt7ch, K—Kt1; 2 P—B7ch, K×P; 3 K—R7 and the Pawn
queens. Instead he tried 1 K—Kt5, B—K8; 2 K—B4 (2 K—R6 still
wins), B—B7; 3 P—Kt7ch??? (3 K—Kt5 was still good enough), K—
B2; 4 K—Kt5, B—R2; 5 K—R6, B—Kt1; 6 K—Kt5, K—Q3; 7 K×P,
K×P; 8 K—Kt4, K×P; 9 K—B4, K—Kt3; 10 K—Q3 and here Black
could have won with 10 .... B—Kt6, transposing into No. 153.

A more exact and pretty illustration of how advanced passed Pawns
win against a Bishop is No. 169b (Troitsky, 1928), White: K at Q6, P's
at QKt2, QKt3, QB2, KR2, KR5; Black: K at KR5, B at QR2, P's at
QKt5, KB3. The solution is 1 P—R6, B—Q5; 2 K—Q5!!, B×P; 3
P—B4!!!, P×P e.p. (if 3 .... P—B4; 4 P—B5, P—B5; 5 K—K4, K—
Kt5; 6 P—B6 and queens with check); 4 P—R7, P—B7; 5 P—R8=
Qch, K—Kt4; 6 Q—Kt7ch, K—B5; 7 Q—Kt3ch, K—B4; 7 Q—Q3ch.

With a large number of Pawns on the board (Bishop plus three or
more) the Bishop almost always wins. There are only two possible
saving chances for Black: advanced passed Pawns, or a complete
blockade. Of these only the first occurs with any degree of frequency
in actual play and here the side with the Bishop is often hard put to
it to hold the game.

It frequently happens that when there is the full equivalent of 3 P's
for the B with a weak Pawn position the Bishop is unable to stem the
tide. E.g., No. 169c (Capablanca-Lasker, New York, 1924) White:
K at KB5, P's at QR3, QKt2, Q4, K3, KB4, KKt5; Black: K at KKt2,
B at KKt1, P's at QR2, QB3, K5. Capablanca won as follows: 1 ....
B—Q4; 2 P—Kt4, P—R3; 3 K—Kt4! (first the Pawns must get to the
fifth. 3 K—K5, K—Kt3 is inferior), B—B5; 4 P—B5, B—Kt6; 5 K—

B4, B—B7; 6 K—K5, K—B2; 7 P—R4, K—Kt2 (7 .... B×P; 8 K×P also leaves Black helpless); 8 P—Q5, B×P (or 8 .... P×P; 9 K×P, B×P; 10 K×P and the three connected passed Pawns cannot be held); 9 P—Q6, P—B4; 10 P×P, B—B3; 11 K—K6, P—R4; 12 P—B6ch, resigns.

Unless these passed Pawns are already in existence such a defense is rarely feasible, for even if the King gets to the enemy Pawns they can usually be defended by the Bishop at a distance (this in contrast to the similar case with the Knight). Pawns are weakest in block positions where they are on the same color as the Bishop. E.g., No. 169d, White: K at K5, P's at QR5, QKt4, QB5, KR4; Black: K at KR2, P's at QR3, QKt4, QB3, B at KR4. White to play wins: 1 K—Q6, K—Kt2; 2 K—B7! (the simplest: it is better to have the Bishop cut off from the Pawns than to be deceived by a mess of wood), K—B2; 3 K—Kt6, K—K2; 4 K×P, K—Q1; 5 K—Kt7, B—Kt5; 6 P—R6, B—B1ch; 7 K—Kt6 and wins. Or here 1 K—Q6, B—Kt5; 2 K—B7, K—Kt3; 3 K—Kt7, K—R4; 4 K×RP, B—B1ch; 5 K—Kt6, K×P; 6 P—R6 etc.

Where Pawns can no longer be stopped a stalemate defense is the only chance. Thus in No. 169e (Duras, 1901), White: K at KKt1, B at K2, P's at QKt6, QB2, Q4, K3, KB4, KKt2, KR3; Black: K at KR5, P's at QR5, QKt2, QB6, Q4, K5, KB4, KKt5, KR4 White just manages to draw by 1 K—B2, P—R6 (not 1 .... P×P??; 2 P—Kt3 mate); 2 B—B1!, P—Kt6ch; 3 K—K1!!, P—R7; 4 K—K2, P—R8=Q (B or Kt draws) stalemate. Another such device is seen in No. 169f (Campbell), White: K at QKt5, B at KKt5, P's at QR4, QKt2, QKt6, Q4; Black: K at KB8, P's at QKt2, Q3, Q4, KKt6, KR6. 1 B—Q2, any; 2 B—R5, any; 3 P—Kt4, any, stalemate! (This is certainly snubbing your opponent with a vengeance.)

III. BISHOP AND PAWNS VS. BISHOP OF THE SAME COLOR WITH AND WITHOUT PAWNS

A. POSITIONS WITH MATERIAL ADVANTAGE

Here we have the same situation noted in Knight endings: one Pawn ahead in general is sufficient but the fewer Pawns there are the harder it is to win. We shall again consider the various possible endings systematically.

1. BISHOP AND PAWN VS. BISHOP

A great deal of work has been done with this finale, notably by L. Centurini towards the end of the last century, and the results are practically exhaustive of all the possibilities. Centurini summed up his investigations in the two following principles:

(1) The game is drawn when the Black King either is on or can occupy any square in front of the Pawn from which it cannot be driven away by the Bishop.

(2) If the Black King is behind the Pawn and the White King near the Pawn, then Black can draw if and only if his King is attacking the Pawn and has the opposition and if and only if his Bishop can manoeuvre on two diagonals on each of which it can occupy at least two squares.

These principles will become clearer from the analysis which follows.

The first case is elementary. With his King in front of the Pawn (No. 170) Black moves his Bishop ad infinitum and draws by exhaustion. *1 K—Q5, B—Q1; 2 K—Q6, B—R5; 3 K—Q5, B—Kt6; etc.* The proviso that the King cannot be driven off the file by the Bishop is important. E.g., No. 170a, White: K at QB6, B at QB5, P at QKt6; Black: K at QKt1, B at Q1. White to play wins with 1 B—Q6ch, K—R1; 2 P—Kt7ch. If the Pawn is farther back when the King leaves the file we get into some other case.

If the Black King is on a rank ahead of the Pawn but not directly in front of it the outcome depends on whether he can reach a crucial square to transpose into No. 170 or not. If not, he must either transpose into some case to be considered later or allow White to promote. E.g., No. 170b (Regence, 1856) White: K at QB6, B at KR2, P at K6; Black: K at QB1, B at QR4. Black to move draws at once by 1 .... K—Q1 and 2 .... K—K1. White to move seems to win with 1 P—K7, but Black has the ingenious rejoinder 1 .... B—Q1!!! and if 2 P—K8=Q or R stalemate, while 2 P—K8=Kt or B both lead to nothing. And if here 1 B—B7!, B—Kt5!; 2 B—Kt6, B—K2!; 3 B—R5, B—R6; 4 K—Q5, K—Kt2; 5 K—K5, B—K2; 6 K—B5, K—B3; 7 K—Kt6, K—Q4; 8 K—B7, B—B4; 9 B—Q8, K—K5; 10 B—K7, B—B7; 11 B—Kt4, B—R5; 12 B—B3, K—B4 and we have reached the drawn position No. 159c.

No. 170c (Berger) is an example of a position where the White Pawn queens by force. White: K at QB6, B at QB5, P at QR6; Black: K at QB1, B at QKt1. 1 B—Q4 and Black must either release the P by a B move, or allow 2 K—Kt7 after 1 .... K—Q1, when he again must allow the Pawn to queen.

If the Black King is not in front of the Pawn and is not near it at all,

No. 170

Draw.

the win is again fairly simple. Thus in No. 171 (Centurini), where Black's King is only two squares away, *1 B—B6* soon decides: *1 ....
B—K7; 2 B—Q5, B—Kt4; 3 B—K6, K—K6; 4 B—Q7, B—B8* (or 4
.... B—R3; 5 P—B6, K—Q5; 6 P—B7, K—B5; 7 B—R3, K—Kt5;
8 K—B6, K—R4; 9 B—Kt4, K—Kt5; 10 K—Kt6); *5 P—B6, K—Q5;
6 P—B7, B—R3; 7 K—B6, K—B6; 8 K—Kt6* and the Pawn promotes.

Even if the White Pawn is still on its original square a win is possible. No. 171a (Grigorieff, 1931), White: K at QB3, B at QB6, P at QKt2; Black: K at KR5, B at KR4. White to play wins. 1 P—Kt4, B—K7 (or 1 .... K—Kt4; 2 P—Kt5, B—K7; 3 P—Kt6, B—R3; 4 K—Kt4, K—B3; 5 K—R5, B—B1; 6 B—Kt5, B—Kt2; 7 B—R6, B—Kt7; 8 B—B8!, K—K2; 9 K—R6, K—Q1; 10 B—Kt7, B—R6;

No. 171

White wins.

No. 172

Draw.

11 K—R7, B—Kt5; 12 B—Kt2, B—B1; 13 B—R3); 2 B—Q5, K—Kt4; 3 B—B4, B—Kt5!; 4 P—Kt5, K—B3; 5 P—Kt6!, B—B1; 6 K—Q4, K—K2; 7 K—B5, K—Q2; 8 B—Kt5ch, K—Q1; 9 K—Q6; B—Kt2; 10 B—Q7, B—Kt7; 11 B—K6!, B—Kt2; 12 K—B5, B—R3; 13 K—B6, B—B1!; 14 B—B4!, B—R6; 15 K—Kt7!, B—Kt7ch; 16 K—R7, K—Q2; 17 B—R6, K—Q3; 18 B—Kt7, B—R6; 19 B—B3, B—B1; 20 B—Kt4 and the Bishop must finally quit the diagonal and allow the Pawn to queen.

When the Black King is near the Pawn, but behind it, we get a more elaborate series of possibilities. First of all, in accordance with our principle, we consider those positions where Black's Bishop has two long diagonals. This is the case when White has either a Bishop Pawn (with the Bishop not of the same color as the queening square) or a center Pawn. In No. 172 (Centurini) the only attempt White can make is *1 B—B7, B—K7; 2 B—Kt6, B—B5,* but *3 B—R7, B—Kt6;*

4 B—Kt8, B✕B! destroys White's illusions. On other moves, such as
1 B—K6 Black can always reply 1 .... B—K1; or 1 B—Kt5, B—Kt3.

From this example we can also see why diagonal opposition is not
enough for Black to draw. The Black Bishop must have at least two
squares available from which he can be driven away only when the
opposing Bishop blocks his Pawn. E.g., in No. 172a, Black K at K4,
other pieces as in No. 172, 1 B—Q3, K—B5; 2 B—Kt6 is conclusive.
Another case where a bad King position, though near the Pawn, is
ruinous is No. 172b (Horwitz, 1880), White: K at KKt5, B at Q5,
P at KB6; Black: K at KR2, B at KKt3. White wins by 1 B—Kt8ch!,
K—R1! (1 .... K✕B; 2 K✕B, White has the opposition); 2 B—K6,
B—K1 (if 2 .... K—R2; 3 B—B5 and again White has the opposition,
while if 2 .... B—Q6; 3 K—B4, B—Kt4; 4 K—K5, B—K1; 5 K—Q6,
K—R2; 6 K—K7; K—Kt3; 7 B—Q7, B—B2; 8 B—B5ch); 3 K—B5,
K—R2; 4 B—Q5, B—R4 (or 4 .... B—Q2ch; 5 K—K5, K—Kt3;
6 P—B7, K—Kt2; 7 K—Q6, B—B4; 8 K—K7); 5 K—K6, K—Kt3;
6 K—K7, K—B4 (6 .... K—Kt4 loses—diagonal opposition!);
7 B—B7, B—Q8; 8 B—K6ch and 9 P—B7.

With a center Pawn we get a position such as No. 172c (Centurini),
White: K at KB7, B at Q8, P at K6; Black: K at KB4, B at QB4.
Draw. 1 B—K7, B—B7; 2 B—Kt4, B—R5; or 1 B—B6, B—Kt5;
2 B—Kt7, B—B4; 3 B—B8, B✕B. Here too the diagonal opposition
would lose, e.g., No. 172d, Black K at Q4, other pieces as in No. 172d.
1 B—K7, B—B7; 2 B—Kt4, B—R5; 3 B—B3, K—Q3; 4 B—B6 and
the Pawn cannot be stopped.

When the Black Bishop has only one long diagonal a KtP always
wins but BP and RP win or draw depending on the King positions.

In No. 173 (Centurini) we have the typical win with a RP. *1 B—*
Kt7, B—Q7; 2 B—R6, B—Kt5
(2 .... B✕B; 3 K✕B, K—B4;
4 K—Kt7); *3 B—K3, B—B1* (or
3 .... B—B6; 4 P—R6, B—R8;
5 P—R7, B—Kt7; 6 B—R6, Kt7);
4 B—Q4, K—R5; 5 B—K5!,
K—Kt5; 6 B—B6, K—B5; 7 B—
Kt7, B—R6; 8 P—R6 and queens in
two moves. It is essential here
to have the square in front of the
Pawn available for the Bishop. For
this reason if we move everything
up two ranks, No. 173a, White: K at
KKt8, B at K7, P at KR7; Black:
K at KKt3, B at K4 the result is
a draw, since White cannot get to

No. 173

White wins.

KR8 with his Bishop. Here again diagonal opposition as in No. 173b. White: K at KKt8, B at KB8, P at KR7; Black: K at K3, B at K4, loses, for 1 B—Kt7 decides at once. Or Black to play, 1 .... B—R1; 2 B—Kt7! (just to be fancy. 2 K×B is of course good enough: 2 .... K—B2; 3 B any), B×B; 3 K×B and queens.

On the other hand, horizontal instead of vertical opposition draws for Black because he could then exchange Bishops and get back to KB2 with his King. E.g., No. 173c, Black K at K3, other pieces as in No. 173, nothing can be done, for if 1 B—Kt7, B—Q7; 2 B—R6, B×B; 3 K×B, K—B2 =.

The KtP, as has been mentioned, always wins, although in No. 174 (Centurini) considerable finesse is required. *1 B—R4, K—Kt3* (if 1 .... B—B5; 2 B—B2, B—R7; 3 B—R7, B—B5; 4 B—Kt8, B—K6; 5 B—Kt3, B—R2; 6 B—B2—this is the variation White is trying to force); *2 B—B2ch, K—R3!; 3 B—B5!!* (to get the Black Bishop out of his corner—the point will soon be apparent), *B—Kt6* (or any other square); *4 B—K7, K—Kt3; 5 B—Q8ch, K—B3; 6 B—R4!* (gaining the decisive tempo. With the B at R7 this was impossible), *B—Q3, 7 B—B2, B--R7; 8 B—R7, B—Q3; 9 B—Kt8, B—B4; 10 B—R2, B—R2; 11 B—Kt1* and wins.

With the Pawn on the sixth the winning idea is exactly the same but easier to execute. No. 174a (Centurini), White: K at KB5, B at K7, P at KKt6; Black: K at KR4, B at KKt2. White to play concludes with 1 B—Kt5, B—B1; 2 K—B6!, K—Kt5 (or 2 .... B—K2ch; 3 K—B7!!, B—B1; 4 B—Q2 and Black cannot maintain his grip on the Pawn with both B and K); 3 B—Q2, B—R6; 4 B—B3, B—B1; 5 K—B7, B—R3 (5 .... K—R4; 6 B—Q2); 6 B—Q2. Or Black to play, 1 .... K—R3 (if 1 .... B—R3; 2 K—B6, B—Kt4ch; 3 K—B7, B—R3; 4 B—B5, K any; 5 B—K3); 2 B—B6, B—B1; 3 B—Q4,

No. 174

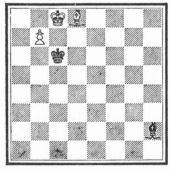

White wins.

B—K2 (or 3 .... B—Kt2; 4 B—K3ch, K—R4; 5 B—Kt5, B—B1; 6 K—B6 as in the variation where White begins); 4 P—Kt7, K—R2; 5 K—K6, and 6 K—B7. (Note that in the analogous position with a center Pawn Black draws by maintaining vertical or horizontal opposition, but not diagonal.)

With a suitable King position, the KtP can even win when it is on the fifth with two squares covered by the opponent's Bishop still to be crossed. Thus in No. 175 (Berger, 1920), after *1 P—Kt4* (Black to

play of course draws by 1 .... K—Kt6), *B—K3* (1 .... B—B2;
2 P—Kt5); *2 P—Kt5, B—B4; 3 B—Kt6, B—K3; 4 B—B2, B—B2;
5 B—Q1, K—B4; 6 B—R5, B—Kt6; 7 P—Kt6, K—B3; 8 P—Kt7,
B—Kt1* (else 9 K—R7); *9 B—Kt6, K—K2* (if 9 .... B—Kt6; 10 K—
R7, B—B5; 11 B—B2, K—Kt4; 12 K—R8, K—R3; 13 B—R7, B—
R7; 14 B—Kt8, B—Kt8; 15 B—Kt3, B—R2; 16 B—B2); *10 B—B2,
K—B3; 11 B—Q3, K—K2; 12 K—Kt6, K—K1; 13 K—B6, K—Q2;
14 B—Kt6, K—Q3; 15 B—B7, B—R2; 16 K—Kt5, K—K2; 17 K—R6*
and wins. The win here is again due to that old rascal, the diagonal
opposition. For in No. 175a, Black K at KR5, other pieces as in No.
175, on 1 P—Kt4, B—B2 draws at once. But even 1 P—Kt4, B—
Kt6; 2 P—Kt5, B—B7 draws, for after 3 B—Kt6, B—R5; 4 B—Q3,

No. 175

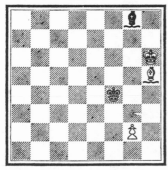

No. 176

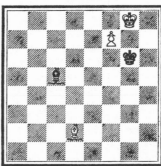

White to play wins.   White wins.

B—K1; 5 B—K2, B—B2; White does not have 6 B—R5 at his
disposal. With a BP the win is conditional upon whether the White
King is on the suitable square or not, although the position of the
Black King this time makes little or no difference.

In No. 176 (Centurini) White always wins because his King covers
the square KKt7. *1 B—B3, B—R6; 2 B—Kt7, B—Kt5; 3 B—B8,
B—Q7; 4 B—R3, B—R3; 5 B—B1, B—Kt2; 6 B—Q2, K—B6;
7 B—B3ch.* But, No. 176a, with the White K at K8, other pieces as
in No. 176, nothing can be done because the Black Bishop has two
long diagonals to manoeuvre on. Thus: 1 B—R5, K—B3; 2 B—Q8ch,
K—K3; 3 B—Kt5, B—Kt5; 4 B—R6, B—B4; 5 B—B8, B—K6;
6 B—Kt4, B—R3; 7 B—Q2, B—Kt2; 8 B—K3, K—Q3, etc.

Applications of this fact are seen in the following two illustrations.
No. 176b (Rabinovitch), White: K at Q6, B at K4, P at QB7; Black:
K at QKt3, B at QB1. Draw. 1 B—B6, B—R3; 2 B—Q7, B—Kt2;

3 B—R3, B—R3; 4 K—Q7, K—B4!; 5 K—Q8, K—Q3 and we are back to No. 176a. With the King positions reversed White of course wins—we get to No. 176. No. 176c (J. Crum, 1921), White: K at KB3, B at KR5, P at QB5. Black: K at Q7, B at KB8. White wins. 1 P—B6, K—B6; 2 P—B7, B—R3; 3 K—K3!, K—Kt5; 4 B—K2, and now:

- a) 4 .... B—B1; 5 K—Q4, B—Kt2; 6 B—B1, B—B1; 7 K—Q5, B—Kt2ch; 8 K—Q6, K—R4; 9 K—B5! (else 9 .... K—Kt3 transposes into No. 176b), B—B1; 10 K—B6, B—Kt5; 11 K—Kt7, B—B4; 12 K—Kt8, and we have No. 176.
- b) 4 .... B—Kt2; 5 K—Q4, B—B1; 6 K—Q5, B—Kt2ch; 7 K—Q6, K—R4; 8 K—B5, B—B1; 9 K—B6, B—R6; 10 K—Kt7, B—B4; 11 K—Kt8 and again wins as in No. 176.

If the White Pawn is still on the sixth, and the seventh rank is covered by the Bishop, the game is a draw (No. 172).

Where the Pawn is only on the fourth or fifth rank and the Black King is near it the result is always a draw except for the RP and some special positions (See No. 175). This will require no elaborate demonstration if we merely recall that with the Pawn on the sixth or seventh the win always (except for a RP) involves a Bishop sacrifice to divert the rival from the queening square. Even when the Pawn can be forced to the sixth or seventh the resulting position is so disadvantageous that a win is out of the question. E.g., No. 176d (Berger, 1920) White: K at QB4, B at K7, P at QKt5; Black: K at QR5, B at QR2. Draw. 1 B—B5, B—Kt1; 2 P—Kt6, K—R4; 3 K—Q5, K—Kt4; 4 P—Kt7, B—B2! but not 4 .... K—R3; 5 K—B6, B—R7; 6 B—K7, B—Kt6; 7 B—Q8, B—Kt1; 8 B—Kt6!, B—B5; 9 B—B7.

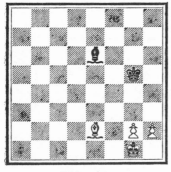

No. 177

White wins.

We can sum up all the above results in the general conclusion that when the Black King is behind the Pawn, RP and BP win on occasion, KtP always, center Pawns never.

2. BISHOP AND TWO PAWNS VS. BISHOP

B+2P win as a rule against B without any trouble. Where the two Pawns are connected, No. 177, White must simply take care to keep the Pawns together. Here an added precaution is necessary: to prevent the sacrifice of Black's Bishop for the White KtP, since the White Bishop is of the wrong color. Nevertheless, there is no special difficulty in the winning process.

1 .... B—R6; 2 P—Kt3, K—R3; 3 B—B1, B—Kt5; 4 P—R4, B—B4; 5 K—B2, B—Kt5; 6 K—K3, B—K3; 7 K—B4, B—Q2; 8 B—Q3, B—R6; 9 B—B5, B—B8; 10 P—Kt4, B—K7; 11 P—Kt5ch, K—R4 (or 11 .... K—Kt2; 12 B—Kt4 and 13 P—R5); *12 K—Kt3* (not 12 P—Kt6?, K—R3; 13 K—K5, B—R4=), *B—Q8; 13 B—K4, B—Kt6; 14 B—B3ch, K—Kt3; 15 K—B4, B—B2; 16 P—R5ch, K—Kt2; 17 K—K5, B—Kt6; 18 B—K4, B—B2; 19 P—R6ch, K—R1; 20 K—B6, B—R4; 21 B—Q5, K—R2; 22 B—B7.*

Black can draw against B+2 connected passed Pawns only if he can effectively blockade the Pawns with his King or force an ending with nothing but RP's and B of the wrong color. The latter case may be seen in a simple transformation in No. 177a, White King at KB1, other pieces as in No. 177. Black to play draws by 1 .... B—R6, since 2 P—Kt3 is impossible.

An example of the former is No. 177b, White: K at QB2, B at K1, P's at QKt4, QB3; Black: K at QB5, B at KKt4. Draw. The attempt 1 K—Kt2, B—B5; 2 K—R3, B—B2; 3 K—R4 is met by 3 .... B—Q1; 4 B—B2, K×P; 5 K—Kt5, K—Kt6; 6 B—B5, K—B6; 7 K—B6, K—B5; 8 P—Kt5, B—R4; 9 B—Kt6, B—K8 and White can do nothing (Compare No. 175a). This type of blockade is by no means always unbeatable, however, since White has the threats of both Bishop and Pawn sacrifices available. E g., No. 177c, White: K at KB3, B at QB1, P's at KB4, KKt5; Black: K at KB4, B at KB1. White wins by 1 K—Kt3, B—Kt2; 2 K—R4, B—B1; 3 K—R5, B—Kt2; 4 P—Kt6, B—B1; 5 B—R3, B—Kt2; 6 B—Q6, K—K3; 7 B—K5, B—B1; 8 P—Kt7.

Two disconnected passed Pawns likewise are enough to win. In No. 178 the decision is brought about by *1 P—B4ch, K—Q3; 2 P—B5, K—K4; 3 P—Q4ch, K—B3; 4 K—B4, B—Kt6; 5 B—B6, B-B7; 6 B—Q7, B—Kt6; 7 K—K4, B—B5* (or 7 .... B—B7ch; 8 K—Q5); *8 P—Q5, B—Kt6; 9 B—K6, B—B5; 10 K—Q4, B—K7: 11 P—Q6, B—Kt4; 12 P—Q7!, K—K2; 13 P—B6ch, K—Q1; 14 P—B7, K—K2; 15 P—B8= Qch, K×Q; 16 P—Q8= Qch.*

If the Pawns are farther apart the win is even simpler: White advances both Pawns as far as possible, brings his King to the support of the Pawn not blockaded by Black's King, meanwhile defending the other Pawn with his Bishop. Black will then have to give up his Bishop for the distant passed Pawn, when White is left with B+P against the lone King. Or he can give up one Pawn to divert the White King and then queen the other Pawn as in one of the variations Nos. 171-176. This latter stratagem was used in No. 178a (Kashdan-Fine, New York, 1936), White: K at KKt2, B at Q2; Black: K at

QKt4, B at QR4, P's at QR3, KR5. The continuation was 1 B—Kt5, B—Kt3; 2 B×P, P—R4; 3 K—B3, P—R5; 4 K—K2, P—R6; 5 B—B6 (if 5 K—Q3; B—Q5!!); K—B5; 6 K—Q2; K—Kt6; 7 K—B1, P—R7 and White resigned, since there is no defense to B—B4— R6ch—Kt7.

Again Black draws only if he can blockade or if he has a favorable position against RP+B of the wrong color. Such a defense against RP+B can usually be set up if White's other Pawn is on the KB or K files (or correspondingly on the Q-side). For to win White will surely have to give up his RP to divert the King, but both B+KP vs. B and B+BP vs. B are almost always drawn (No. 172 and No. 172a).

No. 179 (Goglidze-Kasparyan, Tiflis, 1929) illustrates this point.

No. 178   No. 179

White wins.   Black to play draws.

1 .... B—Kt5ch; 2 K—K7, B—K7; 3 B—Kt6 (if 3 P—K6, B—Kt5 or B—B5 followed by B×P), *B—Kt5; 4 K—Q8, K—R3; 5 B—K8, K—Kt2* (for 5 .... B—K3 see A); *6 K—K7, B—Q8; 7 B—B7, B—K7; 8 P—R6ch, K×P; 9 K—B6, B—Kt5; 10 B—Kt6, B—K7; 11 P—K6, B—B5; 12 P—K7, B—Kt4; 13 K—B7, K—Kt4.* Draw. No. 172c.

A. 5 .... B—K3; 6 K—K7, B—Kt5!; 7 K—B6! (or 7 K—Q6, K—Kt4; 8 B—Q7, B×P etc.), B—R6; 8 B—B7! (if 8 B—Kt6, B—Kt5!; 9 B—B5, B×P; 10 P—K6, B—K1; 11 P—K7, B—Kt4; 12 B—R3, B—R5; 13 K—B7, K—Kt4!=), B—Kt5 (or 8 .... B—Q2; 9 B—K6, B—Kt4; 10 B—Kt4, B—B5); 9 B—Kt6, B—Q2; 10 B—B5, B—Kt4; 11 B—Kt4 (again if 11 P—K6, K×P; 12 P—K7, B—B3; 13 B—K6, B—Kt4; 14 K—B7, K—Kt4—No. 172c), B—B5; 12 B— B3, B—Kt6; 13 K—K7, K—Kt4; 14 K—Q6, B—B5; 15 B—Q5, B—K7; 16 B—B7, B—Kt5 etc.=.

B+3 or more Pawns vs. B is, of course, an elementary win.

3. BISHOP AND TWO PAWNS VS. BISHOP AND PAWN

With all the Pawns on one side this is a draw, as is the similar Knight ending if the Black King is anywhere in front of the Pawns. The best White can do is to exchange one Pawn, when we get to B+P vs. B, No. 170. If, however, the Black King is not near his Pawn and the White King is, then the win is quite simple: White captures the Pawn and remains with B+2P vs. B.

Thus if, as normally happens, the Black King is near the Pawns, White has winning chances only if he has an outside passed Pawn. Whether such a Pawn wins or not depends on the distance from the other Pawn. If it is far away (e.g., both on Kt files) then the Bishop must be sacrificed to stop it, so that White wins; but when it is near (e.g., K and KKt files) then the Black King can blockade the Pawns. Where one of White's Pawns is a RP and the B of the wrong color no general rule is applicable; the position must be judged on its merits.

In No. 180 we have the general win with the outside passed Pawn. After *1 .... B—B5* (or 1 .... P—R4; 2 P—Kt5, P—R5; 3 P×P, B—Q4; 4 P—Kt6, K—Kt3; 5 K—Q4, etc.—Compare No. 178a); *2 B—Kt4, K—K2* (on 2 .... K—B3; 3 B—K2, B—Q4; 4 K—B4, K—Kt3; 5 P—Kt5, B—Kt2; 6 B—B3, B—B1; 7 P—Kt6, P—R4; 8 P—Kt7, B×P; 9 B×B, P—R5; 10 P—Kt4! is decisive); *3 B—K2, B—B2; 4 P—Kt5, K—Q3; 5 K—B4, K—B4; 6 K—B5, P—R4* (sooner or later forced); *7 K—Kt5, B—K1; 8 K—R6, K—Kt3; 9 B×P, B×P; 10 P—Kt4* and wins as in No. 175.

Another such case, this time where the Pawns are closer to one another and where White has a BP, is No. 180a (Santasiere-Kashdan, Boston, 1938), White: K at Q6, P's at QKt6, KB4, B at Q5; Black: K at QKt1, B at KKt5, P at KB3.

White wins. 1 K—K7, P—B4; 2 K—B6, B—R6!; 3 K—K5!! (excellent. If instead 3 K—Kt5, K—B1; 4 B—K6ch, K—Kt2; 5 B×P, B—Kt7; 6 B—Q3, B—R6; 7 B—K2, K×P; 8 B—Kt4, B—B8; 9 P—B5, K—B4; 10 P—B6, B—B5; 11 K—Kt6, K—Q3; 12 K—Kt7, K—K4; 13 B—R5, K—B5; 14 B—B7, B—K7; 15 B—Kt3, B—R4; 16 B—B2, K—Kt4 and Black has just managed to reach No. 172), K—B1; 4 B—K6ch, K—Kt2; 5 B×P, B—B8; 6 B—K6, K×P (Black ᴑlayed 6 .... B—Q6 and resigned

White wins.

after 7 K—Q4); 7 P—B5, B—Q6 (or 7 .... K—B2; 8 P—B6, K—Q1;
9 B—B7, B—Q6; 10 K—B4, K—Q2; 11 K—Kt5, K—Q3; 12 K—R6,
K—K4; 13 K—Kt7, B—Kt4; 14 B—Kt3 and Black loses because he
has only diagonal opposition); 8 P—B6, B—Kt3; 9 K—Q6, B—R4·
10 K—K7, K—B4; 11 B—B7 and again Black loses because he
cannot get the vertical opposition with his King at K4.

Where the Pawns are close together a draw may be expected. In
No. 181 (Euwe-Alekhine, third match game, 1937) the continuation
was *1 K—R5, K—Kt2; 2 P—K4, B—Q6; 3 P—K5, B—Kt3ch;
4 K—Kt4, K—B2; 5 B—Q5ch, K—K2; 6 K—B4, B—R2; 7 P—Kt3,
K—B1* (7 .... K—Q2 is also good enough, e.g., 8 B—K4, B—Kt1;
9 B—B5ch, K—K2; 10 B—B8, B—R2, etc.); *8 B—K4, B—Kt1;*

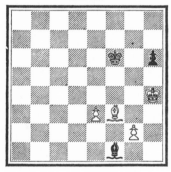

No. 181

Draw.

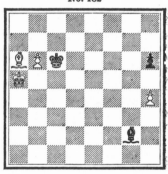

No. 182

White wins.

*9 B—B3, K—K2; 10 K—Kt4, K—K3; 11 K—B4, K—K2; 12 B—Kt4,
B—Kt6; 13 B—B8, K—B2* and a draw was agreed to.

With a RP+B of the wrong color we naturally expect an exception
to the general rules, and we shall not be disappointed. Everything
depends upon where the Kings are. Thus No. 182 (Eliskases-Capablanca, Semering-Baden, 1937) is a win because Black's King cannot
manage to blockade the Pawn and maintain control of the long
diagonal. Eliskases concluded the game as follows: *1 B—B8, B—B8;
2 B—Kt4, B—Q6* (for 2 .... K—Kt2 see No. 182b): *3 B—B3ch,
K—Q3; 4 B—Kt7, B—K7; 5 B—R6, B—B6; 6 B—B1* (threatening
K—R6), *B—Kt2; 7 B—R3!, K—K2; 8 K—Kt5, K—Q3; 9 B—Kt4*
(now Black is in zugzwang), *K—K2; 10 K—B5, B—Kt7; 11 B—B8,
K—Q1* (or 11 .... B—B6; 12 B—R6, B—Kt7; 13 B—Kt5, B—Kt2;
14 B—B6, B—R3; 15 B—B3, K—Q2; 16 B—Kt4ch, K—Q1; 17 K—
B6, etc., as in the game); *12 B—R6* (12 B—K6 was also good enough),

B—B6; 13 K—Q6, B—Kt7; 14 B—B4, K—B1; 15 B—Q5, B—B8
(on 15 .... B×B; 16 K×B, K—Kt2; 17 K—K6 Black gets back
one move too late); *16 K—K6, B—K7; 17 K—B6, K—Q2; 18 K—Kt6,
P—R4; 19 K—Kt5, K—Q3; 20 B—B7, K—B3; 21 B×P* and Capablanca resigned—White wins as in No. 173.

Two further points are noteworthy here. With the Black King at
QKt1, White draws if his King is at QR5, but wins with his King at
QB5. The difference is that in No. 181a, BK at QKt1, other pieces
as in No. 181, on 1 K—Kt5, B—B8ch; 2 K—R5, B—Kt7 is the
rejoinder; if 1 K—Kt4, B—Kt2!!; 2 B—B4, B—Kt7; 3 K—B5,
K—Kt2 and White can make no progress, while finally 1 K—Kt4,
B—Kt2; 2 K—Kt5! is met by 2 .... P—R4!! when, as the reader will
recall, 3 B×B, K×B only draws.

On the other hand, in No. 182b, White: K at QB5, B at QR6, P's at
QKt6, KR4; Black: K at QKt1, B at KKt7, P at KR3, White can win
because 1 .... B—Kt2 can be answered by 2 B×B!, K×B; 3 P—
R5!!, K—B1; 4 K—Q6, K—Kt2; 5 K—K6, and the White King
reaches KKt7 after capturing the Black RP.

Where Black's Pawn is also passed, the win is not difficult, since
White can block the Pawn either with his Bishop or his King and
proceed to exploit his own Pawns. A pretty illustration of a win in an
unusually difficult position is No. 182c (Reti, 1925), White: K at KB1,
B—Q8, P's at QR4, KKt6; Black: K at QB5, B at KKt2, P at QB4.
White wins by 1 B—R5!, K—Kt6 (if 1 .... K—Q4; 2 K—K2,
K—B3; 3 K—Q3, K—Kt2; 4 B—B3, B—R3; 5 K—B4, K—Kt3;
6 K—Q5, B—B1; 7 B—K1, B—Kt2; 8 B—Q2, B—B1; 9 B—K3,
K—R4; 10 B×P, B —Kt2; 11 B—Q4, B—R3; 12 K—K6, and the
Bishop must soon abandon the diagonal KB1—KR3); 2 B—B3!!,
K×B; 3 P—R5, K—Kt7; 4 P—R6, P—B5; 5 P—R7, P—B6;
6 P—R8=Q, P—B7; 7 Q—Kt7ch, K—R7; 8 Q—B7ch, K—R6;
9 Q—B7, K—Kt6; 10 K—K2, B—B6; 11 P—Kt7!, B×P; 12 K—
Q3.

Two connected passed Pawns likewise win against one passed
Pawn without any trouble. If necessary, White can even sacrifice his
Bishop for the Black Pawn and queen his own advanced Pawns. E.g.,
No. 182d (Santasiere-Fine, New York, 1938), White: K at QB6,
B at QB5, P's at QR4, QKt3; Black: K at K3, B at K8, P at KR2.
White wins. After 1 .... P—R4; 2 P—Kt4, P—R5; 3 P—Kt5,
B—Kt6; 4 B—Kt1, P—R6; 5 P—R5, K—B4 (or 5 .... P—R7;
6 B×P, B×B; 7 P—R6, B—Kt8; 8 P—Kt6); 6 P—Kt6, K—K5;
7 P—R6, K—B6; 8 P—R7, K—Kt7; 8 B—B5! (8 P—R8=Q, K×B
gives Black drawing chances, but should also be good enough),
P—R7; 9 P—R8=Q, P—R8=Q; 10 K—Q7 dis ch, K—R7; 11
Q×Qch, K×Q; 12 B—Q6, and Black resigned.

4. POSITIONS WITH TWO OR MORE PAWNS ON EACH SIDE

Unless all the Pawns are on one side, a Pawn ahead normally wins. The winning method, which is essentially the same as that for P and Kt endings, should conform to the following pattern:

1. White first gets his King and Bishop to the best possible squares (centralization).
2. He then sets up a passed Pawn and advances it as far as he can.
3. If this passed Pawn is blockaded by the Black Bishop, an exchange of Bishops is offered. This will either win the Bishop or force a Queen.
4. If the passed Pawn is blockaded by the Black King, the White King goes to the other side, (if necessary sacrificing the passed Pawn), where a decisive superiority in material is established (two Pawns or one passed Pawn which costs Black his Bishop).

We may take No. 183 as a typical position. The win would then proceed in the following way: *1 .... P—Kt3* (1 .... P—B3 is no better; it weakens Black's White squares and makes King entry easier); *2 K—B1, K—B1; 3 K—K2, K—K2; 4 K—Q3, K—Q3; 5 K—B4* (first phase concluded), *K—B3; 6 P—QKt4, B—Kt3; 7 P—B3, B—B2; 8 P—QR4, B—Kt3; 9 B—Q4, B—B2; 10 P—Kt5ch, P×Pch; 11 P×Pch, K—Kt2* (or 11 .... K—Q2; 12 P—Kt6, B—Kt6; 13 K—Q5, B—B5; 14 P—Kt7, B—Kt1; 15 B—K5—this is an example of 3); *12 K—Q5, B—Kt1* (12 .... B—B5; 13 B—K5, B—K6; 13 K—Q6); *13 P—Kt6, B—R7; 14 B—K5, B—Kt8; 15 K—Q6* (fourth phase), *K×P; 16 K—K7, K—B4; 17 K×P, K—Q4; 18 B—Kt7, P—R4; 19 K×P*, and White will come out three Pawns ahead. Or, if he wishes, he can advance his BP until the Black Bishop must be sacrificed for it.

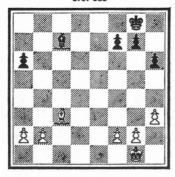

No. 183

White wins.

A similar example, taken from actual play, is No. 183a (Weiss-Blackburne, New York, 1889), White: K at K1, B at Q2. P's at QR2, Q3, KB2, KKt2; Black: K at KKt1, B at QKt7, P's at QR2, QKt2, K2, KB2, KKt3. Blackburne conducted the ending impeccably: 1 B—K3, P—QR3; 2 K —Q2, K—B1; 3 K—B2, B—K4; 4 K—Kt3, K—K1; 5 K—B4, K —Q2; 6 K—B5, B—B2; 7 P—B3, P—K3; 8 P—R4, P—Kt3ch; 9 K —B4, K—B3; 10 B—B2, P—B3;

11 B—K3, B—Q3; 12 B—Q4, P—K4; 13 B—K3, P—QKt4ch; 14 P×P, P×Pch; 15 K—Kt3, K—Q4 (first and second phases concluded); 16 B—B2, P—B4; 17 K—B3, P—Kt4; 18 P—Kt4 (or 18 B—K3, B—K2!; 19 K—Kt3, P—Kt5!), P×P; 19 P×P, B—B4; 20 B—K1, P—K5!; 21 P×Pch, K×P; 22 B—Q2, B—K6; 23 B—K1, K—B6; 24 K—Kt4, K×P; 25 K×P, K—B6; 26 K—B4, P—Kt5; 27 K—Q3, B—B7; 28 B—R5, P—Kt6; 29 B—B7, P—Kt7; 30 B—R2, B—Kt3; 31 K—Q2, K—Kt5 and White resigned.

An illustration where there is already a passed Pawn on the board is No. 183b (Fine-Kashdan, New York, 1938), White: K at KKt1, B at K4, P's at QR3, QB5, K5, KKt3, KR2; Black: K at K2, B at Q2, P's at QR3, K3, KKt2, KR2. The conclusion was 1 .... P—R3; 2 K—B2, K—Q1; 3 K—K3, K—B2; 4 K—Q4 (the first and second steps are now completed), P—QR4; 5 B—Q3, B—K1; 6 B—B4, B—Q2; 7 B—Kt3, B—B1; 8 B—R4, B—Kt2; 9 K—B4, B—R3ch; 10 B—Kt5, B—Kt2; 11 K—Kt3, resigns, for he must now lose a second Pawn.

Very often one or more of these steps may be omitted. E.g., when one already has an outside passed Pawn and one's King is centrally placed, then only one of the last two phases will be required. Again, if one is more than one Pawn ahead, the simple advance of passed Pawns will usually force a Bishop exchange at the expense of a Pawn, when the Pawn ending is routine.

The object of forcing a passed Pawn is to divert the enemy King or Bishop from the scene of action where they are most needed. Where the King is already diverted, of course this step is superfluous. E.g., in No. 183c (Mieses-Schiffers, Breslau, 1889), White: K at KR4, B at QKt7, P's at QR3, KKt4, KR3; Black: K at KB3, B at QKt6, P's at QR5, KB2, KKt3, KR3 all that Black has to do is to go to the Queen's side and capture the Pawn there. The Bishop can defend the KBP from a distance and this in turn defends the KKtP, so that White can do nothing in the absence of Black's King. Thus a simple win is possible by 1 .... K—K4; 2 P—Kt5, P—R4 (Pawn exchanges should be avoided wherever possible. If e.g., 2 .... P×Pch; 3 K×P, K—Q5?; 4 K—B6, K—B6; 5 B—B6, K—Kt7; 6 B×P!, B×B; 7 K×P, B—B7; 8 P—QR4, draws); 3 K—Kt3, K—Q5; 4 K—B4, K—B6; 5 K—K5, K—Kt7; 6 K—B6, K×P; 7 B—B6, K—Kt7 (or 7 .... K—Kt5); 8 B×P, B×B; 9 K×P, B—B7 and Black will come back with his King and capture both White Pawns.

The more Pawns there are the easier the win—the pickings are juicier after the Black King has been driven off. But even with three Pawns against two the win is not difficult. E.g., No. 183d (Kashdan-Fine, New York, 1936), White: K at KB3, B at QR5, P's at QR4, KR3; Black: K at KB4, B at K2, P's at QR3, KB2, KKt4. Black won by 1 .... K—K3; 2 K—Kt4, P—B4ch; 3 K—B3, K—Q4; 4 B—B7, K—B4; 5 B—R5, K—B5; 6 B—B7, K—Kt5; 7 P—R5, K—B4; 8 B—Kt6ch, K—B3; 9 B—K3, B—Q1; 10 B—Q2, K—Kt4; 11 K—B2, P—B5; 12 B—B3, K—B5 (not 12 .... B×P; 13 B—B6); 13 B—Q2, B—K2 (threat 14 .... B—Kt5. If 14 B—B1, K—Kt5; 15 B—Q2ch, K—Kt6); 14 P—R4, P×P; 15 B×P, B—Q1; 16 B—Q2, K—Kt4; 17 K—Kt2, B×P and we have No. 178a.

The most common difficulty encountered in these endings is the blockade. The Pawns are in such an unfortunate position that no passed Pawn can be forced, and the King can always be prevented from piercing the enemy defense. This obstacle may often be overcome by a sacrifice at the proper moment. No. 184 (Lasker-Bogatyrtschuk, Moscow, 1935) is a case in point. The only way White can force a passed Pawn is by exchanging his KP for the Black QP. Lasker consequently played 1 P—K4?, but after 1 .... P—Q5!!; 2 B—B4, B—Kt2; 3 K—Kt5, B—B1; 4 K—B4, K—Q2; 5 K—B3, B—Kt2; 6 K—K2, B—B1; 7 K—Q3, B—Kt2; 8 K×P, B—B1; 9 K—K3; B—Kt2 a draw was agreed to because the blockade can only be broken by an inadequate Bishop sacrifice. 10 K—B4, B—B1; 11 K—Kt5, K—K2; 12 K—Kt6, B—Kt2; 13 K—Kt7, B—B1; 14 K—Kt8, B—Kt2; 15 B×P, K×B; 16 K—B8, K×P; 17 K—K7, K×P; 18 K—Q7, K—Q5; 19 K—B7, B—R1!; 20 K—Kt6!, K—B5; 21 K×RP, K×P; 22 K—Kt6, K—B5; 23 P—R6, K—Kt5; 24 P—R7 (if 24 K—R7??, K—Kt4; and Black wins), K—B5; 25 K—B7, K×P; 26 K—Kt8, K—Kt3; 27 K×B, K—B2 stalemate!

After the game Grigorieff pointed out the following highly ingenious win: *1 K—Kt5!, K—B2; 2 B—Kt6ch, K—K2* (White is trying to reach Q4 with his King without freeing the Black King. If 2 .... K—Kt2; 3 B—K8, B—Kt2; 4 K—Kt4, K—B1; 5 B—R5, K—Kt2; 6 K—B3,

No. 184

White wins.

B—B1; 7 B—K8!, B—Kt2; 9 K—K2, K—B1; 10 B—R5, K—Kt2; 11 K—Q3, B—B1; 12 B—K or 11 .... K—R3; 12 B—B7, B—B1; 13 B—K8, B—Kt2; 14 B—Q7); *3; K—Kt4, B—Kt2; 4 K—B3, K—B1; 5 K—K2, K—Kt2; 6 B—K8!, K— B1* (again if 6 .... K—R3; 7 B— Q7); *7 B—R5, K—Kt2; 8 K—Q3, K —B1* (once more if 8 .... K—R3; 9 B—B7, B—B1; 10 B—K8, B— Kt2; 11 B—Q7); *9 K—Q4, K—K2; 10 P—K4* and now

a) *10 .... P×P; 11 K×P, B— B1; 12 K—B4, B—Kt2; 13 K—Kt5*

B—B1; 14 K—Kt6, B—Kt2; 15 K—Kt7, B—B1; 16 B—B3,
B—Kt2; 17 B—K4!!, B—R1; 18 P—Kt5!, RP×P; 19 P—R6
and with Black's Bishop stalemated he must move his King,
when his KP is lost.

b) *10 .... K—Q2; 11 B—K2, K—K2; 12 P×P, KP×P* (if 12 ....
BP×P; 13 P—Kt5, P×P; 14 B×P, K—Q1; 15 P—B6, B—R1;
16 K—B5, K—B2; 17 P—R6, P—Q5; 18 K×P, B×P; 19 B×B,
K×B; 20 P—R7, K—Kt2; 21 K—B5 and wins); *13 B—Kt4,*
K—B2; 14 B—Q7!!, K—K2; 15 P—K6, K—B3 (15 .... B—R1;
16 B—B8. White now wins by an ingenious triangulation manoeuvre); *16 K—Q3, K—K2; 17 K—K3, K—B3; 17 K—Q4,*
K—K2; 19 K—K5, B—R1; 20 B—B8, and Black's position is
hopeless.

In general a sacrifice (such as that above in variation a) is the knife
which cuts the Gordian knot of a blockade. Two other illustrations
are seen in the following two examples.

No. 184a (Gunsberg-Berger, Nuremberg, 1883), White: K at KKt3,
P's at QKt4, Q4, K3, B at QB2; Black: K at KKt4, B at Q2, P's at
QKt4, QB5, Q4, KB4. Black won by 1 .... B—K7; 2 K—B2, B—R4;
3 K—K7 (if 3 K—Kt3, B—K7; 4 K—B2, B—Q6; 5 B×B, P×B; 6 K—
K1, P—B5), B—Kt5; 4 K—Q2, K—R5; 5 K—B3, K—Kt6; 6 K—Q2,
K—B7; 7 B—Kt1, P—B6ch!!; 8 K—Q3, B—B6!; 9 K×P, B—K5!;
10 B—Q3, B×B; 11 K×B, K—K8; 12 K—B3, K—K7.

Or No. 184b (Bird-Janowski, Hastings, 1895), White: K at QR4,
B at Q2, P's at QR6, QKt5, QB4, KB4, KR4; Black: K at QR2, B
at QB2, P's at QB4, KB3, KB4, KR4. White can decide at once by
1 P—Kt6ch!, B×P (1 .... K×P; 2 B—R5ch, K—B3; 3 P—R7);
2 K—Kt5, B—Q1; 3 B—R5, B—K2; 4 B—Kt6ch, K—R1; 5 B×P
etc. Instead White tried 1 B—K3, B—Q3, but could only manage
to draw.

Wherever a sacrifice or an exchange is contemplated it is essential
to calculate the resulting Pawn vs. Bishop ending with great precision.
A case in point with a bockaded Pawn position is No. 185 (Fine-Kevitz,
New York, 1936). After *1 .... B—R3; 2 B—Q3, P—Q4; 3 K—B1,*
K—B3!; 4 K—K2, P—Q5! (4 .... P×P would leave Black with a
hopeless tripled Pawn, while 4 .... B×P; 5 B×B, P×B; 6 K—K3,
K—K4; 7 P—B3 is an easily won K and P ending); *5 K—Q2, B—Kt2;*
6 B—K2, B—B1 (the exchange of KtP's would clearly be inadvisable,
since White would then have two connected passed Pawns); *7 P—B3,*
B—K3; 8 P—R3, B—Q2; 9 K—B2, B—B4ch; 10 B—Q3, B—K3
(again the exchange of Bishops would be a hopeless loss); *11 K—Kt3,*
P—R4; 12 P× QP, BP×P; and here *13 K—R4* leads to a simple win
because of a finesse in the Pawn ending: *13 .... P—B4* (if 13 .... B—
B4; 14 B×B!, K×B; 15 P—B5!, K—K4; 16 K—Kt3, K—Q4; 17 P—

B6!!, K—B4; 18 P—R4, K—Q4; 19 P×P and it is all over); *14 K×P, B—B4; 15 B—K2* (15 B×B, K×B; 16 K—R4 is simpler, but the text is more systematic) *B—B7; 16 P×P!, P—Q6; 17 B—B3, P—Q7; 18 K—Kt5, P—Q8= Q; 19 B× Q, B×B; 20 K×P, B×P; 21 K—Kt6* and the Bishop cannot hold the three isolated Pawns, e.g., *21 .... K—K2; 22 P—B5, K—Q1; 23 P—B6, K—B1; 24 P—R4, K—Kt1; 25 P—R5, B—B4; 26 P—R6, B—K5* (26 .... B—Q6; 27 P—R7ch, K—R1; 28 P—Kt4!); *27 P—Kt4!, B×P (Kt7) 28 P—Kt5, B—K5; 29 P—R7ch, K—R1; 30 P—B7, B—B4; 31 P—Kt6* etc.

Thus with weak Pawns a Bishop sacrifice is often the shortest road to victory. Another example is No. 185a (Mieses-Gunsberg, Hannover, 1902), White: K at QB7, B at KR7, P's at QR5, QB5, KB5, KR5; Black: K at K2, B at Q4, P's at QR3, QKt2, KKt2. Mieses concluded with 1 B—Kt8!!, B×B (else 2 B—K6—B8); 2 K×P, B—B5; 3 P—B6, B—Q4; 4 K—Kt6, K—Q1; 5 P—B6!, P×P; 6 P—R6, Γ—K5; 7 K—Kt7!! (very pretty: Black is in zugzwang. Compare the Reti problem No. 162), K—K2; 8 K×P, K—B2; 9 K—Kt6 and Black resigned.

Where both sides have passed Pawns the usual rule that the one who gets there first wins is again applicable. Of course, where one side has two passed Pawns, the other only one, he need only blockade his opponent's Pawn and advance his own. A position in which this plan can be executed only after some subtle manoeuvring is No. 185b (Duras, 1906–'07), White: K at QR7, B at QB1, P's at QR5, QKt7, KR2; Black: K at Q6, B at QB2, P's at KKt4, KB5. 1 B—R3, K—B5 (1 .... P—B6; 2 B—B5 is hopeless); 2 B—K7, P—B6; 3 B—Q8!, B×KRP (3 .... P—B7; 4 B×B, P—B8 = Q; 5 P—Kt8 = Q, Q—B7ch; 6 Q—Kt6 gives Black no perpetual check); 4 B—Kt6, K—Kt4! (or 4 .... P—Kt5; 5 B—B2, K—Kt4; 6 P—R6 as in the main variation); 5 P—R6, P—Kt5; 6 B—B2, B—B2; 7 P—Kt8=Qch!!!, B×Qch; 8 K—Kt7!!!, K—R4; 9 B—R4, K—Kt4; 10 B—K1!, P—Kt6; 11 B×P, B×B; 12 P—R7, P—B7; 13 P—R8 = Q, P—B8 = Q; 14 Q—R6ch and the Black Queen will not live long.

Where there are Pawns on both sides of the board Black can draw only by a blockade (Cf. No. 184) or by setting up dangerous counterplay (No. 185). But it should be remembered that such stratagems are possible only either in exceptional cases or where the superior side has made a mistake. These exceptional cases occur, usually, when the Pawn majority is doubled or hopelessly isolated, or when the King is in a terribly cramped position.

When all the Pawns are on one side (3 vs. 2, 4 vs. 3) the ending is drawn. In No. 186 (Stahlberg-Fine, Kemeri, 1937) after *1 .... P—B3; 2 K—B5, B—Q2; 3 B—Kt8, P—R3; 4 K—Q5, B—R5; 5 K—Q4,*

B—Q2; 6 B—B4, B—R5; 7 B—Q3, B—K1; 8 P—R4, P—Kt4 it is
clear that no further progress is possible. The fact that the White
Bishop is of the wrong color here is immaterial. With Black Bishops
Black would merely set up his King at K3 instead of K2. Even in the
most favorable case, No. 186a, White: K at K4, P's at K5, KB4,
KKt3, KR2, B at QB3, Black: K at K3, B at QB4, P's at KB2, KKt3,
KR2, White can make no headway against skillful defense. E.g.,
1 P—Kt4, B—Kt8; 2 P—B5ch, K—Q2; 3 P—R3, B—B7; 4 K—Q5,
B—K6; 5 P—K6ch, P×Pch; 6 P×Pch, K—K1; 7 K—K5, B—Kt4
there is no way for White to get to the K-side Pawns, e.g., 8 B—K1,
B—K2; 9 P—R4, B—Q1; 10 P—R5, B—K2, etc. However, 7 ....

No. 185

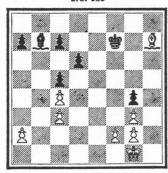

White wins.

No. 186

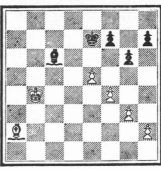

Draw.

P—R4 would have been a mistake here: after 8 P×P, P×P; 9 K—
B5, B—B7; 10 K—Kt5, P—R5; 11 K—Kt4, B—B4!; 12 B—K1!,
B—K2; 3 B×P, B×B; 13 K×B, K—K2; 15 K—Kt5, K×P; 16 K—
Kt6 White just manages to win.

B+3P vs. B+2P is likewise a draw, unless the Black Pawns are
isolated. E.g., No. 186b, White: K at K4, B at QB3, P's at KB4,
KKt4, KR3; Black: K at K3, B at QB4, P's at KKt3, KR2. Draw.
But No. 186c, White: K at KKt4, B at QB3, P's at K4, KB4, KR3;
Black: K at K3, B at QB4, P's at KB2, KR2. White wins. 1 P—
B5ch (if 1 K—R5?, P—B4!!; 2 P×Pch, K×P; 3 B—K5, B—K6=.
But here not 1 .... P—B3!?; 2 K—R6!!, B—K6; 3 K×P, B×P;
4 K—Kt6, B—Kt4; 5 P—K5! and wins), K—K2; 2 P—K5 (2 K—R5,
B—K6) and now Black has two chief lines of defense:
    a) 2 .... P—B3; 3 P—K6! (3 P×Pch?, K—B2; 4 K—R5, B—K6,
       is of course much inferior), B—K6; 4 B—Kt4ch, K—K1; 5 K—

B3!, B—B8; 6 K—K4, B—Kt4 (Black must mark time); 7 K—Q5, B—B8; 8 P—K7!!, K—Q2; 9 P—K8=Qch!!!, K×Q; 10 K—K6, B—Kt7; 11 B—K7, B—B8 (11 .... B—R8; 12 B×P, B×B; 13 K×B is obviously hopeless); 12 B×P, B—R6; 13 B—Kt7 followed by P—B6—B7ch winning the Bishop.

b) 2 .... B—K6; 3 B—K1!, K—Q2; 4 B—R4, K—B3 (or 4 .... K—K1; 5 P—K6); 5 P—K6 (the simplest), P×P; 6 P×P, K—Q3; 7 K—B5 (threatening K—B6), B—Q5; 8 B—K1, K—K2; 9 B—Kt4ch, K—K1; 10 B—Q6, B—B7 (if 10 .... B—Kt3 with the idea of taking the sting out of 11 B—Kt3, K—K2; 12 B—R4ch, K—Q3; 13 K—B6?, B—Q1ch!, White makes a tempo move, 11 B—Kt4! and 11 .... B—B7 is forced; again, if 10 .... B—B6; 11 B—K5, B—K8; 12 B—B6. The point is that White cannot be prevented from getting his Bishop on the diagonal KR4—Q8 with the Black King at K1); 11 B—B4, K—K2; 12 B—Kt5ch, K—K1; 13 K—Kt4, B—Q5; 14 K—R5, K—B1 (or 14 .... B—Kt2; 15 P—R4!, B—B1; 16 B—B6!, B—K2!; 17 K—Kt5!!, B—B1; 18 P—R5, B—R6; 19 K—R6, B—B8ch; 20 K×P, etc.); 15 P—K7ch, K—B2; 16 K—R6, B—B6; 17 K×P, B—Q5; 18 P—R4, B—B6; 18 P—R5, B—Kt7; 20 P—R6, B—Q5; 21 P—K8=Qch!!, K×Q; 22 K—Kt8, B—B6; 23 P—R7, B—Q5; 24 B—R6 and wins.

With a Bishop of the wrong color and the same Pawn position, i.e., No. 186d, White: K at KKt4, B at Q3, P's at K4, KB4, KR3; Black: K at K3, B at QKt6, P's at KB2, KR2, this winning manoeuvre is not possible, so that the result will be a draw. E.g., 1 .... K—B3; 2 P—K5ch, K—Kt2; 3 K—Kt5, P—R3ch; 4 K—Kt4, B—Q8ch; 5 K—Kt3, P—B3; 6 P—K6 (6 K—B2, P×P; 7 P×P=. Compare No. 182), B—Kt6; 7 P—B5 (7 B—B5, K—B1), B—Q8; 8 K—B4, K—B1; 9 B—K4, B—K7; 10 B—Q5, B—Q8 and the extra Pawn is insufficient. White could not win this ending even if he managed to get his Pawn to KB6, e.g., No. 186e, White: K at KB4, B at KB3, P's at K5, KB6, KR3; Black: K at KKt1, B at QB7, P's at KR2, KB2. 1 .... P—R3 (else 2 B—K4 followed by K—Kt5—R6 will win the RP); 2 B—K4, B—Q8; 3 K—Kt3, K—B1; 4 K—R4, K—Kt1; 5 B—B5, K—R1; 6 B—Kt4, B—B7; 7 K—R5, K—R2; 8 P—K6!, B—Kt3ch; 9 K—R4, P×P (else P—K7); 10 B×P, B—K1 (here we have the only winning variation: if 10 .... K—R1?; 11 K—Kt3, B—R2; 12 K—B4, B—Kt1; 13 K—K5!, B—R2; 14 K—Q6, B—Kt3; 15 K—K7, B—R4; 16 B—Q7 and queens the Pawn); 11 K—Kt3, K—Kt3 or 11 B—B5ch, K—Kt1; 12 K—Kt3, K—B2, or 11 P—B7, B×P. But in general neither No. 186c nor 186e can be forced.

B+5P vs. B+4P, all on one side, i.e., Pawns on the Q, K, KB, KKt,

KR files, wins. For White can set up a passed Queen's Pawn and then proceed in exactly the same manner as in the general case No. 183.

B. POSITIONS WITH EVEN MATERIAL

Again such endings are normally drawn, but the significant point to be noted is under what circumstances a win is possible. As for Kt endings, we can group positional advantages under the three general headings of P, B and K superiority with the proviso that these groupings are not completely independent.

1. BETTER PAWN POSITION

This in turn can be broken up into a large number of different types. We shall distinguish the same four classes that we used for Kt endings.

a) The Outside Passed Pawn.

In Kt endings this was the most important group, chiefly because a Knight cannot block a Pawn at a distance. But since a Bishop can, such an advantage is not quite so overwhelming here, although still usually sufficient to win.

No. 187 (Maroczy-Mieses, Monte Carlo, 1903), is an elegant illustration of the typical winning method. White has what is commonly called a Queen's-side majority, which is the same thing as a potential outside passed Pawn. Maroczy established a decisive superiority by *1 P—KKt4!* (His first concern is to force a weakness or an advance on the King's side), *P—B4; 2 P—KR3, P—Kt3; 3 P—R3, P—QR4; 4 P—Kt3, P—K4; 5 B—Q2, P—K5ch; 6 K—K2, K—Kt3* (The threat of the passed Pawn Black's King tied down); *7 B—K3, B—B3; 8 P×P, P×P; 9 P—B3, P—B5?* Hastens defeat. For the most difficult rejoinder, 9 .... B—Q5, see A.); *10 B×KBP, P×Pch; 11 K×P, P—R5; 12 P×P, B—Kt7; 13 K—K4, B×P; 14 K—Q5, B—Kt7; 15 B—Q6, B—Q5; 16 B×Pch* and Black resigned.

A. *9 .... B—Q5; 10 P×P, P×P; 11 B—Q2, B—Kt7; 12 P—QR4, B—Q5; 13 K—B1, P—R4; 14 K—Kt2, K—R3* (if 14 .... P—R5; 15 B—Kt5; if 14 .... B—K4; 15 K—B2); *15 K—Kt3, B—K4ch* (else

No. 187

White wins.

16 K—B4); *16 K—R4, B—Q5!; 17 K—Kt5!!* (not 17 K×P?, B—B7;
18 K—Kt6, P—K6 and Black wins), *P—K6* (on anything else 18 K—
B4 or 18 K—B5 is conclusive); *18 B—K1, B—Kt7* (18 .... K—Kt3;
19 K×P); *19 K—B4, B—B8; 20 K—B3, K—Kt3; 21 K—K2, K—R3;
22 B—R4* followed by *B—Kt5* and since Black's Pawns are all on
Black squares even with the blockade on the Queen's wing the win is
simple.

Thus we see that the chief difficulty in winning with an outside
passed Pawn is that of penetrating the enemy defenses with the King.
For this reason some Pawn exchanges are desirable (this in exception
to the general rule that Pawn exchanges diminish the winning chances
of the superior side). An analogous case to No. 187, where no straight-
forward entry with the King was feasible, is No. 187a (List-Fine,
Ostend, 1937) White: K at K2, B at Q4, P's at K3, K5, KB3, KKt2,
KR2; Black: K at KKt1, B at QR6, P's at QR7, K3, KB2, KKt3,
KR2. Black wins. After 1 K—Q3, B—B4!; 2 B—R1, K—Kt2; 3 P—
Kt4 (3 K—B4, B×P; 4 K—Kt3, K—R3; 5 K×P, K—Kt4; 6 K—Kt3,
B—Kt8; 7 K—B4, B×P; 8 K—Q3, K—B4 is also lost), P—R4; 4 P—
R3, K—B1 (now entry via R3 and Kt4 is not feasible, since White can
play P—KB4); 5 P—K4, B—B7 (again threatening K—Kt2—R3—
Kt4 if White's King should go after the RP); 6 K—K2, B—Kt6;
7 K—K3, K—K2; 8 K—Q4? (a mistake. But on 8 K—Q3, K—Q2;
9 K—B4, K—B3; 10 B—B3, K—Kt3!; 11 K—Kt3, K—B4; 12 K×P,
K—B5; 13 K—Kt2, K—Q6 White is also lost), P—B3!; 9 P×Pch,
K×P; 10 P—Kt5ch (else B—K4), K×P and White resigned.

Sometimes entry with the King is not even necessary until a late
stage. This generally happens when the outside passed Pawn is blockaded by the Bishop. Thus in No. 188 (Tchigorin-Pillsbury, London,
1899) Black decides by *1 .... P—QR4!* (else 2 P—QKt4); *2 K—B3,
K—K3; 3 K—K3, P—KKt5!* (all-important. Not only are the 3 K-
side Pawns now held by Black's two, but the vital square K4 is re-
served for the Black B or K); *4 P×P, P×P; 5 K—Q3, P—R5; 6
P×P, P×P; 7 B—Kt4, B—K4* (threatening .... B—Kt7); *8 B—R3,
B—R8!* (to occupy K4 with the K); *9 B—B1, P—B4* (9 .... K—K4;
10 B—B4ch and Black's K must go right back); *10 B—R3* (or 10
P×Pch, K×P; 11 K—B4, K—K5), *K—K4; 11 P×P, K×P; 12 K—
K3, K—K4; 13 P—B4ch, K—Q4; 14 P—B5, B—K4; 15 K—B2, K—
K5* and Tchigorin abandoned the hopeless struggle.

Ordinarily the important question to be answered when one has an
outside passed Pawn is how and when to force an entry with the King.
Very often this requires considerable care, since any misstep which
reduces the amount of material likewise increases the opponent's drawing chances. Such calculation is at times rather involved, but is al-

ways based on the principle of exchanging as few Pawns as possible.
No. 189 (from Flohr-Loevenfisch, Moscow, 1936) is a case in point.
Loevenfisch could have had this position, but avoided it because he
felt that it should be drawn. However, Black can win by *1 ....
P—QR4; 2 K—B3* (if 2 B—Q6, K—Kt3; 3 K—B3, K—B2; 4 P—K4,
B—K2; 5 B—B7, P×Pch; 6 K×P, P—R5; 7 K—Q4, K—K3; 8 K—
B4, K—B4; 9 P—R3, K—K5; 10 P—Kt4, K—B6; 11 P—B5, K—
Kt7; 12 B—K5, B—B1!; 13 P—R4, K—R6; 14 B×P, B×B; 15 P—
Kt5, P—R4!; 16 P—B6, B—R1!—see No. 163a), *P—R5; 3 K—K2,
P—R6; 4 K—Q3, B—Kt3; 5 K—B2* (or 5 B—Q4, P—R7 and White
must move his Bishop again), *B×P; 6 B—Q6, P—R7; 7 K—Kt2,
K—Kt3; 8 B—K5* (if 8 K×P, K—R4; 9 P—R3—9 B—B8, K—Kt5!;

No. 188

Black to play wins.

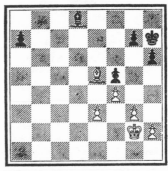

No. 189

Black to play wins.

10 B×P, P—R4; 11 K—Kt3, B—Kt8; 12 K—B2, B×P; 13 K—Q1,
K—B6; 14 K—K1, B×Pch; 15 K—B1, P—R5 as in No. 178a—, B—
B7; 10 B—B8, B×P; 11 B×P, B×P; 12 K—Kt3, K—R5; 13 K—B2,
K×P; 14 K—Q3, K—Kt7 and wins), *B—Kt8; 9 P—R3, P—R4!;
10 K×P, B—B7; 11 K—Kt3, B×P; 12 K—B4, K—B2; 13 K—Q3*
(13 K—Q5, P—R5!; 14 B—Q6, P—Kt4; 15 P×P, B×B; 16 K×B,
P—B5 or 16 .... K—Kt3), *P—Kt4; 14 K—K2, B×P; 15 B×B* (else
the two connected passed Pawns after 15 B—Q4, P—Kt5 will decide),
P×B; 16 K—B3, K—B3; 17 K×P, P—R5 and wins as in No. 26.

That an outside passed Pawn may win when there are as few as two
Pawns on each side is shown by the following problem of Lasker's.
No. 189a, White: K at K2, B at Q2, P's at QKt2, KKt2; Black: K at
KKt1, B at K2, P's at K4, KKt2. The main variation is 1 B—B3,

B—Q3; 2 K—K3, K—B2; 3 K—K4, K—K3; 4 P—QKt4, B—B2; 5 P—Kt5, K—B3; 6 P—Kt4, K—K3; 7 P—Kt5, P—Kt3; 8 B—Kt2, B—Q1; 9 B×P, B×P; 10 P—Kt6! and the Pawn queens.

Finally, how even one passed Pawn may under certain circumstances win is seen in two problems by Troitsky. No. 189b, White: K at K5, B at KKt1, P at QR4; Black: K at KR6, B at KKt4, P at KR4. 1 P—R5, B—R5 (or 1 .... K—Kt6; 2 K—B5!, B—B5; 3 B—R2ch, or 1 .... B—Q1; 2 B—Kt6!); 2 P—R6, B—Kt6ch; 3 K—K4, B—Kt1; 4 K—B3!, K—R5; 5 B—K3!, K—R6; 6 B—B2, K—R7; 7 B—Kt3ch and wins. No. 189c, White: K at K8, B at QR8, P at QR5; Black: K at KR7, B at QB7, P at QB4. 1 P—R6, P—B5; 2 P—R7, P—B6; 3 B—R1!! (the only winning continuation. For if now 3 .... B—Kt3ch; 4 K—K7, P—B7; 5 P—R8=Q, P—B8=Q; 6 Q—Kt2 mate); B—R5ch; 4 K—B7! (after seven more moves the point of going to this square with the King will be clear!), B—B3!; 5 B×B, P—B7; 6 P—R8=Q, P—B8=Q; 7 Q—R2ch, K—Kt6; 8 Q—KKt2ch, K—B5 (or 8 .... K—R5; 9 Q—B2ch, K—Kt5; 10 B—Q7ch, K—R4; 11 Q—R2ch, etc.); 9 Q—B3ch, K—Kt4; 10 Q—Kt3ch, K—B4; 11 Q—Kt6ch (now we see why the King had to be at B7), K—B5 (11 .... K—K4; 12 Q—B6 mate); 12 Q—R6ch and wins the Black Queen.

b) *A Protected Passed Pawn.*

This is a greater advantage here than in the corresponding Knight ending because the Bishop is not as good a blockader. It consequently cramps the mobility of the Black pieces. How it is exploited may be seen in No. 190 (Maroczy-Gruenfeld, Vienna, 1920). *1 B—Q2, B—Q1; 2 P—K6!, B—B3; 3 K—R5!, K—Kt2!* (if 3 .... B×P; 4 K—Kt6); *4 B—K1!, B—Q1ch; 5 K—R4, K—B1; 6 B—Kt3, B—B3!; 7 K—R5!, B×P* (White had gained a tempo. If here 7 .... K—Kt2; 8 B—Q6); *8 K—Kt6, B—B3; 9 K×P, P—Q5; 10 B—K5!!!* and Black resigned, for after 10 .... B×B; 11 P—K7 follows, while 10 .... B—K2; 11 B×P is hopeless.

c) *Qualitatively Superior Passed Pawns.*

In general, when there are pieces on the board, connected passed Pawns are preferable to disconnected ones because they can be more easily advanced. And, of course, the nearer the Pawns are to the eighth rank, the stronger they are. In such cases it is imperative to push one's own Pawns ahead as quickly as possible and take only the most essential precautionary measures against the opponent's Pawns. E.g., in No. 191 (Alatortzeff-Loevenfisch, Leningrad, 1934), White with Pawns on the fifth and sixth has an undeniable advantage, but this will only become decisive if he gets one Pawn to the seventh. The best defense for Black is *1 .... P—K5;* (Compare the alternatives:

a) 1 .... K—Q2 (or 1 .... K—Q1); 2 B—Kt5ch, K—B1; 3 P—B6, K—Kt1; 4 P—Kt5!, B—K5; 5 P—B7ch, K—B1; 6 B—R6ch, B—Kt2; 7 B—B4!, B—B3; 8 B—K6ch, B—Q2; 9 P—Kt7ch, K×KtP; 10 B×B, K×P; 11 B—K6, K—Q3; 12 B—Kt8, K—K2; 13 K—B3, K—B1; 14 B—B4, K—Kt2; 15 K—K4, P—R3; 15 P—R4! and wins.

b) 1 .... P—Kt4 (the game continuation); 2 B—R6, K—Q1; 3 B—Kt5, K—K2; 4 P—B6, K—Q3; 5 P—B7, B—Kt2; 6 B—Q3, K—B4 (6 .... B—B1; 7 B—B5); 7 B—B5, K×P; 8 P—

No. 190   No. 191

White wins.   Black to play; White wins.

B8=Q, B×Q; 9 B×B, P—K5; 10 B—B5, P—K6ch; 11 K—B3, P—R3; 12 B—Q3 and Black resigned, since he loses both Pawns after 13 K—K4);

2 B—R6, K—Q1 (if 2 .... K—Q2; 3 B—Kt5ch, K—B1; 4 P—B6, K—Kt1; 5 P—Kt5! with much the same continuation as in the main variation); *3 B—Kt5, K—B1* (or 3 .... P—Kt4; 4 P—B6, P—R3; 5 P—R3, P—K6ch; 6 K—K2, B—K5; 7 P—B7ch, K—B1; 8 B—R6ch, B—Kt2; 9 B—Q3!, B—B3; 10 B—B5ch, B—Q2; 11 K—Q3! and wins); *4 P—B6!, K—Kt1* (if instead 4 .... P—Q6; 5 B—R6ch, K—Kt1; 6 P—B7ch); *5 P—Kt5!, P—K6ch; 6 K—K2, B—K5; 7 P—R3, B—Kt7; 8 P—R4, B—K5; 9 P—B7ch, K—B1; 10 B—R6ch, B—Kt2; 11 B—B4, K—Q2* (if 11 .... B—B3; 12 K—Q3! and Black must again move a Pawn since either Bishop or King move would be immediately fatal); *12 K—Q3, K—Q3* (12 .... B—B6; 13 B—K6ch or even 13 B—R6); *13 K×P* and it is all over.

We may in fact set up a rule which is applicable to all types of ending: *Advance passed Pawns as rapidly and as far as possible, but take care to avoid a blockade which stalls them.* Another illustration of this principle with Bishop endings is No. 191a (Zukertort, from a game, 1868). White: K at KR5, B at QB1, P's at QB4, Q3, KB5, KKt6; Black: K at KR1, B at QB2, P's at QR6, QB4, QB7, Q5. White wins only by 1 P—B6!, B—K4! (or 1 .... P—R7; 2 P—B7, B—Q3; 3 B—R6; or 1 .... K—Kt1; 2 B—R6 followed by P—B7ch); 2 P—B7, B—Kt2; 3 B×P, B—B1; 4 B—B1, K—Kt2 (on other moves, such as 4 .... B—Kt2; 5 B—B4 would be conclusive); 5 K—Kt5! and now

a) 5 .... B—K2ch; 6 K—B5, B—Q3 (6 .... B—B1; 7 B—B4); 7 B—Kt5, B—B1; 8 B—B4, B—K2; 9 B—K5ch, K—R3 (9 .... K—B1; 10 K—K6); 10 P—Kt7!, P—B8=Q; 11 P—Kt8=Q, Q—B8ch; 12 B—B4ch! and mates in a few.

b) 5 .... B—Q3; 6 K—B5, B—K2 (or 6 .... B—B1; 7 B—B4 as in a)); 7 B—B4, B—B1; 8 B—Kt5, B—Q3; 9 B—B6ch, K—R3; 10 P—Kt7!, P—B8=Q; 11 P—Kt8=Q, Q—B8ch; 12 K—K6, Q—K7ch; 13 K×B and wins.

c) 5 .... K—R1; 6 K—B6, B—Kt2ch; 7 K—K7, B—B1ch; 8 K—K8, B—Kt2 (if 8 .... B—Q3; 9 B—R6 decides. Or 8 .... K—Kt2; 9 B—B4, P—B8=Q; 10 B×Q, B—Q3; 11 B—B4, etc. Or finally 8 .... K—Kt2; 9 B—B4, B—Q3; 10 B×B, P—B8=Q; 11 P—B8=Qch, K×P; 12 B—B4 and wins); 9 B—B4, P—B8=Q; 10 B×Q, B—R3; 11 B—B4!, B—Kt2; 12 B—K5 and mates next move.

A problem of Troitsky's which illustrates mating and other possibilities after both sides have queened is worth mention here. No. 191b, White: K at Q8, B at QB5, P's at KB4, KKt6; Black: K at QR1, B at KR7, P's at QR6, K7. White to play wins by 1 P—Kt7 (1 B—B2??, B—Kt8!), P—K8=Q; 2 P—Kt8=Q (threatening mate beginning with K—B7 dis ch or K—Q7 dis ch) K—Kt2; 3 Q—Kt3ch, K—B3; 4 Q—Kt6ch, K—Q4; 5 Q—Kt5!!! and Black cannot escape the noose.

It must not be supposed that superior passed Pawns win automatically in all cases. They confer an advantage, but whether this is sufficient to win cannot be determined beforehand. E.g., in No. 191c (game Morphy-Loewenthal), White: K at KB1, B at K5, P's at QR2, KB2, KR2; Black: K at KR2, B at QB4, P's at QR2, QKt4, QB2, Black's connected passed Pawns against White's disconnected ones are not quite sufficient. The game was drawn after 1 .... B—Q3; 2 B—Q4! (the Pawn ending after 2 B×B?, P×B would be lost: 3 K—K2, P—R4; 4 K—Q3, P—R5!; 5 K—B3, P—Q4; 6 K—Q4—on Pawn moves Black moves .... K—Kt3 when both White Pawns

are on the fourth, so that the King must move then anyhow—, P—
Kt5!!; 6 P—B4, P—Kt6; 7 P×P, P—R6; 8 K—B3, P—Q5ch; 9 K—
B2, P—Q6ch and queens), P—B4; 3 B—K3, P—R4; 4 K—K2, P—
R5; 5 K—Q3, P—R6 (5 .... P—B5ch; 6 K—B3, B×P; 7 K—Kt4);
6 B—B1!, K—Kt3; 7 K—K4, P—B5; 8 P—B4, P—Kt5; 9 B×P!!,
P×B; 10 K—Q4 and draws, since after all loose Pawns have been
disposed of we get to No. 147c.

Where a winning superiority has already been established one must
be careful to avoid traps which give the opponent counterchances.
Above all, when there are advanced passed Pawns one must be on the
lookout for unexpected sacrificial combinations. E.g., No. 191d
(Bachmann-Mayinger, Augsburg, 1898), White: K at KKt5, B at
K2, P's at QR2, QKt3, QB2, KKt4, KR5; Black: K at KR1, B at
Q2, P's at QKt3, QB4, Q5, K5, K6. White to play could have settled
matters speedily with 1 K—B4, but overlooked the threat and played
1 P—R6?. After 1 .... B—Kt4!!; 2 B×B, P—Q6!; 3 P×P, P—K7
Black forced a Queen and won.

Again to emphasize the point that special positions sometimes occur
which invalidate every rule (Reti's motto is said to have been: "No
rule without exceptions") we quote No. 191e (Kubbel, 1921), where
White draws even though he cannot stop Black from queening and
cannot queen his own Pawn (stalemate theme). White: K at QB6,
B at QR8, P's at KKt6, KR6; Black: K at KR1, B at KKt7, P's at
KKt2, K5. White to play and draw. The solution is 1 K—Q6!!,
P×P!!! (if 1 .... P—K6; 2 K—K7!, K—Kt1; 3 B×B, P—K7; 4 B—
Q5ch, K—R1; 5 K—B8 and mates); 2 K—K5!, P—K6 (2 .... K—
Kt2; 3 B×P=); 3 B×B, P—K7; 4 K—B6!!!, P—K8=Q; 5 P—
Kt7ch, K—R2 (5 .... K—Kt1?; 6 B—Q5ch); 6 B—K4ch!!, Q×B;
7 P—Kt8=Qch!!!, K×Q stalemate!

d) *Qualitatively Superior Pawn Position.*

This comprises all those cases where the superiority does not consist
of some passed Pawn or Pawns, but is rather due to an inherent weakness in the Pawn structure, such as badly isolated doubled Pawns, and
blocked Pawns. It is often exceedingly difficult to draw the line here
and determine whether the advantage comes from the weak Pawns or
the weak Bishop. In fact the two go so closely together that they can
frequently be distinguished only for purely theoretical purposes.

In No. 192 (Rjumin-Kan, Moscow, 1935) we have a typical instance
of Pawns blockaded by a Bishop. White's majority on the Q-side is
worthless and Black can look upon his majority on the K-side as a
potential outside passed Pawn and decide accordingly. The game
continued *1 .... K—K4; 2 B—B6, P—B4; 3 P—QR4, P—KKt4;*

No. 192

Black wins.

4 P—R4 (hastens the end, but other moves are equally useless in the long run. E.g., 4 K—B2, P—R4; 5 K—K2, P—R5; 6 K—B2, P—Kt5, etc. If here 6 K—B3, B—Q 4ch is conclusive: 7 B×B, K×B; 8 P—QKt3, K—K4!; 9 P—Kt4, K—Q4; or 9 K—K2, P—Kt5; 10 P×P, P×P; 11 P—Kt4, P—R6; 12 K—B2, P—R7; 13 K—Kt2, P—Kt6, etc.), *P×P ch; 5 K×P, P—B 5!; 6 K—Kt4* (6 P×P ch, K×P and Black gets to the Q-side), *B—Q8 ch!; 7 K—R3, P×P; 8 K—Kt2* (8 K—Kt3, B—Kt6! and 9 K—B3 is met by .... B—Q4ch), *K—B5; 9 P—Kt4, B—Kt6* and White resigned.

Where the Pawns are absolutely weak (i.e., doubled or hopelessly blocked by Pawns) the win proceeds in exactly the same way as in No. 192, i.e., one simply ignores the extra Pawn (since it is useless in the play) and acts as though one were a Pawn ahead. E.g., No. 192a (Konstantinopolsky-Alatortzeff, Leningrad-Moscow, 1939), White: K at KR1, B at KB3, P's at QB2, QB3, KB4, KKt4, KR3; Black: K at Q2, B at QR3, P's at QB5, K3, KB2, KKt2, KR2. The doubled White QBP is held by one Black Pawn, so that Black need merely set up a passed Pawn on the K-side. The game continued 1 K—Kt1, P—K4!; 2 P×P (2 P—B5, P—Kt4!; 3 K—B2, P—B3 and White has a further weakness: his Pawns are fixed on White squares), K—K3; 3 K—B2, K×P; 4 K—K3, B—B1; 5 P—R4, P—R3; 6 B—K2, B—K3; 7 B—B3, P—Kt3; 8 B—K2, B—Q4; 9 B—B1, P—Kt4 (Black prefers to establish a passed KKtP because it is further from the QBP's and because it can be advanced to the sixth without blocking the Black Bishop); 10 P×P, P×P; 11 B—K2, P—B3; 12 B—B1, P—B4; 13 P×P, K×P; 14 K—Q4, B—K3; 15 K—K3, K—Kt5; 16 K—B2, B—Q4; 17 B—K2ch, K—R6; 18 K—Kt1 and now Black can win by the subtle 18 .... P—Kt5; 19 B—B1ch, K—Kt6; 20 B—K2, B—K3!!; 21 B—Q1 (if 21 B—B1, K—B6; 22 B—Kt2ch, K—K7; 23 K—R2, K—Q7; while if 21 K—R1, K—B7, and if 21 K—B1, K—R7 is conclusive), K—B5; 22 B—K2 (or 22 K—B2, P—Kt6ch; 23 K—Kt1, B—Kt5! and the Pawn ending is easily won), K—K6; 23 B—B1, K—Q7; 24 K—B2, K×P(B7); 25 K—Kt3, K×P and wins.

The isolated Pawn is a serious weakness in Bishop endings only if it is subject to direct attack by the enemy King and if there are additional Pawn weaknesses. E.g., No. 192b (Santasiere-Fine, New York,

1938), White: K at KKt1, B at QKt2, P's at QR4, QKt3, K5, KB2, KKt3, KR2; Black: K at KKt1, B at K2, P's at QR2, QKt5, Q4, KB2, KKt2, KR2. White wins because the Black Q-side Pawns are weak and because he has a Pawn majority on the K-side. The game continued 1 P—B4, P—B3; 2 B—Q4, P—QR3; 3 K—B2, K—B2; 4 K—K3, P×P; 5 B×P, P—Kt3; 6 K—Q4, K—K3; 7 P—Kt4 (White is simply ignoring the Black QP and is proceeding as though he had an outside passed Pawn), B—Q1; 8 P—B5ch, P×P; 9 P×Pch, K×P; 10 K×P, K—Kt5; 11 B—Q6, P—QR4; 12 K—B6, K—R6; 13 K—Q7, B—Kt3; 14 B—K7, K×P; 15 K—B6, B—B7; 16 K—Kt5, K—Kt6; 17 K×P and the two White Pawns are too strong (See No. 182d).

Under certain circumstances a chain of advanced Pawns can become a winning advantage if they go together with a Bishop which by capture or sacrifice can force one through. The most common case is seen in No. 192c (Amateurs, 1775), White: K at KB4, B at Q2, P's at QR6, QKt5, QB4; Black: K at K2, B at Q5, P's at QR2, QKt3, QB4. White to play can either win two Pawns or force a queen with 1 B—R5!!, for if 1 .... P×B; 2 P—Kt6, K—Q3; 3 P×P and queens, while if 1 .... K—Q2; 2 B×P!!!, K—B1; 3 B×RP with a decisive superiority. Black to play can draw here with 1 .... K—Q2; 2 B—R5, K—B2! (but still not 2 .... P×B??; 3 P—Kt6, K—B1; 4 P×P! and queens).

2. BETTER BISHOP

This brings us to the well-known topic of "good" and "bad" Bishops. Any piece is good or bad in proportion to its mobility; this is why, e.g., a Rook is better than a Knight—it can cover more squares. Now, if a Bishop is forced to defend a number of Pawns which are on the same color it becomes cramped and is reduced to the status of a Pawn. In such a case, we speak of a "bad" Bishop, while the opponent's piece, which is free to roam all over the board at will, is the "good" Bishop. This situation is peculiar to Bishops because they are per se confined to squares of only one color and when those squares are occupied by Pawns, they have few moves left.

Even when the Pawn position is not intrinsically weak the bad Bishop may be a fatal handicap. E.g., in No. 193 (game Schelfhout-Menchik). Here we see at once what the trouble is: the Black Bishop

No. 193

White wins.

has to defend two weak Pawns. With Black to play he would have to give up one of them at once, so that White's first task is to lose a move. If he manoeuvres his Bishop along the diagonal Q1—KR5, he will have two reserve squares (Q1 and K2) but Black will also have two (KB2, KKt3). On the other hand if he manoeuvres along the diagonal KR1—QR8, he will have two squares (KKt2, KR1) to Black's one (Q2). Thus the win begins with *1 B—Kt2, B—Q2; 2 B—R1, B—K1; 3 B—B3, B—Q2* (giving up the other Pawn loses much more quickly: 3 .... B—B2; 4 B×BP, B×P; 5 B—K8!, B—Kt6; 6 P—B6, B×P; 7 P—B7 and queens or 6 .... B—K3; 7 B—Q7, B—B5; 8 P—B7); *4 B×RP, B—B1* (4 .... B—K3; 5 B—K8); *5 B—K8, B—Kt2; 6 B— Q7, K—Kt3; 7 K—Kt3, K—B3; 8 K—B3, K—Kt3; 9 K—K3, K—B3;*

<table>
<tr><td>No. 194</td><td>No. 195</td></tr>
</table>

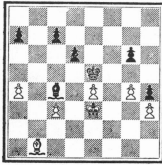

Black wins.

White to play wins.

10 K—Q4, B—R1; 11 B—B8, K—K2; 12 K—K5 and the rest is simple. A noteworthy point in this example is that with the Bishops off the board White just manages to draw, but only because the Pawn position is blockaded.

More often than not the Pawn position is itself intrinsically weak when there is a bad Bishop on the board. This is due to the fact that with all or most of the Pawns on one color, the squares of the opposite color are easily occupied. A fine example of the exploitation of a bad Bishop coupled with weak squares is seen in No. 194 (Winawer-Steinitz, Vienna, 1882). With Black Bishops the game would be a draw, possibly even in White's favor. But as it is, White's Bishop is a do-nothing, while all his Pawns are subject to attack. Steinitz won as follows: *1 .... B—B8; 2 K—B3, P—Kt4!* (not 2 .... B×P; 3 B— Q3!, K—B3!; 4 K—B4!, B—Kt7; 5 P—Kt5ch, K—K3; 6 B—B4ch,

K—K2; 7 B—Q3!, P—R6; 8 K—Kt3, K—K3; 9 P—K5! with good counter-chances, because now it is Black's Bishop which is tied down); *3 B—R2, P—B3* (threatening .... B—Q6); *4 B—B7* (if instead 4 B—Kt1, P—R4; 5 B—B2, B—B5; and Black wins a Pawn because the White Bishop has no moves: e.g., 6 K—K3, B—B2; 7 B—Q1, B—Kt3; 8 B—B3, P—B4; 9 B—Kt2, B—K1 or here 7 K—B3, B—Kt3; 8 K—K3, P—Q4); *B—Q6; 5 K—B2* (if 5 B—Kt6, P—Q4 wins the Pawn), *K—B5; 6 P—R5, B×P; 7 B—B4, P—Q4; 8 B—R6* and the conclusion is not difficult: *8 .... P—B4; 9 B—B8, P—B5; 10 P—R6, K—K4; 11 B—Q7* (11 K—K3, B—Kt7), *P—Q5; 12 P×Pch, K×P; 13 K—K2, B—Q6ch; 14 K—K1, P—B6; 15 B—B8, K—K6; 16 K—Q1, K—B7; 17 B—B5, B×P; 18 K—B2, B—B8; 19 K×P, B×P* and soon queens'

Where the Pawns are already weak (i.e., even without the bad Bishop) a bad Bishop is a straw that will break any chess camels. back. No. 195 (Eliskases-Brauer, correspondence, 1933) is an excellent illustration. The Black Pawns are all isolated and therefore inferior to the White, but the added handicap of a Bishop with three Pawns fixed on its color is fatal. Eliskases continued with *1 P—Kt3!* (to exchange Black's only strong Pawn), *B—Kt5* (the alternatives are no better: a) 1 .... K—B4; 2 B—R3ch, K—K5; 3 B×B, P×Pch; 4 K×P, K×P; 5 K—B4!, K×P; 6 K—K5!, P—Kt4; 7 B—K8, P—Kt5; 8 B×P, P—Kt6; 9 B—Kt6 and the White Pawn queens; b) 1 .... P×Pch; 2 K×P, K—B4; 3 B—R3ch as in a); c) 1 .... B—K3; 2 K—Kt2!!! (but not 2 P×P!, K—B4!; 3 B—R3ch, K—B3!; 4 B×B, K×B; 5 K—Kt3, K—B4; 6 K—B3, K—B3! with a drawn Pawn ending), K—B4; 3 K—B3, P×P; 4 B—Q3ch!, K—B3; 5 K×P, B—B4; 6 B—Kt5, B—Kt3; 7 K—B4, and will win by B—Q7—B8 or B—K8; d) 1 .... P—B6; 2 K—Kt1, B—Kt5; 3 K—B2, K—B4; 4 K—K3 and the Black BP is doomed); *2 B—Kt2!* (but not 2 P×P?, K—B4; 3 B—Kt2, K×P; 4 B×P, B—B1; 5 B—Kt2, K—K6; 6 P—Q5, B—Q2!; 7 P—B6, P×P!!!; 8 P×P, B×P!!!; 9 B×B, K—B5 and draws because the King gets back to R1), *P—B6* (if instead 2 .... B—K3; 3 P×P!, K—B4; 4 K—Kt3, K—B3; 5 K—B3, and will win by B—B3, Q1—R4); *3 B—B1, K—B4; 4 B—Q3ch, K—K3; 5 K—Kt1, K—Q2* (or 5 .... B—B4; 6 B—Kt5); *6 K—B2, K—B3; 7 B—B2!!* (threatening 8 B—Q1 and preparing to answer 7 .... K—Kt4 with 8 B—Kt3!, B—K3; 9 K—K3!!, K—Kt5; 10 B—Q1, K—B6; 11 B×P, B—B2; 12 P—Kt4!, etc.), *P—Kt3; 8 P×P, K×P; 9 B—Q1, B—K3* (9 .... K—Kt4; 10 B×P, B×B; 11 K×B, K—B5; 12 K—K3, K—B6; 13 P—Kt4!, P×P; 14 P—R5! and queens first); *10 B×P, B—B2; 11 K—K3, K—Kt4; 12 K—B4, K—Kt5!; 13 K—K5, K—B5* and now White wins an extra Pawn by the typical tempo-losing manoeuvre we saw in No. 180: *14 B—R1, B—Kt1; 15 B—Kt2!, B—B2; 16 B—B3, K—Q6; 17 B×QP,* and Black resigned.

Where the superior side has an outside or potential outside passed Pawn the win with the good Bishop is quite simple. E.g., in No. 196 (Eliskases-Capablanca, Semmering-Baden, 1937) Black's Bishop not only has to stop the Pawn but must also defend the QRP so as to allow the King to get back. This is too much to ask of one poor chess piece and consequently the loss is inevitable. After *1 .... B—Kt5; 2 P— K5, P×Pch; 3 P×P, P—R3* (3 .... P—QR4; 4 P×Pch, K×P; 5 K— B5 and wins); *4 P—R4, B—R4; 5 P—K6, B—K1* White could have brought the game to a speedy conclusion by *6 P—K7, K—B2; 7 K— K5, K—B1; 8 K—B6, K—B2; 9 K—Kt7, K—B1; 10 K—B8, K—Q2; 11 B—B7.*

In No. 196a (Pillsbury-Billecard, Munich, 1900) we have another illustration of play with a good Bishop and a passed Pawn. White: K at KB4, B at Q3, P's at QKt4, QB3, K5, KKt4; Black: K at K3, B at KB2, P's at QKt4, QB3, Q4, KKt3. After 1 P—Kt5! the Black Bishop is little better than a useless chunk of wood: 1 .... B—K1; 2 B—B1, B—B2 (on 2 .... B—Q2, as in the game, the Pawn ending is easily won after 3 B—R3ch, K—K2; 4 B×B, K×B; 5 K—K3, K—K2; 6 K—Q4, K—K3; 7 K—B5); 3 B—R3ch, K—K2; 4 K—K3, B—K1; 5 P—K6!, K—Q3 (or 5 .... P—B4; 6 P×P, B—B3; 7 K—Q4); 6 K— Q4 and Black's game is hopeless.

It sometimes happens that Pawns which are all on the color of the Bishop are so weak that the opposing King can come in and just pick them off at will. Such a case is seen in No. 196b (Van Scheltinga-Fine, Amsterdam, 1936), White: K at KR2, B at QB3, P's at QKt4, QB5, K5, KB3, KB2, KR3; Black: K at KKt1, B at KKt2, P's at QR3, QKt2, K3, KB2, KKt3, KR3. Black to play. After 1 .... K—B1; 2 K—Kt3, K—K1; 3 K—B4, K—Q2; 4 K—K4, K—B3; 5 K—Q4, K—Kt4; 6 B—Q2, P—KR4; 7 P—B4, B—B1; 8 P—B3, P—R4 White resigned since he must lose at least one Pawn to begin with.

Whenever there is a choice of where to place the Bishop to defend a weak Pawn, the spot which leaves the Bishop most mobility should always be chosen. E.g., in No. 196c (Kashdan-Fine, New York, 1936), White: K at KKt1, B at KKt3, P's at QR4, QB4, KB4, KR3; Black: K at KKt1, B at Q7, P's at QR2, QKt3, KB2, KKt3, after 1 .... K—Kt2; 2 K—B2, K—B3; 3 K—K2, B—B8; 4 K—B3, K—B4; 5 B—R2, B—R6; 6 B—Kt1!, B—Q3; 7 B—K3, B—B1; 8 B—B2! is the only correct continuation for if 8 .... B—Q3; 9 B—K3! defends the Pawn and leaves two good reserve squares for the Bishop. Instead White played 4 K—Q1?, B—R6; 5 K—K2, B—Q3; 6 K—B3, K—B4 and now he must lose a Pawn, for if 7—K3, or 7 B—R2, P—Kt4 and the BP is pinned, while on 7 P—R4, P—B3, and P—Kt4 is still an unanswerable threat.

3. BETTER KING POSITION

This is of greater importance here than in any other ending with pieces because once the King is firmly secured at some vital point he cannot be driven away. In addition, as for Knight endings, once the King manages to attack the enemy Pawns he can invariably reap a plentiful harvest.

Those cases where the King is unopposed and can simply capture all the Pawns need not be considered in any detail. The interesting examples arise only when there is a race to see who gets there first or when some unusual sacrificial defense is offered.

No. 196   No. 197

Black to play; White wins.   White to play wins.

Where one's King can succeed in getting to the bulk of the enemy Pawns, the fact that one is a Pawn (or sometimes even two) behind frequently does not matter. E.g., in No. 197 (Berger) two Pawns win against three. 1 B—B7? is unsatisfactory because of the sacrifice 1 .... P—Kt4!; 2 P×P, P—B5!; 3 P—Kt6 (or 3 P×P, P—Kt6; 4 P—Kt6, P—Kt7; 5 P—Kt7, P—Kt8=Q; 6 P—Kt8=Qch, Q×Q; 7 B×Q, K—Kt1 and the Black King reaches QB1,=.), B—Q5; 4 P—Kt7, B—R2; 5 P×P, P—Kt6; 6 P—B5, K—Kt1; 7 B—K5, K—B2; 8 P—B6, P—Kt7!; 8 B×P, B—Kt1; 9 B—Q4, K—K3; 10 B—Kt6, K—Q3=. The win must begin by attacking the Pawns with the King. Thus *1 K—B3, P—Kt4* (1 .... K—Kt1; 2 K—K4, K—B2; 3 K—Q5, K—K2; 4 K—B6 is hopeless for Black: he loses all his Pawns); *2 P×P, P—B5; 3 P×P, P—Kt6; 4 B—B1,* and now:
  a) *4 .... P—Kt7; 5 B×P, B×B; 6 K—K4, K—Kt2; 7 P—Kt6, B—R6* (or 7 .... K—B3; 8 K—Q5, B—K4; 9 P—B5!, B—Kt6;

10 K—B6, K—K2; 11 K—Kt7, and P—B6); *8 K—Q5, B—B8;*
9 K—Q6, B—B5ch; 10 K—Q7, K—B2; 11 P—B5, B—K6;
12 P—Kt7 and queens.

b) *4 .... K—Kt1; 5 K—K4, K—B2; 6 P—Kt6, K—K3; 7 P—Kt7,*
B—K4; 8 B—Kt2, B—R7; 9 P—B5, B—Kt6; 10 K—Q4, K—Q2;
11 K—Q5, K—B2; 12 P—B6, B—R7 (King moves do not
save the game either. E.g., 12 .... K—Kt3; 13 B—Q4ch,
K—B2; 14 B—R7, K—Q1; 15 B—Kt6ch, K—K2; 16 P—B7,
P—Kt7; 17 B—B5ch, or here 13 .... K—R3; 14 K—K6,
P—Kt7; 15 B×P, K—R2; 16 B—Q4ch, K—Kt1; 17 B—K5ch);
13 K—B5, B—Kt6; 14 K—Kt5, B—R7; 15 B—Q4 (threatening
B—Kt6ch and K—R6), *K—Kt1; 16 B—Kt6, P—Kt7* (if 16 ....
B—B2; 17 K—R6, B×B; 18 K×B, P—Kt7; 10 P—B7 mate);
17 K—R6, P—Kt8= Q; 18 P—B7ch, B×P; 19 B—R7 mate.

Thus we see that although the King may be ready to gobble up a
number of Pawns care must still be exercised to make sure that the
superiority established is a winning one. Here again even chess
Homers sometimes nod. E.g., in the third match game Alekhine-
Bogoljuboff, 1929, the position No. 197a, White: K at KB5, B at
KKt6, P's at QR5, KB3, KKt2, KR3; Black: K at K2, B at KB8,
P's at QR2, KB5, KKt4, KR5 occurred. Alekhine played 1 B—R5?,
B×P; 2 B—Kt4, K—Q3, but after 3 K×P, K—K4; 4 K×P, K—Q5!;
5 K—Kt5, K—K6; 6 P—R4, B×P! could only draw. He could have
won quickly with 1 K×P, B×P; 2 K—Kt4!, K—B3; 3 B—K4,
K—K4; 4 K×P, K—Q5; 5 K—Kt4, K—K6; 6 P—R4, etc.

Even when each side has only one Pawn (not passed) a favorable
King position may be decisive. E.g., No. 197b (Horwitz, 1880),
White: K at KB6, B at QB6, P at KKt3; Black: K at KR4, B at KKt1,
P at KB2. White to play wins by 1 B—B3ch, K—R3; 2 P—Kt4,
K—R2 (2 .... B—R2; 3 P—Kt5 mate); 3 P—Kt5, K—R1; 4 B—K4,
B—R2; 5 B×B, K×B; 6 K×P, etc. Or the Pawn is won and the
opposing Bishop prevented from stopping the passed Pawn created,
as in No. 197c (Teichmann-Marshall, San Sebastian, 1911), White:
K at K4, B at KB1, P at KKt2; Black: K at KKt6, B at KKt5,
P at KR5. Marshall concluded with 1 .... B—B1; 2 K—K3, B—Q2!
(not 2 .... B—Kt2; 3 B—B4!, B×P; 4 B—K6=. No. 173c); 3 K—
K4 (unfortunately necessary. If 3 K—K2, B—B3; 4 K—K1, B×P as
played, while if 3 K—Q2, K—B7!; 4 B—B4, K×P; 5 K—K1, K—
Kt8!; 6 B—B1, B—K3!; 7 B—Kt5, P—R6; 8 B—B6, P—R7; 9 B—
K4, B—R6 and wins), B—B3ch; 4 K—K3, B×P and Black won, for
after 5 B—B4, P—R6 the Pawn queens. An allied case with two
Pawns on each side is No. 197d (Kaiser-Lasker, simultaneous exhi-
bition, Hamburg, 1904), White: K at KKt1, B at QB2, P's at KB3,
KKt2; Black: K at KKt6, B at QB5, P's at QB6, KR5. Lasker

won by 1 .... B—Kt4; 2 K—R1 (White is in zugzwang), B—B8;
3 K—Kt1, B×P; 4 P—B4, P—R6 and mate next move.

IV. BISHOPS OF OPPOSITE COLORS

Because such Bishops cannot possibly attack the same points or be
exchanged the win is considerably more difficult when there is a
material advantage. In fact, one Pawn ahead in general only draws,
while even with two Pawns there are many positions where no win is
possible.

1. BISHOP AND PAWN VS. BISHOP

The simplest case of B+P vs. B is invariably a draw because the

No. 198   No. 199

White to play wins. (Rare exception   White to play wins. Draw with all
to general rule.)   pieces one or two files to the left.

extra White Bishop is useless, so that one has in effect an ending of
P vs. B. The Pawn can then queen only in certain very special
positions, e.g., No. 198, where after *1 P—R6, B—B4; 2 K—B3!,
K—Q4; 3 P—R7, B—K5ch; 4 K—K3* Black must abandon the
Bishop if he wants to clear the diagonal.

2. BISHOP AND TWO PAWNS VS. BISHOP

There is no simple general rule which covers all the cases where
B+2P win against B; we shall have to enumerate a large number of
typical cases.

a) Doubled Pawns.

A doubled Pawn wins only if the Black King cannot reach a square
in front of the Pawn from which he cannot be driven away. Thus in
No. 199 (Berger, 1889) White wins by *1 B—Kt5, B—B4; 2 P—B7!,*

*B—R6; 3 P—B6, B—Kt5; 4 K—B5, B—R6!; 5 K—Kt6, B—B1;
6 K—R7, B any; 7 K—Kt8* followed by 8 P—B8 = Q, etc. But here
2 K—B7?, B—K5! would only draw: 3 K—Kt7, B—B6; 4 K—Kt6,
B—K5; 5 P—B7, K—Q2 and the best White can do is to score a moral
victory by 6 P—B6ch, K—B1; 7 B—Kt3, B×P; 8 K×B stalemate.
Such positions as No. 199 are great exceptions. Even No. 199a,
White: K at QB6, B at KKt6, P's at QKt5, QKt6; Black: K at Q1,
B at KKt6 are drawn since White cannot get to R7 and QR8 unless
he goes off the board.

b) *Connected Passed Pawns.*

This is the most complicated case; the result depends on the files
and ranks that the Pawns are on as well as on the places and colors
of the Bishops. We shall classify the positions according to the ranks
the Pawns are on. It will be well to bear in mind that it is always
desirable for the defender to force the Pawns on to squares of the
opposite color; he can then blockade them and draw with ease. The
superior side must therefore play his Pawns to squares that are of the
same color as the opponent's Bishop. If he can do this he wins; if not
he draws.

(1) *Both Pawns on the Sixth Rank.*

This is always a win (except for certain position with the RP). In
No. 200 after *1 .... K—K1; 2 B—Kt5ch, K—B1* (or 2 .... K—Q1;
3 K—Kt6, B—R6; 4 K—B7); *3 K—K4,* the Black Bishop must stay
on the diagonal KB1—QR6 to prevent the KP from queening, so that
White's King is free to march to Q7 and support the advance of the
KP. *3 .... B—R6; 4 K—Q5, B—Kt5; 5 K—B6, B—R6* (or 5 ....
K—K1; 6 K—B7 dis ch); *6 K—Q7, B—Kt5; 7 P—K7ch.* Where
there is a RP, with a Bishop of the wrong color, the ending is a win if
the Black King is confined to the corner, but otherwise a draw. Thus
No. 200a, White: K at QR5, B at Q2, P's at QR6, QKt6; Black:
K at QR1, B at KB6. White to play wins by 1 B—B4 (but other
moves such as 1 K—Kt4? would lead to a draw after 1 .... K—Kt1!;
2 K—B5, K—B1; 3 K—Q6, B—R8 and Black simply continues to
move his Bishop back and forth along the long diagonal), B—Kt7;
2 K—Kt4, B—B6; 3 K—B5, B—Kt7 (Black has no choice: he must
not move his Bishop off the diagonal, for if he does the KtP will
queen); 4 K—Q6, B—B6 (4 .... K—Kt1; 5 K—Q7 dis ch) 5 K—B7,
B—Kt7; 6 P—Kt7ch. But as we have seen, No. 200b, Black King at
QB1, other pieces as in No. 200a, is drawn, since the White King is
now forbidden access to the key square QB7.

(2) One Pawn on the Sixth Rank; the Other on the Fifth.

This is an immediate draw if the Pawns are blockaded, but otherwise a win, since it transposes into the first case. Sometimes Black has the alternative of getting his King out behind the Pawns but this is of no avail. E.g., No. 200c, White: K at KKt4, B at KB1, P's at KB6, KKt5; Black: K at KB2, B at K8. 1 .... K—K3 (White to play would begin with 1 K—B5; when P—Kt6—Kt7 and B—B4 forces a queen); 2 K—R5, B—Kt5 (or 2 .... K—B4; 3 B—R3ch); 3 B—R3ch, K—K4; 4 K—R6, B—Q7 (or 4 .... K—B5; 5 P—Kt6. Or 4 .... B—B1ch; 5K—R7, B—Kt5; 6 P—B7); 5 P—B7, B—Kt5; 6 P—Kt6, K—B3; 7 P—Kt7! (or 7 K—R7, B—B1; 8 B—B5!, B—Kt2; 9 B—Kt1, B—B1; 10 K—Kt8), K×P; 8 B—K6ch.

<table>
<tr><td align="center">No. 200</td><td align="center">No. 201</td></tr>
<tr><td>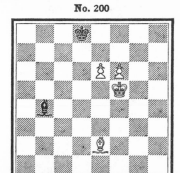</td><td></td></tr>
<tr><td>White wins. (Pawns may be on any file except R and Kt, for which see No. 200a.)</td><td align="center">Draw. Win with Black Bishop at QR6.</td></tr>
</table>

(3) Both Pawns on the Fifth Rank.

When the two Pawns are on the fifth, the outcome depends upon whether they can both get to the sixth or not. This in turn is determined by whether the Bishop can both control the square in front of the Pawn and prevent the White King from entering to cover that square a second time. E.g., in No. 201 the square Q3 is covered by the Bishop and the White King cannot leave the pawn at K5 undefended. Therefore the position is drawn. But in No. 201a, with the Black Bishop at QR6, other pieces as in No. 201, the White King can get to QB6 and support the advance of the QP: 1 K—B4, K—K1 (or 1 .... B—Kt7; 2 P—Q6ch, K—K1; 3 P—K6 or 3 K—Q5—No. 200); 2 P—Q6, K—Q1; 3 K—Q5, K—K1; 4 P—K6 and wins. Or No. 201b, Black: K at QB2, other pieces as in No. 201a, White wins by 1 K—K4, B—B1; 2 K—B5, B—R6; 3 K—K6, B—Kt5; 4 P—Q6ch, etc.

Where White's Bishop is on Black squares, the results correspond to those in No. 201. I.e., if the Black Bishop is at KKt1, where it stops P—K6 and prevents the entry of the King the game is a draw, but if it is at KR6, the White King gets to B6 or the Pawn advances and White wins. Thus No. 201c, White Bishop at KKt3, Black Bishop at KKt1, other pieces as in No. 201 is a draw, while No. 201d, White Bishop at KKt3, Black Bishop at KR6, other pieces as in No. 201 is a win. Here in No. 201d some finesse is required: On 1 B—R4ch, K—Q2; 2 K—K3, B—Kt5; 3 K—B4, B—R6; 4 K—Kt5??, B—Kt7!! draws, for if 5 P—K6ch, K—Q3!; 6 B—Kt3ch, K—K2!!!=. But White can win with 1 B—K1, B—Kt5; 2 B—Kt4ch, K—Q2 (2 .... K—B2; 3 K—B5); 3 K—K3—B4—Kt5—B6, as in No. 201, for if now at any time . . . B—Kt7, then P—K6ch and P—Q6 is decisive.

If we move the Pawns one file over to the left or to the right we get exactly the same situation. If the Bishop can attack one Pawn and prevent the advance of the other White can do nothing. Thus No. 201e, White: K at Q4, B at KKt3, P's at QB5, Q5; Black: K at Q2, B at QR1, is a draw; Black plays simply B—Kt2—R1. But No. 201f, Black Bishop at QR5, other pieces as in No. 201e, White wins after 1 .... B—Kt4; 2 K—B3, B—R5; 3 K—Kt4, B—Q8; 4 P—B6ch, etc. Similarly, if the colors of the Bishops are reversed, Black draws with his Bishop at KB1, but loses with his Bishop at KKt6.

If we move the Pawns two files over to the left or to the right the color of the Bishop, rather than the particular square it is on, is the decisive factor. Thus in No. 202 White wins by *1 B—B3ch, K—R2; 2 K—Q5, B—R4; 3 K—B6*, etc. The position which corresponds to No. 201, No. 202a, Black Bishop at QR2, other pieces as in No. 202, does Black no good here because he has no reserve square for his Bishop. After 1 B—B3ch, K—B2; 2 K—Kt4 he cannot prevent 3 P—Kt6 in any reasonable manner. If the Bishops' colors are reversed, i.e., if White has a Bishop on Black squares, Black a Bishop on White squares, the lack of elbow room militates in Black's favor this time. In No. 202b, White: K at QB4, B at Q2, P's at QKt5, QB5; Black: K at QB2, B at KB6, after 1 B—R5ch, K—Q2! saves the day for Black because White cannot get his King through on the Queen's side —e.g., 2 K—Kt4, B—Kt7; 3 B—Kt6, B—B6; 4 K—R5, B—Kt2! (but not 4 .... B—Kt7?; 5 K—R6, 6 B—R5, 7 K—Kt6 and wins); 5 B—R7, K—B2! and White is at a standstill. Again, it would do White no good to play his King to the King's side after 1 B—R5ch, K—Q2, since that would not cover the crucial square QB6. Similarly 1 B—B4ch is met by 1 .... K—Kt2 (but not 1 .... K—Q2; 2 K—Kt4—R5) and if 2 B—Kt5, K—B2!; 3 K—Kt4, K—Kt2!; 4 B—Q8, K—B1!; 5 B—Kt6 (5 B—R5, K—Q2! as above), K—Kt2! and 6 K—B4 is refuted by 6 .... B—R4; 7 K—Q4, B—K1!, etc. White could only win here if Black made the mistake 1 B—R5ch, K—Kt2?, for then the White King gets to Q6: 2 K—B3, B—Kt7; 3 K—Q4, B—B6; 4 K—K5, B—Kt7; 5 K—Q6, B—B6; 6 P—B6ch, etc.

Again we have the equivalent of the draw in No. 201 here in No. 202c, White: K at QB4, B at QR5, P's at QKt5, QB5; Black: K at QKt2, B at K1, where White can do nothing at all.

RP and KtP which are still on the fifth draw regardless of the positions and colors of the Bishops. Obviously White has winning chances only in the equivalent of No. 201d or No. 201f—No. 202c, White: K at QR4, B at KB3, P's at QR5, QKt5; Black: K at QR2, B at KB7. But here 1 K—Kt3 is answered by 1 .... B—K8!; 2 P—Kt6ch, K—R3!; 3 P—Kt7, K—R2!, or 3 B—K2ch, K×P; or 3 K—R4, B×P.

No. 202

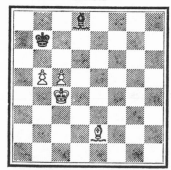

White wins. Draw if the positions of the Bishops are reversed.

No. 203

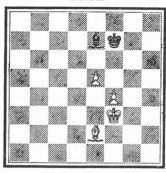

White wins.

(4) One Pawn on the Fifth Rank; the Other on the Fourth.

Ordinarily this merely transposes into the corresponding position with the Pawns on the fifth, but there is one important exception in No. 203. After *1 .... B—B1; 2 B—B4ch, K—K2; 3 K—K4* (but not 3 P—B5?, B—Kt2!=, as in No. 201e), *B—Kt2; 4 K—B5, B—R3; 5 K—Kt4!!* Black is in zugzwang, for if *5 .... B—Kt2; 6 K—Kt5!, K—B1; 7 K—Kt6, B—R1; 8 K—R7, B—Kt2; 9 B—Kt3!!* and the Bishop is lost, while if 5 .... K—K1; 6 P—B5, K—K2; 7 P—B6ch is conclusive.

This possibility occurs uniquely with the KP (or QP) and BP's. E.g., if we take the corresponding position one file to the right (or three files to the left), No. 203a, White: K at K4, B at K2, P's at KB4, KKt5; Black: K at KB2, B at QR4 (with the Pawn at B5 and the White King at KB4 we could have No. 202f), on 1 B—R5ch, K—K2!

still draws, for if 2 P—B5, B—B6 we have No. 202b, while 2 K—B5 or 2 K—K5 are both met by 2 .... B—Q7! There is, however, one special type of position which applies on any file except R and Kt, and that is when the Bishop is blocking the Pawns from the first rank and the White King can manage to attack it without having to advance the Pawns. E.g., No. 203b, White: K at Q6, B at K4, P's at KB4, KKt5; Black: K at KKt2, B at Q1. White to play wins by 1 K—Q7, B—R4; 2 P—B5, B—B6; 3 K—K6 etc. However, this position could only have arisen through an exchange or a blunder. With Black to play, e.g., it can still be held: 1 .... B—R4; 2 K—K6 (2 P—B5, B—Q1), B—Q7; 3 K—K5, B—B8 and White cannot advance. With a RP, even this advantage is inconclusive. E.g., No. 203c, White: K at Q6, B at K2, P's at QR5, QKt4; Black: K at QR2, B at Q1. Draw, for after 1 K—Q7, B—R5; 2 P—Kt5, B—K8! (but not 2 .... B—B7; 3 K—B6+); 3 P—Kt6ch, K—Kt2; 4 B—B3ch, K—R3! etc., one Pawn is lost.

(5) *Both Pawns on the Fourth Rank.*

Here almost all positions are drawn, since Black has time to set up an adequate defense against White Pawns on the fifth. In No. 204 (Henneberger, 1916) we have the unusual possibility of a Bishop sacrifice but Black can stop the Pawns in time. *1 B—K4ch, K×B; 2 K—B4, B—B5!; 3 K—B5, B—K6ch; 4 K—B6, K—Q5; 5 P—Kt5* (or 5 P—R5, K—B5; 6 P—Kt5, K—Kt5; 7 P—R6, K—R4), *K— B5; 6 P—Kt6, K—Kt5; 7 P—Kt7, B—R2.* Or here 3 P—R5, B—K6! (but not 3 .... B—Q7; when 4 K—B5 wins, for if 4 .... B—K6ch; 5 K—B6, B—Q7; 6 P—R6!); 4 P—Kt5, K—K4; 5 P—Kt6, K—Q3; 6 K—Kt5, K—Q2; 7 K—R6, K—B3; 8 K—R7, B—B7 and the Pawns are pinned.

No. 204

Draw.

With a KtP and BP, any reasonable position draws for Black. If his Bishop is on White (Q-side) or Black (K-side) we get No. 204a, White: K at QB3, B at K3, P's at QKt4, QB4; Black: K at QB3, B at K3. 1 P—Kt5ch, K—Kt2; 2 K —Q4, B—B2; 3 K—B5, B—R4; 4 K—Q6, B—K7; or 4 K—Kt4, B —K1 but even the clumsy 3 .... B—K1 draws here after 4 K—Q6, K—B1!; 5 K—K7, B—R4; 6 P— B5, B—K7; 7 P—Kt6, K—Kt2; 8 K—Q6, B—B6. If his Bishop is on

Black (Q-side) or White (K-side) Black must prevent the advance to the fifth to be able to draw (Vide No. 202). Consequently we get a situation similar to that in No. 201: if the Bishop can attack one Pawn and prevent the advance of the other, a draw results; if not he loses. E.g., No. 204b, White: K at QKt3, P's at QKt4, QB4, B at K2; Black: K at QKt3, B at KB7. White wins. 1 B—R5!, B—Kt8 (1 .... B—Kt6; 2 P—B5ch, K—B3; 3 K—B4—No. 202); 2 B—K8, B—B7; 3 K—B2, B—Kt8 (if 3 .... B—K8; 4 P—B5ch, K—B2; 5 K—Kt3! but not 5 P—Kt5?, B—B7; 6 P—Kt6ch, K—Kt2=); 4 K—Q3, B—B7; 5 K—K4, B—K8 (or 5 .... B—Kt8; 6 K—Q5); 6 P—B5ch, K—B2 (6 .... K—R3 is no better; the same continuation is conclusive); 7 P—Kt5, B—R4; 8 K—Q5, K—Kt2; 9 K—Q6, B—B2ch; 10 K—Q7, B—R4; 11 B—R5, B—B2; 12 B—B3ch, K—Kt1; 13 K—B6! and wins. But again No. 204c, Black Bishop at KB1, other pieces as in No. 204b is a clear draw.

With BP and QP much the same results ensue. With a Black Bishop (White Bishop if KP and BP) any reasonable square draws, e.g., No. 204d, White: K at QB3, B at QR4, P's at QB4, Q4; Black: K at QB2, B at KKt8. Draw. After 1 P—B5, B—B7; 2 K—B4, Black has time for 2 .... B—R5; 3 P—Q5, B—K2. And again even so favorable a variation as 3 K—Q5, B—K2; 4 K—K6, K—Q1! (but not now 4 .... B—B1?; 5 K—B7, B—R3; 6 P—Q5 wins) leads to nothing, e.g., 5 B—Kt5, B—B1; 6 K—B7, B—R3; 7 P—Q5, B—K6; 8 P—B6, B—B5 etc. Where White's Bishop is on Black squares, again the position of the Black Bishop is conclusive. Thus No. 204e, White: K at QB3, B at QR3, P's at QB4, Q4; Black: K at QB3, B at KB2, is a draw, but No. 204f, Black Bishop at KKt7, other pieces as in No. 204e, is a win for white.

With center Pawns the results are still the same. When White has a Black Bishop, the game is always a draw. No. 204g (Tarrasch) White: K at K3, B at QB1, P's at Q4, K4; Black: K at Q3, B at QB7. 1 .... B—Q8!; 2 B—R3ch, K—Q2; 3 P—Q5, B—R4; 4 K—B4, B—Kt3; 5 K—K5, B—R2; 6 K—Q4, B—Kt3; 7 P—K5, B—B2 etc. But when White has a White Bishop he wins if Black's Bishop is at KR7, draws if it is at KR1. E.g., No. 204h, White: K at Q3, B at QKt3, P's at Q4, K4; Black: K at Q3, B at KR7. White wins by K—K2—B3—Kt4—B5 and again the attempt .... B—Kt8 is refuted by P—K5ch and K—Q3 or K—K4, or P—Q5, depending on circumstances.

(6) *Pawns on the Second (or Third) Ranks.*

It seems self-evident that such positions must be drawn, since Black has so much time at his disposal to effect one of the adequate defenses

No. 205

White wins.

enumerated above. This is in fact the case, but nevertheless there is still one exception. No. 204i (Berger, 1889), White: K at KKt4, B at Q3, P's at K2, KB2; Black: K at KB2, B at KKt2. White wins. 1 P—B4, B—B1; (there is nothing better: Black must mark time. As we have seen, he can only hope to stop the Pawns by keeping his Bishop in the long diagonal); 2 P —K4, B—Kt2; 3 P—K5, K—K3; 4 B—B4ch, K—K2; 5 K—Kt5 and we have No. 203. With the Black Bishop at Q3 in No. 204i the game is an easy draw. E.g., 1 P—B4, K—B3; 2 P—K4, B—Kt1, etc.

We can sum up in five general rules:

Bishop and two connected passed Pawns against a Bishop of the opposite color:

1. Always win when both Pawns are on the sixth rank (except for RP and B of the wrong color);
2. Win in many positions when both Pawns are on the fifth rank; in some cases regardless of the placement of the opponent's Bishop; in others only when the Bishop cannot attack one Pawn and prevent the advance of the other at the same time. RP always draws;
3. Win only in a number of special cases when both Pawns are on the fourth rank;
4. Win only in a few problem positions when the Pawns are still on the second rank;
5. KBP and KP with a White Bishop and QBP and QP with a Black Bishop offer the most winning chances.

In the above we have always been thinking only of those positions where the Black King is in front of the Pawns (except for No. 204). If the King is behind the Pawns and White's King is supporting them the Bishop cannot hold the position. Thus in No. 205 White concludes with *1 P—R7, B×P; 2 K×B, K—any; 3 P—Kt6* etc. If the King is near the Pawns, but not in front of them the result can only be determined by considering the position which arises when the Black King finally does manage to blockade the Pawns. In general we find that White wins if his Pawns are on the fourth rank or beyond, provided he has at least one center Pawn. E.g., if we move all the pieces in No. 204 one file to the right, the position is still tenable for Black. No. 205a, White: K at Q3, B at K3, P's at QKt4, QB4; Black: K at K4,

B at K3. 1 P—Kt5, K—Q3!; 2 P—B5ch, K—B2; 3 B—B4ch, K—
Kt2 and 4 P—B6ch is refuted by .... K—Kt3, when the KtP cannot
be defended. The sacrifice 1 B—B4ch is met in exactly the same way
as that in No. 204: 1 .... K×B; 2 K—Q4, B—Kt5!; 3 P—Kt5, B—
B6! (3 .... B—K7; 3 K—Q5! again loses); 4 K—B5 (or 4 P—B5,
B—K7; 5 P—Kt6, B—B6), K—K4, etc.=. But if we go one more
file to the right, No. 205b, White: K at K3, B at KB3, P's at QB4,
Q4; Black: K at KB4, B at KB3, White wins: 1 P—B5, B—R5;
2 B—B6!!, K—K3; 3 K—K4, B—B7 (or 3 .... B—Kt6; 4 P—Q5ch,
K—K2; 5 B—R4, transposing into No. 201f); 4 B—R4! (not 4 P—
Q5ch??, K—B2!!=), B—Kt8 (4 .... K—K2; 5 K—Q5); 5 K—Q3,
K—Q4; 6 B—Kt3ch, K—B3; 7 K—B4 and again we have No. 201f.

c) *Disconnected Passed Pawns.*

Here there is a general rule which is applicable to all cases: If the
Pawns are two or more files apart, they win; if they are only one file
apart they draw. The reason is simple: if the Pawns are far apart, the
Bishop must blockade one, while the King stops the other, so that the
White King can support the Pawn held by the Bishop and win that
piece. But if the Pawns are close together the Black King can cover the
advance of both. Thus in No. 206 White wins by *1 B—B3, B—R5;
2 K—K6, K—Q1; 3 P—B6, B—Kt4; 4 P—B7, B—R3; 5 K—B6, B—
B1; 6 K—Kt6, K—K2; 7 K—R7!, K—Q1; 8 K—Kt8, K—K2; 9 P—
B7* and one Pawn will queen.

A RP and B of the wrong color, of course, are an exception to this
rule, since the Bishop can be sacrificed for the other Pawn, when RP+
B draw. E.g., No. 206a, White: K at QKt5, P's at QR5, KB6, B at
K3; Black: K at QR1, B at Q4. Draw, since the Black Bishop stops
the KBP and the Black King takes
care of the KRP.

Again, No. 206b, White Pawn at
K5, other pieces as in No. 206, is
a draw, because in the similar variation, 1 B—B3, B—R5; 2 K—K6,
B—Kt4; 3 K—B7, B—R5; 4 P—K6
Black has the defense 4 .... K—
Q1. White can then win the Bishop
with 5 P—K7ch, B×P; 6 P—
B7ch, but not the game. However,
this fact is in itself of some significance because it shows that when
there are more Pawns on the board,
two such disconnected Pawns as
in No. 206a are sufficient.

No. 206

White wins. Draw with White Pawn
on King file.

It is now quite clear that three passed Pawns will always win, but again there is one exception to be noted. No. 206c, White: K at QR1, B at K5; Black: K at Q6, P's at QR7, QKt6, QB5, B at K3. Draw, for if 1 .... P—B6; 2 B×P! and if 1 .... K—B7; 2 B—R8, B—B4; 3 B—Kt7 etc. Any Pawn advance is immediately refuted by a Bishop sacrifice.

3. BOTH SIDES HAVE PAWNS

One Pawn ahead or a positional superiority which is decisive in other endings is as a rule insufficient here because White can only attack the enemy Pawns with his King. *In general it is necessary to have effective threats on both sides of the board in order to be able to win.*

a) *Positions Where the Defender Can Draw Despite Material or Positional Inferiority.*

This is, as we have just pointed out, the case which most frequently occurs. The drawing method always consists of blockading the enemy's dangerous Pawns with the King and defending one's own Pawn with the Bishop at a distance. No. 207 (Vidmar-Spielmann, St. Petersburg, 1909) is typical of many others. Spielmann tried *1 ....* *B—R6* (to block the K-side Pawns and get some counterplay there), when White could have drawn most simply by *2 K—Q4, P—KKt4; 3 K—B4, B—Q2; 4 P—R4, P×P* (or 4 .... P—Kt5; 5 B—Q6 and the Bishop can hold the two Pawns); *5 P×P, K—K3; 6 K—Kt4* and White can give up the QBP, and still draw the game, since the Q-side Pawns are blocked. Even if White were careless and allowed Black the most favorable position on the King's side, e.g., 2 K—Q4, B—Q2; 3 K—B4, P—KKt4; 4 K—Kt4, K—K3; 5 P—B4, K—B4; 5 B—K7, P—Kt5; 6 B—R4, K—K5; 7 P—B5, K—B6; 8 B—Q8, K—Kt7, thus losing a Pawn, this superiority would be inconclusive. For after 9 B—R4, K×P; 10 K—R3, K—Kt7 (Black can obviously do nothing on the K-side); 11 K—Kt4, K—B6; 12 K—R3, K—K7; 13 K—Kt4, K—Q6; 14 B—B6, K—B7; 15 B—R4!, K—Kt7; 16 B—B6ch, K—R7; 17 B—R4, P—R6; 18 B—B6, B—K1; 19 B—R4, K—Kt7; 20 B—B6ch and still no progress is possible. Black could win this ending only if he

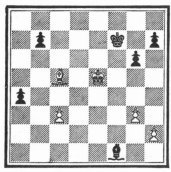

No. 207

Draw.

were allowed to secure a passed Pawn on the King's side. E.g., in the
above variation 12 K—R3, K—K5; 13 B—K7?, K—Q5; 14 B—Q6?,
P—R4; 15 K—Kt4?, P—R5!; 16 P×P, B—K1!; 17 P—R5, B×P;
18 K×P, B—K1ch; 19 K—Kt4, K—K6; 20 K—B3, K—B7 and wins
White's Bishop. Why it is essential to blockade the Black QRP with
the King rather than with the Bishop is seen in the game continuation:
1 .... B—R6; 2 B—R3?, P—Kt4; 3 B—Kt4?, K—Kt3; 4 P—B4,
K—R4; 5 K—B6? (5 K—Q4 was still good enough), K—Kt5; 6 B—
R3, B—Kt7; 7 B—Q6, B—B8; 8 K—Kt7, K—B4!; 9 P—B5 (9 K×P,
B×P and Black will have two active passed Pawns against White's
one; again if the positions of the King and Bishop were interchanged—
K at QKt4, B at KKt7—White could draw), P—R6!; 10 P—B6,
P—R7!; 11 P—Kt4ch, K—K5; 12 B—K5, P×P; 13 B—R1, P—B4;
14 K×P, P—B5; 15 K—Kt6, K—Q6; 16 K×P, P—B6 and White
resigned.

Examples of such positions where the inferior side draws by blockading one wing with his King and defending the other with his Bishop
are legion. The drawing method then consists of two steps: forcing
as many enemy Pawns as possible off the color of one's Bishop in order
to increase the effectiveness of the Bishop and augment the mobility of
the King, and then blockading the side where there is a passed Pawn
or potential passed Pawn with one's King, while the wing where there
is an even number of Pawns is held by the Bishop. A few examples
from tournament practice will further illustrate this point.

No. 207a (Koenig-Landau, Birmingham, 1939), White: K at Q1,
B at KKt2, P's at QR3, QKt2, KKt3, KR2; Black: K at Q3, B at
KB7, P's at QR2, QKt3, K4, KB4, KR3. After 1 B—R3, K—K3;
2 K—K2, B—Q5; 3 P—Kt3, K—B3 (if 3 .... B—Kt8; 4 K—B1!,
B×P?; 5 K—Kt2); 4 P—KKt4, B—Kt8; 5 P×P, B×P; 6 K—B3,
B—Kt8; 7 K—K4, B—B4; 8 P—R4, B—B1; 9 B—B1, B—Kt2;
10 B—K2, K—Kt4; 11 B—Q3, P—R4; 12 B—B1, P—R5; 13 B—R3,
K—B3; 14 B—Kt4 etc. A draw was soon agreed to, since Black's
King cannot get through. Or, a case where the superior side has a
RP and B of the wrong color, No. 207b, Maroczy-Pillsbury, Munich,
1900: White: K at K4, B at QB3, P's at K5, KB5; Black: K at KKt4,
B at QB5, P's at QR5, QR6, QB4, KB2. Draw after 1 P—K6!, P×P;
2 P×P, B×P; 3 K—K5, B—Kt6; 4 K—Q6, P—B5; 5 K—B5, K—
B5; 6 K—Kt4, P—R7; 7 K—R3, K—K6; 8 K—Kt2, K—Q6; 9 K—
R1!!

Once an effective blockade of the Pawns by the King is established,
two connected passed Pawns are not enough to win. In fact, there
is one special case where three connected passed Pawns do not win.
But two blockaded Pawns draw even when there are Pawns on the
other side of the board, while three win.

b) Positions Where Material (or Positional) Advantage Is Decisive.

Despite the common impression to that effect, it is by no means true that Bishops of opposite colors always draw. In a large number of cases one Pawn ahead is a sufficient advantage, while it sometimes even happens that materially even positions are untenable just because the Bishop is of the wrong color. Once more in addition to the general rule we must make certain necessary distinctions. First of all we shall consider only those positions where the material is even or where one side is at most a Pawn ahead.

We have already seen that there must be significant threats on *both* sides of the board if the superior side is to have any winning chances. In addition, it is evident that when one side has two connected passed Pawns, unblockaded, his opponent will have to give up his Bishop to stop them. Then again, it was shown in the discussion of endings with Bishops of the same color that it is a severe handicap to have all one's Pawns on the same color as the Bishop, since that piece is left without any mobility. Such a situation here likewise opens the road for the entrance of the White King.

We can then distinguish five cases in which an ending with Bishops of opposite colors can be won with an advantage of one Pawn or a superior position. In all except the last it is essential to have Pawns on both sides of the board. 1. The King is better placed. 2. The passed Pawns are qualitatively superior (two passed Pawns against one). 3. There is one passed Pawn and sufficient play on the other wing. 4. The Pawns are better placed (all the defender's Pawns are) on the same color as his Bishop and the attacker has the initiative. 5. Special combinations.

(1) BETTER KING POSITION

This usually occurs as a result of previous exchanges. E.g., in No. 208 (Euwe-Fine, AVRO, 1938) the Rooks have just come off. Black wins by playing his King to the Q-side. *1 .... B—Q3* (to prevent P—QKt4 and P—B5 or P—Kt5, when White might be able to defend his Pawns at a distance); *2 B—B2, K—K4; 3 B—Q3, P—R4; 4 K—Kt2, B—B4; 5 B—B2, P—B5* (else this Pawn will be lost when Black's King goes to Q5); *6 B—Kt6, K—Q5; 7 B—B5, K—B6; 8 B—B8, K—Kt7* and White resigned, for after *9 B×P, K×P; 10 B×P, K×P* the QRP decides.

It is the King position which is usually the decisive factor in these endings. To keep one's own King mobile and to prevent the opponent's King from supporting his Pawn majority is often worth a Pawn; in many cases a Pawn sacrifice is required to make sure that the enemy King does not occupy a dominating position. E.g., No. 208a (Pinkus-Fine, New York, 1940), White: K at KB2, B at K3, P's at QR2, QKt2, K5, KB4, KKt2, KR2; Black: K at KB4, B at K5, P's at QKt5, QB2, Q4, KB2, KKt2, KR5. Black to play. Black stands better, but his slight superiority will disappear into thin air unless he can get his King to K5. Accordingly he tries 1 .... B—Kt8 but after 2 K—B3!!! the best he can do is win a worthless Pawn. If White instead makes a routine move such as 2 P—QR3?, P×P; 3 P×P, K—K5 is decisive, e.g., 4 P—R4, P—Q5; 5 B—Q2, P—QB4; 6 P—R5, B—Q6; 7 P—Kt3, P×Pch; 8 P×P, B—R3; 9 P—Kt4, P—B5; 10 K—K1, P—B6; 11 B—B1, P—Q6 etc. But the ingenious

No. 208   No. 209

Black wins.   White to play; Black wins.

2 K—B3 drew: 2 .... B×P; 3 P—Kt4ch, P×P e.p.; 4 P×P, B—Kt6; 5 P—Kt4ch, K—K3; 6 B—B5, B—Q8ch; 7 K—K3!, P—Kt6; 8 P—Kt5, K—B4; 9 B—R7, P—Kt3; 10 B—B5 and the Pawn is worthless because the Black squares are effectively blocked. After the attempt 10 .... K—Kt5; 11 B—R7, B—B7; 12 B—B5, B—B4; 13 B—R7, K—Kt6; 14 B—Q4, K—Kt7; 15 B—R7, B—K3; 16 B—Q4, K—B8; 17 K—Q2! a draw was agreed to.

(2) BETTER PLACEMENT OF PASSED PAWNS

This and a superior King position are the most common reasons for winning finales with opposite Bishops. Where White has two connected passed Pawns against one, the Bishop can both hold the enemy Pawn and support the advance of its own. E.g., in No. 209 (Olland-

Pillsbury, Hanover, 1902) the continuation was *1 P—B4, K—Kt3;
2 P—R4, K×P; 3 B—R3, B—R7!* (to get the White King away from
K3); *4 K—B2, P—R4; 5 B—B1, B—B5; 6 B—R3* (White can do
nothing), *B—B8; 7 P—Q5, P×P; 8 P×P, B—R6; 9 B—B1, B—B4ch;
10 K—K1, P—B5; 11 B—B4, P—Kt3; 12 K—Q2, P—B6; 13 P—Q6*
(else P—K6ch—K7), *B×P; 14 K—K3, K—B4; 15 K—B2, K—B5;
16 B—Kt5, P—K6ch* and White resigned, for the best he can do is
give up his Bishop for the two Pawns.

From the discussion of B+2P vs. B it is clear that in most cases
the presence of a Black passed Pawn there would not change the result.
E.g., if we add a Pawn at Q7 in No. 200, giving us No. 209a, White:
K at KB5, B at K2, P's at K6, KB6; Black: K at Q1, B at QKt5, P at
Q7 White still wins. *1 .... K—K1; 2 B—Kt5ch, K—B1; 3 B—R4,
B—R6; 4 K—K4, B—Kt5; 5 K—Q5, B—R6; 6 K—B6, B—Kt5;
7 K—Q7,* exactly as in No. 200. The only time the extra Pawn makes
a difference is when the Bishop must get off the right diagonal to
block it. E.g., in No. 201, if Black had his Bishop at QKt5 he would
lose, but if he had his Bishop at QKt5 and a Pawn at QR5 he would
draw because the White Bishop must desert the diagonal KR3—QB8.
E.g., No. 209b, White: K at Q4, B at KKt4, P's at Q5, K5; Black:
K at K2, B at QKt5, P at QR5. Draw. For if *1 K—B4, P—R6;
2 K—Kt3, B—B4!; 3 B—B5, B—Kt5; 4 B—Kt1, B—R4!; 5 K×P*
(5 *P—Q6ch, K—K3=*), *B—B2* and we have No. 201; while if *1
B—Q1, P—R6; 2 B—Kt3, K—Q2!; 3 K—B4, B—K2; 4 K—Kt5,
K—B2* or *3 K—Q4, B—B1; 4 K—K4, B—B4; 5 K—B5, K—K2,*
or *3 K—Q4, B—B1; 4 B—R4ch, K—B2* and the White Bishop has
to go right back.

Two connected passed Pawns may at times even win without the
Pawn advantage, e.g., if the enemy Pawns are blocked or doubled.
Thus No. 209c (from a game in the Chess Tournament, 1851) White:
K at K2, B at Q3, P's at QR4, KB2, KB3; Black: K at Q5, B at KB5,
P's at QR3, QKt2, QB4. Black to play can win by *1 .... P—B5;
2 B—B5, P—Kt4; 3 P×P* (or 3 *P—R5, P—Kt5; 4 B—B8, P—Kt6!;
5 K—Q1, P—B6!), P×P· 4 K—Q1, K—B6; 5 B—Q7, P—Kt5;
6 B—K6, P—Kt6; 7 B—B7, K—Kt5; 8 B—K6, P—B6* etc., as in No.
200. In short, one must not confuse the physical fact of the presence
of a piece of wood shaped in the Staunton pattern with the chessic
fact of the presence of a Pawn—in chess a piece or Pawn which
cannot move is as bad as no piece at all, sometimes even worse.

Examples of where two such connected passed Pawns win against
one can be multiplied indefinitely; we shall quote one more which is
particularly instructive. In No. 209d (Bogoljuboff-Ed. Lasker, New
York, 1924) White first blocks the Black Pawn majority, then exploits

his own. White: K at KKt1, B at KB4, P's at QR3, Q3, K4, KKt2, KR2; Black: K at K2, B at QKt2, P's at QR2, QKt4, KKt3, KR2, White to play. 1 B—Q2!, K—K3; 2 K—B2, K—Q3; 3 K—K3, K—B4; 4 B—R5, B—B1; 5 B—Q8, B—Q2; 6 B—R5 (6 B—K7ch followed by P—Q4 is simpler), P—Kt4; 7 B—B3, P—KR4 (or 7 .... P—QR3; 8 B—B6, P—KKt5; 9 B—K7ch, K—B3; 10 P—Q4 and P—Q5 etc.); 8 B—Q4ch, K—Q3; 9 B×P, P—R5; 10 B—Q4, K—K3; 11 B—B3, K—B2; 12 P—Q4, K—Kt3; 13 P—Q5, B—B1; 14 B—R5, B—Q2; 15 B—Q8, P—R6; 16 P×P, B×P; 17 K—Q4, B—Q2; 18 P—K5, K—B4; 19 P—K6, B—K1; 20 B×P Resigns.

It might be expected that disconnected passed Pawns would win more easily than connected ones with a number of Pawns on the board, just as they do in B+2P vs. B, but this is not the case because the extra Pawns complicate the problem of entry for the White King. Thus in No. 210 (Berger-Mackenzie, Frankfurt, 1887) if we removed all the Pawns except White's QP and Black's QKt and KRP the win would be child's play. But as it is Black must evolve some rather complicated manoeuvring to score. The game continuation was 1 .... K—B3!; 2 B—Kt8, P—QR3; 3 B—B7, P—QKt4; 4 K—B2, K—K3; 5 P—Kt3, K—Q4; 6 K—K3, P—KR4; 7 P—R4, B—Q8; 8 B—Q8, K—B5; 9 B—R5, B—B7; 10 K—Q2, B—B4; 11 K—B1, K—Q6; 12 K—Kt2, B—K3; 13 K—R3, P—B3; 14 K—Kt4, P—Kt4; 15 P×P, P×P; 16 B—Q8, P—Kt5 and White drew. Instead, as Berger demonstrated, *1 .... B—Kt6!* would have won, with the following main variations:

a) *2 B—Kt8, P—QR4!!!; 3 B—B7, P—R5; 4 B×P, P—R6; 5 P—Q5, B×P* (but not 5 .... B—B5?; 6 P—Q6!!, P—R7; 7 P—Q7, P—R8ch; 8 K—R2=! since both 8 .... Q—R1; 9 P—Q 8=Q and 8 .... Q×P; 9 P —Q8=Q are inadequate); *6 B—Q4ch, P—B3; 7 P—B4, B×BP; 8 K—B2, K—B2; 9 K—K3, K—K3; 10 P—Kt3, P—Kt4!; 11 P—R4, P×P; 12 P×P, P—B4* and the passed Pawns on both sides of the board decide.

b) *2 B—B7, P—KKt4!; 3 K—B2, P—B4; 4 P—Kt3, B—Q4; 5 B—Q8, K—Kt3; 6 B—B7, P—KR4; 7 K—K3, P—Kt4; 8 B—Q8, P—R3; 9 B*

No. 210

Black to play wins.

—*B7* (or 9 K—B2, P—B5 followed by 10 .... K—B4), *B—Kt7; 10 P—R4, P—B5ch; 11 P×P, P×RP; 12 K —B2* (else 12 .... P—R6 forces 13 P—B5ch), *B—K5; 13 B—Q8* (or 13 P—B5ch; there is nothing really adequate), *P—R6; 14 K—Kt3, B—B4; 15 P—Q5, K—B2; 16 B—B7, K—K2; 17 P—Q6ch* (17 K—R2, K—Q2; 18 B—K5, P—R4 etc.), *K—K3; 18 K—R2, K—Q4; 19 K—Kt3, K—B5; 20 B—R5, K—Kt6; 21 K—R2, K—R5; 22 B—B7, P—R4; 23 B—Kt6, P—Kt5* and wins the Bishop.

c) *2 K—B2, P—QR4; 3 B—Q6, P—QKt4; 4 P—Kt3, B—Q4; 5 K—K3, P—Kt4; 6 K—B2, P—B4; 7 K—K3, K—B3; 8 B— K5ch, K—K3; 9 B—Kt7, P—R5; 10 B—B8, P—R4; 11 B—R3, P—R5; 12 P×P, P—B5ch; 13 K—B2, P×P* followed by K—B4—K5—Q6 etc., for if 14 B—Kt4, K—B4; 15 B—K7, K—K5; 16 B×P, P—R6 the Pawn queens.

d) *2 P—R4, P—QR4; 3 B—Q6, P—R5; 4 K—B2, P—R3; 5 K— K3, B—Q4; 6 P—Kt4* (6 P—Kt3, P—Kt4), *P—B4; 7 P×P, P×P; 8 K—B4, K—B3; 9 B—Kt4, K—K3; 10 B—B8, B—B5!; 11 B—Kt4, P—Kt4; 12 B—B8, P—R4; 13 B—Kt4, B—K7; 14 K—K3, B—Kt5; 15 K—Q3, K—Q4; 16 B—B8, P—B5* and the Bishop will again have to be sacrificed for one of the passed Pawns.

Again where there are fewer Pawns the superior side has much less trouble. E.g., No. 210a (V.d. Lasa-v. Bilguer, 1842) White: K at KKt2, B at Q3, P's at QR5, KB2, KR2; Black: K at KKt2, B at QKt5, P's at Q3, KB3. The win is obvious after 1 P—R6, B—B4; 2 P—B4, K—R3; 3 K—B3, K—R4; 4 K—K4, K—Kt5; 5 P—B5, K—Kt4 (or 5 .... K—R6; 6 K—Q5); 6 K—Q5, K—R3; 7 K—K6!, K—Kt2; 8 P—R3! and Black must sacrifice a Pawn, which deprives him of his only counterchance.

The essential point in all such endings is that two passed Pawns must be set up in order to win. For this reason the inferior side should try to avoid any unbalance in the Pawn structure and any weakness which might create any such unbalance. How such a slight weakness would be exploited may be seen from No. 210b (Rubinstein-Treybal, Carlsbad, 1929), White: K at KKt1, B at Q6, P's at QR2, QB3, K4, KB2, KKt2, KR3; Black: K at KKt1, B at K3, P's at QR3, QB5, KB3, KKt2, KR2. If the Black Pawn were at QKt4 here the game would be a certain draw. But its exposed position at QB5 facilitates the setting up of two passed Pawns. Rubinstein won as follows: 1 .... P—B4; 2 P—B3!, P×P; 3 P×P, B—Q2; 4 K—B2, K—B2; 5 K—K3, K—K3; 6 B—B4 (shuts the Black King out), B—K1; 7 K—Q4, B—Kt4; 8 K—B5 (now White will exchange his QRP for

the Black QBP; but first he wants
to get his KP to K7), K—Q2;
9 P—K5, K—K3; 10 P—Kt4, P—
Kt3; 11 P—R3, P—KR4;12 P×P,
P×P; 13 P—KR4, K—B4; 14 B—
Kt3, K—K3; 15 B—R2, K—K2;
16 K—Q5, K—Q2; 17 P—K6ch, K
—K2; 18 K—K5, K—B1; 19 B—
B4, K—Kt2; 20 B—Kt5, K—Kt3;
21 K—Q5, K—B4; 22 P—K7,
K—Kt3; 23 K—B5, K—B2; 24
K—Kt4 (now the time is ripe),
K—K3; 25 P—R4, B—B3; 26
K×P, B×P; 27 K—B5, K—Q2;
28 P—B4, K—B2; 29 K—Q5, K—
Q2; 30 K—K5, B—Q8; 31 K—B6,

No. 211

White wins.

K—K1; 32 P—B5, P—R4 and Black resigned. The simplest win
now is 33 P—B6, P—R5; 34 P—B7, B—Kt5; 35 B—B1, B—B1;
36 B—R3, B—Q2; 37 K—Kt6, B—Kt5; 38 B—Kt4 and Black is in
zugzwang.

Where the White Bishop cannot both prevent the advance of the
enemy Pawn and support his own he can still usually win once passed
Pawns on both sides of the board have been, or can be, set up which
will cramp the Black pieces. E.g., in No. 211 (Rubinstein-Gruenfeld,
Carlsbad, 1929) the White Bishop cannot support the eventual passed
KKtP effectually, for then Black would advance his QBP and exchange that for the White Pawn. Nevertheless, since the Black
Bishop must guard QR4 and QR2, and the Black King must guard
KKt2, a fairly simple win is possible. First the Black QBP must be
forced to a Black square in order to limit the mobility of the Bishop.
1 K—Kt4, B—K6; 2 B—R4!, P—B4; 3 B—Kt5! (for the game continuation 3 B—Kt3 see A), *K—Kt2; 4 P—R4, B—Q7; 5 P—KR5!,
P×Pch; 6 K×P, B—R4* (or 6 .... K—B2; 7 K—Kt4, K—K3;
8 B—B4ch, and White's King still gets to KB5); *7 K—Kt4, K—Kt3;
8 B—K8ch, K—Kt2; 9 K—B5, P—B5; 10 B—Kt5, P—B6; 11 B—Q3,
B—B2; 12 B—B2, K—B2; 13 B—Q1!* and Black is in zugzwang:
13 .... K—Kt2 (if 13 .... B—R4; 14 K×P, K—Kt3; 15 K—Q6,
K×P; 16 P—K5, B—Kt5ch; 17 K—Q7, K—B4; 18 P—K6, K—B3;
19 P—R5 and wins); *15 B—Kt3, K—R2; 15 K—B6, B—Q1ch* (now
forced); *16 K×P!, B×P; 17 P—R5, B—K6; 18 P—R6, K—Kt2;
19 K—Q6* and the Bishop cannot hold both Pawns.

A. The continuation chosen by Rubinstein is also quite adequate,
but less direct. (*1 K—·Kt4, B—K6; 2 B—R4, P—B4*); *3 B—Kt3,*

B—Q7; 4 B—B4! (Thus blocking the diagonal KKt1—QR7, so that the Black Bishop may never relax his watch on his QR4), *K—Kt2; 5 P—R4, K—B1; 6 K—B3* (6 P—R5 transposes into the above variation after 6 .... P×Pch; 7 K×P, K—Kt2; 8 B—Kt5), *K—K2* (not 6 .... B—K8?; 7 K—K2! and if 7 .... B×P??; 8 P—R5! queening); *7 K—K2, B—R4; 8 K—Q1* (8 B—Q5 looks better but is not, for after the best reply 8 .... B—Kt5; 9 K—Q3, P—B5ch!! Black draws:

a) 10 B×P, B—K8; 11 B—Q5, B×P!; 12 P—R5, B—B7; 13 K—B4, K—Q3!; 14 K—Kt5, B—K6; 15 P—R6, K—B2=.

b) 10 K×P, B—K8; 11 K—Kt5, B×P; 12 P—R5, B×P; 13 P—R6, B—K6; 14 K—B6, K—B3!; 15 K—Kt7, K—Kt4; 16 P—R7, B×P; 17 K×B, K—B5; 18 K—Kt6 and White just manages to draw.

c) 10 K—K2, P—B6; 11 K—Q3, P—B7!; 12 K×P, B—K8 etc.),
B—Kt5; 9 B—K2, K—Q3; 10 K—B2! (but not 10 .... P—R5? as played, for then P×P; 11 B×P, K—K2; 12 K—B2, P—B5!; 13 B—K2, K—B2!!; 14 B×Pch, K—Kt3=, e.g., 15 K—Kt3, B—K8; 16 B—Q5, K×P; 17 K—B4, K—B3; 18 K—Kt5, K—K2; 19 P—R5, K—Q1; 20 K—Kt6, K—B1; 21 P—R6, B—B7ch; 22 K—B6, K—Kt1 etc.), *B—K8* (or 10 .... P—B5; 11 B×P, or 10 .... K—K2; 11 K—Kt3!, B—K8; 12 P—R5, P×P; 13 B×P followed by K—B4—Kt5); *11 P—KR5, P×P; 12 B×P, K—K2; 13 K—Q3, K—B1; 14 K—B4, B—Kt5; 15 K—Q5, B—B6* (15 .... B—Q7; 16 K×KP, B×P; 17 P—R5, P—B5; 18 K—Q4, B—R5; 19 K×P etc.); *16 K×BP, B—Q7; 17 P—Kt6, K—Kt2; 18 K—Kt5* and the rest is simple.

Again in a similar position with fewer Pawns there would be nothing to it. E.g., No. 211a (Reti-Tartakover, Semmering, 1926), White: K at KB3, B at QB4, P's at QKt3, KKt3, KR2; Black: K at KB1, B at QB4, P's at K6, KR4. 1 K—K4, P—R5 (or 1 .... K—Kt2; 2 P—R3!, B—Q3; 3 P—Kt4, P×P; 4 P×P, B—B4; 5 K—Q5, B—R2; 6 P—Kt4, K—Kt3; 7 P—Kt5, K—Kt4; 8 B—K2 etc.); 2 P—Kt4! (not 2 P×P??, K--Kt2= since the Bishop is of the wrong color), K—K2; 3 K—Q5!, B—R2; 4 P—R3, K—Q2; 5 P—Kt4, B—Kt1; 6 K—K4, B—Q3; 7 P—Kt5. B--B4; 8 K—B4, B—Kt3; 9 P—Kt5 and Black soon resigned.

(3) ONE PASSED PAWN (ACTUAL OR POTENTIAL) AND PLAY ON THE OTHER WING

The classical illustration of this type of superiority is No. 212, Nimzovitch-Capablanca, Riga, 1913. If White's Pawn were at QKt2 instead of QB3 there would be no winning hopes for Black at all. As it is, Capablanca evolved the following magnificent conclusion. *1 P—*

QR4, K—K3!!; 2 B—Kt8, P—QR4 (much better than 2 .... P—QR3; the point will soon be clear); *3 K—K1* (if 3 B—B7, P—Kt4!; 4 P×P, P—R5; 5 P—B4, P—R6; 6 B—R5, P—R7; 7 B—B3, K—Q3! and 8 .... B—K3 and both Pawns go the way of all wood, so that Black is left with passed Pawns on both sides of the board), *K—Q4!; 4 K—Q2* (or 4 B—B7, K—B3!; 5 B×P?, P—Kt3), *B—Q2; 5 B—B7, K—B3!; 6 B—Q8, P—Kt3; 7 P—B4, K—Kt2; 8 K—B3, B×P.* The rest is not difficult. *9 K—Kt2, B—Q2; 10 K—Kt3, B—K3; 11 K—B3, P—R5; 12 K—Q3, K—B3; 13 K—B3, P—Kt5; 14 B—R4, P—R4; 15 B—Kt3, P—R6; 16 K—Kt3, B×Pch!!; 17 K×P* (if 17 K×B, P—R7; 18 B—K5, P—R5; 19 K—Kt3, P—Kt6!; 20 P×P, P—R6! or

No. 212	No. 213
	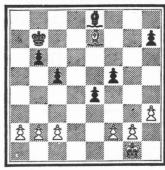
White to play; Black wins.	White to play wins.

20 K×P, P—Kt7! and Black queens), *P—Kt4,* etc. The two Pawns win easily, as in the examples given above.

If White had not started with 1 P—QR4 here, but had tried some other move, e.g., 1 K—K1, Black would still have won, but would not have had such an easy time. E.g., 1 K—K1, B—B4; 2 K—Q2, P—B5! (best; on other moves 3 P—B4 would be very difficult to counter); 3 B—Kt8, P—R3; 4 K—K3 (if White remains passive Black manoeuvres his King to KB6 and advances his K-side Pawns), B×P; 5 K—Q4, P—Kt4; 6 K—B5, K—K3; 7 K—Kt6, K—Q4!; 8 K×P, B—R5; 9 P—QR3 (the threat was P—QKt5), P—R4; 10 B—B7, P—Kt5; 11 B—Kt3, K—K5; 12 K—Kt6, K—Q6!! (to gain a vital tempo); 13 B—K5 (13 B—K1?, P—R5!; 14 K—B5, P—Kt6!; 15 P×P, P—R6), P—R5; 14 K—B5, K—K5; 15 B—Kt8, K—B6; 16 K—Q4, P—Kt6; 17 P×P, P×P!; 18 B—P.7, P—Kt7; 19 K—K5, K—K7 and wins by the one tempo.

(4) PAWNS BETTER PLACED

The only case where this has any real meaning here is when all or most of the Pawns are on the same color as the defender's Bishop. This not only weakens the Pawns and cramps the Bishop but also allows the White King to roam at will all over the board. Because the Pawns are not easily defended the King has to come to the rescue and, as we have seen, this may be fatal because passed Pawns have to be blockaded by a King rather than a Bishop.

Thus in No. 213 (Nimzovitch-Tarrasch, Bad Kissingen, 1928) if Black had his Pawns at KKt2 and KB3 instead of KB4, and K5, he could play 1 .... B—Kt3 and draw without any trouble. But now *1 K—R2* forces Black to shift his King to the other wing. *1 .... P— QB5* (if 1 .... P—KB5; 2 B—Kt5, P—B6; 3 P—KKt4! with potential passed Pawns on both wings); *2 K—Kt3, K—B1; 3 K—B4, K—Q2; 4 B—Kt4, K—K3; 5 B—B3, B—Q2* (5 .... B—Kt3; 6 K—Kt5, K— Q4 costs Black a Pawn after 7 P—KKt3, P—Kt4; 8 K—R6, K—B3; 9 P—R4, K—Q4; 10 P—R5, B—K1; 11 P—Kt3, P×P; 12 BP×P, K—B3; 13 P—R4!, P×P; 14 P×P, K—Kt3; 15 P—R5ch, K—Kt4; 16 K—Kt5!, B—B2; 17 K×P!, etc.—the passed BP decides); *6 P— KKt3, P—Kt4; 7 K—Kt5, K—B2; 8 P—KR4, B—B1; 9 K—R6, K— Kt1; 10 P—Kt3!* (forcing the decisive passed Pawn on the Q-side), *P×P, 11 BP×P, P—B5* (desperation. If 11 .... B—Q2; 12 B—K5! Black is in zugzwang, for if 12 .... B—B1; 13 P—R4 and if 12 .... B—K1; 13 K—Kt5, B—Q2; 14 K—B6, K—B1; 15 B—Q6ch, K—Kt1; 16 K—K7, B—B3; 17 K—K6 winning a Pawn or here 16 .... B—B1; 17 P—R4 and wins); *12 P×P, B—Q2; 13 K—Kt5, K—B2; 14 P—B5, B—B3; 15 K—B4, K—K2; 16 K—K5* and the disconnected Pawns decide. The remaining moves were *16 .... B—K1; 17 K×P, B— B3ch; 18 K—K5, B—K1; 19 K—Q5, B—B2ch; 20 K—B5, B—K1; 21 B—K5, B—Q2; 22 K—Kt6, K—B2; 23 P—B6, B—K1; 24 P—B4, K—K3; 25 K—R6!, K—B2; 26 P—Kt4, K—K3; 27 P—R4!, P×P; 28 P—Kt5* Resigns.

With two connected passed Pawns or two passed Pawns on both sides of the board the win is fairly simple even in blocked positions. We give two illustrations. Disconnected Pawns: No. 213a (V. Bardeleben-Mackenzie, Bradford, 1888), White: K at KB2, B at QR7, P's at QR2, QKt3, Q4, K5, KB4, KKt2, KKt3; Black: K at K3, B at K1, P's at QKt4, QB3, Q4, KB4, KKt2, KR4. Black to play. 1 .... B—Q2; 2 K—K3, B—B1; 3 K—Q3, K—Q2; 4 B—Kt6! (this is important for else the Black King gets to QB2 and impedes the progress of the White King), P—Kt5 (or 4 .... B—R3; 5 K—B3, B—B1; 6 K—Kt4, B—Kt2; 7 K—B5, B—R3; 8 B—R5, B—B1; 9 K—Kt6 and wins. Note how Black's Pawns get in his own way because they are all on White squares); 5 B—B5, B—R3ch; 6 K—B2, B—B8; 7 B×P, B×P; 8 B—K1 (else Black might have counter chances with .... P—Kt4, ... P—B5 and .... P—R5), B—B8; 9 K—B3, B—R3; 10 K—Kt4, P—Kt3; 11 K—B5, B—Q6; 12 K—Kt6, B—B7; 13 P—R4, K—B1 (13 .... B×P transposes into the main variation too); 14 P—R5, B×P; 15 P—R6, K—Kt1; 16 P—K6, P—B4 (desperation); 17 P×P, P—Q5; 18 P—K7 and Black resigns.

In the above example the Pawns on White squares were fatally weak because they limited the mobility of the Bishop and allowed the entrance of the White King. In No. 213b (Cukierman-Monosson, Paris, 1939) against White's connected passed Pawns weak Pawns lose because they are subject to attack by the opponent's King. White: K at KR2, B at K7, P's at QR4, QKt6, K5, KB2, KKt3, KR4; Black: K at KR2, B at QR3, P's at Q5, K3, KB2, KKt3, KR4. White to play won by 1 K—Kt2, P—Q6; 2 B—Kt5, K—Kt2; 3 K—B3, K—B1; 4 K—K4, K—K1; 5 K—Q4, K—Q2; 6 K—B5, P—Q7 (zugzwang. If 6 .... B—Kt2; 7 P—QR5 followed by P—R6 or K—Q6 or K—Kt5, while if 6 .... K—B1; 7 K—Q6, K—Kt2; 8 P—R5 and K—K7 is conclusive); 7 B×P, B—K7; 8 B—R5, B—R3; 9 P—B4, K—B1 (again in zugzwang. On 9 .... B—K7?; 10 P—Kt7 wins, while 9 .... B—Kt2 is answered with 10 K—Kt5); 11 K—B6, B—Kt2ch; 12 K—Kt5! B—K5; 13 B—Kt4, K—Kt2; 14 P—R5, B—Q6ch; 15 K—B5, B—K5; 16 K—Q6, B—B4; 17 K—K7, K—R3; 18 K×P, K—Kt2; 19 K—K7, B—Kt5; 20 K—Q7, B—B4; 21 B—B5, B—Kt5; 22 B—Kt1, B—B4; 23 P—R6ch! (finally breaking the deadlock), K×RP; 24 K—B7, and Black resigned, for if 24 .... B—K5; 25 P—Kt4!, P×P; 26 P—B5!!, KtP×P; 27 P—R5 forces a queen.

We have repeatedly tried to emphasize the point that mobility is the decisive factor in all phases of chess. Nowhere is this more clearly demonstrated than here in endings with Bishop of opposite colors. At times the defender can draw when he is two Pawns down because his opponent's Pawns are blocked. And with weak Pawns the defender can lose when the material is even. E.g., in No. 214 (Rabinovitch-Romanowsky, Leningrad, 1934), after *1 B—Kt3!* Black is lost. (Other moves are inferior because Black could get counter chances by sacrificing his KP) *1 .... K—Kt2* (the game continuation 1 .... P—K4;

No. 214

White to play wins.

2 B×P, K—B2; 3 K—R4, K—K3; 4 K—Kt5, B—K1; 5 K—R6, B—B2; 6 K—Kt7, B—K1; 8 P—Kt5, K—B4; 9 K—B8! is equally hopeless); *2 B—K5ch, K—R2; 3 K—Kt3, B—K1* (or 3 .... K—Kt1; 4 K—B4, K—B1; 5 K—Kt5, K—B2; 6 K—R6! and the Bishop is lost); *4 K—B4, K—Kt3; 5 B—B7, K—B3; 6 B—Q8ch, K—B2; 7 K—K5, B—Q2; 8 K—Q6, B—K1; 9 B—Kt5!, K—B1; 10 K×KP, B—B2ch; 11 K—Q7, B—K1ch; 12 K—Q8, B—B2; 13 B—R6ch, K—Kt1; 14 K—Q7,* and after the capture of the BP the win is routine.

(5) SPECIAL COMBINATIONS

These usually arise when the defender's Bishop must stay at some vulnerable point to protect a vital Pawn. E.g., No. 215 (Horwitz, 1880). *1 B—K1ch, K—Kt4; 2 B—Kt4!* (if 2 P—R4ch?, K—B4; 3 P—Kt4ch, K—B5; 4 K—Kt6, K—Kt6!; 5 P—R5, K—R5!; 6 B—Q2, B—K7!!; 7 K×P, K—Kt4!; 8 P—R6, B—B6ch= because the Pawns are blocked), *P—Kt3; 3 B—K1, K—B4; 4 B—B2ch, K—Q4* (or 4 .... K—Kt4; 5 B—K3!, K—R4; 6 B—Q2ch, K—Kt4; 7 P—R4ch, K—B4; 8 P—Kt4ch, K—B5; 9 K×P, B—B1; 10 P—R5 or 10 P—Kt5 and wins); *5 K×P, B—K7; 6 P—Kt4, K—B5; 7 K—R5, K—Kt6; 8 P—R4, B—B8; 9 P—Kt5, B—K7; 10 P—Kt6, B—B6; 11 K—Kt5, B—K7ch; 12 K—B5, B—R3; 13 P—R5, K—R5; 14 B—K1, B—Kt2; 15 B—Q2, B—R3; 16 K—B6* and wins, for the Bishop is lost and Black's King cannot get back to the corner.

With an advantage of two Pawns the win is relatively simple, unless of course we have one of the positions Nos. 202–205 or something which reduces to them. But the general case presents no real difficulty provided care is taken not to blockade the Pawns. An example of a win with little material left is No. 215a (Klein-Euwe, Hastings, 1938–'39) White: K at QB1, B at QKt8, P at KR2; Black: K at KB2, B at KB6, P's at QKt2, KKt2, KR5. The conclusion was 1 K—Q2, P—KKt4; 2 K—K3, B—B3; 3 B—B7, K—Kt3; 4 B—Kt6, K—R4; 5 K—B2, K—Kt5; 6 B—Q8, P—Kt4; 6 B—K7, B—Kt2; 8 K—K3, B—B1; 9 K—K4, K—R4; 10 K—K3, P—KKt5; 11 K—B2, P—Kt6ch!; 12 P×P, P—R6!; 13 B—Q6, K—Kt5; 14 B—Kt4, B—Kt2; 15 K—Kt1, K×P; 16 resigns.

No. 215

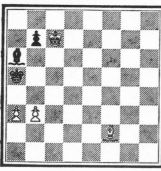

White to play wins.

Chapter V

MINOR PIECE ENDINGS

In this chapter we shall consider all possible combinations of minor pieces, except those with only Knights (Ch. III) and only Bishops (Ch. IV).

I. BISHOP VS. KNIGHT

For many years there has been a theoretical controversy, at times heated, about the respective merits of these two pieces. In the latter part of the last century most experts, apparently intrigued by the romantic and unpredictable powers of the Knight, preferred that piece on the ground that it could get to every square on the board, which a Bishop could not do. Such a great master as Tchigorin openly maintained that to exchange a Bishop for a Knight conferred a definite, even if perhaps intangible advantage, while a player who kept on struggling with two Bishops against two Knights was just being plain pigheaded. Then along came Steinitz who reversed the entire theory: A Bishop is in every respect superior to a Knight. This advantage, he claimed, is so great that when one has a Bishop vs. a Knight, one may be said to have the "minor exchange." This view, systematized by Dr. Tarrasch, was prevalent for a while, but was eventually seen to be much too radical. After the first world war the pendulum swung the other way, when the hypermodern school, with its penchant for exotic chess, showed a marked preference for the Knight. And finally, with the decline of the hypermoderns (from 1930 on) the Bishop again came into his own, but this time the peculiar virtues of the Knight were also given their due.

As far as the endgame is concerned, we may summarize the contemporary views on this topic in four conclusions.

1. The Bishop is in general better than the Knight.
2. Where there is material advantage the values of the two pieces are of minor importance. Nevertheless, a Bishop usually wins more easily than a Knight in such cases.
3. Materially even positions should normally be drawn, but if there

is a slight positional advantage the Bishop will be able to exploit it more effectively.

4. When all or most of the Pawns are on the same color as the Bishop, the Knight is preferable.

We shall now proceed to consider the question more systematically.

A. THE BASIC POSITIONS

1. BISHOP AND PAWN VS. KNIGHT

This is a draw if the Black King is in front of or reasonably near the Pawn, but a win if the King is far away or behind the Pawn. In the simplest case, No. 216a, White: K at Q4, B at KB4, P at K4; Black:

No. 216   No. 217

White to play draws.   White wins.

K at Q2, Kt at KKt5 after 1 B—Kt5 (1 K—Q5, Kt—B3ch and 2 ....
Kt×P), K—K3 White can do nothing to budge the rock at K3. The
Kt cannot be stalemated unless it is on the edge of the board. If the
Black King were at KKt3 in this example, the result would still be a
draw. On the other hand, if the Pawn is far advanced it is essential
for the Black King to be directly in front of it. If it is not, the only
defense is stalemate. E.g., No. 216 (Horwitz, 1880). On *1 Kt—Kt3!!,
B—K4* (or 1 .... B×Kt stalemate); *2 Kt—B1, K—K7; 3 K—Kt2,
B—B5!; 4 K—R1!!, K—B6* (4 .... K×Kt stalemate); *5 Kt—Kt3!,
B—K6; 6 K—R2, B—B5; 7 K—R1* and Black can only wring his
hands in despair because White is so eager to give away his piece. But
if we move the position over one file to the left, No. 216b, White: K
at KKt3, Kt at KKt5; Black: K at K6, B at K5, P at K7 it is clear
that there is no stalemate and that Black's Pawn will queen. If 1 Kt—
B3, then simply B×Kt. But No. 216c, White King at K1, other
pieces as in No. 216b, is a draw.

Where the Black King is behind the Pawn White should in general win if his Pawn is on the sixth rank and if his King can attack the Knight directly. This is due to the fact that by skillful manipulation of his pieces White can force the Knight away from the Pawn. E.g., in No. 217 (Chess Players Chronicle, 1856) the Pawn would be freed by the following manoeuvre. *1 B—B3!* (better than 1 B—K5?, K—Kt3; 2 B—Q4ch, K—Kt4! and White has no good waiting move), *K—Kt3* (if 1 .... K—Q4 or 1 .... K—Kt4, 2 B—Q4!! wins); *2 B—R5ch, K—Kt4; 3 B—Q8, K—B4; 4 B—R4, K—Kt4; 5 B—Kt5, K—B4; 6 B—K3ch, K—Q4; 7 B—Q4!, Kt—Q3; 8 P—B7!* and wins. A similar stratagem is seen in No. 217a (game of Dr. Lasker's), White: K at Q5, B at KB6, P at QB6; Black: K at KB2, Kt at K3. White to play wins. 1 B—K5!, K—K2; 2 B—Kt3! (to answer Kt—Kt4 by B—R4), K—B3 (2 .... K—B2; 3 B—R2!, K—K2; 4 B—K5!, K—B2; 5 K—Q6, etc.); 3 K—Q6, Kt—Q5 (or 3 .... K—B2; 4 B—K5); 4 B—K5ch. But if the Black Knight were at QKt4 in No. 217, the game would be drawn. No. 217b, Black Kt at QKt4, other pieces as in No. 217. 1 B—Kt7, K—Q4; 2 B—R6, K—B4; 3 B—K3ch, K—Q4; 4 B—Kt1, K—K4!; 5 K—B8, K—Q4!; 6 K—Kt7, Kt—Q3ch; 7 K—B7, Kt—K1ch (but not 7 .... Kt—Kt4ch?; 8 K—Kt6, Kt—Q3; 9 P—B7, Kt—B1ch; 10 K—Kt7, Kt—K2; 11 B—B2 and 12 B—R4); 8 K—Kt6 (8 K—Q7, Kt—B3ch), K—Q3; 9 B—R2ch, K—Q4 and White is no nearer his goal. But again if the White King can attack the Knight, the ending is won. No. 217c, White King at QKt7, Black Knight at QKt4, other pieces as in No. 217. 1 B—K5, K—B5; 2 K—Kt6, K—Kt5; 3 B—Kt3, K—B5; 4 B—K1, Kt—Q3; 5 P—B7, K—Q4; 6 B—Kt4, Kt—B1ch; 7 K—Kt7, etc.

The RP wins more easily than any of its colleagues when the King is behind it, chiefly because the Bishop can so often be sacrificed. Thus in No. 218 (Handbuch, 1843) after *1 K—Kt5!* the Pawn cannot be stopped: *1 .... Kt—B7; 2 P—R4, Kt—K5ch* (or 2 .... Kt—Kt5; 3 P—R5 and the Knight must move); *3 K—Kt6, Kt×B; 4 P—R5, Kt—B5; 5 P—R6, Kt—K4ch; 6 K—Kt7, K—B5; 7 P—R7* and Black is one move too late. Or a similar case, No. 218a (from a game Englisch-Wittek, Vienna, 1882), White: K at QKt7, B at Q8, P at QR5; Black: K at QR5, Kt at KR3. White wins. 1 .... Kt—B2;

No. 218

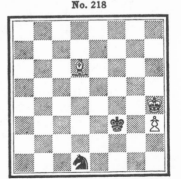

White to play wins.

2 P—R6, Kt—Q3ch (2 .... Kt×Bch; 3 K—Kt6); 3 K—B6, Kt—B1 (3 .... Kt—Kt4; 4 B—K7, Kt—R2ch; 5 K—Kt7, Kt—Kt4; 6 K—Kt6); 4 B—Kt6, K—Kt5; 5 K—Kt7!, Kt—Q3ch; 6 K—B7!, Kt—Kt4ch; 7 K—B6, K—R5; 8 B—B5, K—R4; 9 K—Kt7, K—R5; 10 K—Kt6 and again the Knight must move.

However, when the RP is on the seventh, with the King stalemated, the defender can always draw and sometimes even win. E.g., No. 218b (Richter, 1910) White: K at QR8, P at QR7, B at KKt8; Black: K at QB2, Kt at KR8, White to play just manages to draw: 1 B—B4, Kt—B7; 2 B—Q3!, Kt—Q8; 3 B—B4, Kt—B6; 4 B—Kt3!, Kt—Kt4; 5 B—B4, Kt—Q3; 6 B—R6!, Kt—K1; 7 B—B4, Kt—B3; 8 B—K6!, Kt—K5; 9 B—B4, Kt—B4; 10 B—Kt5!, etc. The Knight can never

No. 219	No. 220

White to play wins.	White to play wins.

get to QKt3. Even where the King is not completely stalemated there are good drawing chances. No. 218c (Schindlbeck, 1911), White: K at K2, Kt at KB1; Black: K at KKt7, B at KB7, P at KR6. Draw. 1 Kt—R2!, B—B4 (1 .... K×Kt; 2 K×B —draw because of the RP); 2 Kt—B3! (but not 2 Kt—B1?, B—Q5!; 3 K—K1, B—B6ch; 4 K—K2, B—Q7!!! and wins), B—Kt5; 3 Kt—R4ch, K—Kt6; 4 Kt—B3, B—B6; 5 K—B1!, K×Kt; 6 K—Kt1=.

Finally, when the Black Knight is stalemated a win is possible even with the King in front of the Pawn. Thus in No. 219 (Calvi, 1847) *1 B—Q5!* is decisive: *1 .... K—K2; 2 K—B5, K—Q2; 3 K—B6, K—K1; 4 P—K6, K—B1; 5 P—K7ch, K—K1; 6 K—K6* (or 6 B—B7ch), *Kt—B3* (or any other Knight move); *7 B×Kt mate.*

2. KNIGHT AND PAWN VS. BISHOP

With the King in front of, or near, the Pawn this too is an elementary draw. The Bishop remains on the diagonal which the Pawn has to cross and it is impossible for the Knight to both block the diagonal and chase the King away.

When the King is not in front of the Pawn there is a win only if the enemy King is far away, except that with a center Pawn a draw is forced. To win the Knight must block the diagonal of the Bishop and allow the Pawn to advance.

The general case with the King near the Pawn may be discussed as a corollary to No. 220 (Kling and Horwitz, 1851). Here the win is achieved by *1 K—K7!, K—R2* (or 1 .... B—R6ch; 2 K—K8, B—B1; 3 P—B7ch, K—Kt2; 4 Kt—Kt6, B—Q3; 5 Kt—K7); *2 P—B7, B—R6ch; 3 K—K8, K—Kt2; 4 Kt—B4, B—Kt5* (if 4 .... B—B4; 5 Kt—Kt6, K—Kt3; 6 Kt—Q5, K—B4; 7 Kt—K7ch); *5 Kt—K3, B—R6; 6 Kt—Q5, B—B1; 7 Kt—K7.*

It is quite obvious however that this example is an exception. E.g., if the Black King were originally in the corner the game would be drawn. No. 220a, Black King at KR1, other pieces as in No. 220. 1 P—B7 (now 1 K—K7 can be answered by 1 .... B×Kt; 2 P—B7, B—Kt2), B—R6; 2 K—Q7, K—Kt2; 3 K—K8, K—B3! and now the White Knight cannot go to K7. And if the Black King is at K1 in the original position (instead of KKt1, KR1) White has no winning prospects at all.

With a RP even this slight winning hope vanishes. No. 220b (Sam Loyd, 1860) White: K at K1, B at QR4; Black: K at KKt7, P at KR6, Kt at KR5. White plays and draws. 1 B—Q7!!, P—R7; 2 B—B6ch, K—Kt8; 3 B—R1!!! (the point to White's first move), K×B (if 3 .... Kt—Kt7ch; 4 K—K2!!, Kt—B5ch; 5 K—K1, etc.); 4 K—B2! =, since the Knight cannot gain a tempo (Vide No. 114). Or No. 220c (Holm, 1911) White: K at Q1, B at QKt6; Black: K at KKt2, Kt at K4, P at KR6. White plays and draws. 1 B—Kt1!,

Kt—B6; 2 B—R2!!, Kt×B; 3 K—K2, K—Kt3 (or 3 .... Kt—Kt5; 4 K—B3); 4 K—B2, Kt—Kt5ch; 5 K—Kt3, P—R7; 6 K—Kt2=, and we again have one of the positions where Kt+P do not win (No. 113).

When the Black King is at a distance from the Pawn the Bishop may be blocked by the Knight and the Pawn will then queen. The general case is No. 221 (Kosek, 1910). The solution is *1 Kt—Q6, B—Kt8; 2 P—B6, B—Kt3; 3 K—K6, B—B2* (the threat was 4 K—Q7

No. 221

White wins.

followed by Kt—B4); *4 K—Q7, B —Kt1; 5 Kt—Kt5, K—Kt7; 6 Kt—B7, K—B6; 7 K—B8, B—R2; 8 Kt—Kt5, B—Kt3* (if 8 .... B—K6; 9 Kt—Q6, B—Kt3; 10 Kt—B4, B—B7; 11 K—Q7, B—Kt6; 12 Kt—Q6); *9 Kt—R3!* (but not 9 K—Kt7?, B—Q1; 10 Kt—R3, K—K5; 11 Kt—B4, K—Q4=), *K—K5; 10 Kt—B4, B—B7; 11 K—Q7, B—Kt6; 12 Kt—Q6ch* and the Pawn can no longer be stopped. Or the similar case with the KtP, No. 221a (Kosek, 1910), White: K at QB5, Kt at Q4, P at QKt5; Black: K at KKt8, B at KKt7. White wins. 1 Kt—B6, B—B8; 2 P—Kt6, B—R3; 3 K—Q6, B—Kt2 (else 4K—B7 and 5 Kt—Kt4); 4 K—B7, B—R1; 5 Kt—R5, K—B7 (5 .... B—B6; 6 Kt—B6); 6 Kt—Kt7!, K—K6; 7 K—Kt8, etc. The difference between this and the similar B+P vs. Kt ending is that here if the defender's King is anywhere near the Pawn (barring certain special stalemate possibilities as in No. 222a) the game is hopelessly drawn, while with B+P vs. Kt there are winning chances as long as the defender's King is not directly in front of the Pawn.

It is evident that White can win only if he can shut the Black Bishop out of either diagonal from which the Pawn can be held. With a center Pawn on the sixth this is not possible, but with one on the seventh it is. Thus No. 222 is a draw, for after *1 K—Q8, B—R5; 2 K—B7, B—K1,* or *1 Kt—B6, K—Q7; 2 Kt—K5, K—K6; 3 Kt—Q7, K—Q5; 4 K—Q8, B—Kt3; 5 Kt—B6* (or 5 Kt—B8, B—B4; 6 K—K7, B—B1!), *B—B4* the Bishop is still covering the vital square. Of course it may happen that as a result of previous exchanges the Knight can block the Bishop. Or again the Black King may be in such a bad position that it facilitates this kind of blockade. Such is the case in a pretty problem by Kling and Horwitz, 1851. No. 222a, White: K at KB7, Kt at KKt1, P at K6; Black: K at KR1, B at KR5. White to play wins. 1 Kt—B3, B—Q1 (forced); 2 Kt—K5!, K—R2 (or 2 .... B—Kt4; 3 Kt—Kt4); 3 Kt—Kt4, K—R1 (3 .... B—R5; 4 Kt—B6ch); 4 Kt—B6! and Black must either capture the Knight or abandon the Pawn at once to its pleasant fate. But note that in the original position Black to play can draw by 1 .... K—R2!; 2 Kt—B3, B—Q1; 3 Kt—K5, K—R3! and with the Bishop free to move wherever he pleases the above winning manoeuvre is out of the question.

On the other hand, with the Pawn on the seventh there is too little leeway for the Bishop. Thus, e.g., No. 222b, White: K at QB7, P at Q7, Kt at Q4; Black: K at KB8, B at KR5. White wins: 1 Kt—B6, K—K7; 2 K—Q6, K—K6; 3 Kt—K7. But, as has been pointed out, if the Black King is near the Pawn this case is likewise a draw. No. 222c, Black King at KB2, other pieces as in No. 222b. Nothing can be done since K7, at which square the Knight blocked the Bishop in No. 222, is now doubly guarded.

With a RP even though the King is relatively near a win may be possible. Thus in an ingenious problem by Horwitz (1885), No. 222d, White: K at QB7, Kt at QKt8, P at QR7; Black: K at QKt5, B at QR1, White wins as follows: 1 K—Kt6!!, K—B5; 2 Kt—R6, K—Q5; 3 Kt—B7, B—Kt7; 4 Kt—K6ch, K—K4; 5 Kt—Q8, B—R1; 6 K—B7, K—Q4!!; 7 Kt—Kt7 (not 7 K—Kt8?, K—Q3!; 8 K×B, K—B2=), K—K3; 8 Kt—R5, K—K2; 9 K—B8, K—K1; 10 Kt—B4!, K—K2; 11 K—Kt8, K—Q1; 12 Kt—R5, K—Q2; 13 Kt—Kt7!, K—B3; 14 K×B, K—B2; 15 Kt—Q6! and the White King gets out of the corner. But if the Black King is favorably placed this is a win or a draw depending on who has the tempo. No. 222e (Horwitz, 1885) White: K at QKt8, P at QR7, Kt at QR5; Black: K at Q1, B at QR1 (this is the position reached in No. 222d after White's twelfth move). White to play can

No. 222	No. 223

Draw. Win if the Bishop is on black squares.   Black wins.

only draw, for after 1 Kt—Kt7ch, (or 1 K×B, K—B2!, but not 1 .... K—B1; 2 Kt—B4, K—B2; 3 Kt—Kt6), K—Q2; 2 K×B, K—B1! the Knight cannot drive the King away from B1—B2. But Black to play loses as in No. 222d.

3. BISHOP AND TWO PAWNS (OR MORE) VS. KNIGHT

Two Pawns in general are a sufficient winning advantage and this case is no exception. The model positions present no difficulties whatsoever—the Pawns are advanced and either queen or cost the defender his piece.

No. 223 (Analysis by W. Ward. From a game in Lancashire, 1915) is one of the most involved wins with two connected passed Pawns, further complicated of course by the fact that the Bishop is of the wrong color. The solution is *1 Kt—B4!* (or 1 Kt—R4!, B—Kt4!; 2 Kt—Kt2, K—K7!), *B—Kt4!* (but not 1 .... K—B6? which would only draw after 2 Kt—Q3, P—Kt7ch; 3 K×P, B—Q3ch; 4 K—Kt1, K—Kt6; 5 Kt—B2!, B—B5; 6 Kt—Kt4!!, K—B6; 7 Kt—K5ch!, etc.); *2 Kt—Q3ch* (again as above if 2 Kt—Kt2, K—K7. Or 2 Kt—R3ch, K—B8; 3 Kt×B, P—Kt7ch; 4 K×P, P—Kt8 = Qch and mates in two), *K—K7; 3 Kt—K5, K—B8!; 4 Kt—B3, P—Kt7ch; 5 K×P, K—B7; 6 Kt—Kt1, B—B5ch*. But if we move this position up two ranks the Knight has more room and the blockade of the Pawns ensures a draw. No. 223a, White: K at KB3, Kt at K4; Black: K at Q6, B at K2, P's at KB5, K4 (we have transferred the position to the center in order to avoid the extra drawing possibility of the RP+B of the wrong color). Draw. For White has eight squares available for his Knight; of these one (KKt3) is made impracticable by the Black Pawn, two are held by the Black King and four by the Black Bishop, but there is still and always will be a residue of one square left to the Knight, so that he will always be able to move to and from K4.

For the sake of completeness we give the model win here when the Pawns are not blocked. No. 223b, White: K at Q3, B at QB3, P's at Q4, K4; Black: K at K3, Kt at QKt3. 1 B—R5, Kt—Q2; 2 P—Q5ch, K—Q3 (or 2 .... K—K4; 3 B—B7ch, or 2 .... K—K2; 3 K—Q4); 3 K—Q4, K—K2; 4 P—K5, K—K1; 5 P—K6, Kt—B3; 6 P—Q6, K—B1; 7 P—Q7, etc.

With two disconnected Pawns White wins just as easily; the idea then is, as usual, to support one Pawn with the Bishop and advance the other with the help of the King. No. 224 (Behting, 1892) presents a number of problems as difficult as any that come up in practical play. The only correct solution is *1 K—K6!!* (the two alternative tries 1 P—R5 and 1 B—R7 are both insufficient:

a) 1 P—R5, Kt—B1; 2 K—K7, K—Kt2; 3 K—K8, Kt—K3!;
   i) 4 B—R7!, Kt—B2ch!; 5 K—K7, Kt—Q4ch; 6 K—Q6, K×P =
   ii) 4 P—R6ch, K—R1!; 5 B—R7, K×B; 6 K—K7, Kt—B5!! =
   iii) 4 P—R6ch, K—R1; 5 K—K7, Kt—B1; 6 B—R7, Kt—Kt3ch!!; 7 K—B6, K×B =
b) 1 B—R7, K×B; 2 P—R5, Kt—K4!!; 3 K×Kt, K—Kt2; 4 K—K6, K—B1! Draw, since both 5 P—R6 and 5 K—B6 are stalemate),

1 .... K—Kt2; 2 P—R5, Kt—B5ch (if 2 .... Kt—B1ch; 3 K—K7, K—R1!; 4 B—R7!, Kt×B; 5 P—R6! and wins); *3 K—Q6!!, K—B1; 4 P—R6, Kt—Kt3; 5 K—K6, Kt—K2; 6 K—K5, Kt—Kt3ch* (if 6 .... Kt×B; 7 P—R7!!! is conclusive); *7 K—B5, Kt—R1; 8 K—B6, Kt×P; 9 P—R7* (not 9 B×Kt?? stalemate), *Kt—R1; 10 B—K6, Kt—B2; 11 K—Kt6, Kt—R1ch; 12 K—R6, K—K2; 13 B—Kt4!, K—B2* (or 13 .... Kt—B2ch; 14 K—Kt7, K—K1; 15 B—R5); *14 B—B3, K—B3; 15 B—R5, K—K2; 16 K—Kt7* and now the Knight may be captured.

Alternative defenses for Black are (after *1 K—K6*);

a) 1 .... Kt—B5ch; 2 K—B5, Kt—Kt3; 3 K—B6, Kt—B1; 4 K—K7, K—Kt2; 5 P—R5, K—R1; 6 B—R7, Kt×B; 7 P—R6.

b) 1 .... Kt—B1ch; 2 K—K7, etc., as in a).

c) 1 .... K—R4; 2 B—R7!, Kt—B1ch; 3 K—B6, K—R3; 4 B—B5, Kt—Kt3; 5 B—K4!, Kt—B1; 6 K—K7, K—Kt2; 7 P—R5, Kt—Q2; 8 P—R6ch, K—R1; 9 B—R7!

The general case with two disconnected passed Pawns is again an elementary win. In a typical position such as No. 224a, White: K at Q4, B at Q3, P's at QKt4, K4; Black: K at Q3, Kt at Q2, a model continuation would be 1 P—Kt5, Kt—K4; 2 B—K2, Kt—Q2; 3 B—Kt4, Kt—K4; 4 B—B5, Kt—B6ch; 5 K—B4, Kt—K4ch; 6 K—Kt4, Kt—Q6ch (6 .... K—B2; 7 K—B5); 7 K—R5, K—B2; 8 P—Kt6ch, K—Kt2; 9 B—K6, Kt—K4; 10 B—Q5ch, K—Kt1; 11 K—Kt5, Kt—Q2; 12 K—B6, Kt—K4ch; 13 K—Q6, Kt—Q6; 14 P—K5 and the Knight has to be sacrificed for the KP.

Black can draw with a Knight against B+2P in one of two cases: 1. blockade; 2. RP+B of the wrong color. Neither of these, however, is foolproof. An example of blockade is seen in No. 223a. A case where the Bishop gets in the way of the Pawns is No. 224b (H. W. Butler, 1889), White: K at QKt5, B at QB7, P's at QB6, Q6; Black: K at K3, Kt at K4. Black to play draws. 1 .... K—Q4; 2 P—Q7, Kt×BP; 3 K—Kt6, Kt—Q1!; 4 B×Kt (or 4 B—Kt3, Kt—B2= as in No. 217b), K—Q3=. With RP+B of the wrong color the game is drawn only if the Knight is in a position to sacrifice itself for the extra Pawn, which in general happens only if the Pawns are connected. For if they are disconnected White can sacrifice the RP to divert the King and then win with the other Pawn as in No. 217 or 218. However, even when they are connected, if the KtP is ahead of the RP a win should be possible. E.g., No. 224c, White: K at KR2, B at K2, P's at KKt3, KR3; Black: K at KKt3, Kt at K4. 1 P—Kt4, Kt—B3 (if 1 .... K—Kt4; 2 K—Kt3, Kt—Kt3; 3 B—Q3, Kt—R5; 4 B—K4!); 2 K—Kt3, Kt—Q5; 3 B—Q3ch, K—B3; 4 P—R4, Kt—K3; 5 B—B4, Kt—B4; 6 K—B4, Kt—Q2; 7 B—Q3, K—Kt2; 8 P—Kt5, Kt—B3!; 9 B—K4, Kt—R4ch; 10 K—Kt4, Kt—B3ch; 11 K—B5, Kt—R4; 12 B—B3, Kt—

No. 224

White wins.

Kt6ch; 13 K—B4, Kt—B8; 14 P—R5, etc. But with the RP too far advanced the sacrifice of the Knight is a serious and often unavoidable drawing threat. No. 224d, White P's at KR4, KKt3, other pieces as in No. 224c is drawn after 1 .... K—R3; 2 K—Kt2, K—Kt2; 3 K —B2, Kt—Kt3!; 4 P—R5 (else .... Kt×P), Kt—K4; 5 K—K3, K—R3; 6 K—B4, Kt—B2; 7 B—B4, Kt—Kt4= (No. 217b).

An example which combines the motifs of blockade and the disadvantage of the RP is No. 224e (Stein, 1789, solution by Walker), White: K at K6, B at QB8, P's at QR6, Q7; Black: K at Q1, Kt at QKt4. Drawn. 1 K—Q5 (if 1 B—Kt7, Kt—B2ch; 2 K—Q6, Kt×P!), Kt—R2; 2 K—Q6, Kt×Bch; 3 K—B6!, Kt—R2ch!; 4 K—Kt7, K×P; 5 K × Kt, K—B2 =.

A doubled Pawn wins unless the defending King is in front of it.

It goes without saying that B+3P vs. Kt is routine, what annotators love to call "simple technique." Nevertheless, even here when the Pawns are blockaded the defender may at times draw. Thus No. 224f (Kling and Horwitz, 1851), White: K at KR2, Kt at K4; Black: K at KB8, B at KKt7, P's at KB6, KKt5, KR6. Draw! 1 Kt—B2!!, P—Kt6ch (or 1 .... K×Kt stalemate); 2 K×P, P—R7; 3 K×P, K×Kt stalemate. Again, a mate with the Kt is not unthinkable either: No. 224g (Horwitz), White: K at QKt3, Kt at QKt4; Black: K at QR8, B at QKt7, P's at QB6, QKt4, QR6. White mates in six: 1 K—B2!, B—B8 (or 1 .... P—R7; 2 Kt—B6, B—R6; 3 Kt—Q4, any; 4 Kt—Kt3 mate); 2 K×B, P—B7; 3 K×P, P—R7; 4 Kt—Q3, P—Kt5; 5 Kt—B1, P—Kt6ch; 6 Kt×P mate.

4. KNIGHT AND TWO PAWNS VS. BISHOP

This too is in general a fairly simple win. The exceptions come only with a blockade.

Sometimes it is necessary to sacrifice one Pawn and win with the other. This is the case in No. 225 (Horwitz, 1885). The solution is *1 Kt—Kt8ch, K—Kt4* (if 1 .... K—R2; 2 P—Kt5); *2 P—R6, B—R1* (or 2 .... K×P; 3 K—Kt6, B—R1; 4 Kt—B6ch, K—B5; 5 Kt—Q8, K—Kt5; 6 Kt—Kt7, K—B5; 7 K—B6!, K—Q5; 8 K—B7, K—Q4; 9 K—Kt8, K—B3; 10 K×B, K—Kt3; 11 Kt—B5); *3 P—R7, B—Kt7* (3 .... K×P; 4 K—Kt6! transposes into No. 222d); *4 Kt—Q7, K×P; 5 K—Kt6, K—B5; 6 Kt—B5, B—R1; 7 Kt—R6,* etc., as in No. 222d.

The general case is illustrated in No. 225a (Lasker-Pillsbury, Paris, 1900), White: K at QR5, Kt at QB7, P's at QR2, QKt3; Black: K at K4, B at Q6. The conclusion was 1 K—Kt4, K—Q3; 2 Kt—Kt5ch, K—B3; 3 P—R4, K—Kt3; 4 Kt—R3, B—K7; 5 Kt—B4ch, K—R3; 6 K—B3, B—Q8; 7 Kt—Kt2, B—R4; 8 P—Kt4, B—K1; 9 K—Kt3,

B—B3; 10 K—B4, B—Q2; 11 K—B5, B—Kt5; 12 Kt—B4, B—Q8;
13 P—Kt5ch, K—R2; 14 P—R5, B—B6; 15 Kt—K5, B—Kt2; 16
Kt—B6ch, K—R1; 17 K—Kt6, B—R3!; 18 Kt—Kt4!, B—Kt2;
19 Kt—R6, B—B6; 20 Kt—B7ch, K—Kt1; 21 P—R6, Resigns.

The blockade is, as we have mentioned, the only drawing weapon at
Black's disposal. It is usually quite effective even though the Kt,
unlike the B, can cover every square. Thus in No. 226 (Fine-Reshevsky, Semmering-Baden, 1937) the win at first blush seems to be a
simple technical problem. But even though the White King can roam
at will all over the board he can never manage to advance his Pawns.
The ending can only be won if White gets his King to KB3 or KR4,

No. 225

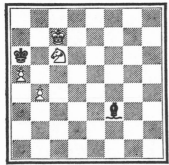

White to play wins.

No. 226

Draw!

but Black is able to prevent this. The concluding moves were *1 ....
B—Kt3; 2 K—Q3* (if 2 K—B1, K—B6!; 3 P—Kt5, B—R4; 4 P—
Kt6, B—B6; 5 P—Kt7, B×P; 6 Kt×B, K—Kt6 and the RP goes),
*B—Q1; 3 K—Q4, B—B3ch; 4 K—Q5, B—R1; 5 K—Q6, B—K4ch;
6 K—K6, B—R8; 7 K—K7, B—Kt7; 8 K—B7, K—Kt4!* and a draw
was agreed to.

That No. 225 is won only because of the favorable position of
White's pieces is clear by comparison with No. 226a (Horwitz, 1880)
where the blockade cannot be broken through. White: K at KR3,
B at K8; Black: K at KB5, Kt at K4, P's at KKt4, KR5. White to
play draws. 1 B—Kt5!, Kt—Kt5! (or 1 .... Kt—B6; 2 B—Q7,
Kt—Q5; 3 B—Kt4, Kt—B4; 4 B—K2. Other alternatives are 1 ....
Kt—Kt3; 2 B—K2, K—K6; 3 B—R6, K—B7; 4 K—Kt4, Kt—K4ch;
5 K×P, K—Kt6; 6 B—B8=. 1 .... P—Kt5ch; 2 K×P, Kt—B6ch;
3 K—R5, P—Kt6; 4 B—B1, K—K6; 5 K—Kt4, K—B7; 6 B—R3,

Kt—Kt8; 7 B—B1! and again Black is at a standstill); 2 B—R6!! (but not 2 B—Q7?, Kt—B7ch; 3 K—Kt2, Kt—Q6 and now

    a) 4 K—R3, K—B6; 5 B—B6ch, K—B7; 6 K—Kt4, Kt—K4ch; 7 K×P, K—Kt6; 8 B—Kt7, Kt—Kt5; 9 K—R5, Kt—K6; 10 B—R1, P—R6; 11 K—Kt5, Kt—Kt7; 12 K—B5, K—B6; 13 K—Kt5, P—R7 followed by K—B7—Kt8 and K×B, as in No. 225.

    b) 4 B—Kt5, K—K6; 5 K—R3, Kt—B7ch; 6 K—R2, P—Kt5; 7 B—Q7, P—Kt6ch; 8 K—Kt2, K—B5; 9 B—B8, P—R6ch; 10 B×P, Kt×B; 11 K×Kt, K—B6, etc.), 2 .... Kt—B7ch; 3 K—Kt2, K—K6; 4 B—B8, Kt—Q6 (4 .... P—Kt5; 5 B×P!, Kt×B; 6 K—R3); 5 K—R3, Kt—B5ch; 6 K—Kt4, P—R6; 7 K×P, P—R7; 8 B—Kt7 with a clear draw.

In the center of the board this type of blockade is just as strong. E.g., No. 226b (Perenny-Loewenthal, 1851), White: K at KKt3, Kt at KR3, P's at KB4, K5; Black: K at K5, B at QB3. Draw. 1 Kt—Kt5ch, K—B4; 2 Kt—B3, B—K1!; 3 Kt—Q4ch, K—K5; 4 Kt—K6, B—Kt4!; 5 K—R4 (5K—Kt4, B—Q2), B—B5=.

With disconnected passed Pawns a blockade cannot be set up, so that exceptions to the general rule that such Pawns win are to be found only in problems. No. 227 (Dr. Neustadtl, 1894) is typical of the winning strategy employed in this kind of ending. *1 Kt—B8* (the simplest: 1 K—B8 is good enough but is more complicated), *K—B4* (if 1 .... K—Kt6; 2 Kt—K6, K×P; 3 Kt—B7, K—B6; 4 K—B8 and we have transposed into No. 221); *2 Kt—K6, B—Kt6; 3 Kt—Q4ch, K—K5; 4 Kt—K2, B—K4; 5 P—B7, B×P; 6 K×B* and the Kt holds the fort until the King gets back. The same idea (sacrifice of one Pawn to deflect the King) is the clue to the solution in No. 227a (Des Guis-Preti, 1849), White: K at Q6, Kt at QB7, P's at QR3, K7;

No. 227

White wins.

Black: K at QR5, B at KB2. White decides as follows: 1 K—K5, B—R4 (if 1 .... K×P; 2 K—B6, B—R4; 3 Kt—Kt5ch, K—Kt5; 4 Kt—Q6, K—B4; 5 Kt—B7); 2 K —B6, K—R4; 3 K—Kt7, K—Kt3; 4 Kt—Q5ch, K—B4; 5 Kt—B6, K —Q3; 6 Kt×B, K×P and now the Kt gets to the Q-side in good time: 7 Kt—B4, K—Q3; 8 Kt—Q3, K—Q4; 9 Kt—Kt2 etc.

A doubled Pawn (unless it is a RP) always wins even when the enemy King is directly in front of it. This is due to the fact that there is no safe haven for the King, no square from which he cannot be chased away. E.g., No. 227b, White: K at QB4, Kt at Q4, P's at QB3, QB5; Black: K at QB2, B at KR6. White wins. 1 K—Kt5, B—B8ch (else P—B6 followed by K—B5 or K—Kt6); 2 P—B4, B—Q6; 3 Kt—K6ch (better than 3 P—B6, K—Q3!; 4 K—Kt6?, B×P; 5 P—B7, K—Q2; 6 K—Kt7, B—R3ch!=), K—Q2; 4 Kt—B4, B—B8; 5 Kt—Q5, B—Q6; 6 P—B6ch, K—B1 (6 .... K—Q3; 7 K—Kt6, B×P; 8 P—B7); 7 K—B5, B—K7; 8 K—Q6!, B—B8 (8 .... B×P; 9 Kt—Kt6ch); 9 Kt—K7ch followed by 10 P—B7ch and 11 P—B8=Q.

5. BISHOP AND TWO PAWNS VS. KNIGHT AND PAWN

The results here are approximately the same as those for the similar case with other minor pieces. With an outside passed Pawn it is usually won—the Pawn either wins a piece or decoys the King, when the decision comes on the other wing. Thus No. 227c, White: K at Q3, B at Q4, P's at QKt5, KKt4; Black: K at Q3, Kt at Q2, P at KKt3. White wins. 1 .... K—Q4; 2 P—Kt6, K—B3 (if 2 .... Kt—Kt1; 3 P—Kt7, K—B3; 4 B—K5, K×P; 5 B×Kt, K×B; 6 K—K4, K—B2; 7 K—K5, etc.); 3 K—K4, K—Kt2; 4 K—B4, Kt—B1; 5 K—K5, Kt—Q2ch; 6 K—K6, Kt—B1ch; 7 K—B7, Kt—Q2; 8 K×P, etc. Of course if the Pawns are closer together or if there is a RP+B of the wrong color all winning efforts will be in vain.

Two connected passed Pawns should likewise win because the Bishop can hold the Pawn from a distance and at the same time support his own Pawns.

But when all the Pawns are together (with or without a passed Pawn) no win is possible if the defending King can place himself in front of the Pawns. Similarly, if the King cannot do this but is too far from "home" to come back in time the Kt cannot hold the fort.

No. 228 (Monke-Heinrich, Westphalia Hauptturnier, 1926) is an example of a complicated win with a RP with the King in front of it. The analogous case with the KtP would offer no trouble at all: Black would merely get his King out of the way and advance his Pawn. But here the King is stalemated and the problem is how to break this deadlock. *1 Kt—K2, B—K6!; 2*

No. 228

Black wins.

Kt—Kt3 (if 2 K×B, K—Kt7 and the Pawn marches triumphantly on), *B—Q7!; 3 Kt—K2* (or 3 Kt—B1ch, K—Kt8; 4 Kt×B, P—R7 and wins, or 3 K—B2, B—K8ch!), *B—K8; 4 Kt—Q4, K—R8; 5 Kt —K2, P—R7; 6 Kt—Q4, K—Kt8; 7 Kt—K2ch, K—B8; 8 Kt— Kt3ch, B×Kt; 9 K×B, P—R8=R!* (not Q, stalemate) and the rest is simple. Of course, if the White King were at R1 in the original position the game would be a fairly certain draw.

Where the Bishop is bottled up the Kt may at times even win with a Pawn down. E.g., Horwitz gives the following position, No. 228a, White: K at QB6, Kt at QB3, P at QKt2; Black: K at QR2, B at QKt1, P's at QB2, QKt3. White wins. 1 Kt—Kt5ch, K—R1 (1 .... K—R3; 2 P—Kt4!, B—R2; 3 Kt×P mate); 2 P—Kt4, B—R2; 3 Kt×Pch, K—Kt1; 4 Kt—Kt5, K—R1; 5 Kt×B, K×Kt; 6 P—Kt5 and wins. Similarly under certain circumstances the road of an advanced passed Pawn may be smoothed by a judicious sacrifice. In No. 228b (Kubbel, 1910), White: K at KKt1, Kt at KKt6, P at QR6; Black: K at KKt5, B at QKt6, P's at Q2, K3, White wins by 1 Kt— K7!, B—B7 (or 1 .... B—Q8; 2 Kt—B6!, B—B6; 3 Kt—K5ch); 2 Kt—Q5!, B—K5; 3 Kt—B6ch.

6. KNIGHT AND TWO PAWNS VS. BISHOP AND PAWN

The results here are surprisingly somewhat different from the analogous cases treated above. This is due to the fact that the Kt is useless at a distance.

An outside passed Pawn does not in general win. For the Kt cannot both defend the extra Pawn and attack the enemy Pawn. In addition if the King wins the Bishop for one Pawn the Knight is very often unable to defend the other Pawn. Consequently the outcome depends on the corresponding Kt+P vs. B ending. Even in a case like No. 229 (O. Hey, 1913) where one wee check would do the trick the Bishop can foil his agile adversary. White can try to reach B7 by a variety of different paths, e.g., 1. Kt—K6 (via Kt5 or Q8); 2. Kt—KB5 (via Q6, KR6); 3. Kt—KB3 (via K5, KKt5); 4. Kt—QKt7 (Q6, Q8); 5. Kt—K4 (Q6, KKt5). But by posting his Bishop on the proper diagonal Black can prevent the realization of any of these plans. E.g., *1 Kt—K6, B—R5; 2 Kt—B5, B—Q1!* (not 2 .... B—K2?; 3 Kt—Kt7! and wins); *3 Kt—Kt7, B—B2; 4 Kt—B5, B—Q1; 5 Kt—K4, B—K2; 6 Kt—Q2* (if 6 Kt—Kt5, B×Kt), *B—Q3; 7 Kt—B3, B—B5; 8 Kt— R4, B—K4; 9 Kt—B5, B—B5*, etc. Obviously going over to the Q-side would offer no chance of ultimate success here. But even if the White KRP were back a few squares such a shift would lead to nothing. E.g., No. 229a, White Pawn at KR5, other pieces as in No. 229. Draw. 1 K—B5, K—R2; 2 K—K4, B—K8; 3 Kt—B5, B—Q7; 4 K—Q5,

B—K8; 5 K—B5, B—Q7; 6 K—Kt5, B—K8; 7 Kt—Q4, K—R3; 8 Kt—B6, K×P; 9 Kt×P, K—Kt3; 10 Kt—B6, K—B2; 11 Kt—Kt4, B×Kt=. Only if the Pawn is all the way back at KR3 can White win this ending. Thus No. 229b, White Pawn at KR3, other pieces as in No. 229. White wins. 1 K—B5, K—R2; 2 K—K4, K—Kt3; 3 K—Q5, K—R4; 4 K—B4, B—K8; 5 K—Kt5, B—B6; 6 Kt—B6, K—R5; 7 Kt×P, K×P; 8 Kt—B6, K—Kt5; 9 Kt—Kt4, K—B4; 10 P—R5, K—K3; 11 P—R6, B—Q5; 12 K—B6! and just manages to keep the King out: 12 .... B—B7 (if 12 .... K—K2; 13 Kt—Q5ch, K—Q1; 14 Kt—Kt6); 13 Kt—Q5, B—R2; 14 K—Kt7, K×Kt (14 .... B—Kt8; 15 Kt—Kt6); 15 K×B, K—B3; 16 K—Kt8.

No. 229   No. 230

Draw.   White to play and win.

Two connected passed Pawns, again unlike the similar case with B+2P vs. Kt+P, are as a rule not a sufficient winning advantage. For the Kt has to guard the enemy passed Pawn, and because its radius of operation is so strictly limited it can do nothing to aid its own Pawns. Clearly the nearer the defender's Pawn is to his rival's the greater are the winning chances.

A type of winning possibility which is uniquely seen in endings with Kt vs. B is that of advancing a passed Pawn to trap a Bishop, despite the large number of moves available to that piece. The most striking and beautiful illustration of this theme that we have ever come across is No. 230 (Reti, 1922). After 1 Kt—Q4ch, K—B4; 2 K—R1!!!! Black has no move with his Bishop which does not cost him that piece (e.g., 2 .... B—B5; 3 Kt—K6ch, or 2 .... B—Q7; 3 Kt—Kt3ch), and only two moves with his King to stay within the square of the RP. But on 2 .... K—Q4; 3 P—R6, the square B3 is taboo, while 2 .... K—Q3; 3 Kt—B5ch again costs him his Bishop. Hence he must try 1 .... K—Kt2 in reply to the Kt check and this loses by exactly one tempo. The solution is *1 Kt—Q4ch!, K—Kt2* (1 .... K—B4; 2 K—R1!!!!); *2 K×P, K—R3; 3 Kt—Kt3, B—B5ch; 4 K—R3, K—Kt4; 5 K—Kt4, B—Kt1; 6 P—B4, K—Kt5; 7 P—B5, K×Kt; 8 P—B6, K—Kt5; 9 P—B7, B—Q3; 10 P—R6* and the B cannot hold both P's. A similar idea is seen in a problem by Kubbel, 1909. No. 230a, White: K at Q1, Kt at Q4, P's at QKt3, Q5; Black: K at QR2, B at QKt8, P at QKt2. White to play and win. 1 P—Q6, K—Kt1 (or Kt3); 2 K—B1!!!, B—Q6 (2 .... B—K5 amounts to the same thing. 2 .... B—Kt3, or R2 is met by 3 P—Q7, K—B2; 4 Kt—K6ch, K×P; 5 Kt—B8ch); 3 P—Q7, K—B2; 4 Kt—K6ch, K×P; 5 Kt—B5ch and the Bishop goes the way of all wood. An analogous case, this time coupled with the theme of blocking the diagonal of the B, is No. 230b (Mattison, 1914), White: K at KKt1, Kt at KB7, P's at QR5, QB5; Black: K at K1, B at KR4, P at Q2. White to play and win. 1 P—B6!, P×P; 2 P—R6, B—B6 (2 .... P—B4; 3 Kt—K5); 3 Kt—·Kt5!!, B—Q4 (or 3 .... K—Q1; 4 P—R7!); 4 Kt—K6!, P—B4 (if 4 .... K—Q2; 5 Kt—B5ch followed by P—R7); 5 Kt—B7ch, K—Q2; 6 Kt×B, K—B1; 7 Kt—B3, K—Kt1; 8 Kt—Kt5, P—B5; 9 K—B2, P—B6; 10 K—K3 and the King is in the square, so that the RP will decide.

Curiously enough, with Kt+2P vs. B+P the winning chances are greatest when all the Pawns are on one side. This for the same reason that Kt+P vs. Kt or Kt+P vs. B is sometimes won even when the enemy King is in front of the Pawn—the Kt can cover all squares. But ordinarily it can force a decision not by queening the Pawn but only by capturing Black's last stalwart. Where this is not possible the ending is drawn.

The most favorable type of case is seen in No. 231 (Romanovsky-Verlinsky, Moscow, 1925). The position suggests a clear winning plan: to attack the BP with the King at K 5 (or Kt5) and the Kt at Q6 or K7 and then force Black either by check or zugzwang to abandon the Pawn. That this is in fact possible is seen in the game continuation. *1 K—K3, K—Kt4; 2 P—Kt3, B—R5* (If 2 .... K—Kt5; 3 K—B2, B—K5; 4 P—R3ch, K—Kt4; 5 K—K3, B—B3; 6 Kt—K6ch, K—B3; 7 Kt—Q4!, B—Kt7; 8 P—R4, K—K4; 9 Kt—B3ch, K—B3; 10 K—B4 and we have transposed into a position that occurred in the game);

No. 231

White wins.

3 Kt—R3ch, K—Kt5; 4 Kt—B2ch, K—Kt4; 5 P—R3 (5 P—R4 at once
is simpler), *B—B3; 6 P—R4ch, K—B3; 7 K—B4!, B—K1; 8 Kt—Q1,
B—Q2; 9 Kt—K3, B—K3; 10 Kt—B2* (not 10 P—R5, B—Q2; 11 P—
R6, B—K3!=), *B—B2* (or 10 .... B—B1; 11 Kt—Q4, B—Q2; 12
Kt—Kt3, B—B1!—or A—; 13 Kt—B5, K—Kt3!; 14 K—K5, K—R4;
15 Kt—Q3!, K—Kt5; 16 Kt—B4, B—Kt2; 17 K—B6, K×P; 18 P—
R5, K×Kt; 19 P—R6 and the ending with Q vs. BP offers Black no
hope. Variation A. 12 .... B—K3; 13 Kt—B5, B—Q4; 14 Kt—Q7ch,
K—K2; 15 K—K5, etc.); *11 Kt—R3!, B—Q4; 12 Kt—Kt5, B—K3* (if
12 .... B—R7; 13 Kt—Q6, B—Kt8; 14 Kt—K8ch, K—B2; 15 Kt—
B7 and now

   a) 15 .... K—Kt3; 16 Kt—Q5, B—B7; 17 K—K5, K—R4; 18
      Kt—B4ch!, K—R3; 19 K—B6, B—Kt8; 20 Kt—K6, K—R4;
      21 K—Kt7!, K—Kt5; 22 Kt—B4, K×P; 23 P—R5 and the
      Pawn cannot be stopped.

   b) 15 .... K—B3; 16 Kt—Q5ch, K—K3; 17 P—R5!, B—K5;
      18 Kt—B3 followed by 19 K—Kt5, etc.); *13 Kt—Q6, B—Q2;
      14 P—R5, B—K3; 15 Kt—K8ch, K—B2; 16 Kt—B7, B—B1;
      17 K—Kt5, B—Q2; 18 Kt—Q5, K—Kt2; 19 Kt—K3, K—R2;
      20 Kt×P* Resigns.

If the superior side's Pawns are far advanced, the possibility of an
exchange or sacrifice may be just as dangerous as that of a capture.
E.g., No. 231a (Horwitz, 1885), White: K at KB8, Kt at QKt1, P's at
K6, KB5; Black: K at Q1, B at QKt5, P at K2. White wins. 1 K—
B7, K—B2 (or 1 .... B—K8; 2 Kt—R3, B—B6; 3 Kt—B4, B—Q5;
4 Kt—Q6!, B—K4—or A—; 5 Kt—B8, B—B3; 6 Kt×P, etc., as in
the main variation. Variation A. 4 .... B—B3; 5 Kt—K4, B—R5;
6 P—B6! and Black is in zugzwang); 2 Kt—Q2, K—Q1 (2 .... B×Kt;
3 P—B6); 3 Kt—B3, B—Q3; 4 Kt—R4, B—R6; 5 Kt—Kt6, B—Kt5;
6 Kt×P!, B×Kt; 7 P—B6, B×P; 8 K×B, K—K1; 9 P—K7 and
White has the opposition.

But without the possibility of a capture or sacrifice as in the above
examples the game is normally a draw. E.g., No. 231b (Capablanca-
Fine, Semmering-Baden, 1937), White: K at KR2, Kt at K1, P's at
KB4, KKt4; Black: K at KKt2, B at Q4, P at KR2. Draw. Capa-.
blanca tried 1 K—Kt3, K—B3; 2 Kt—B3, B—K5; 3 Kt—K5, B—B7·
4 K—R4, P—R3; 5 Kt—Q7ch, K—Kt2; 6 P—B5, B—R5; but after
7 Kt—B5, B—Q8; 8 K—Kt3, K—B2; 9 K—B4, B—K7; 10 Kt—K4,
B—Q8; 11 Kt—B3, B—Kt6; 12 K—K5, B—B5 agreed to a draw.

Of course if the enemy King can attack the Pawn directly and win it
the game is lost. In such cases the defender's only hope lies in simplification. E.g., No. 231c (Judd-Mackenzie, 1888), White: K at KB2,
B at Q6, P at KR5; Black: K at K5, Kt at K6, P's at KKt2, KKt5.
White to play would draw at once by 1 B—B8, Kt—B4; 2 B×P! for if

2 .... Kt×B?; 3 P—R6. Black to play tried 1 .... Kt—B4, when 2 B—B7 and if 2 .... Kt—Q5; 3 B—Q6, K—B4 (or 3 .... Kt—K3; 4 K—Kt3, K—B4; 5 K—R4=); 4 B—B8, Kt—K3; 5 P—R6 was the best defense. Instead White played 2 B—B8? (2 B—B7 was correct) and lost after 2 .... P—Kt6ch; 3 K—Kt1, K—B6!; 4 B×P, Kt×B!!; 5 P—R6, Kt—K3; 6 P—R7, Kt—B5; 7 P—R8=Q, Kt—K7ch; 8 K—B1, P—Kt7ch; 9 K—K1, P—Kt8=Qch; 10 K—Q2, Q—B8ch; 11 K—Q3, Kt—B5ch; 12 K—Q4, Q—Kt7ch and wins Black's Queen.

B. MORE COMPLICATED ENDINGS

We come now to the great mass of finales that are met in practical play but are not immediately reducible to one of the more elementary cases (A1—6). Here again an exhaustive analysis is neither feasible nor desirable; we shall confine ourselves to setting up certain all-important general rules which will serve as a guide through the maze.

1. MATERIAL ADVANTAGE

As we have seen in other endings, the advantage of a Pawn is sufficient for a win. We have also noted what the general winning idea is: either force a queen or gain more material. With two Pawns or a piece up, of course, the technical problem requires merely a judicious advance of the Pawns.

The winning process in the case of Bishop and Knight finales may be most conveniently divided into five steps (compare p. 150 in Bishop endings). These are:

1. Place all the pieces in the most favorable positions available.
2. Weaken the opponent's Pawns as much as possible.
3. Create an outside passed Pawn.
4. If a piece is diverted to stop the Pawn, capture it.
5. If the King is used to block the Pawn, manoeuvre your own King to the other wing and establish a decisive superiority there.

In many cases one or more of these steps has already been carried out. Sometimes one or two steps are superfluous; e.g., in endings where the superior side has a Knight, the *threat* of an outside passed Pawn is just as strong, possibly stronger, than its fulfillment.

The best position for the pieces is the center. A Bishop, however, is just as effective from some other point on a long diagonal (KR1—QR8, QR1—KR8). Pawns are weakened by forcing them to advance too hastily or by forcing them on to squares of the same color as the Bishop. This last statement must be qualified by the further condition that the side which has a Bishop should try to force the Pawns off the Bishop's color.

A model case with a Bishop is No. 232 (Godai-Becker, Vienna, 1926).

The first step requires bringing the King to the center (the B is already well posted at Q4). *1 K—Kt1, K—B2; 2 K—B2* (2 Kt—B5 would be of no avail: Black simply replies 2 .... K—K2 and 3 .... K—Q3), *K—K3; 3 K—K3, K—Q3.* Next the White Pawns must be weakened. Since it is Black who has the B, it is desirable to have the White Pawns on Black squares, for then both Bishop and King will have attained maximum mobility. *4 P—Kt3* (saving his opponent a lot of hard work but, of course, there is no really adequate defense. If White tries to stave off defeat by keeping Black's King out, the win would be achieved by weakening the Pawns on the Q-side. E.g., 4 Kt—B5, K—B3; 5 Kt—R4, K—Kt4; 6 Kt—Kt2, P—KKt4; 7 K—B2,—or A —, P—KR4; 8 K—K3, P—Kt3; 9 K—B2, P—R4; 10 P×P, P×P; 11 K—K3, B—B5; 12 K—B2, K—B4; 13 K—K3, B—Kt4 and White is in zugzwang: 14 P—Kt3, P—B4; 15 P—B4, KP×Pch; 16 P×P, P—Kt5; 17 K—B2, P—KR5; 18 K—Kt1, K—Q5, etc. Variation A. 7 K—Q3, P—Kt3; 8 K—B3, P—KR4; 9 Kt—Q3, P—K5; 10 P×P, B×P; 11 Kt—K1, K—R5; 12 K—Kt2, P—B4; 13 P—Kt3, P—B5; 14 P×P, P×P; 15 K—R2, P—B6 and wins the Kt. Clearly the side where the final blow will fall may vary according to circumstances: it is in general that which happens to be most vulnerable), *4 .... P— QKt3; 5 Kt—B2* (the threat of a passed Pawn is sufficient here. If White offers Black a passed Pawn in the center he will still be unable to prevent the entry of the Black King to one side or the other. E.g., 5 P—B4, B—B5; 6 P×Pch, P×P; 7 Kt—Kt2, B—Kt4; 8 K—K4, P—Kt3; 9 P—KR4, B—B3ch; 10 K—K3, K—Q4; 11 Kt—Q3, B— Kt4; 12 Kt—Kt2, P—KR4 and Black's King must penetrate either via QB5 or via Q5), *K—B3; 6 Kt—Q1, K—Kt4; 7 Kt—Kt2, P—Kt4* (White has in effect stopped the passed Pawn with his King and if he does nothing will allow his rival to gain the decisive material advantage on the Q-side. Instead he plays for a phantom counter-chance, and permits Black a passed Pawn on the KR file); *8 P—B4* (or 8 K—K2, P—QR4; 9 P×P, P×P; 10 K— K3, P—R4; 11 K—K2, K—B4; 12 K—K3, B—B3 and again Black cannot be kept out), *KP×Pch* (to create a protected passed Pawn here by 8 .... P—K5?? would be a serious strategical error not only because the Knight is a born block-ader but also because it places a vital Pawn on the same color as the

No. 232

Black wins.

Bishop); *9 P×P, P—Kt5; 10 P—B5, P—KR4* (threatening to win at once by .... P—R5, ... P—Kt6, ... P—R6 and .... P—R7); *11 K—Q4* (desperation. If 11 K—B4, P—R4; 12 P×P, P×P; 13 K—Kt3, K—B4; 14 K—R4, B—B2! followed by capture of the QRP or KBP, e.g., 15 Kt—Q3ch, K—Q5; 16 Kt—B4, K—K5 or 16 Kt—B1, K—B6), *B—B6* (avoiding the trap. If 11 .... P—R5?; 12 K×B, P—Kt6; 13 P×P, P×P; 14 Kt—Q1!, K—R5; 15 Kt—K3 and wins. Or here 13 .... P—Kt7; 14 Kt—B3 mate!); *12 K—K3, P—R5; 13 P—R3* (preferring the shorter and more painless way out. The move chosen leads to the fourth step—loss of a piece. 13 K—B4 would be an example of the fifth step: 13 K—B4, P—R4; 14 P×P, P×P; 15 K—K3, B—B3; 16 K—B2, K—B4; etc.), *B—B3!; 14 P×P, P—R6; 15 Kt—Q3, P—R7* 16 resigns. After 16 Kt—B2, P—R8=Q all the romance goes out of White's life.

When the superior side has a Knight, it is as a rule not desirable to create an outside passed Pawn at once. For the Bishop can hold it at a distance, while the Knight cannot support it at a distance, so that there is no loss of mobility for the defender. Instead the weakening of the opponent's Pawns and the threat of a potential outside passed Pawn, as a result of which the Bishop is tied down but the Knight is not, are the most important of the three preliminary steps. No. 233 (Spielmann-Maroczy, Carlsbad, 1929) may be taken as a model case. Here the Pawns on the Q-side are irretrievably on squares of the wrong color so that the Pawns on the other wing are the only ones that need be considered. Now, it is clear that if Black does nothing White will march his King to QKt6 or QB7 and capture a Pawn there (if necessary by Kt—B5). Consequently Black must do something against this threat. But all that he can do is to drive the Kt away, which can only be done by fixing his Pawns on White. The game continuation

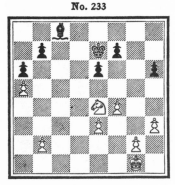

No. 233

White wins.

was *1 K—B2, P—B4* (if 1 .... B—Q2; 2 P—KKt3, B—B3; 3 Kt—B3, K—Q3; 4 P—QKt4, K—K2; 5 P—K4, K—Q3; 6 P—K5ch, K—B2; 7 K—K3, K—Q2; 8 Kt—K4, K—K2; 9 Kt—Q6, K—B1; 10 K—Q4, followed by annihilation of the Q-wing); *2 Kt—B3!* (somewhat surprising. But it is important to keep the Black King out and to preserve the square Q4 for the White King. On 2 Kt—B5?, K—Q3; 3 P—Kt4, K—Q4 Black has excellent counterchances), *P—K4* (Pawn exchanges are as a rule advisable for the defender—the fewer the Pawns the greater the drawing chances); *3 K—K2, P×P* (one may justly inquire why Black voluntarily relinquishes the struggle for the center square: the answer is, as expected, that he has no choice. For if 3 .... K—Q3; 4 P—QKt4, B—K3; 5 K—Q3, B—B2; 6 Kt—R4, B—Q4; 7 P—Kt3, B—Kt7; 8 P—R4, B—Q4; 9 Kt—B5, B—B3; 10 K—B4, B—Kt4ch; 11 K—B3, B—B3; 12 Kt—Q3, P×P; 13 KP×P, K—Q4; 14 Kt—B5!, K—Q3; 15 K—Q4 and we have essentially the same position as that reached in the game); *4 P×P, K—Q3; 5 P— QKt4, B—Q2* (Why doesn't Black try to exchange his weak Q-side Pawns? Because that would permit the entry of the White King to the K-side. E.g., 5 .... K—B3; 6 K—Q3, P—Kt3; 7 P×P, K×P; 8 K—Q4, P—QR4; 9 P×Pch, K×P; 10 K—K5 with a simple win); *6 K—K3, B—B3; 7 P—Kt3, B—Q2; 8 K—Q4.* The first two steps have now been completed. It would be pointless for White now to try to set up a passed Pawn on the K-side. For that would require moving his Kt to K3, and even then he would not be successful, because Black could counter with P—KR4. But the constant threat of a passed Pawn brings about Black's downfall firstly because he can never dare to exchange his B for the Kt and secondly because his B must not stray too far afield but must always keep an eye on the K-side, while the Kt may do as it pleases. The immediate winning idea consists of chasing the Black King away from Q3, so that White may enter via either K5 or QB5. *8 .... B—K3* (8 .... B—B3 makes no difference. After 9 Kt—Q1, B—K5—9 .... B—Q2 transposes back into the game—; 10 Kt—K3, B—Kt8; 11 P—Kt4 gives White his long-coveted passed Pawn, which is conclusive here. E.g., 11 .... P×P; 12 Kt×P, P— R4; 13 Kt—B6, P—R5; 14 Kt—K4ch, K—B3; 15 P—B5, B—R7; 16 P—B6, K—Q2; 17 K—K5 and wins); *9 Kt—R4, P—R4; 10 Kt— B5, B—Q4; 11 Kt—Q7!* (very pretty. But of course 11 Kt—Q3 was just as good), *B—Kt6; 12 Kt—K5, B—B7; 13 Kt—B4ch, K—B3; 14 K—K5* this is simpler than the game continuation 14 Kt—K3, B—Kt8; 15 Kt—Q1!, K—Q3!; 16 Kt—B3, B—B7; 17 K—B4!, K— B3; 18 P—R4!, K—Q3; 19 P—Kt5!, P×Pch; 20 Kt×Pch, K—K2; 21 K—B5, B—K5; 22 Kt—Q6 and Maroczy resigned), *B—Q6* (or 14 .... K—Kt4; 15 Kt—R3ch, K×P; 16 Kt×Bch, K×P; 17 K×P, K—R5; 18 K—K4, K—Kt6; 10 K—Q3, P—Kt4; 20 P—B5, P—R4; 21 P—B6, etc.); *15 Kt—Q6, B—Kt8; 16 Kt×BP, K—Kt4; 17 Kt— Q6ch, K×P; 18 Kt×P, B—Q6; 19 P—B5* and the Bishop will have to be sacrificed for the Pawn without any hope of counterplay on the other wing. E.g., *19 .... B×P* (19 .... K—Kt4; 20 P—B6, B—Kt3; 21 K—K6, K—B3; 22 Kt—Q6, K—B4; 23 K—K7, K—Kt5; 24 Kt— B7, B—Kt8; 25 Kt—Q8, B—Kt3; 26 Kt—B6ch, K—Kt4; 27 Kt—K5, and the Pawn will queen); *20 K×B, K—Kt4; 21 K—K5, K—B3; 22 Kt—Q6* and the rest is simple.

Where there already is an outside passed Pawn, the case where the superior side has a Bishop presents no difficulty—the idea is no different from that in endings with Bishops of the same color (see page 150). Either the Kt tries to stop the Pawn and is captured or the enemy King comes to the rescue and leaves the Pawns on the other wing exposed. Two examples will suffice. No. 233a (Rubinstein-Nimzovitch, Carlsbad, 1907) White: K at KKt1, Kt at QB3, P's at KB4, KKt3, KKt2; Black: K at KB1, B at QB5, P's at QR4, KB2, KKt2, KR2. Black to play wins. The continuation was 1 .... K—K2 (going to the Q-side. 1 .... B—Kt6; 2 Kt—Kt5, P—R5; 3 Kt—R3, would again require a little forceful persuasion by the King to dislodge the recalcitrant cavalier); 2 K—B2, K—Q3; 3 K—K3, K—B4; 3 P—Kt4, K—Kt5; 5 K—Q4, B—Kt6; 6 P—Kt5, P—R5; 7 Kt—Kt1 (now Nimzovitch could have won prosaically by 7 .... P—R6 when 8 Kt×P is necessary. He prefers instead to force the desolate Knight to abandon the Black Pawn and allow it to promote), B—K3; 8 P—Kt3, K—Kt6; 9 Kt—B3, P—R6; 10 K—Q3, P—Kt3; 11 K—Q4, K—B7; 12 resigns. For the Kt cannot be maintained at QB3. No. 233b (Nimzovitch-Janowski, Carlsbad, 1907) is strikingly similar to No. 183. White: K at KKt3, B at QKt3, P's at QKt5, KB4, KKt2, KR3; Black: K at KB3, Kt at Q2, P's at KB2, KKt3, KR3. First: centralization (step No. 1 in our schema). 1 K—B3, K—K2; 2 K—K3, P—B3 (thus incidentally allowing the completion of Step No. 2—but Black has no choice); 3 K—Q4, K—Q3; 4 B—Q1, Kt—Kt3; 5 B—B3, Kt—B1; 6 P—R4 (further softening the K-side), Kt—K2 (if 6 .... Kt—Kt3; 7 B—K4, P—Kt4; 8 BP×P, BP×P; 9 P—R5, Kt—Q2; 10 B—B3, Kt—Kt3; 11 K—K4, K—K3; 12 B—Kt4ch, K—B3; 13 K—Q4 and it is all over: the Kt is lost); 7 B—K4 (not 7 P—Kt6 because of 7 .... Kt—B4ch), P—Kt4 (clearly neither Kt nor K can budge. Alternative Pawn moves are likewise of no avail, e.g., 7 .... P—B4; 8 B—B3, Kt—B1; 9 B—Q5, Kt—K2; 10 P—Kt6!, K—Q2; 11 K—K5, etc. Or 7 .... P—R4; 8 P—Kt6, Kt—B3ch; 9 B×Kt, K×B; 10 P—Kt7, K×P; 11 K—Q5, K—B2; 12 K—K6 and Black has breathed his last); 8 BP×P, BP×P; 9 P×P (the simplest), P×P; 10 P—Kt6, P—Kt5 (again if 10 .... Kt—B3ch; 11 B×Kt, K×B; 12 K—K5 is conclusive); 11 P—Kt7, K—B2; 12 K—K5. Now White captures the other Pawn, which will cost Black his Kt. The rest is simple. 12 .... P—Kt6; 13 K—B4, Kt—Kt1; 14 K×P, Kt—B3; 15 B—B3, Kt—Q2; 16 K—B4, K—Q3; 17 K—B5, K—K2; 18 B—B6, Kt—Kt1; 19 B—Kt5. Resigns. With the Kt "on ice" White will soon queen.

With a Kt an outside passed Pawn is somewhat more difficult to exploit. Ordinarily the most essential step is that of weakening the enemy Pawns by forcing them on to squares of the same color as the Bishop.

No. 234 (Fine-Reshevsky, Semmering-Baden, 1937) is typical of the problems involved. Clearly White can not get his King to any more advantageous post than K2, and his QKtP is hard to support. On the other hand Black's pieces are or will be better placed because the King can occupy a more central square and because the Bishop can both stop the QKtP and keep his eye on the KBP. Consequently the only way White can win is by diverting the Black King to the Q-side and capturing two Pawns on the K-side. To do this he must not only get his QKtP to Kt5 (to make the threat of an advance more real) but also soften up his quarry on the K-side. The continuation was *1 P— QKt3, B—Q5; 2 Kt—B6, B—Kt3; 3 Kt—Kt4* (the Kt would be too exposed at QB6. E.g., 3 P—QKt4, K—B3; 4 P—Kt5, K—K3; 5 K— B1, K—Q3 with excellent counter-chances.), *K—B2; 4 Kt—Q5, B— Q5; 5 K—B1, K—K3; 6 Kt—K3, B—B4; 7 K—K2, P—R4* (to keep the Kt out of an important square. On 7 .... K—K4; 8 Kt—B2, K— Q4; 9 P—QKt4, B—B1; 10 P—Kt5, B—B4—or A—; 11 Kt—K3ch, K—Q5; 12 P—R4, B—Kt3; 13 Kt—Kt4, K—B4; 14 Kt—B6, K×P; 15 Kt×RP, B—Q1; 16 P—Kt3, K—B5; 17 Kt—B8, P—Kt4; 18 P— R5 the Bishop is doomed. A. 10 .... K—B4; 11 K—K3, K×P; 12 K×P, K—B3; 13 K—K5, K—Q2; 14 K—B6, K—K1; 15 Kt—K3 and wins another Pawn. Black is gambling on the possibility of exchanging one or more Pawns); *8 Kt—B2, P—Kt4; 9 P—QKt4, B—Q3; 10 P—Kt3, K—K4; 11 P—Kt5, B—B4; 12 Kt—K3, K—Q5; 13 Kt— B5ch, K—K4* (after 13 .... K—B5 he would inevitably lose two Pawns on the K-side: 14 Kt—Kt7, K×P; 15 Kt×P, K—B5; 16 Kt— B6, K—Q5; 17 P—B3!, P×Pch; 18 K×P, B—K2; 19 Kt—Kt8!, B— Q1; 20 Kt—R6!, B—B3; 21 K—Kt4, K—Q4; 22 Kt—B7); *14 Kt— Kt7, P—R5; 15 P—Kt4* (now all the preliminary spade work is completed), *B—Kt3; 16 Kt—B5, B— B4; 17 Kt—K3, K—Q5; 18 P—B3!* (in the game White made the mistake of postponing this essential freeing move too long: 18 Kt—B5ch, K—B5; 19 Kt—R6, K×P; 20 Kt—B7, K—B5!!; 21 Kt×P, K— Q4; 22 P—B3, P×Pch; 23 Kt×P, K—K5!!!; 24 Kt×P, K—B5; 25 Kt —B5, B—Kt3 and the result is a draw because White's King is only an innocent bystander), *B—Kt3* (or 18 .... P×Pch; 19 K×P, K

No. 234

White wins.

—K4; 20 P—Kt6!); *19 Kt—B1!, K—K4* (if 19 .... P×Pch; 20 K×P, K—B5; 21 K—K4, K×P; 22 K—B5, B—Q1; 23 Kt—Q2 is conclusive); *20 Kt—Q2, P×Pch; 21 K×P, K—B3; 22 Kt—B4, B —B2; 23 P—Kt6, B—B5; 24 P—Kt7, K—K3* (or 24 .... B—B2; 25 Kt—R5—B6—fourth step); *25 K—K4, K—Q2; 26 K—B5* and both Black Pawns are lost.

The lesson which the above example teaches us is that before saicrficing an outside passed Pawn one must be certain that the ensuing ending with all the Pawns on one side will leave sufficient material for a win.

With a potential outside passed Pawn the procedure is essentially the same. Nimzovitch's maxim that the threat is stronger than its fulfillment is quite appropriate here, though one is inclined to qualify it a bit.

In No. 235 (Bernstein-Reshevsky, New York, 1940) we have a case which seems to be relatively unfavorable for the Bishop: the potential passed Pawn is blocked. However, here this makes no difference because the Pawns are stuck on Black squares, so that the Bishop can always come to the rescue and help them advance. Thus P—KKt4— Kt5 is in the long run unavoidable. The fact that all the White Pawns are on White squares is no handicap because they are exposed to attack. In general, if the Pawns of the side which has the B are on the same color, that is always a serious disadvantage, but the other side's Pawns should be placed on that color only if they are not subject to attack.

Reshevsky wound up in No. 235 as follows: *1 .... K—B2; 2 Kt— Kt5* (if 2 Kt—K6, B×BP; 3 Kt×KBP, B—Kt6; 4 Kt—K6, B×P; 5 Kt×BP, P—QKt4 and wins), *B×BP; 3 Kt×BP, B—Q6; 4 Kt—R8, P—QKt4* (4 .... B×P; 5 Kt×P, B—R3 would transpose into the

No. 235

Black wins.

game); *5 P×P, B×P; 6 K—B2, K —B3; 7 Kt—Kt6* (7 K—B3, K—B4; 8 Kt—Kt6, B—Q6 or R3), *B—R3; 8 K—B3, K—B4; 9 Kt—R8, B— Q6; 10 Kt—Kt6, P—Kt4; 11 P— R4, B—R3* (more accurate than 11 .... B—K5ch; 12 K—B2, K—K4; 13 Kt—B4ch); *12 Kt—R8, B—B5; 13 Kt—Kt6, B—Kt6!; 14 K—B2, K —K5;* 15 Resigns, for he must lose at least one more Pawn.

Another illustration with such a potential club is No. 235a (Vidmar-Marshall, Carlsbad, 1929), White: K at KKt1, B at Q1, P's at

QR2, QKt2, KB2, KKt2, KR3; Black: K at KKt1, Kt at KB3, P's at QR2, QKt2, KB2, KKt2. White wins. Vidmar continued as follows: 1 B—B3, P—QKt3; 2 K—B1 (first and second steps), K—B1; 3 K—K2, K—K2; 4 K—Q3, K—Q3; 5 K—Q4, Kt—Q2; 6 B—Q5, Kt—K4; 7 P—B4, Kt—Kt3; 8 P—KKt3 (the preliminaries are over; now the main bout begins), P—B3; 9 B—K4, Kt—B1; 10 B—B5 (stalemating the Knight. Ordinarily it is not good policy to allow enemy Pawns to be placed on the same color as the Bishop, but this case is an exception because the Pawns are subject to attack.), P—Kt3; 11 B—B8, P—QKt4 (a desperate gamble: A Marshall does not like to be choked to death without saying a word); 12 P—KR4 (12 B—Kt4 is safer but not quite as accurate), P—B4; 13 P—R5, K—B2; 14 B×P! (Decisive. However, there were two other satisfactory lines: a) 14 P—R6!, K×B; 15 K—K5, K—Q2; 16 K—B6, K—K1; 17 P—QKt4!, P—R3; 18 K—Kt7, K—K2; 19 P—R7, Kt×P; 20 K×Kt, K—B2; 21 P—R3, K—B3; 22 K—Kt8 and the K and P ending is lost because White has the opposition. b) 14 B—R6, P×P—or 14 .... K—Kt3; 15 P—R6, K×B; 16 K—K5 and will queen the Pawn—; 15 K—K5, P—R5; 16 P×P, Kt—Kt3ch; 17 K×P, Kt×RPch; 18 K—Kt4, Kt—Kt7; 19 B×P, Kt—K8; 20 P—B5, Kt—B7; 21 P—B6, K—Q3; 22 K—B5, etc.), P×B; 15 K—K5, K—Q2; 16 K×P (in the game Vidmar played 16 K—B6 but after 16 .... K—K1 retreated 17 K×P because of the trap 17 K—Kt7, P—R4; 18 P—R6?, Kt—R2; 19 K×Kt??—19 K—Kt6 still wins—, K—B2=), K—K2; 17 P—Kt4 and the three connected passed Pawns are too much for one poor mortal.

Where the passed Pawn is in the center the technical difficulties are greatest, especially with a Bishop. This is due to the fact that it then requires considerable skillful manoeuvring in order to force an entry with the King or an adequate material advantage. Such positions, particularly when coupled with other weaknesses, can frequently be held to a draw by the defender. No. 236 (Euwe-Botvinnik, Nottingham, 1936) is one of the most involved cases of this type which has ever occurred in tournament play. The moves were: *1 .... Kt—Kt1; 2 K—B3, Kt—B3; 3 B—B3* (to prevent Kt—R4), *P—Kt3* (in order to be able to play his K to K3); *4 K—B4, P—R3; 5 P—QR4, K—K3;*

No. 236

Draw.

6 P—R4, Kt—Kt5; 7 K—B3 (the reason why White cannot win is that despite his Pawn plus the exchange of pieces would do him no good. If, e.g., 7 B—Kt7, Kt—Q6ch; 8 K—B3, Kt—K4ch; 9 B×Kt, K×B; 10 P—Kt4, P—KKt4; 11 P—KR5, P—R4 the ending is hopelessly drawn), *Kt—Q6; 8 B—Kt7, Kt—K4ch!* (but not 8 .... P—KR4?; 9 K—K2, Kt—K4??; 10 B×Kt!, K×B; 11 K—B3, P—R4; 12 P—Kt4, P×Pch; 13 K×P, K×P; 14 K—Kt5 and gets there first); *9 K—K2* (now 9 B×Kt would only draw, as in the note to Black's seventh move), *Kt×P; 10 B×P, P—QKt4* (this is the simplest drawing line. In the game there occurred 10 .... Kt—Kt7 when White could have forced a favorable decision by 11 B—Kt7, Kt×P; 12 P—Kt4, P—QKt4; 13 P—R5, P×P; 14 P×P, K—B2; 15 B—R1, Kt—Kt3; 16 K—B3, P—Kt5?; 17 P—K5, Kt—Q2; 18 K—K4, K—K3; 19 P—R6, Kt—B1; 20 K—Q3, K—Q4; 21 P—K4ch, K—B3; 22 K—B4, P—R4; 23 K—Kt3!!, K—Kt4; 24 P—K6, P—R5ch; 25 K—R2, Kt—Kt3; 26 B—B6, K—B3; 27 P—K7, K—Q2; 28 P—K5, P—B5; 29 P—K6ch, K—K1; 30 K—Kt1, P—B6; 31 K—B2, P—R6; 32 K—Kt3 and Black is in zugzwang); *11 P×P, P×P; 12 B—B8, Kt—Q3!; 13 B×Kt, K×B; 14 P—Kt4* but the K and P ending is only a draw despite White's extra Pawn—the doubled KP is no better than a single P.

But if there are no weaknesses, a central passed Pawn wins just as surely, though often not just as quickly, as one on the outside files. No. 237 (Euwe-Spielmann, match, 1932) is an excellent example. The first phase is centralization. *1 .... Kt—B4* (1 .... Kt×P; 2 B×P, P—Kt5; 3 K—K2, Kt—R5; 4 B—B4, Kt—B6ch; 5 K—Q3, Kt—Q8; 6 P—B4 was inferior); *2 B—Q5, P—QR4* (to prevent 3 P—QKt4, which would leave his Pawns hopelessly weak. 2 .... Kt—Q6 is re-

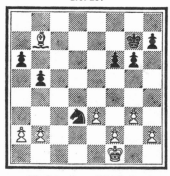

No. 237

Black to play. White wins.

futed by 3 K—K2, Kt×KtP; 4 B—Kt3!, P—QR4; 5 K—Q2, P—R5; 6 B—Q5!, P—R6; 7 K—B2, P—B4; 8 B—B3, Kt—B5; 9 B—K2, Kt—Q3; 10 K—Kt3 and both the QRP and QKtP will be captured); *3 P—K4, K—B1; 4 K—K2, K—K2; 5 K—K3, K—Q3* (or 5 .... Kt—R5; 6 K—Q4, Kt×P; 7 K—B5, Kt—Q6ch; 8 K×P, Kt×P; 9 K×P and wins); *6 K—Q4, P—Kt4; 7 P—B4, P×P; 8 P×P, Kt—Q2; 9 B—B7!* (White will now force a passed Pawn in the center which will function in exactly the same way as an outside Pawn—tie down the

Black King and thus make it possible for White to switch over to the
Q-side), *P—R3* (Euwe gives the following alternatives:
  a) 9 .... Kt—B4; 10 P—K5ch, P×Pch; 11 P×Pch, K—B3; 12
     B—Q5ch, K—Kt3; 13 P—K6, Kt—R3; 14 P—K7, Kt—B2;
     15 B—B7.
  b) 9 .... Kt—Kt3; 10 P—K5ch, P×Pch; 11 P×Pch, K—K2; 12
     B—Kt8, P—R3; 13 P—Kt3, Kt—Q2; 14 K—Q5, P—Kt5; 15
     B—R7, Kt—B1; 16 B—B5, P—R4; 17 P—KR4 with a simple
     win in both cases); *10 B—K8, Kt—B1; 11 P—K5ch, P×Pch;*
     12 P×Pch, K—B2; 13 B×P, Kt—K3ch; 14 K—Q5, Kt—Kt4;
     15 P—K6, K—Q1; 16 P—KR4, Resigns.
In conjunction with a Knight a center Pawn is even stronger than
with a Bishop—chiefly because the function of the passed Pawn is to
constrict the mobility of the enemy King and force an entry to one
side. An apt illustration of the model winning procedure (weakening
the Pawns, forcing an entry with the King) is found in No. 237a
(Botvinnik-Rjumin, 1936), White: K at KB2, Kt at QR4, P's at QR2,
QKt3, K2, KKt3, KR2; Black: K at K3, B at K2, P's at QR2, QB4,
KKt2, KR2. White wins. 1 K—K3, K—B4; 2 K—B3, K—K4;
3 P—K3, B—Q3; 4 Kt—Kt2, K—Q4; 5 Kt—B4, B—B2; 6 K—K2
(threatening to break through on the Q-side by K—Q3, P—K4ch and
Kt—K3 or Q2), K—K5; 7 Kt—Q2ch, K—B4; 8 K—B3, K—K4; 9
P—KKt4 (at the present juncture it is more important to limit the
mobility of Black's King than of Black's Bishop), K—Q4; 10 P—
KR3, B—Q1; 11 K—K2, B—B2; 12 K—Q3 (now that the K-side
Pawns are safe White is going to get his King to QB4), B—Kt6; 13
Kt—K4, (in order to weaken the Black Pawns first—there is no hurry),
B—K8; 14 Kt—Kt5!, P—KR3; 15 Kt—K4, B—R5; 16 Kt—B3ch,
K—K4 (or, as in the game, 16 .... K—B3; 17 K—K4, B—B3; 18
Kt—Kt1, K—Q3; 19 Kt—R3, K—K3; 20 Kt—Kt5!, P—QR4; 21
Kt—B7ch, K—Q2; 22 Kt—Q5, B—Kt7; 23 Kt—Kt6ch and Black
resigned for he must lose a second Pawn after 23 .... K—K3; 24 K—
Q3, B—R6; 25 K—B4, K—K4; 26 K—Kt5, B—Kt5; 27 Kt—B4ch,
etc.); 17 K—B4, B—B7 (or 17 .... B—K2; 18 K—Kt5 and the QRP
is the victim); 18 Kt—Q1, B—Kt8; 19 K×P, with a simple win. He
can even sacrifice the Kt after 19 .... K—K5; 20 P—Kt4!, K—Q6;
21 K—Q5, K—Q7; 22 P—K4, K×Kt; 23 P—K5, B—Kt3; 24 P—K6,
B—Q1; 25 P—QR4, K—B7; 26 P—QKt5, K—Kt6; 27 P—R5 and
Black is just too late to save the bacon.
With only a few Pawns (3 vs. 2) a center Pawn still wins when the
superior side has a Kt, but there will often be difficulty with a B.
E.g., No. 237b (Tartakover-Spielmann, Carlsbad, 1923), White: K at
Q5, Kt at KB3, P's at K3, KKt5, KR4; Black: K at KB2, B at KKt6,

P's at KKt3, KR4. After 1 P—K4! Black resigned and Tartakover gives five variations to show why:

a) 1 .... K—K2; 2 Kt—K5 and the KKtP is lost.

b) 1 .... B—Kt1; 2 Kt—K5ch, B×Kt; 3 K×B with a simply won K and P ending (compare Nos. 54, 54a).

c) 1 .... B—B7; 2 K—Q6, B—Kt6ch; 3 K—Q7, B—B7; 4 P—K5, B—B4; 5 P—K6ch, K—B1; 6 Kt—K5 and the Bishop is lost.

d) 1 .... B—B2; 2 Kt—K5ch, K—Kt2; 3 K—K6, B—Kt3; 4 Kt—B3, B—B2; 5 K—Q7, B—Kt3; 6 P—K5, etc., as in c).

e) 1 .... K—Kt2; 2 K—K6, B—B7; 3 K—Q7 and again continues as in c). Or No. 237c (Euwe-Fine, Bergen a/Zee, 1938), White: K at Q3, Kt at K4, P's at QR2, QKt3, Q4; Black: K at KKt5, B at QB8, P's at QR2, QKt3. White wins. 1 .... B—B5; 2 K—B4, K—B6; 3 Kt—B3, B—R7; 4 P—Kt4, B—B2; 5 P—Kt5, B—Q3; 6 Kt—Q5, K—K5; 7 Kt—B6ch, K—K6; 8 K—Q5, B—K2; 9 Kt—Kt4ch, K—Q6; 10 Kt—K5ch, K—B6; 11 Kt—B6, B—B3; 12 P—R4, B—Kt2; 13 K—Q6 and Black resigned.

Now let us consider a similar case with a Bishop. No. 237d (Carls-Becker, Dresden, 1926), White: K at Q4, B at KKt4, P's at K5, KKt3, KR2; Black: K at KB2, Kt at QB3, P's at KKt4, KR3. The game was adjudicated a win by the Dutch Chess Federation on the basis of the following analysis: 1 K—Q5, Kt—K2ch (or 1 .... Kt—Kt5ch; 2 K—Q6, or 1 .... Kt—R4; 2 B—K2, K—K2; 3 K—K4, K—K3; 4 P—Kt4, Kt—Kt2; 5 B—B4ch, K—K2; 6 K—B5, Kt—B4; 7 P—R3, Kt—R5; 8 K—Kt6, etc.); 2 K—Q6 and now

a) 2 .... Kt—Kt1 (any other Kt move would likewise permit the exchange of pieces); 3 B—K6ch, K any; 4 B×Kt and the rest is routine.

b) 2 .... K—B1; 3 K—K6, Kt—Kt1; 4 B—Q1, K—Kt2; 5 B—Kt3, K—B1; 6 K—B5, Kt—K2ch; 7 K—B6, Kt—Kt1ch; 8 K—Kt6, Kt—K2ch; 9 K×RP and Black can resign.

c) 2 .... K—K1; 3 K—K6, Kt—Kt1; 4 B—R5ch, K—B1; 5 B—B7, Kt—K2; 6 K—B6, Kt—B3; 7 P—K6, Kt—K2; 8 P—Kt4, Kt—Q4ch; 9 K—Kt6, Kt—K6; 10 P—R3, K—K2 (10 .... Kt—Kt7; 11 K—B6!); 11 K×P, K—B3; 12 B—Kt6, Kt—Kt7; 13 P—K7, K×P; 14 K×P, K—B1; 15 K—R6 and we have No. 224c.

So far so good. But if we juggle the pieces around a bit we see that though the Bishop often wins the simplicity of No. 237d is only apparent. E.g., consider the position No. 237e, White: K at Q4, B at K4, P's at K5, KKt3, KR2; Black: K at K2, Kt at Q2, P's at KKt3, KR2. This, which we may take to be more typical than No. 237d, requires considerable manoeuvring before the point is scored. The first step is to force the Pawns to advance, when we shall have transposed back into the easier case. This is made possible by the threat of an effective sacrifice. 1 B—Q5, Kt—Kt1 (if 1 .... Kt—Kt3; 2 B—Kt8, K—B1; 3 B×P!, K—Kt2; 4 K—B5, Kt—B1; 5 K—B6!, K×B; 6 K—Q7, Kt—Kt3ch; 7 K—Q8, Kt—Q4; 8 P—K6 is sufficient); 2 B—Kt8!, P—R3 (again if 2 .... K—B1; 3 B×P!, K—Kt2; 4 K—Q5!, K×B; 5 K—Q6, K—Kt2; 6 P—K6, K—B1; 7 K—B7!, K—K2; 8 K×Kt, K×P; 9 K—B7, K—B4; 10 K—Q6, K—Kt5; 11 K—K6, K—R6; 12 K—B6, K×P; 13 P—Kt4, K—Kt6; 14 P—Kt5 and wins); 3 B—Q5, Kt—Q2; 4 B—K4, Kt—B1 (4 .... P—Kt4; 5 B—Q5 transposes into No. 237d, while 4 .... K—B2 is met by 5 K—Q5, Kt—Kt3ch; 6 K—B6!, Kt—B1; 7 K—B7!, Kt—K2; 8 K—Q7, K—B1; 9 K—K6. If here 7 .... Kt—R2; 8 B—Q5ch, K—K2; 9 B—B4! wins the Kt); 5 K—Q5, K—Q2; 6 P—R4! and now:

a) 6 .... K—K2; 7 P—R5!, P×P; 8 B—B5! (the point: the Kt is stalemated), P—R5 (if 8 .... Kt—Q2; 9 B×Kt!, K×B; 10 P—K6ch, K—K2; 11 K—K5, P—R5; 12 P×P, P—R4; 13 K—B5 is decisive, while if 8 .... K—Q1; 9 K—Q6, K—K1; 10 P—K6, P—R5; 11 P—K7!!, P×P; 12 B—K4 is the refutation); 9 P×P, K—Q1 (or 9 .... P—R4; 10 K—Q4, K—B2; 11 K—B5!—triangulation—, K—K2; 12 K—Q5 and Black's King must give way); 10 K—Q6, K—K1; 11 P—R5 (not 11 P—K6??, Kt×P!!=), K—B2 (11 .... K—Q1; 12 B—Kt6!); 12 B—B2!, K—Kt1 (12 .... K—K1; 13 B—Kt6ch!, Kt×B; 14 P×Kt, P—R4; 15 P—K6, P—R5; 16 P—Kt7 or here 13 .... K—Q1; 14 P—K6); 13 K—K7, K—Kt2; 14 B—B5!, K—Kt1; 15 K—B6, K—R1; 16 K—B7 and if Black could only skip a move he might be able to defend himself, but he can't, so his game is hopeless. E.g., 16 .... Kt—R2; 17 B×Kt, or 16 .... Kt—Kt3; 17 P×Kt.

b) 6 .... P—R4; 7 B—B2!, K—K2; 8 B—Kt1!, K—Q2 (he has no choice); 9 K—K4, K—K2 (if 9 .... Kt—K3; 10 B—R2, Kt—B4ch; 11 K—Q4, Kt—R5; 12 B—B7); 10 B—R2, Kt—Q2; 11 K—B4, K—B1 (11 .... Kt—B4; 12 K—Kt5!, Kt—K5ch; 13 K×P, Kt×P; 14 B—B4, K—B1; 14 K—Kt5, Kt—K5ch;—else the Kt is lost—; 15 K×P, Kt—B4; 16 B—Kt5!, K—K2; 17 K—Kt6, K—K3; 18 P—R5, K×P; 19 P—R6, Kt—K3; 20 B—B4, Kt—B1ch; 21 K—Kt7 and wins); 12 B—Kt1, K—B2; 13 B—B2!, Kt—B1 (13 .... K—Kt2; 14 P—K6, Kt—B4; 15 K—K5); 14 B—Kt3ch, K—Kt2; 14 K—K4, Kt—Q2; 15 K—Q5, K—B1; 16 K—Q6, Kt—Kt3; 17 K—B7, Kt—R1ch; 18 K—Kt7 and wins.

On the other hand, if the Black Pawns were on their original squares here White could do nothing. No. 237f, White: K at Q4, B at Q5, P's at K5, KKt3, KR2; Black: K at K2, Kt at Q2, P's at

KKt2, KR2. Draw. 1 B—K4, P—R3! (the point); 2 B—B5, Kt—
Kt3; 3 B—B2, Kt—Q2; 4 B—Kt3, Kt—Kt3; 5 K—K4, K—B1!;
6 K—B5, Kt—B1; 7 K—K6 (or 7 K—Kt6, Kt—K2ch; 8 K—R7,
Kt—B3; 9 P—K6, Kt—K2—the Kt cannot be stalemated by the
Bishop and can consequently always cover the square K2 and prevent
the only P sacrifice which might give White winning chances), Kt—
K2; 8 K—Q6, Kt—Kt3; 9 P—K6, Kt—K2; 10 B—B2, Kt—B1ch;
12 K—Q7, Kt—K2; 13 P—R4, Kt—Kt1, etc.—again the Kt cannot
be stalemated and White cannot get through.

A protected passed Pawn is not so strong in conjunction with
a Bishop as it is with a Knight. For the B is at home in open positions,
while the Kt is most effective when the Pawns are blockaded.

No. 238 (Petrov-Reshevsky, Semmering-Baden, 1937) is an illustration of the type of ending where the Bishop is effective. Here the
Kt is practically stalemated by the B and as a result the decisive
entry of the White King cannot be prevented. The conclusion was
*1 .... Kt—B1; 2 B—Kt5, K—B2; 3 K—Kt3, Kt—Q2; 4 B—K7,
K—Kt3; 5 B—Q8ch, K—Kt2; 6 K—B3* (6 K—R4, K—R3), *K—B1;
7 B—K7, K—B2; 8 K—Q3* (Now White has reached the position he
was striving for—any Kt move will cost Black a Pawn), *K—B1;
9 K—K3, K—B2; 10 K—B3, K—B1; K—Kt4, Kt—Kt3* (desperation);
12 B✕P, Kt✕P; 13 B—Kt4! (or 13 B—B8, Kt—Q7; 14 B✕P, Kt✕P;
15 B✕P, when White will still win, but there may be some technical
difficulties. The text is simpler.), *Kt—Kt7; 14 K—Kt5, Kt—Q6;
15 K—Kt6!,* and Black resigned, for after *15 .... Kt✕B; 16 K✕P*
the KBP cannot be stopped.

But if the Bishop were on White squares in No. 238, the Kt could
not be stalemated and no entry with the King could be forced. E.g.,
No. 238a, White Bishop at Q3, other pieces as in No. 238. Draw.
First on the Q-side: 1 K—Kt3, K—B2; 2 K—R4, K—Kt3; 3 B—K2,
Kt—B3; 4 B—B3, Kt—K1; 5 B—K2, Kt—Q3; 6 B—Q3, Kt—K1
and White is at a standstill. Similarly on the K-side: 7 K—Kt3,
K—B2; 8 K—B2, K—Q2; 9 K—Q2, Kt—B3; 10 K—K3, Kt—R4;
11 K—B3, Kt—B5; 12 B—B2, K—Q3; 13 K—Kt4, K—K2; 14 K—
Kt5, K—Q3; 15 P—B6, P✕Pch; 16 K✕P and now all that Black
need do is move back and forth until White gets tired.

If the Pawn position is not blocked a protected passed Pawn
is just as great an advantage as an outside Pawn. E.g., No. 238b
(Spielmann-Tarrasch, Gothenburg, 1920), White: K at Q1, Kt at K2,
P's at QR2, QKt2, QB3, KKt2, KR2; Black: K at KKt1, B at QR3,
P's at QR2, QB4, QB5, Q4, KKt4, KR2. Black wins. (The QP is a
potential protected passed Pawn.) 1 .... K—B2; 2 Kt—Kt1, B—B1;
3 K—Q2, B—Kt5 (stalemating the Kt temporarily. To get out of the
straitjacket White must set up new targets for Black to aim at);

4 P—KR3, B—R4; 5 P—KKt4, B—Kt3; 6 Kt—B3, K—B3; 7 K—
K3, B—Kt8; 8 P—R3, B—K5; 9 Kt—Q2, K—K4 (not 9 .... B—
Kt7; 10 K—B2!, B×P?; 11 K—Kt3! and the B is lost); 10 K—B2,
K—B5; 11 Kt—B1, B—Kt8 (to gain time); 12 Kt—Q2, B—B7;
13 Kt—B3, B—Q8; 14 Kt—Q2, P—KR3; 15 K—K1, B—R5; 16 K—
B2, B—B7; 17 Kt—B1, P—QR4 (to block the Q-side completely
before the decisive break on the other wing); 18 Kt—Q2, B—Kt3;
19 Kt—B3, P—R5; 20 Kt—Q2, P—R4; 21 P×P, B×P (now the
KRP is White's Achilles' heel); 22 Kt—B1, B—B2; 23 Kt—Kt3,
B—Kt3; 24 Kt—B1, B—B4 and White soon resigned.

If the superior side had a Kt instead of a B no such difficulties
would arise because the enemy B would be deprived of mobility by
having to guard the passed Pawn.

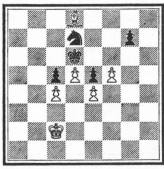

No. 238

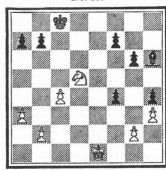

No. 239

White wins. Draw with the White   Black wins.
     Bishop at Q3 instead of Q8.

The defender can draw with a Pawn down or put up a rousing
good fight chiefly in cases of blockade and weak Pawn structure (the
two are not completely independent). For, as we have seen, an
advantage of *one* Pawn wins only because it can be increased to two
Pawns or a piece. This increase is brought about by an attack on
the enemy Pawns with the King. If the position is blocked, this
attack is out of the question, while if one's own Pawns are weak,
one must guard them before venturing out to harass the opponent's.

The blockade is usually most effective when the inferior side
has a Kt. Nevertheless the superiority of the B is such that unless
the position is completely blockaded an entry with the King can
usually be forced. E.g., in No. 239 (Winawer-Blackburne, Nurenberg,
1883) offhand one would say that Black's majority of 4 vs. 2 on the
K-side is counter-balanced by White's 3 vs. 2 on the Q-side because

the KBP is doubled, and that the game should therefore be a draw. But because the long diagonal is still at Black's disposal he can win. *1 .... K—Q2; 2 K—K2, P—B4; 3 K—B3, P—KKt4* (tying the King down); *4 Kt—Kt4, B—Kt2; 5 Kt—Q3, K—Q3* (now the Kt must not move); *6 P—QKt3, B—Q5; 7 K—K2, B—K6; 8 K—B3* (the threat was .... P—Kt5), *P—Kt3; 9 P—QKt4, P—QR3; 10 P—R4, B—Q5* (White's Pawn moves are finally exhausted); *11 K—K2, B—B6; 12 P—Kt5, P—R4; 13 K—B2, B—Q5ch; 14 K—K2, B—Kt8!; 15 K—B3, B—K6!* (He has finally reached his goal. Either the Kt moves, when a Pawn on the Q-side goes by the board, or the K moves, when the advance P—Kt5 is conclusive); *16 P—Kt4* (Desperation. If 16 K—K2, P—Kt5; 17 K—B1, P—B6!; 18 P×BP, P×RP!; 19 P—B4, B—Q5 and the Kt must move), *RP×P e.p.; 17 K—Kt2, B—Q7; 18 P—B5ch* (or 18 K—B3, P—Kt5ch; 19 P×P, P×Pch; 20 K—Kt2, B—K6; 21 K—B1, P—B6), *P×P; 19 P—Kt6, P—B5; 20 Kt—K5, P—B6* (20 .... K×Kt!! is also playable: 21 P—Kt7, K—K5; 22 P—Kt8=Q, P—B6ch; 23 K—B1, P—Kt7ch; 24 K—B2, B—K6ch and mate next move); *21 Kt—B4ch, K—B3; 22 Kt—R3, K×P* and White will soon have to Pawn his Knight.

A somewhat similar case where it is very difficult to penetrate the enemy lines is No. 239a (Spielmann-Krejcik, Vienna, 1930), White: K at KKt3, B at Q3, P's at QR3, QB2, QB4, Q5, KR3; Black: K at KB3, Kt at K4, P's at QR2, QKt2, QB4, Q3. Clearly the problem for White is how to get to the Q-side with his King, for a direct attempt by K—B2—K2—Q2—B3—Kt3—R4 would be frustrated by .... Kt×B and .... K—Kt3—R4. Spielmann solved the problem as follows: 1 K—B4, P—R3; 2 B—K2, P—Kt3; 3 P—KR4, Kt—B2; 4 P—R5, Kt—R3. Now White can make progress only by successively stalemating the Black Kt. 5 B—Kt4, Kt—B2; 6 P—R4, Kt—K4; 7 B—K2, Kt—B2; 8 B—Q3, P—R4; 9 B—K2, Kt—K4 (if 9 .... Kt—R3; 10 B—B1, Kt—B2; 11 B—Q3, Kt—R3; 12 B—Kt6, Kt—Kt1; 13 B—B5, Kt—R3; 14 B—K6); 10 P—R6, Kt—Kt3ch; 11 K—Kt4, Kt—K4ch; 12 K—R5, Kt—B2; 13 P—R7, K—Kt2; 14 B—Q3, K—B3; 15 K—Kt4, Kt—K4ch; 16 K—B4, Kt—B2; 17 B—K2, K—Kt3; 18 B—B3, Kt—R1; 19 B—Kt4, Kt—B2; 20 B—K6, Kt—R1; 21 B—Q7!, K×P; 22 K—B5, K—Kt2; 23 B—K8 (to keep the Kt tied down: the K and P ending is always won because White has an extra tempo), K—B1; 24 B—R5, K—K2; 25 K—Kt5, Kt—B2ch; 26 B×Kt, K×B; 27 K—B5 and Black resigned.

The method of defeating a blockade, then, is that of manoeuvring into a position where the opponent has no good moves—zugzwang. This is accomplished by advancing the King as far as possible and then stalemating the Kt with the B.

Another type of difficulty which frequently arises is that of weak or blocked Pawns. No. 236 is one such example. There the Pawns were so weak that Black could draw with best play. Barring such extreme cases, however, a blocked position causes annoyance and requires technical ingenuity, but there should never be any doubt as to the ultimate outcome. E.g., in No. 240 (Balogh-Eliskases, Budapest, 1934), Black's passed Pawn is so near the enemy King that it implies no real threat, his Bishop is almost wholly ineffective, and his KP is a potential target which makes any long trips with his King rather dangerous. Nevertheless because of the possibilities on the Q-wing he can win. The game continued: *1 .... K—B3; 2 Kt—K1* (pinning his hopes on passive defense. The more active 2 P—KR4!? is met by 2 .... P—Kt5; 3 P—R5, K—Kt4; 4 Kt—R4!?, P—B5!; 5 Kt—Kt6, P—Kt6!; 6 P×P, P×P; 7 K—Q3, K—Kt5; 8 Kt×B, P×Kt; 9 P—Kt5, P—B6; 10 P—Kt6, P—B7; 11 K—K2, P—B8 = Qch!; 12 K×Q, P—Kt7; 13 P—Kt7, P—Kt8 = Qch), *P—Kt5* (not 2 .... P—B5; 3 Kt—B2!, B—Q7; 4 Kt—Q4ch, K—Q2 and Black is nowhere); *3 Kt—Q3, B—R7; 4 Kt—K1* (4 Kt—Kt2, K—Kt4; 5 K—Q3? leaves the KP en prise), *K—Kt4; 5 Kt—B3, B—Kt6; 6 K—Q3, P—B5ch; 7 K—K4, B—B7* (7 .... P—Kt6; 8 P×P, P×P; 9 K—Q3, K—B4; 10 K—B3, K—Q4; 11 K×P, K—K5 was also good enough. If here 8 Kt—Q4ch, K—R5; 9 P×Pch, P×P; 10 K—Q3, B×P; 11 Kt×P, K—R6 is conclusive); *8 Kt—Q2, P—B6; 9 Kt—Kt3, K—R5* (this inroad is decisive); *10 K—Q3, K—R6; 11 K—B4, K×P; 12 K×P, K—Kt7!; 13 Kt—B1, K×Kt; 14 K×P, B—Kt6; 15 K—Q4, K—Q7;* 16 Resigns.

Endings with all the Pawns on one side (4 vs. 3, or 3 vs. 2) are not easy to judge. With 3 vs. 2 if there is no passed Pawn (e.g., BP, KtP, RP vs. KtP, RP) it is surely a draw (compare No. 231b). With a passed Pawn (e.g., KP, KtP, RP vs. KtP, RP) if the superior side has a Kt he should win (No. 237b), but if he has a B he will win only if he can force a weakness in the enemy's Pawn structure (No. 237f). With 4 vs. 3, however (KP, BP, KtP, RP vs. BP, KtP, RP) if the superior side has a Kt he should in general win, since he can convert his KP and BP into an outside passed Pawn by exchanging the enemy BP. But with a B, although he has better prospects than with

No. 240

Black wins.

3 vs. 2, a draw will frequently result because of the inability of the B to cover all squares.

2. POSITIONAL ADVANTAGE

All chess theory is based on the concept of mobility: one piece is stronger than another if it can cover more squares, one position is preferable to another if the pieces act together more harmoniously, do not get in one another's way. This consideration is the key to questions of positional advantage in general, but is especially applicable in the case of B vs. Kt. Thus a Kt in the center covers eight squares; a B thirteen. It is only because the Kt can cover squares which the B cannot reach that the discrepancy is not more marked.

We can distinguish four different types of superiority here, of which the first two are the most important—better Bishop, better Knight, better King position, better Pawn position. By examining all these cases in detail we shall be able to get a clearer picture of why the B is in general superior, even though the Kt is quite often just as strong and stronger.

a) *The Bishop Is Superior.*

It stands to reason that the B needs wide open spaces to show his talents: he can control KR8 from QB3, but if there are enemy Pawns at KKt7, KB6 and K5 this control is only potential and does him no good. Similarly if his own Pawns are at Q4 and K5 the B is almost as useless as a Pawn.

The first type of position then in which we can note the power of the B is one in which the Pawns are balanced and unblocked. I.e., there are just as many Black Pawns on the Q-side as there are White (and

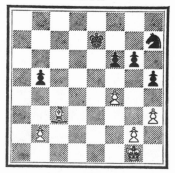

No. 241

White to play wins.

similarly for the other wing) and these Pawns are free to move about. In such cases the B may be exploited in one of three ways:

1. By forcing a direct entry with the King.
2. By creating weaknesses in the enemy Pawn position which will permit the King entry.
3. By capturing one or more Pawns.

Of these the first represents the central idea, for a positional advantage is useless if it cannot be converted into a material advantage.

The third is also important, but usually occurs only in special positions. The second is of course subsidiary to either the first or, less frequently, the third; it almost always goes hand in hand with them.

No. 241 (Flohr-Loevenfisch, Leningrad-Moscow, 1939) is a splendid example of the first case—forcing an entry with the King because of the superiority of the B. After *1 K—B2, K—K3; 2 K—K3, Kt—B1* (Black has little choice: if he tries to oppose the entry of the White King his Kt will be stalemated. E.g., 2 .... K—Q4; 3 K—Q3, P—B4; 4 B—Kt7!, P—Kt4; 5 K—K3, K—K3; 6 P—KKt3, K—B2; 7 B—B3, P×Pch; 8 P×P, Kt—B1; 9 K—Q4, Kt—Kt3; 10 B—Q2, Kt- R5; 11 K—B5, Kt—B6; 12 B—K3, K—K3; 13 P—Kt4, Kt—K8; 14 K×P, K—Q4; 15 K—R6, Kt—B7; 16 B—Q2 and the extra Pawn is decisive. Or 2 .... K—B4; 3 B—Kt4!, K—K3; 4 K—K4, P—B4ch; 5 K—Q4, Kt—B3; 6 K—B5 and again a vital Pawn goes); *3 B—Kt4, Kt—Q2; 4 K—Q4, Kt—Kt3* (If 4 .... K—B4; 5 B—Q2!, Kt—Kt3; 6 P—QKt3!, K—K3; 7 K—B5, Kt—Q4; 8 P—QKt4 and wins); *5 P—Kt4* (not 5 K—B5?, Kt—R5ch), *P×P; 6 P×P, P—B4; 7 P—Kt5!* (One must avoid Pawn exchanges if one is trying to win), *Kt—Q4; 8 B—Q2, K—Q3; 9 P—Kt3!!!* (the point to the previous play: Black is in zugzwang. If the K moves, then either K—B5 or K—K5 is conclusive. If the Kt moves, B—Kt4ch forces the Black monarch to get out of the way. Finally, there is the Pawn move, which was played. It loses a P.), *P—Kt5; 10 K—B4, K—B3; 11 B—B1, Kt—B6* (Costs him the KtP, but there was no adequate defense. If 11 .... K—Q3; 12 B—Q2, K—B3; 13 K—Q4, K—Q3; 14 B—B1, Kt—B6; 15 B—K3!, Kt—Q4; 16 B—Q2, K—B3; 17 K—B4, K—Q3; 18 K—Kt5, K—K2; 19 K—B5, K—K3; 20 B—B1, Kt—B6; 21 B—K3, K—K2; 22 B—Q4, etc., as in the game); *12 B—Kt2* (not 12 K×P?, Kt—R7ch), *Kt—K7; 13 B—K5, Kt—B8!* (highly ingenious, but in the long run unavailing); *14 B—Kt8!* (if 14 K×P, K—Q4; 15 K—B3, K—K5; 16 P—Kt4, Kt—Q6! and both 17 P—Kt5, Kt×B and 17 B—B7, Kt×BP! are not quite adequate), *Kt—R7; 15 B—R7, Kt—B6; 16 B—K3, Kt—K5; 17 B—Q4* (he is in no hurry), *Kt—Kt6; 18 B—K3, Kt—K5; 19 K×P, K—Q4* (now Black's drawing hopes lie wholly in the blockade of the White QKtP); *20 K—R5, K—B3; 21 K—R6, Kt—B6; 22 B—Q2, Kt—Kt4; 23 P—Kt4, Kt—Q3; 24 B—B1, Kt—Kt4; 25 B—Kt2, Kt—B2ch; 26 K—R5, Kt—Kt4; 27 B—B6, Kt—B2; 28 B—K5, Kt—Q4* (28 .... Kt—Kt4 is equally hopeless. There would follow 29 K—R6, Kt—R6; 30 K—R7, K—Kt4; 31 K—Kt7, Kt—B7; 32 K—B7!, Kt×P; 33 K—Q7, K—B5; 34 K—K6, Kt—Q6; 35 K—B6, K—Q4; 36 B—Kt8, K—K5; 37 K×P, Kt×Pch; 38 B×Kt, K×B; 39 K—B6 and the White Pawn gets there just in time); *29 P—Kt5ch, K—Kt2; 30 B—Q6, K—R2; 31 P—Kt6ch, K—Kt2; 33 K—Kt5, Kt×P; 34 K—B5, Kt—R5ch; 35 K—Q5,*

Kt—B6ch; 36 K—K6, K—B3; 37 B—K5, Kt—K5; 38 K—B7, K—Q4; 39 K×P, K—K3; 40 K—R7, Kt×Pch; 41 P×Kt! Resigns.

In the above example the Kt was in an unfortunate position and the danger of having that piece stalemated forced Black to allow the entry of the White King. But even with the Kt solidly entrenched in the center of the board the power of the B may make itself felt. The only conditions are that there should be Pawns on both sides of the board and that they should be mobile. Thus in No. 242 (Stoltz-Kashdan, The Hague, 1928) the greater scope of the B is the reason why Black's King cannot be prevented from attacking the Pawns on one side or the other. The first step is centralization:

No. 242

No. 243

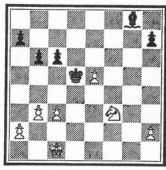

Black to play wins.

Black to play wins.

1 .... K—B1; 2 K—B1, K—K2; 3 K—K2, K—Q3; 4 K—Q3, K—Q4. Now the White King must be driven away from Q3. *5 P—R4* (to evade the danger of losing a P), *B—B1!; 6 Kt—B3, B—R3ch; 7 K— B3* (Or 7 K—K3, K—B4; 8 Kt—Kt5, K—Kt5; 9 Kt×BP, and the Kt will soon have to be given up for the passed Pawn), *P—R3; 8 Kt—Q4, P—Kt3* (first the Pawns must be immunized against attack); *9 Kt—B2, K—K5* (at last! the first point is scored); *10 Kt— K3, P—B4; 11 K—Q2, P—B5; 12 Kt—Kt4, P—R4; 13 Kt—B6ch, K—B4; 14 Kt—Q7* (He has little choice. If 14 Kt—Q5, B—Kt2; 15 Kt—K7ch, K—B3; 16 Kt—Kt8ch, K—B2; 17 Kt—R6ch, K—Kt2 is decisive), *B—B1!; 15 Kt—B8, P—Kt4; 16 P—Kt3* (16 P×P?, K×P costs him his Kt), *P×RP; 17 P×RP, K—Kt5* (Finally Black is ready to pluck the ripened fruit. The Pawn capture is conclusive.); *18 Kt—Kt6, B—B4; 19 Kt—K7, B—K3; 20 P—Kt4, K×P; 21 K— Q3, K—Kt5; 22 K—K4, P—R5; 23 Kt—B6, B—B4ch; 24 K—Q5, P—B6!* (else Kt—K5ch followed by Kt—B3. Now the Pawn queens

by force); *25 P—Kt5, P—R6; 26 Kt×P, P—R7; 27 P—Kt6, P—R8=*
Q; 28 Kt—B6, Q—QKt8; 29 K—B5, B—K5; 30 Resigns.

A case very similar to the above is No. 243 (Bogatyrtchuk-Rabino-
vitch, Leningrad, 1923). The dominating position of the Black
King is deceptive here because he must lose time in order to capture
the KP. Nevertheless after this capture, despite the fact that the
White King will be placed on a Black square (K3), the Bishop will
continue to rule the board and the Black King will be able to effect
a break on one side or the other. The continuation was: *1 .... P—*
B4! (not 1 .... K—K5; 2 Kt—Q4, P—B4; 3 Kt—B6 with excellent
counter-chances); *2 K—Q2, K—K5; 3 K—K2, P—KR3* (to prevent
Kt—Kt5ch. Now the B may move.); *4 Kt—Q2ch* (he agrees before
the proof is furnished. On 4 K—B2, B—B2; 5 K—Kt3, B—R4 was
expected), *K×P; 5 K—K3, B—Q4!* (centralization); *6 Kt—Kt1* (or
6 Kt—B3ch, K—B4!; 7 P—KR3, P—QR4; 8 P—B4, B—K5; 9 P—
R3, B—B7; 10 Kt—Q2, K—Kt4; 11 K—B3, K—R5; 12 K—Kt2,
B—Q8!; 13 K—R2, P—R4; 14 K—Kt2, K—Kt4; 15 K—Kt3, P—
R5ch; 16 K—B2, K—B5 and wins as in the game. White is proceeding according to the sensible idea that he will advance his Pawns only
if there is no alternative—any change in their present status would
inevitably weaken them), *K—B4; 7 Kt—R3, P—R3* (else Kt—Kt5—
Q6 will give White counterplay); *8 Kt—B2, K—Kt5; 9 K—B2, K—B5!*
(the first goal has been reached: the King is firmly entrenched on the
fifth rank. Now a decisive inroad to one side must be prepared.
This is done by weakening the Q-side Pawns.); *10 Kt—K3, B—B2;*
11 K—K2, P—Kt4; 12 K—B2, B—K3; 13 K—K2, K—K5!! (Now
White is in zugzwang. If 14 P—B4, P×P; 15 P×P, K—Q5; 16 K—
Q2, P—KR4! wins a P, while a King move would allow either ....
K—B6 or .... K—Q6); *14 Kt—Kt2, B—Kt5ch* (or at once 14 ....
P—B5!); *15 K—Q2, B—K3; 16 Kt—K1, P—B5!; 17 P×P* (A bitter
pill to swallow. But 17 P—Kt4, B—Kt5! 18 Kt—Kt2, K—B6 is no
sweeter.), *B×P; 18 P—QR3, P—QR4; 19 Kt—B2, P—R5; 20 Kt—Q4*
(20 Kt—K3, K—B6!), *P—R4; 21 Kt—B2, K—B6; 22 Kt—K3, K—*
B7!; 23 Kt—B5, K—Kt7; 24 P—R4, K—B6; 25 Kt—K7, K—Kt6!;
26 Kt—Kt6, B—B2; 27 Kt—K5, B—Q4; 28 Kt—Kt6, B—K5; 29 Kt—
K5, K×P. Now that this vital Pawn is gone the rest is simple.
30 K—K3, B—Q4; 31 Kt—Q3 (on 31 K—B4 the King escapes via
KR6 and KKt7 to the Q-side), *B—B5; 32 Kt—B2, K—Kt6; 33 Kt—*
K4ch, K—Kt7 and White will have to give up his Kt for the RP.

Often it is essential to weaken the enemy Pawn position or to open
the game before the King can enter for the decisive break. A simple
case of this type is No. 244 (Tchekhover-Lasker, Moscow, 1935).
Lasker won as follows: *1 K—B1* (if 1 P—QR4, K—Kt3; 2 P—QKt4,
B—Q3; 3 P—Kt5, K—R4; 4 Kt—B3, B—K4 is conclusive), *P—*

QKt4! (the ending is being conducted with mathematical precision. After 1 .... B—Kt7; 2 P—QR4, K—Kt3; 3 K—K1, K—R4; 4 K—Q2, K—Kt5; 5 K—B2 it is doubtful whether Black can win); *2 K—K1, B—Kt7; 3 P—QR4, P×P; 4 P×P, K—B3!!* (again admirably calculated. On 4 .... K—Kt3; 5 K—Q2, K—R4?; 6 K—B2!, B—K4; 7 P—B4, B—Q3; 8 K—Kt3 White's position is tenable); *5 K—Q2, K—B4!; 6 Kt—B3* (sad necessity. If 6 K—B2, B—Q5!; 7 P—B3, K—B5! is conclusive: a) 8 Kt×B, K×Kt; 9 K—Kt3, P—QR4! and the ending is easy; b) 8 Kt—B1, B—K4; 9 P—R3, K—Kt5 and wins a vital Pawn), *K—Kt5; 7 Kt—Kt5, P—QR4!*

No. 244	No. 245
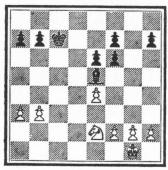	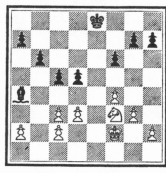
Black wins.	White to play; Black wins.

Now a Pawn is lost without any compensation. The rest involves nothing new. *8 Kt—Q6, K×P; 9 K—B2* (if 9 Kt×P, K—Kt6; 10 Kt—Q8, P—R5; 11 Kt×P, P—R6; 12 Kt—B5ch, K—B5 and the Kt must be given up at once to stop the Pawn), *B—K4; 10 Kt×P, B×P; 11 Kt—Q8, P—K4; 12 Kt—B6, B—Kt8; 13 P—B3, B—B4; 14 Kt—Kt8, K—Kt4; 15 P—Kt4, B—K2; 16 P—Kt5* (the Kt was endangered), *P×P; 17 Kt—Q7, B—Q3; 18 Kt—B6, K—B5!;* 19 Resigns. For after 19 Kt×P, B—K2 White will lose both Pawns and Knight.

But even when the position is more complicated this scheme of weakening the Pawns to open a path for the King is feasible. While it would be exaggerated to say that the B then wins by force in all such balanced Pawn positions, it is true that the slightest unfavorable deviation from the normal will usually cost the side which has the Kt the game. Thus in No. 245 (Reti-Rubinstein, Gothenburg, 1920) the doubled Pawn is fatal. The continuation was *1 Kt—K1, K—K2;*

2 K—K3, K—K3 (to weaken the K-side Pawns. The threat is K—B4—Kt5—R6); *3 P—Kt4, K—Q3* (to answer 4 K—Q2 with 4 .... B—Q2); *4 P—KR3, P—Kt3; 5 K—Q2* (the changing of the guard. But the weak K-side Pawns require the attention of a sovereign), *B—Q2; 6 Kt—B3, K—K2!* (Reculer pour mieux sauter—he threatens 7 .... P—KR4!; 8 P×P, P×P; 9 P—KR4, K—K3. If at once 6 .... P—KR4?; 7 P—Kt5!, B×P; 8 P×P, B—B4—not 8 .... K—K3; 9 Kt—Kt5ch—; 9 Kt—K5, P—R5; 10 K—K3 and should draw.); *7 K—K3, P—KR4!; 8 Kt—R2* (Or 8 P—Kt5, B×P, or 8 P×P, P×P; 9 P—KR4, K—K3; 10 Kt—K1, K—B4; 11 K—B3, P—Q5! etc.), *K—Q3!* (He has done a good day's work on the K-side and now he shifts to the other wing. The weak QBP keeps White's King tied down); *9 K—K2* (On 9 K—B3, B—R5! wins a Pawn, while 9 .... P—Q5!; 10 P×P, P×P; 11 K—K4?, K—B4! threatening .... B—B3 mate is also quite good. 9 P—Q4 is refuted by 9 .... K—B3; 10 K—Q2, K—Kt4; 11 K—Q3, B—B1; 12 K—Q2, K—B5; 13 QP×P, KtP×P; 14 Kt—B1, P—Q5; 15 P×QP, K×P; 16 Kt—K3, K—K5. If here 11 P—B5, P×KtP; 12 BP×P, P—Kt6; 13 Kt—B3, B×P, or 12 Kt×P, B×P costs White a Pawn. The same variations hold against P—B5 at some other stage), *P—Q5* (fixing the Q-side Pawns); *10 BP×P?* (This loses much more quickly than the alternative 10 P—B4!, when Black's best line is 10 .... P×P; 11 P×P—or A—, K—K2 —or B—; 12 K—Q2, P—KKt4; 13 P—B5—or C—, K—Q3; 14 Kt—B3, B—B3; 15 K—K2, P—QR3; 16 K—B2, B×Kt; 17 K×B, P—QKt4!! and the K and P ending is won: 18 K—K4, K—B3; 19 K—B3, K—Q2!; 20 K—K4, K—Q3; 21 K—B3, K—K4; 22 P×P ·—or D—, P×P; 23 P—R3, K—Q4; 24 K—Kt3, P—B5; 25 K—B3, P—B6!; 26 K—Kt3, K—B4; 27 K—B3, P—Kt5; 28 P×Pch, K×P; 29 K—K4, K—R6; 30 K×P, K—Kt7; 31 K—K4, K×P; 32 P—Q4, K—Kt7; 33 P—Q5, P—B7 and gets there just in time.

Variation A. 11 Kt×P?, K—K3; 12 Kt—R6, P—B4.

Variation B. 11 .... P—KKt4?; 12 P×P!, P×P; 13 K—B2!!, B—R5 (or 13 .... K—K4; 14 K—Kt3, B—R5; 15 Kt—B3ch, K—B3; 16 Kt—K1=); 14 Kt—B3, B×P; 15 K—K2!!=.

Variation C. 13 P×P, P×P; 14 K—K2, K—B3!; 15 K—Q2, K—K4 and wins. Or 15 K—B2, B—R5.

Variation D. 22 K—Kt3, P×P; 23 P×P, P—Q6!; 24 P×P, K—Q5, or 22 P—R3, K—Q3; 23 K—K4, K—B3; 24 K—B3, K—Q2! etc., as above.) *10 .... BP×P; 11 K—Q2* (He must do something against the march of the Black King to the Q-side. If 11 P×P, P×P; 12 P—KR4, K—B4; 13 Kt—B3, B—Kt5; 14 K—B2, B×Kt; 15 K×B, P—B4! decides), *P×P; 12 P×P* (again 12 Kt×P, B×Kt leads into a lost Pawn ending), *B—B3; 13 K—K2* (if 13 P—B3, P×Pch; 14

K×P, B—Kt7! and the Kt is stalemated), *B—Q4; 14 P—R3, P—QKt4* (Black has in effect a majority of P's on the Q-side and by advancing them will secure an outside passed Pawn); *15 Kt—B1, P—R4; 16 Kt—Q2, P—R5!; 17 Kt—K4ch* (desperation. If 17 Kt—Kt1, B—K3!; 18 K—B3, B—R7!; 19 Kt—Q2, P—Kt5!; 20 P×P, P—R6 and the Pawn can no longer be stopped), *B×Kt; 18 P×B, P—Kt5!; 19 K—Q2* (19 P×P, P—R6 and the P queens), *P×P; 20 K—B1, P—Kt4;* 21 Resigns, for after 21 P×P, P×P; 22 K—Kt1 both K—K4 and K—B4 are sufficient for Black.

While it is a serious positional handicap for the side which has the Bishop to put all his Pawns on the B's color (because his own pieces are then merely obstructing one another), his opponent should place them on that color only if he has the initiative and if they are not subject to attack. We have already seen several examples (Nos. 235, 245) where the exposed position of the Pawns enhances the value of the Bishop. In No. 245 the White pieces were tied down to the defense of the Pawn and this made a decision on another part of the board possible. But sometimes it is so bad that a Pawn is lost by force. Such is the case in No. 246 (Maroczy-Teichmann, Nurenberg, 1896). In this position a Pawn can be won in various ways but Black must make sure that the resulting ending will not be drawn because of his weak KtP's. E.g., 1 .... K—K4; 2 K—K3, B—K5; 3 Kt—Q1, B—Kt7; 4 Kt—B2, B—B8 but then White holds the game by 5 Kt—K4!, B×BP (or 5 .... P—B3; 6 Kt—Q2!, B—Kt7; 7 Kt—B3ch!); 6 Kt×KtP, B×P; 7 Kt—B3ch!! and the K and P ending is drawn. However, in view of the fact that White's Kt is stalemated and six of his seven Pawns are potential targets, his position is untenable in the long run. *1 .... K—K2; 2 K—K3, K—Q2* (going to the Q-side); *3 K—B3* (If 3 K—Q2, B—K5; 4 Kt—Q3, B—Kt7;

No. 246

Black wins.

5 Kt—B2, B—B8; 6 Kt—K4, B×RP!; 7 Kt×KtP, B×P; 8 Kt×P, B×P and wins), *K—B2; 4 K—K3, K—Kt1; 5 K—B3* (If now 5 K—Q2, B—K5; 6 Kt—Q3, B—Kt7; 7 Kt—B2, B—B8; 8 Kt—K4, B×RP!; 9 Kt×KtP, B×P and the King must lose valuable time to get back to the RP, so that Black comes out a clear Pawn ahead: 10 K—K3, B×P; 11 Kt×P, K—B2 etc. Or here 9 Kt×QP, P—B3!; 10 Kt—K4, B×P; 11 Kt×BP, B×P and the two connected passed Pawns decide), *K—R2; 6 K—K3,*

K—R3; 7 K—Q2 (if 7 P—B6, K—R4; 8 K—B3, B×P; 9 Kt×B, K×Kt; 10 K—K4, K—Kt6; 11 K—B5, K×P(B6); 12 K×P, P—Kt4!; 13 P×P, P—B5; 14 K—R6, K—Q5; 15 K—Kt7, P—B6; 16 K ×P, P—B7; 17 K—Kt7, P—B8 = Q; 18 P—B7, Q—Kt4ch and wins), *B—K5; 8 Kt—Q1, K—R4* and White's Pawns will fall like ripe apples: 9 Kt—B2, B—Kt7; 10 K—K3, K×P; 11 K—Q2, K—Kt6; 12 K —Q3, B—B8ch; 13 K—K3, K×P(B5); 14 Kt—K4, B×P; 15 Kt ×Pch, K×QP; 16 Kt×BP, B×P; 17 Kt×P, B×P and Black is three Pawns ahead.

Even if the defender just manages to hold all his material in this and similar positions where the Pawns are exposed, he is at a definite disadvantage because of the constricted placement of his pieces. "The best defense is a counter-attack" holds just as often in the endgame as in the middle game and opening. Where the superior side has no tempo with which to exploit his control of more terrain, a sacrifice will sometimes do the trick. It should be remembered that it is harder for a Kt to stop Pawns than it is for a B, and in particular that a Kt is especially weak against a passed RP. This fact is utilized in No. 246a (Marco and Faendrich-Charousek and Schlechter, Vienna, 1897), White: K at Q2, Kt at K2, P's at QR3, QKt3, K4, KB3, KKt3, KKt2; Black: K at Q3, B at QB3, P's at QR4, QKt3, K4, KB3, KKt3, KR4. Black won. The conclusion was 1 .... K—B4; 2 K—B3, B—Kt4; 3 Kt—B1, B—B8; 4 Kt—Q3ch, K—Kt4!; 5 Kt—K1, P—Kt4; 6 P—B4, KtP×P; 7 P×P, P—KR5; 8 P×P, P×P; 9 Kt—B3 (else 9 .... B×P anyhow, e.g., 9 K—Q2, B×P!; 10 Kt×B, P—R6; 11 Kt any, P—R7 and queens next move), B×P; 10 Kt×KP, P—R6; 11 Kt—Kt4, B×P; 12 K—Q4, B—B7 and the rest is simple: 13 K—B3, B—B4; 14 Kt—R2, K—B4; 15 K—Q2, K—Q5; 16 Kt—B1, B—K3; 17 Re-signs.

If the superiority of the Bishop is manifest in a balanced Pawn position, it is even more evident in the second case, when the Pawns are not in equilibrium, i.e., when there is a Pawn majority on one side. For the Bishop can support his potential passed Pawn at a distance, which means that he can both support the advance of his own Pawns, and prevent the march of his opponent's.

Even in positions where the material has been greatly reduced, this

No. 247

White to play; Black wins.

power of the Bishop to combine offense and defense is evident. Thus in No. 247 (match game Dubois-Steinitz, 1862) the B stops the White K-side Pawns and at the same time keeps an eye on the square QB8, on which the BP will queen, while the Kt will be exhausted by the task of watching the QBP. The win was achieved as follows: *1 Kt— Q4ch, K—Kt7; 2 P—Kt6, B—R3; 3 P—R4, P—R4; 4 P—R5, P—R5; 5 Kt—B2* (Now we see the trouble. The Kt cannot come to the aid of his Pawns), *P—R6; 6 Kt—Q4, P—R7; 7 Kt—B2* (hoping for 7 .... P—R8=Q??; 8 Kt×Q, K×Kt; 9 K—B2, B—Kt2; 10 P—R6!=), *B—Kt2!!* (now White is in zugzwang); *8 Kt—R1, K×Kt; 9 K—B2, B—R3; 10 P—Kt7, B×P; 11 K—B1, P—B7!!* (the coup de grace); *12 K×P, B—R3* and White resigned since he can no longer keep the Black King from coming out of the corner.

It is clear that the more material there is the easier it is to make the superiority of the Bishop tell. Thus in the above example if there had been more Pawns White would not have had the slightest chance of confining Black's King to the corner. Similarly, in general, where both sides have passed Pawns (or potential passed Pawns) and there are five or six Pawns apiece the Bishop is clearly better. No. 248 (Golombek-Keres, Margate, 1939) may be considered typical. The B in conjunction with the majority of Pawns on the Queen's wing make it possible for the Black King to force an entry. The winning process in fact is exactly the same as though Black were a Pawn ahead, for since the KP is almost automatically blocked Black can ignore it and mobilize his own Pawn majority. Keres continued with *1 .... B—B7!* (first step: weaken the enemy Pawns); *2 P—KKt4* (or 2 Kt—K2, K—B3; 3 K—Q3, K—K4 and both White's pieces are tied down), *K—B3; 3 K—K2, B—Q5; 4 K—B3* (hoping to hold the other wing with his Kt. If instead 4 K—Q3, B—Kt3; 5 P—QR4, K—K4; 6 Kt—K2, P—QR4 and again the Black King enters via KB5), *P—QR4; 5 P—Kt5ch, K—K4* (not 5 .... K×P??; 6 Kt—K6ch); *6 Kt—Q3ch, K—Q3; 7 P—KR4, P—QKt4; 8 Kt—K1* (On King moves .... P—QB4—QB5 will force the Kt away anyhow), *B—B4; 9 Kt—Q3, B—Kt3; 10 Kt—B4, B—Q5; 11 Kt—Q3, P—B4* (Now White is faced by exactly the same dilemma as in the case where he is a Pawn down: either stop the Pawn with the King and lose the Q-side Pawns, or stop the Pawn with his Kt and lose that piece or transpose into a lost K and P ending. He chooses the latter.); *12 Kt—B4* (or 12 K—K2, P—B5; 13 P×P, P×P; 14 Kt—B4, K—K4; 15 Kt— Q5, K×P; 16 Kt—B6ch, K—B4; 17 Kt×P, B—Kt2!; 18 K—Q2, K—Kt5; 19 Kt—B6ch, K×P; 20 Kt—K4, K—Kt5; 21 K—K3, B—K4 and the extra Pawn is decisive), *P—B5; 13 P×P, P×P; 14 Kt—Q5, K—K4; 15 Kt—B6, P—R4; 16 Kt—Q5, P—B6; 17 Kt— B4, P—B7; 18 Kt—Q3ch, K—Q3; 19 K—K2, B—Kt7!!* and White resigned, for after *20 K—Q2, P—B8= Qch; 21 Kt×Q, B×Ktch; 22 K×B, K—K4; 23 K—Kt2, K×P; 24 K—R3, K—B5; 25 K—R4, K—Kt5; 26 K×P, K×P; 27 K—Kt5, K×P; 28 P—R4, P—R5* Black queens first.

If in addition to the unbalanced Pawn structure the defender has further weaknesses the game is as good as lost. E.g., in No. 248a (Rellstab-Bogoljuboff, Swinemuende, 1931), White: K at QB2, B at KKt7, P's at QR2, QKt2, K4, KB5, KKt4, KR3; Black: K at Q2, Kt at KB6, P's at QR5, QKt3, QB5, K3, KKt4, KR2 the Q-side Pawns are hopelessly weak, and the Kt is badly placed. As a result Black is already reduced to desperate measures. The game concluded

No. 248

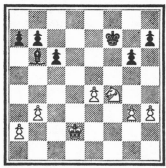

Black wins.

No. 249

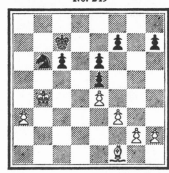

White wins.

with 1 K—B3, P—Kt4; 2 P×Pch (on 2 K—Kt4 he feared 2 .... P—K4!; 3 K×P?, P—R6!, but 3 P—R3 was perfectly all right), K×P; 3 K—Kt4, Kt—Q7; 4 K×P, P—R6; 5 P×P, Kt×P; 6 K×P, Kt—Kt6; 7 P—QR4, P—R4; 8 K—Kt5, P×P; 9 P×P, K—Q2; 10 K—Kt6, K—B1; 11 B—K5, Kt—B8; 12 P—R5, Kt—K6; 13 K—B6, Kt—B5; 14 B—B7 and Black resigned.

In the above examples we find the Bishop in conjunction with a passed Pawn (or potential passed Pawn) which is on the outside because of the relative positions of the Kings. When the passed Pawn is on the R or Kt file, so that it is outside no matter where the Kings happen to be, the speedier manoeuvrability and greater range of the Bishop become even more effective. This is seen in No. 249 (Rubinstein-Johner, Carlsbad, 1929) where the B decides despite the fact that the Pawn position is unfavorably blocked. Rubinstein won as follows: *1 P—QR4* (the first step is to advance the RP as far as feasible in order to constrict the Black pieces. The direct attempt 1 K—B5 is refuted by .... Kt—Q2ch), *Kt—Q2; 2 P—R5, P—R3;*

3 B—Q3, K—Kt2; 4 P—Kt4!! (he can make no further progress on the Q-side and must first weaken the other wing. The text threatens to secure a decisive passed Pawn by P—R4, P—R5, and P—Kt5!), *K—B2; 5 P—R4, Kt—B1; 6 B—B1, Kt—Q2; 7 B—R3!!, Kt—B1; 8 P—R5!, P—B3* (the point to White's manoeuvring has become clear: he has made this weakening unavoidable. For if 8 .... Kt—Q2; 9 P—Kt5!, P×P; 10 P—R6, Kt—B1; 11 B—Kt4!, Kt—R2; 12 B—R5, P—B3; 13 B—B7!, Kt—B1; 14 B×P!!, Kt—Kt3; 15 P—R7, Kt—R1; 16 B—B5, Kt—B2; 17 B—Kt6, Kt—R1; 18 B—R5 and now the entry of the White King is conclusive while if 8 .... Kt—R2; 9 K—B5, Kt—Kt4; 10 B—Kt2, Kt—R2; 11 P—R6!, Kt—B1; 12 P—Kt5!!, Kt—Q2ch; 13 K—Kt4, K—Kt3; 14 P—Kt6, P×P; 15 P×P, P—R4; 16 P—Kt7, Kt—B3; 17 B—R3, P—R5; 18 B×P, K×P; 19 K—B5 with a simple win. Now the Kt is further hampered by the necessity of defending the KP, and this straw is too much for his already overburdened back); *9 B—B1, Kt—Q2; 10 B—B4, Kt—B1; 11 B—Kt3, Kt—R2!; 12 K—B5!!* (not 12 B×P?, Kt—Kt4! followed by Kt×BP), *Kt—B1; 13 B—R2, Kt—Q2ch; 14 K—Kt4, Kt—B1; 15 P—R6!, K—Kt3; 16 P—R7, K×P; 17 K—B5, K—Kt2* (just too late); *18 K—Q6* (decisive), *K—Kt3; 19 K—K7, Kt—R2; 20 B×P, K—B2* (or 20 .... Kt—Kt4; 21 B—Kt3, Kt×BP; 22 K×P, K—B4; 23 K—Kt6, K—Q5; 24 K×P, K×P; 25 P—Kt5 and wins. If here 22 .... Kt—R7; 23 B—Q1! is sufficient); *21 B—B4!* (not 21 B—B5?, Kt—Kt4; 22 K×P, K—Q3!; 23 K—Kt6; P—B4!! and the B cannot get back), *Kt—Kt4; 22 K×P, K—Q3; 23 K—Kt6, K—K2.* Here Black resigned. The conclusion might have been *24 K×P, Kt×BP; 25 P—Kt5* etc., or *24 K×P, K—B3; 25 P—B4, Kt×KP; 26 P—Kt5ch, K—B4; 27 B—Q3!, K×P; 28 B×Kt* etc.

The power of a Bishop together with passed Pawns is so great that sometimes it can even compensate for the absence of a Pawn. Thus in No. 249a (Lasker-Lipke, Breslau, 1889) White: K at KKt4, B at Q2, P's at QKt2, KB4, KKt3, KR4; Black: K at Q2, Kt at Q4, P's at QR3, QKt2, QB2, Q3, KR3. Black to play. White wins. The Bishop can easily hold the Q-side Pawns as long as is necessary while the Knight cannot effectually blockade the K-side Pawns. Lasker wound up as follows: 1 .... Kt—B3ch; 2 K—B5, K—K2; 3 P—KKt4, P—Q4; 4 P—Kt5, P×P; 5 BP×P! (keeping the passed Pawns as far outside as possible), Kt—Q2 (or 5 .... Kt—K5; 6 B—B1, Kt—B4; 7 P—R5, Kt—Kt6; 8 B—B4, P—Q5; 9 P—R6, K—B2; 10 P—Kt6ch); 6 P—Kt6, K—B1; 7 P—R5, P—Q5; 8 P—R6, K—Kt1; 9 P—R7ch, K—R1; 10 K—K6, Kt—B1ch; 11 K—B7 and Black resigned.

One of the most important conclusions that we can draw from the discussion is that *the Bishop is at his best with Pawns on both sides of the board, preferably as far apart as possible.*

We come now to the third kind of position where the B is superior, When all the Pawns are on one side, the only winning chance for the Bishop, even when he is a Pawn ahead (see above), is based on stalemating the Knight. We have already seen examples of this (Nos. 241, 245) with Pawns on both sides, when the object of the stalemate was to divert the enemy King and effect an entry with one's own monarch. But when such an entry is pointless because there are no Pawns to be captured, the stalemate must result in capture of the Knight. It is rather surprising to find that when the Knight strays off (often as a result of exchanges) to the edge of the board the danger of its being lost is quite real.

No. 250 (Marshall-Nimzovitch, Berlin, 1928) is a classic illustration from tournament practice. The Kt can get out only at the cost of a lost King and P ending. After *1 .... K—Q4!* there are three main variations:

a) *2 Kt—Q8, K—Q3; 3 Kt—Kt7ch, K—B3!!!; 4 Kt—R5ch, K— Q4!!; 5 Kt×B* (for 5 Kt—Kt7 see b)), *K×Kt; 6 K—B1* (or 6 P—B3, P—K6!; 7 K—B1, K—Q6; 8 K—K1, P—B4; 9 P—Kt4 P—B5!; 10 K—Q1, P—K7ch; 11 K—K1, K—K6; 12 P—Kt3, P×P and mates in two), *K—Q6; 7 K—K1, P—R4; 8 K—Q1, P—K6!!!; 9 P×P* (if 9 P—B3, P—B4!; 10 P—B4, P—K7ch, 11 K—K1, K—K6 etc.), *K×P; 10 K—K1, K—K5; 11 K—K2, K—B4; 12 K—B3, K—Kt4; 13 K—K3, K—Kt5; 14 K—B2, P—B3; 15 K—B1, K×P; 16 K—Kt1, P—R5; 17 K—B1, P—R6; 18 K—Kt1!, K—Kt5; 19 P×Pch, K×P; 20 K—B2, K—Kt5* and wins because his King is two squares in front of the Pawn, so that he has the opposition.

b) *2 Kt—Q8, K—Q3; 3 Kt—Kt7ch, K—B3!; 4 Kt—R5ch, K—Q4; 5 K—R2* (or 5 Kt—Kt7, B—R7!; 6 Kt—Q8, K—Q3; 7 Kt— Kt7ch, K—B3; 8 Kt—R5ch, K—Kt3 and the Kt is lost), *B—R7!; 6 K—R3, K—B4; 7 Kt—Kt7ch, K—B3!; 8 Kt— R5ch, K—Kt3* and again the Knight has no escape.

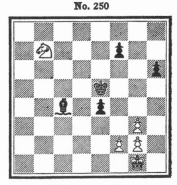

No. 250

Black to play wins.

c) *2 K—R2* (the game continuation), *B—R7!; 3 P—Kt4, P —B 3!* (the simplest); *4 K—K t3, K—B3; 5 Kt—R5ch, K— Kt3; 6 K—B4, K×Kt; 7 K× P* (if instead 7 K—B5, K— Kt5!; 8 K×BP, K—B6; 9 P —Kt5, P×P; 10 K×P, K— Q7; 11 K—B4, B—Kt8!; 12

P—Kt4, K—K7; 13 K—Kt3, B—R7!; 14 P—Kt5, B—B2;
15 K—Kt2, B—Kt3; 16 K—Kt1, K—B6; 17 K—B1, K—B5;
18 K—K2, B—R4ch and wins), *B—K3!; 8 K—B4, K—Kt5;*
9 K—Kt3, K—B4; 10 K—R4, B—B2!; 11 P—B4!, K—Q3;
12 P—Kt5, RP×Pch; 13 P×P, P—B4; 14 P—Kt6!, B—K3!;
15 K—Kt5, K—K4; 16 K—R6, K—B3!; 17 P—Kt3, B—Q2;
18 K—R5, K—Kt2 (simpler 18 .... B—K1); *19 K—Kt5,*
B—K3; 20 K—R5, B—B1!; 21 K—Kt5, B—Q2; 22 K—R5,
K—B3!; 23 K—R6, B—K1!; 24 P—Kt7, B—B2! and White
resigned, for after *25 K—R7, K—Kt4; 26 P—Kt8= Qch,*
B× Qch; 27 K×B, K—Kt5 he cannot catch the BP.

The complete stalemate of the Knight without the help of Pawns
occurs only when the Kt is on the edge of the board and the Bishop
is in or near the center, e.g., Kt at Q1, B at Q5, or Kt at QR1, B at Q8.
When this happens the game is naturally untenable for the Kt side
unless he can free his Kt or exchange enough Pawns. Thus in No.
250a (Englisch-Wittek Vienna, 1882), White: K at K4, B at KKt5,
P's at QR2, QKt2, QB4, KB3; Black: K at KKt6, Kt at KKt1, P's at
QR3, QKt2, QB2, Q3, K4. White wins even though the enemy King
is dangerously near his Pawns: 1 .... K—B7; 2 P—B4, P×P; 3 K×P,
K—K7; 4 K—K4! (he must not go after the Kt), P—B3; 5 P—R4,
P—R4; 6 P—Kt3, P—B4 (forced, for if 6 .... K—B7; 7 K—B5!,
K—K7; 8 K—K6 wins); 7 K—Q5, K—Q6; 8 K×P, K—B7; 9 K×P,
K×P; 10 K—Kt5, K—B6; 11 K×P!, K×P; 12 K—Kt6, K—Kt5;
13 P—R5, K—R5; 14 B—Q8!, Kt—R3; 15 K×P and wins (No. 218a).
Such a stalemate may win even when each side has only one Pawn.
E.g., No. 250b (Berger-Tchigorin, Barmen, 1905), White: K at Q6,
B at KB4, P at QB5; Black: K at KB2, Kt at KR4, P at QB3. White
to play won by 1 B—K5!, K—K1; 2 K×P, K—K2; 3 K—Kt7, K—K3
(too late); 4 P—B6, K×B; 5 P—B7 and wins (Compare No. 219).

However, with one Pawn the win is always nip and tuck. Thus in
No. 250c, a stalemate possibility saves the day: White: K at K4,
Kt at QR8, P at QR2; Black: K at Q1, B at KKt8, P at QR2. White
to play draws! 1 K—Q5, K—Q2!; 2 P—R4, P—R4; 3 K—B4, K—B3;
4 Kt—B7!!, K×Kt; 5 K—Kt5, B—Kt3; 6 K—R6!!!, K—B3 stalemate.

Summary: The Bishop is better than the Knight when the Pawns
are not blocked because it then controls more terrain. This advantage
is exploited by forcing the enemy King to one side and penetrating
to a group of Pawns with one's own King. The Bishop is most
effective when there are Pawns on both sides of the board. In an
unbalanced Pawn position, the superiority of the Bishop is more
marked than in a balanced one. Finally, one should above all avoid
placing one's Pawns on the same color as one's Bishop.

b) The Knight Is Superior.

The type of position where this occurs has already been indicated: one where the Pawns are fixed (immobile) on the color of the Bishop. This solidification results in a loss of mobility for the Bishop, especially when he is blocked by his own Pawns which must be defended, while the Kt hops about as gaily as ever. It must be remembered that although the Bishop is at a handicap when the opponent's Pawns are on the same color, this is not generally serious, but that to have his own Pawns fixed on the same color is usually disastrous. Other illustrations of this fact are found in Chapter IV (Bishop endings), Parts III B, IV b) 4).

The manner in which the Knight makes use of this kind of advantage (bad Pawn position, bad Bishop) may be deduced from our general principles. A positional superiority must be converted into a gain in material. Normally this will be done by attacking a group of Pawns with the King. To get through with the King, both the enemy pieces (K and B) must be diverted either by checks or by a direct attack on Pawns. Sometimes, as in the similar case in a), the Pawns will be so weak that they cannot be defended even when threatened only by the Kt.

This leads us to a threefold classification of the types of positional advantage which a Kt may enjoy against a Bishop:

1. A weak color complex (that opposite to the B) which makes it impossible to put up any effective barrier to the march of the enemy King.
2. The Pawns are subject to a direct attack by the Knight. This immobilizes the Bishop and again facilitates the entry of the King.
3. The Pawns are weak, but not because they are on the same color as the Bishop (e.g., doubled, or isolated). Since the Knight can reach all squares this means that they may be attacked by two pieces (K and Kt) but only defended by one (K). Loss of material cannot be postponed for long.

The first two almost always go together, the chief difference being that in the first the Bishop has much more scope.

1. WEAK COLOR COMPLEXES

The Bishop can cover only half the squares on the board; the other half must be taken care of by the Pawns and the King. But when the Pawns are all on the same color as the Bishop, the opposite-colored squares are governed only by "squatters' rights." In such cases we speak of a *weak color complex*.

No. 251 (Zubareff-Alexandrov, Moscow, 1915) illustrates all the

No. 251

White to play wins.

drawbacks of such a Pawn config-uration. White to play can get his King to QB5, and the best that Black can do is oppose him at QB2. The next step is to force the Black King out of the way. Clearly this can be done only by checking or stalemating the Bishop. The first is not feasible, for all the squares from which the Kt could check are guarded. We must then get the Bishop into a position where he has no good moves. This will be accom-plished if we attack two Pawns on White squares, both of which must be defended by the Bishop, which will then be unable to go away. Finally, a tempo move with a Pawn (there are at least four extra tempo moves on the Q-side) and Black will have to give way. The conclusion —capture of Pawns, exploitation of one or more passed Pawns—is already familiar. With this general outline in mind, the game con-tinuation is naturally broken up into six phases, which are commonly seen in such endings.

1. *Advance the King as far as he can go.* *1 K—B2, K—K2* (it would be even worse for Black to go to the K-side, since he gets no-where there and will then no longer be able to keep the White King out. E.g., 1 .... K—B2; 2 K—K2!, K—Kt3; 3 Kt—K3!, K—Kt4; 4 P—KKt3!, P—KR4; 5 K—Q3!, P—R5; 6 K—Q4! etc.); *2 K—K3, K—Q1; 3 K—Q4, K—B2; 4 K—B5, B—B1.*

The next step is to attack two Pawns both of which must be de-fended by the Bishop. There are no such Pawns available at the moment; hence we must create them. We know that they must be on White and that they must be immobile. So the Kt must start snooping around the K-side. This brings us to the second phase.

2. *Weaken the enemy Pawns by fixing as many as possible on the color of the Bishop.* *5 Kt—Kt4, B—Kt2* (forced: if 5 .... P—QR4; 6 Kt—B2, B—Q2; 7 P—QR3, B—K1; 8 Kt—Q4 and wins a Pawn); *6 P—KKt3* (Black was threatening to get some air by 6 .... P—Q5 and 7 .... B×P), *B—B1; 7 Kt—Q3, B—Q2; 8 Kt—B4, P—Kt3* (he has little choice. If 8 .... B—B1; 9 Kt—R5, P—Kt3; 10 Kt—B6, P—KR4; 11 P—KR4, B—Kt2; 12 Kt—K8ch, K—Q2; 13 Kt—Q6 is immediately conclusive); *9 Kt—R3!, P—R3* (else 10 Kt—Kt5, P—R3; 11 Kt—B7, P—KR4; 12 P—R4 etc., as above); *10 Kt—B4, P—Kt4; 11 Kt—R5, B—K1; 12 Kt—B6, B—B2* (if 12 .... B—B3 13 P—KR4, P×P; 14 P×P, B—Kt2; 15 Kt—Kt8, P—KR4; 16 Kt—-

B6 and wins a Pawn); *13 Kt—Kt4!* (he wants to have the Pawns on White), *P—KR4; 14 Kt—K3* (good enough, but 14 Kt—B2 followed by Kt—R3 was simpler), *B—Kt3* (Black's inability to undertake any counteraction is striking. If here 14 .... P—R5; 15 P×P, P×P; 16 Kt—Kt2, winning a Pawn); *15 P—KR4!* (finally fixing the Pawns), *P×P* (15 .... P—KKt5; 16 Kt—Kt2 is even worse); *16 P×P, B— K5.* Now that the situation on the K-side is cleared up we come to the third phase:

3. *Attack two Pawns with the Knight, both of which must be defended by the Bishop.* The Bishop will thus be immobilized. Here the two Pawns are the KP and the KRP, so that the Kt must get to either KB4 or KKt7, the most practical, of course, being KB4. *17 Kt—B1, B—B6* (if 17 .... B—Kt3; 18 Kt—Kt3, B—B2; 19 Kt—K2—B4); *18 Kt— Q2, B—K7* (or 18 .... B—Q8; 19 P—QR3, B—K7; 20 Kt—Kt3, B—B6; 21 Kt—Q4, B—Kt5; 22 P—Kt3, B—R6; 23 Kt—K2 etc.); *19 Kt—Kt3, B—Kt5; 20 Kt—Q4, B—R6; 21 Kt—K2; B—B4; 22 Kt— B4, B—Kt5.* Now the Bishop is chained to his post, and any tempo will give Black the choice of losing a Pawn on the K-side or the Q-side. Thus the fourth phase is:

4. *Now that the Bishop is immobilized, make any Pawn tempo.* This will force either the B or the K to play with consequent loss of material. *23 P—Kt4, K—Q2;* This accomplished, the fifth and semi-final phase is

5. *Gain of material with either the King or the Knight* (depending on Black's choice). *24 K—Kt6, B—B6; 25 K×P, K—B3; 26 Kt×KP.* Here Black resigned. The final stage would be

6. *Advance the passed Pawns until a piece is won.*

The *double attack* is the key to the ending in weak color complexes. Where there are no reserve Pawn moves a tempo must be gained by the King and if this is not possible the defender will be able to hold the game. Thus in No. 252 (Schlechter-Walbrodt, Vienna, 1898) there are two threats: Kt×BP (if the B moves) and K—Kt5 (if the King moves). If it were Black's turn he could therefore just as well resign. E.g., *1 .... B—B4; 2 Kt×P!, B—Q2; 3 Kt—Q8, B—B1; 4 P—B6, P×P; 5 P—Kt7* etc. But White to move cannot gain a tempo. If *1 K—B3* (1 Kt—Kt6 is pretty but useless: 1 .... B—Kt5!; 2 Kt— B8??, B—B4! But not 1 .... K×Kt?; 2 K—K5, B—Kt5; 3 K—Q6, K—B4; 4 K—B7, K—K5; 5 K×P, K×P; 6 K—B7 and queens first), *K—K2!* (if 2 Kt—Q3, B—B4!, but not 2 .... B—Kt5ch; 3 K—K3, B—B4; 4 Kt—B4, B—Kt5; 5 Kt—Kt6ch, K—B3!; 6 Kt—K5, B—B1; 7 K—B4 and wins); *2 K—K3, K—K3; 3 Kt—Q3, K—B3!; 4 Kt—B4, B—Kt5,* or *4 Kt—Kt4, K—K3; 5 K—B4, K—B3* etc. White can make no headway.

Where the weak color complex is accompanied by an unfavorable

Pawn position (isolated, doubled, blocked Pawns) the win is practically certain. A common case is that of the isolated QP. Such an isolated Pawn is not in itself fatal (see No. 257) but in conjunction with another weakness it is too much for one poor chess player. No. 253 (Capablanca-Reshevsky, Nottingham, 1936) is typical. The weak color complex (squares QB5, QKt4) and the exposed isolani offer White the double target which it would otherwise take him so long to set up. As a result passive play on Black's part would be hopeless. There might follow 1 .... K—B2; 2 Kt—Kt4, B—Kt2; 3 Kt—B2, B—B3; 4 Kt—Q4, B—Q2; 5 K—K2, K—K2; 6 K—Q3, P×P; 7 P×P, K—Q3; 8 K—B3, K—B4; 9 P—Kt4ch, K—Q3;

No. 252   No. 253

White to play draws; Black to play   White wins.
loses.

10 Kt—K2, K—K4; 11 Kt—B1, B—B3; 12 Kt—Q3ch, K—Q3; 13 K—Q4, B—K1; 14 Kt—B4, B—B2; 15 Kt—K2, B—K1; 16 Kt—B3, B—B3 (completion of the first four steps in No. 251); 17 P—Kt4 and Black is already reduced to Pawn moves: 17 .... P—Kt4; 18 P—R5, P—R3; 19 P—B4, P×P; 20 P×P, B—Q2, when the most conclusive is 21 Kt×P, B×P; 22 Kt×P, B—B4; 23 Kt—Kt8, B—Kt5; 24 Kt×P, B×P; 25 Kt—B5ch, K—Q2; 26 K—K5 and the rest is simple. To avoid this variation Reshevsky tried a counter attack on the K-side, but the essential weaknesses in his position could not be disposed of. The game continued *1 .... P—Kt4; 2 P×P, P×P; 3 Kt—Kt4, B—Kt2; 4 P—Kt4!, K—Kt2; 5 K—K2, K—Kt3; 6 K—Q3, P—R4* (if 6 .... P—Q5; 7 P—K4); *7 P×Pch, K×P; 8 K—Q4, K—R5; 9 Kt×P, K—Kt6; 10 P—B4, P—Kt5* (his only hope, but it is a frail reed. If first 10 .... B×Kt; 11 K×B, P—Kt5; 12 P—B5, K—R6; 13 P—B6, P—Kt6; 14 P—B7, P—Kt7; 15 P—B8=Q, P—Kt8=Q; 16 Q—

R6ch and exchanges Queens); *11 P—B5, B—B1; 12 K—K5, B—Q2; 13 P—K4, B—K1; 14 K—Q4, K—B6; 15 P—K5, P—Kt6; 16 Kt—K3, K—B5; 17 P—K6, P—Kt7; 18 Kt×Pch, K×P; 19 K—Q5, K—Kt5; 20 Kt—K3ch, K—B5.* Here the game was adjourned and Black resigned without resuming play.

A weak color complex is often accompanied by a virtual or qualitative Pawn minority on one side—all the Pawns, being on one color, are blocked and a majority is useless. In that event the opponent has a real or potential outside passed Pawn with which he can force the win. This is illustrated in No. 254 (Thomas-Landau, Amsterdam, 1937), where White has three to two on the Q-side, while the Black QP is blocked and practically worthless. White forced the entry of his King as follows: *1 Kt—B2, B—K1; 2 P—QKt4, B—Q2; 3 Kt—Q4* (an ideal position for the Kt), *B—K1; 4 P—QR4, P—QR3; 5 P—R5!!!* (an unusual move; he does not wish to exchange the RP), *B—Q2; 6 P—Kt5, BP×P* (if 6 .... RP×P; 7 P—R6, B—B1; 8 Kt×Pch, K—Q2; 9 K×P!); *7 K×P.* White is now one step nearer his goal. The Black QKtP is, like his erstwhile colleague on the Q-file, blocked and worthless. *7 .... B—K1; 8 Kt—B2, B—Q2; 9 Kt—Kt4, B—B1; 10 K—B6, K—Q1; 12 K—Q6!, B—Kt2; 12 P—B6, B—B1; 13 P—B7ch, K—K1; 14 K—B6, K—B2; 15 K—Kt6, K—K2; 16 Kt×P, K—Q3; 17 Kt—Kt4* and Black gave up.

Even with White's B free to roam the board, he is always kept in check by his weak Pawns and the threat of a K entry. An example where a potential passed Pawn decides in such a case is No. 254a (Michell-v. Scheltinga, Amsterdam, 1937), White: K at K2, B at KB8, P's at QR2, QB3, K3, KB3, KR2; Black: K at K3, Kt at K4, P's at QR3, QB2, KB4, KKt4, KR2. Black to play wins. 1 .... P—Kt5!; 2 P×P (forced: if 2 P—B4, Kt—B6; 3 P—R3, Kt—Kt8ch), P×P; 3 B—R6, K—Q4; 4 K—B 2, K—K5; 5 K—Kt3, P—B4! (to fix the QBP); 6 B—B8, P—B5; 7 B—B5, K—B4; 8 B—Q4, Kt—B6; 9 P—KR3, P—KR4; 10 P×Pch, P×P; 11 B—Kt6, Kt—Kt4; 12 B—Q4, Kt—K5ch; 13 K—R4, Kt—B 7!! (prepares the decisive K break); 14 K—Kt3, Kt—Q8; 15 P—R3, K—K5!; 16 K×P, Kt×Pch; 17 K—Kt5, Kt—B7!; 18 B—B5, K—Q 6; 19 K—B5, K×P; 20 K—K4, K—Kt6; 21 K—Q5, P—B6; 22 K—K4, Kt×P; 23 K—Q3, Kt—B5; 24 B—B8, P—R4; 25 B—Kt7, Kt

No. 254

White wins.

—Kt7ch; 26 K—K2, P—R5 and White gave up the hopeless struggle. Note that in the above example White's passed center Pawn was useless.

2. THE BAD BISHOP

We have already seen examples of this in the pure Bishop endings (see Nos. 193, 195, 214). Against a Kt a bad Bishop—one with all or most of his Pawns on the same color—is even worse. The winning idea is the same as that in weak color complexes: the two, as already mentioned, go hand in hand. The chief difference is that in these examples the B is much worse off. In No. 255 (Henneberger-Nimzovitch, Winterthur, 1931) we see the Kt at his best. With a B Black would not be able to exploit his advantage here. The win is achieved by stalemating the Bishop and then forcing an entry with the King. The first step then is to cramp the B by compelling it to defend the QBP and KKtP. *1 .... Kt—K5; 2 K—K2, K—Q4; 3 K—K3.* What next? Black can stalemate the B completely only by getting his Kt to QKt8. If, when he gets to QKt8, the White B is at Q2, White to play can draw by B—K1, P—R6, B—Q2, for after the exchange of pieces Black does not have the opposition. Hence he must manage to get his Kt to QKt8 only when the B is at K1, for then B—Q2 can be met by .... KtXB, KXKt, K—K5, K—K2, P—R6!, securing the opposition. Consequently he must lose a move with his King. *3 .... K—Q3!; 4 K—K2, K—B3; 5 K—K3, K—Q4; 6 K—K2.* Now the Kt manoeuvre can begin. *6 .... Kt—Q3; 7 K—K3, Kt—Kt4; 8 B—Q2, Kt—R6; 9 B—B1* (as indicated above, if 9 B—K1, Kt—Kt8; 10 B—Q2, KtXB decides), *Kt—Kt8; 10 B—Kt2, P—R6; 11 B—R1.* Now the B has no moves at all and Black need only lose a tempo to get in with his King. Of course the Kt is lost if White

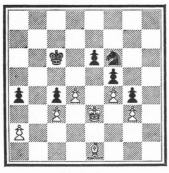

No. 255

Black wins.

goes after it, but as the sequel shows, Nimzovitch has calculated that he will then win on the K-side. *11 .... K—Q3; 12 K—K2, K—B3; 13 K—Q1* (13 K—K3, K—Q4; 14 K—B2!, Kt—Q7!; 15 K—Kt2, K—K5 or 15 K—K2, Kt—K5 is much worse), *K—Q4; 14 K—B2, K—K5; 15 KXKt, K—B6; 16 B—Kt2!, PXB!!!* (not 16 .... KXP?; 17 BXP, K—B6; 18 B—B5!, P—Kt6; 19 P—R4, P—Kt7; 20 P—Q5! and White wins); *17 P—R4, KXP; 18 P—R5, K—R7; 19 P—R6, P—Kt6; 20 P—R7, P—Kt7; 21 P—*

R8= Q, P—Kt8= Qch; 22 K×P, Q—Kt7ch!! (this, it goes without saying, Nimzovitch had foreseen); *23 Q×Qch, K×Q; 24 K—R3, K —B6; 25 K—Kt4, K×P; 26 K×P, K—K6; 27 P—Q5, P×Pch; 28 K×P, P—B5* and White resigns since his Pawn will only be on the sixth when White queens. A masterful example of precise calculation.

The case where the B is hemmed in by the enemy Pawns is almost as bad as the above, the only difference being that the possibility of a sacrifice comes up. However, such a threat is rarely serious. E.g., No. 255a (Riemann-Blackburne, Hamburg, 1885), White: K at KB2, B at QB1, P's at QR2, QB3, Q4, KB3, KKt4, KR4; Black: K at KB3, Kt at QB5, P's at QR2, QKt2, Q4, KB5, KKt4, KR3. Black wins. 1 .... P—QR4; 2 P—R5 (Clearly Black can win only by playing his K to the Q-side. In that event White wishes to have the threat of B×P followed by P—Kt5 in reserve), K—K3; 3 K—K2, K—Q2; 4 K—Q3, K—B3; 5 K—B2, K—Kt4; 6 K—Kt3 (the "threat" turns out to be bluff. If 6 B×P, P×B; 7 P—Kt5, P×P!; 8 P—R6, Kt—Q3; 9 P—R7, Kt—B2.), K—Kt3! (he wishes to lose a move); 7 K—B2, K—B3!; 8 K—Kt3, K—Kt4; 9 P—R4ch (forced), K—B3; 10 K—B2, P—Kt4 (setting up an outside passed Pawn); 11 P×Pch, K×P; 12 K—Kt3, K—Kt3! (another triangulation manoeuvre to lose a move); 13 K—R4, K—R3; 14 K—Kt3, K—Kt4; 15 K—B2, K—R5; 16 K—Kt1, K—Kt6 and White cannot save his B: if 17 K—R1, K—B7 (of course 17 .... K×P also wins without any trouble).

In this example we may note that the winning method consisted of taking advantage of the blockade of the QBP and QP by the Kt by setting up an outside passed Pawn. The inability of the B to undertake any counteraction and the power of the Kt to constrict both the B and the K were equally striking.

A Bishop is a bad defensive piece and when it is glued down to the defense of a Pawn it is just as badly off as when it is blocked by its own or enemy Pawns. Thus in No. 255b (Charousek-Marco, Nurenberg, 1896), White: K at K3, B at KKt4, P's at QR3, QKt3, QB4, K4, KB5, KR3; Black: K at QB3, Kt at KKt4, P's at QR2, QKt3, QB4, K4, KB3, KR5, the B is chained to the KRP while the Kt is able to attack two points. As a result Black can do as he pleases with his King, while White can only mark time. The simplest win is 1 .... P—R3; 2 K—Q3 (if 2 P—R4, P—Kt4; 3 BP×Pch, P×P; 4 P×Pch, K×P; 5 B—K2ch, K—Kt5), P—Kt4; 3 P×Pch (or 3 K—K3, P×P; 4 P×P, K—Kt3; 5 K—Q3, K—R4 etc.), P×P; 4 K—K3, P—B5; 5 P×P, P×P; 6 P—R4, K—B4; 7 P—R5, K—Kt4; 8 B—K2, Kt×RP; 9 B×Pch, K×P; 10 B—B1, Kt—B5 and the Pawn plus is sufficient.

We see then that a Bishop's mobility may be limited either by his own Pawns or the enemy's. The former is worse because there is no resource available to break the straitjacket. It is exploited by attacking the enemy Pawns from an unassailable position (Nos. 255, 255b) and then coming in with the King. With the B stalemated the opponent is virtually a piece ahead. Where the B is blocked by enemy Pawns the possibility of a sacrifice must be taken into account. The method of operation is essentially the same as that in the first case— proper manipulation of the King, setting up an outside passed Pawn and then continuing in the routine manner with such a Pawn, i.e., decoying the enemy King and bringing about a decision on the other wing (No. 255a).

It is well to remember that the Knight is effective against a Bishop only if it is able to set up a double attack, for, unlike the opposite case, a simple threat is too easily parried. As a result the side which has the Kt is interested in fixing the Pawns on the color of the B in order to set up additional targets. This theoretical point is the clue to the defense in a good many endings. E.g., No. 256 (Alekhine-Yates, Hastings, 1925-26). White can win only by fixing a sufficient number of Black Pawns on squares where they can be threatened. Thus *1 P—Q4!*, *P—B5* (not 1 .... P×Pch; 2 K×P, K—K3 when we have an isolated QP in conjunction with a weak color complex. The win is then accomplished by 3 Kt—B3, B—B3; 4 K—B5, B—Kt2; 5 Kt—Kt5, P— R3; 6 Kt—Q4ch, etc.—compare No. 253); *2 P—B5!* and now Black must make a crucial decision: shall he play .... P×P or .... P—Kt4? While it is by no means easy to answer such a question over the board the double target principle is quite helpful. If he plays 2 .... P×P; 3 Kt—B4 (else .... P—B3), B—B3!; 4 Kt×RP leaves him with weak Pawns (this cannot be avoided in any case) but there is no easy double attack by White feasible. On the other hand, if he plays 2 .... P— Kt4, it is clear that White will reply P—KR4, clear the square KB4 for his Kt and that Q4 and KR4 will be obvious and simple points of attack. Consequently, on purely theoretical grounds he should have replied 2 .... P×P. Not having read this book, he chose instead 2 .... P—Kt4, when Alekhine secured an overwhelming position in the following convincing manner: 3 P—KR4, P—B3 (3 .... P×P; 4 P×P, P—B3; 5 Kt—B4 is much worse: 5 .... P×P; 6 P×P, B— B2; 7 K—Q4, K—Q1; 8 P—K6 and it is all over); 4 RP×P!!, BP× KtP; 5 Kt—Kt1!, B—Q2; 6 P—B6ch, K—K1; 7 Kt—B3, P—Kt5; 8 Kt—R4 and now the conclusion is similar to that in the other examples: after a double attack the B will be in zugzwang. 8 .... B— K3; 9 Kt—Kt6, B—B2; 10 Kt—B4, K—Q2; 11 K—K2, P—R4; 12 K—K3 (Voila!) 12 .... B—Kt1 (on a K move 13 P—K6 is conclusive); 13 Kt×RP, B—B2; 14 Kt—B4, B—Kt1; 15 Kt—K2. Now that there is only one target left (Q4) the Kt can do no more and the K is brought up. 15 .... B—K3; 16 K—B4, K—K1; 17 K—Kt5, K—B2; 18 Kt—B3 (forcing the K to move), K—B1; 19 K—Kt6, K—Kt1; 20 P—B7ch!!, K—B1; 21 K—B6, B×P; 22 P—K6, B—R4; 23 Kt×P, B—K1; 24 Kt—B3 and Black resigned.

Let us return to the critical stage. One can give no money-back guarantee that the theoretical reply would have saved the game, but analysis bears out the feeling that it would have offered White a much harder nut to crack. *2 .... P×P!; 3 Kt—B4* (if 3 K—B4, P—B3!!; 4 Kt—B3, B—B3; 5 K×P, B—Q2ch!; 6 K—B4, B—K3 and Black is out of the woods), *B—B3* (he must not let the support of his protected

No. 256

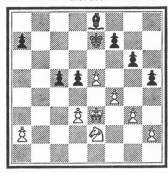

White to play.

No. 257

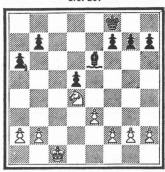

Draw.

passed Pawn go); *4 Kt×RP, K—B1; 5 Kt—B6* (5 Kt—B4, K—Kt2; 6 Kt—K2, K—Kt3; 7 K—B4 is no better: after 7 .... P—R3; 8 Kt—B3, B—Kt2; 9 P—KR4, B—B3; 10 P—R5ch, K×P; 11 K×P, B—B1ch; 12 K—B6, B—K3! Black has all the winning chances, while if 5 K—B4, K—Kt1; 6 K×P?, P—B6; 7 Kt—B4, B—Kt4!! and wins), *K—Kt2; 6 K—B4, K—B1!!* (relying on his passed Pawn); *7 P—KR4, K—Kt2; 8 P—R5, K—R3; 9 Kt—Kt8ch, K×P; 10 Kt—K7, B—R1!; 11 Kt×BP, K—Kt3; 12 Kt—Q6, P—R3* and there is still no clear win in sight. In the above variation the double target Q4 and KB4 could have been attacked only from K7, which White could not reach, or from K3, which would have involved playing the King away from KB4 and thus eased the defense problem for Black.

Where there is only one target the game is normally drawn. Thus the isolated QP without any further weaknesses is not fatal. This was shown in No. 257 (Flohr-Capablanca, Moscow, 1935). After *1 .... K—K2; 2 K—Q2, K—Q3; 3 K—B3, P—QKt3!; 4 P—B4, B—Q2;*

5 Kt—B3, P—B3! (keeping his Pawns on Black squares); *6 K—Q4, P—QR4!; 7 Kt—Q2, B—B1; 8 Kt—Kt1, B—K3; 9 Kt—B3, K—B3.* This is the best that White could obtain. Now his only winning hope lies in creating a second threat (besides the QP). This might be done by Kt—Kt1—Q2—B3—R4, P—B5, P—KKt4, Kt—Kt2—B4. Then Black's B at B2 would be tied down to the defense of two points, for if .... B—Kt1, Kt—R5 wins a Pawn, while his King would be unable to leave Q3, since Kt—K6!, B×Kt, P×B, K—Q3, P—K7! would then decide. Consequently Black would have to weaken his K-side Pawns. This need not necessarily be fatal, but it would give White something to aim at. However, Capablanca sees through this plan and it dies a-borning against his careful defense. *10 P—QR3, P—KR3* (this move makes no difference); *11 P—KKt3, P—KR4* (he is going to block the K-side); *12 P—QKt4, P×P; 13 P×P, K—Q3; 14 P—Kt5, P—Kt3* (Now the plan sketched above is impossible and a speedy draw may be expected); *15 P—B5!* (a sacrifice in order to get his Kt to KB4), *P×P; 16 Kt—K2, B—Q2!; 17 Kt—B4, B—K1!!* (the point: he does not mind losing the worthless QP, but the KRP is vital); *18 Kt×QP, B×P; 19 Kt×KtP* (19 Kt×BP, B—K7), *B—B3; 20 Kt—B4ch, K—K3* and it is clear that there is no longer any real danger. This ending should be compared with No. 253, where the presence of an extra weakness provides the needed additional threat.

Any blocked position is bad for a Bishop, however. At times (as in the analogous case with B vs. Kt) immediate material loss may be unavoidable. E.g., No. 257a (Horowitz-Fine, New York, 1934), White: K at KKt4, B at QB1, P's at QR4, QKt3, Q4, K3, KB2, KKt3, KR4; Black: K at Q2, Kt at QKt5, P's at QR4, QKt3, QB2, K5, KB6, KKt2, KR2. White to play resigned, because he cannot save his Pawn at KB2.

3. WEAK PAWNS

There are many cases in which such Pawns are more effectively exploited by the Kt than by the B. They occur chiefly when a Pawn majority is blocked and when Pawns are exposed on squares not covered by the B. A B can capture Pawns only when they are on his color; a Kt can snare them anywhere.

No. 258 (Rubinstein-Alekhine, London, 1922) is typical of the first case—a blocked Pawn majority. The B cannot break the blockade, while the Kt and P keep the White King out. Black wins by simply marching his K over to the support of his passed P. The continuation was *1 .... K—B1; 2 K—Kt2, K—K2; 3 B—Kt8, K—Q3; 4 B—B7, K—B4; 5 B×P, Kt×P; 6 K—B3* (if 6 P—Kt4, Kt—Q5; 7 P—Kt5, P×P; 8 P×P, Kt×P is sufficient), *K—Q5; 7 B—B7, K—Q6; 8 B×Kt, K—Q7; 9 B—B4, P—Kt6; 10 B×P, P—K7* and White resigned.

The case where the B is unable to defend exposed Pawns is more common. No. 259 (Gilg-Spielmann, Carlsbad, 1929) may be taken as a model. The KP is exposed and can only be defended by a P. This is prevented by *1 .... P—KKt4!*, when the Pawn is lost. The continuation was *2 K—Kt2, Kt—Q2; 3 P—KR4, P—R3; 4 P×P, P×P; 5 P—B4, P×P; 6 K—B3, Kt×Pch; 7 K×P, P—B3*, when the two connected passed Pawns win. The game went on *8 K—K4, K—B2; 9 K—Q4, Kt—B3ch; 10 K—B3, K—K2; 11 P—Kt4, P×Pch; 12 P×P, K—Q3; 13 B—Q1, P—K4; 14 B—Kt4, Kt—K2; 15 B—B3, P—B4; 16 B—Kt2, P—K5; 17 B—R3, K—K4; 18 P—B5, P—Kt4!* (to preserve an extra Pawn against the possibility of a sacrifice); *19 B—*

No. 258

Black wins.

No. 259

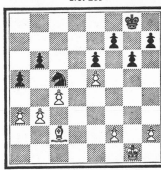

Black to play wins.

B1, Kt—Q4ch; 20 K—Q2, Kt—B2; 21 B—R3, P—B5; 22 K—K2, P—B6ch; 23 K—B2, K—B5; 24 B—Q7, P—K6ch; 25 K—B1, K—Kt6; 26 B—B6, P—K7ch; 27 K—K1, Kt—K3 and White resigned.

In No. 259a (Dake-Fine, Chicago, 1934) the case is somewhat more complicated. White: K at K4, Kt at QKt6, P's at QR2, QKt2, QB2, KKt4, KR3; Black: K at K2, B at K1, P's at QR3, QB3, QB4, KKt3, KR2. After *1 .... B—B2; 2 K—K5!, B×P; 3 P—Kt5!, B—Kt8; 4 P—B3, B—B7; 5 Kt—B4, K—Q2; 6 Kt—K3, B—Q6; 7 Kt—Kt4, K—B2; 8 Kt—B6, K—Kt3; 9 Kt×P* the White K-side Pawns won. Here White was able to sacrifice a Pawn on the Q-side because with Black's QBP doubled the extra Pawn was meaningless.

Summary: The Knight is preferable to the Bishop in positions where the Pawns are blocked. It is especially bad for the player with the Bishop to have all or most of his Pawns on the color of the Bishop. Weak color complexes and a bad Bishop go together. The key to the winning method in both cases is the double attack, placing the Bishop in zugzwang. The Knight then either captures a Pawn or allows the entry of the King. If the Pawns are weak or exposed the Knight is likewise in a better position to take advantage of the inferiority.

c) Better Pawn Position.

It must not be supposed that all B vs. Kt endings are determined by the superiority of one of the minor pieces. On the contrary: in a great number other factors loom just as large, and in a good many it makes no difference whatsoever which piece one has. This is the salient fact which distinguishes these last two rubrics from the first two: the positional advantage could be exploited with equal success by either piece, and it is merely an accident that one rather than the other is present.

The outside passed Pawn is again the principal kind of superiority which we must note. Ordinarily a Bishop is somewhat more effective here than a Knight, but the strength of such a Pawn is so great that either piece will usually win with equal ease. We may recall how the Pawn is used: to decoy the enemy King and penetrate to the Pawns with one's own King. An example with a Kt is No. 260 (Loevenfisch-Ragosin, Leningrad-Moscow, 1939). The continuation was *1 .... K—B1* (if 1 .... P—K5; 2 Kt—Q2 wins a P); *2 Kt—Q2, K—K1* (the White King cannot be kept out. If 2 .... B—K2; 3 P—B6, K—K1; 4 K—B3, P—B4; 5 P×P, P×P; 6 Kt—B4, B—B3; 7 Kt—Q6ch, K—Q1; 8 P—B7ch and wins); *3 K—B3, B—K2; 4 P—B6, K—Q1; 5 K—K4, K—B2; 6 K—Q5, P—B4* (hoping to create a diversion on the K-side. 6 .... P—B3; 7 Kt—K4 is hopeless); *7 P×P, P×P; 8 K×P* (the simplest), *K×P; 9 Kt—Kt3, B—Q3ch; 10 K—K6, B—R7; 11 Kt—Q4ch, K—B4; 12 Kt×P, P—R4; 13 Kt—Kt3, K—Q5; 14 K—B5, P—R5; 15 Kt—R5, B—Kt8; 16 P—B3, B—B7; 17 Kt—B4, B—K8; 18 Kt—Kt6, K—Q4; 19 K—Kt4* and the rest is routine (See No. 227).

No. 260

White wins.

With two outside passed Pawns (one for each side) one must get going as fast as one can, sit tight and hope for the best. In No. 260a (Pillsbury-Lasker, St. Petersburg, 1895–'96) White: K at Q4, Kt at QKt6, P's at QR4, QKt3, KKt2, K R3; Black: K at KB5, B at KB4, P's at QB3, KB2, KKt3, KR5 this rule was ignored by Black, who had to pay the penalty. He could have drawn by 1 .... P—Kt4!; 2 P—R5 (or 2 K—B5, B×P!; 3 P×B, P—

Kt5; 4 P—R5, P—Kt6=), B×P!; 3 P×B, P—Kt5; 4 P—R6, P—K
t6; 5 P—R7, P—Kt7; 6 P—R8=Q, P—Kt8=Qch; 7 K—B3, Q—K6
ch; 8 K—Kt2, Q×Kt with an even position. Instead Lasker played
1 .... B—K5? when 2 P—R5, P—B4ch; 3 K×P, B×P; 4 P—R6, P
—Kt4; 5 Kt—Q5ch!, K—K4; 6 Kt—K3!!, B—B6; 7 P—Kt4, K—K3;
8 P—Kt5, B—K7; 9 Kt—Q5 forced him to resign.

Advanced passed Pawns when not blocked by the King almost invariably cost the defender a piece, especially with Kt vs. B. No. 261
(Naegeli-Colin, Berne, 1932) is an illustration. White to play can win
by *1 P—B6!, K—Kt4* (if 1 .... B—B6; 2 Kt—B5ch!, K—Kt4; 3 P—
B7 and queens); *2 P—B7, P—K4; 3 P—B5!!!* (3 Kt—Q6ch, K—B3;

No. 261   No. 262

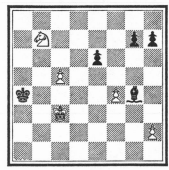   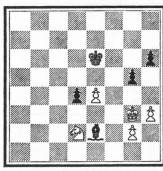

White to play wins.   Black to play wins.

4 P—B8=Qch?, B×Q; 5 Kt×B, P×P would only draw), *B×P; 4
Kt—Q6ch, K—B3; 5 Kt×B, K×P; 6 Kt×P* and the rest is routine.
With the Kt such combinations occur much more frequently than with
the B. E.g., No. 261a (Berger) White: K at KKt1, Kt at QB7, P's at
QKt6, QB4; Black: K at KB6, B at QR7, P's at QKt2, KB2. White
to play wins. 1 P—B5, B—Kt8 (forced: P—B6 must be met); 2 Kt—
K6!!, P×Kt (2 .... B—K5; 3 Kt—Kt5ch); 3 P—B6 and will queen,
for if 3 .... B—K5; 4 P—B7 and if 3 .... B—B4; 4 P×P.

Exposed Pawns often cannot be defended, especially when they are
attacked by a B and defended by a Kt. Thus in No. 262 (Walbrodt-
Charousek, Nuremberg, 1896) the KP must go. Charousek played
1 .... K—K4, and after *2 K—B2, B—Q6; 3 K—B3, P—R4; 4 P—Kt3*
(4 P—Kt4, P—R5), *B×Pch!* won quickly, for if 4 .... Kt×B, P—
Kt5ch; 5 P×P, P×Pch; 6 K×P, K×Kt; 7 K—R4, P—Q6. The
conclusion was *5 K—K2, P—R5!* (fixing the KRP); *6 P×P, P×P;
7 K—B2, K—B5; 8 Kt—Kt3, P—Q6; 9 Kt—Q2, B—Q4; 10 Kt—B1,*

B—K3; 11 Kt—Q2, B×P; 12 Kt—B3, B—Kt5; 13 Kt×P, P—Q7 and it is all over.

Doubled Pawns which are isolated are born but to die. Even if they are not captured they are no better than one Pawn, so that the enemy is virtually one Pawn ahead. Usually, however, they cannot even be defended. E.g., No. 262a (Hanauer-Fine, New York, 1938), White: K at QKt1, Kt at Q5, P's at QB6, KB6, KKt5; Black: K at KB2, B at K4, P's at QR3, QR5, KR2. Black must lose both his RP's. The game went: 1 .... B—R7; 2 K—Kt2, B—Q3; 3 K—R2, K—Kt3; 4 Kt—K7ch, K—B2; 5 Kt—B5, B—B2; 6 K—R3, K—Kt3; 7 K×P, K—B2; 8 K—Kt3, P—QR4; 9 K—R4, B—Q1; 10 K—Kt5, K—K3; 11 K—B4, K—B2; 12 K—Q5, B—Kt3; 13 Kt—Q6ch, K—B1; 14 K—K6, P—R5; 15 Kt—B4, B—B2; 16 Kt—K5 Resigns.

d) Better King Position.

Here again we may omit the obvious case where one King is so near that he can capture a large number of Pawns. A more refined method is required when one King is merely near enough to threaten the Pawns and cramp his rival's style. This too will normally result in material gain but only after considerable juggling. No. 263 (Tchigorin-Charousek, 4th game of tie match, Pest, 1896) is typical. The White King can get to QR6 or QB6 but cannot win anything directly. Nevertheless the strong post at QB6 is sufficient to win. Tchigorin concluded as follows: *1 .... B—K2; 2 K—B4, K—B1; 3 K—Kt5, K—K1; 4 K—R6, B—B4; 5 K—Kt5* (5 Kt—B3 was also good), *B—K6; 6 K—B6, K—Q1; 7 P—QKt4, P—KR4; 8 P—QR4, B—Q7; 9 P—Kt5, P—R5; 10 Kt—Q4, P—Kt4; 11 Kt—B5, B—K8; 12 Kt—R6, P—B3; 13 Kt—B5, B—Kt5; 14 Kt—Q4, K—B1; 15 Kt—K6, B—Q3; 16 P—R5, B—Kt6; 7 P—Kt6, RP×P; 18 P×P, P×P; 19 P—Q6* and Black had to give up his B and soon resign.

II. BISHOP, KNIGHT AND PAWNS VS. BISHOP, KNIGHT AND PAWNS

Almost all such endings are governed by the same principles as simple B or simple Kt endings, or a combination of the two. There are only two questions then which need be considered—Bishops of opposite colors and reduction (exchange).

A. BISHOPS OF OPPOSITE COLORS

As we noted, there are many cases in which a Pawn plus does not win with only such Bishops on the board. These all involve positions where the superior side can take the initiative on only one side of the board. In such positions it is essential to avoid exchanging Knights, although exchange of Bishop for Knight, or Knight for Bishop are both permissible.

Except for some very unusual cases, the win is impossible in materially even positions. Where one side is a Pawn ahead the winning method differs in no essential respect from that in pure Kt or pure B endings—place one's pieces as well as possible, secure a passed Pawn, tie up the enemy pieces, divert the King, switch over to the other side of the board and establish a decisive superiority there. Usually the win is somewhat easier because with a Pawn down the defender's other Pawns are exposed and often lost. Most of the time a suitable exchange (Kt for B, or B for Kt) is feasible.

No. 264 (Marshall-Nimzovitch, New York, 1927) is a model for the superior side. The game continued *1 P—KB4* (the defender as usual

No. 263

White wins.

No. 264

Black wins.

tries to exchange as many Pawns as possible), *Kt—R6!* (holding the QRP and threatening 2 .... Kt—Kt4; 3 Kt—Kt1, B—Q6); *2 P×P, P×P; 3 K—B2, B—R4; 4 B—K5, P—Kt5* (to clear up the situation on the K-side. If 4 .... Kt—Kt4; 5 P—Kt4, B—Kt3; 6 P—B4, P×P; 7 Kt×P, B—B2; 8 P—QR4, B×Kt; 9 P×Kt, B×P; 10 B—B6 and wins a Pawn on the K-side, so that it becomes doubtful whether Black can win); *5 P×P, B×P; 6 K—K3, B—B4; 7 B—Kt7, B—K3* (threatening 7 .... Kt—Kt4; 8 Kt—Kt1, B—B4); *8 B—B8* (loses a Pawn. But even after 8 K—Q3, K—Q2; 9 B—B8, Kt—Kt4; 10 P—B4, P×Pch; 11 Kt×P, P—QR4; 12 P—R3, B—B4ch; 13 K—K3, K—B3; 14 Kt—K5ch, K—Q4; 15 Kt—B3, P—R5!; 16 B—K7, P—B4; White must lose another Pawn), *Kt—Kt4; 9 Kt—Kt1, P—QR4; 10 K—Q2* (if 10 P—R4, Kt—R2 followed by B—Q2), *B—B4; 11 Kt—R3, Kt×Kt; 12 B×Kt, B—Kt8; 13 B—B8, B×P* and the rest is not difficult: *14 B—Kt7, B—B5; 15 K—K3, K—Kt2; 16 B—R6, K—R3; 17 K—Q2, B—B8; 18 P—Kt3, K—Kt4; 19 K—B1, K—B5; 20 K—*

Kt2, P—B4; 21 B—K3, P×P!; 22 B×P, P—Kt4; 23 B—Kt6, P—R5; 24 B—R5, P—Q5!; 25 P×P, P—Kt5; 26 B—Kt6, P—R6ch; 27 K—R2, K—Kt4; 28 B—B5, K—R5 and White resigned.

The winning chances are greatest when the Pawns are unevenly distributed, i.e., 3 to 1 on one side and 2 to 3 on the other. In fact, in such unbalanced Pawn positions with a Pawn ahead the game is normally a win despite the opposite-colored Bishops. No. 265 (Kan-Flohr, Leningrad-Moscow, 1939) is typical. The weakness of White's position lies not so much in the fact that he must lose a Pawn but rather in the danger of the remote passed Pawn that Black will secure. The game continued *1 Kt—Kt6, B×P; 2 B—Kt3* (if 2 B—B2, P—QR4; 3 B×P, P—R5; 4 Kt—B4, P—R6; 5 Kt—Q3; B—Kt8 and wins a piece), *B—Kt8; 3 Kt—K5, Kt—Q7* (Black must of course avoid the exchange of Knights); *4 Kt—B6, B—K5; 5 Kt—R5, B—Q4!* Now White's Knight is stalemated and we have in effect an ending of Kt vs. B. *6 B—Q6, P—B5; 7 B—Kt4, Kt—K5; 8 K—R2, K—B2; 9 K—Kt1, P—R4!* (he has a winning advantage on the other wing, so he wants to rid himself of the danger on the K-side); *10 P×P, Kt—Kt6; 11 K—B2, Kt×BP; 12 B—R3, K—B3; 13 B—B1, K—K3; 14 B—B4, B—K5; 15 B—B7, K—Q4; 16 B—Kt8, K—B4; 17 B—R7ch, K—Q3; 18 B—Kt8ch, K—K3; 19 B—B4, B—R1; 20 B—B7, Kt—K2; 21 B—Kt6, Kt—Q4; 22 B—Q4, Kt—B3* (decisive); *23 K—K3, Kt×P; 24 P—R4, Kt—Kt6; 25 K—Q2, P—Kt3; 26 B—Kt6, Kt—B4; 27 B—Q8, K—Q4; 28 K—K2, K—K5; 29 K—Q2, K—B6; 30 K—B2, K—Kt5; 31 K—Kt2, Kt×P; 32 K—R3, Kt—B4; 33 K—Kt4, Kt—Kt2!* and White soon resigned, for if 34 K—B5, Kt—K3ch.

Again the fewer Pawns there are the greater is the likelihood of a draw. E.g., No. 265a, (Winawer-Pillsbury, Nuremberg, 1896), White: K at KB2, B at QR1, Kt at KKt5, P's at KKt2, KR4; Black: K at K2, B at QR7, Kt at QB3, P's at QR2, QKt5, KKt3. White to play draws. 1 P—Kt4! (1 K—K2 was played and lost after 1 .... P—R4; 2 Kt—B3, P—R5; 3 Kt—Q4, Kt×Kt; 4 B×Kt, K—Q3 because the K-side Pawns had not yet been exchanged), P—R4 (or 1 .... B—B2; 2 P—R5, P×P; 3 Kt×B, K×Kt; 4 P×P, K—Kt1; 5 K—K2, K—R2; 6 K—Q3 and Black cannot win with his King so far away); 2 P—R5, P×P; 3 P×P, P—R5; 4 P—R6, B—Kt8; 5 P—R7, B×P; 6 Kt×B, P—R6; 7 K—K2, P—Kt6; 8 K—Q2=.

B. BISHOPS OF THE SAME COLOR

These endings ordinarily differ in no essential respect from the corresponding simple cases of B vs. B, Kt vs. Kt, or B vs. Kt. It is important to exchange the right piece. Thus if the opponent has all his Pawns on the color of his Bishop, one will not exchange the Bishop, but if he has not, one will. The rule to follow is that *one should ex-*

change the opponent's most active piece. E.g., in No. 266 (Eliskases-Capablanca, Semmering-Baden, 1937) it is all right to exchange Black's Knight, but not his Bishop, although even the exchange of Knights should be permitted only at the proper moment, i.e., when it will not facilitate a break on the Q-side. Thus Eliskases won after *1 B—B1!* (preventing the freeing move 1 .... P—QR4), *Kt—K3* (1 .... P—QR4; 2 Kt—R4ch); *2 Kt—R4ch!* (no exchange yet! After 2 Kt×Kt, B×Kt, either 3 .... P—QR4 or 3 .... P—B4 will get Black out of the woods), *K—B2; 3 K—B2, P—Kt4; 4 K—K3, P×Pch; 5 P×P, Kt—Kt2; 6 Kt—B5!, Kt—K3; 7 Kt×Ktch!* (now it is all right

No. 265

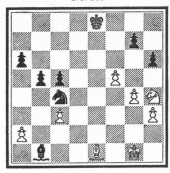

White to play; Black wins.

No. 266

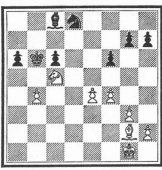

White to play wins. He should exchange Kt for Kt, or B for Kt, but *not* Kt for B, or B for B.

because White's King is centralized), *B×Kt; 8 K—Q4!, K—Kt3; 9 B—B4!*, etc. For the continuation see No. 196.

Summary: In endings where each side has a Bishop and a Knight the basic principles remain the same as for the corresponding simpler endings. If the Bishops are of opposite colors, the superior side should be careful not to exchange Knights. If the Bishops are of the same color, the superior side should try to exchange his opponent's most active piece. As a rule, it is to the advantage of the superior side to exchange pieces, but to his disadvantage to exchange Pawns, and conversely the inferior side should avoid the exchange of pieces, but should try to reduce the number of Pawns.

III. THE TWO BISHOPS

The superiority of the Bishops in any more or less normal Pawn position is now universally recognized. Steinitz was the first to point it out and since his day countless tournament games have demonstrated it time and again. In this section we shall analyze the nature of this advantage and lay down some general rules for its proper exploitation.

In the case of Bishop vs. Knight we saw that the Bishop helped the King penetrate the enemy lines. With an extra piece on the board, this penetration is not often feasible. Nevertheless, we also saw that a Bishop can limit the mobility of a Knight, and this constriction idea is the one which is the key to endings of two Bishops against B+Kt or two Knights. The Bishops must be made to work together and cramp the enemy position; wherever possible they then facilitate the entry of the King; otherwise they create weaknesses and hammer away at them until some more tangible advantage (King entry, material gain) materializes.

The strength of the outside passed Pawn with one Bishop was clear enough; with two Bishops it is almost a winning advantage. For the Bishops in unison can control every square on the queening file. Thus there are two chief reasons why the two Bishops are so strong: 1. They can cramp the enemy position, and 2. they can provide a perfect escort for an outside passed Pawn.

In order to examine the winning process in greater detail we shall consider unbalanced and balanced Pawn positions separately. Of course, we are interested only in positional advantage here; material advantage is exploited according to the principles set up in Chapter IV, and Chapter V, Part I.

A. THE PAWN STRUCTURE IS UNBALANCED

By this we mean that the Pawns are not distributed on the same files, i.e., that there is at least one file on which there is a greater number of Pawns (either 2 to 1, or 1 to 0) for one side or the other. E.g., White has one Pawn on each of the QKt, QB, KKt, KR files; Black

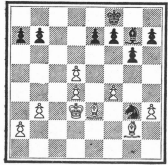

No. 267

White to play wins.

one Pawn on each of the QR, QKt, KKt, KR files. In such cases the power of the two Bishops is tremendous; very often this alone is sufficient to win. The winning process in these endings may be divided into four steps.

1. Place the pieces in the best possible positions. These will be squares from which they cramp the mobility of the enemy pieces.

2. Set up an outside passed Pawn, or a potential outside passed Pawn. In other

words advance the Pawns as far as you can. Black stops them.

3. If Black goes to the threatened sector with his King, turn your attention to the other wing, where you will be able to either capture material with the Bishops or force an entry with the King.

4. If Black does not try to stop the Pawn with his King the advance of the passed Pawn will cost him a piece.

It will be noticed that this method differs in no essential respect from that of B vs. Kt. In actual play, however, it will be found that it works much more smoothly and easily.

No. 267 (Leonhardt-Bernstein, Barmen, 1905) illustrates the great strength of the outside passed Pawn. We may take it that the first step has been completed here. Thus White first tries to set up a 2–1 majority on the Q-side. *1 P—Q6!, P×P* (forced: if 1 .... P—Kt3; 2 P—Q7!); *2 B×P, Kt—B4; 3 B—B2, B—R3; 4 K—K4, Kt—K2; 5 P—Q5!* (cramping the enemy pieces and at the same time threatening to win the QRP), *P—B4ch; 6 K—B3, P—R3* (if 6 .... P—R4; 7 B—Kt6); *7 P—R4* (threatening P—Kt4—Kt5, and if then P×P, P—R5!—R6—R7—R8=Q. If the Pawn once gets to R5 it will be impossible for Black to stop it), *B—Kt2; 8 K—K2* (not 8 P—Kt4?, B—B6; 9 P—Kt5, P×P; 10 P×P, K—K1; 11 B—R7, K—Q2; 12 P—Kt6?; B—Q5 and Black still has some fight left), *B—B6.* The second step is all over; now we have the fourth. If 8 .... K—K1; 9 K—Q3, K—Q2; 10 K—B4, wins a P); *9 K—Q3, B—Kt5; 10 B×P, P—R3* (if 10 .... Kt×P; 11 K—B4, Kt—B2; 12 K×B, Kt×B; 13 K—Kt5, Kt—B2ch; 14 K—Kt6, Kt—Q4ch; 15 K—Kt7, and the advance of the QRP will decide); *11 B—Kt7, P—Kt4; 12 P×P, P×P; 13 K—B4, B—Q7; 14 P—Kt4* and soon won. The advance of the QKt and QRP's will cost Black at least a piece, while Black's KKtP is easily stopped.

It sometimes happens that a passed Pawn cannot be secured by simple advances and exchanges. In such cases a cramped position can often be exploited by means of a sacrifice which sets up a passed Pawn. An example is No. 267a (Perlis-Baird, Barmen, 1905), White: K at Q2, B's at QB2, QKt6, P's at QR3, QKt4, K4, KB3, KKt3, KR2; Black: K at K1, B at K3, Kt at Q1, P's at QKt2, QB3, K4, KB3, KKt2, KR2. White won as follows: 1 P—B4, P×P; 2 P×P, B—R7; 3 K—B3, Kt—K3; 4 B—K3, Kt—B1; 5 P—QR4, Kt—Q2; 6 B—Q3, K—Q1; 7 K—Q4, Kt—B1; 8 P—B5!, Kt—Q2; 9 B—KB4, K—K2; 10 P—R4, B—Kt6; 11 P—QR5, P—R3; 12 B—K2, B—R7; 13 B—Q1, B—B2; 14 B—B7!, B—R7; 15 B—R4, B—B2. This is the critical position. White cannot improve his position any more and breaks through by means of a sacrifice. 16 B×P!, P×B; 17 P—R6, P—B4ch and now the simplest win was 18 P×P, Kt—Kt1; 19 B×Kt, B—K1; 20 K—Q5, although 18 K—K3, Kt—Kt3; 19

B×Kt, B—K1; 10 B×Pch as played in the game is of course also good enough.

Against a doubled Pawn the two Bishops will generally be able to force the gain of material or the creation of an outside passed Pawn. This is illustrated in No. 268 (Soultanbeieff-Flohr, Folkestone, 1933). The weakness of White's QKtP is the key to Black's winning plan. First he will force the P to Kt4. Then he will play his K to the Q-side. To prevent the entry of the King White will have to play his Kt to QB3, for his King is kept impotent by the iron grip of the two Bishops. And finally Black will capture the QKtP and establish an outside passed Pawn. In the absence of White's King, such a Pawn is sure to cost White a piece. Flohr worked out his plan as follows: *1 ....* *K—Kt3; 2 K—Kt2* (2 K—B1, B—Kt4ch and poor White has to go right back), *B—Q4; 3 P—Kt4, K—B2* (first and second steps are now in progress); *4 Kt—Kt3, K—K1; 5 Kt—K2, K—Q2; 6 Kt—B3, K— B3; 7 K—R2, B—QKt6* (a few moves to gain time on the clock. 7 .... B—K2 at once was perfectly all right); *8 K—Kt2, B—B5; 9 K—Kt1, B—Q6; 10 K—Kt2, B—B5; 11 Kt—Kt1, P—Kt3; 12 K— Kt1, B—Q6; 13 Kt—B3* (if 13 Kt—R3, P—Kt4!; 14 K—Kt2, B—K2; 15 K—B2, P—QR4!; 16 P×P, P—Kt5 wins the Kt), *B—K2; 14 K— B2, B×P; 15 Kt×P, B—K2; 16 Kt—B3, B—R5ch* (confining the King to the K-side); *17 K—Kt1, B—B5; 18 K—Kt2, P—QR4; 19 K—Kt1, P—Kt4; 20 K—Kt2, P—R4; 21 K—Kt1* (the impotence of the King makes this an illustration of the fourth step in our schema), *B—QKt6; 22 K—Kt2, P—Kt5; 23 Kt—K2, B—Q4ch; 24 K—B1, B—B5; 25 B—K1* (desperation. 25 B—B1, P—R5; 26 B—Q2, P—R6 is likewise hopeless), *B×B; 26 K×B, B×Kt; 27 K×B, P—QR5* and White resigned. For if 28 K—Q3, K—Q4; 29 K—Q2, P—R6; 30 P×P, P×P; 31 K—B3, K—K5 he loses three Pawns on the K-side.

Against an isolated QP, a single Kt is more effective than a single B, although with no extra weaknesses the game should be a draw in either case. But with two Bishops an isolated QP may be serious enough to cause a loss, although one cannot demonstrate this with any degree of certainty. In No. 268a (Rubinstein-Gajdos, Barmen, 1905) Rubinstein did work out a win, but he was helped by some inferior play on his opponent's part. White: K at KKt1, B's at Q4, K2, P's at QR2, QKt2, K3, KB3, KKt2, KR2; Black: K at KB2, B at QB1, Kt at Q3, P's at QR3, QKt2, Q4, KB3, KKt2, KR2. The game continued: 1 K—B2, B—Q2; 2 K—K1, Kt—Kt4 (better is 2 .... B— Kt4); 3 B—B5, K—K3; 4 K—Q2, P—B4?? (a horrible positional blunder: it immobilizes his own Bishop and strengthens the opponent's Bishop on Black squares); 5 P—QKt3, Kt—Q3; 6 P—QR4, Kt—B1; 7 K—B3, Kt—K2; 8 B—Q4, P—KKt3; 9 K—Kt4, B—B3; 10 K— B5, K—Q2; 11 P—R5, Kt—B1; 12 B—Q1, Kt—R2; 13 P—R4, Kt—

Kt4; 14 B—B2, Kt—B2; 15 P—Kt3, Kt—K1; 16 B—K5!, K—K3;
17 P—B4, K—Q2; 18 P—QKt4, Kt—B2; 19 B×Kt!, K×B; 20 B—
Kt3, P—R4; 21 B—R2, K—Q2; 22 B×P, B×B; 23 K×B, K—B2;
24 K—K5 Resigns.

Where there is a weak color complex the two Bishops can usually
clear a path for the King by stalemating or constricting the enemy
pieces. E.g., No. 268b (Hasenfuss-Fine, Kemeri, 1937), White: K
at KKt1, B at K3, Kt at QB2, P's at QR4, QKt3, Q4, K5, KB4,
KKt3, KR2; Black: K at KKt1, B's at Q2, K2, P's at QR2, QKt2,
Q4, KB2, KKt2, KKt5, KR4. Black won as follows: 1 .... B—KB4;
2 Kt—K1, B—Kt8!; 3 B—Q2, K—R2; 4 K—B2, K—Kt3; 5 K—K3,

No. 268   No. 269

Black wins.   Black to play wins.

K—B4; 6 P—R5, P—KKt4! (setting up a potential outside passed
Pawn); 7 Kt—Q3, B—B7; 8 Kt—B5, P×Pch; 9 P×P, P—Kt3;
10 P×P, P×P; 11 Kt—Q7, P—Kt4; 12 P—Kt4, P—R5!; 13 Kt—B5,
P—Kt6; 14 P×P, P×P; 15 K—B3, B—KR5; 16 B—K3, B—Q8ch;
17 K—Kt2, K—Kt5; 18 B—Q2, B—B6ch; 19 K—Kt1, K—B4;
20 B—K3, B—K5; 21 B—Q2, P—Kt7; 22 Kt×B, K×Kt; 23 K×P,
K×QP; 24 K—R3, B—K2; 25 K—Kt4, K—Q6 and the QP decides.

The possibility of stalemating or cramping the mobility of Knights
is one of the most important stratagems at the disposal of the player
with the Bishops. This is the reason why the Knights may never
venture to stray far afield. If a Knight is not lost directly, an exchange
at the judicious moment is usually available to transpose into a simpler
ending. An example is No. 269 (Walbrodt-Charousek, Nuremberg,
1896). Charousek won by *1* .... *B—Kt4!* (threatening 2 .... B—
R3! and 3 K—K3); *2 Kt—R3* (if 2 K—Kt4, K—K3; 3 Kt—R3, B—
K7ch; 4 Kt—B3, P—Q6!; 5 Kt—Kt1, B—K4; 6 K—R5, B—B5; and

wins), *B—B8!; 3 Kt(K5)—B4* (if 3 K—B2, B×P!, while if 3Kt(R3)—B4, K—K3; 4 Kt—Q2, B×Pch), *K—K3; 4 Kt—Q2, B—Q6; 5 Kt(R3)—B4, B—B1; 6 Kt—Kt2, B—R3; 7 Kt(Kt2)—B4* (The Kt's cannot find a haven. If 7 Kt(Q2)—B4, B—KKt2; 8 K—K2, P—Q6ch!; 9 K—Q2!, B—Q5!; 10 K—Q1, B×Kt(Kt7); 11 Kt×B, K—K4 and wins), *B—Kt5; 8 K—Kt4, B×Kt(Q7)!* This is the decisive exchange. *9 Kt×B, B—K7ch; 10 K—Kt3, K—K4* and Black won (See No. 262). While there is no precise analogy with two Bishops against B+Kt, if the Pawns are on the color of the lone B an exchange of B for Kt would leave one with a better B ending. E.g., No. 269a (Scheltinga-Fine, Amsterdam, 1936), White: K at KR2, B at Q2, Kt at KB3, P's at QKt4, QB5, K4, KB2, KKt2, KR3; Black: K at KKt1, B's at Q6, KKt2, P's at QR3, QKt2, K3, KB2, KKt3, KR3. After 1 P—K5 (forced), B—K5!; 2 B—B3, B×Kt!; 3 P×B, K—B1 White has the bad Bishop and his game is untenable (No. 196b).

B. THE PAWN STRUCTURE IS BALANCED

Here the defender's drawing chances are much greater than in a), but even so he often finds it impossible to hold the game. For the B's working together can usually manage to weaken the enemy Pawns and cramp the enemy pieces. Once this is done the rest is not too difficult.

No. 270 (Berger-Tchigorin, Carlsbad, 1907) is a model case. The winning process consists of five steps. *1. Weakening the opponent's Pawns.* This is the most important of all—on it hinges the outcome of the game. In the illustration before us this took place voluntarily, although it could have been forced. *1 .... K—K2; 2 B—K5* (correct is 2 B—B8), *Kt—K1; 3 K—K2, B—Q3; 4 B—B3, P—QKt3?* (4 ....

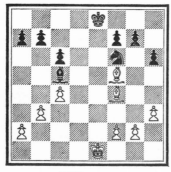

No. 270

White won.

K—Q1 was better. Whether Black could hold the game in that event is not certain, but it would have offered better chances than the course actually chosen); *5 P—Kt3, P—B3?* (better P—Kt3). From here on we may take it that there is a forced win. The next step is *2. Cramping the opponent's pieces. 6 P—B4, B—B4; 7 B—K4, K—Q2* (now the K is tied down to the defense of the QBP); *8 P—QKt4, B—K2; 9 K—B3, Kt—Q3; 10 B—Q3, K—K3; 11 P—Kt4, P—KKt4.* This move is so obviously weakening that one is forced to inquire how it happened that a player of Tchigorin's strength chose it. The reason is that he wished to prevent the entry of the White King. E.g., if 11 .... K—Q2; 12 K—Kt3, K—B2; 13 K—R4, P—B4ch; 14 K—R5 and wins. On the other hand, if 11 .... K—B2; 12 B—Q4, K—K3; 13 P—R3, K—B2; 14 P—QB5, P×P; 15 B×P, Kt—B1; 16 B—B5!, B×B; 17 P×B, Kt—K2; 18 B—Q7 Black is in zugzwang and has no defense against the march of the White King to the Q-side. In other words, the cramping effect of the Bishops, which can attack both sides of the board simultaneously, has already made itself felt. The next step is 3. *Clearing a path for the entrance of the King. 12 P—R3, Kt—B2; 13 B—B5ch* (Not 13 K—K4, Kt—Q3ch), *K—Q3; 14 B—Kt6, Kt—Q1; 15 P×P!, RP×P,* (forced, for if 15 .... BP×P; 16 B—Kt7 wins the RP); *16 K—K4.* The game is approaching a climax. To keep the White King out Black must stalemate his Kt. *16 .... Kt—K3; 17 B—B7!, Kt—Kt2* (17 .... Kt—Q1?; 18 B—Kt8!, or 17 .... Kt—B5; 18 K—B5, Kt×P; 19 B×P, B×B; 20 K×B and the KtP cannot be held.); *18 B—K1, K—Q2; 19 B—B3, B—Q1; 20 P—Kt5!* (opening the way on the Q-side as well), *K—K2; 19 B—Kt8, K—B1; 20 B—R7, P×P; 21 P×P, K—K2.* Thus Black has held the White King out, but he has had to submit to a terrific battering and now gets into zugzwang. This brings us to the fourth step. 4. *After the White King has penetrated as far as possible, forcing the exchange of the piece which is holding him off. 22 B—Kt4ch, K—K3; 23 B—Kt8ch, K—Q2; 24 K—Q5!* Now he is in zugzwang. *24 .... B—K2* (forced, for if 24 .... K—B2; 25 B—B8, Kt—K1; 26 B—K6, K—Kt2; 27 B—Q7!, Kt—B2ch; 28 K—K4, P—R3; 29 P—R4, P×P; 30 P×P, K—Kt1; 31 B—Q6, K—Kt2; 32 B—B6ch, K—B1; 33 K—B5 and Black must lose his K-side Pawns); *25 B×B, K×B.* And now the fifth and final phase. 5. *Penetrating with the King and capturing material. 26 K—B6, Kt—K1; 27 P—QR4* (27 K—Kt7, Kt—Q3ch; 28 K—R6! was also good enough), *Kt—Q3; 28 K—B7, Kt—K5; 29 B—Kt3, Kt—B4; 30 B—B2, K—K3; 31 K—Kt8* (in the game there occurred 31 K—B6?, K—K4; 32 P—R5, Kt—K3; 33 P×P, Kt—Q5ch; 34 K—Kt7, P×P; 35 B—Q3, when 35 .... P—B4!; 36 P×P, Kt×KtP!! would have drawn), *K—Q3* (if 31 .... P—R3; 32 K—B7, P×P; 33 P×P, K—K3; 34 K×P, K—Q3; 35 K—R7, K—B2; 36 P—Kt6ch, K—B3; 37 B—K4ch wins); *32 K×P, K—B2; 33 P—R5!, P×P; 34 P—Kt6ch, K—B3; 35 B—K4ch, Kt×B; 36 P—Kt7* and wins.

The idea of *stalemating the Kt* is central in these endings. A classic illustration is No. 271 (Tarrasch-Rubinstein, San Sebastian, 1912). Clearly the first three steps above have been completed. Rubinstein now concludes as follows: *1 .... K—K4; 2 P—Kt4, B—K6!; 3 K—B3* (if 3 Kt—B2, B×Kt; 4 K×B, K—B5), *K—Q5; 4 B—Kt3, B—Kt2* (4 .... B×P; 5 B×P, B—KB8 was simpler. If then 6 B—Kt7!,

B×Kt!; 7 B—R6!!, K—B6!!!; 8 K—Kt3!, K—Kt7; 9 B—B4, B—
KB8; 10 B×B, K×P; 11 K—B3, B—R3; 12 B—Kt5, K—Kt6;
13 K—K4, P—R5; 14 K—Q4, P—R6 wins); *5 K—K2, B—QR3;
6 B—B2* (6 B×P, B×Pch; 7 K×B3, B—KB8 transposes into the
note to Black's 4th move), *B—QKt4* (to provoke P—R4. 6 .... K—
B6; 7 K×B, P—Q5ch was also good enough); *7 P—R4, B—Q2;
8 K—B3, K—B6; 9 K×B, P—Q5ch; 10 K—K2, K×B; 11 Kt—B4,
B×RP* and it is all over. The last moves were *12 Kt—K6, B—Kt6!;
13 Kt×Pch, K—Kt7; 14 Kt—Kt5, P—R5; 15 K—K3, P—R6; 16
Kt×P, K×Kt; 17 K—Q4, K—Kt5;* 18 Resigns.

The Bishops are seen at their worst in blocked positions and where all

No. 271	No. 272
Black to play wins.	Black to play. Drawn.

the Pawns are on one side. With a combination of these two even a
Pawn up may not be sufficient to win. Thus in No. 272 (Euwe-
Alekhine, 3rd match game, 1937) Alekhine held his opponent to a
draw. After *1 .... K—B2; 2 P—R4, P—Kt4!* (essential to prevent
B—B4 and P—R5, which would free the King); *3 B—R5ch, K—K2!*
(not 3 .... K—B3?; 4 B—Q8ch, K—B4; 5 P—Kt4ch winning a
Pawn, or 3 .... K—Kt2?; 4 B—Q8!, P×P; 5 B×P followed by B—
Kt3—B4 and marching the King to the Q-side); *4 B—Kt4, B—Kt2.*
Now White can make no further progress with his Bishops, so he
offers an exchange of B for the strong Kt, but his winning hopes are
soon dissipated. *5 B—K5, Kt×B; 6 P×Kt, P×P; 7 K—Kt1, B—R3;
8 K—R2, K—B2* and the game was eventually drawn (No. 181).

Endings with all the Pawns on one side are almost always drawn
if the superior side has three Pawns or less, usually drawn if he has
four Pawns. An example where 2B's+2P's hold B+Kt+3P's is No.

272a (Gygli-Alekhine, Berne, 1932), White: K at KR3, B's at QB8, KB8, P's at KB3, KR2; Black: K at KR1, B at Q5, Kt at Q8, P's at KR2, KKt2, KB4. Drawn. 1 .... Kt—K6; 2 B—K6, P—B5; 3 B—R3, B—K4; 4 B—B1, Kt—B7; 5 B—Kt3, Kt—K8; 6 B—Q5, Kt—Q6; 7 B—Q2, P—Kt3; 8 B—B4, Kt—Kt7; 9 B—K2, P—R4; 10 B—QB1, Kt—R5; 11 B—Q2, K—Kt2; 12 B—Kt4, K—B3; 13 B—R5, Kt—B4; 14 B—Q8ch, K—B4; 15 B—K7, Kt—Q2; 16 B—Q3ch, K—K3; 17 B—Q8, K—B2; 18 B—KKt5 and Alekhine soon admitted that he could make no headway against White's stubborn defense.

Summary: The two Bishops are better than two Knights or Bishop and Knight in most normal Pawn positions. If the Pawns are unbalanced, so that the side with the two Bishops can set up an outside passed Pawn the game is practically a forced win. If the Pawns are balanced, the slightest weakness in the Pawn structure may prove fatal. The three ideas which are the key to all such endings are: 1) Limiting the opponent's mobility. 2) Stalemating the Kt (or Kt's). 3) Exchanging one set of pieces to transpose into a favorable simple ending (especially a Bishop ending where the opponent's Pawns are on the same color as his Bishop).

IV. TWO PIECES VS. ONE

The advantage of a piece in general wins only if there are Pawns on the board and there are less than three Pawns for the piece.

A. NO PAWNS

Just as one minor piece cannot mate a lone King, so two minor pieces against one cannot in general win. But there are a number of exceptions to be noted.

It is always bad for the defender to have his King in the corner. Such positions give rise to most of the exceptions to our general rule that two pieces only draw against one. The reason of course is the threat of checkmate.

An example with 2 Kt's vs. 1 Kt is No. 273 (Berger). The solution is *1 Kt—KB7!* (1 Kt×Kt?? of course would only draw), *Kt—Q3* (any other Kt move amounts to the same thing: the point is that Black cannot give check in less than three moves); *2 Kt—R6ch, K—R1;*

No. 273

White to play wins. The Black Kt may be on any square marked ×.

3 Kt—Kt3! Now we see what difference the extra Black piece makes: if it were not on the board Black would be stalemated. *3 .... Kt— B5; 4 Kt (Kt5)—B7* mate.

An analogous case with two B's vs. one is No. 273a (Berger), White: K at KKt5, B's at K4, KB8; Black: K at KR1, B at K1. White to play wins. 1 K—R6 (threatening B—R7!), K—Kt1; 2 B— R3, B—Kt4 (there is nothing to be done. If 2 .... K—B2; 3 B— Kt6ch and 4 B×B; if 2 .... K—R1; 3 B—R7!, any; 4 B—Kt2 mate, and finally if 2 .... B—B2; 3 B—R7ch, K—R1; 4 B—Kt2 mate); 3 B—Q5ch, K—R1; 4 B—Kt2 mate.

No. 274 (Kling and Horwitz, 1851) illustrates the mating possibilities with B+Kt vs. B. The solution is *1 B—K5ch, K—Kt1; 2 B— Kt7!, B—R5!; 3 Kt—B4, B—K2; 4 Kt—Q5, B—Kt4* (if 4 .... B— Q1; 5 B—R6, B—R5; 6 Kt—K3, B—K2; 7 Kt—B5, B—Q1; 8 B— Kt7 and wins); *5 B—B3, B—R5* (or a) 5 .... B—B8; 6 Kt—B6ch, K—R1; 7 Kt—K4ch, K—Kt1; 8 B—Kt7, B—Kt4; 9 Kt—Q6, B— K2; 10 Kt—B5. b) 5 .... B—Q1; 6 B—Kt4, B—R5; 7 Kt—K3, B—Kt6; 8 Kt—B5, B—B5; 9 Kt—K7ch, K—B1; 10 Kt—Q5ch, winning the B); *6 B—Kt4, B—B7* (he must prevent Kt—K3); *7 Kt— B6ch, K—R1; 8 B—B8, B any; 9 B—Kt7* mate.

With B+Kt vs. Kt another kind of winning threat appears: trapping the Kt. E.g., No. 274a (Berger), White: K at K5, B at QB4, Kt at KB5; Black: K at KR1, Kt at K1. White to play wins. 1 B— B7!, Kt—B2 (if 1 .... Kt—Kt2; 2 Kt—R6!, K—R2; 3 Kt—Kt4!, K—R1; 4 Kt—B6! and the Kt is lost); 2 K—Q4, Kt—R3 (if 2 .... Kt—Kt4ch; 3 K—B4, Kt—R6ch; 4 K—Kt4, Kt—B7ch; 5 K—B3, Kt—R6; 6 B—K8, Kt—Kt8ch; 7 K—Q3, Kt—R6; 8 Kt—K3, K— Kt1; 9 K—B3, K—B1; 10 B—R4, K—K2; 11 K—Kt2); 3 K—B4, Kt—Kt1; 4 B—K8, K—Kt1; 5 K—Q5, Kt—R3; 6 K—Q6, Kt—Kt5; 7 B—Kt5, Kt—B7; 8 B—Q3, Kt—K8; 9 B—K4, K—B2; 10 K—K5, K—Kt3; 11 K—B4, K—B3; 12 Kt—Q4, K—K2; 13 Kt—B5ch, K— K3; 14 Kt—Kt3, K—B3; 15 K—K3, K—Kt4; 16 Kt—K2, K—Kt5; 17 K—B2 and the Kt will finally pay the penalty for not being a B.

A mating attack with B+Kt vs. Kt is seen in No. 274b (Amelung, 1896), White: K at KKt6, B at KR6, Kt at KB6; Black: K at KR1, Kt at Q5. 1 .... Kt—B4; 2 B—B8, Kt—R5ch; 3 K—B7, Kt—B4; 4 Kt—K4, K—R2; 5 Kt—Kt5ch, K—R1; 6 B—B5, Kt—Q3ch; 7 K— B8, Kt—B4; 8 B—Kt6, Kt—Kt2; 9 B—R5, Kt—B4; 10 B—B3ch, Kt—Kt2; 11 B×Kt mate. However here the Kt could draw if it were on one of a number of other squares: QB3, QB5, Q6, KR6 and of course any square from which a capture is possible.

Two B's against Kt offer the best winning chances of all. No. 275 (Kling and Horwitz, 1851) differs from the other examples in that there is no immediate threat, either of mate or of capturing the Kt.

The solution is *1 B—QKt4, Kt—R2* (If 1 .... Kt—Q2; 2 B—Q5ch, K—Kt2; 3 B—B4, Kt—B1; 4 B—B3ch, K—R3; 5 B—B7, Kt—R2; 6 B—K8, Kt—B1; 7 B—Kt2, Kt—R2; 8 B—Q4, Kt—B1; 9 K—B6, Kt—R2ch; 10 K—B7, Kt—Kt4ch; 11 K—Kt8, Kt—B6; 12 B—K3ch, Kt—Kt4; 13 K—B8 and wins the Kt. Or 1 .... Kt—Kt1; 2 B— Q5ch, K—Kt2; 3 K—Kt5!, K—R2; 4 B—B8!, K—R1; 5 B—K4, Kt any; 6 K or B×Kt. Or finally 1 .... Kt—K1; 2 B—R5ch); *2 B— B3, K—K1* (if 2 .... K—B1; 3 K—Kt6, while if 2 .... K—Kt1; 3 B—Q5ch, K—B1; 4 K—Kt6. A Kt move likewise does not help: 2 .... Kt—B1; 3 B—R5ch, K—Kt1; 4 B—K8, K—R2; 5 K—B6,

No. 274

White to play wins.

No. 275

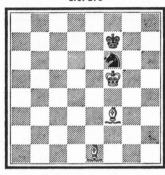

White to play wins.

K—R3; 6 B—Q2ch, K—R2; 7 B—Kt4, K—Kt1; 8 B—B7ch, K any; 9 B×Kt); *3 B—R5ch, K—B1* (or 3 .... K—Q1; 4 B—QKt4 followed by B—Kt6); *4 K—Kt6, K—Kt1; 5 B—KKt4, Kt—B1ch; 6 K—B6, Kt—R2ch* (if 6 .... K—R2; 7 K—B7, Kt—Kt3; 8 B—B5, etc.); *7 K—K7, Kt—Kt4* (on 7 .... Kt—B1; 8 B—KR5, Kt—Kt3ch; 9 K— B6, Kt—R1; 10 B—K2, K—R2; 11 B—B4, K—R3; 12 B—Q3, K— R4; 13 K—Kt7 decides); *8 B—B6* (8 B—B5, Kt—K5! is harder), *Kt—K5!; 9 B—K6ch, K—R2; 10 B—B5ch, K—Kt1; 11 B—R4!* (not 11 B×Kt?? stalemate), *Kt—B6* (or a) 11 .... Kt—B4; 12 B—KB2, Kt—R3; 13 K—Q6; b) 11 .... Kt—Q7; 12 K—B6, K—B1; 13 B— Q3, Kt—Kt6; 14 B—KB2 and the Kt is trapped in both cases); *12 K—K6, Kt—Kt4; 13 B—KB2, Kt—B2ch; 14 K—Q7, Kt—Kt4; 15 B—Q3* and again the cavalry must make its last stand.

Attempts have been made to show that two B's win against Kt in all positions, but the proofs are inconclusive.

Summary: Without Pawns two pieces win against one only in certain special positions. These occur chiefly when the defender's

King is in the corner. The win is accomplished by checkmating. When the lone piece is a Kt, there is the additional possibility of trapping it. Endings with two B's vs. Kt offer the best winning chances.

B. WITH PAWNS

1. WHITE HAS ONE PAWN

a) *If Black has no Pawns* the win is routine. No. 276 may be taken as the general case. The continuation could be *1 K—K5, B—*

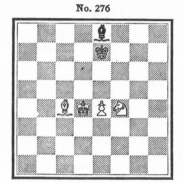

No. 276

White wins.

No. 277

White wins.

Q2; 2 Kt—Kt6ch, K—Q1; 3 K—Q6, B—Kt5; 4 P—K5, B—B4; 5 Kt—B4, K—K1; 6 P—K6 and *6 .... B×P* is necessary, when *7 Kt×B* gives the elementary mate with B+Kt (No. 4).

Difficulties come up for one of three reasons: 1. The superior side has two Knights. 2. The Pawn is on the seventh. 3. There is a RP+B of the wrong color. All of these may make the win more complex, but prevent it only in problem positions. The first is shown in No. 277 (Berger), the solution to which is *1 P—R6, B—Kt6!; 2 Kt—Q6!!* (not 2 P—R7ch, K—R1; 3 Kt—Q6?, B—B7ch; 4 K—R6, B×P!=), *B—B7ch; 3 Kt—B5!, B—Kt6; 4 P—R7ch, K—R1; 5 Kt—K7!, B—B7ch; 6 K—R6, B×P; 7 Kt—B7* mate. Similarly two Kt's+ P vs. Kt also win: No. 277a (Berger), White: K at KB6, Kt's at K4, KB5, P at KR5; Black: K at KKt1, Kt at KR6. 1 Kt—Kt5!, Kt—B7 (if 1 .... Kt—B5; 2 Kt—K7ch, K any; 3 Kt—Kt6ch, while if 1 .... Kt—Kt8; 2 Kt—K7ch, K—R1; 3 K—Kt6); 2 Kt—R6ch, K—B1 (or 2 .... K—R1; 3 K—Kt6, any; 4 Kt—B7 mate); 3 Kt—

K6ch, K—K1; 4 Kt—Kt8, K—Q2; 5 K—Kt7!, K×Kt; 6 P—R6 and
wins. In the second case, when the Pawn is on the seventh, the danger
of stalemate is always present. Nevertheless with accurate play it
can normally be obviated. One example will suffice. No. 277b
(Horwitz, 1880), White: K at KB5, B at KB8, Kt at KB6, P at KR7;
Black: K at KR1, Kt at QB3. White wins. The main variation is
1 B—Q6!, K—Kt2; 2 K—Kt5, Kt—Q5; 3 B—B8ch, K—R1; 4 K—
Kt6, Kt—K3; 5 B—R6, Kt—B1ch; 6 K—B7, Kt—K3!; 7 Kt—Kt4!!!,
Kt—Q1ch; 8 K—Kt6, Kt—K3; 9 B—Kt7ch!!!, Kt×B; 10 Kt—K5,
any; 11 Kt—B7 mate. In the third case—RP+B of the wrong color—
one must take care not to exchange the other piece or to push the
Pawn too hastily. E.g., No. 277c (Alekhine-V. Scheltinga, Amster-
dam, 1936), White: K at KR6, B at QB2, Kt at KR5, P at KR3;
Black: K at KR1, Kt at QB5. White wins. 1 .... Kt—K6; 2 B—
Q3, Kt—Q4; 3 K—Kt5, Kt—K2; 4 P—R4, Kt—Q4; 5 Kt—Kt3,
Kt—K2; 6 B—B4, K—Kt2; 7 Kt—R5ch, K—R1; 8 Kt—B4, K—
Kt2; 9 P—R5, Resigns, for if 9 .... K—R1; 10 Kt—Kt6ch, Kt×Kt;
11 P×Kt, etc. The ending with two B's+P vs. B is not quite as
easy. Here one must not advance the RP to the seventh rank too
early. No. 277d (Berger), White: K at KB5, B's at QR2, QR3, P at
KR5; Black: K at KR3, B at QB6. White to play wins. 1 B—B1ch!,
K—R2 (1 .... K×P?; 2 B—Kt5!, any; 3 B—B7 mate); 2 P—R6,
B—R4; 3 K—Kt5, B—Q1ch; 4 K—R5, B—B3; 5 B—Kt1ch, K—R1;
6 K—Kt6 (now 6 P—R7?? would only draw, for Black plays his Bishop
back and forth along the long diagonal and refuses to budge his King),
B—B6; 7 B—R3, B—Q5; 8 B—R2, B—B6; 9 B—B8, B—Q5; 10 B—
Kt7ch, B×B; 11 P×B mate.

b) *If Black has one Pawn* the win is achieved by first capturing that
Pawn, when we are back to the
previous case. No. 278 (Alek-
hine-V. Scheltinga, Amster-
dam, 1936) may be taken as a
model. Alekhine won as fol-
lows: *1 .... P—R3; 2 Kt—
K4, Kt—Kt5; 3 B—Kt1, Kt
—Q4; 4 K—B3, Kt—B3; 5
Kt—Q6, Kt—Kt1; 6 Kt—
B5ch, K—Kt3; 7 K—B4, Kt
—B3; 8 Kt—Kt3 dis ch, K
—Kt2; 9 K—B5, K—B2; 10
B—R2ch, K—Kt2; 11 B—
Kt3!* (a tempo move), *Kt—
K1; 12 Kt—R5ch, K—R2;
13 B—B2, Kt—B2; 14 K—*

No. 278

White wins.

B6 dis ch, K—R1; 15 K—Kt6, Kt—Q4; 16 K×P. For the rest of the game see No. 277c.

The most difficult type of position here is that with RP+B of the wrong color with B's of opposite colors. For if Black defends his Pawn White can capture it only at the cost of exchanging a piece, which would leave him with a drawn ending. No. 279 (Kohtz and Kockelkorn) illustrates the problem. White must begin with *1 K— Q3* to prevent K—B4—Kt5, for if now 1 .... K—B4; 2 B—K7ch forces the K back. *1 .... P—R5* is then forced, since the threat was 2 P—R4 and 3 B—Q8. Now if White gets his King to QR3 or QKt4, Black defends his P with his B, so that if White captures with the Kt he can reply B×Kt and draw. Consequently White can only win by driving the Black King away. Thus the solution is: (1 K—Q3, P—R5) *2 K—B2, K—B4; 3 K—Kt2, B—Q2; 4 K— R3, K—Kt3* (not 4 .... K—B5; 5 Kt×P!, B×Kt; 6 K×B and wins because the Black K cannot get back to the R file); *5 K— Kt4, K—R3; 6 P—R3, B—K1; 7 K—B5, K—Kt2* (if 7 .... B— Q2; 8 K—Q6, B—K1; 9 K—B7, K—R2; 10 B—K3ch, K—R3 (10 .... K—R1; 11 Kt—Q5 and captures the Pawn with discovered check); 11 B—B2, B—Kt4; 12 Kt×B!, K×Kt; 13 K—Kt7 and wins —we have transposed into No. 147); *8 B—Q8, B—Q2; 9 K—Q6!, K—B1; 10 B—Kt6!, B—K1; 11 K—K7, B—B3; 12 B—R5, B—Q2; 13 Kt—K4, B—Kt5; 14 Kt—Q6ch, K—Kt1; 15 B—Kt6, B—R6; 16 K— B6, B—Kt5; 17 K—K5, B—Q8; 18 K—Q4, B—B7; 19 K—B5, B— Kt6; 20 K—Kt4, B—Q8; 21 K—Kt5, B—B7; 22 K—B6, B—Q8; 23 B—B2, B—B7; 24 K—Kt6, B—Q8; 25 B—R4, B—Kt6; 26 B—Q8, B—B7; 27 B—B7ch, K—R1; 28 Kt—Kt5, B—Q6; 29 Kt—Q4, B— K5; 30 B—Kt3, B—Q6; 31 Kt—B6, B—K5; 32 Kt—Kt4, B—B6; 33 K—B7, K—R2; 34 B—B2ch, K—R1; 35 Kt—R2, B—K5; 36 Kt— B3, B—B7; 37 Kt—Q5, B—Kt6; 38 Kt—Kt6ch, K—R2; 39 Kt×P dis ch* and the rest is simple. Similar variations offer the solution in the analogous case with two KtP's. E.g., No. 279a (Horwitz, 1885), White: K at Q7, B's at QR5, KB1, P at QKt6; Black: K at QKt1, B at QB4, P at QKt2. White wins. 1 B—R3, B—Kt8; 2 K—Q6, B—R7ch; 3 K—B5, B—Kt8ch; 4 K—Kt5, B—R7; 5 B—Q2, B—Kt6; 6 B—Kt5, B—R7; 7 B—Q8, B—Kt6; 8 K—B5, B—R7; 9 K—Q5, B—Kt6; 10 K—K6, B—B7; 11 K—Q7, B—K6; 12 B—Kt2, B—B7; 13 B—B7ch, K—R1; 14 K—B8, B×P; 15 B—Kt8, any; 16 B×P mate.

c) *If Black has two Pawns,* the winning method is still that of capturing them (unless the White Pawn is passed). This can very often be done by means of mate threats. E.g., No. 279b (Alekhine-V. Scheltinga, Amsterdam, 1936), White: K at KB2, B at QKt3, Kt at KB3, P at KR3; Black: K at KR4, Kt at

QKt5, P's at KKt4, KR2. White wins. 1 Kt—K5!, Kt—R3 (if 1 .... K—R5; 2 K—Kt2, Kt—R3; 3 B—B7! threatening mate and forcing P—Kt5); 2 B—B2!, K—R3 (if 2 .... P—R3; 3 K—Kt3 mates in a few); 3 Kt—B7ch, K—Kt2; 4 Kt×P, etc. (No. 278). It stands to reason, however, that with two Pawns there will be many positions where Black can exchange the last Pawn and draw.

d) *If Black has three Pawns,* he should be able to draw as a rule unless his Pawns are badly blockaded. E.g., No. 279c (Fine Keres, Semmering-Baden, 1937), White: K at KB1, B at KKt3, P's at KB4, KKt2, KR2; Black: K at K3, B at QKt7, Kt at

No. 279   No. 280

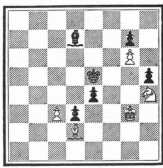

White to play wins.   White wins.

KKt5, P at KB4. Draw. 1 P—R3, Kt—B3; 2 B—B2, Kt—Q4; 3 P—Kt4 and Black cannot win.

e) *If Black has four Pawns or more* he should at least draw. Usually, as in the analogous case with B+P (or Kt+P) vs. 4 P's, he will win.

2. WHITE HAS TWO OR MORE PAWNS

Here we can apply the same rule as in the analogous cases with one piece: three Pawns for the piece draw, anything less loses, anything more wins.

The win with a piece for two Pawns often presents some difficulty. The general idea is that of first blockading the Pawns, and then attacking them. Eventually further material must be lost because the defender simply does not have enough pieces to hold his opponent off. Where no direct attack is successful, zugzwang will often do the trick. No. 280 (Schwan-Fahrni, Barmen, 1905) is a good example.

White can win by *1 K—B2, K—Q4; 2 K—K3, B—B1* (The alternatives are no better: a) 2 .... K—K4; 3 P—B4, B—K3; 4 B—B3ch, K—Q3; 5 K×P, B×P; 6 K—K3, K—K3; 7 B×P, B—Kt4; 8 B—B3, B—B5; 9 P—Kt7, K—B2; 10 Kt—B3, K—Kt1; 11 Kt—K5, B—Kt4; 12 Kt×P, etc., as in No. 276. b) 2 .... B—K1; 3 K—B4, B—Q2; 4 Kt—Kt2, B—K1; 5 K—Kt5, K—K4; 6 Kt—B4, P—R5; 7 K×P, K—B4; 8 K—Kt3, B×P; 9 Kt×B, K×Kt; 10 K—B4 and after capturing both K and QP's the rest is routine.); *3 K—B4, B—Kt5; 4 Kt—Kt2, B—B6* (if 4 .... K—B5; 5 Kt—K3ch, K—Kt6; 6 P—B4 or 6 K×P); *5 Kt—K3ch, K—K3; 6 K—Kt5, K—K2; 7 Kt—B5ch, K—B1; 8 P—B4, B—Kt5; 9 B—Kt4ch, K—Kt1; 10 Kt—K3, B—B6; 11 P—B5, K—B1; 12 P—B6 dis ch, K—K1; 13 B—B3, K—Q1; 14 B×P, P—Q7; 15 B—B6ch, K—K1; 16 P—B7, B—Kt5; 17 Kt×B* and wins.

Summary: If there are less than three Pawns for the piece, the superior side wins. The method consists of capturing as many Pawns as possible, always being careful to retain one's own Pawns. The minimum necessary for a win is shown in No. 276: two pieces plus Pawn vs. one piece.

No. 281

White to play wins.

No. 282

White to play wins; Black to play draws. Win No. 282a with White King at QKt2 and No. 282b with White Rook at QKt8.

Chapter VI

ROOK AND PAWN ENDINGS

I. ROOK VS. PAWNS

The results here are quite different from those for B and Kt endings because the Rook is a sufficient mating force. Consequently if it manages to capture all the Pawns it will win. In general, if the White King is near the Pawns, one and two Pawns lose, three or four draw; if the White King is not near the Pawns, but the Black King is, one Pawn draws, two or more Pawns win.

A. ROOK VS. ONE PAWN

To have any prospects at all Black's King must be near the Pawn and must be able to stay near it. For this reason both King and Pawn must be at least on the fourth rank. What happens if they are only on the third is seen in No. 281. *1 R—R5!, P—R4; 2 K—B7, P—R5; 3 K—Q6, P—R6; 4 R—R3!, P—R7; 5 R—R3.*

But when the Black King and Pawn are both on the fourth rank or beyond, the outcome depends on the position of the White King. Of course, if the White King can manage to occupy some square directly in front of the Pawn it is all over, since he can attack the Pawn with both King and Rook and capture it. Problems arise only when the White King cannot reach the queening file. This gives us our basic *Rule 1: White can win with Rook vs. Pawn if and only if both King and Rook can cover some square which the Pawn must still cross.* It is difficult if not impossible to set up exact subsidiary rules. Those which are given below, however, hold in the great majority of cases.

Rule 2. If the White King is in front of the Pawn, but to one side, the game is won if it is two files from the square of the Pawn (White to play). No. 282 is the general case. Black to play draws by *1 .... P— R4; 2 K—Kt2, P—R5; 3 K—B2* (if 3 R—Kt1ch, K—B6; 4 R—KR1, K—Kt6 does not alter matters), *P—R6; 4 K—Q2, P—R7; 5 K—K2, K—Kt6; 6 R—KR1,* (there is nothing better), *K—Kt7; 7 R×Pch=.* But with White to play, he can impede the advance of the Pawn and gain time to get his King to the KR file. *1 R—Kt1ch, K—B4; 2 R—*

R1, K—Kt3; 3 K—Kt2, P—R4; 4 K—B3, K—Kt4; 5 K—Q2, P— *R5; 6 K—K2, K—Kt5; 7 K—B2, P—R6; 8 R—R1, K—B5; 9 R—* *R4ch, K any; 10 K—Kt3* and the Pawn goes the way of all pawns. The crucial question here is whether the White King can reach K2 before the Pawn gets to the seventh or not. If it is at QKt2, No. 281a, other pieces as in No. 281, it can and the game is won. 1 .... P—R4; 2 R—Kt1ch, K—B6; 3 R—R1, K—Kt5; 4 K—B3, P—R5; 5 K—Q3, P—R6; 6 K—K2, K—Kt6; 7 R—Kt1ch (but not 7 K—B1??, P—R7=), K—R7; 8 R—Kt8, K—R8; 9 K—B2, P—R7; 10 K—Kt3!!, K—Kt8; 11 K—R3 dis ch, K—R8; 12 R—QR8, K—Kt8; 13 R—R1ch, K—B7; 14 K×P.

With the White Rook behind the Pawn, the King can be one square further away because White gains time by attacking the Pawn. Thus *No. 282b, White Rook at Q Kt8, other pieces as in No. 282,* is a win: *1 .... P—R4; 2 R—Kt8ch, K—B6* (or 2 .... K—R6; 3 K—Kt2, P—R5; 4 K—B2, K—R7; 5 K—Q2, P—R6; 6 K—K2, K—R8; 7 K—B3, as in the main variation); *3 R—KR8, K—Kt5; 4 K—Kt2, P—R5; 5 K—B2, P—R6; 6 K—Q2, K—Kt6; 7 K—K2!* (not 7 K—K3, K—Kt7!!; 8 R—Kt8ch, K—B8!!=, or 8 K—K2, P—R7=), *K—Kt7* (if 7 .... P—R7; 8 K—B1! and the King must abandon the Pawn to its fate); *8 R—Kt8ch, K—R8; 9 K—B3!* (not 9 K—B1?, P—R7!=), *P—R7; 10 K—Kt3!!, K—Kt8; 11 K—R3 dis ch, K—R8; 12 R—QR8,* etc.

When the White King is behind the Pawn, various cases must be distinguished.

With a RP or KtP it is better to have the Rook behind the Pawn (on the eighth rank). We then have

Rule 3. If both the White Rook and the White King are behind the Pawn (RP or KtP) White wins if his King is two ranks from the square of the Pawn. To be more precise, one should add the further proviso that the King need not lose a tempo to stay within two ranks of the square. No. 283 (Euwe, 1934) illustrates this rule. There are two ways to win:

A. *1 K—Q6, P—Kt5* (or 1 .... K—K5; 2 R—KKt8, K—B5; 3 K—Q5, etc., as in the main variation); *2 K—Q5, K—B5; 3 K—Q4, K—B6* (if 3 .... P—Kt6; 4 R—B8ch, K—Kt5; 5 K—K3 etc.); *4 K—Q3, P—Kt6* (or 4 .... K—B7; 5 R—B8ch, K—Kt7; 6 K—K2, K—R7; 7 R—KKt8, P—Kt6; 8 K—B3); *5 R—B8ch, K—Kt7; 6 K—K2, K—Kt8* (or 6 .... K—R7; 7 R—KKt8, P—Kt7; 8 K—B2, K—R8; 9 R—R8 mate); *7 K—B3* (or 7 R—KKt8), *P—Kt7; 8 R—KKt8, K—R8; 9 K—B2!* (but not 9 R×P?? stalemate), and White mates in at most three.

B. *1 R—B8ch, K—K5* (or 1 .... K—Kt5; 2 K—B6, K—B5; 3 K—Kt6 dis ch, K—Kt5; 4 R—B5); *2 K—B6, P—Kt5; 3 K—Kt5,*

P—Kt6; 4 K—R4, P—Kt7; 5 R—KKt8, K—B6; 6 K—R3 and wins the P.

In both the above variations it is essential for the White King not to have to lose a tempo on his way back, i.e., to stay near the square without loss of tempo. This is why No. 283a, White Rook at Q6, other pieces as in No. 283, is drawn. On 1 R—B6ch, K—K5; 2 K—K6, P—Kt5; 3 R—Kt6, K—B6!; 4 K—B5, P—Kt6 White has no good tempo move: if 5 K—Kt5, P—Kt7; 6 K—R4, K—B7 and he is one move too late, for if 7 R—B6ch, K—K7; 8 R—KKt6, K—B7! etc. The best try for White is 1 R—Q5ch, K—B5; 2 K—B6, P—Kt5; 3 R—Q4ch, K—B6; 4 K—B5, P—Kt6; 5 R—Q3ch, K—B7; 6 K—B4, P—Kt7; 7 R—Q2ch, K—B8; 8 K—B3, P—Kt8=Kt!!ch; 9 K—K3, Kt—R3!!=(No. 496). With the Rook at QR3, No. 283b, other pieces as in No. 283, the trouble is that one must lose time with the Rook. Thus after 1 K—Q6 (or 1 K—B7, P—Kt5! and White must mark time: 2 K—Kt7, K—B5; 3 K—Kt6, P—Kt6; 4 K—R5, P—Kt7; 5 R—R1, K—Kt6 etc.), P—Kt5; 2 K—Q5, K—B5; 3 R—R8 is the only chance, but then 3 .... P—Kt6; 4 R—B8ch, K—K6; 5 R—KKt8, K—B7; 6 K—K4, P—Kt7 makes the draw clear.

All of these endings are *critical positions*, in the sense that if White is any nearer he wins easily, while if he is not as well placed, the draw is certain. E.g., in No. 283c, White: K at KB7, other pieces as in No. 283a, White wins: 1 R—B6ch, K—K5 (or 1 .... K—Kt5; 2 K—Kt6, K—R5; 3 K—B5); 2 K—Kt6, P—Kt5; 3 K—R5!, P—Kt6; 4 K—R4, P—Kt7; 5 R—KKt6, K—B6; 6 K—R3, K—B7; 7 R×Pch etc. Similarly in No. 283d, White King at KB7, other pieces as in No. 283b, the win is clear after 1 R—R5ch, K—B5; 2 K—Kt6, P—Kt5; 3 K—R5, P—Kt6; 4 K—R4, P—Kt7; 5 R—KKt5, K—B6; 6 K—R3.

A RP forms an exception, as usual. Thus in the case analogous to No. 283a, No. 283e, White: K at KB7, R at K6; Black: K at KKt4, P at KR4, White wins by the checking sequence: 1 R—K5ch, K —Kt5; 2 K—Kt6, P—R5; 3 R—K4ch, K—Kt6; 4 K—Kt5, P—R6; 5 R—K3ch, K—Kt7; 6 K—Kt4, P —R7; 7 R—K2ch, K—Kt8; 8 K—Kt3!!, P—R8=Ktch; 9 K—B3, K— B8; 10 R—KKt2!! and wins the Kt.

With a BP or center P the play is somewhat different. Here we

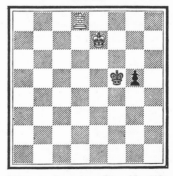

No. 283

White to play wins. Draw No. 283a with White R at Q6; draw No. 283b with White R at QR3.

have *Rule 4. If the Black King is on the same rank as the Pawn, and the White Rook is on the first rank, White to play always wins when the Pawn is on the second, third, or fourth ranks, wins if and only if his King is three ranks behind the Pawn on the fifth rank, two ranks behind the Pawn on the sixth, and on the same rank as the Pawn on the seventh. In addition, if the Kings are on the same side of the Pawn, White must never have to move into a position in which the Black King has the opposition.*

When the Kings are on opposite sides of the Pawn, the win is simpler. The critical position is No. 284 (Euwe, 1934). *1 K—B6,*

No. 284   **No. 285**

White to play wins; Black to play draws.   White to play wins. Black to play draws. Draw No. 285a with White King at QKt7.

P—Q6; 2 K—B5, K—K6; 3 K—B4, P—Q7; 4 K—B3, K—K7; 5 K—B2. Or Black to play, *1 .... P—Q6; 2 K—B6, P—Q7; 3 K—B5, K—K6; 4 K—B4, K—K7; 5 R—R2, K—K8.* Draw. With the Pawn on the second, third or fourth ranks we really have a trivial case, since the White King can be at most three ranks behind. With the Pawn on the sixth rank the White King must be nearer because his rival has gained an extra move. Thus here the critical position is No. 284a, White: K at QKt5, R at QR1; Black: K at K6, P at Q6. White to play wins; Black to play draws. 1 K—B4, P—Q7; 2 K—B3, K—K7; 3 K—B2. Or 1 .... P—Q7; 2 K—B4, K—K7. In addition, when the Pawn is on the sixth White's King must not be more than two files from the square of the Pawn (Rule 2). Thus if the Black King is at KKt6, P at KB6, White Rook at QR1, White King at QKt5 wins, but at QR6 only draws.

Where the Kings are on the same side of the Pawn there is the added difficulty of giving Black the opposition and having to lose a valuable tempo. The critical position is No. 285 (Euwe, 1934). The solution is *1 K—Q6, P—K6* (or 1 .... K—Q5; 2 K—K6, P—K6; 3 K—B5 and we have No. 284); *2 K—K5, P—K7; 3 K—B4, K—Q6; 4 K—B3, K—Q7; 5 K—B2.* Or *1 .... P—K6; 2 K—Q6, P—K7; 3 K—K5, K—Q6; 4 K—B4, K—Q7; 5 R—R2ch, K—Q6!* or even 5 .... K—Q8. But No. 285a, White King at QKt7, other pieces as in No. 285, is drawn because after 1 K—B6, P—K6 Black has the opposition and White must waste a move. Similarly, with the Pawn on the fourth rank, No. 285b, White: K at QR8, R at QR1; Black: K at K4, P at KB4, White to play can only draw because after 1 K—Kt7, P—B5; 2 K—B6, P—B6; 3 K—B5, K—K5; 4 K—B4, P—B7 Black has the opposition. The stratagem of gaining the opposition is of the utmost importance in such endings. E.g., No. 285c, White: K at QKt5, R at QR1; Black: K at K4, P at KB5. Black to play. According to the rule White wins unless his opponent holds him off with the opposition. This is in fact what happens. 1 .... K—Q5!; 2 R—Q1ch (2 K—Kt4, P—B6), K—K6; 3 R—K1ch, K—Q7!, or 3 K—B4, P—B6; 4 K—B3, P—B7 and again the King cannot approach.

With the Pawn on any one of the four central files, to have the White Rook on the eighth is equivalent to the loss of a move. E.g., if we place the R at QR8 in No. 285, the game is a draw. For 1 R—K8, K—Q5; 2 K—Q6, P—K6; 3 K—K6, P—K7 (or even 3 .... K—K5!); 4 K—B5, K—Q6; 5 K—B4, K—Q7 gets there one move too late.

Where the Kings are on the same file the win is achieved by going to the opposite side. This of course requires gaining the opposition as a preliminary step. Thus in No. 286 (Reti, 1928) White has the opposition and must hold it while his Rook is on the first rank. So the solution is *1 R—Q2!, P—Q5; 2 R—Q1!!!*. Now Black will have to lose according to Rule 4 because White has the opposition. All that is necessary is to go to the opposite side of the Pawn. *2 .... K—Q4; 3 K—Q7!!!* (but not 3 K—B6?, K —K5; 4 K—K6, P—Q6 and Black has the opposition!), *K—B5* (or 3 .... K—K5; 4 K—B6); *4 K—K6* and we have No. 284.

Finally we must note that in certain rare cases the Rook cannot stop the Pawn on the seventh. A classic problem with this idea is

No. 286

White to play and win.

No. 286a (from a game Potter-Fenton, 1895. Solution by Lasker),
White: K at QKt6, P at QB6; Black: K at QR8, R at Q4. White to
play wins by 1 P—B7, R—Q3ch; 2 K—Kt5 (not 2 K—Kt7, R—Q2, or
2 K—B5, R—Q8), R—Q4ch; 3 K—Kt4, R—Q5ch; 4 K—Kt3, R—
Q6ch; 5 K—B2, R—Q5!!; 6 P—B8=R!!! (if 6 P—R8=Q, R—B4ch;
7 Q×R stalemate), R—QR5 (necessary to stop mate); 7 K—Kt3!
and either mates or captures the Rook.

B. ROOK VS. TWO PAWNS

As usual, three different types must be distinguished.

1. *Two connected passed Pawns, in the absence of the Kings, win if*

No. 287

White wins.

No. 288

White wins.

they are both on the sixth, but otherwise lose. This is shown in No. 287.
With White to play *1P—Kt7, R—Kt5; 2 P—R7* forces a Queen, (For
the ending Q vs. R see No. 597). Or Black to play, *1 .... R—Kt1;
2 P—Kt7, R—Kt1; 3 P—R7* etc.

*If the enemy King can reach any square in front of the Pawns the
game is a win.* This is to be expected, since the Rook can then capture
the two Pawns. No. 288 illustrates the point. The method is to
blockade the Pawns and then capture them: *1 R—R4, K—Kt4; 2 K—
B2, K—R4; 3 K—K3, P—R6* (if 3 .... K—Kt4; 4 R—R5ch, K—Kt3;
5 K—B4, P—Kt6; 6 K—Kt4, P—Kt7; 7 R—Kt5ch, K—R3; 8 K×P);
4 K—B2!, K—R5; 5 R—Kt4, K—Kt4 (5 .... P—R7; 6 K—Kt2);
6 K—Kt3, K—R4; 7 R×P, P—R7; 8 R—R4ch.

Normally such endings arise as a result of a sacrifice which draws
the enemy King away from the Pawns and allows one's own King to
approach them. The crucial question then is how near the King must

be to the Pawns to be able to stop them. The critical position is No. 289. White to play queens the KP, captures the Rook and then queens his BP. *1 P—K8 = Q, R × Q; 2 K × R, K—K3; 3 P—B7, etc.* Black to play blockades the Pawns and then captures them. *1 .... K—Q2; 2 K—Kt6, K—K3!; 3 K—Kt7, R—QKt1; 4 K—Kt6* (if 4P—K8=Q, R×Q; 5 P—B7, R—K2); *R—Kt1ch; 5 K—R7, K—B2; 6 K—R6, K×P.* The win for Black, however, does not hold when White has BP+KtP because of a stalemate possibility. No. 289a, White: K at KKt7, P's at KKt6, KB7; Black: K at K3, R at QR1. Black to play can only draw. 1 .... K—K2; 2 K—R6, K—B3; 3 K—R7, R—QKt1; 4 P—B8 = Qch!!!, R × Q; 5 P—Kt7, R—B2; 6 K—R8!!, R×P stalemate. The same holds true for BP+RP. No. 289b,

No. 289

Whoever moves wins. Black King at K4, KB4 or KKt4 draws.

No. 290

White to play wins.

White: K at KR7, P's at KKt7, KR6; Black: K at KB3, R at QR1. Black to play. Draw. 1 .... K—B2; 2 P—Kt8=Qch; 3 R×Q stalemate. Note that if Black has his Rook behind the Pawn in No. 289, i.e., on the K-file, he can only draw at best. No. 289c, Black Rook at K8, other pieces as in No. 289. White to play wins as before. Black to play can only draw by 1 .... K—Q2; 2 K—B8!, R—K3; 3 K—B7, or even 3 P—B7!, R×P; 4 K—Kt8. 2 K—Kt7, in the hope of provoking 2 .... K—K1??; 3 P—B7ch is met instead by 2 .... R—KB8; 3 K—B7, R—K8, or 3 .... R×Pch; 4 K×R, K—K1.

To decide the outcome of any ordinary ending with K+2P vs. K+R we must compare it with Nos. 287, 288 and 289. Thus in No. 290 (Tarrasch-Janowski, Ostend, 1907) White wins because he forces both Pawns to the sixth. *1 K—Q4, K—Kt6* (if 1 .... R—B4; 2 K—K4!! R×KtP; 3 P—B7 and queens after 3 .... R—Kt5ch; 4 K—K3, R—Kt6ch; 5 K—B2); *2 K—K5, K—B5; 3 P—Kt6, R—K8ch; 4 K—*

Q6, R—KKt8 (the game continuation was 4 .... R—Q8ch; 5 K—K7, R—K8ch; 6 K—B7 Resigns—we have No. 289 after 6 .... R—KKt8; 7 P—Kt7, K—Q4; 8 P—Kt8=Q); *5 P—Kt7!!* (but not 5 P—B7?, R×Pch; 6 K—K5, R—Kt4ch=, for if 7 K—K4, R—Kt8!; 8 P—B8= Q??, R—K8ch; 9 K—B5, R—B8ch), *K—Q5!; 6 K—B6!!* (6 K—K6, K—K5; 7 K—B7, K—B4 gives No. 289, while 6 P—B7 is refuted by **6 ....** R—Kt3ch!; 7 K—K7, R×P and the BP is pinned), *K—B5!* (the only move: if 6 .... K—K4; 7 P—B7, R—Kt3ch; 8 K—Kt5, while if 6 .... R—Kt3; 7 K—Kt5 is again the answer); *7 K—Q7!!!* (the point: White will reach K8), *K—Q4; 8 K—K8, K—K3; 9 P— B7, R—QR8; 10 P—B8=Ktch!!, K any; 11 P—Kt8= Q.*

Two Pawns on the fifth cannot win if the enemy King is right near. No. 290a (Kling and Horwitz, 1851), White: K at Q5, R at KR5; Black: K at QB6, P's at QR5, QKt5. Draw. 1 R—R3ch, K—Kt7; 2 K—B4, P—Kt6; 3 R—R2ch (or 3 K—Kt4, K—R7; 4 K×P, P— Kt7; 5 R—R3ch, K—Kt8; 6 R—Kt3, K—R8=), K—R6! (but not 3 .... K—B8?; 4 K—B3!, K—Kt8; 5 R—K2, K—R8; 6 R—K4!, P—Kt7; 7 R×Pch, K—Kt8; 8 R—QKt4, K—R8; 9 K—B2! and wins); 4 K—B3, P—Kt7!; 5 K—B2, K—R7; 6 R—R1, P—R6 and we have No. 289b. Or No. 290b (Keidanski, 1914), White: K at QKt5, R at QB2; Black: K at Q4, P's at K6, KB5. White to play draws. 1 R—B8!!, P—K7; 2 R—Q8ch, K—K5; 3 K—B4, K—K6 (or 3 .... K—B6; 4 R—K8, K—B7; 5 K—Q3, No. 289); 4 R—K8ch, K—Q7 (or 4 .... K—B7; 5 K—Q3, P—B6; 6 K—Q2=); 5 R— Q8ch, K—B7; 6 R—K8, P—B6; 7 R—K3!! and Black cannot do better than wear White out by allowing perpetual check.

When the King of the Pawns is on or near the edge of the board, the threat of checkmate may often be an adequate defense against two Pawns on the sixth and seventh, while if both Pawns are on the sixth, or one is on the seventh and the other on the fifth, the Rook may even win.

No. 291 (Keres-Eliskases, Noordwijk, 1938) is the typical drawing case. The continuation was *1 .... K—B6!; 2 K—Kt1, R—R3!; 3 P—Kt7, R—Kt3ch; 4 K—B1* (the only way to escape the checks: if 4 K—R1, R—R3ch), *R—KR3!!* and here a draw was agreed to. If *5 K—Q1, K—Q6; 6 K—K1, K—K6; 7 K—B1, K—B6; 8 K—Kt1, R—Kt3ch* and the best White can do is try again on the other side, since *9 K—B1, R—KR3!; 10 K—K1, K—K6!* etc., is the only way to avoid perpetual check. There are innumerable variations on this theme. One where the threat is used to allow the King to approach the Pawns is No. 291a (Kling and Horwitz, 1851), White: K at KB6, R at QKt1; Black: K at KR4, P's at QR6, QKt7. White to play draws. 1 K—B5, K—R5 (the only chance: if 1 .... K—R3; 2 K— B6); 2 K—B4, K—R6; 3 K—B3, K—R7; 4 K—K3!!, K—Kt7 (the win is a mirage. On 4 .... K—Kt6; 5 R—Kt1ch!, K—R6; 6 K—B3, K—R7?; 7 R—Kt1 wins for White, while 4 .... P—R7?? is likewise answered by 5 R×Pch, destroying Black's hopes); 5 K—Q3!!! (the point), K—B6; 6 K—B2, P—R7; 7 K×P (or 7 R—B1ch, K—Kt7)=. In No. 291b (Freeborough, 1898) the threat almost wins but Black just manages to escape by underpromoting. White: K at QB3, R at KB1; Black: K at QR6, P's at QR7, QKt6. Draw. 1 .... P—Kt7; 2 R—B8!, P—Kt8=Ktch!; 3 K—B2, P—R8=Q; 4 R—R8ch, K—Kt5; 5 R×Q, Kt—R6ch; 6 K—Q3, Kt—Kt4= (See No. 496).

Where the Pawns are still on the sixth or disunited (one on fifth, other on seventh) the Rook usually wins. In No. 292 (Shapiro,

No. 291

Black to play draws.

No. 292

White to play wins.

1914) the solution is *1 R—Q2ch, K—Kt8* (if 1 .... K—R8; 2 K—Kt3 and mate next move); *2 K—B3!, K—B8* (or 2 .... P—Kt7; 3 R—Q1ch, K—R7; 4 R—KKt1!! and wins, as in No. 291a); *3 R—QR2, K—Q8* (3 .... K—Kt8; 4 R—K2, P—Kt7; 5 R—K1ch, K—R7; 6 R—KKt1); *4 K—Q3, K—B8; 5 K—K3!, P—R7* (if 5 .... P—Kt7; 6 K—B2); *6 R—R1ch, K—Kt2; 7 R—R1!, K—B6; 8 K—B3* and wins. A more complicated instance is seen in No. 292a (Sackmann, 1920), White: K at Q6, R at KB1; Black: K at KKt3, P's at KKt2, KR5. White wins. The main variation is 1 .... K—R4; 2 K—K5, K—Kt5!; 3 K—K4!, K—Kt6; 4 K—K3, K—Kt7; 5 K—K2, P—R6; 6 R—B2ch, K—Kt6; 7 R—B7!, P—Kt4; 8 K—B1, K—R7; 9 K—B2, P—Kt5; 10 R—KKt7, K—R8; 11 K—Kt3, K—Kt8; 12 R×P, P—R7; 13 K—R3 dis ch, K—R8; 14 R—Q4 and the last Pawn will go.

2. Two disconnected passed Pawns, in the absence of the Kings, have a chance against a Rook only if both are at least on the sixth. In that case they hold the Rook if it is on the eighth rank, but win against the Rook if one is on the seventh and the Rook is stopping it on the file.

The critical position in the general case is shown in No. 293 (Rabinovitch). Black to play moves *1 .... R—KB2* and captures both Pawns. White to play gets his King nearer and succeeds in supporting the BP after the RP is gone: *1 K—B4, R—KB2* (1 .... K—B7; 2 K—Q5, K—Q6?; 3 K—K6, K—K5; 4 P—B7 wins); *2 P—R7!!, R×RP; 3 K—Q5, K—B7; 4 K—K6, K—Q6; 5 P—B7=*.

If the King of the Pawns is near enough, and the enemy King is not, two Pawns on the sixth, or on the fifth and sixth may win against a Rook. This is illustrated in No. 294 (Berger). The solution is *1 P—*

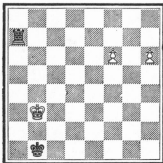

No. 293

White to play draws. Black to play wins.

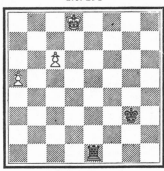

No. 294

White to play wins.

R6!, R—Q8ch (if 1 .... R—QR8; 2 P—B7, R—Q8ch; 3 K—K7, R—QB8; 4 K—Q7!, R—Q8ch; 5 K—K6, R—K8ch; 6 K—B6, R—B8ch; 7 K—Kt6, R—B8; 8 P—R7 and wins); *2 K—B8, R—QR8; 3 K—Kt7!* (for 3 P—B7 see A.), *R—Kt8ch; 4 K—R8!!!, R—QB8; 5 P—R7!, K—B5* (or 5 .... R×P; 6 K—Kt7); *6 K—Kt7, R—Kt8ch; 7 K—R6, R—R8ch; 8 K—Kt6, R—Kt8ch; 9 K—B5, R—QR8; 10 P—B7, K—K4; 11 K—B4, K—K5; 12 K—B3, K—K6; 13 K—Kt2* and wins. Variation A. 3 P—B7, K—B5!; 4 K—Q7 (if 4 K—Kt7, R—Kt8ch; 5 K—B6, R—B8ch; 6 K—Kt6, K—K4!; 7 P—R7, K—Q3!!; 8 K—Kt5, R—Kt8ch!; 9 K—B4, R—QR8!!!=, for if 10 P—B8=Q, R—B8ch), R—Q8ch; 5 K—K7, R—K8ch; 6 K—B8 (not 6 K—B7?, R—QB8!, or 6 K—B6, R—QB8; 7 P—R7, R—B3ch! and Black wins in both cases), R—KR8!!!; 7 P—R7 (not 7 K—Kt7, R—QB8. If 7 K—Kt8, R—Kt8ch), R—R1ch; 8 K—K7 (or 8 K—Kt7, R—R1!; 9 K—B6, K—Kt5; 10 K—K6, K—Kt4; 11 K—Q6, K—B3; 12 K—

B6, K—K2; 13 K—Kt7, K—Q2!; 14 K×R, K×P=), R—R1!; 9 K—
Q6, K—B4!; 10 K—B6, K—K3; 11 K—Kt7, K—Q2!!! (the point to
Black's defense); 12 K×R, K×P and both monarchs sleep peace-
fully ever after.

However, where the Pawns are far apart, if the Rook reaches the
first rank they cannot win. Thus No. 294a, White: K at K5, P's at
QKt7, KKt7; Black: K at QR8, R at Q1. Draw. For if 1 K—B6,
R—QKt1!; 2 K—Kt6, K—Kt7 and the White King cannot approach
without allowing the capture of one Pawn either with check or with
a pin on the other Pawn.

Where the Pawns are not yet on the sixth it is always better to
attack the Pawn which is further advanced. For in R vs. P the nearer
the P is to the eighth rank the better the drawing chances. E.g., No.
294b (Mandelbaum, 1881), White: K at QKt6, R at KR8; Black: K
at Q3, P's at KB5, KR2. White to play and win. 1 R—KB8!!! (not
1 R×P?, K—Q4!; 2 R—KB7, K—K5=—No. 283b), K—K4; 2 K—
B5, K—K5! (2 .... P—R4; 3 R—K8ch, K—B4; 4 K—Q4 is worse);
3 K—B4, K—K6; 4 K—B3, P—B6 (He has little choice. On 4 ....
P—R4; 5 R—K8ch, K—B7; 6 K—Q2, P—R5; 7 K—KR8, K—Kt6;
8 K—K1!, P—R6; 9 K—B1, P—B6; 10 R—Kt8ch, K—R7; 11 K—
B2, K—R8; 12 K×P, P—R7; 13 R—QR8 decides); 5 R—K8ch, K—
B7; 6 K—Q2, P—R4; 7 K—KR8, K—Kt7; 8 R×P, P—B7; 9 R—
Kt5ch, K—B6; 10 R—B5ch and wins.

3. *Doubled Pawns* cannot defend themselves in the absence of the
Kings. With their King nearby and the enemy King not directly in
front of them they normally draw. But even if the enemy King is far
away they can rarely win. The general case is seen in No. 295. White
draws by *1 R—B7ch, K—Kt7; 2*
R—Kt7ch, K—R7 (not 2 ....
K—R6?; 3 K—Kt1!); *3 R—R7ch,*
K—Kt6; 4 R—Kt7ch, K—B5;
5 R—B7ch (not 5 R—Kt1, K—
B6), *K—Q5; 6 R—Q7ch, K—*
K6; 7 R—K7ch, K—B6; 8 R—
B7ch etc. Neither side can do
better than perpetual check. But
if the White King is at KR3 (or
any square on the fourth-seventh
ranks except KB4, K4) his Black
rival can escape to KR8 and
when White has no more checks
he must resign. Thus in No.
295a, White King at KR3, other
pieces as in No. 295, Black wins.

No. 295

White to play draws. White King at
KR3 loses No. 295a. White Rook at
KB6 loses No. 295b.

1 R—B7ch, K—Q5; 2 R—Q7ch, K—K6; 3 R—K7ch, K—B7; 4 R—B7ch, K—Kt8; 5 R—Kt7ch, K—R8 and the Pawn queens. Similarly if the Rook is on the sixth (or fifth or nearer) rank the checks are soon exhausted. No. 295b, White Rook at KB6, other pieces as in No. 295. Black wins. 1 R—B6ch, K—Q5; 2 R—Q6ch, K—K5; 3 R—K6ch, K—Q4 and White has no checks.

Summary: In the absence of the Kings, two connected passed Pawns on the sixth or beyond win against the Rook, two disconnected passed Pawns on the sixth or beyond hold the Rook, but neither side can make any progress, while two doubled Pawns lose. Pawns that are not yet on the sixth always lose. If the King of the Pawns is supporting them,

No. 296

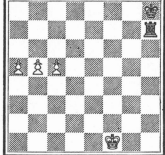

Black to play; White wins.

No. 297

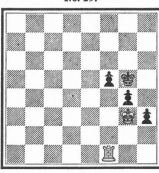

Draw. Pawns on 6th, 5th, 4th lose. Pawns on 4th, 3rd, 2nd win.

but the other King is far away, two connected Pawns win, disconnected and doubled Pawns only draw. If the enemy King is directly in front of the Pawns, connected and doubled Pawns lose, but disconnected may draw. Finally, if both Kings are near the Pawns, but the enemy King is not directly in front of them, the result is normally a draw. It is always best to have the Rook on the first rank.

C. ROOK VS. THREE PAWNS

1. ALL CONNECTED

Three Pawns on the fifth or beyond win against the Rook in the absence of the Kings. In No. 296 after *1 .... R—R4* (on 1 .... R—QKt2; 2 P—Kt6 is murderous: 2 .... K—Kt2; 3 P—B6, R—Kt1; 4 P—B7 and White should not be satisfied with anything less than two Queens); *2 P—Kt6, R×P; 3 P—R6* we have No. 287. If the King of the Pawns is supporting them, while the other King is away on vacation, three Pawns on the fourth may also win. But without the aid of the King three Pawns which are not all on the fifth lose.

With the enemy King directly in front of the Pawns, the critical position is No. 297 (Handbuch)—if we move all the pieces back one rank, the Rook wins, if we move them up one rank the Pawns conquer. In No. 297 best play for both sides is *1 R—B2, K—Kt3; 2 K—B4, K— B3* (but not 2 .... K—R4; 3 R—Q2, K—R5??; 4 R—Q6, K—R4; 5 R—K6, P—R7; 6 R—K8 and wins); *3 R—K2, K—B2; 4 R—K5* (4 K×P?, P—Kt6! and Black wins), *K—Kt3*. Black need only keep away from KR4 and KR2, and prevent the capture of the BP with check. *5 R—K6ch* (if 5 R×P?, P—R7!; 6 R—Kt5ch, K—R3 and the RP promotes), *K—Kt2* (not 5 .... K—R4; 6 R—Q6! as in the note to Black's second move, or 5 .... K—R2; 6 K—Kt5!, K—Kt2; 7 R—Kt6ch, K—R2; 8 R—R6ch, K—Kt2; 9 R—R5 followed by K× P. If 9 .... P—Kt6; 10 R×P, P—Kt7; 11 R—KKt3); *6 R—Q6* (6 K—Kt5?, P—R7; 7 R—K7ch, K—B1 just draws: 8 R—KR7, P— Kt6; 9 R—B6, K—Kt1; 10 R—R3, P—B5; 11 R—R5, P—B6; 12 R— Kt5ch, K—B1; 13 R—KR5, K—K1; 14 K—K6 etc.—the mate threat saves White), *K—B2; 7 R—KR6, K—Kt2; 8 R—R5* (if 8 K—Kt5, P—B5!; 9 K×KtP, K×R; 10 K×RP then leads to an elementary draw), *K—Kt3; 9 R—Kt5ch, K—R3!; 10 R—Kt8* (on either K or R×BP, P—R7 wins for Black), *K—R2; 11 R—Q8, K—Kt3; 12 R— Q6ch, K—B2* and White is beginning to move around in circles.

If the Pawns are not yet advanced to the position in No. 297, e.g., No. 297a, White: K at KKt4, R at KB1; Black: K at KKt3, P's at KB3, KKt4, KR5 White wins because he can afford to capture the BP. 1 R—B2, K—Kt2; 2 K—B5, K—B2; 3 R—K2, K—Kt2; 4 R—K6, K—R2; 5 R×P, P—R6; 6 K×P, P—R7; 7 R—B1. In intermediate positions the following trap must be noted. No. 297b (Berger), White: K at KB2, R at KKt8; Black: K at KR3, P's at KB4, KKt5, KR5. White wins. The solution is 1 K—K2!!, P—R6; 2 K—K3, K—R4 (2 .... P—R7; 3 R—R8ch, or 2 .... K—R2; 3 R—Kt5); 3 K—B4, K—R3; 4 K×P and wins. If Black replies 1 .... P—Kt6 (instead of 1 .... P—R6); 2 K—B3, K—R4; 3 K—B4 decides.

With the Pawns further up, No. 297c, White: K at KKt2, R at KB1; Black: K at KKt5, P's at KB5, KKt6, KR7, Black wins with or without the move. 1 .... P—B6ch; 2 R×P, P—R8=Qch; 3 K× Q, K×R. Or 1 R—QR1, P—B6ch; 2 K—R1, K—R6. However, if the White Rook were at QR4 here, the game would be drawn: the Rook holds the BP and if the Black King gets too close checks him away. Another exception to the rule that when the Pawns are on the 7th, 6th and 5th they win is No. 297d, White: K at QB3, R at KR1; Black: K at QR6, P's at QB5, QKt6, QR7. Draw. 1 .... P—Kt7;

2 R—R8!!, P—Kt8=Ktch; 3 K×P, Kt—B6!; 4 R—R8ch, Kt—R5; 5 K—Kt5!, P—R8=Q; 6 R×Ktch, K—Kt7; 7 R×Q.

In the absence of the King of the Pawns, when the other King is blocking them the Rook of course wins: it can capture at least one Pawn to begin with. An exception to this is the case when two Pawns are on the seventh. Thus No. 298 (Rinck, 1914) is drawn because the Black Rook cannot get to the first rank quickly enough. The solution is *1 P—K6, R—QB6* (Black must get to the first rank. If 1 .... R—K6; 2 P—K7, K—B2; 3 K—Kt5, K×P? is impossible because of 4 P—Kt8=Q, while 3 .... R—K3; 4 K—B5 likewise is useless, since 4 .... R×BP? is refuted by 5 P—K8=Qch, K×Q; 6 P—Kt8=Qch);

No. 298

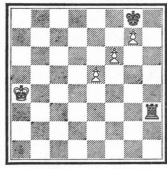

White to play draws.

No. 299

White to play draws. Pawns on 5th, 4th, 3rd win.

2 K—Kt5, R—B1; 3 K—Kt6! (not 3 P—K7?, R—K1; 4 K—B6, K—B2; 5 K—Q7, R—QR1! and wins), *K—R2* (threatening 4 .... R—K1); *4 K—Kt7, R—K1; 5 P—Kt8=Qch!!* (but not 5 P—K7?, K—Kt1; 6 K—B7, K—B2, or 5 P—B7, R—K2ch; 6 K—B6, K×P and Black wins in both cases), *R×Q* (or 5 .... K×Q; 6 P—B7ch); *6 P—B7, R—B1; 7 K—B6!, K—Kt2; 8 P—K7, K×P=*.

Where the enemy King is to one side of the Pawns, the critical position is No. 299 (Meyer, 1890). After *1 K—K5, R—Q1; 2 P—Q5, R—K1ch* nothing can be done: *3 K—B6, K—B6; 4 P—Q6, K×P; 5 P—Q7, R—B1ch!; 6 K—K7, R—QR1; 7 P—K4, K—K6; 8 P—K5, K—Q5; 9 K—Q6* (9 P—K6, K—K4 is No. 289), *R—R3ch; 10 K—B7* (10 K—K7, R—R1), *R—R2ch; 11 K—B8, K×P; 12 P—Q8=Q, R—R1ch.* On the other hand, in No. 299a, White: K at K5, P's at Q5, K4, KB3; Black: K at KKt4, R at Q2, White to play wins. For after 1 K—K6, R—Q1; 2 P—Q6, K—B5; 3 K—Q5, K×P; 4 P—K5 the two Pawns decide.

2. ONLY TWO PAWNS ARE CONNECTED

Here it is practically impossible to set up any explicit rules or even critical positions. With the King far away, the Rook normally cannot hope to stop the Pawns, while with the King nearby the Pawns draw only if the King can succeed in bringing about one of the earlier positions with R vs. 2 P's. An interesting example of the strategy involved is No. 300 (Reti, 1929). The only correct solution is *1 R—KKt8!, P—Kt6!* (1 .... P—B6; 2 R×P, P—Kt5; 3 R—KB4 offers no hope at all); *2 R—Kt4, P—Kt5; 3 R×BP, P—Kt6; 4 R—B1!, P—KKt7; 5 R—KKt1, P—Kt7; 6 K—Kt7, K—Q5; 7 K—B6, K—K6; 8 R—Kt1!, K—Q6; 9 R—Kt1!* and both sides must keep on repeating moves.

3. ISOLATED PAWNS

The results are the same as usual: the P's must be far advanced. If the King of the Pawns is nearby, but the other is not, the Pawns win; if the other King is nearby, the Rook wins. In all cases it is essential to have the R on the first line. Two examples will illustrate the strategy involved in winning with the Rook. No. 300a (N. N.-Tartakover, Paris, 1933), White: K at QR4, P's at QB7, KB4, KR4; Black: K at KB2, R at KKt5. Black to play wins. 1 .... R—Kt1!; 2 K—Kt5, K—K2; 3 K—B6, R—KR1!; 4 P—B5 (4 K—Q5, K—Q2), R—KB1!; 5 P—R5, R—KR1; 6 P—B6ch, K—K3!!; 7 P—B7, K—K2!; 8 P—R6, R—QB1; 9 P—R7, R—KB1; 10 K—Kt7, K—Q2; 11 K—Kt6, R—QB1; 12 K—B5, K×P; 13 K—Q5, K—Q2 and wins. No. 300b (Reti 1928) White: K at KKt1, R at QB1; Black: K at KB4, P's at QB7, K7, KKt7. White to play wins. The main variation is 1 K—B2!, K—K5; 2 K×KP (White has the opposition), K—Q5; 3 R—KKt1, K—K5; 4 R—K1!!, K—Q5 (4 .... K—B5; 5 K—B2 or 4 .... K—K4; 5 K—K3!!); 5 K—Q2 and wins.

Summary: Three connected passed Pawns, in the absence of the King, win against the Rook if they are on the fifth rank or beyond. When the enemy King is in front of them they draw if they are on the fourth, fifth, and sixth rank, respectively, win on the fifth, sixth, and seventh, lose on the third, fourth and fifth. Where only two Pawns are connected the result depends entirely on the relative positions of the

No. 300

White to play draws.

Kings and Pawns. Where all the Pawns are isolated Rook on the first rank and King stopping the Pawns will generally win.

D. ROOK VS. FOUR OR MORE PAWNS

As is to be expected, four Pawns will normally win against the Rook. However, when they are not far advanced, the Rook will be able to stem the tide. No. 301 (Euwe-Capablanca, Carlsbad, 1929) is a case in point. After *1 .... R—R3ch; 2 K—B5, K—Q5; 3 P—K5, K—Q4; 4 P—Kt3* (4 P—Kt4, R—R1; 5 P—R4, R—B1ch; 6 K—Kt5, R—Kt1ch does not win either), *R—R1; 5 K—B6, R—R3ch; 6 K—B5, R—R1* a draw was agreed to. A possible alternative continuation, given by Tartakover, is *7 P—R4* (7 P—Kt4, R—B1ch; 8 K—Kt5,

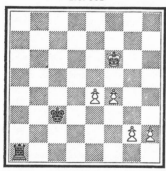

No. 301

Drawn.

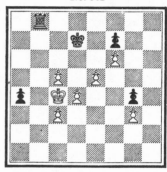

No. 302

Black wins.

R—Kt1ch; 9 K—R4??, K—K5; 10 K—Kt3, R—QR1! and Black will win), *R—KKt1; 8 K—B6,* (8 P—Kt4, R—B1ch and draw by perpetual check), *R×P; 9 P—K6* (9 P—R5? R—KR6; 10 K—Kt5, K—K3; is worse), *R—Kt5; 10 P—B5, R×P; 11 P—K7, R—K5; 12 K—B7, K—Q3!; 13 P—B6* (P—K8=Q, R×Q; 14 K×R, K—K5), *K—Q2=* (No. 298).

More than four Pawns should win without any trouble.

E. ROOK AND PAWNS VS. PAWNS

There is no real equivalent here of the Rook to so and so many Pawns because if the Rook supports the passed Pawn it can force a Queen. An illustration is No. 302 (Marco-Maroczy, Vienna, 1903). The White Pawns look strong, but there is no stopping the Black QRP. The game continued *1 P—Q5, P—R6; 2 P—B6ch, K—B2; 3 K—B5, P—R7; 4 P—Q6ch, K—B1; 5 P—K6, P—R8= Q; 6* Resigns. Without a passed Pawn the Rook is much less effective, and the Pawns, just as in the cases A to D, can often draw or win. An example of an interesting draw with Rook plus Pawn vs. three Pawns is No. 302a (Neumann-Steinitz, Baden-Baden, 1870), White: K at QB4, P's at QB6, QB7, KKt5; Black: K at KB6, R at K1, P at KKt3. Neumann played 1 K—Q5 (if 1 K—Kt5, K—K5; 2 K—Kt6?, K—Q4; 3 K—Kt7, K—Q3; 4 P—B8=Q, R×Q; 5 K×R, K×P and wins the K and P ending), when 1 .... R—QR1; 2 K—K5, K—K6; 3 K—B6, R—QB1; 4 K×P, K—B5; 5 K—B6, R×P; 6 P—Kt6, R×Pch; 7 K—B7₂ K—B4; 8 P—Kt7 gives a clear draw.

II. ROOK AND PAWN VS. ROOK

General rule: *If the Black King can reach the queening square, the game is drawn; if not the game is lost.* While this holds in most cases, it must be looked upon as a convenient rule of thumb and not adhered to too rigidly. In particular, the RP forms an exception to the second part.

Since it is difficult to grasp the essence of this ending without knowing a number of examples, and since the ending is so basic in all R and P play, we shall give a fairly exhaustive analysis. To begin with, we shall give the ideal drawing position, according to our general rule.

A. THE BLACK KING IS ON THE QUEENING SQUARE

If the Pawn is not far advanced, the King cannot be driven away. This has been known since the time of Philidor. No. 303 is the standard position. Black keeps his R on the third rank until the P reaches the sixth, and then goes to the eighth. When the square K6 is no longer available for the White King he will not be able to occupy Q6 or KB6 and will be unable to drive the Black King out. The moves might be *1 P—K5, R—QR3; 2 P—K6, R—R8* (2 .... R—Kt3?? would be a bad blunder—3 K—B6, K—Q1; 4 R—R8ch, K—B2; 5 K—B7 wins); *3 K—B6, R—B8ch; 4 K—K5, R—K8ch; 5 K—Q6, R—Q8ch, etc.*

There are three traps that the defender must avoid—immobilizing his Rook, unnecessarily allowing his King to be driven away from the queening square, and going to the wrong square with his King when

No. 303

Draw.

he must leave. *These are the only three cases in which one can lose with the King on the queening square.*

1. IMMOBILIZING THE ROOK

The idea of the defense in No. 303 was not to allow the White King to reach the sixth rank unmolested. This can only be prevented by keeping the R mobile, here, playing it to the eighth rank. What happens if it is kept on the first rank is shown in No. 304. Black to play can only mark time, since he must keep his R on the first rank to prevent mate. White then wins as follows: *1 .... R—B1* (or 1 .... K—Kt1; 2 R—Kt2ch, K—B1; 3 P—K7ch, K—K1; 4 R—

No. 304   No. 305

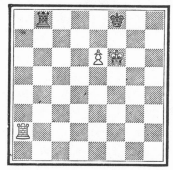   

White wins. Win in analogous posi-   Black to play loses. Draw with Black
tions with QP and BP, but draw with   Rook anywhere else along the eighth
KtP and RP.   rank except K8.

Kt8ch, K—Q2; 5 R×R); *2 R—KR2, K—Kt1; 3 R—Kt2ch, K—R1* (or 3 .... K—B1; 4 P—K7ch, etc.); *4 K—B7, R—B2ch; 5 P—K7* and the R must be sacrificed for the P. *With the BP* we do not have this mating threat at a distance because there is not enough elbow room, but there is an alternative which is good enough. No. 304a, White: K at KKt6, R at QR2, P at KB6; Black: K at KKt1, R at QKt1. White wins. 1 .... R—QB1 (again he can only twiddle his thumbs); 2 R—R7, R—Kt1; 3 R—Kt7ch, K—B1 (or 3 .... K—R1; 4 R—R7ch, K—Kt1; 5 P—B7ch, K—B1; 6 R—R8ch); 4 R—KR7, K—Kt1; 5 P—B7ch, K—B1; 6 R—R8ch, K—K2; 7 R×R. *With a KtP or RP* there is no effective mating threat possible, so that the game is a draw even when the Black R is on the first rank. E.g., No. 304b, White: K at KR6, R at QR2, P at KKt6; Black: K at KKt1, R at QKt1. Draw. For if 1 R—R7, R—QB1; 2 R—Kt7ch, K—R1; 3 R—R7ch, K—Kt1 the advance 4 P—Kt7?? would be a boomerang because of the crushing reply 4 .... R—B3ch. With a RP one cannot even make an unsound combination.

2. ALLOWING THE KING TO BE DRIVEN FROM THE QUEENING SQUARE

With proper play this need never be permitted. What happens if it is, is illustrated in No. 305 (Dr. Emanuel Lasker). The mate threat forces Black's K to move. *1 .... K—B1* (or 1 .... K—K1; 2 R—R8ch, K—B2; 3 K—Q7, R—QR8; 4 P—Q6, R—R2ch; 5 K—B6, R—R3ch; 6 K—B7, R—R2ch; 7 K—Kt6!, R—Q2; 8 K—B6 and wins); *2 R—R8ch, K—Kt2; 3 K—Q7, R—KKt8; 4 P—Q6, R—Kt2ch; 5 K—K6, R—Kt3ch; 6 K—K7, R—Kt2ch* (or 6 .... K—B3; 7 R—B8ch, K—Kt2; 8 P—Q7); *7 K—B6!, R—Q2; 8 K—K6, R—Kt2; 9 P—Q7* and wins the R for the P. If the Black R were at Q8 in the diagrammed position, 1 .... K—B1; 2 R—R8ch, K—Kt2 would draw (No. 328). If it were at QR8, QKt8, KB8 or KKt8, a check on the third line would transpose back into No. 303. Finally, we must note that the win is not possible if the White R is at KKt7 or on the Q-side. E.g., No. 305a, White R at KKt7, other pieces as in No. 305. Black to play draws. 1 .... K—B1; 2 R—Kt8ch, K—Kt2; 3 K—Q7, R—KR8!; 4 R—Kt7 (if now 4 P—Q6, R—R2ch; 5 K—K6, R—R3ch; 6 K—K7, R—R2ch; 7 K—B6, K—B3=), R—R1!!; 5 P—Q6, K—Kt3!!! and draws (No. 326). Or No. 305b, White Rook at QR7, other pieces as in No. 305. 1 .... K—B1; 2 R—R8ch, K—Kt2; 3 R—R8, R—Q8! and draws. (No. 328). But not here 1 .... K—K1?; 2 R—R8ch, K—B2; 3 K—Q7 and wins as in No. 305. The difference is that White's King must guard the Pawn.

An example from actual play shows a series of elementary blunders which are easier to prevent than to cure. No. 305c (Salve-Burn, St. Petersburg, 1909), White: K at Q5, R at KB6, P at Q4; Black: K at Q2, R at K6. The game went 1 R—B7ch, K—K1; 2 R—KR7, R—Q6? (2 .... R—QR6; 3 K—K6, R—R3ch gives us No. 303); 3 K—K6!, R—K6ch? (3 .... K—Q1; 4 P—Q5, R—Q8 was simpler); 4 K—Q6, R—QR6; 5 R—R8ch, K—B2; 6 R—QB8 and here 6 .... R—Q6! was the only move to draw.

With a RP two drawing methods are feasible for Black. No. 305d, White K at QR6, R at KR7, P at QR5; Black: K at QR1, R at QKt8. Draw. If Black keeps his R on the Kt file White can obviously do nothing. E.g., 1 .... R—Kt2! (why not be fancy?); 2 R—R8ch, R—Kt1; 3 R—R3, R—Kt6!, etc. But even 1 .... K—Kt1 is good enough: 2 R—R8ch, K—B2; 3 K—R7, R—Kt4; 4 P—R6, R—Kt7; 5 K—R8, R—Kt6; 6 P—R7, R—Kt8; 7 R—R2, R—B8!—the Black King will always stay at either QB2 or QB1.

3. PLAYING THE KING TO THE WRONG SIDE

We have already seen one example of this in No. 305b. The most common case, however, is that with the BP. Although it is fairly frequent, even masters go astray: in 1931 Capablanca won two games with it despite the fact that a "book" draw had been reached. The trap is seen in No. 306 (Analysis by Kashdan in the Chess Review, 1933). After *1 K—Kt6* there is only one drawing move: *1 .... R—QB8!* (the alternatives 1 .... R—Kt3ch???; 2 P—B6, R—Kt1—No. 304a, and 1 .... R—Kt8ch; 2 K—B6, K—Q1; 3 R—R8ch, K—K2; 4 K—B7—No. 329 are both fatal); *2 K—B6* (on 2 R—R8ch, K—Q2;

<table>
<tr>
<td align="center">No. 306</td>
<td align="center">No. 307
The Lucena position</td>
</tr>
<tr>
<td>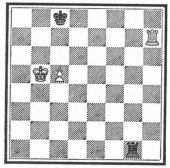</td>
<td></td>
</tr>
<tr>
<td align="center">White to play. Draw.</td>
<td align="center">White wins; win in all analogous
positions except with RP.</td>
</tr>
</table>

3 P—B6ch? is met by 3 .... R×Pch), *K—Kt1!!* (this is the critical point where the error is most likely to be made. 2 .... K—Q1; 3 R—R8ch, K—K2; 4 R—QB8!!! wins. No. 329); *3 R—R8ch, K—R2; 4 R—QB8, R—KR8!* (now we see the difference: the Black K is on the R file and does not block the check); *5 R—Q8, R—QB8!; 6 R—Q5, K—Kt1; 7 K—Q7, K—Kt2=*. White has made no progress.

B. THE KING IS CUT OFF FROM THE QUEENING FILE

By this we mean that the White R occupies the file between the P and the K so that the Black K is unable to blockade the P. There are three questions to be considered here—the ideal position (known as the Lucena position), when it can be reached, what the exceptions are.

1. THE LUCENA POSITION

This is the key to all these endings. It was first discovered by Lucena, a Spanish author who wrote towards the end of the fifteenth century. The solution to No. 307 is *1 .... R—R6; 2 R—B4!* ("building a bridge" is an apt description of the winning method), *R—R8; 3 R—K4ch, K—Q2; 4 K—B7, R—B8ch; 5 K—Kt6, R—Kt8ch; 6 K—B6, R—B8ch* (if 6 .... R—Kt7; 7 R—K5 followed by R—KKt5, while if 6 .... K—Q3; 7 R—Q4ch, K—B3; 8 R—Q8, R—B7ch; 9 K—K5, R—K7ch; 10 K—B4, etc.); *7 K—Kt5, R—Kt8ch; R—Kt4* and wins.

If the Black R leaves the R file, say 1 .... R—K7, then 2 R—KR1 allows the exit of the White K to KR8 or KR7, freeing the P. If the Black K goes to K2 and B3, the White K gets to B8, e.g., 1 .... K—K2; 2 R—K1ch, K—B3 (2 .... K—Q3; 3 R—K4 as above); 3 K—B8.

Clearly, these lines are not applicable to a RP, since there the exit of the White K is blocked on the one side he can go to by both K and R. The case of the RP will be discussed under 3) (Nos. 319–323).

2. WHEN THE LUCENA POSITION CAN BE REACHED

In general, if the White Pawn is on the fifth and the Black King is cut off, White always wins, but if the White P is on the fourth, White *always* wins only if the Black K is kept at a distance of at least three files from the P. Thus if the P is on the QKt file, the K must be on the KB file. There are, however, a number of cases where White wins even though the King is much nearer. These occur when there is a distance of two or more ranks between the King and the Pawn.

Rule 5: If the Pawn is on the fifth rank with its King near it and the Black King is cut off from the queening file, White wins. This is. illustrated in No. 308. It makes no difference whose move it is. The win proceeds: *1 K—R5, R—R1ch* (or 1 .... K—Q2; 2 P—Kt6); *2 K—Kt6, R—Kt1ch; 3 K—R6, R—R1ch* (if 3 .... K—Q2; 4 P—Kt6, R—KR1; 5 P—Kt7 followed by 6 K—R7, winning the Rook); *4 K—Kt7, R—R7; 5 P—Kt6, R—QKt7; 6 K—R7, R—R7ch; 7 K—Kt8, R—QKt7; 8 P—Kt7,* and we have the Lucena position.

No. 308

White wins.

An exception to this rule *with the KtP* occurs when Black has time to oppose Rooks. No. 308a, Black King at Q2, other pieces as in No. 308, is a draw, for after 1 .... R—QB1! White cannot afford to exchange, and on 2 R—K1, K—B2; 3 K—R5, R—R1ch; 4 K—Kt4, K—Kt3 gives No. 303. The only other exception occurs when the White King is cut off from the Pawn by the Black Rook on the intermediate rank. Thus No. 308b, White: K at QKt3, R at QB2, P at QKt5; Black: K at Q1, R at KB5. Draw. 1 K—R3, R—KR5; 2 P—Kt6, R—R3; 3 P—Kt7, (or 3 R—Kt2, K—B1), R—R3ch!; 4 K—Kt4, R—Kt3ch=.

With the KP or BP, if the Black King is on or near the edge of the board, it must be held at least two files away from the Pawn. Thus the critical position is No. 309. White to play decides by *1 R—Kt2!, R—K1; 2 K—B5, R—B1ch; 3 K—K6*, etc. as above. But Black to play draws by *1 .... K—Kt2!!; 2 R—KB2, R—R5ch; 3 K—Q5, R—R4ch; 4 K—Q6, R—R3ch; 5 K—K7, R—R2ch; 6 K—K6, R—R3ch*, etc. If *7 K—B5, K—B2*. The point is that the White King cannot escape perpetual check unless he plays his Rook to the Q-side, in which case the Black King goes in front of the Pawn. The proviso that the Black King must be at a distance of two files from the Pawn holds even when the Pawn is on the sixth. E.g., No. 309a, White: K at K7, R at KB6, P at K6; Black: K at KKt2, R at QR4 is a draw: 1 R—B7ch, K—Kt1; 2 R—B4 (if 2 R—B8ch, K—Kt2; 3 R—Q8, R—R2ch; 4 R—Q7, R—R1!=), R—R2ch; 3 K—B6 (or 3 K—Q6, R—R3ch; 4 K—K5, R—R2!), K—B1!; 4 R—QKt4, R—B2ch!! (the point); 5 K—K5, R—B8=.

As long as the White King is not more than one square away from the Pawn it makes no difference whether the Black Rook is on the rank or the file. E.g., No. 309b, White: K at K3, R at KKt1, P at K5; Black: K at KR3, R at QR5. White wins. 1 K—Q3, R—QKt5; 2 P—K6, R—Kt3; 3 R—K1, R—Kt1; 4 P—K7, R—K1; 5 K—Q4, K—Kt2; 6 K—Q5, K—B2; 7 K—Q6, R—QR1; 8 R—B1ch, K—Kt2; 9 R—QR1! and wins.

Rule 6: If the Pawn is on the third or fourth rank and its King is near it, White can always force a win if and only if the Black King is cut off at a distance of three files from the Pawn (KtP) or two files from the Pawn (BP or QP or KP). If the Pawn is on the second rank, and Black's King is on the fourth or fifth, White wins if and only if the King is cut off at a distance of five files from the Pawn.

At first sight it seems surprising that the same distance holds good even though the Pawn is farther back. The reason for this will become clear from the examples. However, in some cases it does make a difference because at times it is essential for the Black King to attack the Rook.

The critical position for Rule 6 *with the Pawn on the fourth* rank is No. 310. Here the win is *1 R—K1!, K—B4* (or 1 .... K—B2; 2 R—K5!, K—B3; 3 R—QB5, K—K3; 4 P—Kt5, K—Q2; 5 K—Kt4, R—B1; 6 P—Kt6! and wins—No. 308); *2 K—B4, R—B1ch; 3 K—Q5, R—QKt1* (3 .... R—Q1ch; 4 K—B6, R—B1ch; 5 K—Kt7); *4 R—QKt1, K—B3; 5 P—Kt5, K—K2; 6 K—B6!, K—Q1; 7 P—Kt6, K—B1; 8 R—KR1* and wins. On the other hand, with Black to play, we get *1 .... K—K3!; 2 R—Q4, K—K4!; 3 R—Q7* (3 R—QB4, K—Q4), *K—K3!; 4 R—Q4* (4 R—B7, K—Q3), *K—K4; 5 K—B3, R—KR1* (5 .... R—QR1 is also good: 6 R—QB4, R—QKt1; 7 R—B6, K—Q4; 8 R—QR6, R—QB1ch; 9 K—Kt3, R—B3!=); *6 P—Kt5* (6 R—

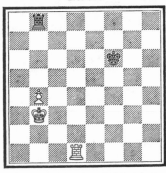

No. 309   No. 310

White to play wins; Black to play   White to play wins; Black to play
draws.   draws.

Q7, K—K3!; 7 R—QR7, K—Q4); *R—QKt1; 7 R—KR4* (7 R—QKt4, K—Q4=), *K—Q3!; 8 K—Kt4, K—B2* and we have the standard draw of No. 303.

The ending in No. 310 is very delicate and the slightest misstep may be fatal. E.g., if Black retreats to K2 he loses. No. 310a, Black King at K2, other pieces as in No. 310. White to play wins. 1 R—Q4!, K—K3 (or 1 .... R—Q1; 2 R×R, K×R; 3 K—R4!, K—B1; 4 K—R5); 2 K—B4!, R—B1ch (if 2 .... K—K4; 3 R—Q5ch, K—K3; 4 P—Kt5, R—B1ch; 5 R—B5, K—Q2; 6 P—Kt6!); 3 K—Kt5, R—Kt1ch; 4 K—B6, R—B1ch; 5 K—Kt7, R—B8; 6 P—Kt5 and wins.

The point that is most essential for the defense is that the Black King must be able to attack the Rook whenever the Rook threatens to let the Pawn advance or to free the King. Thus we get another critical position in No. 311 (Grigorieff, 1937). White to play wins by *1 K—R4!, R—R1ch* (1 .... K—Q3; 2 P—Kt5, or 1 .... R—B1; 2 R×R, K×R; 3 K—R5, or 1 .... R—Kt2; 2 K—R5!!, R—Kt1; 3 P—Kt5); *2 K—Kt5, R—Kt1ch; 3 K—R6!, K—Q3* (3 .... R—R1ch; 4 K—Kt7); *4 P—Kt5* and again we have No. 308. On the other hand Black to play can attack the Rook and prevent the advance. *1 .... K—Q3!; 2 K—R4, K—Q4!!; 3 R—B5ch, K—Q3; 4 K—R5* (4 R—B1, R—R1ch and the King has to return: 5 K—Kt3, R—QKt1, etc., while if 4 R—Kt5, R—R1ch; 5 R—R5, R—QKt1; 6 P—Kt5, K—B2=.), *R—R1ch!; 5 K—Kt5* (5 K—Kt6, R—Kt1ch), *R—Kt1ch; 6 K—B4, R—KR1!* (an alternative is 6 .... R—Kt2; 7 P—Kt5, R—QB2!=, but not 6 .... R—Kt3??; 7 P—Kt5, R—Kt2; 8 R—B6ch, K—Q2; 9 K—B5!, R—B2; 10 K—Kt6! or 9 .... R—Kt1; 10 P—Kt6!; R—QB1; 11 R×R, K×R; 12 K—B6, K—Kt1; 13 P—Kt7 and wins); *7 R—KKt5* (there is nothing he can do: if 7 P—Kt5??, R—R5ch or 7 K—Kt5, R—Kt1ch), *K—B3=.*

No. 311

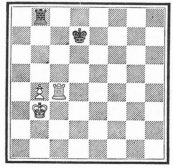

White to play wins; Black to play draws.

No. 312

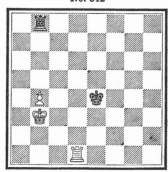

White to play wins; Black to play draws.

Again if the Black King is too far down (on the same rank as the Pawn), White's Rook can penetrate to the sixth and cut off the Black King on a rank, which is another winning stratagem. The critical position is No. 312 (Grigorieff, 1937). White to play wins by *1 R—Q6!, K—K4; 2 R—QR6, K—Q4; 3 K—R4, R—KR1* (or 3 .... R—Kt2; 4 P—Kt5, or 3 .... K—B5; 4 R—B6ch, K—Q4; 5 P—Kt5); *4 P—Kt5, R—R8; 5 R—QB6* and we have No. 308.

The rule does not hold unchanged when the Black Rook cuts off the White King from the Pawn by occupying the third rank. In that case the Black King must be at a distance of four files from the Pawn.

The critical position is No. 313 (Grigorieff, 1937). Here the win is possible only because the sixth rank is available to the Rook. Thus: *1 K—B2!!, K—B4* (1 .... R—KKt6; 2 P—Kt5, R—Kt4; 3 P—Kt6, R—B4ch; 4 K—Q3, R—QKt4; 5 R—K6 is just as bad: 5 .... K—B4; 6 R—B6, K—K4; 7 K—B4, R—Kt8; 8 K—B5, R—Kt7; 9 R—B7, K—K3; 10 P—Kt7, R—B7ch; 11 K—Kt6, R—Kt7ch; 12 K—R7, R—R7ch; 12 K—Kt8, etc., we have Lucena's position); *2 P—Kt5, K—B3* (if instead 2 .... R—KKt6; 3 P—Kt6, R—Kt2; 4 K—B3, R—Kt2; 5 R—QKt1, K—K3; 6 K—B4, K—Q2; 7 K—Kt5!, K—B1; 8 R—KR1!, R—Q2; 9 K—R6, R—Q1; 10 K—R7, R—Q2ch; 11 K—R8 and wins: 11 .... R—KKt2; 12 P—Kt7ch, R×P; 13 R—R8ch, etc.); *3 P—Kt6, K—B2* (or 3 .... R—R1; 4 K—B3, R—QKt1; 5 R—QKt1, K—K3; 6 K—B4, K—Q2; 7 K—Kt5!!, K—B1; 8 R—B1ch!, K—Q2—8 .... K—Kt2; 9 R—B7ch, K—R1; 10 R—R7 mate—; 9 K—R6 and wins); *4 R—QKt1!, R—R1; 5 K—B3, K—K3; 6 K—Kt4!, K—Q2; 7 R—QB1!, R—QB1; 8 R—B5!!, R—B3* (8 .... R×R; 9 K×R, K—B1; 10 K—B6 and White has the opposition); *9 K—Kt5, R×Rch; 10 K×R, K—Q1; 11 K—Q6!* and wins.

But with Black to move in the diagrammed position he can prevent the winning stratagem, for, as the reader has doubtless noticed, White always noses in by exactly one move in the above variations. *1 .... K—B4!; 2 P—Kt5* (if 2 K—B2, K—B3!; 3 P—Kt5, R—R4!; 4 P—Kt6, R—B4ch!; 5 K—Q3, R—QKt4), *R—Q6!!!* (the only reply: if 2 .... R—KKt6; 3 K—B2, while if 2 .... K—B3; 3 P—Kt6, both transposing into variations given above); *3 R—QKt1!!* (or 3 K—B2, R—Q4; 4 R—QKt1, R—B4ch; 5 K—Q3, K—K4; 6 P—Kt6, K—B1; 7 P—Kt7, R—QKt1; 8 K—B4, K—Q3=), *K—K3!; 4 P—Kt6, R—Q1!!* (but not 4 .... K—Q2??; 5 P—Kt7, K—B2; 6 P—Kt8=Qch, K×Q; 7 K—B2 dis ch); *5 K—R3, K—Q2; 6 R—Q1ch, K—K1!!* (6 .... K—B1??; 7 P—Kt7ch, K—B2; 8 R× R. 6 .... K—K2 is equally good, however.); *7 R—QB1, R—Q3; 8 R—QKt1, K—Q2!!* (the saving clause. 8 .... R—Q1?; 9 K—Kt 4, K—Q2; 10 R—Q1ch or simply 10 R—QB1, R—QB1; 11 R—B5 would be a blunder); *9 K—R4* (Such is life on a chess board, 9 P—Kt7 looks good but is refuted by 9 .... R—R3ch; 10 K—Kt2, R—Kt3ch; 11 K—B2, R×R; 12 K×R, K— B2), *K—B1; 10 K—R5, K—Kt2=.* We see that the winning ma-

No. 313

White to play wins; Black to play draws.

noeuvre with the Pawn on the fourth involves playing the Rook behind the Pawn and advancing with one's King. With a KtP there is not enough room to get near the Pawn, but with a more central Pawn there is. This fact accounts for the second part of the rule.

With a center Pawn we have the same situation as before—if Black's King is on or near the edge of the board he draws; if not he loses. No. 314, which is equally applicable to a BP, illustrates this point. Unlike the analogous case in Nos. 310 and 312 White can get his King to the sixth. The solution is *1 .... K—Kt3; 2 K—B4, R—B1ch; 3 K—Kt5, R—Q1; 4 K—B5, R—B1ch; 5 K—Kt6, R—Q1; 6 R—Q1, K—B2; 7 K—B7!!* (the point. 7 P—Q5?, K—K2; 8 K—B7, R—Q2ch only draws), *R—Q4* (or 7 .... R—QR1; 8 R—K1, R—R2ch; 9 K—B6, R—R3ch; 10 K—Kt5, etc.); *8 K—B6, R—Q1* (8 .... R—QR4; 9 R—K1, R—R3ch; 10 K—Kt5, R—Q3; 11 K—B5, or 10 .... R—K3; 11 R×R, K×R; 12 K—B6); *9 P—Q5, R—QR1* (9 .... K—K1; 10 R—K1ch); *10 R—K1, R—R3ch; 11 K—Kt5, R—R7; 12 P—Q6* and wins (No. 308). The win here is made possible by the fact that the checks on the rank are soon exhausted. Consequently when the Black King is on the QR file the game will be drawn. Thus in No. 314a, Black King at QR4, White Rook at QKt1, other pieces as in No. 314, Black holds everything by the threat of perpetual check. At the moment Black's King is on the best square, but even with Black to move he can draw with best play. 1 .... K—R5!! (not 1 .... K—R3?; 2 K—K4, R—K1ch; 3 K—Q5, R—Q1ch; 4 K—B6!!!, K—R2; 5 P—Q5 and wins—No. 309); 2 K—K4 (2 R—Kt6, K—R4!; 3 R—K6, K—Kt4; 4 K—K4, R—KR1; 5 P—Q5, R—R5ch; 6 K—K5, R—R4ch; 7 K—Q6, K—Kt3!!; 8 K—Q7 dis ch, K—Kt2; 9 P—Q6, R—R2ch; 10 R—K7, R—R1!=—see also No. 324), R—K1ch; 3 K—B5, R—Q1; 4 K—K5, R—K1ch; 5 K—B6, R—Q1; 6 R—Q1, K—Kt4; 7 K—K7, R—KR1!!; 8 P—Q5, R—R2ch; 9 K—Q8, R—R1ch; 10 K—Q7, R—R2ch; 11 K—K6, R—R3ch; 12 K—K5, R—R4ch; 13 K—B4, K—Kt3!!; 13 P—Q6, R—R1=. No. 309. The distance between the White King and the Black Rook (two squares on the Q-side; three squares on the K-side) makes all the difference in the world.

With a BP once Black's King is on the edge of the board, the game is a hopeless draw, but with the King on the other side it works in exactly the same way as a QP or KP.

When the Pawn is on the third rank the rule still holds, but there are fewer exceptions. The reason why the Black King need not be one file further from the Pawn is that a new winning method is available: defending the Pawn on the rank. The general case is shown in No. 315 (Grigorieff, 1937). With White to play the continuation is *1 R—K4!!* (gaining a tempo. Inferior is the method of No. 310—1 K—B3, R—B1ch; 2 K—Q4, R—QKt1; 3 K—B4, R—B1ch; 4 K—Q5, R—QKt1;

5 R—QKt1, K—K2!; 6 K—B6, R—Kt5!!; 7 R—K1ch (7 K—B5, R—Kt1), K—Q1; 8 R—K3, R—KR5!!; 9 R—K5, R—R3ch; 10 K—Kt7, R—R2ch; 11 K—Kt8, K—Q2; 12 R—QB5, R—R5; 13 R—QKt5 (13 K—R7, R—Kt5! =), K—B3; 14 R—Kt7, K—B4 followed by R—QKt5 with a clear draw), *K—B4* (Or:

a) 1 .... R—Kt2; 2 K—B3, R—B2ch; 3 K—Q4, R—QKt2; 4 K—B4, R—B2ch; 5 K—Q5, R—QKt2; 6 P—Kt4, K—B4; 7 R—QB4, K—B3; 8 K—B6, R—Kt1; 9 P—Kt5 and wins.

b) 1 .... K—B2; 2 P—Kt4—No. 310); *2 R—K3!, K—B5* (2 .... K—B3; 3 K—B3, R—B1ch; 4 K—Q4, R—QKt1; 5 K—B5!, R—B1ch; 6 K—Q6, R—QKt1; 7 R—B3ch, K—Kt3—or A—; 8 K—B5,

No. 314

White wins. Draw with Black King at QR4.

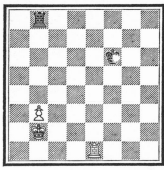

No. 315

White wins.

R—B1ch; 9 K—Q4, R—QKt1; 10 K—B3, R—B1ch; 11 K—Kt2, R—QKt1; 12 R—B1, K—Kt2; 13 K—B3, R—B1ch; 14 K—Q4, R—QKt1; 15 K—B4, R—B1ch; 16 K—Q5, R—QKt1; 17 R—QKt1!, K—B2; 18 P—Kt4, K—K2; 19 K—B6!, K—Q1; 20 R—Q1ch!! and wins, for if 20 .... K—B1; 21 R—KR1. Variation A. 7 .... K—Kt4; 8 K—B5, K—Kt5; 9 R—Q3!!, R—B1ch; 10 K—Kt6, R—Kt1ch; 11 K—B7, R—Kt5; 12 K—B6, K—B5; 13 K—B5, R—Kt1; 14 P—Kt4, R—B1ch; 15 K—Kt5, R—Kt1ch; 16 K—B4, R—B1ch; 17 K—Kt3, R—QKt1; 18 R—Q5, K—K5; 19 R—KR5, K—Q5; 20 P—Kt5 with a simple win—No. 330); *3 R—K1, K—B4* (or 3 .... K—B6; 4 K—B3, R—B1ch; 5 K—Q4, R—QKt1; 6 R—QKt1!, K—K7; 7 P—Kt4, K—Q7; 8 P—Kt5, K—B7; 9 R—Kt4); *4 K—B3, R—B1ch; 5 K—Q4, R—QKt1; 6 K—B4, R—B1ch; 7 K—Q5, R—QKt1* (ingenious but unavailing is 7 .... R—Q1ch; 8 K—B6, R—B1ch; 9 K—Kt7, R—B6; 10 R—QKt1!!!, K—K3; 11 P—Kt4, etc.); *8 R—QKt1, K—B3*

(the point to the long manoeuvre: Black's King is one move too late);
9 P—Kt4, K—K2; 10 K—B6, K—Q1; 11 P—Kt5 and wins.

The difficulty with the Pawn on the third rank is that it is not enough to merely get the King to the fifth or the sixth, for Black can then still prevent the advance of the Pawn. But it turns out that in the best defensive position Black is in zugzwang, so that the stratagem of losing a tempo always provides a solution.

It is essential to keep the pieces integrated until a clear win is in sight. Thus if White plays his King out too early he may get into the

No. 316

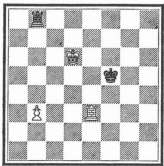

White to play wins; Black to play draws.

No. 317

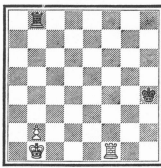

White to play wins; Black to play draws. With Black King at KKt2 win no matter who moves.

critical position No. 316 (Grigorieff, 1937). The win is achieved by
1 K—B5, K—B5 (if 1 .... R—B1ch; 2 K—Q4, R—QKt1; 3 K—B3, R—B1ch; 4 K—Kt2, etc.—No. 315); *2 R—R3, K—K4; 3 R—R5ch!* (not 3 P—Kt4?, R—B1ch; 4 K—Kt5, R—Kt1ch—the King is forced back to QKt3, when .... K—Q3 draws), *K—K3; 4 R—R6ch, K—Q2; 5 R—R7ch, K—K3; 6 P—QKt4, R—B1ch; 7 K—Kt6, R—Kt1ch; 8 R—Kt7, R—KR1; 9 P—Kt5* and wins. Black to play draws by *1 .... K—B5!; 2 R—R3, K—B4!* (not 2 .... K—K5; 3 K—B7!, R—Kt4; 4 K—B6, R—Kt1; 5 P—Kt4!! and wins); *3 K—B7, R—Kt5; 4 K—B6, R—Kt1!; 5 K—B5, R—B1ch; 6 K—Kt4, R—Kt1ch; 7 K—B3, K—K3=.*

With a center Pawn or a BP White can only win if the Black King is at the required distance of three files. This means that when White has a KP, if Black's King is on the KR file he draws, if it is on the QKt file he loses.

When the Pawn is on the second rank if the Black King is properly placed, i.e., in a position to attack the White Rook on the third, White can win only if the King is cut off at a distance of five files from the Pawn. Thus the critical position is No. 317. White to play wins by *1 R—Kt1, K—R4; 2 K—B2, R—B1ch; 3 K—Q3, R—QKt1; 4 K—B3, R—B1ch; 5 K—Q4, R—QKt1; 6 R—QKt1, K—Kt3; 7 P—Kt4, K— B2; 8 K—B5!, K—K2; 9 K—B6* and wins. But since White wins by only one tempo it is clear that if the Black King were one file nearer that would save the game. Thus Black to play draws by *1 .... K— Kt4!; 2 R—B3, K—Kt5!* (not 2 .... K—Kt3?; 3 P—Kt3 and wins); *4 R—B1, K—Kt4; 5 K—B2* (the only chance), *R—B1ch; 6 K—Q3, R—QKt1; 7 K—B3, R—B1ch; 8 K—Q4, R—QKt1; 9 R—QKt1, K— B3; 10 P—Kt4, K—K2; 11 P—Kt5, K—Q2=.*

If the Black King is on the second rank (with White to play) White can win even though the King is at a distance of only three files. For he can play his Rook to the third rank, his Pawn to the third, King to the second and thus transpose into No. 315.

3. EXCEPTIONS

There are two principal types of exceptions to the general theory— one when the Pawn has already reached the seventh, and the second with a RP.

a) The Lucena Position.

Exceptions here occur with the Pawns on the four center files when the Kings are on opposite sides of the Pawn. White must use his Rook to cut off the Black King, and this allows perpetual check on the other side.

The case with the KP is seen in No. 318. Black to play can force the King to the QKt file and then attack and capture the Pawn. *1 .... R—R1ch; 2 K—Q7, R—R2ch; 3 K—K6, R—R3ch; 4 K—K5, R— R4ch; 5 K—Q4, R—R5ch; 6 K—B5, R—R4ch; 7 K—Kt6* (7 K—Q6, R—R3ch), *R—K4=.* White to play wins quite simply by *1 R— Kt1ch, K—R2* (1 .... K—B3; 2 K —B8); *2 R—K1, R—Q7; 3 K—B7, R—B7ch; 4 K—K6*, etc. If the

No. 318

White to play wins; Black to play draws. Always win with Black King at KKt1 or Black Rook at QKt7.

Black King is at KKt1 in the original position, No. 318a, BK at KKt1, other pieces as in No. 318, the check at KB8 decides: 1 .... R—R1ch; 2 K—Q7, R—R2ch; 3 K—Q6, R—R3ch; 4 K—B5, R—K3; 5 R—B8ch, K—Kt2; 6 P—K8=Q. Similarly, if the Black Rook is at QKt7, the checks are exhausted too soon. No. 318b, BR at QKt7, other pieces as in No. 318. White wins. 1 .... R—Kt1ch; 2 K—Q7, R—Kt2ch; 3 K—Q8, R—Kt1ch; 4 K—B7, R—QR1 (4 .... R—K1; 5 K—Q7); 5 R—QR1!!!, R—K1; 6 K—Q7 and wins for if 6 .... K—B2; 7 R—B1ch.

No. 319	No. 320
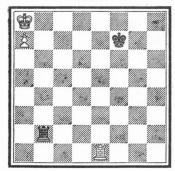	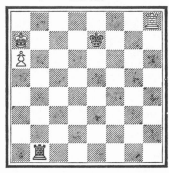
White wins. Draw with Black King any nearer the Pawn.	White to play wins; Black to play draws.

b) *The RP.*

This case presents an unusual problem: that of extricating the White King once the Pawn has reached the seventh. It is to be expected that the Black Rook will occupy the Kt file; the White Rook will then have to oppose his rival in order to free the King. When the Black King is on the first or second rank it will normally take the White Rook three moves to get to QKt8. This accounts for

Rule 7. With a RP on the seventh White wins if and only if the Black King is no nearer than the KB file (QRP), or QB file (KRP).

This rule is illustrated in No. 319. The win here hangs on a thread: **1 R—KR1** (tempo moves are meaningless), *K—K2;* **2 R—R8** (2 R—R7ch?, K—Q3; 3 R—QKt7 is a mistake because of 3 .... R—QR7!, for if then 4 K—Kt8??, R—R1 mate!), *K—Q3* (if 2 .... K—Q2; 3 R—QKt8, R—KR7; 4 K—Kt7, R—Kt7ch; 5 K—R6, R—R7ch; 6 K—Kt6, R—Kt7ch; 7 K—B5, etc.—the checks are soon exhausted);

3 R—QKt8, R—QR7; 4 K—Kt7, R—Kt7ch; 5 K—B8 (5 K—R6 does not get the King out: 5 .... R—R7ch; 6 K—Kt6, R—Kt7ch; 7 K—R5, R—R7ch and 8 K—Kt6 is necessary), *R—B7ch; 6 K—Q8, R—KR7!* (with a rather annoying threat); *7 R—Kt6ch, K—B4* (7 .... K—K4; 8 K—B7); *8 R—B6ch!* (the quickest, though 8 R—Kt2! is also good enough. E.g., 8 .... R—R1ch; 9 K—B7, R—R2ch; 10 K—Kt8 and the White King escapes to QR6), *K—Kt4* (or 8 .... K×R; 9 P—R8=Qch. Or 8 .... K—Q4; 9 R—QR6, R—R1ch; 10 K—B7, R—R2ch; 11 K—Kt6, R—R3ch; 12 K—Kt5); *9 R—B8, R—R1ch; 10 K—B7, R—R2ch; 11 K—Kt8* and wins.

If the Black King is any nearer in the diagrammed position the White King can never get out of the corner. No. 319a, White: K at QR8, R at Q1, P at QR7; Black: K at K2, R at QKt7. Draw. 1 R—KR1, K—Q2; 2 R—R8, K—B2; 3 R—QKt8, R—KR7; 4 R—Kt7ch, K—B1!; 5 R—Kt1, R—QB7; 6 R—Kt8ch, K—B2, etc.

With the Pawn on the sixth rank White's prospects are somewhat better because his King is not completely stalemated. Nevertheless the rule holds. This may be seen from the critical position No. 320. The win is *1 R—QKt8!, R—QB8; 2 K—Kt7, R—Kt8ch* (2 .... K—Q2; 3 P—R7 and 2 .... K—Q3; 3 P—R7 both transpose into No. 319 and notes); *3 K—R8, R—QR8; 4 P—R7, K—Q3; 5 K—Kt7,* etc.—we have the main variation of No. 319. But Black to play: *1 .... K—Q2; 2 R—QKt8, R—QR8; 3 K—Kt7, R—Kt8ch; 4 K—R8, R—QR8; 5 P—R7, K—B2=*. No. 319a.

If the White Rook has command of the Kt file, the critical position occurs one file closer, i.e., Black's King must be on the Q file (QRP) or K file (KRP) to draw. This is seen in No. 321 (Rabinovitch). White to play moves *1 P—R7,* when Black can resign. Black to play can save himself by *1 .... R—B3ch; 2 K—R5* (2 K—Kt5, K—B2!!; 3 P—R7, R—Kt3ch; 4 K—B5, R—R3=. If here 4 K—R5??, R×R; 5 P—R8=Q, R—R7ch wins for Black. If 2 K—Kt7, R—B2ch; 3 K—Kt8, R—B1ch; 4 K—R7, R—B8!=. No. 320), *R—B4ch* (not 2 .... R—B1?; 3 P—R7! R—QR1; 4 K—R6 and wins); *3 K—R4* (or 3 K—Kt4, R—B3!), *R—B3!!* (3 .... R—B1? is a mistake: 4 R—Kt7ch, K—B3; 5 K—R5, R—KR1; 6 R—Kt6ch, K—B2; 7 P—R7, R—R4ch; 8 K—R6, R—KR8; 9 R—B6ch!, K—Q2; 10 R—B5 and wins. Again, 3 ....

No. 321

Black to play draws; White to play wins.

R—B5ch? also loses: 4 K—Kt5!, R—B2; 5 R—KR2, R—B8; 6 P—
R7, R—QR8; 7 R—R8!!, etc.); *4 R—Kt7ch, K—B1; 5 K—Kt5, R—
B8* (5 .... R—KR3; 6 K—R5, R—KKt3; 7 R—Kt1, R—Kt2; 8 K—
Kt6, K—Kt1 is also good enough); *6 K—Kt6, R—Kt8ch; 7 K—R7,
R—QB8=.* Once more it is clear that with Black's pieces one file
further away, the game is won in any case. No. 321a, White: K at
QKt6, R at QKt2, P at QR6; Black: K at K2, R at Q2. White wins.
1 .... R—Q3ch; 2 K—R5, R—Q4ch; 3 R—Kt5!, R—Q8; 4 P—R7,
K—Q2; 5 K—R6!, R—R8ch; 6 R—R5 and wins.

With the Pawn on the fifth or fourth rank White has winning chances
only if Black is unable to oppose Rooks. This means that with the
Pawn on the fifth the White Rook must be on the K file, while if it is
on the fourth the White Rook must be on the KB file. Thus in the
best possible position for the Black pieces—Rook on the first rank,
King on the first or second—the rule holds as above. This is shown in
No. 322 (Cheron, 1926). After *1 K—Kt5, R—Q1!!* (not 1 .... R—
Kt1ch?; 2 K—B6, R—Kt8; 3 P—R6, R—QR8; 4 K—Kt6, R—Kt8ch;
5 K—R5!!!, R—R8ch; 6 R—R4 and wins); *2 R—QB4* (2 R×R ob-
viously leads to nothing but a draw, while 2 R—QR4, K—Q2; 3 K—
Kt6, R—Kt1ch; 4 K—R7, R—Kt8; 5 R—B4, R—Kt7 is also insuffi-
cient—Nos. 320, 321), *R—Kt1ch!* (tempting but erroneous is 2 ....
K—Q2; 3 P—R6, R—QB1; 4 P—R7!! and wins); *3 K—R4* (3 K—R6,
K—Q2 transposes back into the well-known draws), *K—Q2; 4 P—
R6, R—QB1!* (or 4 .... R—Kt8; 5 K—R5, R—R8ch; 6 K—Kt6, R—
Kt8ch=), *5 R—QKt4, R—KR1!* (inferior is 5 .... K—B2?; 6 R—
Kt7ch, K—B3; 7 K—R5); *6 K—R5, K—B2; 7 P—R7* (if now 7 R—
Kt7ch, K—B1!; 8 K—Kt6, R—R3ch; 9 K—R7, R—KB3 or 9 ....
R—R8=), *R—R4ch; 8 K—R6, R—R3ch; 9 K—R5, R—R4ch; 10 K—
R4, R—R1=.*

If the Black King is on the KB file, the White Rook on the K file,
opposing Rooks is impossible because after the exchange the Black
King is outside the square of the Pawn. Consequently White wins by
advancing his Pawn to the seventh and continuing as in No. 320.

Again, if the Black pieces are not on the best squares in No. 322 he
will lose. No. 322a, Black Rook at QR2, other pieces as in No. 322.
White to play wins. 1 K—Kt5, R—Q2; 2 R—QR4!, K—Q1 (or 2 ....
R—Q1; 3 P—R6, R—QR1; 4 P—R7, K—Q2; 5 K—Kt6, K—B1; 6
R--R4); 3 P—R6, R—QR2; 4 K—Kt6, R—R1; 5 P—R7 and wins the
Rook. Or No. 322b, Black King at K3, other pieces as in No. 322.
White to play wins. 1 K—Kt5, R—Kt1ch; 2 K—B6, K—K4 (if 2
.... R—QR1; 3 R—K4ch, K—B4; 4 R—QR4, R—B1ch; 5 K—Kt7,
R—B8; 6 R—QKt4! and wins); 3 R—QR4, R—B1ch!; 4 K—Kt7!,
R—B8; 5 P—R6, R—Kt8ch; 6 K—B6, R—B8ch; 7 K—Kt5, R—
Kt8ch; 8 K—R5, R—Kt1; 9 P—R7, R—QR1; 10 K—Kt6 and wins.

With the Pawn on the fourth rank when the Black pieces are on the
best possible squares White wins only if the Black King is on the KKt
file (QRP) or the QKt file (KRP) for otherwise Black can oppose
Rooks. Where the Black King is not on the best square (first or second rank) the critical position is No. 323 (Rabinovitch). Black to
play transposes into the draw of No. 322 by 1 .... K—K3; 2 K—Kt4,
K—K2; 3 P—R5, R—Q1!. White to play can force the Black King to
a more unfavorable position (KB file or 5th rank). *1 K—Kt4, R—
Kt1ch; 2 K—B5, R—QR1* (if 2 .... R—B1ch; 3 K—Kt6, R—Kt1ch;
4 K—B7, R—QR1; 5 R—QR1!, R—R4; 6 K—Kt6, R—R1; 7 P—R5
and wins); *3 K—Kt5, R—Kt1ch; 4 K—B6!, R—QR1; 5 R—K1ch!*

No. 322

Draw. Black King at K3 or R at QR2
loses.

No. 323

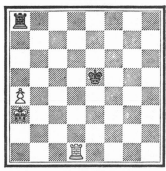

White to play wins; Black to play
draws.

(the only move to win. If 5 R—QR1, R—B1ch; 6 K—Kt7—or A—,
R—B7; 7 R—QKt1, K—Q3; 8 P—R5, K—Q2; 9 P—R6, R—B2ch=.
No. 321. Variation A. 6 K—Q7, R—B7; 7 P—R5, R—Q7ch; 8 K—
K7, R—KR7!; 9 P—R6, R—R2ch; 10 K—Q8, K—Q3; 11 R—Q1ch,
K—B3=), *K—Q5* (or 5 .... K—B3; 6 R—QR1, R—B1ch; 7 K—
Kt7, R—B7; 8 P—R5, R—Kt7ch; 9 K—B6, R—B7ch; 10 K—Kt5,
R—Kt7ch; 11 K—B4, R—B7ch; 12 K—Kt3, R—B1; 13 P—R6, K—
K3; 14 P—R7, R—QR1; 15 K—Kt4, K—Q3; 16 K—Kt5, K—B2;
17 K—R6, R—R1; 18 R—B1ch, K—Q3; 19 K—Kt7 and wins); *6 R—
QR1, K—B5; 7 P—R5, R—R1; 8 R—R4ch!, K—Kt6* (there is nothing
better: 8 .... K—B6; 9 P—R6, R—R3ch; 10 K—Q5, R—R4ch;
11 K—Q6, R—R3ch; 12 K—K5, R—R4ch; 13 K—B6, R—R1; 14 P—
R7, R—R1; 15 K—K5, K—Kt6; 16 R—R1, K—Kt5; 17 K—Q6,
K—Kt4; 18 K—B7 and again Black is one move too late); *9 R—Q4,*

K—B6; 10 R—Q7, R—R3ch; 11 K—Kt7, R—R8; 12 P—R6, R—Kt8ch; 13 K—B8 and the Pawn marches on: *13 .... R—QR8; 14 P—R7, K—B5; 15 K—Kt8, R—Kt8ch; 16 R—Kt7.* Again, since White always manages to win by a nose, it is clear that if the Black King is one file nearer in the diagrammed position the draw is simple.

B1. THE BLACK KING IS NOT ON THE QUEENING FILE BUT IS NOT DIRECTLY CUT OFF

This is complementary to B, for obviously in many cases transpositions are possible. What we are interested in are those positions where

No. 324

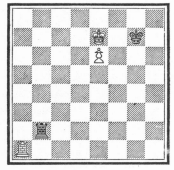

Black to play draws. White Rook at QR8 or K1 wins.

No. 325

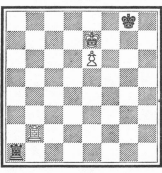

Black to play, White wins. White Rook may be anywhere on QKt, QB, Q, and KR files. Draw with Black King at KKt2 or KKt3.

no such simple transposition is available—chiefly where the Black King is at a distance of one file from the Pawn. In order to win White's King must be in front of his Pawn, which must be on the fifth rank or beyond.

With a KP or QP it is always better for the defense to have his King on the short side of the Pawn, i.e., with a KP, on the K-side, with a QP, on the Q-side. *When the Pawn is on the sixth* Black draws only if his King is at Kt2. Thus the ideal defensive position for Black is No. 324 (Grigorieff, 1937). Here the defense is *1 .... R—Kt2ch; 2 K—Q6, R—Kt3ch!* (but not 2 .... K—B1?; 3 R—R8ch, K—Kt2; 4 P—K7 and wins); *3 K—Q7, R—Kt2ch!* (King and Pawn must part); *4 K—Q8* (if 4 K—B6, R—Kt7!!; 5 R—KB1—else K—B1—, R—K7!; 6 K—Q7, R—QR7!!; 7 P—K7, R—R2ch; 8 K—K6, R—R3ch=. No. 318.),

R—Kt1ch!; 5 K—B7, R—Kt7; 6 R—KB1 (else 6 .... K—B1), *R—QR7; 7 P—K7, R—R2ch=* (No. 318). With the White Rook on the eighth, the Rook checks are not sufficient, for in No. 324a, White Rook at QR8, other pieces as in No. 324, after 1 .... R—Kt2ch; 2 K—Q6, R—Kt3ch (2 .... K—B3; 3 R—B8ch, K—Kt2; 4 P—K7); 3 K—Q7, R—Kt2ch; 4 K—B6!, R—K2 (or 4 .... R—Kt8; 5 P—K7); 5 K—Q6, R—Kt2; 6 P—K7 is decisive. Similarly, if the White Rook is at K1 the checks are ineffectual: No. 324b, WR at K1, other pieces as in No. 324. White wins. 1 .... R—Kt2ch; 2 K—Q8!, R—Kt1ch; 3 K—Q7!, R—Kt2ch; 4 K—B8, R—K2; 5 K—Q8, K—B3 (5 .... R—R2; 6 P—K7); 6 R—B1ch, KXP; 7 R—K1ch. However, to have the Rook at R7 does White no good: Black plays 1 .... R—Kt1! and discovered checks are pleasant but meaningless. Finally, if the Black King is at KKt1 or KKt3, White always wins. No. 324c (Grigorieff, 1937), BK at KKt3, other pieces as in No. 324. White wins. 1 .... R—Kt2ch; 2 K—Q8, R—Kt1ch; 3 K—B7, R—Kt7; 4 R—K1!, R—B7ch; 5 K—Q7, R—Q7ch; 6 K—K8, R—QR7; 7 P—K7 and the King can get out.

It is important to note, however, that with the positions of the Rooks reversed Black always draws, even when the White Rook is on one of the ideal squares. This is shown in No. 325 (Tarrasch, 1906). On *1 .... K—Kt2; 2 R—Kt2ch* wins at once (No. 309). Likewise after *1 .... R—R2ch; 2 K—B6, R—R1* (forced); *3 R—Kt2ch* is decisive. If the White Rook is on the K or KB files, R—R2ch will force the King away from the Pawn and allow the approach of either the Rook or the King. With the King at Kt2 or Kt3 the situation, however, is different (Compare No. 324c). For then on 1 .... R—R2ch White cannot escape the checks easily; he must go to the Q-side, when .... K—B3 will draw.

With the Black Rook attacking the Pawn, we get the critical position No. 326 (Tarrasch, 1906). White to play wins by *1 R—QB8, R—QR8* (1 .... R—K7; 2 K—Q 7, R—Q7ch; 3 K—K8); *2 K—K8!, K—B3; 3 P—K7, K—K3* (3 .... R—R2; 4 R—B6ch); *4 R—B6ch, K—Q4; 5 K—Q7* and wins. Black can draw by *1 .... R—QR8!; 2 R—Q8, R—R2ch; 3 R—Q7* (3 K—K8, K—B3), *R—R1* (but not 3 .... R—R3?; 4 K—K8 dis ch, K—B3; 5 P—K7, R—R1ch; 6 R—Q8, R—R2; 7 R—Q6ch and wins

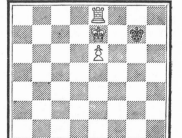

No. 326

White to play wins; Black to play draws.

—No. 318); *4 R—Kt7, K—Kt3!* (not 4 .... K—Kt1?; 5 K—B6—
No. 325); *5 K—Q7* (or 5 R—B7, K—Kt2!; 6 R—Q7, K—Kt3; 7 R
—Q1, R—R2ch; 8 K—Q6, R—R3ch, etc. Or 5 R—Kt1, R—R2ch;
6 K—B8, R—R1ch=), *K—B3!; 6 R—B7* (6 P—K7, K—B2; 7 R—
B7, R—K1; 8 K—Q6, R—QR1!=, but not 8 .... R—KR1?; 9 P
—K8=Q!db1 ch, K×Q; 10 R—Kt8ch), *K—Kt2!* (a mistake is 6
.... R—R8?; 7 P—K7, R—Q8ch; 8 K—K8!); *7 K—Q6 dis ch, K—
B1; 8 R—KR7, R—R3ch=*.

But with the Black King on the long side of the Pawn, the Rook
does not have enough room for checks and consequently always loses.
This is seen in No. 327. For after *1 .... R—QR8; 2 R—KR8, R—*

No. 327

White wins.

No. 328

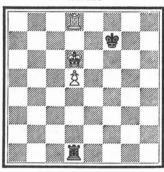

White to play wins; Black to play
draws. Black King at QKt2 always
draws.

R2ch; 3 K—B6, R—R3ch; 4 K—B7, R—R2ch; 5 K—Kt6 both Black
and the checks are exhausted: *5 .... R—Q2; 6 K—B6, K—K3;
7 R—R6ch.* Or 6 .... R—R2; 7 P—Q7. Of course, if Black could
give check in the diagrammed position he would manage to draw.
No. 327a, Black Rook at QR8, other pieces as in No. 327. Black to
play draws. 1 .... R—R2ch; 2 K—B6, R—R3ch; 3 K—B7, R—
R2ch; 4 K—Kt6, R—R8!; 5 P—Q7, K—K2=.

With the Pawn on the fifth Black may have his King on the long side
and still draw, but he must be able to prevent an advantageous advance to the sixth. The critical position is No. 328. The win is
rather unusual. *1 K—B7, R—QR8* (or 1 .... R—B8ch; 2 K—Q7,
R—QR8; 3 R—B8!, R—R2ch; 4 R—B7, R—R1; 5 P—Q6, etc., as in
the main variation); *2 R—QKt8!* (the only move: if 2 P—Q6?, R—
R2ch; 3 K—Kt6, R—R8=), *R—R2ch* (2 .... K—K2; 3 P—Q6ch,
K—K3; 4 R—K8ch, or 3 .... K—B2; 4 P—Q7, R—B8ch; 5 K—Q8!);

3 R—Kt7, R—R1; 4 K—Q7!!! (4 P—Q6?? is a mistake, for the reply
4 .... K—K3! draws: 5 P—Q7, K—K2!, or 5 R—Kt1, R—R2ch;
6 K—Kt6, R—Q2), *K—B3!; 5 P—Q6, K—B2!* (so that if now 6 K—
B6 dis ch, K—K1!; 7 R—KR7, R—R3ch!=, and if 6 K—B7, K—K3;
7 P—Q7, K—K2=), *6 R—B7!!* (now we see why the "short" side is so
bad for Black: the Rook cannot maintain the position), *R—QKt1;
7 R—B1!, R—Kt2ch; 8 K—B6, R—Kt7; 9 R—K1!* and we have
transposed into No. 308. Black must check on the short side and
cannot prevent the Lucena position. Black to play has time to ob-
struct the advance of the Pawn: *1 .... R—QR8!; 2 R—QB8* (if
2 K—B7, R—R2ch; 3 K—Kt6, R—R8; 4 P—Q6, K—K3=), *R—Q8!*
(but not 2 .... R—R3ch; 3 K—Q7!, R—R2ch; 4 R—B7, R—R1;
5 P—Q6, etc., as above); *3 R—B2* (3 K—B6, K—K2), *K—K1; 4 R—
KR2, R—Q6; 5 R—R8ch, K—B2; 6 R—Q8, R—QR6!* etc. White's
King cannot leave Q6 without allowing the approach of the Black
King.

With the Black King at QKt2, i.e., on the short side the game is
always drawn, because the Black Rook then has plenty of room to
move about in. Even if White gets his Pawn to the sixth, in a relatively favorable position such as No. 326, Black will always be able to
retain the move and draw. In practice it is essential to keep the Black
Rook active.

With the BP it makes no difference whether the Pawn is on the
fifth or the sixth: if Black's King is on the short side he draws, if not
he loses. No. 329 illustrates the situation. The continuation might
be *1 .... R—KR8; 2 K—Kt7, R—Kt8ch; 3 K—B7, R—KB8; 4 P—
B6, R—KR8* (4 .... R—KKt8; 5 R—K8); *5 R—QR8, R—KB8*
(5 .... R—R2ch; 6 K—Kt8, R—R8; 7 P—B7, etc.); *6 R—R2, R—
K8; 7 R—Q2ch,* etc. But if the
Black King is on the KR file the
Rook has checks galore and can
draw. Thus No. 329a: *1 R—K8,
R—QKt8; 2 K—B7, R—Kt2ch; 3
R—K7, R—Kt1; 4 P—B6, R—
QR1; 5 R—K8* (now there is no
question of stalemating the Black
Rook), *R—R2ch; 6 K—B8* (or 6
K—K6, R—R3ch; 7 K—B5, R—
R4ch; 8 R—K5, R—K3, etc.), *K
—Kt3; 7 R—K6, R—R1ch=.*

If the Pawn is on the sixth there
is one winning position which must
be noted: No. 329b, White: K at
KB7, R at KB8, P at KB6; Black:

No. 329

White wins. Draw No. 329a with
Black King at KR2.

K at KR2, R at KB8, White to play wins. 1 R—K8!, R—QR8; 2 K—B8!, K—Kt3; 3 P—B7, K—B3; 4 R—QKt8, R—R3; 5 K—Kt8.

Cases with the RP and KtP would be essentially the same as those where the Black King is cut off, for all the difference is due to the position of the Black King on the long or short side of the Pawn and there is no such thing with the Pawn on the side of the board.

C. THE BLACK KING IS CUT OFF ON A RANK

In this case the Black King is behind the Pawn. As we saw in the positions where the Black King was to one side of the Pawn, if the

No. 330

No. 331

White to play wins; Black to play draws.

White to play wins; Black to play draws. Pawn on R5 always draws.

Pawn is on the fifth or beyond, the King can escort it to the eighth, but if not, the Black Rook can impede its forward march. Consequently the general rule that a Pawn on the fifth wins, but one on the fourth only draws, holds good here too.

The critical position, then, is No. 330. *1 P—B5, R—KB1; 2 K—K5, R—K1ch; 3 K—B6, R—QKt1* (or 3 .... R—B1ch; 4 K—Kt6, R—Kt1ch; 5 K—B7, etc.); *4 K—Kt6, R—Kt3ch; 5 P—B6, R—B3* (Black can do nothing to get a commutation of sentence); *6 K—Kt7, R—B2ch; 7 P—B7, R—Kt2; 8 K—Kt8*. Black to play checks until the White King is forced back and then attacks the P: *1 .... R—K1ch; 2 K—Q3* (2 K—B5, R—B1ch; 3 K—Kt5, R—Kt1ch; 4 K—R6, R—KB1; 5 R—R4, K—B6 is no better), *R—Q1ch; 3 K—B2, R—KB1; 4 R—R4, K—B6=.* Again, if the Rook is nearer, or if the King is further away, White will win. No. 330a, Black Rook at QKt2, other pieces as in No. 330. White wins. 1 .... R—K2ch;

2 K—Q5, R—KB2; 3 K—K5, R—K2ch; 4 K—B6, etc. And No. 330b, Black King at KKt8, other pieces as in No. 330. White wins. 1 .... R—K1ch; 2 K—Q5, R—KB1; 3 K—K5, R—K1ch; 4 K—Q6, R—KB1; 5 R—R4, K—B7; 6 K—K7!, R—B4; 7 K—K6, R—B1; 8 P—B5, etc.

With a RP these variations do not work because the White King cannot escape checks by hiding behind the Pawn. To have winning chances White's Pawn must be on the sixth and the Rook must be on the Kt file. No. 331 is a critical position. The simplest win is *1 P— R7, R—QR1;* (if 1 .... R—Kt8; 2 K—R5!, R—R8ch; 3 R—R4, or 2 .... R—Kt4ch; 3 R—Kt5, R—Kt8; 4 K—R6); *2 R—Kt7, K—B5; 3 K—R5, K—B4; 4 K—R6, K—B3; 5 R—Kt8.* Black to play draws by *1 .... R—Kt3; 2 R—Kt3ch* (2 K—R5, R×Pch), *K—B5; 3 R— Kt4ch, K—B6; 4 K—Kt5, R×P=.* With the Pawn on the fifth White cannot do better than draw because the Pawn cannot advance. E.g., No. 331a, White Pawn at QR5, other pieces as in No. 331, draw. 1 R—Kt6 (1 P—R6; R—Kt3 or 1 R—R4, R—Kt3=), R—Kt5ch (not 1 .... K—B5?; 2 R—B6ch, K—Q4; 3 K—Kt5, R—Kt8; 4 R— KR6, R—Kt8ch; 5 K—R6, R—Kt8; 6 K—Kt6, R—Kt8ch; 7 K—R7, K—B4; 8 P—R6, R—Kt7; 9 K—R8, R—Kt8; 10 P—R7, R—Kt7; 11 R—R8, K—B3; 12 R—B8ch, K—Q2; 13 R—Kt8, R—QR7; 14 K— Kt7 and wins: No. 320); 2 K—Kt5, R—Kt4ch; 3 K—R6, K—B5; 4 R—Kt1 (4 R—B6ch, K—Q4; 5 R—B1, R—Kt7, etc.), R—Kt3ch; 5 K—R7, R—Kt2ch; 6 R—Kt7, R—Kt8; 7 P—R6, K—B4; 8 R— Kt2, K—B3; 9 R—B2ch, K—Q2; 10 K—Kt7, R—Kt8ch=.

From the above we see that when White's King is in the corner, he can win only if Black's King is confined to the fourth rank.

A common case is that where the White Rook is on his seventh rank, the Black King on his third (i.e., cut off from the first) and the White King not confined to the R file. This is normally a draw if the Black King is on the K file or nearer unless the Pawn is on the seventh or can reach there without abandoning the control of the rank by the Rook. No. 332 occurred in the 16th match game Euwe-Alekhine, 1935 (the colors are reversed). Later analysis showed that this is a critical position. It is interesting to observe that despite its apparent simplicity, this ending was bungled by both sides. Alekhine played

No. 332

White to play wins; Black to play draws.

1 R—R7?, when 1 .... R—QR8!; 2 K—Kt6, K—Q3!; 3 P—R6, R—Kt8ch; 4 K—R7, K—B3 draws. Euwe actually replied 1 .... R—B8ch?, when after 2 K—Kt7!, R—Kt8ch; 3 K—B8, R—B8ch; 4 K—Kt8!, R—Kt8ch; 5 R—Kt7, R—QR8; 6 R—Kt6ch, K—Q4; 7 P—R6, K—B4; 8 K—Kt7, R—R8; 9 R—B6ch Black resigned. The correct play (Grigorieff) is *1 P—R6!, R—B8ch* (if 1 .... R—QR8; 2 R—R8 wins: 2 .... R—B8ch; 3 K—Kt5, R—Kt8ch; 4 K—B4, R—B8ch; 5 K—Kt3, R—QR8; 6 P—R7, K—Q2; 7 R—R8!, or 2 .... K—B2; 3 K—Kt6, R—Kt8ch; 4 K—R7, K—K2; 5 R—QKt8, etc. No. 320); *2 K—Kt7* with the following possibilities:

a) *2 .... R—Kt8ch; 3 K—B8, R—QR8; 4 R—R7, K—Q3; 5 P—R7, K—B3; 6 R—B7ch* (an amusing alternative which occurred in a problem of Ponziani's 150 years ago is 6 R—R6ch, K—B4; 7 K—Kt7, R—Kt8ch; 8 K—B7, R—QR8; 9 R—R5ch, K—B5; 10 K—Kt7, R—Kt8ch; 11 K—B6, R—QR8; 12 R—R4ch, K—B6; 13 K—Kt6, R—Kt8ch; 14 K—B5, R—QR8; 15 R—R3ch, K—B7; 16 R—R7, K—B6; 17 K—Kt6, K—B5; 18 R—R8.), *K—Kt3; 7 K—Kt8.*

b) *2 .... K—Q3; 3 K—Kt8, R—QR8; 4 R—KR7, R—Kt8ch; 5 R—Kt7, R—QR8; 6 P—R7.*

c) *2 .... K—Q4; 3 K—Kt8, R—QR8; 4 R—Q7ch, K—K3; 5 R—KR7, R—Kt8ch; 6 R—Kt7, etc.*

d) *2 .... K—Q2; 3 K—Kt8 dis ch, K—Q1!; 4 R—KR7, R—Kt8ch; 5 R—Kt7, R—QB8; 6 R—Kt2, R—B1ch; 7 K—Kt7, R—B2ch; 8 K—Kt6, K—B1; 9 R—KR2, K—Kt1; 10 R—R8ch, R—B1; 11 P—R7ch.*

e) *2 .... R—KR8; 3 R—R8, K—Q2; 4 P—R7, R—Kt8ch; 5 K—R6, R—R8ch; 6 K—Kt6!, R—Kt8ch; 7 K—B5!, R—B8ch; 8 K—Q4, R—Q8ch; 9 K—K3, R—K8ch; 10 K—B2, R—QR8; 11 R—R8!*

f) *2 .... R—QR8; 3 R—R8, K—Q3; 4 R—Q8ch!, K—K2; 5 R—Q5, R—Kt8ch; 6 K—B6, R—QR8; 7 K—Kt6, K—K3; 8 R—QR5, R—Kt8ch; 9 R—Kt5.*

Black to play can draw in the diagrammed position by the odd tempo: *1 .... R—B8ch; 2 K—Kt7, K—Q2!; 3 K—Kt8 dis ch, K—Q1; 4 R—KR7* (or 4 P—R6, R—B1ch; 5 K—Kt7, R—B2ch; 6 K—Kt6, R×R; 7 K×R, K—B2), *R—QR8!; 5 R—R5, R—Kt8ch; 6 K—R7, K—B2=.* (No. 320).

As a rule, it is worse for the defense to be cut off on a rank than on a file. If the Black King cannot get in front of the Pawn, a win may be possible even with the Pawn on the third rank. The critical position with the KtP is No. 333 (Grigorieff, 1937). The win is *1 K—R3 R—R1ch* (1 .... K—B6; 2 R—B5ch, K—Q5; 3 P—Kt4); *2 K—Kt4,*

R—Kt1ch (or 2 .... K—Q6; 3 R—R5, R—Kt1ch; 4 K—R4); *3 K— R4, R—R1ch; 4 R—R5, R—QB1; 5 P—Kt4, K—B5* (if 5 .... R—B8; 6 R—R5, R—R8ch; 7 K—Kt5, R—R1; 8 K—B6); *6 R—R7, K—Q4; 7 P—Kt5, K—B4; 8 K—R5, K—Q3; 9 P—Kt6, K—B3; 10 K—R6, K—Q3; 11 R—R7, R—R1ch; 12 K—Kt7, R—R8; 13 R—QB7* with a standard win (No. 308). Black to play holds everything with *1* .... *R—QR1!; 2 R—QKt5* (2 P—Kt4, K—B5), *R—R2; 3 R—Kt8, K— B4!*, etc.

No. 333

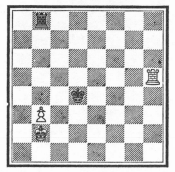

No. 334

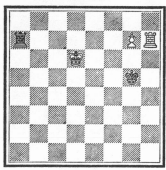

White to play wins; Black to play draws. Always win with Black King at Q6.

White wins.

C1. THE BLACK KING IS BEHIND THE PAWN, BUT NOT DIRECTLY CUT OFF

This is the analogue of B1, but the results are different. There is nothing resembling the case of the "long" and "short" sides of the Pawn, but there are certain other special features which are worth considering.

When the Pawn is on the seventh the trap exemplified in No. 334 is worth watching for. The threat is of course P—Kt8=Q (the fact that the Pawn queens with check is of no real importance, since Q vs. R is a theoretical win). Against the only plausible defense *1* .... *R— R3ch* (1 .... R—R1; 2 R—R8); White continues *2 K—Q5!!, R— KKt3; 3 K—K5!!!*, when Black is in zugzwang: *3* .... *K—Kt5; 4 R— R1!, K—Kt4; 5 R—Kt1ch, K—R3; 6 R×Rch.* It is always bad to try to stop a passed Pawn from the side.

With the Pawn on the sixth the trap No. 335, pointed out by Kling

and Horwitz in 1851, must be noted. The saving clause is *1 .... R—
Kt3!!; 2 P—K7* (if instead 2 R—KR8, R×P!; 3 R—R5ch, K—Kt5,
while on 2 R—K7 Black merely tempoes on the rank), *R—B3ch;
3 K—Kt7, R—Kt3ch; 4 K—R7* (4 K—R8, R—R3ch), *K—B3!!* (the
point); *5 R—B8ch* (else 5 .... R—Kt2ch and 6 .... R×P), *K×P=*.
When the Pawn is on the Q file, or further "west," this combination

No. 335   No. 336

 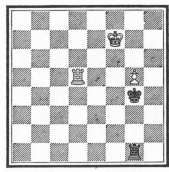

Black to play draws. Win with Pawn   Black to play draws. Win with Pawn
         on the Q-file.   on B or center files.

does not work because the White Rook has more room. No. 335a,
White: K at K7, R at Q8, P at Q6; Black: K at K4, R at QR4.
White wins. 1 .... R—R3; 2 R—KR8!! (but not 2 P—Q7?, R—
K3ch; 3 K—B7, R—B3ch; 4 K—Kt7, K—K3=), R×P (2 .... R—
R2ch; 3 P—Q7 is hopeless: there follows simply 4 K—K8); 3 R—R5ch,
K any; 4 K×R.

With the Pawn on the fifth there is a different type of trap, shown
in No. 336. Here the catch comes after *1 .... K—R4!; 2 P—Kt6 dis
ch* (or 2 K—B6, R—Kt7; 3 R—Q1, R—B7ch), *K—R3; 3 R—Q6*
(again if 3 R—Q2, R—B8ch, while 3 R—B5 is of course answered by
3 .... R×P), *R—Kt7; 4 R—B6.* Now Black is faced by the apparently irresistible attack beginning with 4 R—B1—but he has something up his sleeve. *4 .... R—Kt4!; 5 R—B1, R—B4ch!!; 6 R×R,*
stalemate!!! With a center or B Pawn there is no stalemate and consequently no defense. E.g., No. 336a, White: K at K7, R at QB5,
P at KB5; Black: K at KB5, R at KB8. White wins. 1 .... K—
Kt4; 2 P—B6 dis ch, K—Kt3; 3 R—B6, R—B7; 4 R—K6, R—B8
(now 4 .... R—B4; 5 R—K1 leads to nothing, since 5 .... R—K4ch;
6 R×R is brilliant but useless); 5 R—K2, R×P; 6 R—Kt2 ch and
wins.

With the Pawn on the fourth Black can only draw if his Rook is on
the first rank, so that it can drive the White King away. An example
is No. 337 (Rabinovitch) which, as we have seen (No. 330) would be
a draw with the Black Rook at QKt1. Now White can win as follows:
1 .... R—Kt1 (or 1 .... R—Kt5; 2 K—R5!, R—Kt1; 3 P—Kt5);
*2 R—R3ch, K—K5; 3 K—R6!, K—B5; 4 P—Kt5, R—R1ch; 5 K—
Kt7* and wins. With the Pawn on the third Black can get to No. 330.
E.g., No. 337a, White: K at KKt4, R at QR1, P at KKt3; Black:
K at KB7, R at QKt7. Draw. 1 .... R—Kt1; 2 R—R2ch, K—K6;
3 R—R5, K—B7; 4 R—KKt5, K—Kt7!; 5 K—R5, R—R1ch=.
White to play cannot improve his position: e.g., 1 R—R4, R—Kt1;

No. 337	No. 338

White wins. Draw with similar position and Pawn on the third rank.	White to play wins; Black to play draws.

2 K—R3, R—R1ch; 3 R—R4, R—KKt1; 4 R—B4ch, K—K6, etc.=.

Where the White King is not directly near the Pawn, the problem is
always one of transposing back into the standard positions. Thus in
the critical position No. 338 (Salvioli, 1887) White wins by *1 K—
Kt4!, R—B1* (if 1 .... R—B8; 2 R—Q5, K—B5; 3 R—Q8, R—B8;
4 P—K5, etc., or 1 .... R—K7; 2 K—B5, K—B4; 3 K—K6ch, K—
Q5; 4 P—K5, K—B4; 5 K—K7—No. 330, or 1 .... R—Q7; 2 K—B5,
K—B4; 3 K—K6 dis ch, K—B3; 4 R—Q5!, R—KR7; 5 R—Q1, R—
R3ch; 6 K—B5, R—R4ch; 7 K—B6, R—R3ch; 8 K—Kt5, R—K3;
9 K—B5, R—K1; 10 P—K5 and wins—No. 309); *2 R—Q5!, K—B5;
3 R—Q6!, R—Kt1ch; 4 K—B5, R—B1ch; 5 R—B6!, R—Q1; 6 R—
B7!, K—Q5; 7 P—K5, K—Q4; 8 P—K6, K—Q3; 9 K—B6, R—QR1;
10 R—Q7ch, K—B3; 11 R—Q1* and wins—No. 309. The variation is
essentially the same as that of No. 333.

D. THE WHITE ROOK IS IN FRONT OF THE PAWN

This type of position normally occurs where both Kings are at a distance, so that the Pawn has to be defended by the Rook. The best place for the Black Rook to be is then behind the Pawn, because this preserves his freedom of action.

When the Pawn is on the seventh White can win only in the special case where he can remove his Rook with check or the threat of check. This is illustrated in No. 339. White to play can do nothing, for if he gets his King to QKt7 the Black Rook checks him until he leaves the neighborhood of the Pawn. But if the Black King is not on a

No. 339   No. 340

Draw. Black to play loses only if his King is beyond the heavy line.   White to play wins; Black to play draws.

safe square, the White Rook will be able to leave R8 with check, and then queen the Pawn. Or, with the Black King at K2, 1 R—R8 follows, when 1 .... R×P; 2 R—R7ch wins the Rook. The fact that we have a RP here makes no difference whatsoever. On the contrary, any other Pawn would be much less promising because the Black King is then so much nearer. Unlike the similar ending where there are more Pawns on the board, the Black King cannot hide behind his rival here. E.g., No. 339a (Troitzky, 1896), White: K at KKt4, R at QR8, P at QR7; Black: K at KKt7, R at QR8. White wins. 1 K—B4 (threatening R—Kt8ch), K—B7 (hide-and-go-seek on the chess board); 2 K—K4, K—K7; 3 K—Q4, K—Q7; 4 K—B5, K—B6 (if 4 .... R—B8ch; 5 K—Kt4, R—Kt8ch; 6 K—R3, R—R8ch; 7 K—Kt2 and wins); 5 R—QB8!!, R×P; 6 K—Kt6 dis ch.

With the Pawn further back we have either a horse race to see who gets there first, or a transposition into some other case. No. 340 is a critical position. White to play continues *1 K—B4, K—Kt3; 2 K— K5, K—B2; 3 K—Q6, R—Kt7; 4 K—B6, K—K2; 5 R—R8, R—B7ch; 6 K—Kt7, K—Q2; 7 R—R1, R—Q7; 8 R—QB1* (No. 309). It would be a fatal mistake to advance the Pawn here, e.g., 3 P—Kt7?? (instead of 3 K—Q6), K—Kt2!! (not 3 .... K—K2?; 4 R—KR8) and draws as in No. 339. Black to play can get to the Pawn in time: *1 .... K— Kt3; 2 K—B4, K—B3; 3 K—K4* (3 P—Kt7, K—Kt2 and the White King will never be able to approach.), *K—K3; 4 P—Kt7* (or 4 K—Q4, K—Q3; 5 K—B4, K—B3, or 4 R—KR8, K—Q3!; 5 R—R6ch, K—B4 or even 4 .... K—Q2; 5 K—Q5, R—Kt7; 6 K—B5, R—Kt8; 7 R—KR8, R—Kt7 and White still cannot win), *K—Q2!* (of course not 4 .... K—B2; 5 R—KR8); *5 K—Q5* (or 5 R—KR8, R×P; 6 R—R7ch, K—B3), *K—B2=*.

With a RP the case is somewhat different, again because of the threat of a series of checks. The critical position No. 341 is one which at first sight seems such more favorable for White than the corresponding case with the KtP because the Black King is confined to the first rank. White to play wins in an unusual manner: *1 K—K2!* (not 1 K— K3?, R—K8ch; 2 K—Q4, R—K3=), *K—Kt1* (or 1 .... R—R6; 2 K—Q2, K—Kt1; 3 K—B2, K—B1; 4 K—Kt2, R—R4; 5 R—R8ch, K—Kt2; 6 K—Kt3, R—KB4; 7 R—QKt8, R—QR4; 8 R—Kt6, K— B2; 9 K—Kt4, R—R8; 10 K—Kt5, K—K2; 11 K—B6 and wins. Or 1 .... R—R4; 2 K—Q3, R—Q4ch; 3 K—B4, R—Q3; 4 K—Kt5, or finally 1 .... R—KR8; 2 R—Kt7, R—R8; 3 P—R7, R—R6; 4 R— Kt8ch); *2 K—Q3, K—B1* (2 .... R—Q8ch; 3 K—B4, R—B8ch; 4 K—Kt5, R—Kt8ch; 5 K—B6, R—B8ch; 6 K—Kt6, R—Kt8ch; 7 K—B7, R—B8ch; 8 K—Kt8, R—QR8; 9 R—R8!, K—Kt2; 10 K— Kt7, R—Kt8ch; 11 K—R7 and wins—No. 320); *3 R—R8ch, K—Kt2; 4 K—B4, R—KB8; 5 R—K8!, R— QR8; 6 K—Kt5, K—B2; 7 R—K4* and we have transposed into No. 320. Black to play can draw in a variety of ways, of which the simplest is *1 .... R—R4!; 2 K—K3, R—K4ch; 3 K—Q4, R—K3; 4 K —Q5, R—KB3; 5 K—B5, K—Kt1; 6 K—Kt5, R—B4ch; 7 K—B6, R —B3ch; 8 K—B7, R—B2ch; 9 K— Kt8, R—B1ch,* etc. White's King must leave the neighborhood of the Pawn.

The best position for the Black Rook is behind the Pawn. To guard the Pawn from the side is

No. 341

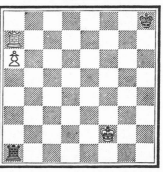

White to play wins; Black to play draws.

bad because the Rook does not cover the queening square. The threat of getting the White Rook out with check is then so strong that both Black pieces are tied up and the White King can approach. An example is No. 342 (Grigorieff, 1934). The threat of R—Q8ch is decisive. *1 .... R—B2ch* (1 .... R—Q2; 2 K—K4, R—K2ch; 3 K—Q4, R—Q2; 4 K—B4, R—B2ch; 5 K—Kt5); *2 K—K3!* (but not 2 K—K4?, R—Q2! when Black can draw!!: 3 K—K3, K—Q4!; 4 K—B4, R—B2ch, etc., or 3 K—B4, K—Q4; 4 K—B5, R—B2ch; 5 K—Kt6, R—Q2!; 6 K—B6, K—Q3! etc.), *R—Q2; 3 K—K4* (now Black is in zugzwang again), *R—K2ch; 4 K—Q4, R—Q2* (4 .... K—K3; 5 K—B5, K—K4; 6 K—B6, K—K3; 7 K—

No. 342   No. 343

White wins.   White to play wins; Black to play draws.

Kt6); *5 K—B4, R—B2ch; 6 K—Kt5!, R—Q2; 7 K—Kt6* and now Black is defenseless against the removal of the White Rook.

E. THE WHITE ROOK IS BEHIND THE PAWN

Of course there are winning chances here only when the Black Rook is blockading the Pawn. There are few finesses: the win or draw depends on who gets there first. No. 343 (Seyburth, 1899) is a critical position. After *1 K—Q6, K—Kt4; 2 K—B7, K—B4; 3 K—Kt7* it is all over. Black to play can hold everything by an ingenious defense: *1 .... K—B4!; 2 K—Q7, K—Kt3; 3 R—Kt1ch!, K—B4!!* (not 3 .... K×P?; 4 K—B7 when White wins. Or 3 .... K—R3?; 4 K—B7!, R×Pch; 5 K—B6! and again the threat of mate is fatal); *4 R—Kt7, R—KR1!!* (the Black defense is not easy: if here 4 .... K—Q4?; 5 R—Kt5ch, K—B5; 6 R—QR5, K—Kt5; 7 R—R1, K—Kt4; 8 K—B7 wins); *5 K—B7, R—R1!* (if 5 .... R—R2ch; 6 K—B8, R—R1ch;

7 K—Q7, R—R1! is still all right, but not 7 .... R—R2ch?; 8 K—K6, R—R1; 9 R—Kt8); *6 K—Q7, R—R1!* Draw.

III. ROOK AND TWO PAWNS VS. ROOK

Just as in the simpler cases with B's and Kt's this is normally a win, but, as usual, there are a number of exceptions. We must distinguish the three possible combinations of the Pawns.

A. CONNECTED PAWNS

Connected Pawns always win unless they are blockaded. The only case which presents any real difficulty is that of the KtP+RP, partly because of the lack of hide-outs for the White King, and partly because of the threat of stalemate when the Pawns reach the seventh. The model win is shown in No. 344 (Zukertort-Steinitz, London, 1883. Of course, it might just as well have been taken from one of a dozen other games.). White must take care to advance his Pawns cautiously in order to avoid either an unpleasant blockade or an annoying series of checks. *1 R—QKt8, K—Kt3* (on R checks the White King gets to KR4); *2 R—Kt5, R—QB6; 3 R—K5!* (not 3 P—R4 at once because of the checks, when White has no good flight square), *R—R6; 4 P—R4* (if now 4 .... R—R7ch; 5 K—B3, R—R6ch; 6 R—K3), *R—QKt6; 5 P—R5ch, K—R3; 6 R—KB5* (preparing the entry of his King), *R—QR6; 7 R—B3, R—R8; 8 K—Kt3, R—Kt8ch* (the best chance: if the Rook stays on the R file the Pawns advance more easily. E.g., 8 .... R—R7; 9 R—B6ch, K—Kt2; 10 P—Kt5, R—R5; 11 P—R6ch, K—R2; 12 R—B4, R—R4; 13 K—Kt4, etc.); *9 K—R4, R—R8ch; 10 R—R3, R—KKt8; 11 R—R2!* (Black is in zugzwang), *R—QR8; 12 P—Kt5ch, K—Kt2;*

No. 344

13 R—KB2!, R—R8ch; 14 K—Kt4, R—Kt8ch; 15 K—B5, R—KR8; 16 P—R6ch, K—R2; 17 R—B4! (the most systematic. An alternative is 17 P—Kt6ch, K×P; 18 K—B6, K—R4; 19 P—Kt7, R—KKt8; 20 R—R2ch. But 17 .... K—Kt1 gets back to the main variation), *R—KKt8; 18 R—K4!, R—B8ch; 19 K—Kt4, R—Kt8ch; 20 K—R5, R—R8ch; 21 R—R4, R—KKt8; 22 R—R2!* (again Black is in zugzwang), *R—Kt6; 23 R—K2, R—R6ch; 24 K—Kt4, R—R6; 25 R —K7ch, K—Kt1; 26 P—Kt6, R—*

White wins.

R5ch; 27 K—B5, R—R4ch; 28 R—K5, R—R1. This position can be won in various ways, of which the safest is leaving the Pawns intact and exchanging Rooks. *29 K—B6, R—R3ch; 30 R—K6, R—R1; 31 R—Q6, R—K1; 32 R—Q5, R—R1; 33 K—K7, R—R2ch; 34 R—Q7, R—R1; 35 R—Q8ch* and the rest is simple.

As long as one remembers the two principles that the Pawns must not be blockaded and that there must always be a safety square for the King (or a method of avoiding checks) one cannot go wrong here.

A variant which often arises is that where the King is at a distance, and the Rook must defend the Pawns. This can only be done with the R on the R file, so that there may be some difficulty extricating it. But the win is always possible. E.g., No. 344a, White: K at QKt3, R at KR6, P's at KKt6, KR5; Black: K at KKt2, R at KKt5. White to play wins. 1 R—R7ch, K—Kt1 (or A); 2 K—B3, R—KR5: 3 K—Q3, R—KKt5; 4 K—K3, R—KR5; 5 K—B3, R—QKt5; 6 K—Kt3, R—QR5; 7 K—K7, R—R6ch; 8 K—Kt4, R—R5ch; 9 K—Kt5, R—R4ch; 10 K—B6, R—R1; 11 P—R6 and we have No. 334. A. For 1 .... K—B3 see No. 344c.

Another type of problem which may occur is that where the White King cannot find a haven without blockading his Pawns. Sometimes this problem is insoluble (No. 350) and White cannot win. Usually, however, if the Pawns are not blockaded, a way out can be found. E.g., No. 344b (Chess Players' Chronicle, 1872–73), White: K at QB7, R at Q5, P's at QR5, QKt5; Black: K at QR2, R at QKt8. The trouble here is not only that any Pawn advance would be bad, but also that the King cannot easily get out of the way to let the Rook hold the Pawns (as in No. 344a). The only solution is 1 .... R—B8ch; 2 K—Q6!, K—Kt2 (if 2 .... R—QR8; 3 K—B6!!, R×P; 4 P—Kt6ch wins, while 3 .... R—B8ch is refuted by 4 R—B5, R—KR8; 5 R—B4! followed by K—B5—Kt4); 3 R—Q4, R—QR8; 4 K—B5!!, R×P (else 5 R—Q7ch); 5 R—Q7ch, K—B1; 6 R—KR7, R—R8; 7 K—Kt6, R—QKt8; 8 R—R8ch, K—Q2; 9 R—QKt8! and wins.

Still another difficulty that comes up is that where the Pawns are stopped by the combined efforts of the enemy K and R. In such cases the win again involves holding the Pawns with the Rook and approaching with the King. E.g., No. 344c (Thomas-Alekhine, Hastings, 1922), White: K at KB3, R at KKt7; Black: K at QB3, R at KR7, P's at KKt6, KR5. For the time being Black cannot push either Pawn, nor is it at once clear just how the King can approach. Still, the method chosen by Alekhine is a forced win. 1 R—Kt6ch, K—Q4; 2 R—Kt7, K—Q5; 3 R—Kt8, K—Q6; 4 R—Q8ch, K—B6; 5 R—KKt8, K—Q7; 6 R—QR8!, R—B7ch!; 7 K—Kt4, P—Kt7; 8 R—R1!, K—K6! (8 .... R—B8??; 9 R—R2ch and 10 R×P=); 9 K—R3, R—K7!; 10 R—KKt1 (10 R—R3ch, K—B7. If 10 K—R2, K—B7;

11 R—KKt1, P—R6 as in the game), K—B6; 11 K—R2, P—R6; 12 R—QR1 (White resigned here. On 12 K×P, R—K1!; 13 K—R4, R—R1ch; 14 K—Kt5, R—R8 forces the win), K—B7; 13 R—QKt1, R—K8; 14 R—Kt2ch (14 R×R, K×R; 15 K—Kt1, K—K7, etc.), K—K6; 15 R—Kt3ch, K—Q5; 16 R—Kt4ch, K—B4; 17 R—Kt4, R—R8ch and wins.

When the Pawns are blockaded by the King, the game is usually a draw. An exception occurs when one Pawn is on the seventh. Thus No. 345 (Kling and Horwitz, 1851) is won, but if the Pawns were on the fifth and sixth the game would be drawn. Here the win is *1 K—*

<table>
<tr><td align="center">No. 345</td><td align="center">No. 346</td></tr>
<tr><td>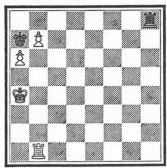</td><td>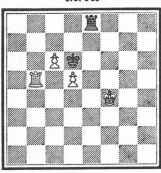</td></tr>
<tr><td align="center">White wins. Draw with Pawns on
5th and 6th.</td><td align="center">White wins.</td></tr>
</table>

R5, R—R4ch; 2 R—Kt5, R—R1; 3 R—Kt6! (the R must not leave the Kt file yet: if 3 R—B5?, R—R3! draws), *R—R4ch; 4 K—Kt4, R—R5ch; 5 K—B5, R—R4ch; 6 K—Q4, R—R5ch; 7 K—K5, R—R4ch; 8 K—B4, R—R5ch; 9 K—Kt5, R—R1; 10 R—QB6!!* (the winning move), *K—Kt1* (the threat was 11 R—B8); *11 K—Kt6, R—KB1; 12 K—Kt7, R—Q1; 13 K—B7, R—R1; 14 K—K7, R—R2ch; 15 K—Q6, R—R3ch; 16 K—B5, R—R4ch; 17 K—Kt6, R—R1; 18 P—R7* mate.

Black may draw with R vs. R+2P for one of three reasons: blockade, stalemate, bad position of the White Rook.

a) Blockade.

If neither Pawn has reached the sixth this is always a draw; but if one is on the sixth and the other on the fifth, a win is possible provided there are no RP's.

The two main cases are shown in the adjoining two diagrams. In No. 346 (Cheron, 1926) White wins by getting his King to (*R8!!* The solution is *1 .... R—K8* (relatively best. The alternatives are:

a) 1 .... R—K2; 2 R—Kt7
b) 1 .... R—K4; 2 P—B7!, R—K1; 3 R—Kt8
c) 1 .... R—K7; 2 R—Kt8!, R—B7ch; 3 K—K3, R—B2; 4 R—Kt7!, R×R; 5 P×R, K—B2; 6 K—K4, K×P; 7 K—K5, K—B2; 8 K—K6, K—Q1; 9 K—Q6.
d) 1 .... R—QR1; 2 K—K4, R—R5ch; 3 K—Q3, R—R1; 4 K—B4, R—R1; 5 R—Kt7, R—R5ch; 6 K—Kt5, K×P; 7 R—Q7ch); *2 R—Kt8!!, R—B8ch* (2 .... K×P; 3 P—B7, or 2 .... R—

No. 347

Draw.

No. 348

Draw. Win with White King at QB6.

QB8; 3 R—Q8ch); *3 K—Kt5, R—Kt8ch; 4 K—B5, R—B8ch; 5 K—Kt6, R—Kt8ch; 6 K—B7, R—B8ch; 7 K—K8, R—K8ch; 8 K—Q8, R—KR8; 9 K—B8!, R—R2* (if 9 .... K×P; 10 R—Kt6!!, K—B4; 11 K—Kt7, R—R3; 12 R—Kt1 and wins, but not 10 P—B7??, K—B3!; 11 K—Q8, R—R1ch; 12 K—K7, R—R2ch=); *10 R—Kt5, R—KKt2; 11 K—Kt8, R—KR2; 12 K—R8!, R—R8* (or 12 .... R—R1ch; 13 R—Kt8, or 12 .... R—KKt2; 13 R—Kt7, R—Kt1ch; 14 R—Kt8); *13 R—Kt8!, R—R8ch: 14 K—Kt7, R—Kt8ch; 15 K—B8, R—QB8* (to prevent P—B7); *16 R—Kt7, K×P; 17 P—B7, K—B3; 18 K—Kt8* and wins.

That this is not possible with a RP is due to the fact that in the R+P vs. R ending, a RP forms an exception to the ordinary rules. Thus in No. 347 (Cheron, 1926) after *1 K—B8, R—KKt2; 2 R—Q7, R—Kt1ch; 3 R—Q8, R—Kt2; 4 K—Kt8!* (4 R—Q6ch, K×P; 5 K—

Kt8, R—Kt1ch=), *R—KR2; 5 R—Q6ch!* (or 5 R—K8, R—KKt2;
6 R—K6ch, K×P!; 7 P—R7, R—Kt1ch=. If now 5 .... K×P?;
6 P—R7, R—R1ch; 7 K—B7, R—R2ch; 8 R—Q7 wins), *K—B4!!!;*
6 P—Kt6 (if 6 R—K6, K×P!; 7 P—R7, R—R1ch; 8 K—B2, R—
R2ch; 9 K—Kt8, R—R1ch=, while if 6 P—R7 then simply 6 ....
K×R; 7 P—R8=Q, R—R1ch; 8 K—Kt7, R×Q; 9 K×R, K—B4),
K×R; 7 K—R8, R—R1ch!; 8 K—R7, K—B3; 9 P—Kt7, K—B2;
10 P—Kt8= Qch, R×Q stalemate!

In other cases it is essential to prevent the chief winning attempt of
the sacrifice of one Pawn to force a won R+P vs. R ending. Thus
No. 348 is drawn by keeping the Rook on the Q file and shutting the
White King out of the K-side. The only possibility is *1 R—R8,*
K×P; 2 P—Kt5, R—QKt8; 3 R—QKt8, K—B5; 4 P—Kt6, K—
Kt4!! (but not 4 .... K—B4??; 5 R—B8ch!!, K—Kt4; 6 P—Kt7
and wins); *5 K—Q6, K—R3; 6 K—B7, R—B8ch; 7 K—Q7, R—B7=.*
With the White King at QB6, the advance of the KtP is secured by a
sacrifice. No. 348a, WK at QB6, other pieces as in No. 348. White
wins. 1 .... R—KKt8; 2 R—R4ch, K×P; 3 P—Kt5, etc.

b) Stalemate.

This defense is seen chiefly with the RP, and is one of the reasons
why that ending is so much more difficult than the corresponding one
with center Pawns. All the important points are seen in No. 349 (Horwitz, 1881). The draw is held by *1 .... R—R3!!; 2 K—Kt6* (2 R×R
stalemate), *R—Kt3* (not 2 .... R×Rch?; 3 K×R!, K×P; 4 K—B7!,
K—R1; 5 K—Kt6 and wins); *3 K—R5, R—Kt4* (again 3 .... R×R?
loses after 4 P×R, K×P; 5 K—Kt5, K—R1; 6 K—R6, K—Kt1;
7 K—Kt6); *4 R—KR6* (if 4 R—B7, R×Pch!; 5 K—R6, R—Kt3ch!),

R—R4; 5 K—Kt4, R—R5ch; 6 K—
B3, R—R6ch; 7 K—K4, R—R5ch;
8 K—Q3, R—KKt5; 9 P—Kt6, R—
Kt8 and White cannot win because
there is no haven in the neighborhood of the Pawns. The only
win for White besides those mentioned comes after 2 .... R—Q3?
(instead of 2 .... R—Kt3); 3 K—
B7!, R—Q2ch; 4 K—K6, R—R2;
5 P—Kt6 and now that the stalemate threat is lifted White wins:
5 .... R—R1; 6 K—B5, K—Kt2;
7 R—B7ch, K—R1; 8 K—Kt5,
R—R4ch; 9 R—B5!, R—R1; 10 K
—R6, R—R3; 11 R—B8 mate.

No. 349

Black to play draws.

A somewhat different stalemate may occur with the Pawns further back. E.g., No. 349a, White: K at KB3, R at Q7, P's at K6, KB5; Black: K at KB3, R at QR5. Black to play draws. 1 .... R—B5ch!!; 2 K—K3 (2 K×R stalemate), R×P; 3 P—K7, R—K4ch, etc. If here 1 .... K×P??; 2 P—K7, R—R1 (or 2 .... R—R6ch; 3 K—K2, R—R7ch; 4 R—Q2); 3 R—Q8 and White wins.

c) The White Rook Is Badly Placed.

This occurs only in conjunction with Pawns on the same rank, i.e., Pawns which are not defending one another. The chief type is seen

No. 350   No. 351

White to play. Draw.   White wins.

in No. 350. *1 R—Kt6ch, K—R2* does White no good, because the King still cannot approach. As soon as it gets near the Pawns it is checked away. The similar case with center Pawns would be won because the White King could escape to one side or the other.

B. DISCONNECTED PAWNS

This too is generally a fairly simple win. The idea is the same as that in the similar cases with B's and Kt's discussed earlier: one Pawn is sacrificed to force one of the winning positions with R+P vs. R.

No. 351 may be taken as the general case. The most difficult continuation for White is *1 .... R—Kt1; 2 R—B4ch, K—Q4; 3 P—Kt4, K—B4; 4 K—Q3, K—Q4; 5 P—B4ch, K—K4; 6 R—K4ch, K—Q3* (if the K goes to the K-side, K—B3 will win); *7 K—K3, K—B3; 8 K—B4, R—B1ch; 9 K—Kt3, R—KKt1; 10 R—K5, K—Q3; 11 R—KB5, K—K3; 12 P—B5, R—Kt2; 13 K—B4, R—QR2; 14 R—K5ch, K—Q2; 15 P—Kt5, K—B3; 16 K—B5* and now that the Pawns are on the fifth the QBP is of no importance. White sacrifices it and wins by advancing his KKtP (No. 309).

When the Pawns are close together the same method prevails, except for the case of the RP+BP discussed below. E.g., No. 351a (Ercole Del Rio, 1831), White: K at Q3, R at QR4, P's at Q4, KB4; Black: K at K3, R at Q3. White wins. 1 .... K—B4; 2 R—R8, K×P; 3 R—B8ch, K—Kt4; 4 K—K4, R—K3ch; 5 K—Q5, R—K8; 6 K—Q6, R—Q8; 7 P—Q5, etc.

Black can draw against two RP's and against RP+BP. With other Pawns he can draw only in special cases, chiefly when the White Rook is immobilized.

a) RP+BP.

This ending has been notorious ever since the famous game Marshall-Rubinstein, San Sebastian, 1911, although it had already occurred in a game Steinitz-Blackburne, Vienna, 1898. The drawing idea is simply this: White cannot hold on to both Pawns if he wishes to try to win, but must sacrifice one of them to divert the Black King. It stands to reason that he will sacrifice the RP. But we have already seen that R+BP vs. R is a draw when the Black King is on the edge of the board (No. 329a) except for one special position. Consequently Black need only avoid this special position (No. 329b) to draw.

The best continuation for both sides may begin from No. 352 (Schlechter-Tarrasch, Cologne, 1911). *1 R—K3* (threatening to exchange Rooks), *K—B3; 2 R—KKt3, R—QR8; 3 K—Kt4, R—R1; 4 R—Kt3* (or 4 P—R4), *R—Kt1ch; 5 K—B3, R—Kt8; 6 R—Kt8, R—B8ch; 7 K—Kt4, R—Kt8ch; 8 K—R5, K—B2!* (in the game there occurred the inferior 8 .... R—Kt2; when 9 R—B8ch, K—K2; 10 R—B5, K—K3; 11 R—KKt5, R—R2ch??; 12 K—Kt6, R×P; 13 R—K5ch won (No. 329). 11 .... R—KB2! would still have saved everything: 12 K—Kt4, R—QR2; 13 P—R4, R—R8; 14 R—Kt6ch, K—B2; 15 R—Kt6, K—Kt2!; 16 K—B5, R—R4ch; 17 K—Kt4, R—R8; 18 K—Kt5, R—Kt8ch; 19 K—R5, R—KB8, etc., as in the main variation. A trap to be avoided here is 11 .... R—KB2; 12 K—Kt4, R—QR2; 13 P—R4, R—R8; 14 R—Kt6ch, K—B2; 15 R—Kt6, R—R2?; 16 K—Kt5, R—R4ch; 17 P—B5, R—R2; 18 P—R5, K—Kt2; 19 P—

No. 352

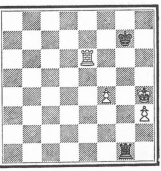

Draw!

R6ch, K—R2; 20 R—K6, R—QKt2; 21 R—K5!, R—R2; 22 P—B6, R—R8; 23 R—K7ch, K—Kt1; 24 P—R7ch, K—R1; 25 P—B7 and wins.); *9 R—Kt6, K—Kt2; 10 P—R4, K—B2* (Black must take care to keep the White Pawns and King as far back as possible. Another trap comes up after 10 .... R—KB8; 11 K—Kt5, R—Kt8ch; 12 K—B5, R—KR8; 13 R—Kt6ch, K—R2?—13 .... K—B2! is correct—; 14 R—Kt4, K—R3?; 15 K—B6, K—R4??—15 .... R—R8 is essential and was still good enough. Now Black is lost—; 16 R—KKt8!, R—QR8; 17 R—QB8!, K×P; 18 P—B5, R—R3ch; 19 K—Kt7, R—R2ch; 20 K—Kt6 and wins); *11 R—Kt5, K—B3; 12 R—Kt5, R—KB8; 13 R—Kt6ch, K—B2!* (if 13 .... K—B4; 14 R—Kt8 and the King will be driven to the wrong side of the Pawn); *14 R—Kt4, R—QR8* (we are now following the Marshall-Rubinstein game with colors reversed. If here 14 .... K—B3; 15 K—R6, K—B4?; 16 R—Kt8! drives Black's King away from the all-important squares B2 and B3); *15 K—Kt5* (if instead 15 K—R6, R—R3ch!!; 16 K—R7, R—KB3!!!; 17 P—R5, K—B1; 18 P—R6, K—B2; 19 R—R4, K—B1; 20 K—R8, K—B2; 21 P—R7, K—B1, etc.=. The BP plays no significant part at all in the proceedings here, since it hampers White's Rook as well as Black's), *R—R1!* (obstructing the threatened advance of the BP. However, 15 .... R—R4ch was a good alternative: 16 P—B5, R—R8!; 17 P—R5, K—Kt2!; 18 P—R6ch, K—R2; 19 R—K4, R—Kt8ch; 20 K—B6, R—QR8!; 21 R—K8, R—R7!—not A—; 22 K—B7, K×P; 23 P—B6, R—R2ch; 24 R—K7, R—R1=. No. 329a. A. 21 .... R—R3ch?; 22 K—Kt5, R—R2; 23 R—K5!, R—Kt2; 24 P—B6, K—Kt1; 25 K—Kt6, R—Kt1; 26 R—K7 and wins); *16 P—R5, K—Kt2; 17 R—Kt1* (Rubinstein tried 17 P—R6ch, but after 17 .... K—R2!; 18 K—R5, R—KB1!!!; 19 R—R4—or A—, R—KKt1!; 20 P—B5, R—Kt8; 21 R—B4, R—R8ch; 22 K—Kt5, R×P; 23 P—B6, R—Kt3ch; 24 K—B5, R—Kt8; agreed to a draw. A. 19 R—Kt7ch, K—R1; 20 K—Kt5, R—B4ch!; 21 K—Kt6, R—B3ch, etc.=), *R—R4ch; 18 K—Kt4, R—R7!* (The Black King is happy where he is and sees no reason for moving. Inferior would be 18 .... K—R3?; 19 R—Kt1!, R—R3; 20 R—Kt4, R—QB3; 21 R—K4!, R—R3; 22 P—B5, R—R8; 23 P—B6!!, R—Kt8ch; 24 K—B5, R—B8ch; 25 K—K6, K×P; 26 P—B7, K—Kt3; 27 R—Kt4ch, K—R2; 28 R—Kt8 and wins. Or here 23 .... R—R1; 24 K—B5, R—R4ch; 25 K—K6, R—R3ch; 26 K—K7, R—R2ch; 27 K—B8, K×P; 28 P—B7, K—Kt3; 29 R—KB4!, R—R1ch; 30 K—K7, R—R2ch; 31 K—K6, etc.); *19 R—Kt1, R—Kt7ch; 20 K—B5, R—KR7; 21 R—Kt7ch, K—R3; 22 K—B6, R×P; 23 P—B5, R—R8; 24 R—Kt2, R—R6!* (both 24 .... K—R2; 25 K—B7 and 24 .... K—R4; 25 R—Kt8! lose); *25 K—B7, R—R6; 26 R—Kt7, R—R1=* (No. 329a).

Another trap with the two Pawns which cannot come out of the main variation is nevertheless worth noting. No. 352a (Reshevsky-Apscheneek, Kemeri, 1937), White: K at KB3, R at Q4, P's at KB5, KR5; Black: K at KR1, R at KKt4. White to play wins. 1 P—B6!!, R—R4 (1 .... R×P; 2 R—Q8ch, K—R2; 3 K—Kt4!, R—R8; 4 P—B7, or 1 .... R—B4ch; 2 R—B4 or 1 .... K—Kt1; 2 R—Kt4); 2 R—Q8ch, K—R2; 3 K—Kt4, R—R5ch; 4 K—B5, R—R4ch; 5 K—K6, R—R3ch; 6 K—K7, R—R2ch; 7 R—Q7, R—R8; 8 K—K8 dis ch, K—R1; 9 P—B7, R—K8ch; 10 R—K7, R—KB8; 11 R—K6! and Black resigned.

No. 353

Draw.

No. 354

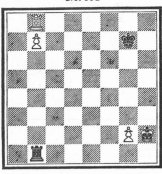

Draw. Win with Pawn at QKt6.

b) The Two RP's.

This depends on the transposition into the corresponding R+RP vs. R ending. If the Pawns are not beyond the middle of the board a draw will normally result. No. 353 (Gothenburg-Stockholm) illustrates the possibilities. The draw was achieved by *1 .... R—R5!; 2 R—B3ch* (or 2 P—R5, K—Kt4), *K—Kt3; 3 K—B2, R×KRP; 4 K—K2, R—R5; 5 K—Q2, R—R3; 6 K—B2, R—KB3; 7 R—Q3, K—B2; 8 K—Kt3, K—K2; 9 K—Kt4, R—Q3* and a draw was agreed to. Or No. 352a (Tchigorin-Salve, Carlsbad, 1907), White: K at KR6, R at Q3, P's at QR4, KR5; Black: K at K4, R at QR7. Draw. The conclusion was 1 R—KB3, R×P; 2 K—Kt7, R—Kt5ch; 3 K—B7, R—KR5; 4 R—QR3, R—B5ch; 5 K—K7, R—QKt5; 6 R—R5ch, K—B5; 7 P—R6, K—Kt5; 8 R—R7, K—Kt4; 9 P—R7, R—Kt1; 10 K—B7, K—R3. Drawn.

c) *The Rook Immobilized.*

We have already seen that it is not advisable to have the Rook in front of the Pawn. In No. 354 this lack of mobility makes it impossible to win. For the Black King remains at KKt2, from which square he can be driven away only by an earthquake, while the Rook plods patiently to and fro along the Kt file. The White King of course can not approach the QKtP: as soon as he gets to QB7 checks drive him away again. With the Pawn at QKt6, White can win by marching his King in. If Black's King goes over to the Q-side the KKtP advances and calls him back. E.g., No. 354a, White P at QKt6, other pieces

No. 355

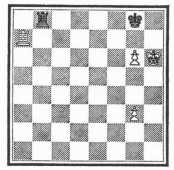

White wins.

No. 356

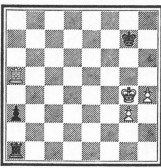

White to play wins; Black to play draws.

as in No. 354. White wins. 1 K—Kt3, K—B2; 2 K—B4, K—Kt2 (if 2 .... K—K2; 3 P—Kt7!, K—Q2; 4 R—KR8, R×P; 5 R—R7ch and the KKtP wins); 3 K—K5, K—B2; 4 K—Q6, etc.

C. DOUBLED PAWNS

Doubled Pawns are not much better than a single Pawn in R and P endings. With a few exceptions exactly the same rules hold, whether the Black King is in front of the Pawn or cut off from the Pawn. The chief exception occurs with a KtP on the sixth and the Black Rook confined to the first rank (No. 355). Without the extra Pawn this is a draw, but now White can force the exchange of Rooks. *1 R—R6!* (but not 1 P—Kt4, R—QB1; 2 P—Kt5?, R—Kt1; 3 P—Kt7??, R—Kt3ch!; 4 P—Kt6, R×Pch!; 5 K×R stalemate), *R—KB1; 2 P—Kt4!* (or a Rook tempo along the rank. 2 P—Kt7? at once allows the unpleasant rejoinder 2 .... R—B3ch!!; 3 R×R stalemate), *R—K1;*

3 R—KB6, R—R1; 4 P—Kt7, R—Kt1; 5 R—B8ch, R×R; 6 P×R= *Qch, K×Q; 7 K—R7* and wins. A Pawn on one of the four center files which reaches the sixth and confines the Black Rook to the first rank wins even if it is single, so that the rules remain the same. It is worth observing that this winning position with the Pawn on the sixth cannot be forced from any normal beginning; again the extra Pawn makes no difference.

In the Lucena position the extra Pawn may even be in the way! E.g., No. 355a (Duras, 1903), White: K at QKt8, R at KKt2, P's at QKt6, QKt7; Black: K at Q2, R at QR6. White has to resort to the problem continuation 1 R—Q2ch, K—K2!; 2 R—Q6!! (normally 2 R— Q4 would decide, but not here, for after 2 .... R—R8; 3 K—B7, R—B8ch the King has to go back to his cubby hole), R—QB6 (or 2 .... K×R; 3 K—B8, R—B6ch; 4 K—Q8, R—KR6; 5 P—Kt8= Qch); 3 R—QB6!!, R×R; 4 K—R7 and wins.

IV. ROOK AND TWO PAWNS VS. ROOK AND PAWN

As usual, the extra Pawns create more and different winning possibilities. Roughly, we may say that R+2P always win against R+P when White has two passed Pawns, win most of the time when White has one passed Pawn, but always draw when there is no passed Pawn. It will be recalled that exactly the same situation holds in minor piece endings.

The various combinations of Pawn positions give us three cases.

A. WHITE HAS TWO PASSED PAWNS

1. Only *connected passed Pawns* win here with any great regularity. In practice the two connected Pawns vs. one on the other side of the board occur most frequently. The winning idea is to get the Rook behind the enemy Pawn and thus be able to use it to stop that Pawn and support one's own.

First of all we shall consider the most usual case, that where the Black Rook is in front of the Pawn, the White Rook behind it. In that event we get the critical position No. 356. The point is that the White King must be able to ensconce himself behind his Pawns without allowing the exchange of Black's QRP for his KKt or KRP. White to play can just manage to do this: *1 K—R5, P—R7* (1 .... R— KKt8; 2 P—Kt4, R—Kt6; 3 P—Kt5 is worse); *2 P—Kt4, K—R2* (to go out with the King is no better: 2 .... K—B3; 3 P—Kt5ch, K—K3; 4 K—Kt6!, K—Q3; 5 P—R5, K—B3; 6 P—R6, K—Kt3; 7 R—R8, K—Kt4; 8 P—R7, R—R8; 9 R×P and wins); *3 P—Kt5, K—Kt2; 4 R—R7ch, K—B1* (4 .... K—Kt1; 5 K—Kt6, threatening mate); *5 P—Kt6!* (the simplest; 5 K—Kt6 is also good enough), *K— Kt1* (5 .... R—Kt8; 6 R×P, K—Kt2; 7 R—R7ch, K—B3; 8 R—

B7ch, or 5 .... K—K1; 6 P—Kt7, R—KKt8; 7 K—R6!, P—R8=Q; 8 R×Q, etc.); *6 K—R6!, R—KB8; 7 R×P* and it is all over. Black to play can prevent White from advancing his Pawns side by side. *1 .... P—R7!; 2 R—R7ch, K—Kt3; 3 P—R5ch, K—R3; 4 R—R8, K—Kt2; 5 R—R3, K—B3!* (but not 5 .... K—R3??; 6 R—R7! and the Rook must move); *6 P—R6* (there is no way of making progress: if 6 R—R6ch, K—Kt2; 7 K—Kt5, R—KKt8!; 8 R×P, R×Pch= or 6 R—R7, K—K3; 7 P—R6, K—B3; 8 P—R7, R—R8, etc.), *K—Kt3; 7 R—R6ch, K—R2; 8 K—Kt5, R—KKt8; 9 R—R7ch, K—Kt1; 10 R× P, R×Pch.* Draw.

With a BP+KtP we have the same critical position, for R+KtP vs. R does not win even when the Black Rook is confined to the first rank, while R+BP vs. R does not win if the Black King is on the side of the board. Even the most favorable case, that with two center Pawns, is only a draw with correct defense. For a R+KP (or QP) ending will result, where Black has a simple draw if he goes to the short side of the Pawn with the King (Nos. 325–328).

With his rook defending the Pawn from the side (e.g., on the seventh rank), Black has no threat of a check, so that even Pawns on the second rank may win. The only resource for the defense is then to come to the aid of the Pawn with his King (see No. 358). The result in such cases depends on how far advanced the Pawns are: normally the two Pawns will win unless the enemy Pawn is on the sixth or beyond, supported by the King.

If the two Pawns are supported by the Rook, and stopped by the enemy King and Rook, it may sometimes be difficult to approach with the King. As a rule, however, Black will get into zugzwang—either allow the enemy King to get close or the Pawns to advance. E.g., No. 356a (Thomas-Alekhine, Hastings, 1922, with colors reversed), White: K at KKt2, R at QR7, P's at QR5, QKt6; Black: K at QB3, R at QKt6, P at KKt5. White to play wins. First we note that Black is in zugzwang: if his King leaves QB3, or if his Rook leaves the Kt file, P—Kt7 will win at once. Consequently White need only tempo with his King to get through. The win is 1 K—B2, R—Kt8; 2 K— Kt3, R—Kt5; 3 K—R4! and now Black must give up his KtP. For the resulting ending see No. 344c.

The ending is far more difficult when the Black Rook is behind the Pawn, the White Rook in front of it. Then, with the Pawn on the seventh, KtP+RP do not win at all, while other Pawns win only if both are on the sixth. No. 356b, White: K at KR5, R at QR1, P's at KKt6, KR6; Black: K at KR1, R at QR1, P at QR7. Draw. The only plausible attempt is 1 P—R7 so that if 1 .... R—R3?; 2 R—Q1!, R—R1; 3 K—R6!, P—R8=Q; 4 R×Q, R×R; 5 P—Kt7 mate. But in reply to 1 P—R7, K—Kt2 draws, for if 2 K—Kt5, R—R4ch; 3 K—Kt4, R—R1! threatening K×P, while 2 R—KB1?, P—R8=Q is only a brilliant blunder. With other Pawns the Rook has a'mate threat when the Pawns are on the sixth: No. 356c: White: K at KKt6, R at QR1, P's at K6, KB6; Black: K at KKt1, R at QR1, P at QR7. White wins. 1 .... K—B1; 2 R—R1!, K—Kt1; 3 P—B7ch, K—B1; 4 R—R8ch or 4 K—B6.

A model case from practical play may be seen in No. 357 (Marshall-Euwe, Bad Kissingen, 1928) (The colors have been reversed). To determine whether this position is won or not, we must compare it with No. 356. Thus 1 .... R—Kt8; 2 R—QR6, R—QR8; 3 K—Kt4, P—R5; 4 P—B4, P—R6; 5 P—K4, P—R7; 6 K—B5, and now we see that White wins. As a result Black feels compelled to offer a different defense. The winning method may then be divided into four phases:

1. White guards the Black passed Pawn by placing his Rook behind it.
2. With the help of both King and Rook he advances his own Pawns as far as possible, taking care to avoid a blockade.
3. If Black prevents the further advance by manipulation of his Rook White will either capture the Black Pawn or the Black Rook.
4. If the Black Rook does not try to stop the Pawns a Queen will be forced by their steady advance.

The game continuation in No. 357 was as follows: *1 .... K—Kt2; 2 K—Kt3; K—B2; 3 P—B4, K—K2; 4 P—K4, K—Q2* (an example of the third phase: the Black King is trying to drive the White Rook away from the R file, he is speculating on the strength of his own Pawn.

This is in point of fact the only defense which gives him any chance whatsoever, but here he is much too late); *5 R—QR6, K—B2; 6 P—B5, K—Kt2; 7 R—R6, P—R5; 8 P—B6!, K—B2* (now the King has to come back, else the R will be lost); *9 R—R7ch, K—Q3; 10 R—K7!!* (a vital move, for else his Pawns will be blockaded), *R—Kt8!* (there is a cute tactical refutation of 10 .... P—R6: 11 P—K5ch, R×P; 12 R×R, K×R; 13 P—B7, P—R7; 14 P—B8=Q, P—R8=Q; 15 Q—KR8ch, and wins); *11 K—B2* (to keep the Black Rook out of KB8),

No. 357

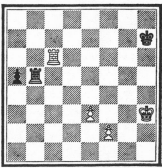
White wins.

R—Kt7ch; 12 K—K3, R—Kt6ch (or 12 .... R—Kt8; 13 K—Q4!, R—Q8ch; 14 K—B4, etc., as in the main variation); *13 K—Q4, P— R6; 14 P—K5ch, K—B3; 15 R—QR7; R—Kt5ch; 16 K—B3, R— KB5; 17 K—Kt3!* (better than 17 R×P, K—Q4!), *K—Q4; 18 R—K7, R—B6ch; 19 K—R2; K—B5; 20 P—B7, K—Kt5; 21 R—Kt7ch, K— R5; 22 R—R7ch, K—Kt5; 23 P—K6, R—B7ch; 24 K—Kt1, K—Kt6; 25 R—Kt7ch, K—R5; 26 R—Kt8* Resigns.

It will be noticed that when the Black King left the White Pawns their advance was secured by the Rook, while the White King held the Black Pawn. This is a subsidiary phase which is frequently seen. If Black's Rook and King together stop the Pawns White must bring up his King, since the R alone cannot force any progress; but if only one of the two tries to stop the Pawns either a queen will be forced or the Rook will be lost.

If the defender's Rook is in front of the Pawn as in No. 356, so that he threatens to advance to the seventh and queen, it is essential for the superior side to keep his King in front of one of his Pawns in order to make sure that the White Rook cannot get out with check. E.g., No. 357a (Janowski-Yates, New York, 1924), White: K at KR5, R at K8, P at QR4; Black: K at KB3, R at KB6, P's at KB4, K5. The winning line adopted was 1 K—R4, R—QR6; 2 R—QR8, K—K4; 3 K— Kt5, R—Kt6ch; 4 K—R5, P—K6; 5 P—R5, K—B5!; 6 P—R6, R— Kt8; 7 P—R7, R—QR8 (now White has no check); 8 K—Kt6, R— R3ch; 9 K—R5, P—K7!; 10 R—K8, K—B6!! resigns for if 11 P— R8=Q, R×Q; 12 R×R, P—K8=Q.

Black can draw this ending only if he succeeds in making his own Pawn a threat, or if he can blockade the two Pawns. The lone Pawn becomes a threat by advancing to the seventh and being supported by the King. If it is merely aided by the Rook, the White Rook can preserve its freedom of action; the only conceivable threat of a Rook check is easily warded off (Cf. No. 357a). But if the King comes up too White may run the danger of losing his Rook. Of course such a defense is feasible only when the White Pawns are not far advanced, for else White can sacrifice his Rook and win with two Pawns vs. Rook. An example of such a drawing resource is No. 358 (Reshevsky-Alekhine, AVRO, 1938). After *1 P—Kt4, K—B3!* saved the day (1 .... K—K3??; 2 K—Kt3, K—B3; 3 P—R3, K—Kt3; 4 K—R4 is hopeless: No. 357); *2 K—Kt3* (on 2 P—Kt5, K—Kt4!; 3 R—R6ch, K—Kt2; 4 R×P, R×P; 5 R—QB2, R—Kt1 is the simplest drawing line), *K— Kt3; 3 R—R8, K—Kt4; 4 P—R3* (if 4 P—Kt5, K—Kt5 threatens 5 .... R—Kt6ch and 6 .... R—R6, so that the White King must leave the third rank and lose his RP), *K—Kt5; 5 K—B4, R—QB7!* (threatening 6 .... R—B5ch followed by either 7 .... R—B6ch and

8 .... R—QR6, or 7 .... R—B4ch and 8 .... R—QR4. Since there is no defense to this threat White is compelled to take a draw by perpetual check); *6 R—Kt8ch, K—B6!; 7 R—QR8, K—Kt5!* Drawn. It would have been folly for Black to try to play for a win here by 7 .... K—Kt7, for after 8 P—R4, P—R8=Q; 9 R×Q, K×R; 10 P—R5, K—Kt7; 11 P—Kt5, K—B6; 12 P—Kt6, R—KKt7; 13 K—B5 the Pawns win.

If the King is blockading the Pawn, a similar type of drawing stratagem is available: Black advances the Pawn to the seventh and threatens either mate or queening, which compels White to accept perpetual check. E.g., No. 358a (Reshevsky-Capablanca, AVRO, 1938), White: K at QB2, R at QKt5, P's at QR3, QKt2; Black: K at KKt6, R at

No. 358   No. 359

Draw.   Draw.

KR8, P at K6. Draw. 1 K—Q3, K—B5!; 2 R—Kt8, R—Q8ch; 3 K—K2, R—Q7ch; 4 K—K1, K—B6; 5 R—B8ch, K—K5; 6 P—Kt4, R—QR7; 7 R—QR8 (or as in the game: 7 R—K8ch, K—B6; 8 R—B8ch, K—K5 Draw agreed to), K—Q6 (or even 7 .... P—K7; 8 P—Kt5, K—K6; 9 R—K8ch, K—B6; 10 R—B8ch, etc.); 8 R—Q8ch, K—K5; 9 R—QR8, K—Q6=.

The blockade is of course an effective weapon even with R+2P vs. R. But there are many cases (especially with one Pawn on the sixth) where White may still win. When Black has an extra Pawn the added counterplay may neutralize even those advanced Pawn positions which would otherwise be won. Thus in No. 359 (Steinitz-Lasker, match 1894) without the Black KtP the game would be lost, despite the blockade (See No. 346), but as it is, Black can draw. *1 K—Q4* (the normal move 1 R—QKt1, is not good here, because

White cannot afford to exchange Rooks: 1 .... R—R5ch; 2 R—Kt4??, R×Rch; 3 K×R, P—Kt5 and the White King is outside the square. Consequently 2 K—Kt5 is forced in answer to 1 .... R—R5ch, but then 2 .... R—Q5; 3 R—K1, R×Pch; 4 K—B4, R—B4ch; 5 K—Q4, R—B2 destroys all White's winning hopes), *R—R5ch!* (best: if instead 1 .... R—KB1; 2 R—K5!!, P—Kt5; 3 R—Kt5, R—QR1; 4 K—K3, R—R6ch; 5 K—B4, R—R5ch; 6 K—Kt3! White has excellent winning chances. White's second move here is based on a pretty trap: 2 .... R—B5ch?; 3 K—Q3!!, K×R?; 4 P—K7, R—Q5ch; 5 K—B3 and the Pawn queens); *2 K—Q3, R—R1!!* (in the game Lasker played 2 .... R—R6ch? and resigned after 3 K—K4, P—Kt5; 4 K—B5, R—R1; 5 P—K7, R—K1; 6 K—B6, P—Kt6; 7 K—B7, K—Q2; 8 P—Q6!, P—Kt7; 9 R—KKt1); *3 K—K4, R—KB1!!; 4 K—Q4!* (or 4 R—KKt1, R—B5ch; 5 K—K3, R—B4!=, if now 6 R—Q1, R—B1; 7 K—K4, R—B5ch; etc.), *P—Kt5!* (not 4 .... R—B5ch?; 5 R—K4, R—B1; 6 R—K5!, P—Kt5; 7 R—Kt5, etc., as above); *5 R—KKt1* (or 5 R—QR1, R—B5ch; 6 K—K3, R—B1!; 7 R—R5, P—Kt6, or 5 K—K4, P—Kt6; 6 R—QB1, P—Kt7; 7 R—KKt1, R—KKt1; 8 K—B3, K×P), *R—B5ch; 6 K—K3, R—B4=*.

Another game from a world championship match which shows the use of the weapon of the blockade is No. 359a (Alekhine-Euwe, 13th match game, 1935), White: K at Q4, R at QB7, P at QR7; Black: K at KKt3, R at QR8, P's at KB2, KKt5. Draw. The simplest drawing line here is 1 K—K3!, P—B4 (1 .... R—R5; 2 R—B4!); 2 K—B4, R—R5ch; 3 K—Kt3, K—B3; 4 R—QKt7!, K—K4; 5 R—Kt5ch, K—K3; 6 R—Kt6ch, K—Q4; 7 R—Kt5ch, etc. Instead the game continued 1 K—K5?, P—B3ch?? (correct was 1 .... R—R5! and if then 2 R—B4, P—B3ch; 3 K—Q6, R—R3ch; 4 K—Q5, K—Kt4 and

No. 360

White to play draws; Black to play wins.

wins—the blockade is lifted); 2 K—B4, R—R5ch (now it is too late); 3 K—Kt3, P—B4 (or 3 .... K—Kt4; 4 R—Kt7ch, K—B4; 5 K—R4!); 4 K—R4!, K—B3; 5 R—QKt7! and a draw was agreed to, for if 5 .... K—K4; 6 R—Kt5ch, K—K3; 7 R—Kt6ch, etc.—if the Black King goes to the Q-side the BP will fall.

We see that *two connected passed Pawns win against one Pawn unless either the single Pawn is far advanced and supported by both King and Rook or the two Pawns are blockaded.*

2. *Disconnected passed Pawns* win only if a transposition ,to a simpler case with R+P vs. R is feasible. In other words the normal state of affairs is that the Rooks will capture one Pawn each. Frequently of course, one passed Pawn or set of Pawns will be much more dangerous than the rival set. In such cases one Pawn may even win against two.

No. 360 (Leonhardt-Spielmann, San Sebastian, 1912) is typical of a great number of such endings. In the game it was White's move, and after *1 P—Kt6!, K—Q6; 2 R—Q7!* (not 2 R—Kt8, P—Q5; 3 P—Kt7, P—Kt6; 4 R—Kt8, R—Kt8ch!; 5 K—Kt2, R×P; 6 R×Pch, K—Q7; 7 R—KR3, R—Kt2ch and wins. It is imperative for White to preserve his Rook's freedom of action), *P—Q5; 3 P—Kt7, R—Kt3* (Black can find no really satisfactory solution because the White King is too near the Pawns. If, e.g., 3 .... R—Kt8ch; 4 K—Kt2, K—K6; 5 K—Kt3, P—Q6; 6 K×P, P—Q7; 7 K—B3!, K—K7; 8 R—K7ch, K—Q8; 9 R—QR7, R—Kt6ch; 10 K—Kt2, K—K7; 11 R—K7ch, etc. The trouble is that Black must give up one Pawn to get the White King out of the way); *4 K—Kt2, R—Kt8; 5 K—Kt3,* and a draw was agreed to, for if *5 .... R—Kt8ch; 6 K—R4* and the Black Rook has to return. But obviously the result in such cases depends on the positions of the Pawns. For this reason Black to play wins—he can advance his Pawns more quickly. E.g., *1 .... K—B6; 2 R—B7ch, K—Kt6; 3 R—KKt7, P—Q5; 4 P—Kt6* (4 R—Q7, R×P; 5 R×P, R—Kt8ch; 6 K—Q2, K—R6 is lost—No. 309), *P—Q6; 5 R—Kt8, P—Q7ch; 6 K—Q1, K—Kt7; 7 P—Kt7, P—Kt6; 8 R—Q8, R×P; 9 R×Pch, K—Kt8* and wins.

The defending side must choose the moment for the exchange of Pawns carefully. An example similar to No. 359 which illustrates a number of the traps which occur is No. 360a (Spielmann-Landau, 3rd match game, 1936), White: K at KB1, R at QR6, P at KR6; Black: K at K4, R at QKt5, P's at QKt4, Q4. Draw. The game continued 1 .... R—B5ch; 2 K—K2, K—Q5; 3 R—Kt6, K—B4; 4 R—Kt8 (keeping the Rook on the seventh rank, as in No. 360, would also do), R—KR5; 5 R—KR8, K—Q5; 6 P—R7, R—R7ch; 7 K—Q1! (but not 7 K—B3, K—Q6! and Black will win, for if 8 R—Q8, R×P; 9 R×Pch, K—B5 the White King is too far away), K—Q6; 8 K—B1, P—Q5; 9 K—Kt1, P—Kt5 (9 .... K—Q7 is met by 10 R—Q8); 10 K—R1! (the simplest: if 10 K—B1?, R—B7ch; 11 K—Kt1, R—B2! and will win), K—Q7; 11 K—Kt2! (again the safest. If 11 R—Q8?, R×P; 12 R×Pch, K—B6!; 13 R—Q8, R—R8ch; 14 K—R2, P—Kt6ch; 15 K—R3, R—R8 mate, or 13 R—Q1, K—B7!), P—Q6; 12 K—Kt3, R—R5; 13 K—R4!, K—Q8; 14 R—Q8, R×P; 15 R×Pch. Drawn.

Where the Pawns are far apart, the King should take care of one and the Rook of the other, always of course with an eye on the resulting R+P vs. R ending. E.g., No. 360b (Spielmann-Capablanca, Moscow,

1925), White: K at K2, R at QB5, P at Q4; Black: K at KKt3, R at KKt6, P's at KKt5, QB6. Draw. 1 K—B2!! (not 1 K—Q1?, R—Q6ch; 2 K—K2, R×P; 3 R×P, R—B5 and wins—No. 309), R—R6; 2 K—Kt2, R—Q6; 3 K—R2, K—B3; 4 K—Kt2, K—K3; 5 K—R2, K—Q3; 6 K—Kt2, R—Q7ch; 7 K—Kt3, P—B7; 8 K—R4! (of course not 8 K×P??, R×Pch. Similarly 8 R—B3?, K—Q4; 9 K×P, K×P is bad), R—Kt7; 9 K—Kt5!! (the Black King must be kept out at all costs), R—Kt8; 10 R×P, K—Q4; 11 K—B4, K×P; 12 R—Q2ch. Drawn.

In the above examples the defender's King is always directly in front of one of the Pawns. But even where this is not the case, a draw may be secured by utilizing the counterchances which the single passed Pawn confers. Thus the Pawn at B5 guarantees the draw in No. 361 (Bogoljuboff-Thomas, Hastings, 1922). After *1 .... R—R3* (on 1 .... P—Kt5; 2 P—B6, P—Kt6; 3 R×P, P—R6; 4 R—Kt1, P—R7; 5 R—QR1 draws easily enough, but even 4 R×P!, R×R; 5 P—B7, R—QB6; 6 K—Q6 is sufficient); *2 P—B6, K—K2; 3 K—B5, K—Q1; 4 K—Q6, P—Kt5; 5 R—KKt3, P—R6; 6 R×P.* Black's advantage is dissipated and a draw is the natural result. If the passed Pawn is blockaded by the Rook (instead of the King as in the above example) the superior side is in effect fighting with one active piece against two, so that a win is out of the question. E.g., No. 361a (Loewenfisch-Pirc, Moscow, 1935), White: K at QB6, R at KB1, P's at QKt4, Q4; Black: K at KB2, R at KB5, P at KB7. Black to play draws. 1 .... K—K1! (it would of course take much too long for the King to come to the aid of the Pawn, while 1 .... R×P?; 2 R×Pch, K—K1; 3 P—Kt5 transposes into a loss); 2 P—Kt5, R—B3ch!; 3 K—B7, R—B2ch; 4 K—B8, K—K2! (the only move. If now 5 P—Kt6, K—Q3!; 6 P—Q5, R—B1ch; 7 K—Kt7, K×P, etc.); 5 K—B7, K—K1 dis ch; 6 K—B6 (6 K—Kt8, R—B3), R—B3ch; 7 K—Kt7, R—B2ch; 8 K—R6, K—Q2; 9 P—Kt6 (or 9 P—Q5, K—Q3; 10 P—Kt6, R—B6!; 11 P—Kt7, R—R6ch; 12 K—Kt6, R—Kt6ch; 13 K—R7, R—R6ch; 14 K—Kt8, R—KB6=), K—B1; 10 P—Q5, R—B6! and White can only wring his hands in despair.

The single Pawn may even win against the two Pawns if it is supported by both King and Rook and the superior side's forces are disorganized. E.g., No. 361b (Tarrasch-Schlechter, 8th match game, 1911), White: K at Q6, R at QR8, P at K6; Black: K at KR2, R at KB4, P's at QR6, KKt2. White wins. 1 .... R—B3 (or 1 .... R—B8; 2 P—K7); 2 K—Q7!, K—Kt3; 3 P—K7, R—B2; 4 K—Q6, R×P; 5 K×R, K—B4; 6 K—Q6!, P—Kt4; 7 K—Q5, K—B5; 8 K—Q4, P—Kt5; 9 R—B8ch!!, K—Kt6; 10 K—K3, P—R7; 11 R—QR8, K—R6; 12 R×P, P—Kt6; 13 K—B3, Resigns.

3. Doubled Pawns practically never win. For if the Black King is near them, even without Black's extra Pawn the game would be drawn, while if the Black King is supporting his own Pawn, the likely result is a R vs. 2P ending, which is a draw in this case.

Summary: Rook and two passed Pawns vs. Rook and Pawn is normally a win when the Pawns are connected, but a draw when they are disconnected or doubled.

B. WHITE HAS ONE PASSED PAWN

Unlike the similar cases with minor pieces the Pawn plus here is normally not enough. The theoretical reason is that the Rook is so strong that it need not permit the enemy King to cross over and cap-

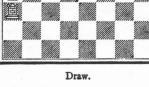

No. 361   No. 362

Draw.   Draw.

ture the last Pawn (it will be recalled that this was the winning method with Bishops). Still it is worth our while to examine the major possibilities.

The passed Pawn may be blocked either by the King or by the Rook. It is far better to block it with the King, for the Rook is immobilized in front of a Pawn. The basic rule of all Rook endings is that Rooks belong behind Pawns.

When the Pawn is blocked by the King a draw is to be expected. No. 362 (Lasker-Steinitz, 14th match game, 1896) may be taken as the general case. The simplest drawing line is *1 .... R—K6; 2 R— Q4ch* (if 2 R—B2, R×P!; 3 R—B4ch, K—R6; 4 R—B3, R×R; 5 P×R, K—Kt5; 6 K—Q3, K—B4 =, or 3 R×P, R—Kt6; 4 R—B2, K—B5 =), *K—B4* (better than 2 .... K—R6; 3 R—R4 mate); *3 R— Q3, R—K7ch; 4 R—Q2, R—K6; 5 R—B2, P—B5!; 6 K—Kt2, R— Kt6; 7 K—R3, K—Kt4; 8 K—Kt2, K—B4!; 9 K—B2, K—Kt4; 10 K—Q1, R× QKtP; 11 R×P, R—Kt6; 12 R—B2, K—B4; 13 K—K1,*

K—Q3; 14 K—B1, K—K2 and White cannot win. An alternative defense is 1 .... R—K5; 2 R—B2, R—Kt5; 3 K—Kt2, P—B5! (in the game there occurred 3 .... R—K5??; 4 P—Kt3!, R—K4; 5 R—B4ch and now Lasker could win: 5 .... K—Kt4; 6 K—R3, R—Q4; 7 R—B3, K—R4; 8 P—Kt4ch, K—Kt4; 9 K—Kt3, K—Kt3; 10 K—B4, K—B3; 11 R—Kt3!, R—K4; 12 P—Kt5ch, K—Kt3; 13 K—Q4, R—K5ch; 14 K—Q5, R—K1; 15 K—Q6, R—K8; 16 R—KB3, K×P; 17 R×Pch, K—B5; 18 P—Kt4 and Steinitz soon resigned; 4 K—B2, K—B4!; 5 K—Q3, R—Kt6ch; 6 K—K4, R×P; 7 K×P, K—Q3; 8 R—K2, R—Kt1 = (No. 310).

It is clear that if he wishes to win White must rely upon the possibility of giving up his passed Pawn to capture the enemy Pawn and secure a won R+P vs. R ending. The outcome thus depends on whether this plan can be carried out. As usual, the RP is harder to capitalize on than other Pawns, and if the Black King is in any reasonable position a draw is unavoidable. E.g., No. 362a (Teichmann-v. Bardeleben), White: K at KB5, R at QR5, P at QR3; Black: K at KR5, R at QKt6, P's at QKt4, KR4. Draw. The correct defense is 1 K—B4, K—R6; 2 P—R4, P×P; 3 R×Pch, K—Kt7; 4 R—R5, P—R6; 5 K—K4, K—B7; 6 K—Q4, K—K7; 7 K—B4, R—R6; 8 K—Kt4, etc. Or here 2 .... R—Kt5ch; 3 K—B3, R×P; 4 R×P, P—R5; 5 R—Kt5 with a theoretical draw. Of course, with a KtP this ending would be won.

To blockade the Pawn with the Rook is less favorable. It is relatively best to have the Rook behind the Pawn. In that event, the defender draws if his King can find a haven behind the Pawns, but loses if he cannot. As a rule the King can find a safe spot only if the two remaining Pawns are on the same file. No. 363 (Steinitz-Gunsberg, 9th match game, 1890–91) is typical. Against the threat of the removal of the Black Rook with check White is defenseless, for on 1 K—R6, P—Kt4! compels him to expose his King. Consequently the only hope lies in driving the Black King as far away from the K-side as possible, giving up the Rook for the RP, and taking one's chances on the ensuing R vs. P ending. This stratagem is bound to be unsuccessful here because the Black King is too near. The win is *1 R—R4ch, K—Q4* (in the game there occurred 1 .... K—B6?; 2 R—R3ch, K—B7??; 3 K×P, R—Kt8ch; 4 K—B7, P—R8=Q; 5 R×Q, R×R; 6 P—R5 and drew because the Black King is too far behind the Pawn); *2 R—R5ch, K—B3; 3 R—R6ch* (if 3 K—R6, P—Kt4! 4 P×P, R—R8ch; 5 K—Kt7, P—R8=Q; 6 R×Q, R×R; 7 P—Kt6, K—Q2; 8 K—B6, R—B8ch; 9 K—Kt5, K—K2 and wins, while 3 K×P, R—Kt8ch is essentially the same as the main variation), *K—Kt2; 4 R×RP, R×R; 5 K×P, K—B3; 6 P—R5, K—Q2; 7 P—R6, K—K3; 8 P—R7, R—Kt7ch; 9 K—R6, K—B2* and wins.

If the Pawns are on the same file here, the check could be prevented. Thus No. 363a, White Pawn at KKt4, other pieces as in No. 363, is drawn. For after 1 K×P the only sensible continuation is 1 .... R—KKt8; 2 R×P, R×Pch followed by a handshake.

It is far worse for the defense to have his Rook in front of the Pawn. For then he has no moves with it, and his opponent can either capture the Rook or the last Pawn. E.g., No. 363b, White: K at KB4, R at QR1, P's at QR7, KR4; Black: K at KB3, R at QR1, P at KKt3. White wins. 1 .... K—B2; 2 K—K5, K—K2; 3 R—R2! (tempo), K—B2; (or 3 .... K—Q2; 4 K—B6, K—B3; 5 K×P, K—Kt2; 6 P—R5, etc.); 4 K—Q6, K—B3; 5 K—Q7, K—B4; 6 K—B7, K—Kt5; 7 R—R4ch, K—Kt6; 8 K—Kt7 and it is all over.

Where the superior side has any choice in the matter, he should naturally try to force the Rook to blockade the Pawn. If he can, as is likely, cut the King off, the ending may not differ in any essential respect from that of R+P vs. R. The historic ending Morphy-Riviere, Paris, 1863, is an example. No. 363c, White: K at KB3, R at QB3, P at QR3; Black: K at Q3, R at QR5, P's at QKt4, Q4. Black to play wins. The shortest and most logical road to victory is 1 .... R—K5! and now:

a) 2 R—B8, R—K3; 3 R—Q8ch, K—B4; 4 R—B8ch, K—Q5; 5 R—QKt8, K—B5; 6 R—B8ch, K—Q6; 7 R—QKt8, P—Q5!; 8 R×P, R—B3ch; 9 K—Kt2, K—B5!; 10 R—Kt8, P—Q6; 11 R—Q8, K—B6; 12 R—B8ch, K—Kt6; 13 R—Q8, K—B7!; 14 R—B8ch, K—Q8; 15 P—R4, R—B4!; 16 R—B7, P—Q7; 17 R—B8, K—K7; 18 R—K8ch, K—Q6; 19 R—Q8ch, K—B6; 20 R—B8ch, K—Q5; 21 R—Q8ch, R—Q4.

b) 2 R—Kt3, K—B4; 3 R—B3ch, K—Q5; 4 R—Kt3, R—K3; 5 R×P, K—B5; 6 R—Kt8, P—Q5; 7 P—R4, P—Q6; 8 P—R5, P—Q7; 9 R—Q8, K—B6; 10 K—B2, K—B7; 11 R—B8ch, K—Q8; 12 K—B1 (if 12 R—QR8, R—QB3 followed by .... K—B7), R—B3ch; 13 K—Kt2, R—QR3; 14 R—B5, K—K7; 15 R—K5ch, K—Q6; 16 R—Q5ch, K—K6; 17 R—K5ch (else simply .... R×P), K—Q5; 18 R—K8, R—Q3 and the Pawn queens.

Where the Pawns are close to one another (just as in the analogous

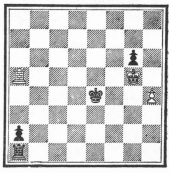

No. 363

Black wins.

case with Bishops) the game is tenable. For the Black King will necessarily stay nearby, so that there can be no question of forcing a won R+P vs. R ending. No. 364 (Reti-Breyer, Baden, 1914) is a relatively favorable case, yet even here White could do nothing. The game continuation was *1 R—B4, R—R7; 2 P—R4, R—R4; 3 K—Kt4, K—B1; 4 R—B5, R—R5ch; 5 K—Kt5, R—R6; 6 P—Kt4, K—Kt2; 7 P—R5, R—R3; 8 R—Q5, R—QKt3; 9 K—B4, R—Kt8; 10 P—Kt5, R—B8ch; 11 K—K4, R—KR8; 12 P—R6ch, K—Kt3* Drawn. Or No. 364a (Reshevsky-Apscheneek, Kemeri, 1937), White: K at KB4, R at K5, P's at KB3, KKt4; Black: K at KB3, R at QR6, P at KR3. White tried 1 R—K4, R—Kt6; 2 R—R4, R—Kt3;

No. 364

Draw.

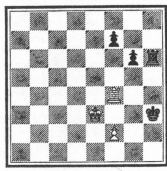

No. 365

Black to play wins; draw with Black King at KKt2.

3 K—Kt3, R—Kt6; 4 R—R6ch, K—Kt4; 5 R—R5ch, K—B3; 6 R—B5ch, K—Kt3; 7 R—B5, R—R6; 8 R—Q5, K—B3; 9 K—B4, R—R5ch, etc., but no real progress could be made. Black later lost by making an incorrect sacrifice at the wrong time.

In order to win the superior side must capture the last Pawn. As a rule this cannot be done without help from the opponent. E.g., No. 364b (Gruenfeld-Wagner, Breslau, 1925), White: K at KKt4, R at QR7, P at KR4; Black: K at KR3, R at KB8, P's at KB2, KKt3. White to play. 1 R—R8 draws quite simply, for if 1 .... P—B4ch; 2 K—Kt3, R—Kt8ch; 3 K—R3, R—Kt8; 4 R—R8ch! the Black King cannot get through. Instead there occurred 1 R—QKt7?, P—B4ch; 2 K—Kt3, R—Kt8ch; 3 K—R3, R—QR8; 4 R—Kt8, R—R6ch; 5 K—R2, K—R4; 6 R—R8ch, K—Kt5; 7 R—R6, R—R3!; 8 K—Kt2, P—B5; 9 K—B2, P—B6; 10 K—K3, K—Kt6; 11 Resigns.

C. WHITE HAS NO PASSED PAWN

In view of No. 364, this must inevitably be a draw with any normal K position. Still, the superior side may win if his King manages to penetrate to the enemy Pawn. But beginning from scratch this can never be forced.

The exception to the rule is seen in No. 365 (Spielmann-Alekhine, New York 1927). The win here is possible only because Black can capture the KBP. Alekhine played *1 .... P—B4!;* and after *2 R—B3ch* (or 2 K—K2, K—Kt7; 3 P—B3, K—Kt6; 4 R—QR4, R—R7ch; 5 K—K3, R—KB7; 6 R—KB4, R—B8. Or 2 R—QR4, K—Kt7; 3 R—R6, R—R6ch; 4 K—B4, R—R5ch; 5 K—K5, R—K5ch; 6 K—B6, R—KKt5; 7 P—B4, R×P; 8 K×P, R—B8; 9 K—Kt5, P—B5; 10 K—B5, P—B6 and wins.), *K—R7!* (threatening to exchange Rooks by .... R—R6. 2 .... K—Kt7?; 3 R—Kt3ch is inferior); *3 R—B4, R—R6ch; 4 K—K2* (Spielmann resigned here), *K—Kt7; 5 R—QR4* (or 5 P—B3, R—R1!; 6 K—K3, R—K1ch; 7 K—Q2, K—Kt6 and the Pawn cannot be saved), *R—KB6; 6 R—R6, P—Kt4* and again the Pawn falls.

This then is the chief winning chance in such endings: capturing the last Pawn. In the above case Spielmann could have saved the game as late as one move before the diagrammed position if he had attacked the White Pawns from behind. Another such example is No. 364b.

The only other type of win occurs in a position such as No. 366. White to play decides at once by *1 K—B6, R—Kt3ch; 2 P—K6* threatening both 3 R—R8ch and 3 R×Pch. The best defense is *1 .... R—Kt3* (if 1 .... K—Kt2; 2 P—K6, R—B1; 3 P—B6ch, K—Kt1; 4 P—K7, R—K1; 5 R—Q7); *2 R—R8ch, K—K2* (or 2 .... K—Kt2; 3 P—B6ch, K—R2; 4 R—R7!, K—Kt1; 5 K—R6, R—Kt1; 6 P—K6!!, P×P; 7 K—Kt6, P—K4; 8 R—Kt7ch, K—B1; 9 R—KR7, K—Kt1; 10 P—B7ch); *3 P—B6ch, K—K3* (or 3 .... K—Q2; 4 R—KB8); *4 R—K8ch, K—Q4; 5 K—R6, R—Kt8* (5 .... R—K3; 6 R×R, K×R; 7 K—Kt7); *6 K—Kt7, R—Kt2; 7 R—K7.* Of course, such a position as No. 366 can be reached only through extremely passive play on the defender's part. With the Pawns on the R and Kt files even this chance does not exist. E.g., No. 366a, White: K at KB5, R at QR7, P's at KKt5, KR5; Black: K at KKt1, R at QKt1, P at

No. 366

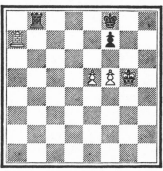

White wins.

KR2. Draw. For the Rook cannot be driven off the first rank. Exchanging Pawns leads to nothing, and a move such as 1 P—R6 is similarly fruitless.

V. MATERIAL ADVANTAGE (IN GENERAL)

There is no ending in which more mistakes in the transformation of a won position into a point scored are made than in R endings. Even the games of the greatest masters are often chock full of inaccuracies and sometimes outright blunders. And yet there is no type of ending which is more common and more important. We shall follow our usual system of classification according to material and position. Unfortunately it is hardly possible to set up one general winning schema (as in Bishop endings) which would be applicable to all varieties of material advantage; we shall have to be content with one for each of the specific classes.

In all of the following cases we are referring to positions where one side is one Pawn ahead.

A. WHITE HAS AN OUTSIDE PASSED PAWN

Even here there is such a variety of possibilities that one general winning plan is still impossible.

In the first place we must consider those cases *where the Pawns are otherwise evenly balanced.* This means that the only passed Pawn (or potential passed Pawn) is that which confers the advantage. Now, this Pawn must be stopped by the defender. This gives us a second division, depending on whether the Rook or the King is watching the Pawn.

The most usual state of affairs is that where the Pawn is held by the Rook. In that event the game is drawn if the defender's Rook is behind the Pawn, but lost if it is in front of the Pawn. An exception occurs when the Black King is cut off and White can move his King to the support of the passed Pawn, for then we have a situation which differs in no essential respect from that of R+P vs. R.

When the Black Rook is behind the Pawn, the White Rook in front of it, we get the typical draw in No. 367. The idea of the draw is this: In order to win, White will have to keep his P at R6, and march his King to the Q-side. He will thus expose his K-side and have to lose at least one Pawn. Once Black has captured a Pawn, he will advance his King and will then win Black's Rook for the QRP, but White will emerge with a R vs. P ending in which his King is too far away to be able to effect a win. If White gets too frisky and sacrifices more than one Pawn, Black may even win.

The model continuation in No. 367 is *1 K—B3, P—R4; 2 P—R4* (2 K—K4, R×P; 3 R—QB8, R—R7; 4 R—B6, R×P; 5 K—Q5,

R—R7; 6 K—B5, P—Kt4; 7 K—Kt6, P—R5; 8 P×P, P×P; 9 P—
R7, P—R6; 10 K—Kt7, P—R7; 11 R—B1, R—Kt7ch; 12 K—R6,
R—R7ch; 13 K—Kt7 etc. = . But if here 4 R—QR8?, R×P; 5 P—R7,
R—R7 Black will win), *K—B3* (Black may only play his King out if,
as in this position, he is not exposed to a check. See also No. 339);
3 K—K3 (if now 3 K—K4, R×P; 4 R—QB8, R—K7ch!; 5 K—Q5??,
R—QR7; 6 R—B6ch, K—B4; 7 K—B5, K—Kt5; 8 K—Kt6, K×P
and again Black has all the winning chances), *K—B4; 4 P—B3,
R—R6ch; 5 K—Q4, R×P; 6 R—KB8, R—R6; 7 R×Pch, K—Kt5;
8 R—B6, K×P; 9 R×Pch, K×P; 10 K—B5, K—R6; 11 K—Kt6,
P—R5; 12 P—R7, K—R7; 13 K—Kt7, R×Pch* (even 13 .... P—R6

No. 367

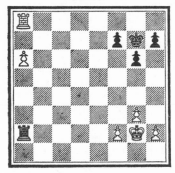

Draw.

No. 368

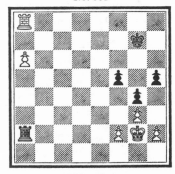

White wins.

draws now: Q vs. RP cannot be won); *14 K×R, P—R6; 15 K—Kt6,
K—R8* etc. = .

If the White King is stalemated there are no winning possibilities at
all. E.g., No. 367a, White: K at KR3, R at QR8, P's at QR6, KB4,
KKt3, KR2; Black: K at KKt2, R at QR7, P's at KB4, KKt3, KR2.
Draw. The only chance is 1 P—Kt4, but then 1 .... P×Pch; 2 K×P,
R×P; 3 P—R7, R—R7, etc., is all right. The White King cannot
approach his Pawn because of the strong KRP, but even if he could
it would do him no good (No. 339).

White has winning chances in positions analogous to No. 367 in
two cases: when the Black Pawns are too far advanced or too widely
scattered and consequently subject to capture or when (usually with
Pawns other than a RP) White can afford to give up one Pawn on the
K-side, blockade the remaining Pawns and win his opponent's Rook.

The first of these eventualities is seen in No. 368. Here White can

succeed in capturing at least one Pawn to begin with, and then winding up with a R+2P vs. R ending. The process is: *1 .... R—R6.*
Any Pawn sacrifice would be futile:

a) 1 .... P—B5; 2 P×P, P—R5; 3 P—R7, R—R8; 4 P—B5, R—R7 (4 .... K—B2; 5 R—R8! or 4 .... K—R3; 5 R—R8ch); 5 P—B6ch, K—B2 (or 5 .... K×P; 6 R—B8ch, or 5 .... K—R2; 6 P—B7); 6 R—R8, R×P; 7 R—R7ch.

b) 1 .... P—R5; 2 P×P, P—B5; 3 P—R7, K—R2 (or 3 .... R—R8; 4 P—R3); 4 K—B1, P—B6; 5 K—K1, K—Kt2; 6 K—Q1, K—R2 (6 .... R×P; 7 R—Kt8 or 7 R—Kt8ch); 7 K—B1, K—Kt2; 8 K—Kt1, R—R3; 9 K—B2, K—R2; 10 K—Q3, K—Kt2; 11 K—K4, R—R5ch; 12 K—B5, K—R2; 13 P—R5, K—Kt2; 14 P—R6ch, K—R2; 15 K—Kt5. White now wins both Black Pawns, and the march of the BP, as in a), decides.

c) 1 .... P—R5; 2 P×P, R—R6 (i.e., Black tries to keep his Pawns intact); 3 P—R7, K—R2; 4 P—R5, R—R8 (4 .... P—B5; 5 K—B1 as in b); 5 K—Kt3, R—R5; 6 P—R6, R—R4; 7 K—B4, R—R7!; 8 K—Kt3 (8 K×P??, R×Pch only draws: No. 354), R—R4; 9 P—R3!, R—R6ch; 10 K—Kt2!, P×Pch; 11 K—R2, R—R7; 12 K×P, R—R5; 13 P—B4!, R—R8; 14 K—R4, R—R7; 15 K—Kt5, R—R4; 16 K—B6, R—R8; 17 K×P, etc. · The point to be remembered is that once the Pawn is on the seventh, White must be two Pawns ahead to win, and this second Pawn must be able to lure the King from his corner, for which reason it must not be either a RP or a KtP. The continuation after 1 .... R—R6 is *2 P—R7, R—R8; 3 P—B4!* (the only way to get the King out), *R—R6; 4 K—B2, K—R2; 5 K—K2, K—Kt2; 6 K—Q2, K—R2; 7 K—B2, K—Kt2; 8 K—Kt2, R—R3; 9 K—Kt3, K—R2; 10 K—B4, K—Kt2; 11 K—Q5, R—R8; 12 K—K5, R—R4ch; 13 K—K6, K—R2* (Black is in zugzwang); *14 K—B6* (an alternative win is 14 R—K8, R—R3ch; 15 K×P, R×P; 16 K—Kt5, R—R7; 17 K×P, R×Pch; 18 K×P. Or here 14 .... R×QRP; 15 R—K7ch, R×Rch; 16 K×R, K—Kt3; 17 K—K6), *R—R8* (an advocate of euthanasia would recommend 14 .... K—R3; 15 R—R8 mate, but not everybody prefers such a painless death); *15 K×P, R—R4ch; 16 K—K4* (the other Pawns can also be won in the same manner, but why be greedy? The BP is enough), *R—R8; 17 P—B5, K—Kt2; 18 P—B6ch, K—B2; 19 R—R8, R×P; 20 R—R7ch, K×P; 21 R×R.*

If Black has a KP or QP, the ending is just as bad. For White advances the Pawn to the seventh, and then marches in and captures the Pawn. E.g., No. 368a, White: K at KB2, R at QR8, P's at QR6, K2, KKt2, KR2; Black: K at KKt2, R at QR7, P's at K3, KKt3,

KR3. White wins. 1 P—R7, R—R6; 2 P—K3, R—R7ch; 3 K—B3, R—R5; 4 P—K4, R—R6ch; 5 K—B4, R—R4; 6 K—K3, R—R5; 7 K—Q3, K—R2; 8 K—B3, K—Kt2; 9 K—Kt3, R—R8; 10 K—Kt4, K—R2; 11 K—Kt5, K—Kt2; 12 K—B6, K—R2; 13 K—Q7, R—R5; 14 P—K5, R—R3; 15 K—K8!, K—Kt2; 15 K—K7, R—R8; 16 K×P, etc.

The second possibility—that of giving up one Pawn and blockading the others—occurs much less frequently because the defender will not voluntarily consent to a blockade. But if the Pawns are already in that position (No. 369) the win may be forced in the following manner: *1 .... R—R6ch; 2 K—Q4!, R×KtP; 3 R—QB8!* (but not 3 P—R7??, R—QR6=`), *R—QR6; 4 R—B7ch, K—B3* (4 .... K—B1; 5 P—R7 and 6 R—B8ch); *5 P—R7, K—K3; 6 K—B5, R—R8; 7 K—Kt6, R—Kt8ch* (or 7 .... K—Q4; 8 R—B5ch, K—K5; 9 R—R5); *8 K—B6, R—QR8; 9 K—Kt7, K—Q4* (9 .... R—Kt8ch; 10 K—B8 is equally useless); *10 R—K7!, K—Q3; 11 R—K5!, R—Kt8ch* (11 .... R×Pch is hopeless); *11 K—R6, R—R8ch; 12 R—R5* and wins.

With other Pawns this second winning stratagem is much less likely to succeed because the Black King is necessarily so much nearer the passed Pawn.

Summary: If White's Rook is in front of his passed Pawn, and Black's Rook behind it, the game is drawn unless the Black Pawns are exposed to attack or blockaded.

This conclusion is in accordance with our fundamental rule *that Rooks belong behind Pawns*, not in front of them.

If we reverse the positions of the Rooks in No. 367, we get another verification of our rule, for White now wins. This case with the White Rook behind the passed Pawn, and the Black Rook in front of it, is seen in No. 370 (Alekhine-Capablanca, 34th match game, 1927—the game with which Alekhine won the title). The win here consists of four steps.

1. Centralization of the King.

Black will eventually have to allow the penetration of the White King to one side, since his Rook must not move (if it does, the Pawn advances), while his White rival has an inexhaustible number of tempi. We then get

2. The Black King will go to blockade the Pawn, for if he stays

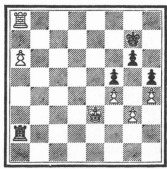

No. 369

White wins.

on the other wing White will attack and capture the Rook.
3 White's King will attack the group of Pawns on the other wing.
4. At the proper moment the White Rook will abandon the passed
   Pawn and establish a decisive material superiority (two Pawns,
   or R+P vs. R in a theoretical win) on the other wing.

All these steps are exemplified in the model No. 370. The game
continued *1 .... R—R3* (1 .... R—B4; 2 R—QR4 is worse); *2 R—
QR4* (actually two harmless but meaningless moves were interspersed
here), *K—B3; 3 K—B3, K—K4; 4 K—K3, P—R4; 5 K—Q3, K—Q4;
6 K—B3, K—B4; 7 R—R2!* (completion of the first step: Black's
King must now give way), *K—Kt4; 8 K—Q4* (again two meaningless
moves intervened), *R—Q3ch* (to blockade the Pawn with his King.
On 8 .... K—Kt5; 9 R—R1! is simplest: 9 .... K—Kt6; 10 K—B5,
K—Kt7; 11 K—Kt5!, R—B3; 12 R—R4!, K—Kt6; 13 R—KB4!,
R—K3; 14 R×P and it is all over); *9 K—K5, R—K3ch; 10 K—B4,
K—R3* (second step); *11 K—Kt5, R—K4ch; 12 K—R6* (third step),
R—KB4 (more accurate was 12 .... R—K2); *13 P—B4* (Alekhine
points out that there is a quicker win: 13 K—Kt7!, R—B6; 14 P—R4,
R—B4; 15 P—B4 and Black must give up the BP), *R—Q4!; 14 K—
Kt7, R—Q2* and now the shortest and most logical road to victory
(again pointed out by Alekhine) is *15 K—B6* (the variation adopted is
also good enough: 15 P—B5, P×P; 16 K—R6, P—B5; 17 P×P, R—
Q4; 18 K—Kt7, R—KB4; 19 R—R4, K—Kt4; 20 R—K4!, K—R3;
21 K—R6, R×RP; 22 R—K5, R—R8; 23 K×P, R—KKt8; 24 R—
KKt5, R—KR8; 25 R—KB5, K—Kt3; 26 R×P, K—B3; 27 R—K7
Resigns), *R—B2; 16 P—B5, P×P* (if 16 .... R—B3ch; 17 K×P,
P×P; 18 R—KB3); *17 K×P, R—B4ch; 18 K—B6, R—B2; 19 R—
KB2!, K×P; 20 R—B5ch, K—Kt3; 21 R×P, K—B3; 22 R—R7,
K—Q3; 23 R×P* and the rest is simple.

A similar case with the KtP is No. 370a (Fine-Reinfeld, New York,
1940), White: K at KR2, R at QKt2, P's at QKt4, KKt2, KR3;
Black: K at KR3, R at QKt2, P's at KR2, KKt3. White wins. 1 K—
Kt3, K—Kt4; 2 P—Kt5, R—Kt3; 3 K—B3, K—B4; 4 K—K3,
K—K4; 5 K—Q3, K—Q4; 6 K—B3, K—B4; 7 P—R4 (first step com-
pleted), P—R3; 8 R—Kt1, P—R4 (Note that the K and P endings are
always lost for Black); 9 R—Kt2, K—Q4; 10 K—Kt4, R—Kt1;
11 R—Q2ch, K—K4 (now White wins as in R+P vs. R—the Black
King is cut off); 12 R—Q3, K—B4; 13 R—KKt3, R—K1; 14 P—Kt6
Resigns.

Black has drawing chances in such positions only if his King can
manage to squeeze in among the enemy Pawns and scare up some
counter-chances. This is a tactical resource for which no general
rules can be laid down. An example is No. 371 (Lasker-Loewenfisch,

Moscow, 1925). Lasker could have drawn by setting up a passed RP:
1 P—B5!!, KP×P (1 .... KtP×P?; 2 P—R5 is obviously bad for
Black); *2 P—K6!!, P×P dis ch; 3 K×P, K—Kt4; 4 R—R1, P—B5*
(4 .... R—Q2; 5 P—R5, R—Q7; 6 R—R1!, P—B5; 7 P—R6, P—B6;
8 P—R7, R—Q1; 9 P—R8=Q, R×Q; 10 R×R, P—R5; 11 R—R3 is
likewise insufficient: Black just manages to draw); *5 P—R5, P—K4*
(against 5 .... P—B6 there is the ingenious defense 6 R—KB1!,
P—R5; 7 R×P, P—R6; 8 R—B1, P—R7; 9 R—QR1, K—B5; 10 P—
R6, K—Kt6; 11 P—R7, R—R1; 12 R—K1!!, K—Kt7; 13 R—K2ch,
K—Kt8 (13 .... K—B6; 14 R—K1); 14 R×KP!, P—R8=Q; 15 R—
K1ch=); *6 R—K1!!* (this saves everything), *P—R5* (6 .... R—K2;

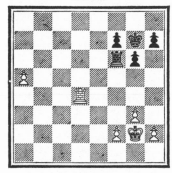 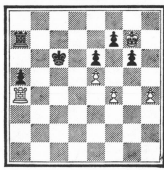

No. 370   No. 371

White wins.   White to play can draw.

7 K—B6, R—K1; 8 K—B7); *7 R×Pch, K—Kt5* (7 .... K—B3;
8 R—K1, P—R6; 9 P—R6, P—R7; 10 P—R7=); *8 R—K4ch, K—
Kt6; 9 R×P, P—R6* and both sides will enjoy the satisfaction of winning a Rook for a Pawn. Lasker chose the inaccurate defense 1 K—
B6? and lost after 1 .... K—Kt4; 2 R—R1, P—R5; 3 P—B5, KP×P;
4 P—K6, P×P; 5 K×KtP, P—B5!; 6 P—R5, P—B6!; 7 P—R6 (if
now 7 R—KB1, P—R6!; 8 R×P, P—R7; 9 R—B1, P—R8=Q wins),
P—K4!!; 8 R—K1!! (8 P—R7, R×P!!!; 9 K×R, P—K5; 10 R—KB1,
P—R6; 11 K—Kt6, P—R7; 12 K—B5, P—K6!; 13 K—K4, P—K7
followed by P—B7), P—R6; 9 R×Pch, K—B5; 10 R—K1, P—R7;
11 P—R7, R—R1; 12 K—Kt7 (or 12 R—QR1, K—Kt6; 13 R—KB1!,
P—B7!; 14 K—Kt7, P—R8=Qch!; 15 R×Q, R×Q; 16 P—R8=Q,
R—Kt8ch!! and either Black will promote with check or capture his
opponent's new-born Queen), P—B7!; 13 R—QR1 (if 13 R—KB1,

P—R8=Qch!; 14 R×Q, R×R; 15 P—R8=Q, R—Kt8ch as above), K—Kt6; 14 R—KB1, P—R8=Q!; 15 R×Q, R×R; 16 Resigns.

Still another application of our basic rule that Rooks belong behind Pawns is seen in the third type of Rook position with an outside passed Pawn: the Pawn is defended by its Rook from the side and attacked by the enemy Rook from behind. While this case is more favorable than that where the White Rook is in front of the Pawn (No. 367) it is not as favorable as the second type (No. 370) and is in general a draw unless the Pawn has reached the seventh.

This case (with the Rook defending the Pawn from the side) is seen in No. 372 (Euwe-Alekhine, 23rd match game, 1937). The game continued *1 K—K2, R—KB6; 2 K—K1!!* (the only move: White must keep the Black King out of the Q-side. If, e.g., 2 R—Kt7, K—B4!; 3 R—Kt5ch, K—K5!; 4 R×RP, K—Q5; 5 R—QKt5, K—B6!; and the Pawn reaches the seventh and costs White his Rook: 6 P—R5, P—Kt7; 7 P—R6, R—B4!!; 8 R—Kt7, R—K4ch; 9 K—Q1, R—Q4ch; 10 K—K2, R—Q2!!; 11 R—Kt8, K—B7; 12 R—B8ch, K—Kt8; 13 K—K3, R—Kt2! etc.), *P—B4; 3 R—Kt6ch, K—B2; 4 R—KR6!* (forcing the issue), *R—QB6!* (on 4 .... P—B5, as played, White had an easy equalizing line: 5 R×P, R—B6—or A—; 6 R—QKt5, P—B6; 7 K—Q2, R—B7ch; 8 K—K3, P—Kt7; 9 K—B4, R—B5ch; 10 K—K3, R—B7. Drawn. Variation A: 5 .... P×P; 6 P×P, R×P; 7 K—B2, R—B6ch; 8 K—Kt2, K—K3; 9 R—QKt5=—compare No. 360b); *5 K—Q2!* (freeing the King. 5 R×P??, P—Kt7; 6 R—R7ch, K—Kt3; 7 R—Kt7, R—B8ch loses), *R—B7ch; 6 K—K3, P—Kt7; 7 R—QKt6, K—K2; 8 P—B4!!* (not 8 P—B3?, K—Q2; 9 K—B4, K—B2; 10 R—Kt5, K—B3; 11 R—Kt8, R—K7; 12 P×P, BP×P; 13 R—Kt3, K—B4; 14 R—Kt8, K—B5 and wins), *K—Q2; 9 K—Q4!!* (the point: the Black King cannot get through), *K—B2; 10 R—Kt3, K—B3; 11 R—Kt8, R—Kt7; 12 R—Kt3, R×P* (12 .... R—Q7ch; 13 K—K3!); *13 R×P, R—KR6; 14 K—K5!, R×P; 15 K×P* and in view of White's strong Pawn and Black's lack of coordination of his pieces no win is possible.

If the Pawn were on the seventh, however, White would be doomed to passive defense and Black could win by simply marching his King to the Q-side. No. 372a, White: K at KB1, R at QKt5, P's at KB2, KKt3, KR2; Black: K at KKt3, R at Q7, P's at QKt7, KB3, KKt5, KR4. Black wins. 1 K—Kt2 (forced: on 1 K—K1, R—B7; 2 K—Q1, R—B8ch White can resign), K—B2; 2 R—Kt6, K—K2; 3 R—Kt5, K—Q2; 4 R—Kt6, K—B2; 5 R—Kt3, K—B3; 6 R—Kt8, K—B4; 7 R—Kt3, K—B5; 8 R—Kt8, K—B6; 9 R—B8ch, K—Kt6; 10 R—Kt8ch, K—B7; 11 R—B8ch, K—Q8; 12 R—QKt8, K—B8; 13 R—B8ch, R—B7.

When the Pawn is on the seventh, and the defender's King is out in the open air (not confined to a dungeon as in No. 371a) the win is far more difficult. Its outlines, however, remain the same as those in No. 370, where the White Rook is behind the Pawn: First the White King gets to the center of the board (or near it). Then the Black King must stay near the Pawn, for else the White King can march in and capture the Rook. But now there is the all-important difference that Black has just as many tempi as White. Consequently, the only way to win is to capture two Pawns with the Rook, or to capture one Pawn and get to a theoretical win either by threatening to capture a second or by transposing into the equivalent of one of the R+2P vs. R+P wins.

No. 372   No. 373

Draw. Win No. 371a with Pawn on   White wins.
seventh.

This process is illustrated in No. 373 (Tartakover-Nimzovitch, Bad Kissingen, 1928). First White centralizes his King. *1 .... K—B3; 2 K—K1, P—Kt3!* (essential, else the King will be tied down to the K-side forever—which is too long here); *3 K—Q1, K—K4; 4 K—B1, K—Q4; 5 K—Kt1, R—R3; 6 K—Kt2, K—B3; 7 R—Kt7, K—B4.* Now the problem is how to continue, for the Black King cannot be driven away from B4 and the White King can get no nearer than Kt3 or B3. The only attempt that he can make is to secure a winning advantage on the K-side. But 8 R×P, R×P; 9 R—Kt5ch, K—Q5; 10 R×P, R—KB2! is not good enough, since Black will have a strong passed Pawn supported by both King and Rook. After further preparatory moves have been made, we find that the only way out of the dilemma is to get the White King back to defend the KBP, but not to allow the Black King to return. *8 P—R4!* (first fixing the Pawns), *R—R4; 9 P—Kt3* (the move chosen was 9 P—Kt4?!, but this is based on a trap and turns out to be strategically premature: 9 P—Kt4, P×P; 10 P—R5!, P—Kt6!!; 11 BP×P, P—K6!; 12 R×P, R×P; 13 K—B2, R—R7ch; 14 K—Q1, K—Q5; 15 P—R6, P—K7ch; 16 K—K1, K—K6; 17 R—K6ch, K—B6; 18 P—R7, R—R8ch; 19 K—Q2, R—Q8ch; 20 K—B2, R—Q1 and obviously nothing can be done), *9 .... R—R3; 10 K—Kt3, R—R8* (10 .... K—Q4; 11 K—Kt4, R—R8; 12 K—Kt5, K—K4; 13 K—Kt6, K—B4; 14 K—Kt7, K—Kt5 is hopeless); *11 K—B3!!, R—R6ch* (essential: if 11 .... R—R7; 12 R×P, R—R6ch; 13 K—Q2, R×RP; 14 K—K3!, R—K2; 15 R—Kt5ch decides, while a King move allows the entrance of the White monarch); *12 K—Q2, K—Q5* (12 .... K—Q4; 13 R×P transposes back into the main variation after 13 .... R×P; 14 R—Kt5ch, K—Q5; 15 R×P); *13 R—Q7ch!* (White must see to it that the Black KP does not become too strong. If 13 R×P, R—R7ch!; 14 K—K1, P—K6!!; 15 R—Q6ch, K—K4; 16 R—Q8, P×Pch; 17 K—B1, R×P; 18 R—KR8, K—K5; 19 K×P, R—R4 and draws), *K—B4* (on 13 .... K—K4 White wins by one vital tempo: 14 K—B2, K—K3; 15 R—KKt7, K—Q4; 16 K—Kt2!, R—R3; 17 K—B3!!, K—B4; 18 R×P, R—R6ch; 19 K—Q2, R×P; 20 K—K3, etc.,); *14 K—K2, K—B3; 15 R—KKt7, K—B4; 16 R×P, R×P; 17 K—K3, R—K2; 18 R— Kt5ch* and it's all over but the scoring.

If the defender's Rook were in front of the Pawn in any of the above examples, it is obvious that the superior side could simply walk in with his King and capture at least several extra Pawns.

Finally, we must consider those positions where the Pawn is blocked by the King. In that event, if the White King is nearby the win is fairly easy, but if the Pawn can only be defended by the Rook Black should draw.

No. 374 is a model case where the Black King is blockading the passed Pawn. It will be recalled that the drawing method in R+P vs. R was to keep the Black Rook on the third rank until the Pawn reached the sixth and then play it to the eighth. While this was good enough when there was nothing to capture but empty and tasteless squares, when there are Pawns around a King let loose among them always manages to have a satisfying repast. The winning method in such positions is:

1. The Pawn is advanced as far as convenient.
2. If Black's Rook leaves the third rank White will win as in the case of R+P vs. R.
3. If Black's Rook keeps the White King out, the White Rook will sneak behind the Black Pawns and, aided later by the King, capture at least one or two.

No. 374 (Eliskases-Keres, Semmering-Baden, 1937) illustrates the method with a BP. Keres tried *1 .... P—R4,* when *2 R—R2, K—B1; 3*

K—Kt5 soon decided. The immediate threat is 4 K—B6, R—B2ch; 5 K—Q6, so that Black is forced to stake everything on a counterattack—second step above. *3....* *P—R5; 4 K—Kt6* (simpler is 4 K—B6, K—Kt1; 5K—Q6 but the move played is also good enough), *R—B6; 5 P×P, P×P; 6 R—R8ch, K—Q2; 7 P—B6ch, K—K2; 8 R—KR8* (simpler than 8 P—B7, R—Kt6ch; 9 K—R7, R—R6ch; 10 K—Kt8, R—Kt6ch; 11 K—B8, R—Kt7, but 12 R—Kt8 is also quite adequate), *R—Kt6ch; 9 K—B7, R—Kt7; 10 R—R7ch, K—B3*

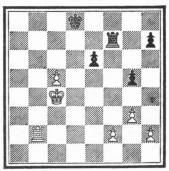

No. 374

White wins.

(or 10 .... K—K1; 11 K—Q6, R—Q7ch; 12 K×P, R—K7ch; 13 K—Q6, R—Q7ch; 14 K—B7, R×P; 15 R×P etc.); *11 K—Q8, R—Q7ch; 12 R—Q7, R×P; 13 P—B7, K—Kt4; 14 P—B8=Q, R—B1ch; 15 K—B7, R×Qch; 16 K×R, P—K4; 17 R—K7* and Black soon recognized the futility of further resistance.

The similar position with the KtP would be won by setting up a decisive material superiority on the other wing. No. 374a, White: K at QKt4, R at QR2, P's at QKt5, KB4, KKt3, KR2; Black: K at QB1, R at K2, P's at KB2, KKt3, KR4. White wins. 1 .... K—Kt2; 2 R—Q2, K—B2; 3 K—B5, K—Kt2; 4 R—Q6, K—B2 (if the Rook leaves the second rank, the Black King will be smoked off the Kt file: 4 .... R—K7; 5 R—Q7ch, K—B1; 6 R×P, R×P; 7 K—B6, R—B7ch; 8 K—Kt6, R—KKt7; 9 R—KKt7, R×P; 10 P—B5, P—Kt4; 11 P—B6, R—KB6; 12 P—B7, K—Q2; 13 R×P, R×P; 14 R×P, K—B1; 15 R—R8ch and wins); 5 R—KB6, K—Kt2; 6 P—B5!, P—Kt4 (6 .... P×P; 7 R×P, P—R5; 8 P×P is hopeless); 7 P—R4!, P×P; 8 P×P, K—B2; 9 K—Q5!, K—Kt2; 10 K—Q6, R—K5 (10 .... R—B2; 11 K—K5, R—B4ch; 12 K—B4, R×P; 13 R×Pch, K—B1; 14 K—Kt5 is likewise lost: 14 .... K—Q1; 15 K—Kt6!, K—K1; 16 R—QR7, R—Kt8; 17 R—R8ch, K—Q2; 18 R—R8 and we have one of the won positions with a BP, since the Black King is on the wrong side); 11 R×Pch, K—Kt3; 12 R—KR7, R×P; 13 P—B6, R—KB5; 14 P—B7, P—R5; 15 K—K7, R—K5ch; 16 K—B6, R—B5ch; 17 K—Kt7, R—Kt5ch; 18 K—R8, R—KB5; 19 K—Kt8, R—Kt5ch; 20 R—Kt7 and wins.

With a RP the case is not so clear because Black need not fear having his King chased out. Still, by concentrating the major forces on the other wing enough material can be won to assure victory.

If the Black King is cut off from the passed Pawn, White will always win. For with the extra Pawns on the board, if the White Pawn is on the third or fourth rank White can always sacrifice it to capture one or two Pawns on the other wing. Thus No. 375, which would be drawn if there were no Q-side Pawns, is a fairly elementary win here. The best defense is *1* .... *P—QKt4* (1 .... K—B2; 2 K—B4, R—B1ch; 3 K—Q5, R—Q1ch; 4 K—B5, R—B1ch; 5 K—Q6, R—Q1ch; 6 K—B7, R×P; 7 K×P, P—R4; 8 K—Kt6, P—R5; 9 P—R3, K—B3; 10 K—R5, K—B4; 11 R—K8, R—Q7; 12 R—QKt8, R—Q5; 13 R—Kt4 likewise leads to a loss); *2 K—B3, P—QR4; 3 R—K5, R—QKt1; 4 K—Q3, P—R5; 5 K—K4, R—Kt2; 6 K—Q5, R—QB2* (6 .... P—Kt5; 7 K—B4, P—R6; 8 P×P, P×P; 9 R—QR5, or even 8 P—Kt3 followed by R—QKt5); *7 R—K6ch, K—B2; 8 R—QKt6, P—R6; 9 R×P* and the two passed Pawns decide.

When the Black King is cut off at some distance from the Pawn, the simplest winning method is to set up a position where the remaining Pawns are held by the Rook, while the King is free to go to the support of the passed Pawn. E.g., No. 375a (Rabinovitch-Ragosin, Tiflis, 1937), White: K at KB2, R at KKt6, P's at KKt2, KR4; Black: K at KB5, R at K2, P's at QR2, KKt2, KR3. Black wins. 1 .... R—KB2; 2 K—Kt1 (or 2 K—K2, K—B4; 3 P—R5, P—R4!; 4 R—R6, K—Kt5; 5 R×P, K—Kt6 and Black will win both Pawns—compare No. 375), K—B4; 3 P—R5, K—K5; 4 R—R6, (if instead 4 R—Q6, K—K4; 5 R—Q8, K—K3; 6 K—R2, R—Q2; 7 R—QB8, K—Q3; 8 K—R3, R—QB2; 9 R—QKt8, K—B3; 10 K—Kt4, P—R4 and the Black Pawn will cost White his Rook, while he can do nothing but bite his nails in despair on the K-side), K—Q4; 5 K—R2, K—B4; 6 R—R1, K—Kt3; 7 R—Kt1ch, K—B3; 8 R—B1ch, K—Kt2; 9 R—Kt1ch, K—R1!; 10 R—QR1, R—B4!; 11 P—Kt4, R—KKt4; 12 K—Kt3, P—R4; 13 K—B3, K—R2; 14 R—R4, K—Kt3; 15 K—K3, R—Q4! (now the White King is cut off again and the Pawn marches triumphantly on); 16 R—KB4, R—Q2; 17 R—B5, P—R5; 18 P—Kt5, P×P; 19 R×P, P—R6; 20 K—K4, P—R7; 21 R—Kt1, K—Kt4; 22 R—QR1, R—R2; 23 K—Q3, K—Kt5; 24 K—B2, K—R6; 25 R—KKt1, R—B2ch; 26 K—Q3, K—Kt7; 27 Resigns.

Sometimes this defense of the remaining Pawns is not essential, but it is feasible to give one up and win with the passed Pawn. Such is the case in No. 375b (Vidmar-Dus-Chotimirsky, Carlsbad, 1907), White: K at K5, R at QKt5, P's at QR5, KKt4, KKt6; Black: K at KB1, R at QR7, P's at KKt2, KR3. White wins. 1 K—Q6, R—Q7ch; 2 K—B7, K—K2; 3 R—KB5!, (he must keep the Black King out; to have the Rook capture a Pawn is not harmful since that costs Black so much time), R—Q2ch; 4 K—B6, R—Q3ch; 5 K—Kt5, R×P; 6 P—R6, R—Q3; 7 P—R7, R—Q1; 8 K—Kt6, P—Kt3;

9 R—QKt5, K—B3; 10 K—B7, R—KR1; 11 K—Kt7, R—R2ch; 12 K—R6, R×Pch; 13 K×R, P—Kt4; 14 K—R6, K—K3; 15 K—R5, Resigns.

Black has drawing chances when his King is cut off only when the enemy Pawn structure is weakened and he can get his King in to attack the Pawns. This is seen in No. 376 (Alatortzeff-Tchekhover, Tiflis, 1937). In order to win White must play his King to the Q-side, but this leaves the K-side exposed. The continuation was *1 K—K3* (1 K—K4 does not threaten anything, while 1 P—QR4?, R—QR8; 2 R—K4, R—R6ch; 3 K—K2, K—B4 is inferior—No. 367), *K—B4*

No. 375

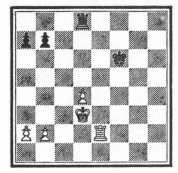

White wins.

No. 376

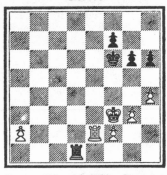

Draw. Win with White Pawns at KKt2, KR3.

(the saving counteraction); *2 R—Q2, R—QB8; 3 K—Q3, K—Kt5!; 4 R—B2, R—Q8ch; 5 K—K2* (a psychological retreat. If 5 K—B3, P—B4; 6 K—Kt3, R—Kt8ch; 7 R—Kt2, R—K8; 8 P—R4, P—B5!; 9 P×P, K×RP; 10 P—R5, K—Kt5; 11 P—R6, R—K1=, since the Black KRP is just as dangerous as his playmate on the QR file), *R—QR8; 6 K—K3, R—K8ch; 7 K—Q2* and now *7 .... R—K4!* was the most direct drawing line. In the game Black tried 7 .... R—QR8; 8 K—B3, P—Kt4? (8 .... P—B4 was better); 9 P×P, P×P; 10 K—Kt2, R—K8 when White evolved the problem-like finish 11 P—R4, P—B4; 12 K—Kt3, P—B5; 13 P×P, P×P; 14 P—R5, P—B6; 15 P—R6, K—R6; 16 P—R7, R—K1; 17 R—R2, R—QR1; 18 K—B4, K—Kt7; 19 K—B5!, R—B1ch (equally inadequate is 19 .... R×P; 20 R×R, K×P; 21 K—Q4); 20 K—Kt6, R—K1; 21 K—B6!!! (but not now 21 P—R8=Q, R×Q; 22 K×Q, R×P=—the White King is too far away), K—B8 (or 21 .... R—KR1; 22 K—

Kt7, R—R2ch; 23 K—Kt6, R—R1; 24 R—B2!, R—K1; 25 K—Kt7!
and Black will have to give up the Rook for the passed Pawn without
capturing the KBP for if 25 .... R—K2ch; 26 K—Kt8!, R—K1ch;
27 R—B8 and queens); 22 R—B2, K—Kt7; 23 K—B7!, R—K2ch;
24 K—Kt8 and wins: after 24 .... R—K1ch; 25 R—B8, R×Rch;
26 K×R, K×P; 27 P—R8=Q Black's Pawn is only on the sixth.
But after the defense given above (7 .... R—K4) Black can afford to
give up his Rook at the appropriate moment because he will capture
a Pawn on the K-side: *8 P—R4* (8 R—B4ch, K—R6!; 9 R—B4,
P—B4; 10 K—B3, P—Kt4; 11 P×P, P×P; 12 R—QKt4, K—Kt7;
13 R—Kt2, P—B5; 14 P×P, P×P; 15 K—Kt4, P—B6; 16 P—R4,
R—K7!!, etc.=), *P—B4; 9 R—R2, R—QR4; 10 K—B3, P—B5;
11 K—Kt4, R—R1; 12 R—R3* (despite the Pawn up White's position
is no bed of roses. If, e.g., 12 P×P, K×RP; 13 R—R3?, R—KB1!;
14 P—R5, R×Pch; 15 K—Kt5, R×P and Black may even win),
R—Kt1ch!; 13 K—B5, R—Kt7; 14 P—R5, R×P; 15 P×P! (essential:
if 15 P—R6?, P×P; 16 P—R7, R—B1; 17 P—R8=Q, R×Q; 18
R×R, P—Kt7; 19 R—R1, K×P; 20 K—Q4, K—Kt6; 21 K—K3,
P—R4 the Pawns are too strong and will win), *R×P!; 16 P—R6,
R—B1!; 17 P—R7, R—QR1!* (it is important to draw White's King
as far as possible away from the Pawns); *18 K—Kt6, P—Kt4!* (again
not to lose time); *19 P×P, P×P; 20 K—Kt7, R×Pch; 21 K×R,
K—B5; 22 K—Kt6, P—Kt5; 23 K—B5, P—Kt6=.*

If the Pawns were not weakened, White could win because Black
would have no counterplay. The White King would march over to
the Q-side (as in the above example) and the advance of the Pawn
would be conclusive.

Note that the important point about the weakness of the Pawns is
that Black must be able to capture one and then transpose into a
drawn R vs. P ending. Where the Pawns are merely exposed, but not
capturable, there is no real defense. One more example will help to
make the winning method clear. No. 376a (Marshall-Capablanca,
9th match game, 1909), White: K at KKt5, R at Q4, P's at QR4, K3,
KR3; Black: K at K3, R at KB7, P's at QR4, KB2. White wins.
Marshall played 1 R—K4ch, K—Q4; 2 R—KB4, R—Kt7ch; 3 K—
B6, R—Kt6; 4 P—K4ch, K—Q5; 5 P—K5 dis ch, K—Q4 (5 .... K—
K6; 6 R—B1!, R×P; 7 K×P, R—R5; 8 P—K6, R×P; 9 P—K7, R—
K5; 10 R—K1ch) and now the most precise win was 6 P—R4 (against
6 R—B5, as played, Capablanca succeeded in drawing after 6 ....
K—K5!; 7 R—R5, R—B6ch; 8 K—K7, R—B5; 9 R—Kt5, K—Q5;
10 R—R5, K—B6; 11 R—R7, R—B4; 12 K—Q6, K—Kt6?; 13 R—
R4, R—B6; 14 K—K7, R—K6; 15 K×P, R×P; 16 K—KKt4?, R—
QB4; 17 R—KB4, R—B2ch; 18 K—Kt6, R—QKt2!!; 19 P—R4, R—
Kt5!! for after the exchange of Rooks or the capture of White's RP

White can no longer win), R—K6 (or 6 .... R—KR6; 7 R—B5!, K—K5; 8 P—R5, R—R8; 9 P—K6!, P×P; 10 K×P and with the Black King cut off on a rank the win with the two RP's is only a question of time); 7 R—B5, K—K5 (else 8 K×P); 8 R—B1!, R—QR6 (8 .... R—KR6 is met in the same way); 9 R—K1ch, K—Q4; 10 K×P, R—B6ch (10 .... R×P; 11 P—K6, R—B5ch; 12 K—Kt6, R—B1; 13 P—K7, or 11 .... R×P; 12 P—K7, R—R1; 13 R—QR1, R—R2ch; 14 K—B6!, R—R1; 15 R×Pch, K—Q3; 16 R—R6ch, K—Q2; 17 R—R7ch, K—Q3; 18 K—B7, R—R2ch; 19 K—B8, R—R1ch; 20 K—Kt7, R—K1; 21 K—B7); 11 K—K7, R—B5; 12 P—K6, R×QRP; 13 K—Q7, R×P; 14 P—K7, R—R1; 15 R—QR1 and wins. The point here is that Black could bring about exchanges, but could never actually win any material, so that the whole ending became a more complicated version of No. 375.

If the Pawns are not otherwise balanced (e.g., 3 to 1 on one side, 1 to 2 on the other), *the winning method consists of setting up two connected passed Pawns.* Of course, one must make sure that the enemy Pawn does not become too dangerous. The position reached will be the same structurally as the R+2P vs. R+P ending—the extra Pawns will make no difference. This is why one must set up *connected* passed Pawns, for disconnected Pawns do not win with any great degree of frequency (See Nos. 356–363 for the elementary cases). No. 377 (Euwe-Alekhine, 1st match game 1937) is typical of such endings with 3 Pawns vs. 2. Euwe's conduct of the final phase is exemplary. *1 R—QB4!* (first tying the Black Rook down and also hindering the advance of the Pawn), *R—Kt3; 2 K—K2, K—B2* (2 .... K—K2; *3 R—KR4 is hopeless); 3 R—KR4, K—Kt3; 4 R—KB4, R—Kt6; 5 R—QB4, R—Kt3; 6 K—K3!* (now the Pawns will soon start rolling), *K—B4; 7 P—Kt4ch, K—K3* (if 7 .... K—Kt4; 8 P—B3, K—R5; 9 R—B5!, R—Kt6ch; 10 K—K2!, R—Kt7ch; 11 K—Q1!, R—Kt8ch; 12 K—B2, R—Kt4; 13 R×P, K—Kt4; 14 K—Q3 and wins); *8 P—B4, K—Q4* (hoping to get his Pawn going. The alternative 8 .... P—R4 loses prettily after 9 P—Kt5!, K—B4; 10 R—B5ch, K—K3 or A—; 11 P—B5ch, K—Q3; 12 P—Kt6!, K×R; 13 P—Kt7, R—Kt1; 14 P—B6 and the Black King is one move too late. Variation A. 10 .... K—Kt5; 11 P—Kt6, R—Kt1; 12 R—Kt5ch, K—R5; 13 P—

No. 377

White wins.

Kt7, R—KKt1; 14 R—Kt3 followed by the march of the BP); *9 R—Q4ch!, K—K3* (on 9 .... K—B4; 10 P—B5 is conclusive); *10 P—B5ch, K—K2* (10 .... K—B3; 11 K—B4); *11 R—K4ch, K—B2; 12 P—R4* (there are various satisfactory alternatives hereabouts: the line chosen is the most direct), *R—Kt8; 13 K—B4, R—QB8* (if 13 .... P—R3; 14 R—QB4, R—B8ch; 15 K—Kt3, P—R4; 16 K—Kt2, R—K8; 17 P—Kt5 and the win is only a question of time); *14 R—R4, P—R3; 15 R—R7ch, K—Kt1; 16 P—Kt5, R—B5ch; 17 K—K5, R×P* (Alekhine resigned here); *18 P—Kt6, R—R8; 19 K—B6* and mate cannot be postponed for more than one move.

Where the Black Pawns are weak White is ordinarily in a position to come out two Pawns ahead. E.g., No. 377a (Lasker-Bogoljuboff, New York, 1924), White: K at KB3, R at KR7, P's at QR2, KKt2, KR2; Black: K at QKt4, R at QR1, P's at KB4, KB5. White wins. 1 .... R—R6ch! (the only way to hang on to his last Pawn for a while. On 1 .... R×P; 2 R—KB7 he loses both Pawns in short order); 2 K×P, R×P; 3 R—KKt7, R—B7ch; 4 K—K3! (the game continuation 4 K—K5, P—B5! gives Black excellent counterchances, since the sacrifice .... P—B6 always threatens to lead into the R+BP+RP vs. R ending), R—B8 (or 4 .... R—R7; 5 R—Kt5, K—B5; 6 K—B3, R—R4; 7 K—B4); 5 R—Kt5, K—B3; 6 K—K2, R—B5 (6 .... R—KR8; 7 P—R3, P—B5; 8 R—KB5, R—KKt8; 9 K—B2); 7 P—Kt3, R—K5ch; 8 K—B3, R—K4; 9 K—B4!, R—K7; 10 P—R4, R—B7ch; 11 K—K3, R—B8; 12 K—K2, R—KKt8; 13 K—B2 and despite Black's stubborn defense White will capture the BP and secure two connected passed Pawns.

The defender can normally draw if his Pawn has become a serious threat. When White does not have two passed Pawns as yet, a Pawn on the seventh defended from the side or from behind is surely sufficient. This is seen in another Alekhine-Euwe game: No. 377b (13th match game, 1935), White: K at K1, R at QB7, P's at QR7, KR3; Black: K at KKt2, R at QR5, P's at KB2, KKt3, KR2. Draw. The difficulty with Black's position is that his King cannot leave the neighborhood of the BP and his Pawns cannot advance quickly enough. After 1 K—Q2, P—Kt4; 2 K—B3, P—R4; 3 K—Kt3, R—R8; 4 K—B4, P—Kt5 (if 4 .... K—Kt3; 5 K—Kt5!, P—B3; 6 K—Kt6, P—Kt5; 7 P×P, P×P; 8 R—B8, K—B4; 9 P—R8=Q, R×Q; 10 R×R, K—K5 is a draw.); 5 P×P, P×P; 6 K—Q4, K—Kt3; 7 K—K3 draws (No. 359a).

Again, if the Pawn majority is blockaded or devaluated, no wins possible. Thus in No. 377c (Schlechter-Janowski, Ostend, 1907) where the Pawns are doubled, a draw is the normal result. White: K at KKt3, R at QR5, P's at QR4, KR3; Black: K at KR2, R at QKt7, P's at KB4, KKt2, KKt3. Draw. 1 R—R8, P—Kt4; 2 P—R5, R—

Kt6ch; 3 K—R2, R—Kt7ch; 4 K—R1, R—Kt2; 5 P—R6, R—Kt8ch;
6 K—Kt2, R—QR8; 7 P—R7 and now the Black King dare not expose
himself to a check, while Black is unable to set up two passed Pawns.
Janowski tried 7 .... K—Kt3; 8 K—R2, P—B5; 9 K—Kt2, R—
R7ch; 10 K—R1, P—Kt5!; but the reply 11 R—KB8! (11 P×P?,
K—Kt4! loses, since Black gets two connected passed Pawns), R×P;
12 R×P, P×P; 13 R—Kt4ch, K—R4; 14 R—Kt3, K—R5; 15 R—
Kt6! made the draw plain.

Summary: With an outside passed Pawn and an otherwise balanced
Pawn position White wins easily if the Black King is cut off, or if his
Rook is behind the Pawn, but can in general only draw if his Rook is
in front of or to the side of the Pawn and the Black King is free to
roam about. A weak Pawn structure, however, is usually fatal for
Black, while it destroys White's winning chances. If the Pawn position is not balanced White must set up two connected passed Pawns
as quickly as possible and then proceed in exactly the same manner
as in R+2P vs. R+P—advancing his own Pawns but at the same
time guarding the enemy Pawn.

B. WHITE HAS A POTENTIAL OUTSIDE PASSED PAWN

This of course is the same as saying that White has a majority of
Pawns on a wing.

We shall first consider *those positions where the Pawn position is
otherwise balanced.* Unlike the analogous cases with minor pieces, the
winning method does not involve merely setting up a passed Pawn,
for, as we saw in A, there are a number of positions where such a Pawn
does not win. The superior side must not exchange before he is
certain that the resultant ending is won. In general, the two most
common reasons why he can have this certainty are a) that the enemy
King is cut off from the passed Pawn and b) that his Rook is behind
the passed Pawn.

*If the defending King is not near the potential passed Pawn, i.e., is
on the side where the Pawns are in equilibrium, the winning method consists of three steps:*

1. Placing the King and Rook on the best possible squares.
2. Advancing the Pawns which are in the majority as far as convenient without actually setting up a passed Pawn.
3. Transposing to one of the won positions with an outside passed
   Pawn. On occasion this may mean that one should secure two
   connected passed Pawns against a single passed Pawn.

In the first step, the Rook should be placed aggressively (with as
much freedom of action as possible), while the King should defend
any weak Pawns.

A case where two connected passed Pawns are set up is seen in No. 378 (Mieses-Dus-Chotimirsky, Carlsbad, 1907). The King and Rook are placed well enough (.... K—K3 and .... R—Q1 or .... R—Kt1 may be played at an opportune moment) so Black starts his Pawns rolling. *1* .... *P—KKt4; 2 R—KKt1, P—Kt5; 3 R—QB1* (if 3 P—KR3, R—KKt1 gives us the win with the Rook behind the passed Pawn: No. 369), *R—Q1; 4 R—KB1, R—Q6ch; 5 K—B2* (in the game there occurred 5 K—B4, R—Q5ch; 6 K—B5, R×P and with two Pawns up the rest was simple: 7 R—B5, P—R5; 8 R—R5, P—Kt6; 9 P×P, P×P; 10 K—Q5, R—K7; 11 R—Kt5, P—Kt7; 12 P—Kt4, K—B3; 13 R—Kt8, K—B4; 14 R—Kt7, R—Q7ch; 15 K—B4, K—

<table>
<tr><td>No. 378</td><td>No. 379</td></tr>
</table>

<table>
<tr><td>Black wins.</td><td>Black wins.</td></tr>
</table>

B5; 16 Resigns), *R—K6!* (the most direct); *6 R—B5, R—K7ch!* (far better than the alternative 6 .... R×P; 7 R×RP); *7 K—Q3, R×RP; 8 R×Pch, K—B3; 9 R—B5ch, K—K3* (on 9 .... K—Kt3; 10 R—B1, R×P; 11 P—K5 the KP may become dangerous); *10 P—Kt3, P—Kt6; 11 R—KKt5, P—R5; 12 K—K3, P—Kt7; 13 K—B2, P—R6; 14 R—Kt7, R—R8; 15 R—Kt5, R—B8ch* and wins White's Rook.

A 3–1 complex, where the passed Pawn is supported by the King, is just as good as two connected passed Pawns. Thus in a case analogous to the above, No. 378a (Opocensky-Fahrni, Baden, 1914), White: K at KR3, R at K3, P's at QR4, QKt3, KKt3, KR4; Black: K at KB3, R at QKt5, P's at QR4, QKt3, QB4, KKt3, KR4 the quickest way to win is 1 .... K—B4; 2 R—B3ch, K—K5; 3 R—B6, R×KtP; 4 R×KKtP, P—B5; 5 R—QB6, P—B6; 6 K—Kt2, K—Q6 and White will soon lose his Rook.

The transposition to a won ending with an outside passed Pawn may occur either when the defending King is cut off, or when the Rook of the passed Pawn gets behind it, or when the Pawn is on the seventh and defended from the side. Of course special cases with other varieties of outside Pawn endings may also be won.

In No. 379 (Teichmann-Schallopp, Nuremberg, 1896) Black exchanges when he can force his Pawn to the seventh and defend it with his Rook on the seventh. Schallopp wound up as follows: *1 R—B4, R—Kt3* (1 .... R—Q7; 2 P—B3, R—Kt7; 3 P—Kt4 is not as accurate, for 3 .... P—Kt6?; 4 P×P, R×P; 5 R—R4 should not do better than draw); *2 K—Kt1, K—B3; 3 K—B1, K—K3* (Black will not exchange before his Pawn can reach the seventh); *4 K—K2, P—Kt6!; 5 P×P, R×P; 6 R—QR4, R—Kt7ch; 7 K—K3, P—R7* and the rest is routine: *8 P—Kt4, K—Q4; 9 P—Kt5, K—B4; 10 P—Kt4, K—Kt4; 11 R—R8, K—Kt5;* 12 Resigns.

The transposition with the Rook behind the Pawn is seen in No. 380 (Breyer-Johner, 1914). The extra Black Pawn at KKt2 makes no difference since it is doubled: Black is for all practical purposes only one Pawn ahead. The conclusion was both simple and straightforward: *1 .... P—Kt3; 2 R—R3, P—R4; 3 R—Q3, P—QKt4; 4 R—Q6, K—B2; 5 P—R3, R—K3; 6 R—Q7ch, R—K2; 7 R—Q5, R—Kt2; 8 K—K3, P—Kt5!; 9 P×P* (9 P—QR4, P—Kt6 is worse), *P×P; 10 K—Q2, P—Kt6; 11 K—B1, P—Kt7ch; 12 K—Kt1, R—Kt6; 13 P—R4, R—Kt5; 14 R—Q6, R×P; 15 K×P, R—QB5 and the rest is* academic: *16 K—Kt3, R—B2; 17 R—Q1, P—Kt4; 18 R—B1ch, K—Kt3; 19 R—KKt1, K—B4; 20 R—B1ch, K—K5; 21 R—KKt1, K—B5* (21 .... P—Kt5!; 22 R×Pch, K—B4; 23 R—Kt1, P—Kt4 is shorter but the text is of course adequate); *22 R—B1ch, K—K6; 23 R—KKt1, R—B4; 24 K—Kt4, R—B4; 25 K—B3, K—B7; 26 R—Kt4, K—B6; 27 R—Q4, P—Kt5; 28 R—Q3ch, K—Kt7* and White soon abandoned the hopeless struggle.

The most common error in this type of ending is to transpose at the wrong time—usually too early, sometimes too late. A few examples will illustrate this.

No. 380a (Reggio-Przepiorka, Barmen, 1905), White: K at KB3, R at Q1, P's at QR2, QKt2, QB4, KB4, KKt3, KR3; Black: K at KB3, R at K1, P's at QR3, QKt2, K2, KKt3, KR4. 1 .... R—K2; 2 R—Q6, R—QB2; 3 P—Kt3, P—QKt4; 4 R×RP?

No. 380

Black to play wins.

(the correct refutation was 4 R—Q4, P×P; 5 R×P, R—Q2; 6 R—B6, P—R4; 7 P—KKt4!, R—Q6ch; 8 K—K4, R×RP; 9 P—Kt5ch, K—B2; 10 R—B7ch, K—K1; 11 K—K5, etc.), P×P; 5 P×P, R×P; 6 P—Kt4, R—B6ch; 7 K—Kt2, P×P; 8 P×P, R—B5; 9 K—B3, R—B6ch; 10 K—B2 and White tried everything but it was too late.

No. 380b (Fine-Thomas, Nottingham, 1936), White: K at KKt2, R at Q3, P's at QR2, QKt3, KKt3, KR2; Black: K at K3, R at KB4, P's at QKt4, KKt2, KR3. Here 1 P—QR4!, P×P; 2 P×P, R—QR4; 3 R—R3, K—Q4; 4 K—B3, K—B5; 5 P—R4, K—Kt5; 6 R—R1, K—Kt6; 7 R—Kt1ch!, K—B5; 8 R—Kt7!, P—Kt4; 9 P×P!, P×P; 10 R—K7, K—Q4; 11 K—Kt4, R×Pch; 12 K×P, R—R1; 13 P—Kt4, R—Kt1ch; 14 K—B5, R—B1ch; 15 K—Kt6, R—Kt1ch; 16 R—KKt7 would have decided. Instead White delayed the advance too long and Black built up an ingenious counter-threat on the other wing: 1 R—Q2, R—B4; 2 K—B3, K—K4; 3 R—Q7, P—Kt3; 4 R—K7ch, K—B4; 5 R—K2, R—B6ch; 6 K—B2, P—R4; 7 K—K1, K—Kt5; 8 K—Q2, R—B4; 9 K—Q3, P—Kt4; 10 R—QB2, R—B4; 11 K—B3, P—R5; 12 P×P, P×P; 13 K—Kt4, P—R6; 14 P—R4 (ten years overdue), P×P; 15 K×P, K—B6; 16 P—Kt4, R—KKt4; 17 P—Kt5, R—Kt7! Drawn, for both sides will queen.

No. 380c (Opocensky-Fahrni, Baden, 1914), White: K at KKt2, R at QB3, P's at QR4, KKt3, KR4; Black: K at KB3, R at QKt5, P's at QR4, QKt3, KKt3, KR4. After 1 .... R×QRP (on 1 .... K—B4; 2 R—B6 also gives White excellent drawing chances: Black had clarified the situation on the Q-side too soon); 2 R—B6ch, K—B4; 3 R×QKtP, R—QKt5; 4 R—R6, P—R5; 5 K—R3, R—QB5; 6 R—R5ch, K—K5; 7 R—R6, K—Q6; 8 R×KtP, P—R6; 9 R—QR6, R—B6; 10 R—R5, K—B7; 11 R×KRP, P—R7; 12 R—R5, K—Kt7; 13 R×Pch, K×R; 14 P—R5 a draw was agreed to.

No. 381

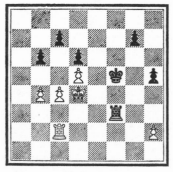

Black wins.

Often the defender prefers not to wait for the transposition to a won ending with an outside passed Pawn, and resorts to some tactical sortie. In that event more material can usually be won. No. 381 (Janowski-Rubinstein, Carlsbad, 1907) is a case in point. After *1 .... R—QKt6!!* (to fix the Q-side Pawns); *2 R—B2ch, K—Kt3; 3 R—Kt2ch, K—R3; 4 P—Kt5, R—KB6* Janowski reasoned that against a

Rubinstein it was useless to try to hold the position by any passive defense, such as 5 R—QB2, P—Kt4; 6 R—KKt2, P—R5; 7 R—QB2, P—Kt5; 8 R—KKt2, K—R4, etc., so he goes out to do or die. *5 K— K4, R—B3; 6 R—R2, P—Kt4; 7 R—R7, R—B5ch!!* (essential: the point will soon be clear); *8 K—Q3, R—B2; 9 P—B5, QP×P; 10 P— Q6, R—Q2!* (now we see why the King had to be driven to the Q file); *11 R×P, R×Pch; 12 K—K4, R—Q5ch!; 13 K—B5, P—R5; 14 R— B8* (or 14 R—B6ch, K—R4; 15 R×KtP, R—B5ch; 16 K—K5, R— B7; 17 R—QB6, R×P; 18 R×P, R—QKt7 and the two passed Pawns march on), *R—B5ch; 15 K—K5, P—B5; 16 R—R8ch, K—Kt2; 17 R— QB8, K—Kt3; 18 R—Kt8ch, K—R4; 19 P—R3, P—B6; 20 R—R8ch, K—Kt3; 21 R—Kt8ch, K—R3; 22 R—R8ch, K—Kt2; 23 R—QB8, R—B6; 24 R—B6, R×P; 25 R×P, R—B6;* 26 Resigns.

Two other examples of the refutation of tactical counterattacks will further illustrate this important practical point. It is of course hardly possible to set up any general rules, but in a position where the major pieces do not cooperate loss of material is inevitable.

No. 381a (Rubinstein-Duras, Pistyan, 1912), White: K at K2, R at QB5, P's at QR2, QKt3, K3, KB2, KKt3, KR2; Black: K at Q3, R at QKt2, P's at QR3, Q2, KB4, KKt3, KR2. White to play. 1 R— B8, R—Kt3; 2 K—Q3, K—Q4; 3 P—KR4, P—R3; 4 R—B4, P— Kt4; 5 P×P, P×P; 6 P—KKt4!, R—Kt4 (or 6 .... P×P; 7 R×P, R—Kt3; 8 P—B4); 7 P×P, K—K4; 8 R—QR4, P—R4; 9 K—B4, R—Q4; 10 P—B3!, P—Q3; 11 P—K4, R—B4ch; 12 K—Q3, P—Q4; 13 R—Q4, P×Pch; 14 P×P, P—Kt5; 15 R—Q8 and Black soon gave up.

No. 381b (Foltys-Fine, Margate, 1937), White: K at K3, R at Q2, P's at QKt2, QB3, K4, KKt2; Black: K at QB3, R at KKt5, P's at QB4, Q3, K4, KKt2, KR4. 1 K—B3, R—B5ch; 2 K—K3, P—R5; 3 R—Q1, P—Kt4; 4 P—KKt3 (giving Black a passed Pawn. But against passive play the advance of the Pawns on the K-side and of the King on the other wing would win easily), P×P; 5 R—KKt1, P—Kt5; 6 R×P, P—B5!; 7 R—Kt1, K—Kt4; 8 R—KR1, P—Kt6!; 9 R—KKt1, R—B7! (Black has carefully calculated that he will be able to win both Q-side Pawns); 10 R×P, R×P; 11 R—Kt8, R— QB7; 12 R—Kt8ch, K—R3; 13 R—R8ch, K—Kt2; 14 R—R3, K— B3; 15 R—R6ch, K—Q2; 16 R—R3, K—K3!; 17 K—B3, K—B3; 18 K—Kt3, K—Kt4; 19 K—B3, K—R5; 20 R—R6, R×Pch; 21 K— K2, R—Q6; 22 R—B6, R—Q5; 23 K—K3, K—Kt6; 24 R—B8, R— Q6ch; 25 K—K2, K—B5 Resigns. For if 26 R×P, R—Q5; 27 R×R, P×R; 28 K—Q3, K—K4.

In all the above examples the defending King was on the side where the Pawns are balanced. *If the King is on the side of the potential passed Pawn* the winning method is essentially the same as that given above. The chief difference is that as a rule the step which involves transposition to a won ending with an outside passed Pawn is of minor importance because any such Pawn is already blocked by the King. Instead the entrance of the King to the other wing is the decisive manoeuvre.

No. 382 (Lawrence-Mieses, Cambridge Springs, 1904) is typical. The winning idea is simplicity itself: after adequate preparation (safe-guarding the R position and the Pawns) White will march his King to the Q-side and win at least one more Pawn there. The game continued *1 .... K—B3; 2 P—KB4, P—KR3; 3 K—B3, P—QR4; 4 K—K4* (this is step 1 in our schema on page 355; the remainder is a variant of the third step), *R—Q2; 5 P—B3, R—QKt2; 6 K—Q5, R—Q2ch; 7 K—B4, R—Q1* (or 7 .... P—Kt4ch; 8 K×KtP, R×P; 9 R×P, R×RP; 10 P—Kt5ch, P×P; 11 P×Pch, K—K3; 12 K×P); *8 R—Q5, R—K1; 9 P—B5* (super-cautious: 9 R—Q6ch, K—Kt2; 10 R×QKtP, R—K6; 11 R—Kt5, R×RP; 12 R×RP, R—B6; 13 R×P, R×Pch gives Black splendid counterchances, but the simple 9 K—Kt5, R—K6; 10 P—Kt5ch, K—K3; 11 R—K5ch!, R×R; 12 P×R, P×P; 13 P—Q4 puts an end to all resistance), *P×P; 10 R×Pch, K—Kt3; 11 P—R4* (first safeguarding the K-side Pawns), *R—K6; 12 P—R5ch, K—Kt2; 13 P—Kt5, P×P; 14 R×Pch, K—B2; 15 R—Q5* (now that Black has been deprived of his last chance on the K-side the inroad on the other wing is conclusive), *K—K2; 16 K—Kt5* (or as played: 16 P—Q4, P×P; 17 P×P, R—K3; 18 R—K5, Resigns), *R—K3; 17 P—B4, K—B3; 18 R—Q7, K—Kt4; 19 R—QKt7, R—Q3; 20 R×P, R×P; 21 K×RP, K×P; 22 R—Kt5, K—Kt3; 23 K—Kt6* and the rest is routine.

A simpler example from recent tournament practice is No. 382a (Flohr-Vidmar, Nottingham, 1936), White: K at K4, R at K5, P's at QR3, QKt4, KKt3, KR5; Black: K at QKt3, R at KR2; P's at QR3, KKt4, KR3. White wins. After 1 .... K—B3; 2 R—K6ch, K—Kt4; 3 K—B5, R—B2ch; 4 R—B6 Black resigned because he must lose both Pawns on the K-side: 4 .... R—KR2; 5 K—Kt6, R—R1; 6 K—Kt7, R—K1; 7 K×P, R—K6; 8 R—B5ch, K—Kt3; 9 R×P, R×KtP; 10 K—Kt7, etc.

The transposition to a won ending with an outside passed Pawn is seen in No. 382b (Loevenfisch-Botvinnik, 11th match game, 1937), White: K at K3, R at Q3, P's at QR3, QKt2, KB4, KR2; Black: K at KB3, R at QB1, P's at QR4, QKt4, KKt3. White to play wins. The game concluded 1 R—Q6ch, K—B2; 2 R—Q5, P—Kt5; 3 P×P, P×P; 4 R—Q4, P—Kt6; 5 R—Q3, R—KR1; 6 K—K4, R×P; 7 R×P, R—K7ch; 8 K—Q3, R—KB7; 9 K—K3, R—KKt7; 10 R—Kt5, R—Kt8; 11 K—Q3, R—KB8; 12 R—Kt4, R—B7; 13 P—Kt3, R—B6ch; 14 K—K4, R—Kt6; 15 R—Kt5, R—Kt8; 16 R—Kt4,

R—Kt8; 17 R—Kt7ch, K—B3; 18 R—Kt6ch, K—B2; 19 P—Kt4,
R—K8ch; 20 K—Q4, R—KB8; 21 K—K5!, R—K8ch; 22 K—Q6,
R—K5; 23 P—Kt5, R×P; 24 R—B6, Resigns, for if 24 .... P—Kt4;
25 P—Kt6, P—Kt5; 26 P—Kt7, R—Kt5; 27 K—B7, P—Kt6; 28 P—
Kt8=Q, etc.—the KtP is lost.

With an unbalanced Pawn position, we again have the same chief
winning possibilities: reduction to a more elementary case with an
outside passed Pawn, and setting up two connected passed Pawns vs.
one. In addition, if the Pawns are weak, as is apt to be the case, more
material may be won.

No. 382

White wins.

No. 383

Black wins.

The only one of these eventualities which differs from anything that
we have had before is that where both players can secure sets of connected passed Pawns. The superior side will then have an extra Pawn
somewhere else, but the speed with which the Pawns can be advanced
is the decisive factor. Such endings often end in hair-raising spectacles,
where one player wins by a chessic nose. No. 383 (Kostitch-Gruenfeld,
Teplitz-Schoenau, 1922) is illustrative. Against passive defense Black
would win by a judicious advance of his Q-side Pawns. E.g., 1 R—
Q2, R—K5; 2 R—QB2, P—Kt4; 3 R—Q2, P—R4; 4 R—QB2, P—
Kt5; 5 R—Q2, P—QR5; 6 R—QB2, K—Q4; 7 R—KB2, P—Kt6;
9 P×P, P×P; 10 R—QKt2, R—QKt5, etc. For this reason Kostitch
tried *1 R—Kt5,* when Gruenfeld won by pushing his Q-side Pawns
with both hands: *1 .... R×P; 2 R×RP, R—QKt7!*. Black has two
advantages: 1. his King is protected from checks; 2. the White King
and Rook have to get out of the way of the Pawns. These advantages
make the ending an example of the well-known Manhattan Chess Club

rule that Black Pawns travel more quickly than White ones. *3 R—R8, P—R4; 4 K—Kt4* (if 4 R—R8, K—B4! is the most precise:

a) 5 P—Kt4ch, K—Kt4; 6 R—Kt8ch, K—R3!; 7 P—Kt5ch, K—R4; 8 P—Kt6, R—Kt5 and wins for if 9 P—Kt7, K—R3 and 10 R—K8, K×P gives a simple win (No. 356).

b) 5 R—B8ch, K—Kt3; 6 R—Kt8ch, K—B2; 7 R—QR8, R—Kt5; 8 P—Kt4, P—R5; 9 K—R4, P—Kt4; 10 K—Kt5, R—Kt6; 11 P—R4, P—R6; 12 P—R5, P—Kt5!; 13 K—R6 (13 P—R6, R—KR6), R—KKt6; 14 P—Kt5, R—Kt7; 15 P—Kt6ch, K—B3; 16 R—B8ch, K—K4!; 17 P—Kt7, P—R7; 18 R—QR8, P—Kt6; 19 R—R5ch (19 K—R7, P—Kt7), K—B3; 20 R—R6ch, P—K3 and will queen), *P—R5; 5 R—R8, R—Kt5ch; 6 K—B3, P—Kt4; 7 P—R4, K—B3; 8 P—Kt4, R—Kt6ch; 9 K—K4, P—R6; 10 R—R6ch, K—Kt2; 11 K—B5, P—Kt5; 12 R—R7, R—B6ch; 13 K—K4, R—B7; 14 K—K3, R—QKt7!;* 15 Resigns. For if now *15 R×Pch, K—B1; 16 R—QR7, P—R7; 17 P—R5, P—Kt6; 18 P—R6, R—R7; 19 P—Kt5, P—Kt7; 20 R×P, R—R6ch!; 21 K any, P—Kt8= Q.*

C. THE EXTRA PAWN IS IN THE CENTER

It makes little or no difference whether there is actually a passed Pawn on the board, or whether it is merely potential. If the Pawn is not yet passed, it is usually best to exchange it and make it passed as soon as possible. This is in contrast to the cases with outside Pawns, chiefly because the drawing dangers (enemy Rook behind the Pawn) which an outside Pawn involves are much more remote here.

We must again distinguish otherwise balanced and unbalanced Pawn positions. If the Pawn position is balanced, it is best for the defense to have the passed Pawn blockaded by the King. This leaves the Rook free to annoy the opponent in other quarters.

With such a set-up, i.e., a balanced Pawn position (except for the extra Pawn) and the Black King in front of the Pawn the win consists of five steps.

1. Weakening the Black Pawns by compelling them to advance and be blockaded.
2. Tying up the Black Rook by attacking the weakened Pawns.
3. Advancing the King and passed Pawn as far as is convenient— usually Pawn on the fifth rank.
4. Putting Black in zugzwang by threatening to march in with the King or to capture more material.
5. Transposing to an elementary win by either the win of additional material, an advantageous exchange, or a reduction to one of the standard positions.

One will of course rarely see all these steps carried out in their entirety. Black will most often resort to some tactical sortie which forces his opponent to discard the plan temporarily and ward off the opponent's threats. But against a passive defense, which usually staves off defeat longest in such endings, the win will always conform to the pattern given.

There are two classic endings which illustrate the whole winning process beautifully.

The first is No. 384 (Tarrasch-Thorold, Manchester, 1890). Tarrasch's handling of the ending is exemplary. *1 K—B2, P—Kt3* (Black is very obliging and advances his Pawn voluntarily. But on 1 .... K—Q3; 2 R—Kt3, R—B5ch; 3 K—K3, R—B2; 4 R—R3, P—Kt3; 5 R—B3 White would likewise have achieved his object); *2 R—R3, P—KR4* (first step completed); *3 K—K3, R—Q3; 4 P—Q4* (the order in which the second and third steps are carried out is of secondary importance—it varies with the position), *R—K3ch; 5 K—Q3, R—K8; 6 R—Kt3!* (The Rook's short-lived freedom is at an end—the second step is now completed), *R—K3* (6 .... R—QKt8?; 7 K—B2 loses a Pawn, while 6 .... R—Q8ch; 7 K—B3, R—B8ch; 8 K—Q2, R—B3 transposes back into the game); *7 R—K3* (White makes a few useless moves here, but they do no harm. 7 P—QR4 is more direct), *R—Q3; 8 R—K5, R—KB3; 9 P—QR4* (to safeguard the Pawns on the Q-side and prepare the advance of the QP and the King. In effect Tarrasch is executing the fourth step, which is, as a rule, the most difficult of all), *R—B7* (this Rook is a kind of jack rabbit—it pops out and then goes right back); *10 R—K2, R—B3; 11 P—QKt4, R—B8; 12 R—K5, R—B7; 13 R—KKt5!* (forcing the Rook to return—note the effect of the weakening of the Black Pawns), *R—B3; 14 P—R3* (14 P—Q5 at once was also possible, but the text is more methodical), *K—Q3* (or 14....R—Q3;15P—Q5,R—KB3; 16 K—K4, K—Q3; 17 R—K5 as in the game); *15 K—K4, R—K3ch; 16 R—K5, R—B3; 17 P—Q5!!* (Black is finally forced to give way with the King. If the R moves, R—K6ch wins a Pawn, while if 17 .... P—R4; 18 P×P, P×P; 19 K—Q4!, R—B5ch; 20 R—K4, R—B3; 21 R—K6ch!!, R×R; 22 P×R, K×P; 23 K—B5 with a simply won Pawn ending.), *17 .... K—Q2; 18 R—Kt5* (to allow the King to occupy K5. The fourth step is not

No. 384

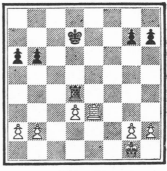

White wins.

yet wholly completed), *K—Q3; 19 R—Kt3, K—K2* (he must prevent the exchange of Rooks which White was threatening); *20 R—KB3, R—Q3; 21 K—K5.* Now we have the second key position. The Black Rook is forced to abandon the third rank and White's Pawn advances to the sixth. *21 .... R—Q1; 22 P—Q6ch!!* (a pretty tactical finesse: if 22 .... R×P; 23 R—B7ch, K×R; 24 K×R and the Pawn ending is hopeless for Black), *K—Q2.* This finally finishes the fourth step: the Black pieces have been driven back as far as possible. White can now win in a variety of ways; Tarrasch chooses to cut off the Black King from the QP and capture Black's Rook. *23 R—B7ch, K—B1* (more merciful was 23 .... K—B3; 24 R—B7 mate); *24 R—B7ch, K—Kt1; 25 R—B2, R—K1ch; 26 K—B6, P—QKt4; 27 P—Q7* (anything goes), *R—R1; 28 K—K7, R—R2ch; 29 K—Q6, R—R1; 30 R—K2* Resigns.

It is clear from this example that the chief problem is to force Black into zugzwang (fourth step). In the other classic ending we shall see how the consummate artistry of a Rubinstein solves this problem. No. 385 (Rubinstein-Lasker, St. Petersburg, 1909). The first and second steps are already completed, since the Black Rook is tied down to the defense of the exposed QRP. First, then, Rubinstein advances the Pawn. *1 R—R6* (1 P—K4 at once is also good, but to have the Black King confined is helpful), *K—B1; 2 P—K4, R—QB2* (Lasker wisely marks time—playing the King to the Q-side in order to free the Rook would lose more quickly); *3 P—KR4* (as in the previous example: before he goes out into the world with his King he wants to have his Pawns insured), *K—B2; 4 P—Kt4, K—B1; 5 K—B4, K—K2; 6 P—R5, P—R3* (the crisis. Why, one naturally asks, does Lasker create

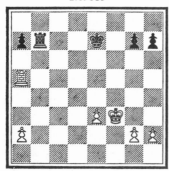

No. 385

White wins.

a hole at KKt3 with his Pawn move? The answer is that he cannot afford to let the White Pawn get to KKt6. E.g., 6 .... K—B2; 7 K—B5, K—K2; 8 P—Kt5, K—B2; 9 P—K5, K—K2; 10 P—Kt6, P—R3; 11 R—K6ch!! and Black is on the horns of a dilemma: shall he lose beautifully or prosaically? The beautiful variation is 11 .... K—Q2; 12 R—KB6!!!, K—K1—12 .... P×R; 13 P—Kt7, R—B1; 14 P×P and will queen—; 13 R—B7!!, R×R; 14 P×Rch, K×P; 15 P—K6ch, K—K2; 16 K—K5, K—K1; 17 K—Q6, K—Q1; 18 P—K7ch, K—K1,

19 K—K6, P—R3; 20 P—R3, P—R4; 21 P—R4, P—Kt4; 22 P×P, e.p., and mates in two. The prosaic line is 11 .... K—B1; 12 R—Q6, K—K2; 13 R—R6, R—Kt2; 14 R—QB6, R—Q2; 15 R—B8—threatening R—KKt8—, R—Q7; 16 R—B7ch, K—Q1; 17 R×RP, R—R7; 18 R×P, R×Pch; 19 K—K6 and Black can resign.); *7 K—B5, K— B2* (now Black's King is also in zugzwang because he cannot allow his White rival to get to Kt6); *8 P—K5, R—Kt2; 9 R—Q6, K—B1; 10 R—QB6* (10 K—Kt6, R—Kt5; 11 R—Q8ch, K—K2 attacking the Rook. Now White is threatening this inroad), *K—B2; 11 P—R3!!!* Zugzwang! The various unpleasant alternatives are:

a) *11 .... K—B1; 12 K—Kt6, R—Kt6* (note that the Rook cannot go to Kt5); *13 R—B8ch, K—K2; 14 R—B7ch, K—K3; 15 R× KtP, R×P; 16 K×P* and the two connected Pawns are irresistible.

b) *11 .... R—K2; 12 P—K6ch, K—Kt1; 13 K—Kt6!, R—K1; 14 P—K7!!, K—R1; 15 R—Q6, K—Kt1; 16 R—Q8* and mates.

c) *11 .... R—Q2; 12 P—K6ch.*

There remains only the variation chosen by Lasker: Resigns.

In positions where there is no obvious target by attacking which the opponent's Rook can be tied down, the only resource is simplification. If everything is exchanged on one side, the center Pawn is in effect an outside passed Pawn and should be exploited as such. An example of such a case where there is no other winning possibility is No. 385a (Schlechter-Tchigorin, Hastings, 1895), White: K at K3, R at KR3, P's at QKt4, QB4, QB5, KKt4; Black: K at KKt3, R at KKt2, P's at QR3, QKt2, QB3, K4, KB3. The only winning chance is 1 .... P—B4; 2 P×Pch, K×P; 3 R—R5ch, K—K3, and because of the weakness of the White Q-side Pawns it turns out to be sufficient: 4 R—R6ch, K—Q2; 5 P—Kt5, RP×P; 6 P×P, P×P; 7 K—K4, R—K2; 8 R—QKt6, K—B2; 9 R×P, K—B3; 10 R—R5. Now Black wins a second Pawn 10 .... R—K1; 11 R—R7, R—K3; 12 R—R5, R—K2; 13 R—R1, K×P. The rest is not difficult. 14 R—B1ch, K—Q3; 15 R—Q1ch, K—B3; 16 R—B1ch, K—Q2; 17 R—Q1ch, K—B1; 18 R—Q5 (or 18 R—B1ch, K—Kt1; 19 R—QKt1, K—B2; 20 R— B1ch, K—Q3; 21 R—Q1ch, K—B4; 22 R—B1ch, K—Kt5; 23 R— Kt1ch, K—B5!!; 24 R—B1ch, K—Kt6; 25 R—B5, K—Kt5; 26 R— B1, P—Kt4, etc.), K—B2; 19 R—B5ch, K—Q3; 20 R—Kt5, K—B3; 21 R—Kt1, P—Kt4 and White soon resigned.

If the Pawn is not yet passed, it is well to exchange it and create a passed Pawn, unless it will land on the sixth rank. For there it is too easily blockaded and will only be in the way. Instead, the constant threat of forcing a passed Pawn will usually be sufficient to tie up the White pieces and secure the required plus elsewhere.

A model ending with a potential passed Pawn on the fourth rank is No. 385b (Tartakover-Kashdan, Folkestone, 1933), White: K at KR1, R at K1, P's at QR2, QKt3, KB3, KKt2, KR3; Black: K at KKt2, R at Q6, P's at QR3, QKt5, K4, KB3, KKt3, KR2. Black won as follows: 1 R—K2, K—B2; 2 R—QB2, R—B6 (the White Rook must not be freed: if the Q-side Pawns were exchanged the game would be drawn); 3 R—Q2, K—K3; 4 K—Kt1, P—B4; 5 K—B2, P—Kt4; 6 K—K2, P—QR4; 7 K—Q1, P—K5; 8 P×P, P×P; 9 R—Q8 (White prefers to take a chance with his Rook out in the open. Against passive play Black wins as in Nos. 384 and 385), R—Kt6 (9 .... R—Q6ch wins but the R ending is surer); 10 R—QR8, R×KKtP; 11 R×P, K—B3; 12 K—K1, R—R7; 13 R—R4, K—B4; 14 R×P, R×QRP; 15 R—Kt7, P—R4; 16 R—B7ch, K—K4; 17 P—Kt4, R—R7; 18 P—Kt5, R×P; 19 P—Kt6, R—QKt6 and the rest is routine (No. 356).

It often happens that the schema which we have set up is not feasible because there is no way to force Black into zugzwang. This usually occurs when the Black King and Rook are near the passed Pawn on the fifth or sixth rank. In such cases the game is sometimes a forced draw. Where a win is possible, the method is that of transposition to some other type (outside passed Pawn) by giving up the center Pawn in return for one of the opponent's wing Pawns. The most valuable subsidiary stratagem is that of getting the Rook to the seventh rank, where it always plays a predominant role.

A model example for this type of reduction is No. 386 (Book-Reshevsky, Kemeri, 1937). It is at once apparent that our general winning scheme is not applicable chiefly because there are no obvious targets to attack and tie up the Black Rook, but also because with the Pawn on

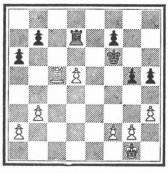

No. 386

White wins.

the fifth and White's King so far away the Black King has too much freedom. In fact the only reason Black loses is that his KKtP and KRP are weak. The game continued *1 K—B1, R—Q3* (if 1 .... K—K4; 2 P—Q6 dis ch, K—B3; 3 R—B7, R×P; 4 R×QKtP is good enough, e.g., 4 .... R—Q8ch; 5 K—K2, R—KKt8; 6 R—Kt6ch, K—B4; 7 R×P, R×P; 8 P—QR4 and we have the same basic structure as in No. 356); *2 K—K2, P—Kt3* (against passive play White wins by marching his King to the Q-side); *3 R—B7!* (not 3 R—B6?, K—

K4!=), *K—K4* (the best chance. On 3 .... R×P; 4 R—B6ch, K—K4; 5 R×P, P—R4; 6 P—QR4, K—Q5; 7 P—QKt4, P×P; 8 R×Pch, K—K4; 9 R—Kt5 and the Pawn ending is easy); *4 R×P, R×P; 5 P—KKt4!* (White has thus secured a highly favorable variation of the ending with a potential outside passed Pawn: the Q-side Pawns are weak and the White Rook attacks everything all over the board), *P×P; 6 P×P, K—K3* (if 6 .... K—K5; 7 R—B6, R—Kt4; 8 P—B3ch, K—Q5; 9 P—B4!, P×P; 10 R×Pch, K—B6; 11 K—B3, K—Kt7; 12 R—R4, P—R4; 13 K—B4 and the passed KtP decides); *7 R—KKt7, K—B3; 8 R—QB7, R—Q3; 9 P—B3, R—K3ch; 10 K—Q3* (White is headed for the Q-side. Compare No. 382), *R—Q3ch; 11 K—K4, R—K3ch* (passive defense is futile: 11 .... P—Kt4; 12 R—QR7, K—K3; 13 R—KR7 and Black must give way); *12 K—Q5, R—K7; 13 R—B6ch, K—B2; 14 P—R4, P—Kt4* (or 14 .... R—K6; 15 R×P, R×KBP; 16 P—R5!, R—B5; 17 R×P, R×P; 18 R—QKt6, R—Kt8; 19 P—R6, P—Kt5; 20 P—R7, R—QR8; 21 R—Kt7ch, K—Kt3; 22 K—K4!, K—Kt4; 23 P—Kt4, R—R6; 24 P—Kt5, P—Kt6; 25 P—Kt6, P—Kt7; 26 R—Kt7ch); *15 R×P, P×P; 16 R×P, R—K6; 17 P—Kt4, R×P; 18 P—Kt5, K—K2; 19 R—K4ch, K—Q2; 20 R—K5* and after the last Pawn is gone the win is academic (No. 351).

If the Pawn is on the sixth, unsupported by the King, this sort of transition is much less favorable. A successful ending which shows some of the difficulties involved is No. 386a (Euwe-Bogoljuboff, Zurich, 1934), White: K at K3, R at QB6, P's at QR3, Q6, K4, KKt2, KR4; Black: K at KB2, R at Q2, P's at QR2, K4, KKt3, KR2. Black to play. After 1 .... K—K3; 2 R—R6, P—R4; 3 P—R4, R×P; 4 R×P, R—Kt3!; 5 P—R5, R—Kt6ch; 6 K—B2, R—Kt7ch (or 6 .... R—Kt5; 7 K—K3, R—Kt6ch; 8 K—Q2, R—Kt7ch; 9 K—B3, R×P; 10 R—R8 and wins. If here 7 .... R—R5; 8 R—R8, K—B2; 9 P—R6, K—Kt2 White wins by capturing the KP—No. 368); 7 K—Kt3, R—Kt6ch; 8 K—R2, R—R6; 9 P—R6, K—Q3! Bogoljuboff evolved a dangerous counter-attack against the White KP which Euwe could only refute with a great deal of ingenuity: 10 R—KKt7!, K—B4; 11 R×P, K—Q5; 12 P—Kt4!!, P×P (on 12 .... R—R7ch; the main variation of the win is 13 K—Kt1, R—R8ch; 14 K—B2, R—R7ch; 15 K—K1, R—R8ch; 16 K—Q2, R—R7ch; 17 K—B1, P×P; 18 K—Kt1!, R—R4; 19 P—R5, P—Kt6; 20 P—R6, P—Kt7; 21 R×P, R×P; 22 R—KR2, R—R1; 23 P—R7, R—R1; 24 R—R4 and White will eventually capture the KP since Black can only move his King: 24 .... K—K6; 25 K—B2, K—B6; 26 K—Q2, K—Kt6; 27 R—R6, K—B6; 28 K—Q3, K—B5; 29 R—R1, R—Q1ch; 30 K—B4, R—KR1; 31 K—Q5, etc.—White wins the Rook and gets back in time to stop the Pawn); 13 P—R5, K×P; 14 P—R6, K—B4; 15 R—Kt6, P—K5; 16 K—Kt2, R—R7ch; 17 K—B1 and the White

Pawns got there first: 17 .... R—R8ch; 18 K—K2, R—R7ch; 19 K—K3, R—R6ch; 20 K—Q2, P—Kt6; 21 P—KR7, P—K6ch; 22 K—K2, P—Kt7; 23 P—R8=Q, P—Kt8=Ktch (a chess joke); 24 K—B1, P—K7ch; 25 K—K1, Resigns. The difficulty in this and similar endings is that the passed Pawn is so exposed that White does not have the freedom of choice that he has in the other cases.

To block the Pawn with the Rook is much less favorable for the defense. That passed Pawns should be blockaded by the King, and not by a piece is a rule which holds for all endings.

Where the Black King is not near the Pawn there is a valuable new winning method (in addition to those given above) available: cutting off the King and then continuing as in the elementary cases, disregarding the extra Pawns. In No. 387 (Alekhine-Euwe, Amsterdam, 1936) this method is seen quite clearly. The key to Black's strategy is to keep the White King away from the QP. His winning plan against passive defense then consists of playing his King to the Q-side and advancing the QP. To such a scheme White could offer no effective resistance, so Alekhine decides to try to win the Black QRP and get enough compensation in his passed QRP. But this involves giving up the KKtP, and the two disconnected passed Pawns vs. one prove to be too much. The game continued: *1 K—Kt4, K—B2; 2 R—B3, P—R4; 3 K—B3* (not 3 R—R3 directly because of 3 .... R—K5ch and 4 .... P—R5), *K—Kt3;* (3 .... P—R5 holds on to everything, for if 4 R—R3, R—K5 but the course Black chooses is somewhat more direct); *4 R—R3, K×P; 5 R×P, K—B4; 6 P—R4, P—Kt4* (with a view to using this Pawn to decoy the White King and facilitate the advance of the QP); *7 R—R8, R—K5; 8 R—B8ch!* (apparently forcing Black where he wants to go, but the entrance of the King could not be prevented anyhow and White wishes to block the QP temporarily), *K—K4; 9 R—K8ch, K—Q5; 10 R—QKt8* (threatening to set up a drawn position by 11 P—Kt4! and 12 P—R5—the Black Rook would then have to return and free the White King), *P—B4!; 11 P—R5* (in the game the variation 11 P—Kt4 led to a speedily loss because the White Pawns are easily stopped: 11 .... P—B5; 12 P—R5, R—K6ch; 13 K—B2, R—QR6; 14 R—KKt8, P—B6; 15 R×P, R—R7ch; 16 K—B3, P—B7; 17 Resigns); *R—K8; 12 P—R6, R—QR8; 13 R—QR8,*

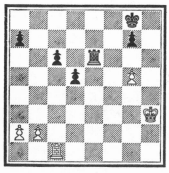

No. 387

Black wins.

K—Q6; 14 P—R7, P—Q5! (better than 14 .... P—B5; 15 R—Q8, R×P; 16 R×Pch, K—B7; 17 R—Kt5!); *15 P—Kt3* (or 15 R—QB8, R×P; 16 R×P, R—B2ch; 17 K—Kt4, R—QKt2; 18 R×P, R×P; 19 K—B3, R—Kt1 with a standard win—the King is on the long side of the Pawn), *R—B8ch!; 16 K—Kt4, R—B2; 17 K×P, K—B7!; 18 R—QB8* (18 K—Kt6, R—B2! and the Pawn marches on), *R×P; 19 R×Pch, K×P; 20 K—B5, R—K2; 21 R—Q5, K—B5; 22 R—Q8, P—Q6* and wins.

Where the Black King is at some distance from the Pawn, whether directly cut off or not, it is often advisable to sacrifice material in order to support the passed Pawn with the King and advance it to the sixth or seventh. For with the enemy King out of the way, the Rook will have to be given up to stop the Pawn. Of course the resulting ending with R vs. P's must be carefully appraised but if the superior side retains at least one Pawn he will usually win.

An example of an ending which abounds in such sacrificial possibilities is No. 388 (Alekhine-Euwe, Berne, 1932). Against the obvious 1 .... R—B4ch White gives up three Pawns but just manages to capture Black's Rook and get back in time: 1 .... R—B4ch; 2 K—K3, R—KR4; 3 P—Q5!, R×Pch; 4 K—Q4, R—R8; 5 R—Q7, K—Kt2; 6 R×RP, R—KB8; 7 P—Q6, R×P; 8 K—Q5!! (not 8 P—Q7?, R—Q7ch; 9 K—B4, K—B3!!; 10 K—Kt5, R×Pch; 11 K—B6, K—K2 with an easy draw), R—Q7ch (on 8 .... K—B3; 9 R—R8, R—Q7ch; 10 K—B6, R—B7ch; 11 K—Q7, P—Kt4; 12 K—Q8, P—Kt5; 13 P—Q7, K—Kt4; 14 K—K7, R—Q7; 15 P—Q8=Q, R×Q; 16 R×R, P—B4; 17 K—K6 wins as in the main variation); 9 K—B6, R—B7ch; 10 K×P, R×Pch; 11 K—B7, R—B7ch; 12 K—Q8, P—Kt4; 13 P—Q7, P—Kt5; 14 K—K8, R—Q7; 15 P—Q8=Q, R×Qch; 16 K×R, K—Kt3 (16 .... P—Kt6; 17 R—R3); 17 K—K7, P—B4; 18 R—R6ch!!!, K—Kt4 (18 .... K—Kt2; 19 R—KB6); 19 K—B7!!, P—B5 (or 19 .... K—B5; 20 K—B6); 20 R—Kt6ch, K—R5 (if 20 .... K—B4; 21 P—R4, P—B6; 22 P—R5, K—B5; 23 P—R6, P—Kt6; 24 P—R7, P—B7; 25 P—R8=Q, P—B8=Q; 26 R—B6ch); 21 K—B6, P—B6; 22 K—B5, P—Kt6 (22 .... P—B7; 23 R×Pch and 24 R—KB4); 23 R—Kt4ch!, K—R6; 24 K—B4, P—B7; 25 R×Pch, K—R7; 26 R—KB3, K—Kt7; 27 P—R4 and wins.

Possibly inspired by this or a similar exciting variation, Euwe in-

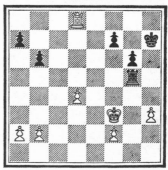

No. 388

Black to play. Draw.

stead tried *1 .... R—QR4* with the continuation *2 P—R3* (the sacrificial line 2 P—Q5! is answered by 2 .... R×P!; 3 K—K4, R×P; 4 K—K5, K—Kt2!; 5 K—Q6, R×P; 6 R—QR8, P—KKt4; 7 K—B7, R—B7ch; 8 K—Q7, P—B4; 9 R×P, K—B3; 10 P—Q6, P—Kt5; 11 P×P, P×P; 12 K—K8, K—Kt4; 13 P—Q7, R—Q7 with a draw as the result), *R—QKt4; 3 R—Q7!* (3 P—Kt4?, P—R4), *K—Kt2* (3 .... R×P?; 4 R×Pch, K—R3; 5 R×P); *4 R×RP, R×P; 5 R—K7!* (to keep the Black King cut off), *K—B3; 6 R—K2, R—Kt6ch; 7 R—K3, R—Kt7; 8 P—KR4* (the only way to make any progress is to sacrifice a Pawn in order to permit the advance of the QP. 8 P—Q5, R—Q7; 9 K—K4, R×BP lets the Black King out. The most enterprising, and dangerous for Black, is 8 R—K8!, R—Kt6ch; 9 K—K4! but by advancing his own Pawns rapidly Black can manage to hold the game: 9 .... R×QRP; 10 K—Q5!, R×P; 11 K—B6, R—B6ch; 12 K×P, R—Q6; 13 K—B5, R—Q7; 14 P—Q5 (14 P—B4, K—B4), R×P; 15 P—Q6, R—Q7; 16 K—B6, R—B7ch; 17 K—Kt6, R—Q7; 18 K—B7, R—B7ch; 18 K—Q8, P—Kt4; 19 P—Q7, P—Kt5; 20 R—K4, K—Kt4; 21 R—Q4, R—QR7; 22 K—K7, R—R1; 23 P—Q8=Q, R×Q; 24 R×R, P—Kt6; 25 K×P, K—B5=), *R—Q7!* (now White does not have to sacrifice—he loses a Pawn anyhow); *9 K—K4, R×BP; 10 R—QKt3,* (On 10 K—Q5, R—B5; 11 R—QKt3, R×RP; 12 R×Pch, K—B4 the connected Black Pawns are dangerous and may even win), *R—K7ch; 11 K—Q5, R—K3; 12 R—QB3* (threatening R—B6), *K—K2; 13 R—B7ch, K—K1; 14 P—R4* and although White still has a minimum positional advantage he cannot win.

To have the defending Rook in front of the passed Pawn, the attacking Rook behind it, is the worst possible position for the defense, even when the Pawn is in or near the center. E.g., No. 388a (Maroczy-Marshall, New York, 1924), White: K at KKt4, R at QB2, P's at QR2, QKt4, QB5, KR4; Black: K at K5, R at QB3, P's at QR2, QKt3, KKt2. White won by reducing to an ending with R+2P vs. R+P. The first step is to fix the Black QRP by P—QKt5; next the QBP is exchanged for the QKtP, the White Rook reaches the seventh rank and captures the QRP. The conclusion was: 1 R—QB1 (not 1 P—R4, K—Q6; 2 R—B1, K—Q7 with "perpetual check" to the Rook), K—K6; 2 R—K1ch, K—Q5 (if now 2 .... K—Q7; 3 R—K7, P×P; 4 P×P, P—R4; 5 R×P, R×P; 6 P—R5, R—B5ch; 7 K—Kt5, R—B4ch; 8 K—R4!, R—B5ch; 9 R—Kt4, R—B3; 10 R—R4!, R—QR3; 11 K—Kt5, and wins); 3 R—Q1ch, K—K4; 4 R—QB1, K—K5; 5 P—R4! (by the checks White has gained the tempo necessary for this important move), K—K6; 6 P—Kt5!, R—Kt3ch (6 .... R×P?; 7 R×R, P×R; 8 P—R5, P—B5; 9 P—Kt6, P—B6; 10 P—Kt7!, P—B7; 11 P—Kt8=Q, P—B8=Q; 12 Q—B4ch); 7 K—R3, P×P; 8 R×P, R—KB3 (cn 8 .... P—R3, R—B6 is decisive); 9 R—B3ch,

K—B7; 10 R—B7, P—R3; 11 R—B2ch, K—B6; 12 R—B6, R—B5; 13 R×P, R—KKt5; 14 R—R7, and the rest is simple: 14 .... R— Kt6ch; 15 K—R2, R—Kt7ch; 16 K—R1, R—Kt5; 17 P—Kt6, R× Pch; 18 K—Kt1, P—Kt4; 19 R—B7ch, K—Kt6; 20 P—Kt7!, R— QKt5; 21 K—B1, P—Kt5; 22 P—R5, K—R6; 23 R—R7ch, K—Kt6; 24 P—R6, Resigns.

Where the Pawn position is otherwise unbalanced, much more attention must be paid to tactical considerations. As a rule the winning method involves weakening the opponent's Pawns, centralization of the pieces, and then either capture of material or reduction to an elementary case. But because the Pawns are scattered, simplification, especially to R+2P's vs. R+P, is always a possibility. Where exchanges are unavoidable, White should always try to set up two connected passed Pawns, while Black's best chance lies in a strong passed Pawn defended by his King.

No. 389 (Loevenfisch-Rjumin, Moscow, 1935) is a model win. The first step is to weaken the Queens side Pawns. *1 R—QB5!* (preparing P—QR4), *K—Kt1* (if 1 .... R—Q1; 2 P—Q5, K—Kt1; 3 K—B3, K—B2; 4 K—B4, K—K2; 5 K—K5, K—Q2; 6 P—Q6, R—K1ch; 7 K—Q5, R—K7; 8 R—B7ch, K—Q1; 9 R×P, R×KtP; 10 K—B6, is conclusive); *2 P—QR4!, R—Q1* (2 .... P×P; 3 R×P, R—Kt1 4 R×P is hopeless); *3 P×P!* (not 3 P—Q5?, P×P!!), *P×P; 4 P—Q5, R—Kt1.* Now that the Black Rook and Pawns are tied up, the next step is to bring the King to the Q-side. *5 K—B3, K—B2; 6 K—K3, K—K2; 7 K—Q4, K—Q2; 8 K—B3, K—Q3; 9 K—Kt4.* Next, in view of his powerful R and K positions White will win another Pawn. *9 .... R—KB1;* (or 9 .... R—K1; 10 R×KtP, R—K7; 11 K×P, R×BP; 12 R—Kt6ch, and if 12 .... K—K4 to save the Pawn, 13 R— K6ch, K—B4; 14 R—K3 cuts off the Black King from the QP and decides quickly); *10 P—B4, P— Kt4; 11 P×P, P×P; 12 R×KtP, R—B7; 13 K×P, R×RP; 14 R— Kt6ch, K—Q2; 15 R—KKt6, R×P; 16 R×P.* With R+2P's vs. R the rest is routine. (No. 351).

As a rule, the extra Pawn in such cases exercises a restraining influence on the opponent's pieces, and in the early stages of the ending this is frequently its chief value. With the mobility of one of the enemy pieces restricted Pawn weakening and reduction to simpler cases are in

No. 389

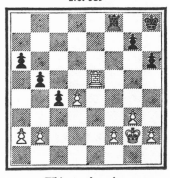

White to play wins.

order. E.g., in No. 389a (Schlechter-Teichmann, Vienna, 1904), White: K at QB1, R at KB1, P's at QR3, QKt2, QB2, KB3, KKt3; Black: K at KKt3, R at KB1, P's at QR2, QKt2, QB3, Q4, KKt2, KR2 the only immediate effect of the extra Pawn is to allow the Black Rook to get to the seventh rank, and this is sufficient here: After 1 .... R—B4; 2 K—Q2, R—R4; 3 R—K1 (3 R—B2, R—R6; 4 R—Kt2, K—B4; 5 K—K3, P—KKt4; 6 K—B2, P—Kt5); R—R7ch; 4 K—Q3 (4 R—K2 is impossible because of Black's extra Pawn which would win without any trouble in the pure Pawn ending), K—B2; 5 P—QKt4, P—KR4; 6 R—K5, P—KKt3; 7 P—R4, R—Kt7; 8 R—Kt5, R—B7; 9 P—KB4, K—B3; 10 P—B3, P—R5!; 11 K—K3 (11 P×P, R×P and also wins the RP), R—B7; 12 K—Q3, P—R6!!; 13 R—Kt4, R—KKt7; 14 K—Q4, R—Kt8! and Black soon won because White must lose another Pawn to begin with.

D. ALL THE PAWNS ON ONE SIDE

We have already seen that R+2P vs. R+P, all on one side, is drawn. The two other cases which occur most frequently are those where the superior side has three and four Pawns, respectively.

1. ROOK AND THREE PAWNS VS. ROOK AND TWO PAWNS

Unless White has a KP, there are no winning chances at all. No. 390 is the general case. The White King cannot get through to R6, for if 1 K—R4, R—Kt4. If the Pawn advances and exchanges, 1 P—B5, P×P; 2 P×P we have in effect the ending with R+BP vs. R. Black can then again cut the White King off. This is however the best try. *1 P—B5, P×P; 2 P×P, R—QB3* (more dangerous, but also good if correctly continued, is 2 .... R—Kt5; 3 P—B6, R—Kt3, etc.=. A trappy continuation is 3 .... R—QB5; 4 R—Kt7ch, K—R1?; 5 R—Kt4, R—B3?; 6 P—B7, R—B1 but after all these doubtful and inferior moves on 7 R—K4, K—Kt2; 8 R—K8, R—B6ch still draws); *3 K—Kt4, R—QKt3; 4 K—Kt5, P—R3ch; 5 K—R5, R—KB3; 6 K—Kt4, R—QKt3*, etc. Another attempt is seen in No. 390a (Saemisch-Spielmann, Teplitz-Schoenau, 1922), White: K at QR1, R at KKt4, P's at QR2, QKt3; Black: K at QKt2, R at K3, P's at QR2, QKt5, QB4. Black got his RP to R6, but even that did not help: 1 .... R—K8ch; 2 K—Kt2, R—K7ch; 3 K—Kt1, K—B3; 4 R—Kt5, R—Q7; 5 K—R1, P—R4; 6 K—Kt1, R—Q4; 7 R—Kt8, R—R4; 8 R—Q8, R—R8ch; 9 K—B2, R—R7ch; 10 K—Kt1, P—R5; 11 R—Q1! (11 P×P?, P—B5 creates winning chances), K—Kt4; 12 R—Q6, R—R8ch; 13 K—B2, K—R4; 14 R—Q8, P—R6; 15 R—Q1! (adding insult to in-

jury—a Pawn down and he dares to exchange!), R×R; 16 K×R, P—
B5; 17 K—B2, P—B6; 18 K—B1 and a draw was agreed to.

White can win this ending only if the Black King is cut off from the
Pawns. No. 390b, White: K at KB3, R at K2, P's at KB4, KKt4,
KR2; Black: K at Q4, R at QR2, P's at KKt2, KR2. White wins.
1 .... R—Kt2; 2 P—B5, R—R2; 3 P—Kt5, K—Q3 (3 .... R—R5;
4 R—K7); 4 P—R4, R—R5; 5 R—K4, R—R8; 6 R—K8, R—B8ch;
7 K—Kt4, R—Kt8ch (7 .... P—Kt3; 8 P×P, P×P; 9 R—KKt8);
8 K—R5, R—KB8 (8 .... R—QR8; 8 R—KR8); 9 R—KKt8, R×P;
10 R×P and wins the second Pawn as well. Or No. 390c, White: K
at KB3, R at K3, P's at KB4, KKt2, KR2; Black: K at Q4, R at QR2,

No. 390

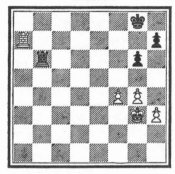

Draw.

No. 391

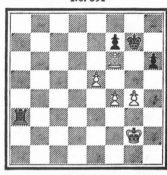

White wins.

P's at KKt3, KR4. White wins. *1 R—K5ch, K—Q3; 2 K—Kt3!*
(but not 2 R—KKt5?, R—R6ch; 3 K—B2, K—K3!!; 4 R×Pch, K—
B4; 5 R—Kt5ch, K×P; 6 R×P, R—R7ch; 7 K—B1, R—R8ch; 8 K—
K2, R—R7ch, etc.=), K—Q2; 3 R—KKt5, R—R3; 4 P—B5, P×P;
5 R×BP, R—R3; 6 K—R4, R—KKt3; 7 P—Kt3 and again the last
Pawn goes.

When White has a KP, his prospects are brighter, but except for
certain positions the game is a draw. The chief of these won cases is
No. 391 (Capablanca-Yates, Hastings, 1930–31). Capablanca's conduct of the ending is flawless. *1 R—QKt6, R—K6* (hoping to prevent
the advance); *2 R—Kt4, R—QB6* (if 2 .... P—B3; 3 R—Kt7ch wins
a P); *3 K—B2, R—QR6; 4 R—Kt7* (threatening P—K6), *K—Kt1* (or
4 .... K—Kt3; 5 P—B5ch, K—Kt4; 6 R×P, K×P; 7 P—K6 and
wins); *4 R—Kt8ch, K—Kt2; 5 P—B5* (the threat is now 6 P—B6ch,
K—R2; 7 R—KB8, K—Kt3; 8 R—Kt8ch, K—R2; 9 R—Kt7ch), *R—
R7ch* (or 5 .... K—R2; 6 R—K8, R—QKt6; 7 P—B6, R—QR6;

8 R—KB8, R—R2; 9 K—K3 and White wins as in the game by march-
ing his King to QB6); *6 K—K3, R—R6ch; 7 K—K4, R—R5ch; 8 K—
Q5!!, R—R4ch* (on 8 .... R×P; 9 P—B6ch, K—R2; 10 R—KB8,
K—Kt3; 11 R—Kt8ch, K—R4; 12 R×R, K×R; 13 P—K6 queens);
9 K—Q6, R—R3ch; 10 K—B7, K—R2 (there is nothing better. On
the alternative 10 .... R—R8; 11 P—B6ch ends with a bang: 11 ....
K—R2; 12 R—KB8, R—R2ch; 13 K—Q8, K—Kt3; 14 R—Kt8ch,
K—R2; 15 R—Kt7ch, K—R1; 16 P—Kt5!!, P×P; 17 K—K8, R—
R4; 18 R×KtP, R—R2; 19 P—K6!, P×P; 20 P—B7, R—R1ch; 21
K—K7, R—R2ch; 22 K—B6, R—R1; 23 R—R5 mate!); *11 K—Q7!,
R—R2ch; 12 K—Q6, K—Kt2* (or 12 .... R—R3ch; 13 K—K7, R—
R2ch; 14 K—B6); *13 R—Q8, R—R4* (or 13 .... R—Kt2; 14 P—
B6ch, K—Kt3; 15 K—B6!—the simplest—, R—R2; 16 K—Kt6,
R—R5; 17 R—Kt8ch, K—R2; 18 R—Kt7ch, K—R1; 19 R×P);
14 P—B6ch, K—R2; 15 R—KB8, R—R2; 16 K—B6!!!! (the magnifi-
cent point to Capablanca's previous play: Black is in zugzwang),
*K—Kt3; 17 R—Kt8ch, K—R2; 18 R—Kt7ch, K—R1; 19 K—Kt6, R—
Q2; 20 K—B5!* (threatening P—K6), *R—B2ch; 21 K—Q6, R—R2;
22 P—K6!* (the most precise: if 22 P—Kt5, P×P; 23 R×KtP, K—
R2; 24 R—Kt7ch, K—R1; 25 P—K6, R—R3ch; 26 K—K7, R×Pch!!;
27 K×P, R×Pch!!!; 28 K×R stalemate), *R—R3ch; 23 K—K7,
R×Pch* (23 .... P×P; 24 P—B7!!, R—R2ch; 25 K—B6, R—R1; 26
K—Kt6 and mate next move); *24 K×P, R—K5; 25 P—Kt5!!* (a
splendid conclusion), *P×P; 26 K—Kt6,* Resigns. The immediate
threat is 27 R—R7ch, K—Kt1; 28 P—B7ch, K—B1; 29 R—R8ch.
To this there is no adequate defense, for if 26 .... R—K3; 27 R—
R7ch, K—Kt1; 28 R—QR7, K—B1 (28 .... R—K1; 29 P—B7ch);
29 R—R8ch, R—K1; 30 R×Rch, K×R; 31 K—Kt7, P—Kt5; 32
P—B7ch.

An alternative method of winning is seen in a game Duras-Capa-
blanca, New York, 1913. No. 391a, White: K at KKt2, R at QR4,
P's at KB2, KR3; Black: K at KKt4, R at Q6, P's at KKt2, KB4, K5.
Black wins. 1 R—R5, P—Kt3; 2 R—Kt5 (on 2 R—R6 to prevent
K—B5 2 .... P—B5! decides: 3 R—R5ch, K—B3; 4 R—R6ch, K—
B4; 5 R—R5ch, K—K3; 6 R—R6ch, R—Q3, etc., as in the game), K—
B5!; 3 R—R5, R—Q7; 4 R—R4, P—Kt4; 5 R—Kt4, K—K4; 6 R—
Kt5ch, R—Q4; 7 R—Kt8, P—B5; 8 R—Kt8, K—Q5!; 9 K—B1, K—
Q6; 10 R—QR8, P—K6!!; 11 R—R3ch (after 11 P×P, K×P; 12 R—
R3ch, R—Q6; 13 R—R5, P—B6!; 14 K—Kt1, R—Q8ch; 15 K—R2,
P—B7 is conclusive), K—K5; 12 P×P, P—B6!! (not 12 .... P×P?;
13 R—R8!, R—B4ch; 14 K—K2!, R—B7ch; 15 K—K1, K—B6; 16
R—B8ch, K—Kt6; 17 R—K8!, R—B6; 18 K—K2=.); 13 K—Kt1,
R—Q6!; 14 R—R8 (the exchange of Rooks would also lose after 14
R×R, K×R; 15 K—B2, K—K5, etc. On 14 R—R5 the answer is

simply 14 .... K×P! as in the note to White's 11th move or as in the game), K×P; 15 R—K8ch, K—B5; 16 R—KKt8, R—Q8ch; 17 K—B2, R—Q7ch; 18 K—B1 (18 K—Kt1, P—Kt5!!!; 19 R×Pch, K—K6; 20 R—Kt8, R—Q8ch; 21 K—R2, P—B7; 22 R—K8ch, K—Q7; 23 R—Q8ch, K—B7; 24 R×R, K×R; 25 K—Kt2, K—K8 and wins), R—KR7; 19 K—Kt1 (19 R—R8, K—Kt6; 20 K—Kt1, P—B7ch), R×P; 20 R—Kt7, P—Kt5; 21 R—Kt8, K—Kt6; 22 Resigns.

Despite the imposing character of Capablanca's play if we examine the ending closely we find that Black can draw if he gets his Pawn to KB3 (i.e., prevents P—K5). This is seen in No. 392. All appearances to the contrary, not even *1 R—Kt7* wins. The reply is *1 .... P—R4!; 2 P—B5ch* (if 2 P—Kt5, P×P; 3 R—Kt6ch, K—Kt2; 4 P×P—or A—, R—KKt5; 5 R—Kt5, K—Kt3=. Variation A. 4 P—B5, P—Kt5ch; 5 K—Kt3, R—K5; 6 K—R4, R×P; 7 K×P (7 K—Kt5, K—B2), K—B2; 8 K×P, R—K2, etc.=. Or here 2 P×Pch, K×P; 3 R—KKt7, hoping to get a passed KP, but then 3 .... K—R3!; 4 R—Kt2, P—B4!; 5 R—Kt5, R—R4 makes the draw clear—the White King cannot get near the Pawn without giving up the KP), *K—R3; 3 P×P, K×P; 4 R—KKt7, R—QKt5; 5 R—Kt6, R—Kt3; 6 K—K4* (6 P—K4 is no better: e.g., 6 .... R—R3; 7 P—K5, R—R6ch; 8 K—K4, P×P; 9 K×P, R—R4ch=. Note that Black's King is always on the short side of the BP—No. 329a), *R—R3; 6 K—Q5, R—R6!; 7 P—K4, R—R3!; 8 P—K5, R—R4ch; 9 K—K6, R×Pch; 10 K×P,* R—R4=, since the White King will be checked away from its dominating position: 11 R—Kt1, R—R3ch; 12 K—Kt7, R—R2ch; 13 K—R8, R—KB2, etc. The other possible attempt by White is the advance of his KP: 1 R—Kt6, R—R4; 2 P—K4, R—R6ch; 3 K—B2, K—Kt2!; 4 R—Q6, R—QKt6; 5 P—K5 (5 K—K2, R—Kt6; or 5 R—Q7ch, K—Kt1! and White can make no progress), P×P; 6 P×P, R—Kt4; 7 R—K6 (7 P—K6, K—B3), K—B2; 8 R—B6ch, K—K2; 9 R—B5, K—K3; 10 K—Kt3, R×P=, or 10 R—R5, R×P; 11 R×Pch, K—B2=.

If the White Pawn is not at KKt4 (compare No. 391a) Black can still play his Pawn to KB3 and prevent the entrance of the White King by deploying his Rook along the fourth rank. The only real danger to Black in all variations of this ending arises from the advance of the White Pawn to KB6.

Draw.

We have purposely chosen positions which are much more favorable for White than the average one secured in tournament play. In the games quoted, Capablanca's opponents could have staved off defeat time and again had they realized the importance of preventing the march of the KBP. Once the Black Pawn is at KB3 with any normally active Rook position White has no real winning chances at all. E.g., No. 392a (Reshevsky-Apscheneek, Kemeri, 1937), White: K at KR4, R at KKt8, P's at KKt2, KB3, K4; Black: K at KR3, R at K7, P's at KB3, KR2. Draw. The game continued 1 .... R—KB7; 2 K—Kt3, R—R7; 3 K—B4, R—R4! (keeping the White King out); 4 P—Kt4 (4 R—Q8, K—Kt3; 5 R—Q5, R—R7 gets White nowhere quickly), R—R6! (again ties down the White King); 5 R—Q8, K—Kt2; 6 R—Q5, P—R3 and White saw nothing better than 7 P—K5, P×Pch; 8 R×P, when 8 .... K—B3 makes the draw plain (No. 364).

Where the defender has a KP, if he can get his Rook on the seventh rank, the game is a fairly certain draw. One example will suffice. No. 392b (Kashdan-Alekhine, Folkestone, 1933), White: K at K2, R at KR5, P's at KB2, KKt3, KR2; Black: K at K4, R at QR4, P's at K5, KB4. Black to play draws. 1 .... R—R7ch; 2 K—B1 (2 K—K3, R—R6ch), P—K6! (more risky but still good enough was 2 .... R—R8ch; 3 K—Kt2, R—R7; 4 P—Kt4!, K—B5!; 5 R×Pch, K×P; 6 R—K5, K—B5; 7 R—K8, R—Kt7=); 3 P×P, K—K5; 4 K—Kt1 (if 4 P—R4, R—R6! equalizes), R—K7; 5 R—R4ch, K—K4! (but not 5 .... K×P?; 6 R—KB4, although even here 6 .... R—K8ch; 7 K—Kt2, R—K7ch; 8 K—R3, R—KB7!! would probably draw); 6 R—R8, K—B3!; 7 R—B8ch, K—Kt3; 8 R—K8, K—B2; 9 R—QB8 (9 R—K5, K—B3), R×KP=.

2. ROOK AND FOUR PAWNS VS. ROOK AND THREE PAWNS

Many writers have assumed that this ending is normally won, chiefly because of two famous games of Capablanca's. Analysis of these games reveals that in both Capablanca's opponents made the mistake of allowing the exchange of their KtP for the enemy RP, thus remaining with R+BP+RP vs. R+KP+BP+KtP. But even after this error was committed a draw could have been held by proper handling of the sequel, for, as we have just seen, this ending is won only if the White King can reach K5 and prevent the advance of the Black KBP. In view of all this, it is certain that in any usual position the four Pawns will not win against the three.

The Capablanca-Yates position (Hastings, 1930–31), No. 393, is typical. The simplest drawing line is 1 .... P—R4!, when we have No. 394. But even as played by Yates, quite a few inaccuracies were required to drift into a loss. The game continuation was *1 R—R6,*

R—Kt5; 2 P—R3, R—QB5; 3 K—B3 (on 3 P—Kt4, R—B4 followed by .... P—R4 was still strong), *R—QKt5; 4 R—R5!, R—QB5* (now the advance of the RP will be prevented once and for all, but even that should not be fatal); *5 P—Kt4, P—R3* (this move is not necessary to prevent P—Kt5, since it could always be played then. But it does come in handy against the advance of the enemy RP. E.g., if Black plays passively, White may play P—R4—R5, K—Kt3, P—B4, K—B3, and finally R—R7, threatening P—K4—K5, P—B5 and P—R6ch.

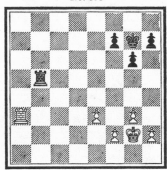

Draw.

In that event, ... P—R3 at some future date would certainly be forced); *6 K—Kt3* (preparing the advance of the BP), *R—B8* (if 6 .... P—Kt4; 7 P—R4 with a position similar to that in the game); *7 K—Kt2, R—B5; 8 R—Q5, R—R5* (on 8 .... P—Kt4; 9 K—Kt3 and 10 P—R4 follows); *9 P—B4, R—R7ch; 10 K—Kt3, R—K7; 11 R—K5, R—K8; 12 K—B2, R—KR8; 13 K—Kt2, R—K8; 14 P—R4, K—B3* (more exact was 14 .... R—QR8; 15 P—R5, P×P!; 16 R×P, P—B3; 17 R—QKt5, K—Kt3; 18 K—B3, R—R5=. 16 P×P is no better for White: the RP will only be a target later); *15 P—R5, K—K7ch; 16 K—B3, R—K8?* (pointless: 16 .... R—R7 was in order); *17 R—R5, K—Kt2; 18 P×P, K×P* (if 18 .... P×P; 19 R—R7ch, K—Kt1—or A—; 20 P—K4!, R—B8ch; 21 K—K3, R—KKt8; 22 P—B5!!, R×P; 23 P—B6!!, R—Kt8; 24 P—K5 and White's passed Pawns win because they are much nearer the eighth. Variation A. 19 .... K—B3; 20 R—R7!, R—B8ch; 21 K—Kt2, R—K8; 22 K—B2, R—KR8; 23 P—Kt5ch or even 23 R×P); *19 P—K4* (a slight tactical inaccuracy: 19 R—Q5, R—B8ch; 20 K—Kt2, R—K8; 21 K—B2, R—QR8 would have forced P—K4 with a better King position), *R—B8ch; 20 K—Kt3, R—Kt8ch; 21 K—R3, R—KB8; 22 R—KB5, R—K8??* The final, but this time decisive, blunder. 22 .... P—B3 would have drawn without much trouble. On 23 K—Kt2, R—K8; 24 P—K5, P×P is sufficient: 25 P×P (25 R×P, R×R!; 26 P×R, P—R4! and the King gets back in front of the KP), R—K6; 26 K—B2, R—QR6!; 27 R—B3 (27 P—K6, R—R3!; 28 R—K5, R—R1; 29 K—K3, K—B3; 30 R—K4, R—K1=), R—R4!; 28 R—B6ch, K—Kt2; 29 R—B5, R—R6!, etc.—the White King cannot get through. *23 P—K5!, R—K6ch; 24 K—Kt2!* (but not 24 K—R4?, R—KB6; 25 R—B6ch, K—Kt2; 26 P—B5, R—K6, or 26 P—Kt5, P×Pch; 27 K×P, R—B8; 28 R—QR6, R—K8;

29 R—R7, R—K7=: 30 R—K7, R—K8!; 31 K—B5 (31 P—B5; R×P!), R—QR8; 32 P—K6, R—R4ch; 33 K—K4, K—B3!, etc.=), *R—QR6; 25 R—B6ch, K—Kt2* and now we have No. 391.

The simplest draw beginning from the original position in No. 393 is, as we have mentioned, playing the RP to R4. The resultant ending is seen in No. 394, which occurred in the game Mikenas-Alekhine, Warsaw, 1935. (The colors are reversed; Alekhine had the four Pawns). It makes no difference whether White retains his Pawn at K3 or not—

No. 394

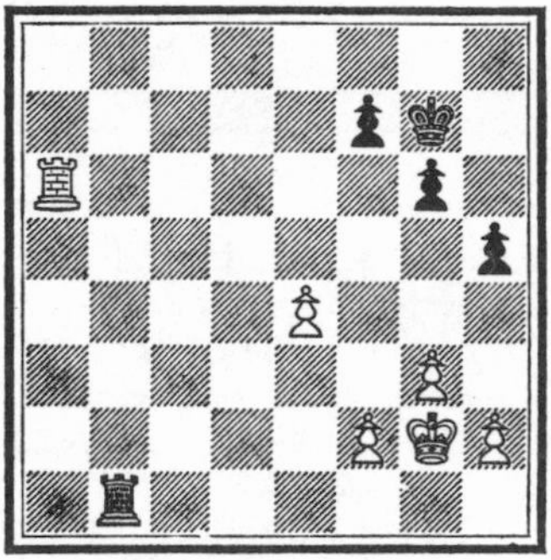

Draw.

No. 395

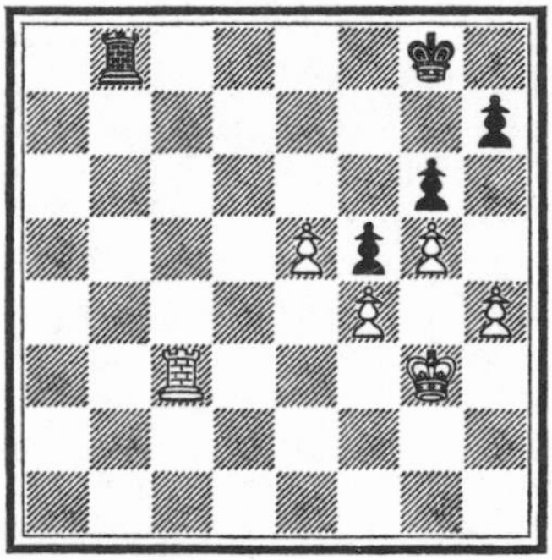

White wins.

he can only make progress by the advance of his KP. P—R3 and P—Kt4 is met by .... P×P, P×P, when Black draws easily in the absence of weak Pawns. The only reasonable try is *1 P—B4,* since K or R moves do not threaten anything, when there follows *1 .... R—Kt7ch; 2 K—R3, R—K7!; 3 P—K5.* Now Black can draw by shifting his Rook back and forth along the seventh rank, but Mikenas found a tactical resource which soon put an end to White's winning attempts: *3 .... P—Kt4; 4 P×P* (If 4 R—KB6, as played, then 4 .... P—Kt5ch; 5 K—R4, R×Pch; 6 K—Kt5, P—R5!=) *R×P; 5 K—R4, R—K7!; 6 P—R3, R—K6!* and with White's King bottled up the two Pawns do not win: *7 R—KR6, R—R6; 8 R×P, R—R5ch; 9 P—Kt4, R—R6!; 10 R—R6, R—QKt6; 11 R—Q6, R—R6; 12 P—Kt6!, P—B3!* (the simplest) and a draw was agreed to.

Again against careful play from a usual position White will not be able to build up any real winning threats. E.g., No. 394a (Reshevsky-Apscheneek, Kemeri, 1937), White: K at KKt1, R at QR6, P's at K4, KB3, KKt2, KR3; Black: K at KB1, R at K1, P's at KB2, KKt2, KR2. Draw. The continuation was: 1 .... R—B1; 2 R—R7, R—

B8ch; 3 K—R2, R—B7; 4 P—R4, R—K7; 5 K—R3, P—Kt3; 6 P—
R5, P×P; 7 R—R5, P—R5!; 8 R—R5, K—Kt2; 9 R—Kt5ch, K—R3;
10 K×P, P—B3! and nothing can be done. The defense .... P—Kt3
and .... P—R4 was likewise strong here.

White can win by force only if he has a passed KP. The model for
this point is No. 395 (Vidmar-Menchik, Carlsbad, 1929). There is
nothing to stop White from getting his King to Q6, R on the QB file,
and then advancing his KP. Miss Menchik tried to hinder this plan
by playing her King to the Q-side, but then her K-side Pawns proved
to be irretrievably weak. After *1* .... *R—Kt2; 2 K—B3, K—Kt2;
3 K—K3* Black tried 3 .... R—R2, when the conclusion was 4 R—
Kt3, K—B2; 5 R—Kt4, K—K2; 6 R—Kt5, R—Q2; 7 R—Kt6, R—
R2; 8 R—QB6, K—Q2; 9 R—Q6ch, K—K2; 10 P—R5!, R—R6ch;
11 K—Q4! (but not 11 R—Q3?, R×Rch; 12 K×R, P×P; 13 K—K3,
K—B2; 14 K—B3, K—Kt2!; 15 K—Kt3, P—R3; 16 K—R4, K—
Kt3!; 17 P—K6, P×Pch; 18 P×P, P—B5=), R—R5ch; 12 K—Q5,
R—R4ch; 13 K—B6, R—R3ch; 14 K—B5 (now 14 .... R—R4ch
will be answered by 15 K—Kt4, when Black has no more checks),
14 .... R—R5; 15 P×P, P×P; 16 R×P, R×P; 17 K—Q5, R—QR5;
18 R—Kt7ch, K—B1; 19 R—QKt7, R—R3; 20 P—K6, P—B5; 21
K—K5, P—B6; 22 K—B6, R—R1; 23 P—Kt6, P—B7; 24 P—Kt7ch,
K—Kt1; 25 R—Kt1, P—B8=Qch; 26 R×Q, R—R7; 27 R—K1,
Resigns. Against the best defense *3* .... *R—Kt5!* the win is more
difficult: *4 R—B7ch, K—Kt1; 5 R—B6!, R—K5ch* (or a) 5 .... R—
Kt6ch; 6 K—Q4, R—Kt5ch; 7 K—Q5, R×P; 8 P—K6, R—K5; 9 K—
Q6, R—Q5ch; 10 K—K5, R—Q1; 11 P—K7, R—K1; 12 K—K6, P—
B5; 13 R—Q6, P—B6; 14 R—Q8 and mates. b) 5 .... K—B2; 6
R—B6ch, K—K2; 7 P—R5, P×P; 8 R×P, P—R5; 9 R—B6, R—
Kt6ch; 10 K—K4, R—Kt5ch; 11 K—B5 and the rest is routine);
6 K—B3, R—R5; 7 R—B6, K—Kt2 (or 7 .... R—R6ch; 8 K—K2,
R—R5!; 9 K—K3!, R—K5ch; 10 K—B3, etc., as in the main varia-
tion. If here after 7 .... R—R6ch; 8 K—K2, R—R7ch; 9 K—Q3,
R—R6ch; 10 K—Q4, R—R5ch; 11 K—Q5, R×P; 12 P—K6, R—K5;
13 R—B7, R—K8; 14 K—Q6, R—K5; 15 R—R7, P—B5; 16 R—
R8ch, K—Kt2; 17 P—K7, K—B2; 18 R—B8ch and wins); *8 P—R5!,
R—Kt5* (8 .... P×P; 9 R×P, R—R6ch; 10 K—Kt2, P—R5; 11 R—
B6, etc., or 8 .... R—R6ch; 9 K—K2, R—R7ch; 10 K—Q3, R—
R6ch; 11 K—Q4, R—R5ch; 12 K—Q5, P×P; 13 R×P, P—R5; 14
R—B6, P—R6; 15 P—K6, P—R7; 16 R—R6, R×P; 17 R×P, R—
B8; 18 P—K7, R—K8; 19 K—Q6, R—Q8ch; 20 K—B7, R—K8; 21
K—Q8, R—Q8ch; 22 K—K8, R—Q4; 23 R—KB2, R—Q6; 24 R—
B7ch, K—Kt1; 25 R—B6, K—Kt2; 26 R—B6, R—Q4; 27 R—B8,
K—Kt3; 28 R—Q8, R—K4; 29 K—Q7, K×P; 30 P—K8=Q, R×Q;
31 R×R, P—R4, 32 K—K6, K—B5; 33 R—KR8, K—Kt5; 34 K—

K5, P—R5; 35 K—K4, K—Kt6; 36 K—K3 and wins); *9 P—R6ch!, K—Kt1; 10 P—K6, R—K5; 11 K—B2!!* (the point: by sacrificing the KBP White's King gets into the game), *R×Pch; 12 K—K3, R—QR5; 13 K—Q3, R—K5* (on 13 .... R—R1; 14 K—Q4, R—KB1; 15 K—K5!, R—R1; 16 R—B7 decides, or 14 .... R—R5ch; 15 K—B5, R—R4ch; 16 K—B6!, R—R1; 17 R—B7, R—R3ch; 18 K—Q5, etc.—the King gets to B6); *14 K—Q2!!, R—Q5ch* (or 14 .... R—K4; 15 K—B3!, R—K5; 16 K—Q3); *15 K—B3, R—QR5!; 16 R—B7!* (not 16 P—K7, R—R1!), *R—K5; 17 R—Kt7ch, K—B1* (17 .... K—R1; 18 P—K7, P—B5; 19 R—B7); *17 R×RP, R×P; 18 R—R8ch!!, K—B2; 19 R—R8!, R—K6ch; 20 K—Q2, R—KR6; 21 R—R6* and wins the KKtP, when the two connected passed Pawns decide.

E. SPECIAL DIFFICULTIES THAT ARE ENCOUNTERED IN THE CONVERSION OF A MATERIAL ADVANTAGE INTO A WIN

1. WEAK PAWNS

This is the most common type of handicap for the superior side. It nullifies the material plus quite often. There are two chief subdivisions: isolated and doubled Pawns.

Isolated Pawns are a weakness peculiarly exploitable by Rooks. In endings with minor pieces they make practically no difference. No. 396 (Capablanca-Alekhine, New York, 1924) is a splendid example of how such Pawns may be pounced upon by the defense to hold a seemingly lost position. Capablanca tried *1 R—Q2, K—K3; 2 K—K3, P—QB3!; 3 P—KR4* (not 3 P—B5, R—Kt4!; 4 R—Q6ch, K—K4; 5 R×P, R—R4=. Alekhine rec-

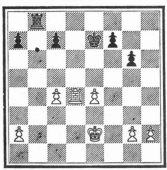

No. 396

Draw.

ommends 3 P—KR3! in order to continue with K—Q4—B3 and then P —B5. But Black has the resource 3 .... K—K4!, for if 4 R—Q7, R —Kt7; 5 R×BP, R×RP; 6 P—Kt4, R—R6ch he will at least draw. The weakness of the White Pawns makes any Black counterattack too effective, *R—KR1!!; 4 P—Kt3, R—R4!!* This is the point. With the Rook on the fourth rank White can no longer win. The conclusion was *5 R—R2* (threatening P—Kt4), *R—R4!; 6 K—B4* (6 P—Kt4?, K—K4), *P—B3!* (again if

now 7 P—Kt4, P—Kt4ch; 8 P×P, P×Pch; 9 K—K3, K—K4; and
White will be lucky to draw!); *7 R—QB2, R—K4* (the threat was 8 P—
B5); *8 P—B5, R—R4; 9 R—B3* (with a view to R—R3), *P—R4; 10
K—B3, K—K2; 11 K—Kt4, K—B2; 12 R—B4, K—Kt2; 13 R—Q4*
(a last attempt), *R×BP; 14 R—Q7ch, K—B1; 15 K—B4, K—Kt1;
16 R—QR7, K—B1; 17 P—QR4, K—Kt1; 18 P—Kt4, P—Kt4ch;
19 P×P, R×P; 20 R—R6, R—QB4; 21 K—K3, K—B2; 22 K—Q4,
R—KKt4; 23 R×BP, R×P; 24 R—B5, R—Kt4* and a draw was agreed
to, for if 25 R×R, P×R; 26 K—K5, K—Kt3!; 27 K—Q6, K—B2!
(the simplest) and if now 28 K—Q7, K—B3! while if 28 P—K5, K—
K1!; 29 K—Q5, K—K2; 30 K—Q4, K—K3; 31 K—K4, P—Kt5; 32
K—B4, P—Kt6; 33 K×P, K×P, etc.=.

An example where two Pawns are not enough to win is No. 396a
(Reti-Tartakover, Baden, 1914), White: K at K2, R at QR6, P's at
QR4, QB3, KB2, KB4; Black: K at KKt2, R at KR7, P's at KB3,
KR2. The doubled KBP and the isolated Q-side P's make the win
impossible. The conclusion was 1 .... R—R8; 2 P—R5, P—R4!;
3 R—R7ch, K—Kt3; 4 P—R6, R—R8; 5 R—R8, K—B4; 6 K—K3
(if 6 K—B3, R—R6), P—R5; 7 P—R7, P—R6; 8 P—B4, P—R7;
9 R—KR8, R×P; 9 R×P, R—K2ch; 10 K—Q4, R—Q2ch; 11 K—
B5, K×P!; 12 K—B6, R—Q7; 13 P—B5, P—B4; 14 K—B7, K—B6;
15 P—B6, P—B5; 16 K—Kt6, R—Kt7ch and the game was called a
draw. White can get his Pawn to the seventh, but cannot queen without removing his Rook from R2. Black then captures the BP, gives up
his Rook for the BP and draws by advancing his own Pawn.

Note that the drawing method in both the above examples is essentially the same: limit the mobility of the opponent's Pawns, advance
one's own passed Pawn as rapidly as possible, finally reduce to an
elementary draw.

The cases where two Pawns do not win are rare exceptions, although
there may often be difficulties. Ordinarily it is possible to reduce
to a standard win. E.g., No. 396b (Steinitz, 1895), White: K at
K1, R at QR2, P's at QR4, KB3, KR2; Black: K at KR6, R at QKt5,
P at QR4. Although the ending is not easy White can win in the
following manner: 1 K—B2!, K×P; 2 R—R1, R—Kt6 (if 2 .... R—
QB5; 3 K—K3, K—Kt6; 4 R—Kt1ch, K—R6; 5 P—B4!, R×RP;
6 P—B5, R—QKt5; 7 P—B6, R—Kt1; 8 K—B4 and wins); 3 R—K1,
R—R6; 4 R—K4, K—R6; 5 R—KKt4, R—R7ch; 6 K—K3, R—
R6ch; 7 K—K2, R—R7ch; 8 K—Q3, R—R6ch; 9 K—B2, R×P;
10 R—Kt5, R—B5; 11 R×P, K—Kt5; 12 R—R8! and the rest is
routine: 12 .... K—Kt4; 13 P—R5, K—B3; 14 P—R6, R—QR5!;
15 K—Q3! (No. 341).

Doubled Pawns are a handicap in all types of ending, especially where two Pawns are held by one. An example from tournament practise is No. 397 (Tarrasch-Johner, Teplitz-Schoenau, 1922). The four White Pawns on the K-side are held by Black's two. After *1 P—QR4, P—R4; 2 K—Kt2, P—Kt3; 3 P—R3, K—B4; 4 R—QB7, R—Kt5; 5 R—B6, R—Kt7; 6 K—B1, R—Kt5; 7 K—K2, R—Kt6; 8 K—Q2* Black can draw by moving back and forth with his Rook. Instead he chose to try for more by 8 .... P—R5?, which gave White a chance to undouble his weaknesses and win: 9 P×P, R×P; 10 R×QKtP, K×P; 11 R—B6ch!, K—K5; 12 R×P, R×P; 13 R—Kt5, K—B6; 14 R—B5ch, K—Kt7; 15 R×P, K×P; 16 R—R8 and wins by marching the Pawn on to the seventh.

If the doubled Pawns are not liquidated, and there is a disadvantage on the other wing, one may even lose with a Pawn plus. E.g., No. 397a (Belavienetz-Ebralidze, Tiflis, 1937), White: K at KKt3, R at Q1, P's at QR2, QKt2, Q5, KB3, KKt4; Black: K at KKt2, R at K1, P's at QR2, QKt3, QB4, KB2, KB3, KR2. Here Black must get rid of the doubled Pawn at once by 1 .... P—B4; 2 P×P, K—B3 when he will surely at least draw and may win. Instead he played passively and lost after 1 .... P—B5?; 2 K—B4!, P—Kt4; 3 R—Q4, R—QB1; 4 P—Q6, K—B1; 5 P—R3, P—QR4; 6 K—K4, P—Kt5; 7 P×P, P×P; 8 K—Q5, P—B6; 9 P×P, P×P; 10 P—Q7!, R—Q1; 11 K—Q6, R—R1; 12 R—QB4, R—R3ch; 13 K—B7, R—R2ch; 14 K—B8, R—R1ch; 15 K—Kt7, R—Q1; 16 K—B7, Resigns.

In order to win one must be able to either exchange the doubled Pawns or transform them into a more concrete advantage. How one may win by exchanging them may be seen in No. 397b (Keres-Capablanca, Semmering-Baden, 1937), White: K at QB3, R at KB5, P's at QR3, QKt2, KKt2, KKt5; Black: K at KKt1, R at K8, P's at QR5, QKt4, KR2. After 1 .... R—K6ch; 2 K—Kt4! is necessary: 2 .... R—Kt6ch; 3 K—R5, R×KtP; 4 R×P, R×P; 5 K×P, K—B2; 6 R—K5!, K—Kt3; 7 K—Kt5 White wins by the odd tempo. Transforming doubled Pawns into an outside passed Pawn supported by the Rook behind it is seen in No. 397c (Colle-Alekhine, Scarborough, 1926), White: K at KR2, R at K3, P's at QR2, QKt3, QB4, KKt2, KR3; Black: K at KB2, R at KB8, P's at QR4, QKt3, QB2, QB4, KKt3, KR2. Alekhine secured a clear advantage by 1 .... P—R5!; 2 P×P, R—B8; 3 P—R5!, R×P; 4 R—R3, R—Q5!; 5 R—QKt3, P×P!; 6 R—Kt5, P—B5!; 7 R×P, K—K3; 8 K—Kt3, R—Q4!; 9 R—R4, R—QB4, after which the rest is routine: 10 R—Kt4, P—B6; 11 R—Kt1, P—B7; 12 R—QB1, K—Q4; 13 K—B3, K—Q5; 14 Resigns.

Blockaded Pawns are of little importance in this connection because they are so easily disposed of with Rooks on the board. Nevertheless, the defender must be careful not to exchange Rooks or unblock the Pawns.

2. STRONG ENEMY PASSED PAWN

This may be just as great an obstacle for the winning side as weak Pawns. It should be securely blockaded as early as possible, preferably by the King, but if there is no alternative, by the Rook.

The danger that one distant passed Pawn may create, together with the manner of combatting it, are clearly illustrated in No. 398 (Euwe-Capablanca, Carlsbad, 1929). If we remove the Black QRP and the White KP it is all over. But here White is hard put to it to take care of the QRP. The game went *1 .... K—B4* (the threat was P—K5); *2 R×RP, K—Q5* (if 2 .... P—R4; 3 P—K5, P×P; 4 R×R, K×R;

No. 397   No. 398

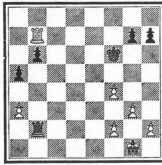   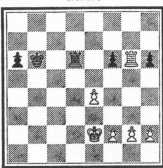

Draw.   Black to play. White wins.

5 K—Q3 and the King is in the square of the RP); *3 K—B3, P—R4; 4 K—B4* (better than 4 P—K5, K×P; 5 R—R5ch, P—B4; 6 P—Kt4, R—KB3; 7 K—K3, P—R5!; 8 K—Q3, R—Q3ch; 9 K—B4, K—B5!=), *P—R5* and now the most direct winning variation is *5 R—R3!* (in the game Euwe played 5 R—R5? and could only draw after 5 .... R—R3; 6 R—Q5ch, K—B6; 7 R—Q1, P—R6; 8 K—B5, P—R7; 9 P—B4, P—R8=Q; 10 R×Q, etc.,—see No. 301), *R—R3* (or 5 .... R—K3; 6 R—K3, P—R6; 7 R×P, R×Pch; 8 K—B5, etc.); *6 R—R3, K—B5* (the difference between this and the line played is that Black requires five more moves to win the White Rook); *7 P—R4, K—Kt5; 8 R—R1, P—R6; 9 K—B5, P—R7; 10 P—Kt4, K—Kt6; 11 P—R5, K—Kt7; 12 R×Pch, R×R; 13 K×P, K—B6; 14 P—B4, K—Q5; 15 P—K5, R—R1; 16 P—B5, R—KKt1; 17 P—K6, R×P; 18 P—K7, R—K5; 19 P—R6* and the Pawns are too much for the poor Rook.

With the White Rook behind the Pawn this type of sacrifice may be more difficult, but if two or three connected passed Pawns remain it is usually a fairly simple matter to calculate whether they will be successful against the lone Rook. An example from a world's championship match is No. 398a (Bogoljuboff-Alekhine, 1st match game, 1934), White: K at KB3, R at QB8, P's at KB4, KKt3, KR3; Black: K at Q6, R at QR7, P at QKt6. White wins. The main variations are 1 R—QKt8, P—Kt7; 2 P—B5 and now:

a) 2 .... K—B7; 3 K—K4, R—R5ch; 4 K—K5, R—R4ch; 5 K—K6, R—R3ch; 6 K—B7, R—R2ch; 7 K—Kt6, R—R6!; 8 R×Pch!, K×R; 9 P—Kt4, R×P; 10 P—B6, K—B6; 11 P—B7, R—B6; 12 K—Kt7, K—Q5; 13 P—Kt5! (but not 13 P—B8= Q?, R×Q; 14 K×R, K—K4=), K—K4; 14 P—Kt6, K—K3; 15 P—B8=Q—just in time!—and wins.

b) 2 .... K—B6; 3 P—Kt4, R—R8; 4 P—Kt5, P—Kt8=Q; 5 R×Q, R×R; 6 K—K4, K—B5; 7 K—K5, K—B4; 8 P—Kt6, R—K8ch; 9 K—B6, K—Q3; 10 P—Kt7, R—KKt8; 11 P—R4 and wins by advancing the RP.

A passed Pawn can often save the game for Black when it is supported from behind by the Rook and blockaded by the enemy Rook. For then the enemy Rook is stalemated and unable to come to the aid of the Pawns. A case in point is No. 399 (Leonhardt-Schlechter, Nuremberg, 1906). The essential stratagem in such endings is to blockade the passed Pawn as early as possible. For this reason White plays *1 R—R4!* and after *1 .... K×P; 2 K—B3, K—Kt4; 3 P—Kt3, K—B3; 4 K—B4, R—R3; 5 P—K5ch, K—Kt2; 6 P—Kt4, K—Kt3; 7 P—R4, K—R3; 8 P—Kt5ch!, K—Kt2* (or 8 .... K—R4; 9 K—B5, R—R1; 10 K—B6, R—R2; 11 P—Kt6!, P×P; 12 P—K6, R—R3; 13 K—B7, R—Kt3; 14 P—K7, R—Kt2; 15 K—B8 and wins); *9 K—B5,*

No. 399

White to play wins; Black to play draws.

K—R2; 10 P—R5, K—Kt2; 11 P—R6ch, K—R2 White can afford to free his Rook. *12 R—QB4!, P—R5* (or 12 .... R—R2; 13 P—K6!, P×Pch; 14 K—B6, P—K4; 15 P—Kt6ch and mate next move); *13 R—B7, K—Kt1; 14 R—B8ch, K—R2; 15 R—B8, R—R2* (15 .... P—R6; 16 R×Pch, K—Kt1; 17 P—Kt6, R—R1; 18 P—R7ch, K—R1; 19 K—Kt5!!, P—R7; 20 K—R6, P—R8=Kt; 21 P—Kt7 mate); *16 P—K6, P—R6* (16 .... P×Pch; 17 K—B6); *17 R×Pch, R×R; 18 P×R, P—R7; 19 P—B8=Q, P—R8=Q; 20 P—Kt6* mate. Since both the main line and a number of sub-variations succeed by only one tempo, it is reasonable to suppose that Black to play can draw. This is in fact borne out by the game and analysis. *1 .... P—R5!; 2 R— R3, K×P; 3 K—B3* (if White goes after the RP with his King Black will win the KP and the resulting R+2P vs. R+P will be drawn), *K—Kt4; 4 P—Kt3, K—B3; 5 K—B4, R—R4; 6 P—Kt4, K—Kt3; 7 P—K5, R—R3; 8 P—R4, K—R3; 9 P—Kt5ch, K—Kt3; 10 K—Kt4, R—R4; 11 P—R5ch, K—Kt2; 12 K—B5, R—R3; 13 P—R6ch, K— R2*=for now the above manoeuvre comes too late: 14 R—B3?, P—R6; 15 R—B7, P—R7; 16 R×Pch (16 P—Kt6ch, K×P), K—Kt1; 17 P— Kt6, R—R1 and Black has saved himself.

An application of the same idea is seen in No. 399a (Koehnlein-Spielmann, Hamburg, 1910), White: K at KKt2, R at K2, P's at QKt2, K4, KB5, KKt4, KR4; Black: K at KR2, R at KB1, P's at QR4, QKt5, KKt2, KR3. Black to play draws. 1 .... P—R5; 2 R—QB2 (if 2 P—K5, P—R6; 3 P×P, P×P; 4 P—K6, R—QR1; 5 P—K7, P—R7! and since 6 R×P??, R×Rch! loses, 6 R—K1, R— K1; 7 R—R1, R×P; 8 R×P=is forced), P—R6; 3 P×P, P×P; 4 R— R2, R—QR1; 5 P—Kt5, P×P; 6 P×P, K—Kt1; 7 K—B3, K—B2; 8 K—Kt4, R—R5!; 9 K—B4, R—R4; 10 K—K3, P—Kt3! (forcing the draw); 11 K—B4, P×P; 12 P×P, R—R5ch; 13 K—K5, R—R4ch; 14 K—B4, R—R5ch, etc. Drawn. The King cannot get to the QRP without losing both K-side Pawns.

Where the Pawns are advanced, their number dwindles in importance because of the threat of promotion. For that reason it is essential for the superior side to nip any such counterattacks in the bud by stopping the passed Pawn at an early moment. We have already seen illustrations of this above. Three other examples will make the technique and the kind of trap to be expected clear.

No. 399b (Alekhine-Euwe, 5th match game, 1927), White: K at KR2, R at K6, P's at QR5, QKt4, QB5, K5; Black: K at KR1, R at K6, P's at QR3, QKt2, QB3, Q4, K5. Black to play. The first consideration must be to stop the dangerous KP. With this in mind 1 .... R—KB6! seems the natural move and it does in fact win. The main variation is 1 K—Kt2, R—B4; 2 P—Kt5!, P—K6!; 3 P×RP, P×P; 4 R×P, P—K7; 5 R—R6ch, K—Kt2; 6 R—R1, P—Q5!; 7 P— B6, P—Q6; 8 P—B7, R—B1; 9 R—KKt1!!!, K—R3!!! (not 9 .... P— Q7?; 10 P—B8=Q, R×Q; 11 K—B2 dis ch); 10 R—R1ch, K—Kt4; 11 R—KKt1, K—B5!; 12 K—B2, K×P dis ch; 13 K—K1, K—Q5; 14 K—Q2, R—B8; 15 R—Kt4ch, K—Q4; 16 R—Kt5ch, K—Q3; 17 P—B8=Q, P—K8=Qch and either wins the White Queen or mates. Euwe chose instead 1 .... P—Q5, when 2 R—Kt6!, threatening the advance of the KP, drew: 2 .... R—KB6 (or 2 .... K—R2; 3 R—Kt2, P—Q6; 4 P—K6, R—K7; 5 P—K7, etc.,) and a draw was agreed to, since 3 R—Kt4, P—Q6; 4 R×P, R—B1; 5 K—Kt3, R—K1 gets rid of all the passed Pawns.

No. 399c (Reshevsky-Alekhine, AVRO, 1938) is a perfect example of a case where extra material is more of a hindrance than a help. White: K at KB2, R at KR5, P's at Q4, KKt2, KR2; Black: K at KB2, R at Q6, P at QR5. Without the QP, White would surely have placed his Rook behind the Black RP and pushed on his Pawns as quickly as possible. This would doubtless have won since the Black King is at quite a distance from his Pawn, while if the Rook gets in front of the Pawn White could reach the favorable position in No. 356. In this position, White can win by following out the same principle: 1 R—R5!, R×P (1 .... P—R6; 2 K—K2, R—QKt6; 3 P—R4, K—K3; 4 P—Kt4, K—Q3; 5 P—R5 is worse); 2 K—K3! (to facilitate the advance of his Pawns), R—QKt5; 3 K—B3, K—K2 (the only chance: if 3 .... R—Kt6ch; 4 K—Kt4, R—QR6; 5 P—R4, R—R8; 6 K—R5, P—R6; 7 P—Kt4, P—R7; 8 P—Kt5 and wins—No. 356); 4 P—Kt4, K—Q2; 5 P—R4, K—B2; 6 P—R5, K—Kt3; 7 R—R8, K—Kt2 (7 .... K—Kt4; 8 P—R6, K—B5; 9 P—R7); 9 R—K8, P—R6; 10 R—K1, P—R7; 11 R—QR1, R—R5; 12 P—R6, K—B3; 13 P—R7, R—R1; 14 R×P, R—R1; 15 R—R7, K—Q3; 16 P—Kt5, K—K3; 17 P—Kt6 and wins. Instead Reshevsky tried to hold on to his extra Pawn and this gave his ingenious opponent sufficient time to come over to the support of his RP with his King. The game continuation was 1 P—Q5, P—R6; 2 R—R7ch, K—B3; 3 R—R7, K—K4; 4 R—R5 (more loss of time but now it was too late to get the Pawns going), R—Q7ch; 5 K—B3, R—Q6ch; 6 K—K2, R—QKt6; 7 K—B2, R—Kt7ch; 8 K—Kt3, R—Kt6ch; 9 K—R4, R—Kt7; 10 K—R3, P—R7; 11 P—Q6 dis ch (to get the Black King out of the way: if 11 P—Kt4, K—B5!; 12 R—R4ch, K—K4, or 12 R—R3?, R—Kt6ch), K×P; 12 P—Kt4, K—B3! and now the Black King can draw by approaching the passed RP (No. 358).

No. 399d (Gilg-Mattison, Carlsbad, 1929), White: K at KB3, R at KB5, P's at K3, KB2, KKt2, KR2; Black: K at QB3, R at QR5, P's at QR4, QKt3, KB3. Black to play. After the capture at KB6 White will have no less than four passed Pawns. Nevertheless by marching on with his own QKt and QRP Black is assured of a draw. The best line is 1 .... P—Kt4!; 2 R×Pch, K—B4; 3 R—B8, P—Kt5; 4 R—QKt8, (else .... P—Kt6 and .... R—Kt5), K—B3!; 5 P--Kt4, K—B2!; 6 R—Kt5, K—B3! and White does best to take a draw. Instead Black gilded the lily and lost after 1 .... R—QB5?; 2 R×Pch, K—Kt4; 3 R—B8, P—R5; 4 R—QR8, K—Kt5; 5 P—Kt4!, R—B4; 6 P—R4, R—QR4; 7 R×R, P×R; 8 P—Kt5. Both sides promoted but White won the Q and P ending.

Finally, positions occur where a strong passed Pawn wins despite a material minus of one or two Pawns. Such a case is seen in No. 399e (Capablanca-Thomas, Carlsbad, 1929), White: K at KKt3, R at QB7 (ch), P's at K3, KB2, KKt2, KR3; Black: K at QB4, R at QKt3, P's at QKt5, KKt2, KR3. Here 1 .... K—Q3! decides without much trouble because White has no time to go Pawn-grabbing: 2 R—B1 (2 R×P, P—Kt6; 3 R—Kt8, P—Kt7; 4 R—Q8ch, K—K2; 5 R—Q1, P—Kt8=Q; 6 R×Q, R×R and wins because he still has one Pawn), P—Kt6; 3 R—QKt1, P—Kt7; 4 K—B4, K—Q4; 5 P—K4ch, K—Q5; 6 P—K5, K—B6; 7 K—B5, P—Kt3ch; 8 K—K4, K—B7 and the rest is simple. Instead the game continued 1 .... R—B3?; 2 R×P, P—Kt6; 3 R—Q7, R—Q3 and a draw was agreed to because White now has too many Pawns on the K-side.

3. STRONG ENEMY ROOK POSITION

This is usually a Rook on the seventh or sixth rank attacking a mass of Pawns. Such a Rook can often save the day for the inferior side by capturing material directly or by forcing the sacrifice of material to avoid perpetual check or a mating combination.

No. 400 (Nimzovitch-Marshall, New York, 1927) is typical of those cases which go hand in hand with strong King positions. The White King is confined to the side of the board, and the connected passed Pawns can advance only with the greatest of difficulty. As a result Black has strong counterplay which assures him of a draw. Marshall tried *1* .... *P—R4* (necessary to keep the White King confined); *2 R—R7* (not 2 K—R4?, K—B4!; 3 P—R3??, R—QR7!!; 4 P—Kt4ch—forced to stop mate—P×P; 5 K—Kt3, R×Pch and Black might win. Similarly if 2 P—Kt4, P×Pch; 3 K—Kt3, P—B4; 4 R—Q6ch?, K—K5; 5 R—KB6, P—Kt4; 6 P—K6?, K—Q6!; 7 P—B5?, R—K8; 8 K—Kt2, P—B5 Black will win). Now the most exact drawing continuation was *2* .... *K—B3!,* for if then 3 R—K7 to prepare P—B5, 3 .... P—Kt4!; 4 P—Kt4 (necessary to stop mate), P×Pch; 5 K—Kt3, R—K6ch; 6 K—B2, R—KB6; 7 R—B7, K—Q4; 8 R—B6, P—B4 the result is an exciting draw: 9 P—K6, P—B5; 10 P—B5, P—Kt6ch; 11 P×P, P ×Pch; 12 K—Kt2, K—B5; 13 P—K7, R—B7ch; 14 K—Kt1!, R—B8ch; 15 K—Kt2=, but not 15 .... R—B7ch; 16 K—B1??, P—Kt7ch; 17 K—Kt1, K—Kt6 and mates.

No. 400

Black to play. Draw.

Thus the normal continuation would be *3 R—R6ch, K—Q4; 4 R—R7, K—B3,* etc. The game continuation was 2 .... R—QB7 (hoping for a mating attack); 3 R—K7 (if 3 K—R4!?, R×Pch; 4 K—Kt5, P—B3ch; 5 K—Kt6, R—QKt7; 6 K×RP, R×P; 7 R—K7, K—B4!; 8 K—R4!, R—Kt8; 9 P—B5, K—B5; 10 K—R3 a draw should still result), P—Kt4; 4 P—Kt4 (or 4 P—B5, P—Kt5ch; 5 K—R4, R×Pch; 6 K—Kt5, P—B3ch; 7 K—Kt6, P—R5!=), P—R5? (the simple 4 .... P×Pch; 5 K×P, R—B5ch; 6 K×P, P—B3ch; 7 K—Kt6, R×P draws at once); 5 P—B5, P—B4; 6 P—B6? (and now 6 P—K6 would have won: 6 .... R—B6ch; 7 K—Kt2, P×P; 8 R—Q7ch, K—B3; 9 R—Q8, P—R6ch; 10 K—Kt1, R—K6; 11 P—B6, P—Kt6; 12 P×P, R—K8ch; 13 K—R2, P—Kt5; 14 P—K7, R—K7ch; 15 K—Kt1, R—K8ch; 16 K—B2, P—R7; 17 R—QR8, K—Q2; 18 P—B7! and queens or wins the Rook), R—B6ch; 7 K—Kt2, P×P and now a draw was agreed to, for after the only try 8 P—B7, P—R6ch; 9 K—Kt1, R—KB6; 10 P—K6, R—B8ch; 11 K—B2, R—B7ch; 12 K—Q3, P—Kt6; 13 P×P, P—R7; 14 R—R7, K×P; 15 R×P, R×P there is too little wood for a fire.

The normal position where a well-placed Rook yields perpetual check is No. 400a (Keres-Fine, Semmering-Baden, 1937), White: K at K3, R at QKt6 (ch), P's at KB4, KKt3, KR3; Black: K at KB3, R at QR5, P's at QR4, KB4, KKt3, KR3. Here the game was called a draw, since the winning attempt 1 .... K—B2; 2 R—Kt7ch, K—K3; 3 R—Kt6ch, K—Q4?; 4 R×P might win for White, but not for Black.

A Rook on the seventh rank is usually sufficient compensation for a Pawn. Sometimes the "pig"—as Janowski used to call it—even counterbalances the loss of two Pawns. A classic instance of such "piggishness" is seen in No. 401 (Tarrasch-Rubinstein, San Sebastian,

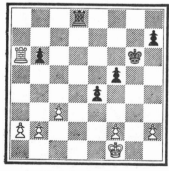

No. 401

Black to play draws.

1911). Passive defense would be hopeless: White merely sets up two passed Pawns on the Q-side and walks in. So Rubinstein plays va banque. *1 .... R—Q7!!; 2 R× Pch, K—Kt4; 3 K—K1* (or 3 P— QR4, P—B5; 4 P—R5, P—B6; 5 K—K1, R—K7ch and on 6 K—Q1? R×BP; 7 P—R6, P—K6!; 8 P— R7, R—Q7ch; 9 K—B1, P—B7 White will lose, so that he must allow perpetual check by 6 K—B1, R—Q7; 7 K—K1, R—K7ch etc.), *R—B7; 4 R—Kt5, K—Kt5!* (he must not block his Pawn. The threat is now ⊞P—B5—B6); *4 P—R3ch* (the only chance), *K×P; 5 R×P, R×KtP; 6 R—B4* (or 6 P—R4, 3̶—R7; 7 P—R5, K—Kt5; 8 R—K5, K—B6, etc. If 6 R—R5ch, K—Kt5; 7 R×P, R×RP=), *R×RP; 7 R×P, P—R4!; 8 P—QB4, K—Kt7!; 9 R—KB4* (9 P—B4?, P—R5! might well lose), *R—QB7; 10 R—KR4, K—B6!* (Rubinstein's play is a model of precision. On 10 …. R×KBP?; 11 R—R2ch!, K×R; 12 K×R, K—R8; 13 P—B5 White wins: 13 …. P—R5; 14 P—B6, P—R6; 15 P—B7, P—R7; 16 K—Kt3!, K—Kt8; 17 P—B8=Q, P—R8=Q; 18 Q—B1 mate); *11 K—Q1, R×KBP; 12 P—B5, K—K6; 13 R×P* (or 13 P—B6, R—B3!! and 14 P—B7, R—B3=is forced, for if 14 R—QB4??, K—Q6!! and Black wins the Rook), *K—Q5* Drawn.

Against a Rook which has assumed a strong position the old adage that the best defense is a counterattack is applicable. For passive play in such cases usually yields nothing (compare Nos. 400, 401). An example of a successful counterattack is No. 401a (Alekhine-P. Frydman, Podebrady, 1936), White: K at K3, R at QR5, P's at QKt2, QB2, K4, KB5, KR2; Black: K at QB3, R at KKt2, P's at QKt2, K4, KB3, KR2. White to play. Alekhine, aggressive as usual, scored in the following interesting manner: 1 R—R8!, R—Kt7; 2 R—KB8!, R×RP; 3 R×Pch, K—B4; 4 P—Kt4ch!!! (the point: Black's King is diverted and one Pawn is removed from the second rank), K—B5; 5 R—Q6!!, R—R6ch (if 5 …. R×P; 6 R—Q5!, K×P; 7 R×P and White's two connected passed Pawns will decide); 6 K—K2, R—R5; 7 K—B3, P—R4 (if instead 7 …. R—R6ch; 8 K—Kt4, R—K6; 9 P—B6, R×Pch; 10 K—B5, R—B5ch; 11 K×P, R—B7; 12 R—Q4ch, K—B6; 13 R—KB4, R—K7ch; 14 K—Q6, R—K1; 15 P—B7, R—KB1; 16 K—K7 and wins); 8 R—K6, R—B5ch; 9 K—K3, P—R5; 10 R×P, P—R6!; 11 R—Q5! (not 11 K×R?, P—R7! and queens), R—R5; 12 R—Q4ch!, K—B6; 13 R—Q1, P—R7; 14 R—KR1, R—R6ch; 15 K—B4, R—R5ch (15 …. K—Q5; 16 P—B6); 16 K—K5, K—Q7; 17 P—B6, K—K6; 18 K—Q6!, R×KP (or 18 …. K×P; 19 P—B7, R—B5; 20 K—K7, R—B7; 21 R×P); 19 R×P, R—Q5ch; 20 K—K5, Resigns.

Care must always be exercised to keep the Rook as mobile as possible. An example where a bad (cramped) Rook is fatal despite a Pawn plus is No. 401b (Saemisch-Treybal, Teplitz-Schoenau, 1922), White: K at K4, R at QR7, P's at Q5, KB5; Black: K at KKt2, R at KB3, P's at QKt3, KB2, KKt5. White to play wins. 1 K—K5, R—R3; 2 R—R4!, K—B1; 3 P—Q6, K—K1; 4 R—R8ch, K—Q2; 5 R—R7ch, K—Q1 (5 …. K—K1; 6 R—K7ch, K—B1; 7 P—B6 and 8 P—Q7); 6 R×P, R—R8; 7 R—KKt7, R—KKt8; 8 P—B6, R—K8ch; 9 K—Q5, R—Q8ch; 10 K—B6, K—K1; 11 P—Q7ch, K—B1; 12 R—K7!, P—Kt4; 13 R—K8ch, K—B2; 14 P—Q8=Q, R×Q; 15 R×R, K×P; 16 K—Q5 Resigns.

VI. POSITIONAL ADVANTAGE

As usual, we shall divide the material into the three subdivisions of better Rook, Pawns and King respectively, although it is again largely a theoretical task to dissociate the three groupings in any given case. Pawn position and Rook superiority in particular are practically inseparable.

A. BETTER ROOK POSITION

The criterion by which we can judge whether one Rook is better than another is its *degree of mobility:* its freedom of action, the number of squares it can control. It is this which justifies our basic maxim that *Rooks belong behind Pawns.* We shall distinguish five types of superiority.

1. THE ROOK ON THE SEVENTH RANK

Normally there are a number of Pawns on the seventh rank which the White Rook is attacking. To defend them with the Black Rook would be to immobilize that piece, while if there are Pawns on both sides of the board, the King cannot possibly defend them all. In any event, Black is severely handicapped and must always weaken his position, often lose a Pawn.

The simplest case where the Rook captures material without any real compensation is No. 402. The Black King is tied down to the defense of the K-side Pawns, the Rook to the QRP. Against passive play White will march his King to QKt7 and capture a Pawn. The best chance is *1 .... R—QKt1* (the defense 1 .... R—K1ch; 2 K— Q4, R—K3, which would work in the absence of too many K-side Pawns, fails here after 3 R×RP, K—Kt2; 4 P—B4!, K—B3; 5 K— B5, for the White King gets to QKt5, supports the Pawn and frees the Rook. Compare No. 341); *2 R×RP, R—Kt6ch; 3 K—Q4, R— R6; 4 K—B5, R—R7; 5 K—Kt6, R×P; 6 R—B7, R×P; 7 P—R7, R—Kt7ch; 8 K—B5!, R—QR7; 9 R—B8ch, K—Kt2; 10 P—R8=Q, R×Q; 11 R×R, P—R4; 12 K—Q4* and with the White King so near the win is simple. With the White Pawn at QR3 or QR4 here, the game may likewise be won, but other complications arise (see No. 406).

A more complicated variant on the same idea is No. 402a (Thorvaldsson-Feigin, Folkestone, 1933), White: K at KKt1, R at QKt1, P's at QR2, QB3, KB3, KKt2, KR2; Black: K at KKt1, R at K7, P's at QR2, QB2, Q3, KKt3, KR2. Black to play wins. 1 .... R— QB7!! (best: 1 .... R×RP; 2 R—Kt8ch, K—B2; 3 R—Kt7 gives White a certain draw); 2 R—Kt3 (now 2 R—Kt8ch, K—B2; 3 R—

Kt7 would be met by 3 .... R×BP; 4 R×RP, P—Q4, when the two connected passed Pawns would decide), K—B2; 3 P—KR4, K—K3; 4 R—R3, P—QR4!; 5 K—R2, P—B4; 6 K—R3, P—Q4; 7 K—Kt3, K—K4 and White resigned. This may seem a bit premature, but he has no way of preventing the decisive entry of the Black King: e.g., 8 K—R3, K—Q3!; 9 P—B4, K—B3; 10 P—Kt4, K—Kt4!; 11 P—B5, P×P; 12 P×P, R—B7; 13 K—Kt4, P—B5!!; 14 K—Kt5, P—R4!; 15 K×P, R×Pch; 16 K—Kt4, R—K4; 17 P—R5, R—K5ch; 18 K—Kt5, R—K6; 19 P—R6, R—R6; 20 K—Kt6, P—Q5; 21 P—R7, P—Q6, etc.

If there is a mass of Pawns undefended by the King a Rook on the

No. 402

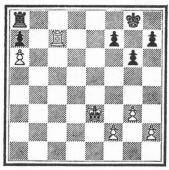

White wins.

No. 403

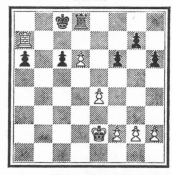

White to play wins.

seventh just eats them up. One enemy passed Pawn on the other wing can then be disregarded. An elementary illustration of the idea is seen in No. 403 (Euwe-Capablanca, Carlsbad, 1929). After *1 R—B7ch!, K—Kt1; 2 R×BP* (first getting rid of one potentially dangerous passed Pawn), *K—Kt2; 3 R—B7ch, K—Kt3; 4 R×P, R×P; 5 R—Kt6* (the sixth rank functions here in exactly the same manner as the seventh in other cases), *K—B4; 6 R×RP* should win (see No. 398).

Where the Pawns must be lost it is better to allow the opponent disconnected ones than connected. E.g., No. 403a (Bogoljuboff-Maroczy, Carlsbad, 1929), White: K at QB3, R at QR5, P's at QR4, KB2, KKt2, KR3; Black: K at KB3, R at QR8, P's at QR2, K3, KKt3, KR3. Black to play. 1 .... R—R7; 2 R×P, R×P; 3 R—KR7, P—R4 and now White, seeing that a Pawn goes no matter what he does, played 4 P—R5? and lost. Instead 4 P—Kt4! would have drawn, for if 4 .... P×P; 5 P×P, R—B5; 6 P—R5!, R—R5 (or 6 .... R×P; 7 P—R6, R—QR5; 8 R—R7, P—Kt4; 9 R—R8, P—Kt5; 10 P—R7, K—Kt2; 11 K—Q2, P—Kt6; 12 K—K2=); 7 R—R7, K—Kt4; 8 P—R6, K×P; 9 R—R8, P—Kt4; 10 P—R7, K—Kt6; 11 K—Kt3, R—R8; 12 K—Kt4, P—Kt5; 13 K—B5, K—Kt7; 14 K—Kt6 with a simple draw, while if 4 .... R—B6ch; 5 K—Kt4, R×P; 6 P×P, P×P (6 .... R×P??; 7 R×R, P×R; 8 P—R5 and queens first); 7 P—R5, R—R8; 8 R—R6ch!, K—B4; 9 P—R6, P—K4; 10 P—R7, R—R8; 11 R×Pch=. After the game continuation 4 P—R5?, Maroczy ensconced his King behind his Pawns and won handily: 4 .... R×P; 5 P—R6, R—QR7; 6 P—R7, K—Kt4; 7 R—K7, K—R5; 8 K—Kt3, R—R8; 9 R×P, R×P; 10 R×P, K×P; 11 K—B2, R—Q2 and we have No. 319.

To avoid such loss of material the defender often resorts to a counterattack with his Rook. Normally such tactics are far more promising than passive defense. No. 403b (Alekhine-Euwe, 27th match game, 1935) is typical. White: K at KB2, R at Q1, P's at QR2, QKt4, QB3, KB3, KKt2, KR2; Black: K at KKt1, R at K1, P's at QR2, QKt3, K3, KB2, KKt2, KKt3. White to play. After 1 R—Q7!, R—QB1!; 2 R×RP, R×P; 3 R—R8ch, K—R2 Black has fair counterchances—for the continuation see No. 423—, but 1 .... R—R1; 2 K—K3, P—R4; 3 P—Kt5, R—QB1; 4 K—Q3 leaves him with a hopeless loss.

When the Rook has unchallenged control of the seventh rank, and the enemy King is on the eighth rank, confined there by the Rook, White is said to have the "absolute seventh." In conjunction with the King and a passed Pawn the absolute seventh is murderous. Witness No. 404 (Capablanca-Tartakover, New York, 1924), where White sac-

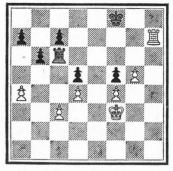

No. 404

White to play wins.

rifices two Pawns to get his King to the sixth. *1 K—Kt3!!, R×Pch; 2 K—R4, R—B6* (this loses quickly. He could have put up much stiffer resistance with 2 .... R—B8!, for if 3 P—Kt6?, R—R8ch; 4 K—Kt5, R×R; 5 P×R, K—Kt2; 6 K×P, P—B4!; 7 K—K6, P×P; 8 P—B5=. The most exact line after 2 .... R—B8 is 3 K—R5!, P—B4—or A—; 4 R—Q7!, P×P (5 .... P—B5; 6 K—Kt6); 5 R×QP, R—Q8; 6⁺K—Kt6, P—Q6; 7 K—B6, K—K1; 8 P—Kt6, P—Q7; 9 P—Kt7, R—KKt8; 10 R×QP and wins. Variation A.

3 .... R—R8ch; 4 K—Kt6, R×R; 5 K×R, P—B4; 6 P—Kt6 and queens too soon); *3 P—Kt6!, R×Pch; 4 K—Kt5, R—K5* (Black must be able to return to the first rank. If 4 .... R×P; 5 K—B6, K—Kt1; 6 R—Q7 and mates, or 5 .... K—K1; 6 R—R8ch, K—Q2; 7 P—Kt7, winning the Rook); *5 K—B6, K—Kt1; 6 R—Kt7ch, K—R1; 7 R×P* (Now White gets all his Pawns back with interest), *R—K1; 8 K×P* (the simplest), *R—K5; 9 K—B6, R—B5ch; 10 K—K5, R—Kt5; 11 P—Kt7ch, K—Kt1* (after 11 .... R×P; 12 R×R, K×R; 13 K×P the Pawn ending is hopeless); *12 R×P, R—Kt8; 13 K×P, R—QB8; 14 K—Q6, R—B7; 15 P—Q5, R—B8; 16 R—QB7, R— QR8; 17 K—B6, R×P; 18 P—Q6* Resigns.

If there is little material left, a Rook on the seventh is usually much less effective, since there is much less to be captured. E.g., No. 404a (Kashdan-Alekhine, Folkestone, 1933), White: K at KB1, R at KKt7, P's at KB2, KKt3, KR2; Black: K at K3, R at QR4, P's at K4, KB3, KR2. Black to play. 1 .... P—R4; 2 R—KR7, P—K5; 3 K—K2 and now 3 .... P—B4 demonstrated the draw quickly (if instead 3 .... R—K4?; 4 K—K3, K—Q4; 5 P—R4, K—K3; 6 R—R7, K—Q4; 7 K—B4, K—K3; 8 R—R6ch, K—K2; 9 R—R4 and Black loses the Pawns in worse circumstances); 4 R— R6ch (or 4 R×P, R—R7ch; 5 K—B1, R—R8ch; 6 K—Kt2, R—R7!; 7 R—R8, K—B2 and the threat .... P—K6 equalizes), K—K4; 5 R×P, R—R7ch; 6 K—B1, P—K6!, etc.—see No. 392b. A some- what more complicated case, though with only two Pawns on each side, is No. 404b (Tchekhover-Romanovsky, Leningrad, 1934), White: K at QKt1, R at KB7, P's at K3, KKt3; Black: K at QB3, R at QB7, P's at QKt6, K5. Black to play. Here the seventh rank is meaningful only to the extent that the Rook confines the White King. The game continued 1 .... R—K7; 2 R—B5? (correct was 2 P—Kt4, R×P; 3 P—Kt5, R—Kt6; 4 R—K7, K—Q4; 5 K—Kt2, K—Q5!; 6 R— KKt7!, P—K6!; 7 P—Kt6!, P—K7; 8 R—Q7ch, K—K6; 9 R—K7ch, K—Q7; 10 R—Q7ch, and draws, for if 10 .... R—Q6; 11 R×Rch, K×R; 12 P—Kt7 and there is no mate after both have queened), R×P; 3 P—Kt4, R—Kt6 (or 3 .... R—K7; 4 P—Kt5, K—Q3; 5 P—Kt6, P—K6; 6 R—B3, K—K4; 7 P—Kt7=); 4 P—Kt5? (4 R— K5, R×P; 5 K—Kt2, K—Q3; 6 R—K8, K—Q4; 7 K×P, K—Q5; 8 K—B2 is a standard draw—No. 305), K—Q3; 5 K—Kt2, P—K6; 6 R—B1, K—K4!; 7 R—B8, R×P; 8 K×P, K—K5; 9 K—B2, R—Q4 and wins, for the White King is on the long side of the Pawn.

2. THE OPEN FILE

Unchallenged control of an open file always confers an advantage. Where there are weak Pawns in the enemy camp, and the Rook can penetrate to the seventh rank, material can usually be won. The method of exploiting an open file involves branching off to one of the wings at the appropriate moment.

No. 405 (Marshall-Euwe, Bad Kissingen, 1928) is a typical instance. Place the White Rook at QB1 and Black will have to fight hard to draw. But now he can first cramp the White pieces and then secure a decisive material superiority. Euwe won as follows: *1 .... R—QB1; 2 R—B3!* (relatively best. If 2 R—B2, R—B8ch; 3 R—B1, R—B5!; 4 R—Q1, R—B7; 5 P—Kt4, R—B6 and wins a Pawn), *R—B8ch!* (driving the White King away. On 3 R—B1?, R—B5!; 4 R—Q1, R—B7 wins a Pawn); *3 K—R2, R—Q8; 4 R—QKt3, R×P; 5 R×P, R×P; 6 R×RP, R—B7.* Let us pause to consider. The material is still even but the White Pawn at KKt5 is hopelessly weak. White has two connected passed Pawns on the Q-side, Black in the center. This in itself is of no great moment, but here it makes all the difference in the world because Black is in a position to support his Pawns, while White is not. *7 P—QKt4, R—Kt7; 8 R—Kt7, R—R7; 9 R—R7, K—Kt3; 10 P—Kt5, P—Q5!* (This advance will force the exchange of the Black QP for the White QKtP or QRP and leave Black with two connected passed Pawns vs. one); *11 P—Kt6* (White has no time to advance his Pawns methodically. If 11 P—R4, P—Q6; 12 P—Kt6, P—Q7 and 13 R—Q7, R×P; 14 R×P, R—QKt5; 15 R—Q6, R—Kt7 is necessary, when Black will win as in the game. Similarly, to try to stop the Black Pawns with the King would be suicidal: 11 K—Kt1?, P—K4; 12 K—B1?, P—Q6; 13 P—R4, R—R8ch; 14 K—B2, P—Q7 and wins), *R—Kt7; 12 R—R4, R×P; 13 R×P, R—Kt6!* (to be sure to get behind the passed Pawn); *14 R—QR4, K×P* (Now Black need only rid himself of the doubled Pawn, which is easily done); *15 R—R8, P—B5; 16 P—R4, P—B6!; 17 R—Kt8ch!* (if 17 P×P, R×P; 18 P—R5 Black has time to force the crucial position of No. 356 because his Pawn is still on the second rank: 18 .... R—QR6; 19 P—R6, K—B5!; 20 P—R7, P—K4! and if 21 R—KB8, R×P and the BP is protected), *K—R3!; 18 P×P, R×P; 19 R—Kt3, R—B4; 20 R—Kt4* (20 R—QR3, R—R4 is somewhat more difficult, but the QRP is so far back that Black will still win), *R—B4; 21 R—Kt4, R—B6; 22 K—Kt2, K—Kt3* and wins. For the conclusion see No. 357.

The strength of the open file lies in the fact that it can be used as a springboard to get the Rook to other parts of the board. Consequently where there is no available jumping-off place on the fifth, sixth or seventh ranks, the open file will not be of much use. An illustration of this principle is seen in No. 405a (Bogoljuboff-Johner, Carlsbad, 1929), White: K at KB3, R at QB1, P's at QR2, QB3, QB4, Q5, KB4, KKt4, KR2; Black: K at KKt3, R at K2. P's at QR2, QKt3, QB2, Q3, KB2, KB3, KR3. White to play. 1 P—B5ch,

K—Kt2 (1 .... K—Kt4 is enterprisingly fatal: 2 P—R4ch, K×RP;
3 R—R1ch, K—Kt4; 4 R—R5 mate); 2 P—QR4, P—QR4 makes the
draw certain—the open file gets Black nowhere because the Rook
cannot occupy any square beyond the fourth rank. Instead Bogoljuboff played 1 P—QR4? and after 1 .... P—KB4! realized that the
threat 2 .... R—K5 would cost him at least one Pawn. He chose
the counteroffensive 2 P—B5, but after the series of peaceful exchanges: 2 .... KtP×P; 3 R—QKt1, P×Pch; 4 K×P, R—K6;
5 R—Kt7, P—R4ch; 6 K—R4, R×P; 7 R×BP, R—B6; 8 P—R5,
R×Pch; 9 K—Kt3, R—Kt5ch; 10 K—B3, K—B3; 11 R×RP, R—
QR5; 12 R—Q7, K—K4!; 13 R×BP, R×P; 14 R—KR7, K×P the
Black connected passed Pawns carried the day.

No. 405

No. 406

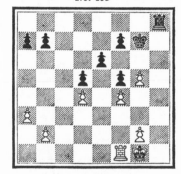

Black to play wins.   Black to play.

3. THE WHITE ROOK IS ATTACKING A PAWN OR PAWNS DEFENDED BY THE BLACK ROOK

Pawns should be defended by the King because only the monarch
does not thereby lose mobility. A Rook which defends any Pawn
(except for strong passed Pawns) is cramped and much inferior to its
rival which is attacking those Pawns. The seventh rank is but one
illustration of this general fact: in No. 402 Black loses only because
his Rook is chained to a defensive post.

The usual type of position in which this advantage is seen is No. 406
(Match St. Petersburg-London, 1886-88). The game was adjourned
here and was not played to a finish. Tchigorin later published
analysis to support his claim that White should win, but he appears
to have been over-optimistic.

There are two important guiding principles that are displayed in this ending:

1. Purely passive play loses for Black.
2. An adequate counterattack at the proper moment will suffice to draw.

The first is illustrated in the following variations:

a) 1 .... R—R2?; 2 K—K4, R—R3; 3 K—Q4, R—R2; 4 P—B4 and now:

    1) 4 .... R—R3; 5 R—Kt7ch, K—Q3 (5 .... K—K3; 6 K—B5, R—R1; 7 R—Kt6ch, K—B2; 8 K—Kt5); 6 P—B5, P×P; 7 P×P, R—R1; 8 R—Kt6ch, K—K2; 9 K—B5, R—R1; 10 R—Kt5!, K—Q2; 11 R×P and wins.

    2) 4 .... K—Q3; 5 R—Kt6ch, K—K2; 6 K—B5, R—B2ch; 7 K—Kt5, R—B8; 8 P—Kt5, P—B4 (8 .... P×P would lose both P's); 9 R×P, R—KB8; 10 K×P, R×P; 11 R—K B6!, R—B8; 12 K—Kt6, P—B5; 13 P—R5, R—KKt8; 14 R×P, R×P; 15 P—R6, R—Kt8; 16 P—R7, R—QR8; 17 R—B5 and wins.

b) 1 .... R—R1; 2 K—K4, R—R2; 3 K—Q4, K—Q3; 4 P—Kt5, K—K2 (4 .... P×P; 5 R—Kt6ch, K—K2; 6 R×P again wins two Pawns for if 6 .... R—Kt2?; 7 R—Kt7ch); 5 R—Kt6, R—Q2ch; 6 K—K4, P—B4ch; 7 K—K5, R—Q6; 8 R×P,R×P; 9 R—Kt7ch, K—B1; 10 R—QR7 and wins for if 10 .... P—B5; 11 K—B6, K—K1; 12 P—Kt6, R—KKt6; 13 R—R8ch, K—Q2; 14 R×P, P—B6; 15 R—KB5, K—K1; 16 P—Kt7, etc.

c) 1 .... K—K3; 2 K—K4, K—Q2; 3 K—Q4, K—B2; 4 K—B4, K—B3; 5 R—B5ch!, K—Q3; 6 K—Kt5, R—R2; 7 R—B3!, R—R1; 8 R—B6ch, K—K4; 9 K—Kt6!, R—Kt1ch (forced: 9 .... P—Kt4 is answered by 10 R—B5ch, K—K3; 11 K—Kt7, R—Q1; 12 R×P, R—Q5!; 13 R—R8!, R—KB5; 14 P—R5, R×BP; 15 P—R6, R—QR6; 16 P—R7 and wins); 10 K×P, R—Kt6; 11 P—B4ch, K×P; 12 R×Pch, K—Kt4 (12 .... K×P; 13 R×Pch, K—B4; 14 R—Kt6 and wins because the Black King is cut off on the fourth rank); 13 R—Kt6!, R—K6!; 14 R—Kt4, K—R5; 15 K—Kt5, R—K4ch; 16 K—B6, R—K3ch; 17 K—B5, R—K4ch; 18 K—Q6, R—K8; 19 R—QB4!, P—Kt4; 20 K—B5, R—K4ch; 21 K—Kt4, R—K1 (21 .... R—K8; 22 P—R5, R—Kt8ch; 23 K—B5, R—QR8; 24 K—Kt5, R—Kt8ch; 25 R—Kt4, R—QR8; 26 R—R4, etc.); 22 P—R5, R—Kt1ch; 23 K—B5, R—B1ch; 24 K—Q5, R—Q1ch; 25 K—K6, R—K1ch; 26 K—Q7, R—QR1; 27 R—QR4!, R—R2ch; 28 K—B6, R—R1; 29 P—R6, R×Pch; 30 R×R, K×P; 31 K—Q5, K—B6; 32 R—B6ch, K—K6; 33 R—KKt6; K—B5; 34 K—Q4, P—Kt5; 35 R—B6ch and wins.

It follows that Black's only chance lies in getting his Rook behind the White QRP. In fact, the immediate sacrifice seems to draw most effectively. *1 .... R—B3!; 2 R×P, R—B5ch; 3 K—K3* (if 3 K—Kt3, P—Kt4; 4 R—R7ch, K—K3; 5 P—R5, R—B7; 6 P—R6, R—R7; 7 R—R8, K—B2!=), *R—B6ch; 4 K—K4, R—B5ch; 5 K—Q5, R—B5; 6 K—B6* (on 6 R—R7ch, K—Q1! draws), *R×BP; 7 R—QB5, P—B4!; 8 P×P* (8 P—Kt5, P—B5; 9 P—R5, R—B8; 10 P—R6, P—B6; 11 P—R7, R—QR8; 12 K—Kt7?, P—B7), *R×P!; 9 R—B2* (9 R×R, P×R; 10 P—R5, P—B5 and both queen), *P—Kt4; 10 K—Kt6* (10 R—QR2, K—B2; 11 P—R5, K—Kt3; 12 P—R6, R—B3ch and the White King must retreat), *R—B3ch; 11 K—Kt7* (11 R—B6?, R×Rch; 12 K×R, P—Kt5 and Black wins), *R—B4; 12 R—QR2, K—B3; 13 P—R5, K—Kt3; 14 P—R6, R—B2ch; 15 K—B6, R—B3ch; 16 K—B5, R—B4ch; 17 K—Q4, R—B5ch; 18 K—K3, R—B1; 19 P—R7, R—QR1; 20 K—B4, K—B3,* etc.=.

A similar instance where an aggressive counteraction can save a seemingly lost ending is No. 406a (Tarrasch-Janowski, Ostend, 1907), White: K at Q2, R at QKt6, P's at QR4, QKt3, Q4, KB2, KKt4; Black: K at KB2, R at Q2, P's at QR4, QKt5, Q4, KB3, KKt4. Black to play. A Pawn must go, for if 1 .... R—R2; 2 R—Q6. Janowski instead played 1 .... R—B2! when 2 R—Q6, R—B6; 3 R×QP, R×P; 4 R×QRP, K—K3; 5 R—KB5, R—QR6; 6 P—R5, K—K2! should have drawn. The continuation was 7 K—B2, K—K3; 8 R—Kt5, K—Q3; 9 K—Kt2, K—K3; 10 R—Kt6ch (10 R×P, R×P will hardly win: the Black King is too near the passed Pawn), K—Q4; 11 R×BP, K—B5!; 12 R—B5! (or 12 P—R6, R—Kt6ch; 13 K—B2, R—B6ch and it is dangerous for White to try to avoid perpetual check, e.g., 14 K—Q2, R—Q6ch; 15 K—K2, R—QR6; 16 R—KKt6, P—Kt6!; 17 R×P, P—Kt7; 18 R—B5ch, K×P; 19 R—QKt5, K—B6; 20 P—B4, R×P; 21 P—B5, R—R5!; 22 R×P, K×R; 23 K—B3, K—B6; 24 P—B6, K—Q5; 25 K—B4, K—Q4 dis ch; 26 K—B5, R—R8; 27 P—Kt5, R—B8ch; 28 K—Kt6, K—K3! and wins), R—Kt6ch; 13 K—B2, R—B6ch; 14 K—Q2, R—Q6ch; 15 K—K2, R×P; 16 P—R6, R—Q1; 17 R×P, P—Kt6; 18 R—Kt7, P—Kt7; 19 R—Kt7, K—B6; 20 P—B4, R—QR1; 21 P—B5, R×P; 22 K—K3 and now 22 .... R—R8! draws: 23 R×P, K×R; 24 P— B6 R—KB8; 25 P—Kt5, K—B6; 26 K—K4, K—B5; 27 K—K5, K —B4; 28 K—K6, R—K8ch; 29 K—B7 (if 29 K—Q7, R—Q8ch; 30 K—B7, R—KB8! threatening .... R—B4), K—Q3; 30 P—Kt6, R—KKt8; 31 P—Kt7, K—K4=. No 289. Black instead played 22 .... R—R5? and lost after 23 R×P!, K×R; 24 P—B6!!—see No. 290.

An instance where passive play was fatal is No. 406b (Dake-Campolongo, Folkestone, 1933), White: K at KKt1, R at QR1, P's at QR4, K5, KKt3, KR2; Black: K at KKt1, R at Q5, P's at QR3, KB2,

KKt2, KR2. White to play can draw by 1 R—Kt1!, P—Kt3 (the best chance); 2 R—Kt8ch, K—Kt2; 3 R—Kt7!, K—B1; 4 R—Kt8ch, K—K2; 5 R—Kt7ch, K—K3; 6 R—Kt6ch, etc. Instead he tried 1 K—B2?, when 1 .... R—K5; 2 K—B3, R×KP cost him a Pawn and the game.

The superior side should likewise play aggressively and attempt to convert his positional advantage into something decisive at the earliest possible moment. Connected passed Pawns and an outside passed Pawn supported by the King or by a Rook behind it are the chief types of superiority outside of simple capture of material. E.g., No. 406c (Spielmann-Alekhine, New York, 1927), White: K at KB1, R at K4, P's at QKt4, KB2, KKt3, KR4; Black: K at KB3, R at QR5, P's at QKt2, QB4, KB2, KKt3. White to play. After 1 R—B4ch, K—K3; 2 R—K4ch (or 2 P×P, R×R; 3 P×R, K—Q4; 4 P—B5!, K×P; 5 P×P, P×P; 6 P—B4, K—Q4! wins) and now Alekhine, as he later demonstrated, could have scored by 2 .... K—Q4!; 3 R—K7, P×P!; 4 R×KtP, K—B5; 5 R—B7ch, K—Q6; 6 R—Q7ch, K—B7; 7 R—B7ch, K—Kt7; 8 R×P, P—Kt6; 9 R—B6, K—R6!; 10 R—Kt6, P—Kt7 and 11 R×P is forced, when Black's King gets back very quickly. Instead the passive 2 .... K—Q2; 3 P—Kt4!, P×P; 4 P—R5! should have led to a draw.

Where the White Rook is attacking Pawns on the file rather than on the rank, the case is usually easier because any such counterattack as in the above examples is necessarily less successful. A classic exploitation of this type of advantage is No. 407 (Flohr-Vidmar, Nottingham, 1936). In this position White stands better for two reasons: firstly because his Rook is active, while his opponent's is passive, and secondly because the Black Pawns on the Q-side are

blockaded and therefore weak. But in Rook endings such advantages are not permanent. Black threatens to play his King to Q3 and ultimately QKt3, free his Rook and obtain counterplay. To hold on to his superiority White must play both energetically and accurately. With this in mind his plan of campaign consists of five steps: 1. Definite prevention of the freeing .... P—QB4. 2. Centralization of his King. 3. Weakening the Black K-side Pawns. 4. Forcing an entry with his King. 5. Capture of material. Whether all this

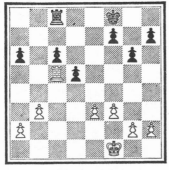

No. 407

White to play.

will be possible, i.e., whether the ending is a forced win or not, is hard
to say beforehand, but if White can win he must proceed in the manner
indicated. The main variation which we give is the course the game
took. *1 K—K2, K—K2; 2 K—Q3, K—Q3; 3 R—R5, R—QR1; 4 K—
Q4* (the first two steps go together), *P—KB4?* (This is played with
a view to exchanging as many Pawns as possible, but it voluntarily
weakens his Pawn structure and hastens defeat. Passive play certainly
would have held out longer and might well have staved off defeat in
the long run. The principal alternatives are:

a) 4 .... R—R2; 5 P—KKt4, P—KB4! (Black must not allow
the crippling of his Pawn position by P—KKt5. 5 .... P—B3;
6 P—KR4, R—R1; 7 P—K4, P×P; 8 P×P, R—R2; 9 P—
KKt5 is thus also bad); 6 P—Kt5 (after 6 P×P, P×P; 7 P—K4
is the last chance, but 7 .... BP×P; 8 P×P, P×P; 9 K×P,
K—K3 should draw, since Black has exchanged so many Pawns),
R—R1; 7 P—KR4, R—R2; 8 P—K4, BP×P; 9 P×P, P×P;
10 K×P, K—K3; 11 K—B4, K—Q3; 12 K—Kt4, K—K3;
13 P—R5, K—Q3; 14 P—R6, K—K3; 15 K—B4, K—Q3;
16 K—K4, K—K3; 17 R—K5ch, K—Q3 (17 .... K—B2;
18 K—Q4—B5); 18 R—R5 (there is no good continuation: if
18 P—R4, R—QKt1), K—K3; 19 K—Q4, K—Q3 and although
White still has his advantage there is no forced win.

b) 4 .... K—B2?; 5 K—B5, K—Kt2; 6 R—R4, P—QR4 (if 6 ....
R—K1; 7 R—Kt4ch, K—B2; 8 R—Kt6, while if 6 .... K—B2;
7 R—KB4, P—B4; 8 P—KKt4, R—KB1; 9 P—K4!, QP×P;
10 BP×KP, R—K1; 11 KP×P, P×P; 12 P×P and the extra
Pawn will win); 7 R—KB4, P—B4 (7 .... R—KB1; 8 R—B6);
8 P—KKt4, P×P (or 8 .... R—KB1; 9 P—K4 as above);
9 R—B7ch, K—R3; 10 P×P, R—K1 (the best chance); 11 R×P,
R×P; 12 K×BP, P—Q5; 13 R—R8, K—R2; 14 R—Q8, R—
K7; 15 R×P, R×QRP; 16 R—R4!, R—B7ch!; 17 K—Kt5,
R×P; 18 R×Pch, K—Kt2; 19 R—R6, R—QKt7; 20 R×P,
R×Pch; 21 K—B4, R—Kt6; 22 K—Q5, K—B2; 23 K—K4,
K—Q2; 24 K—B4, R—Kt8; 25 R—B6, K—K2; 26 R—B5!,
R—QR8; 27 K—Kt5, R—R1; 28 K—R6 and wins—just in
time.

After the move chosen Flohr demonstrates that White can win by
force. We now begin the fourth step. *5 P—QKt4!* (permanent prevention of the liberating .... P—QB4), *R—QKt1; 6 P—QR3, R—
QR1* (6 .... R—Kt3 immobilizes the Rook altogether); *7 P—K4!*
(compelling a favorable exchange. White's King now threatens to get
to the other wing), *BP×P; 8 P×P, P×P; 9 K×P, R—R2* (if 9 ....
K—K3; 10 K—B4, K—B3; 11 R—QB5, R—QB1; 12 P—QR4, K—
K3; 13 K—Kt5, K—Q3; 14 K—R6, R—QKt1; 15 R—B4, will win—

the immediate entry of the White King can be stopped only at the
cost of a further weakening of the Pawn position); *10 K—B4, P—R3*
(to allow the White King to get to R6 is equally fatal: 10 .... R—R1;
11 K—Kt5, R—R2; 12 K—R6, K—K3; 13 P—KKt4, K—Q3; 14 P—
Kt5, K—K3; 15 P—QR4, R—QKt2; 16 R×P, R×P; 17 R×Pch,
K—B2; 18 R—B7ch, K—K3; 19 R×P and wins); *11 P—KR4, K—
K3* (11 .... K—B2; 12 K—K5, K—Kt3; 13 K—B6 is worse);
12 K—Kt4, R—R1 (on 12 .... K—B2; 13 P—R5 is equally effective);
13 P—R5! (fixing the K-side Pawns), *P—Kt4* (13 .... P×Pch;
14 K×P, R—KKt1; 15 P—Kt4!, K—Q3; 16 R—KB5!, K—B2;
17 R—B4! is no better); *14 P—Kt3* (the Black Pawns have been
sufficiently "softened": now the King will try to get in), *R—R2;
15 K—B3, R—R1; 16 K—K4, R—R2; 17 R—K5ch!!* (forcing the
reluctant Black monarch to make up his mind), *K—Q3* (The other
side was no better: 17 .... K—B3; 18 R—QB5, R—QB2; 19 R—R5,
R—QR2; 20 K—Q4, K—K3; 21 K—B5, R—Q2; 22 R×P, R—Q6;
23 R×Pch, K—Kt2; 24 P—Kt5, R×P; 25 R—Kt6ch, K—R2; 26 P—
Kt6, etc.); *18 R—K8!* (threatening both R—KR8 and K—B5), *P—B4*
(Desperation. On 18 .... R—K2ch; 19 R×R, K×R; 20 K—K5,
the win is routine); *19 R—Q8ch!!* (again chasing the Black King to
where he does not want to go), *K—B3* (on 19 .... K—B2 or 19 ....
K—K2 the answer is 20 R—KR8 threatening both R—R7 and R×P.
E.g., 19 .... K—B2; 20 R—KR8, P×P; 21 R—R7ch!, K—Kt3;
22 R×R, K×R; 23 P×P, K—Kt3; 24 K—B5, K—Kt4; 25 K—Kt6,
K×P; 26 K×P, P—R4; 27 K×P, P—R5; 28 P—R6 and queens first,
preventing the opposing RP from promoting); *20 R—B8ch, K—Kt3*
(or 20 .... K—Kt4; 21 R×Pch, K—R5; 22 R—R5ch, K—Kt6;
23 K—B5); *21 R×P* (the rest is simple), *R—R2; 22 R—K5* (22 K—B5
is also strong), *K—B3; 23 R—K6ch, K—Kt4; 24 K—B5, R—B2ch;
25 R—B6* Resigns, for he must lose both K-side Pawns.

4. WHITE ROOK BEHIND A PASSED PAWN, BLACK ROOK IN FRONT OF IT

As we saw in the case of material advantage, to have the Rook
behind the passed Pawn is the strongest possible position. It so
happens that it is so strong that with even material it likewise confers
a marked and at times winning superiority. For the enemy Rook is
then bottled up, while the enemy Pawns can be taken care of by the
King.

The type of position where this advantage is sufficient to win is
seen in No. 408 (Lasker-Rubinstein, St. Petersburg, 1914). Black's
Rook is tied up (the Pawn will be passed in a moment) while his
passed Pawn is securely blockaded. Lasker won as follows: *1 P—B5,*

P×P; 2 P×P, R—B3 (if 2 .... P—Q5; 3 P—B6, K—Q4; 4 P—B7,
K—K4; 5 P—Kt4!, K—Q4; 6 R—B4!, K—K4; 7 R—K4ch!!, K—B4;
8 R—K1!, R×P—the only chance—; 9 R—B1ch, K—K3; 10 R×R,
K×R; 11 K×P, K—K3; 12 K—B5, K—Q2; 13 K×P, K—B2;
14 K—R6 and wins); *3 R—B4!, P—Kt5* (3 .... P—Q5; 4 K—K4,
K—B5; 5 K—K5, R—B1; 6 P—B6, K—Q6; 7 R×Pch, etc.); *4 P—
Kt3, R—B2; 5 P—B6, K—Q3; 6 K—Q4, K—K3; 7 R—B2!, K—Q3*
(7 .... R×P; 8 R×Rch, K×P; 9 K×P is likewise lost); *8 R—QR2!,
R—B2; 9 R—R6ch, K—Q2; 10 R—Kt6* resigns. After 10 .... R—B6;
11 R×P, R—B6; 12 K—K5, R—B8; 13 R—KB4, R×R; 14 K×R,

No. 408

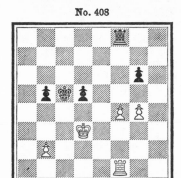

White wins.

No. 409

White to play.

K—K3; 15 P—B7, K×P; 16 K—K5, K—K2; 17 K×P the win is
routine.

Where Black's Pawn majority is not adequately blocked the win is
more difficult, although in the absence of the Black King it is quite
certain. E.g., No. 408a (Kashdan-Steiner, Pasadena, 1932), White:
K at KKt2, R at QB2, P's at QB5, KKt3, KR3; Black: K at KR2,
R at Q5, P's at QR4, KKt2, KR3. White to play wins. 1 P—B6,
R—Q1; 2 K—B3! (2 P—B7? would be inaccurate: 2 .... R—QB1;
3 K—B3, P—R5; 4 K—K4, P—R6; 5 K—Q5, P—R7=), P—R5 (or
2 .... K—Kt3; 3 K—K4, K—B3; 4 P—B7, R—QB1; 5 K—Q5, K—
K2; 6 K—B6, etc.); 3 K—K4, P—R6; 4 K—K5! R—Q6 (4 ....
R—QB1; 5 K—Q6); 5 P—B7, P—R7; 6 R×P, R—QB6. The rest
is simple. 7 K—Q6, R—Q6ch; 8 K—B6, R—B6ch; 9 K—Kt7, R—
Kt6ch; 10 K—R8, R—QB6; 11 R—R7 resigns. Black must give up
his Rook in two moves and has no counterplay on the King's side.

5. THE WHITE ROOK IS MORE ACTIVE

This division is a residue of everything not contained in the previous ones. It is generally due to possession of a semiopen file. Ordinarily such a superiority is not decisive: it leads to a win only if one is successful in blockading the enemy Pawns.

A famous instance of the exploitation of enemy inaccuracies in such an ending is No. 409 (Marshall-Tarrasch, match, 1905). We shall again follow the game continuation. But first let us analyze the position.

Black has a slight superiority because his Rook is more aggressively posted and because his center Pawn exerts a bind on the White position. Against purely passive play this could be exploited in the following manner: advance on the Q-side, exchange Rooks, play the King to QR5, fix the Pawns on the K-side, and break on the Q-side at the appropriate moment. E.g., 1 K—B2, K—K2; 2 K—Kt3, P—K4; 3 K—B3, P—QKt4; 4 K—K2, P—Kt5; 5 K—B2, R—R5; 6 K—K2, P—QKt4; 7 K—B2, K—Q3; 8 K—K2, P×P; 9 R×P (9 P×P, P—Kt5), R×R; 10 P×R, K—B4; 11 K—Q2, K—Kt3; 12 K—B1, K—R4; 13 K—Kt2, K—R5; 14 K—R2, P—B4; 15 K—Kt2, P—B5; 16 K—R2, P—Kt4!; 17 K—Kt2, P—Kt5; 18 K—R2, P—B6; 19 P—R3, P—Kt6!; 20 P—R4, P—R4; 21 K—Kt1, K×P and wins by advancing the KtP. It goes almost without saying that all this is by no means forced, but it does show that there are some real dangers for White. To avoid them he should play his King to the Q-side and try to get his Rook into the game. Followed out properly, this idea should draw. *1 R—B1ch* (the alternative 1 R—QB1, K—K2; 2 P—B3, P×P; 3 R×P, K—Q2!; 4 R—B4, P—QKt4; 5 R—B2, R—R5! threatening .... P—Kt5 is not wholly satisfactory), *K—K2; 2 R—B4?* (But this is an unnecessary loss of time. 2 K—B2, R—R4; 3 K—K2, R—QB4; 4 K—Q2 would have held the position. The exchange of Rooks need not be feared, for White can block the Q-side on .... P—QKt4 by P—QKt4 and besides, he can secure counterplay on the K-side), *R—R4!!* (preparing to weaken the Q-side Pawns); *3 K—B1* (not 3 P—K5, R×KP; 4 R×P, R—K7; 5 R—QB4, P—B4; 6 P—QKt4, K—Q3 and White's Rook is tied to the defense of the BP, while Black's is powerfully posted on the seventh), *R—QB4; 4 R—B2, R—QKt4!; 5 P—QKt3, R—KR4!* (to gain time to blockade the Black QRP); *6 P—R3, P—QKt4!; 7 P—QKt4?* (a second mistake, after which the Rook must defend the QRP. The correct move was 7 K—K2 and if then 7 .... R—R3; 8 K—Q2, P—K4; 9 K—B1, R—R3; 10 K—Kt2, R—KB3; 11 R—K2, and, although Black retains an undeniable advantage there is no forced win in sight), *K—R3!; 8 R—B4* (a better defensive opportunity was 8 P—K5!, e.g., 8 .... R—R4;

9 R—K2, P—QKt3; 10 K—K1, K—Q2; 11 R—K4, P—B4; 12 K—
Q2, K—B3; 13 P—B4!, P×Pch; e.p.; 14 K×P, K—Q4; 15 P—QR4!,
KtP×P; 16 P×P, P×P; 17 R×P, R×KP; 18 R—R7, R—Kt4;
19 P—Kt4 and in view of Black's scattered Pawns it is doubtful
whether he can win. If, e.g., 19 .... K—K4; 20 R—KB7, P—R3;
21 K—B4, K—Q3; 22 P—Q4, P×P; 23 K×P=), *P—K4; 9 R—B5,
R—K3; 10 K—K2, P—KKt3; 11 R—B1, R—R3; 12 R—QR1, P—
Kt3; 13 K—Q2, R—R5; 14 P—B3* (if now 14 K—B1, R—R1!; 15 K—
Kt2, R—KB1; 16 R—KKt1, R—B7; 17 K—Kt3, K—K3 and the
White pieces are all tied up), *P—B4; 15 P×QP* (it is too late to do
anything but weep. On 15 P×BP, KtP×P; 16 K—B2, P—B5!
leaves White just as badly pickled as ever. E.g., 17 P×QP, P×Pch;
18 K×P, R×Pch; 19 K—K3, R—R5 and a Pawn is lost. After
20 R—Kt1, R×Pch; 21 K—B2, R—R4; 22 K—K3, K—Q3; 23 R—
Q1ch, K—B3; 24 R—Q5, R—R7; the extra Pawn will decide since
Black gets passed Pawns on both sides and his King is near the passed
White King Pawn), *P×KtP!; 16 P×KP, K—K3; 17 P—Q4, P×P*
("Black Pawns are faster than White." The Black passed Pawns
are farther advanced and better protected); *18 K—B3, P—R7!; 19 P—
Kt4* (zugzwang!. If 19 K—Kt3, R×P; 20 R×P, K×P; 21 R—R7,
P—R4; 22 R—K7ch, K—B5; 23 R—K6, P—Kt4; 24 R×P, R×P;
25 R×P, R—K4; 26 R—Kt8, K—Kt6; 27 R—KR8, P—R5, while
if 19 K—Q3, R—R6ch; 20 K—B2, R—KKt6!; 21 R×P, R×Pch;
22 K—Kt3, R×R; 23 K×R, P—Kt4; 24 K—Kt3, P—R4; 25 K—
Kt4, P—Kt5; 26 P×P, P×P; 27 K×P, P—Kt6; 28 P—Q5ch, K×P;
29 K—B6, P—Kt7 winning easily in both cases), *19 .... P—Kt4;
20 K—Q3, P—Kt5* (20 .... R—R6ch is also strong); *21 K—B4, P—
Kt6 dis ch; 22 K×P* (22 K—B3, R×P!), *R×P; 23 R×P, R×P;
24 R—R6, R—K6ch; 25 K—B2, R×RP; 26 R×Pch, K×P; 27 R—
Kt4, R—K6; 28 K—Q2, R—K5* and White resigned. After 29 R—
Kt7, K—B5; 30 R×P, K×P; 31 R—R1, K—B6!; 32 K—Q3, R—K1;
33 R—B1ch, K—Kt7; 34 R—B5, P—Kt5 we have No. 308.

Where the Pawns are scattered and exposed the aggressive Rook is
sure to bring in some booty, although the exploitation of the material
won may not be so simple. E.g., No. 409a (Zukertort-Mason, Vienna,
1882), White: K at KKt1, R at KR3, P's at QR2, QKt2, QB2, KB2;
Black: K at KKt1, R at KB3, P's at QR2, QB3, Q5, KKt4. White
to play wins! 1 R—R3!, R—B2; 2 R—R5, R—Kt2; 3 K—Kt2, K—
R2; 4 K—Kt3, K—R3; 5 R—QB5 (an inaccuracy. 5 R—R6, R—
QB2; 6 K—Kt4, K—Kt3; 7 P—Kt4, threatening P—Kt5, wins a
Pawn by force. But even after the move played White should win),
R—Kt3; 6 K—Kt4, R—B3; 7 P—B3, R—B5ch; 8 K—Kt3, R—B3;
9 R—B4, R—Q3; 10 K—Kt4, P—B4! (the best way to give up the
Pawn. There was no way to save everything. E.g., 10 .... R—B3;

11 R×QP, or 10 .... K—Kt3; 11 R—B5, R—Q4; 12 R×Pch);
11 R×BP, P—Q6; 12 P×P, R—Q5ch!; 13 K—Kt3, R×P; 14 R—R5,
R—Q2; 15 R—R6ch, K—R4!; 16 P—Kt4, R—KB2; 17 P—Kt5, R—
K2; 18 P—R4, R—Q2; 19 R—K6! (in the game there occurred 19 P—
R5?, R—Q4; 20 R×P, R×P; 21 P—R6, R—R4 and Black has a
theoretical draw. If the Pawn advances to the seventh the King
backs up to Kt2 and the Rook holds the Pawn at KKt4), R—Q5 (or
19 .... R—QKt2; 20 R—K4, P—R3!; 21 P×P!, R—Kt3; 22 P—R5,
R×P; 23 R—K5, R—KB3; 24 R—Kt5! and Black is in zugzwang:
if 24 .... K—Kt3; 25 R—Kt6); 20 R—K4!, R—Q2 (20 .... R—Q8;
21 R—K7, P—R3; 22 P—Kt6!, R—QKt8; 23 R—QKt7!, K—Kt3;
24 R—Kt8, K—Kt2; 25 K—Kt4 and wins); 21 R—QKt4, R—QKt2;
22 P—R5, R—Kt1; 23 P—Kt6, P×P; 24 P×P, R—Kt2; 25 R—Kt5,
K—Kt3; 26 K—Kt4, K—B3; 27 R—Kt1!, K—Kt3; 28 R—Kt2!,
K—B3; 29 R—Kt5!, R—Kt1—else the Pawn goes with check—;
30 P—Kt7 and Black must still lose the KtP, when the rest is routine.

B. BETTER PAWN POSITION

In most of the above examples the superior side had better Pawns,
but the decisive factor was the Rook position. Here we shall consider
those cases where the Rook position makes little or no difference.

1. BETTER PASSED PAWNS

In general the more advanced and better protected passed Pawns
are superior. They should wherever possible be supported by the
King. This rule is in agreement with other cases noted, e.g., that
where a strong passed Pawn supported by the King counterbalances
two or even three connected passed Pawns.

No. 410

Black to play wins.

With one passed Pawn, a Pawn
on the seventh will normally win
against one on the third. Black will
have to give up his Rook for the
Pawn and take his chances in the
R vs. P ending, which, with the
Pawn so far back will not as a
rule offer him much solace. With
the Pawns differently distributed,
e.g., one on the fifth, the other on
the sixth, the King positions will
be decisive.

A typical case from a tournament
game is No. 410 (Betbeder-Flohr,
Folkestone, 1933). After *1 .... R
—Q6ch; 2 K—B4* (2 K- -B2, R—

R6; 3 P—R4, K—B7), *R—Q5ch!!* (but not 2 .... K—B7?; 3 R×Pch, K×R; 4 P—R5, K—B6; 5 P—Kt6, P—R3; 6 K—B5, R—R6; 7 P—Kt7!, R×Pch; 8 K—Kt6, R—Kt4ch; 9 K×P=); White resigned. The main variation is *3 K—Kt3, K—B7; 4 R—B8ch, K—Kt6; 5 R—Kt8ch, K×P; 6 R×P* (else 6 .... R—Kt5), *K×R; 7 P—R5, K—B6* and wins, for if *8 P—Kt6, P×P; 9 P×P, R—Q3.*

If the Pawn is not yet on the seventh in such positions there may still be time to utilize the more backward Pawn. E.g., No. 410a (Tarrasch-Bluemich, Breslau, 1925), White: K at KR3, R at QR5; P at KR5; Black: K at QKt7, R at QKt5, P at QR6. White to play. Dr. Tarrasch resigned here, but it was later demonstrated that 1 P—R6! should have drawn: 1 P—R6!, R—Kt3 (or 1 .... R—Kt1; 2 K—Kt4, P—R7; 3 K—Kt5 and both sides lose their Rooks); 2 R—R5!, R—Kt1 (if 2 .... P—R7; 3 P—R7, R—Kt1; 4 R—Kt5ch!!, R×R; 5 P—R8=Qch,=); 3 P—R7, R—KR1; 4 K—Kt4!, P—R7; 5 R—Kt5ch, K—B6; 6 R—QR5, K—Kt6; 7 R—Kt5ch, K—R5; 8 R—Kt7!=.

As these examples indicate, the results of such endings frequently depend upon tactical finesses and intermezzos. Two problems will further illustrate some of the typical traps which may arise.

In No. 410b (Dr. Lasker, 1890) a Pawn on the seventh wins against another on the seventh because of an unfortunate King position. White: K at QB8, R at KR7, P at QB7; Black: K at QR4, R at QB7, P at KR7. White to play wins. 1 K—Kt7!, R—Kt7ch; 2 K—R7, R—QB7; 3 R—R5ch, K—R5 (if the King ever goes to the Kt file, K—Kt7 does not permit a check, and the Pawn queens); 4 K—Kt7, R—Kt7ch; 5 K—R6, R—QB7; 6 R—R4ch, K—R6; 7 K—Kt6, R—Kt7ch (if instead 7 .... K—Kt6; 8 K—Kt7, or 8 .... K—R7; 9 R×P or 8 .... R—B8; 9 R×P); 8 K—R5, R—QB7; 9 R—R3ch, K any; 10 R×P and the Pawn queens.

In No. 410c (Horwitz, 1881) a Pawn on the sixth wins against one on the fifth by means of mate threats. White: K at KKt2, R at QB1, P at KKt6; Black: K at KR5, R at QR6, P at KB5; White to play wins. After 1 R—KKt1!!! Black is lost. 1 .... R—R1 (on 1 .... R—Kt6ch; 2 K—B2 the Pawn marches on; on 1 .... R—R7ch or 1 .... P—B6ch the Black Pawn is captured and the White one supported); 2 P—Kt7, K—R4; 3 K—B3, R—KKt1; 4 K×P, K—R3; 5 K—B5, K—R2 (or 5 .... R×P; 6 R—R1 mate); 6 K—B6, R—B1ch (or 6 .... R—QR1; 7 P—Kt8=Qch, R×Q; 8 R—R1 mate); 7 P×R=B or Kt or R and mates in a few, but not =Q? stalemate.

A protected passed Pawn on the seventh is stronger than one that is unprotected, even when the King is far away. This is seen in No. 411 (Fleischmann-Leussen, Barmen, 1905). White brings his King up to the aid of the QKtP and wins easily. The conclusion was

1 K—K3, P—B8= Qch; 2 R×Q, K×R; 3 K—Q4, K—Q7; 4 K—B5, K—K7; 5 K—B6, K×P (if instead 5 .... R—KR1; 6 K—B7, R—R2ch; 7 K—Kt8, K×P; 8 K×P, K—Kt7; 9 K—Kt6, R—R1; 10 P—R7 and queens); *6 K—B7, R—KB1; 7 P—Kt8= Q, R×Q; 8 K×R, K—Kt7* (or 8 .... P—Kt5; 9 K×P, P—R4; 10 K—Kt6, P—R5; 11 P—R7, P—Kt6; 12 P×P, P×P; 13 P—R8=Q and wins); *9 K×P, K×P; 10 K—Kt6, P—Kt5; 11 P—R7, P—Kt6; 12 P—R8= Q* and the rest is routine.

It goes without saying that in any normal position two passed Pawns, especially if they are connected, are far superior to one. The outcome, however, may then often be determined by other factors, chiefly the degree of advancement of the Pawns.

<table>
<tr><td align="center">No. 411</td><td align="center">No. 412</td></tr>
<tr><td>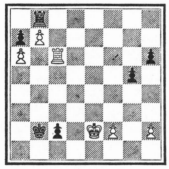</td><td></td></tr>
<tr><td align="center">White to play wins.</td><td align="center">White to play wins.</td></tr>
</table>

Where both sides have two connected passed Pawns, certain essential distinctions must be made. Other things being equal, *connected passed Pawns are superior to disconnected.* An elegant demonstration of this fact with a minimum of material on the board is No. 412 (Alekhine-Alexander, Margate, 1937). White's superiority lies in the fact that he can both stop the opponent's Pawns from advancing and facilitate the march of his own Pawns. After *1 R—R5!* (preventing .... P—Kt4 and .... K—B3), *R—QKt3* (loses time but there is not much to be done. If 1 .... K—Kt3; 2 P—K5, R—QKt3; 3 K—K4, K—B2; 4 P—Q4, P—Kt4; 5 K—B5, R—Kt3; 6 P—Q5, P—Kt5; 7 P—K6ch, K—Kt2; 8 R×P, P—Kt6; 9 P—K7 and wins); *2 P—Q4, R—Kt6ch* (only to go right back. But even if 2 .... K—B3; 3 K—B4, R—K3; 4 P—K5ch, K—B2; 5 P—Q5 decides quickly); *3 K—B4, R—Kt5; 4 P—Q5, R—Kt3; 5 R—B5!, R—Kt5* (or 5 .... R—Kt2; 6 P—K5,

R—R2; 7 R—B8!, P—R4; 8 P—K6ch, K—B3; 9 R—B8ch, K—Kt3; 10 P—Q6, and wins); *6 R—B7ch, K—B1* (if the King goes to the third rank the Rook checks and captures the RP); *7 R—R7*, Resigns. The conclusion might be *7 .... R—R5; 8 P—Q6, K—K1; 9 K—K5, P—Kt4; 10 K—Q5, P—Kt5; 11 P—K5, P—Kt6; 12 P—K6* and queens earlier.

When the Pawns are far advanced, the rule that connected passed Pawns are stronger than disconnected ones may not hold, for the position may well be such that the disconnected ones queen earlier. A case in point is No. 412a (Mattison-Rubinstein, Carlsbad, 1929), White: K at QB3, R at K3, P's at QR4, QB4, KB3, KKt4; Black: K at Q2, R at KB1, P's at QR3, QB4, Q3, KR5. Black to play wins. 1 .... R—K1!!; 2 K—Q2 (2 R—Q3, P—R6; 3 R—Q1, R—K6ch wins a Pawn), R×R; 3 K×R, P—Q4! and White resigned, because Black queens first.

Where both sides have connected passed Pawns, it is often a good old-fashioned horse race—whoever gets there first wins. In such cases it is essential to cut off the enemy King whenever possible, for a Rook alone cannot stop two passed Pawns supported by a Rook or King. No. 413 (Keres-Alekhine, AVRO, 1938) is typical. The simplest win is *1 P—B6, K—K2* (the only chance to get the King to the Pawns. If 1 .... R—QB7; 2 P—Kt5, R—QKt7; 3 R—QB4, or 2 .... K—K2; 3 R—Kt4! as in the main variation); *2 R—Q4!* (it is essential to cut off the King. In the game there occurred 2 P—Kt5?, R—QKt7!; 3 R—QB4, K—Q1; 4 R—B5, P—Kt5; 5 K—B4, R—Kt5ch; 6 K—Kt3, K—B2; 7 K—R4, K—B1; 8 R—R5, K—B2; 9 R—R7ch, K—B1!; 10 R—QKt7, R—QB5!!; 11 K—Kt3, P—B4; 12 K—R4, R—B4! Drawn because the White King has no time to come to the aid of the Pawns), *R—QB7* (if instead 2 .... R—QKt7; 3 K—Q3 threatening P—B7, and on 3 .... R—Kt8; 4K—B2, R—QR8; 5 P—B7, R—R1; 6 P—Kt5, etc., queening soon); *3 P—Kt5, R—B4* (the only chance: if 3 .... R—QKt7; 4 P—B7, R—QB7; 5 P—Kt6, or 3 .... P—B4; 4 R—QKt4, K—Q1; 5 P—Kt6 as in the main variation); *4 R—QKt4!* (the most precise. On 4 R—Q7ch, K—K1; 5 R—QKt7, K—Q1; 6 K—Q4, R—B8; 7 K—Q5 White will however also win), *K—Q1; 5 P—Kt6!, K—B1; 6 P—Kt7ch, K —Kt1; 7 R—Kt6, P—-B4* (there is no defense: 7 .... R—R4; 8 P

No. 413

White to play wins.

—B7ch, K×P; 9 P—Kt8=Qch); *8 R—R6, K—B2; 9 R—R8, P—B5ch* (spite check); *10 K—K4, R—Kt4; 11 R—B8ch, K—Q3; 12 P—Kt8= Qch* and wins.

With the Pawns far advanced, the superior side may sometimes be involved in a mating net, but it is usually not difficult to extricate himself. E.g., No. 413a (Metger-Caro, Berlin, 1897), White: K at QB6, R at KR7, P's at K3, KKt2, KR2; Black: K at QB1, R at QR7, P's at QR6, QKt7, K5. Black to play wins. 1 .... K—Q1! (but not 1 .... K—Kt1?; 2 R—R8ch, K—R2; 3 R—R7ch, K—R3; 4 R—R8!, K—R4; 5 K—B5 and Black cannot avoid perpetual mate threat); 2 K—Q6, K—K1; 3 K—K6, K—B1; 4 K—B6, K—Kt1; 5 R—QKt7 (5 R—Kt7ch, K—R1; 6 R—Kt7, R—R8 and now 7 R—Kt8ch, K—R2; 8 R—Kt7ch is refuted by 8 .... K—R3; 9 R—Kt8, R—B8ch; 10 K any, P queens, while 7 K—Kt6 is likewise met by 7 .... P—Kt8= Qch), R—R8 and wins.

Where both sets of Pawns are far advanced, tactical considerations, such as who manages to queen first, determine the result. We may take as an instance one of the most hair-raising encounters ever recorded. No. 413b (Walbrodt-Zinkl, Leipzig, 1894), White: K at QKt3, R at Q1, P's at QKt7, QB7; Black: K at KKt1, R at KB1, P's at KB7, KKt7. White to play wins. 1 P—B8=Q, P—B8=Q (if 1 .... P—Kt8=Q; 2 Q×Rch!, K×Q; 3 P—Kt8=Qch, K—B2; 4 Q—R7ch, K any; 5 R×Q, P×R=Q; 6 Q×Q—three Queens do a disappearance act in six moves!); 2 Q—Kt4ch, K—R1 (or 2 .... K—B2; 3 R—Q7ch, K—B3; 4 R—Q6ch, K—K4; 5 R—K6ch, K—Q4; 6 Q—K4ch and mates in a few); 3 Q—R3ch, K—Kt2 (he must not allow the QKtP to queen with check: 3 .... K—Kt1; 4 R×Q, P×R= Q; 5 Q×Q, R×Q; 6 P—Kt8=Qch. After the text this combination would not work because Black has .... R—Kt8ch at the end); 4 R—Q7ch, R—B2 (King moves lead to mate); 5 Q—Kt4ch, K—R2 (or 5 .... K—R3; 6 R—Q6ch, R—B3; 7 R×Rch, Q×R; 8 P—Kt8=Q and Black has only one check); 6 Q—K4ch, K—Kt2; 7 P—Kt8=Q!, P—Kt8=Q; 8 Q(Kt8)—K5ch, Q—B3; 9 Q×Qch, K×Q; 10 Q—B4ch and wins!

Finally, where both sets of Pawns are not yet beyond the center of the board, they must march on as quickly as possible and hope for the best. E.g., No. 413c (from Treybal-Reti, Teplitz-Schoenau, 1922), White: K at KR1, R at KR5, P's at KKt2, KR4; Black: K at KB1, R at QR7, P's at QR3, QKt4. Black to play. Draw. 1 .... P—Kt5; 2 R—R8ch, K—Kt2; 3 R—QKt8, P—R4; 4 K—R2! (on 4 P—Kt4 Black does best to play 4 .... R—Q7; 5 R—Kt5, R—Q5 and exchange a Pawn. If, e.g., 4 .... R—QKt7?; 5 P—Kt5, P—R5; 6 P—R5, P—R6; 7 P—R6ch, K—Kt3; 8 R—Kt6ch, K—R2; 9 R—Kt7ch, K—Kt1; 10 P—Kt6, R—KB7; 11 R—Kt8ch, R—B1; 12 P—R7ch and wins), R—Kt7!; 5 R—QR8, R—R7! and both sides are well advised to take the draw by repetition of moves. E.g., 6 K—R3?, P—Kt6; 7 P—Kt4, P—Kt7; 8 R—QKt8, P—R5; 9 P—Kt5, R—R6ch; 10 K—Kt4, R—QKt6 and Black wins, or 6 R—QKt8, R—R6; 7 P—Kt4, P—Kt6; 8 R—Kt7ch, K—B3; 9 R—Kt6ch, K—K4; 10 P—R5, P—R5; 11 P—R6, R—R7ch; 12 K—Kt3, R—QB7; 13 P—R7, R—B1; 14 P—Kt5 and White wins!

Where there are more Pawns on the board, it is in general impossible to stop them in any rational manner. The only thing to do is to advance as rapidly as possible. No. 414 (Perlis-Nimzovitch, Carlsbad, 1911) illustrates some of the possibilities. The game continued *1 P—R4, P—R5; 2 P—R5, R—R8; 3 R—R8ch, K—K2; 4 R—R8* (4 P—R6, P—R6; 5 P—R7, R—R8; 6 R—R8, R×P; 7 R×P=. Or here 6 R—KKt8, P—R7!; 7 R—KR8, etc. But 4 .... P—Kt4? instead of 4 .... P—R6 is weak: after 5 P—R7, R—R8; 6 R—KKt8!, R×P; 7 R×P White has two connected passed Pawns while Black's Pawns are scattered and exposed), *P—Kt4; 5 P—Kt4, R—R8; 6 K—K4?* (fatal loss of time. Correct was 6 P—B4! threatening 7 P—Kt5, R×P; 8 P—Kt6. On 6 P—B4 the best reply is 6 .... K—Q3; when 7 P—B5ch, K—B3; 8 K—B4, R—B8ch; 9 K—Kt3, R—QR8; 10 K—B4 leads to a draw by repetition of moves), *K—Q3; 7 P—B4* (now it is too late because the Black Pawns advance with tempo), *P—B4ch; 8 K—Q3* (if instead 8 K—B3, P—Kt5ch; 9 K—B4, R—B8ch; 10 K—Kt5, P—Kt6, or 9 K—B2, P—R6; 10 P—B5ch, K—B3; 11 R—B8ch, K—Kt2; 12 R—KR8, R—R5 and wins), *P—Kt5!* (a pretty combination: if 9 R×P, P—Kt6 costs White his Rook); *9 P—B5ch* (or 9 P—Kt5, P—Kt6!; 10 P—Kt6, K—B3; 11 R—B8ch, K—Kt2; 12 R—B7ch, K—Kt1; 13 P—B5, P—Kt7 and Black gets there first), *K—B3; 10 R—B8ch* (there is no defense: if 10 K—K2, P—R6; 11 K—B2, R—R5), *K—Q2; 11 R—KR8, P—Kt6; 12 P—Kt5, P—Kt7; 13 P—B6ch, K—Q3; 14 R—Q8ch, K—B2; 15 R—KKt8, P—Kt8 = Q* and White soon resigned.

No. 414

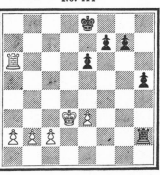

White to play. Draw.

A similar instance where dilatory tactics prove fatal is No. 414a (Spielmann-Vidmar, Carlsbad, 1907), White: K at KB 1, R at QB4, P's at QKt2, QB2, KB2, KKt2, KR2; Black: K at QB1, R at QR7, P's at QR2, QKt2, QB2, Q5, KR2. White to play. It is clear that White must first safeguard the Pawn on the Q-side (for any Black passed Pawn threatens to queen with check) and then get his own majority on the K-side going. Instead he first allows Black two passed Pawns and then jockeys around trying to stop the Pawns with King and Rook and of course loses. 1 P—QKt4? (1 P—Kt3, P—Kt4; 2 R—B5, P—Kt5; 3 K—K2 will give Black at most one passed Pawn), P—QKt4; 2 R×P? (This too is weak. 2 R—B5, R—Kt7; 3 R×P, R×BP; 4 K—K1, while none too good, was far better than the line chosen), R×P; 3 R—Q5?? (a third mistake, after which no more are necessary. 3 P—B4!, P—B4; 4 P×P, P—QR4?; 5 P—B5! was still good enough to draw at least), P—QR3; 4 R—Q4? (4 P—B4 was still better), P—B4; 5 P×P, P—QR4; 6 K—K1, P—R5; 7 R—Q2, R—B8ch; 8 R—Q1, R×P; 9 K—Q2, K—Kt2. And now the advance comes too late. The rest is simple. 10 R—QB1, R—B4; 11 P—B3, K—Kt3; 12 K—B3, R—B4ch; 13 K—Q2, R—R4; 14 P—R3, P—Kt5; 15 K—B2, K—Kt4; 16 R—K1, R—Q4; 17 P—B4, P—Kt6ch; 18 K—Kt1, P—R6; 19 P—Kt4, R—Q5; 20 R—KB1, K—Kt5; 21 Resigns. Against the threat of 21 .... P—R7ch; 22 K—R1, K—R6 there is no defense.

On the basis of the above discussion we may set up four rules:

1. Passed Pawns must be advanced as quickly as possible. What Nimzovitch called their "lust to expand" must be satisfied.
2. Other things being equal, the Pawns which are more advanced win.
3. Two or more connected passed Pawns cannot be stopped by a King alone or by a Rook alone; *both* pieces are required to stem the tide.
4. It is advisable to support passed Pawns with the King rather than with the Rook.

2. EXPOSED PAWNS

This is a type of weakness which first becomes important in Rook endings, largely because minor pieces, especially singly, cannot attack such Pawns easily. The chief disadvantage which attaches to them is not so much that material is lost sooner or later—sometimes this happens only after long and complicated maneuvering—but *that their defense limits the mobility of the defending pieces.*

The simplest case is that where a number of Pawns are exposed and fall like ripe fruit. The only chance in such endings is a counterattack, but with a number of Pawns behind, such an attack should fail. A typical instance is No. 415 (Alekhine-Bogoljuboff, 8th match game, 1934). White's position is so badly crippled that he must lose a Pawn no matter what he does. E.g., 1 K—Kt4, R—R7; 2 R—B1, R—B7; or 2 P—B3, R—Kt7ch; 3 K—R3, R—Q7, or finally 2 P—KB4, R—

Kt7ch; 3 K—B3, R—KR7. But
this is not the worst: after the first
Pawn is gone White's remaining
Pawns are still so scattered and
feeble that another will probably
fall before long. Accordingly Alekhine chooses a line which may
give him a passed Pawn and some
counterplay. The main variation up
to move 11 is the game continuation. *1 R—K1!, R—R5?* (this is a
good chess move, but a psychological blunder. The simplest was
1 .... R—K 2 which wins the
Pawn and gives Black no compensation at all. For if then 2 R×R,

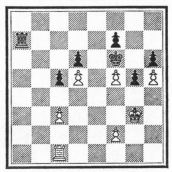

No. 415

White to play. Black wins.

K×R; 3 K—B3, K—B3; 4 K—K4, P—Kt5!; 5 K—B4—or A—,
P—B5; 6 K×P, K—K4; 7 P—B4ch, K×P; 8 K—B3, P—B3; 9 K—
K3, K—B4; 10 K—K4, P—Q4ch; 11 K—K3, P—Q5ch; 12 P×Pch,
K—Q4 and it is all over. Variation A. 5 P—QB4, K—Kt4; 6 P—
B6!, K×RP!; 7 K—B5, K—R5; 8 K—B4, K—R6; 9 K—B5, P—Kt6;
10 P×P, K×P; 11 K—K4, K—Kt5 and the win is routine. Nor can
White hope for anything by avoiding the exchange of Rooks—e.g.,
2 R—QR1, R—K4; 3 P—QB4, R×BP; 4 R—R6, K—K4; 5 R—R8,
K—Q5; 6 R—R8, R—B3, etc. But from a purely objective point of
view the move chosen is just as good, since it should likewise win.);
2 R—K8, R—QB5 (embarras de richesse—2 .... R—QR6, 2 ....
R—KR5 and 2 .... K×P are all just as strong); *3 R—KR8, R×Pch;
4 K—Kt2* (or 4 K—Kt4, R—B5ch; 5 K—Kt3, R—KR5; 6 R×Pch,
K—K4, etc.), *K×P; 5 R×P, P—B3; 6 R—R7, K—K4; 7 P—R6,
R—QR6; 8 R—K7ch, K×P; 9 P—R7, R—R1; 10 K—Kt3, P—B4;
11 P—B4* (Alekhine has indeed with his customary ingenuity secured
some counterthreats, but with accurate play Bogoljuboff could still
have won by the odd tempo), *P—Kt5!* (in the game there occurred
11 .... P×Pch??; 12 K×P, P—B5; 13 K×P, P—B6 and the game
is drawn: 14 R—Q7, R—QB1; 15 R—QB7, R—B1ch; 16 K—Kt6,
K—Q5; 17 K—Kt7, R—QKt1; 18 P—R8=Q, etc.); *12 K—R4* (the
best chance), *P—B5; 13 K—Kt5, P—B6; 14 K×P, P—Kt6; 15 K—
Kt6* (15 K—Kt4, P—Kt7; 16 R—K1, K—Q5; 17 K—Kt3, P—B7;
18 K×P, K—Q6; 19 K—Kt3, K—Q7 .... R—KR1 at any intermediate stage here is also strong), *P—Kt7; 16 R—K1, P—B7; 17 K—
Kt7, K—Q5; 18 P—R8=Q, R×Q; 19 K×Q, K—Q6; 20 R—KKt1!,
K—K6!; 21 P—B5* (with two KtP's White could keep on playing
hide-and-go-seek—see No. 294a), *K—B7; 22 P—B6, K×R; 23 P—B7,*

P—B8= Q; 24 P—B8= Q, Q—B6ch; 25 K—Kt8, Q—KKt6ch; 26 K—
R7, K—R7 and queens since White has no good checks and cannot
pin the Pawn.

Endings in which the counterplay is a serious danger and does in
fact assure the draw occur frequently. They almost always involve
(as in No. 415) the utilization of strong passed or advanced Pawns.
We give two examples.

No. 415a (Tartakover-Bogoljuboff, New York, 1924), White: K at
QB5, R at QKt4, P's at QR3, QB3, Q5, KKt2, KR3; Black: K at Q2,
R at QKt1, P's at QR2, QKt4, KB3, KKt6, KR5. Black to play.
Obviously Black cannot hold on to everything; in fact he apparently
loses a Pawn without compensation. But by making use of his strong
Pawn he can secure a draw. The game continued 1 .... P—B4!!
(so that if now 2 R×KtP??, R×Rch; 3 K×R, P—B5 and Black wins,
while if 2 R×RP, R—B1ch; 3 K×P (3 K—Kt4?, R—B5ch! and again
Black wins), R×P; 4 R—KB4, R×P; 5 R×P, R—R7=); 2 P—QR4,
P—QR3; 3 K—Q4, R—K1! (the threat was 4 P—B4); 4 K—Q3 (not
4 P×P??, R—K5ch; 5 K—Q3, R×R; 6 P×R, P×P and again Black
wins), P×P; 5 R×QRP, R—K8; 6 R×QRP and now 6 .... R—
Q8ch draws without any difficulty, for if 7 K—B4, R—Q7; 8 K—B5?,
R×P; 9 R—R7ch, K—K1; 10 K—Q6, R—K7; 11 P—B4, R—Kt7;
12 R—KKt7, P—B5; 13 P—B5, P—B6; 14 P—B6, R—QB7; 15 K—
K6, K—B1; 16 R—Kt4, P—B7 and Black wins, while if 7 K—K3,
R×QP; 8 R—KR6, R—K4ch; 9 K—B3, R—K5 with an even game.
Instead Bogoljuboff played 6 .... R—KKt8? and lost after 7 R—
R2!, K—Q3; 8 P—B4. The remaining moves were 8 .... K—K4;
9 R—K2ch, K—Q3; 10 R—QB2, K—B4; 11 R—Q2, R—KB8; 12 K—
K2, R—KKt8; 13 K—K3, K—Q3; 14 P—B5ch!, K×P; 15 P—Q6,
R—K8ch; 16 K—B4, R—K1; 17 P—Q7, R—Q1; 18 K×P, Resigns.

No. 415b (Thomas-Alekhine, Hastings, 1922), White: K at KR4,
R at K4, P's at QKt3, Q5, KB4, KR3; Black: K at KR2, R at KKt3,
P's at QB2, Q3, KKt2, KR3. Black to play. Alekhine secured two
connected against disconnected passed Pawns, but the position was
such that his opponent could have held the draw. The game went
1 .... R—Kt8; 2 R—B4, K—Kt3; 3 R×P, K—B4; 4 R—Q7, K×P;
5 R×QP, R—Kt6!; 6 R—Q8, P—Kt4ch; 7 K—R5, R×Pch; 8 K—
Kt6, K—K4; 9 P—Q6, K—K3; 10 P—Kt4, P—Kt5; and here 11 P—
Kt5! would have drawn, for if 11 .... P—Kt6; 12 K—R7!!, P—Kt7;
13 R—KKt8 and 13 .... K×P is forced, since 13 .... R—R7?;
14 P—Kt6, K×P; 15 P—Kt7 loses. Instead White played 11 P—Q7?
and lost after 11 .... P—Kt6; 12 R—KKt8, K×P; 13 K—B5, P—
R4—see No. 356a.

Where the Pawns are not just hanging in the air, the conversion of
the positional advantage into a win is far more complicated. In

general it involves first tying up the enemy pieces, and then advancing on the side where one has a majority. Once more we have a classic to guide us—No. 416 (Schlechter-Rubinstein, San Sebastian, 1912). Now, offhand one would not suppose that this position is lost for White. The Black majority on the K-side can be matched with a White one on the Q-side. The two Pawns are easily defended. Yet it is precisely this last point which is the rub: White has to *defend* his Pawns, while Black can *attack* them. If it does nothing else, this assures Black of the initiative and in chess this is of central importance. Accordingly, Rubinstein's plan of campaign here may be summarized in four steps.

1. By attacking the K-side Pawns he will immobilize the White Rook.
2. Centralization of the King.
3. Advance on the K-side with his Pawns.
4. If the White King goes to the K-side Black will capture material; if the White King stays on the Q-side and assists his own potential passed Pawn Black will create a passed Pawn and force White to sacrifice his Rook for it.

The actual moves were as follows: *1 .... R—K3!; 2 R—K1* (2 R—Kt3, R—KB3; 3 R—Kt2, R—B6; 4 R—K2 loses a tempo), *R—KB3; 3 R—K2* (the threat was .... R—B7). Now the first step is completed, since the White Rook dare not leave either the KP or the RP to its fate. *3 .... K—K3; 4 K—B2, K—K4; 5 P—B4* (At this early stage Schlechter is already desperate. And not without reason, for the passive line 5 K—Q2, K—K5; 6 K—K1, R—B6 is hopeless: e.g., 7 K—Q2, P—KKt4; 8 P—B4, P—Kt5; 9 P—Kt4, P—R5; 10 P—B5, P×P; 11 P×P, R—B4 and after the loss of the Pawn White is just as badly off as ever), *K—K5; 6 P—Kt4, P—KKt4; 7 K—B3, P—Kt5; 8 P—B5, P—R5; 9 R—KKt2, R—Kt3.* Black will soon have a strong passed Pawn with the Rook behind it. The third step is completed, and now the second part of the fourth step will be carried out. The rest is simple. *10 K—B4* (10 P—B6, R×Pch), *P—Kt6; 11 RP×P, RP×P; 12 K—Kt5, P×P; 13 P×P, K—B6; 14 R—Kt1, P—R3ch!!* White resigns. For after 15 K—B4, P—Kt7; 16 K—Q5, K—B7; 17 R×Pch, R×R; 18 P—B6, K×P the win is child's play.

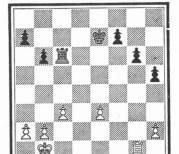

No. 416

Black to play wins.

Even where the defending side has a passed Pawn, if his remaining Pawns are weak he is in a bad way. No. 417 (Spielmann-Rubinstein, St. Petersburg, 1909) is a striking example of this. According to all the ordinary rules, White should have the better of it: he has an outside passed Pawn behind which he can place his Rook, and his two Pawns on the K-side hold Black's three. But the weakness of all his Pawns nullifies everything else and swings the pendulum the other way. The procedure is similar to that in the previous example: first tie up the White pieces, then centralize. After that it will be found that White's position is so full of holes that he must lose a Pawn. We follow the game continuation. *1 .... R—R1!; 2 R—B3* (The "natural" move 2 R—R2, placing the Rook behind the passed Pawn was rejected by Spielmann because it would have immobilized that piece after 2 .... R—R5! Nevertheless the Black Rook is likewise none too free to move about then, so that 2 R—R2 was preferable on theoretical grounds. And analysis indicates that it might well have saved the game, for Black can then capture material only at the cost of allowing the White RP to advance and become dangerous. E.g., 2 R—R2, R—R5; 3 K—Kt3, K—K2; 4 K—B3, K—K3; 5 K—K4, P—Q4ch; 6 K—Q3, K—Q3; 7 K—B3, K—B3; 8 K—Q3, K—Kt4; 9 K—B3!, R—B5ch; 10 K—Q3, K—R5; 11 R—Kt2, R—B2; 12 R—Kt6, K×P; 13 R—Q6, K—Kt6; 14 R×P, R—B6ch; 15 K—K2, R×P; 16 R—Q7=. Or (instead of 5 .... P—Q4ch) 5 .... P—Kt4; 6 R—R1, P—B3; 7 R—R2, P—B4ch; 8 K—Q3, K—Q4; 9 K—B3, R—B5ch; 10 K—Kt3!, R×P; 11 P—R4, R—Q6ch; 12 K—Kt4, K—B3; 13 P—R5, K—Kt2; 14 R—K2, R×P; 15 R—K7ch, K—R3; 16 R×P, R—R5ch; 17 K—B3, K×P; 18 R×P, R—KB5; 19 R—Kt6, P—Q4; 20 R—Q6=. From here on the game is a forced win.); *2 .... R—R5!; 3 R—Q3* (first step completed), *K—K2; 4 K—Kt3, K—K3; 5 K—B3, K—Q4; 6 K—K2!* (Black dare not go into a K and P ending because of White's outside passed Pawn. That Rubinstein can still evolve a winning scheme borders on the miraculous. The key to his following maneuvers is to get to a position where White will be in zugzwang and have to move his Rook, abandoning the defense of one of the Pawns); *6 .... P—Kt4* (solidifying his K-side position); *7 R—QKt3*

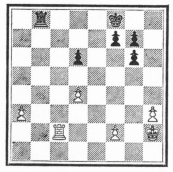

No. 417

Black to play.

(a tactical intermezzo which does not affect the outcome), *P—B3!* (avoiding the traps and setting one on his own hook! If 7 .... R×QP?; 8 R—Q3 and White may win, while if 7 .... K×P?; 8 R— Kt7 with a fairly certain draw.); *8 K—K3* (if now 8 R—Kt7?, R×P; 9 R×RP, R×P and the QP will fall, so that Black will be two Pawns ahead), *K—B5; 9 R—Q3, P—Q4* (now the Rook has no moves); *10 K—Q2, R—R1!; 11 K—B2* (on 11 K—K3, R—QKt1!; 12 K—Q2, R—Kt7ch; 13 K—K3, R—R7 wins a P), *R—R2; 12 K—Q2, R—K2!* (now White is finally compelled to move his Rook away. If 13 K—B2, R—K7ch; 14 R—Q2, R×Rch; 15 K×R, K—Kt6!; 16 K—K3, K×P; 17 K—B3, K—Kt6; 18 K—Kt4, K—B5, etc., while if 13 P—QR4, R—R2; 14 R—R3, K×P. Or finally 13 R—K3, R—Kt2!!; 14 R—Q3, R—Kt7ch; 15 K—K3, R—R7); *13 R—B3ch, K×P; 14 P—QR4, R— R2; 15 R—R3, R—R4!* (Blockading at an early moment to prevent the Pawn from becoming dangerous); *16 R—R1, K—B5; 17 K—K3, P— Q5ch; 18 K—Q2, R—KB4!* (the beginning of the end. First the King will replace the Rook as a blockader. Once the Rook is free it will establish a decisive superiority on the K-side); *19 K—K1* (To give up the BP would be immediately fatal: 19 P—R5, R×Pch; 20 K—K1, R—QKt7; 21 P—R6, R—Kt1; 22 P—R7, R—R1; 23 K—Q2, K—B4; 24 K—Q3, K—Kt3; 25 K×P, R×P and wins on the K-side), *K— Kt5; 20 K—K2, K—R4!* (20 .... R—R4?; 21 K—Q3, R×P; 22 R×Rch!, K×R; 23 K×P=); *21 R—R3, R—B5; 22 R—R2* (Loses a second Pawn. But if 22 K—B1, R—R5; 23 K—Kt2, K—Kt5; 24 R—R1, P—Q6; 25 P—R5, P—Q7; 26 P—R6, R—R1; 27 P—R7, R—R1; 28 K—B3, R×P! and it is all over), *R—R5; 23 K—Q3, R×Pch; 24 K×P, R—R5ch; 25 K—Q3, R×P; 26 R—K2* (the Rook cannot reach the seventh: if 26 R—B2, R—KB5; 27 K—K3, K—Kt3; 28 R—B8, R—QR5!, etc., transposing back into the game), *R—KB5.* The rest is not difficult—Black need only exchange the KtP for the BP. *27 K—K3, K—Kt3; 28 R—B2, K—Kt2; 29 R—B1, R—QR5* (preparing to get his King over to the Pawns); *30 R—KR1, K—B3; 31 R— R7, R—R2; 32 K—K4, K—Q3; 33 K—B5* (Loses quickly, but on other moves the Rook gets back and the steady Pawn advance decides. E.g., 33 K—B3, K—K3; 34 K—K4, R—R5ch; 35 K—B3, P—Kt3; 36 R—R6, K—B4; 37 R—R1, P—Kt5ch; 38 K—Kt3, K—Kt4; 39 R—QKt1, P—B4; 40 R—Kt5, R—R6ch; 41 K—Kt2, K—R5; 42 R— Kt4, R—R7; 43 R—KB4, R—Kt7; 44 R—R4, P—Kt4; 45 R—R8, P—Kt6, etc.), *P—Kt3ch!; 34 K×KtP, R×R; 35 K×R, K—K4; 36 K—Kt6, P—Kt5.* 37 Resigns (For the Pawn ending see No. 42).

If there were no weaknesses in Black's position in the above example, the win would have been much simpler, since he could afford to exchange Rooks. The speed with which material is lost in such cases is seen in the similar ending No. 417a (Marshall-Tchigorin, Barmen, 1905), White: K at K3, R at QKt2, P's at QR3, Q4, KB4, KKt3, KR2; Black: K at KB2, R at QB5, P's at QR3, QKt4, KB3, KKt2, KR2. Black to play. After 1 .... K—K3! (if 1 .... R—B6ch; 2 K— K4, White's QP might become dangerous); 2 R—Kt3, K—Q4; 3 R— Q3, P—B4! White is already in zugzwang, for if 4 R—Q2, R—B6ch; 5 R—Q3, R×Rch; 6 K×R, P—QR4 and the outside passed Pawn is decisive. Marshall tried 4 P—R3, P—KR4; 5 K—K2, but 5 .... R×P; 6 R—QB3, R—K5ch; 7 K—Q2, P—R5 left him without any real hope. The remaining moves were 8 R—B7, P×P; 9 R×P, R×P; 10 R×P, K—K4; 11 K—K2, R—QB5; 12 R—Kt6, R—QR5; 13 R—Kt3, P—B5; 14 R—Kt3, R—B5; 15 K—Q1 (Note the uselessness of the White KRP), K—K5; 16 P—KR4, P—B6; 17 K—K1, K—B5; 18 P—R5, R—B8ch; 19 K—B2, R—B7ch; 20 K—K1, K— Kt6; 21 P—R6, R—K7ch; 22 K—Q1, R—KR7; 23 P—R4, P—Kt5 (23 .... P×P is also good enough); 24 R×P, R—R8ch; 25 K—Q2, P—B7 and White soon resigned.

No. 418 (Flohr-Petrov, Semmering-Baden, 1937) illustrates a different kind of winning possibility: attacking a Pawn mass with the King. If we examine the position, we find that Black has two isolated and exposed Pawns (QR3, Q4) and one exposed at KR4 which weakens the K-side. If we place the Black Rook at R2 or Q3, the Black King at KB1, we have substantially the same type of ending as in No. 417 and 417a. But here Black's King is supporting his passed Pawn and cannot come to the defense of the K-side. Accordingly the winning plan that suggests itself for White is to hold the QRP with the Rook and to set up a passed Pawn on the K-side. It is also clear that Black's only chance lies in advancing his QRP.

No. 418

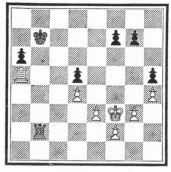

Black to play.

The game continuation was *1 .... R—Kt4* (The alternative 1 .... K —Kt3 seems to offer better drawing chances, but appearances are deceptive: 2 R×QP, P—R4; 3 R— Q6ch!, K—Kt2!; 4 R—Q7ch, K —Kt3; 5 R×P, P—R5; 6 P—Q5, P—R6; 7 R—B4, K—R4—or A—; 8 R—B8, R—Kt3—or B—; 9 R— R8ch, R—R3; 10 R—QB8, P—R 7; 11 R—B1, K—Kt5; 12 R—QR1, K—Kt6; 13 P—K4, K—Kt7; 14 R ×Pch, R×R; 15 P—K5!! and the Pawns win: 15 .... K—B6; 16 P —K6, R—R1; 17 P—K7, K—Q5;

18 P—Q6, etc. Or 15 .... R—R8; 16 K—K4, R—K8ch; 17 K—B5, K—B6; 18 P—Q6, K—B5; 19 P—Q7, R—Q8; 20 P—K6, etc. Variation A. 7 .... P—R7; 8 R—R4, R—Kt4; 9 R×P, R×P; 10 R—R8 and wins. Variation B. 8 .... P—R7; 9 R—R8ch, K—Kt4; 10 P— K4, K—Kt5; 11 K—B4!, K—Kt6; 12 P—Q6, R—Q7; 13 P—K5 and wins); *2 R—R2!* (guarding the second rank and thereby freeing his King), *P—Kt3?* (this passive continuation is, however, quite inferior. Since the best that White can do at the moment is to capture the KRP, Black should have played 2 .... P—R4! and if then 3 K—B4, K—Kt3 with two possibilities:

a) 4 K—Kt5?, R—Kt8; 5 K×P, K—Kt4; 6 K—Kt4, P—R5; 7 K—B5, K—Kt5; 8 K—K5, K—Kt6; 9 R×P, K×R; 10 K×P, K—Kt4; 11 P—K4, R—Kt6!; 12 P—K5, R—KB6 and Black should win.

b) 4 K—K5, K—B3!—not A—; 5 R—B2ch, K—Q2!; 6 R—R2, K—B3; 7 P—B3, K—Q2! and White cannot do anything, for if 8 R—QB2, P—R5; 9 R—R2, R—R4 the Black RP is too dangerous, while if 8 P—Kt4, P×P; 9 P×P, K—K2; 10 P—R5, P—B3ch; 11 K—B5, K—B2; 12 R—QB2?, R—R2! with at least a draw. Variation A. 4 .... R—Kt5?; 5 K×P, K—Kt4; 6 K—K5!, P—R5; 7 P—Q5, R—Kt8; 8 R—Q2 and White's passed Pawn is too strong); *3 K—B4!, P—B3* (he must stop the entry of the King. Now White's threats are so immediate that Black has no time to nurse his Pawn along.); *4 P—Kt4!, P×P; 5 K×P* (threatening P—R5), *R—Kt8* (so that if 6 P—R5, R—Kt8ch); *6 R—R5!* (driving the Rook back again), *R—Kt4?* (after this mistake the game is lost. 6 .... K—Kt3! was necessary, for if then 7 R×P, P—R4; 8 R—Q6ch, K—Kt2; 9 R×P, P— R5 White's Rook cannot get back (10 P—Q5, P—R6) and he can at best draw after giving up the Rook for the Pawn. Consequently after 9 .... P—R5 White must take the draw by 10 R—B7ch, K—Kt3; 11 R—B6ch, K—Kt2—but not A—; 12 R—B7ch, etc. Variation A. 11 .... K—R2?; 12 R—B6, P—R6; 13 R—B3 and will win. Nor can White take only one Pawn and retain any real winning chances: 6 .... K—Kt3; 7 R×P, P— R4; 8 R—QB5, P—R5; 9 R—B2, K—R4; 10 R—B8, R—Q8; 11 P—R5, R—Kt8ch; 12 K—B4, P×P; 13 P—Q5, P—R6; 14 K—B5, K—Kt5; 15 P—Q6, R—Q8 and Black cannot lose.); *7 R—R1!!* (the first rank must be controlled now rather than the second), *R—Kt7* (or 7 .... P—R4; 8 P—R5, P×Pch; 9 K×P, R—Kt7; 10 P—B4, K—Kt3; 11 K—Kt6 and White will win); *8 K—B3, R—Kt3* (it is too late—if 8 .... K—Kt3; 9 R—KKt1, P—R4; 10 R×P, P—R5; 11 R—Kt1!, P—R6; 12 R—QR1, P—

R7; 13 P—R5 and Black's Rook must go after the KRP, giving up his own QRP, when the resultant ending with R+3P vs. R+2P is lost because of the weakness of the Black Pawns. If here 10 .... R—Kt8 instead of 10 .... P—R5, then 11 R— Kt8, K—Kt2; 12 K—B4, P—R5; 13 P—B3, P—R6; 14 R—Kt2, R—Kt7; 15 R—Kt1, P—R7; 16 R—QR1, K—Kt3; 17 P—R5 and wins as above); *9 R—KKt1!, P—B4* (9 .... P—R4; 10 R×P, P—R5; 11 R—Kt1, P—R6; 12 R—QR1, etc., as in the last note); *10 K—B4, R—K3; 11 R—Kt1ch* (11 P—R5 at once was also strong), *K—R2; 12 P—R5!, R—K5ch* (or 12 .... P×P; 13 K×P, R—R3; 14 K—Kt5, R—R1; 15 P—B4 and the advance of the BP will be decisive, as in the game); *13 K—Kt5, R—Kt5ch* (The alternative was 13 .... P×P; 14 K×BP, P— R4, but then 15 R—Kt5, K—R3; 16 R×QP, R—Kt5; 17 R— Q6ch, K—Kt2; 18 R—KR6, P—QR5; 19 R×P, R—Kt7; 20 P—B4, P—R6; 21 R—R1, P—R7; 22 P—K4 wins without any trouble); *14 K—B6, P×P; 15 K×P, R—Kt7; 16 K—K5, R— Kt4ch* (after 16 .... R×P; 17 K×P, P—R5; 18 P—K4 the two connected Pawns win easily, e.g., 18 .... P—R6; 19 P—K5, P—R7; 20 P—K6, P—R4; 21 P—K7, R—K7; 22 K—Q6, P— R5; 23 P—Q5, P—R6; 24 K—Q7, P—R7; 25 R—QR1, etc.); *17 K—K6, P—R5; 18 R—KR1!* (So that if 18 .... P—R4; 19 R×P, P—R5; 20 R—R2!, P—R6; 21 P—B4 and it is all over), *R—R4; 19 P—B4, K—Kt3; 20 P—B5, K—B2; 21 P—B6, K— Q1* (a futile attempt to get back in time); *22 R—KB1, R—R3* (there is nothing to be done. On 22 .... K—K1; 23 R—QKt1, K—Q1; 24 R—Kt8ch, K—B2; 25 P—B7 is murderous); *23 K— B7,* Resigns. There is no stopping the BP. On 23 .... P—R6; 24 K—Kt7, R—R5; 25 P—B7, R—Kt5ch; 26 K—B6 poor Black does not even have a respectable spite check.

Unless they are passed, Pawns which are too far advanced are weak. Even if only one Pawn has stuck its neck out that may be enough to provide the opponent with a tangible advantage. A strtagem often employed in such cases is the sacrifice of a Pawn to disrupt the Pawn position completely.

No. 419 (Eliskases-Keres, Semmering-Baden, 1937) is typical. There is a slight advantage in White's favor because of the Black Pawn at QKt4. At the moment nothing can be done about it because the Pawn is adequately defended. The first step therefore is to remove the support, i.e., exchange Pawns. This is done by *1 P—QR4!, R— Kt2* (1 .... P×P; 2 R—QR1, R—R2; 3 R×P, P—QR4; 4 K—B4, R—B2ch; 5 K—Kt3!, R—R2; 6 R—B4 is much weaker—White succeeds in blockading the RP with his King and Black's Rook is occupying a useless post); *2 P—Q5!* (preparing to bring the King in), *P—K3;*

3 P×KP, BP×P; 4 P×P, P×P. Now that Black's Pawns have been scattered and separated, the next step is to get the King or Rook in to attack them. *5 K—K4!* (threatening 5 P—QB4, which would not be good at the moment because of the check at Q2), *K—B2?* (After this Black is lost. The best defense was 5 .... R—QB2!; 6 R×P, R×P; 7 R—Kt7, when 7 .... R—B4!, cutting the White King off, draws without much trouble. If here 6 K—Q4, R—B5ch; 7 K—K5, R×P; 8 R×P, R—B2!; 9 K×P, K—B1; 10 K—B6, R—B2ch is an easier theoretical draw); *6 P—QB4, P—Kt5; 7 K—Q4, K—K2* (there is not much he can do: on 7 .... R—Q2ch; 8 K—B5, R—Q7; 9 K—Kt6, R×P; 10 P—B5, R×P; 11 P—B6 he loses his Rook and the White

No. 419

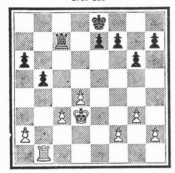

White to play.

No. 420

Black to play. White wins.

King gets back in time, especially since the Black Pawns are so scattered); *8 P—B5, P—Kt4; 9 K—B4, K—Q1; 10 R×P, R—KB2; 11 R—Kt2* and the rest is not difficult (No. 374).

Where there is one exposed Pawn, if it is not adequately defended by the King it may well cost the player the game. No. 420 (Capablanca-Reti, New York, 1924) is an instance. After *1 .... K—B2; 2 K—B3, R—Q1* (the threat was 3 K—B4 or 3 R—K1. If 2 .... P—KKt4; 3 R—K2, K—K3; 4 K—K4, R—KB1; 5 K×P, R—B5ch; 6 K—B5 White will have no trouble winning); *3 R—Kt4, P—KKt4; 4 P—KR4* (he is in no hurry), *K—Kt3; 5 P×P, P×P; 6 K—K4* the win is straightforward: *6 .... K—R4; 7 R—Kt1, K—R5; 8 P—K6, P—Kt5; 9 P—K7, R—K1* (Reti resigned here); *10 K—B5!, R×P* (or 10 .... P—Kt6; 11 R—R1 mate); *11 R×Pch, K—R4; 12 R×P, R—K7; 13 R—QKt4!* (not 13 R—Q7, R—B7ch), *P—Kt3; 14 P—Q4, K—R3; 15 P—Q5, K—Kt2; 16 R—K4!, R×P; 17 K—K6, R×P; 18

P—Q6, P—R4; 19 P—Q7, R—Q7; 20 K—K7 and wins easily because the Black Pawns are still far back.

Usually some tactical finesses must be countered before the Pawn can be won in similar positions. E.g., No. 420a (Tchekhover-Budo, Tiflis, 1937), White: K at KB3, R at K2, P's at QR2, QKt2, Q5, KB2, KKt3, KR2; Black: K at Q2, R at QKt4, P's at QR2, QB4, Q3, KB2, KKt2, KR2. Black to play wins. The Pawn at Q5 is exposed and weak but Black must chop down a lot of wood before he can get to it. Black's play is exemplary: 1 .... R—Kt5; 2 R—Q2, K—K2; 3 K—K3, K—B3; 4 P—B4 (to prevent .... K—K4. Now Black must get rid of this Pawn), K—B4; 5 K—B3, P—KR4; 6 P—Kt3 (if 6 P—KR3, P—Kt4!; 7 P—Kt4ch, P×Pch; 8 P×Pch, K—B3 and the KBP must be exchanged, when Black wins a Pawn. E.g., 9 P—B5, R—B5ch; 10 K—Kt3, K—K4; 11 P—Kt3, R—Q5; 12 R—K2ch, K—B3! or 9 P×Pch, K×P; 10 R—K2, R—B5ch!., etc.), P—QR4; 7 R—Q3 (if instead 7 R—K2, P—R5; 8 P×P, R×RP; 9 R—K7, R—R6ch, etc.), P—R5; 8 P×P, R×RP; 9 P—QR3, P—Kt4!; 10 P×P, K×P. Now White has two badly exposed Pawns and Black has a strong passed Pawn to boot. The rest is thus not difficult. 11 K—K2, K—B4; 12 K—Q2 (or 12 R—K3, R—K5; 13 P—KR4, R—Q5, or 13 R×R, K×R; 14 P—KR4, P—B4), K—K5; 13 K—B2, P—B5; 14 R—QB3, K×P; 15 K—B3, K—B3; 16 K—Kt2, R—R2; 17 R—B5, P—Q4; 18 R×RP, R—Kt2ch; 19 K—B2, R—Kt6; 20 R—R6ch, K—B4; 21 R—R6, R—KB6; 22 P—KR4, R×KtP; 23 P—R5, R—KR6; 24 P—R6, P—B3!; 25 R×P, R×QRP and now we have a standard ending: No. 356.

Attention should be paid to the ending which results after the weak Pawn has been captured. In particular, critical Pawn endings must be counted out carefully. E.g., No. 420b (Kostitch-Gruenfeld, Teplitz-Schoenau, 1922), White: K at KB3, R at K2, P's at QR2, K6, KKt3, KR2; Black: K at KB4, R at QR4, P's at QR2, QKt3, K2, KR4. Black to play wins. The simplest line is 1 .... R—K4; 2 R×Rch, K×R; 3 P—Kt4, P×Pch; 4 K×P, P—Kt4!; 5 K—Kt5, P—R4; 6 P—KR4, K×P! (threatening to get back); 7 K—Kt6, P—Kt5; 8 P—R5, P—R5; 9 P—R6, P—Kt6; 10 P×P, P×P; 11 P—R7, P—Kt7; 12 P—R8=Q, P—Kt8=Qch; 13 K—Kt5, Q—B4ch; 14 K—R4, Q—B3ch and after the exchange of Queens Black has the opposition. Gruenfeld, who was in time pressure, did not have time to examine the niceties of this ending, and instead played 1 .... R—R6ch; 2 K—Kt2, R—R4, when White tried 3 K—R3. Now 3 .... R—K4? would be a blunder because after 4 R×Rch, K×R; 5 K—R4! Black can at best draw: the main variation is 5 .... K×P; 6 K×P, K—B2; 7 K—R6, K—Kt1; 8 P—QR4!, P—R3; 9 K—Kt6, P—Kt4; 10 P×P, P×P; 11 K—B5!, K—B2!; 12 P—R4, P—Kt5; 13 K—K4, P—K4; 14 K—

Q3!, K—K3; 15 K—B4, K—B4!; 16 K×P, K—Kt5; 17 K—B3, K—B6; 18 K—Q2, K—B7; 19 K—Q3, K—B6=. But instead 3 .... R—R5! puts White in zugzwang, for if 4 K—Kt2, R—K5 wins, while the Rook is stalemated. For the ending after 4 R—Kt2, K×P; 5 R—Kt5, R×P; 6 R×P, R—QKt7 see No. 383.

An isolated Pawn in the center is a handicap, but, as in similar endings with minor pieces, if there is no further weakness it should not lose. This is seen in No. 420c (Rubinstein-Cohn, Carlsbad, 1907), where, despite a bad Pawn on the Q-side Black can draw. White: K at K3, R at Q3, P's at QR5, QKt2, QB3, KKt2, KR2; Black: K at K2, R at QB4, P's at QR3, QKt4, K4, KKt2, KR2. Black to play. After 1 .... R—B5; 2 P—QKt3, R—B4! should have been played with two main variations:

a) 3 K—K4, P—Kt5!; 4 P×P (4 P—B4, R×RP; 5 R—Q5?, R×R; 6 K×R, P—QR4; 7 K×P, P—R5; 8 P×P, P—Kt6 and Black wins), R—Kt4; 5 R—QB3, R×Pch; 6 K×P, R—Kt4ch; 7 K—K4, R×RP; 8 R—B7ch, K—B3; 9 R—R7, R—R6=.

b) 3 P—QKt4, R—B5; 4 K—Q2, R—B5; 5 R—Q5?, R—B7ch; 6 K—K3, R×P; 7 R×Pch, K—Q3; 8 R—KB5, R×P with at least a draw.

In the game there occurred instead 2 .... R—B3, when Rubinstein won as follows: 3 K—K4, K—K3; 4 R—R3, P—R3; 5 R—Kt3, K—B3 (5 .... P—Kt4; 6 P—R4!); 6 K—Q5, R—K3; 7 R—B3ch, K—K2; 8 P—Kt3, P—Kt3; 9 R—K3, K—B3; 10 P—B4 and White's passed Pawn is far superior to Black's. The remaining moves were 10 .... P×P; 11 P×P, R—K1; 12 R—B3ch, K—Kt4; 13 P—B5, P—K5; 14 P—R4ch, K—Kt5; 15 R—B4ch, K×P; 16 R×P, R—QR1; 17 P—B6, R—Kt4; 18 P×P, P×P; 19 P—B7, K—B6; 20 R—K1 and Black resigned. White wins the Black Rook for his BP, gives up his Rook for the KtP, captures the Black QRP, and then queens the last Pawn.

3. DOUBLED PAWNS

In Pawn endings doubled Pawns which are qualitatively inferior, i.e., are held in check by a smaller number, are a serious handicap, but even when they do not permit a passed Pawn their lack of mobility is often fatal. With pieces on the board, again, and especially with Rooks, any deviation from the normal Pawn position is a disadvantage because it offers the enemy new targets. Besides, reduction to a Pawn ending where less mobile and doubled Pawns are bad is always a possibility.

In No. 421 (Alekhine-Spielmann, New York, 1927) Black loses because he cannot afford to exchange Rooks. The main variation is the game continuation. After *1 R—K1ch, K—Q2* is necessary because the Q-side P's must be defended by the King. On 1 .... K—B2 White

No. 421

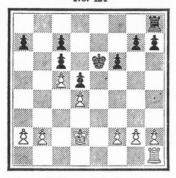

White to play wins.

has a forced win with 2 K—B3!, R—QKt1; 3 R—K3, R—Kt2; 4 P—QR3, R—Kt1; 5 K—B2, R—K1 (else 6 R—Kt3 will compel the exchange under less favorable circumstances); 6 R×R, K×R; 7 K—Kt3, K—Q2; 8 K—R4, K—B1; 9 K—R5, K—Kt2; 10 P—B3!, P—Kt3; 11 P—KKt3, P—KR3; 12 P—KR3, P—R4; 13 P—B4!, P—B4; 14 P—KR4, P—R3 (or 14 .... K—Kt1; 15 K—R6, K—R1; 16 P—QKt4, K—Kt1; 17 P—Kt5, K—R1—or A—; 18 P—R4, K—Kt1; 19 P—R5, K—R1; 20 P—Kt6, RP×P; 21 RP×P, P×P; 22 K×P and wins, or here 20 .... K—Kt1; 21 P—Kt7!, P—Kt4; 22 RP×P, P—R5; 23 P—Kt6 and queens with mate. Variation A. 17 .... P×P; 18 K×P, K—Kt2; 19 P—B6ch and wins); 15 P—QKt3, K—R2; 16 P—QKt4, K—Kt2; 17 P—R4, K—R2; 18 P—Kt5, RP×P; 19 P×P, P×P; 20 K×P, K—Kt2; 21 P—B6ch followed by K—B5 with a simple win. *2 K—B3* (2 R—K3 at once is also strong), *R—QKt1; 3 R—K3, R—KB1; 4 R—Kt3, R—B2; 5 R—R3, P—KR3; 6 K—Q2!* Now the double threat of R—QR3 and R—K3—K8 can only be parried by playing the King to QKt2 and the Rook to the King file. *6 .... R—K2* (or 6 .... K—B1; 7 R—R3, K—Kt2; 8 R—K3, R—Q2; 9 R—K8 and the march of the White King to the K-side decides—Black's King is a prisoner of his Pawns on the other wing); *7 R—K3!* (for the game continuation see A.), *R×R* (7 .... R—B2; 8 R—QR3, R—K2; 9 P—B3! is hopeless); *7 K×R, K—K3; 8 K—B4, P—Kt3; 9 P—KKt4* (White is trying to seal the K-side because he can win on the Q-side), *P—Kt4ch; 10 K—K3, K—Q2; 11 K—Q3, K—B1; 12 K—B3, K—Kt2; 13 K—Kt4, K—R3; 14 K—R4, K—Kt2; 15 K—R5, P—QR3* (if 15 .... K—Kt1; 16 K—R6 and wins as in the note to Black's first move); *16 P—QR4, K—R2; 17 P—QKt3!, K—Kt2; 18 P—QKt4, K—R2; 19 P—Kt5, RP×P; 20 P×P, K—Kt2!; 21 P—Kt6!!* (not 21 P×Pch??, K—R2!!= because the position is completely blockaded), *P×Pch* (21 .... K—Kt1; 22 K—R6 is worse); *22 P×P, K—Kt1; 23 K—R6!, P—B4* (23 .... K—R1; 24 P—Kt7ch, K—Kt1; 25 K—Kt6); *24 P×P, P—Q5; 25 P—Kt7, P—Q6; 26 K—Kt6, P—Q7; 27 P—B6, P—Q8=Q; 28 P—B7 mate.*

A. Alekhine played 7 R—R3, when 7 .... R—K5! should have proved to be an adequate defense: 8 R—R4, K—B1; 9 P—B3, R—R5; 10 P—KR3, K—Kt2; 11 K—K3, P—B4!; 12 R—Kt4ch, K—B1; 13

P—R4 and now 13 .... P—B5ch; 14 K—B2, R—R4 draws. Spielmann instead tried 13 .... P—Kt4?, bottling up his Rook, when Alekhine won in the following ingenious manner: 14 P—R5, P—Kt5; 15 RP×P, P×P; 16 P—R6!, P×P; 17 P×P, R—R8; 18 R—Kt7, R—K8ch; 19 K—B4!, R—Q8; 20 K—K5, R—K8ch; 21 K—B5, R—Q8; 22 R×RP!, R×P; 23 R—R8ch, K—Q2; 24 P—B4, R—R5; 25 P—R7, P—R4; 26 P—Kt3!!, R—R8; 27 K—K5, R—K8ch; 28 K—Q4!, R—Q8ch; 29 K—B3, R—QR8; 30 P—B5, K—K2; 31 K—Q4, P—R5; 32 K—K5, R—K8ch; 33 K—B4, R—QR8; 34 K—Kt5, R—Kt8ch (or 34 .... P—R6; 35 R—R8, R×P; 36 R×P, R—R8; 37 P—B6ch, K—B2; 38 R—R7ch winning easily); 35 K×P, R—QR8; 36 K—Kt5, R—Kt8ch; 37 K—B4, R—QR8; 38 K—K5, R—K8ch; 39 K—Q4, R—QR8; 40 K—B3, R—R6; 41 K—Kt2, R—R3; 42 P—Kt4, K—B2; 43 K—Kt3, R—R8; 44 P—B6! (to stalemate the King), R—R3; 45 P—Kt5!, P×P; 46 K—Kt4, Resigns. For if 46 .... P—B3; 47 R—R8! and if 46 .... R—R8; 47 K×P, P—Q5; 48 K—B4, R—R5ch; 49 K—Q3, P—B3; 50 K—K4 winning the QP, after which White can capture the BP with his King.

4. A PROTECTED PASSED PAWN

Since a Rook is not an effective blockader (a Kt is) it stands to reason that a protected passed Pawn will be quite powerful in Rook endings. We have already seen one example (No. 404) where such a Pawn shows its strength in conjunction with a Rook on the seventh. In No. 422 (Capablanca-Eliskases, Moscow, 1936) we have an instance where only the inferior position of the Black pieces, caused by the strong White Pawn at K5, is the reason for losing. At first sight the position does not seem to be any too good for White, but Capablanca uses the temporary sacrifice *1 P—B5!!* to demonstrate his superiority. After *1 .... P×P* (1 .... K—B2; 2 K—B4, R—K1; 3 R—KKt3 is no improvement); *2 K—B4, R—K3* (the alternative was 2 .... K—B2; 3 K×P, R—K3; 4 R—KKt3, R—R3 but on 5 R—Kt5 Black is in zugzwang for if his Rook moves on the Rook file, he allows the ruinous P—K6ch); *3 K×P, R—Kt3* (or 3 .... K—B2; 4 R—KKt3 as in the last note); *4 P—K6!* (Capablanca's winning line is simplicity itself),

No. 422

White to play wins.

R—Kt5; 5 K—K5, R—K5ch; 6 K—Q6, R×QP (Spite nibble. If
6 .... K—B1; 7 K—Q7 and Black must lose his Rook for the KP regardless of how he continues); *7 R—K3* Resigns. For now the Pawn
queens by force: 7 .... R—K5; 8 R×R, P×R; 9 P—K7, K—B2;
10 K—Q7, etc.

5. QUALITATIVE PAWN MAJORITY

This occurs (see Chapter II, pages 48, 62–69) when an extra Pawn on
one wing is meaningless either because it is blockaded or doubled. As a
result the opponent is in effect a Pawn ahead. King and Pawn endings
in such cases are almost always lost, but in R endings there is often
counterplay available.

    a) If the Pawns are doubled, there is no way (excepting a blunder by
    the opponent) of straightening the Pawns. The only chance
    then is to try to keep the disadvantage at a minimum by seeking
    compensation elsewhere.

No. 422A (Eliskases-Loevenfisch, Moscow, 1936) is typical of the
endings where the doubled Pawns are a fatal handicap. For all practical purposes White is a Pawn behind because his three Pawns on the
K-side are held by Black's two. But with his Rook so well placed,
White can still manage to draw with the proper continuation. After
1 R—B7!, P—Kt4! (the best chance: if he abandons the KtP White
will have a passed KBP); *2 R×P, P—B5; 3 R—K7!!* draws by keeping
the Black King from the Pawns (for the game continuation see A.),
P—B6 (or 3 .... K—B3; 4 R—K3, P—B6; 5 P—R4, P—B7; 6 R—
B3=); *4 P—R4!, R—QR8* (if instead 4 .... P—B7; 5 R—QB7, K—
K4; 6 P—R5, K—Q5; 7 P—R6, K—Q6; 8 R—Q7ch and the Black
King will never be able to remain in the neighborhood of the Pawn—
even without the White RP the game would then be drawn); *5 R—
QB7, R—R6; 6 P—R5, K—K4; 7 P—R6, K—Q5; 8 P—R7, K—Q6;
9 P—B4, P—B7; 10 R—Q7ch!* (10 P—B5?, R×P!), *K—K7; 11 R—
QB7, K—Q7; 12 R—Q7ch=,* since 12 .... K—B8?; 13 P—B5! forces
Black to take the draw at once or lose.

A. In the game Eliskases played 3 R—R5ch? and lost because he
could not get his K-side Pawns going in time: 3 .... K—K3!; 4 R—
R6ch, K—Q4; 5 R×P, P—B6; 6 R—R8, R—QR8!; 7 R—QB8, R×P;
8 K—R3 (the cramped Pawns make progress too slow. If 8 P—B4,
P—Kt5!; 9 K—Kt1, K—Q5; 10 K—B2, R—R7ch; 11 K—B1, R—Q7!;
12 R—Q8ch, K—K6; 13 R—K8ch, K—Q6; 14 R—Q8ch, K—B7; 15
R—QB8, K—Kt7; 16 R—Kt8ch, K—B8; 17 P—B5, P—B7; 18 P—
B6, K—Q8; 19 P—B7, P—B8=Q; 20 P—B8=Q, K—B7 dis ch and
mate), K—Q5; 9 K—Kt4 (or 9 P—B4, P×P; 10 P×P, P—B7 dis ch;
11 K any, R—QB6), R—R4!!; 10 P—B4, R—QB4; 11 R—Q8ch,

K—K6; 12 R—Q1, P—B7; 13 R—QB1, P×P; 14 P×P, K—Q7; 15
R—QR1, P—B8=Q; 16 R×Q, R×R and the rest is simple: 17 K—
Kt5 (17 P—B5, K—K6; 18 P—B6, R—KB8; 19 K—Kt5, K—K5;
20 K—Kt6, K—K4; 21 P—B7, K—K3), K—K6; 18 P—B5, K—K5;
19 P—Kt4, K—K4; 20 K—Kt6, R—B3ch; 21 K—Kt7, R—QR3!; 22
K—B7, K—B5; 23 K—Kt7, K—Kt4!! and White resigned for if 24
K—B7, K×P; 25 P—B6, K—B4 and the last Pawn goes.

Where the passed Pawn is far advanced, or where there is no such
counterplay as in the previous example, the superior side wins by proceeding as though he were a Pawn ahead. E.g., No. 422a (Rabino-

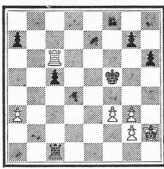

No. 422A

White to play.

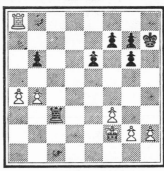

No. 423

Black to play. Draw.

vitch-Kan, Moscow, 1935), White: K at K4, R at Q3, P's at QR3,
QB3, QB4, QB5, KB4; Black: K at KB3, R at KR7, P's at QR3,
QKt2, QB3, KB2, KR6. Black to play wins. He gives up his KRP
in order to establish a decisive material superiority on the other wing:
1 .... R—K7ch; 2 K—B3, P—R7!; 3 R—Q1, R—QB7; 4 K—Kt3,
K—B4; 5 R—K1, P—B3; 6 K—B3, R×Pch; 7 K—Kt2, R×BP;
8 R—QKt1, R×QBP; 9 R×P, K×P and with two clear Pawns to the
good the rest is simple: 10 K×P, P—B4; 11 K—Kt2, R—B6; 12 R—
Kt4ch, K—K6; 13 K—Kt3, R×P; 14 R—QB4, P—R4; 15 R×P,
K—K5 dis ch; 16 K—B2, R—R7ch, etc.

Where there is no clear or strongly supported passed Pawn there
may often be time to put the doubled Pawn complex to some good use,
and save the game in that way. It should always be remembered that
there are a great many cases where a Pawn ahead does not win in Rook
endings.

An interesting example from a world's championship match is No.
423 (Alekhine-Euwe, 27th match game, 1935). If the QKtP's were off

the board and White's RP were at R7 he could win by playing P—
KR4, P—KKt4, P—Kt5 and then getting his King around to K7
(see No. 368a). But now Black can dictate the terms on which a Q-
side passed Pawn will be permitted. The game continuation will give
us a hint as to what these terms should be: 1 .... R—Kt6?; 2 P—
Kt5!, P—Kt4; 3 K—K2, P—K4; 4 K—Q2, P—B3; 5 K—B2, R—
Kt5; 6 K—B3, R—Q5; 7 R—R6, K—Kt3; 8 R×P, R×P; 9 R—R6,
R—Q5; 10 P—Kt6! and Black resigned. If 10 .... R—Q1; 11 P—
Kt7, R—QKt1; 12 R—Kt6, K—B2; 13 K—B4, K—K2; 14 K—Kt5,
K—Q2; 15 K—R6, K—B2; 16 K—R7, etc. It is clear that Black's
mistake lay in not mobilizing his K-side Pawns early enough. Conse-
quently, as later analysis showed, *1 .... P—K4!* would have drawn:
2 P—Kt5 (The alternatives are a) 2 K—K2, P—B4; 3 K—Q2, R—B5;
4 P—Kt5, P—K5!; 5 P×P, P×P; 6 K—K3, P—Kt4; 7 K—B2, K—
Kt3; 8 R—R6, K—B4; 9 R×P, R×P; 10 R—QB6, R—Kt5; 11 P—
Kt6, K—B5; 12 P—Kt3ch, K—Kt5=. b) 2 P—Kt4, P—Kt4!; 3
P—Kt5, P—Kt3; 4 R—R6, R—R6; 5 K—K2, P—B4; 6 K—Q2, P—
K5; 7 P×KP, P×KP; 8 K—B2, P—K6 and again the Black passed
Pawn prevents the White King from supporting the Q-side), *P—B4;
3 R—K8, R—B5; 4 R×P, R×P; 5 R—K6, R—R7ch!; 6 K—Kt3* (On
6 K—K3, R×P; 7 R×QKtP, R×P; 8 R—K6, R—QKt7; 9 P—Kt6,
P—Kt4 Black's passed Pawn again saves the game), *P—Kt4!; 7 R×P,
R—QKt7* (White has won a Pawn but the cramped position of his
King and the strong Black Rook nullify the advantage); *8 R—Kt8,
K—Kt3; 9 P—Kt6, K—B3; 10 P—Kt7* (10 P—R4, P×Pch; 11 K×P,
K—Kt3; 12 K—Kt3, R—Kt5=. No. 367. White's King cannot get
to the Pawn without sacrificing a valuable Pawn on the K-side), *P—
B5ch; 11 K—Kt4!, K—Kt3!* (not 11 .... R×Pch?; 12 K—R3, R—
Kt7; 13 R—B8ch); *12 P—Kt3* (or 12 P—R4, P×P; 13 K×RP, K—
R2!; 14 K—R3, P—Kt3; 15 K—R2, R—Kt8!, etc., 12 R—QB8, R×P;
13 R—B6ch, K—R2; 14 K×P, R—Kt7 is likewise only a theoretical
draw), *P×P; 13 P×P, R—Kt5ch; 14 P—B4* (14 K—R3, R—Kt7),
P×P; 15 P×P, R—Kt8=.

An analogous instance where aggressive counteraction counterbalances the weakness of the doubled Pawn and which incidentally shows
once more that a passed Pawn in the center is not quite as strong as one
on the side is No. 423a (Spielmann-Reti, Baden, 1914), White: K at
Q3, R at QKt1, P's at QR4, QB2, QB4, Q5, KKt2, KR2; Black: K at
KB2, R at KB5, P's at QR2, QKt3, QB2, K4, KKt2, KR2. White to
play draws. 1 P—R5!, K—K2; 2 P—B5!!, P×BP; 3 R—Kt7, K—Q3;
4 R×RP, R—Q5ch; 5 K—K3, R—QB5; 6 P—R6, R×P; 7 R—R8,
R—B6ch; 8 K—K4, R—B5ch; 9 K—Q3, R—QR5; 10 P—R7, K—Q2;
11 R—KKt8! (the simplest. On 11 P—Q6!?, R—R6ch; 12 K—K4,
P—B5 Black retains winning chances), R×P; 12 R×Pch, K—Q3;

13 R×RP, R—R5; 14 R—R8 and now the Black doubled Pawns are worthless, so that a draw is the legitimate result.

b) If the Pawns are blockaded the opponent is likewise temporarily a Pawn ahead. For practical purposes, an immobile Pawn is as bad as one that is doubled. As a rule, however, it is necessary to proceed with more energy here than in the previous case because a blockade is not permanent, but depends on a certain position of the pieces.

A clasic example of the exploitation of such a Pawn block is No. 424 (Rubinstein-Alekhine, Carlsbad, 1911). The White advantage is threefold: 1. the single Pawn at QKt5 holds the two Black Pawns at QR2 and QKt3; 2. Black's Pawn at Q4 is isolated and his K-side Pawns are weakened; 3. Black's Rook is passive, White's active.

Accordingly Rubinstein formulates a winning plan which consists of four steps.

1. Preventing the liberating .... P—QR3.
2. Tying the Black Rook down permanently to the defense of a Pawn.
3. Breaking through on the K-side to clear the way for the King.
4. Establishing a decisive material advantage.

Rubinstein's treatment of the ending is beyond all praise. *1 P—B3!!* A subtle prophylactic measure. If in reply 1 .... R—QB1??; 2 R×R, K×R; 3 P—K4! and the Pawn ending is won: 3 .... BP×P (or 3 .... K—Kt2; 4 P×BP, P×P; 5 P—Kt4, P×P; 6 P×P, P—QR4; 7 P×Pch, K×P; 8 P—B5 and queens); 4 P×P, P×P; 5 P—Kt4, K—Q2 (5 .... P—KR4; 6 P—B5!, P×P; 7 P×RP! and promotes first); 6 K—K3, K—K3; 7 K×P and since the two Black Pawns on the Q-side are no better than one White is a Pawn ahead and wins with his two passed Pawns. *1 .... R—K1* (at any rate preventing P—K4. On the desperate 1 .... P—QR4?; 2 R×QKtP, P—R5; 3 R—R6! wins at once. If here 2 .... K—B2; 3 R—B6ch; K—Kt2; 4 K—Q3, P—R5; 5 K—B2, P—R6; 6 K—Kt1, R—R4; 7 R—K6!, R×Pch; 8 K—R2, R—Kt7ch; 9 K×P, R—Kt7; 10 P—Kt4!, P×P; 11 P×P, R×P; 12 K—Kt4!, P—R4; 13 K—B5, P—R5; 14 K×P, P—R6; 15 R—K7ch,K—Kt3; 16 R—KR7, R—Kt6; 17 P—K4 and White's

No. 424

White to play wins.

connected passed Pawns win); *2 K—Q3, R—K2; 3 P—Kt4* (first and third steps—the second is being carried out indirectly), *R—K3!; 4 R—B1!* (to exchange Rooks would be a mistake because Black is threatening to set up a passed KRP), *R—K2* (thus the Rook is tied down: the threat was R—QR1); *5 R—KR1, K—K3; 6 R—QB1, K—Q2* (6 .... P—KR4; 7 P×RP, P×P; 8 R—B6ch, K—Q2; 9 R—R6 and wins a Pawn; *7 R—K1* (tempo moves to gain time), *R—B2* (7 .... P—KR4; 8 P×RP, P×P; 9 K—K2, P—R5; 10 K—B2 and White's Rook can then go around to the loose Pawns, while his King blocks the KRP. Still, this line probably was more promising than the passive one chosen); *8 R—QR1, K—Q3; 9 R—QB1, K—Q2; 10 R—B6, R—B1; 11 K—K2!* (the third step now enters its second phase: the White King threatens to reach KKt5), *R—B2* (11 .... R—B1; 12 R×R, K×R; 13 P×P, P×P; 14 P—K4, K—Kt2; 15 K—B2 and wins); *12 K—B2, R—B1; 13 K—Kt3, R—K1; 14 R—B3, R—K2; 15 K—R4!, P—KR3* (To allow the King to enter would be fatal. The most direct win would be 15 .... R—B2; 16 K—Kt5, K—Q3; 17 K—R6, K—Q2; 18 P—Kt5, R—K2; 19 R—B6, R×P (the only chance); 20 K×P, R×P; 21 K×P, R×P; 22 K—B7, R×P; 23 P—Kt6 and wins the Rook. Now that all the Pawns have been uprooted White is bound to capture material); *16 K—Kt3!* (threatening K—B2, R—B1, R—KKt1, P×P, R—Kt6 and R—KB6), *P—KR4; 17 K—R4!, R—R2; 18 K—Kt5!* (the simplest), *BP×P!* (a trap: if 19 K×P?, P—Kt6!; 20 K×R, P—Kt7; 21 R—B1, P—R5 and Black wins); *19 P×P, P×P; 20 K×P (Kt4), R—R8* (he has no choice. On 20 .... R—K2; 21 K—Kt5, R—K3; 22 K—R6!—Kt7—B7 and eventually Black will have to play .... R—Q3, when R—R3 will decide); *21 K—Kt5, R—QKt8* (21 .... R—Kt8ch; 22 K—B6, K—Q3; 23 R—B6ch, K—Q2; 24 K—K5 is hopeless); *22 R—R3, R×P; 23 R×Pch, K—Q3; 24 K×P, R—Kt6; 25 P—B5* (25 R—QKt7, K—B3; 26 R—K7 holds on to the extra Pawn, but the move chosen is more forceful), *R×P; 26 P—B6, R—Kt6ch; 27 K—R7, R—KB6; 28 P—B7, R—B5* (the last chance); *29 K—Kt7, R—Kt5ch; 30 K—B6!* (30 K—B8, R×P; 31 R—R8, R—B5; 32 K—Kt7, P—Q5 is less clear), *R—B5ch; 31 K—Kt5!, R—B8; 32 K—Kt6* (threatening R—R8), *R—Kt8ch; 33 K—B6, R—B8ch; 34 K—Kt7, R—Kt8ch; 35 K—B8, R—Q8; 36 K—K8, R—K8ch; 37 K—Q8, R—KB8; 38 R—Q7ch, K—B3; 39 K—K8, R—B7; 40 R—K7!, K—Kt4; 41 R—B7!* (again the simplest), Resigns. The conclusion might be 41 .... R—K7ch; 42 K—Q7!, R—B7; 43 K—K6, R—K7ch; 44 K×P, R—KB7; 45 K—K6, R—K7ch; 46 K—Q7, R—KB7; 47 K—K8, R—K7ch; 48 K—Q8, R—KB7; 49 P—Q5, etc.

Where the blockade remains effective, and there are no doubled Pawns or other weaknesses, the superior side is in effect a Pawn ahead and should proceed accordingly: centralize, advance his majority, tie up the enemy pieces, secure a decisive material advantage. A perfect example of this process is No. 425 (Naegeli-Alekhine, Zurich, 1934). The game continuation was *1 .... K—K4* (centralization); *2 R—K3, P—B4* (second step: advancing the Pawn majority in order to tie up the enemy pieces); *3 P—KR4* (If instead 3 P—B4ch, K—Q5!; 4 R—Kt3, R—B1!; 5 R—K3, R—B7ch; 6 KxR, KxR; 7 P—QR4, PxP; 8 P—Kt5, K—B7; 9 P—Kt6, P—K6; 10 P—Kt7, P—K7; 11 P—Kt8=Q, P—Kt8=Q; 12 Q—R7ch, K—Kt7 and Black will emerge with two Pawns plus on the K-side), *K—Q5; 4 R—Kt3, P—R3; 5 R—K3* (White's Rook is tied down to the weak Q-side Pawns. If 5 R—Kt1, R—B6; 6 R—QR1, P—K6ch; 7 PxPch, RxP; 8 P—R4, PxP; 9 RxP, RxP and wins), *P—Kt4; 6 PxP, PxP; 7 R—Kt3, R—B1* (the Rook has performed nobly on the QB file and now switches over to the other wing); *8 R—K3, R—KR1; 9 R—K2, P—B5; 10 PxP, PxP; 11 K—B2* (he must give his Rook some leeway), *R—R7; 12 K—Kt3* (Desperation. After 12 K—Q2, RxP!; 13 RxR, P—K6ch; 14 K—K2, PxR; 15 KxP, K—B5!; 16 K—B3, K—Kt6; 17 KxP, KxP; 18 K—K3, KxP the win is routine), *R—R6ch* (to centralize the Rook. An alternative win which however had to be calculated to a nicety was 12 .... P—B6; 13 R—B2, RxP!!; 14 RxR, K—K6; 15 R—B1, P—B7; 16 P—R4, PxPch; 17 KxP, K—K7!; 18 R—KR1, P—B8=Q; 19 RxQ, KxR; 20 P—Kt5, P—K6; 21 P—Kt6, P—K7; 22 P—Kt7, P—K8=Q; 23 P—Kt8=Q, Q—R8ch; 24 K—Kt5, Q—Kt8ch and wins White's Queen.); *13 K—Kt2, R—Q6* (Now the White King will not be able to stop the eventual passed KP or BP. The rest is simple.); *14 R—B2, P—B6; 15 K—B1, P—K6; 16 PxPch, KxP;* 17 Resigns. After 17 R—B8, P—B7 White's Rook is lost.

An analogous case where straight-forward exchanging leads to an elementary win because of the cramped position of the enemy pieces and Pawns is No. 425a (Vidmar-Dus-Chotimirsky, Carlsbad, 1907), White: K at KKt1, R at K6, P's at QR4, QKt3, Q6, KKt6,KKt2; Black: K at KB1, R at Q2, P's at QR4, QKt3, KB4, KKt2, KR3. Black to play. The three Black K-side Pawns are held by White's two so that the QP is in effect an extra Pawn. After 1 .... R—Q1; 2 K—B2, R—K1!; 3 P—Q7!, R —Q1; 4 RxP, RxP; 5 R—Kt5,

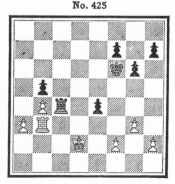

No. 425

Black to play wins.

R—Q7ch; 6 K—B3, P—B5; 7 R×P, R—Q6ch; 8 K×P, R×P; 9 R—
QKt5, R—QB6; 10 P—R5, R—B5ch; 11 K—B5, R—B7; 12 P—Kt4
Black can reestablish material equality, but the strong RP decides (see
No. 375b).

C. BETTER KING POSITION

One King may be better placed than another for one of two reasons:
either on general principles, i.e., one is centralized, while the other is
not, or on the special principle that one is nearer the vital Pawns.
The second category is really the basic one because a centralized King
is strong only to the extent that it can switch over to one side or the
other and capture material or support a strong passed Pawn.

1. CENTRALIZATION

Examples of this in conjunction with other advantages may be found
throughout the previous discussion—see, e.g., Nos. 416, 419, 422.
Here we are concerned with positions where centralization alone is the
decisive factor.

A typical instance of where such centralization is conclusive is No.
426 (Treybal-Mattison, Carlsbad, 1929). The fact that White is a
Pawn behind is of no consequence since the two Black RP's are
doubled. The first point that we notice is that Black cannot afford
to exchange Rooks because White's King is too near the RP. Thus
after 1 .... R×R; 2 P×R, P—R6; 3 K—B3, P—B5; 4 KtP×P,
K—B4; 5 P—B5, K—B3; 6 P—Q4 and wins. Thus *1 .... R—B2* is
forced. But now White can advance his center Pawns which, in the
absence of Black's King will win a Rook. The game continued *2 P—
B5, P—Kt4* (or 2 .... P—B5; 3 P×P, K×RP; 4 P—K6, P×P;
5 P×P, K—Kt5; 6 K—Q5, P—R4; 7 R—Kt3ch, K—R5; 8 P—B5
and wins easily. If here 3 .... R×Pch; 4 R—Q4, exchanging Rooks
and queening the KP); *3 P×P, P×P; 4 P—K6, P×P; 5 P×P, P—
B5; 6 R—K3!* (but not 6 R—Q7?, R—B1; 7 P—K7, R—K1; 8 K—
K5, P—R6; 9 K—B6, P—R7; 10 R—Q1, P×P=), *R—KKt2; 7 P×P,
P×P; 8 K—B4, R—Kt1; 9 P—K7, R—K1; 10 K—B5, P—R6; 11 K—
K6, P—R7; 12 R—KR3,* Resigns. Black's King is unable to capture
the BP. If the Black King had been at K2 in the diagrammed position
he would have drawn quite easily. In fact White would then not have
dared to oppose Rooks, for with the King in the center Black would
win the Pawn ending.

A similar instance is No. 426a (Stahlberg-Fine, 2nd match game,
1937), White: K at Q5, R at QR1, P's at QKt5, QB6, K3, KKt2,
KR2; Black: K at QKt1, R at QB2, P's at QR2, K5, KB4, KKt2,
KR2. White to play wins. After 1 R—KB1, R—B2 (1 .... P—

Kt3; 2 P—Kt4, P×P; 3 R—B8ch, R—B1; 4 R×Rch, K×R; 5 K×P
and White has two passed Pawns to Black's one. Nevertheless the
Pawn ending is won only by the odd tempo: 5 .... P—R4; 6 K—B4,
K—B2; 7 P—K4, K—Q3; 8 P—K5ch, K—K3; 9 K—Kt5!, K—K2;
10 P—B7!, K—Q2; 11 P—K6ch, K×P; 12 K—B6, P—R5; 13 P—
K7, P—Kt6; 14 P—K8=Q and Black is one move too late); 2 P—
Kt4, Black is already reduced to the desperate 2 .... P—B5!?, since
2 .... P—Kt3; 3 K—K6 is hopeless. 2 .... P—B5 was refuted by
3 P×P, P—K6; 4 P—B5, P—KR4; 5 P—R3, P×P; 6 P×P, K—B2;
7 R—K1, R—K2; 8 R—K2, K—Kt3; 9 P—Kt5, K×P; 10 P—B6,
P×P; 11 P×P, R—QB2 (if 11 .... R—KB2; 12 R×P, R×P;

No. 426   No. 427

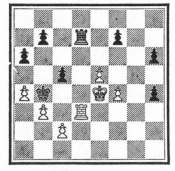   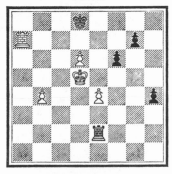

Black to play. White wins.   White to play wins.

13 P—B7, R—B1; 14 R—Kt3ch, K any; 15 R—Kt8); 12 R×P,
P—R4; 13 R—K7 and Black resigned—the two passed Pawns are too
much.

2. ONE KING IS NEARER THE VITAL PAWNS

The "vital" Pawns may be either a strong (advanced) passed Pawn
or simply a mass of Pawns. In the former case one either queens
or wins a Rook; in the latter one simply captures material with the
King or King and Rook combined.

The more important case is that where one King is nearer its passed
Pawn. Here we have two typical positions. The first is seen in No.
427 (Schlechter-Perlis, Carlsbad, 1911). It is obvious that if White
could get his King to K6 or QB6 without being checked away that
he could escort his Pawn to the eighth. But if at once 1 K—K6,
R×Pch and if 1 K—B6, R—B7ch. Accordingly he must block the

files by a sacrifice: *1 P—K5!!* after which Black is lost in all variations:
a) *1 .... P×P; 2 K—K6, R—QB7* (2 .... K—B1; 3 P—Q7ch and
queens at once. After 3 .... K—Kt1; 4 P—Q8ch, K×R;
5 Q—R5ch, K—Kt2; 6 Q—Kt5ch the Rook goes); *3 R—R8ch,
R—B1; 4 R×Rch, K×R; 5 K—K7, P—R6; 6 P—Q7ch, K—
Kt2; 7 P—Q8 = Q, P—R7; 8 Q—Q5ch* and wins.
b) *1 .... R×Pch; 2 K—B6, K—K1; 3 R—R8ch, K—B2; 4 P—Q7*
and queens.
c) *1 .... R—Q7ch; 2 K—K6, K—B1; 3 P—Q7ch!* (the simplest),
*K—Kt1; 4 R—R6!, K—B2; 5 R—Q6, R×Rch; 6 P×Rch, K—
Q1; 7 P—Kt5, P—R6; 8 P—Kt6, P—R7; 9 P—Kt7, P—R8 = Q;
10 P—Kt8 = Q* mate!
d) *1 .... P—R6; 2 P—K6, K—B1; 3 P—Q7ch, K—Q1; 4 R—
R8ch* and mates.

The second typical position occurs when one Rook is tied up. No.
428 (Apscheneek-Petrov, Kemeri, 1937) is a good example. By constant mate threats Black will eventually force the White King to
abandon the immediate neighborhood of the passed Pawn. Best play
for both sides is *1 K—B1* (1 K—K3?, P—B6; 2 R—Kt8, R×P;
3 R×P, P—B7 is hopeless), *K—B6!!* (not 1 .... P—B6?; 2 R—Kt8,
R×P; 3 R×P and will draw); *2 R—Kt8* (On 2 K—Q1, R—Q3ch;
3 K—K2, R—Q2 the threat of .... K—Kt6, ... P—B6—B7 forces
White to get his Rook out of the way under much less favorable circumstances), *R×P; 3 R×P, R—K2!* (better than 3 .... R—R2;
4 K—Q1, R—R8ch?; 5 K—K2, K—Kt7; 6 R—Kt6ch, K—B7; 7 R—
Kt5, P—B6; 8 R×P, K—Kt6; 9 R×P, P—B7; 10 R—QB5, P—
B8=Q; 11 R×Q, R×R; 12 K—B3 and Black will be unable to win
against the three passed Pawns), *4 K—Q1* (relatively best. On 4 K—
Kt1, R—K8ch; 5 K—R2, K—B7; 6 R—Kt5, P—B6; 7 R×BP, K—
Q6; 8 R×P, P—B7; 9 R—QB5, P—B8=Q Black wins because his
King is near the Pawns, while 4 R—Q6, R—K8ch; 5 R—Q1, R×Rch;
6 K×R, K—Kt7 is immediately fatal), *R—K6!!* (4 .... K—Kt7;
5 R—Kt6ch gets Black nowhere); *5 R—QR6* (The alternative is
5 R—Kt5, K—Kt7; 6 R×BP, R—Q6ch as in the main variation),
*K—Kt7!; 6 R—R5, R—Q6ch; 7 K—K2, R×P; 8 R×P, P—B6; 9 R—
Kt5ch, K—B8; 10 R×P, P—B7; 11 R—QB5, K—Kt7!; 12 R×Pch*
(the threat was .... R—QB6), *K×R; 13 P—R5, K—B6; 14 K—B2,
R—R6; 15 K—Kt2, R×P; 16 K—B3, K—Q5* and wins.

Positions where one King is nearer a set of Pawns are as a rule
rather simple: a material advantage must soon result. One fairly
complicated example will suffice. No. 428a (Loevenfisch-Lissitzin,
Moscow, 1935), White: K at KB4, R at QB6, P's at QR4, QKt5,
KKt3, KR2; Black: K at KR2, R at K2, P's at QR2, QKt3, KB4,
KR3. Black to play; White wins. The game went 1 .... R—KB2

(if 1 .... R—K5ch; 2 K×P, R×P; 3 R—B7ch, K—Kt1; 4 K—Kt6,
K—B1; 5 K×P and White has two connected passed Pawns); 2 P—
R4, R—KKt2; 3 P—KR5! (Now Black must lose the BP no matter
how he plays, for if 3 .... R—KB2; 4 R—K6, K—Kt2; 5 R—K5),
R—Kt5ch (the only chance); 4 K×P, R×RP (if instead 4 ....
R×KtP; 5 R—B7ch, K—Kt1; 6 R×P, R—Kt4ch; 7 K—B6, R×RP;
8 P—R5!!!, R×P—or A—; 9 P—R6, R—QR4; 10 R—Kt7ch!, K—

No. 428	No. 429

 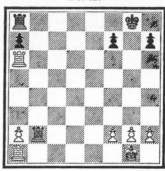

White to play; Black wins.	Draw.

B1; 11 P—R7, K—K1; 12 K—K6, K—Q1; 13 R—Kt8ch and wins.
Variation A. 8 .... P×P; 9 P—Kt6, R—QKt4; 10 P—Kt7 followed
by 11 R—R8ch winning the Rook); 5 R—B7ch, K—Kt1; 6 K—Kt6,
R—Kt5ch; 7 K×P, R×P; 8 R×P, R—Kt6; 9 R—QKt7!! (the point:
White either captures the second Pawn or forces his RP through),
R×P; 10 K—Kt6, K—B1; 11 P—R6, R—K4 (or 11 .... R—Kt8;
12 R—Kt8ch, K—K2; 13 P—R7); 12 R—Kt8ch Resigns.

VII. TWO ROOK ENDINGS

Most of the time such endings differ in no essential respect from
those with single Rooks on the board; often the exchange of one pair
is unavoidable. The superior side must take care to reduce to an
ending which is favorable for him—e.g., get his Rook behind a passed
Pawn.

If no exchange is feasible there are several respects in which these
endings may differ from those previously considered. The most important of these is that where both Rooks reach the seventh. Other
things being equal, they will then draw with a Pawn down, and will
force the capture of material in even positions.

The typical position where they compensate for the loss of a Pawn is No. 429 (Schlechter-Maroczy, Carlsbad, 1907). Black gives up his RP to get both Rooks on the seventh: *1 .... R—Q1!; 2 R×P, R(Q1)—Q7; 3 R—R3* (or 3 R—KB1, R×RP=), *K—B1!* (the safest. After 3 .... R×BP; 4 R—Kt3ch, K—B1; 5 P—QR3 Black might have trouble.); *4 R—KB1* (now 4 R—KKt3 is met by 4 .... R×RP), *R×RP; 5 R×R* (if he does not exchange Black will double on a file and force it that way), *R×R* and the game was eventually drawn. White to play in the diagrammed position cannot improve his game in any way. E.g., 1 P—QR3, R—Q1; 2 R×P, R(Q1)—Q7; 3 R—KB1, R—R7; 4 R—R4, K—B1; 5 P—Kt3, R—Q6, etc.

A more complicated variant on the same theme is No. 429a (Capablanca-Fine, AVRO, 1938), White: K at KKt3, R's at QR7, KR1; P's at QR3, QKt4, K3, KB2, KKt2, KR2; Black: K at KKt1, R's at Q1, Q7, P's at QKt3, K3, K5, KB2, KR2. Black to play. After 1 .... R—R7; 2 R—R6, R(Q1)—Q7; 3 R—KB1, R(Q7)—Kt7; 4 R×P (the threat was .... R×KtP), R×RP; 5 P—Kt5, K—Kt2; 6 P—R4, R(R6)—Kt6; 7 K—B4, R×P; 8 R×R, R×R; 9 P—Kt4, R—Kt5 the game should be drawn, since Black can afford to give up his KP.

An instance where one Rook on the seventh coupled with the threat of getting the other in suffices to tie up the enemy pieces is No. 429b (Botvinnik-Loevenfisch, 6th match game, 1937), White: K at KKt1, R's at QR7, KKt3, P's at QR2, QKt3, KKt2, KR5; Black: K at KKt1, R's at QKt1, Q4, P's at QKt3, K3, KB2, KKt2, KR3. White to play draws. 1 R—KB3, R—KB1 (after 1 .... R—KB4; 2 R×R, P×R; 3 P—R4, R—Q1; 4 R—Kt7, R—Q3; 5 P—Kt4 Black is in effect only one Pawn ahead on the K-side and this is more than counterbalanced by the extra White Pawn on the other wing); 2 P—R4, R—Q5; 3 R—Kt7, R—QKt5; 4 K—B2 (Despite the Pawn minus, 4 R—K7 forces the draw at once, but the move played is also good enough), P—K4; 5 K—K2, P—K5; 6 R—QB3, R—Q1; 7 P—Kt4, R—KB1; 8 R(Kt7)—B7, P—B4 (or 8 .... R—Q5; 9 R(B7)—B4, R(B1)—Q1; 10 R×R, R×R; 11 R—B4!, R—Q6; 12 R—Kt4, R—Q3; 13 R×P); 9 R—K7, P—B5!; 10 R(B3)—B7, P—B6ch; 11 K—B1, R—Q1; 12 P—Kt5 and now Black to play can compel White to take perpetual check after 12 .... P—K6!; 13 R×Pch, K—R1; 14 R—R7ch, K—Kt1. Instead Black tried 12 .... R—Q8ch? and lost after 13 K—B2, R—Q7ch; 14 K—K1, R—K7ch; 15 K—B1, P×P (the threat was 16 R—B8ch and 17 P—Kt6 mate); 16 R×Pch, Resigns. If 16 .... K—B1; 17 P—R6 and mate is forced.

Two Rooks on the seventh draw only because the enemy pieces are tied down to the defense of a vital Pawn. But where the enemy Rooks can defend the Pawn and the checks from an active position, or where counterthreats are available, the Rooks on the seventh will not save the game.

An illustration of a position which just manages to win is No. 430 (Grob-Fine, Ostend, 1937). White's conduct of the ending may be taken as a model. *1 .... K—B1* (the conbination of No. 429 does not work now: 1 .... R—Q3; 2 P—QR4, R(Q3)—Q7; 3 R×P, R×KtP; 4 R×R, R×R; 5 R—R1 and wins); *2 K—Kt2, K—K1; 3 K—Kt3,* (lifting the pin. The threat is now P—B3 and R—Kt3 followed by R—B2), *R—Q3; 4 P—QR4* (4 P—B3?, R(Q3)—Q7, threatening mate), *P—KKt4; 5 K—B3, R—B7; 6 K—Kt2, K—Q2; 7 R—Kt5, K—B3; 8 R—KB5!* (liberating the other Rook), *R×KtP; 9 R—B1ch, K—Kt2; 10 R×Pch, K—R3; 11 R—QB8, K—R4; 12 R—QB4* (again threatens mate), *K—R3; 13 R—K4* (The ending now enters its second phase: White has succeeded in freeing both Rooks and his next objective is to set up a passed Pawn on the K-side), *R—R7; 14 P—R4!, P×P; 15 K—R3, R—Q8; 16 K×P, R—R8ch* (Black has no real counterplay: he can only harass his opponent), *17 K—Kt3, P—R4* (rather exchange than lose it for nothing); *18 P×P, R×P;* Now we have an ending which is quite simple with only one Rook, but the extra pieces produce complications. *19 K—Kt4, R—KR8; 20 P—B4, R—Kt8ch; 21 K—B5, R(Kt8)—QR8; 22 R—B8!, R—QB8* (if instead 22 .... K—Kt2; 23 R—K7ch, K—B3; 24 R—B6ch, K—B4; 25 R—K5ch, K—Q5; 26 R×P, R×P; 27 R—K4ch, K—Q4; 28 R×R, R×R; 29 K—Kt5 with an elementary win (No. 330) while on 22 .... R×P; 23 R×R, R×R; 24 R—R8ch, K—Kt4; 25 R×R, K×R; 26 K—K6, P—Kt4; 27 P—B5 White queens first and wins Black's Queen by checking at R8 and Kt8); *23 R(B8)—K8, R(B8)—QR8; 24 R—Kt4!, K—Kt2; 25 R—K7ch, K—B3; 26 R—B4ch* (26 R—K6ch is not so clear), *K—Q4; 27 R—B8* (threatening mate), *K—Q5; 28 R—Q8ch, K—B6; 29 R—B7ch, K—Kt6; 30 R—QKt8, R×P; 31 R×Pch.* The rest is routine, but requires a little more care than the corresponding ending with one pair of Rooks. *K—R6; 32 R—B3ch, K—R7; 33 R—K6, R—KB8; 34 R—K4, R—R4ch; 35 K—K6, R—KR8; 36 R—K5, R—KR3ch; 37 K—B5, R—R4ch; 38 K—B6, R—QR3ch; 39 K—Kt7, R—KR8; 40 P—B5, R—QKt8; 41 R—K2ch, K—R8; 42 R—K6, R—Kt8ch; 43 K—B7, R—R2ch; 44 R—K7, R—R3; 45 R(B3)—K3* Resigns. The march of the Pawn cannot be halted.

A similar instance which is somewhat easier for the winning side is

No. 430

White wins.

No. 430a (Nimzovitch-Spielmann, Carlsbad, 1929), White: K at KKt1, R's at QR1, K4, P's at QR3, QKt4, KKt2, KR2; Black: K at QB1, R's at Q1, QKt6, P's at QB2, QB3, KR2. The game continued 1 .... R—Q7; 2 R—K7, P—R4; 3 R—B7! (to force the Rook away from the Pawn: the threat is R—B2), R(Kt6)—Kt7; 4 R—Kt7, K—Kt2; 5 P—R3, R(Q7)—QB7; 6 R—Kt5 (to prevent or at least postpone .... P—B4), K—Kt3; 7 R—KB1, P—B4; 8 R—B4!!, P—B5 (8 .... P×P; 9 P×P, R—Kt8ch; 10 K—R2, R(B7)—Kt7; 11 R×P, R×P; 12 R—B6ch is worse); 9 P—KR4 (to have an eventual flight square for his King. E.g., 9 R—B6ch, P—B3; 10 R(Kt5)—Kt6, P—R5!; 11 R×Pch, K—Kt4; 12 R—B8??, R—B8ch; 13 K—R2, R(Kt7)— Kt8 and mate is unavoidable), R—R7; 10 R—B6ch, K—Kt2; 11 R— Kt5ch, K—B1; 12 R—KKt6!, R—Q7; 13 R—QB5 (Now further simplification in White's favor will decide quickly), R(R7)—QB7; 14 R—Kt7, K—Kt1; 15 R(B5)×P, R×Pch!; 16 R×R!, R—B8ch; 17 K—B2, K×R; 18 R—Kt5!, P—B6; 19 R×P, R—KR8; 20 R— B5ch and the rest is simple.

Two Rooks on the seventh may not only compensate for the loss of a Pawn; if proper steps are not taken against them they will often win. This is especially true when there is an absolute seventh, i.e., when the King is confined to the first rank and cannot escape behind his Pawns.

An example where overcautious defense proves fatal is No. 431 (Lasker-Eliskases, Moscow, 1936). We shall follow the course of the game. *1 R—QB1!*(better than 1 R—K1, K—R1; 2 R(K1)—K7, R— KKt1; 3 R×RP, R—Q7=), *K—R1?* But now this obvious move loses. The only defense was the cold-blooded 1 ...., P—QR4!!; 2 R(B1)— B7, P—R5; 3 R×Pch, K—R1; 4 R×Pch, K—Kt1; 5 R(B7)— Kt7ch, K—B1 and White is well-advised to take perpetual check, since any winning attempt may be a boomerang. E.g.:

No. 431

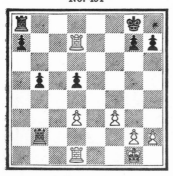
White to play.

a) 6 P—R4?, P—R6; 7 P—R5, P—R7; 8 P—R6, P—R8= Qch; 9 K—R2, R×Pch!!; 10 R×R, R—R7 and wins.

b) 6 R—R7?, R×R; 7 R×R, R —Kt6; 8 P—R4, P—R6; 9 P —R5, P—Kt5; 10 P—R6, K —Kt1; 11 P—B4 (or 11 P— Kt4, R—Kt7; 12 P—Kt5, P —R7; 13 P—Kt6, R—Kt8ch; 14 K—R2, P—R8=Q), R —B6! (now 11 .... R—Kt7? is bad: 12 P—B5, P—R7; 13 P—B6, R—Kt8ch; 14 K—

R2, P—R8=Q; 15 P—B7ch!!, K—B1; 16 R×Q, R×R; 17 P—R7 and White wins); 12 K—R2 (there is nothing to be done: if 12 K—B2, R—B7ch; 13 K—B3, P— R7; 14 P—B5, P—Kt6; 15 P—B6, R—B1! and one of Black's Pawns will queen, or 12 P—B5, P—Kt6!!; 13 R×P (on 13 P—B6, P—Kt7 Black queens with check), P—Kt7; 14 R— R8ch, K—R2; 15 R—QKt8, R—B8ch and wins the Rook), R—B3!; 13 P—Kt4, R×Pch; 14 K—Kt3, R—QKt3!; 15 P— Kt5, P—Kt6; 16 P—B5, P—Kt7 and White's Pawns are too far back to save the game.

2 R(B1)—B7, R—KKt1 (now 2 .... P—QR4, is too late. There would follow 3 R—R7!, R—QB1 (.... R×R?; 4 R—Q8 mate); 4 P— R4, P—R5; 5 R×KtP, P—R6!; 6 R×Pch, K—Kt1; 7 R(KR7)— QKt7 (holding up the advance of the Pawn and preventing the Black Rook at QB1 from going to the seventh), P—R7; 8 K—R2!, P—Kt5; 9 P—R5, P—Kt6; 10 R—Kt7ch!, K—B1; 11 R—R7, K—Kt1; 12 R(QR7)—Kt7ch, K—B1; 13 P—R6 and mate can be postponed only by problem moves); *3 R×RP, P—R3; 4 P—R4!* (not 4 R×P?, R— K1! threatening both .... **R**—K8 mate and doubling on the seventh), *P—Kt5; 5 R(R7)—Kt7, P—Kt6; 6 K—R2, R—Q7* (else simply R×QP and R(Q5)—Kt5); *7 R×KtP, R—K1; 8 R(Kt3)—Kt7!* (to reply R×KtP to .... R(K1)—K7), *R× QP* (desperation: after 8 .... R— KKt1; 9 R×QP; he is two Pawns down); *9 R×KtP, R—Q1* (or 9 .... R—K3; 10 R(KKt7)—Q7!, R—K1; 11 R—R7ch, K—Kt1; 12 R×P); *10 R—R7ch, K—Kt1; 11 R×P, R—K6; 12 R(R6)—R7, P—Q5; 13 R(R7)—Q7, R(K6)—K1; 14 P—R5!, P—Q6; 15 P—R6!* (threatening mate in four), *R×R; 16 R×R, R—K3; 17 R×P* Resigns.

With two Rooks on the absolute seventh the case is usually hopeless, especially if the King is in the center. An example is No. 431a (Eliskases-Fine, Hastings, 1936–'37), White: K at K1, R's at QKt6, K4, P's at QR5, K3, KKt3, KR2; Black: K at KB3, R's at QR7, KKt7, P's at QR3, K3, KKt2, KR2. White to play. Black wins. The game concluded: 1 R(Kt)×Pch (if 1 R(K)×Pch, K—B2 and White has no check. After 2 K—B1, R(Kt7)—QB7 the only move to stop mate then is 3 R—Kt1, which costs him a Rook), K—Kt4; 2 R(K6)— K5ch (or 2 R(K4)—K5ch, K—Kt5; 3 R—K4ch, K—R4; 4 R(K4)— K5ch, P—Kt4), K—R3; 5 R—R4ch, K—Kt3; 6 K—B1, R(Kt7)— Kt7. To stop mate White must now lose a Rook. 7 R—Kt4ch, K—B3, 8 resigns. White could have staved off mate in the beginning by 1 K—B1, but then 1 .... R×KRP; 2 K—Kt1, R (R7)— QB7; 3 R—Kt1, R×P leaves him two Pawns down with a hopeless position.

When the King is in the neighborhood there is usually no defense at all against a Rook on the absolute seventh. An example from a tournament game is No. 432 (Englisch-Gunsberg, Hamburg, 1885). After *1 R—Q1!,* threatening R—R1ch and R—QR8 mate, Black is defenseless. *1 .... R(R4)—R7* is the only chance, but then *2 R— R8ch* mates: 2 .... *K—R2* (or 2 .... R—Kt1; 3 R—R1ch, R—R7; 4 R×R mate); *3 R—Q7ch, K—R3; 4 R—R8* mate. A somewhat more complicated instance is No. 432a (Berger), White: K at QB6, R's at QR2, Q3, P at KR6; Black: K at QB1, R's at QKt5, KR1, P at KB4. White to play wins. The main variation is 1 P—R7!, K—Kt1 (the threat is R—R7—Kt7. If 1 .... R×P; 2 R—R8ch, R—Kt1; 3 R— Q8ch, K×R; 4 R×Rch, K—K2; 5 R—Kt7ch wins); 2 R—Q7, R— B5ch; 3 K—Q5, R—B8; 4 R(R2)—R7, P—B5; 5 R(Q7)—Kt7ch,

No. 432

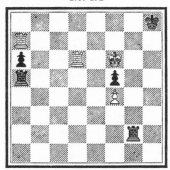

White to play wins.

No. 433

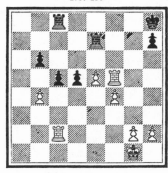

White to play wins.

K—B1; 6 R—Kt7, K—Kt1; 7 R(R7)—B7, R—Q1ch; 8 R—Q7 and wins. Still another type of mating possibility is that where the King is at R3. E.g., No. 432b (Zukertort-Steinitz, Vienna, 1882), White: K at KR3, R's at QB6, K7, P's at QR4, KB4, KKt3; Black: K at KKt1, R's at QKt7, KKt7, P's at QR4, KB2, KKt3, KR2. Black to play wins. 1 .... P—R4; 2 K—R4 (2 P—Kt4, R—R7ch; 3 K—Kt3, P—R5ch; 4 K—B3, R(R7)—B7ch; 5 K—K3, R(B7)—K7ch and wins a Rook), R—Kt6!; 3 K—Kt5 (or 3 R—B8ch, K—Kt2; 4 R(B8)—B7, R—R7ch; 5 K—Kt5, R×P mate, or 3 R—B6, R(Kt7)×P; 4 R(B6)× BP, R—Kt5 mate), K—Kt2!; 4 R×KtPch, K—B1!! and wins a Rook!

Other cases in which an extra pair of Rooks makes any difference are of little importance; a few may be mentioned briefly.

In No. 433 (Rabinovitch-Loevenfisch, Moscow, 1935) the advantage of having a Rook behind a passed Pawn is nullified. After *1 R—B6!, P—Q5* (or 1 .... R—Q2; 2 R×KtP, P—B5; 3 P—K6, R(Q2)—Q1; 4 R—Kt7!, P—Q5; 5 R—R2!, R—R1; 6 P—K7!, R—K1; 7 R×R,

R×R; 8 R—Q7 and wins); *2 R—Q6!, R(K2)—QB2; 3 P×P, P×P; 4 K—B2, R—B3; 5 R—Q5!, K—Kt2; 6 K—B3, K—B2; 7 P—Kt4, K—K2; 8 P—B5, P—R3; 9 P—R4, R—Q1; 10 P—B6ch,* Resigns. Note how the two Rooks completely blockaded the enemy Pawns—something which one Rook alone cannot do.

An example where an extra outside passed Pawn is insufficient because of the extra pair of Rooks is No. 433a (From Anderssen's games), White: K at KKt1, R's at QR1, KR2, P's at QR2, QKt2, QB2, KKt2; Black: K at QB1, R's at KKt1, KKt5, P's at QR2, QKt2, QB3. Black to play draws. 1 .... R—K5!; 2 R—KB1 (or 2 K—R1, R—K7; 3 P—KKt3, R—K6, or 2 K—B2, R—B1ch; 3 K—Kt3, R—K6ch; 4 K—Kt4, R—Kt1ch; 5 K—B4, R—K7=), R—K7; 3 R—B2 (on 3 R—QB1, K—B2 White has no way to go forward), R—K8ch; 4 R—B1, R—K7; 5 R—B2, R—K8ch, etc.

No. 434 (Euwe-Alekhine, 23rd match game, 1937) illustrates the play with disconnected vs. connected passed Pawns. Normally connected Pawns are better, but the two Rooks counterbalance this slight superiority. After *1 .... R—Kt1; 2 P—Q7, P—Kt3* (or 2 .... KR—Q1; 3 R—K3, P—R5; 4 R—Q4!, K—B1; 5 R×RP, R×KtP; 6 R(R4)—K4, R(Kt4)—Kt1; 7 R—K8ch, R×R; 8 P×R=Qch, R×Q; 9 R×P=); *3 R—K3!* is the simplest drawing line (for the game continuation see A.): *3 .... P—R5; 4 R—Q4!, P—Kt7!* (but not 4 .... R—R1?; 5 P—Kt6!, P—R6; 6 P—Kt7!, R(R)—Kt1; 7 R×P, P—R7; 8 R—R4, KR—Q1; 9 R×P, R×QP; 10 R—R8 and wins); *5 R—QKt4, KR—Q1; 6 R—Q3, R—Kt2; 7 R×KtP* (the winning attempt 7 P—Kt6, R(Q1)×P!; 8 R×R, R×R; 9 P—Kt7? wins for the wrong side: 9 .... R×P!; 10 R×R, P—R6 and one Pawn queens), *R(Q1)×P; 8 R×R, R×R=. A.* 3 R—QR1, R×P; 4 R—K8, R—Q4!; 5 R×P, R×P; 6 R×Rch, K×R; 7 R—QKt5, R—Q6; 8 R—Kt7, K—Kt2. Black has won a Pawn but the game is drawn (see No. 372).

Finally, there are some positions where the extra pair of Rooks creates winning chances which would not otherwise be present. This may occur when there are slight weaknesses on both sides of the board which one Rook alone cannot exploit. A classic example is No. 435 (Kan-Capablanca, Moscow, 1936). Here Black has an undeniable advantage because of his possession of two semi-open files

No. 434

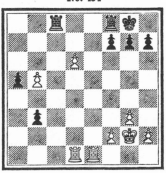

Black to play. Draw.

(see No. 409). If there were only one Rook on the board he could make use of only one of the files, but not both. With two Rooks he can attempt to use them simultaneously. We shall follow the game continuation. *1 R—Q3, P—QKt4; 2 R(B2)—Q2* (2 P—KB4, P×P; 3 R×BP, R—R5; 4 R—K3, R—B5; 5 P—B3, P—Q4 loses a Pawn), *P—B4; 3 K—B2, R—R5* (preparatory to centralization); *4 K—K2, K—B2; 5 R(Q2)—Q1, K—K3; 6 K—Q2, R—QKt1* (maneuvering); *7 R—QB3, P—Kt4!* (to break through on the K-side: the other semi-open file); *8 P—R3, P—R4; 9 R—KR1, R—Q5ch; 10 K—K2, R—KKt1; 11 R—Q3, R—R5!* (he must not yet exchange); *12 R(R1)—Q1?* (Inferior. 12 K—B2 or 12 K—K3 would have held the game more easily; now Black gets the open file), *P—Kt5; 13 RP×P, P×P; 14 K—K3* (if 14 R—KR1, P×Pch; 15 P×P, R—Kt7ch; 16 K—Q1, R—KB7 and White's pieces are tied up), *R—KR1!; 15 R—Kt3* (15 P×P? is weak: 15 .... R—KKt1; 16 K—B3, R—B1ch; 17 K—K3, R—KB5 with a clear advantage), *R—R7; 16 R—Q2, R—Q5!; 17 R—K2* (obviously he cannot afford to exchange now), *P—B3; 18 R—QB3, P—Kt6!; 19 R—Q3?* (19 P—B4! draws: 19 .... R—KR5; 20 P×P, R(Q5)×Pch; 21 K—B3, R(R5)—B5ch; 22 K×P, R—Kt5ch; 23 K—B3, R×R; 24 K×R(K2), R×Pch; 25 K—B3, R—R7; 26 K—Kt3, R—Q7; 27 P×P=), *R—R8!; 20 P—KB4, R—KB8!; 21 P—B5ch, K—B3* and now White must lose a Pawn: *22 P—B3, R×Rch; 23 K×R, P—Q4; 24 P—Kt3, P—B5ch; 25 P×BP, KtP×Pch; 26 K—K3, R—QR8!; 27 K—B3, R×P.* The rest is simple. *28 K×P* (28 R—K3, R—Kt6!; 29 K×P, P—Q5), *R×Pch; 29 K—R4, R—B8; 30 P—Kt4, R—R8ch; 31 K—Kt3, P—Q5; 32 R—QR2, P—Q6; 33 K—Kt2, R—K8; 34 K—B2, R×P;* 35 Resigns.

No. 435

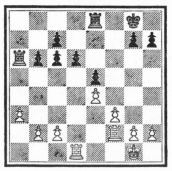

White to play.

Chapter VII

ROOKS AND MINOR PIECES

While it is customary to speak of an ending where each side has two Rooks and two minor pieces, we shall have to confine ourselves to the most indispensable positions. Anything that is more complicated may as a rule be reduced to the simpler cases contained in this book.

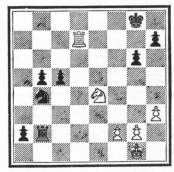

White to play draws.

White to play draws. Mate with White Pawn at KR5.

I. ROOK AND KNIGHT VS. ROOK AND KNIGHT (OR BISHOP)

The only type of position where any new element is introduced is that where the Rook is on the seventh or eighth and can conjure up threats of mate or perpetual check.

No. 436 occurs frequently. The draw is forced after *1 Kt—B6ch, K—B1* (1 .... K—R1?; 2 R×P mate); *2 Kt×Pch, K—K1; 3 Kt—B6ch, K—B1; 4 Kt—R7ch,* etc., perpetual check. The White Rook must be at Q7 here: if it were at QB7 Black could get out of checks via Q1. Thus: 1 Kt—B6ch, K—B1; 2 Kt×Pch, K—K1; 3 Kt—B6ch, K—Q1; 4 R—Q7ch, K—B1. If the Black King were at R1 in the original position, Kt—B6 would mate despite the fact that Black can queen with check.

Another kind of perpetual check with R+Kt is seen in No. 437. *1 R—B8ch, K—R2; 2 Kt—B8ch, K—Kt1; 3 Kt—K6 dis ch, K—R2;*

4 Kt—B8ch, etc. In No. 437a, White Pawn at KR5, other pieces as in No. 437, this sequence leads to mate. 1 R—B8ch, K—R2: 2 Kt—B8ch, K—Kt1; 3 Kt—Kt6 dis ch, K—R2; 4 R—R8 mate. Of course if the White Kt at KKt6 is otherwise defended the same mate follows.

There is one other position which comes up time and again—No. 438. After *1 R—B7!* Black will be mated as soon as his checks are exhausted.

No. 438

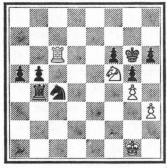

White to play wins.

No. 439

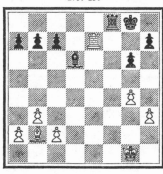

White to play wins.

II. ROOK AND BISHOP VS. ROOK AND BISHOP (OR KNIGHT)

GENERAL

There is only one position where the whole is more than simple addition of the parts: No. 439. *1 R—Kt7ch, K—R1; 2 R×KtP dis ch* mates in two more moves: *2 .... B—K4; 3 B×Bch, R—B3; 4 B×R* mate. If he is sadistically inclined, White may mop up the Q-side before putting an end to his opponent's misery: 2 R×BP dis ch, K—Kt1; 3 R—Kt7ch, K—R1; 4 R×QKtP dis ch, K—Kt1; 5 R—Kt7ch, K—R1; 6 R×QRP dis ch, K—Kt1; 7 R—Kt7ch, K—R1; 8 R×KtP dis ch, etc.

BISHOPS OF OPPOSITE COLORS

A. MATERIAL ADVANTAGE

As we saw in Chapter III a Pawn ahead in general wins with Bishops of opposite colors only if there is play on both sides of the board. For this reason a simple outside or center passed Pawn with no subsidiary weaknesses in the enemy camp only draws. With Rooks on the board however the ending is much more favorable for the winning side. We shall consider only those cases which would be drawn if the Rooks were off the board.

1. OUTSIDE PASSED PAWN

This is a draw unless play on the other wing with Rook and Bishop may be obtained. Of course this is much more frequently the case with two pieces than with only one, so that even though the game may be a theoretical draw, the defense will be far more difficult.

In No. 440 (Euwe-Alekhine, 8th match game, 1935) White has two advantages in addition to the outside Pawn: his Pawn has only one Black square to cross before queening and he can secure command of the open QB file. We shall follow the game continuation. *1 ....* *B—R2* (there is no time to get the Rook to QB2. On 1 .... R—Q1; 2 P—R6 threatens 3 R×B! and the B has to "scram."); *2 P—R6, R—Q1; 3 R—Kt2!* (just in time!), *R—Q2; 4 R—Q2ch, K—K2; 5 R—B2, R—Q3* (On 5 .... K—Q1; 6 R—B8ch, K—K2; 7 B—B6! forces the exchange of B's favorable for White. After 7 .... R—Q3; 8 R—B7ch, K—Q1 (8 .... K—B3; 9 B—K8); 9 R×B, R×B; 10 R×P the win is routine); *6 P—B4!* (threatening P—K4—K5), *P—B4* (Black cannot afford to allow his Rook to be driven away from Q3 and Q1. E.g., 6 .... R—Q1; 7 P—K4, R—Q5; 8 P—Kt3, R—Q1; 9 P—K5, R—Q5; 10 B—B6, R—Q1; 11 B—Kt5, B—Kt3; 12 R—B6, R—QKt1; 13 R×B!); *7 R—B7ch, R—Q2; 8 R—B3, R—Q3; 9 P—R4!!* Black is in zugzwang! On all waiting moves White has a forced win:

  a) 9 .... R—Q2; 10 B—B8, R—Q3; 11 R—B7ch, K—Q1; 12 R×B, K×B; 13 R×P.

  b) 9 .... R—Q1; 10 B—B8!, K—Q3 (or 10 .... B—Kt1; 11 R—B6, R—Q3; 12 R—B7ch!, K—Q1; 13 P—R7, B×P; 14 R×B, K×B; 15 R×P); 11 R—Q3ch, K—B2; 12 R×R, K×R; 13 B×P with an easy win because now there are passed Pawns on both sides.

  c) 9 .... B—Kt3; 10 R—B8, R—Q1; 11 R—B6, R—Q3 (or 11.... B—R2; 12 B—B8 as above); 12 R×B!, R×R; 13 P—R7.

No. 440

Black to play; White wins.

Since White has an easy win in all three cases, after his Pawn moves are exhausted Black will be compelled to stake everything on a counterattack. *9 .... P—Kt3; 10 R—B2, P—R4; 11 R—B3* (the simplest was 11 R—B8 for if 11 .... R—Q1; 12 R×R, K×R; 13 P—K4, K—K2; 14 P×P, KP×P; 15 K—Q3 and will win since Black must keep his King at K2 to defend the K-side Pawns and the White King can then march in. But the move chosen is more methodical and good enough.), *R—Kt3; 12 R—B7ch, K—Q3; 13 R—Kt7, R—Kt7ch; 14 K—Q3!!* (the KKtP is defended by the B), *R—R7; 15 R×P, R—R6ch; 16 K—B4, B×P; 17 B—Q5!, B×P; 18 R×Pch, K—B2; 19 R—B6ch, K—Kt1; 20 R—KKt6* (if 20 R—Kt6ch?, K—R2; 21 K—Kt5?, R—R4ch!!; 22 K×R, B—B2=), *B—B2; 21 B—Kt7, K—R2* (there is no defense: if 21 .... R—R4; 22 K—Kt4!, R—K4; 23 B—B3!, K—R2; 24 R—Kt7, K—Kt3; 25 P—R7 and wins. If here 22 .... P—B5; 23 R—Kt8ch, K—R2; 24 R—Kt7, B—Q1; 25 R—Q7, B—Kt3; 26 B—B3 dis ch, K×P; 27 B—K2 ch and mate next move); *22 R—Kt5* (wins a second Pawn: if 22 .... R—R5ch; 23 K—Kt5, R×P; 24 R—Kt8, B—Kt1; 25 B—B3 Black has to sacrifice at least a piece to avoid mate), *B—Q1; 23 R×RP, B×P; 24 R×P.* The rest is simple: with the Rooks off the board it would also be won. *24 .... K—Kt3; 25 R—Kt5ch, K—B2; 26 R—Kt3, R—R4; 27 K—Q4, B—B7ch; 28 K—K4, K—Q3; 29 R—Q3ch, K—K3; 30 B—B8ch, K—K2; 31 R—Q5, R—R5ch; 32 K—B5, B—Kt6; 33 R—Q7ch, K—B1; 34 P—R7, B—B7; 35 B—R6!* Resigns.

But if there are no such additional weaknesses the game should be drawn with best play. No. 441 (Keres-Fine, Zandvoort, 1936) may be taken as a model. *1 B—Kt4!* prevents the advance of the Pawn. To try to get the King over to the Q-side would be futile, since Black cannot cross the QB file. Nor can Black attempt to advance the QRP by .... R—Q8ch and .... R—QR8, for White would then reply R—B7 and get up a dangerous counterattack against the Black K position. Consequently the only chance is to secure some advantage on the K-side. The game continuation was *1 .... P—KR4; 2 P—R4!* (.... P—R5! would cramp him too much), *P—K4; 3 K—R2, K—Kt3; 4 K—Kt3, B—Q6; 5 R—B6, R—Kt2; 6 B—B3* (threat: 7 B×P), *B—Kt4; 7 R—B8, K—B2; 8 P—B3* (necessary to allow the K to get to the other wing if the Rooks are exchanged), *R—Q2; 9 K—B2, R—Q8; 10 R—B7ch, K—Kt1; 11 P—Kt4!* (The strongest defense. If instead 11 R—B8ch, K—R2; 12 R—B7 threatening B—Kt4—B8, then Black has a curious win in 12 .... R—QB8; 13 B—R5?, R—B8ch; 14 K—Kt3, R—QR8; 15 B—Kt4, R—R7!!; 16 B—B8, K—Kt1!!; 17 B×P, B—B8 and transposes into a won R and P ending: 18 R—B1!, R×Pch; 19 K—R3, R×B dis ch; 20 R×B, R—QR2, etc.), *R—B8ch; 12 K—Kt2?* (But this loses. 12 K—Kt3! was essential. If then 12 .... P—K5 as in the game, there is the surprising rejoinder 13 P×KP, P×P!; 14 P—K5!!, R—B6ch; 15 K×P, B—K7; 16 P×P!!! and Black has nothing to discover, so that after 16 .... P×P; 17 K—R5!! a draw must result), *P—K5!; 13 P×KP* (13 P—Kt5, P×Pch; 14 K—Kt3,

B—K7!; 15 P×P, P×P; 16 B×P, R—Kt8ch; 17 K—B2, R—Kt7ch; 18 K—K1, B—Kt4 and wins), *P×P; 14 P—K5, R—B6!* (this mating combination is disastrous for White); *15 P×P, P×P; 16 K—Kt1, B—B8!* (threatening .... P—Kt6, ... B—R6 and .... R—B8 mate so that White must beat a hasty retreat). The game would still be a draw with the Rooks off the board, but now Black has a mating attack. *17 R—B6, K—B2; 18 P—K4, P—Kt6; 19 P—K5, P×P; 20 B×P, B—R6; 21 R—B1, P—R4; 22 K—R1, P—R5; 23 B—Q4, P—R6; 24 R—B2, R—Kt6!; 25 P—R5, R—Kt8ch; 26 B—Kt1, R—Kt7; 27*

No. 441

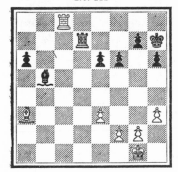

White to play. Draw.

No. 442

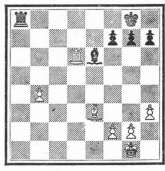

Black to play. Draw.

R—B7ch, K—K3; 28 B—Q4, R—Kt8ch; 29 B—Kt1, P—R7; 30 Resigns.

With fewer Pawns the winning prospects are even more meager. An example from a world's championship match is No. 442 (Tarrasch-Lasker, 14th game, 1908). The same considerations apply here as in the previous example: White must attempt to win on the K-side, but nothing can be forced. The game continuation was *1 .... K—B1; 2 P—Kt5, K—K2; 3 R—Q1, R—Q1; 4 R—Kt1, B—Q4; 5 B—Kt5ch, P—B3; 6 B—B4, B—Kt2; 7 R—K1ch, K—Q2; 8 R—QB1, K—K3; 9 P—Kt6, R—Q2; 10 R—K1ch, K—Q4; 11 R—K8, K—B3; 12 B—K3, B—R3; 13 R—QR8, B—Q6; 14 R—QKt8, B—R3; 15 K—R2, B—Q6; 16 P—KKt4, B—Kt3; 17 K—Kt3, P—KR4; 18 P—B4, P×P; 19 P×P, R—K2* (an inaccuracy. 19 .... P—B4 practically forces the draw); *20 R—B8ch, K—Kt2; 21 R—B3, B—K5; 22 P—B5, P—Kt3?* (Should lose. 22 .... B—Q4 was still good enough); *23 P—Kt5, R—KB2* (23 .... BP×P; 24 P—B6); *24 KtP×P??* (24 R—R3 wins, for if then 24 .... K—Kt1; 25 R—R7, R×R; 26 P×Rch, K—R1 27 P×BP, etc. Or 24 .... B—Q4; 25 P×KtP, etc.); *R×P; 25 R— B7ch, K—R3; 26 R—R7ch, K—Kt4; 27 P—Kt7, B×P* and after the exchange of the last Pawn a theoretical draw results.

2. POTENTIAL OUTSIDE PASSED PAWN

There is a great difference between this classification and the previous one because the superior side can not only try to create a passed Pawn in a favorable position, but he can also attempt to get two connected passed Pawns or to set up an unbalanced Pawn position where even the Bishop alone might win. No. 443 (Keres-Fine, Warsaw, 1935) is a rather difficult example which illustrates this point. If we remove the two RP's the game is undeniably drawn. But with the extra Pawns White is always tied down to the Q-side for fear of allowing two connected passed Pawns. The game continued *1 .... R—B5* (1 .... R—B6; 2 B—K7); *2 B—K7, B—K5; 3 R—KB2, B—Q4; 4 B—Q6, K—R2; 5 K—R3, K—Kt3; 6 P—Kt3, B—K5; 7 R—B4, P— R4; 8 R—B2, R—B6; 9 R—B4, B—B6; 10 B—K7, B—Q4; 11 R— Kt4ch, K—B2; 12 B—Q6, R—B8!* Now the following break cannot be prevented. *13 R—B4ch, K—Kt3; 14 R—Kt4ch, K—R2; 15 R— R4ch, K—Kt1; 16 R—KB4, R—QR8; 17 K—Kt4!!* (the only chance— a mating attack!), *P—Kt5!; 18 P×P, P—R5!; 19 K—Kt5, R—KKt8; 20 P—Kt4, P—R6; 21 K—Kt6, B—K5ch!; 22 R×B, P—R7; 23 R— KB4, R×Pch!; 24 R×R, P—R8= Q* and should win.

It is always wise in such endings to play aggressively and to upset the balance of the Pawn position whenever possible. E.g., No. 443a (Capablanca-Tartakover, Bad Kissingen, 1928), White: K at KKt1, R's at QR1, KB1, B at KB5, P's at QR2, QKt2, QB4, KB2, KKt2, KR2; Black: K at QB2, R's at Q1, KR1, B at KB3, P's at QR2, QKt2, QB3, KR2. White to play wins. 1 QR—Q1! (1 QR—Kt1?, R—Q7, or 1 QR—K1?, R—Q7; 2 R—K6, R—KB1!), B×P; 2 R×R, R×R; 3 B×P, R—Q5; 4 P—Kt3!, R×P; 5 P—KR4 and White won by advancing his three connected passed Pawns.

3. THE EXTRA PAWN IN THE CENTER

The situation here is worse for the superior side than that where he has the Pawn on the wing because it is much harder to get play on two wings. The best chance is to try to get two connected passed Pawns.

An example with a classic finish is No. 444 (Johner-Rubinstein, Carlsbad, 1907). White to play can draw at once by 1 P—B4! for if 1 .... P—B3; 2 P×P, P×P; 3 P—R3!, B—B1 (any other square is just as bad); 4 R×P, R—Q8ch; 5 K—R2, R×B; 6 R—K8ch, K—B2; 7 R×B=, while if 1 .... P×P; 2 B×P, P—B3; 3 P—QKt4, P—R3;

4 B—K3 the position is too simplified to offer any real chances. White instead played too passively and lost as follows: *1 P—B3?, B—K3; 2 K—B2, R—Q4; 3 P—QKt4, P—R3; 4 P—Kt3, B—Q2; 5 B—K3, P—KB4; 6 R—QB1, P—B3; 7 R—B2, K—B2; 8 K—K2* (8 R—Q2, K—K3! and if White exchanges he gives Black two connected passed Pawns), *P—Kt4; 9 B—B5, P—B5; 10 R—R2, B—B4; 11 P×P, B—Q6ch; 12 K—K1, KtP×P; 13 R—R7ch, K—Kt3; 14 R—K7, B—Kt4!; 15 R—K6ch, K—Kt2!!; 16 B—Q6, K—B2!!!; 17 R×RP, R—Q6!!!!* (the point: White gets two passed Pawns in the center); *18 K—B2, R—K6; 19 B—B5, R—K7ch; 20 K—Kt1, B—B5; 21 R×BP,*

No. 443

Black wins.

No. 444

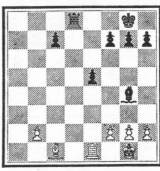

White to play. Draw.

B—Q4; 22 R—Q6, B×P; 23 P—R4, P—K5; 24 B—Q4, R—Q7; 25 B—K5, P—K6!; 26 B×P, R—Kt7ch; 27 Resigns—Black queens by force.

Summary: Material advantage is always more easily exploited with Rooks on the board. In some cases, though not all, the presence of the Rooks is the deciding factor.

B. POSITIONAL ADVANTAGE

With only Bishops on the board, the positional advantage must be quite great to be sufficient for a win. But the Rooks alter the situation and introduce two new elements: easier exploitation of weak Pawns, and mating combinations.

1. WEAK PAWNS

When there are no Rooks it is rarely possible to attack and capture enemy Pawns; even if one is won, a draw usually results. Consequently weak Pawns are fatal as a rule only if they block the action of the Bishop (see No. 214). But with Rooks the case is quite different because the Pawns can be attacked twice (B and R) or three times, (B, R and K) but defended only twice (R, K) at most.

No. 445 (Alekhine-Euwe, 21st match game, 1935) is an excellent illustration. Without the Rooks, Black could win two Pawns by .... B×BP, but the reply B—R3—B8 then gives White more than enough to draw. With Rooks Black can also win a Pawn to begin with but his position will remain just as powerful. The game continuation is exemplary: *1 .... R—Kt5!* (1 .... B×BP; 2 R—Kt3 gives White counterplay. 1 .... R×QP?; 2 R×R, R×R; 3 R—Q1 is bad for

No. 445   No. 446

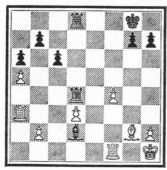

Black to play wins.   Black to play.

Black); *2 R—B2* (or 2 R—R2, R×QP; 3 R—Q1, R(Q6)—Q5), *R×KtP; 3 B—B1* (better 3 B—K4, R—Kt8ch; 4 K—Kt2, B—K6; 5 R—KB3, R—Kt7ch; 6 K—Kt3, though 6 .... B—Kt8 will still win), *R—Q5; 4 P—B5, R—B5!; 5 R×R, B×R; 6 P—R3, B—Q3; 7 R—R1, K—B2.* With so many weak Pawns the entry of the King is conclusive. Even without Rooks the win would now be only a question of time. *8 P—Q4, K—B3; 9 R—K1, B—Kt5; 10 R—R1, R—Q7; 11 B—B4, R×P; 12 B—K6, R—Q1* (preventing B—B8); 13 Resigns.

2. MATING COMBINATIONS

These occur far more frequently with opposite-colored Bishops than with those of the same color because the Bishop cannot be opposed.

One of the most common types is seen in No. 446 (Yates-Rubinstein, Moscow, 1925). Rubinstein played *1 .... R—Q7??* and lost after

2 B—Kt4!!, B—Kt3 (the threat was R—KR7 and R×P mate);
3 R×B, P×B; 4 RP×P, R—Kt7!!; 5 R—B6!! (but not 5 R×P?,
R—Kt3!; 6 R—Q7, R—Kt2; 7 R—Q8, R—Kt1; 8 R—Q6, R—Kt3,
etc.=. Now White has time to move his King and lift the stalemate),
R—Kt8; 6 R—B4! (threatening R—K4—K6), *R—K8; 7 R—K4,
R×R* (desperation. If 7 .... R—K7; 8 R—K6 wins at once); *8 P×R,
K×P; 9 P—K5!, P—B6ch; 10 K—Kt1, K—B4; 11 P—K6,* Resigns.
The correct defense was 1 .... B—K8!; 2 R—Kt2, R—Q7=.

A more complicated instance is No. 447 (Nimzovitch-Wolf, Carlsbad, 1923). Here Nimzovitch evolved the following ingenious idea:
1 P—KR4! (preventing P—Kt4), *K—Kt1* (if 1 .... R—QKt2; 2 R—

No. 447	No. 448
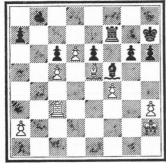	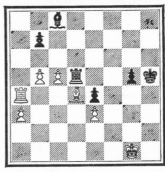
White to play wins.	Black to play draws.

Kt3! and Black cannot exchange Rooks); *2 R—QKt3, R—Q2;
3 R—Kt8ch, K—B2; 4 R—QB8, B—K5; 5 K—Kt3, P—KR4; 6 K—B2,
B—Q4; 7 K—K3, B—Kt7; 8 K—Q4, B—R8; 9 B—R8!!!* (the point
to White's plan. The idea is K—K5, B—B6—Kt5—R6 and R—B8
mate. If then in reply .... K—Kt2, R—B7 wins. Black has no
choice but to give up a Pawn), *P—K4ch; 10 K×P, B—Q4; 11 B—B6,
B—B6; 12 B—Kt5, K—Kt2* (now 13 R—B7 can be met by 13 ....
B—Kt5); *13 P—B5!!* (the coup de grace: the immediate threat is
K—K6), *B—Kt5; 14 P—B6ch, K—R2; 15 R×P* Resigns.

A mating threat may also be used as a drawing combination.
An example of this is No. 448 (Keres-Romanovsky, Leningrad-
Moscow, 1939), where the mating set-up is the same as that in No. 441.
After *1 .... B—R6; 2 R—Kt4* (trying to win. On 2 K—R2, K—Kt5;
3 R—R8, R—B4; 4 P—B6, R—B7ch; 5 K—Kt1, R—B8ch; 6 K—R2,
R—B7ch Black has perpetual check), *P—Kt5; 3 P—B6* (If instead

3 K—R2?, R—B4; 4 P—B6, K—R5; 5 R—Kt1, P—Kt6ch; 6 K—Kt1, P—Kt7; 7 K—R2, R—B8; 9 R—R1, P—Kt8=Q mate), *R—KB4; 4 B—K5!, R✕B!; 5 P✕P, R—K1; 6 R✕P, R—QKt1; 7 R—K7, P—Kt6!* (renewing the mate threat); *8 R—R7ch, K—Kt5; 9 R—Kt7ch, K—B6; 10 R—B7ch, K✕P; 11 R—KKt7, K—B5; 12 R—B7ch, B—B4; 13 P—R4, R—Q1; 14 K—Kt2, R—QKt1; 15 K—Kt1, K—Kt5; 16 R—K7, K—R6!; 17 P—R5, R—Q1; 18 R—K1, B—K5; 19 P—Kt8=Q!,* Drawn. After 19 .... R✕Q; 20 R✕B, R✕P; 21 R—K1, R✕P we have a theoretical draw.

III. ROOK VS. TWO MINOR PIECES

In the ending, two pieces are approximately equivalent to a Rook plus one Pawn. However, the nature of the Pawn configuration may force a change in this estimate. Where the Pawns are scattered, or offer convenient targets, the pieces are superior; where the Pawns are solid a Rook will usually be able to hold its own. A great deal depends on who has the initiative; this consideration is much more prominent here than in any other ending.

If there are no Pawns on the board, the game is drawn. Passing over this trivial case, these endings fall into three groups, according to the amount of material each side has.

A. EVEN PAWNS

This will usually be a draw, but the two pieces win more often than the Rook. They are especially effective when the enemy Pawns are exposed and cannot be defended with Pawns. For then the two pieces can pile up on a Pawn, which is held by R and K, and exchange B+Kt (or B+B, or Kt+Kt) for R+P, when they have in effect captured a Pawn. Sometimes the King is far away, or there are too many weaknesses, and a Pawn cannot be defended at all.

An excellent illustration of this type of position where the two pieces win is No. 449 (Marco-Blackburne, Nuremberg, 1896). One glance shows us that White's advantage is considerable. His pieces occupy excellent, impregnable squares. No open file is of any earthly use to the Rook. Black has a motley assortment of weak Pawns and is condemned to a policy of watchful waiting. The game continued as

No. 449

White to play wins.

follows: *1 P—B3* (releasing the pin and preparing to centralize his King), *R—QB1* (threatening .... R—B6 with some counterplay); *2 Kt(Kt3)—K2, P—QR4?* (suicidal. The only chance was the patient 2 .... K—Kt2; 3 K—B2, P—KR3, although after 4 K—K3, K—B2; 5 K—Q2, K—K2; 6 B—Kt3, K—Q3; 7 Kt—B4 Black is almost completely tied up and should lose in the long run.); *3 B—Q3!* (not 3 K—B2?, P×P; 4 P×P, R—B5!; 5 P—Kt5, B×P!=), *P×P; 4 P×P, R—R1* (another open file but it is just as useless as all the others); White now sets out to capture the KtP. *5 K—B2, R—R5* (this loses quickly. On 5 .... R—QKt1; 6 K—K3, K—Kt2; 7 Kt—B3 White will likewise win but it will take more time: 7 .... P—R3; 8 Kt—Q5, K—B2; 9 B—B4, K—Kt2; 10 P—Kt5, R—Kt2; 11 Kt—B6, B—K1; 12 B—Q3, B—Q2; 13 K—B4, K—B2; 14 B—K4, K—K3; 15 Kt—Q4ch, K—Q3; 16 Kt×BP, etc.); *6 P—Kt5, R—Kt5; 7 K—K3, K—Kt2; 8 Kt—B4, R—Kt7; 9 B—K2, R—Kt8; 10 Kt—Q5!, B—B1* (or 10 .... R—KR8; 11 Kt×KtP, B—K1; 12 Kt—Q5, R×P; 13 P—Kt6, R—R8; 14 P—Kt7, R—QKt8; 15 B—Kt5 and wins); *11 Kt×KtP, B—Kt2.* The rest is simple: by advancing the KtP White will capture material. *12 Kt—B4, K—B1; 13 Kt—Q6, B—R1; 14 Kt(Q4)—B5, R—Kt5; 15 P—R4, B—Q4; 16 P—R5, B—K3; 17 B—Q3, B×Kt; 18 Kt×B, K—B2; 19 B—B4ch!, K—K1* (19 .... R×B; 20 Kt—Q6ch); *20 K—Q4, R—Kt8; 21 K—B5, K—Q2; 22 P—Kt6, R—KR8; 23 P—R6, R—R4; 24 B—Kt5ch, K—B1; 25 B—Q3, K—Kt2; 26 B—K4ch, K—Kt1; 27 K—Q6, R—Kt4; 28 Kt—K7, R—KR4; 29 Kt—Kt8, P—B4; 30 B—Q5, P—B5; 31 B—K4, R—QKt4; 32 P—Kt7, K—R2; 33 Kt—B6, R—Kt3ch; 34 K—K7, R—Kt5; 35 Kt—Q7* and Black eventually gave up.

Where there are no serious weaknesses, the initiative in conjunction with the two Bishops may be decisive. No. 450 (Bernstein-Alekhine, Berne, 1932) is an example. Without any obvious blunders or even mistakes of judgment on his opponent's part Alekhine methodically conducted the game to a successful conclusion. Black first rids himself of his doubled Pawn on the Q-side, then exchanges Knights, and then creates targets for his King and Bishops. The game continued: *1 R—KR1, Kt—K4; 2 R—KB1, B—K6; 3 P—QKt3, P—QB4; 4 Kt—B1, B—Q5ch; 5 K—Q2, P—B5; 6 P—B3, B—B4; 7 P—QKt4,*

No. 450

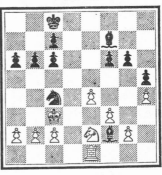

White to play; Black won.

B—B1!; 8 Kt—K2, P—QB4; 9 P—R3, K—Q2; 10 K—B2, Kt—Q6; 11 P—B4, B—K3; 12 Kt—B1, B—Kt5!; 13 Kt×Kt, B—K7; 14 Kt— K5ch, P×Kt; 15 R—B2, B—Q6ch; 16 K—Kt2, P×KtP; 17 RP×P, P×P; 18 R×P, B—Q3 (now that the position has been opened the rest is simple. White must lose at least one Pawn to begin with.); *19 R—B7ch, K—K3; 20 R—B3, B×KP; 21 R—K3, K—Q4; 22 P— Kt3, P—R4; 23 P×P, P×P;* 24 Resigns.

The side with the Rook can win only if he has the initiative and can convert that into material gain. As a rule this happens where the enemy pieces are scattered and not well coordinated.

No. 451 (Canal-Capablanca, Budapest, 1929) is an example where the two pieces are helpless because they do not work together. After *1 .... R—Kt8!; 2 B—Q5, R(B1)—Kt1; 3 K—Kt2, R(Kt1)—Kt6!; 4 R×R, R×R; 5 Kt—Q2* (5 P—QR4, R—Kt5), *R×RP* Black's two passed Pawns win: *6 Kt—K4, P—QR4!; 7 Kt×P, P×P; 8 K—B1, P—R5; 9 K—K2, R—R8; 10 Kt—Q3, P—R6; 11 P—B5, P—R7; 12 K—B3, R—Q8; 13 B×P, R×Ktch; 14 K—K4, R—Q7; 15 B—B4, K—B1!* and Black won. The speed with which the White position fell apart is rather surprising, but there does not seem to be anything that he could have done.

From this illustration we can conclude that the Rook will win if there is a distant passed Pawn which is not adequately blockaded. Since this is rather unusual, one is naturally inclined to try to set up some more general rule. One such rule is that *wherever there are two widely separated passed Pawns the Rook will win*. For two pieces can cooperate to control one given square, but not two. However, to make sure that there will be no counterplay, the above rule holds in general only when the side with the Rook is a Pawn ahead. We already know that if the two pieces are not properly coordinated material will be lost.

Another ending which helps to make this theory clearer is No. 452 (Reti-Bogoljuboff, Bad Kissingen, 1928). First of all it is evident that Black must win a Pawn, chiefly because of the unfortunate position of the White Kt. *1 .... R—QKt8; 2 Kt—K3, R×P; 3 P— R5* (else he loses this Pawn too), *P—Kt4!* (he must avoid the blockade B—Q8); *4 P×P e.p., R×P.* Now White's primary concern must be to blockade the QRP. But in addition there is an obvious target in Black's camp—the KP—and this must be kept under observation. The most logical line then was 5 Kt—B4, R—Kt5 (Black's KP is only a handicap: after 5 .... R—Kt4; 6 K—K3, R—B4; 7 K—Q3, K—B2; 8 B—Q2, K—K3; 9 B—B3 the game is a hopeless draw); 6 Kt×P, R×P; 7 Kt—B6, K—B2; 8 B—K3, K—K3; 9 K—K2, K—Q4; 10 Kt—R5, R—QR5; 11 B—Q2, K—B4; 12 K—Q3, K—Kt4;

13 Kt—Kt7 and since the Black Pawn still cannot advance a draw must result. Instead White played *5 K—K2?, R—Kt5!; 6 K—B3, K—B2; 7 B—R4, R—Kt8* (7 .... P—QR4 at once was simpler); *8 Kt—B4, K—K3; 9 B—Kt3, R—QB8!; 10 Kt—R5* (not 10 Kt×P?, R—B6ch and 11 .... R×B), *R—QR8; 11 Kt—B4, R—R5; 12 Kt—K3, P—QR4; 13 B—K1, R—R6; 14 K—K2, P—R5; 15 Kt—B2, R—QKt6; 16 B—Kt4.* Opportunity knocks twice in this ending. The forward march of the Pawn is securely stopped and Black's only chance now lies in securing threats on the K-side. *16 .... P—R4;*

No. 451

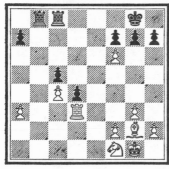

Black to play won.

No. 452

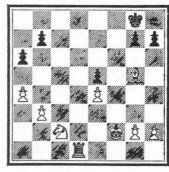

Black to play.

17 B—B8, P—Kt4; 18 P—R3, R—Kt8; 19 K—Q2, R—KB8; 20 B—B5, R—B5; 21 K—Q3, R—B2; 22 B—K3, R—Q2ch; 23 K—K2, R—KKt2; 24 P—Kt4?? (gives Black his long-sought chance to get play on the K-side. After 24 B—B1, or 24 Kt—R3 the game is drawn, since 24 .... P—Kt5; 25 P×P is meaningless), *P—R5!!; 25 B—B1, R—QB2; 26 K—Q3, R—QKt2!!; 27 B×P, R—Kt6ch; 28 K—B4, R×P* and now White must lose a piece. The remaining moves were *29 K—Kt4, P—R6!!; 30 Kt×P, R×Kt!!; 31 B×P* (31 K×R, P—R6 and queens), *R—K6; 32 K—B4, R×Pch; 33 K—Q3, R×P; 34 B—B2, K—B4; 35 K—K3, R—QR5; 36 K—B3, R—R6ch; 37 B—K3, R—Kt6;* 38 Resigns.

Where all the Pawns are on one side, without any weaknesses the game is drawn. The model for this is No. 453 (Capablanca-Lasker, St. Petersburg, 1914). The game continued *1 .... R—K7; 2 B—B2, P—B3; 3 K—B1, R—R7; 4 P—Kt4, K—B2; 5 Kt—K4, P—R3; 6 K—Kt2, R—R6; 7 P—B4, R—QKt6; 8 Kt—Kt3, R—R6; 9 Kt—*

*B1, R—Q6; 10 Kt—K3, R—B6; 11 K—B3, R—R6; 12 P—B5, R—R7;
13 Kt—Q5, R—Kt7; 14 Kt—B4, R—R7; 15 P—R4, R—R4.* After
a long series of tempo moves which are equivalent to *16 Kt—K6,
R—Kt4; 17 K—K4, R—Kt7; 18 B—Q4, R—Kt5; 19 K—Q5, R—Kt8*
Capablanca tried the break *20 P—Kt5* which is the only possible
winning chance, but still could do no more than draw. Lasker
replied *20 .... RP×P; 21 P×P, P×P; 22 Kt×Pch* (if 22 Kt×P
(Kt7), P—Kt5; 23 Kt—K6, P—Kt6; 24 Kt—Kt5ch, K—Kt1; 25 P—
B6, R—Kt4ch; 26 B—B5, R×Bch!; 27 K×R, P—Kt7; 28 Kt—B3,
K—B2=), *K—Kt1; 23 Kt—K6, R—Q8* but White can never succeed
in winning the KKtP under favorable circumstances.

No. 453

Draw.

No. 454

White wins.

B. THE PLAYER WITH THE TWO PIECES IS ONE OR MORE PAWNS AHEAD

When there are a number of Pawns on the board, two pieces plus
one Pawn vs. Rook always win. This is shown most simply by the
fact that when there is nothing else left, two pieces P still win, unless
there are a RP+B of the wrong color or two Knights.

The general case is seen in No. 454. The winning method is nothing
more than the methodical advance of the Pawn. *1 Kt—Kt2, R—
QKt5; 2 K—K3, R—Kt6; 3 P—B4ch, K—B3; 4 Kt—K1, R—R6;
5 Kt—B3, R—Kt6; 6 Kt—R2, R—B6; 7 Kt—Kt4ch, K—K3; 8 Kt—
B2!, R—R6; 9 K—B3, K—B3; 10 K—Kt4, R—Kt6; 11 Kt—K4ch,
K—K2; 12 B—K2, R—K6; 13 B—B3, R—R6; 14 P—B5, R—R3;
15 K—Kt5, R—R8* (15 .... R—R4; 16 K—Kt6 does not help any);
16 P—B6ch, K—B2; 17 B—R5ch, K—B1; 18 K—Kt6, R—Kt8ch

(if 18 .... R—R3; 19 Kt—Kt5, R—Kt3; 20 B—Kt4, R—R3; 21 B—K6 and wins); *19 Kt—Kt5, R—Kt7* or 19 .... R—KB8; 20 B—Kt4, R—B7; 21 B—R3!, K—Kt1; 22 B—K6ch, K—B1—or A—; 23 Kt—R7ch, K—K1; 24 B—B7ch, K—Q2; 25 K—Kt7, R—Kt7ch; 26 B—Kt6 and the Pawn cannot be stopped. Variation A. 22 .... K—R1; 23 B—B5, R—KKt7; 24 P—B7, R×Ktch; 25 K×R, K—Kt2; 26 B—K6 or here 23 .... R—QR8; 24 Kt—K6, R—Kt8ch; 25 K—B7, R—QR8; 26 B—Kt4, R—R2ch; 27 K—K8, R—R1ch; 28 Kt—Q8, etc.); *20 B—B3!, R—Kt8; 21 K—B5, R—KB8* (if 21 .... R—Kt6; 22 B—Q5, while if 21 .... K—Kt1; 22 B—Q5ch, K—B1; 23 Kt—R7ch, K—K1; 24 P—B7ch, etc.); *22 K—K6, R—K8ch; 23 B—K4!, R—KB8; 24 Kt—R7ch, K—Kt1* (24 .... K—K1; 25 P—B7ch, R×P; 26 B—Kt6); *25 K—K7, R—B5; 26 Kt—Kt5, R—B8; 27 Kt—K6, R—B7; 28 B—Kt6, R—B8; 29 P—B7ch, K—R1; 30 P—B8= Q, R×Q; 31 Kt×R!* (not 31 K×R stalemate) and the rest is standard.

Exceptions to No. 454 occur with RP+B of the wrong color, with two Knights, and in certain special positions where the two pieces are for one reason or another not working together satisfactorily. Such a special case is No. 454a (Fine-Appel, Lodz, 1935), White: K at QB5, R at K7; Black: K at KB4, B at Q4, Kt at KB3, P at K5. White to play draws. After 1 K—Q4! the Pawn cannot advance: 1 .... K—B5; 2 R—K5, B—Kt6; 3 R—QKt5!, B—B7 (if 3 .... B—K3; 4 R—Kt6, K—B4; 5 R—Kt1); 4 R—Kt2, B—Q8; 5 R—Kt7! (now 5 R—Kt1, B—B6; 6 R—KB1, Kt—Kt5 loses), B—R4; 6 R—K7!, B—Kt3 (there is no good alternative); 7 R—K6, K—Kt4 (7 .... K—B4; 8 R—K5ch); 8 K—K5, Kt—Kt5ch; 9 K—Q4, Kt—B7 (or 9 .... Kt—B3; 10 K—K5); 10 R×Bch and a draw was agreed to, since 10 .... K×R; 11 K—K3 is routine.

While two Knights plus Pawn only draw vs. a Rook because the Rook can be sacrificed for the Pawn, where there are more Pawns the two Knights will usually win. Such an ending is seen in No. 455 (Tchekhover-Euwe, Leningrad, 1934). We shall follow the game continuation. *1 P—B4* (there are no wholly satisfactory alternatives, e.g.:

a) 1 R—Q1, P—K4; 2 P—B4, K—Q3; 3 P—B5, Kt—B5!; 4 R—KKt1, Kt×RP; 5 R×

No. 455

White to play. Black wins.

P, K—K2; 6 R—R7, Kt—B5; 7 R×P, Kt—Q3; 8 R—R4, Kt—Kt6 and will win the KP.

b) 1 P—R4, Kt—B3!; 2 R—QR1, Kt—R4 and the RP is a constant headache.), *Kt—Kt4; 2 R—QKt1, K—B3; 3 R—B1ch, K—Q3; 4 R—Q1ch, K—B4; 5 R—KKt1, P—Kt3; 6 R—KR1, P—R4; 7 P—B5* (seeking salvation in exchanges. But the Kt's can hold everything.), *KtP×P; 8 P×P, P—K4!* (with this strong passed Pawn the win becomes routine. Of course Black takes care not to allow the exchange of BP's); *9 R—B1ch* (or 9 R×P, Kt×P; 10 R—R7, P—B3; 11 R—R6, Kt—Q4), *Kt—B5; 10 P—R4, Kt—Q3; 11 P—R5, K—Kt4; 12 P—B6, Kt×P.* Now the win is straightforward. *13 K—Kt3, Kt(R4)—B5; 14 K—R4, K—B4; 15 K×P, K—Q4; 16 K—Kt5, K—K3; 17 R—B1, Kt—K5ch; 18 K—R6, Kt×P; 19 K—Kt7, Kt—R4ch; 20 K—B8, P—B4;* 21 Resigns.

C. THE PLAYER WITH THE ROOK IS ONE OR MORE PAWNS AHEAD

Rook plus one Pawn vs. two pieces is usually a draw, though either side may have winning chances. Rook plus two Pawns always win.

When there is nothing else on the board, R+P offers no winning prospects at all, since the opponent can if he wishes even give up one of the pieces for the Pawn. With more material the game is still normally drawn, but positional considerations may weigh the scale in favor of one side or the other.

No. 456 (Flohr-Keres, Semmering-Baden, 1937) illustrates the chances and counterchances. White must rely first on his KBP which will eventually be passed and second on the attempt to win material by aiming at some weak point (e.g., QB6). But for the time being neither of these ideas can be realized successfully. For if:

No. 456

White to play.

a) 1 B—R4, P—KR4!; 2 Kt—Kt6! (2 Kt×BP??, P—R5; 3 K—B1, P—R6; 4 K—Kt1, P—R7ch; 5 K—R1, R—KB1; 6 Kt—K7, R×P; 7 Kt×Pch, K—Kt2: 8 B—Q7, R×P and Black has all the winning chances—9 P—K4?, R—Q7, or 9 Kt—B6, P—R4; 10 P—K4, P—R5; 11 P—K5,

P—R6; 12P—K6, R—K7, etc.), R—R3; 3 Kt—K5, P—R5! (better than 3 .... P—B4; 4 Kt—Q7ch, K—R4; 5 Kt×P, P—R5; 6 B—Kt3, P—R6; 7 B×P, P—R7; 8 B—R1 and White should win); 4 B×P, R×B!; 5 Kt×R, K×Kt; 6 K—B3, K—Kt4!; 7 K—Kt4, K—B5; 8 P—B4!, P×P; 9 P×P!, K×P; 10 K×P, K—K5; 11 K—Kt5!. P—Q5; 12 P—B5 and the resultant Q ending is drawn.

b) 1 P—B4??, P×P; 2 P×P, R—K1. Good (K)night! Consequently White must improve his position before he can make any winning attempt. Black's prospects, on the other hand, lie first in his passed KRP, and second in securing a passed Pawn on the Q-side. The first is of more defensive than offensive value, for White can easily blockade the Pawn, while the second cannot be forced. We must conclude then that White has the better of it and that Black may well be satisfied with a draw. The game continued *1 Kt—Kt6, R—QKt1!; 2 K—B3* (hoping to stop the KRP and capture the QBP, but Black has enough counterplay on the Q-side. The alternative 2 Kt—K5, K—B2; 3 B—Kt3, P—QR4; 4 K—Q3, R—KB1!; 5 K—K2, R—QKt1 is no improvement, since the winning attempt 6 P—B4?, P×P; 7 P×P, R—Kt5 is far too dangerous: 8 K—Q3, P—R5; 9 B—Q1, P—R6; 10 K—B3, R—Kt7; 11 B—Kt3, P—R4, etc.), *P—B4!* (threat-ning to secure another passed Pawn, so that White has no time for K—Kt4—R5. E.g., 3 K—Kt4?, P—B5!; 4 K—R5, K—B2; 5 K×P, R—Kt7; 6 B—B5, R×BP; 7 K×P, P—B6 and Black will win); *3 Kt—K5, R—Q1; 4 P×Pch, K×P; 5 B—Kt3!* (fastening on the new target. 5 Kt—B7?, R—KB1; 6 B—Kt6, K—Kt5; 7 K—Kt4, K—R6; 8 P—B4, P×P; 9 P×P, P—QR4 is much too dangerous), *R—K1; 6 Kt—Q3ch, K—Q3; 7 Kt—Kt4* (leads to simplification, but 7 K—Kt3, P—QR4 offers no real winning chances), *P—QR4!; 8 Kt—B2* (8 Kt×P?, P—R5; 9 B×P, R—B1ch; 10 K—K4, R×P; 11 B—Kt3, P—Kt5 should win for Black because his Pawns are unimpeded), *R—B1ch; 9 K—Kt2, R—QR1!; 10 Kt—Q4, P—R5; 11 B—Q1, K—B4* (or 11 .... P—R6; 12 B—Kt3); *12 P—R3, K—B5; 13 Kt—B6, K—B6; 14 B—B3.* Here a draw was agreed to. A likely conclusion is 14 .... K—Kt7; 15 B×P, K×P; 16 P—B4, P×P; 17 P×P, K—Kt7; 18 K—Kt3, P—R6; 19 K—R4, P—R7; 20 B×P, K×B; 21 K—R5, K—Kt6; 22 Kt—K5, etc.

The Rook is seen at its best when (as above, Nos. 451, 452) there are passed Pawns on both sides of the board. Two Rooks may be superior to R+B+Kt when they have strong files at their disposal. This type of advantage is seen in No. 457 (Pillsbury-Tarrasch, Vienna, 1898). Pillsbury's winning continuation is as simple as it is

No. 457

Black to play. White wins.

convincing. *1 .... B—B1; 2 R—Q4* (threatening to threaten R×P), *P—Kt3* (if 2 .... K—Kt1; 3 R—K5, P—Kt3; 4 R—QB4, Kt—R5; 5 P—QKt3, Kt—B6; 6 R—B6, etc., much as in the game); *3 R(K1)—Q1, Kt—Kt2* (Black cannot afford to allow the exchange of Rooks because he would then lose one of his Q-side Pawns. E.g., 3 .... R—Kt1; 4 R—Q8, R×R; 5 R×R, K—Kt2; 6 R—Kt8, Kt—R5; 7 P—Kt3, Kt—B6; 8 R—Kt6. The counter-combination 8 .... Kt—K7ch; 9 K—B1, Kt—Q5 is of no use because he will have to give up a piece for White's passed RP); *4 R—Q7!* (a nice tactical point), *R—Kt1* (on 4 .... Kt×P there is the pretty refutation 5 R—QB7!! threatening R—Q5. 5 .... R—Kt1 is forced, when 6 R—Q5, R—Kt4; 7 R—Q8, K—Kt1; 8 R(B7)—B8 wins a piece); *5 R(Q1)—Q5, K—Kt1; 6 K—B1, Kt—B4; 7 R—R7, R—B1; 8 P—KKt3, B—Kt2; 9 P—Kt3, B—B1* (he has little choice: on Kt moves the RP and the game fall together. If the Bishop sticks to the long diagonal P—KR4—R5 induces a fatal weakening of the K-side Pawns); *10 P—R4, R—B3* (passive play is hopeless: 10 .... K—R1; 11 P—R5, K—Kt1! 12 P×P, P×P; 13 K—Kt2, K—R1; 14 R—Q4, Kt—K3; 15 R—Q1!, Kt—B4; 16 R—R1ch, K—Kt1; 17 R(R1)—R7, etc., as in the game); *11 R—Q8, R—B3; 12 R—Kt8, P—B5; 13 R—Kt6, R—B4; 14 P—Kt4.* Puts an end to Black's attack. The rest is easier. *14 .... R—Q4; 15 K—Kt2* (the threat was .... P—B6), *R—Q5; 16 R—Kt8* (intending 17 R(R7)—R8, Kt—K3; 18 R×RP, or 17 .... Kt—Q2; 18 R—Q8), *R—Q2; 17 R×R, Kt×R; 18 R—Kt7, Kt—B4; 19 R×KtP.* After the loss of this second Pawn Black might just as well resign since he must lose a piece to stop White's passed Pawn. The remaining moves were *19 .... B—Q3; 20 R—Kt6, B—K2; 21 P—QKt4, Kt—R5; 22 R×RP, B×P; 23 R—R8ch, K—B2; 24 P—R6,* Resigns.

Rook plus two Pawns vs. two minor pieces is always a win, subject to the inevitable exceptions of blockade and special cases, such as drawn R+P vs. B or Kt endings (see Nos. 472, 473, 505, 506).

The general case when there is no other material on the board is seen in No. 458 (Steinitz-Zukertort, 13th match game, 1886). The game continuation was *1 .... B—Q5?* when White wins by force: *2 K—R6, B—Kt2ch; 3 K—R7, B—Q5; 4 P—Kt6ch, K—B3; 5*

R×Kt!, K×R; 6 P—Kt7, etc.
But against the best defense *1 ....
B—Kt2!* White cannot force his
King through to R6 because he
cannot gain a tempo with his Rook.
On 2 R—B7, B—K4; 3 R—R7,
B—Q5; 4 R—Q7, B—K4! follows,
for if now 5 K—R6?, K—K1 =.
There remains then the alternative
of trying to force the advance of
the Pawns. While this is a
long and arduous process, analysis,
chiefly by Berger, shows that it can
be done. After 1 .... B—Kt2;

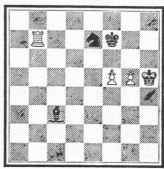

White wins.

the most forceful win is *2 K—Kt4!*
(not 2 R—Kt5, B—Q5; 3 K—R6?,
Kt—Kt1ch; 4 K—R7?, Kt—B3ch!!; 5 P×Kt, B—K6!! = because the
White King is trapped in the corner), *B—B6* (The White King is
trying to reach K4. On other B moves K—B3—K4 at once may
follow); *3 R—Kt3!* (now 3 K—B3?, B—Q7! is useless for White),
B—Kt2 (the alternatives are:

a) 3 .... Kt—Q4; 4 K—B3, K—K2; 5 K—K4, K—Q3; 6 R—
   QR3, K—B3; 7 R—R6ch, K—B4; 8 P—B6.

b) 3 .... B—K4; 4 R—Kt5, B—B6; 5 R—Kt7!, B—K4; 6 K—B3,
   B—B6; 7 K—K4, B—Q7; 8 P—Kt6ch, K—B3 (8 .... K—B1;
   9 K—K5); 9 R—Kt6ch, K—Kt2; 10 P—B6ch!!, K×P; 11
   P×Kt dis ch, K—B2; 12 R—K6!, K—K1; 13 K—B5, B—Kt5;
   14 R—K4, B×P; 15 K—K6 with a standard win (No. 466));
4 K—B4 (not 4 P—B6?, B×P!; 5 R—KB3, Kt—Kt1; 6 P×B,
K—Kt3!; 7 P—B7, Kt—R3ch and 8 .... Kt×P=), *B—R1;
5 K—K4, B—Kt2.* Now that the King is centralized White
can set about advancing his Pawns. *6 R—Kt6, B—B6* (If
instead 6 .... B—R1; 7 P—Kt6ch, K—B1—or A—; 8 R—
Kt8ch, K—Kt2; 9 K—B4 followed by K—Kt5. Variation A.
7 .... K—Kt2; 8 R—Kt8, Kt—Kt1; 9 K—K5, Kt—B3;
10 R×B, etc.); *7 P—B6, Kt—Kt3* (or 7 .... Kt—B1; 8 R—B6,
or 7 .... B×P; 8 R×Bch, K—Kt2; 9 R—QR6, or finally
7 .... Kt—Kt1; 8 K—B5 and neither sacrifice 8 .... Kt×P;
9 P×Kt nor 8 .... B×P; 9 P×B, Kt—R3ch; 10 K—Kt5 is of
any use); *8 R—Kt7ch, K—K3* (8 .... K—K1; 9 K—B5 is
worse); *9 R—KKt7!, Kt—R5* (on other Kt moves 10 R—K7ch
and 11 K—B5 follows); *10 R—K7ch, K—Q3; 11 R—KR7,
Kt—Kt3; 12 K—B5, Kt—B1; 13 P—Kt6!* and Black must give
up both pieces for the two Pawns.

If the Pawns are further back, a methodical advance will get them to their goal. Disconnected Pawns win even more easily because both pieces are needed to stop one Pawn. The King and Rook then support the advance of the other Pawn. If one piece alone stops a Pawn, the Rook can force its sacrifice and then go back to the other wing. Of course drawn positions with R+P vs. B or Kt must be avoided. Where there is additional material the win is much easier because a piece sacrifice is then unavailing.

Summary: Two pieces plus one Pawn always win against a Rook. Rook plus one Pawn vs. two pieces is normally a draw, while Rook plus two Pawns vs. two pieces is always won. With more material on the board, positional considerations may alter these rules.

IV. THREE PIECES VS. TWO ROOKS

This is normally a draw, but in favor of the pieces because they have more play. With a Pawn to the good the pieces will win. One example will illustrate this point. No. 459 (Capablanca-Alekhine, Nottingham, 1936). The pieces are highly effective here because Black's Pawns offer so many convenient targets and because the Black Rooks are so passive. The game continued *1 Kt—Q2!* (threatening Kt—K4—B3—Q5 which would tie Black down to the defense of the QKtP), *P—B4* (on 1 .... P×P; 2 P×P, P—QR4; 3 P—Kt5!, P—R5; 4 Kt—Kt1! Black must defend his KtP and still has no real counterplay); *2 P—Kt5!* (fixing the Q-side Pawns), P—QR4 (2 .... P×P?; 3 P×P, R—Q1; 4 B—Q5ch is much worse); *3 Kt—B1, K—B2; 4 Kt—Kt3, K—Kt3* (on 4 .... K—K3; 5 B—R3 Black's King cannot move any nearer the Q-side); *5 B—B3, R—K2; 6 K—B1, K—B3; 7 B—Q2, K—Kt3; 8 P—QR4.* Here the game was adjourned and Alekhine resigned without resuming play. The reason is that he

No. 459

White to play wins.

has no counterchances whatsoever and is defenseless against the White threats. A likely conclusion would be *8 .... R—K3; 9 B—B3, R—K2; 10 P—R4, R—K3; 11 P—R5ch, K—R3; 12 K—Kt2, R—K2; 13 K—R3, R—K3; 14 K—R4, R—K2; 15 B—KKt2, R—Q2; 16 B—R3, R(Q2)—KB2; 17 B—QKt2* and Black is in zugzwang so that he must lose at least a Pawn and the exchange. After the further 17 .... R—K2; 18 Kt×Pch, R×Kt; 19 B×R, R—K7; 20 B—B6, R—QR7 (the only chance); 21 B—Kt5ch,

K—Kt2; 22 P—R6ch he must also lose the KRP, since 22 ....
K—Kt1; 23 B—K7!, R×RP? allows mate in two: 22 B—K6ch and
23 B—B6 mate. Note the helplessness of the Rooks in this ending.

V. THE ADVANTAGE OF THE EXCHANGE

A. ROOK VS. BISHOP (NO PAWNS)

In the general case (pieces arbitrarily placed) this is a draw. It can
be won by force only if the Black King is in the "wrong" corner or in
the center with his opponent having the opposition.

The "wrong" corner is that which has the same color as the Bishop;

No. 460

Draw.

No. 461

White to play wins.

the "right" corner is of the opposite color.

It is always possible to force the King to the side of the board
by successively pinning the Bishop. But the Black King should head
for the right corner as fast as his legs will carry him, and once arrived
there nothing can happen to him. The normal draw is seen in No.
460. The Bishop may be anywhere where it does not allow mate or
capture. The attempt *1 R—R8ch, B—Kt1* leads to nothing because
2 K—Kt6 or 2 R—Kt8 both stalemate.

Though this position is a fairly easy draw, there are a number of
traps into which the unwary may fall. All of these arise when the
Bishop cannot get back to the square directly next to the King. An
example is No. 461 (Maestre, 1939). Here there are two solutions:

I. *1 R—Q4!* and Black is in zugzwang!

  a) 1 .... B—Kt5 or 1 .... B—Q2, 2 R×B. b) 1 .... B—B4
  or 1 .... B—K3, 2 K×B. c) 1 .... B—B1; 2 R—Q8ch

and 3 R×B.   d) 1 .... B—Kt7; 2 R—Kt4ch and 3 R×B.
e) 1 .... B—B8; 2 K—Kt6! and either mates or if 2 ....
K—B1; 3 R—B4ch and wins the Bishop.   f) 1 .... K—B1;
2 R—Q8 mate.   g) 1 .... K—R1 or 1 .... K—R2, 2 R—
R4ch and 3 R×B.   An interesting illustration of the power
of the centralized Rook!

II. *1 R—K8ch, K—R2; 2 R—K7ch, K—Kt1* (on 2 .... K—R1;
3 K—Kt6 wins at once. If 2 .... K—R3 White wins as follows:
3 R—K3!, B—Kt5 (best); 4 R—K1!, B—B6; 5 R—KB1!, B—
B3!; 6 R—QB1, B—B6; 7 R—B3, B—Kt5; 8 R—B2!, B—R4;
9 R—KR2 and the Bishop must go); *3 K—Kt6!* (3 R—Kt7ch,
K—R1; 4 R—Kt1!, B—Q2!; 5 K—B7, B—B3! does not win),
K—B1 (forced); *4 R—K3, B—Q2; 5 K—B6, K—Kt1* (on a B
move the Rook attacks the B and gets to the eighth with tempo.
E.g., 5 .... B—Kt5; 6 R—KKt3, B—K7!; 7 R—Kt2!, B—
B6!; 8 R—KB2! and now both 8 .... B—K5 and 8 .... B—
Kt5 are out because of the discovered check, so that Black
must submit to the inevitable: 8 .... B—B3; 9 R—B2, B—
Q2; 10 R—QKt2!, B—K1; 11 R—Kt8 or here 10 .... K—Kt1;
11 R—Kt8ch, K—R2; 12 R—Kt7); *6 R—Kt3ch, K—R1* (again
on 6 .... K—B1; 7 R—QKt3 wins as in the last note); *7 K—
B7!!, K—R2* (or 7 .... B—B4; 8 R—Kt8ch, K—R2; 9 R—
Kt5); *8 R—Kt7ch!!, K—R3* (a cruel dilemma: on 8 .... K—
R1; 9 R—Kt5! leaves him defenseless against the mate);
9 K—B6! (now we have the same position as in the note to
Black's 5th move), *B—B3; 10 R—QB7, B—B6; 11 R—B3,
B—Kt7* (or 11 .... B—Kt5; 12 R—B2); *12 R—B2, B—B6;
13 R—R2ch, B—R4; 14 R—R1.*   For a fuller analysis of this
position see No. 466.

With the King in the other corner, Black loses because he has an
extra move with his Bishop.   Thus in the case analogous to No. 460,
No. 462, White wins as follows: *1 .... K—Kt1; 2 K—Kt6, B—Kt5;
3 R—KKt7, B—K3; 4 R—K7, B—Kt5; 5 R—K8ch, B—B1; 6 R—
KR8, K—R1; 7 R×B* mate.   The difference is manifest: in the right
corner a tempo move by the Rook stalemates Black; in the wrong
corner it does not.   Often the position is not quite so clearcut.
E.g., if the White Rook is at KKt7 in No. 462, Black to play can draw
by 1 .... K—Kt1; 2 K—Kt6, K—B1; 3 K—B6, K—Q1; 4 K—Q6,
K—K1 and now 5 K—K6 is impossible.   The crux of the matter lies
in whether White can secure a position where a check on the eighth
(or on a Rook file) would be mate and it is his turn to move.   He can
then gain the needed tempo for the mate threat by attacking the B.
One further illustration will make this all-important point clearer.

In No. 463 Black loses because his King cannot escape the noose and he is confined to B moves. The best defense is *1 .... B—R7!* (so that White cannot threaten mate and attack the Bishop simultaneously); *2 R—QR3, B—Kt8* (2 .... B—B5; 3 R—R4, or 2 .... B—Q4; 3 R—R5, B—B2; 4 R—KB5, B—Kt3; 5 R—B6, etc.); *3 R—QKt3, B—B7; 4 R—Kt2, B—Q6; 5 R—Kt8!* and now 5 .... K—R6; 6 R—Kt3 loses the Bishop, so that Black must again move the B and loses after *5 .... B—B4; 6 R—R8ch, B—R6; 7 R—R7, K—R8; 8 R×B* mate. White to play wins with the Rook anywhere else on the board. However, if his Rook is at KB1 the win is rather difficult. No. 463a (Maestre, 1939), White: K at KB2, R at KB1; Black: K at KR7,

No. 462

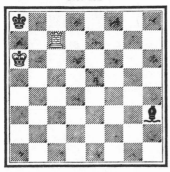

White wins.

No. 463

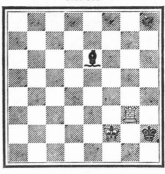

White wins regardless of whose move it is.

B at KB4. White to play wins. 1 R—KKt1, K—R6 (or 1 .... B—K5; 2 R—Kt4); 2 K—B3, K—R7 (2 .... K—R5; 3 K—B4, B—R6; 4 R—R1); 3 R—Kt3, B—K5ch; 4 K—B2 and we are back to No. 463. But No. 463b, Black Bishop at KB2 or KR4, other pieces as in No. 463a, is drawn because White cannot force the winning position: e.g., 1 R—KKt1, K—R6 and 2 K—B3 is impossible so that Black can get back to the right corner.

Where no immediate mate is threatened White will win only if he can transpose into Nos. 462 or 463. This is seen in No. 464 (Maestre, 1939). Here White to play wins only if his Rook can get to one of five different squares:

1. *1 R—QKt6, B—Kt7ch; 2 K—B7* as in No. 463.
2. *1 R—QKt2, B any; 2 R—QKt6*, again No. 463.
3. *1 R—QR2ch, K—Kt1; 2 R—QKt2ch, K—B1; 3 R—KB2.*
4. *1 R—KKt3, K—Kt1* (or 1 .... B—K7; 2 R—QKt3! and 3 R—

QKt6); *2 R—Kt7, B any; 3 R—QB7* followed by 4 K—Kt6 when we have No. 463.

5. *1 R—Q2, B—B5* (if 1 .... B—R6 or 1 .... K—Kt1, then 2 R—QKt2 as in 3)); *2 R—QKt2, K—R3; 3 R—Kt4 and wins.*

Where the King is not yet confined to the corner, the game is always drawn. An example is No. 465 (Maestre, 1939). The best try is *1 R—K3,* when *1 .... B—Kt3!* is the only reply (if, e.g., 1 .... B—B7 or Kt8, 2 R—K7ch, K—Kt1; 3 K—Kt6 or 3 K—B6 wins because the King cannot escape); *2 K—B6, K—Kt1* (not 2 .... B—R4?; 3 K—B7! or 2 .... B—B4; 3 R—K7ch); *3 K—Q7* (3 R—K6, B—R4=. Black always moves the Bishop to a square from which he can

No. 464   No. 465

White to play.   Draw.

check the White King away from QB6 and allow his own King to escape via R3 and R4), *K—Kt2; 4 R—QKt3ch, K—R3!*=(but not 4 .... K—R2?; 5 K—B7! and wins because 5 .... K—Kt3; 6 R—Kt6ch loses the B). Of course there are some special positions here where Black is lost because he does not have enough squares for his Bishop. E.g., No. 465a (Dehler, 1909), White: K at KKt4, R at QR1; Black: K at KR2, B at QKt1. White to play wins! 1 K—B5, K—Kt2 (the B has no moves for if 1 .... B—B2; 2 R—R7 and if 1 .... B—Kt6; 2 R—R1ch, K—Kt2; 3 R—KKt1); 2 R—QKt1, B—R7; 3 R—Kt2!, B—Q3; 4 R—Kt7ch, K—B1 (forced, since 4 .... K—R3; 5 R—Kt6 wins the B); 5 K—K6, B—B4 (or any other square: the winning combination cannot be prevented); 6 R—B7ch, K—Kt1 (if 6 .... K—K1; 7 R—B7, B—Kt3; 8 R—B8ch, B—Q1; 9 R—R8); 7 K—B6, B—Q5ch; 8 K—Kt6 and again we have No. 463.

With the Kings in the center (B,K,Q files or 3–6 ranks) White can win only if his King bars his rival's exit to the second rank (or Kt file), so that a Rook check on the eighth rank (or R file) would be mate. A model case is seen in No. 466 (Kling and Horwitz, 1851). The idea is the same as that encountered in a number of previous instances: to gain a tempo for the mate threat by attacking the B. Here the solution is *1 R—Kt3, B—K5* (the best chance. If 1 .... B—Q4, 1 .... B—B3, 1 .... B—Kt2, 1 .... B—R1 or 1 .... B—R8, then the reply 2 R—Q3, or 2 R—QB3, or 2 R—QKt3, or 2 R—QKt3!, or 2 R—KR3, respectively, gets the Rook to the eighth without allowing the King to move. The only variation worth mentioning is 1 .... B—B3; 2 R—QB3, B—Q2; 3 R—QKt3! and the B must

No. 466

White to play wins.

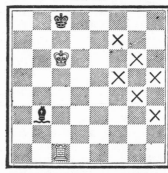

No. 467

White to play. Draw with Bishop on any marked square regardless of position of White Rook, provided no checkmate or capture is possible.

play, for if 3 .... K—K1; 4 R—Kt8ch and if 3 .... K—Kt1; 4 R—Kt8ch, K—R2; 5 R—Kt7, winning the B in both cases); *2 R—K3, B—Kt7!* (or 2 .... B—R2; 3 R—QKt3! and if 3 .... K—Kt1; 4 R—Kt8 mate); *3 R—K2, B—B6; 4 R—KB2!, B—B3* (his last feeble chance. On 4 .... B—K5 or 4 .... B—Kt5, 5 K—K5 or 5 K—Kt5 dis ch wins the B); *5 R—QB2, B—Q2* (5 .... B—Kt2; 6 R—QKt3); *6 R—QKt2!, B—B3* (K moves also lose the B); *7 R—Kt8ch, K—B1; 8 R—R8, K—Kt1; 9 R×Bch* and mates in two.

Any Rook position except that at KKt6 will win in all cases. With the Rook at KKt6, the Black B at QB3, QB1 or QR3 draws. E.g., No. 466a, White: K at KB6, R at KKt6; Black: K at KB1, B at QR3. Draw. 1 R—Kt7, K—K1; 2 K—K6, B—B5ch and the King can be confined to the eighth rank only by the combined efforts of

King and Rook. If the Kings are at Q6 and Q1 we get similar variations.

Where the White King is on a White square the case is far more difficult because only about half the possible positions win. No. 467 is given by Maestre (1939). With the Bishop on any square as shown the game is drawn. E.g., in the position given *1 R—QR1, K—Q1; 2 K—Q6, K—K1.* Or White Rook at QB5, Black Bishop at KKt3. 1 R—K5, ˙B—B2; 2 R—K7, B—R4; 3 R—KR7, B—B6ch; 4 K—Q6, K—Kt1, etc. A trap here is 3 K—Q6, B—Kt5?; 4 R—B7ch! and 4 .... K—Q1 gives No. 466, while 4 .... K—Kt1; 5 K—B6 and 6 K—Kt6 gives No. 463. The correct reply is 3 .... K—Kt1 and if 4 R—QB7, B—B6! To have the B on some other square would not necessarily lose, but might give rise to lost positions. E.g., No. 467a, White Rook at QKt7, Black Bishop at Q6, Kings as in No. 467. White to play wins. 1 R—B7ch and since 1 .... K—Q1; 2 R—Q7ch loses the B, 1 .... K—Kt1 is forced, when 2 K—Kt6 wins as in No. 463. Or No. 467b, White R at QB2, Black B at KB8, Kings as in No. 467. 1 R—KB2 wins at once.

With the King at K6 we get similar results. No. 467c (Maestre, 1939), White: K at K6, R anywhere provided it cannot checkmate or capture a B; Black: K at K1, B at KR4, KB6, KB8, Q6, QKt2, QKt4, QR3, QR5. Draw. The variations are similar to those in No. 467. E.g., White Rook at K5, Black Bishop at QR3. 1 R—QR5, B—B5ch or 1 R—QB5, K—Q1; 2 K—Q6, K—K1.

The point in all these examples is that if the Rook can attack the Bishop and threaten mate *and* prevent a B check, White wins; if not the game is a draw.

B. ROOK PLUS PAWN VS. BISHOP

No. 468

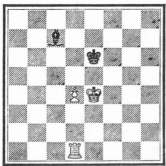

White wins.

As is to be expected this is a win, but there are some special drawing positions which must be avoided, and some unforeseen difficulties may arise especially with the RP. The investigations of Philidor, Lequesne, Centurini, v. Guretzky-Cornitz, Berger and others have practically reduced this finale to a mathematical exercise.

First of all the general win is seen in No. 468 (Philidor, 1777). The idea is to get the King to the sixth rank after which the Pawn advances and the finish is routine. *1 R—QR1, B—Kt6* (or any other square); *2 R—R6ch, B—Q3; 3 R—Kt6.* This is the *key maneuver:* whenever the B is pinned the R tempoes and allows the King to come forward. *3 .... K—Q2; 4 K—Q5, B—Kt6; 5 R—Kt7ch, K—B1* (or 5 .... B—B2; 6 R—R7); *6 R—KB7, B—R7; 7 K—B6, K—Q1; 8 P—Q5, K—K1; 9 R—KR7, B—K4; 10 P—Q6, K—Q1; 11 R—QR7, K—K1; 12 R—R8ch, K—B2; 13 P—Q7,* etc.

With a B of the other color the win may be somewhat more difficult. No. 468a (Berger), White: K at Q3, R at KB8, P at Q4; Black: K at Q3, B at QKt6. The winning idea now is different: sacrifice of the Rook at the appropriate moment. *1 R—B6ch, K—Q4; 2 K—B3, B—Q8!; 3 R—B2!, B—Kt5; 4 R—B8, K—Q3; 5 R—Q8ch, K—K2; 6 R—KKt8, B—K3; 7 R—KKt6, K—Q3; 8 K—Kt4, K any; 9 R×B, K×R; 10 K—B5, K—Q2; 11 K—Q5* and White has the opposition so that the Pawn will queen.

If the Pawn has been advanced to the fifth too hastily (e.g., 1 P—Q5ch in No. 468) the ending is still won but far more difficult. No. 468b (v. Guretzky-Cornitz), White: K at K4, R at Q1, P at Q5; Black: K at Q2, B at QB2. White wins. The idea is this: White must get his King to K5 or QB5 and then either play his Rook to the seventh or advance P—Q6. To effect this combination he must force the Bishop into a position from which it will not be able to check the King away from one of the two vital squares. The solution is 1 K—Q4 (there are various alternative sequences which are equally good), B—Kt6; 2 R—QR1, B—B5; 3 R—R7ch, K—Q3; 4 R—R6ch, K—Q2; 5 R—KB6, B—B8 (The alternatives are:

a) 5 .... B—Q7; 6 R—B2, B—K8; 7 R—B7ch, K—Q3; 8 R—B6ch, K—Q2; 9 K—B5.

b) 5 .... B—Kt4; 6 R—KKt6, B—B8; 7 R—Kt7ch, K—Q3; 8 R—Kt2, B—B5; 9 K—K4, B—B8; 10 R—QR2, B—Kt4; 11 R—R6ch, K—Q2; 12 K—K5.

c) 5 .... B—R7; 6 R—KKt6, B—B5; 7 R—Kt4 as in b).

d) 5 .... B—Kt1; 6 R—B7ch, K—Q3; 7 K—B4, B—B2; 8 R—B6ch, K—K2; 9 R—KKt6, B—Q3; 10 K—Kt5, K—Q2; 11 R—Kt7ch, B—K2; 12 K—Kt6, K—Q3; 13 R×B!, K×R; 14 K—B7 and queens); 6 R—B2!, B—R6; 7 R—QR2, B—Kt5; 8 R—QKt2, B—R6; 9 R—Kt7ch, K—Q3; 10 R—Kt6ch, K—B2 (10 .... K—Q2; 11 K—K5); 11 R—QR6, B—B1; 12 K—K5, B—Kt2ch; 13 K—K6, etc.

If the Pawn is still on the second or third rank, one may have to maneuver a bit before being able to advance. E.g., No. 468c (v. Guretzky-Cornitz), White: K at Q1, R at QKt3, P at Q2; Black: K at Q5, B at KB4. White wins. *1 R—Kt8, B—Kt5ch; 2 K—B1,*

B—B4; 3 R—Q8ch, K—B5; 4 K—Q1, B—Q6; 5 K—K1, B—B4; 6 K—B2, B—Q6; 7 K—K3, B—B4; 8 P—Q4, etc.

Once the Pawn has reached the sixth ahead of the King, complications may arise. The winning stratagem then involves the sacrifice of the Pawn at an appropriate moment. This is seen in No. 469 (v. Guretzky-Cornitz). Here the solution is *1 R—Kt4, B—R3* (if the B stays on the KKt1—QR7 diagonal the R goes over to the other side: 1 .... B—B2; 2 R—Kt4, B—R7; 3 R—Kt8ch, K—Q2; 4 R—Kt7ch, K—Q1; 5 P—Q7, K—K2; 6 R—Kt2!, B—B5; 7 R—Q2 or 6 .... B—K3; 7 P—Q8=Qch); *2 R—Kt8ch, K—Q2; 3 R—Kt7ch, K—Q1; 4 K—Q5!* (the Pawn must not be advanced prematurely),

No. 469

White wins.

No. 470

White wins.

B—Kt4 (or 4 .... B—Q6; 5 R—Kt3, B—B4; 6 K—K5, B—Kt8; 7 R—Kt8ch, K—Q2; 8 R—Kt7ch, K—Q1; 9 P—Q7, K—B2; 10 K—K6—K7 and wins, or here 5 .... B—Kt4; 6 K—B5, B—R5; 7 R—Kt4, B—Q8; 8 R—Q4, B—B6; 9 P—Q7); *5 K—B5, B—Q6; 6 P—Q7, K—B2; 7 R—K7!!, B—B4; 8 P—Q8= Qch, K×Q; 9 K—Q6, K—B1; 10 R—B7ch, K—Kt1* (10 .... K—Q1; 11 R—B7); *11 K—B6* and *12 K—Kt6,* when we have No. 463.

With a KtP the same idea of forcing the B to unfavorable squares is conclusive. Thus in No. 470 (Centurini) the solution is *1 R—Kt2, B—Q6* (1 .... B—B4; 2 R—Q2, B—B1; 3 R—Q6ch, K—Kt2; 4 P—Kt6, K—R3; 5 R—Q8, B—K3; 6 K—K5—B6, or 5 .... B—R3; 6 K—B5. Or here 2 .... B—R6; 3 R—Q3, B—B8; 4 R—Q6ch, K—Kt2; 5 P—Kt6, K—R3; 6 K—B5, etc.); *2 R—Q2, B—Kt8; 3 R—Q6ch, K—Kt2; 4 K—Kt4, B—K5; 5 R—Q4, B—Kt7; 6 R—Q7ch, K—Kt3; 7 R—Q6ch, K—Kt2; 8 P—Kt6, K—R3; 9 K—B5, B—R6ch;*

10 K—B6, etc. Note that here the K cannot get through directly, but must follow the P. A KtP on the sixth wins by sacrificing itself to force No. 463. E.g., No. 470a (Salvio), White: K at KB5, R at QKt7, P at KKt6; Black: K at KR1, B at QR8. White wins. 1 P—Kt7ch, K—R2; 2 R—KB7!, B—Kt7 (or 2 .... B×P; 3 K—Kt5); 3 P—Kt8=Qch, K×Q; 4 K—Kt6, etc.

The win with the BP on the fifth is shown in No. 471 (v. Guretzky-Cornitz). *1 R—B7ch, K—B3; 2 R—B2, B—R5!* (or 2 .... K—B2; *3* K—Kt5, or 2 .... B—Kt5; 3 R—B6ch, K—B2; 4 K—K5 or finally 2 .... B—R4; 3 R—B6ch, K—B2; 4 P—B6, K—Kt3; 5 K—K5, B—Q1; 6 R—QR6, etc.); *3 R—B6ch, K—B2; 4 R—B1, K—B3* (again

No. 471 No. 471   No. 472

 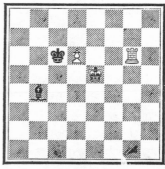

White wins.   Draw.

there is no good alternative. If 4 .... B—B7; 5 R—B2, B—R5; 6 R—KR2, B—K2; 7 R—R7ch, K—B3; 8 R—R6ch, K—B2; 9 K—K5, while if 4 .... B—K2; 5 R—B7, K—B3; 6 R—B6ch, K—B2; *7* K—K5); *5 R—KKt1, B—B7; 6 R—Kt6ch, K—B2; 7 R—Kt2, B—K8* (or 7 .... B—Kt3; 8 R—Q2, B—R4; 9 R—Q7ch, K—B3; 10 R—Q6ch, K—B2; 11 K—Kt5); *8 K—Kt5, B—R4* (If 8 .... B—B6; 9 R—QB2, B—B3ch; 10 K—B4, B—Q1; 11 R—B3, B—R5; 12 R—KR3, B—K8; 13 K—K5); *9 R—QB2, B—Q1ch; 10 K—B4, B—R5; 11 R—KR2, B—Q1; 12 R—R7ch, K—B3; 13 R—QR7, B—B2ch!; 14 K—Kt4!, B—Q1; 15 R—R6ch, K—B2; 16 K—R5, K—Kt2; 17 R—Q6, B—K2* (17 .... B—R4; 18 P—B6ch, K—B2; 19 K—Kt5); *18 R—Q7, K—B2; 19 R×Bch, K×R; 20 K—Kt6* and wins. This is perhaps the most difficult case.

There are two trap positions which White must avoid. The first of these is No. 472, which may occur with any Pawn. If the Rook leaves the sixth, or the King moves, the Pawn is captured. A tempo move does White no good, since Black has two more good squares for his Bishop. A similar case with the BP is No. 472a (Vianna, 1883), White: K at QKt7, R at QR6, P at QB6; Black: K at Q3, B at K5. Draw. Again neither King nor Rook has any good moves. The second trap draw occurs with the BP and is seen in No. 473 (Del Rio, 1831). The trouble is not only that the White King cannot approach without being checked away (this was also the case in No. 469) but also that no winning position can be forced by sacrificing the Pawn. Black keeps his B on the diagonal KKt1—QR7, but always retains the possibility of a check if the K goes to Kt6. On *1 P—B7, K—Kt2!* followed by 2 .... B×P is the proper answer, but not 1 .... B×P?;

<table>
<tr><td>No. 473</td><td>No. 474</td></tr>
</table>

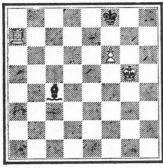

Draw.

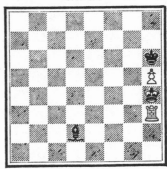

White wins.

2 K—B6! (No. 466). Another trap here is 1 .... B—Kt6; 2 R—QKt7, B—B5; 3 R—QB7, B—Kt4? (3 .... B—R7 or Q4 is correct); 4 P—B7!, K—Kt2; 5 K—B5, B—R5; 6 R—Kt7, B—Q8; 7 K—K6, B—R4; 8 R—B7, B—Kt3; 9 P—B8=Qch!, K×Q; 10 K—B6 and wins.

The RP is an exception to the other rules. If the queening square is of the same color as the B, the Black K is in the wrong corner and the game is always won. This is shown in No. 474 (v. Guretzky-Cornitz). White gives up the Pawn at the appropriate moment in order to transpose into one of the favorable R vs. B cases. *1 K—Kt4, B—B8; 2 K—B5, B—Q7; 3 R—QKt3!, B—B8* (for 3 .... K×P at any stage see No. 466); *4 R—Kt6ch, K—R2; 5 P—R6!, B—Q7* (5 .... B×P; 6 R—Kt7ch, B—Kt2; 7 K—Kt5, K—Kt1; 8 K—Kt6); *6 R—KB6* (the point will soon be clear), *B—K6* (or 6 .... B—B6; 7 R—Q6. B—Kt5; 8 R—Q4, B—B6; 9 R—Q3, B—Kt7; 10 K—Kt5, B—B8ch;

11 K—R5, B×P; 12 R—Q7ch, B—Kt2; 13 R—Kt7, K any; 14 K—Kt6, etc.); *7 K—Kt4, B×P; 8 K—R5, B—K6; 9 R—B7ch, K—Kt1; 10 K—Kt6* and wins (No. 463). Now we see why the R went to the KB file!

If the queening square is not of the same color as the B, the Black K is in the right corner and the problem is far more complicated. In general White can win if his Pawn is not beyond the fourth rank.

The main variations are seen in No. 475 (v. Guretzky-Cornitz). The winning idea is to chase the Black King to the KB file, but the execution of this idea is not simple. Best play for both sides is: *1 .... B—B4; 2 K—Kt5, B—Kt8; 3 K—R6, K—Kt1* (or 3 .... B—R7; 4 R—R7ch, K—Kt1; 5 R-Kt7ch as in the main line); *4 R—Kt7ch* and now there are two branches:

a) *4 .... K—R1; 5 P—R4, B—Q6; 6 P—R5, B—Kt8.* Now White must wriggle the Pawn on to R7. *7 R—Kt7, B—R7; 8 R—Kt8ch, B—Kt1; 9 K—Kt5, K—Kt2; 10 R—Kt7ch, K—R1!* (10 .... K—B1; 11 P—R6 and 12 P—R7); *11 K—Kt6, B—B5* (or Q4, or R7—White's Rook moves are always designed to prevent B checks); *12 R—R7ch, K—Kt1; 13 R—Q7* (or K7, QKt7 if the B is at Q4, QR7), *K—R1* (or 13 .... K—B1 if the R is at K7, when 14 K—B6, B—R7; 15 P—R6, K—Kt1; 16 P—R7ch gets back to the main line); *14 P—R6, B—R7; 15 P—R7, B—Kt8ch; 16 K—R6* and wins.

b) *4 .... K—B1; 5 P—R4, B—Q6; 6 R—Kt3, B—K5; 7 R—Kt5!, K—B2!* (White is threatening to get his King back to Kt4 via R5. If 7 .... B—Q6; 8 K—R5, B—K7ch; 9 K—Kt6, K—Kt1; 10 R—Q5, K—B1; 11 P—R5 wins, and similarly for other B moves); *8 R—Kt3, B—B7; 9 K—R5.* The winning idea now is to drive the Black King to the K file. *9 .... K—B3* (or 9 .... B—Kt8; 10 R—Kt5, B any; 11 K—Kt4 followed by K—B4 and the advance of the RP to R6 and the eventual penetration of the White King. E.g., 9 .... B—Kt8; 10 R—Kt5, B—B7; 11 K—Kt4, B—Kt3; 12 P—R5, B—Kt8; 13 P—R6, B—Kt3; 14 K—B4, K—B3; 15 R—QKt5, B—Q6; 16 R—Kt7! and 17 P—R7. If 9 .... B—Q8ch; 10 K—Kt5! K—Kt2; 11 R—QB3! and Black cannot get on to the

No. 475

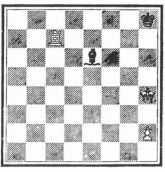

White wins.

right diagonal: 11 .... B—K7; 12 P—R5, B—B8; 13 P—R6ch, K—R2; 14 R—B7ch, K—R1; 15 P—R7 and 16 K—R6.); *10 R —Kt5, B—Q8ch* (else 11 K—Kt4 as in the last note); *11 K— R6, K—B2; 12 R—Kt7ch, K—B3* (if 12 .... K—B1; 13 K —Kt6, B—K7; 14 K—B6 and 15 R—Kt5, 16 P—R5, 17 P— R6, 18 R—Kt7, 19 P—R7 decides); *13 R—Kt1, B—K7; 14 R —Kt2, B—Q6; 15 R—B2ch, B—B4* (or 15 .... K—K2; 16 P —R5, B—Kt8; 17 K—Kt7 and the Pawn goes forward); *16 P —R5, K—K3; 17 R×B* (the simplest), *K×R; 18 K—Kt7* and queens.

Once the Pawn is on the fifth only a special position such as those above is sufficient to win. The draw is seen in No. 476 (Berger). After *1 R—Kt7, B—B7; 2 K—Kt5, B—Q6; 3 K—R6, K—Kt1!; 4 R—Kt7ch, K—B1!!* (4 .... K—R1?? loses because it transposes into variation a) of No. 475) White cannot win because he does not have the square KKt5 at his disposal. If the Pawn is at R6 even this slight hope is out because White's King cannot get to R6. Black keeps his Bishop on the diagonal KR2—QKt8 and nothing can touch him.

Summary: Rook and Pawn always win against a Bishop except for certain positions. These occur when the Pawn has been advanced to the sixth too hastily (Nos. 472, 473) or with a RP which queens on a square not of the same color as the Bishop. Such a RP in general draws if it is on the 5th or 6th but wins on the 4th. In the winning process it is advisable to remember that the Pawn should not be too far in front of the King.

C. ROOK VS. BISHOPS AND PAWNS

In general, a Rook is equivalent to a little less than Bishop plus two Pawns. The ending with R vs. B+2P is ordinarily a draw, but where the Pawns are far advanced the B will win. Where there is no other material on the board, R vs. B+P will draw because R vs. B is in general drawn. However, with three Pawns the Bishop will always win.

1. ROOK VS. BISHOP AND PAWN

Since the game is in general drawn without the Pawn, its presence does not change the theoretical result. But two new considerations come up:

1. If the R vs. B ending is won, the extra Pawn will not save Black.
2. Where the Pawn is far advanced it may in certain special positions force a Queen with the help of the B.

The simplest case which illustrates the first remark is No. 477 (Berger). After *1 R—Q2, B—B4; 2 R—Q8ch, B—B1; 3 R—QKt8* the Pawn sacrifice still leaves Black in a mess. *3 .... P—Kt4; 4 R×P, B—Q3; 5 R—Q5, B—K2; 6 R—QR5,* etc. Even if the Pawn reached Kt5 White would win because he has so many extra tempi. E.g., 3 R—QR8 (instead of 3 R—QKt8), P—Kt4; 4 R—QKt8, P—Kt5; 5 R—QB8, P—Kt6; 6 R—QKt8, P—Kt7; 8 R×P and again he still wins.

A more complicated instance is No. 477a (Sackmann), White: K at KKt6, R at KB3; Black: K at KKt1, B at QKt5, P at QB4. White to play wins. Here the problem is to force the Pawn to advance so that the B will not be defended. Accordingly the solution is 1 R—B5!, B—R6; 2 R—B1!!, B—Kt5; 3 R—B3!!! (the point: now the B has

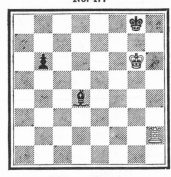

No. 476

No. 477

Draw.

White to play wins.

no moves which do not permit an immediate attack), P—B5; 4 R—B5!, B—B6 (hiding behind the Pawn. If 4 .... P—B6; 5 R—QKt5, P—B7; 6 R×B, P—B8=Q; 7 R—Kt8 and mates); 5 R—B7!! Now he has no less than eight squares at his disposal, but not a single one can save him. E.g., 5 .... B—Q5; 6 R—Q7, B—B4; 7 R—Q8ch, B—B1; 8 R—B8, etc., or 5 .... B—R1; 6 R—QB7, K—B1; 7 R—B8ch, etc.

There are even positions where the Pawn only gets in Black's way. E.g., No. 477b (Sackmann), White: K at QB6, R at QB1; Black: K at QKt1, B at KB1, P at KR3. White to play wins despite the fact that the Black King is in the right corner. The reason is that the Black B cannot go to KR3. 1 R—K1, K—R2 (or 1 .... B—R6; 2 R—Kt1ch, K—B1; 3 R—QR1. 1 .... B—KR3 is the only saving move when the Pawn is off); 2 R—KB1 and now the B is lost, for if 2 .... B—Kt5; 3 R—R1ch, K—Kt1; 4 R—QKt1.

The type of position where the B+P win is seen in No. 478 (Deutsche Schachzeitung, 1887). After *1 .... P—B7; 2 R—QB8, B—B6; 3 R—Q8ch, K—K7!; 4 R—K8ch, K—B7!!* (but not the retreat on the K and Q files: 4 .... K—Q6; 5 R—Q8ch, K—K5; 6 R—K8ch, K—Q4?; 7 R—K1!!, B×R; 8 K—Kt2=); *5 R—B8ch, K—Kt7; 6 R—Kt8ch, K—R7* White has no good checks and cannot get back to the first rank, so that the Pawn queens.

2. ROOK VS. BISHOP AND TWO PAWNS

This is a draw unless the Pawns manage to advance so far that the Rook must be given up for one of them. In general this is not possible.

No. 478   No. 479

Black to play wins.   Draw.

Connected passed Pawns draw if they are on the fourth rank but win on the fifth or beyond. (An exception must be made for RP's.) The draw is seen in No. 479. The most promising attempt is *1 .... K—B4* (if 1 .... B—K2; 2 R—R1! and now:

a) 2 .... P—K5ch; 3 K—Q4, B—B3ch; 4 K—K3, B—Kt7 (4 .... K—B4; 5 R—R5ch, B—Kt4ch; 6 K—Q4); 5 R—R4!, K—K4; 6 R—R5ch, K—Q3; 7 R—R4!, B—B8ch; 8 K—Q4!, etc.=.

b) 2 .... P—K5ch; 3 K—Q4, B—B3ch; 4 K—K3, B—Q1; 5 R—R6ch, K—K4; 6 R—R5ch, K—Q3; 7 R—R6ch, K—B4; 8 R—K6!, B—Kt4ch; 9 K—K2, B—B5; 10 K—B2!, K—Q5; 11 K—K2! Black cannot advance without blockading the Pawns and his King cannot get back to KB4.

c) 2 .... K—B4; 3 R—B1ch, K—Kt5; 4 R—Kt1ch, K—B6; 5 R—B1ch, K—Kt7; 6 R—B5, B—Q3; 7 R—B6, etc.); *2 R—R5ch, K—B5; 3 R—R4ch, K—B6* (if 3 .... K—Kt4; 4 R—QR4, K—B4; 5 R—R5=); *4 R—R5, P—K5ch; 5 K—B2, P—K6;*

6 R×P, P—K7; 7 R—Q1! and the Rook is sacrificed for the last Pawn.

If we move all the pieces down one rank, so that the Pawns are on the fifth, the Pawns will win. No. 479a, White: K at Q2, R at KR3; Black: K at K4, B at QB5, P's at Q5, K5. Black wins. After 1 . . . . K—B5; 2 R—R4ch, K—B6; 3 R—R3ch, K—B7; 4 R—R4, P—K6ch; 5 K—B2, P—K7 White has no time to take the P. However Pawns on the fifth in general do not win if the opposing Rook is on the eighth (No. 480a).

Two Pawns on the sixth will win regardless of the Rook position. In No. 480 (Handbuch), White's Rook is favorably placed, but still cannot stem the Pawns. The solution is *1 K—K1, K—B4; 2 R—B8ch* (or 2 R—K8, P—Q7ch; 3 K—K2, B—B6ch; or 2 R—Q1, B—Kt6ch; 3 K—K1, K—B5; 4 R—B8ch, K—Q5; 5 R—Q8ch, K—B6; 6 R—B8ch, B—B5 as in the main line), *K—Kt5; 3 R—Kt8ch, K—B6; 4 R—B8ch, B—B5; 5 R—Q8, P—Q7ch; 6 K—Q1, P—K7* mate or here 5 R—K8, P—Q7ch; 6 K—Q1, B—Kt6ch and queens. To have the Rook on the second rank is worse, since Black plays . . . . K—B6 and the Pawns go right on through. If we move the position back one rank, No. 480a, White: K at Q2, R at Q8; Black: K at Q4, B at Q3, P's at Q5, K5, the game is drawn because the B cannot be sacrificed. 1 K—K2, K—B3; 2 R—K8, P—Q6ch (2 . . . . K—Q4; 3 R—Q8); 3 K—K3 and now 3 . . . . B—B5ch? as above is a plain blunder because after 4 K×B the Pawn does not queen. An exception to the rule that Pawns on the sixth win occurs when the B is not mobile. No. 480b (Goudjou, 1881), White: K at KB1, R at QR2; Black: K at KKt6, B at KB7, P's at K6, KB6. Draw. If the Black King moves, R×B simplifies. The best try is 1 . . . . B—Kt8! but it remains unsuccessful for after 2 R—QKt2, B—R7; 3 R—KB2!, B—Kt 8; 4 K×B, P—K7!; 5 R—Kt2ch!, K—B5; 6 R×P, P×R; 7 K—B2 the Kings are left to do battle alone.

The RP (as usual!) likes to be different. Except for certain special cases RP+KtP never win because of a peculiar stalemate possibility. In No. 481, which is surely the best that Black can do, the Rook plays along the second rank until the Black King leaves the QKtP, and then offers itself at QKt2: *1 . . . . K—B5; 2 R—KKt2, B—Q5; 3 R—KR2,*

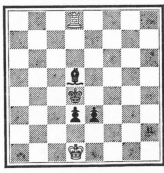

No. 480

Black wins.

K—Q6; 4 R—QKt2!, K—B6 (either capture is stalemate); *5 R—K2!* (the brilliant 5 K—R1!!??? loses after 5 .... B—K6!; 6 R—KR2, B—Q7; 7 R—R1, K—B7; 8 R—B1ch!, K—Q6!; 9 R—Q1, K—K7; 10 R—R1, B—B6ch; 11 K—Kt1, P—R7ch), *B—B4!; 6 R—QKt2, B—K6; 7 R—KR2, B—Q7; 8 R—R3ch, K—B5; 9 R—R4ch, K—Kt4; 10 R—R3,* etc. To have the Rook behind the Pawn is dangerous but not fatal. Thus No. 481a (Handbuch), White: K at QR1, R at QKt8; Black: K at QR5, B at QR4, P's at QR6, QKt6 is drawn. 1 R—QR8, K—Kt4; 2 R—Kt8ch, K—B5; 3 R—QR8!, K—Kt4; 4 R—Kt8ch, B—Kt3; 5 R—QR8, etc. The Rook sticks to the QR

No. 481   No. 482

Draw.   Draw.

file whenever the Pawn threatens to check. A special win is No. 481b (Steinitz, 1880), White: K at QKt1, R at QR8; Black: K at Q7, B at QR4, P's at QR6, QKt6. Black to play wins. 1 .... P—R7ch; 2 K—Kt2, P—R8=Qch!!; 3 K×Q, K—B7; 4 R—B8ch, B—B6ch; 5 R×Bch, K×R; 6 K—Kt1, P—Kt7 and wins.

Disconnected passed Pawns win only if one can queen, capturing the Rook, while the other is held by the Bishop. This again is in general not possible. The drawing idea is seen in No. 482 (Berger). The only try Black can make is to approach the KP with his King, when the Rook is given up for the KP and the King captures the QP: *1 .... B—Q6; 2 R—K7, K—B5; 3 R—K8, K—Q5; 4 R×P!* (but not 4 K×P?, B—K5!). Where one Pawn is not directly attacked by the King, the defender must get his King as near to it as possible in order to make the Rook sacrifice effective. E.g., No. 482a (Cozio, 1766), White: K at KKt2, R at QR2; Black: K at KR5, B at Q3, P's at QR6, KKt5. Draw. 1 .... K—Kt4; 2 R—R1, K—B5; 3 R—R2,

K—K5; 4 R—R1, K—Q5; 5 R×P!, B×R; 6 K—Kt3=. If the White King stays at KKt1 here the game is lost.

The type position where the Rook loses is No. 483 (Stamma, 1745). *1 B—K5, R—R8; 2 P—B7, R—KB8; 3 K—R7, R—R8ch; 4 K—Kt6, R—Kt8ch; 5 K—B7, R—B8ch; 6 B—B6!, R—KKt8; 7 B—Q8, R—B8ch* (or 7 .... R—Kt7; 8 P—Kt8=Q); *8 K—Kt6, R—Kt8ch; 9 B—Kt5!* and queens. The characteristic of this ending is that Black has permitted the White King to come too near his KtP.

Positions which would be won without the Pawns are sometimes but not always, won with Pawns. E.g., No. 483a (Sackmann, 1915) White: K at QB6, R at KB5; Black: K at QR2, B at KKt1, P's at KB2, KKt4. White to play wins. 1 R—B1!!, P—B3 (if 1 .... K—Kt1; 2 R—Kt1ch, K—R2; 3 R—Kt7ch, K—R3; 4 R—Kt8 or 3 .... K—R1; 4 R—K7, B—R2; 5 K—Kt6); 2 R—R1ch, K—Kt1; 3 R—Kt1ch, K—B1 (or 3 .... K—R2; 4 R—Kt7ch as above); 4 R—KR1! and wins the B. Or No. 483b (Berger), White: K at KB6, R at QB7; Black: K at KKt1, B at KB1, P's at QR6, QB4 (compare No. 477). White to play wins. 1 K—Kt6!, P—R7; 2 R—QR7, P—B5; 3 R×P, P—B6; 4 R—R8, P—B7; 5 R—QB8, etc.

3. ROOK VS. BISHOP AND THREE (OR MORE) PAWNS

This is of course always a win for the Pawns. The Rook can be sacrificed for at most two, and a third is left to bring home the bacon. A rare exception is No. 483c (from a game Schiffers-Ascharine, 1875), White: K at KR4, B at QB5, P's at QR2, Q4, K5; Black: K at K3, R at Q2. Black to play draws. 1 .... R—Q4!; 2 P—R4, R×P!!; 3 P×R, K×P; 4 P—R5, K—Q4; 5 P—R6, K—B3; 6 K—Kt5, K—B2; 7 B—R7, K—B3!, etc.=.

D. ROOK AND PAWNS VS. BISHOP AND PAWNS

The presence of extra Pawns makes a vast difference. Now, when there are no Pawns for the exchange, the Rook wins easily, when there is one Pawn for the exchange the Rook wins, but with difficulty, when there are two Pawns for the exchange, the game is normally a draw, and finally when there are three or more Pawns for the exchange the Bishop wins, though not always too easily.

No. 483

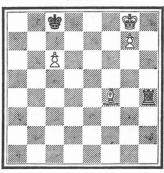

White to play wins.

In general the side with the Rook (usually the superior side) should bear these points in mind:

1. The central winning idea is to get the King through to a mass of Pawns and in that way capture material.
2. As many Pawns as possible should be forced on to squares of the same color as the Bishop.
3. A few Pawn exchanges may be necessary to clear files, but *one must always retain Pawns on both sides of the board.*
4. Try to keep the Pawn position *unbalanced.* In particular any passed Pawn practically confers a winning advantage immediately.

1. NO PAWNS FOR THE EXCHANGE

This is usually easily won. With three or four Pawns the King can force his way to one side or the other at once. With more Pawns a few must first be exchanged. Whenever the chance offers itself, to give up the Rook for Bishop and Pawn is an effective simplification.

We may take No. 484 (Adams-Fine, Dallas, 1940) as typical. Here Black's winning plan consists of four steps:

1. Centralization.
2. Advance of his Pawn majority on the K-side, forcing a passed Pawn.
3. Penetration with his King or Rook or both.
4. Capture of material.

After *1 .... K—K2; 2 B—Kt5, P—B4; 3 K—K3, K—B3; 4 P—QR4, K—K4* (first step completed); *5 P—B3, P—QR4; 6 B—B6, P—Kt4* (second step) the most difficult line is *7 P—R3* (the game continuation was 7 K—Q2, R—Q3; 8 Resigns, since 8 B—Kt5, P—Kt5 wins a Pawn), *P—R4; 8 B—B3, P—Kt5; 9 P×P, RP×P; 10 B—K2, P—B5ch; 11 K—B2* (if 11 K—Q2, P—B6; 12 P×P, P—Kt6; 13 B—B1, K—B5; 14 B—Kt2, R—KR1; 15 K—K2, R—R7; 16 K—B1, K—K6, etc.), *K—B4; 12 B—B1* (note that the B is tied down to the QP), *R—K1* (third step begins); *13 B—K2, P—Kt6ch; 14 K—B1* (if 14 K—K1, P—B6; 15 P×P, P—Kt7, winning the B), *R—K6; 14 B—Q1!, K—K4!; 15 B—B2* (after 15 B—K2, K—Q3 White must move—and lose—a Pawn), *P—B6; 16 P×P, R×Pch; 17 K—Kt1, R—B7; 18 B any, R×P* and the rest is routine—Black can capture every White Pawn if he is so minded.

Even with only one Pawn apiece a win may be secured by skillful manipulation of the Rook. The case where Black has a passed Pawn on the seventh may prove exceedingly difficult, but if the Pawn is not supported by the King the game is lost against best play. No. 485 (Chess Players Chronicle, 1856) is an example of this. The winning idea is to place Black in zugzwang, so that he will have to either give up his own Pawn or allow the White Pawn to queen. With this in mind, the quickest solution is *1 R—R7, B—Kt1; 2 R—R8!, B—Q4!; 3 R—R5!* (White has lost a move), *B—Kt1; 4 R—R7!, B—Q4* (if 4 .... B—B5; 5 R—R4, B—Kt6; 6 R—Kt4ch, K—R2; 7 R—Kt1 followed by P—B6—B7); *5 K—Q6 dis ch, B—B2; 6 K—K5, K—R3* (6 .... K—R1 or 6 .... K—Kt1 leads to the same or similar variations. 6 .... K—B1; 7 K—B6 loses at once); *7 K—B6* and now:

a) *7 .... B—Kt1; 8 R—R8, K—R2; 9 K—K7, B—Q4; 10 R—R5, K—R3* (if 10 .... K—Kt2; 11 P—B6ch, K—Kt3; 12 R—R4! and Black is in zugzwang); *11 R—R6ch, K—Kt2* (if 11 .... K—R2; 12 P—B6, K—Kt3; 13 P—B7 dis ch or 12 .... K—Kt1, as

<table>
<tr><td>No. 484</td><td>No. 485</td></tr>
</table>

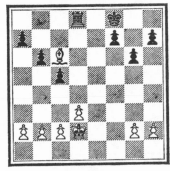

Black wins.   White wins.

in the main variation); *12 P—B6ch, K—Kt1* (12 .... K—Kt3; 13 P—B7 dis ch); *13 R—R3* (or R5, R4, R7) and now Black is in zugzwang. If the King moves 14 P—B7 wins the B. If 13 .... B—Kt6 (or anywhere else along this diagonal), 14 R—R8ch, K—R2; 15 P—B7 again wins the B. Finally if 13 .... B—K5; 14 P—B7ch and queens.

b) *7 .... B—Q4; 8 R—R3!, B—Kt6; 9 R—R8, K—R2; 10 K—K7, B—Q4; 11 R—R6, B—B5; 12 R—R4, B—Kt6; 13 R—R4ch, K—Kt1; 14 R—R1, B—B7; 15 P—B6, B—Kt8; 16 P—B7ch, K—Kt2; 17 P—B8 = Qch* and mate next.

c) *7 .... B—Kt6 (or B5); 8 K—K7,* etc., as in a) and b).

Where there is no passed Pawn, the game is won if the Pawns are in the center, but may be drawn with the Pawns on the Kt or R files. No. 486 is the model case in the center. The winning idea consists of giving up the Rook for B+KP at a moment when the Black King cannot reach K2 (since this is the only draw with K+P vs. K). Best play for both sides is *1 .... K—K3* (if 1 .... K—B4; 2 R—R8!, K—B3; 3 R—Q8!, B—B4; 4 K—K2, B—Q5; 5 K—B3, B—B4; 6 K—Kt4, etc.); *2 K—B4, K—Q3; 3 R—R6ch, K—Q2; 4 K—Q5, K—K2; 5 R—R7ch* (but not 5 R—K6ch?, K—Q2; 6 R×P??, B×R; 7 K×B, K—K2=), *K—B3* (if 5 .... K—K1; 6 K—K6, K—B1; 7 R—R8ch, K—Kt2; 8 R—QKt8, B—B6; 9 K—K7, B—Q5; 10 R—Kt1, B—B6; 11 R—KB1, etc., as in the main variation—the idea is to get the Black King at a distance of one file from the Pawn); *6 K—Q6, B—B6; 7 R—QKt7!, B—Q5* (or 7 .... B—Q7; 8 R—Kt8, B—B5; 9 R—B8ch, etc.); *8 R—Kt3, K—B2; 9 K—Q7, K—B3; 10 R—B3ch, K—Kt3; 11 R—B5,*

No. 486

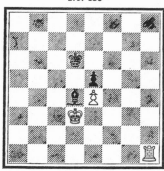

White wins.

No. 487

White wins.

B—B6; 12 K—K6, B any; 13 R×P and wins for after 13 .... B×R; 14 K×B, K—B2; 15 K—Q6 White has the opposition. Two RP's only draw because White is stalemated after the sacrifice. No. 486a, White: K at QKt7, R at Q3, P at QR6; Black: K at K2, B at KKt8, P at QR2. Draw. After 1 R—QB3, K—Q2; 2 R—B8, B—B7; 3 R—QR8, B—Kt8; 4 R×P, B×R; 5 K×R, K—B2 White's King is stuck. The attempt to drive Black's King to the other edge of the board would not prove successful because White's King can always be checked off Black squares. A KtP vs. a RP should win because the resulting P ending is won. E.g., No. 486b, White: K at QR4, R at KB1, P at QKt5; Black: K at QKt2, B at QKt3, P at QR2. White to play wins. 1 R—B7ch, B—B2; 2 K—Kt4, K—Kt3; 3 R—B6ch, K—Kt2; 4 K—B5, B—Kt3ch and now 5 R×Bch is already good enough: 5 .... P×R; 6 K—Q6, K—Kt1; 7 K—B6, etc. If 4 .... B—Q1; 5 R—B7ch, B—B2; 6 R—R7, K—Kt1; 7 K—B6 is conclusive. A B on

White squares is worse here because the Black King is then in the wrong corner. Two KtP's draw with a B of the same color as the Pawn on the second, but White may win if the B is of the opposite color. No. 486c, White: K at QKt4, R at KB6, P at QKt5; Black: K at QR2, B at K6, P at QKt2. Draw. The White King cannot get to either QKt5 or QB5 and stay there, nor can he work his way around to QB8 because the moment the K is on the sixth Black's K gets to QKt3. But in No. 486d, Black: B at K7, other pieces as in No. 486c, White to play wins. 1 P—Kt6ch, K—R3; 2 K—B5 and Black is in a mating net. However, Black to play draws by 1 .... P—Kt3 because White must then guard his KtP and cannot move about too freely with both K and R. If the Black Pawns are not on their original squares the defense is far more difficult and Black will usually lose.

This brings us to the interesting question of R+2P vs. B+2P, all on the Kt and R files (on the center files the ending would be a fairly easy win, as in No. 486). Here the situation is worse for Black: with a normal Pawn position he will always lose. No. 487 is favorable for the defender because the King is in the right corner, but still White can win by penetrating with his King. *The basic weakness of Black's position is that he cannot defend his White squares.* Consequently the entry of the White King is bound to be decisive. *1 K—B3, K—B2; 2 K—B4, P—QR3* (the best chance. If 2 .... K—B3; 3 R—Kt6, P—Kt4ch?; 4 K—Q4, K—B2; 5 K—Q5, B—B1; 6 R—KB6, B—K2; 7 R—B7, K—Q2; 8 R×Bch, K×R; 9 K—B5 with an easily won K and P ending); *3 K—Q5, B—B5; 4 R—KB2, B—K6; 5 R—B7ch, K—Kt3* (or 5 .... K—B1; 6 K—Q6, or 5 .... K—Kt1; 6 K—Q6 and 7 K—Q7. The point is that the White King cannot be prevented from reaching QB8); *6 K—Q6, B—Q5; 7 P—Kt3, B—B4ch* (7 .... K—R2; 8 K—B7 and 9 K—B8 is hopeless); *8 K—Q7, K—Kt4; 9 K—B7, P—Kt3; 10 R—B4!, B—K6; 11 R—K4, B—B4; 12 K—Kt7, B—Kt8* (if 12 .... B—B1; 13 R—K5ch, B—B4; 14 P—R3!, P—R4; 15 R—R5, P—R5; 16 P—Kt4 and wins; 12 .... P—R4; 13 P—R4 mate may be the easiest way out); *13 P—R3!, K—B4* (or 13 .... B—B4; 14 R—K5 and wins a piece); *14 K×RP* and the rest is simple. This march of the King is always the key to the winning process in all such endings.

A B on White is even worse for Black because White can afford to exchange one pair of Pawns (see No. 486d). No. 487a, White: K at QB2, R at KR2, P's at QR2, QKt2; Black: K at QB1, B at QB3, P's at QR2, QKt2. White wins. 1 K—B3, P—R3 (the best chance again. On 1 .... K—B2; 2 K—B4, K—Kt3; 3 R—R6, K—B2; 4 K—B5, P—Kt3ch; 5 K—Q4, B—Q2; 6 K—Q5 it is practically all over); 2 K—B4, K—Kt1; 3 K—-B5, K—R2. Now this position looks impregnable because the King march to the eighth would not threaten anything im-

mediate, but even so White can win. 4 R—R3, B—Kt4; 5 R—QKt3,
B—B3; 6 K—Q6, B—R8 (6 .... K—Kt1; 7 R—Kt3); 7 P—R3, B—
B3; 8 K—B7, B—R8; 9 R—Kt6, B—Kt7 (if 9 .... P—R4; 10 P—
Kt4 as in the main variation); 10 P—Kt4, B—B6; 11 P—R4, B—Kt7;
12 P—Kt5, P×P (12 .... P—R4; 13 R—KB6, B—K5; 14 P—Kt6ch,
K—R3; 15 R—B8 and mates. If 12 .... B—B6; 13 R—B6 again
threatening P—Kt6ch); 13 P×P, B—B6; 14 R—KB6, B—K5; 15
R—B4 and wins.

Any earlier weakening of the P position in these examples would
merely hasten Black's downfall.

Black has drawing chances in endings with even Pawns only if he
has a strong passed Pawn which is not adequately (i.e., by the enemy
King) blockaded. A typical instance is No. 488 (Vidmar-Bogoljuboff,
Nottingham, 1936). After *1 .... K—Kt6; 2 K—K1, P—Kt4!* draws
(for the game continuation see A.). *3 P—R4* (if 3 R—Q2, P—Kt5!
White might even lose, e.g., 4 R—KB2, B—Kt2; 5 R—Q2, P—K4;
6 R—QB2, P—K5; 7 R—B2, B—R3; 8 R—Q2, B—Q6!; 9 R—KB2?,
B—K7!; 9 R×B, P×R; 10 K×P, K—Kt7, etc.), *P×P; 4 P×P,
B—B5; 5 P—R5, P—K4; 6 R—B2* (or 6 P—K4—it makes no real
difference because the Rook can never leave the second rank), *B—
Kt4; 7 P—K4, B—R3; 8 R—QR2, B—B5!* = for the attempt 9 P—
R6??, B×R; 10 P—R7, P—B7ch! loses for White.

A. Bogoljuboff played 2 .... B—K5? which allows the White Rook
to get behind the B Pawn and win: 3 P—R4!, B—B3; 4 R—QKt2,
P—K4; 5 R—Q2, B—K1; 6 K—B1!, B—B3 (6 .... B—B2; 7 R—Q7,
B×P; 8 R—Kt7ch, K—R5; 9 P—R5, etc., as in the game); 7 R—Q6!,
B—K5; 8 R—KB6 (now Black can just as well resign), B—Q6ch;
9 K—K1, B—B7; 10 P—R5!, B×P; 11 R—Kt6ch, K—R5; 12 K—B2,
P—K5; 13 R—Q6!, B—B5 (he must lose a Pawn. If 13 .... B—R5;
14 R—QKt6, B—B3; 15 P—R6 or 15 R×B); 14 R—Q4, B—Kt4;
15 R×Pch, K—R6; 16 R—K7, B—B3; 17 R—Kt7, K—R5; 18 R—
Kt3 (this part is routine), K—R4; 19 R×P, K—Kt4; 20 R—B4, B—
R8; 21 K—K1, Resigns.

With two Rooks vs. Rook and Bishop it is essential for the superior
side to exchange a pair of Rooks, a task which is usually none too difficult. One example will suffice. No. 488a (Duras-Cohn, Carlsbad,
1907), White: K at KB2, R's at QR1, Q4, P's at QR2, K5, KB4,
KKt2, KR2; Black: K at KKt1, R at QR3, B at K3, P's at QKt4,
QB7, KB4, KKt2, KR2. White wins. The conclusion was 1 K—K3,
R×P; 2 R—QB1, R—Kt7; 3 K—Q2, B—Kt6; 4 R—Kt4, R—Kt8;
5 R×KtP, K—B2; 6 R—Kt7ch, K—Kt3; 7 P—Kt3, K—R3; 8 R—
R7!, P—Kt3; 9 R—QR1, R×R(B8) (or 9 .... R—Kt7; 10 K—B3);
10 K×R, P—Kt4; 11 R—R3, Resigns. After his Rook went Black's
game just fell apart.

2. ONE PAWN FOR THE EXCHANGE

As a rule this is a win for the Rook, but the practical difficulties are many. Again the central ideas are to gain an entry with the King or Rook and to set up an unbalanced Pawn position. The defense must rely chiefly on blockade possibilities. An important point to remember is that with all the Pawns on one side the game is drawn.

No. 489 (Lasker-Ragosin, Moscow, 1936) illustrates the play for both sides. We shall follow the game continuation. *1 B—Q3, K— Kt2; 2 K—B2, K—B3; 3 K—K3, K—K4!* (This centralization is necessary because the tempting 3 .... K—Kt4 leads to nothing after

No. 488	No. 489
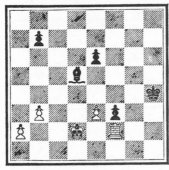	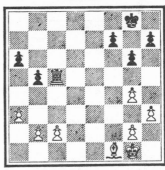
Black to play draws.	White to play. Black wins.

4 K—Q4!, R—B2; 5 P—B4, P×P; 6 B×P, P—QR4; 7 P—Kt4, P×P; 8 P×P and White has some winning chances!); *4 P—Kt5* (to prevent .... P—KB4—B5, but it weakens the Pawn position. 4 B— K4, P—B4; 5 P×P, P×P; 6 B—Q3, R—B2; 7 K—B3 was preferable), *K—Q3!; 5 P—KR4, P—R3?* (Now was the time to force the issue with the Rook. After 5 .... R—K4ch; 6 K—Q4, R—K8; 7 P—B4, R—Q8; 8 K—B3, K—B3 or 6 K—B4, R—K8; 7 P—R5, R—QKt8; 8 P—QKt3, R—QR8 Black not only wins a Pawn, but sets up a passed Pawn for himself); *6 P×P, R—R4; 7 P—KKt3, R×P(R3); 8 P—B4!, R—R4; 9 P×P?* (and now White could have blocked the position and drawn by force. 9 P—QKt4!, R—K4ch; 10 K—B4, P—B4; 11 P×P, P×P; 12 P—R5!, P×P; 13 B×BP, R—K8; 14 B—Kt6, K—Q4; 15 B×P, R—QR8; 16 B—K8=), *P×P; 10 P—QKt3, R—K4ch; 11 K— B4, R—Q4; 12 B—K4, R—Q7* (wins a Pawn); *13 P—KKt4* (if 13 P— QR4, P—Kt5!), *R—QR7; 14 P—R5, R×P; 15 P—Kt4* (if instead 15 P—R6, R×P; 16 P—R7, R—R6 while if 15 P×P, P×P; 16 B—B2,

R—R7!; 17 B—Q3!, P—Kt5!; 18 K—Kt5, R—QKt7; 19 B—B4, R—Kt7; 20 B—Q3, R—Kt6; 21 B—B2, K—K2!; 22 K—B4, R—QB6; 23 B—Q1, R—B4; 24 P—Kt5, R—B4ch; 25 K—Kt4, R—B7 and will win), *P—B4!!* (a splendid move which gives Black a strong passed Pawn—an example of the strength of the unbalanced Pawn position); *16 B—Kt1* (16 B—B3, R×Bch!; 17 K×R, P×Pch; 18 K×P, P×Pch; 19 K×P, K—Q4 and wins), *P×RP; 17 P×RP, R—KR6; 18 K—Kt5, K—K4; 19 K—Kt6* (again 19 B×P, R×Pch! leads to a simple win), *R—Kt6ch; 20 K—B7, R—QKt6* (decisive); *21 B—B2, R×P; 22 P—R6, R—KR5; 23 K—Kt6, P—Kt5; 24 B—Q1, P—B5; 25 P—R7, R×P!; 26 K×R, K—K5; 27 K—Kt6, P—B6; 28 K—Kt5, K—K6;* 29 Resigns.

No. 490   No. 491

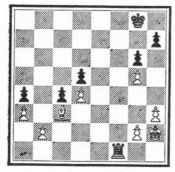 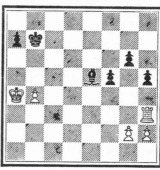

Black to play. Draw.   Black to play draws.

An example of the strength of the blockade as a drawing weapon is No. 490 (Blackburne-Mason, Nuremberg, 1883). Black tried *1 ....* *P—R4,* when White could have forced a draw by 2 P×P, e.p., K—R2; 3 P—KKt4!, K×P; 4 P—R4, when there is no weak spot through which the Black King can enter. Instead he played *2 P—KKt4?* and this gave Black the needed opportunity: he can now force his opponent into a zugzwang position. *2 .... R—B6; 3 K—Kt2, R—K6; 4 K—R2* (if 4 P×P, P×P; 5 K—R2, K—B2; 6 K—Kt2, K—Kt3; 7 P—R4, K—B4; 8 K—R2, R—K5; 9 K—Kt3, R—Kt5ch; 10 K—R3, K—K5 and White must lose a Pawn), *R—K7ch; 5 K—Kt3* (if 5 K—Kt1, P×P; 6 P×P, R—K5 wins), *P—R5ch!! 6 K×P* (6 K—B3, R—R7), *R—Kt7!; 7 B—R5, R×QKtP* and White must lose too much material.

Black may also draw and even win when he secures a strong passed Pawn. An interesting example of a draw is No. 491 (Alekhine-Rell-stab, Kemeri, 1937). The game continued *1 .... K—B3; 2 K—R5,*

K—Q4; 3 K—R6, P—B5!; 4 R—R3 (trying to win. 4 K×P, K—B5 is the simplest draw), *P—Kt4; 5 K×P, P—Kt5; 6 P—Kt5, K—K5; 7 P—Kt6, P—B6!* Now White is hard put to it to find a draw, but the B is not quite strong enough to win. *8 P×Pch, P×P; 9 R—R4ch, K—Q6* (or 9 .... K—B4; 10 R—R5, P—B7; 11 R×Bch, etc.); *10 R—R3ch, K—K7; 11 R—R5!, B—B5; 12 R—R2ch, K—K8; 13 R—R1ch, K—K7; 14 R—R2ch,* etc. Neither side can do better than accept the perpetual check.

Where the defender has an outside passed Pawn, with all the other Pawns on one side of the board, the game should be drawn. This is seen in No. 491a (Ragosin-Eliskases, Moscow, 1936), White: K at KB1, B at QKt7, P's at QB6, KB2, KKt3, KR3; Black: K at KB1, R at QB4, P's at KB2, KKt2, KR3. Draw, because Black must always keep an eye on the BP. The game continued 1 K—K2, K—K2; 2 K—K3, K—Q3; 3 K—B3, R—B5; 4 K—K3, P—Kt4; 5 K—Q3, R—QR5; 6 K—K3, P—R4; 7 K—B3, P—R5; 8 K—Kt2, R—QB5; 9 K—B3, R—QKt5; 10 K—Kt2, R—Q5; 11 K—B3, R—QB5; 12 B—R8, K—K4; 13 B—Kt7, P—B4; 14 P×P, R—B6ch; 15 K—K2!, P×P; 16 K—Q2!, R—B4; 17 K—K3, R—B6ch; 18 K—Q2, K—Q5; 19 P—B4!, etc.—Black could do nothing.

3. TWO PAWNS FOR THE EXCHANGE

Since two Pawns are usually a full equivalent for the exchange, such an ending should normally be drawn. But if the side with the B has two passed Pawns, strongly supported by the King, he will generally win, while conversely if the Pawns are weak and subject to attack the R will win.

The effect of the presence of extra Pawns may be seen in No. 492 (from a game Wittek-Schwarz, Graz, 1890). Without the Q-side Pawns the game would be drawn because the White Pawns are too far back. But now there is the added possibility of capturing another Pawn. Best play for both sides is *1 P—B4!, R—R3ch; 2 K—K5, K—Q2; 3 P—B5, R—R8* (the Rook must get behind the Pawns); *4 K—B6, R—R7; 5 P—K5, K—K1; 6 K—K6* (if 6 P—K6, R—K7! and the Pawns cannot advance), *R—R8; 7 K—Q5, R—R4.* A critical position. 7 .... R—KB8 is apparently more natural but it loses after

No. 492

White to play wins.

8 P—B6, R—B7; 9 K—B6!, R—K7; 10 B—Q6, since Black loses his last Pawn: e.g., 10 .... R—QKt7; 11 P—K6, R—KB7; 12 P—B7ch, R×P; 13 P×Rch, K×P; 14 K×P, K—K1; 15 K—B6, K—Q1; 16 P—R4, etc.—the Black King cannot get to QR1. *8 P—B6, K—B2* (if 8 .... R—Kt4; 9 K—K6, R—Kt3; 10 K—B5, R—Kt8; 11 P—K6 and wins as in the last note); *9 B—B3, K—K1* (or 9 .... R—Kt4; 10 K—Q6); *10 K—B6, R—R6; 11 B—Kt4, K—B2; 12 K×P, K—K3; 13 B—Q6* and the rest is simple: *13 .... R—Kt6ch; 14 K—B4, R— Kt8; 15 P—R4, R—QR8; 16 K—Kt3* (so that if 16 .... K—B2; 17 B—R3), *R—Kt8ch; 17 K—R2, R—Kt2; 18 K—R3, R—Kt8; 19 P— R5, R—R8ch; 20 K—Kt4, R—Kt8ch; 21 K—B5, R—QR8; 22 K—Kt6, R—Kt8ch; 23 K—B6, R—QR8; 24 B—B7!* (White must not advance too hastily: after 24 K—Kt7, R—Kt8ch; 25 K—R7, R—QR8; 26 P— R6, R—R7; 27 K—Kt7, R—Kt7ch; 28 K—R8?, R—QR7; 29 P—R7, R—QKt7 his King can never get out and the game is drawn), *R— B8ch; 25 K—Kt7, K—Q2; 26 B—Kt6, K—K3; 27 P—R6, K×P; 28 P—R7, R—QR8; 29 P—B7* and queens.

Similarly, if we add an extra set of Pawns to No. 479 Black will win because the sacrificial drawing possibilities would disappear. If the two Pawns are disconnected the win is even simpler.

Where the Pawns are weak or not well supported the Rook will win. A typical case is seen in No. 493 (Blackburne-Mason, Berlin, 1881). White's position is so badly riddled with holes that he cannot avoid the loss of several Pawns. The game continued *1 P—Kt4* (if 1 K—Kt2, R—B7ch; 2 K—Kt1, K—B6; 3 B—K5, R—K7 and White must give up one Pawn immediately, with more to follow); *P×P; 2 K—Kt2, R—Q8; 3 P—R5, R—Q6; 4 P—R6, R—R6; 5 B—Kt7, K—B4; 6 K—*

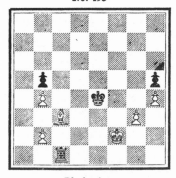

No. 493

Black wins.

B2, K—Kt4; 7 K—Kt2, R×P; 8 B×Rch, K×R; 9 K—Kt3, K—Kt4 and the rest is routine: *10 K—Kt2, K—B5; 11 K—B2, K—K5; 12 K—Kt3, K—Q6!* (but not, as in the game, 12 .... K—Q5?; 13 K×P, K—B5; 14 K—B3, K×P; 15 K —K3, K—Kt6, when 16 K—Q4! draws); *13 K×P, K—B7; 14 K —B3, K×P; 15 K—K3, K—Kt6; 16 K—Q2, K×P*, etc.

Two Pawns can be defended by the B alone only when they are both on the same color, in which case they lose in mobility. E.g., No. 493a (Tchigorin-Olland, Carlsbad, 1907),

White: K at KKt2, R at KB1, P's at KKt3, KR2; Black: K at K Kt2, B at KB2, P's at QR2, QKt3, KKt4, KR3. Black to play; White wins. The game continuation was 1 .... P—QR4 (or 1 .... P—QR3; 2 R—QKt1, P—Kt4; 3 R—QR1, B—Q4ch; 4 K—B2, B—Kt2; 5 R—QB1, K—Kt3; 6 R—B7, B—Q4; 7 R—QR7); 2 R—QKt1, P—R5; 3 R×P, P—R6; 4 R—R6, P—R7; 5 K—B3 and the rest is not difficult: White's King marches in and wins a Pawn on the K-side. 5 .... B—K3; 6 K—K4, P—R4; 7 K—K5, B—B5; 8 R—R5, K—Kt3; 9 P—R4, P—Kt5; 10 R—R7, B—B2; 11 R—R6ch, K—Kt2; 12 K—B5, K—R2; 13 K—Kt5, K—Kt2; 14 R—R7, K—Kt1; 15 K—R6, K—B1; 16 K—R7!, K—K1; 17 K—Kt7, B—Q4; 18 K—B6!, B—B5; 19 R—R8ch, K—Q2; 20 K—Kt6 and wins.

<table>
<tr><td>No. 494</td><td>No. 495</td></tr>
</table>

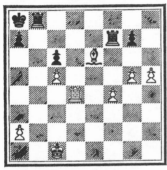

Black to play. White wins.

Black wins.

With two Rooks vs. R+B, the B+2P are superior to the Rook because there are now other ways of defending the Pawns. No. 494 (Alekhine-Flohr, Nottingham, 1936) is typical. Black is helpless against the Pawns even though they are unsupported by the White King (compare No. 493a). The game concluded: *1 .... R(B2)—Kt2; 2 B—Kt3, R—R1; 3 P—R6!, P×P; 4 P—Kt6, R—Kt2; 5 P—B5, R—KB1* (5 .... P—KR4; 6 B—B2, R(R1)—Kt1; 7 P—B6, R×P; 8 B×R, R×B; 9 P—B7, R—B3; 10 R—Q8ch and wins); *6 B—B2, P—KR4; 7 R—Q6, R—K2; 8 P—B6, R—K8ch; 9 K—Q2, R—KB8; 10 P—B7, P—R5; 11 R—Q7,* Resigns.

This example is but another instance of a basic rule for all such endings: *In all endings with two Rooks vs. Rook and minor piece the person who is the exchange ahead should try to exchange one pair of Rooks.*

4. THREE PAWNS (OR MORE) FOR THE EXCHANGE

This is usually a simple and straightforward win: the Rook is unable to hold back the Pawns. An example where the winning side experiences a little difficulty because his Pawns are blockaded is No. 495 (Fine-Keres, AVRO, 1938). The game continued *1 R—R1, P—Kt4; 2 R—K1, K—B3; 3 R—KKt1, K—Kt3; 4 R—K1, B—B3; 5 R—KKt1!, P—Kt5!!* (the simplest); *6 P×P, P—B5; 7 P—Kt5, B—Q5; 8 R—Q1, B—K6!; 9 K×P, B—B8; 10 R—Q6ch, K×P; 11 R—QKt6, P—B6; 12 K—Q3, K—B5; 13 R—QKt8, K—Kt6;* 14 Resigns. White must lose his Rook for the KBP.

No. 496

Black to play draws.

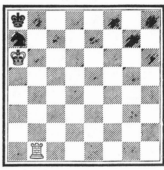

No. 497

White to play wins; Black to play draws.

E. ROOK VS. KNIGHT (NO PAWNS)

This too is in general a draw. However, Black must stay in the center of the board, because all the won cases occur with the King in the corner.

The general draw is seen in No. 496. After *1 .... Kt—Q1ch; 2 K—Q6, Kt—Kt2ch; 3 K—Q5, Kt—Q1* White can do nothing. If, e.g., 4 R—R8, K—Q2, or 4 R—K7, Kt—Kt2 White can never set up a mating position and can never drive the King into the corner.

What happens when the King gets to the corner is seen in No. 497. White to play wins by *1 K—Kt6!, K—Kt1* (or 1 .... Kt—B1ch; 2 K—B7, Kt—R2; 3 R—Kt8 mate); *2 R—Kt2!!, Kt—B1ch; 3 K—B6 dis ch, K—R1* (or 3 .... K—R2; 4 K—B7); *4 K—B7* and mate in at most two moves. Black to play can draw by getting his Kt out of the noose. *1 .... Kt—B1; 2 R—Kt2* (there is nothing better: on 2 R—Kt7, Kt—Q3; 3 R—Q7, Kt—B1; 4 R—Q8, K—Kt1 White is no where), *Kt—K2!!* (but not 1 .... Kt—R2?; 2 K—Kt6 as above, or 1 .... Kt—Q3; 2 K—Kt6 and if 2 .... K—Kt1; 3 K—B6 dis ch) and if now *3 K—Kt6, K—Kt1; 4 K—B5 dis ch, K—B2* = or 3 R—K2, Kt—B1=.

Where White wins endings with R vs. Kt he must use one or more of three stratagems:

1. Mating threats;
2. Pinning the Kt in positions where the Black King must abandon it;
3. Stalemating the Kt and capturing it.

These three usually go together, but generally one is of outstanding importance.

<table>
<tr><td align="center">No. 498</td><td align="center">No. 499</td></tr>
<tr><td></td><td>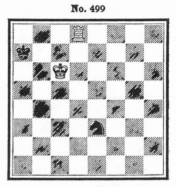</td></tr>
<tr><td align="center">White wins.</td><td align="center">White to play wins.</td></tr>
</table>

A relatively simple example which illustrates all three is No. 498 (Berger). After *1 .... Kt—Kt2* (if 1 .... Kt—Kt6; 2 R—Q1 and the Kt is lost: 2 .... K—Kt2; 3 K—Kt4, etc.); *2 R—Q7, K—Kt1; 3 K—Kt6, K—R1!; 4 R—R7!* (better than 4 R×Kt? stalemate) and now if *4 .... Kt—Q1; 5 R—R8* and if *4 .... Kt—Q3; 5 R—R8ch* with mate in both cases.

The most complicated variations occur when the Kt is in the center of the board, but can be stalemated because it is separated from the King. Mate threats are always involved in such cases. Since the play is quite difficult we shall give several instances in order to illustrate the procedure. In all cases the central idea is to drive the Kt to the edge of the board.

In No. 499 (Berger) the solution is *1 R—Q7ch, K—R3* (if instead 1 .... K—Kt1; 2 R—Kt7ch, K—R1; 3 R—Kt3, Kt—B5; 4 R—QB3, Kt—K4ch; 5 K—B7 and mates, or 1 .... K—R1; 2 R—Q3, Kt—B5;

3 R—QB3 with the same mate. If here 4 .... Kt—R4ch; 5 K—Kt6 wins the Kt); *2 R—Q3, Kt—B5; 3 K—B5, Kt—K4* (forced: on 3 .... Kt—R4; 4 R—QR3, or 3 .... Kt—Kt3; 4 R—R3ch, K—Kt2; 5 R—QKt3 wins the Kt); *4 R—Q5!, Kt—B6* (relatively best: if 4 .... Kt—Kt5; 5 K—Q4, Kt—B7; 6 R—KKt5, Kt—R6; 7 R—Kt6ch, K—Kt4; 8 K—K3 and the Kt is caught. Similarly after 5 .... Kt—R7; 6 R—KB5, Kt—Kt5; 7 R—B4, Kt—R7; 8 K—K3 the Kt does not come out alive. And if here 5 .... K—Kt2; 6 R—Q6, Kt—R7; 7 R—KB6, Kt—Kt5; 8 R—KKt6, Kt—B7; 9 K—K3, etc. Finally if 4 .... Kt—B2 instead of 4 .... Kt—Kt5, then 5 K—B6, Kt—R3; 6 R—Q4, K—R4; 7 R—KB4, Kt—Kt1; 8 K—Q6 followed by K—K6—B7 captures the luckless horse); *5 R—B5!, Kt—Q7* (there is nothing better:

a) 5 .... Kt—R5; 6 R—B6ch, K—Kt2; 7 K—Q4, Kt—Kt7; 8 K—K4, K—B2; 9 R—KR6, K—Q2; 10 R—R2, Kt—K8; 11 R—K2.

b) 5 .... Kt—Kt8; 6 R—B6ch, K—Kt2; 7 K—B4, Kt—K7; 8 R—B2, Kt—Kt6; 9 K—Q4, Kt—R4; 10 K—K5, Kt—Kt6; 11 R—KKt2, Kt—R4; 12 R—Kt5, or 11 .... Kt—B8; 12 K—B4 and 13 R—KB2.

c) 5 .... Kt—K8; 6 K—B4, Kt—B7; 7 R—B3, K—R4; 8 R—B3, Kt—K8; 9 R—R3ch, K—Kt3; 10 R—KKt3!, Kt—B7; 11 R—QB3, Kt—K8; 12 K—Q4, K—Kt4; 13 K—K4, K—Kt5; 14 R—B1, Kt—Kt7; 15 R—KKt1, Kt—R5; 16 R—Kt4.

d) 5 .... Kt—K8; 6 K—B4, Kt—-Kt7; 7 K—Q3, Kt—K8ch; 8 K—Q2, Kt—Kt7; 9 K—K2, Kt—R5; 10 R—B6ch followed by 11 K—B2 and 12 K—Kt3); *6 R—B4, K—R4; 7 R—QKt4!!, K—R3* (if 7 .... Kt—B8; 8 R—Kt1 and if 7 .... Kt—B6; 8 R—Kt3, winning the Kt in either event); *8 R—R4ch, K—Kt2; 9 R—KB4, Kt—Kt6ch* (or 9 .... K—R3; 10 K—Kt4, K—Kt3; 11 K—B3, Kt—Kt8ch; 12 K—Kt2, Kt—Q7; 13 K—B2); *10K—Kt4, Kt—B8; 11 K—B4!, Kt—K7 12 R—Kt4, K—B3; 13 K—Q3, Kt—B8ch; 14 K—B2, Kt—R7* (or 14 .... Kt—K7; 15 K—Q2); *15 R—QR4.*

No. 500

White wins.

Similarly, if the Kt is on some other square on the K-side it will inevitably be caught and captured. E.g., in No. 500 (Berger) Black's wide choice of moves still cannot save him:

a) *1 .... K—Kt1; 2 K—Q4, K—B2; 3 R—KB6, Kt—K7ch; 4 K—Q3, Kt—B8ch* (or 4 .... Kt—Kt6; 5 R—B3, Kt—R4; 6 R—B5, Kt—Kt6; 7 R—KKt5, etc.); *5 K—B4, Kt—K7; 6 R—B2, Kt—Kt6; 7 K—Q5, K—Q2; 8 K—K5, K—B3; 9 R—KKt2, Kt—B8* (or 9 .... Kt—R4; 10 R—Kt5); *10 K—B4 and 11 R—KB2.*

b) *1 .... Kt—K7; 2 K—B4, Kt—B5* (or 2 .... Kt—Kt6; 3 K—Q3, Kt—B4; 4 R—KB6, or 2 .... Kt—Kt8; 3 R—KB6, Kt—K7; 4 R—B2); *3 R—KB6, Kt—K7; 4 R—B2, Kt—Kt6; 5 K—Q4, etc., as in a).*

c) *1 .... Kt—Kt7; 2 R—KB6, Kt—K6* (2 .... Kt—K8; 3 K—B4, Kt—Kt7; 4 K—Q3, Kt—K8ch; 5 K—Q2, Kt—Kt7; 6 K—K2, etc.); *3 R—B3, Kt—Kt5* (3 .... Kt—B7; 4 R—B3, Kt—K8; 5 K—Q4, Kt—Kt7; 6 K—K4); *4 K—Q4, K—Kt2; 5 R—B4, Kt—R3; 6 K—K5, K—B2; 7 K—B6, Kt—Kt1ch; 8 K—B7, Kt—R3ch; 9 K—Kt7.*

d) *1 .... Kt—R6; 2 R—KB6, Kt—Kt8* (2 .... Kt—Kt4; 3 K—Q5 followed by R—B5); *3 R—B2, Kt—R6; 4 R—B5, Kt—Kt8; 5 K—Q4, Kt—K7ch; 6 K—K3, Kt—B6; 7 K—Q3, Kt—Q8; 8 R—R5ch, K—Kt2; 9 R—R2 and 10 R—Q2.*

e) *1 .... Kt—R4; 2 K—Q4, Kt—Kt6* (2 .... Kt—B5; 3 K—K3, Kt—Kt7ch; 4 K—K4, K—Kt2; 5 R—Q2, Kt—R5; 6 R—Q7ch, 7 R—KKt7 and 8 R—Kt4); *3 R—K6, Kt—B4ch* (or 3 .... Kt—B8; 4 R—KKt6, or 3 .... Kt—R4; 4 K—K5, Kt—Kt6; 5 K—B4); *4 K—K4, Kt—Kt6ch; 5 K—B4, Kt—R4ch; 6 K—Kt4, Kt—Kt2; 7 R—K7ch.*

Now we can see why positions with King and Kt next to one another in or near the corner usually lose: if the Kt stays near the King it will be pinned and captured; if it does not it will be stalemated and captured.

No. 501 (Berger) is the most favorable position that White can have without winning immediately, and its variations include everything that has been considered. *1 .... Kt—R4ch; 2 K—Kt5, Kt—Kt2* (if 2 .... Kt—Kt6; 3 R—Q8! and the Kt is lost—see No. 498); *3 R—KB8!* (not 3 R—R7?, K—Kt1; 4 K—Kt6, Kt—Q1 = —No. 497), *Kt—Q3ch; 4 K—B6, Kt—B5* (if 4 .... Kt—Kt2; 5 R—B7, K—R1; 6 K—Kt6! and wins. For 4 .... Kt—

No. 501

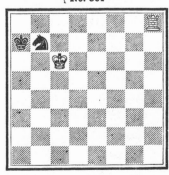

White wins. Black to play.

K5 see Variation A.); *5 R—Q8!, Kt—K4ch* (relatively best. The alternatives are:

a) 5 .... Kt—Kt3; 6 R—Q4, Kt—B1; 7 K—B7, Kt—Kt3; 8 R—Q1, Kt—R1ch; 9 K—B6, K—Kt1; 10 R—KR1, K—R2; 11 R—QKt1 and wins the Kt.

b) 5 .... Kt—R6; 6 R—Q4, Kt—B7; 7 R—K4, K—Kt1; 8 K—Kt6, K—B1; 9 R—B4ch.

c) 5 .... Kt—Kt7; 6 R—Q4, K—R1; 7 K—Kt6.

d) 5 .... Kt—R4ch; 6 K—Kt5—No. 498.

e) 5 .... Kt—K6; 6 R—Q7ch, etc.—No. 499); *6 K—B5* (No. 502),

No. 502

No. 503

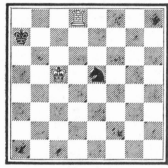
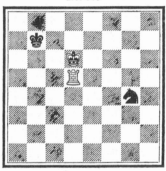

Black to play; White wins.   Black to play; White wins.

K—Kt2 (for alternatives see Variation B.); *7 R—Q5, Kt—Kt5* (for 7 .... Kt—Kt3 see Variation C. 7 .... Kt—B6 transposes into Variation B, line a)); *8 K—Q6!* (No. 503), *K—Kt3* (for alternatives see Variation D); *9 R—Q2!, Kt—K6* (or 9 .... Kt—B3; 10 R—Kt2ch, K—R4; 11 R—K2, K—Kt4; 12 R—K6, Kt—Kt5; 13 K—Q5, Kt—B7; 14 K—Q4, K—Kt5; 15 R—Kt6ch, K—R6; 16 R—Kt1!, Kt—Kt5; 17 R—KB1, K—Kt5; 18 R—B4, Kt—R3; 19 K—K5 dis ch, K—B4; 20 K—B6, K—Q3; 21 R—Q4ch, K—B4; 22 R—KR4, Kt—Kt1ch; 23 K—B7); *10 R—Kt2ch, K—R4* (the best chance); *11 K—B5!, K—R5!; 12 R—Q2!* (No. 504), *Kt—B4* (For 12 .... Kt—B8 see Variation E.); *13 R—Q3, Kt—K2; 14 R—KB3, Kt—Kt3* (14 .... Kt—B1; 15 R—B7 or 14 .... Kt—Kt1; 15 K—Q6, Kt—R3; 16 K—K6); *15 K—Q6, K—Kt4; 16 R—B5ch, K—Kt3; 17 R—B6, Kt—R5; 18 K—K5 dis ch, K—B4; 19 K—K4*, etc.
Variation A. 4 .... Kt—K5; 5 R—B7ch, K—Kt1 (5 .... K—R3;

6 R—B4, Kt—B6; 7 R—B4, or 5 .... K—R1; 6 K—Kt6); 6 R—Kt7ch, K—R1 (6 .... K—B1; 7 R—K7, Kt—B3; 8 R—K6); 7 R—Kt4 and now:

a) 7 .... Kt—B3; 8 R—KB4, Kt—R4 (8 .... Kt—R2; 9 K—B7, or 8 .... Kt—K1; 9 R—B8); 9 R—B5, Kt—Kt6 (9 .... Kt—Kt2; 10 R—B8ch and 11 R—B7ch); 10 R—B3, Kt—K5; 11 K—Kt6 and mates in at most two moves.

b) 7 .... Kt—Kt4; 8 R—Kt4, Kt—K3; 9 K—Kt6! and mates.

c) 7 .... Kt—B6; 8 R—QB4, Kt—Q8; 9 K—B7, Kt—Kt7; 10 R—Kt4 and wins the Kt.

On other Kt moves 8 K—B7 decides.

Variation B. There is no way to save the Kt.

a) 6 .... Kt—B6; 7 R—Q5 and now

   1) 7 .... Kt—K8; 8 R—B5, Kt—Q6ch; 9 K—B4, Kt—Kt7ch; 10 K—Kt3, Kt—Q6; 11 K—B3. If here 8 .... Kt—B7; 9 R—B3, Kt—K8; 10 R—KKt3, K—Kt2; 11 K—B4, Kt—B7; 12 R—QB3, Kt—K8; 13 K—Q4 and 14 K—K4.

   2) 7 .... Kt—Kt8; 8 R—B5, Kt—K7; 9 R—B3, K—Kt2; 10 K—B4, Kt—Kt8; 11 R—K3 or 10 .... Kt—B8; 11 R—B2.

   3) 7 .... Kt—R7; 8 R—B5, Kt—Kt5; 9 K—Q4, K—Kt2 (or 9 .... Kt—R3; 10 R—B6, Kt—Kt5; 11 R—KKt6); 10 R—B4, Kt—R3; 11 K—K5, K—B2; 12 K—K6, K—Q1; 13 R—KR4.

   4) 7 .... Kt—R5; 8 R—KKt5, Kt—B6; 9 R—B5, Kt—Q7 (9 .... Kt—R5; 10 R—B6, K—Kt2; 11 K—Q4, K—B2; 12 K—K4, Kt—Kt7; 13 R—KR6!, K—Q2; 14 R—R2, Kt—K8; 15 R—K2); 10 R—B4, K—R3; 11 K—Kt4, K—Kt3; 12 K—B3, Kt—Kt8ch; 13 K—Kt2, Kt—Q7; 14 K—B2.

No. 504

b) 6 .... Kt—Kt5; 7 K—Q4, K—Kt2 (or 7 .... Kt—B3; 8 R—KB8); 8 R—KB8, K—B2; 9 R—KB4, Kt—R3; 10 K—K5, K—Q2; 11 K—B6, Kt—Kt1ch; 12 K—B7, Kt—K2; 13 R—Q4ch.

c) 6 .... Kt—Kt3; 7 R—Q4!, K—Kt2; 8 K—Q6, Kt—R1; 9 K—K6, Kt—Kt3; 10 R—KKt4, Kt—B1ch; 11 K—K7, Kt—R2; 12 R—Kt7.

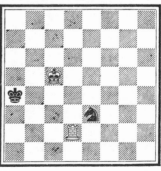

Black to play; White wins.

Variation C. 7 .... Kt—Kt3; 8 K—Q6 and now
a) 8 .... Kt—B5; 9 R—Q2, K—Kt3; 10 K—K5, Kt—Kt3ch; 11 K—B6, Kt—B5; 12 K—B5, Kt—R4; 13 R—Kt2.
b) 8 .... K—B1; 9 R—KB5, Kt—R5; 10 R—B4, Kt—Kt7; 11 R—K4.
c) 8 .... K—Kt3; 9 R—Q4 and 10 R—KKt4.
d) 8 .... Kt—B1; 9 R—KKt5 and 10 R—Kt7.
e) 8 .... Kt—R1; 9 K—K6, Kt—Kt3; 10 R—Q4, K—B2; 11 R—KKt4, Kt—B1ch; 12 K—K7, Kt—Q2; 13 R—B4ch.
f) 8 .... Kt—R5; 9 R—KR5, Kt—Kt7; 10 K—K5, Kt—K6 (or 10 .... Kt—K8; 11 R—R3, Kt—B7; 12 R—QB3, Kt—K8; 13 K—K4 and 14 R—K1); 11 K—Q4, Kt—B7ch (if 11 ...., Kt—Kt5; 12 R—KB5, K—B2; 13 R—B4, Kt—R3; 14 K—K5, K—Q2; 15 K—B6, Kt—Kt1ch; 16 K—B7); 12 K—B5, Kt—K8 (12 .... Kt—K6; 13 R—KKt5); 13 R—B5, Kt—Kt7 (or 13 .... Kt—Q6ch; 14 K—B4, Kt—Kt7ch; 15 K—Kt3, Kt—Q6; 16 K—B3, Kt—K8; 17 R—B2); 14 K—Q4, Kt—R5; 15 R—B6 and 16 K—K4 followed by R—R6—R2—K2, as usual.

Variation D.
a) 8 .... Kt—B3; 9 R—K5 transposes back into the main line.
b) 8 .... Kt—K6; 9 R—Kt5ch, K—R3; 10 K—B5 and now the chief branch lines are:
  1) 10 .... Kt—B7; 11 R—Kt2, Kt—K6; 12 R—Kt6ch, K—R2; 13 R—Kt3 as in the main line.
  2) 10 .... Kt—B8; 11 R—QKt3, Kt—R7; 12 R—Kt3, Kt—B8; 13 R—R3ch, K—Kt2; 14 K—Q4, K—B3; 15 R—KB3, Kt—Q7; 16 R—Q3, etc.
  3) 10 .... Kt—Kt5; 11 R—Kt6ch, K—R2; 12 K—K6, Kt—R7; 13 R—KB6, Kt—Kt5; 14 R—B7ch, K—Kt1; 15 K—Q4, K—B1; 16 R—B4, Kt—R3; 17 R—B6, Kt—Kt5; 18 R—KKt6.
  4) 10 .... Kt—B4; 11 R—Kt6ch, K—R4 (or 11 .... K—R2; 12 R—KB6, Kt—Kt6; 13 K—Q5, Kt—K7; 14 K—B4, Kt—Kt6; 15 K—Q3); 12 R—KB6, Kt—R5; 13 K—Q4.
  5) 10 .... Kt—Q4; 11 R—Kt3, Kt—B5; 12 R—Kt6ch, K—R2; 13 R—Q6—No. 500.
c) Other Kt moves lead to familiar variations. E.g., 8 .... Kt—B7; 9 R—Q4, K—Kt3; 10 K—K6, Kt—R6 (10 .... K—B4; 11 K—K5); 11 K—B5, Kt—Kt8; 12 R—Q2, Kt—B6; 13 R—Q3, Kt—K8 (13 .... Kt—Kt8; 14 R—K3); 14 R—QB3, K—Kt4; 15 K—K4, K—Kt5; 16 R—B1, Kt—Kt7; 17 R—KKt1, etc.

Variation E. 12 .... Kt—B8; 13 R—Q3, Kt—R7; 14 K—Q5,

K—Kt5; 15 K—K4, K—B5; 16 R—Q1, Kt—Kt5; 17 R—KB1, K—B4; 18 R—B5ch, K—Kt5; 19 R—B4, Kt—R3; 20 K—K5 dis ch, K—B6; 21 K—B6, etc.

F. ROOK AND PAWN VS. KNIGHT

This, like the similar case with a B, is won but there are a few positions where the Kt can manage to draw. No. 505 (Handbuch) is the simplest draw. After *1 K—Kt2, K—K7!; 2 R—Kt3* (hoping to play his K to R3, Kt4, B4, K4, etc.), *Kt—B4!* forces the draw for on *3 R—R3, Kt—Q5* repeats the position.

No. 505   No. 506

Draw.   Draw.

The most typical draw occurs when the Pawn is too far advanced and cannot be supported by the King. No. 506 (Dr. Em. Lasker-Ed. Lasker, New York, 1924—the colors have been reversed) is a classic instance. White is helpless because he cannot approach the Pawn with his King. E.g., *1 .... Kt—Kt2; 2 K—K5, Kt—R4; 3 K—Q5, Kt—Kt2; 4 R—KB6, Kt—R4; 5 R—K6, Kt—Kt2; 6 K—K5, Kt—R4; 7 K—B6, K—R3!; 8 K—K5* (8 K—K7, K—Kt2 and 9 .... Kt—B5), *K—Kt4; 9 K—Q5*, etc.

With a RP the similar ending is won because of the mate possibilities. Thus in No. 507 (Lewis, 1835) White can win by *1 R—R4!, Kt—B3; 2 K—Q5, Kt—R2; 3 K—Q6.* The winning idea is to get the King to QKt8 and advance the Pawn. *3 .... Kt—Kt4ch; 4 K—Q7, K—R2* (or 4 .... Kt—R2; 5 K—Q8, Kt—Kt4—or A—; 6 K—B8, K—R2; 7 R—R5, Kt—Q3ch; 8 K—B7, Kt—B5; 9 R—R4, Kt—Kt3;

10 R—Q4, Kt—R1ch; 11 K—B6, Kt—Kt3; 12 R—QKt4, Kt—B1; 13 K—B7, Kt—K2; 14 R—Q4!, K×P; 15 K—Q7, Kt—B4; 16 R—K4, K—Kt3; 17 K—K6, Kt—Kt6; 18 R—K1 and wins the Kt as in No. 501. Variation A. 5 .... Kt—B3ch; 6 K—B8, K—R2; 7 K—B7, Kt—Kt1; 8 R—R5, K—R1; 9 P—R7, Kt—R3ch; 10 K—Q6, Kt—Kt5; 11 R—R4, Kt—Q6; 12 K—Q5 and again the Kt has strayed too far); *5 K—B6, Kt—B6; 6 R—QB4, Kt—Kt8* (to prevent 7 K—Kt5); *7 R—B1, Kt—Q7* (7 .... Kt—R6; 8 K—B5); *8 K—Kt5* followed by *9 R—B7ch,* etc.

Similar positions with the Pawn on the 4th, 5th, or 7th are likewise

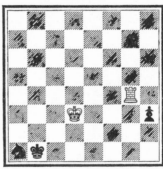

No. 507	No. 507A
White wins.	White to play wins.

won. No. 507a (Amelung, 1907), White: K at QB3, R at QR1, P at QR5; Black: K at QKt4, Kt at QR3. White wins. 1 R—R3, Kt—B4; 2 K—Q4, Kt—R3; 3 K—Q5, Kt—Kt5ch; 4 K—Q6, Kt—R3; 5 R—R1, Kt—Kt5; 6 K—B7, K—R3; 7 R—R4, Kt—Q4ch; 8 K—B6, Kt—K2ch; 9 K—B5, Kt—B1; 10 R—R1, Kt—R2; 11 R—QB1, K—Kt2; 12 K—Kt4, Kt—B3ch; 13 K—R4, Kt—R2; 14 R—B2, Kt—B3; 15 R—KR2. But No. 507b (Berger), White: K at QB1, R at QR1, P at QR3; Black: K at QKt6, Kt at QR5, is drawn because as soon as the White King leaves QB1, ... K—Kt7 will capture the Pawn.

G. ROOK VS. KNIGHT AND PAWNS

Again we have the same general results as with a Bishop: one Pawn draws, but may lose; two Pawns draw, but may win; three Pawns always win.

1. ROOK VS. KNIGHT AND PAWN

This is of course a draw in general, but there are some special positions which win. Thus in No. 507A (Salvioli, 1887) White can first capture the Pawn and then transpose into a won R vs. Kt ending: *1 K—B3!, P—R7; 2 R—KR4, Kt—B7; 3 R×P, Kt—K6!; 4 K—Q3, Kt—Q4* (if 4 .... Kt—Q8; 5 R—R1 and if 4 .... Kt—Kt5; 5 R—K2, while if 4 .... Kt—B4; 5 R—R5, winning the Kt in all variations); *5 R—R4, K—Kt7; 6 R—Q4* and will win as in No. 503.

Again there are special cases where the Pawn may win. An example is No. 508 (Berger). After *1 .... P—B7; 2 R—Kt1, K—Q7!* Black

No. 508

Black to play wins.

No. 509

Draw.

will queen for if *3 K—R2, Kt—B6ch; 4 K—R3, Kt×Rch* (anything but 4 .... P×R=Q or R or Kt), etc.

2. ROOK VS. KNIGHT AND TWO (OR MORE) PAWNS

With the White King in front of the Pawns this is always a draw, but if the King is far away the game is untenable.

No. 509 (Handbuch) is the counterpart to No. 480. Black cannot win here because he cannot advance the Pawns without blockading them. E.g., *1 K—K1, P—Q7ch* (or 1 .... K—B5; 2 R—B8ch, K—Kt6; 3 R—Q8!, Kt—B5; 4 R×P!, Kt×Rch; 5 K—K2) *2 K—K2, K—B5; 3 R—B8ch, K—Kt6; 4 R—Q8, Kt—B6ch* (or 4 .... K—B5; 5 R—B8ch, K—Q5; 6 R—Q8); *5 K×P,* etc. However, if the Rook were not behind the Kt here White would lose. E.g., No. 509a (Berger), White Rook at QR2, other pieces as in No. 509. Black wins.

1 K—B1 (or 1 R—R4ch, K—B4; 2 R—R5ch, K—B5; 3 R—R4ch, K—Kt6; 4 R—Q4, Kt—B6ch; 5 K—K1, K—B7), Kt—B6; 2 R—QKt2, K—B5; 3 R—KR2, Kt—K5; 4 R—R4, P—Q7ch; 5 K—B2, K—Q4; 6 R—R5ch, K—K3; 7 R—R6ch, K—B4; 8 R—R1, P—K7. Disconnected Pawns are still less promising here, since the short-stepping Kt cannot defend two widely separated P's and there are quite a few positions where it cannot even defend ŏne Pawn.

However, if the White King is not near the Pawns, the Rook alone will not be able to hold them. An instance is No. 510 (Berger). After *1 .... K—Kt4; 2 K—B3, Kt—Kt6; 3 R—R1, P—R6; 4 R—R2, K—Kt5; 5 K—K3, P—Kt4!; 6 R—QB2!* (to prevent 6 .... K—B6. If 6 K—Q3, P—R7!; 7 R×P, Kt—B8ch), *Kt—B4; 7 K—Q2* (or 7 K—

No. 510	No. 511
	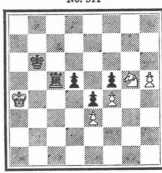
Black to play wins.	White to play. Black wins.

Q4, Kt—R5; 8 K—Q3, K—Kt6; 9 R—B1, P—R7, etc.), *Kt—K5ch; 8 K—B1, Kt—B6!; 9 R—KR2, K—Kt6* followed by .... P—R7.

More than two Pawns will practically always win by straightforward advancing.

H. ROOK AND PAWNS VS. KNIGHT AND PAWNS

The general results here are the same as those for the Bishop (p. 477). In the ending the exchange is worth a little less than two Pawns.

1. NO PAWNS FOR THE EXCHANGE

R vs. Kt in such cases is normally a somewhat simpler win than R vs. B. In the general case, corresponding to No. 484, the entrance of either the White King or the White Rook can never be prevented. Furthermore the Kt cannot defend anything that is far away, so that with Pawns on both sides of the board Black is certain to lose material in short order. The chief danger for the winning side is not (as with the B) getting all the Pawns on one side, but blockading the Pawn position so that the Kt can both attack and defend at the same time.

An example where the side with the Kt has counterchances—No. 511—will illustrate the ease with which such endings can usually be decided. After *1 P—R6, R—B1; 2 K—Kt4* (or first 2 P—R7, R—KR1), *P—Q5!* exchanges the KP and QP for the obstructing RP. The noteworthy feature of this sacrifice is that White will have to lose all his Pawns in the long run. *3 P×P, P—K6; 4 P—R7, P—K7; 5 Kt—B3, R—KR1; 6 K—B3, R×P; 7 K—Q2, K—B3!* (7 .... R—Q2; 8 Kt—K5 is pointless); *8 K×P, K—Q4; 9 K—B2, R—R2!; 10 Kt—Kt5* (desperation: if 10 K—K3, R—R6ch; 11 K—B2, K—K5 and it is all over), *R—R6!; 11 K—Kt2, K×P (No. 512); 12 K—B2, R—K6!* (White gets into zugzwang and is unable to hold on to his Pawn); *13 K—Kt2, K—Q6; 14 K—B2, R—K7ch; 15 K—B3, R—K8!; 16 K—B2, R—Q8; 17 K—B3* (if the Kt moves, 17 .... K—K5 decides), *R—B8ch; 18 K—Kt3* (White played 18 K—Kt2, R×P; 19 Kt—K6, R—K5!; 20 Resigns), *K—K6; 19 Kt—K6* (or 19 Kt—R3, R—B6ch; 20 K—Kt2, R×Kt; 21 K×R, K×P), *R—B7!* and White must give up the Pawn. The last point is *20 Kt—B7* (20 K—R3, R×P), *R—B6ch!; 21 K—Kt2, K—K5; 22 Kt—K6, R—B6; 23 K—B2, R—B3,* etc.

This brings us to the question of R+P vs. Kt+P. With a passed Pawn the Rook of course wins quite easily, since a Rook can both stop the enemy passed Pawn and support its own, while a Kt cannot. With no passed Pawn, unlike the similar B ending it makes no difference whether the Pawns are in the center or on the side: the game is drawn only if the Kt can both attack the Pawn and prevent the enemy King from coming in. This is possible only in certain positions where the Pawn is blockaded.

The general win has already been seen in No. 512. The case with RP vs. KtP or RP is just as easy because a Kt is seen at its worst when it is on the edge of the board. E.g., No. 512a (Tarrasch-Reti, Bad Kissingen, 1928), White: K at KKt2, Kt at KB4, P at KR4; Black: K at KKt2, R at QKt7 (ch), P at KR2. Black wins. Black's King just walks in and captures the Pawn. The conclusion was 1 K—Kt3, K—B3; 2 Kt—R3, R—Kt6ch; 3 K—Kt2, K—B4; 4 Kt—B2,

No. 512

Black wins.

K—B5; 5 Kt—R3ch, K—Kt5; 6 Kt—B2ch, K×P; 7 Kt—K4, R—
K6; 8 Kt—B2, R—Kt6ch; 9 K—R2, P—R3; 10 Kt—K4, R—Kt5;
11 Kt—B2, R—Kt2; 12 Kt—K4, K—Kt5; 13 Kt—B2ch, K—B6;
14 Kt—R3, R—Kt7ch; 15 K—R1, R—QR7; 16 Resigns.

The typical draw is seen in No. 513. If Black's King leaves the QP
(say via QKt3), White releases the pin on his Kt and threatens Kt×P.
Black must then defend the Pawn with his Rook, only to find that his
King can get nowhere because of the strongly centralized Kt. E.g.,
1 .... K—B3; 2 K—Q2, R—R4; 3 K—Q3, K—Kt3; 4 K—Q2
(4 K—K2, K—B3; 5 K—B3? is bad: 5 .... R—R5; 6 Kt—B5, R—K5
and Black wins), *K—Kt4; 5 K—Q3, K—Kt5; 6 K—Q2, K—Kt6;*
7 K—Q3, K—Kt7; 8 K—Q2, R—R7ch; 9 K—Q3, R—R6; 10 K—Q2,

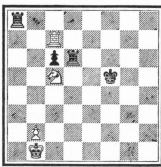

No. 513	No. 514
Draw.	Black wins.

R—R4; 11 K—Q3, K—B8; 12 K—B3!, R—R6; 13 K—Q3, R—Kt6;
14 K—K2, R—Kt4; 15 K—Q3, etc.=.

With all the Pawns on one side the win proceeds in exactly the same
manner as in Nos. 487 and 487a—the White King marches in, the
Black pieces are constricted, eventually material is won. Since few
R+P vs. Kt+P endings need be feared, the pitfalls with the B do not
come up and the technique of the win is simpler. The chief danger to
be avoided is a blockade.

Difficulties come up in this ending chiefly with two R's vs. R+Kt.
The reason is that with the extra material White's King cannot penetrate the enemy defense. Accordingly whenever possible the superior
side should exchange Rooks.

The technical problem is hardest when each side has only one Pawn—
illustrated in No. 514 (Alekhine-Lasker, St. Petersburg, 1914). As
long as White's Rook is on the board there is very little that Black can

do; but once the Rook is exchanged White may just as well resign
(No. 512). How can Black force the exchange? Chiefly by the utilization of the *pin* of the Kt and the creation of *mating threats*. With
this in mind, the following moves are intelligible. *1 R—B7ch, K—K4;
2 K—B2, R—KR3; 3 Kt—Q3ch, K—Q3; 4 R—B5, R—QKt1; 5 K—
B3, K—B2; 6 R—B7ch, K—Kt3; 7 R—Q7,* (the threat was .... R—
R6 and .... R—Q1), *R—R6; 8 R—Q4, R(Kt1)—KR1; 9 R—Kt4ch*
(if 9 R—Q7, R(R1)—R4; 10 R—Q4, P—B4; 11 R—Q6ch, K—B2;
12 R—QR6, R—Q4 and wins), *K—B2; 10 K—B2, R(R1)—R5;
11 R—Kt3, R—R7ch* (somewhat quicker was 11 .... P—B4!; 12 R—
B3, K—Q3; 13 R—R3, P—B5; 14 R—R6ch, K—Q4; 15 Kt—B1, R—
R7ch; 16 K—Kt1, R—R8; 17 R—R3, R(R5)—R6; 18 R×R, R×R,
for after 19 K—B2, K—B4!; 20 Kt—R2, K—Q5; 21 Kt—Kt4, R—
R7ch; 22 K—Kt1, K—B4; 23 Kt—B2, K—Kt4 the Black King
reaches QKt6). Here there ensued a good deal of maneuvering
(doubtless with an eye on the clock!) which is equivalent to *12 K—B3,
R—R4; 13 R—R3, R—Q4; 14 R—Kt3, R—Kt7; 15 R—R3, K—Kt3.*
Now Alekhine is virtually compelled to bring his Rook around to Q1,
which will permit the Black King to get to QKt4. *16 R—R1* (if
16 K—B4, R—Kt5ch; 17 K—B3, P—B4; 18 K—B2, R—Kt7ch;
19 K—B3, R—Kt6; 20 K—B2, P—B5), *R—Kt6; 17 R—Q1* (Lasker
has improved his position because his opponent's Kt is doubly pinned),
K—Kt4; 18 K—B2 (if now 18 R—Q2, R—B4ch; 19 K—Kt3, R(B4)—
Kt4 forces the exchange of Rooks. Here 19 K—Q4, R—B5ch; 20 K—
K5, R—K6ch; 21 K—B5, R—Q5 wins more quickly for Black), *K—
B5* (compelling a weakening of the P position), *19 P—Kt3ch, K—Kt4;
20 R—Q2, R—R6; 21 R—Q1, R—R7ch; 22 K—B3, R—Q1; 23 R—
KKt1, R—R6; 24 R—Q1, R(Q1)—KR1; 25 R—KKt1* (the threat
was .... R—R8, ... R—Q2, ... R(R1)—R7, exchanging Rooks),
R(R1)—R4; 26 K—B2, R—Q4; 27 R—Q1, R—Kt4; 28 R—KB1 (for
the game continuation see A.), *R—Kt7ch; 29 K—B3, R(R6)—R7;
30 R—B1* (there is nothing better: if 30 Kt—Kt4, P—B4, if 30 Kt—
K1, R—R7!; 31 R—Kt1, P—B4; 32 R—B1, R—QR8, while finally
the aggressive 30 R—B5ch is refuted by 30 .... K—Kt3; 31 K—Q4,
R—QB7; 32 P—Kt4, R—R5ch; 33 K—K3, R—R6ch and 34 R—B3,
R×Rch; 35 K×R is forced, when 35 .... K—Kt4 wins quickly),
P—B4. Now all the White pieces except the Kt are tied to their posts.
31 Kt—B4, R—R7!; 32 Kt—Q3 (if 32 K—Q3, R(R7)—KB7; 33 K—
K3, R(B7)—QKt7; 34 R—B3, R—R6 winning a Pawn), *R—QR6!*
(threatening .... P—B5); *33 R—QKt1* (if 33 Kt—K5, R—R6ch;
34 Kt—Q3, P—B5! The exchange of Rooks by 33 R—B2 would
doubtless hold on longest, but the win would then be merely a question of time), *P—B5; 34 Kt—B1* (the only chance), *K—B4!; 35 R—
Kt2, R—R6ch; 36 K—B2, P—B6; 37 R—Kt1* (or 37 R—R2, R×Rch;

38 Kt×R, K—Q5), *R—QR1!; 38 Kt—Q3ch* (or 38 Kt—K2, R—
R7ch; 39 K—Q1, R—R8ch, or 38 P—Kt4ch, K—B5), *K—Q5; 39 R—
Q1* (39 Kt—B1, R—KR7ch; 40 K—Q1, P—B7ch), *R—QR7ch* and
wins for if 40 Kt—Kt2ch, K—B4 costs White the Knight, and if
40 K—Kt1, P—B7ch.

A. Alekhine played 29 R—Q2, whereupon 29 . . . . R(R6)—Kt6
forced the exchange of Rooks: 30 Kt—B1, R—Kt7; 31 Kt—K2, K—
Kt3! and White resigned, for since he has no checks the threat of . . . .
R—K4 is fatal.

This stratagem of slowly constricting the enemy forces until the ex-
change of Rooks is unavoidable is the key to all such endings with only
one or two Pawns left. Another illustration is No. 514a (Tarrasch-
Reti, Bad Kissingen, 1928), White: K at KB3, R at QR2, Kt at KR3,
P at KR2; Black: K at KKt3, R's at K3, Q4, P at KR2. Black wins.
After 1 . . . . R—B4ch; 2 Kt—B4ch (tit for tat!), K—Kt4; 3 P—R4ch,
K—R3; 4 K—Kt4, R(K3)—KB3; 5 R—R4, R—QKt4; 6 R—B4,
R(B3)—QKt3; 7 R—B7, R—Kt5; 8 R—B7, R—Kt2!; 9 R—B5, K—
Kt2; 10 K—Kt3, R(Kt5)—Kt4; 11 Kt—K6ch, K—Kt3; 12 R—B2,
R—Kt6ch White can no longer postpone the exchange, for if 13 K—
Kt4, P—R4ch; 14 K—B4, R—B2ch wins a R. For the ending after
13 K—Kt2, R—Kt7; 14 R×R, R×Rch see No. 512a.

With more Pawns on the board, the winning strategy involves re-
stricting the mobility of the Kt, weakening the Pawn position, and
either penetrating with the King or setting up a passed Pawn. Of
course, whenever the exchange of Rooks is possible it should be
adopted, for the win then involves nothing more difficult than walking
the King in. An excellent example of the model procedure when no
passed Pawn can be set up immediately is No. 515 (Alekhine-Kashdan,

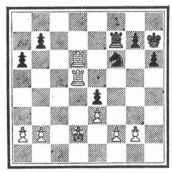

No. 515

White to play wins.

Pasadena, 1932). White's plan
against passive play is to advance
his QKtP to QKt6, R to QB5, and
then R—B7, which would force the
exchange of Rooks. To prevent this,
Black must undertake some desperate counteraction. The game
continued *1 R—KB5, K—Kt3;
2 R—B5, K—R2; 3 K—K2* (the
threat was . . . Kt—Kt5), *P—KKt4;
4 P—QKt4, K—Kt2; 5 P—R4, Kt
—Kt5* (his only chance: after 5 . . . .
K—R2; 6 P—Kt5, P×P; 7 P×P,
K—Kt2; 8 P—Kt6 Black can give
up); *6 P—B3, P×Pch; 7 P×P,
Kt—R7; 8 P—B4!, P×P; 9 P×P.*

Now that a passed Pawn has been set up the technical problem is much simpler. *9 .... Kt—Kt5* (9 .... R×P; 10 R—B7ch is worse: Black loses both his Q-side P's); *10 K—B3* (simpler was 10 P—Kt5), *Kt—B3; 11 P—Kt5, Kt—Q2* (a trap: if 11 R—B7?, Kt—K4ch!); *12 R(B5)— Q5, Kt—B3; 13 R—KB5, K—Kt3; 14 R—B5.* Now that the Kt is pinned Black is defenseless. *14 .... P×P; 15 R×P* (15 P×P was also good enough: but the move chosen wins a P), *R—B2; 16 R(Kt5)— Kt6, R—B2; 17 P—R5, K—Kt2; 18 R—Kt5, R—B2; 19 R(Q6)—Kt6, R—B6ch; 20 K—K2.* The rest is routine. *20 .... R—B5; 21 R×Pch, K—Kt3; 21 P—B5ch* (or 21 R—Kt4), *K—Kt4; 22 P—R6, R—QR5; 23 P—R7, Kt—K5; 24 K—K3* Resigns.

Where White has a passed Pawn or can set one up the win is chïld's play because the Kt cannot both defend against the Pawn and support its own Pawns. E.g., No. 515a (Tartakover-Dus-Chotimirski, Carlsbad, 1907), White: K at QKt2, R's at QB4, KR2: P's at QR2, QKt3, QB2, KKt5; Black: K at KKt2, R at K2, Kt at KB4, P's at QR2, QKt2, KKt3, KR2. White wins. Here he need only advance his Q-side Pawns. 1 R—B3, Kt—K6; 2 R—Q3, Kt—Kt5; 3 R—R4, P— KR4; 4 P×P, e.p. ch, Kt×P; 5 P—B4, Kt—B4; 6 R—Kt4, K—B3; 7 P—B5, P—KKt4; 8 P—Kt4, K—Kt3; 9 P—Kt5, K—R4; 10 R— QB4, P—Kt5; 11 P—B6, P×P; 12 P×P, R—QB2; 13 R—Q5, K— Kt4; 14 R(B4)—B5, K—R5 (14 .... R—B2; 15 P—B7); 15 R×Kt and it is all over.

2. ONE PAWN FOR THE EXCHANGE

Again this is won, but the technical difficulties are considerable. And, of course, there are quite a few drawn cases.

First of all we must note that in unbalanced Pawn positions the Rook will usually win. A passed Pawn is set up and normally cramps the opponent's game so badly that either Kt or K becomes worthless. An instance where one lone passed Pawn decides is No. 516 (Dr. Em. Lasker-Dr. Ed. Lasker, New York, 1924). White's Pawns are not quite far enough, so that Black has time to exploit his Q-side majority: *1 .... R—Q2* (for the game continuation see A); *2 Kt—K3* (or 2 Kt —B6, R—Q1; 3 P—Kt5, P—R4; 4 P×P, P—Kt5; 5 P—Kt6, P—Kt6 and queens), *P—R4!; 3 P×P, P— Kt5; 4 P—Kt5, K—B4!; 5 Kt—B2,*

No. 516

Black to play wins

P—Kt6; 6 Kt—R3, K—Kt5; 7 Kt—Kt1, P—Kt7; 8 P—Kt6, R—Q8!; 9 P—Kt7, R—Kt8; 10 K—Q3, R×P; 11 K—B2, R—Kt7ch; 12 K— Q3, K—Kt6; 13 P—R6, R—Kt3 and wins. White must lose first his Pawns and then his Kt.

A. Black lost a tempo by *1 .... R—R1,* after which Dr. Lasker found the justly celebrated draw: *2 Kt—K3, P—R4; 3 P×P, P—Kt5; 4 P—R6, K—B4; 5 P—R7, P—Kt6; 6 Kt—Q1, R—QR1; 7 P—Kt5, R×P; 8 P—Kt6, R—Q2; 9 Kt—Kt2, R—Q7; 10 K—B3, R—Q1; 11 K—K4, K—Q3; 12 K—Q3!!, R—QB1; 13 P—Kt7, K—K3; 14 P— Kt8=Qch!, R×Q; 15 K—B4, R—Kt6; 16 Kt—R4,* etc., (No. 506).

Similarly, if the Pawns are balanced but there is a sufficient number

No. 517

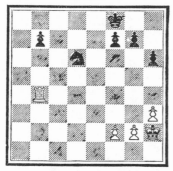

White to play. Draw.

No. 518

White to play.

on both sides White will normally be able to win, for the march of the King is bound to lead to the capture of material.

But with all the White Pawns on one side, the game may often be drawn. By manipulating his extra Pawn properly Black should be able to divert either the Rook or the King and thus guard against material loss. An example of this strategy is No. 517 (Steinitz-Zukertort, match, 1886). Zukertort drew by advancing his QKtP. The game continuation was: *1 K—Kt3, K—K2; 2 K—B4, K—K3; 3 P— R4, K—Q4; 4 P—Kt4, P—QKt4; 5 R—Kt1, K—B4; 6 R—B1ch, K— Q4; 7 K—K3, Kt—B5ch;* 8 K—K2 (if 8 K—Q3, Kt—K4ch), *P—Kt5; 9 R—QKt1, K—B4; 10 P—B4, Kt—R6; 11 R—B1ch, K—Q5; 12 R— B7, P—Kt6; 13 R—Kt7, K—B6;* (Black still draws even though the White Rook is on the seventh); *14 R—B7ch, K—Q5!* (but not 14 .... K—Kt7?; 15 R×P, K—R7; 16 R×P, P—Kt7; 17 'R—Kt7, P— Kt8=Q; 18 R×Q, K×R; 19 P—R5 and the Pawns decide); *15 R— QKt7, K—B6* and a draw was agreed to.

If we examine this ending carefully, we come to the conclusion that Black drew only because his Kt can both attack (support the advance of the QKtP) and defend (the K-side Pawns). Consequently where the Pawns are farther apart or otherwise weakened Black must lose. With all the Pawns on one side, one would naturally expect the game to be a draw. Yet the defender must still play with care and the slightest weakness may be fatal. No. 518 (Vidmar-Alekhine, San Remo, 1930) is instructive because one is surprised to find such an ending lost no matter what White does. We shall follow the game continuation. *1 P—R4.* While such a move is bad on the general principle that any advance weakens the Pawn structure it apparantly cannot be avoided in the long run. E.g., 1 Kt—B5, K—B2; 2 Kt—Q6ch, K—K3; 3 Kt—K4, P—R3; 4 Kt—B2, K—K4; 5 Kt—Kt4ch, K—Q5; 6 Kt—B2, K—K6; 7 Kt—Kt4ch, K—K7 and now if 8 K—B4, K—B8; 9 Kt—K3ch, K—B7 wins without much trouble: 10 Kt—B5, R—R2!; 11 P—Kt4, R—R5ch; 12 K—K5, K×P; 13 Kt×KtP, K×P, etc. From this variation one is compelled to conclude that Dr. Vidmar's move is best, despite the violation of a basic rule. *1 .... K—K2; 2 Kt—K4, P—R3* (not 2 .... K—K3?; 3 Kt—Kt5ch); *3 Kt—B2, K—K3; 4 Kt—Q3, K—B4; 5 Kt—B4, R—R5; 6 Kt—Q3, R—QB5; 7 Kt—B2, R—B3; 8 Kt—R3, K—K4.* A critical position. If White keeps on stalling with his Knight Black's King will get to the eighth and win a Pawn. E.g., 9 Kt—B4, R—B7; 10 Kt—R3, R—Q7; 11 Kt—B4, R—R7; 12 Kt—R3, K—Q5; 13 Kt—B4, K—K6; 14 Kt—K6!, R—R2! (if 14 .... P—Kt3; 15 Kt—B4 would draw because now White's Knight attacks KKt6 and defends KKt2 at the same time); 15 Kt—B4, R—R3!; 16 Kt—R3 (if 16 K—Kt4, R—R5; 17 P—Kt3, R—B5 wins a Pawn. 16 Kt—R5 does not threaten anything), K—K7; 17 Kt—B4ch, K—B8 and White cannot hold on to everything. E.g., 18 P—R5, R—R4; 19 K—R2, K—B7; 20 K—R3, R—KKt4; 21 K—R4, K—K6; or 18 Kt—R3, R—R7; 19 Kt—B4, P—Kt4; 20 P×P, P×P; 21 Kt—K6, R×Pch; 22 K—R3, K—B7 with an easy win in both cases. Vidmar accordingly tried *9 P—R5,* but Alekhine now ingeniously demonstrated a forced win: *9 .... R—B7; 10 Kt—B4, R—Q7!; 11 Kt—R3, K—Q5; 12 Kt—B4, K—K6; 13 Kt—K6* (relatively best. After 13 Kt—R3, R—Kt7; 14 Kt—B4, R—Kt4; 15 Kt—K6, R—K4! wins a Pawn, while on 13 K—Kt4, R—Q5; 14 P—Kt3, R—R5 is quite adequate: 15 K—B5, R—R4ch!; 16 K—Kt6, R—Kt4ch; 17 K—B7, K×P; 18 Kt—K6, R×KtP; 19 Kt×P; K—B5; 20 K—B6 and now 20 .... R×Kt!; 21 K×R, K—Kt4 makes the win routine), *R—Q4!; 14 P—B4!* (a clever try, but it comes too late. If 14 K—Kt4, R—K4; if 14 K—R4, R—K4; 15 Kt×P, R—KKt4; 16 Kt—K6, R×KtP; 17 P—B4, K—K5 and White will lose all his Pawns), *R—KB4!* (but not 14 .... R×P?; 15 Kt×P, R—R4;

16 K—Kt4, K—K5; 17 Kt—R5 and White will draw); *15 K—Kt4, R—B3!; 16 P—B5* (if now 16 Kt×P, R×Pch as in the main varia-tion), *K—K5!* (the game conclusion was 16 .... R—B2; 17 P—Kt3, K—K5; 18 Kt—B5ch, K—Q5!; 19 Kt—Kt3ch, K—K4 Resigns. On 16 .... R—B2; 17 Kt—Q8 makes matters more difficult, however); *17 Kt×P* (if 17 Kt—B5ch, K—Q4; 18 Kt—Q3, K—Q5; 19 Kt—B4, K—K5), *R—B2; 18 Kt—K6* (best. After 18 Kt—K8!, K—K4!; 19 P—B6, R—B1; 20 Kt—B7, R×P the Knight will be lost), *R×P.* Now White is unable to consolidate his position and must lose both remaining Pawns: *19 K—R4* (if 19 P—Kt3, R—K4; 20 Kt—Q8, R—Kt4ch; 21 K—R4, K—B6; 22 Kt—B7, R—Kt5ch; 23 K—R3, R×Pch; 24 K—R4—or A—R—Kt8; 25 Kt×P, K—B5; 26 K—R3, R—Kt6ch; 27 K—R4, R—Kt2!!; 28 K—R3, R—KR2 and wins the Knight. A. 24 K—R2, K—B5; 25 Kt×P, R—Kt2! and wins as above), *K—K4; 25 Kt—B5* (if instead 25 Kt—Q8, K—Q4! wins the Kt), *R—B5ch; 26 K—R3, R—Q5; 27 P—Kt3, K—Q3!; 28 Kt—Kt3* (28 Kt—R6, R—QB5), *R—Q8; 29 K—R4, K—Q4; 30 P—Kt4, R—Q6; 31 P—Kt5!* (the best chance: if 31 Kt—B1, R—K6; 32 P—Kt5, R—K5ch, etc.), *R×Kt; 32 P×P, K—K3; 33 P—R7, R—Kt1; 34 K—Kt5, K—B2* and wins.

Even though it seems almost incredible, no wholly satisfactory de-fense for White in the diagrammed position can be found and No. 518 must be considered a win for Black.

With two Rooks it stands to reason that with a normal Pawn struc-ture some kind of impregnable position can usually be set up by the defender. However, the slightest deviation from the normal may well cost the Kt the game. E.g., No. 517a (Pillsbury-Napier, Hanover, 1902), White: K at QB2, R at K2, Kt at QKt4, P's at QR3, QKt2, Q4, KKt5; Black: K at KKt3, R's at KB8, KR6, P's at QKt2, QKt3, Q4. Black won by a mating attack: 1 .... R—B5; 2 R—K6ch? (better 2 Kt×P, R×P; 3 Kt×P which would probably draw), K×P; 3 R×P, R—B7ch; 14 K—Kt1, R—QKt6!; 5 R×P (or 5 Kt×P, R(B7)×Pch), R(Kt6)×Pch; 6 K—B1, R—Kt6; 8 R—Kt7ch, K—R3; 8 R—QB7, R×P; 9 Kt—B2, R—QKt6!!; 10 R—B5, K—Kt3!!! (White is now in zugzwang); 11 Kt—R1, R—B8ch; 12 K—B2, R—QR6; 13 Kt—Kt3, R—B7ch and White resigned because his Kt is lost.

3. TWO (OR MORE) PAWNS FOR THE EXCHANGE

Two Pawns are roughly somewhat more than an equivalent for the exchange. Nevertheless, in endings with only one Rook and one Knight on the board, the result is usually a draw, with the chances in favor of the side with the Rook. The reason for this is that the Knight alone is unable to defend a large number of Pawns.

The helplessness of the Knight in protecting widely scattered Pawns is clearly demonstrated in No. 519 (Euwe-Capablanca, 8th match game, 1931). Black cannot avoid the loss of a Pawn, for if 1 .... K—B3; 2 R—Q7 and either R×RP or R—Q6ch and R×QKtP. Capablanca tried *1 .... P—K5ch!* and after *2 K—B4* (not 2 K×P?, Kt—B6ch. 2 K—Kt2 would win a P too, but after 2 .... Kt—B6; 3 R—Q7, Kt—Kt4; 4 R—K7, K—B3!; 5 R×KP, P—QR4; 6 R—K8,

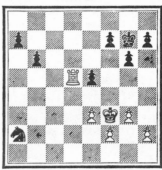

Black to play. White wins.

Kt—Q3; 7 R—QKt8, P—QKt4; 8 R—Kt6, K—K4; 9 P—B4ch, K—Q4 Black's Pawns would be dangerous), *Kt—Kt5!* (if 2 .... Kt—B6; 3 R—Q7, P—QR4; 4 K—K5! and Black will lose two and possibly three Pawns); *3 R—QKt5* (3 R—Q7?, Kt—Q6ch and if 4 K×P?, Kt—B4ch, but 3 R—Q4 would have gained an invaluable tempo: 3 .... Kt—Q6ch; 4 K×P, Kt×Pch; 5 K—B3, Kt—R6; 6 R—Q7 and Black will lose both Q-side Pawns), *Kt—Q6ch; 4 K×P, Kt×Pch; 5 K—Q4* (if now 5 K—B3, Kt—Q8 makes matters difficult), *P—B4* (or 5 .... Kt—R6; 6 R—Q5, K—B3; 7 R—Q7, Kt—Kt4; 8 P—R4. Black cannot reach the kind of impregnable position exemplified in No. 517); *6 R—Kt2, Kt—Kt5; 7 P—R3, Kt—B3; 8 R—QB2.* Black has preserved material equality all this while, but now he can no longer hold on. The game continued: *8 .... Kt—K5; 9 P—Kt4, K—B3; 10 P×P, K×P* (or 10 .... P×P; 11 R—B6ch, K—Kt4; 12 R—B7, P—KR4; 13 K—K5, Kt—B7; 14 R—Kt7ch, K—R5; 15 R×P, Kt×P; 16 K×P with an easy win); *11 R—B7, Kt—Kt4; 12 R×QRP, P—R4.* Here *13 P—R4* wins most convincingly (for the line chosen see A.), *Kt—B6ch; 14 K—Q5, P—KKt4* (or 14 .... Kt×P; 15 R—B7ch, K—Kt5; 16 P—K4, Kt—Kt7; 17 P—K5, P—R5; 18 P—K6, P—R6; 19 P—K7, P—R7; 20 P—K8=Q, P—R8=Q; 21 Q—K6ch, K—Kt4; 22 Q—B6ch and wins); *15 P×P!, K×P* (if 15 .... Kt×P; 16 R—R4!, P—Kt4; 17 R—B4ch, K—Kt3; 18 R—QKt4 wins); *16 K—K4, Kt—Q7ch; 17 K—Q3, Kt—B6; 18 K—K2, Kt—K4; 19 R—QKt7, Kt—B5; 20 K—Q3, Kt—K4ch; 21 K—K4, Kt—Kt5; 22 R×P, P—R5; 23 R—Kt5ch, K—Kt3; 24 K—B4, Kt—B3; 25 R—Kt5ch, K—B2* (25 .... K—R3; 26 R—Kt1); *26 P—K4* and Black will soon lose his Pawn. A. Euwe played 13 R—R3, Kt—B6ch; 14 K—Q3? (14 K—Q5, P—KKt4; 15 R—R8 still wins), when *14 ....*

Kt—Kt8; 15 K—Q2, P—KKt4; 16 R—Kt3, P—R5 led to a draw: 17 R×P, Kt×P; 18 K—K2, P—Kt5; 19 R—Kt5ch, K—K5; 20 R— Kt4ch, K—B4; 21 K—B1, K—Kt4; 22 R—Kt5ch, K—Kt3; 23 R— Kt4, K—R4; 24 R—Kt5ch, K—Kt3. White's King cannot get into the game because of the strong Black passed Pawns.

With the King near the passed Pawns, the Knight should not lose, but the winning chances are practically nil. An example is No. 520 (Fine-Reshevsky, New York, 1940). The game continued *1 .... K— Q4; 2 Kt—B4ch, K—B3; 3 K—B4* (a desperate winning attempt. 3 Kt—K2 is of course a routine draw), *R×P; 4 P—Kt5ch, K—Q2; 5 K—Q5, R—Kt8; 6 Kt—Q3, R—Q8; 7 K—B4, R—QKt8=*. Noth-

No. 520   No. 521

Black to play. Draw.   Black to play. White wins.

ing could be done even if the Pawns got to the sixth (No. 509).

Again, however, R+Kt+2P vs. 2 R's (with more material on the board) is usually a pretty easy win for the Knight because the Rook helps to defend the Pawns.

An illustration is No. 521 (Euwe-Alekhine, 26th match game, 1935). Black's best chance is 1 .... R×Kt; 2 P×R, K—Kt1; 3 R—K3, K— B1; 4 R—QR3, R×P; 5 R×P, R×P; 6 P—Kt3!, R—K7; 7 R×P, R×P; 8 R—QKt7, when White will barely manage to win. Alekhine chose not to sacrifice and the Pawn roller proved to be irresistible. The game concluded *1 .... P—KR3* (if 1 .... K—Kt1; 2 R—Kt1ch, K—R1; 3 R—Kt5!, R×R; 4 Kt×R, K—Kt2; 5 P—Q6!, R×P; 6 P— Q7, R—K8ch; 7 K—Kt2, R—Q8; 8 P—Q8=Q!, R×Q; 9 Kt—K6ch. Or here 5 .... R—Q2; 6 Kt—K6ch, K—B2; 7 Kt—B4, K—K1; 8 K— Kt2, R—Kt2ch; 9 K—B3, K—Q2; 10 K—K4, K—B3; 11 Kt—Q5, followed by Kt—K7ch, K—Q5, etc.); *2 Kt—Q8!, R—B7* (2 ....

R(B4)×P; 3 R×R, R×R; 4 Kt—B7ch); *3 P—K6, R—Q7; 4 Kt—B6, R—K1; 5 P—K7, P—Kt4* (desperation. Note that without the Rooks Black could get his King to KB2 and blockade the Pawns, which would surely draw, and might even win); *6 Kt—Q8, K—Kt2; 7 Kt—Kt7, K—B3; 8 R—K6ch, K—Kt4; 9 Kt—Q6, R×KP; 10 Kt—K4ch* Resigns.

A similar instance with disconnected Pawns is No. 521a (Botvinnik-Loevenfisch, 2nd match game, 1937), White: K at KR1, R's at QKt2, KB3, P's at QR2, QKt4, KR2; Black: K at KR1, R at KKt1, Kt at KKt5, P's at QR2, QKt3, QB4, KB5, KR2. Black to play wins. 1 .... Kt—K4!; 2 R—KB1(2 R×P, Kt—Q6), Kt—Q6; 3 R—Kt2

No. 522

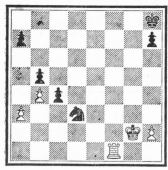

Black to play wins.

No. 523
Philidor's Position

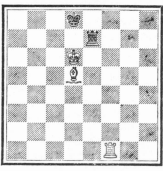

White to play wins.

(or 3 R—Q2, P—B5; 4 P—Kt5, R—Kt4), P—B5; 4 R—QB2, P—Kt4; 5 P—QR3, P—KB6!; 6 R—Q2 (6 R×KBP, Kt—K8), R—Kt7!!; 7 R×R, P×Rch; 8 K×P (Diagram No. 522). Black now wins by a combination which frequently occurs in endings with Kt vs. R. *8 .... P—B6!; 9 K—B3* (if 9 R—B8ch, K—Kt2; 10 R—B8, P—B7!! and 11 R×P, Kt—K8ch costs White his Rook), *P—B7; 10 K—K2, P—B8=Q; 11 R×Q, Kt×Rch; 12 K—Q2, Kt—R7; 13 K—B2, K—Kt2; 14 K—Kt2, Kt×P; 15 P×Kt, K—B3,* with an easily won P ending.

VI. ROOK AND BISHOP VS. ROOK

For some strange reason this ending occurs far more frequently than the similar one with the Knight. It has been analyzed exhaustively ever since the days of Philidor and it has now been definitely established that the general case is a draw. The difficulty which attaches to it, however, is due not only to the fact that there are a number of important exceptions where White wins but also to the complicated nature of the drawing variations.

The general win is seen in No. 523 (Philidor's Position). Here the solution is *1 R—B8ch, R—K1; 2 R—B7, R—K7!* (best. As will be seen from the further course of the analysis, ... R—K6 or .... R—K8 would transpose into the main line. If 2 .... R—R1; 3 R—QR7, R—R3ch; 4 B—K6 wins at once); *3 R—KKt7!* (to force the Black Rook to a less favorable square), *R—K8* (3 .... R—K6; 4 R—QKt7 again gets into the main line); *4 R—Kt7, R—QB8* (forced: if 4 .... K—B1; 5 R—QR7!, R—QKt8; 6 R—R7!, K—Kt1; 7 R—R8ch, K—R2; 8 R—R8ch, K—Kt3; 9 R—Kt8ch and wins the R. Or here 6 .... R—Kt3ch; 7 B—B6 and mates soon); *5 B—Kt3!!* (a tempo move to get the Rook to the unfavorable sixth rank), *R—B6!* (best. On 5 .... K—B1; 6 R—Kt4, threatening mate in three beginning with B—K6ch, forces 6 .... K—Q1 when 7 R—KB4, R—K8; 8 B—R4, K—B1; 9 B—B6, R—Q8ch; 10 B—Q5, K—Kt1; 11 R—QR4 decides. If here 7 .... K—B1; 8 B—Q5, K—Kt1; 9 R—QR4, etc.); *6 B—K6, R—Q6ch; 7 B—Q5, R—QB6* (7 .... K—B1; 8 R—QR7 and wins); *8 R—Q7ch!, K—B1* (if now 8 .... K—K1; 9 R—KKt7 and wins because the Black Rook cannot get to the KB file. This was one reason why the Rook had to be forced to go to the sixth); *9 R—KB7, K—Kt1; 10 R—Kt7ch, K—B1; 11 R—Kt4!, K—Q1* (or 11 .... R—Q6; 12 R—QR4 and now the R cannot go to the QKt file); *12 B—B4!!!* (the point), *K—B1* (there is no way to stop mate); *13 B—K6ch, K—Q1; 14 R—Kt8ch, R—B1; 15 R×R* mate.

Philidor's position is won with the Kings on any file except the Kt. But when the Black King is near the edge of the board the win is more difficult.

In No. 524 (Lolli) Black has an additional defense which was not

No. 524

White to play wins.

available in Philidor's position. *1 R—K8ch, R—Q1; 2 R—K7* and now:

a) *2 .... R—Kt1* (in No. 523 this led to an immediate mate) *3 R—QR7, K—Kt1; 4 R—Kt7ch, K—R1* (4 .... K—B1; 5 B—Q6); *5 B—Q6, R—B1ch* (if 5 .... R—Kt8; 6 R—Kt8ch, K—R2; 7 R—KR8 and if 7 .... R—Kt3; 8 R—R1, while if 7 .... R—B8ch; 8 B—B5ch and 9 R—R8 mate); *6 B—B7, R—KKt1* (6 ....

R×Bch; 7 R×R!); *7 R—Kt1, R—Kt3ch; 8 B—Q6, R— Kt2; 9 R—K1, R—KR2; 10 R—K8ch, K—R2; 11 B—B5ch* and mates in two. An alternative win here is 3 R—K6, R—R1; 4 B— Q6, K—Q1; 5 B—K5, R—B1; 6 B—Kt7, R—Kt1; 7 B—B6ch, K—B1; 8 R—K4, R—B1 (or 8 .... K—Kt1; 9 B—K5ch, K— B1; 10 R—QKt4, R—Kt3ch; 11 B—Q6); 9 B—Kt7, R—Kt1; 10 R—QR4, and either wins the Rook or mates.

b) *2 .... R—Q7; 3 R—KB7, R—Q1* (if 3 .... R—Q8; 4 R—QR7, as in No. 523, with the continuation 4 .... R—QKt8; 5 B—R3, K—Kt1; 6 R—K7!, K—R1; 7 R—K4, R—Kt2; 8 R—K5!! and Black is in zugzwang: 8 .... K—R2 or 8 .... R—Kt8, then 9 R—R5ch, K—Kt1; 10 B—Q6ch, and mates in two); *4 B—K7, R—Kt1; 5 R—B5, K—Kt1* (5 .... R—Kt3ch; 6 B—Q6, R— Kt1; 7 R—QKt5); *6 B—Q6ch, K—B1; 7 R—QR5 (or Kt5), any; 8 R—R8* mate.

With the Kings on the R file Black has additional drawing chances due to the stalemate possibilities, but here too there is a win with best play. In No. 525 (Kling and Kuiper, 1846) it makes no difference whose turn it is to move. There are two main variations:

a) *1 .... R—Kt7; 2 R—R6, R—Kt8; 3 B—Kt6, R—R8ch; 4 K— Kt5, K—Kt2; 5 R—R7ch, K—B1; 6 B—B5, R—Q8; 7 K—B6* and continues as in No. 524.

b) *1 .... R—K1; 2 B—B7, R—K3ch; 3 B—Kt6, R—K1; 4 R—R6, K—Kt1; 5 R—QB6, K—R1!; 6 B—Q4! R—QKt1* (if 6 .... K— Kt1; 7 K—Kt6, R—K8; 8 R—KB6, R—Kt8ch; 9 K—B6, etc.); *7 R—K6, R—QB1; 8 B—B3!, R—QKt1* (or 8 .... K—Kt1; 9 B—K5ch, K—R1; 10 K—Kt6); *9 R—K2, R—Q1; 10 K—Kt6, K—Kt1!; 11 B—Kt4, K—B1* (or 11 .... K—R1; 12 K—B7.

Or 11 .... R—Kt1; 12 B —Q6ch, K—B1; 13 K—B6 and 14 R—QR2); *12 K—B6, R—Q2; 13 R—K8ch, R— Q1; 14 R—K7, R—Kt1* and either *15 R—QR7* or *15 B —Q6* transposes into No. 524 line a).

On the Kt file the game is drawn because Black has just enough room to wiggle around in. Best play for both sides in No. 526 is *1 R— Q8ch, R—B1; 2 R—Q7, R—B7; 3 R—KB7, R—B6; 4 B—R4, R—B8* (4 .... R—B5?; 5 B—B6, R— Kt5ch; 6 B—Kt5); *5 B—B6, R—*

No. 525

White wins.

Kt8ch; 6 K—B5, R—Kt7! (Black must stay on the Kt file); *7 B—Q5, R—KR7* (the threat was 8 K—Q6); *8 R—Kt7ch, K—B1; 9 R—K7, K—Kt1!; 10 K—B6* (or 10 K—Kt6, R—QB7!; 11 B—Kt3, R—B8!; 12 R—Q7, K—B1!; 13 R—Q2, R—QKt8 (13 .... K—Kt1?; 14 B—B2); 14 R—Q3, R—QKt7; 15 K—B6, R—QKt8; 16 B—K6ch, K—Kt1; 17 R—Q8ch, K—R2; 18 R—Q7ch, K—Kt1; 19 B—Q5, R—B8ch; 20 K—Q6, R—B2!=. Or here 16 B—Q5, R—B8ch; 17 K—Q6, R—B2; 18 R—QR3, R—Q2ch; 19 K—K6, R—Q1; 20 R—R7, K—Kt1!, etc.), *R—R3ch; 11 B—K6, R—R8!; 12 R—Kt7ch, K—R1; 13 R—Kt2* (or 13 R—Kt7, K—Kt1!; 14 B—B5, R—R3ch; 15 B—Kt6, R—R1!; 16 K—Kt6, K—B1!; 17 B—K4, R—R3ch; 18 B—B6, K—Q1, etc.,=), *R—B8ch; 14 K—Kt6, K—Kt1; 15 B—B5, R—B5!; 16 R—Kt5, R—KR5; 17 K—B6ch, K—R2; 18 B—Q3, R—KB5; 19 R—Kt7ch, K—R1; 20 R—Kt7, K—Kt1!* (not 20 .... R—B3ch?; 21 K—B7—see No. 526a), etc.

An exception to this position is No. 526a (Zytogorsky, 1843), White: K at QB7, R at K7, B at Q3; Black: K at QR2, R at KB3. White wins. The main variation is 1 .... R—B1; 2 B—Kt5, R—KKt1; 3 R—K1, R—Kt2ch; 4 B—Q7, R—Kt3; 5 B—K6, R—Kt2ch; 6 K—B6, R—Kt3; 7 R—R1ch, K—Kt1; 8 R—Kt1ch, K—R2; 9 R—Kt7ch, K—R1 (9 .... K—R3; 10 R—K7 leads to Philidor's position); 10 R—K7, R—Kt7; 11 B—B5, R—KB7; 12 R—K5, R—B6; 13 B—K6, K—Kt1; 14 R—Kt5ch, K—R2; 15 R—R5ch, K—Kt1; 16 B—Q5, R—KKt6; 17 R—Kt5ch, K—R2; 18 R—Kt7ch, K—R1; 19 R—KR7, R—Kt3ch; 20 K—B7 dis ch, K—R2; 21 B—B4, R—Kt5; 22 K—B6 dis ch, K—Kt1; 23 R—R8ch, K—R2; 24 B—Q5, R—Kt8 (24 .... R—Kt4; 25 R—R1!); 25 R—R7ch, K—Kt1; 26 B—K4, R—Kt4—or A—; 27 K—Kt6, K—B1; 28 B—B6, K—Q1; 29 R—

No. 526

Draw.

Q7ch, K—B1; 30 R—K7, R—Kt1; 31 R—QR7 and wins.

A. 26 .... R—B8ch; 27 K—Q6, R—B2!; 28 R—R2, R—B1; 29 R—QR2, R—Q1ch; 30 K—B6, R—K1; 31 B—Q5, R—K3ch; 32 K—Q7, R—QR3; 33 R—Kt2ch, K—R2; 34 R—Kt7ch, K—R1; 35 R—B7 dis ch, K—Kt1; 36 R—B8ch, K—R2; 37 K—B7 and mates.

Other drawn positions where the Black King is on the edge of the board fall into one of the four classes typified by the following positions.

In No. 527 (Szen) the Black Rook can always interpose on a check and there is no way for White to improve his position. E.g., *1 R— Kt8ch, R—B1; 2 B—B6ch, K—B2; 3 B—K5ch, K—Q1; 4 R—Kt1, R—B7*, etc. An exception occurs only in the similar positions where the Black King is at QB1 or KB1 and the Black Rook has no effective check. I.e., No. 527a, White: K at Q6, R at QR6, B at Q5; Black: K at QB1, R at QKt7. White wins. 1 .... R—Kt8; 2 R—R8ch, R—Kt1; 3 R—R1, R—Kt7; 4 R—R1!, K—Kt1; 5 R—R8ch, K—R2; 6 R—R8ch, K—Kt3; 7 R—Kt8ch, and wins the Rook. This variation occurs repeatedly in Philidor's Position.

No. 527	**No. 528**
	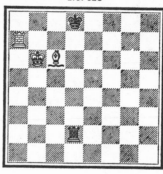
Draw.	Draw.

The other drawn cases come up when White's King is on the sixth, but there is no direct mate threat. In No. 528 (Kling and Kuiper) after *1 K—B5!, R—KB7* is the correct reply (but not 1 .... R—Q8?; 2 B—Q5! and we get either the Philidor position after 2 .... R— B8ch; 3 K—Q6 or the Szen (No. 527a) position after 2 .... K—B1; 3 K—Q6, R—QKt8); *2 B—Q5, R—B3!* or *2 R—Q7ch, K—B1; 3 R—K7, R—B3; 4 K—Kt6, R—Q3*. (No. 529). Exceptions to this occur as in No. 527a, and with the Rook too near the center. E.g., No. 528a (Berger), White: K at K6, R at QR7, B at Q6; Black: K at QB1, R at QB5. White to play wins. 1 K—Q5, R—B8; 2 B—B5, K—Q1; 3 K—B6, K—K1; 4 R—K7ch, K—Q1; 5 R—K2, R—B5 (5 .... R—B6; 6 R—KB2; and 6 .... R—K6 is impossible); 6 R— Q2ch, K—K1 (or 6 .... K—B1); 7 R—KB2 and wins.

No. 529 (Kling and Kuiper) is similar. If *1 R—K7, R—Q3; 2 R—K2, R—Q8* we have No. 527. Exceptions to this occur when the Black Rook has less than three squares at its disposal. E.g., No.

529a (Centurini, 1867), White: K at Q6, R at KB7, B at K6; Black: K at K1, R at KR3. White to play wins. 1 R—B1, R—Kt3; 2 R—B2!, R—R3; 3 R—QR2, K—B1; 4 R—KKt2, R—R1; 5 K—Q7!, R—R2ch; 6 K—Q8, R—R1; 7 R—Kt3, R any; 8 R—Kt8, mate.

Finally, No. 530 (Cochrane) is perhaps most important of all because there are no exceptions to it. White cannot threaten mate by 1 K—Q6 because of 1 .... R×Bch, while other moves threaten nothing at all. The simplest drawing rule for Black to follow is to wait until the White King has moved to one side, and then play to the other.

No. 529

Draw.

No. 530

Draw.

No. 531 (Flohr-Reshevsky, Semmering-Baden, 1937) illustrates the method of handling this ending in over-the-board play. The game continuation was: *1 .... R—K7; 2 R—R4, R—K8; 3 R—R6ch, K—K2; 4 K—Q4, K—Q2; 5 B—B4, R—Q8ch; 6 K—B4, R—K8; 7 B—Q2, R—Q8; 8 B—Kt4, R—KKt8; 9 B—B5, R—B8ch; 10 K—Q5, R—Q8ch; 11 B—Q4, K—Q1* (No. 530); *12 R—R7, R—Q7; 13 K—K5, K—B1!; 14 B—B5, R—Q2; 15 B—K7, K—Kt2; 16 K—K6, K—B3; 17 R—R1, R—Q7; 18 R—B1ch, K—Kt4; 19 B—Q6, R—K7ch; 20 K—Q7, R—K5; 21 R—B5ch, K—R5; 22 K—B6, K—Kt6; 23 K—Q5, R—K1; 24 R—Kt5ch, K—B7; 25 B—B5, K—Q6; 26 R—Kt3ch, K—K7; 27 B—Q4, R—Q1ch; 28 K—K4, R—K1ch; 29 B—K5, K—K8; 30 R—Kt2, R—K2* (No. 530! again) and a draw was agreed to.

When there are Pawns on the board, the ending is exactly the same as B vs. P's, except that R+B+P always win, even with RP+B of the wrong color. In No. 532 (Capablanca-Tarrasch, St. Petersburg,

1914) we have the model winning procedure. The White King will be forced out of the corner by getting the Black King to QKt6 and the Rook to the seventh. *1 R—B1ch, K—Kt4; 2 R—Kt1ch, K—B4; 3 R—B1ch, K—Q3; 4 R—Q1ch, B—Q4ch; 5 K—Kt2, P—R6ch; 6 K—R1, K—B4* (6 .... P—R7?; would be a mistake after which Black could only draw); *7 R—B1ch, B—B5; 8 R—KKt1, R—R7; 9 R—Kt5ch, K—Kt5; 10 R—Kt1, R—R7ch; 11 K—Kt1, R—Q7!* and White resigns for if *12 R—K1, K—Kt6; 13 R—K3ch, B—Q6ch* and if 14 K—R1, R—R7 mate or 14 .... R—Q8 mate.

No. 531   No. 532

Draw.   Black wins.

VII. ROOK AND KNIGHT VS. ROOK

This too is in general a draw. However, there are only a few won positions and the defense is much easier.

There are five typical wins, in all but one of which both Black's Rook and King are confined to the first rank.

The simplest case is No. 533 (Centurini, 1850). The idea is to get the K to Kt6 and the Kt to KB6, when R—R7 will be mate, or the K to KR6, the Kt to KKt6, when R—KKt7 mates. To do this White must guard the sixth rank. *1 K—Kt6* (if Black plays, 1 .... R—R3; 2 R—K7, K—Kt1; 3 K—Kt6 transposes into the main line). *K— Kt1* (The alternatives are:

    a) 1 .... R—Kt1ch; 2 K—R6, R—QB1 (2 .... R—Kt8; 3 Kt— Kt5); 3 Kt—B4, K—Kt1; 4 Kt—Kt6, R—B2; 5 Kt—K7ch and wins.

    b) 1 .... R—QB1; 2 R—QR7, R—QKt1; 3 R—QB7, R—R1;

4 R—B6, R—K1; 5 K—B7, R—R1; 6 R—B5, R—R2ch;
7 Kt—B7 and mates.
c) 1 .... R—K1; 2 Kt—Kt5, R—Kt1ch; 3 K—R6, R—QB1;
4 R—R7ch, K—Kt1; 5 R—Kt7ch, K—B1; 6 Kt—R7ch, K—K1;
7 Kt—B6ch, K—B1; 8 K—Kt6, R—B2; 9 R—Kt8ch, K—K2;
10 Kt—Q5ch and wins); *2 R—Kt6, R—K1; 3 R—B6, R—R1;
4 Kt—Kt5, K—B1; 5 R—K6!, R—Kt1; 6 Kt—R7ch, K—Kt1;
7 R—K7, R—Kt3ch; 8 Kt—B6ch* and will mate in a few.
No. 534 (Centurini, 1850) is similar. After *1 R—QB7* (again if
Black moved first it would make no difference), there are two main
variations:

No. 533

White wins.

No. 534

White wins.

a) *1 .... R—Kt1; 2 R—QR7, R—Q1* (or 2 .... K—Kt1; 3 K—
Kt6, K—R1; 4 R—R7ch, K—Kt1; 5 R—Kt7ch, K—B1; 6 K—
R7, R—Kt2; 7 Kt×R); *3 Kt—B5, R—Kt1; 4 R—B7ch, K—
Kt1* (or K1); *5 Kt—K7ch, K—R1; 6 Kt—Kt6ch, K—Kt1;
7 R—Kt7* mate.
b) *1 .... K—Kt1; 2 K—Kt6, K—R1; 3 R—R7ch, K—Kt1;
4 R—Kt7ch, K—B1; R—B7ch, K—Kt1; 6 Kt—K4,* and mates
in a few.
In No. 535 (Centurini, 1887) White wins even though the Black
pieces have a fair degree of liberty. But appearances are deceptive,
for again it is to White's advantage to have his opponent move first.
1 R—K3, R—B7 (1 .... K—B1; 2 Kt—R7ch, K—Kt1; 3 R—K8ch.
Or 1 .... R—B1; 2 Kt—R7, etc.); *2 R—K1, R—B5* (now forced);
3 R—QR1, R—B7 (the point to forcing the Black Rook to B5 was
that now 3 .... K—B1 is refuted by Kt—K6ch); *4 Kt—K4!, R—
Kt7ch, 5 K—B6, K—R1* (or 5 .... R—Kt5; 6 R—R8ch, K—R2;

7 Kt—Kt5ch and mates); *6 R—R3* (again tempo moves to get the Black Rook to the fourth rank), *R—Kt8; 7 R—R2, R—Kt5; 8 Kt—Kt5, R—B5ch; 9 K—Kt6, K—Kt1; 10 Kt—K6!, R—Kt5ch; 11 K—B6, K—R1; 12 K—B7!, R—R5; 13 K—Kt6, R—Kt5ch; 14 Kt—Kt5* and Black must give up his Rook to ward off immediate mate.

The most complicated of all is No. 536 (Centurini, 1878) where the Black King is stalemated. The solution is *1 .... R—Kt6ch; 2 K—B7, R—Kt2ch; 3 K—K6, R—QKt2* (if 3 .... R—Kt8; 4 R—Q7!, R—K8ch; 5 K—B7, and mates); *4 R—KKt2* (not 3 R—R2ch, K—Kt2; 5 R—R7ch, K—B1! since 6 R×R? is stalemate), *R—Kt3ch; 5 K—B5,*

No. 535

No. 536

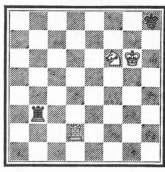

White wins.

White wins.

R—Kt4ch; 6 K—Kt6, R—Kt7; 7 R—Kt5, R—Kt4; 8 Kt—Q5, R—Kt2; 9 K—B6 (the threat is now 10 Kt—K7, R—Kt3ch; 11 K—B7, K—R2; 12 R—QR5 when we have No. 535), *R—KR2* (for the alternatives see A); *10 Kt—K7, R—R3ch* (if 10 .... R—Kt2; 11 R—QR5, R—R2; 12 R—R8 mate); *11 K—B7, R—R2ch; 12 K—B8, R—R6; 13 R—Kt8ch, K—R2; 14 R—Kt7ch, K—R3; 15 Kt—Kt8ch, K—R4; 16 Kt—B6ch* and either wins the Rook or mates.

A. There are three other choices:

a) 9 .... R—Q2; 10 Kt—K7, R—Q3ch; 11 K—B7, K—R2; 12 R—Kt7ch, K—R3 (12 .... K—R1; 13 Kt—Kt6ch); 13 Kt—B5ch and wins.

b) 9 .... R—QR2; 10 R—Kt1, R—QKt2; 11 R—QR1!, R—Q2; 12 Kt—K7, R—Q3ch; 13 K—B7, K—R2; 14 Kt—B5, R—Q2ch; 15 K—B6, R—QKt2; 16 R—R1ch, K—Kt1; 17 Kt—K7ch, K—B1; 18 R—R8 mate.

c) 9 .... R—KKt2!; 10 R—K5!, R—Q2 (10 .... R—QR2; 11 R—K1 transposes into b)); 11 Kt—K7, R—Q3ch; 12 K—B7, K—

R2; 13 R—K1, R—QR3 (13 .... K—R3; 14 Kt—B5ch); 14 R—
R1ch, R—R3; 15 R—R1, R—R6; 16 Kt—Kt8!, K—R1 (if
16 .... R—R7; 17 Kt—B6ch, K—R3; 18 R—KKt1, R—KKt7;
19 Kt—Kt8ch); 17 Kt—B6, and mates in two.

Finally we have No. 537 (Centurini, 1887) where White wins despite
the relatively inoffensive placement of his pieces. The solution is
1 .... K—B1 (if 1 .... K—R1; 2 Kt—K7!, R—QKt1; 3 K—R6,
R—Q1; 4 Kt—Kt6ch, K—Kt1; 5 R—R7 and mates. Or 1 .... R—
KB1; 2 Kt—K7ch, K—R1; 3 R—R1 and mates. Or 1 .... R—
QKt1; 2 R—KB6, K—R1; 3 K—R6 and 4 Kt—K7 or R4 as in the

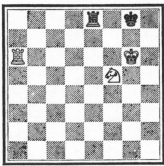

No. 537

White wins.

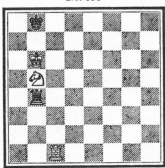

No. 538

Draw.

main variation); *2 R—B6ch, K—Kt1; 3 Kt—R6ch, K—R1; 4 K—B7!,
R—R1; 5 Kt—B5, R—R2ch; 6 K—Kt6, R—R1; 7 K—R6, R—K1;
8 Kt—K7!, R—R1; 9 R—B7, R—R3ch; 10 Kt—Kt6ch* and mates in
three.

Except for these five positions (and their offshoots) White can win
only in problem cases or with the willing cooperation of his opponent.
The idea of the draw in general is this: to pin the Knight and prevent
a mating threat which forces the Rook back to the first rank or the
King into the corner. The pin is equally effective on either the rank
or the file.

In No. 538 (Centurini) Black holds the game because White's
pieces are not free to move about as they please. If, e.g., *1 K—B6,
R—Kt7!* (but not 1 .... K—B1?; 2 Kt—Q6ch, K—any; 3 R—K1
and wins); *2 Kt—Q6, R—Kt6; 3 R—B2, R—Kt8!* (Black must choose
his Rook moves carefully. If here 3 .... R—Kt5?; 4 R—KR2
followed by R—R8ch, and Kt—Kt5ch wins, while if 3 .... R—KR6;

4 R—Kt2ch, K—R1; 5 R—Kt2, R—R1 (5 .... R—B6ch; 6 K—Kt6, R—Kt6ch!; 7 Kt—Kt5); 6 R—Kt7, and we have No. 533); *4 Kt—B4, R—KR8; 5 R—KKt2, R—R3ch; 6 Kt—Q6, K—R2* and again White cannot win because his Knight is pinned.

The second typical draw is No. 539 (Centurini, 1878). The best try is *1 R—B7ch, K—Kt1; 2 R—B6* (if 2 R—Kt7ch, K—B1!, but not 2 .... K—R1??; 3 R—K7, R—R1; 4 Kt—Q4 and wins), *R—R8; 3 Kt—Q4, R—Kt8ch; 4 Kt—Kt5, R—Kt7; 5 R—B1, R—Kt5,* etc.— No. 538.

A tricky position which must be handled with care is No. 539a (Salvioli, 1887), White: K at Q6, R at KB3, Kt at KKt5, Black: K at K1, R at KR5. Draw. 1 Kt—K6, R—R1; 2 R—B6 (if 2 R—B4, R—Kt1; 3 R—B2, R—R1; 4 Kt—Kt7ch, K—Q1; 5 R—QB2, R—R8! is the only saving move), R—Kt1; 3 Kt—B7ch, K—Q1; 4 R—KR6 (or 4 R—B7, R—Kt3ch; 5 Kt—K6ch, K—B1; 6 R—K7, K—Kt1; 7 K—B6, R—R3; 8 K—Kt6, K—B1!, etc.—No. 539), K—B1; 5 K—B6, K—Q1! (on 5 .... K—Kt1; 6 Kt—Kt5! wins: 6 .... K—B1; 7 Kt—Q6ch, K—Q1; 8 R—R7, R—Kt2; 9 Kt—Kt7ch, or here 7 .... K—Kt1; 8 R—R7 as in No. 533); 6 Kt—Q5, R—K1! (the only line: if 6 .... R—KB1?; 7 R—R7 wins: 7 .... K—B1; 8 R—B7ch, K—Kt1; 9 K—Kt6, followed by Kt—Kt4—B6 or 7 .... K—K1; 8 R—K7ch, K—Q1; 9 R—Q7ch, and mates); 7 R—Q6ch, K—B1; 8 Kt—Kt6ch, K—Kt1; 9 Kt—Q7ch, K—R2 (but not 9 .... K—R1; 10 R—Q1, R—K3ch; 11 K—B7, and wins); 10 K—B7, R—K8; 11 R—Q5, R—B8ch; 12 Kt—B5, R—B7; 13 K—B6, R—B8; 14 R—R5, K—Kt1!; 15 R—R8ch, K—R2; 16 R—R3, K—Kt1; 17 R—Kt3ch, K—B1!, etc.=.

Thus White can win this ending only in certain favorable positions where the Black King is in or near the corner.

The general draw where the Black King is not confined to a corner is exemplified in No. 540 (Berger). The continuation might be *1 R—R6ch, K—K2; 2 K—Q5, R—B1!; 3 Kt—K4, R—Q1ch* (3 .... R—B8; 4 R—R7ch, K—K1; 5 K—K6, R—B3ch; 6 Kt—Q6ch, K—B1 = (No. 539) is also good); *4 K—K5, K—B2; 5 R—B6ch, K—Kt2;* (or 5 .... K—K2. A trap is 5 .... K—K2; 6 Kt—Q6, R—KB1; 7 Kt—

No. 539

Draw.

B5ch, K—K1; 8 R—K6ch, K—B2?; 9 R—K7ch, K—Kt3??; 10 R—
Kt7ch, K—R4; 11 K—B4 and wins); *6 Kt—Q6, R—QR1; 7 Kt—
B5ch, K—Kt1; 8 R—Kt6ch, K—B1; 9 R—QKt6, K—B2* (or even
9 .... K—K1; 10 K—K6, K—Q1; 11 R—B6, R—Kt1); *10 R—
Kt7ch, K—Kt3; 11 R—Kt7ch, K—R4; 12 K—B4, R—R5ch,* etc.=.

With Pawns the ending is in no essential respect different from that
with Kt vs. P's.

VIII. MISCELLANEOUS COMBINATIONS OF ROOKS AND MINOR PIECES WITHOUT PAWNS

Since these endings occur so rarely in practical play we shall have

No. 540

Draw.

No. 541

White to play wins.

to confine ourselves to the general outlines of the theory and a few
outstanding examples. *Rule: In general, endings without Pawns can
be won only if White is at least a Rook or two minor pieces ahead.*

A. THE DOUBLE EXCHANGE

Two Rooks always win against two minor pieces (unlike the elementary draw with only one exchange). The winning idea is to pin
one piece and trap or capture the other. As is to be expected, the
most difficult case is that where Black has two Bishops.

In No. 541 (Kling and Horwitz, 1851) the win is accomplished by
pinning the QB: *1 R—KB2ch, K—Kt2* (if 1 .... K—K3; 2 R—K1,
B—R4; 3 R—QR2, K—B3; 4 R×B, K×R; 5 R—R5 ch, etc.);
2 R—KKt2, B—B5ch; 3 K—Kt2, B—K4ch; 4 K—Kt3, K—R3 (or
4 .... K—B3; 5 R—B1ch, K—Kt2; 6 R(B1)—KKt1. On 5 ....
B—B4 the Rooks double on the KB file); *5 R—R1ch, B—R4; 6 R—
Q2, B—B5* (6 .... K—Kt4; 7 R×B and 8 R—Q5); *7 R—Q5, B—*

Kt4; 8 R—Q6ch and wins a Bishop. With B+Kt or 2 Kt's the situation is even more hopeless for Black.

B. ROOK AND MINOR PIECE VS. TWO MINOR PIECES

All such positions are as a rule drawn, but there are quite a few exceptions, especially with R+B vs. 2 Kt's.

An unusual ending where Black has two B's is No. 542 (Berger, 1921). The main variation is *1 B—K4!* (threatening K—B4 and R—R7), *B—Q1* (best: e.g., 1 .... B—QKt6; 2 K—B4, B—K8; 3 R—R7ch, K—Kt8; 4 R—R1ch, K—B7; 5 R—R2ch, K—Kt8; 6 R—Kt2ch, K—B8; 7 R—Kt2, B—Q8; 8 K—K3 followed by R—QKt1);

No. 542

No. 543

White to play wins.   White to play wins.

2 K—B2, B—Kt3ch (if 2 .... K—R6; 3 K—B3, K—R5; 4 K—B4); *3 K—B3* (with the double threat of 4 R—Kt6 and 4 R—Kt2ch, K—R6; 5 R—Kt6), *B—Kt6; 4 R—QKt7!, B—Q8ch; 5 K—B4, B—QB4; 6 R—R7ch, K—Kt8; 7 R—R1ch,* and *8 R×B.*

C. ROOK VS. THREE MINOR PIECES

Since a Rook is approximately equivalent to a little less than two minor pieces such endings are theoretically drawn. Nevertheless, it stands to reason that White disposes of a large number of tactical possibilities, so that there will not be any smooth sailing for the defender.

A curious instance of a forced win is No. 543 (Rinck, 1920) 1 B—Q6?, K—B4 leads to nothing, since it would be madness to take the exchange! But *1 B—Q2ch,* leads to the capture of the Rook by a Knight: *1* .... *K—B4; 2 Kt—Q7, R—K3* (the only square where he can avoid immediate capture or a check and capture); *3 K—B3!, R—QR3* (on other R or K moves, a Kt check decides); *4 Kt—K7ch, K—K3; 5 Kt—B5ch, K×Kt; 6 Kt×R,* etc.

Chapter VIII

QUEEN ENDINGS

The powers of the Queen are so extraordinary that these endings are unique in a number of respects. To a great extent tactical considerations are predominant. Mating attacks, combinations to win pieces abound. It is chiefly for this reason that the strategical bases of other endings are in large part not applicable here, so that Queen endings are in a class by themselves.

I. QUEEN VS. PAWNS

A Queen, unlike a Rook or a minor piece, can win against any number of Pawns. It is not the number, but the *degree of advancement* and the file that the Pawns are on that count. Thus eight Pawns on the second rank will surely lose, but one Pawn on the seventh may draw and two Pawns on the seventh may win.

A. QUEEN VS. ONE PAWN

It is obvious that Black has a chance only if his Pawn is on the seventh, threatening to promote, and his King right next to it. For if the White Queen ever manages to get in front of the Pawn and blockade it, the Black King can never drive her away, and the White King majestically walks up and takes charge of the booty. When the Pawn is on the seventh with the King nearby, in general RP or BP draw, but any other Pawn loses.

The general win is seen in No. 544. The winning idea is to force the Black King to occupy the square in front of the Pawn, which gives the White King time to approach and help capture the luckless peon. This is done by successively check- ing and attacking the P. *1 Q—*

No. 544

White to play wins.

522

B7ch, K—Kt7 (1 .... K—K8; 2 K—B6); *2 Q—K6, K—B7; 3 Q—B5ch, K—Kt7; 4 Q—K4ch, K—B7; 5 Q—B4ch, K—Kt7; 6 Q—K3, K—B8; 7 Q—B3ch!* (the crucial position), *K—K8* (now forced, since 7 .... K—Kt8 is met by 8 Q×P); *8 K—B6, K—Q7; 9 Q—B2, K—Q8; 10 Q—Q4ch, K—B7; 11 Q—K3, K—Q8; 12 Q—Q3ch, K—K8; 13 K—Q5, K—B7; 14 Q—Q2, K—B8; 15 Q—B4ch, K—Kt7; 16 Q—K3, K—B8; 17 Q—B3ch!, K—K8; 18 K—K4* (an alternative win is 18 K—Q4, K—Q7; 19 Q—B2, K—Q8; 20 K—Q3, P—K8=Q; 21 Q—B2 mate); *K—Q7; 19 Q—Q3ch, K—K8; 20 K—B3, K—B8; 21 Q×Pch, K—Kt8; 22 Q—Kt2* mate.

Exceptions to this occur only where the White King gets in his

No. 545

White to play. Draw.

No. 546

Draw.

Queen's way and bars a check. E.g., No. 546a, White: K at K5, Q at Q8; Black: K at K7, P at Q7. Draw. White has no checks at all and cannot prevent the Pawn from queening on the next move.

This zigzag manoeuvre will not be successful against a BP or RP because Black has a stalemate defense there. Thus in No. 545 after *1 Q—Kt3ch,* the reply is *1 .... K—R8!* and since 2 Q×P is stalemate White cannot gain the necessary tempo for the approach of his King. Similarly in No. 546 after *1 Q—Kt3ch, K—R8!* White must release the Black King to avoid immediate stalemate.

Exceptions to these draws occur only when the White King is near the scene of action and can set up a mating position after the Pawn has queened. In No. 547 proper the stalemate is first avoided by getting the White King in front of the Queen. *1 K—Kt6!, K—Kt7; 2 K—B5 dis ch, K—B7* (best: if 2 .... K—R8; 3 K—Kt4!, etc.); *3 Q—K4ch, K—Kt7; 4 Q—K2ch, K—Kt8* (4 .... K—Kt6; 5 Q—K5 and 6 Q—R1); *5 K—B4!!, P—R8 = Q* (any other promotion is just as bad); *6 K—Kt3!* (the point), *Q—Q5* (the trouble is that Black has no check); *7 Q—K1ch* and mate next. A variant on this theme is No. 547a, White: K at K4, Q at KR8; Black: K at QKt8, P at QR7. White to play wins. 1 Q—KR1ch, K—Kt7; 2 Q—Kt2ch, K—Kt8 (if 2 .... K—Kt6 again 3 Q—KKt7 and 4 Q—QR1); 3 K—Q3!, P—R8 = Kt (or 3 .... P—R8 = Q; 4 Q—B2 mate, or 3 .... K—R8; 4 K—B3 and mate next); 4 K—B3 and mates in two. For Pawn endings from which these positions may come about see Nos. 14, 31A, 80b, etc.

With the BP there are similar mating positions. An example is No. 548 (Lolli). Here the King must be prevented from getting to

No. 547

White to play wins. White King may be anywhere in marked-off area.

No. 548

White to play wins.

the Q-side. *1 Q—Kt3!, K—Q7; 2 Q—Kt2, K—Q8; 3 K—B3!, K—Q7* (3 .... P queens; 4 Q—K2 mate); *4 K—B2, K—Q8; 5 Q—Q4ch, K—B8; 6 Q—QKt4!, K—Q8; 7 Q—K1* mate. The position which corresponds to No. 547 is No. 548a, White: K at QR4, Q at QB8; Black: K at QKt7, P at QB7. White to play wins. 1 Q—R8ch, K—R7 (1 .... K—Kt8; 2 K—Kt3, P—B8 = Q; 3 Q—R7ch, K- R8; 4 Q—R7ch, K—Kt8; 5 Q—R2 mate); 2 Q—R2, K—Kt7; 3 Q—Q2, K—Kt8 (or 3 .... K—R8; 4 K—Kt3 or 4 Q—B1ch); 4 K—Kt3, P—B8 = Q; 5 Q—R2 mate. A variant on this is No. 548b, White: K at Q5, Q at K8; Black: K at Q8, P at QB7. White to play wins. 1 Q—R4, K—Q7; 2 Q—Q4ch, K—K7; 3 Q—B3, K—Q8; 4 Q—Q3ch, K—B8; 5 K—B4, etc., as in No. 548a (5 .... K—Kt7; 6 Q—Q2, K—Kt8; 7 K—Kt3). White may also win if his King is near enough to cover the queening square. E.g., No. 548c, White: K at K3, Q at KB3; Black: K at QKt8, P at QB7. White to play wins. 1 Q—K4,

K—Kt7 (if 1 .... K—R8; 2 K—Q2! If 1 .... K—B8; 2 Q—QKt4, K—Q8; 3 Q—Q2 mate); 2 Q—Kt4ch, K—R8 (2 .... K—B8; 3 K— B2!, K—Q8; 4 Q—K1 mate); 3 K—Q2 and wins the Pawn without allowing stalemate.

If the Pawn is not yet on the seventh White will always win because there is no stalemate threat. The case with the BP is seen in No. 549. After *1 .... K—Kt7; 2 Q—Kt4ch, K—B7; 3 K—Kt7, K—K6;* even *4 K—B6* wins: *4 .... P—B7; 5 Q—Q1, K—B5; 6 Q—KB1,* etc. Of course White can check the Black King, force it in front of the Pawn and use the time gained to approach with his King, exactly as in No. 544. The case with the RP is even simpler. No. 549a, White: K at QR8, Q at QR6; Black: K at KKt7, P at KR6. White to play wins. 1 Q—K2ch. If now 1 .... K—Kt8; 2 Q—Kt4ch, K—R7; 3 K—Kt7 and the Pawn goes. If 1 .... K—Kt6; 2 Q—B1, K—R7 (or 2 .... P—R7; 3 K—Kt7, K—R5; 4 Q—Kt2); 3 Q—B2ch, K— R8; 4 K—Kt7!, P—R7; 5 Q—B1 mate. Finally, if 1 .... K—R8; 2 Q—KB2!, P—R7; 3 Q—B1 mate. Note that in both these and all similar endings it is possible to prevent the Pawn from reaching the seventh.

Exceptions occur only when the White King is blocking a file or diagonal so that White cannot give enough checks or prevent the Pawn from getting to the seventh. E.g., No. 549b (The Chess World, 1865), White: K at KKt7, Q at QKt7; Black: K at QB8, P at QB6. Draw. After 1 Q—R1ch, K—Kt7 the only check White has which does not permit the Pawn to advance is 2 Q—Kt7ch, when 2 .... K— B8 repeats the position. With the White King elsewhere White can pin the Pawn and use the time gained to approach first with his Queen and then with his King.

B. QUEEN VS. TWO PAWNS

No. 549

With two Pawns Black is worse off than with one, for in order to have drawing chances, he must have *both* Pawns on the seventh.

The case where the extra Pawn is the cause of Black's downfall is seen in No. 550 (Berger). After *1 Q—Kt4ch, K—R8; 2 Q—R3ch, K—Kt8; 3 Q—Kt3ch, K—R8* (or 3 .... K—B8; 4 K—B4, K—K8; 5 K—Q3, K—B8; 6 K—Q2, P— R4; 7 Q—R2, P—R5; 8 Q—R1 mate); *4 Q×P* is not stalemate now so that Black can resign.

White wins.

However, if the Black Pawn were at R5, White can check at KKt4 but can only draw because he does not have the square KKt3 at his disposal.

With the Pawns widely separated White wins if he can capture the one on the seventh. This usually depends on the position of his King. Thus No. 551 is a draw because the White King is so far away. E.g., *1 Q—Kt7ch, K—R8; 2 Q—B6, K—Kt7; 3 Q—Kt5ch, K—R8; 4 Q—*

No. 550

White to play wins. No. 550a: Draw with Black Pawn at R5.

No. 551

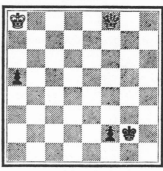

Draw.

B4, K—Kt7; 5 Q—Kt4ch, K—R7; 6 Q—B3, K—Kt8; 7 Q—Kt3ch, K—B8; 8 K—Kt7, P—R5; 9 K—B6, P—R6 and draws because White must first capture the QRP. If the White King were at, say, Q4 here, he could approach and capture the BP.

This drawing stratagem exists only with the BP. In the analogous case with the RP Black gets mated. No. 551a (Berger), White: K at QKt6, Q at KR8; Black: K at KKt7, P's at QR5, KR7. White to play wins. *1 Q—Kt8ch, K—B7* (not 1 .... K—R8; 2 Q—Kt3!, P—R6; 3 Q—B2, P—R7; 4 Q—B1 mate); *2 Q—R7, K—Kt6!; 3 Q—Q3ch* (the zigzag win of No. 544 is not possible here because the Black King stays in the triangle KKt7—KKt6—KR6. E.g., *3 Q—Kt7ch, K—R6; 4 Q—R5ch, K—Kt6!; 5 Q—Kt5ch, K—R6!; 6 Q—K3ch, K—Kt7!; 7 Q—K2ch, K—Kt6!* Black need only prevent checks at either KKt4 or KB3. Thus 4 .... K—Kt7?? is a fatal blunder because of *5 Q—Kt4ch, K—B7; 6 Q—R3, K—Kt8; 7 Q—Kt3ch, K—R8; 8 Q—B2 and mate next*), *K—Kt7; 4 Q—K4ch, K—Kt6!; 5 K—B5, P—R6; 6 K—Q4, P—R7; 7 Q—R1, P—R8=Q; 8 Q×Q, K—Kt7; 9 Q—Kt2ch and wins as in No. 547.* If Black's Pawn is one square further, the game is drawn. No. 551b, Black Pawn at QR6, other pieces as in No. 551a. Draw. After the above maneuver we get 5 K—B5, P—R7!; 6 Q—R1, P—R8 = Q!; 7 Q×Q, K—Kt7 and White's King is not in the winning zone. With other Pawns White decides by capturing one, since the Q vs. P case is won.

With doubled Pawns we get a peculiar situation if one Pawn is on the seventh and the other on the fifth. In No. 552 (Bekey, 1906), White cannot win despite the proximity of his King because the square QB3 is not available. On *1 Q—R3ch, K—B7; 2 Q—R2ch, K—B8,* if 3 K—Q3 the Pawn promotes with check. No. 552a, White: K at Q4, Q at QB4; Black: K at Q8, P's at K5, K7 is won however because White's Queen can get around to the other side. 1 Q—R4ch, K—Q7; 2 Q—R5ch, K—Q8; 3 Q—KR5, K—Q7; 4 Q—Kt5ch, K—Q8; 5 Q—Kt4, K—Q7; 6 Q—Kt2, K—Q8; 7 K×P!, P—K8 = Qch; 8 K—Q3 and mates in a few.

The most difficult case with the White King in some other part of the board is No. 552b (Bekey, 1906), White: K at QR8, Q at QKt8; Black: K at QKt6, P's at QKt5, QKt7. White to play wins. The idea is to capture the P at Kt5 when the Black King is at QKt8, so that No. 544 will result. The solution is then 1 Q—Kt3ch, K—R7 (if 1 .... K—R5; 2 Q—Kt6 and 3 Q—QKt1; if 1 .... K—B7; 2 Q—B2ch, K—B8; 3 Q—QB5ch, etc.); 2 Q—B2, K—R8 (or 2 .... K—R6; 3 Q—KB5, K—R7; 4 Q—QB2 as in the main line, or 2 .... P—Kt6; 3 Q—Q2, K—R8; 4 Q—R5ch, K—Kt8; 5 Q—Kt4, K—B7; 6 Q—B4ch, etc.); 3 Q—Q4, K—R7 (if 3 .... K—Kt8; 4 Q×P; if 3 .... P—Kt6; 4 Q—R4ch); 4 Q—Q5ch, K—Kt8 (the alternatives are a) 4 .... K—R6; 5 Q—Q1, K—R7; 6 Q—R4ch; b) 4 .... K—R8; 5 Q—R5ch; c) 4 .... P—Kt6; 5 Q—R5ch, K—Kt8;

No. 552

6 Q—Kt4 winning the back Pawn in all cases); 5 Q—B6, P—Kt6 (or 5 .... K—R7; 6 Q—R4ch); 6 Q—Kt5, K—B7; 7 Q—B4ch, K—Kt8 (or 7 .... K—Q7); 8 Q×P and we have No. 544.

Black will often be able to draw with two disconnected Pawns on the seventh, but only if he has a BP or RP. Thus in No. 553, where neither Pawn alone could draw, the zigzag approach wins. *1 Q—B7ch, K—K8; 2 Q—Kt6, K—B7* (or 2 .... K—Q8; 3 Q—Q3ch, K—B8!; 4 Q—B3ch!, K—Q8; 5 Q—Q4ch!, K—B8; 6 Q—Kt1ch, etc.); *3 Q—*

Draw. Win only with Pawns on QKt, QB and K files. Win except with Bishop and RP's if White King is elsewhere.

B5ch, K—K8 (if 3 .... K—Kt6; 4 Q—Kt5ch, K—B6; 5 Q—B1!, K—B7; 6 Q—B4ch, etc., as in the main line); *4 Q—Kt4, K—B7* (if 4 .... K—B8; 5 Q—B3ch and captures one of the Pawns; if 4 .... K—Q8; 5 Q—Q4ch as in the note to Black's 2nd move); *5 Q—B4ch, K—K8* (or 5 .... K—Kt8; 6 Q—Kt3, K—R8; 7 Q—R4ch, K—Kt8; 8 Q—K1ch, K—R7; 9 Q×P); *6 Q—K3, K—Q8; 7 Q—Q4ch, K—B8; 8 Q—Kt1ch, K—Q7; 9 Q×P,* etc.

But if one of the Pawns draws, Black can afford to abandon the other. No. 554 (Kling and Horwitz) is an illustration. After *1 Q— B5ch, K—Q8; 2 Q—Q4ch, K—K7* White must capture the KtP, when

No. 553   **No. 554**

White to play wins.   Draw.

the BP alone will draw. It is curious to see that if the Black King is not near by the BP the game is lost. No 554a (Kling and Horwitz, 1851), Black King at QR8, other pieces as in No. 554. White to play wins. 1 Q—R3ch (not 1 Q—B6?, P—B8=Q!); K—Kt8; 2 Q—R6!, K—B7 (or 2 .... K—B8; 3 Q—B1ch); 3 Q—K2ch, K—B6 (3 .... K—B8; 4 Q—B1ch); 4 Q—B1 and the White King approaches. An unusual type of draw is seen in No. 554b (Kling and Horwitz, 1851), White: K at K1, Q at KR8; Black: K at K6, P's at QR7, KR7. White must take perpetual check, since Black is threatening to win by 1 .... P—KR8=Qch and 2 .... P—QR8=Q or vice versa. Black need only avoid the capture of one of his Pawns with check.

Two connected passed Pawns on the seventh, supported by the K, draw unless the White King is nearby or one of the Pawns is lost. The general case where either Pawn alone would lose is seen in No. 555 (Berger). After *1 Q—Kt3ch, K—K5!* (not 1 .... K—Q5?; 2 Q— B4ch, K—Q6; 3 Q—B3ch); *2 Q—Kt4ch, K—K6!; 3 Q—K6ch, K—*

B7!; 4 *Q—B6ch, K—K8;* 5 *Q—R4ch, K—Q8;* 6 *Q—KKt4, K—B8!,*
etc., it is clear that White can get nowhere. But a position such as
No. 555a (Kling and Horwitz, 1851), White: K at QKt1, Q at KR2;
Black: K at K6, P's at K7, Q7 is won because the White King re-
stricts Black's moves and can help to build up an attack. The solution is 1 Q—R6ch, K—Q6!; 2 Q—Q6ch, K—B6 (if 2 .... K—K6;
3 Q—B5ch, K—Q6; 4 Q—B2ch!, K—K6; 5 Q—B3ch wins. Note
that the check at QB2 could not be given in No. 555); 3 Q—B5ch,
K—Q6; 4 Q—B2ch, K—K6; 5 Q—B3ch, K—B7; 6 Q×P and wins.

If one of the Pawns alone would draw, White can win only if his

No. 555	No. 556

White to play. Draw.	White to play wins.

King is nearby. E.g., No. 555b (Lewis), White: K at QR5, Q at
Q5; Black: K at QB7, P's at QR7, QKt6. White to play wins. 1 Q—
Kt2ch, K—B8 (1 .... K—B6; 2 Q—Kt7ch and 3 Q—R1 or 1 ....
K—Q6; 2 Q—QKt2!); 2 Q—B1ch, K—B7; 3 Q—K2ch, K—B8; 4 K—
Kt4!, P—Kt7 (or 4 .... P—R8=Q; 5 Q—K1ch, K—Kt7; 6 Q—
Q2ch, K—Kt8; 7 K×P and wins); 5 K—B3, P—Kt8=Ktch; 6 K—
Q3!, P—R8=Kt; 7 Q—QR2 puts an end to Black's picturesque de-
fense.

C. QUEEN VS. THREE (OR MORE) PAWNS

As we mentioned in the introduction the number of Pawns makes
no great difference. Four passed Pawns on the second rank are deci-
mated before you can say checkmate. Black has chances only when
his Pawns are far advanced.

No. 556 (Berger, 1914) is in a sense a critical position. The winning
idea is to blockade the Pawns and gain time to bring up the King.

With this in mind we begin with *1 K—Kt2* with the following possibilities:

a) *1 .... P—B6; 2 Q—QKt8, K—Kt4* (2 .... P—B7; 3 Q—B4, or 2 .... P—Kt6; 3 Q—B4ch); *3 Q—KKt3* and the King can now march in.

b) *1 .... P—Kt6; 2 Q—B3, K—Kt4* (the only hope); *3 K—B3, P—Kt7; 4 Q—B2, K—Kt5* (or 4 .... P—B6; 5 Q—Kt3ch and one Pawn goes with check); *5 K—Q3, P—B6; 6 K—K3, P—R7; 7 Q×₿Pch*, etc.

c) *1 .... P—R7; 2 Q—Kt2, P—Kt6; 3 Q—B3, P—R8 = Q* (else the White King again gets to K5 and captures every Pawn); *4 Q×Qch, K—Kt5; 5 K—B3, P—B6; 6 K—Q2, P—Kt7; 7 Q—R2!* and wins.

d) *1 .... K—Kt4* (or *R4*); *2 Q—Q5ch, K—R5* (2 .... K—B3; 3 Q—K4); *3 K—B3* and White is a tempo ahead of all of the above variations.

e) *1 .... K—Kt6* (threatening .... P—B6); *2 Q—R1, P—B6; 3 K—B2, P—B7* (If 3 .... K—R5; 4 K—Q2, P—B7; 5 K—K2, P—Kt6; 6 Q—K4ch, K—Kt4; 7 K—B1. Or 3 .... K—B7; 4 K—Q2, P—Kt6; 5 Q×RP, P—Kt7; 6 Q—R4ch, K—Kt8; 7 K—K3, K—B8; 8 Q—B2 mate); *4 K—Q2, P—R7; 5 K—K2* and wins.

No. 556 may be called critical because if the position is moved down one rank, the Pawns will win. No. 556a (Berger), White: K at QR1, Q at QKt8; Black: K at KR6, P's at KB6, KKt6, KR7. Black wins. After 1 Q—B8ch, K—Kt7; 2 Q—B2ch, P—B7; 3 Q—B6ch, K—Kt8 White has no check (except 4 Q—B1ch, P—B8=Q) and cannot prevent one of the Pawns from queening.

An example of how the Queen may win against four relatively advanced Pawns is No. 556b (Kling and Horwitz, 1851), White: K at QKt2, Q at QR3; Black: K at KKt8, P's at KKt7, QB5, QKt6, QR7. White to play wins. The main variation is 1 Q—B5ch, K—R7—or A, B—; 2 Q—K5ch, K—R8 (if 2 .... K—Kt8; 3 Q—K1ch, K—R7; 4 Q—R4ch, K—Kt8; 5 Q×P); 3 Q—R8ch, K—Kt8; 4 Q—B6, K—R7; 5 Q—R4ch, K—Kt8; 6 Q×P, K—B7; 7 Q—B4ch, K—Kt8; 8 Q—Kt3, K—B8; 9 Q—B3ch, K—Kt8; 10 Q×QKtP followed by capture of the QRP by the K when we have No. 544. Variation A. 1 .... K—B8; 2 Q×Pch, K—B7; 3 Q—B4ch, etc., as above, 7th move on. Variation B. 1 .... K—R8; 2 Q—R5ch, K—Kt8; 3 Q—R3 (.... P—B6ch must be prevented), K—B7 (if 3 .... K—B8; 4 Q—B3ch, K—Kt8; 5 Q—KB6! as in the main line); 4 Q—R4ch, K—B6; 5 Q—K1, K—Kt5; 6 Q—B2!, K—R6 (if 6 .... P—B6ch; 7 K—R1, K—R6; 8 Q—K3ch, K—Kt5; 9 Q—Q4ch, K—B6; 10

Q×Pch and wins. Or here 8 .... K—R7; 9 Q—K5ch, K—R8; 10 Q—R8ch and 11 Q×P); 7 K—R1!, P—B6 (7 .... K—R7; 8 Q—R4ch, etc.); 8 Q—K3ch, K—Kt5 (8 .... K—R7; 9 Q—K5ch, K—R8; 10 Q—R8ch, etc.); 9 Q—Q4ch, K—R6 (9 .... K—R4; 10 Q—R8ch and 11 Q—Kt7ch. If 9 .... K—B4; 10 Q—Q5ch); 10 Q×Pch, K—R7; 11 Q—K5ch, etc., as in the main variation.

D. QUEEN AND PAWNS VS. PAWNS

This is practically always a win, regardless of the number or position of Black's Pawns. No. 557 exemplifies the general method. Here there are two ways to win: 1) sacrificing the Queen for the BP; 2) capturing the QP and then exchanging Queens after Black has promoted.

1. *1 Q—B2ch* (but not 1 Q×Pch??, K×Q; 2 K—Kt4, K—Q6; 3 K—B5, K—K5 and Black wins!), *K—Q8; 2 Q—B1ch, K—Q7; 3 K—Kt5, P—B8=Q; 4 Q×Qch, K×Q; 5 K—B5*, etc.
2. *1 Q×QP, P—B8=Q; 2 Q—Kt5ch, K—Q8; 3 Q×Qch, K×Q; 4 P—Q5.*

Where Black has extra Pawn moves the win is simpler because stalemate need not be feared.

The chief type of drawing position is that where the P ending is not won. E.g., No. 557a, White: K at QR5, Q at KB3, P at KR4; Black: K at KKt8, P's at KR4, KB7. Draw. If 1 Q×RP, P—B8=Q; if 1 Q—Kt3ch, K—R8!, etc., and finally if 1 K—Kt4, P—B8=Q; 2 Q×Qch, K×Q; 3 K—B4, K—Kt7; 4 K—Q3, K—Kt6 White can just manage to draw the P ending.

II. QUEEN AND PAWN ENDINGS

No. 557

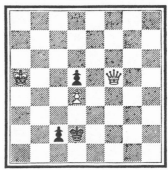

White to play wins.

Endings where both sides have Queens and Pawns are notoriously difficult. One Pawn ahead wins even less frequently than in Rook endings, while with two Pawns the win is still not smooth sailing. *The general rule is that one Pawn wins only if the White King is not exposed, while two Pawns always win.* This of course must be qualified by the more detailed analysis which follows.

A. QUEEN AND PAWN VS. QUEEN

This is a draw unless White has a BP or center P on the seventh supported by the King. As a rule, it is best to have the Black King as far away from the Pawn as possible, unless, of course, it can occupy a square in front of the Pawn, in which case the game is a hopeless draw.

In the first place we must note that in general it is impossible to advance a Pawn very far. Black keeps on checking and when he runs out of checks pins the Pawn. In view of the terrific number of possible positions of the Kings and Pawns, all of which require individual attention, it is out of the question to subject this statement to a precise analysis. At any rate, in actual practice it is usually found that the Pawn can be held back.

We shall confine ourselves to the question of what happens if and when the Pawn gets to the seventh. In that event RP and KtP draw, but BP or center P wins.

In No. 558 we have the interesting problem of the QP. It makes no essential difference where the Black King is: it will always cut down the number of checks and at KR6 it is placed as well as anywhere else. Here it is possible to exhaust the checks and queen the Pawn. *1 .... Q—B4ch* (If 1 .... Q—K6ch; 2 Q—K6ch; if 1 .... Q—B2; 2 K—K8, winning at once in both cases); *2 K—K8, Q—QKt4* (again forced: if 2 .... Q—K6ch; 3 Q—K7 and there are no checks at all, while on 2 .... Q—R4ch; 3 K—B8, Q—B4ch; 4 K—Kt7, Q—Kt8ch —or A—; 5 K—R8! Black has again run out of checks. Variation A. 4 .... Q—B2; 5 Q—B5ch and now a) 5 .... K—Kt6; 6 K—R6! and there are no checks which do not permit a Q interposition with check. b) 5 .... K—Kt7; 6 K—R6, Q—R7ch; 7 Q—R5! and wins. c) 5 ....

No. 558

Black to play. White wins.

K—R5; 6 K—Kt6, Q—Kt6ch; 7 K—B7, Q—Kt6ch; 8 Q—K6, Q—Kt2; 9 Q—K7ch and 10 P—Q8=Q, or here 7 .... Q—B2; 8 Q—B6ch and 9 K—K8. d) 5 .... K—R7; 6 K—B8, Q—Q1ch; 7 K—B7, Q—B2; 8 K—K8, Q—B3; 9 K—K7, Q—B2; 10 Q—Q5!, Q—R2; 11 K—K6! and wins); *3 Q—K6ch, K—R7* (if 3 .... K—Kt6; 4 K—B7, Q—B8ch; 5 K—Kt8 or 4 .... Q—Kt2; 5 K—Kt6, Q—Kt8ch; 6 Q—B5, Q—Kt3ch; 7 K—R5); *4 K—B7, Q—R4ch* (if 4 .... Q—B8ch; 5 K—K7, while if 4 .... Q—Kt2; 5 K—Kt6, Q—Kt7ch; 6 K—

B6!, Q—B6ch; 7 Q—B5, Q—B3ch; 8 K—K7, Q—B2; 9 Q—Q5! and if 9 .... K any; 10 K—K8 decides, while 9 .... Q—R2 is met by 10 K—K6!); *5 K—Kt7, Q—Kt4ch; 6 K—R7, Q—Q1* (forced, since he has no good checks); *7 K—Kt6!, K—R8* (or 7 .... Q—B2; 8 Q—K2ch followed by either Q—Q3ch or Q—Q1ch and P—Q8=Q); *8 K—B7, K—R7* (if 8 .... Q—B2; 9 K—K8); *9 Q—K7* and wins.

The case of the BP is more difficult. Philidor (1803) gave No. 559 as a draw, but subsequent analysts have established a win. The best defense is *1 .... Q—K4ch* (for alternatives see A.); *2 K—Kt8, Q—Kt4ch* (if 2 .... Q—K3; 3 Q—Q4ch, K—Kt6; 4 K—Kt7, Q—K2; 5 Q—Q5ch and 6 K—Kt8); *3 K—B8* and now:

1. *3 .... Q—B4ch; 4 K—K8, Q—QB1ch* (if 4 .... Q—K4ch; 5 K—Q7, Q—Kt2; 6 Q—Q6ch, K any; 7 K—K8); *5 K—K7, Q—B2ch; 6 K—K6, Q—B1ch; 7 Q—Q7, Q—B5ch* (all this is forced); *8 Q—Q5, Q—Kt5ch* (if instead 8 .... Q—B1ch; 9 K—B6, Q—B1; 10 K—Kt6, Q—K2; 11 Q—B6, Q—B1; 12 Q—K6, K any; 13 K—R7, Q—Q1; 14 Q—K4ch, 15 Q—B5 (or B3) ch and 16 P—B8=Q); *9 Q—B5, Q—B5ch* (or 9 .... Q—K7ch; 10 K—B6, Q—Kt7ch; 11 K—Kt6, Q—Kt7ch; 12 K—R5, Q—R7ch; 13 K—Kt5); *10 K—K5, Q—B4ch* (or 10 .... Q—B6ch; 11 K—B4 and when the K gets to Kt5 there are no more checks); *11 K—K4, Q—K2ch; 12 K—B3, Q—B1; 13 K—B2!, K—Kt6* (what Black does is immaterial); *14 K—B1!, K—Kt5; 15 Q—K4ch* and *16 Q—K8* wins.

2. *3 .... Q—R3ch; 4 K—K7, Q—Kt4ch; 5 K—K6, Q—Kt5ch* (or 5 .... Q—R3ch; 6 K—Q7, Q—Kt2; 7 Q—Q6ch, K any; 8 K—K8); *6 Q—B5, Q—B5ch; 7 K—K5*, etc., as in 1).

3. *3 .... Q—K4; 4 Q—KB3!* (in order to free the King), *Q—B4ch* (Or a) 4 .... Q—Kt1ch; 5 K—Kt7, Q—R2; 6 K—R7!, K—Kt4; 7 Q—Kt3ch, K—B3; 8 Q—QB3ch, K any; 9 Q—Kt7 and queens. b) 4 .... Q—R1ch; 5 K—K7, Q—K4ch; 6 K—Q7, Q—Q5ch; 7 K—K6, Q—B5ch; 8 Q—Q5 transposing into 1), or here 6 .... Q—Kt4ch; 7 K—K6, Q—Kt3ch; 8 K—B5, Q—B4ch; 9 K—Kt4 as in the main variation of 3). c) 4 .... K—B4 (or any other K move); 5 K—Kt8!, Q—K3; 6 K—R7, Q—Q2;

No. 559

Black to play. White wins.

7 K—Kt6, Q—Q3ch; 8 Q—B6, Q—B1; 9 K—R7, K any; 10 Q—Kt7 and wins); *5 K—Kt7, Q—Kt8ch; 6 K—R6, Q—B8ch* (if 6 .... Q—R7ch; 7 K—Kt5, Q—K4ch; 8 Q—B5, Q—K2ch; 9 K—R5, Q—B1; 10 Q—Q5, etc., as in 1), note to Black's 8th move); *7 K—R5, Q—B4ch; 8 K—Kt4, Q—KB1* (8 .... Q—B1ch; 9 Q—B5 is merely a transposition); *9 Q—B5, K—B5; 10 K—R5, K—Q5* (if 10 .... K—Kt5; 11 Q—Q5, K—Kt6—R7, etc.); *11 Q—B6ch, K any; 12 K—Kt6, K any; 13 K—R7, K any; 14 Q—Kt7* and wins.

4. *3* .... *Q—B3; 4 Q—K4ch, K any; 5 K—K8* and queens.
5. *3* .... *K—B4* (on other K moves 4 Q—KB3 as in 3) decides); *4 K—K8, Q—R4!; 5 K—K7, Q—Kt4ch; 6 K—K6, Q—R3ch; 7 K—Q7, Q—QB3ch* (if 7 .... Q—KB3; 8 P—B8 = Qch, Q×Q; 9 Q—R3ch); *8 K—K7, Q—B2ch* (or 8 .... Q—Kt2ch; 9 Q—Q7, Q—K5ch; 10 K—Q8); *9 Q—Q7, Q—K4ch; 10 K—Q8, Q—R1ch; 11 Q—K8, Q—Q5ch; 12 K—B8, Q—Kt5ch; 13 Q—Q7, Q—Kt2* (or 13 .... Q—B6; 14 Q—K7ch); *14 Q—K7ch, K—B3; 15 P—B8 = Q, Q—Kt5ch; 16 K—Kt8, Q—Kt6ch; 17 K—R8* and Black has no more checks.

A. The alternatives on Black's first move are easily disposed of:
a) 1 .... Q—B2; 2 K—Kt8! and wins because Black can neither check nor pin.
b) 1 .... Q—K2; 2 Q—B5, Q—R2; 3 K—R7, K—Kt6; 4 Q—B3ch, K any; 5 Q—Kt2 (Kt4) ch, K any; 6 Q—Kt7 and promotes.
c) 1 .... Q—R2; 2 Q—B5, K—R6; 3 Q—B3ch, K—Kt5; 4 K—R6, Q—Kt3ch; 5 K—R7, Q—R2; 6 Q—Kt4ch, K any; 7 K—Kt8 and wins.
d) 1 .... Q—Kt4ch; 2 Q—Kt6, Q—K4ch (2 .... Q—K2; 3 K—Kt8); 3 K—Kt8, Q—Q4; 4 K—R7, Q—R8ch (4 .... Q—Q2; 5 Q—K4ch and 6 K—Kt8); 5 K—Kt7, Q—R8ch; 6 K—Kt8, Q—R7; 7 Q—Kt6ch, K—B6; 8 K—Kt7, Q—Kt7ch; 9 Q—Kt6, Q—Kt2; 10 K—Kt8, Q—Q4; 11 K—R7, Q—R8ch; 12 Q—R6, Q—K5ch; 13 K—R8! and Black has no good checks.

With a KtP White cannot win because he is exposed to perpetual check, even with two Queens. No. 560 (Lolli) demonstrates this. *1* .... *Q—R5ch; 2 Q—R7* (if 2 K—Kt8, Q—Q1ch; 3 K—B7, Q—Q2ch; 4 K—B6, Q—Q5ch, etc. White cannot do better than the main line), *Q—Q1ch!; 3 P—Kt8 = Q, Q—B6ch; 4 Q(R7)—Kt7, Q—R5ch; 5 Q(Kt8)—R7, Q—Q1ch*, etc., with perpetual check.

It is essential for Black in this ending to have his King all the way on the other side of the board since otherwise it will merely get in his way and prevent perpetual check. E.g., No. 560a (Kling and Horwitz, 1851), White: K at QR8, Q at QKt3, P at QKt7; Black: K at QR3, Q at QB3. White to play wins. 1 Q—Kt4!, Q—R8 (or

1 .... Q—Q4; 2 Q—R4ch, K—Kt6; 3 Q—Kt3ch!!, Q×Q; 4 P—
Kt8=Qch and wins. Similarly for 1 .... Q—KB6 or 1 .... Q—
Kt7); 2 Q—R3ch, K—Kt3 (or 2 .... K—Kt4; 3 Q—Kt2ch, K—B5;
4 K—R7, Q—Kt8ch; 5 K—R6, Q—Kt3ch; 6 Q—Kt6); 3 Q—Kt2ch,
K—B4 (3 .... K—R6; 4 Q—R2ch and 5 Q—Kt1 as above); 4 K—
R7, Q—R2; 5 Q—Kt6ch, K—Q4; 6 K—R6 and wins.

But even with the King at a distance from the Pawn there are
some special positions which win. One of these which also shows that
there are other cases besides those already mentioned where Q vs.
Q with no Pawns may win is No. 560b (Lesehalle, 1887), White: K
at K4, Q at QR2, P at QKt4; Black: K at KR8, Q at Q3. White to
play wins. 1 Q—Q5!, Q—Kt3ch (if 1 .... Q×Pch; 2 K—B3!! and

No. 560   No. 561

Black to play draws.   Black wins.

Black is lost. E.g., 2 .... K—R7; 3 Q—R5ch, K—Kt8; 4 Q—Kt5ch
and mates in two, or 2 .... Q—Kt7; 3 K—Kt3 dis ch, K—Kt8;
4 Q—Q1 mate); 2 K—B4 dis ch! (it would be a bad mistake for White
to let Black out of the mating net, since he would then get to No.
560), K—R7; 3 Q—K5!!, Q—Q6; 4 P—Kt5 and wins because any
check either allows mate or the exchange of Queens. E.g., 4 ....
Q—B8ch; 5 K—Kt4 dis ch, K—R8; 6 Q—K4ch, K—Kt8; 7 Q—K3ch,
K—Kt7; 8 Q—R3ch, or 4 .... Q—Q7ch; 5 K—B3 dis ch, K—R8;
6 Q—K4, Q—Kt4; 7 K—B2 dis ch, K—R7; 8 Q—R7ch and mates.
After 4 .... Q—Q8; 5 K—K3 dis ch, K—Kt7; 6 Q—K4ch, K—Kt8;
7 Q—Q4!, Q—R4; 8 P—Kt6, K—R8; 9 Q—R1ch, K—Kt7; 10 Q—
Kt2ch, K—R8; 11 P—Kt7 Black will soon run out of checks.

A RP draws just as simply as a KtP: once the Pawn gets to R7,
the K to R8, perpetual check is unavoidable.

It is extremely difficult to determine in general whether a Pawn will be able to reach the seventh rank by force. That it is possible in some instances is shown by No. 561 (Game, 1911, adjudicated by Dr. Lasker). The first few moves are forced: *1 K—B5, Q—B4ch; 2 K—B6, Q—Q3ch; 3 K—B5, P—B4.* The White King is still badly placed and Black can march his Pawn on. *4 Q—Kt1, P—B5; 5 Q— Kt1ch* (if 5 Q—Kt4, Q—Q2ch), *K—B4; 6 Q—Kt1ch, Q—Q5.* Again there are no more checks; the Pawn advances and eventually we get to No. 561.

Summary: Queen and Pawn vs. Queen wins only with a BP or center Pawn on the seventh. Black's King should be as far as possible from the Pawn. A bad King position may cost Black the game in otherwise drawn positions.

No. 562

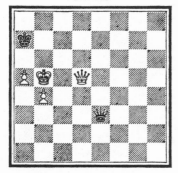

Black to play. White wins.

No. 563

Black to play. White wins.

B. QUEEN AND TWO PAWNS VS. QUEEN

An advantage of two Pawns will always win, but the ever-present danger of perpetual check makes the process tedious and complicated.

1. CONNECTED PAWNS

Here Black has drawing chances only if his King is in front of the Pawns. For else the White King will find a haven behind the Pawns and Black will never be able to give more than a few meaningless checks.

With the Black King well-placed White's task is most difficult with a KtP and RP, chiefly because neither Pawn alone can win. The crucial position which White should then try to secure is shown in No. 562. The idea is to get the King to QB7, interpose the Queen on a check on the rank, and then discover check. The best defense is

1 .... Q—K1ch; 2 K—B4!, Q—K7ch; 3 K—B5, Q—K2ch (or *3 ....*
Q—KB7ch; 4 K—B6, Q—B3ch; 5 K—B7, Q—Kt2ch; 6 Q—Q7, etc.);
4 Q—Q6, Q—Kt4ch (*4 ....* Q—K6ch; 5 Q—Q4); *5 K—B6, Q—*
Kt7ch; 6 K—B7, Q—Kt2ch; 7 Q—Q7 and wins easily: *7 ....* Q—
B6ch (on other moves such as *7 ....* Q—B3; 8 K—B8 leads to mate);
8 K—Q6 dis ch, K—Kt1; 9 Q—Kt5ch and either *10 Q—B6ch* (on
.... K—R1 or *....* K—B1) or *10 Q—B5ch* (on *....* K—R2) will
force the exchange of Queens.

The question then naturally arises whether this can be forced from
any position, and the answer is yes. In No. 563 it is at once obvious
that the proper Pawn position can be secured in a few moves. *1 ....*
Q—B2ch; 2 P—Kt3, Q—Q2; 3 Q—B3ch, K—R3; 4 P—R4, Q—K2;
5 P—Kt4, Q—K7ch; 6 K—R3, Q—K5; 7 P—R5. In all this Black
has no meaningful checks and can only mark time. *7 .... Q—Kt8*
(there does not seem to be anything better. If, e.g., *7 ....* Q—Q4;
8 Q—B8ch, K—Kt4; 9 Q—Kt8ch, K—B5; 10 Q—B7ch, K—Kt4;
11 Q—Kt6ch, K—B5; 12 Q—K3!, K—Kt4; 13 Q—K2ch, K—B3;
14 Q—R6ch, K—B2; 15 Q—Kt6ch, K—Q2; 16 Q—B5 and now the
White King will be able to find a shelter at QKt7 or QR7, while if
7 .... Q—R8; 8 Q—Q3ch, K—R2; 9 K—R4, Q—B3ch; 10 P—Kt5
and the Pawn gets to Kt6 with check after which White has all sorts
of mating threats); *8 Q—B6ch, K—R2; 9 Q—Q5, K—R3* (checks get
the King to Kt5 and transpose into No. 562); *10 Q—Q6ch, K—R2*
(10 .... K—Kt4; 11 Q—Kt6ch, K—B5; 12 Q—B6ch and wins Black's
Queen, which is, as a matter of fact, unimportant, for after 12 ....
K—Q6; 13 K—R4 also wins without any trouble); *11 K—R4, Q—*
KB8 (else K—Kt5); *12 Q—Q7ch, K—R1; 13 Q—Q4, Q—K7; 14 P—*
Kt5, Q—R7ch; 15 K—Kt4, Q—Kt8ch; 16 K—B5, Q—B7ch; 17 K—
Kt6, Q—Kt3ch; 18 K—B7, Q—
B2ch; 19 Q—Q7, Q—KB5ch; 20 K
—B8, Q—B1ch; 21 Q—Q8, Q—
B2!; 22 P—R6! and the discovered
check or a Queen check will be fatal.

2. DISCONNECTED PAWNS

These will, as a rule, win just as
easily as connected Pawns. The
reason is the same: the extra Pawn
shelters the White King from
perpetual check. A classic instance
is No. 564 (Morphy-Anderssen,
Paris, 1858). Black's conduct of
the ending is straightforward and

No. 564

Black to play wins.

requires little explanation. *1 .... Q—Q5ch; 2 K—B1, P—R5; 3 Q—B5ch, K—B3; 4 Q—QB8, K—Kt4!; 5 K—K1* (if 5 Q×P, Q—B5ch and the RP will queen! Similarly, if 5 Q—Kt7ch, Q—Kt3; 6 Q—Q5ch, P—B4; 7 Q—Q3ch, K—R4; 8 Q—Q2ch, K—R3 and White has no checks), *P—B4; 6 Q—Kt7ch, K—B5; 7 Q—B7ch, K—B6; 8 Q—B3ch, Q—Q6; 9 Q—B6ch, K—Kt6; 10 Q—Kt6ch, K—B7!; 11 Q—R7* (again if 11 Q×Pch, Q—B6ch wins), *Q—B6ch; 12 K—K2, P—R6; 13 Q—R4ch, K—Kt7; 14 Q—Kt5ch, Q—Kt6!* (once more the same combination: 15 Q×P, Q—B7ch); *15 Q—R6, P—B5; 16 Q—B6ch, P—B6* and White is lost.

An example where the defender's King is at a greater distance from the Pawns is No. 564a (Horwitz-Staunton, London, 1851), White: K at Q5, Q at QR5, P's at QR4, K5; Black: K at KKt6, Q at K6. The conclusion was 1 Q—Kt4, Q—B6ch; 2 Q—K4, Q—B2ch; 3 P—K6, Q—Kt2ch; 4 K—K5, Q—Kt1ch; 5 K—B6, Q—B1ch; 6 K—Kt5!, Q—Kt2ch; 7 Q—Kt6, Q—K4ch; 8 K—R6 dis ch, K—R5; 9 K—R7, Q—B2ch; 10 K—R6, Q—B5ch; 11 K—Kt7, Q—QB2ch; 12 Q—B7, Q—Kt6ch; 13 K—R7, Q—Q6ch; 14 Q—Kt6, Q—Q3; 15 Q—R6ch, K—Kt5; 16 P—K7!, Q—Q2! (16 .... Q×Pch; 17 Q—Kt7ch); 17 Q—Kt7ch, K—R4; 18 P—K8=Qch!, Q×Q; 19 Q—R6ch, K—Kt5; 20 Q—Kt6ch and wins.

3. DOUBLED PAWNS

While this is not a win with the Black King in front of the Pawns, it is in all cases (except the RP) if the Black King is at a distance. No. 565 shows the difference that the extra Pawn makes (compare No. 560). After *1 .... Q—B1ch* (1 .... Q—B5ch; 2 K—R7, Q—R5ch; 3 K—Kt6, Q—KB5; 4 Q—R7ch, 5 Q—Kt8ch and 6 P—Kt8=Q) the quickest win is *2 K—R7, Q—B7ch; 3 P—Kt6, Q—R7ch; 4 Q—R6, Q—B2* (forced); *5 Q—K2ch, K any; 6 K—R6, Q—B1* and White gets to the diagonal KR2—QKt8 with check and queens his Pawn.

No. 565

White wins.

More than two Pawns as usual win quite simply.

C. MATERIAL ADVANTAGE

Although one Pawn should in general win there are many exceptions and the winning process itself is as a rule long and intricate. *The basic rule of all Queen endings is that the superior side must always be on his guard against perpetual check.*

It will be most convenient to divide these endings into three groups, according to the position of the Pawns and the Kings.

1. THE DEFENDING KING IS NOT NEAR THE OPPOSING PAWN MAJORITY (OUTSIDE AND POTENTIAL OUTSIDE PASSED PAWNS)

No. 566

White wins.

No. 567

White to play. Draw.

This is the simplest case of all. White wins if his King is not exposed, but only draws if it is. Consequently the more Pawns there are the easier it is to win.

The ideal type of winning position is No. 566. The White Queen fulfills her marital duties by defending the King from checks and the Pawn then stolidly marches on. After *1 .... P—R4; 2 P—Kt5, P—R5; 3 P—Kt6, P—Kt4* (a desperate counterattack: else he might just as well resign); *4 Q—B7ch, K—Kt3; 5 P—Kt7, P—Kt5; 6 P×P* is decisive. It is clear that with more Pawns on the board even the faint counterchance that Black has above would disappear.

But the slightest weakness in the White Pawn structure may make it impossible for him to do any better than draw. An example of this is No. 567 (Alekhine-Reshevsky, AVRO, 1938). If the White P were at KB2 instead of KB3, Q—K4 followed by Q—R8 or P—QR4—R5 would win quite easily, using the same procedure as No. 566. But now 1 Q—K4? is answered by 1 .... Q—Q7ch; 2 K—R3, Q—Q2ch; 3 P—Kt4, Q—Q8, etc., with eventual perpetual check. Other attempts are likewise insufficient, as the course of the game shows. *1 Q—R2, K—Kt1; 2 P—QR4, Q—B3; 3 P—R5, Q—R3!* (again 4 Q—Q5 is the "natural" move in such positions, but here it leads to nothing because 4 .... K—Kt2!; 5 Q—K5ch, K—Kt1; 6 Q—Kt8ch, K—Kt2; 7 Q—Kt6, Q—K7ch; 8 K—R3, Q×BP already threatens perpetual check); *4 P—Kt4, P—Kt4!; 5 K—B2* (hoping to be able to get to the Q-side), *Q—Q3!; 6 K—B1, Q—R3ch; 7 K—Kt2, K—Kt2; 8 Q—Kt2ch, K—Kt1; 9 Q—Kt8ch, K—Kt2; 10 Q—K5ch, K—Kt1; 11 K—B2, Q—R2ch; 12 K—K2, Q—R3ch; 13 K—Q2, Q—B5!; 14 Q—KB5, Q—Q5ch; 15 K—K2, Q—Kt7ch; 16 K—Q3, Q—Kt6ch; 17 K—K2, Q—Kt7ch* and a draw was agreed to.

Where the King is exposed it is frequently hard to win with two Pawns to the good. This is illustrated in No. 568 (Alekhine-Euwe, Nottingham, 1936). White can always straighten out his Pawns by P—B4, but in most cases that would allow perpetual check. Accordingly he must postpone this advance until the right moment. The main variation is the game continuation. *1 .... Q—K8; 2 Q—B5ch, K—B2; 3 K—Kt2, Q—QR8* (if 3 .... Q—K7ch; 4 Q—B2); *4 Q—QB2* (not 4 P—R5?, Q—R7ch; 5 K—R3, Q—R8, etc.=because White's Queen must defend the QRP. On the tempting 4 Q×P, the reply 4 .... Q—Kt7ch; 5 K—R3, Q—R8; 6 Q—B4ch, K—Kt2!; 7 Q—B7ch, K—Kt1; 8 K—R4, Q—B3ch!; 9 P—Kt5, Q×BP would suffice to save Black), *K—B3; 5 Q—Kt3, K—K4?* (A mistake in time-pressure. Now 6 Q—Kt8ch wins at once, for if 6 .... K—B3; 7 Q—R8ch and if 6 .... K—Q4; 7 Q—Kt8ch, K—B4; 8 Q×P, Q×P; 9 Q×Pch with an elementary win in both cases); *6 K—B2?, K—B3; 7 Q—Kt6ch* (if 7 P—B4, P×P!; 8 P×P, Q—R8!; 9 Q—Kt2ch, K—

No. 568

Black to play.

B2 and White will have to lose either a Pawn on the K-side or his QRP), *K—Kt2; 8 Q—Kt4, Q—R8!; 9 Q—K1, Q—R7ch; 10 K—K3, K —R2* (if 10 .... Q—R7 then likewise P—R5. The object of the Black K move is to prevent any effective check); *11 P—R5, Q—R7; 12 Q—Q2, Q—R8; 13 K—K2!, K —R3* (this allows P→B4 but there is nothing better. If 13 .... Q— R8; 14 Q—K3!, Q—QKt8—or A—; 15 Q×P, Q—B7ch; 16 Q—Q2, Q— B5ch; 17 K—B2! and wins. Variation A. 14 .... Q—Kt7ch; 15 Q —B2, Q—R8; 16 P—R6, Q—QKt8.

17 Q—B1! and White will soon get out of check, so that his Pawn has advanced one more vital square); *14 P—B4!, P×P* (or 14 .... Q—R5; 15 P×Pch, K—Kt2; 16 Q—B3ch, K—Kt1; 17 Q—B8ch, K—Kt2; 18 Q—B7ch and will win the KKtP with check: 18 .... K—Kt1; 19 Q—Q8ch, K—Kt2; 20 Q—B6ch, K—R2; 21 Q—B7ch, K—R1; 22 Q—B8ch, K—R2; 23 Q—R6ch, etc.); *15 P×P.* Now White's winning plan consists first of driving the Black King back to the first rank, and then of playing his King over to the support of the QRP. With the Black King exposed it will be found that White can escape perpetual check. *15 .... Q—R5; 16 K—B2* (preparing P—Kt5ch, which at once would be answered by .... K—R4), *K—R2* (or 16 .... Q—R8; 17 K—Kt2, Q—R5; 18 P—Kt5ch and if 18 .... K—R4?; 19 Q—K3! will conclude quickly); *17 P—Kt5, Q—R6.* Now the problem is to get the White King to the Q-side. *18 Q—Q7ch, K—R1; 19 Q—B8ch, K—R2; 20 Q—B7ch, K—R1; 21 K—K2, Q—R7ch; 22 K—K3, Q—Kt6ch; 23 K—Q4, Q—Kt5ch; 24 K—Q5, Q—Kt4ch; 25 K—Q4, Q—R3* (on 25 .... Q—Kt5ch the quickest win is 26 K—K5, Q—Kt4ch; 27 K—Q6, etc.); *26 Q—Kt6, Q—B1; 27 Q—Q6!* (the ideal spot for the Queen. 27 Q×P was also good enough), *Q—B7; 28 P—R6, Q—Q7ch; 29 K—K5, Q—B6ch; 30 K—K6, Q—B1ch; 31 K—K7, K—R2; 32 Q—Q7!* (the now familiar maneuver: he will win by giving a discovered check), *Q—B6; 33 K—K6 dis ch,* Resigns. For White can now force the exchange of Queens: 33 .... K—R1; 34 Q—Q8ch, K—R2; 35 Q—K7ch, K—Kt1; 36 Q—B7ch, K—R1; 37 Q—B6ch, etc.

A potential passed Pawn is exploited in precisely the same manner, since one passed Pawn is just about as good as two in Queen endings.

No. 569 (Alekhine-Maroczy, New York, 1924) exemplifies this and also shows how beneficial to the superior side additional Pawns are. The quickest win here (for the game continuation see A.) is *1 Q—B8ch, K—Kt2; 2 Q×P, Q—R8ch; 3 K—K2, Q×KtP; 4 P—QR4, Q×RP* (if instead 4 .... P—Kt4; 5 P—R5, P—R4; 6 P—R6, P—Kt5; 7 P×P, P×P; 8 Q—K7, Q—B6ch; 9 K—K1, Q—R8ch; 10 K—Q2, Q—R8; 11 Q—R3 and wins); *5 P—R5, Q—Kt5ch; 6 K—Q2, Q—B6; 7 P—R6, Q×BPch; 8 K—Q3, Q—B8ch; 9 K—Q4, Q—Q8ch; 10 K—*

No. 569

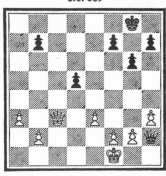

White to play wins.

B5, Q—B8ch; 11 K—Q6, Q×KP; 12 P—R7, Q—Kt6ch; 13 K—Q7,
Q—Kt5ch; 14 K—Q8, Q—R5ch; 15 Q—K7, Q—R5; 16 Q—K5ch,
K—R3; 17 Q—Kt8, Q—R4ch; 18 K—K8, Q—R5ch; 19 K—B8 and
Black has no checks.

A. Alekhine played 1 P—B3 and after 1 .... Q—R8ch; 2 K—B2,
Q—Q8; 3 Q—B8ch, K—Kt2; 4 Q×P?? (4 Q—B3ch, K—Kt1; 5 Q—
Q4 was still good enough), Q—Q7ch; 5 K—Kt3, P—Q5!! draws: 6
P×P, Q—Kt4ch and Black has perpetual check.

A similar instructive error is seen in No. 569a (Maroczy-Alapin,
Barmen, 1905), White: K at KR1, Q at Q2, P's at QR2, QKt2, KKt2,
KR3; Black: K at KR2, Q at KB2, P's at QR3, QKt4, QB5, KKt2,
KR3. Black to play wins. After 1 .... Q—B4; 2 P—R3, Q—Q6;
3 Q—Kt4, Q—QKt6; 4 Q—Q2, P—QR4! wins most simply, e.g., 5 Q—
Q7, Q×KtP; 6 Q—B5ch, P—Kt3; 7 Q—Q7ch, Q—Kt2; 8 Q×P,
Q—QB2; 9 Q—Kt1, P—B6; 10 Q—B2, P—R4; and .... Q—B4—
Q5—Q7. Instead Black played 3 .... Q—Q5; when 4 K—R2, Q—
B5ch; 5 K—R1, Q—KB8ch; 6 K—R2, Q—B8; 7 P—QR4!, P×P;
8 Q×RP, Q×P; 9 Q×BP, Q—Kt1ch; 10 K—R1, P—QR4; 11 Q—
Q3ch only drew because Black cannot both defend against perpetual
check and support his Pawn.

2. THE DEFENDING KING IS NEAR THE OPPOSING PAWN MAJORITY (PAWNS ON BOTH SIDES OF THE BOARD)

Such endings are much more complicated than the foregoing because
a straightforward Pawn advance (as in No. 566 or No. 569) simply will
not do. For the King is secure against perpetual check only when sur-
rounded by Pawns, so that playing them out of the way merely invites
a draw.

The two chief winning stratagems in these cases are 1) playing the
King over to the other side of the board and 2) a mating attack. Of
course the capture of more material is a device that must be used frequently, but this is common to all types of ending.

No. 570 (Pillsbury-Burn, Vienna, 1898) is a splendid illustration of
the difficulties ordinarily encountered and the first method of over-
coming them. The first point to notice is that the natural advance
1 .... P—B4? allows 2 Q—B7ch, K—R3; 3 Q—Kt8 with a practically
certain draw. Black must find a safe spot for his King which will not
be weakened by the Pawn advance and only the Q-side offers such a
haven. Burn of course was quite well aware of all this and since Pillsbury puts up the best defense we may take the game continuation as a
model. *1 .... Q—Q4; 2 K—Kt2, K—B3; 3 Q—B3, Q—B4; 4 Q—*

Q3, K—K2; 5 Q—Q2 (note that White's King must not follow suit because of the danger of exchange of Queens), *Q—Q5; 6 Q—K2, P—B4!* (Now this may be played with impunity); *7 Q—Kt5, P—K5!; 8 P×P, P×P* (the advantage that the passed Pawn confers is clear: the movements of the White Queen are restricted because she must not only watch the Pawn but must also guard against exchange); *9 Q— Kt5ch, K—B2; 10 Q—B4ch, K—K3; 11 Q—Kt5, Q—Kt7ch; 12 K— R3, Q—B3; 13 Q—K3, K—Q4!; 14 Q—Q2ch, Q—Q5; 15 Q—Kt5ch, Q—K4!!* (the point: 16 Q×KtP? is refuted by 16 .... Q—K3ch; 17 Q×Qch, K×Q; 18 P—Kt4, P—K6!, etc., so that Black has gained a

No. 570

Black wins.

No. 571

White to play wins.

valuable tempo); *16 Q—K3, K—B3; 17 K—Kt2, Q—Kt7ch; 18 K— R3, Q—QB7; 19 Q—Kt5, Q—K7!!* (this is Black's real object: the KKtP makes little difference because White cannot set up a passed Pawn, and meanwhile the Black KP is a nasty threat); *20 Q×Pch, K—B4; 21 P—Kt4ch* (desperation. If 21 P—KKt4, Q—B6ch, while if 21 Q—B5ch, K—Kt5; 22 P—Kt4, P×Pch; 23 Q×KtP, Q×Qch!; 24 K×Q, K—B6!; 25 P—R5, P—K6; 26 P—R6, P—K7; 27 P—R7, P—K8=Q; 28 P—R8=Qch, K×P; 29 Q—Kt8ch, K—R6!! and White has no more checks—30 Q—B8ch, Q—Kt5ch—so that he will lose his last Pawn, after which the win is routine), *P×P; 22 Q—Kt5ch, K— Q5; 23 Q—B6ch, K—B5; 24 Q×P* (White now also has a passed Pawn but Black's travel more quickly), *Q—B6!* (threatening mate); *25 Q— K6ch, K—B6; 26 Q—K5ch, K—Kt6; 27 Q—Q5ch, K—R6!* (note how the Pawns defend the King from checks. 27 .... K×P?? would be a serious mistake since the Pawn is only in White's way); *28 K—R2, P—Kt6; 29 Q—B5ch, K—R7; 30 P—R5, P—Kt7; 31 Q—Q5ch, Q—*

Kt6; 32 Q—Q2, Q—Q6; 33 Q—KB2, P—K6; 34 Q—B7ch, Q—Kt6; 35 Resigns.

Sometimes this stratagem of playing the King over to the other wing is used in conjunction with a mating attack or the possibility of an exchange. This is seen in No. 571 (Konstantinopolsky-Budo, Tiflis, 1937). Although White's King appears to be favorably placed, he must regroup his pieces before he can really penetrate to the Q-side. The game continuation was *1 Q—B8ch, K—R2; 2 Q—B5ch, K—R1; 3 Q—K4, Q—B2ch; 4 K—B5, Q—Q2ch; 5 K—K5, Q—K2ch; 6 K—B5, Q—B3ch; 7 K—Kt4, Q—Kt4ch; 8 K—R3, Q—R4ch; 9 Q—R4, Q—B4ch; 10 Q—Kt4, Q—QB4; 11 Q—Kt6!* (after this the King threatens to start going back), *Q—KB7!* (preventing K—Kt4); *12 Q—K8ch, K—R2; 13 Q—K4ch, K—R1; 14 P—B4!* (again intending K—Kt4), *K—Kt1; 15 K—Kt4, Q—Kt8; 16 Q—Q5ch, K—R2; 17 P—R3, Q—B7; 18 K—B5, Q—B7ch; 19 Q—K4, Q—B2; 20 K—K6 dis ch, K—R1; 21 P—Kt3!* (protecting the Pawn and freeing the Queen), *Q—B1ch; 22 K—K7, Q—B2ch* (if 22 .... Q×P; 23 Q—K3!, Q—B4; 24 Q×P, Q—K5ch; 25 Q—K6, Q×RP; 26 K—B7 and wins or here 25 .... Q—Kt2ch; 26 K—B8, Q—Kt1ch; 27 K—B7, Q—B2ch; 28 K—Kt6, Q—B7ch; 29 P—B5ch and wins); *23 K—K6, Q—B1ch; 24 K—B7!, Q—Kt1ch* (or 24 .... Q—B2ch; 25 K—K7, Q—B5ch; 26 Q—K6!, Q—B2ch; 27 K—Kt6, Q—Q1; 28 P—B5, Q—QKt1; 29 P—Kt4, Q—QR1; 30 P—B6 and wins); *25 K—K7, Q—Kt6; 26 P—Kt4!* (the mating attack commences), *P—R4* (if instead 26 .... Q×KRP; 27 K—B7!, Q—Kt6ch; 28 Q—K6!, Q×Qch; 29 K×Q with a won P ending: 29 .... K—Kt1; 30 P—B5, K—B1; 31 K—Q7, etc., or 29 .... P—Kt3; 30 P—B5, K—Kt2; 31 K—K7!, etc.); *27 P×P, Q×KRP* (or 27 .... Q—Kt5ch; 28 Q×Q, P×Q; 29 P—R5 and White will queen with check and come out two Pawns ahead); *28 Q—K5!, K—R2* (or 28 .... Q—R6ch; 29 K—B7, Q—Kt6ch; 30 Q—K6); *29 Q—K4ch, K—R1; 30 Q—Q5!* (if now 30 .... K—R2; 31 K—B7!, Q—B1; 32 Q—K4ch, K—R1; 33 Q—K8ch), *Q—R5ch; 31 Q—Kt5, Q—R8; 32 Q—K5, K—R2; 33 K—B8!, Q—KKt8* (or 33 .... Q—R1ch; 34 Q—K8, Q—Kt7; 35 P—B5 followed by Q—Kt6ch); *34 Q—B5ch, K—R1* (34 .... K—R3; 35 K—Kt8!); *35 Q—Q5!* Resigns. Mate cannot be prevented.

An example where the mating factor is the main element (not in conjunction with playing the King over to the other wing) is No. 572 (Alexander-Reshevsky, Nottingham, 1936). Here there is little hope of being able to play the King over because Black's Pawns are scattered and could become weak. Accordingly Reshevsky prepares to advance on the K-side. The game continued *1 .... Q—Kt4!; 2 Q—K6* (if 2 Q—B7ch, K—R3; 3 Q×RP, P—R5!; 4 P×P, Q—B5ch; 5 K—Kt2, Q×Pch Black then wins the QKtP and eventually the KRP as

well), *K—R3; 3 Q—B8, Q—B3ch; 4 K—Kt2* (if 4 K—K2, P—KKt4
followed by either .... P—Kt5 or .... P—R5, when Black's K-side
Pawns will decide), *P—R5!; 5 P×P, K—R4!* (the point); *6 Q—Q7,
P—R4; 7 Q—Q1ch, K×P; 8 Q—R1ch* (or 8 Q—K1ch, K—R4; 9
Q—Q1ch, K—R3, etc.), *K—Kt4; 9 Q—Q1, K—R3; 10 Q—R1ch,
K—Kt2* (as soon as he has had a chance to post his Queen more effec-
tively the King will come right back); *11 Q—QB1, Q—Q1; 12 Q—B2,
Q—Kt4ch; 13 K—R3, Q—K6ch; 14 K—Kt4, Q—B5ch; 15 K—R3,
Q—B6ch; 16 K—R2* (if 16 K—R4, K—R3!), *K—R3; 17 Q—B6, Q—
B7ch; 18 K—R3, K—R4; 19 Q—Kt7, Q—K6ch; 20 K—Kt2, Q—
Q7ch; 21 K—Kt3, Q—Q6ch; 22 K—B2, Q—Q3; 23 K—Kt3, K—Kt4;*

No. 572

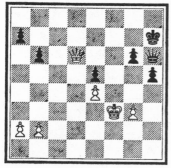

Black to play wins.

No. 573

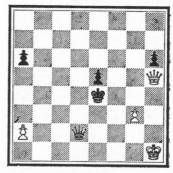

White to play.

*24 K—B3, Q—Q1; 25 K—Kt3, Q—B3; 26 Q—Q5, Q—B5ch; 27
K—Kt2, K—R5!; 28 Q—B6, Q—Kt6ch; 29 K—B1, Q—B6ch; 30
K—K1, Q—K6ch; 31 K—B1* (if 31 K—Q1, P—KKt4), *P—KKt4;
32 K—Kt2, Q—Q7ch* and White resigned, for after 33 K—B1 (or Kt1),
K—Kt6! he must exchange Queens to avoid being mated.

The direct advance of the plus Pawn can win only in special positions where the enemy King is exposed. Thus in No. 573 (Marshall-
Tarrasch, Ostend, 1907) the bad position of the White King is the
only reason why Black will be able to win. After *1 Q—Kt6ch, K—Q4;
2 Q×QRP, P—K5; 3 Q—Kt5ch, K—Q5; 4 Q—Kt6ch, K—Q6; 5 Q—
R6ch, K—K6!; 6 Q×Pch, K—K7; 7 Q—R5ch, K—K8* White is lost
despite his extra Pawn. *8 P—Kt4, P—K6; 9 Q—QB5* (preventing
P—K7), *K—Q8; 10 Q—B5* and now *10 .... P—K7!* wins (Tarrasch
played 10 .... Q—KB7 and Marshall then gave perpetual check beginning with 11 Q—Kt1ch, K—K7; 12 Q—Kt5ch, etc.); *11 Q—Kt1ch,*

Q—B8; 12 Q—Q3ch, K—K8; 13 K—Kt2, Q—B3ch; 14 K—Kt1, Q—B4ch; 15 K—Kt2, Q—B7ch; 16 K—R3, K—B8; 17 P—Kt5, K—Kt8. Now White has no checks and the Pawn will queen.

The most effective *drawing device* (besides perpetual check) is an advanced passed Pawn. No. 574 gives the typical position. Black is forced to take perpetual check, since any such attempt as *1 .... P—R4; 2 P—R6; P—R5; 3 P—R7, P—R6?; 4 Q—Kt7*, might lose, but would surely not win. Against such a strong Pawn the only recourse that the superior side has is an equally strong Pawn. E.g., No. 574a (Lasker-Capablanca, Moscow, 1936), White: K at QB1, Q at QB3, P at QR5; Black: K at KR1, Q at KB7, P's at QB5, K4, KB3, KKt2,

No. 574

No. 575

Draw.

Draw.

KR3. After *1 Q—R3 (1 Q×P, Q—K8ch), K—R2; 2 P—R6, P—B6!* is immediately decisive, for if *3 P—R7, Q—Q7ch; 4 K—Kt1, P—B7ch; 5 K—Kt2, P—B8 = Q dbl ch*, and if *3 Q×P, Q—B8ch; 4 K any, Q×P* with a simple win in both cases.

3. ALL THE PAWNS ARE ON ONE SIDE

As is the case with other endings, if there are not Pawns on both sides of the board, a win with an advantage of one Pawn is rarely, if ever, possible. 2 vs. 1 and 3 vs. 2 are both practically hopeless draws, so that we need only consider 4 vs. 3 and 5 vs. 4.

No. 575 (Sämisch-Maroczy, Carlsbad, 1929) is of value because White made every conceivable attempt to get something out of the position, but without success. The game continued: *1 Q—B7ch, K—Kt1; 2 P—B3, Q—Q6; 3 P—K4, Q—Q7; 4 K—R2, Q—Kt7; 5 Q—Kt3, K—B2; 6 P—B4, Q—K7; 7 Q—Kt3ch (if 7 P—K5, P×P;*

8 P×P, Q—K5; 9 Q—Kt5, K—K3; 10 Q—B6ch, K—Q2; 11 K—Kt3, Q—K6ch, etc., or here 11 Q—B7ch, K—Q1; 12 P—K6, Q—K4ch, etc.=), *K—B1; 8 Q—Kt8ch, K—B2; 9 Q—B7ch, K—K3; 10 P— B5ch* (in the game White checked around for a while, but it led to nothing), *P×P; 11 Q—B8ch, K—K2; 12 Q×P, K—B2;* (even now White has nothing); *13 K—R3, Q—Q6ch; 14 Q—B3, Q—Q2ch; 15 K—R2, Q—Kt4; 16 P—Kt4, P×P; 17 Q×KtP, Q—Kt7ch; 18 K—Kt3, Q—B6ch; 19 Q—B3, Q—B2ch; 20 K—Kt4, Q—Q2ch; 21 K—R5, Q—K1!; 22 Q—B5, Q—R1ch; 23 K—Kt4, Q—Kt1ch; 24 K— B4, Q—Kt8; 25 Q—Q7ch, K—B1; 26 Q—Q5, Q—Kt3; 27 P—R5, Q—R3ch; 28 K—Kt4, K—K2; 29 Q—B5ch, K—Q2; 30 Q—B5ch, K—K2; 31 Q—B4, Q—Kt2ch; 32 K—R4, Q—Kt7; 33 P—R6, K—B2; 34 Q—B7ch, K—Kt1; 35 Q—Q8ch, K—R2!; 36 Q—K7ch, K×P; 37 Q×Pch, K—R2; 38 Q—B7ch, K—R1, 39 Q—R5ch, K—Kt1=.* White has done everything in his power but the game is still drawn. If 40 Q—Kt4ch, Q×Qch; 41 K×Q, K—B1!; 42 K—B4, K—K1!; 43 K—B5, K—B2, etc.

Endings with 4 vs. 3 can be won only when the inferior side's Pawns are weak and subject to attack. Thus in No. 576 (Flohr-Keres, Kemeri, 1937) White can win because either Black's KKtP or KP will be lost in the long run. After *1 .... K—R4; 2 K—K1; K—Kt3; 3 Q—Kt5, Q—R7* (This should lose, but there is little choice. If, e.g., 3 .... K—B3; 4 K—Q2, K—Kt3; 5 P—B5ch!, Q×P; 6 Q×Qch, K×Q; 7 K—B3, with a won P ending, or 4 .... Q—R7ch; 5 K—B3, Q×P; 6 Q—K5ch, K—B2; 7 Q—B5ch, K—Kt2; 8 Q×Pch, K—R2; 9 P—B5, Q—KB7; 10 Q—Kt6ch, K—R1; 11 K—Q4, with a simple win since Black must lose at least one more Pawn); *4 Q—K8ch, K— Kt2; 5 Q—Q7ch!, K—B3!* (the best chance. If 5 .... K—B1; 6 Q— B5ch or 5 .... K—R1; 6 Q—B8ch, K—R2; 7 Q—B5ch, K—R1; 8 Q×KP, Q×P; 9 Q—K5ch, K— R2; 10 Q—B5ch, K—R1; 11 Q×P and with two Pawns the win is relatively simple. The attempt to give perpetual check by 8 .... Q— R8ch (instead of 8 .... Q×P), fails here after 9 K—Q2, Q—R4ch; 10 K—B2, Q—R7ch; 11 K—B3, Q— R6ch; 12 K—B4, Q—R5ch; 13 K—Q5!, Q—Q2ch; 14 K—B5!, Q— R2ch; 15 K—Q6, Q—Kt1ch; 16 K—K7, Q—B2ch; 17 K—B6, Q— Kt2ch; 18 K—K6, Q—Kt1ch; 19 K—Q7 and now the White Queen

No. 576

White wins.

will be able to interpose); *6 Q×P!* wins: *6 .... Q×P* (6 .... Q—R8ch; 7 Q—Q1 and Black has nothing for the two Pawns); *7 Q—R4ch, Q×Q; 8 P×Q, K—B4; 9 K—Q2!, K—Kt5; 10 K—B3, K×P; 11 K—Q4, K—Kt6; 12 K—K5!, P—R4; 13 P—B5, P—R5; 14 P—B6, P—R6; 15 P—B7, P—R7; 16 P—B8=Q, P—R8=Q; 17 Q—B4ch, K—Kt7* (or 17 .... K—R6; 18 Q—R6ch); *18 Q×Pch, K—R7; 19 Q×Qch* and wins.

With 5 vs. 4 the winning chances are much greater. One would normally expect such an ending with Queens to be a draw, but No. 577 (Reshevsky-Fine, Nottingham, 1936) shows that White has real winning possibilities. The game continued: *1 Q—K5ch, K—Kt1; 2 K—*

No. 577

White to play.

No. 578

Black to play.

Kt2, Q—K8; 3 Q—Kt8ch, K—Kt2; 4 Q—Kt2, K—Kt1; 5 Q—B2, Q—Kt5; 6 Q—Q3, K—B1; 7 K—R3, Q—R4; 8 P—K4, Q—R4ch (all this seems to be the best defense Black can put up); *9 K—Kt2, Q—R4; 10 P—Q5!, K—K2; 11 Q—Q4!, P×P; 12 P×P, K—Q3; 13 Q—B4ch, K×P* (13 .... K—K2; 14 Q—K5ch, K—Q2; 15 P—B4 is no better); *14 Q×Pch, K—Q5!; 15 Q—Q7ch!* (in the game there occurred 15 Q× RP?, Q—R7ch; 16 K—R3, Q—K3ch; 17 P—Kt4, K—K6!; 18 Q—QKt7, K—B7! and White cannot win), *K—K6; 16 Q—K7ch, K—Q5; 17 P—R4!, Q—R4* (17 .... Q—R7ch; 18 K—R3); *18 Q—Kt5!, Q×Q; 19 P×Q, K—K6; 20 P—B4, K—K5* (20 .... K—K7; 21 P—Kt4); *21 K—B2, K—Q4; 22 K—K3, K—K3; 23 K—K4, K—B2; 24 K—Q5, K—K2; 25 K—K5, K—B2; 26 K—Q6, K—B1; 27 K—K6, K—K1; 28 K—B6, K—B1; 29 P—Kt4, K—Kt1; 30 K—K7, K—Kt2; 31 P—B5,* and wins.

D. POSITIONAL ADVANTAGE

Queen endings are in some respects similar to those with Bishops of opposite colors. In both two or three Pawns may not be enough to win (though for different reasons) and in both positional advantages may be surprisingly overwhelming. But here the analogy stops; Queen and Pawn endings are really in a class by themselves.

We shall use our customary division.

1. BETTER PAWN POSITION

Here there are three categories which must be considered.

a) One Side Has a Passed Pawn While the Other Does Not.

This is by far the most important because a Queen alone can escort the Pawn to the eighth (See No. 566). The passed Pawn must be at a distance from the Kings in order to be of any great value. No. 578 (Euwe-Reshevsky, Nottingham, 1936) is an interesting example of the power of such an outside passed Pawn. Black's only chance is to secure perpetual check somehow or other. With a view to this he should have played 1 .... Q—B6!, for if then 2 P—R5?, P—K5!; 3 P—R6, Q—B6ch; 4 K—Kt1, Q—Q8ch; 5 K—R2, P—K6!; 6 P×P, Q—K7ch; 7 Q—Kt2, Q×RP and White cannot win (Compare No. 567). After 1 .... Q—B6; 2 Q—Kt7, P—K5; 3 Q×P, Q×QKtP; 4 Q—R8!, P—K4!; 5 P—R5, Q—R7; White is one move behind the line chosen and the game should be drawn. Black played *1 .... Q—Kt3?* and lost as follows: *2 P—R5, Q×KtP; 3 P—R6, Q—R6; 4 P—R7, P—K5; 5 Q—Kt8, Q—B6ch; 6 K—Kt1, Q—Q8ch; 7 K—R2!, Q—K7* (7 .... Q—Q5; 8 K—Kt2. This triangulation manoeuvre is typical); *8 Q—K5ch* and Black resigned. On 8 .... K—R2; 9 Q—B6, Q—R7; 10 Q×Pch, K—R3; 11 Q—B8ch is conclusive, while 8 .... P—B3 is refuted by 9 Q—B7ch, K—R3; 10 Q—B4ch, K—Kt2; 11 P—R8=Q.

b) Qualitatively Superior Passed Pawn.

As usual this means that the Pawns are more advanced. Queen endings are distinctive in that one strong Pawn is just as good as two or three.

An example of the exploitation of such a minimal advantage is No. 579 (Stahlberg-Euwe, Stockholm, 1937). After *1 .... Q—Q5!* it is clear that White's situation is hopeless. There followed *2 K—Kt3, P—Kt6; 3 Q—QKt5, P—Kt7; 4 Q—Kt3, K—Kt2!; 5 P—B4* (or 5 Q—

No. 579

Black to play wins.

B2, Q—K4ch; 6 P—B4, Q—K8ch or 6 K—R3, Q—B4ch); *Q—Q7* and White resigned since he must lose his Queen. The only defense in these cases is perpetual check. E.g., No. 579a (Kashdan-Reshevsky, New York, 1940) White: K at K2, Q at KB6, P's at Q4, KB4, KKt5, KR4; Black: K at KR2, Q at QB2, P's at KB2, K6, Q7. White to play draws. 1 P—Kt6ch!, P×P; 2 P—R5, Q—B5ch; 3 K×P, P—Q8=Q; 4 Q—K7ch, K—R3; 5 Q—Kt5ch, K—Kt2; and 6 Q—K7ch, is still a perpetual: 6 .... Q—B2; 7 P—R6ch, K—Kt1; 8 P—R7ch, Q×P; 9 Q—K8ch, K—Kt2; 10 Q—K7ch, etc.

c) Superior Pawn Structure.

Quiet positional advantages, such as a slightly weaker Pawn skele-

No. 580

White to play.

No. 581

White to play wins.

ton, or blockaded Pawns are of little or no importance in Q-endings. Yet one can surprisingly enough find many cases in which a minimal Pawn weakness is fatal. These almost always occur in conjunction with an exposed King position.

No. 580 (Lissitzin-Capablanca, Moscow, 1935) is an example of this genre which is deceptively simple. We shall follow the game continuation. The position is by no means as easy for White as it looks: he has two weak Pawns to watch. *1 Q—B4, P—R4; 2 K—B1, P—Kt3; 3 K—Kt1, K—Kt2; 4 K—B1, Q—Q3; 5 K—Kt1, Q—B5!; 6 Q—B3, K—R2; 7 K—B1, Q—B4; 8 Q—B4, K—Kt2* (Black is trying to get his King to the center and prevent White from following suit); *9 K—B2, Q—Kt4!; 10 Q—K2, K—B3; 11 Q—Kt2, Q—Q4!; 12 K—K3?* (12 Q—Kt4 was necessary), *P—K4?* (12 .... Q—B5! wins a Pawn, for if 13 P—Q5ch, P—K4! and if 13 Q—Kt1, K—K2; 14 Q—Kt2, K—Q2; 15 Q—Kt1, K—Q3; 16 Q—Kt2, K—Q4 and White is in zugzwang); *13 P—B4?* (the correct reply was 13 Q—Kt4!, P×QPch; 14 Q×Pch, Q×Qch; 15 K×Q, K—K3; 16 P—B4, P—B3; 17 K—B4=), *P×BPch; 14 K×P, K—K3; 15 P—R4, P—B3; 16 K—K3, Q—B5!; 17 P—Kt3, P—Kt4; 18 P×P, P×P.* Now White is in zugzwang and must lose a Pawn. E.g., 19 K—K4, P—Kt5!; 20 K—B4, K—B3; 21 K—K4, Q—K3ch; 22 K—Q3, Q—Q4, etc., *19 Q—KR2, Q—Kt6ch; 20 K—K4, P—Kt5!; 21 Q—K2, Q×KKtP; 22 Q—B4ch, K—K2; 23 Q—B8, Q—B6ch; 24 K—K5, Q—B3ch; 25 K—Q5, Q—Q3ch* and White resigned since his Queen will be exchanged.

2. BETTER QUEEN POSITION

This goes hand in hand with the other categories, but it is instructive to consider it separately.

The most common type of superiority is that where one Queen is more active than her rival. The classic ending with this theme is No. 581 (Maroczy-Marshall, Carlsbad, 1907). Of course, the greater mobility of the White Queen is due in part to the fact that the White King is safe from checks and in part to the weakness of the Black Pawns. After *1 Q—R4!* one expects Black to lose a Pawn soon but Marshall manages to maintain material equality for quite a while. The game continued (1 Q—R4), *1 .... K—Kt2; 2 Q—Kt4ch, K—B2; 3 Q—R5ch!* (getting to the eighth), *K—Kt2; 4 Q—K8, Q—K7.* Black now apparently has enough counterplay but the exposed position of his King spoils everything. *5 Q—K7ch, K—Kt3; 6 Q—B8* (more solid than the spectacular 6 Q×QBP, Q×KtP; 7 Q×KtP, Q×RP; 8 Q×P, P—R4; 9 P—R4, P—R5; 10 P—R5, P—R6; 11 Q—Kt8!! Q—R8; 12 P—R6, P—R7; 13 P—R7, Q×P; 14 Q—Kt8ch, K—B4; 15 Q—R7ch, K—Kt5; 16 Q×P and wins), *P—K4; 7 Q—Kt8ch, K—R3; 8 P—KR4!, Q—B7; 9 Q—B8ch, K—Kt3; 10 P—R5ch!* (the point to White's last few moves), *K×P; 11 Q—Kt7!, Q—Q7* (relatively best. Both 11 .... P—KR3?; 12 Q—Kt4 mate and 11 .... Q—R5; 12 P—Kt4ch are not to be recommended. The chief alternative is 11 .... P—KB4 but 12 Q×RPch, K—Kt4; 13 Q—Kt7ch then wins: 13 .... K—B5 or A—; 14 Q—R6ch, K—Kt6; 15 Q—Kt5ch, K—R7; 16 P—KKt4, P×P; 17 P×P, P—K5; 18 Q—R6ch, K—Kt8; 19 P—Kt5, P—K6; 20 P—Kt6, P—K7; 21 Q—Kt5ch, K—B8; 22 P—Kt7, P—K8=Q; 23 P—Kt8=Q, Q—Q8; 24 Q—R7 and Black cannot avoid the loss of at least two Pawns. Variation A: 13 .... K—R4; 14 P—Kt4ch, P×P; 15 P×Pch, K—R5; 16 P—Kt5, P—K5; 17 Q—R6ch, K—Kt6; 18 P—Kt6, P—K6; 19 P—Kt7 with an easy win); *12 Q×Pch, Q—R3; 13 P—Kt4ch* (simpler is 13 Q×P), *K—Kt4; 14 Q×P, K—B5; 15 Q×KtP, Q—R8; 16 Q—Kt4ch!!* (excellent. He sets up a passed QBP and exposes the Black King), K×P; 17 Q×P, K×P; 18 P—B4! (in Q and P endings one passed Pawn is as good as two. The Black KBP is unimportant), P—K5; 19 P—B5, P—B4 (unavoidable loss of time. If 19 .... P—K6?; 20 Q—Q4ch wins the Pawn since 20 .... K—B6??; 21 Q—Q5ch loses the Q); 20 P—B6, Q—R1ch (again if 20 .... P—K6; 21 Q—Q4ch, Q—K5; 22 Q×Qch, P×Q; 23 P—B7, P—K7; 24 P—B8=Qch and wins); 21 P—B3, P—K6; 22 Q—Kt6ch, K—B5; 23 P—B7, P—K7; 24 Q—K6, K—B6; 25 Q×BPch, K—Kt7; 26 Q—Kt4ch, K—B7; 27 Q—B4ch, K—Kt7; 28 Q—K3!, K—B8; 29 Q—B3ch, K—K8; 30 Q—B4 (good enough, but 30 Q—B5, K—Q7; 31 P—B8=Q, Q×Q; 32 Q×Q; P—K8=Q;

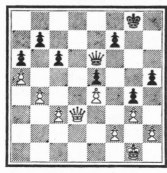

No. 582

White to play wins.

No. 583

White to play wins.

33 Q—Q7ch, K—K6; 34 Q—K6ch was more direct), Q—QB1; 31 Q—Q6, K—B7; 32 Q—Q8, P—K8=Q (if 32 .... Q×Q; 33 P×Q=Q, P—K8; 34 Q—R4ch); 33 Q×Q, Q—Q7ch; 34 K—R3, Q—B8ch; 35 K—R4, Q—B5ch; 36 P—B4 Resigns.

Against a weak Pawn formation even so slight an advantage as a centralized Queen may on occasion be transferred into a win. Thus in No. 582 (Lasker-Bird, Match, 1892), White wins a Pawn to begin with. 1 Q—Q8ch, K—R2; 2 Q—Kt5, P—B3; 3 Q×RPch, K—Kt1; 4 K—Kt2. But Black's remaining Pawns are still just as weak as ever, so that White wins by a straightforward advance on the K-side: 4 .... Q—Q2; 5 P—R3, P×Pch; 6 Q×P, Q—Q6; 7 Q—Kt4ch, K—B2; 8 Q—B3, Q—B5; 9 Q—K3, K—K3; 10 P—B3, K—Q3; 11 K—B2, Q—R7ch; 12 Q—K2, Q—K3; 13 Q—Q2ch, K—B2; 14 P—Kt4!, Q—B5; 15 Q—K3, Q—R7ch; 16 K—Kt3 and the K-march decides. The game concluded: 16 .... Q—R8; 17 P—KKt5, P×P; 18 K—Kt4,

Q—Kt7; 19 K×P, K—Q2; 20 K—Kt4 (or 20 K—B6), *Q—KR7; 21 K—B5, Q—Kt6; 22 K—B6! P—B4* (desperation: if 22 .... K—B2; 23 K—K6! or 22 .... Q—R7; 23 Q—Q3ch); *23 Q—Kt5, Q—R7; 24 Q—B5ch, K—B3; 25 Q—B8ch, K—Kt4; 26 Q×BPch, K—R5; 27 Q×P*, Resigns.

3. BETTER KING POSITION

This can mean either that one King is safe behind a wall of Pawns while the other is buffeted about by unfeeling checks, or that there is a mating position. The first has been seen a number of times in previous examples (e.g., No. 581) so that it will be sufficient to give an example of the second.

In No. 583 (Kling and Horwitz, 1851) White to play forces the win by successive mate threats. *1 Q—Kt2ch, K—B1* (1 .... K—R1; 2 Q—R8ch, Q—Kt1; 3 Q×Qch, and 4 P—Q7); *2 Q—R8ch, Q—K1; 3 Q—Kt7!, Q—Q1* (or 3 .... Q—B2; 4 Q—B8ch! Q—K1; 5 P—Q7); *4 K—Kt6!, Q—K1ch; 5 K—B6!, Q—Q1ch; 6 K×P, Q—K1ch; 7 Q—K7ch, Q×Qch; 8 P×Qch, K—K1; 9 K—Q6* and wins.

III. QUEEN AND MINOR PIECE VS. QUEEN

There is a basic rule (see No. 1, ch. IX) that in endings without Pawns one must be at least a Rook ahead in order to be able to win in general. This holds here as well. Unlike the similar case with Rooks, however, there are only a few exceptions to the general rule. These occur when a series of checks either leads to mate or to the capture of the enemy Queen.

No. 584 (Horwitz, 1872) is an interesting example with a Bishop.

The solution is *1 Q—K3ch, K—B4* (1 .... K—Q4; 2 Q—Kt3ch); *2 Q—B3ch, K—K3; 3 Q—Kt3ch, K—K2* (not 3 .... K—B3; 4 B—Kt5ch); *4 B—Kt5ch, K—B1* (again forced, for if 4 .... K—K1; 5 Q—Kt8ch, K—Q2; 6 Q—Kt7ch Black is either mated or loses his Queen); *5 Q—Kt8ch, Q—K1; 6 Q—Q6ch, K—Kt1* (6 .... K—B2 allows mate in two); *7 B—K7!!* and Black cannot prevent mate, e.g., 7 .... Q—B2; 8 Q—Q8ch, etc.

No. 585 (Dehler, 1908) illustrates some of the possibilities with a

No. 584

White to play wins.

Kt. After *1 Kt—B6ch, K—B4!; 2 Q—B2ch, K—K5!!* offers the best chance, since 3 Q×Q? is stalemate! But *3 Q—K3ch* is good enough: *3 .... K—Q4!; 4 Q—Kt3ch, K—K5!; 5 Q—Q3ch!, K—B5; 6 Q— K3ch, K—B4; 7 Q—B3ch,* and this time he really wins the Queen (7 .... K—K3; 8 Kt—Q8ch or 7 .... K—Kt3; 8 Kt—K5ch).

With Pawns the ending differs in no essential respect from that of B or Kt vs. P's except that again Q+B+P vs. Q wins in all cases.

No. 585

White to play wins.

No. 586

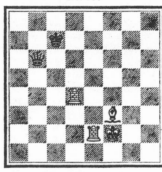

White to play wins.

IV. QUEEN VS. ROOKS AND PIECES

A. QUEEN VS. TWO ROOKS AND PIECE

The advantage accruing to the three pieces here is so great that the ending is as a rule won even without Pawns.

A rather simple example of the helplessness of the Queen is No. 586 (Kling and Horwitz, 1851). After *1 R—B2ch, K—Kt1; 2 R(B2)—B4!* Black must release the pin and suffer the fury of two unchained Rooks: *2 .... Q—KB3* (If 2 .... Q—Kt7ch; 3 K—Kt3 Black has no checks and loses his Queen. On 2 .... Q—R2; 3 K—B1! is quickest: 3 .... Q—R8ch; 4 R—Q1, Q—Kt2; 5 R—Kt1ch, etc., or here 4 .... Q—R3; 5 R—Q8ch and 6 R—R8ch); *3 R—Kt4ch, K—B1; 4 R(Q4)—B4ch, K—Q1; 5 R—Kt8ch, K—Q2; 6 R—Kt7ch, K—Q1* (6 .... K—Q3; 7 R—B6ch); *7 R—QR4!* and wins.

B. QUEEN VS. ROOK AND TWO MINOR PIECES

Without Pawns this is in general a draw, although there are many positions which are in favor of the pieces. But with Pawns, the Queen will usually be unable to defend everything against any direct attack. Thus if R and B threaten an immovable Pawn, it cannot be defended.

No. 587 (Zukertort-Minckwitz, Berlin, 1881) illustrates the power of the pieces. After *1 B—Q4!* the KKtP must fall. The best defense is then *1 .... Q—Kt4ch; 2 K—Kt4, Q—B5* (if 1 .... Q×KtP; 2 R×Pch, K—B1 3 B—B5ch!, Q×B; 4 Kt—K6ch); *3 R×Pch, K—B1; 4 B—B6!, Q—K5* (or 4 .... Q×P; 5 B—K7ch, Q×B; 6 Kt—Kt6ch, K×R; 7 Kt×Q, K—B3; 8 Kt—Q5ch, K—K4; 9 Kt—Kt4, K—Q3; 10 Kt×P, K—B3; 11 Kt—Kt4ch and wins); *5 P—Kt5!, P×P; 6 P— R6, P—Kt5; 7 P—R7, P—Kt6; 8 R—KR7!* and wins. Another possibility here is 4 .... Q—B1ch; 5 K—Kt5, Q—B8; 6 R—QB7!, Q— Kt8ch; 7 K—B5, Q—Kt8ch; 8 K—K6, Q—R7ch; 9 Kt—Q5, Q— K7ch; 10 B—K5, Q—Kt5ch; 11 K—Q6, Q—Kt3ch; 12 K—B5, Q— Kt8ch; 13 B—Q4 and Black is out of checks.

C. QUEEN VS. ROOK AND ONE MINOR PIECE

This is seen relatively frequently, unlike the other groups in this section.

Without Pawns the ending is draw, though it is to be expected that there will be problem positions where one side or the other may win.

With Pawns, the Queen is equivalent to R+B+P. If the Pawns are even, the Queen will win (though not without difficulty); but R, B and two Pawns are required to conquer the Q.

Where the Pawns are even, the win is easier for the Q if they are not balanced. For then the superior side will be able to set up a passed Pawn and capture one of the op-ponent's pieces or tie him up so badly that some other part of the board will be left defenseless.

No. 588 (Alekhine-Thomas, Hastings, 1922) is typical. After *1 Q— Kt5* Black must lose a Pawn: *1 .... R—Q3; 2 P—Kt3, R—Q8ch; 3 K—Kt2, R—QR8; 4 Q—R4* (4 Q×P, P—Kt6; 5 Q—B3 is also good enough but leaves only Pawns on the K-side), *B—K2; 5 Q×RP* (threatening Q—K5, for which reason 5 .... P—Kt6 is not possible), *R—QB8; 6 Q—R8ch, B—B1.* Now that he has done everything

No. 587

White to play wins.

possible on the Q-side, he must turn his attention to the other wing. The steady advance of K and P's is bound to win there. *7 Q—K4, R—B6; 8 Q—Kt1* (to prevent the exchange by .... P—Kt6), *R—R6; 9 K— B3, R—R3; 10 P—K4, R—B3ch* (if 10 .... R—R6ch; 11 K—B4, B—Q3ch; 12 P—K5, B—B1; 13 K—K4, etc., as in the game); *11 K— K2, R—R3; 12 P—B4, P—Kt3* (12 .... R—R6 is better, but after 13 P—K5 White would likewise win by the K-side advance); *13 K— Q3, R—Q3ch; 14 K—K3, R—Q2; 15 Q—B2, R—R2; 16 P—K5, R—R3; 17 K—K4, R—Kt3* (note that Black is reduced to complete passivity); *18 P—Kt4, R—Kt4; 19 K—Q4, R—R4; 20 P—KR4, R— Kt4; 21 P—R5, P×P; 22 P×P, R—Kt3* (or 22 .... R—R4; 23 P—

No. 588   No. 589

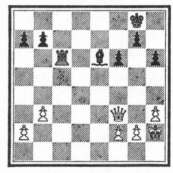

White to play wins.   White to play wins.

B5, R—Kt4; 24 Q—Kt2ch, K—R1; 25 Q—R8, K—Kt1; 26 P—K6, P×P; 27 P×P and wins); *23 P—B5, K—Kt2; 24 Q—B7, R—Kt4* (24 .... R—R3; 25 P—K6); *25 K—B4!* Resigns, since 25 .... R—B4 ch is forced, when 26 Q×R is overwhelming.

The typical ending with balanced Pawns is seen in No. 589 (Fine-Stahlberg, 3rd match game, 1937). After *1 Q—B4!, P—QR3; 2 Q— Kt8ch, B—B1; 3 P—QR4!* (in the game there occurred the less accurate 3 P—QKt4, when 3 .... P—QKt4! might draw), *K—R2; 4 P— QKt4* Black loses because he has too much to defend. White's chief threat is to march his King to Q8 and win the QKtP. Black can at best delay the execution of this plan. The game continued: *4 .... P—B4* (a further weakness, but in the long run unavoidable because of the danger of a check along the diagonal. E.g., 4 .... R—B5; 5 P—Kt5, P×P; 6 P×P, R—B4; 7 Q—Q6!, R—B8; 8 K—Kt3 and the King can get through); *5 Q—K5, R—B3; 6 Q—B7, R—QB3; 7*

Q—K7, R—KKt3; 8 P—B3, R—QB3 (if 8 .... P—QKt4; 9 Q—K8);
9 P—Kt5, P×P; 10 P×P, R—B5; 11 P—R4, R—B7; 12 P—R5, R—
B5; 13 K—Kt3, R—B6; 14 Q—Q6, R—B7. All the preparations are
finished and now the final assault commences. *14 Q—Kt6ch, K—R1;*
15 Q—K8ch, K—R2; 16 K—B4, R—B8; 17 Q—Kt6ch, K—R1; 18
K—K5, B—Q2; 19 Q—QKt6!, B—B1 (19 .... R—QKt8; 20 Q—
Q8ch); *20 K—Q6, K—Kt1; 21 Q—K3!* Resigns for he must lose his B:
21 .... R—Q8ch; 22 K—B7, B—Q2; 23 Q—Kt3ch.

The type position where R, B and P win is seen in No. 590 (Shipley-
Lasker, Philadelphia, 1902). After .... *1 .... R—B7; 2 Q—Kt1,*
K—B6!; 3 Q—R1ch, R—Kt7; 4 Q—B1ch, K×P; 5 Q—Q1ch, K—
Kt5; 6 Q—Kt4, B×Pch; the Queen is unable to stop both Pawns. The
remaining moves were *7 K—Q1, B—Q5!; 8 Q×P, P—B4; 9 Q—K1ch,*
K—R5; 10 K—B1 (note how easily the Black King sidesteps perpetual
check), *R—KB7; 11 Q—Q1ch, K—R6; 12 Q—Q3ch, K—Kt5; 13 Q—*
R6, P—R5; 14 Q—Kt6ch, K—R6; 15 Q—Kt5, R—QKt7; 16 Q—
R6, B—K6ch; 17 K—Q1, R—Q7ch; 18 K—K1, R—Q5; 19 Q—K6, B
—Q7ch; 20 K—Q1, K—Kt7; 21 Q—KKt6, B—B6 dis ch; 22 K—K2, P
—R6; 23 Resigns.

V. QUEEN VS. ROOK (OR ROOKS)
A. QUEEN VS. TWO ROOKS

Queen and Pawn are normally equivalent to two Rooks. This
means that Q+P vs. 2 R's is drawn, but Q+2 P's vs. 2 R's is won,
while with even Pawns or one Pawn to the good, the two Rooks will
win.

Without Pawns the game is as a rule drawn. If the enemy King is
confined to the edge of the board,
the Rooks may win; if the Rooks
are not adequately defended the
Queen may win.

No. 591 (Centurini, 1858) is a
relatively favorable situation which
is still not good enough. After *1*
.... K—R2; 2 Q—Kt1ch, R—Kt3;
3 Q—B5, R—KR1; White can
prevent the fatal discovered check:
4 Q—B7ch, R—Kt2; 5 Q—K6,
R—Kt3; 6 Q—B7ch, K—R3; 7 Q—
K7, R—R2; 8 Q—B8ch, R(R2)—
Kt2; 9 Q—B4ch, K—R2; 10 Q—B5,
K—R1; 11 Q—QB8ch, R—Kt1;
12 Q—B3ch, K—R2; 13 Q—B7ch,

No. 590

Black to play wins.

R(Kt3)—Kt2; 14 Q—B2ch, K—R1; 15 Q—B3, etc. But in No. 591a (Centurini), Black King at KR2, other pieces as in No. 591, Black to play does win. 1 .... R—KR1; 2 Q—R2 (he must stop .... K—Kt1 dis ch), K—Kt3 dis ch wins the Queen: 3 K—Kt2, K—B4 dis ch; 4 K—B3, R—R6ch; 5 K—K2, R—R7ch, etc.

With Pawns on the board, two R's and one Pawn always win, unless there are so few Pawns left that a perpetual check is possible. Thus when there is nothing else, two R's+P only draw; two P's are required to win. No. 592 (Berger) illustrates the difficulties. Best play is

No. 591

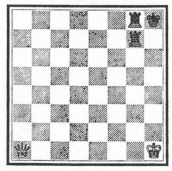

Draw. Win No. 591a with Black King at KR2.

No. 592

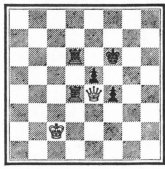

White to play. Black wins.

1 Q—R7, R—Q7ch; 2 K—B1, P—B6; 3 Q—R6ch, K—B4; 4 Q—R5ch, K—B5; 5 Q—R4ch, K—K6; 6 Q—Kt5ch, K—K7! (6 .... K—K5; 7 Q—Kt4ch); *7 Q×Pch, K—B8; 8 Q—Kt5ch* (or 8 Q—Kt3, R—Q8ch; 9 K—B2, R(Q3)—Q7ch; 10 K—B3, P—B7; 11 Q—R3ch, K—K8; 12 Q—R4, R—Q6ch; 13 K—B2, R(Q8)—Q7ch; 14 K—B1, R—Q5; 15 Q—K7ch, R—K7, etc.), *R(Q3)—Q6; 9 Q—KR5, P—B7; 10 Q—R1ch, K—K7; 11 Q—R5ch, K—K8; 12 Q—K5ch, R—K7; 13 Q—R5ch, R(Q6)—Q7; 14 Q—Kt4, K—B8* (14 .... P—B8=Kt also wins); *15 Q—KR4, R—B7ch; 16 K—Kt1, K—K8; 17 Q—Kt3, R(B7)—Q7 and wins.*

The minimal position where 2 R's+P vs. Q win is shown in No. 593 (Steinitz-Pillsbury, Nuremberg, 1896). Yet even here Black cannot advance his Pawn by any straightforward series of moves: he must combine the possibility of the advance with a threat against White's K-side Pawns. The game continued: *1 Q—K6, R(B1)—Q1; 2 Q—QR6, P—R3; 3 P—R4, R—KB1; 4 K—R3* (4 P—Kt4, R—B7ch; 5 K—Kt3, R(Q2)—B2! is worse for White), *K—R2; 5 Q—QB6*

R—Q6ch; 6 P—Kt3, R—K6; 7 Q—B2ch (the threat was R—B3—
KKt3), *K—R1; 8 P—R5, R—K4; 9 K—R4, P—R4!* (at last!); *10 Q—
R4, R—QKt1; 11 P—Kt4, R—KKt4; 12 Q—B6, R—KKt1* (not 12
.... R—Kt5; 13 Q—B8ch; K—R2; 14 Q—B2ch); *13 Q—R6, R—Q1;
14 Q—B6, R(Kt4)—Q4; 15 Q—R4* (if now 15 Q—R6, R—KB1; 16
Q—K6, R—Q6; 17 Q—R6, R—K6!; 18 Q×P, R(B1)—B6 and White
has only one useless check); *R—R1!; 16 K—R3* (or 16 Q—B6, R(Q4)—
Q1; 17 Q—R4, R—Q6 as in the game), *R—Q6ch; 17 K—R4* (Better
17 K—Kt2, though 17 .... R—B6!, 18 K—B2, R—B1ch; 19 K—K2,

No. 593

No. 594

Black wins.

Black to play wins.

R—QB4; will then eventually win the K-side Pawns), *R—K6; 18 Q—
B6, R—KB1;* 19 Resigns, since he is defenseless against R(B8)—B6—
R6 mate (if 19 P—Kt5, R—B5 mate).

The superiority of the two Rooks when the Pawns are even is seen
quite clearly in No. 594 (Tchigorin-Janowski, Carlsbad, 1907). Here
White's Pawns are isolated and cannot be supported by the Rooks.
The continuation was *1 .... R(B3)—Q3!; 2 K—B4, P—R5; 3 K—B5,
K—Kt4!; 4 P—Q5, P—R6; 5 Q—K8, K—B5; 6 Q—K1, R—KR3;
7 Q—B2ch, K—Kt5; 8 Q—Kt1ch, K—B4; 9 Q—B2ch, K—Kt3!!;
10 Q—B2ch* (if 10 K×R, P—R7; 11 Q—Kt3ch, K—B2 dis ch wins),
K—B3; 11 Q—Kt2ch, K—B2; 12 Q—Kt7ch, K—Kt1; 13 P—R6!
(manages to stop the KRP, but leads into a loss with 2 R's+P vs. Q
because of the bad position of the Queen), *R×P; 14 Q—Kt8ch, K—
R2; 15 Q—Kt1ch, R(QR3)—Kt3; 16 P—Q6!, P—R7; 17 P—Q7, P—
R8=Q; 18 Q×Q, R×Q; 19 P—Q8=Q, R—Kt5!* (forcing the King
into a mating net); *20 K—Kt5, R—R4ch; 21 K—Kt6, R—Kt3ch;
22 K—R7, R—KB4; 23 Q—Q3, R(Kt3)—B3.* Now the ending is won
because the White Queen must guard against the mate possibilities

and consequently cannot pay attention to the Pawn. *24 K—Kt7, P—Kt3; 25 K—B7, K—Kt2; 26 Q—Q4, R—B5; 27 Q—B3* (among other things White has no checks), *R—K5; 28 K—Q7, R—QR5; 29 K—K7, R—R3; 30 Q—Kt2, P—Kt4; 31 Q—B3* (if 31 Q—Q4, R(R3)—· K3ch; 32 K—Q7, R—Q3ch), *P—Kt5!; 32 K—K8, R(R3)—B3; 33 Q—KKt3, R(QB3)—K3ch; 34 K—Q7, R—K5!; 35 Q—R4, K—Kt3; 36 Q—R8, K—B4; 37 Q—R5ch, K—B5; 38 Q—R2ch, K—Kt4; 39 Q—Q2ch, R(B3)—B5* (releases the King in order to advance the P); *40 Q—KKt2, R—Q5ch; 41 K—B6, R—B6; 42 Q—K2, R(Q5)—KB5;* 43 Resigns. Once the Pawn gets to the sixth the game is hopeless.

Queen and two Pawns can win against the Rooks only when the

No. 595   No. 596

 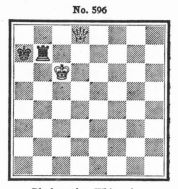

White to play.   Black to play, White wins.

Rooks are not united, or when there are *connected passed Pawns*. No. 595 (Ed.-Lasker-Fine, New York, 1940) illustrates proper play with Queen and Rooks. We shall comment upon the course of the game. *1 K—R1?* (waste of time. The correct saving idea is to exchange one Pawn on the Q-side, then double Rooks against that Pawn and finally win it. E.g., 1 QR—Kt1, P—QKt3; 2 P—QR4, P—K4; 3 P—R5!, P×P; 4 R—QR1, Q—QB6; 5 R—R4, P—B4; 6 P×P, P×P; 7 R(Q1) —QR1, P—K5; 8 R×RP, P—K6; 9 R(R5)—R3, Q—K4ch; 10 K—R1 and if 10 .... P—K7?; 11 R—K1, Q—Kt7; 12 R—K3! will eventually win both Pawns), *Q—QR6; 2 R—Q7* (2 KR—QKt1 was still better. To get both Rooks to the seventh is useless in these endings), *P—QKt4; 3 R—K1, Q×QRP; 4 R(K1)×P, P—QR4; 5 R—Q8ch, K—Kt2; 6 P—Kt5* (threatening R(K7)—K8), *Q—B5!; 7 R(Q8)—Q7* (7 R(K7)—K8, Q—B8ch; 8 K—R2, Q×P), *P—R5; 8 R—B7, Q—KB8ch; 9 K—R2, Q—B5ch; 10 K—Kt1, P—Kt5* and wins.

B. QUEEN VS. ROOK

1. WITHOUT PAWNS

This is a win, but from the general position the process is rather complicated.

In order to have drawing chances Black must keep his Rook near his King, for otherwise a check will capture the Rook. *The basic winning idea is to force Black into zugzwang, so that he will have to move his Rook away from his King.*

The fundamental zugzwang position is seen in No. 596. Here Black loses his Rook very quickly in all variations.

a) *1 .... K—R3; 2 Q—QB8.*

b) *1 .... R—Kt1; 2 Q—R5* mate.

c) *1 .... R—Kt5; 2 Q—R5ch* and *3 Q×R.*

d) *1 .... R—Kt6; 2 Q—Q4ch, K—Kt1; 3 Q—B4ch, K—R2* (3 .... K—B1; 4 Q—B8 mate); *4 Q—R4ch* and *5 Q×R.*

e) *1 .... R—Kt7; 2 Q—Q4ch,* etc.

f) *1 .... R—Kt8; 2 Q—Q4ch, K—Kt1; 3 Q—B4ch, K—R1; 4 Q—B8ch* (or 4 K—B7, leading to mate), *K—R2; 5 Q—B2ch, K—Kt1; 6 Q—R2ch, K—R2; 7 Q—R2ch,* etc.

g) *1 .... R—KB2; 2 Q—Q4ch, K—Kt1* (or 2 .... K—R1; 3 Q—R1ch); *3 Q—Kt2ch, K—R1; 4 Q—R2ch.*

h) *1 .... R—Kt2; 2 Q—Q4ch.*

i) *1 .... R—R2; 2 Q—R5ch, K—Kt1; 3 Q—Kt4ch, K—R2; 4 Q—R3ch, K—Kt1; 5 Q—Kt3ch, K—R2; 6 Q—R2ch, K—Kt1; 7 Q—Kt8ch.*

The general case is shown in No. 597 (Berger). Black is forced to retreat to the edge of the board because he must keep his Rook near his King, but once further retreat is cut off zugzwang is inevitable. Best play is *1 K—Kt2, R—B5; 2 K—B3, R—K5; 3 K—Q3, R—Q5ch; 4 K—K3, R—Q4* (he must let the King through. If, e.g., 4 .... R—QB5; 5 Q—R5ch, K—K3; 6 Q—QKt5, R—KKt5; 7 Q—QB5, R—KR5, 8 K—B3, K—B3; 9 Q—Q5, K—Kt3 and now any move along the fourth rank will cost Black his Rook); *5 Q—R2ch, K—B4; 6 Q—B4ch, K—K3* (or 6 .... K—Kt3; 7 K—K4, R—KKt4; 8 Q—Q6ch, K—Kt2; 9 K—B4, R—Kt3; 10 Q—K7ch, K—Kt1; 11 K—B5,

No. 597

White wins.

R—Kt2; 12 Q—K8ch, K—R2; 13 K—B6—No. 596. Black's best bet is to stay in the center); *7 K—K4, R—Q3; 8 Q—B5ch, K—K2; 9 K— K5, R—Q2; 10 Q—B6ch, K—K1; 11 Q—R8ch!* (but not 11 K—K6??, R—Q3ch!!; 12 K×R stalemate), *K—B2!; 12 Q—R7ch, K—K1; 13 Q—Kt8ch, K—K2; 14 Q—QB8!* and now Black's Rook and King must part. The various defenses are:

a) *14 . . . . R—Q1; 15 Q—K6ch, K—B1; 16 K—B6* and mates.

b) *14 . . . . R—R2; 15 Q—B5ch,* or *14 . . . . R—Q3; 15 Q—B5.*

c) *14 . . . . R—Q6; 15 Q—K6ch, K—Q1; 16 Q—Kt8ch, K—B2* (or 16 . . . . K—Q2; 17 Q—R7ch); *17 Q—B4ch.*

d) *14 . . . . R—Q7; 15 Q—B5ch, K—Q2* (or 15 . . . . K—B2; 16 Q—B4ch, K—Kt2; 17 Q—Kt4ch, K—R1; 18 Q—R5ch, K— Kt1; 19 Q—Kt5ch, or 15 . . . . K—K1; 16 Q—Kt5ch, K—B2; 17 Q—B4ch, etc.); *16 Q—Kt5ch, K—B1; 17 K—K6!, R—QB7!; 18 K—Q6, R—KR7!; 19 Q—K8ch, K—Kt2; 20 Q—K4ch, K— Kt3* (or 20 . . . . K—Kt1; 21 Q—KB4!, R—R2; 22 K—B6 dis ch, etc., as in No. 596 (i)); *21 Q—KB4, R—R4!; 22 Q—K3ch, K—R4; 23 K—B6* and mates or wins the Rook.

e) *14 . . . . R—Q8; 15 Q—B5ch, K—Q2* (or other moves, as in d)); *16 Q—Kt5ch, K—Q1; 17 Q—R5ch, K—B1; 18 Q—B3ch, K—Q2; 19 Q—Kt4, K—B2; 20 Q—B4ch, K—Q1; 21 K—K6, R—K8ch; 22 K—Q6, R—Q8ch; 23 K—B6, R—Q7; 24 Q—B5,* again with either mate or Rook capture.

Black's only drawing chance lies in stalemate. The long-range draw is exemplified in No. 598 (Philidor, 1782). The Black Rook keeps on checking on the R and Kt files. Since the White King cannot go to the K file without permitting . . . . R—K2, his only other winning chance lies in playing his King to KB6, but then . . . . R—Kt3ch stalemates. Thus: *1 . . . . R—R2ch; 2 K—Kt2, R—Kt2ch; 3 K—B3, R—B2ch; 4 K—Kt4, R—Kt2ch; 5 K—B5, R—B2ch; 6 K—Kt6, R—Kt2ch; 7 K—B6, R—Kt3ch!; 8 K×R* stalemate. This can only arise on B, Kt and R files. The analogous case on the Kt and R files is No. 598a; White: K at KR6, Q at KB6, Black: K at KKt1, R at KKt2. Black to play draws because of the stalemate threat. No. 598b, White Queen at KB1 (or KB2, KB3, KB4), other pieces as in No. 598a. Black to play draws without a stalemate threat: perpetual check at KKt2 and KR2.

2. QUEEN VS. ROOK AND PAWN

This is likewise one of the most intricate endings that can come up. In general KtP and BP always draw, but center Pawn and RP usually lose. The problems involved have been completely solved, and we shall outline the results.

a) Center Pawn.

On the third and fourth this is always lost. The best defensive positions for Black is shown in No. 599 (Philidor, 1803). White wins by attacking the Pawn with his King. This is done by continually forcing the Black King to move. The solution is *1 Q—R7ch, K—K3* (if instead 1 .... K—Q1; 2 Q—KB7, K—B1; 3 Q—QR7, K—Q1; 4 Q—Kt8ch, K—Q2; 5 Q—Kt7ch, K—Q1; 6 Q—B6!, K—K2; 7 Q—B7ch, K—K3; 8 Q—Q8, R—B4ch; 9 K—Kt4, R—K4; 10 Q—K8ch, K—Q4; 11 Q—QB8, etc., as in the main variation); *2 Q—QB7, R—QB4; 3 Q—Q8, R—K4; 4 Q—K8ch, K—Q4* (or 4 .... K—B3; 5 Q—Q7,

No. 598

Black to play draws.

No. 599

White wins. Draw with Pawn on second, sixth or seventh.

R—K3; 6 K—Kt4, K—K4; 7 K—Kt5, etc. Once the White King crosses the center of the board the rest is comparatively simple); *5 Q—QB8, R—K5ch* (or 5 .... K—Q5; 6 Q—B6, R—Q4; 7 K—B3, K—K4; 8 Q—B3ch, K—B4; 9 Q—B4, R—K4; 10 Q—B7ch, K—Kt4; 11 Q—Q7, R—Q4; 12 Q—Kt7ch, K—B4; 13 Q—B7ch, K—K4; 14 Q—B4ch, K—K3; 15 Q—B4!, K—K4; 16 Q—K4ch, and wins the Rook); *6 K—B5, R—K4ch; 7 K—B6, R—K5* (on other R moves the P goes, e.g., 7 .... R—K8; 8 Q—Kt7ch, K—Q5; 9 Q—Kt6ch, etc.); *8 Q—B3!* (an alternative win is 8 Q—B5ch, R—K4; 9 Q—Q3ch, K—B4; 10 Q—Q2, K—B3; 11 Q—Q4, K—Q2; 12 Q—QB4, R—QB4; 13 Q—B7ch, K—B3; 14 K—K7!, R—K4ch; 15 K—Q8, R—QB4; 16 Q—Q7ch, K—Q4; 17 K—K7, R—B3; 18 Q—B5ch, K—B5; 19 K—Q7, R—B4; 20 Q—K4ch, etc.), *R—K3ch; 9 K—B7, R—K4; 10 K—B8, R—K5* (on 10 .... R—K3; 11 Q—Kt3ch, K—K4; 12 K—B7, wins); *11 Q—Q3ch, R—Q5* (if 11 .... K—K4; 12 K—K7, P—Q4; 13 Q—

Kt3ch, K—Q5 dis ch; 14 K—Q6, K—B5; 15 Q—Kt2, R—Q5; 16 Q—B2ch, K any; 17 K—K5, etc.); *12 Q—B5ch, K—B5; 13 K—K7, P—Q4; 14 Q—B2ch, K—Kt5; 15 K—Q6* and Black must abandon the Pawn. A similar position with the White King on the seventh or eighth rank wins with any Pawn.

White wins here only because his King can get behind the Pawn. When the Pawn is on the second and the Rook on the third this is impossible. Thus No. 599a (Philidor, 1803), White: K at Q5, Q at QKt3; Black: K at Q1, R at K3, P at Q2 is drawn. E.g., 1 Q—Kt8ch, K—K2; 2 Q—KKt8, R—QB3; 3 K—K5, R—K3ch, etc.—the Black King cannot be forced away from his Pawn. With the Pawn on the fourth rank White wins in exactly the same manner as in No. 599. With the Pawn on the fifth rank we get the critical position No. 599b (Guretzky-Cornitz), White: K at KB5, Q at QB1; Black: K at Q6, R at K6, P at Q5. White to play can only draw. Black to play loses. The win is 1 .... R—K7 (or 1 .... R—K1; 2 Q—R3ch, K—K7; 3 Q—R4, R—Q1; 4 Q—R5, R—B1ch; 5 K—K4, P—Q6; 6 Q—R5ch, K—Q7; 7 Q—R6ch and wins the Rook. Or 1 .... K—K7; 2 Q—B2ch, K—K8; 3 K—B4, R—K7; 4 Q—B1ch, K—B7; 5 Q—Q1, and wins the Pawn); 2 Q—Q1ch, K—K6 (There is no real defense. If, e.g., 2 .... R—Q7; 3 Q—B3ch, K—B7; 4 K—K4, K—Kt7; 5 Q—B7, K—B7; 6 Q—B4ch, K—Q8; 7 K—B3!, K—K8; 8 Q—Kt4 and if 8 .... P—Q6; 9 K—K3, while if 8 .... K—Q8; 9 Q—Kt1 mate); 3 K—K5, P—Q6; 4 Q—Kt1ch, K—Q7 dis ch; 5 K—Q4, K—B7; 6 Q—Kt6, R—Q7; 7 Q—B6ch, K—Q8 (or 7 .... K—Kt8; 8 Q—QB3, R—Q8; 9 Q—Kt3ch, K—B8; 10 K—B3); 8 K—K3 and wins. White to play cannot gain a tempo to force the decisive line. The Pawn on the sixth always draws. This is readily understandable, since White can only win if he has lots of leeway for his Queen. An exception to this rule occurs where the White King is directly in front of the Pawn. Thus in No. 599c (Kling and Horwitz, 1851), White: K at Q1, Q at KB3; Black: K at Q5, R at QB7, P at Q6, White to play wins. The main variation is 1 Q—B4ch, K—Q4; 2 Q—K3, K—B5; 3 Q—K4ch, K—B6; 4 Q—Q5, R—Q7ch; 5 K—K1, R—K7ch; 6 K—B1, K—Q7; 7 Q—QB5, R—K5; 8 K—Kt2, K—K7; 9 Q—B2ch, K—Q8; 10 Q—KB5, R—Q5 (or 10 .... R—K7ch; 11 K—B3, K—B7; 12 Q—B8ch, K—Q7; 13 Q—QB5, R—K8; 14 Q—R5ch, K—Q8; 15 Q—Kt4 and wins); 11 K—B2, R—Q1; 12 K—K3, K—B7; 13 Q—B5ch, K—Q8; 14 Q—K5, P—Q7; 15 Q—QR5!, R—Q3 (If 15 .... K—K8; 16 Q×R!, P—Q8=Q; 17 Q—R4ch, and mate next. On 15 .... K—B8; 16 Q—B7ch, decides. Similarly, after 15 .... R—Q2; 16 Q—R4ch, wins the Rook in a favorable position: 16 .... K—K8; 17 Q—R4ch, K—Q8; 18 Q—R1ch, K—B7; 19 Q—B6ch, etc.); 16 Q—Kt4! and wins for if 16 .... R—Q1; 17 Q—Kt1 mate, if 16 .... R—K3ch; 17 K—Q3 and wins the Pawn, while 16 .... K—B8; 17 Q—B5ch and 16 .... K—K8; 17 Q×R win as above.

b) Knight Pawn or Bishop Pawn.

For once these two obey the same laws!

An unfavorable analogue of No. 599 is seen in No. 600 (v. Guretzky-Cornitz). Although the defense is difficult here, Black can always hold his own because White's King cannot cross the B file. Berger gives the following continuation, which illustrates the winning attempts that White may make. *1 Q—QR2, K—Kt3; 2 Q—R3, R—B3!; 3 K—Q4, R—B5ch; 4 K—Q5, R—B3; 5 Q—K7, R—B2; 6 Q—Q6ch, K—Kt2; 7 Q—K6, R—B5; 8 Q—K5, R—B3; 9 Q—K1, K—Kt3; 10 Q—Kt3, K—Kt2; 11 Q—K5, R—B5; 12 K—Q6, K—Kt3; 13 K—Q7, K—R3; 14 Q—Kt8, R—Q5ch; 15 K—B6, R—B5ch; 16 K—Q5, R—B7* (not 16 .... R—B8; 17 Q—R8ch, K—Kt3; 18 Q—Q8ch, K—R3; 19 Q—B6ch, K—Kt2?; 20 Q—Kt2! and wins); *17 Q—Q6ch, K—Kt2; 18 Q—R3, K—Kt3; 19 Q—K3ch, K—R3; 20 Q—K6ch, K—R4* (but not 20 .... K—R2?; 21 Q—K8, K—Kt3?; 22 Q—Kt6ch); *21 Q—KKt6, R—B5; 22 Q—KR6, R—B1; 23 Q—K3, R—B2; 24 K—Q6, R—B1; 25 Q—R7ch, K—Kt5; 26 Q—R6, R—B5; 27 Q—R2, R—B1; 28 K—Q7, R—B4,* etc.=.

But if the White King can manage to attack the Pawn (as a result of a favorable initial position due to previous exchanges) the game is won. No. 600a (v. Guretzky-Cornitz), White: K at Q5, Q at QKt5; Black: K at Q7, R at QB6, P at QB4. White wins. The main variation is 1 K—K4, K—B7; 2 Q—R6, K—Kt7; 3 Q—R4, K—Kt8; 4 Q—R5, K—Kt7; 5 K—Q5, K—B7; 6 Q—R2ch, K—Q6; 7 Q—QKt2, R—B7; 8 Q—Kt3ch, K—Q7; 9 K—K4, R—B6; 10 Q—Kt2ch, R—B7; 11 Q—Kt5, R—B6; 12 Q—R5, K—B7; 13 Q—R2ch, K—B8; 14 Q—K2, R—B7; 15 Q—K1ch, K—Kt7; 16 K—Q3, P—B5ch; 17 K—Q4, P—B6; 18 K—B4, R—Q7; 19 Q—K3, R—QB7; 20 Q—Kt6ch, K—R7; 21 Q—Kt3ch, K—R8; 22 Q—R3ch, K—Kt8; 23 K—Kt3, R—K7; 24 Q—R6, P—B7; 25 Q—R2ch, K—B8; 26 Q—R1ch, K—Q7; 27 Q—Q4ch, K—B8; 28 Q—Kt1ch, K—Q7; 29 K—Kt2, K—Q6; 30 K—B1, K—K5; 31 Q—Kt3, K—Q5; 32 Q—KB3 and wins the Pawn.

No. 600

Draw. Holds for BP as well. Pawn may be on any rank.

c) Rook Pawn.

The results here are rather peculiar: draw with the Pawn on the third, sixth or seventh, but loss on the second, fourth or fifth.

The win with the Pawn on the fourth is shown in No. 601 (v. Guretzky-Cornitz). After *1 Q—Q5, K—R3* (if 1 .... R—Kt4; 2 Q—Q6ch, K—Kt2; 3 K—B4, R—Kt3; 4 Q—Q5ch, wins the Pawn, for on 4 .... K—R3; 5 Q—R8 mates); *2 Q—B6ch, K—R2* (on 2 .... R—Kt3; 3 Q—R8ch wins: 3 .... K—Kt4; 4 K—Kt3, R—QR3; 5 Q—Q5ch, K—Kt3; 6 K—R4, R—R2; 7 Q—Q6ch, K—Kt2; 8 K—Kt5, K—B1; 9 Q—B8ch, K—Kt2; 10 Q—K7ch, K—Kt1; 11 Q—Q8ch, K—Kt2; 12 Q—Kt6ch, K—R1; 13 K—B6, etc.); *3 K—Q3, R—Kt3; 4 Q—B7ch, K—R3; 5 Q—B8ch, K—R2; 6 K—B4, R—Kt2; 7 Q—Q8, K—R3; 8 Q—R8ch, K—Kt3; 9 K—Kt3, R—QR2* (9 .... K—B3 dis ch; 10 K—R4); *10 Q—Kt8ch, K—R3* (or 10 .... R—QKt2; 11 Q—Q6ch, K—Kt4; 12 Q—Q3ch, and K—R4); *11 K—R4* and wins the Pawn, for if 11 .... R—QKt2; 12 Q—R8ch, R—R2; 13 Q—B6 mate. The win with the Pawn on the fifth is achieved in the same manner. With the Pawn on the second Black will likewise soon lose his last soldier. No. 601a (Berger), White: K at QB5, Q at K5; Black: K at QR1, R at QKt3, P at QR2. White wins. 1 Q—Q5ch, K—Kt1 (or 1 .... R—Kt2; 2 Q—B6, K—Kt1; 3 Q—K8ch, K—B2; 4 Q—QR8, and the Pawn goes); 2 Q—Q7!, R—QR3 (if the Rook moves anywhere along the Knight file checks will soon decide: e.g., 2 .... R—Kt7; 3 Q—K8ch, K—Kt2; 3 Q—B7ch, K—R3; 4 Q—B1ch, K—Kt2; 5 Q—R1ch, and wins the Rook either by Q—R8ch, or Q—R1ch. On 2 .... R—KR3; 3 Q—K8ch, K—Kt2; 4 Q—B7ch, K—R3; 5 Q—KKt7, R—QKt3; 6 Q—Q7! is conclusive); 3 K—Kt5, R—Kt3ch; 4 K—R5 and now Black is compelled to play

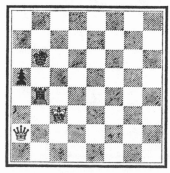

No. 601

White wins.

4 .... K—R1 (the Rook is lost if it moves), when 5 Q—B8ch, R—Kt1; 6 Q—B6ch, K—Kt2; 7 K—R6 follows. The Pawn on the third draws because there are no mate threats (as with the Pawn on the second) and because White's Queen cannot drive the Black King away (as with the Pawn on the fourth). No. 601b (v. Guretzky-Cornitz) White: Q at QR3, K at QB4; Black: K at QKt2, R at QKt4, P at QR3. Draw. White might try 1 Q—K7ch, K—Kt1; 2 Q—K8ch, K—Kt2; 3 Q—Q8, K—R2; 4 Q—QB8, R—Kt2; 5 Q—B5ch,

K—Kt1; 6 Q—Q6ch, K—R2; 7 Q—Q4ch, K—R1; 8 K—B5, K—R2; 9 K—B6 dis ch, K—R1; 10 Q—Q8ch (if 10 Q—KB4, K—R2! is the correct reply, but not 10 .... R—Kt4?; 11 K—B7, R—Kt2ch; 12 K—B8, K—R2; 13 Q—Q6, R—Kt4; 14 Q—Q7ch, K—R1; 15 Q—QB7 and will win the Rook), R—Kt1; 11 Q—Q5, R—Kt2 (11 .... K—R2? loses after 12 K—B7, R—Kt4; 13 Q—Q4ch, K—R1; 14 Q—Q6, K—R2; 15 K—B8, R—Kt2; 16 Q—Q4ch), etc.=. The Pawn on the sixth draws as usual.

It is essential for Black to keep his King, Rook and Pawn close together—any deviation will usually cost him the game. E.g., No. 601c (Berger), White: K at KKt3, Q at QR5; Black: K at KB2, R at KKt2, P at KKt5. White wins. 1 Q—Q5ch, K—B3; 2 Q—B6ch, K—K2 (if 2 .... K—B4; 3 Q—B8ch, K—Kt4; 4 Q—KR8, R—Kt3; 5 Q—K5ch, K—R3; 6 K—R4, K—R2; 7 K—R5!, R—Kt1; 8 Q—B5ch, K—R1; 9 Q—B6ch, R—Kt2; 10 K—R6 and mate next); 3 Q—B5ch, K—B2; 4 Q—B4ch, K—K2; 5 Q—KB1!, R—Kt4; 6 Q—B2, R—Kt3; 7 Q—B4, R—Kt2; 8 Q—B5, R—Kt1; 9 Q—K5ch, K—B2; 10 Q—Q5ch, K—B1; 11 Q—K6, R—Kt2; 12 K—R2, P—Kt6ch; 13 K—Kt2, R—Kt1; 14 Q—B6ch, K—K1; 15 K—R1, P—Kt7ch; 16 K—Kt1 and wins the Pawn.

Summary: With Queen vs. Rook and Pawn, Black must have Rook, King and Pawn close together to have any drawing chances at all. If White gets his King behind the Pawn he will always win. Where the Black Rook prevents the immediate entry of the White King, any Pawn on the second rank (except a RP) draws; RP, KtP and BP on the third rank draw, but a center Pawn loses; KtP and BP on the fourth rank draw, all others lose; RP on the fifth rank loses, KtP and BP draw, center Pawn may lose or draw depending on whose move it is (No. 599b); while all Pawns on the sixth or seventh draw.

3. QUEEN VS. ROOK AND TWO OR MORE PAWNS

Two connected Pawns should ordinarily draw; two disconnected or doubled Pawns lose unless the position with one of the Pawns is drawn.

The type draw is seen in No. 602. Note that here either Pawn alone would lose. If we try to apply the winning method of No. 599 we see that White gets nowhere because the Rook and two Pawns mutually defend one another, so that Black has an inexhaustible supply of tempo moves. But if the Pawns are weakened, White will be able to win. E.g., No. 602a (Kling and Horwitz, 1851), White: K at K3, Q at KB4; Black: K at KB3, R at K2, P's at KB4, K5. White to play wins. The solution is 1 Q—R4ch, K—K3; 2 Q—Kt5,

R—KB2; 3 K—B4, R—B3; 4 Q—Kt8ch, K—K2; 5 K—K5! and will soon capture both Pawns. Or here 2 .... R—Q2; 3 Q—Kt6ch, K—K4; 4 Q—K8ch, K—Q3; 5 K—Q4, R—K2; 6 Q—Kt8ch, K—Q2; 7 K—Q5, P—K6; 8 Q—Kt5ch, K—B2; 9 Q—B6ch, K—Kt1; 10 Q—Q6ch, R—B2; 11 Q—K5 and again both Pawns go.

Three or more Pawns will usually draw, but here too there are many cases where White wins. Of course, the Pawns may also win on occasion, just as three connected passed Pawns may sometimes be stronger than a lone Queen.

4. QUEEN AND PAWNS VS. ROOK AND PAWNS

Barring a few unusual or problem positions the Queen will always

No. 602

No. 603

Draw.   White wins.

win because the Rook cannot possibly defend everything. No. 603 (Colle-Becker, Carlsbad, 1929) is a difficult example from tournament play. Black to play would lose at once because he is in zugzwang. E.g., 1 .... R—QB5; 2 Q—Q7ch, K—R3; 3 Q—K6, R—B6ch; 4 K—K4, R×P; 5 Q×Pch, K—R4; 6 Q×Pch, K—R5; 7 K—B5, R—B6ch; 8 K—Kt6, etc. (No. 600a). Consequently White need only lose a move. The game continued: *1 K—K2!, R—Q4; 2 Q—R5, R—Q5; 3 K—B2! R—Kt5* (if 3 .... R—Q7ch; 4 K—K3, R—Q5; *5 Q—K8!); 4 Q—K8!, R—K5* and now *5 Q—Q7ch!* decides: *5 .... K—Kt3* (5 .... K—R3; 6 Q—B5 is hopeless); *6 Q—Q3, P—B4; 7 Q—Q6ch, K—Kt4; 8 Q—K6, P—B5; 9 Q—Kt8ch, K—B3; 10 Q×P, P×Pch; 11 Q×P* and wins (No. 599).

With one Pawn apiece, the only type of position which might offer any difficulty is No. 603a (Salvioli), White: K at QR5, Q at Q3, P at Q5; Black: K at QKt1, R at QKt3, P at QB2. White wins as follows: 1 Q—B5, K—Kt2; 2 Q—KB8, R—R3ch; 3 K—Kt5, R—Kt3ch; 4 K—B5, R—QR3; 5 K—Q4, R—QKt3; 6 K—K5, R—QR3; 7 Q—K8, R—Q3; 8 Q—K6!, R—Kt3 (8 .... R×Qch; 9 P×R, K—B1; 10 K—B6!); 9 K—B6, R—R3; 10 K—K7, R—Kt3; 11 K—Q7, R—R3; 12 Q×Rch, etc.

VI. QUEEN VS. MINOR PIECES

A. QUEEN VS. ONE PIECE

This is a simple win in all cases, regardless of the number of Pawns that go with the piece.

The case without Pawns is seen in No. 604 (Berger). By exercising a modicum of caution White will soon force mate. Best play is *1 K—Kt2, K—Q4; 2 K—B3, Kt—K5ch; 3 K—Q3, Kt—B4ch; 4 K—K3, Kt—K3; 5 Q—B5ch, K—Q3; 6 K—K4, Kt—B4ch; 7 K—Q4, Kt—K3ch; 8 K—B4, Kt—B2; 9 Q—B5ch, K—Q2; 10 Q—Kt6, Kt—K3; 11 K—Q5, Kt—B2ch; 12 K—K5, Kt—K1; 13 Q—K6ch, K—Q1; 14 Q—B7, Kt—B2; 15 K—Q6, Kt—Kt4ch; 16 K—B5* and Black must already sacrifice his Kt to ward off immediate mate. The win against the B is just as simple.

An example of a win against B+3 P's is No. 604a (Kling and Horwitz, 1851), White: K at KKt1, Q at KB7; Black: K at KKt6, B at QKt8, P's at QR7, KKt7, KR6. White to play wins. 1 Q—B2ch, K—Kt5; 2 Q—B6, K—Kt6; 3 Q—Kt5ch, K—B6; 4 Q—K5, K—Kt5; 5 K—B2!, K—R5 (or 5 .... B—B4; 6 Q—K2ch); 6 Q—Kt3ch, K—R4; 7 Q×Pch, K—Kt4; 8 Q×Pch, K—B3; 9 Q—B3ch, K—K3; 10 Q—B3 and now the mate can proceed in the routine manner.

B. QUEEN VS. TWO PIECES

Without Pawns this is normally a draw, but there are a number of exceptions where the Queen wins, especially with the Black King on the edge of the board.

1. TWO BISHOPS

The Bishops must be set up in such a way that the White King cannot attack either. One such position is No. 605 (Lolli, 1763). After *1 Q—Q7ch, K—Kt1!* (but not 1 .... B—B2? when 2 K—B5

No. 604

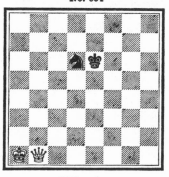

White wins

wins: e.g., 2 .... B—B6; 3 Q—B7, B—R8; 4 Q—QR7, B—Kt7;
5 Q—Kt6!, B—R6; 6 Q—Q4ch, K—B1; 7 Q—R8ch, K—K2; 8 Q—
K5ch, K—B1; 9 K—B6, B—K1!; 10 Q—B7, B—R4; 11 Q—Kt7ch,
K—K1; 12 Q—R8ch, etc.); *2 Q—K6ch, K—Kt2; 3 K—B4, B—R2;*
4 Q—Q7ch, K—Kt3; 5 Q—K8ch, K—Kt2 White can make no
progress. E.g., 6 K—Kt4, B—Kt3; 7 Q—K6, B—R2; 8 Q—Q7ch,
K—Kt3; 9 Q—K8ch, K—Kt2; 10 K—R5, B—B4; 11 Q—B6, B—
Kt3ch, etc.

No. 605

Draw.

No. 606

White wins.

2. TWO KNIGHTS

This too is a draw, because the Knights can keep the White King
out. E.g., No. 605a (Handbuch), White: K at KKt3, Q at K2;
Black: K at KB1, Kt's at KB3, KKt3. Draw. A plausible try is
1 Q—K6, K—Kt2; 2 K—B3, Kt—R2; 3 K—Kt4, but after 3 .... Kt
(R2)—B1; 4 Q—Q6, K—B2; 5 K—Kt5, Kt—K3ch; 6 K—R6,
Kt—K2 White is nowhere.

3. BISHOP AND KNIGHT

This is the worst case for the defender: it is won most of the time
because the pieces cannot be made to cooperate.

No. 606 (Berger) is typical. The main variation is *1 .... K—Kt4;*
(there is nothing better, e.g., 1 .... Kt—K3; 2 K—Q5! and wins a
piece); *2 K—Q5* (2 Q—Kt3ch is also good), *B—B3; 3 Q—Kt3ch,*
K—B4; 4 Q—Kt2, B—Kt4!; 5 Q—QB2ch, K—B3; 6 Q—B2ch, K—
Kt3; 7 K—K5, B—Q1; 8 Q—Kt2ch, K—B2; 9 Q—Q5ch, K—K2;
10 Q—Kt7ch, K—B1; 11 K—Q6, B—B3; 12 K—Q7, K—B2; 13 Q—
K4, K—B1; 14 Q—Kt6!, B—R5; 15 Q—Q6ch, K—B2; 16 Q—Q5ch,

K—Kt3 (16 .... K—B1; 17 Q—QB5ch and 18 Q—B4ch); *17 Q—K4ch, K—R4; 18 Q—R7ch* and wins.

The type of drawn position is seen in No. 606a, White: K at K8, Q at KR5; Black: K at KKt1, B at KKt2, Kt at K4. The White King cannot reach any effective square. E.g., 1 K—K7, B—R1; 2 K—K6, B—Kt2; 3 K—B5, B—R1; 4 K—Kt5, B—Kt2; 5 Q—K8ch, K—R2; 6 K—R5, B—R1; 7 Q—K7ch, B—Kt2; 8 Q—QB7, K—Kt1, etc.

With Pawns the Queen will usually win because the pieces will not be able to defend everything.

C. QUEEN VS. THREE PIECES

Without Pawns this is drawn, but there are a few positions where the pieces win. E.g., No. 606a (Berger), White: K at KR2, Q at KKt2; Black: K at Q3, B's at QB1, QB2, Kt at KR6. Black to play wins. 1 .... K—B4 dis ch; 2 K—R1; B—B4!!; 3 Q—B3 (White has no checks and cannot pin the B), B—K5!; 4 Q×B, Kt—B7ch, etc.

With Pawns the two forces are roughly equivalent. However, with no other material Q+P vs. 3 pieces is drawn, while 3 pieces+ Pawn win vs. Queen.

D. QUEEN VS. FOUR PIECES

Here the pieces always win: the Queen is unable to prevent mate. The helplessness of the Queen is shown in No. 607 (Kling and Horwitz, 1851). It makes no difference whose move it is: Black cannot improve his position.

The solution is *1 B—B5, K—R2; 2 Kt—Q7, Q—R8ch; 3 B—Q4, Q—R3ch; 4 B—K6, Q—R1; 5 K—B7!, Q—Kt1ch; 6 K—K7, Q—QR1* (or any other square); *7 Kt—B8ch, Q×Ktch; 8 K×Q*, etc.

No. 607

White wins.

Chapter IX

CONCLUSION AND SUMMARY

At the close of a book of this kind one is inevitably reminded of the story of the player who was asked by a friend how he had managed to win a position which was a "book" draw. "What good is the book," he replied, "if you don't know it and your opponent doesn't play it?"

It is of course impossible for anybody to know even a small part of what is contained in this book by heart. But the exact amount of specific knowledge is relatively unimportant; what counts is how well the principles are grasped. For this reason I have throughout tried to set up typical positions (for these are merely shorthand for general principles) and have always preferred helpful rules to mathematical exactitude. Anyone who indulges in a little practice at ordinary endings and who relies on the rules set forth will soon find that the individual positions will fall into well-recognized patterns and that a large number of the basic diagrammed endings will steadily become more familiar.

There are three points which are so fundamental that they must always be borne in mind:

1. Without Pawns one must be at least a Rook ahead in order to be able to mate. The only exceptions to this which hold in all cases are that the double exchange wins and that a Queen cannot defend successfully against four minor pieces.

2. Where one is two or more Pawns ahead the win is routine. By this we mean that a straightforward advance of the Pawns will net considerable material gain, usually at least a piece. With a piece to the good one can then capture more Pawns, then more pieces, and finally mate.

3. The theory of the ending proper is concerned to a large extent with the conversion of an advantage of one Pawn into a win. *The basic principle is that one Pawn wins only because it can be used to capture more material.* Straightforward advance will as a rule not do the trick (as it will with two Pawns). The chief devices to be used in the winning process are forcing an entry with the King, keeping the opponent busy on *both* sides (outside passed Pawn) and simplification.

FIFTEEN RULES FOR THE END-GAME

Most of the following rules have been mentioned in the body of the work. We have gathered them here in order to impress upon the reader the necessity of proceeding according to general principles rather than trial and error.

1. Doubled, isolated and blockaded Pawns are weak: Avoid them!
2. Passed Pawns should be advanced as rapidly as possible.
3. If you are one or two Pawns ahead, exchange pieces but not Pawns.
4. If you are one or two Pawns behind, exchange Pawns but not pieces.
5. If you have an advantage do not leave all the Pawns on one side.
6. If you are one Pawn ahead, in 99 cases out of 100 the game is drawn if there are Pawns on only one side of the board.
7. The easiest endings to win are pure Pawn endings.
8. The easiest endings to draw are those with Bishops of opposite colors.
9. The King is a strong piece: Use it!
10. Do not place your Pawns on the color of your Bishop.
11. Bishops are better than Knights in all except blocked Pawn positions.
12. Two Bishops vs. Bishop and Knight constitute a tangible advantage.
13. Passed Pawns should be blockaded by the King; the only piece which is not harmed by watching a Pawn is the Knight.
14. A Rook on the seventh rank is sufficient compensation for a Pawn.
15. Rooks belong behind passed Pawns.